Praise for *1,000 Indian Recipes* by Neelam Batra

"To savor a proper curry is to feel your palate awakened to an explosion of flavor. Neelam's recipes simmer with the fire of life."

—Michael Jackson, bestselling, award-winning singer, songwriter, music and video producer, and Indian food lover

"Collections of Indian recipes seem to run effortlessly into the hundreds, and here are a thousand recipes! Yet Neelam Batra has succeeded in making a new compilation that is completely intriguing, filled with many recipes I've never seen before. I can't wait to sample her many recipes for paneer, her salads and flatbreads, and of course, the chutneys and curries. In short, the whole book looks terrific. Make room for Neelam Batra's book on your kitchen bookshelf!"

—Deborah Madison, author of *Local Flavors, Cooking and Eating From America's Farmers' Markets* and *Vegetarian Cooking for Everyone*

"Neelam's perfect translations of Indian street foods had us wanting to get into the kitchen and cook. Neelam captures all the flavor and complexity of this amazing cuisine and makes it accessible to the home cook."

—Susan Feniger and Mary Sue Milliken, chefs and owners of Border Grill and Ciudad

"Neelam's passion and knowledge of her homeland's cuisine and history shine through on every page. Both experts and novices alike will find this encyclopedic compendium of Indian dishes refreshing and insightful."

—Nancy Silverton, executive pastry chef of Campanile and owner of Campanile and La Brea Bakery (Los Angeles)

"In all of my travels in over 30 years, I have found no comparison to a great Indian meal, and what Neelam Batra has given us is the amazing variety of Indian foods that we can enjoy. *1,000 Indian Recipes* is a magnificent book on anything and everything you may want to know on Indian cuisine and recipes."

—Vijay Amritraj, international tennis star, actor, entrepreneur, and United Nations Messenger of Peace

Dedication

To my father who showers blessings from the heavens above

To my mother for being the silent force behind me and what I am

To my mother-in-law for loving and believing in me

To my husband for making all my dreams come true

To my son-in-law Monti, you're the son I never had

To my daughters Sumita and Supriya for telling me,

"because you're Mumma"

I love you all

1,000 INDIAN Recipes

Alexandra & Eliot

Have fun with this book!

Neela

1,000
INDIAN
Recipes

❀ ❀ ❀

NEELAM BATRA

Wiley Publishing, Inc.

Library of Congress Cataloging-in-Publication Data:

Batra, Neelam.
    1,000 Indian recipes / Neelam Batra.
        p.   cm.
Includes bibliographical references and index.
    ISBN 0-7645-1972-7 (hardcover : alk. paper)
    1. Cookery, Indic.   I. Title.
TX724.5.I4 B3597 2002
641.5954—dc21   2002008124

Publisher: Jennifer Feldman
Executive Editor: Anne Ficklen
Senior Editor: Linda Ingroia
Production Editor: Helen Chin
Cover Design: Edwin Kuo
Interior Design: Holly Wittenberg
Manufacturing Buyer: Kevin Watt
Cover Illustration: Elizabeth Traynor

Manufactured in the United States of America
10   9   8   7   6   5   4   3   2   1

First Edition

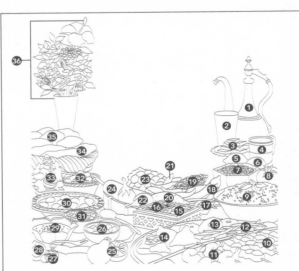

Key to Cover Illustration

1: ewer
2: Mango Milkshake
3: Pure Pistachio Fudge
4: Masala Chai Tea
5: lemon
6: lime
7: Red Lentils with Bengali 5-Spices
8: tomato
9: Ginger-Mint Pilaf with Potatoes and Roasted Cumin Seeds
10: Chicken Tikka Kabaabs
11: Grilled Shrimp Kabaabs
12: String Bean Pakora Fritters
13: South Indian Croquettes with Curry Leaves
14: Traditional Stuffed Triangular Pastries (Samosas); open: Mung Bean and Spinach Samosa
15: cardamom
16: cumin seeds
17: string beans
18: Chinese or Japanese eggplant
19: bitter melon
20: sweet potato
21: okra
22: Indian eggplant
23: cauliflower
24: opo squash
25: pomegranate
26: Sun-cured Pickled Lemon Wedges
27: whole nutmeg (with mace)
28: nutmeg fruit, cut open
29: Ginger and Scallion Raita
30: Zucchini Balls in Creamy Tomato Sauce (curry)
31: Basic Green Chutney
32: Potatoes with Peas and Sesame Seed Powder
33: statue of Ganesh
34: Basic Oven-Grilled Leavened Breads (Naans)
35: Deep-Fried Puffed Breads (Poories)
36: (from top): hibiscus (red), marigold (orange), jasmine (purple), bougainvillea (yellow)

Acknowledgments

I am overwhelmed by the love and inspiration I get from my family and my friends, having them right by my side sharing my experiences. Their words of encouragement and creative comments, and their enthusiastic support every time I raised my hand, means everything. This book is as much theirs as it is mine. I will always remain thankful for all the ideas, insight, special tips, and authentic recipes that have made this book so complete.

Many thanks to my mother, Rani Bhatla, and my mother-in-law, Prakash Batra, for guiding me with their encyclopedic knowledge. Thanks to my dear husband, Pradeep, who made this book possible by making me sign on the dotted line, and for his unflagging confidence in me. That's what really kept me going! And thanks to my darling daughters, Sumita and Surpiya, and my son-in-law, Monti, who continued to encourage my intense work over the four-year period it took to create this book!

Thanks to my brothers and sisters, Rakesh and Renu Bhatla, Veena and Sushil Dua, Raj and Asha Puri, Amita Batra, Virender and Reita Bhalla, Pushpa and Giri Khatod, and to Sanjokta Bhanji for their ideas and recipes and the numerous cups of tea to keep me going.

Special thanks to Sunil and Anita Vora and to Bharti and Ashwani Dhalwala for being my advisors and culinary pillars of support. A warm thanks also to Vivek Bhaman for running to my side everytime I had a computer panic attack. Am I glad they had all the answers!

My heartfelt thanks to my cousins and friends who shared their recipes, knowledge, and part of themselves: Sunita and Romesh Chopra, Billoo and Poonam Bhatla, Mini and Rajan Aneja, Upma and Vikram Budhraja, Poonam and Lalit Pant, Neelam and Raghu Rai, Kiran and Ashok Malik, Ranjana and Ranbir Wasu, Raj and Baljit Ahluwalia, and Madhu and Anoop Sharma, Naina and Madhukar Kapadia, Chitra and Sudesh Arora, Dimple and Raju Patel, Yasmin and Hadi AliKhan, Rosita and Ajit Dighe, Anu and Ravi Khatod, Falguni and Ajay Jalota, Neelam and Naresh Malhotra, Anju and Ashok Khanna, Madhu and Harish Seth, Shahina and Balinder Bhalla, Rita Bhalla, Kanta Kaytee, Shanti Aneja, Nimmi Sawhney, Rita Sawhney, Khushnoor Chugh, Prabha Chauhan, Amita Molloy, Jaywanti Thakar, Bharti Mahendra, Promella Dhar, Sushi Mysoor, Manju Bansal, Nirmala Bhavnani, Moyne Puri, Rama Srinivasan, Raghu Nanjappa and his family in Coorg, and Apurva Chandra.

Many thanks to Sanjay Bargotra, Steve Edwards, Akshay Dhalwala, Nitin Bhatla for all your technical support, from setting up my computer to making sure I knew how to use it. Sohini Baliga, thanks for helping with the writing during the initial stages of the book.

My thanks also, of course, go to Maureen Lasher, my agent. And last but not the least, many thanks to Linda Ingroia, my editor and my friend at Wiley, for making my dream a reality. Linda, your queries and comments have made all the difference. Thanks also go to the diligent and creative team that whipped this book into shape: Erin Connell, assistant editor; Helen Chin, production editor; Holly Wittenberg, designer; Kristi Hart, managing editor; Beth Adelman, copy editor; and Edwin Kuo, art director.

Contents

Introduction

Indian cuisine offers an astounding variety—from simply spiced salads and yogurt dishes (*raitas*) to complex curries, breads, and layered rice dishes (*biryanis*). These dishes, with their unique flavors, aromas, and textures, represent the culinary creativity of one of the earliest and most complicated melting pots of the world—India.

While north India excels in flatbreads, south India has an entire genre of food based on rice in various forms. Both coasts are famous for their seafood preparations, which vary depending on where you are on the coasts. The ways in which Bengalis, from the eastern state of Bengal, prepare fish—with mustard and turmeric—differ radically from how the people from the southwestern state of Kerala do it, with coconut and more coconut. And in the central parts of India, where people are mostly vegetarian, they have created culinary wonders with their primary sources of protein—grains, and beans, lentils, and peas—most commonly referred to as *dal*.

There was a time when all roads led to India—whether it was a stop on the way to equally exotic China, or a final destination. The Greeks, Huns, Persians, Chinese, Jews, Zoroastrians (now Parsis from Iran) French, Dutch, and finally, the British, all traveled through or to India. Some came to visit, some sought refuge, some came to trade, and some to conquer.

They brought their cultures and traditions along with them, some of which influenced India's local cuisines. Add to this India's size and its complex mix of communities based on religion, language, geography, and economic and social status, and the result is a truly multicultural cuisine.

Evidence of the cuisine's variety is only touched upon in America's Indian restaurants. Indian food is not limited to what's served in these restaurants—from the many fast food joints that dot Venice Boulevard in West Los Angeles to the delicious but intricate and elaborate preparations taking gourmands in New York by surprise. But as more Indians come to the United States, bringing their food customs with them, and as more restaurant chefs experiment with varied Indian ways of cooking, this fascinating realm of food is slowly being explored.

In *1,000 Indian Recipes*, I've bridged the gap, capturing recipes from all over the country. Even 1,000 recipes doesn't cover all the wealth I discovered in my travels and in preparing recipes in my kitchen, but you have in this book a wonderful collection of recipes that will make Indian home cooking a pleasure. The average Indian meal is delicious, and, contrary to popular belief, not at all complicated or difficult to make. If you can cook at all, you can cook Indian food. It just takes practice and having the right ingredients.

This book provides the lover of Indian food—by birth or by taste—a wide variety of choices, serving suggestions, and background information that enable you to enjoy and experience Indian food the way Indians do in their own kitchens.

Although the recipes aren't hard, many may require allowing extra time to make the various components of the dishes, or to go stock up at your local Indian or ethnic market for ingredients crucial to the cuisine. You'll see that there are numerous recipes made with a pressure cooker, which enables me to make traditionally slow-cooked dishes such as *dals*, soups, curries, even desserts with much less effort and in less time. I highly recommend that if you don't have a pressure cooker, you invest in one; it will change the way you think about and cook Indian food. Even traditional cooks in India use pressure cookers daily to simplify their lives. So don't worry about sacrificing authenticity. It will still be there in the taste and texture of every dish you make. *Look for the* P *symbol near the recipe title. It signifies that a pressure cooker is used.*

Many people also rightfully think of Indian cuisine as a source for healthful foods full of flavor. Indian meals are nutritionally balanced and are largely vegetarian, offering many options for people looking to improve their health by eating a meat-free diet. In fact, because so many of the recipes in this book are meat-free—as representative of the cuisine—I go a step further in helping you plan healthful meals by identifying which recipes are vegan—meaning free of meat, fish, poultry, eggs, and dairy products. *Look for the* V *symbol near the recipe title. It indicates vegan recipes.*

I strive for a healthful diet. Most of my recipes are as low in fat as they can possibly be: I pan-fry foods that are normally deep-fried, and in most dishes, I use vegetable and other oils instead of *ghee*. Even in cases where I do draw the line at keeping some things authentic—like deep-frying pakoras or using cream as in Butter-Cream Sauce with Fresh Tomatoes, I exercise moderation rather than compromising or giving them up entirely.

I have been cooking Indian food in American kitchens for more than 30 years and I know that every cook needs to adapt meals to her or his lifestyle—to time on hand, to what cooks conveniently, to satisfy various family food preferences, to eat healthfully—because I have lived and do live through those same experiences. I hope you find that these recipes fit your needs for everyday meals, for family gatherings, for parties, and just for experimenting with the great flavors of Indian cooking.

The Indian Philosophy of Food and Menu Planning

I have lived (and have enjoyed living) in the United States for 30 years, but I will always be connected to India. Memories of the natural beauty of the mountains and shores, the tranquility and comforts of family and spiritual rituals, and the sensory joys of preparing and sharing food are indelibly etched in my mind, heart, and soul and inspire me to visit India as often as I can.

Welcoming and sharing with others is paramount to Indian culture and eating together helps develop and strengthen bonds with our family and friends. Indeed, the ancient Sanskrit saying is telling about India: "Atithi Devo Bhava." This literally means that your guest (*Atithi*) is your God (*Devo*), and God will treat you just like you treat your guests. And that is the guiding force of Indian philosophy and hospitality—from the way we receive guests and entertain them to the way we feed them.

Mealtimes in India are steeped in tradition. They are a time for closeness and catching up (and a time for complaining and for gossip, too). Children, husbands, and in-laws feel loved and cherished by the mother and wife of the house. The meals themselves are prepared fresh, with recipes passed from mothers to daughters through the generations—not on paper but in the kitchen, when you are side by side. With a memory of countless recipes, the cook's job then is to imagine and plan the menus carefully, keeping the family's preferences in mind.

A typical everyday meal includes a "wet" dish with a sauce, such as a curry; a "dry" vegetable dish; *chapatis* (whole-wheat griddle breads) and/or rice; and plain yogurt, which serves as a soother, a palate cleanser, and a digestive aid. An array of pickled vegetables, chutneys, and chopped vegetable salads are standard accompaniments.

Meals for company tend to be more elaborate. Special drinks and appetizers are served, the number of the wet and dry dishes increases, *paranthas* (griddle-fried breads) and elaborate rice *pullaos* (pilafs or seasoned rice dishes) take the place of everyday *chapatis*, and plain yogurt transforms into a seasoned or enhanced *raita* or a *pachadi*. Desserts complete the meals with distinction.

Indian food is traditionally served "family style," meaning multiple dishes are brought to the table, from which each person takes her or his share. There is no one main dish; rather, each dish complements the others, and no flavors collide. For example, you would not serve two *dal* (legumes) dishes together or two soupy vegetable curries together, rather, you would choose a dal and a vegetable curry.

For your own meals, before you plan a menu, think always of balance—balance of nutrition with flavor, of "wet" (with sauce) and "dry" (without sauce), and of aesthetics and color.

Make nutritionally balanced meals according to your eating preferences, vegetarian or non-vegetarian. It's important to note that vegetables play an important part of every Indian meal, even when the meals are primarily non-vegetarian.

So, to serve an Indian meal, consider or plan a menu with foods from all the major food groups, buy and use them as fresh as possible, and for the most part, even if varied eating preferences surface, make a few vegetarian dishes—it will follow tradition and usually be better for everyone's health.

For flavor elements, the natural flavors of ingredients are important as well as the results when ingredients are combined. Determine whether you want to serve simple, light flavors or rich, complex tastes. Will spicy or mild dishes satisfy, and how much chile-pepper heat will be bearable for all?

The "wet" and the "dry" factor is particular to Indian cuisine. The "wet" curries or saucy dishes give necessary moisture to the meal. Though there is no set standard, the full-bodied, thicker curries pair well with breads, and the soupy, thinner ones are good served over rice, which soaks up all the juices.

Equally important to a meal are the aesthetics and color. Nothing stimulates the senses and appetite as vibrant colors and a beautifully presented meal. We savor the perceived flavors of foods first with our eyes and nose before actually tasting them. So make your meals as pleasantly fragrant as possible, and attractive too. Even for dull-colored dishes, try simple garnishes of contrasting colors—adding chopped cilantro on a few dishes and a sprinkle of *garam masala* or paprika on others.

Please remember (and gently remind your family from time to time), although it is far more fun to eat what captures the senses—and rich, golden-fried appetizers and desserts or creamy curries are often the most enticing—don't go overboard on high-fat and calorie-rich dishes. Indulge in moderation and give yourself a chance to eat well for the rest of your life.

Menus

Here are some menu suggestions to try out the elements of balance in menu planning, or just to get dinner on the table. Use my recipes as they appear in the book, or be inventive and treat them as points of departure to create new dishes.

A Meal from the American Pantry

Pastry Swirls with Roasted Red Bell Peppers and Potatoes (page 101)

Basic Green Chutney (page 58)

Multi-Colored Warm Tomato Salad (page 201)

Ginger Chicken with Citrus Juices (page 449)

Minty Pot-Roasted Potato Curry (*Pudina Dum-Aalu*) (page 404)

Baby Yellow Patty Pan Squash with Chopped Tomatoes (page 274)

Stir-Fried Mushrooms and Red Chard Pilaf (page 548)

Mango or any other Ice Cream Dessert (pages 637 to 638)

Easy Make-Ahead Meal

Cauliflower, Potato, or Green Bean Pakora Fritters (pages 112 to 114)

Yogurt Chutney with Puréed Greens (page 68)

Chopped Salad with Yogurt (*Cachumbar Pachadi*) (page 243)

Chicken Curry with Dry-Roasted Spices (page 458)

Kashmiri Small Red Beans (page 372)

Simple Cumin Basmati Rice (page 535)

Griddle-Fried Layered Mint, Ajwain, and Black Pepper Breads (page 584)

Pistachio or any other Indian Ice Cream (*Kulfi*) (pages 634 to 638)

Light Weeknight Dinner

Mixed Greens with Pan-Roasted Tomatoes (page 214)

Broiled Indian Swordfish Steaks (page 518)

Yellow Mung Beans with Sautéed Onion and Ginger (page 342)

Quick Garlic and Chile Pepper Eggplant (page 269)

Steamed Turmeric and Red Peppercorn Basmati Rice (page 534)

Whole-Wheat Griddle Breads (*Chapati*) (page 577)

Fresh Seasonal Fruits

Summer Party Menu

Fresh Lime Soda with Berries (page 657)

Griddle-Fried Chicken Skewers with Mango-Ginger Sauce (page 446)

Spinach Salad with Roasted Cumin Seeds (page 214)

Pan-Fried Fish Fillets with Ajwain Seeds (page 520)

Nine-Jewel Paneer Cheese Curry (page 336)

Pomegranate Potatoes (page 254)

Smoked Sugar-Snap Peas (page 298)

Grilled Bell Pepper Fried Rice (page 549)

Indian Vermicelli Pudding (*Seviyan ki Kheer*) (page 626)

Winter Dinner Menu

Traditional Stuffed Triangular Pastries (*Samosae*) (page 103)

Chutney Chickpeas with Tamarind (page 380)

Carrot-Ginger Soup (page 187)

Yogurt Chicken Curry with Caramelized Onions (page 464) or Punjabi Black Urad Beans (page 360)

Hyderabadi Spicy Eggplants with Roasted Peanut and Sesame Sauce (page 400)

Sautéed Spinach Raita (page 227)

Royal Fresh and Dried Fruits Pilaf (*Shahi Pullao*) (page 554)

Simple Carrot Halva (page 621)

Holiday Brunch

Sweet Mango-Yogurt Cooler (*Aam ki Lussi*) (page 653)

Spicy Chickpeas with Pomegranate Seeds (page 377)

Lemon-Marinated Red Onion Rings (page 204)

Baked Semolina Breads (*Kulchae*) (page 597)

Nani Mama's Yogurt Curry with Onion Fritters (page 426)

Spicy Potatoes with Onions and Tomatoes (page 251)

Steamed Basmati Rice (page 533)

Any Halva (pages 618 to 622) or Kheer Pudding (pages 622 to 627)

Orange Pekoe Tea (page 660)

Fourth-of-July Barbecue

Fire-Roasted Green Mango Cooler (*Ammbi-Panna*) (page 658)

Yogurt Coleslaw (page 203)

Spicy Rack of Baby Lamb (page 491)

Grilled Tandoori Chicken (page 445)

Spicy Grilled Shrimp (page 511)

Spicy Smashed Potatoes with Chaat Masala (page 252)

Fire-Roasted Corn-on-the-Cob (page 302)

Rolls with Oat Bran and Fresh Mint (page 606)

Mango or any other Ice Cream or *Kulfi* (pages 634 to 638)

A Thanksgiving Meal

Fresh Lime Soda with Berries (page 657)

Curried Chicken or Lamb Turnovers (page 103)

Deep-Fried Lamb Kabaab Patties (*Shaami Kabaabs*) (page 152)

Vinegar-Marinated Green Chile Peppers (page 84)

Cranberry Chutney Preserve (page 75)

Quick Puréed Root Vegetable Soup (page 186)

Potato Salad with Yogurt (page 211) or Roasted Turkey with Indian Flavors (page 451)

Spicy Pumpkin Purée (page 271)

Taro Root Salad with Ajwain Seeds (page 213)

North Indian–Style Mixed Cauliflower, Carrots, and Green Beans (*Uttar ki Jhalfrezi*) (page 306)

Cranberry Pilaf (*Karonda Pullao*) (page 555)

Decadent Carrot Halva with Evaporated Milk and Jaggery (page 621)

Pure Pistachio Fudge (*Pistae ki Burfee*) (page 641)

A Vegetarian Diwali Celebration

Flour Chips with Yogurt and Mango Powder Chutney (*Papri Chaat*) (page 142)

Potato and Cashew Patties (*Aalu aur Kaaju ki Tikki*) (page 146)

Yogurt Chutney with Puréed Greens (page 68)

Split Urad Beans and Yellow Split Chickpeas with Spinach (page 368)

Stir-Fried Paneer Cheese with Onions and Bell Peppers (page 331)

Creamy Mashed Eggplant with Peas (page 263) or Spicy South Indian Potatoes (page 252)

Morel Mushroom Pilaf with Pistachios and Silver Leaves (*Gucchi-Pista Pullao*) (page 548)

Traditional Urad Dal Croquettes Raita (page 237)

Basic Griddle-Fried Breads (*Saada Parantha*) (page 581)

Saffron Paneer Cheese Triangles (*Cham-Cham*) (page 646)

An Indian Banquet

Basic Fish, Chicken, or Grilled Lamb Tikka Kabaabs (pages 148 to 161)

Stuffed Phyllo Baked Pastry Pouches (page 107)

Bell Pepper Pakora Fritters with Ajwain Seeds (page 114)

Yogurt Chutney with Puréed Greens (page 68)

Mughlai Lamb Curry with Cashews and Coconut Milk (page 476)

Black Urad Beans in a Slow Cooker (page 362)

Royal Paneer Cheese Curry (page 334)

Potato-Stuffed Oval Eggplant (page 267)

Hyderabadi Layered Rice with Mixed Vegetables or Marinated Chicken (*Biryani*) (page 559 or 561)

Griddle-Fried Mughlai Breads with Almonds and Poppy Seeds (*Paranthae*) (page 586)

Spicy Mung Bean Croquettes Raita with Sonth Chutney (page 236)

Paneer Cheese Patties in Creamy Thickened Milk (*Ras-Malai*) (page 645)

Pressure-Cooked Caramel Custard (page 632)

Helpful Hints

This book covers all types of Indian foods—dishes you may have eaten in restaurants, regional and classic home-cooked Indian foods, street foods, as well as modern dishes with Indian flavorings and universal appeal. So there are a range of recipe options to cook and enjoy.

You'll find that the recipes balance traditions with real-world cooking concerns. Although I always strive for authenticity in my dishes, I have strayed from old-world traditions of hand-grinding, sun-drying, and of course, cooking in a tandoor; modern conveniences allow for wonderfully suitable substitutions. I rely on the stove and the oven, on a grill and a pressure cooker, and even get a little help from the microwave. I gravitate toward the food processor, the blender, and the spice grinder, and I use the freezer a lot—not to pull out store-bought frozen foods, but to freeze my spice pastes, puréed chutneys, and other basic ingredients—so when I'm actually cooking, most of the busy work has been done and my time is focused on cooking and creating. As a general rule, I keep my home recipes quick and healthy, and this is how you too probably prefer to cook. Here are some hints and shortcuts for using my recipes and for being an efficient cook of Indian cuisine:

- Always read and understand the recipe before you start. Some recipes have cross-references to other recipes—for needed ingredients such as spice blends, chutneys, and sauces, or for suggestions for accompaniments. Decide if you need to coordinate making them or if you can substitute a store-bought item. (I mention if a purchased product can substitute for homemade.)

- Ingredients to keep on hand, preferably fresh or homemade: cilantro; dry-roasted cumin, sesame seeds, and black peppercorns; ginger paste, garlic paste, and ginger-garlic paste; green chutney; crispy fried ginger and crispy fried onions; fresh lemon juice; *paneer* cheese; pickles, especially mango and lemon; chutney preserves, especially mango and tomato.

- Have all the ingredients ready so you're not opening drawers and bottles when your attention should be on food on the stove or in the oven, or that you have to stop cooking to make a basic preparation.

- To make food go further in the event of unexpected company, make an extra vegetable or quickly cook some frozen peas, chopped fresh vegetables, potatoes, or rice in the microwave, then add them to an existing dish to increase its volume.

- To salvage over-salted or over-spiced foods, add a peeled and chopped cooked or mashed potato; the spud will absorb most of the extra salt and/or chile heat. Or, mix in some yogurt, cooked plain white rice, or another vegetable—the idea is to increase the volume of the dish, so the saltiness and/or heat dissipate.

Spices and Other Seasonings

Spices and Herbs
(a guide) 8

Spice Blends 15

Curry Powders 15

Basic Curry Powder

15-Spice Curry Powder

Kashmiri Curry Powder
with Fennel Seeds and Ginger

South Indian Curry Powder
with Rice and Dal

Gujarati Curry Powder
with Coriander and Cumin

Marathi Curry Powder
with Coconut and Sesame Seeds

Goan Curry Powder

Garam Masalas 18

Garam Masala

Hyderabadi Garam Masala
with Black Cumin Seeds

Mughlai Garam Masala
with Nutmeg and Mace

Parsi Garam Masala with Star Anise

Kashmiri Garam Masala

Savory Spice Blends 20

Chaat Masala

New Delhi Street Food Masala

Bombay Bread-Snack Masala

Minty Cumin-Water Masala

Masala for Griddle-Fried Breads

Masala for Stuffed
Griddle-Fried Breads

Roasted Chile Pepper and
Red Peppercorn Masala

Roasted Cumin and
Fenugreek Masala

Roasted Cumin-Pepper Masala

Punjabi Raita and
Buttermilk Masala

Kashmiri Raita Masala

Masala Blends
for Special Dishes 24

Chickpea Masala
with Pomegranate Seeds

Fragrant Masala with Nuts

Indian Grilling Masala

Spicy Masala
for Wok-Cooked Foods

Gujarati Lentil Masala

Bengali 5-Spices

Meat Masala
with Cumin and Peanuts

Goan Vindaloo Powder

Special South
Indian Blends 28

South Indian Sambar Powder

South Indian Soup Powder

South Indian Lentil Paste

South Indian Coconut
Chutney Powder

South Indian Chutney Powder

South Indian Peanut Powder

South Indian Sesame Seed Powder

Dessert and Tea
Masalas 32

Dessert Masala

Chai Tea Masala

When European explorers went to India in the 16th century, they found the country fragrant with spices and they capitalized on the opportunity for trade and wealth. What they didn't realize was that the Indian people held the secret to the true value of these spices—it lay not in their monetary worth, but in the way the spices could be altered, blended, and coaxed into producing intensely flavorful and satisfying foods.

Even today, the first encounter with the colorful, fragrant Indian spice rack is a beguiling experience. But, once you get past their unusual names, Indian herbs and spices are quite easy to use and, for the most part, are readily available. Look for them in well-stocked supermarkets, in local Indian markets and other ethnic markets, and from catalogs or reputable Internet sites (see the Sources list, page 669).

The following is a list of popular Indian seasonings. (I include ayurvedic—health-affecting—properties because this is integral to how Indians cook.) Buy what is needed for specific recipes and then expand your collection as you feel more comfortable.

Ajwain Seeds

This spice is known by various names—carom, lovage, omum, or Bishop's weed, with no one single English name. However, the name *ajwain* or *ajowan* is universal, so *ajwain* is what I call it throughout the book. These tiny brown or green-brown, ridged, celery seed look-alikes are deceptively fragrance-free, but when crushed, they release a strong and highly aromatic, thyme-like fragrance, which mellows down after cooking. When eaten raw, they have a hot, strong, pungent bite. *Ajwain* seeds are prized as a home remedy to relieve gas and stomachaches, and are often chewed raw by people with seasoned palates.

Asafoetida

Hing or *heeng.* Asafoetida is the dried milky sap (resin) from the rhizome or root-stalk of a giant fennel-like perennial herb. It is dull yellow-brown, has a bitter taste and a very strong, pungent, and disagreeable odor—almost like rotten eggs—from the sulfur

compounds that are present in it. But after cooking, this aroma adds a surprisingly pleasant garlic-onion flavor to the foods. Loaded with therapeutic benefits (carminative, digestion-stimulating, and antibiotic, to name just a few), asafoetida is indispensable to Indian cuisine. Buy your asafoetida in lumps (or fine granules) and then grind them at home. (That is what I have used in my recipes throughout the book.) The commonly available ground version has a mild flavor, because it comes mixed with rice flour and turmeric to mellow it.

Bay Leaves

Tej patta, tejpat, or *tej patra.* Bay leaves come in two types: the leaves of the bay laurel found mostly in the Western world, and those of the Indian cassia tree. Used in much the same way as their western cousins, Indian bay leaves are deep green, long, and elliptical with pointy tips. They have a delicate and sweet, cinnamon-like fragrance, a bitter taste, and are valued as an appetite stimulant and for gas relief. The bark of this tree is often dried and used as cinnamon in many parts of the world, including the United States. (True cinnamon, however, is made from the bark of a different tree—see the entry on cinnamon on page 9.)

Black Salt

Kaala namak. Black salt, a rock salt, comes in irregular rock-candy-type pieces, with smooth facets. The pieces are actually grayish-pink and almost odor-free but it has quite an unpleasant odor when ground—almost like hard-boiled egg yolks, from the sulfur and other mineral compounds in the salt. However, when it is added to foods, it dramatically heightens their flavors and imparts a pleasant tang and fragrance. Black salt is prized for its digestive and anti-gas properties. Do not use interchangeably with table salt.

Cardamom Pods

Illaichi. Cardamom pods, a signature Indian spice and also the world's third most expensive spice after saffron and vanilla, are the dried capsules of a perennial herb in the ginger family. There are two distinct types of cardamom pods in India: the small green and large black. Green cardamom pods (*hari* or *choti illaichi*), are small triangular ovals, ⅓- to ½-inch long, each containing 3 segments with 18 to 20 tiny, sticky, mildly fragrant, brown-black seeds. When crushed or ground, they release a highly aromatic perfume with a hint of eucalyptus and camphor. Their initial bite is very strong, but mellows into a delicate and refreshing fragrance.

Black cardamom pods (*kaali* or *bari illaichi*), are large black, somewhat hairy, triangular ovals ½- to ⅔-inch long. Each pod contains 3 segments, with 30 to 40 sticky seeds. When crushed, they have a strong, nutty and delicate woody-smoky aroma and are much milder than green ones.

Both cardamom pods are considered carminative (gas-relieving) and digestive, and are a popular home remedy for nausea and vomiting. Chewing the green pods also refreshes the mouth and sweetens the breath.

Chiles, Fresh Green and Dried Red

Mirch or *mirchi*. Chile peppers—fresh green (*hari mirch*) and dried red (*laal mirch*)—are part of the capsicum species. There are more than 150 varieties of chile peppers in the world, and as a general rule, the smaller ones are hotter than the larger ones. Most chiles start off green and turn to a shade of red as they age. The red ones are dried (in the shade or the sun) until all their moisture evaporates, leaving behind the wrinkled and brittle red chiles that we are familiar with. Indian cuisine uses both, the fresh green and the dried red.

When dried red chiles of any type (such as cayenne, chile de arbol, or those from the Indian markets) are finely ground the result is called *pisi hui laal mirch,* or dried red chile powder. In your cooking, you can use any pure ground chile powder. My recipes specify cayenne powder because it is easily available.

Chiles stimulate the taste buds and aid digestion. They are considered potent sinus, cough, and cold remedies. Common knowledge though this might be, it bears repeating: Basic common sense should be used when preparing or cooking with the hot chile peppers. Capsaicin and other oils in chiles will make the hardiest soul miserable if they come in contact with delicate membranes around the eyes and nose or skin. Wear plastic kitchen gloves or protect your hands in some way before handling them, and be sure to wash your hands thoroughly afterwards.

Cinnamon and Cassia

Dalchini or *darchini*. Cinnamon, known to cooks in ground or stick form, is the dried inner bark of the branches and young shoots of a tropical evergreen tree. There are 2 types of cinnamon: true cinnamon with tightly rolled "quills" or tubular sticks, with a rich fragrance and a warm and sweet aroma and taste that comes from Sri Lanka, the Seychelles Islands and southern India; and cassia-cinnamon, with thicker, loosely rolled, almost flat quills and a less sweet and an intense and mildly bitter flavor and aroma. (This cinnamon comes from the Indian bay leaf and other cassia trees.) Cinnamon imparts a pleasant fragrance to foods, and aids overall digestion and other stomach ailments, such as gas and nausea.

Cloves

Laung or *lavang*. Cloves are the air-dried, brown-black, nail-shaped, unopened flower buds of a tropical mid-sized evergreen tree. Cloves, usually used whole or ground, are highly aromatic, with a sharp and pungent, yet sweet and almost bitter bite. They are carminative (gas-relieving), and aid digestion, colic, nausea, and vomiting.

Coriander Seeds and Greens

Dhania, sookha, and *patta* or *hara*. Coriander seeds are the peppercorn-sized, ribbed, spherical, pale-green to beige-brown seeds of an annual, fern-like plant of the parsley family. All parts of the plant are used in cooking—the seeds, leaves, stems, and even the roots of the young plants.

Two varieties of coriander seeds are available in the United States: the pale green-beige Indian variety that has a sweet, citrusy aroma (especially when crushed or ground), and the brown Moroccan variety, which is not quite as flavorful. Buy the seeds and grind them yourself, do not make them into a powder—a bit of texture remarkably increases the flavor of the foods. Coriander seeds are believed to be a body-cooling and strengthening spice. Like many other spices, they are also believed to be a carminative (gas-relieving) and digestive tonic, a diuretic, and a mild sedative.

Coriander greens (*hara dhania*), commonly called cilantro or Chinese parsley, are the leaves of the coriander plant. They are prized culinary herbs in Indian cuisine, as well as in other cuisines of the world. The greens have a distinctive, sweet and citrus-like flavor, and a pleasantly fragrant aroma. Although highly perishable and prone to wilting, I find that with a little care, cilantro keeps well in the refrigerator. Trim and wash the cilantro, then spin in a salad spinner and spread on kitchen or paper towels to air-dry until most of the moisture has evaporated. Transfer to zip-closure bags, toss in a small paper towel to absorb excess moisture, and store in the refrigerator about 1 week or longer if the leaves are fresh to start with. Chopped cilantro can be stored in a similar manner in airtight containers. Its best to use fresh leaves, the dried or frozen ones are totally flavorless.

Cumin and Black Cumin

Jeera or *zeera*. Cumin seeds are the small, gray-brown, ridged, elongated, curved, dried fruits of a small annual herb of the parsley family. India grows two types of cumin seeds: the familiar brown seeds called *sufaid jeera* (*sufaid* is white) and the more exotic variety known as *kaala, siyah,* or *shah jeera* (*kaala* and *siyah* mean black and *shah* is royal).

Cumin seeds have a strong, musky, spicy aroma and a pungent, bitter taste. Considered to be another cooling spice, cumin aids digestion, and relieves flatulence, colic, and other stomach disorders, including morning sickness and diarrhea. Cumin seeds are rich in thymol, which is a powerful antiseptic. Black cumin (not to be confused with caraway seeds, even though it is sometimes mistakenly called black caraway) is a rare cumin variety that grows in Kashmir (India), Pakistan, and Iran. These seeds are thinner and much darker than regular cumin and have a delicate and sweet aroma.

Curry Leaves

Meethi neem or *kari patta*. Curry leaves are the small, oval leaves of a tropical shrub or small tree native to southern India and Sri Lanka. Lightly aromatic when whole, they release an exotic, warm, nutty, yet citrusy aroma when they are crushed, bruised, or chopped. In one of those interesting quirks of culinary terminology, curry leaves, while used in a wide variety of curries, are not indispensable to them.

Curry leaves are slightly bitter, and therefore they are believed to be a tonic that removes toxins from the body, helps digestion, and acts as a mild laxative. Their refreshing flavor is almost indescribable to the uninitiated, but unforgettable to those who try it. Once you get used to it, there is no turning back.

Fennel Seeds

Saunf. Fennel seeds—the long, ridged, oval or curved, green-yellow seeds of a tall, annual, feathery shrub—belong to the anise, dill, cumin, and caraway family. There are many varieties of fennel around the world and within India, each different in color, size, and aroma. Fennel seeds look like plumped-up cumin, taste somewhat like anise, and have a licorice-camphor aroma. They have a pleasantly fragrant bite and are often eaten raw, dry-roasted, or sugar-coated to aid digestion, relieve gas, and ease other digestive ailments, including colic in infants.

Fenugreek Seeds and Greens

Daana-methi or *metharae* and *patta* or *hari methi*. Fenugreek seeds are the dried, angular, yellow-brown seeds of a strongly scented annual herb of the legume family. Native to southeastern Europe—mainly the Mediterranean countries, where it is called Greek hay—fenugreek is now grown extensively in India and in other parts of the world. Fenugreek seeds, with their distinctive bouquet and a strong curry flavor, are very bitter when eaten raw. However, with a little stir-frying or dry-roasting, they are transformed into something quite unusual and exciting. These seeds are a natural home remedy believed to stimulate digestion and metabolism, purify the blood and to control sugar levels in diabetic patients.

Fenugreek greens (*methi patta*), the clover-like green leaves, though extremely aromatic and curry-flavored, are quite bitter. Despite this, Indians have a remarkable fondness for them. They are used fresh to make side dishes, added to other green purees, or air-dried (*sookhi* or *kasoori methi*) and used as a flavoring herb. To dry, place rinsed, blotted leaves on towels and air-dry outdoors in shade until crisp.

Ginger

Adrak, taaza, and *sookha*. Ginger is the knobby, buff-colored rhizome (underground stem) of a perennial tropical plant. Ginger rhizomes are dug out after the greens have died. When the ginger is young (often called green ginger), it is very juicy and has a transparent papery-thin skin that needs no peeling, but as it matures, the juices dry up and the skin hardens somewhat, losing its shine over time. This is the type we see most often in markets.

Choose large, plump pieces with as thin and shiny skin as you can find. Any shriveling, dryness, or mold on the edges is a sign of age and excess fiber. Fresh ginger has little or no aroma, but once you peel or cut it, ginger emits a refreshingly warm, woody aroma with citrus undertones and has a pleasantly fragrant and peppery-hot bite.

Topping the list of India's therapeutic spices—and called *maha-aushadhi* or the greatest medicine by the *Ayurvedic* school of natural healing—ginger is highly valued as a stimulant to the digestive and circulatory systems. It is believed beneficial for nausea, fever, muscle aches and pains, and respiratory disorders. It is also considered a home remedy for flatulence, colic, indigestion, vomiting, morning and travel sickness, and similar ailments.

Dried ginger, called *sonth* or *sund*, is the sun-dried ginger rhizomes. Available in pieces or ground into a sand-colored powder, dried ginger has a sharp, sweet, lemony aroma and a pronounced peppery bite.

Kalonji

This spice is known by various names—nigella, onion seeds, black onion seeds, black caraway seeds, and black cumin seeds, with no one English name as the standard. However, the name *kalonji* is widely recongnized, so that is what I call it throughout the book.

Kalonji are tiny, charcoal black, triangular seeds strongly resembling onion seeds. They have a mild, oregano-like flavor and a fragrant, peppery, and slightly bitter bite which, after roasting or cooking, is transformed into a distinct nutty aroma and taste. *Kalonji* seeds are considered an appetite stimulant and are good for digestion.

Kokum

Also *cocum, cocamful,* fish tamarind. *Kokum* is the sun-dried rind of a ½- to 1-inch fruit of the mangosteen-oil tree (not to be confused with other mangosteen trees or fruits). The ripe fruits are enjoyed locally, but most of them are dried into the somewhat sticky, sour, purple-black pieces of *kokum*, as Indians call the spice. Tamarind is a good substitute.

Mango Powder

Amchur. Mango powder is a pale, finely ground powder made from sun-dried, unripe, tart green mangoes. As they dry in the sun, the flesh of the green mangoes shrivels up and turns buff-brown in color. Mango powder is extremely sour and acidic, with a touch of fruity sweetness and fragrance. *Amchur* is also available as small, thin, dried pieces and is considered a stimulating tonic for the stomach. Mango powder is a cooling spice that may also aid digestion.

Mint

Pudina, taaza, and *sookha*. Mint is one of the most valuable and popular herbs in the world. Native to temperate Europe and now grown almost everywhere, mint is an aromatic perennial herb with dark green, oval leaves. With about 40 varieties of mint in the world, it is difficult to distinguish and classify each one of them. They all belong to the *mentha* family and all have essentially similar characteristics.

The fresh leaves (*taaza pudina*) are quite strong, pungent, and very aromatic, and the dried ones (*sooka pudina*) are somewhat mellow, yet full of minty flavor.

Prized as appetite stimulants and believed to be an indispensable home cure for indigestion and stomach disorders, mint leaves are a natural antiseptic that keep the mouth fresh and the taste buds healthy. Mint juice and mint tea are considered effective cold and sore throat remedies.

Mixed Melon Seeds

Char-magaz. This special mixture of seeds comes from four different summer melons—cantaloupe, watermelon, cucumber, and pumpkin (*char* means four and *magaz* means brain). The seeds are almost fragrance-free and their taste is very delicate and mild, similar to pumpkin and sunflower seeds. As the Indian name suggests, this seed combination, rich in iron, zinc, and potassium, ranks high as brain food. It is believed to have body-cooling properties and considered to be mildly diuretic.

Mustard Seeds and Greens

Raayi or *rai*, and *sarson.* Mustard seeds, the small round seeds of an annual plant of the cabbage family, are also one of the important Indian oilseed sources; that is, the seeds are widely used to make oil. Mustard seeds grow in small 1-inch pods that must be collected when they are ripe—but before they burst—then dried and threshed. There are many mustard varieties worldwide, though three—the black, brown, and white (or yellow)—are the most popular.

Mustard seeds in India are usually tiny—much smaller than the types found in the United States—and come in colors ranging from reddish brown to a dark brown and are generally called black. In this book, I refer to the Indian variety simply as black mustard seeds. However, in most recipes the varieties are interchangeable because they have the same essential oils. I often make a colorful mustard seed mixture, similar to multi-colored peppercorn mixtures. Mustard seeds are almost fragrance-free and taste somewhat sharp, bitter, and hot. Once pan-cooked, they impart a mild, tangy flavor and a toasty, nutty fragrance. They are considered a good overall

therapeutic spice. They are believed to stimulate the appetite, act as a carminative (gas-reliever) and a diuretic, as well as relieve respiratory trouble.

Mustard greens (*sarson*) are generously endowed with vitamins A and C, and with iron and calcium. They are very strong tasting and are generally combined with other mild greens, such as spinach, to balance flavors. Mustard oil (*sarson ka tael*) is a natural preservative and is used extensively in chutneys and pickles, and for cooking.

Nutmeg and Mace

Jaiphul and *javitri.* Nutmeg and mace are two distinct spices obtained from the same apricot-like fruit of a tall evergreen tree. (The fruit itself is not eaten.) Nutmeg is a wrinkled, medium brown, 1-inch oval nut that lies nestled inside the thin, brittle, shiny outer shell of a ripe nutmeg seed. To get to the nutmeg, the shell has to be cracked open.

Mace is the lacy, web-like covering wrapped around the outside of the nutmeg shell. This brilliant scarlet-red aril is skillfully removed after the fruit bursts open, and is then flattened and dried to become brittle yellow-orange mace, as we know the spice.

Nutmeg has a rich, warm, citrusy, antiseptic fragrance and balances a bitter, yet sweet, flavor. Mace has a similar but much more defined and slightly more bitter flavor. Nutmeg and mace are both considered quite valuable in pharmaceutical preparations. They are narcotic and should not be consumed in large quantities. When used in moderation, they are considered a stimulant, carminative (gas-reliever), astringent, and aphrodisiac.

Paprika

Kashmiri degi mirch or *rang vaali mirch.* Indian paprika is the brilliant red powder made from mild, non-pungent red chiles. Used mainly for its color, this powder is almost devoid of heat because, even from these mild chiles, all the seeds and veins are removed before they are dried and ground. Most of the Indian paprika comes from Kashmir, hence the name, *Kashmiri degi mirch.* The mild Hungarian paprika is a good substitute. Rich in vitamin C and considered an appetite stimulant, paprika holds a place of honor in the Indian spice rack. It has a sweet chile-like aroma and a bitter aftertaste, which mellows dramatically after it is sizzled in oil.

Peppercorns

Kaali mirch. Black pepper, often known as the king of spices, is one of the oldest and probably the most popular spice known to humanity. The pepper plant is a branching evergreen creeper found mainly in the hot and humid monsoon forests of southwest India. The berries of this plant are called peppercorns. Ranging in color from green, black, and red to white, the peppercorns grow in clusters and are initially green. As they mature, they turn from green to yellow to orange to red. (They do not however, turn to black, as one would expect.) Black peppercorns are actually processed green peppercorns. This manual process involves picking the fully mature (but still unripe) green berries and drying them in the sun. As they dry, they shrivel up and take on the familiar brown-black color.

Green peppercorns are the small, soft, immature, caper-like berries, which are freeze-dried or brine-packed while they are still unripe and green. They have a very delicate flavor. White peppercorns are the fully ripe yellow-red berries, with their outer skin removed. They have a milder flavor but a stronger bite. Black peppercorns have a strong, fragrant, peppery hot bite and a rich, earthy aroma. Their heat, though, does not linger for too long. Their aroma and flavor increases dramatically after they are lightly dry-roasted and then coarsely ground. Prized as a home remedy for flatulence and sore throats (especially when mixed with honey), they are believed to clear the sinuses, stimulate the appetite, and aid digestion.

Pomegranate Seeds, Dried

Anaardana. Pomegranate seeds, used as a spice, are actually the sun-dried or dehydrated, fruity seeds and the flesh of a wild pomegranate tree. As they dry, the juicy flesh around the seeds forms a reddish-brown,

sticky coating with a tangy, fruity, sweet aroma and a predominantly sour, acidic taste. Pomegranate seeds are believed to cool the body, aid digestion, and relieve gas.

Poppy Seeds

Khas-khas. Indian poppy seeds are the tiny, pale yellow-white seeds of the opium-producing poppy plant. Contained in a capsule-like head that develops after the flower dies, the best poppy seeds in India come from the capsules from which opium has not been extracted. (Opium is the milky sap that oozes out once the capsule is open.) The seeds, however, are opium-free.

Poppy seeds come in three different colors: the familiar blue-gray from Europe, the brown from Turkey, and the pale yellow-white from India. All these are very similar in taste and flavor and can be used interchangeably in recipes where color is not important. Raw poppy seeds have a light and sweet aroma, and a pronounced, nutty, almond-like flavor. They are cooling to the body, high in protein, and are considered cures for fever, thirst, stomach irritation, and insomnia.

Rose Water and Essence

Gulaab jal and *ruh gulaab.* Rose water and rose essence are made from the petals of specially cultivated, highly fragrant, deep pink-red roses, called *succha* or pure *gulaab.* Rose water, as the name suggests, looks just like water but exudes a strong, sweet, rosy fragrance. Rose essence is a concentrated version of rose water and, like other flavors and essences, is available in small bottles. Two drops of rose essence are equivalent to 1 tablespoon of rose water.

Saffron

Kaesar or *zaffron.* Saffron threads are the dried orange to deep-red stigmas and tips of the saffron crocus, a member of the iris family. Most of the Indian saffron comes from Kashmir. Saffron has a distinctly warm, rich, powerful, and enticing bouquet and a characteristic bitter taste. It imparts an exotic fragrance and a favored yellow color to all dishes. This color shows up best in the paler milk-based desserts and sauces, and in *pullaos* (pilafs). Saffron is believed to be cooling to the body and, in addition to other things, acts as a stimulant, especially for the heart and brain. In large doses, however, saffron is a narcotic.

Screwpine Essence

Kewda or *ruh kewra*. Screwpine is the essence made from the flowers of a tropical tree with narrow, sword-like leaves. This concentrated clear liquid exudes a delicate floral or piney perfume, which is subtly different from rose essence but is used in much the same way.

Sesame Seeds and Oil

Til or *gingelly*. Sesame seeds are the tiny, smooth, oval, flat seeds of an annual tropical herb. These popular oilseeds (they are used for making oil) come in white, brown, and black colors, are almost fragrance-free and mildly sweet, but when dry-roasted, they provide a rich, nutty fragrance and taste. They are high in protein and calcium and are believed to have a warming effect on the body. They are considered beneficial to the respiratory, digestive, and female reproductive systems.

Sesame oil, also known as *gingelly* oil, is a popular oil used in cooking in southern Indian cuisine and has properties similar to olive oil.

Silver Leaves

Chandi ka verk or *vark*. Not a true spice, but used as a garnish the way some other seasonings are, silver leaves are an integral part of North Indian cuisine. These 4- to 6-inch squares, made with pure silver, are formed by sandwiching thin sheets of silver between layers of ordinary paper and pounding them until they are paper thin, weightless, and indescribably delicate. Today it is done with rollers.

When a recipe calls for *verk*, pick up one sheet of paper with its clinging silver leaf and carefully lay it,

silver side down, on the dish to be garnished. As you do this, the silver will adhere to the dish and the paper can then be lifted off.

Star Anise

Badian, badiyan, dodhful, dodphul, and *anasphal*. Star anise is the dried mahogany-colored, 8-pointed, star-shaped fruit of a large evergreen tree. Each of the eight tips of this star has a bead-like seed. Star anise has a sweet flavor, reminiscent of fennel and anise, even though it is no relation to them. Star anise is considered to be carminative (gas-relieving) and good for the stomach and intestines.

Tamarind

Imli. Tamarind, also known as Indian dates, are the buff to dark brown, sticky fruits contained inside the bean-shaped pods of the evergreen tamarind tree. Covering the fruit is a brittle, buff-brown shell and inside the pulp are flat, shiny, ½-inch seeds. Tamarind has a mild, fruity, sweet and sour fragrance, and a predominantly acidic, sour, and slightly sweet taste. Tamarind is rich in minerals and vitamins, especially vitamin C, and is considered a natural body cooler. It may aid digestion, and can relieve colds and throat infections (especially when used as a gargle). It is a mild laxative and stomach soother.

Turmeric

Haldi. Turmeric, a bright yellow-orange powder in the form we know, is actually the boiled, peeled, sun-dried rhizome of a tropical plant of the ginger family. The rhizome, similar in size and shape to fresh ginger, has short "fingers" and bright orange flesh. Turmeric has a warm, peppery aroma, reminiscent of ginger, and a strong, bitter taste that really mellows upon cooking. This spice is also probably one of the most valuable everyday spices of Indian cuisine. Considered a natural antiseptic, an anti-inflammatory, and a blood purifier, turmeric is used as a home cure to relieve everything from upset stomachs to aches and pains.

Spice Blends

Authentic Indian cooking is about using spices to the dictates of your own taste, and about understanding how to combine them to create a variety of flavors, whether cooking with blends made from scratch or with pre-packaged blends. Indian cuisine features many, many different spice combinations, each for a specific purpose—to impart a specific flavor, or to provide therapeutic benefits, or even a little of both. This is the essence of Indian cuisine.

Here, I give you a few useful spice combinations—some classic, some of my own making—that will make life in the kitchen a little more interesting and a lot more convenient, because once you have the spices mixed and ready to go, you can use them whenever the need arises. Remember that all the recipes I've included here are meant to be guidelines. Once you are comfortable with making your own blends, feel free to improvise.

Curry Powders

Curries (dishes with a sauce) are characterized by unique flavors that are achieved by combining selected wet and dry ingredients. The "wet" comes from grinding fresh ingredients such as onions, ginger, garlic, tomatoes, and fresh herbs into a paste. The "dry" comes from dried spices, herbs, and nuts. Curry powder is not a single spice from the curry plant but a mixture of anywhere from 5 to 15 spices that adds flavor and interest to curries. The primary blend was put together by the British to recreate the flavorful curries they had come to enjoy during they stay in India. Indian cooks, however, prefer the creative freedom of adding spices by the spoonful, at different stages during cooking, to achieve a range of flavors which would otherwise be impossible. Be aware that there are plenty of curry powder blend possibilities and each one is different from the other.

Basic Curry Powder
Kari ka Masala

Makes about 1¹/₂ cups

You can buy your curry powder at the market or make this simple mixture of spices that I use in my kitchen.

1 cup ground coriander seeds
¹/₃ cup ground cumin seeds
2 tablespoons ground turmeric
1 tablespoon ground paprika
1 tablespoon ground cayenne pepper (optional)
1 tablespoon ground dried fenugreek leaves

Put all the spices in a bowl and mix them together with a spoon. Store in an airtight container in a cool, dark place, about 1 month at room temperature or about 1 year in the refrigerator.

15-Spice Curry Powder
Kari ka Masala

Makes about 2 cups

Try this fragrant curry powder when you want complex flavors in everyday home dishes, such as Minty or any other Potato Curry (pages 403 to 407), Spinach or any other Kofta Balls Curry (pages 417 to 419), or any chicken or meat curry. It starts with my Basic Curry Powder, but has a lot more spices.

1 recipe Basic Curry Powder (above)
1 tablespoon ground fennel seeds
1 tablespoon ground black cardamom seeds
1 tablespoon ground green cardamom seeds
1 tablespoon ground dried ginger
1 tablespoon ground fenugreek seeds
1 tablespoon ground black peppercorns
1 teaspoon ground cinnamon
1 teaspoon ground cloves
1 teaspoon ground nutmeg

Put all the spices in a bowl and mix them together with a spoon. Store in an airtight container in a cool, dark place, about 1 month at room temperature or about 1 year in the refrigerator.

Kashmiri Curry Powder with Fennel Seeds and Ginger

Kashmiri Kari ka Masala

Makes about 2 cups

Foods from the northern state of Kashmir tend to have a distinct taste, built upon the flavors of fennel seeds and dried ginger. Saffron, nutmeg, and mace are other favorite Kashmiri spices.

2 tablespoons mustard or vegetable oil
8 to 12 dried red chile peppers, such as chile de arbol, broken
4 to 5 large cloves fresh garlic, minced
1/2 cup fennel seeds
1/4 cup cumin seeds
1/4 cup fenugreek seeds
2 tablespoons black cardamom seeds
2 tablespoons green cardamom seeds
10 bay leaves, coarsely broken
1 teaspoon saffron threads
3 tablespoons ground ginger
1 tablespoon ground paprika
2 teaspoons ground cinnamon
1 teaspoon ground cloves
1 teaspoon ground mace
1 teaspoon ground nutmeg

1. In a medium cast-iron or nonstick wok or skillet, heat the oil over medium heat and stir the red chile peppers and garlic until golden, 1 minute. Add the fennel, cumin, fenugreek, black and green cardamom, bay leaves, and saffron, and roast, stirring and shaking the pan, until the mixture turns a few shades darker, about 2 minutes.

2. Let cool, then grind in a spice or coffee grinder to make a very fine powder. Place in a bowl and mix in the ginger, paprika, cinnamon, cloves, mace, and nutmeg. Store in an airtight container in a cool, dark place, about 1 week at room temperature or about 1 year in the refrigerator.

South Indian Curry Powder with Rice and Dal

Kootupodi

Makes about 2 cups

Popularly called kootupodi, *this blend, which has a delicate aroma and a hot chile pepper punch, is used more as a thickener for curries and soups than as a stand-alone flavor enhancer. It may seem strange to use rice and legumes (*dal*) as spices, but they have been used this way for centuries in India—they add texture, substance, and flavor to the dishes. Parboiled rice is available at Indian markets (and some supermarkets).*

1 cup parboiled (converted) rice
1/4 cup dried white urad beans (dhulli urad dal), sorted
1/4 cup fenugreek seeds
10 to 12 dried red chile peppers, such as chile de arbol, broken
1/2 cup coriander seeds

1. In a medium cast-iron or nonstick skillet, roast the rice, dal, fenugreek seeds, and red chile peppers over medium-low heat, stirring until golden, about 10 minutes. Mix in the coriander seeds and stir until heated through.

2. Cool and grind in a spice or coffee grinder to make a powder. Store in an airtight container in a cool, dark place, about 1 month at room temperature or about 1 year in the refrigerator.

Gujarati Curry Powder with Coriander and Cumin

Dhana-Jeera Masala

Makes about 1 1/4 cups

One of the most basic blends found in northwestern India, dhana-jeera, or coriander and cumin blend, is almost like a curry powder. Use it liberally in just about all curries and side dishes. Sizzle the blend lightly in oil and mix in whatever vegetables and meats you desire.

1/4 cup cumin seeds
1 cup coriander seeds
1 tablespoon cayenne pepper

1. In a medium cast-iron or nonstick skillet, roast the cumin seeds, stirring and shaking the pan over medium heat until a highly fragrant smoke arises and the seeds are a few shades darker, 2 to 3 minutes. Add the coriander seeds and roast until they are just heated through, about 1 minute.

2. Let cool, then grind in a spice or a coffee grinder to make a fine powder. Transfer the mixture to a bowl and mix in the cayenne pepper. Store in an airtight container in a cool, dark place, about 1 month at room temperature or about 1 year in the refrigerator.

Marathi Curry Powder with Coconut and Sesame Seeds

Goda Masala

Makes about 2 cups

This complex blend of spices, with its touch of coconut, is specific to the western state of Maharashtra, where Mumbai (Bombay) is the largest city. Sizzle it in oil and use it to make curries and dry-cooked vegetable dishes.

1/4 cup shredded unsweetened dried coconut
1 cup coriander seeds
1/4 cup cumin seeds
1/4 cup white sesame seeds
2 tablespoons black mustard seeds
1 teaspoon black cumin seeds
1 tablespoon cayenne pepper
1 tablespoon salt, or to taste
1 teaspoon ground turmeric
1 teaspoon ground asafoetida

1. In a medium cast-iron or nonstick skillet, roast the coconut, coriander seeds, cumin seeds, white sesame seeds, black mustard seeds, and black cumin seeds, stirring constantly, initially over high and then over medium heat until golden and fragrant, 2 to 3 minutes. Let cool, then grind in a spice or coffee grinder to make a fine powder.

2. Return to the skillet, mix in the cayenne pepper, salt, turmeric, and asafoetida, and stir over medium heat until heated through, about 1 minute. Let cool completely and store in an airtight container in a cool, dark place, about 1 month at room temperature or about 1 year in the refrigerator.

Goan Curry Powder

Goa ka Shakuti Masala

Makes about 1 1/2 cups

Shakuti, often spelled xacuti, *is a traditional Goan meat or chicken curry that calls for coconut and many, many spices. Because of the number of spices, I make this blend in large quantities so it's ready whenever I wish to make this curry. To use, pan-cook in oil, add the meat, then stir until the meat browns and finishes cooking.*

3/4 cup grated fresh or frozen coconut or shredded unsweetened dried coconut
1/4 cup thinly sliced fresh garlic cloves
8 to 10 quarter-size slices of peeled fresh ginger
3 to 5 fresh green chile peppers, such as serrano, thinly sliced
1/4 cup coriander seeds
2 tablespoons white poppy seeds
1 tablespoon cumin seeds
1 tablespoon black peppercorns
1 teaspoon black cumin seeds
1 teaspoon fennel seeds
1 teaspoon ajwain seeds
15 dried red chile peppers, such as chile de arbol, broken
8 to 10 green cardamom pods, lightly crushed to break the skin
8 to 10 star anise, broken
1 2-inch stick cinnamon, broken
10 whole cloves
1 teaspoon ground turmeric
1 teaspoon ground nutmeg

1. In a medium cast-iron or nonstick wok or skillet, roast the coconut, stirring and shaking the skillet over medium-low heat, until the coconut is crispy and golden, 7 to 10 minutes. If the coconut is not crispy after 10 minutes, lower the heat further to avoid browning, and carefully watch for the next few minutes until the coconut becomes crispy. Transfer to a bowl.

2. In the same skillet, place the garlic, ginger, and green chile peppers and dry-roast, stirring and shaking the pan over low heat until most of the moisture evaporates and the mixture is golden, 7 to 10 minutes. Add to the coconut.

3. Place the remaining spices in the skillet and dry-roast over medium-low heat, stirring and shaking the pan until golden and highly fragrant, 7 to 10 minutes. Let cool, mix all ingredients together, and grind in a spice or coffee grinder to make a fine powder. Store in an airtight container about 3 months in the refrigerator or about 1 year in the freezer.

Garam Masalas

Garam Masala
Garam Masala

Makes about 1¹/₂ cups

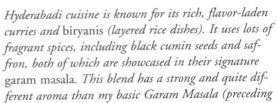

Garam masala, *meaning hot spices in Hindi, is a dark brown, spicy-hot blend that is believed to induce internal heat in the body. Made with four basic spices—cloves, cinnamon, black and/or green cardamom, and black peppercorns—garam masala is available in many different forms. Every region—in fact, every family—has its own unique variation. Just a pinch of this* masala, *sprinkled over dishes as a garnish before serving, adds tremendous fragrance and flavor. It also adds complex nuances to dry-rubs and marinades. Garam masala is now found even in supermarkets, but homemade is always preferred.*

¹/₃ cup ground cinnamon
¹/₃ cup ground freshly black pepper
¹/₄ cup ground black cardamom seeds
¹/₄ cup ground cloves
3 tablespoons ground green cardamom seeds

In a medium cast-iron or nonstick skillet, roast together all the spices, stirring and shaking the pan

over medium heat until heated through, about 2 minutes. Let cool, then store in an airtight container in a cool, dark place, about 1 month at room temperature or about 1 year in the refrigerator.

Hyderabadi Garam Masala with Black Cumin Seeds
Hyderabad ka Garam Masala

Makes about 1¹/₂ cup

Hyderabadi cuisine is known for its rich, flavor-laden curries and biryanis *(layered rice dishes). It uses lots of fragrant spices, including black cumin seeds and saffron, both of which are showcased in their signature garam masala. This blend has a strong and quite different aroma than my basic Garam Masala (preceding recipe), but the two can be used interchangeably.*

2 teaspoons saffron threads dry-roasted and ground (Dry-Roasting Spices, page 35)
¹/₄ cup freshly ground black pepper
¹/₄ cup ground black cumin seeds
¹/₄ cup ground cloves
¹/₄ cup ground cinnamon
¹/₄ cup ground green cardamom seeds

Prepare the saffron. Then, in a medium cast-iron or nonstick skillet, roast together all the spices, stirring and shaking the pan over medium heat until heated through, about 2 minutes. Let cool, then store in an airtight container in a cool, dark place, about 1 month at room temperature or about 1 year in the refrigerator.

Mughlai Garam Masala with Nutmeg and Mace
Mughlai Garam Masala

Makes about 1¹/₂ cups

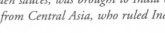

Mughlai cuisine, featuring tandoori *foods and fragrant cream-laden sauces, was brought to India by the Moghuls from Central Asia, who ruled India from*

1526 to 1857. Their characteristic richness also comes from this vibrant garam masala.

- **1 tablespoon saffron threads, dry-roasted and ground (Dry-Roasting Spices, page 35)**
- **¼ cup freshly ground black pepper**
- **¼ cup ground cumin seeds**
- **2 tablespoons ground black cumin seeds**
- **2 tablespoons ground cinnamon**
- **2 tablespoons ground cloves**
- **2 tablespoons ground green cardamom seeds**
- **2 tablespoons ground black cardamom seeds**
- **2 tablespoons ground ginger**
- **1 tablespoon ground bay leaves**
- **1 teaspoon ground mace**
- **1 teaspoon ground nutmeg**

Prepare the saffron. Then, in a medium cast-iron or nonstick skillet, roast all the spices together, stirring and shaking the pan over medium heat until heated through, about 2 minutes. Let cool, then store in an airtight container in a cool, dark place, about 1 month at room temperature or about 1 year in the refrigerator.

Parsi Garam Masala with Star Anise

Parsi Garam Masala

Makes about 1½ cups

This distinctive spice blend comes from one of India's most historic communities—the Zoroastrians, popularly known as the Parsis, who migrated to India from Iran and settled near Bombay in the west-central part of India. The Parsis are avid meat, chicken, fish, and egg eaters, and their foods reflect a strong Iranian influence, shown in their use of rice and nuts, mingled with the locally available coconut and spices.

- **⅓ cup ground green cardamom seeds**
- **¼ cup ground cinnamon**
- **¼ cup ground black peppercorns**
- **¼ cup ground cumin**
- **3 tablespoons ground star anise**
- **2 tablespoons ground cloves**

In a medium cast-iron or nonstick skillet, roast together all the spices, stirring and shaking the pan over medium heat until heated through, about 2 minutes. Let cool, then store in an airtight container in a cool, dark place, about 1 month at room temperature or about 1 year in the refrigerator.

Kashmiri Garam Masala

Kashmir ka Garam Masala

Makes 1½ cups

Situated on the northernmost tip of India, the valley of Kashmir is full of natural beauty, with mountains, small streams, and lakes dotting the countryside. This vibrant, complex garam masala mixture evokes this rich and fragrant land. Use it sparingly, with hearty meat, poultry, and seafood preparations.

- **½ cup fennel seeds**
- **¼ cup black cumin seeds**
- **¼ cup black peppercorns**
- **2 tablespoons green cardamom seeds**
- **1 teaspoon saffron threads**
- **1 tablespoon ground cinnamon**
- **1 tablespoon ground ginger**
- **1 tablespoon ground cloves**
- **1 teaspoon ground mace**
- **1 teaspoon ground nutmeg**

1. In a medium cast-iron or nonstick skillet, roast together the fennel and cumin seeds, peppercorns, cardamom seeds, and saffron threads, stirring and shaking the pan over medium heat until heated through, about 2 minutes.

2. Let cool, then grind in a spice or coffee grinder to make a fine powder. Transfer to a bowl and mix in the cinnamon, ginger, cloves, mace, and nutmeg. Transfer the mixture back to the skillet and roast over medium heat until heated through once more. Let cool, then store in an airtight container in a cool, dark place about 1 month at room temperature or about 1 year in the refrigerator.

Chaat Masala

Chaat Masala

Makes about 1¹/₂ cup

Chaat is the term to describe salads or snack dishes infused with a complex mix of sweet, salty, tangy, and spicy flavors, and always seasoned with some form of the spice blend called chaat masala. *This classic spice blend is made with an unrivaled combination of some of India's most intriguing herbs and spices, featuring mango powder, dry-roasted cumin seeds, and black salt at its base. Of course, there are count- less variations throughout India. Home cooks and professional chefs also use it to jazz up salads, fresh fruits, and fruit juices, and it can be added to dishes to "save" them when their flavors don't seem to be quite right. In this one rare instance, if not using homemade, I recommend trying commercially pack- aged* chaat masala *sold at Indian supermarkets. I like the MDH brand.*

¹/₃ tablespoons cumin seeds, dry-roasted and ground (Dry-Roasting Spices, page 35)
¹/₄ cup mango powder
3 tablespoons dried mint leaves, ground
2 tablespoons tamarind powder
2 tablespoons ground ginger
2 tablespoons ground ajwain seeds
1 to 2 tablespoons salt, or to taste
1 tablespoon ground black salt
1 tablespoon citric acid
1 to 3 teaspoons cayenne pepper, or to taste
1 teaspoon ground asafoetida

Prepare the cumin seeds. Then, in a medium cast-iron or nonstick skillet, roast together all the spices, stirring and shaking the pan over medium heat until heated through, about 2 minutes. Let cool, then store in an airtight container in a cool, dark place, about 1 month at room temperature or about 1 year in the refrigerator.

New Delhi Street Food Masala

Papri Chaat Masala

Makes 1¹/₂ cups

Papri Chaat *(Flour Chips with Yogurt and Mango Powder Chutney, page 142)* is a special snack made with crispy flour chips, yogurt, and a spicy sauce. Its incredible flavors come from a set of spices that are sprinkled on top after the dish has been assembled. This mixture is also delicious in other chaats, *such as Crispy Puffs with Potatoes and Spicy Yogurt (page 140)* as well as in salads and raitas *such as Crispy Urad Dal Croquettes in Yogurt (page 238).*

¹/₂ cup cumin seeds
1 tablespoon ajwain seeds
3 tablespoons mango powder
3 tablespoons tamarind powder
3 tablespoons ground dried mint leaves
1 tablespoon ground ginger
1 tablespoon ground black salt
1 tablespoon salt, or to taste
1 tablespoon cayenne pepper, or to taste

1. In a medium cast-iron or nonstick skillet, roast together the cumin and ajwain seeds, stirring and shaking the pan over medium heat until the spices are a few shades darker, about 2 minutes. Transfer to a bowl.

2. Let cool, then grind in a spice or coffee grinder to make a fine powder. Return the mixture to the skil- let and add the mango and tamarind powder, mint leaves, ginger, black salt, salt, and cayenne pepper.

3. Roast once again over medium heat until heated through, about 1 minute. Let cool, then store in an airtight container in a cool, dark place, about 1 month at room temperature or about 1 year in the refrigerator.

Bombay Bread-Snack Masala

Pav-Bhaji ka Masala

Makes about 1½ cups

From the streets of Mumbai (Bombay) comes an immensely popular snack, called pav-bhaji *(bread and vegetables), which gets its uniqueness from this special spice blend.*

½ cup freshly ground black pepper
1 to 2 tablespoons cayenne pepper, or to taste
⅓ cup ground coriander seeds
⅓ cup ground cumin
1½ teaspoons ground turmeric
1½ teaspoons ground cinnamon
1½ teaspoons ground black cardamom seeds
1½ teaspoons ground cloves
1½ teaspoons ground asafoetida

In a medium cast-iron or nonstick skillet, roast all the spices, stirring and shaking the skillet over medium heat, until the mixture is fragrant and golden, about 2 minutes. Let cool, then store in an airtight container in a cool, dark place, about 1 month at room temperature or about 1 year in the refrigerator.

Minty Cumin-Water Masala

Jeera Paani Masala

Makes 1½ cups

This blend is specifically used for making Spicy Tamarind Water with Mint and Roasted Cumin, or jeera paani *as it is called in Hindi—which literally means "cumin water." Occasionally it is used in place of* chaat masala *over special* chaats, *salads, and* yogurt raitas. *Also try it over fresh fruit juices. To use, mix 1 to 2 teaspoons of this masala into a tall glass of ice water, and add 1 to 2 teaspoons minced fresh mint leaves. Serve as a spicy summer beverage with brunch, or at your next cook-out.*

⅓ cup cumin seeds
1 tablespoon black cumin seeds
2 teaspoons ajwain seeds
1 teaspoon vegetable oil
1 teaspoon ground asafoetida
½ cup dried mango or tamarind powder, sifted
¼ cup ground dried mint leaves
1 tablespoon ground ginger
2 teaspoons ground black salt
1 teaspoon dried cayenne pepper, or to taste
1 tablespoon salt, or to taste
1 teaspoon freshly ground black pepper, or to taste

1. In a medium cast-iron or nonstick wok or skillet, roast together the cumin seeds, black cumin seeds, and ajwain seeds, stirring and shaking the pan over medium heat until heated through, about 2 minutes. Remove the skillet from the heat. Let cool, then grind in a spice or coffee grinder to make a fine powder.

2. Heat the oil in a small nonstick saucepan over medium-high heat and add the asafoetida. It will sizzle upon contact with the hot oil. Quickly add the ground spice mixture and all the remaining spices. Mix well and stir until heated through, about 2 minutes. Let cool, then store in an airtight container in a cool, dark place, about 1 month at room temperature or about 1 year in the refrigerator.

Masala for Griddle-Fried Breads

Parantha Masala

Makes 1½ cups

A visually appealing green herb blend, this masala *flavors* parantha *(griddle-fried breads). To use, add this spice blend inside each* parantha *bread as you roll it, or sprinkle about ¼ teaspoon over each* parantha *just as you remove it from the griddle.*

⅓ cup ground dried fenugreek leaves
⅓ cup ground dried mint leaves
⅓ cup black peppercorns, coarsely ground
¼ cup ajwain seeds, coarsely ground
1 tablespoon black salt (optional)
1 tablespoon salt, or to taste

In a small bowl, mix together all the spices with a spoon and store in an airtight container in a cool, dry place, about 1 month at room temperature or about 1 year in the refrigerator.

Masala for Stuffed Griddle-Fried Breads

Bharvaan Parantha ka Masala

Makes 1¹/₂ cups

Made specifically as a seasoning to be added to various stuffings for griddle-fried parantha *breads, this spice blend is also exceptional as a last-minute garnish on non-Indian dishes such as mashed potatoes, fajitas, and hamburger patties.*

¹/₂ cup ground coriander seeds
¹/₄ cup ground dried pomegranate seeds
2 tablespoons ajwain seeds, coarsely ground
2 tablespoons mango powder
2 tablespoons ground dried mint leaves
1 tablespoon cayenne pepper
1 tablespoon garam masala
1 tablespoon ground ginger
1 tablespoon black salt
1 tablespoon salt, or to taste
1 teaspoon ground nutmeg
1 teaspoon ground mace

In a small bowl, mix together all the spices with a spoon and store in an airtight container in a cool, dry place, about 1 month at room temperature or about 1 year in the refrigerator.

Roasted Chile Pepper and Red Peppercorn Masala

Bhuna Mirchi ka Masala

Makes about ¹/₂ cup

This one has a lot of heat, so use it carefully and sparingly, adding as much or as little as you or your

guests can tolerate. It is indispensable as a last-minute perker-upper for soups, sandwiches, salads, or anything else you care to add it to.

1 tablespoon vegetable oil
15 to 20 dried red chile peppers, such as chile de arbol, broken
2 tablespoons red peppercorns
2 to 4 tablespoons ground paprika
1 teaspoon salt, or to taste

1. In a medium cast-iron or nonstick wok or skillet, heat the oil over medium heat and roast the chile peppers, stirring and shaking the pan, until crispy and a few shades darker, 1 to 2 minutes. (This process is best done outside the house, if possible, as the rising smoke may spread and linger, causing throat irritation. Otherwise, use a stove vent and keep windows open.) Transfer to a bowl.

2. Add the red peppercorns and roast until heated through, but do not brown them. Add to the chile peppers. Let cool, then grind in a spice or coffee grinder to make a fine powder. Mix in the paprika and salt and store in an airtight container in a cool, dark place, about 1 month at room temperature or about 1 year in the refrigerator.

Roasted Cumin and Fenugreek Masala

Bhuna Jeera aur Methi ka Masala

Makes about 1 cup

Used primarily in spicy tamarind-based sauces, this is another one of India's prized spice blends. The combination of the smoky dry-roasted cumin seeds, the bitter fenugreek seeds, and the spicy red chile peppers creates a perfect balance with the fruity sweet-and-sour tamarind, and makes for a delicious sauce. Try adding a teaspoon or two to vegetables such as Anaheim or bell peppers, tomatoes, okra, and eggplants.

1/4 cup cumin seeds

2 tablespoons fenugreek seeds

12 to 15 dried red chile peppers, such as chile de arbol, broken

2 teaspoons salt, or to taste

1 teaspoon ground turmeric

1. In a medium cast-iron or nonstick skillet, roast together the cumin seeds, fenugreek seeds, and red chile peppers over medium heat, stirring and shaking the pan until a few shades darker and highly fragrant, about 2 minutes.

2. Let cool, then grind in a spice or coffee grinder to make a fine powder. Mix in the salt and turmeric and store in an airtight container in a cool, dark place, about 1 month at room temperature or about 1 year in the refrigerator.

Roasted Cumin-Pepper Masala

Bhuna Jeera aur Kaali-Mirch ka Masala

Makes 1/2 cup

The flavor of this mixture is superb on salads and yogurt raitas, *as well as over freshly made, hot* paranthas *(griddle-fried breads) and grilled sandwiches. My mother roasted and ground her spices every time she needed them, but in America I keep a ready supply of roasted spices in a separate pepper mill. With a few twists of the wrist, you get fresh flavor in a flash.*

1/4 cup cumin seeds

3 tablespoons black peppercorns

1 tablespoon hot red pepper flakes, or to taste

1. In a small cast-iron or nonstick skillet, roast separately the cumin seeds, the peppercorns, and the red pepper flakes, over medium heat, stirring and shaking the pan until fragrant and a few shades darker, about 2 minutes each for the cumin and the peppercorns, and just a few seconds for the red chile flakes.

2. Mix together the roasted cumin, peppercorns and red pepper flakes. Let cool, then put in your pepper mill. Grind and use as necessary. Or, grind coarsely in a spice or coffee grinder, store in an airtight container in a cool, dark place, about 1 month at room temperature or about 1 year in the refrigerator.

Punjabi Raita and Buttermilk Masala

Punjabi Raita aur Lussi ka Masala

Makes about 1/3 cup

Meant to liven up dairy dishes and beverages, the fragrance of this blend is very uplifting. I also love it as a last-minute sprinkle over pakoras *(batter-fried fritters) and grilled foods. Or, sprinkle some over freshly chopped salad vegetables such as cucumber, daikon radishes, or tomatoes, and then top with fresh lime or lemon juice.*

1/4 cup cumin seeds, dry-roasted and coarsely ground (Dry-Roasting Spices, page 35)

1 tablespoon black peppercorns, dry-roasted and coarsely ground (Dry-Roasting Spices, page 35)

1 tablespoon coarsely ground dried mint leaves

1 teaspoon ground paprika

1 teaspoon salt, or to taste

In a bowl, mix together all the spices with a spoon and store in an airtight container in a cool, dry place, about 1 month at room temperature or about 1 year in the refrigerator.

Kashmiri Raita Masala

Kashmir ka Raita Masala

Makes about ¹/₂ cup

Kashmiri foods have a unique fragrance about them, coming from fennel seeds and dried ginger (called sund). Here is a mixture that will lend that aroma to your food. It's added by the spoonful to raitas *and pan-cooked vegetables, to lend them that special scent.*

¹/₄ cup coriander seeds
2 tablespoons fennel seeds
2 tablespoons cumin seeds
2 rice-size pieces asafoetida
1 tablespoon black mustard seeds
2 teaspoons ground ginger
¹/₂ to 1 teaspoon cayenne pepper
1 teaspoon salt, or to taste

1. In a medium cast-iron or nonstick skillet, roast together the coriander seeds, and fennel seeds and cumin seeds, stirring and shaking the pan over medium heat until heated through, about 2 minutes. Transfer to a bowl.

2. In the same skillet, dry-roast the asafoetida and the mustard seeds until they start to pop, about 1 minute. (Cover pan momentarily to contain popping, if needed.) Mix into the coriander-fennel-cumin mixture.

3. Let cool, then grind in a spice or coffee grinder to make a fine powder. Mix in the ginger, cayenne pepper, and salt. Store in an airtight container in a cool, dark place, about 1 month at room temperature or about 1 year in the refrigerator.

Masala Blends for Special Dishes

Chickpea Masala with Pomegranate Seeds

Channa Masala

Makes about 1¹/₂ cups

Used throughout India, channa masala *is a popular spice mixture mainly because* channas *(chickpeas), though a specialty of the north, are well-liked in all parts of the country. My* channa masala *is different from the prepackaged blends available in Indian markets because I dry-roast some of the spices. Dry-roasting brings out the complex flavors of the combination of tangy, aromatic, and hot spices. What you find in the markets is more like a curry powder perked up with lots of hot chile powder and a few other spices.*

   Channa masala, *though primarily used to flavor chickpea dishes, is versatile enough to be used in other dishes as well, such as Chickpea Masala Chicken (page 451).*

¹/₂ cup ground cumin
2 tablespoons ground dried pomegranate seeds
2 tablespoons tamarind or mango powder
1 tablespoon ground black cardamom seeds
1 tablespoon ground dried fenugreek leaves
1 tablespoon freshly ground black pepper, or to taste
1 tablespoon cayenne pepper, or to taste
2 teaspoons ground ajwain seeds
1 teaspoon ground cinnamon
1 teaspoon ground cloves
1 teaspoon ground ginger
1 teaspoon ground asafoetida
1 teaspoon ground nutmeg
¹/₂ teaspoon ground mace
¹/₂ cup ground coriander seeds
1 tablespoon ground black salt
1 teaspoon ground turmeric

In a medium cast-iron or nonstick skillet, roast together all the ingredients except the coriander, black salt, and turmeric, stirring and shaking the pan over medium heat until heated through, about 2 minutes. Reduce the heat to low and stir until dark brown and fragrant, about 3 minutes. Remove from the heat and mix in the coriander, black salt, and turmeric. Let cool completely, then store in an airtight container in a cool, dark place, about 1 month at room temperature or about 1 year in the refrigerator.

Fragrant Masala with Nuts
Korma Masala

Makes about 1¹/₂ cups

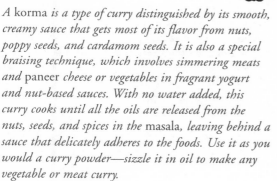

A korma *is a type of curry distinguished by its smooth, creamy sauce that gets most of its flavor from nuts, poppy seeds, and cardamom seeds. It is also a special braising technique, which involves simmering meats and* paneer *cheese or vegetables in fragrant yogurt and nut-based sauces. With no water added, this curry cooks until all the oils are released from the nuts, seeds, and spices in the* masala, *leaving behind a sauce that delicately adheres to the foods. Use it as you would a curry powder—sizzle it in oil to make any vegetable or meat curry.*

¹/₄ **cup each: shelled and finely ground raw pistachios, almonds, and cashews nuts**
2 **tablespoons white poppy seeds**
2 **tablespoons ground ginger**
2 **tablespoons ground green cardamom seeds**
1 **tablespoon ground black cardamom seeds**
1 **tablespoon ground cinnamon**
1 **tablespoon ground black pepper**
1 **teaspoon ground cloves**

In a medium cast-iron or nonstick skillet, roast together all the ingredients, stirring and shaking the pan over medium heat until heated through, about 2 minutes. Let cool, then store in an airtight container in a cool, dark place, about 1 week at room temperature or about 1 year in the refrigerator.

Indian Grilling Masala
Tandoori Masala

Makes about 1¹/₂ cups

A tandoor *is a barrel-shaped clay oven that was introduced to India by the Moghul emperors (of Mughlai cuisine fame). Today,* tandoors *have become an integral part of Indian cuisine, not so much in the home, but in eateries and restaurants specializing in North Indian cuisine, all over India and the world.* Tandoori *foods are usually associated with a specific flavor, which comes from the live coals in the* tandoor *and from a special set of spices that are specially blended for them.* Tandoori masala *brings these flavors closer to home cooks. Try this* masala *as a dry-rub for chicken, meat, or seafood, or in a tangy yogurt and lime juice marinade for* paneer *cheese, or for vegetables such as cauliflower, bell peppers, and mushrooms. Authentic* tandoori masala *colors every food red—which may or may not be to your liking (it isn't to mine), so it pays to make your own. For the red effect, add a few drops of red or orange food coloring to the actual marinade.*

1 **cup Mughlai Garam Masala with Nutmeg and Mace (page 18)**
¹/₄ **cup ground dried fenugreek leaves**
2 **tablespoons ground fenugreek seeds**
1 **to 2 tablespoons cayenne pepper, or to taste**
1 **tablespoon ground paprika**
1 **teaspoon ground turmeric**

Prepare the Mughlai masala. Put all the spices in a bowl and mix them together with a spoon. Store in an airtight container in a cool and dark place, about 1 month at room temperature or about 1 year in the refrigerator.

Spicy Masala for Wok-Cooked Foods
Kadhai Masala

Makes about 1¹/₄ cups

Associated with meat, vegetable, and paneer *cheese dishes made in a heavy, round-bottomed wok known as the* kadhai, *this blend, though very much like a curry powder, is known and marketed specifically for its outstanding fragrance. To use, pan-cook sliced onion, ginger, garlic, and bell peppers, add 1 to 2 tablespoons of the spice mixture, and cook, stirring, until fragrant. Add your choice of meat, vegetable, or* paneer *cheese and finish cooking.*

¹/₂ cup coarsely ground coriander seeds
2 tablespoons ground dried fenugreek leaves
2 tablespoons ground dried mint leaves
2 tablespoons ground cumin seeds
1 tablespoon ground fennel seeds
1 tablespoon ground ginger
1 tablespoon mango powder
1 tablespoon ground dried pomegranate seeds
1 tablespoon cayenne pepper
1 teaspoon ground paprika
1 teaspoon ground black cardamom seeds
1 teaspoon ground nutmeg
1 teaspoon ground black salt

Put all the spices in a small bowl and mix them together with a spoon. Store in an airtight container in a cool, dark place, about 1 month at room temperature or about 1 year in the refrigerator.

Gujarati Lentil Masala
Dhansak Masala

Makes about 2¹/₂ cups

Dhansak *is a signature Parsi dish made primarily with* dal *(legumes) and vegetables. Dhan means dal in the Gujarati language, which is spoken by the Parsis, and sak means vegetables. In addition to these two basics, most* dhansak *dishes also contain chicken, lamb, or some other meat. This unique blend is the underlying taste in all* dhansak *dishes. Try it in place of curry powder in other recipes.*

1 cup coriander seeds
¹/₄ cup cumin seeds
1 tablespoon black cumin seeds
¹/₄ cup black peppercorns
¹/₄ cup fenugreek seeds
¹/₄ cup dried red chile peppers, such as chile de arbol, broken
¹/₄ cup dried curry leaves
1 tablespoon white poppy seeds
1 tablespoon mustard seeds
4 star anise, broken
10 bay leaves, coarsely broken
1 tablespoon ground cinnamon
1 tablespoon ground cloves
2 teaspoons ground black cardamom seeds
2 teaspoons ground green cardamom seeds
2 teaspoons ground nutmeg
1 teaspoon ground mace

1. In a medium cast-iron or nonstick skillet, roast together the coriander, cumin, black cumin, peppercorns, fenugreek, and chile peppers, stirring and shaking the pan over medium heat until the mixture is a few shades darker, about 2 minutes. Mix in the curry leaves, poppy seeds, mustard seeds, anise, and bay leaves and roast another minute. Remove from heat.

2. Let cool, then grind in a spice or coffee grinder to make a fine powder. Mix in the cinnamon, cloves, black and green cardamom seeds, nutmeg, and mace. Store in an airtight container in a cool, dark place, about 1 month at room temperature or about 1 year in the refrigerator.

Bengali 5-Spices
Panch-Phoran

Makes about 1¹/₂ cups

A distinctive east Indian blend, panch-phoran *(which literally means 5 spices) is a mixture of highly fragrant whole spices that adds incredible flavor to food. This mixture is also popular in the north, where it is more often used as a pickling mixture, or* achaari masala *(*achaar *is Hindi for pickle), for an array of pickles—especially raw green mangoes, which is a staple in Indian kitchens. This blend is also used in selected chutneys, as well as some vegetarian and non-vegetarian curries and side dishes.*

²/₃ cup cumin seeds
¹/₃ cup fennel seeds
¹/₄ cup black mustard seeds
3 tablespoons kalonji seeds
2 tablespoons fenugreek seeds

In a medium cast-iron or nonstick wok or skillet, roast all the ingredients together, shaking and stirring the pan over medium-high heat, until heated through, about 2 minutes. Let cool, then store in an airtight container in a cool, dark place, 1 month at room temperature or about 1 year in the refrigerator.

Variation: For a Punjabi version, mix the spices and grind them in a spice or coffee grinder until coarsely ground.

Meat Masala with Cumin and Peanuts
Gosht ka Masala

Makes about 1¹/₄ cups

Use this masala *in conjunction with any of the basic curry pastes (pages 50 to 52) to customize your meat curries. Or simply sprinkle a spoonful or two over cooked dishes as a last-minute garnish—it is especially delicious over steamed* basmati *rice.*

¹/₄ cup shelled raw peanuts, with papery red skin removed
10 to 15 dried red chile peppers, such as chile de arbol, broken
2 tablespoons dried yellow split chickpeas (channa dal), sorted
2 tablespoons cumin seeds
1 tablespoon fenugreek seeds
1¹/₂ tablespoons sesame seeds
1 tablespoon coriander seeds
1 teaspoon white poppy seeds
1 tablespoon black mustard seeds

1. In a medium cast-iron or nonstick skillet, roast the peanuts, stirring and shaking the pan over medium heat until the mixture is a few shades darker, about 1 minute.

2. Add the chile peppers, dal, cumin seeds, and fenugreek seeds and roast until golden, 2 to 3 minutes. Mix in the sesame, coriander, poppy, and mustard seeds and continue to roast until a few shades darker, 2 to 3 minutes. Let cool, then grind in a spice or coffee grinder to make a fine powder. Store in an airtight container in a cool, dark place, about 1 week at room temperature or about 1 year in the refrigerator.

Goan Vindaloo Powder
Vindaloo ka Masala

Makes about 1¹/₂ cup

This masala *reflects the Portuguese influence in the western state of Goa, which was under Portuguese rule from 1510 to 1961. It is primarily used in a unique Goan curry called* vindaloo, *meaning "with vinegar." The vinegar is not part of this dry mixture of spices, but is an essential, separate ingredient that gives vindaloo curries a unique taste, distinguishing them from other curries.*

4 to 6 dried red chile peppers, such as chile de arbol, broken
³/₄ cup coriander seeds
¹/₄ cup cumin seeds
2 tablespoons black cumin seeds
2 tablespoons black peppercorns
1 tablespoon fenugreek seeds
2 teaspoons mustard seeds
1 teaspoon ground turmeric
1 teaspoon ground black cardamom seeds
1 teaspoon ground cloves
1 teaspoon ground cinnamon

1. In a medium cast-iron or nonstick skillet, roast together the red chile peppers, coriander, cumin, black cumin, peppercorns, fenugreek, and mustard seeds, stirring and shaking the pan over medium heat until a few shades darker, about 2 minutes.

2. Let cool, then grind in a spice or coffee grinder to make a fine powder. Transfer to a bowl and mix in the turmeric, cardamom, cloves, and cinnamon. Store in an airtight container in a cool, dark place, about 1 month at room temperature or about 1 year in the refrigerator.

Special South Indian Blends

South Indian Sambar Powder
Sambar Podi

Makes about 1¹/₂ cups

Sambars *are soupy* toor dal *(split pigeon pea) preparations made throughout the southern states of India. All* sambars *are flavored with a version of* sambar powder, *and are usually served with steamed rice, or with* dosas *(crispy rice and lentil crepes, page 607),* iddlis *(steamed rice and lentil cakes, page 133), and* vadai *(deep-fried legume croquettes, page 128). Packaged* sambar *powders are very hot, because the bulk of the blend's weight comes from red chile peppers. At home, you can control the heat of the* sambar *powder you make. Use as a dry-rub, in curries, or as a last-minute flavor enhancer.*

1 tablespoon sesame or peanut oil
10 to 15 dried red chile peppers, such as chile de arbol, broken
2 tablespoons fenugreek seeds
1 tablespoon each: dried yellow split pigeon peas (toor dal), dried yellow split chickpeas (channa dal), dried white urad beans (dhulli urad dal), sorted
1 teaspoon ground asafoetida
¹/₄ cup shredded, unsweetened, dried coconut
¹/₂ cup coriander seeds
¹/₃ cup dried curry leaves
1 teaspoon ground turmeric

1. In a medium cast-iron or nonstick skillet, heat the oil over medium heat and stir-fry the red chile peppers until a few shades darker, about 1 minute. Add the fenugreek seeds, all the dals, and the asafoetida and stir until golden, about 2 minutes.

2. Mix in the coconut and stir until golden, about 2 minutes. Then add the coriander seeds, curry leaves, and turmeric, and stir until heated through, about 1 minute. Let cool, then grind in a spice or coffee grinder to make a fine powder. Store in an airtight container in a cool, dark place, about 1 month at room temperature or 1 year in the refrigerator.

South Indian Soup Powder
Rasam Podi

Makes about 1¹/₂ cups

Rasams, *a specialty of southern India, are spicy, brothy soups. All* rasams *are typically associated with the specific flavors found in this unique blend of spices.* (Rasams *are often called "pepper-water," because black pepper is a core ingredient.*)

 Consumed any time of day, even first thing in the morning, they are potent sinus cleansers, and even the "mild" rasams are meant to be hot. This blend will make a spicy rasam. *Like packaged* sambar *powders, the store-bought* rasam *powders are very hot. At home, you can control the heat of this blend; see the variation below. Caution: Protect your eyes and nose when you roast and grind these spices.*

10 to 15 dried red chile peppers, such as chile de arbol, broken
²/₃ cup coriander seeds
¹/₄ cup dried curry leaves
3 tablespoons black peppercorns
3 tablespoons dried yellow split pigeon peas (toor dal), sorted
2 tablespoons dried yellow split chickpeas (channa dal), sorted
2 tablespoons cumin seeds
1 tablespoon fenugreek seeds
1 tablespoon cumin seeds
1 tablespoon black mustard seeds
¹/₂ teaspoon ground turmeric
4 to 6 rice-size pieces asafoetida

In a medium cast-iron or nonstick wok or skillet, roast together all the ingredients, stirring and shaking

the skillet over medium heat until fragrant and golden, about 3 minutes. Let cool, then grind in a spice or coffee grinder to make a powder. Store in an airtight container in a cool, dark place, 1 month at room temperature or about 1 year in the refrigerator.

Variation: Mild Rasam Powder can be made by excluding or reducing the number of red chile peppers. The black peppercorns may be reduced in quantity, but do not omit, because they are essential to this blend.

South Indian Lentil Paste
Dal Podi

Makes about 1¹/₂ cups

At the base of this blend are three dals—*yellow split chickpeas, yellow split and skinned pigeon peas, and white urad beans—which act not only as flavoring agents, but also as thickeners. Traditionally used in* sambars *(south Indian soupy pigeon pea dishes) and* rasams *(watery south Indian soups), you can also sizzle it in hot* ghee *or oil and then use it as a topping over steamed rice or boiled vegetables.*

1 tablespoon peanut oil
¹/₂ cup dried yellow split chickpeas (channa dal), sorted
¹/₄ cup dried split pigeon peas (toor dal), sorted
¹/₄ cup dried white urad beans (dhulli urad dal), sorted
1 tablespoon cumin seeds
10 to 12 dried red chile peppers, such as chile de arbol, broken
¹/₂ teaspoon ground asafoetida
2 teaspoons salt, or to taste

In a medium cast-iron or nonstick wok or skillet, heat the oil over medium-high heat and stir-fry the dals, cumin seeds, and red chile peppers until a few shades darker, about 2 minutes. Add the asafoetida and stir about 30 seconds. Let cool, then grind in a spice or coffee grinder to make a fine paste. Mix in the salt and store in an airtight container in a cool, dark place, 1 month at room temperature or about 1 year in the refrigerator.

South Indian Coconut Chutney Powder

Chutni Nariyal Podi

Makes about 1¹/₂ cups

Sprinkle over rice or steamed, microwaved, or grilled vegetables, or broiled fish or chicken. Mix it with plain yogurt, adding salt as necessary, to make an almost instant coconut chutney.

1 cup grated fresh or frozen coconut or
    shredded unsweetened dried coconut
2 tablespoons each: dried split pigeon peas (toor dal),
    dried white urad beans (dhulli urad dal),
    dried yellow split chickpeas (channa dal), sorted
6 to 10 dried red chile peppers, such as chile de arbol,
    broken
¹/₄ cup coarsely ground dried curry leaves
1 teaspoon ground asafoetida
1 to 2 tablespoons tamarind powder
1 tablespoon ground jaggery (gur) or
    dark brown sugar

1. In a medium cast-iron or nonstick wok or skillet, roast the coconut, all the dals, red chile peppers, and curry leaves over medium heat, stirring and shaking the pan until golden, about 4 minutes.

2. Add the asafoetida, stir 30 seconds, and remove from the heat. Mix in the tamarind powder and jaggery. Let cool, then grind in a spice or coffee grinder until as fine a powder as possible. Mix in the salt and store in an airtight container in a cool, dark place, about 1 week at room temperature or about 1 year in the refrigerator.

South Indian Chutney Powder

Chutni or Thenga Podi

Makes about 1¹/₂ cups

This hot, sour, and sweet powder comes to me courtesy of my friend Rama Srinivasan, who lives in the southern city of Bangalore. It is almost like a chutney, and that is how it is used to perk up the flavors of otherwise bland foods. Serve alongside steamed rice, iddlis (steamed rice cakes, page 133), or plain dosas (rice and lentil crepes, page 607). Use it sparingly, because the flavors of grated or shredded dried coconut (called kopra, *available in Indian markets) and red chile peppers are quite concentrated. A little bit goes a long way.*

¹/₂ cup dried yellow split chickpeas (channa dal),
    sorted
¹/₄ cup dried white urad beans (dhulli urad dal),
    sorted
2 teaspoons peanut oil
7 to 10 dried red chile peppers, such as chile de arbol,
    broken
1-inch ball of seedless tamarind pulp, broken into
    small bits or 1 tablespoon tamarind powder
¹/₄ cup ground coriander seeds
¹/₄ cup grated or shredded dried coconut (kopra)
¹/₄ cup ground jaggery (gur) or dark brown sugar
2 teaspoons salt, or to taste
1 teaspoon ground turmeric
¹/₄ teaspoon ground asafoetida

1. In a medium cast-iron or nonstick wok or skillet, roast together the dals, stirring and shaking the skillet over medium heat until golden, 2 to 3 minutes. Transfer to a bowl.

2. In the same pan, add the oil and stir-fry the red chile peppers and tamarind until a few shades darker, about 2 minutes. Transfer to the bowl with the roasted dal.

3. Still using the same pan, add the coriander and coconut and roast until a few shades darker, 2 to 4 minutes. Mix in the jaggery, salt, turmeric, and asafoetida, and roast until the jaggery melts, 1 to 2 minutes. Mix in the roasted dals, chile peppers and tamarind.

4. Let cool, then grind in a spice or coffee grinder until coarsely ground. Store in an airtight container in a cool, dark place, about 3 months in the refrigerator or 1 year in the freezer.

South Indian Peanut Powder

Moong-Phalli or Nilakkadala Podi

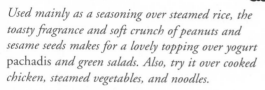

Makes about 1¹/₂ cups

Used mainly as a seasoning over steamed rice, the toasty fragrance and soft crunch of peanuts and sesame seeds makes for a lovely topping over yogurt pachadis *and green salads. Also, try it over cooked chicken, steamed vegetables, and noodles.*

¹/₃ cup white sesame seeds, dry-roasted (Dry-Roasting Spices, page 35)
1 teaspoon sesame or peanut oil
5 to 7 dried red chile peppers, such as chile de arbol, broken
3 to 4 tablespoons dried curry leaves
1 teaspoon ground asafoetida
1 cup roasted peanuts, papery skin removed

1. Prepare the sesame seeds. Then, in a medium cast-iron or nonstick wok or skillet, heat the oil over medium-high heat and stir-fry the chile peppers until a few shades darker, about 1 minute. Add the curry leaves and asafoetida, and stir 30 seconds. Let cool, then grind in a spice or coffee grinder to make a fine powder. Transfer to a bowl.

2. Coarsely grind the peanuts and sesame seeds in a spice or coffee grinder (you may have to do this in 2 or 3 batches). Add to the ground chile pepper mixture and mix well. Store in an airtight container in a cool, dark place, about 1 week at room temperature or about 1 year in the refrigerator.

South Indian Sesame Seed Powder

Til or Ellu Podi

Makes about 1¹/₂ cups

This masala *is delightful as a last-minute garnish over cooked vegetables, meats, or rice. Or stir-fry some with minced ginger and garlic and use as a* masala *base for vegetable side dishes.*

1 teaspoon Asian sesame oil
2 tablespoons fenugreek seeds
1 tablespoon hot red pepper flakes, or to taste
1 teaspoon ground asafoetida
1¹/₄ cups white sesame seeds

1. In a medium cast-iron or nonstick wok or skillet, heat the oil over medium-high heat, add the fenugreek seeds, red pepper flakes, and asafoetida and stir until golden, about 1 minute.

2. Add the sesame seeds, reduce the heat to medium, and roast, stirring and shaking the skillet, until golden, about 3 minutes. Let cool, then grind in a spice or coffee grinder to make as fine a powder as possible. Store in an airtight container in a cool, dark place, about 1 week at room temperature or 1 year in the refrigerator.

Dessert and Tea Masalas

Dessert Masala
Mithai ka Masala

Makes about 1¹/₂ cups

*Along with raisins and nuts, certain fragrant seasonings are crucial to Indian desserts—cardamom, saffron, rosewater, and, occasionally, a touch of black pepper. Although each dessert can be customized, the following standard mixture can be added to almost all desserts. This pale green mixture is also a spectacular garnish over entrees such as rice, casseroles, and white curry dishes. A tablespoon of this stirred into hot milk is also really delicious. I often sprinkle it over vanilla, strawberry, or other fruit-flavored ice creams, and even over Indian banana fudge (*burfee*) and crème brûlées.*

**1 teaspoon saffron threads, dry-roasted and coarsely
    crushed (Dry-Roasting Spices, page 35)**
1 cup shelled raw pistachios
¹/₂ cup shelled raw almonds, coarsely broken
¹/₄ cup cashews, coarsely broken
1 tablespoon coarsely ground green cardamom seeds
1 teaspoon coarsely ground black cardamom seeds

1. Prepare the saffron. The, in a spice grinder or in a small food processor, pulse together the pistachios, almonds, and cashews in one or two batches, to make a coarse powder.

2. Mix in the green and black cardamom seeds and the saffron. Store in an airtight container, about 3 months in the refrigerator or 1 year in the freezer.

Chai Tea Masala
Chai ka Masala

Makes about 1¹/₂ cups

Every family has its own recipe for chai *tea masala, but the following blend has the basic ingredients, which you can add to or alter to your own taste. Use about ¼ to ½ teaspoon per cup of water to make* chai *tea. See the variation in Spicy Chai Tea (page 662).*

¹/₂ cup fennel seeds
¹/₃ cup green cardamom seeds
2 tablespoons black cardamom seeds
2 tablespoons dried mint leaves
1 tablespoon black peppercorns
1¹/₂ tablespoons ground ginger
1 tablespoon ground cinnamon
1 tablespoon ground cloves

1. In a spice or coffee grinder, grind together the fennel seeds, green and black cardamom seeds, mint, and peppercorns to make a fine powder.

2. Mix in the ginger, cinnamon, and cloves, and grind once more to mix the spices. Transfer to a small container and store in a cool, dark place, about 1 month at room temperature or about 1 year in the refrigerator.

Kitchen Basics

Basic Techniques 35

Dry-Roasting Spices, Nuts,
and Flours

Blanching Raw Nuts

Slivering Blanched Nuts

Roasting and Grilling Vegetables

Deep-Frying, Indian-Style

Preparing Mangoes

Reconstituting Dried
Wild Mushrooms

Sprouting Beans and Seeds

Shelling a Coconut

Basic Ingredients 41

Indian Clarified Butter (*Ghee*)

Homemade Yogurt

Yogurt Cheese

Paneer Cheese

Coconut Milk

Crispy Fried Onions

Crispy Fried Fresh Ginger

Crispy Chickpea Batter Drops

Basic Flavoring
Pastes 46

Basic Ginger Paste

Basic Garlic Paste

Roasted Garlic Paste

Basic Ginger-Garlic Paste

Hyderabadi Ginger-Garlic Paste

Basic Ginger and Green Chile
Pepper Paste

Gujarati Green Paste

Basic Onion Paste

Boiled Onion Paste

Fried Onion Paste

Kerala Fried Onion Paste

Basic Curry Paste with Onion

Basic Curry Paste without Onion

Minty Green Curry Paste

Spicy Yellow Curry Paste

Almond and Poppy Seed Paste

Basic Cashew Paste

Chile Pepper Paste

Mughlai Curry Paste with Nuts

Goan Vindaloo Paste

Tamarind Paste

 = Vegan   P = Pressure-Cooker Quick

While it is true that Indian cuisine excites the senses and satisfies the palate with complex flavors, it is also true that with a little guidance and practice, achieving those results, especially for everyday home cooking, is simple.

Generally, most Indian meals are prepared fresh, but what simplifies matters is knowing some basic techniques and having some preparations and ingredients pre-made. If you understand these basic techniques and preparations, know your way around a kitchen, and allow yourself time for chores such as chopping, grinding, roasting, and the like, you can cook Indian food. If this is all new, it's like doing anything else you do for the first time: There's a learning curve, but the experimental journey in the kitchen is stimulating and rewarding.

To cook Indian recipes, you don't need to outfit your kitchen with many gadgets and tools. I offer basic equipment and pan substitutions in recipes, but for true Indian cooking, it is useful to have a concave cast-iron *tava* griddle to make breads, and a nonstick or cast-iron, round-bottomed wok or *kadhai,* as it is called in India. (You can buy both at Indian grocery stores or markets.) Also, it makes sense (and doesn't cost much) to have an additional spice or coffee grinder for the express purpose of grinding spices. (That is, unless you don't mind your spices tasting of coffee, and vice versa!)

In this chapter, you'll find information on basic techniques used in Indian cooking, specific directions on important and classic techniques such as dry-roasting seasonings and grilling and roasting vegetables, and recipes for essential preparations such as clarified Indian butter (*ghee*), *paneer* cheese, and seasoning pastes such as ginger paste and tamarind paste, used in many Indian recipes in this book.

Basic Techniques

Modern Indian cuisine is prepared both with techniques that date back centuries, such as making yogurt and grilling, and with modern adaptations such as pressure cooking and broiling. Although these days you may not crack a coconut very often or dry-roast all your spices, I offer the following preparations for when you want to follow traditional methods for the most authentic results.

Dry-Roasting Spices, Nuts, and Flours
Sookha Bhunna

Makes about ¹/₂ cup

Dry-roasting (sookha bhunna) specifically for dry spices, herbs, nuts, dals (legumes), and selected flours is done by browning them in a skillet, without adding any cooking fat or liquid. This process cooks out the raw smell that untreated spices tend to have and intensifies the flavors by heating the essential oils. Here are some specifics:

Spices (*Masalae*)

All spices can be dry-roasted, but the most popular ones are cumin, black peppercorns, coriander, fennel, sesame, and mustard seeds. This is how—place ¹/₂ cup of any one type of whole seeds in a small, cast-iron skillet, saucepan or *tava* and roast over medium heat, stirring and shaking the pan, until a highly fragrant smoke arises and the seeds are a few shades darker, about 2 minutes. Remove from the heat and let cool. With a rolling pin, the back of a large spoon, or in a mortar and pestle, crush them until coarsely ground. Or, grind them finely in a spice or coffee grinder. Store in an airtight container in a cool, dark place, about 1 month at room temperature or about 6 months in the refrigerator. Roasted black peppercorns can be transferred to a pepper mill to grind fresh for every use.

Nuts and Seeds (*Maevae*)

Starting with ¹/₂ cup whole, sliced, or slivered nuts, place them in a small, cast-iron skillet or saucepan and roast over medium heat, stirring and shaking the pan, until golden (do not brown), about 2 minutes. Remove from the heat and let cool. Use immediately or store in an airtight container in a cool, dark place, about 1 week at room temperature or about 1 month in the refrigerator. It is better not to roast different types of nuts and seeds together or some will darken and burn before others are roasted, but if you need to roast together for convenience, try to roast pieces of the same size at the same time and watch closely for proper color and aroma.

Chickpea and Other Flours (*Besan aur Doosrae Aatae*)

Sift ¹/₂ cup flour and place it in a nonstick skillet or saucepan. Roast over medium-low heat until fragrant and golden, about 3 minutes. Stir constantly and shake the pan often to prevent lumping and burning. Let cool, then store in an airtight container in a cool, dark place, about 1 week at room temperature or about 1 month in the refrigerator.

Blanching Raw Nuts
Bhiguna aur Cheelna

Makes ¹/₂ cup

Almonds (*Badaam*)

Blanching generally means to soften or lighten in color, but in the case of almonds, it means removing the brown skin to reveal the pure, creamy-white color underneath and a softness similar to that of pistachios.

In America you can buy blanched almonds, which are fine for cooking but are nothing compared to the real thing. In India, we peel each soaked nut individually. Luckily, in a country of almost a billion people, there are many hands! The entire process works your fingers to the proverbial bone, but the end result is, in itself, a reward. You may be inspired one day to try it, but if not, at least you know about the authentic preparation. There are two ways of blanching almonds.

Traditional Method

Soak ½ cup shelled raw almonds 8 to 24 hours in enough water to cover by at least 2 inches. (This allows the nuts to absorb the water and soften.) Drain and peel the skin from each one with your fingers.

Quick Method

Boil ½ cup almonds in water to cover until the skins absorb the water and loosen, about 5 minutes. Let cool, then peel. The skin of these almonds comes off quite easily, because the skin absorbs the moisture and expands, but the almond itself remains almost dry. Almonds blanched this way are fine for cooking, where they get a second chance to absorb the moisture.

Pistachios (*Pista*)

When the thin outer covering of shelled pistachios is removed, a brilliant green color is revealed. This process is not quite as labor-intensive as that for almonds, mainly because pistachios are a softer nut to start with and a quick boil releases the dull green skin, which can then be rubbed off.

Place ½ cup shelled, raw pistachios in a small stainless steel (not nonstick) saucepan, with enough water to cover by at least 1 inch, and bring to a boil over high heat. Remove from the heat and set aside to soften, about 1 hour. Drain and place them on a clean kitchen towel. Cover with another towel (or fold the first one over) and rub on the towel with your hands. As you do this, the loosened skin will fall off.

Slivering Blanched Nuts

Mavae Kaatna

Makes ¹/₂ cup

In the West, nuts are slivered by machines, but Indians do each one by hand. Granted, this is a tedious process and is quite taxing on the hands, but what you get in return is delicate shreds of paper-thin nuts.

Start with 1 cup blanched almonds, pistachio, or other nuts. Hold each nut, one at a time, between the thumb and forefinger of your left hand (or the right hand, if you are left-handed) and scrape gently along the length with a sharp paring knife in very small top-to-bottom motions. As you do this, delicate slivers or shavings will fall from the nut. (Be very careful as you do this.)

Roasting and Grilling Vegetables

Sabziyan Bhunna

Indian home cooks routinely roast and grill their vegetables. These roasted vegetables are basically the first step of a recipe—not a dish in themselves. Vegetables that are popularly roasted are eggplants, summer squashes, pearl onions, fresh green chile peppers, unripe green mangoes, and sweet potatoes. In America, I also roast my garden zucchinis and bell peppers of all colors.

Eggplants (*Baingan*)

Makes about 1¹/₂ cups of pulp from each pound of eggplant

No matter which type of eggplant you buy, choose young ones that are light for their size. These will have whiter flesh and fewer seeds. The skin of the eggplant should be shiny and silky smooth with no signs of decay. Also, as a general rule, choose smaller ones in every variety, because the smaller ones have more surface area to be charred, and hence will lend a smokier aroma to a dish, cup for cup.

Traditionally, eggplants are roasted over home-style coal-burning stoves (sigri or angeethi) until their skin is completely charred and the flesh is very soft. But today, people roast them directly over their gas burners. This process messes up the stove, which is why I nearly always char my eggplants over a grill.

To Fire-Roast Eggplants

1. Wash, dry, and lightly oil your hands, and rub them over the surface of each eggplant. Then, with the tip of a sharp kitchen knife, puncture the skin in a few places. Place them, preferably over the hot coals of a grill or over the direct flame of a kitchen stove burner (cover the bottom plate with aluminum foil), and roast, turning with kitchen tongs as the sides blacken, until the eggplant is very soft and the skin is completely charred, 5 to 7 minutes. Transfer to a bowl and let cool.

2. When cool enough to handle, peel off the charred skin and discard. Work close to the kitchen sink, because you may need to rinse your fingers as you go along. Do not wash the eggplants. Mash the pulp with your hands or a fork until somewhat smooth but still lumpy. Do not make a completely smooth purée; a little texture is very desirable. Strain and mix in any juices that may have collected in the bowl. (Some people say these are bitter, but I hate to discard good juices.) Store in the refrigerator about 5 days or about 4 months in the freezer.

To Oven-Roast Eggplants

Lightly oil and puncture the skin in a few places with the tip of a knife and bake in a preheated 400°F oven until the eggplants are tender, 35 to 40 minutes. You can wrap them in aluminum foil before baking.

To Broil Eggplants

Cut into half lengthwise and place, skin side up, on a baking tray lined with aluminum foil. Broil 8 to 10 inches from the heat source until the eggplants are tender and the skin is charred. (Do not cover the eggplants, or there will only soften and not char.)

Bell Peppers (*Shimla Mirch*)

Makes about ²/₃ cup of pulp from each pound of peppers

Roasted bell peppers are not commonly used in Indian cooking. I learned about and came to love them in America, and found it easy to incorporate them into my Indian cooking.

For Indian readers who don't understand why I'm so passionate about them, I say try it once. Roast them, mash them, and then make your bharthas,

raitas, *salads, sauces, and dressings, and remember each different colored bell pepper will yield a visual variation and intrigue your guests.*

To Fire-Roast Bell Peppers

1. Place whole bell peppers, preferably over the hot coals of a grill or over the direct flame of the kitchen stove (cover the bottom plate with aluminum foil) and roast, turning with kitchen tongs as the sides blacken, until the skin is lightly charred, 2 to 3 minutes. (There is no need to oil the bell peppers or poke any holes in them, or to char them completely.)

2. Remove to a bowl, cover (or seal in a zip-closure bag), and set aside about 15 minutes. This allows the peppers to sweat and cool down, making them easy to peel. Peel the peppers, removing as much of the really charred skin as possible. (I leave some lightly charred skin on for flavor.) Do not wash them in water, because this washes away most of the juices and flavor from the peppers. Rinsing your hands as you go along is adequate. Remove the stems and seeds and chop or purée the peppers; strain and add to the purée any juice that may have accumulated in the bowl.

To Oven-Roast Bell Peppers

1. Wash, dry, and cut each bell pepper into halves or quarters, lengthwise. Place on a baking sheet, with the cut side down. Place the sheet on the center rack of the oven, turn on the broiler, and roast until charred, 7 to 10 minutes. Turn once.

2. Put ¼ cup water on the baking sheet to dissolve most of the browned juice and use it in soups, rice, breads, or vegetables.

To Broil Bell Peppers

Wash, dry, and seed the bell peppers, then cut them into 1-inch or larger pieces. Place on a baking sheet lined with aluminum foil. Broil 4 to 5 inches from the heat source, turning once or twice until the pieces are lightly charred.

Deep-frying, Indian Style
Talna

Makes 20 to 30 pieces

Deep-frying is cooking foods (such as cut vegetables or meats) by submerging them in generous amounts of hot oil. This is best done in an Indian kadhai-*wok (or a Chinese wok).*

1¹/₂ to 2 cups oil
20 to 30 pieces of food

1. Heat the oil over medium-high heat until it reaches 325°F to 350°F on a frying thermometer or put a small piece of food into the hot oil. If it takes 15 to 20 seconds before it rises to the top, then it is ready. This is crucial—if the oil is too hot, the outsides will brown quickly, leaving the insides uncooked and if it is not hot enough, the foods will absorb oil.

2. Place food pieces in the wok; do not overcrowd. Fry until golden, about 1 minute. Using a slotted spatula, hold each piece against the edge of the wok for a few seconds, to allow excess oil to drain back into the wok. Then remove to a tray lined with paper towels.

Preparing Mangoes

Mangoes are often called the king of fruits in India, enjoyed in multiple ways, both when sour and unripe and when lusciously sweet and ripe.

Unripe Mangoes

Sour, unripe green mangoes are integral to Indian cuisine, for pickles, chutneys, and other dishes, but they are not the source of rapture that ripe mangoes are. They are prepared as a vegetable. Use a vegetable peeler to remove the skin from unripe mangoes, and slice the flesh around the large center seed.

Ripe Mangoes

To make sure a mango is ripe, sniff it—it should be highly aromatic and sweet-smelling, with no hint of sourness. Ripe mangoes give to light pressure when held in your hand, much like an avocado. The heavier it is for its size, the juicier the mango.

Ripe mangoes are prepared in a number of ways. There are deliciously indelicate ways to eat a mango, but for serving others, one way to prepare a mango is to hold it upright and establish where the "cheeks" are. The cheeks are the fattest sides of the fruit, on both sides of the center seed. Slice off the two cheeks, and serve them with a spoon as you would a papaya. Peel off whatever skin is left on the seed then cut off the fruit around it.

For preparing fruit salads, ice creams, and other sweet treats, you can first remove the peel with a peeler or a knife, then slice off the fruit around the center seed and cut as needed. Or, slice off the cheeks, cut a cross-hatch pattern in the flesh of each mango cheek (without cutting through to the peel), then push the mango cheek inside out and cut off the fruit.

Reconstituting Dried Wild Mushrooms
Sookhi Khumbon ko Bhigona

Makes 1 cup reconstituted mushrooms

In India and the rest of the world, fresh wild mushrooms are very expensive because they only grow in certain places and are very perishable. Most of the wild mushrooms found in India (mainly morels, called gucchi or gucchiyan, and chanterelles, called dhingri) come from Kashmir. People in India, particularly in the north, are fond of them, but use mostly the more readily available and affordable dried form. There and elsewhere, if dried mushrooms are in your pantry, you can easily make a special mushroom dish by reconstituting them. (Always wash them well.)

1 ounce dried wild mushrooms

1. Wash the mushrooms, then soak in water to cover by at least 2 inches until they absorb the water and puff up, about 1 hour. (Keep the soaking water.) Wash them again under running water to remove all dirt that may still be clinging to them. Chop and use as needed.

2. Strain the mushroom-soaking water through a coffee filter or paper towels until it looks completely clean and free of grit. Use it in soups, rice *pullaos* (pilafs), and curries.

Sprouted Beans vs. Bean Sprouts

Sprouted beans and bean sprouts are the delicate-looking beans with wispy tendrils attached, often seen at salad bars and in local produce markets. When dried beans are kept under moist conditions, they germinate—burst open and tiny shoots, or sprouts, as they are called, emerge from them. (These shoots are the beginnings of new plants.) At this stage what you see are soft, juicy beans with about 1/4-inch or smaller white shoots. These are sprouted beans.

When these shoots are allowed to grow (as in alfalfa and mung bean sprouts), they become much longer and the bean itself hollows out and often falls off. These long, tender shoots are called bean sprouts.

In my opinion, sprouted beans and bean sprouts are two different products with two different purposes, even though they both come from the same dried beans. It's the sprouted beans, the ones with tiny white shoots attached and with a delicate flavor and substantial bite, that are routinely used in Indian homes. The long,

thin, white sprouts filled with water are more popular in Asian cooking and are unheard of in Indian cooking. Indians use sprouted beans to make numerous salads, such as Mixed Sprouted Bean Salad with Potato Vermicelli (page 207).

When selecting dried beans and seeds, make sure they come from a reliable source and are not treated with fungicides, as is commonly done to seeds that have to be planted. Also, if the seeds you are sprouting are accidentally left outside for a longer time than is necessary, there is a chance they may spoil. Check to ensure that they are not slimy or bad smelling.

Although all types of dried beans, seeds, and grains, including whole wheat and barley, can be sprouted and used in Indian cuisine, mung beans, lentils, and dew beans (*moth dal*) are Indian favorites.

Be aware that while sprouts from smaller beans can be eaten raw, the larger ones, like chickpeas, should be cooked at least 5 minutes or longer to increase their digestibility.

Sprouting Beans and Seeds
Sookhi Dalonko Phutana

Makes about 4 cups

This is an almost foolproof way of making sprouted beans at home. No special jars, bowls, or pots and pans are needed. Sprouts can only be made with whole beans and seeds. All others (such as the skinned and split dals) *can be soaked 4 to 6 hours to get a lovely and almost sprout-like flavor, but they have none of the nutritional benefits associated with sprouted beans.*

Once beans are sprouted they stay fresh in the refrigerator about 10 days. Sprinkle them in salads or make special salads, like Mixed Sprouted Bean Salad with Potato Vermicelli (page 207), add them to sandwiches, or cook the sprouted beans to make substantial salads, such as Parsi-Style Sprouted Bean Salad (page 208).

**1 cup any variety whole beans and seeds,
    picked over and washed**
1 thick kitchen towel

1. Soak the beans overnight, in water to cover by at least 2 inches.

2. Drain well, cover the bowl with a lid, then wrap with a thick kitchen towel and place in a warm spot in the kitchen, such as a kitchen closet, or in a turned-off oven. Check at least once a day and stir them lightly if you wish to. Keep the beans lightly moist at all times. There is enough moisture when the inside surface of the lid is covered with tiny droplets of water; the beans themselves should feel dry. The beans will sprout in 2 to 3 days.

Shelling a Coconut
Nariyal Cheelna

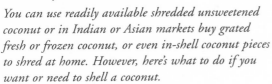

Makes ³/₄ pound coconut meat

You can use readily available shredded unsweetened coconut or in Indian or Asian markets buy grated fresh or frozen coconut, or even in-shell coconut pieces to shred at home. However, here's what to do if you want or need to shell a coconut.

Start with a crack-free, clean-looking coconut with all the "eyes" completely free of any mold. It should feel heavy and full of water (test by shaking the coconut). The uninitiated discard this delicate-tasting coconut water (this is not coconut milk), but anyone who knows coconuts, drinks it, or adds it to soups, rice, and other dishes. South Indians consider coconut water to be as good for you as milk. It is supposed to cool the body in the hot summer months and is considered ideal for convalescents. Before you drink this water, make sure it has no overpowering or rancid smell—that is a sure sign of a spoiled coconut.

1¹/₂ to 1³/₄ pounds whole coconut

Method 1

1. Pierce the 3 "eyes" at the top of the coconut with an ice-pick, the tip of a sturdy, sharp knife (don't break the knife), or a clean screwdriver that you use for no other purpose. Collect all the coconut water in a cup. (Skip this step if you do not want to save the water.)

2. Working outside the house, place the coconut on a clean concrete block or a wooden cutting board. While holding it with one hand, tap the coconut lightly on all sides with a hammer to dislodge the insides from the hard brown shell.

3. Then carefully hit the shell a bit harder with a hammer and crack it open. The hard shell should separate from the coconut. (It may fly off the board, but it won't go far.) If it does not, break the coconut into smaller pieces and very carefully, with the tip of a well-rounded blunt knife, pry off the shell.

Method 2

1. Pierce the 3 "eyes" as you would in Method 1 and collect all the coconut water in a cup.

2. Preheat the oven to 400°F and put the coconut in it until the shell cracks open, 10 to 15 minutes. Remove from the oven, wait until it is cool enough to handle, and tap lightly all around to release the coconut from the shell.

3. Then carefully hit the shell with a hammer and crack it open. The hard shell should separate from the coconut. If it does not, break the coconut into smaller pieces and very carefully, with the tip of a well-rounded blunt knife, pry off the shell.

Basic Ingredients

The following ingredients are used in countless ways by Indian cooks and are frequently cross-referenced throughout the book.

Indian Clarified Butter

Ghee

Makes about 2 cups

Ghee, *interchangeably called* desi, usli, *or* khara ghee *in India, is very easy to make at home and can also be purchased at Indian markets. It translates in English to Indian clarified butter, but in this book, for the sake of brevity, I refer to it in all cases as* ghee.

1 pound unsalted butter
One 1-foot-square piece of fine muslin
        or 4 layers of cheesecloth

1. Place the butter in a heavy, medium saucepan and simmer, stirring occasionally, over medium-low heat until the milk solids turn golden and settle to the bottom of the pan, 15 to 20 minutes. (At first the butter will start to foam, but as it simmers, the foaming will eventually subside.) Once this happens, pass everything through the cheesecloth or a fine-mesh strainer into a sterilized jar.

2. Do not discard the leftover milk solids. Store them at room temperature about 2 days or in the refrigerator about 6 months. Or combine with whole-wheat flour to make paranthas (griddle-fried breads) or add by the teaspoon to flavor soups, rice, or steamed vegetables.

Variation: To make flavored-infused ghee, add any of the following herbs, spices, or combinations to the pan along with the butter. After straining the ghee and removing any large spices, such as cardamom pods and cinnamon, use the milk solids in other dishes.

1/4 cup minced fresh mint leaves
1/2 cup minced fresh curry leaves plus 1/4 teaspoon ground asafoetida
1 teaspoon dried fenugreek leaves
2 tablespoons peeled and minced fresh ginger
1 tablespoon coarsely chopped garlic
2 teaspoons cumin seeds, 2 black cardamom pods, crushed lightly to break the skin, and 2 (1-inch) sticks cinnamon
1 teaspoon black peppercorns and 1 teaspoon ajwain seeds

Clarified Butter and Indian Clarified Butter

(Ghee)

The terms clarified or drawn butter and *ghee* are often used interchangeably, but, in my opinion, these fats are quite different.

Clarified butter is the fat that floats to the top when butter is heated, leaving the pale milk solids settled at the bottom of the pan. *Ghee,* on the other hand, is this same clarified butterfat that is further cooked over low heat until the milk solids at the bottom of the pan turn a rich golden color. As this happens, the butterfat gets infused with a characteristic smoky aroma that comes from the browned milk solids.

Clarified butter, more a concept of the Western world, is generally used as a dipping sauce and cannot be stored at room temperature for extended periods of time. *Ghee,* however, is (or should I say used to be) one of the primary cooking mediums for all foods in India. It stays fresh for a long time at room temperature (4 to 6 months), which explains why, in a tropical climate with no refrigeration, the ingenious Indians cooked all their excess butter into *ghee*. With the quick-spoiling milk solids completely removed, they always had a ready supply. Its shelf life in cool temperatures is even longer.

Besides filling the air with its intoxicating fragrance, *ghee* is believed to have some wonderful healthful benefits. The Indian *Ayurvedic* school of medicine uses it extensively in food preparations. However, today's conventional wisdom encourages moderation, and so do I. A little bit of *ghee* infuses food with a delicious, decadent aroma and flavor. I often sneak a teaspoon into dishes at the last minute. As a side note, authentic Indian *ghee* is much lighter in color than what you see in the United States because it is made from milk of the water buffalo, not from cow's milk.

Homemade Yogurt
Ghar ki Dahi

Makes about 4 cups

Yogurt-making is a simple, easy, and very gratifying art. With very little work, you can have fresh yogurt or curd, as it is called in India every day—the kind that is naturally sweet and has active cultures. Furthermore, you can rest assured that homemade yogurt is free of all the unnecessary and artificial additives added to prolong the shelf life of its store-bought counterpart.

Any and all types of pots and pans may be used, though I find terra-cotta and ceramic ones to be the best. But this is partly sentiment—my mother always maintained that these containers added a certain calming and cooling effect to the body-warming yogurt.

Made with milk and a starter (store-bought yogurt with live cultures or yogurt from a previous homemade batch), homemade yogurt is delicate, sweet, and smooth. It can be made with any type of milk—whole, 2 percent, 1 percent, or nonfat. For health reasons, I generally make mine with nonfat milk.

4 cups milk
2 tablespoons plain yogurt, nonfat or any kind, with active culture
1 pot holder
1 or 2 large, thick kitchen towels

1. Bring the milk to a boil, stirring frequently with a metal spatula in a heavy aluminum saucepan. (Do not use lightweight stainless steel or nonstick Teflon or Silverstone-coated saucepans; stainless steel is not a good conductor of heat, invariably burning the milk, and in the coated pans a layer of brown skin forms at the bottom of the pot, ruining the entire project.)

2. Alternately, put the milk in a large microwave-safe bowl and boil, uncovered, on high power until bubbles rise to the top, 9 to 10 minutes. Remove form the microwave as soon as it boils.

3. Transfer to a yogurt pot (preferably ceramic, though any container will do), and cool until the milk registers 118°F to 120°F on a meat thermometer. Stir in the yogurt starter and cover with a loose-fitting lid.

4. Put a pot holder on a shelf in a kitchen cabinet. Place the yogurt pot on top of the pot holder, fold the towels in half and cover the yogurt pot snugly on every side. This insulates the pot and helps maintain the ideal temperature necessary for the multiplication of the yogurt bacteria. (You can also place the yogurt pot in a turned-off gas oven with a pilot light to achieve the same effect.)

5. Allow the milk to rest undisturbed 3 to 4 hours. Then check to see if the yogurt is set. When you do this, do not pick up the pot or place a fork in the yogurt. Simply uncover the pot and see if the yogurt is firm—almost like gelatin. You may see some watery liquid over the yogurt; disregard it. (You may remove it after chilling the yogurt.) Once the yogurt is set, refrigerate it immediately. The longer freshly made, fully developed yogurt sits unchilled, the stronger and more sour it gets. Serve chilled.

Note: To sweeten yogurt that has soured over time, Indians routinely drain out the whey and then mix in some milk (any type will do). The milk adds its sweetness and lends a freshly made flavor to yogurt.

Yogurt Cheese
Dahi ka Paneer

Makes about 2 cups

Yogurt cheese, dahi ka paneer in Hindi, is also called "hung curd" or "hung yogurt" because it is made by putting yogurt in a cheesecloth and then hanging it (generally from the kitchen faucet) until all the liquid whey drains out, leaving behind a thick, almost cheese-like yogurt. This delicate yet tangy cheese can be used as is, or placed under a heavy object to obtain a block that can be cut into small pieces. You can find cheesecloth in cooking supply stores, or use fine muslin from a fabric store.

Yogurt cheese is flavored with herbs and spices to make special raitas *and chutneys, and also mousse-like desserts called* shrikhand *(Yogurt Mousse with*

Saffron, page 633). Today, I find it irreplaceable in salad dressings and sandwich spreads, and can, on occasion, use it to replace cream cheese and sour cream in recipes that are not subjected to intensive heat. It's a great topping for soups and freshly made parantha *breads (page 579), too.*

1 (32-ounce) container nonfat plain yogurt
1 (2-foot-square) piece of fine muslin
        or 4 layers of cheesecloth

Place yogurt in the muslin or cheesecloth, then twist the cloth snugly around the cheese and tie the ends of the cloth around the kitchen faucet, making sure that the yogurt is a few inches above the bottom of the sink. Allow to drain 4 to 6 hours. The cheese is now ready to be used.

Or, set a large colander or fine-mesh strainer into a large bowl (to catch the whey), and line it with muslin or 4 layers of cheesecloth. Put the yogurt in the strainer and allow to drain 4 to 6 hours in the refrigerator.

Paneer Cheese

Paneer

Makes 8 ounces or about 30 1¹/₄-inch pieces

Paneer *cheese, made by curdling milk with something sour, such as yogurt, lemon juice, or vinegar, and then separating the curds from the whey, is also called Indian cottage cheese or farmer's cheese. This soft, spongy cheese with its sweet, milky aroma is preservative-free, has no artificial additives, and can be made with low-fat or whole milk (nonfat milk will not work; you'll end up with a hard and leathery cheese).*

Paneer *cheese doesn't melt when heated, although too much stirring will cause it to break. Freshly made* paneer *cheese, warm and right out of the cheesecloth, is much prized for its own taste. Indians love it just by itself, or dressed with a little* chaat masala, *a savory and spicy seasoning blend that instantly perks up flavors, and fresh herbs. I even serve* paneer *cheese as part of an antipasto platter, giving it an Italian*

twist with salt, pepper, chopped fresh basil, and balsamic vinegar. Paneer *is easy to scatter over salads, or add to pizza, lasagna, sandwiches, and rice, which can be used in curries, stews, and even desserts.*

When making paneer *cheese, use only heavy-bottomed aluminum or anodized metal pans, and to avoid accidental spills, add the curdling agent almost as soon as you see bubbles rising in the milk.*

Paneer *cheese stays fresh in the refrigerator about 5 days and can also be frozen. To freeze, cut into desired size pieces, stand each piece on a plate in a single layer and freeze. When frozen, transfer to plastic freezer bags and freeze 3 to 4 months. This enables you to remove and use only the number of pieces you need for the recipe.*

As an alternative, you can buy paneer *cheese in the refrigerator section of Indian markets.*

¹/₂ gallon lowfat or whole milk
2 cups plain yogurt, nonfat or any kind,
        whisked until smooth, or ¹/₄ cup fresh
        lemon juice, or a mixture of both
1 (2-foot-square) piece of fine muslin
        or 4 layers of cheesecloth

1. Place the milk in a large, heavy saucepan and bring to a boil, stirring gently, over high heat. Before the milk boils and the bubbles spill over, mix in the yogurt or the lemon juice, and continue to stir until the milk curdles and separates into curds and whey, 1 to 2 minutes. Remove from the heat.

2. Drape the muslin or cheesecloth over a large pan and pour the curdled milk over it. As you do this, the whey drains through the cloth into the pan, and the curdled paneer cheese remains in the cloth.

3. With the paneer cheese still inside it, pick up the cloth from the pan and tie the ends of the cloth around the kitchen faucet to drain, making sure that the cheese is a few inches above the bottom of the sink. Allow to drain 3 to 5 minutes.

4. Remove from the faucet and gently twist the cloth snugly around the cheese, then place the cheese between two salad-size plates (or any other flat surfaces), with the twisted cloth edges placed to one side, out of the way. Place a large pan of water on the top plate and let the cheese drain further, 10 to 12 minutes. (Do this close to the sink or within a baking pan, or you'll have a mess to clean up.)

5. Remove the pan of water from the paneer cheese (which, by now, should have compressed into a chunk), cut into desired shapes and sizes and use as needed. Store in an airtight container in the refrigerator 4 to 5 days or freeze up to 4 months.

Variations: Paneer cheese can also be made with about ¹/₂ cup fresh or bottled lemon or lime juice, 3 to 4 tablespoons white or any other vinegar, or 1 quart buttermilk. Lemon juice and vinegar will yield about 6¹/₂ ounces of paneer cheese, and the buttermilk will yield about 8 ounces. Paneer cheese can also be made with non-dairy soy milk (made from bean curd or tofu) or with a mixture of soy milk and milk. Make both these variations as you would with milk, and follow the directions above.

Coconut Milk
Nariyal Doodh

Makes 1 cup thick coconut milk

Coconut milk is not the water found inside the coconut. It is the milky liquid obtained when the freshly (or sometimes dried) grated or ground white meat of a mature coconut is blended with water and then strained.

In India, coconut milk is usually made from scratch, so I offer the recipe that follows. I do often use canned (unsweetened) coconut milk, which you can find in Indian or Asian markets, and American supermarkets with well-stocked ethnic food aisles.

1¹/₂ cups grated fresh coconut meat
1 cup hot water

1. In a food processor or a blender, process together the coconut and ¹/₂ cup of the water to make as smooth as possible. Leave the processed coconut to soak in this water about 30 minutes. Then, pass everything through the fine mesh of a food mill or a strainer.

2. Return the leftover coconut to the food processor. Add the remaining ¹/₂ cup water, then process and strain again. Mix into the first coconut milk. For a thinner extract, add another cup of water and repeat the process once again. Use immediately, or store in the refrigerator about 4 days or freeze up to 2 months.

Crispy Fried Onions
Bhuna Pyaz

Makes about 3 cups

Deep-fried and drained on paper towels, these onions have a long refrigerator life. They are great additions to all curries and dry-cooked vegetables, and also work well as a last-minute garnish and flavor booster for plain foods. Scatter them over rice pullaos *(pilafs),* biryanis *(layered, baked rice dishes), or any light-colored dishes for an elegant, crispy brown garnish. Use the leftover onion-flavored oil in salads, pastas, and curries.*

6 to 8 small onions, cut in half lengthwise
**   and thinly sliced**
1¹/₂ cups peanut oil for deep frying

1. Heat the oil in a large wok or saucepan over medium-high heat until it reaches 325°F to 350°F on a frying thermometer. (Put a small piece of onion into the hot oil. If it takes 15 to 20 seconds before it rises to the top, the oil is ready.) Add the onions in 1 or 2 batches and fry, stirring and lowering the heat if needed, until deep brown, 5 to 7 minutes per batch.

2. Leaving as much oil as you can in the wok, remove the onions with a slotted spoon to paper towels and set aside until crispy and cool. Transfer to an airtight container and refrigerate up to 2 months.

Variation: A popular technique, and one that uses less oil, is to first dry thinly sliced onions in the sun (4 to 6 hours on a hot summer day) until most of their moisture evaporates, and then fry them.

Crispy Fried Fresh Ginger

Bhuna Adrak

Makes about 1 cup

Cut into thin matchsticks and deep-fried until golden, this ginger is a common last-minute garnish and flavor enhancer. Sprinkle some over rice pullaos *(pilafs), curries, and salads, or roll it within freshly made and generously buttered* chapati *(griddle-cooked breads). Use the leftover ginger-flavored oil in salads, pastas, stews, and curries.*

¹/₂ pound fresh ginger, peeled and cut into thin matchsticks
1¹/₂ cups peanut oil or melted ghee for deep-frying
¹/₂ teaspoon salt, or to taste

1. Heat the oil in a large wok or saucepan over medium-high heat until it reaches 325°F to 350°F on a frying thermometer. (Place a small piece of ginger into the hot oil. If it takes 15 to 20 seconds before it rises to the top, the oil is ready.) Add the ginger in 1 or 2 batches and fry, stirring and lowering the heat if needed, until rich gold in color, 3 to 5 minutes per batch.

2. Leaving as much oil as you can in the wok, remove the ginger with a slotted spoon to a bowl, toss with salt, and set aside until crispy and cool. Transfer to an airtight container and refrigerate up to 2 months.

Crispy Chickpea Batter Drops

Boondi

Makes about 1¹/₂ cups

Boondi *drops are savory, light, crispy ¼-inch rounds made by deep-frying drops of chickpea flour batter. Making* boondi *drops at home is quite easy. All you need is some chickpea flour batter and a large,* round spatula with holes. The spatula is held about 6 inches above the hot oil and the batter is slowly poured through the holes. The batter falls into the wok as tiny drops, which firm up almost immediately upon contact with the hot oil. These drops are called boondi.

The versatile boondi *drops (also called* pakoriyan*) are used to make* raitas *and curries, and are often added to savory trail-mix type of snacks or sprinkled over* chaats *(layered salads). Sometimes they are dipped in saffron-flavored sugar syrup to make special desserts. (In these cases, no salt is added to the batter.)*

²/₃ cup chickpea flour, sifted
¹/₄ teaspoon salt, or to taste
A scant pinch baking soda
¹/₂ cup water, or as needed
1 cup peanut oil for deep frying

1. In a bowl, mix together the chickpea flour, salt and baking soda. Add the water and whisk to make a smooth and creamy batter. Set aside about 10 minutes then whisk again.

2. Heat the oil in a small wok or saucepan over medium-high heat until it reaches 325°F to 350°F on a frying thermometer or until a drop of the batter rises to the top almost immediately. Hold a round spatula with holes over the oil and gradually pour the batter through the holes, while shaking and tapping the spatula to make sure the batter falls as drops into the hot oil and not as one long noodle. Stop pouring when the wok seems to have enough drops.

3. Fry one batch until golden, about 45 seconds, then remove the drops with another slotted spatula to a tray lined with paper towels, before starting the next batch. Repeat until all the batter has been used. Let cool, then store in an airtight container in the refrigerator about 3 months or in the freezer about 6 months.

Basic Flavoring Pastes

Basic Ginger Paste
Pissa Adrak

Makes about 2 cups

Many Indians do not eat any garlic (or onions, for that matter), relying primarily upon ginger, fresh herbs, and spices to flavor their foods. Added to dishes in all forms, shapes, and sizes, each addition of ginger lends a delicate, citrus-like flavor, and it is believed to have countless health benefits.

Select young and juicy rhizomes with shiny skin. Peel the skin and cut the ginger across the grain into thin, quarter-size slices before you purée it. This way, you will be cutting all the fibers into bits, ensuring a smooth paste.

1 pound fresh ginger, peeled and cut crosswise into thin round slices
1 to 3 tablespoons water, as needed

1. Put the ginger slices in a blender (not a food processor, or the paste will not be smooth) and process, adding 1 tablespoon of water at a time, using only the minimum amount necessary to make a smooth paste. (If the ginger is juicy, you will need less water.)

2. Transfer to an airtight container and refrigerate up to 5 days or freeze pre-measured quantities (because it is almost impossible to break off small bits from frozen ginger without thawing all of it) about 3 months. Pre-measured portions can go straight from the freezer into the pan. Another way to freeze is to place the paste in a small zip-closure bag, remove excess air, seal the bag, and press on it lightly to spread the paste into a thin layer. When frozen, pieces can then simply be snapped off.

Masala Pastes

The word *masala* is used for two kinds of seasoning pastes. One is dry *masala*, which is the general word for all spices or spice blends (covered in the Spice Rack chapter), and the other is wet *masala*, which is a paste made with ground onions, ginger, garlic, green chile peppers, and other moisture-containing ingredients that distinguishes curries from other dishes (covered in this chapter). Dry *masalas* and wet *masalas* are the linchpins of Indian cuisine as we know it today.

To remove the raw taste and intensify the inherent flavor and aroma of wet *masala* pastes, they are always slow-roasted in *ghee* or oil (*bhunna*) before the next set of ingredients is added.

A word of caution: Adding any *masala* paste to hot oil will cause the oil and ingredients to splutter, so stand far away from the pan and lower the heat just before adding the ingredients to hot oil, then gently raising the heat to the necessary temperature.

Basic Garlic Paste

Pissa Lussan

Makes about 1 cup

Although it is acceptable to use oil- or water-packed bottled minced garlic that is available in supermarkets all over America (though I personally do not care for it), nothing can replace the true flavor (and the nutritional benefits) of fresh garlic. It is true that peeling fresh garlic cloves can be a chore, but these days even the peeled ones are readily available. Buy yours at the local farmers' markets, where you can guarantee freshness.

1¹/₂ cups fresh garlic cloves, peeled
2 to 3 tablespoons water, as needed

1. Put the garlic in a blender (not a food processor, or the paste will not be smooth) and process, adding 1 tablespoon of water at a time, using only the minimum amount necessary to make a smooth paste.

2. Transfer to an airtight container and refrigerate up to 15 days. Because garlic paste is pungent, be sure to seal it very tightly with plastic wrap under the lid. This will ensure that the rest of your refrigerator doesn't smell garlicky. You can also freeze premeasured quantities (because this paste freezes as one big block that is almost impossible to break without thawing) about 3 months. Pre-measured portions can go straight from the freezer to the pan. Another way to freeze is to place the paste in a small zip-closure bag, remove excess air, seal the bag, and press on it lightly to spread the paste into a thin layer. When frozen, pieces can then simply be snapped off.

Roasted Garlic Paste

Pissa Bhuna Lussan

Makes about 1 cup

This is not a true Indian basic, but it lends itself well to our cuisine. When a recipe calls for flame-roasting whole heads of garlic, I turn to this method—it's a lot less messy. You can do this for any quantity of garlic cloves.

1¹/₂ cups fresh garlic cloves, peeled

Preheat oven 400°F. Place the garlic cloves in a small pie dish or any other baking pan and roast until golden brown, about 15 minutes. Let cool, then process in a blender or coarsely mash with a fork. Or just put the roasted cloves in an airtight container and refrigerate up to 1 month or freeze up to 6 months. With no water added, puréed roasted garlic is easy to separate even when it is frozen.

Basic Ginger-Garlic Paste

Pissa Adrak-Lussan

Makes about 1¹/₂ cups

Used universally in India and ground fresh every time the need arises (which is 2 to 3 times on an average day), this paste is almost the first task of the morning cooking ritual. Once made, it gets added to breakfast breads and to whatever else is the savory call of the morning. In America, I find that making it in bulk at one time and having it available to me makes cooking easier. When making this paste, there's one thing I do that is out of the norm—I mix in some oil. The purists may not agree, but I find that it increases the refrigerator life of the paste and, more importantly, the paste does not darken but retains its original color.

A word of caution: Cut the ginger crosswise, across the grain, into thin slices, or you'll get long fibers in the paste. Also, make sure the storage containers you use are really airtight, so your whole refrigerator doesn't smell of garlic.

1 cup quarter-size slices peeled fresh ginger
1 cup fresh garlic cloves, peeled
1 to 3 tablespoons water

In a food processor or a blender, process together the ginger and garlic to make a smooth paste, adding the water as needed for blending. Transfer to an airtight container, mix in some oil (vegetable, peanut, or olive) until it forms a ⅛-inch layer on top of the paste, and refrigerate up to 15 days or freeze up to 6 months.

Hyderabadi Ginger-Garlic Paste
Hyderabad ka Pissa Adrak-Lussan

Makes about 1¹/₂ cups

From my friend Yasmin AliKhan's Hyderabadi kitchen comes this fragrant variation of the basic ginger-garlic paste, with three times more ginger than garlic. This is a well-guarded secret that gives the southeastern Muslim-style Hyderabadi cuisine its characteristic flavors and silky smooth sauces.

³/₄ pound fresh ginger, peeled and cut crosswise into thin round slices
¹/₄ pound fresh garlic cloves, peeled
1 to 3 tablespoons water

In a blender (not a food processor), blend together the ginger and garlic until smooth, adding the water as needed for blending. Transfer to an airtight container and refrigerate up to 10 days or freeze up to 6 months.

Basic Ginger and Green Chile Pepper Paste
Pissi hui Adrak-Hari Mirch ka Masala

Makes about 1 cup

For the people who don't eat garlic or onions (because they are associated with the base desires of life), this paste is their flavoring basic—along with an array of spices, of course.

6 ounces fresh ginger, peeled and cut crosswise into thin round slices
10 to 15 fresh green chile peppers, such as serranos, coarsely chopped

In a food processor or blender, process together the ginger and chile peppers to make them as smooth as possible. Transfer to an airtight container and refrigerate up to 10 days or freeze up to 4 months.

Gujarati Green Paste
Gujerati Hara Masala

Makes about 1¹/₂ cups

Hara means green, and in this case the word does not indicate the color, but the fact that the masala paste is made from fresh ingredients. Whatever green color there is comes from the fresh green chile peppers that my friend Naina Kapadia adds very generously to the traditional ginger and garlic in this paste. This paste stays fresh in the refrigerator about 15 days, but to extend its refrigerator life even further, she mixes in some oil.

This paste can be a little time-consuming to make, especially in a blender (a food processor works better) because, unlike most other freshly ground pastes, no water is added. However, the lack of water is exactly what makes the paste keep longer. Use it carefully; it is very strong and spicy hot, and even a spoonful goes a long way.

8 ounces fresh ginger, peeled and cut crosswise into thin round slices
6 ounces fresh garlic cloves, peeled
4 to 6 ounces fresh green chile peppers, such as serrano, coarsely chopped
¹/₄ cup vegetable oil

In a food processor or a blender, process together all of the ingredients until very smooth. Transfer to an airtight container and refrigerate up to 1 month, or freeze up to 6 months.

Basic Onion Paste
Pyaz ka Masala

Makes about 1 cup

This is the most commonly used onion paste. Many of the everyday Indian curries start with this basic masala and then mix in the selection of herbs and spices needed for specific dishes.

To use, pan-cook the paste in ghee or oil over medium heat until browned, then add puréed or finely chopped tomatoes to make vegetarian and non-vegetarian curries.

2 tablespoons water
10 to 12 quarter-size slices of peeled fresh ginger
3 to 5 fresh green chile peppers, such as serrano, coarsely chopped
4 large cloves fresh garlic, peeled
1 large onion, coarsely chopped (about 8 ounces)

In a blender, put the water, ginger, and garlic and blend until smooth. Then add the onion and process again until smooth. Transfer to an airtight container and refrigerate up to 10 days or freeze up to 3 months.

Boiled Onion Paste
Ublae Pyaz ka Masala

Makes about 1½ cups

Here, boil the onions in water until they are soft, then process them into a fine paste. Curries made with this paste are very smooth and delicate. A lot of Indian restaurants rely on this paste as their basic, because it is easy to make, stores well, and can be added to just about all curries.

To use, pan-cook the paste in ghee or oil over medium heat until browned, then add puréed or finely chopped tomatoes to make vegetarian and non-vegetarian curries.

1¼ pounds onions, coarsely chopped
3 bay leaves
2 black cardamom pods, pounded lightly to break the skin
4 whole cloves
1 (1-inch) stick cinnamon, broken lengthwise into 2 pieces
½ cup water

1. Place all the ingredients in a medium nonstick saucepan. Cover and bring to a boil over medium-

high heat. Reduce the heat to medium-low and simmer until all the water evaporates and the onions are soft, about 15 minutes.

2. Discard the whole spices, then process the onions in a blender or a food processor until very smooth. Transfer to an airtight container and refrigerate up to 5 days or freeze up to 3 months.

Fried Onion Paste
Talae Pyaz ka Masala

Makes about 1 cup

This paste, used mostly for the richer northern, Mughlai-type dishes, gives everyday curries a distinctive rich quality that sets them apart from the usual fare. Even though the onion, ginger, and garlic are deep-fried, this paste is not as rich as the word "fried" implies. The fried ingredients are drained on paper towels and then ground to make a paste.

To use, add spices to the paste and then simmer with water, buttermilk, whisked yogurt, or light cream, for all types of meats, especially kofta *(fried minced meat balls).*

1 cup melted ghee or vegetable oil for deep-frying
6 to 8 quarter-size slices of peeled fresh ginger
4 large cloves fresh garlic, peeled
1 large onion, cut in half lengthwise and thinly sliced
½ cup nonfat plain yogurt

1. Heat the oil in a large nonstick saucepan over medium-high heat and fry the ginger and garlic until golden, about 2 minutes. Add the onion and fry until everything is well browned, about 5 minutes. (Reduce the heat if the browning occurs too quickly.) Remove to paper towels to drain and reserve the ghee or oil for another purpose.

2. Transfer to a blender or a food processor, add the yogurt and process to make a thick, smooth paste. Transfer to an airtight container and refrigerate up to 5 days or freeze up to 3 months.

Kerala Fried Onion Paste
Kerala ka Talae Pyaz ka Masala

Makes about 2 cups

Popular mostly in the coastal, southwestern state of Kerala, where coconut palm trees grow in abundance, this paste has an incredible smoky and rich bite, that is somewhat mellowed with the addition of coconut milk.

To use, sauté meats, poultry, seafood, or vegetables, along with your favorite herbs and spices, in the paste and then add more coconut milk, water, or broth to make curries of distinction. Drizzle some over grilled foods or simply stir some into steamed rice or vegetables for a flavor boost.

1 cup Coconut Milk (page 44 or store-bought)
1/2 cup peanut oil
5 to 8 dried red chile peppers, such as chile de arbol, broken
2 large onions, coarsely chopped
5 large cloves fresh garlic, peeled
6 to 8 quarter-size slices of peeled fresh ginger
15 to 20 fresh curry leaves

1. Heat the oil in a large nonstick saucepan over medium-high heat and fry the red chile peppers and the onion until golden, 3 to 4 minutes. Add the garlic, ginger, and curry leaves and fry until everything is well-browned, 3 to 5 minutes. (Reduce the heat if the browning occurs too quickly.)

2. Cool, drain, and reserve the oil for another purpose. Then transfer to a blender or a food processor, add the coconut milk and process to make a thick, smooth paste. Transfer to an airtight container and refrigerate up to 5 days or freeze up to 3 months.

Basic Curry Paste with Onion
Pyaz vaala Kari Masala

Makes about 1/2 cup

This is the basic wet masala *curry paste upon which Indians build most of their vegetarian and non-vegetarian curries. Variations stem from adding other ingredients.*

There are two parts to making this paste, each of which has two steps—but it's not complicated, really! First, grind together the ingredients in two groups. Then brown the paste, also in two steps. The masala *is ready when traces of oil are visible on the sides and the top.*

To use, heat the paste and pan-fry spices and whatever vegetables and meats you wish to use, then mix in water, yogurt, buttermilk, coconut milk, cream, or vegetable or chicken broth in varying proportions, for the volume and consistency of the actual sauce and to tenderize the foods being cooked.

7 to 10 quarter-size slices of peeled fresh ginger
3 large cloves fresh garlic, peeled
1 large onion, coarsely chopped
2 large tomatoes, coarsely chopped
1/2 cup coarsely chopped fresh cilantro, including soft stems
1 to 3 fresh green chile peppers, such as serrano, stemmed
1/4 cup peanut oil

1. In a food processor, process the ginger, garlic, and onion to make a smooth paste. Transfer to a bowl. Then process the together the tomatoes, cilantro, and green chile peppers to make a smooth purée.

2. Heat the oil in a large nonstick wok or saucepan over medium-high heat, add the ginger-onion paste and cook, over medium-high heat the first 2 to 3 minutes and then over medium heat until golden brown, 5 to 7 minutes.

3. Mix in the puréed tomato mixture and cook, stirring until all the juices evaporate and the oil separates to the sides. Let cool and store in an airtight container and refrigerate up to 5 days or freeze up to 3 months.

Basic Curry Paste without Onion
Bina Pyaz ka Kari Masala

Makes about 1 cup

For the millions of Indians who eat no onion or garlic (believing them to be associated with the base desires of life), this peppery hot, yet delicate curry paste is their basic. Use it as you would the Basic Curry Paste with Onion (page 50).

1/2 pound fresh ginger, peeled and thinly sliced
5 to 10 fresh green chile peppers, such as serrano, coarsely chopped
1 cup coarsely chopped fresh cilantro, including soft stems
2 large tomatoes, coarsely chopped
1/4 cup peanut oil
1 tablespoon cumin seeds
1/4 cup plain yogurt (nonfat or any kind), whisked until smooth

1. In a food processor, process together the ginger, chile peppers, cilantro, and tomatoes to make a smooth paste.

2. Heat the oil in a large nonstick wok or saucepan over medium-high heat and cook the cumin seeds (they should sizzle upon contact with the hot oil). Quickly add the paste and cook over medium heat the first 2 to 3 minutes, then over low heat until all the juices evaporate.

3. Add the yogurt, a little at a time, stirring constantly to prevent it from curdling, until all of it is incorporated into the sauce. Let cool and store in an airtight container about 15 days in the refrigerator or up to 3 months in the freezer.

Minty Green Curry Paste
Pudinae vaala Hara Kari Masala

Makes about 1 cup

This vibrant paste, used primarily to make minty curries, is wonderfully fragrant with the refreshing herb. Use it as you would the Basic Curry Paste with Onion (page 50). You can also use it in large quantities for marinades or add it to soups 1 tablespoon at a time.

4 to 5 large cloves fresh garlic, peeled
6 quarter-size slices of peeled fresh ginger
1 to 3 fresh green chile peppers, such as serrano, stemmed
5 to 6 scallions, coarsely chopped with greens
1 cup coarsely chopped fresh cilantro, including soft stems
1/2 cup coarsely chopped fresh mint leaves
1 tablespoon fresh lime juice
1 1/2 teaspoons garam masala
1 teaspoon salt, or to taste
1/4 cup peanut oil

1. In a food processor, process together the garlic, ginger, chile peppers, and scallions until minced. Add the cilantro, mint, and lime juice and process to make a smooth paste. Remove to a bowl and mix in the garam masala and salt.

2. Heat the oil in a large nonstick wok or saucepan over medium-high heat, add the green paste and cook, stirring over medium heat for the first 2 to 3 minutes and then over medium to low heat until well browned, 10 to 12 minutes. Let cool, then store in an airtight container for about 1 month in the refrigerator or 6 months in the freezer.

Spicy Yellow Curry Paste
Masaladar Peela Kari Masala

Makes about 1 cup

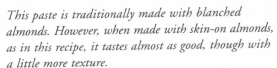

This paste gets its heat from the fresh green chile peppers and its brilliant yellow color from the turmeric. Be sure to store it in a non-porous container so the turmeric doesn't leave permanent stains. Use it to make classic Indian curries.

10 quarter-size slices of peeled fresh ginger
4 to 5 large cloves fresh garlic, peeled
1 to 3 fresh green chile peppers, such as serrano, coarsely chopped
1 large onion, coarsely chopped
1 tablespoon fresh lime juice
1 teaspoon ground turmeric
1 teaspoon cayenne pepper
1 teaspoon garam masala
1 teaspoon salt, or to taste
1/4 cup peanut oil

1. In a food processor, process together the ginger, garlic, chile peppers, onion, lime juice, turmeric, cayenne pepper, garam masala, and salt to make a smooth paste.

2. Heat the oil in a large nonstick wok or saucepan, add the paste, and cook, stirring over medium-high heat the first 2 to 3 minutes and then over medium to low heat until well browned, 10 to 12 minutes. Let cool, then store in an airtight container about 1 month in the refrigerator or 6 months in the freezer.

Almond and Poppy Seed Paste
Pissa Badaam aur Khas-khas ka Masala

Makes about 1 cup

This paste is traditionally made with blanched almonds. However, when made with skin-on almonds, as in this recipe, it tastes almost as good, though with a little more texture.

To use, roast the paste in oil or ghee *and use it along with any of the curry pastes to make unique rich and creamy sauces—as we do in Mughlai Pot-Roasted Lamb with Almonds and Poppy Seeds (page 477). For a richer variation, grind with milk, yogurt, or coconut milk instead of water.*

1/2 cup white poppy seeds
1/2 cup warm water
1/2 cup shelled raw almonds, coarsely chopped
Seeds from 10 to 15 green cardamom pods

Soak the poppy seeds in the water 2 hours. Transfer to a blender (not a food processor), add the almonds and cardamom seeds, and grind everything to make a fine paste, adding more water if needed. Transfer to an airtight container and store in the refrigerator 4 to 6 days or 4 months in the freezer.

Basic Cashew Paste

Pissa Kaaju ka Masala

Makes about 1 cup

On its own, cashew paste forms the base for rich desserts and fudges. Combined with ginger, garlic, and other aromatic spices, it is frequently used to thicken and flavor special sauces. For a variation in flavor, try grinding the cashews with milk, yogurt, or coconut milk instead of the water.

1¹/₄ cups raw cashews
1 cup warm water plus more for the paste

Soak coarsely chopped cashews in the warm water to cover, about 45 minutes. Drain and process in a blender (not a food processor) adding 2 to 3 tablespoons water, as needed, to make a smooth paste. Transfer to an airtight container and store in the refrigerator 4 to 6 days or 4 months in the freezer.

Chile Pepper Paste

Pissi Mirchon ka Masala

Makes about ¹/₃ cup

Definitely not for the faint of palate, much less the faint of heart, this paste could make you sweat for days. Use this paste sparingly, as it tends to be very intense in color as well as flavor. With salt to taste, it can also be used as a chutney or a sandwich spread. Or reduce its potency by mixing in some yogurt and use as a marinade for meat, poultry, and seafood.

10 dried red chile peppers, such as chile de arbol, broken
¹/₄ cup distilled white vinegar or water
5 fresh green chile peppers, such as serrano, coarsely chopped
2 teaspoons black peppercorns, dry-roasted and coarsely ground

Soak the red chile peppers in the vinegar about 1 hour to soften. Transfer to a blender. Mix in the green chile peppers and the peppercorns and blend until smooth. Transfer to an airtight jar and refrigerate up to 6 months.

Mughlai Curry Paste with Nuts

Korma ka Geela Masala

Makes about 1 cup

A blend of two of the best things in life—cream and nuts—kormas are rich curries, traditionally prepared in the dum *(Indian pot-roasting) style of cooking, where the pan and the flavors of the foods are completely sealed and the foods cook slowly. The following paste is what gives most* kormas *their distinctive flavor.*

To use, pan-fry chopped onions until golden, add any meats, mixed vegetables, or paneer *cheese and cook until golden. Then add the paste and finish cooking, adding more yogurt if the meat needs further tenderizing.*

2 tablespoons Basic Ginger-Garlic Paste (page 47)
¹/₂ cup Fragrant Masala with Nuts (page 25)
2 tablespoons melted ghee or vegetable oil
¹/₄ cup heavy cream
¹/₂ cup nonfat plain yogurt

1. Prepare the paste and then the masala. Heat the ghee in a large nonstick saucepan over medium-high heat, add the ginger-garlic paste and korma masala and cook, stirring, until lightly browned.

2. In a bowl, whip together the cream and yogurt with a whisk or an electric beater, then add it to the saucepan in a thin stream, stirring constantly to prevent curdling, until it is completely incorporated into the paste. Let cool, then store in an airtight container in the refrigerator 7 to 10 days or 3 months in the freezer.

Goan Vindaloo Paste

Goa ka Vindaloo Masala

Makes about 1 cup

Vindaloo, *meaning "with vinegar," is a curry to be made spicy, or not at all. It's character comes from vinegar and dried red chile peppers that will clear your sinuses faster than anything from the pharmacy.*

Use with water or broth to make special meat and vegetable curries, such as Hot and Tangy Goan Mixed Vegetables (page 415) and Spicy Goa-Style Lamb Curry (page 502).

3 to 4 dried red chile peppers, such chile de arbol, broken

1/4 cup distilled white vinegar

1/2 cup Goan Vindaloo Powder (page 28 or store-bought)

8 to 10 quarter-size slices of peeled fresh ginger

5 to 7 large cloves fresh garlic, peeled

1 large onion, coarsely chopped

30 to 40 fresh curry leaves

2 teaspoons salt, or to taste

3 tablespoons peanut oil

1. Soak the red chile peppers in the vinegar, 1 to 2 hours. Meanwhile, prepare the vindaloo powder. In a food processor, process together the red chile peppers, plus the vinegar, ginger, garlic, onion, curry leaves, and salt to make a smooth paste. Mix in the vindaloo masala and process once again.

2. Heat the oil in a large nonstick wok or saucepan over medium-high heat and stir-fry the paste, over medium-high heat the first 2 to 3 minutes, and then over medium heat until rich brown, 7 to 10 minutes. Let cool, then store in an airtight container about 1 month in the refrigerator or 6 months in the freezer.

Tamarind Paste

Imli Ras

Makes about 1 1/2 cups

Tamarind, in all its forms, including paste, is available in Indian, Asian, and Mexican markets, but it is worth having made from scratch. You extract the paste from fresh tamarind pods, yielding a delicate flavor and the best color. Or you can simply use the store-bought tamarind paste or powder, as I sometimes do.

If you're using the fresh pods, remove the brittle shell and break the soft and sticky, seed-filled insides into small pieces before you start the recipe.

6 ounces shelled fresh tamarind pods with seeds or 5 ounces tamarind pulp without seeds

1 1/2 cups warm water

1. Soak the shelled tamarind pods or pulp in 1 cup of the water, 1 to 2 hours to soften. With your fingers, gently rub and mash the tamarind to loosen the pulp from the fibrous parts and to separate any seeds.

2. Discard the seeds and pass the softened pulp through a fine-mesh strainer or a food mill to make a smooth paste. (I prefer the food mill, especially when preparing large quantities). Remove the fibrous leftovers to a bowl, mix the remaining 1/2 cup water into the pulp and mash once again. Then pass through the sieve or food mill to extract more paste. Mix into the already extracted paste. Store in an airtight container about 1 week in the refrigerator or freeze measured amounts into ice cube trays and store the cubes in zip closure bags up to 6 months in the freezer.

Chutneys and Pickles

Green Chutneys 58

Basic Green Chutney

Mint Chutney
with Pomegranate Seeds

Mint-Garlic Chutney
with Peanuts and Tamarind

Cilantro-Lime Chutney

South Indian Cilantro Chutney

Scallion-Ginger Chutney

Coconut Chutneys 61

Fresh Coconut Chutney
with Cilantro

Hazram's Coconut-Tamarind
Chutney with Mint

Roasted Coconut Chutney

Shahina's Shredded
Coconut Chutney

Semolina-Coconut Chutney

Garlic and Chile Pepper Chutneys 64

Green Garlic and Nuts Chutney

Peanut and Garlic Chutney

Garlic and Fresh Red Chile
Pepper Chutney

Bean and Legume Chutneys 66

Roasted Dal and Fresh Green
Chile Pepper Chutney

Roasted Black Chickpea
Chutney with Peanuts

Classic Hyderabadi
Ginger-Sesame Chutney

Sesame-Peanut Chutney

Yogurt Chutneys 68

Yogurt Chutney
with Puréed Greens

Yogurt Chutney
with Roasted Dals and Spices

Yogurt Cheese Chutney
with Minced Greens

Yogurt-Almond Chutney

Puréed Fruit Chutneys 70

Puréed Green Mango Chutney

Puréed Fresh
Mango-Ginger Chutney

Tart Apple-Ginger Chutney
with Green Tomatoes

South Indian Tomato Chutney

Preserved Chutneys 72

Tomato Chutney Preserve
with Cashews and Raisins

Red Tomato Chutney Preserve
with Sesame Seeds

Fragrant Mango Chutney Preserve

Spicy Apricot Chutney Preserve

Spicy Apple-Ginger
Chutney Preserve

Cranberry Chutney Preserve

Sonth Chutneys 76

Sonth Chutney
with Dried Mango Slices

Minty Sonth Chutney with Mango
(or Tamarind) Powder and Jaggery

Sonth Chutney
with Fresh and Dried Fruits

Sweet Sonth Chutney with Dates

Mango Pickles 79

Quick Mango Pickle

Mama's Punjabi Mango Pickle

Mama-in-Law's Mango Pickle
with Roasted Spices

Cooked South Indian Mango Pickle

Rama's Grated Mango Pickle

Lime and Lemon Pickles 82

Sun-Cured Pickled Lime
(or Lemon) Wedges

Sweet and Sour Fresh Lime Pickle

Crushed Lemon and
Fresh Red Chile Pepper Pickle

Lemon-Pickled Fresh Ginger Sticks

Minced Ginger-Lime Pickle

Green Chile Pepper Pickles 84

Vinegar-Marinated
Green Chile Peppers

Pickled Chile Pepper Purée
with Tamarind

Prabha's Green Chile Pepper Pickle

Other Vegetable Pickles 86

Crunchy Cucumber Pickle

Water Pickle with Crispy
Cauliflower and Carrots

Spicy Cranberry Pickle

Pearl Onions in Pickling Spices

Pickled Turnips
with Black Mustard Seeds

Pickled Turnips and Cauliflower

Mixed Vegetable Pickle with Garlic

Eggplant and Malanga Root Pickle

rimming with layers of flavor, in often surprising combinations, Indian chutneys and pickles are the pantry and refrigerator essentials that can be made once and eaten all year long. They are perfect for exploring the promise of Indian cuisine. Alone or with other foods, they are tasty and stimulating with every bite.

While an Indian meal can depend solely on chutneys and pickles, when served with *paranthas* (griddle-fried flatbreads) or other breads, or with rice, they are generally meant to be eaten as relishes and condiments, in small portions alongside other foods—some no more than a teaspoon at a time. (Most of the long-lasting pickles and chutneys are preserved with a lot of sodium and/or sugar and fat—something to be aware of, but don't let that be a deterrent.)

Chutneys and pickles range from sweet to fiery hot, and can differ in texture from smooth herbal blends to meltingly soft or crisp-tender chunks of fresh vegetables and fruits. And while they may seem similar to the uninitiated, to Indians each one is very different.

Indian chutneys fall into two broad categories: fresh and preserved. The fresh, perishable kind are the tangy purées of fresh herbs, spices, fruits, and yogurt, such as Basic Green Chutney (page 58) or Yogurt-Almond Chutney (page 69). These chutneys stay fresh about 10 days in the refrigerator. Except the chutneys that contain yogurt, all the fresh puréed ones can also be frozen. To freeze, place the chutneys in serving-size containers or in ice-cube trays. Once they freeze, transfer to plastic zip-closure bags and freeze up to 6 months. Thaw at room temperature, or if you are in a hurry, in the microwave.

In the preserved category are the non-perishable fruit chutneys, such as Fragrant Mango Chutney Preserve (page 73), which have tremendous staying power even at room temperature.

Indian pickles are quite unusual. Most people in the United States think of pickles as solely the sour or garlicky cucumber pickles served in diners and delis. But pickles are made with a variety of fruits and vegetables, mango being a favorite, and with a variety of seasonings. There are no herb and spice pickles (as there are chutneys), though we do have some water pickles that, like the herb chutneys, are more perishable than the regular ones.

Most pickles keep well for long periods of time at room temperature. Some pickles stay fresh for 2 to 3 years, and others, like the lemon pickles, last 10 to 15 years. They actually improve as they age, and the long-aged lemon pickles are considered therapeutic home remedies for stomach ailments.

Green Chutneys

Basic Green Chutney
Hari Chutni

Makes about 1¹/₂ cups

This puréed blend of herbs, spiked with fresh green chile peppers and lime juice, is universal all over India, with each family adding its own special touch and ingredients. Though you can use any onions, I prefer using just the scallion greens for their mild flavor and their deep green color. Another popular addition to this chutney is garlic, but to me it overpowers the flavors, so I generally don't use it. Add 1 to 3 fresh cloves, if you wish.

2 to 5 fresh green chile peppers, such as serrano, stemmed
6 to 8 scallions, just the green parts, coarsely chopped
1 cup fresh mint leaves, trimmed
2 to 3 cups coarsely chopped fresh cilantro, including soft stems
3 to 4 tablespoons fresh lime or lemon juice
1 teaspoon sugar
1 teaspoon salt, or to taste
¹/₂ teaspoon freshly ground black pepper, or to taste

1. In a food processor or blender, process together the green chile peppers and scallion greens until minced. Add the mint and cilantro to the work bowl and process, stopping a few times to scrape the sides with a spatula, until puréed. As you process, drizzle the lime juice through the feeder tube into the work bowl and process until the chutney is smooth.

2. Add the sugar, salt, and pepper and process once again. Adjust the seasonings. Transfer to a bowl and serve immediately, refrigerate about 10 days, or freeze up to 6 months.

Mint Chutney with Pomegranate Seeds
Pudina-Anardana Chutni

Makes about 1¹/₂ cups

My father's favorite—a green chutney made primarily with fresh mint, made tart with the dried seeds of unripe pomegranates. This is the way my mother always makes it, except hers comes out of a mortar and pestle and mine, the blender. I prefer to use the blender (instead of the food processor) to make this chutney because mint leaves are generally tough and the blender does a better job of puréeing them.

Since the tang comes primarily from the pomegranate seeds, add very little lemon juice to this chutney.

1 small red onion, coarsely chopped
3 to 5 coarsely chopped fresh green chile peppers, such as serrano, stemmed
1 tablespoon fresh lemon juice
2 to 4 tablespoons water
2 cups fresh mint leaves
1 cup coarsely chopped fresh cilantro, including soft stems
2 teaspoons ground dried pomegranate seeds
¹/₂ teaspoon freshly ground black pepper
1 teaspoon sugar
1 teaspoon salt, or to taste

1. Put the onion, chile peppers, lemon juice, and 2 tablespoons of water in a blender and blend until smooth. Add the mint and cilantro in 2 batches, adding more as the first batch is reduced to a smooth purée, blending until thoroughly puréed. Add the remaining 2 tablespoons of the water, if needed.

2. Add the pomegranate seeds, pepper, sugar, and salt and blend again. Adjust the seasonings. Transfer to a bowl and serve immediately, refrigerate about 10 days, or freeze up to 6 months.

Mint-Garlic Chutney with Peanuts and Tamarind

Pudina, Lussan, Moong-Phalli aur Imli ki Chutni

Makes about 1½ cups

This strongly flavored chutney, with flavors of the south, goes well with most finger foods, such as pakoras (batter-fried fritters).

2 to 3 tablespoons Tamarind Paste (page 54)
½ cup roasted peanuts, red skins removed
10 large cloves fresh garlic, peeled
4 to 6 fresh green chile peppers, such as serrano, stemmed
2 cups packed fresh mint leaves
1 teaspoon sugar
1 teaspoon salt, or to taste
1 tablespoon peanut oil
1 teaspoon black mustard seeds
5 to 6 fresh curry leaves
⅛ teaspoon ground asafoetida

1. Prepare the tamarind paste. Then, in a food processor or a blender, process together the peanuts, garlic, chile peppers, and mint until minced. Add the tamarind paste, sugar, and salt and process again to make a smooth purée. Add a spoonful or 2 of water if needed for blending. Adjust the seasonings. Transfer to a serving bowl.

2. Heat the oil in a large nonstick wok or saucepan over medium-high heat and add the mustard seeds; they should splutter upon contact with the hot oil, so lower the heat and cover the pan until the spluttering subsides. Add the curry leaves and asafoetida, stir about 30 seconds, transfer to the chutney and swirl lightly to mix, with parts of it visible as a garnish. Transfer to a bowl and serve immediately, refrigerate about 10 days, or freeze up to 6 months.

Cilantro-Lime Chutney

Dhania Chutni

Makes about 2 cups

Join the countless millions of Indians (including me) for whom this mild chutney, powered with the fragrance and taste of fresh cilantro, is the ultimate. You'll find a version of it in every home, no matter where you are in India.

It's so good, it shouldn't be limited to Indian food, either. Try it in sandwiches, tacos, and burritos, with fresh vegetables, fried or baked appetizers, in salads, steamed vegetables, or rice pullaos *(pilafs), or simply serve it on the side with grilled foods.*

½ teaspoon cumin seeds, dry-roasted and coarsely ground (Dry Roasting Spices, page 35)
1 teaspoon Chaat Masala (page 20 or store-bought)
3 to 5 fresh green chile peppers, such as serrano, stemmed
4 quarter-size slices peeled fresh ginger
1 small green bell pepper, coarsely chopped
5 to 6 scallions, green parts only, coarsely chopped
3 cups firmly packed, coarsely chopped fresh cilantro, including soft stems
½ cup fresh mint leaves
2 to 3 tablespoons fresh lime or lemon juice
1 teaspoon sugar
1 teaspoon salt, or to taste

1. Prepare the cumin seeds and the chaat masala. Then, in a food processor or a blender, blend together the green chile peppers, ginger, bell pepper, and scallion greens until minced. Add the cilantro and mint to the work bowl and process, scraping the sides with a spatula a few times, until puréed. As you process, drizzle the lime juice through the feeder tube into the work bowl and process to make a smooth chutney.

2. Add the chaat masala, sugar, and salt and process again. Adjust the seasonings. Transfer to a bowl and lightly mix in the cumin with some of it visible as a garnish. Serve immediately, refrigerate about 10 days, or freeze up to 6 months.

South Indian Cilantro Chutney

Kothmir ki Chutni

Makes about 1¹/₂ cups

Kothmir *chutney, as this is called in southern India, is nothing like any you'll find in the northern parts. The southern version is sharper and more intense in flavor from the addition of sizzled spices and tamarind paste. This is typically a very smooth chutney, so combining with a blender is preferred.*

¹/₄ cup Tamarind Paste, or to taste (page 54)
1 tablespoon peanut oil
2 teaspoons black mustard seeds
4 to 6 dried red chile peppers, such as chile de arbol, coarsely broken
1 tablespoon dried white urad beans (dhulli urad dal), sorted
¹/₈ teaspoon ground asafoetida
3 cups firmly packed, coarsely chopped fresh cilantro, including soft stems
1 teaspoon salt, or to taste

1. Prepare the tamarind paste. Then, heat the oil in a small nonstick saucepan over medium heat and add the mustard seeds, red chile peppers, dal, and asafoetida. Cook, shaking the pan until the dal is golden, about 1 minute. Let cool and transfer to a blender (not a food processor) and blend until as fine as possible.

2. Add the tamarind paste and then add the cilantro in 2 or 3 batches, adding more as the first batch is reduced to a smooth purée. Add 2 to 3 tablespoons water, if needed. Mix in the salt. Adjust the seasonings. Transfer to a bowl and serve immediately, refrigerate about 10 days, or freeze up to 6 months.

Scallion-Ginger Chutney

Harae Pyaz aur Adrak ki Chutni

Makes about 1¹/₂ cups

Simultaneously sharp and gingery-hot, this chutney can also be made with regular onions. I prefer scallions because they are milder, and because they give this chutney a lovely, bright green color, which makes it all the more appealing. To make a smooth chutney, pick the youngest and most tender scallions—the greens tend to be less fibrous.

2 to 4 fresh green chile peppers, such as serrano, stemmed
1 (2¹/₂-inch) piece fresh ginger, peeled and cut into thin quarter-size rounds
12 to 15 young scallions, with green parts included, coarsely chopped
2 to 3 tablespoons fresh lime or lemon juice
2 to 3 tablespoons nonfat plain yogurt
1 teaspoon sugar
1 teaspoon salt, or to taste
1 cup fresh mint or cilantro leaves

1. Place the chile peppers, ginger, scallion greens, lemon juice, and yogurt in a food processor or a blender and process until minced.

2. Add the sugar, salt, and mint or cilantro leaves, and process to a smooth purée. Adjust the seasonings. Transfer to a bowl and serve immediately, refrigerate about 10 days, or freeze up to 6 months.

Coconut Chutneys

Fresh Coconut Chutney with Cilantro
Nariyal aur Dhania Chutni

Makes about 2¹/₂ cups

This authentic chutney is best made with fresh coconut. Time- and labor-intensive though this might be, don't skimp here. The result: a naturally sweet coconut chutney that stays fresh about 10 days in the refrigerator and about 6 months in the freezer. To choose the best coconut, see page 40.

2 to 3 tablespoons South Indian Sambar Powder (page 28 or store-bought)

1 fresh coconut

3 to 5 fresh green chile peppers, such as serrano, stemmed

3 quarter-size slices of peeled fresh ginger

3 tablespoons fresh lemon juice

1 cup plain yogurt, nonfat or any kind, whisked until smooth

1 cup coarsely chopped fresh cilantro, including soft stems

1 teaspoon salt, or to taste

1 tablespoon coconut or peanut oil

1 teaspoon black mustard seeds

2 tablespoons minced fresh curry leaves

¹/₈ teaspoon ground asafoetida

1. Prepare the sambar powder. Then, shell the coconut (page 40). Then, with a vegetable peeler, remove the brown skin from the flesh and discard. Coarsely chop the coconut meat into ¹/₂- to 1-inch pieces. In a food processor or a blender, process together the coconut, green chile peppers, and ginger until minced.

2. Add the lemon juice, yogurt, and cilantro and process, scraping the sides of the work bowl a few times with a spatula until as smooth as possible. Add the salt and sambar powder and process again. Adjust the seasonings, then transfer to a serving bowl.

3. Heat the oil in a small nonstick saucepan over medium-high heat and add the mustard seeds, curry leaves, and asafoetida; they should splutter upon contact with the hot oil, so lower the heat and cover the pan until the spluttering subsides. Quickly add to the chutney and stir lightly with parts of it visible as a garnish. Transfer to a bowl and serve immediately, refrigerate about 10 days, or freeze up to 6 months.

Hazram's Coconut-Tamarind Chutney with Mint
Hazram ki Nariyal Chutni

Makes about 1¹/₂ cups

Hazram is my friend Neelam Malhotra's cook in India, and Neelam swears this chutney is the best in the world. You be the judge. Although this chutney is traditionally ground on a grinding stone (not a mortar and pestle) until it turns into a fine paste, I make mine in a blender. Its texture is not quite as fine, but it still is irresistible.

1 teaspoon coarsely ground dry-roasted cumin seeds (Dry-Roasting Spices, page 35)

¹/₄ cup Tamarind Paste (page 54)

1 fresh coconut

6 to 8 quarter-size slices peeled fresh ginger

3 to 5 fresh green chile peppers, such as serrano, stemmed

2 large cloves fresh garlic, peeled

¹/₂ cup coarsely chopped fresh cilantro, including soft stems

¹/₄ cup fresh mint leaves

1 teaspoon salt, or to taste

1. Prepare cumin and tamarind paste. Then, shell the coconut (page 40). With a vegetable peeler, remove the brown skin from the meat and discard. Coarsely chop the coconut meat into ¹/₂- to 1-inch pieces. In a food processor a blender, process together the coconut, ginger, green chile peppers, and garlic until minced.

2. Add the cilantro, mint, tamarind, and salt and process, scraping the sides of the work bowl a few times with a spatula, until smooth. Adjust the seasonings, then transfer to a serving bowl. Garnish with the cumin and serve immediately, refrigerate about 10 days, or freeze up to 6 months.

Variation: Add about ¹/₂ cup skinned, dry-roasted peanuts or cashews (page 35) along with the coconut in Step 1.

Roasted Coconut Chutney

Bhunae Nariyal ki Chutni

Makes about 1¹/₂ cups

No fresh coconut to deal with here. This traditional chutney, found all over the southern parts of India, is simple to make because it calls for packaged shredded coconut. Its flavor is very nicely concentrated.

2 to 3 tablespoons Tamarind Paste (page 54)
1 cup shredded or grated unsweetened dried coconut
7 dried red chile peppers, such as chile de arbol, 5 broken and 2 with stems
1 tablespoon dried white split urad beans (dhulli urad dal), sorted
1 tablespoon dried yellow split chickpea (channa dal), sorted
2 large cloves fresh garlic, coarsely chopped
1 tablespoon coriander seeds
1 teaspoon cumin seeds
¹/₂ teaspoon fenugreek seeds
1 tablespoon coconut or peanut oil
1 teaspoon black mustard seeds
1 scant pinch ground asafoetida
5 to 7 fresh curry leaves

1. Prepare the tamarind paste. Then, preheat the oven to 250°F. Spread the coconut on a baking tray and roast until golden, 20 to 30 minutes (depending on the moisture content).

2. In a small nonstick saucepan, dry-roast together the broken red chile peppers, urad and channa dals, garlic, coriander, cumin, and fenugreek over medium heat until a few shades darker, about 2 minutes. Let cool, then grind in a spice or coffee grinder, in two batches if necessary, to make a fine powder. Remove spices to a bowl. In the same grinder, grind the coconut, in two batches if necessary, to make it as fine as possible. Mix with the spices.

3. Heat the oil in a medium nonstick wok or saucepan over medium-high heat and add the whole red chile peppers and mustard seeds; they should splutter upon contact with the hot oil, so lower the heat and

cover the pan until the spluttering subsides. Add the asafoetida and curry leaves, then mix in the coconut-spice mixture. Add the tamarind paste and the salt, and stir over medium heat until well mixed. Transfer to a bowl and serve immediately, refrigerate about 10 days, or freeze up to 6 months.

Shahina's Shredded Coconut Chutney

Kopra Chutni

Makes about 1¹/₂ cups

When my friend Shahina Bhalla made this one in front of me, I was amazed at how simple it was, and how good. She described countless ways of serving this chutney, but that day my taste dictated using it as a filling for parantha *(pan-fried) bread. Since that day, I have used it as a filling in puff pastry appetizers and other appetizers, as a topping over* pullaos *(pilafs), and even in tacos.*

3 to 4 tablespoons Tamarind Paste (page 54)
1¹/₄ cups shredded or grated unsweetened dried coconut
2 fresh green chile peppers, such as serrano, stemmed
3 large cloves fresh garlic, peeled
³/₄ cup fresh mint leaves
¹/₂ cup coarsely chopped fresh cilantro, including soft stems
¹/₂ teaspoon salt, or to taste
¹/₄ to ¹/₃ cup water

1. Prepare the tamarind paste. Then, place the coconut in a medium size nonstick skillet and roast, stirring and shaking the pan over medium heat until golden, 2 to 3 minutes.

2. Place all the remaining ingredients in a blender or a food processor and process to make a smooth purée. Mix in the roasted coconut and process again until smooth. Transfer to a bowl and serve. This chutney stays fresh in the refrigerator about 10 days, or in the freezer about 6 months.

Semolina-Coconut Chutney

Sooji-Kopra Chutni

Makes about 1¹/₂ cups

This is mostly semolina, flavored with a tablespoon of dried coconut. I stumbled upon this preparation in my kitchen when I was trying a different recipe, and now I often serve it in place of a traditional coconut chutney with iddlis *(steamed fermented rice cakes) and* dosas *(griddle-fried fermented rice and* dal *crepes). It is practically fat-free, so you can enjoy every spoonful—guilt-free.*

The yogurt in this chutney means it will only stay fresh for about a week, so make just what you need or find different ways to enjoy it within a few days.

¹/₃ cup fine-grain semolina
1 teaspoon peanut oil
1 tablespoon shredded or grated unsweetened dried
    coconut
¹/₈ teaspoon ground asafoetida
1 cup nonfat plain yogurt
15 to 20 fresh curry leaves
3 quarter-size slices of peeled fresh ginger
1 fresh green chile pepper, such as serrano, stemmed
1 teaspoon salt, or to taste
¹/₂ cup finely chopped fresh cilantro,
    including soft stems

1. Place the semolina and oil in a small nonstick wok or saucepan and roast, stirring and shaking the pan over medium-low heat, until the semolina is golden, about 5 minutes. Add the coconut and asafoetida and cook, stirring, another 2 minutes.

2. In a blender, blend together the yogurt, curry leaves, ginger, green chile pepper, and salt until smooth. Add the roasted semolina and coconut mixture, and blend again until smooth. Allow to rest about 30 minutes so the semolina can absorb the yogurt and expand. Transfer to a serving dish and refrigerate at least 2 hours. Mix in the cilantro and serve chilled. This chutney stays fresh in the refrigerator about 1 week. Do not freeze.

Garlic and Chile Pepper Chutneys

Green Garlic and Nuts Chutney

Harae Lussan aur Nuts ki Chutni

Makes about 1¹/₂ cups

Green garlic is to garlic what green onions (also called scallions) are to onions—they are the younger, milder, and fresher versions of these aromatics. Here, I purée together the tender white garlic bulbs with nuts, herbs, and green chile peppers to make a pesto-like chutney. Garlic lovers will savor it on the side with most Indian appetizers and meals, and especially with pakoras *(batter-fried fritters) and* iddli *(steamed fermented rice cakes). This chutney is also useful in many non-Indian dishes, including dips, salad dressings, pizzas, and pastas.*

Look for green garlic (with shoots and bulbs) at farmers' markets or specialty produce stores. Pick the youngest and most tender green garlic—they tend to be less fibrous. If you can't find green garlic, use 3 to 5 cloves of regular fresh garlic and the greens from 4 scallions.

³/₄ cup shelled and coarsely chopped mixed raw nuts, such as walnuts, almonds, cashews, and pine nuts

3 to 5 fresh green chile peppers, such as serrano, stemmed

5 to 7 green garlic shoots (with bulbs), bottom 3 to 4 inches only, thinly sliced

1¹/₂ cups coarsely chopped fresh cilantro, including soft stems

¹/₂ cup fresh mint leaves

¹/₄ cup fresh lime or lemon juice, or to taste

1 teaspoon sugar

1¹/₂ teaspoons salt, or to taste

¹/₂ teaspoon freshly ground black pepper, or to taste

1 tablespoon vegetable oil

¹/₂ teaspoon cumin seeds

¹/₂ teaspoon black mustard seeds

¹/₈ teaspoon ground asafoetida

¹/₄ teaspoon ground paprika

1. In a food processor or a blender, process together the nuts, green chile peppers and garlic until minced. Add the cilantro and mint to the work bowl and process, stopping a few times to scrape the sides with a spatula, until puréed. As you process, drizzle the lime juice through the feeder tube into the work bowl and process until the chutney is smooth. Add the sugar, salt, and black pepper and process again. Adjust the seasonings. Remove to a bowl.

2. Heat the oil in a large nonstick wok or saucepan over medium-high heat and add the cumin and mustard seeds; they should splatter upon contact with the hot oil, so lower the heat and cover the pan and reduce the heat until the splattering subsides. Stir in the asafoetida and paprika just to blend, then transfer the spice mixture to the chutney and swirl lightly to mix, with parts of it visible as a garnish. Transfer to a bowl and serve immediately, refrigerate about 10 days, or freeze up to 6 months.

Peanut and Garlic Chutney

Moong-Phalli aur Lassun ki Chutni

Makes about 1½ cups

This could be India's answer to peanut butter, if it weren't for the bold flavors—delicious, but these flavors require some getting used to. With every bite a hot and tangy mouthful, this chutney is best served with dosas *(griddle-fried fermented rice and* dal *crepes) and plain flat breads.*

¼ cup Tamarind Paste (page 54) or lemon juice

4 to 5 dried red chile peppers, such as chiles de arbol, broken

1¼ cups roasted unsalted peanuts, without red skin

½ cup dried shredded unsweetened coconut

2 large cloves fresh garlic, peeled

½ teaspoon salt, or to taste

1 tablespoon peanut oil

1 teaspoon black mustard seeds

5 to 7 fresh curry leaves

1. Prepare the tamarind paste. Then, in a small skillet, dry-roast the red chile peppers until a few shades darker. Place the peppers in a food processor or a blender. Add the peanuts and process until fine. Then add the coconut, garlic, tamarind (or lemon juice), and salt, and process to make a thick, smooth paste, adding up to ¼ cup water, as necessary.

2. Transfer to a serving bowl. Heat the oil in a small saucepan over medium-high heat. Add the mustard seeds and curry leaves; they should splutter upon contact with the hot oil, so cover the pan until the spluttering subsides. Quickly add the spice mixture to the chutney and swirl lightly to mix, with parts of it visible as a garnish. Transfer to a bowl and serve immediately, refrigerate about 10 days, or freeze up to 6 months.

Garlic and Fresh Red Chile Pepper Chutney

Lussan aur Laal Mirch ki Chutni

Makes about 1½ cups

Although an innocuous-looking red purée, this chutney should be eaten in small doses, unless you have a hearty constitution. It is indispensable with bhel-pooris *(a savory snack made with puffed rice, potatoes, and many chutneys),* dhokla *(steamed chickpea* dal *cakes), and other savory street snacks, and is also lovely in sandwiches and pizzas, or as a rub for meats.*

2 tablespoons black peppercorns, dry-roasted and ground (Dry Roasting Spices, page 35)

6 to 8 large cloves fresh garlic, peeled

6 to 8 quarter-size slices of peeled fresh ginger

15 to 20 fresh green chile peppers, such as serranos, coarsely chopped

2 to 3 red bell peppers, chopped

¼ cup fresh lime juice, or to taste

1 tablespoon ground paprika

1½ tablespoons ajwain seeds, coarsely ground

1 teaspoon cayenne pepper

2 to 3 teaspoons salt, or to taste

1. Prepare the peppercorns. Then place the garlic, ginger, red chile peppers, bell peppers, and lime juice in a food processor or a blender and process until smooth. Add the paprika, ajwain, 1½ tablespoons pepper, and the salt and process again until smooth.

2. Transfer to a serving bowl, garnish with the remaining pepper, and serve. This chutney stays fresh in the refrigerator about 1 month or in the freezer about 6 months.

Variation: Make a simpler garlic chutney by processing together 2 large peeled heads fresh garlic, 2 teaspoons ground cayenne pepper, 1 small tomato, 1 teaspoon ground cumin seeds, and 1 teaspoon salt to make a smooth paste.

Bean and Legume Chutneys

Roasted Dal and Fresh Green Chile Pepper Chutney
Bhel-Puri ki Chutni

Makes about 1¹/₂ cups

This chutney is the one carried all over India by vendors of bhel-puri *(a snack made with puffed rice, potatoes, and many chutneys). Even after we had gobbled down our plates of* bhel-puris, *we used to walk over for extra chutney because it was so good on its own. Very spicy and hot, but very good. Have a cold drink handy.*

³/₄ cup dried yellow split chickpeas (channa dal),
    sorted and washed in 3 to 4 changes of water
2 cups coarsely chopped fresh cilantro,
    including soft stems
20 to 25 fresh green chile peppers, such as serrano,
    stemmed
4 large cloves fresh garlic, peeled
3 to 4 tablespoons fresh lemon or lime juice
1¹/₂ teaspoons salt, or to taste

1. Place the dal in a small cast-iron or nonstick skillet and dry-roast over medium heat, stirring and shaking the pan until golden, 1 to 2 minutes. Let cool, then grind in a spice or coffee grinder to make a fine powder.

2. Place the cilantro, green chile peppers, garlic, and lemon juice in a blender or a food processor and process until smooth. Add the ground dal and the salt and process once again to mix. Transfer to a bowl and serve immediately, refrigerate about 10 days, or freeze up to 6 months.

Roasted Black Chickpea Chutney with Peanuts
Kaalae Channae ki Chutni

Makes about 1¹/₂ cups

This dry chutney, made with store-bought roasted black chickpeas, is used mainly as a garnish with dhoklas *(steamed chickpea* dal *cakes, page 135). Black chickpeas are by themselves a popular and healthy snack, similar to popcorn. Parents always have a supply in the pantry, because this low-calorie food is also high in protein, calcium, and other minerals. Roasted black chickpeas are available at Indian markets.*

¹/₂ cup roasted black chickpeas (bhunae channae)
¹/₂ cup dry-roasted unsalted peanuts,
    red skin removed
¹/₂ cup coarsely chopped fresh cilantro,
    including soft stems
1 to 2 fresh green chile peppers, such as serrano,
    stemmed
1 to 2 tablespoons fresh lime or lemon juice
¹/₂ teaspoon sugar
¹/₄ teaspoon salt, or to taste

1. Rub off the black outer coating from the chickpeas (it comes off easily). In a spice or coffee grinder, grind together the chickpeas and peanuts until smooth.

2. In a food processor or a blender, process together the cilantro, chile peppers, and lime juice, and then add the ground dal, peanuts, sugar, and salt. Process until well mixed. Transfer to a bowl and serve immediately, refrigerate about 10 days, or freeze up to 6 months.

Classic Hyderabadi Ginger-Sesame Chutney
Hyderabad ki Adrak-Til Chutni

Makes about 1¹/₂ cups

Ginger and sesame seeds are used extensively in Hyderabadi cuisine, and this chutney is a classic example. It is made by sautéing ginger and sesame seeds until they are fragrant and then mixing in some jaggery (thickened sugar cane juice), which adds a rustic, molasses-like flavor—yet another dimension to puréed chutneys.

Serve this chutney as a condiment with a meal, use it as a base to make spicy curries, or serve it with crackers as you would serve hummus.

¹/₄ cup Tamarind Paste, or to taste (page 54)

2 teaspoons Indian sesame oil

1 cup peeled and coarsely chopped fresh ginger

1 large clove fresh garlic, peeled

1 to 3 fresh green chile peppers, such as serrano, chopped with seeds

2 dried red chile peppers, such as chile de arbol, broken

1 teaspoon cumin seeds

1 teaspoon black mustard seeds

8 to 10 fresh curry leaves

1 tablespoon white sesame seeds

¹/₈ teaspoon ground asafoetida

1 teaspoon salt, or to taste

2 tablespoons grated jaggery (gur)

1. Prepare the tamarind paste. Then, heat the oil in a small nonstick saucepan over medium-low heat and cook the ginger, stirring, until golden, about 5 minutes. Using a slotted spoon, remove the fried ginger to a blender jar, leaving the oil behind in the pan.

2. In the same oil, add the garlic and the green and red chile peppers and cook, stirring, until golden. Tilt the pan to gather the oil to one side and add the cumin and mustard seeds; they should splutter upon contact with the hot oil, so lower the heat and cover the pan until the spluttering subsides. Quickly add the curry leaves, sesame seeds, and asafoetida.

3. Transfer to the blender jar, add the jaggery, tamarind paste, and the salt, and process until coarsely puréed. Add a tablespoon or 2 of hot water, if needed, for blending. Transfer to a bowl and serve immediately, refrigerate about 10 days, or freeze up to 6 months.

Variation: Mix some of this chutney into Yogurt Cheese (page 42), adjust the seasonings, and make yet another outstanding chutney.

Sesame-Peanut Chutney
Til aur Moong-Phalli ki Chutni

Makes about 1 cup

This is a terrific body-warming chutney (sesame seeds and peanuts are considered warming ingredients in Ayurvedic *medicine), intense in flavor and high in protein—but also high in calories. Enjoy it with popular southern Indian fare such as* dosas *(griddle-fried, fermented rice and* dal *crepes), iddli (steamed, fermented rice cakes), and steamed rice. Also try it in sandwiches, with grilled meats, or mix some into* hummus.

¹/₂ cup Tamarind Paste (page 54)

¹/₄ cup white sesame seeds

¹/₂ cup dry-roasted unsalted peanuts, red skins removed

1 to 3 fresh green chile peppers, such as serrano, stemmed

1 large clove fresh garlic, peeled

¹/₄ cup hot water

¹/₂ cup coarsely chopped fresh cilantro, including soft stems

1 teaspoon salt, or to taste

Prepare the tamarind paste. Then, in a small skillet, roast the sesame seeds over medium heat, stirring and shaking the pan until golden, about 1 minute. Transfer to a blender along with all the other ingredients and blend until smooth. Adjust the seasonings. Transfer to a bowl and serve immediately, refrigerate about 10 days, or freeze up to 6 months.

Yogurt Chutneys

Yogurt Chutney with Puréed Greens
Dahi ki Hari Chutni

Makes about 1¹/₂ cups

This basic chutney is one of the most versatile and crowd-pleasing—the ultimate companion to all types of Indian appetizers and meals. Made simply by mixing puréed fragrant greens (herbs, scallions, and chiles) and spices with plain yogurt, this chutney can also be enjoyed with non-Indian appetizers, as a dipping sauce with vegetables, or as a salad dressing. Also try it as a marinade for fish and chicken.

1 teaspoon Chaat Masala, or to taste
    (page 20 or store-bought)
4 quarter-size slices of peeled fresh ginger
5 to 6 scallions, coarsely chopped
1 to 3 fresh green chile peppers, such as serrano,
    stemmed
2 cups coarsely chopped mixed fresh herbs in any
    proportion, such as cilantro, mint, parsley, dill,
    basil, or lemon basil
2 tablespoons fresh lime or lemon juice
1 teaspoon salt, or to taste
¹/₂ teaspoon coarsely ground black pepper
1 cup nonfat plain yogurt, whisked until smooth
Minced fresh greens of your choice
    (scallions, chile peppers, or herbs)

1. Prepare the chaat masala. Then, in a food processor or a blender, process together the ginger, scallions, and green chile peppers until minced. Add the fresh herbs and lime juice and process again until smooth, scraping the sides of the work bowl with a spatula, as needed. (If you need more liquid while processing, mix in some of the yogurt.) Add the chaat masala, salt, and pepper, and process again.

2. Place the yogurt in a serving bowl and add the puréed greens. Swirl lightly to mix, with parts of the greens visible as a garnish. Scatter the additional minced greens on top, and serve. This chutney stays fresh in the refrigerator about 1 week. Do not freeze.

Yogurt Chutney with Roasted Dals and Spices
Dahi aur Bhuni Dal ki Chutni

Makes about 1¹/₂ cups

Although very ordinary looking, this south Indian chutney's flavor seems to explode at first bite. Try it as a dip with vadai *(deep-fried, fermented lentil dumplings) or with* pakoras *(chickpea flour batter-fried vegetable fritters), or mix in some boiled and chopped potatoes and present it as a* raita *with any rice* pullao *(pilaf).*

1 tablespoon each, dried yellow split chickpeas
    (channa dal), split white urad beans (dhulli
    urad dal), yellow mung beans (dhulli mung dal),
    dry-roasted and ground (Dry-Roasting Spices,
    page 35)
2 teaspoons cumin seeds, dry-roasted and coarsely
    ground (Dry-Roasting Spices, page 35)
1 tablespoon vegetable oil
2 dried red chile peppers, such as chile de arbol,
    with stems, broken
1 teaspoon black mustard seeds
¹/₄ teaspoon ground asafoetida
15 to 20 fresh curry leaves
1 to 2 fresh green chile peppers, such as serrano,
    coarsely chopped
¹/₄ cup grated fresh or frozen coconut
2 tablespoons peeled and coarsely chopped
    fresh ginger
¹/₂ cup coarsely chopped fresh cilantro,
    including soft stems
1 cup nonfat plain yogurt, whisked until smooth
1 teaspoon salt, or to taste

1. Prepare the dals and the cumin. Then heat the oil in a small nonstick wok or saucepan over medium-high heat and add the red chile peppers and mustard seeds; they should splutter upon contact with the hot oil, so lower the heat and cover the pan until the spluttering subsides.

2. Quickly add the asafoetida, curry leaves, green chile peppers, coconut, and ginger, and cook, stirring, until the coconut is golden, about 5 minutes. Add the cilantro and stir another 5 minutes. Transfer to a blender or a food processor and process to make a smooth paste.

3. Place the yogurt in a serving bowl, mix in the processed herb and coconut paste, then add the roasted dals, cumin (save some cumin for garnish), and the salt, and stir to mix well. Sprinkle the reserved cumin on top and serve. This chutney stays fresh in the refrigerator about 1 week. Do not freeze.

Yogurt Cheese Chutney with Minced Greens
Gaadhi Dahi ki Hari Chutni

Makes about 1¹/₂ cups

Yogurt cheese, made by simply draining the water out of yogurt, has the texture and consistency of sour cream and even cream cheese if it is further drained by being pressed under a heavy object. And, like its popular relatives, this cheese is very versatile.

Here we add some pretty common Indian flavors, which, in America fall into the exotic category. The trick here is to mince all the ingredients so that they merge well into the smooth yogurt cheese, yet retain their individuality and delicate crunch. Do not purée.

Serve this one as a dip with crisp vegetables or mix in some chopped hard-boiled eggs, cooked chicken, or even a can of water-packed tuna and present in sandwiches or over salads.

1 teaspoon dry-roasted and coarsely crushed cumin seeds (Dry-Roasting Spices, page 35)
1 teaspoon Chaat Masala, or to taste (page 20 or store-bought)
1¹/₂ cups nonfat plain yogurt
1 (2-foot-square) piece of fine muslin or 4 layers of cheesecloth
10 to 12 scallions, white parts only, minced
¹/₄ cup minced fresh cilantro, including soft stems
¹/₄ cup minced fresh mint leaves
1 tablespoon peeled and minced fresh ginger
1 fresh green chile pepper, such as serrano, minced with seeds
2 tablespoons fresh lemon juice
¹/₄ teaspoon ground paprika

1. Prepare the cumin and the chaat masala. Then, place the yogurt in a colander or a fine-mesh strainer lined with muslin or 4 layers of cheesecloth set over a bowl. Allow to drain about 2 hours in the refrigerator. Transfer to a serving bowl, then whisk with a fork until smooth.

2. Add the scallion, cilantro, mint, ginger, green chile pepper, lemon juice, chaat masala, sugar, and half the cumin, and mix well. Adjust the seasonings. Garnish with the remaining cumin seeds and the paprika, and serve immediately or refrigerate about 1 week. Do not freeze.

Yogurt-Almond Chutney
Dahi-Badaam ki Chutni

Makes about 1¹/₂ cups

As the almonds soak, they absorb some of the yogurt and soften, to lend an interesting texture and a delicate bite to this refreshing, chile-fired chutney. For a change of flavors, instead of the almonds, add walnuts, cashews, or pistachios, or add a mixture of nuts.

1 cup nonfat plain yogurt, whisked until smooth
¹/₂ cup shelled and coarsely ground raw almonds
1 tablespoon fresh lemon juice
¹/₄ cup minced fresh cilantro, including soft stems
1 tablespoon peeled and minced fresh ginger
1 fresh green chile pepper, such as serrano, minced with seeds
1 teaspoon salt, or to taste
Freshly ground black pepper, to taste
1 teaspoon Chaat Masala (page 20 or store-bought)

In a serving bowl, mix together all the ingredients except the chaat masala and chill at least 4 hours. Before serving, prepare the chaat masala then add it to the chutney and swirl lightly to mix, with parts of it visible as a garnish. This chutney stays fresh about 1 week in the refrigerator. Do not freeze.

Puréed Fruit Chutneys

Puréed Green Mango Chutney
Harae Aam ki Chutni

Makes about 1¹/₂ cups

Come summer, when the first mangoes hit the market, there is an air of infectious excitement—let the mango craze begins! Besides devouring mangoes out-of-hand by the dozens, cooks all over the country begin preparing numerous incarnations of mango dishes. This chutney, with its southern flavors of mustard seeds, curry leaves, and asafoetida, is just one of the popular ones.

Serve it with the standard south Indian foods, such as iddlis *(steamed fermented rice cakes),* dosas *(griddle-fried, fermented rice and* dal *crepes), or with any Indian finger foods or rice* pullaos *(pilafs).*

2 large unripe green mangoes (about ³/₄ pound each), washed and wiped dry
3 quarter-size slices peeled fresh ginger
1 to 3 fresh green chile peppers, such as serrano, stemmed
4 scallions, coarsely chopped
15 to 20 fresh curry leaves
¹/₂ teaspoon salt, or to taste
1 to 2 teaspoons sugar (optional)
1 tablespoon peanut oil
2 whole dried red chile peppers, such as chile de arbol
1 teaspoon black mustard seeds
¹/₂ teaspoon coarsely ground fenugreek seeds
¹/₈ teaspoon ground asafoetida

1. With a vegetable peeler, peel the mangoes, then cut the fruit around the center seed into ½- to 1-inch pieces. Place the mango pieces and the ginger, green chile peppers, scallions, curry leaves, and salt in a food processor or a blender, and process until minced. Remove to a serving bowl. Add some of the sugar if the chutney seems too tart.

2. Heat the oil in a small nonstick saucepan over medium-high heat and add the red chile peppers and

mustard seeds; they should splutter upon contact with the hot oil, so lower the heat and cover the pan until the spluttering subsides. Quickly add the fenugreek seeds and asafoetida, stir 30 seconds, then add this seasoning mixture to the chutney, with parts of it visible as a garnish. Transfer to a bowl and serve immediately, refrigerate about 10 days, or freeze up to 6 months.

Puréed Fresh Mango-Ginger Chutney
Pakkae Aam ki Chutni

Makes about 1¹/₂ cups

A textured mash of ripe mangoes and fresh ginger makes for a delicate salsa-like sauce that is as lovely with grilled foods and sautéed fish fillets as it is over salads and steamed vegetables.

Buy fragrant, ripe mangoes that "give" slightly to gentle pressure when held in your hand, (don't poke with your finger or you could damage the flesh). Canned mango pulp from Indian markets is a very good substitute. Use 1 cup of canned mango pulp (preferably the Alphonso variety of mango) in place of each large mango.

3 large ripe mangoes (about ³/₄ pound each), washed and wiped dry
2 tablespoons peeled and minced fresh ginger
¹/₄ cup fresh lime or lemon juice
¹/₄ cup finely chopped fresh cilantro, including soft stems
1 to 2 fresh green chile pepper, such as serrano, minced with seeds
¹/₂ teaspoon salt, or to taste
Freshly ground black pepper

1. With a knife, peel the mango, then coarsely cut the fruit around the center seed. Place the mango pieces in a large serving bowl and mash with a fork to make the fruit as smooth as possible.

2. Mix in all the remaining ingredients. Garnish with black pepper and serve immediately, or refrigerate up to 1 week.

Variation: Mix in ¹/₂ cup yogurt, or substitute peaches, plums, nectarines, pineapples, and other soft fruits for the mangoes.

Tart Apple-Ginger Chutney with Green Tomatoes

Saeb, Adrak aur Harae Tamatar ki Chutni

Makes about 2 cups

Fresh ginger gives this spicy-sour chutney a refreshing piquancy that can perk up even the blandest of dishes. Much as I love this chutney on the side with grilled fish, I think it is unrivaled as a salad dressing.

1 teaspoon black peppercorns, dry-roasted and coarsely ground (Dry Roasting Spices, page 35)
1 tablespoon peanut oil
1 tablespoon coriander seeds
6 to 8 quarter-size slices of peeled fresh ginger
2 fresh green chile peppers, such as serrano, stemmed
2 large tart green apples, such as Granny Smith or pippin, cored and coarsely chopped
2 small green tomatoes, coarsely chopped
1 teaspoon sugar
1 teaspoon salt, or to taste
Fresh cilantro sprigs

1. Prepare the peppercorns. Then heat the oil in a small saucepan over medium-high heat and add the coriander seeds; they should sizzle upon contact with the hot oil. Quickly add the remaining ingredients and cook, stirring, about 5 minutes.

2. Transfer to a food processor or a blender and process to make a coarse purée. Transfer to a bowl, garnish with cilantro sprigs, and serve. This chutney stays fresh in the refrigerator about 10 days, and in the freezer about 6 months.

Variation: Stir some of this chutney into whisked yogurt. Top with dry-roasted, coarsely ground cumin seeds and serve as a raita.

South Indian Tomato Chutney

South ki Tamatar Chutni

Makes about 1¹/2 cups

My friend Sushi Mysoor makes her native Bangalore-style tomato chutney the easy way, using canned

tomato sauce—something the purists would scoff at, but all of us in America are really thankful for. The spicy flavors of this chutney are quite captivating and very versatile. Try it with sandwiches and paranthas *(griddle-fried breads) or with* dosas *(griddle-fried fermented rice and* dal *crepes) and other crepes.*

1 teaspoon Tamarind Paste (page 35)
1 tablespoon coriander seeds
1 teaspoon cumin seeds
1 teaspoon dried yellow split chickpeas (channa dal), sorted
1 teaspoon dried white urad beans (dhulli urad dal), sorted
¹/2 teaspoon black peppercorns
¹/4 cup peanut oil
1 teaspoon black mustard seeds
1 teaspoon dried curry leaves
2 to 3 whole dried red chile peppers, such as chile de arbol
2 large cloves fresh garlic, minced
¹/2 cup finely chopped red onion
1 teaspoon cayenne pepper, or to taste
1 teaspoon salt, or to taste
1 (15-ounce) can tomato sauce

1. Prepare the tamarind paste. Then, in a spice or a coffee grinder, grind together coriander and cumin seeds, dals, and peppercorns to make a fine powder.

2. Heat the oil in a small nonstick saucepan over medium heat and add the mustard seeds, curry leaves, and red chile peppers; they should splutter upon contact with the hot oil, so lower the heat and cover the pan until the spluttering subsides. Quickly add the garlic and onion, stir a few seconds, then add the ground spice and dal mixture, cayenne pepper, and salt and cook, stirring, another 2 minutes.

3. Add the tomato sauce and tamarind paste, cover the pan, reduce the heat to low, and cook, stirring occasionally, until the chutney is thick and fragrant and reduced to about 1 cup, about 20 minutes. Let cool, then serve immediately, refrigerate about 2 months or freeze about 6 months.

Preserved Chutneys

Tomato Chutney Preserve with Cashews and Raisins

*Tamatar, Kaaju aur Kishmish
ki Chutni*

Makes about 2 cups

I got this recipe from my mother-in-law about 20 years ago, and have been making it ever since. Made with fresh tomatoes and preserved with vinegar, this chutney can be enjoyed over hot griddle-fried parantha *breads or presented at your next barbecue. Try it in sandwiches and pita pockets or mix some into yogurt cheese or light sour cream to make a dip for an appetizer platter.*

1 tablespoon vegetable oil
2 tablespoons peeled and minced fresh ginger
2 large fresh garlic cloves, minced
2 to 4 fresh green chile peppers, minced with seeds
1 teaspoon fennel seeds
1/2 teaspoon coarsely crushed fenugreek seeds
1/2 cup coarsely chopped raw cashews
1/2 cup golden raisins
3 large tomatoes, finely chopped (about 1 1/2 pounds)
2 cups sugar, or more to taste
1 tablespoon salt, or to taste
1 teaspoon ground paprika
1/2 teaspoon cayenne pepper
1/2 cup distilled white vinegar

1. Heat the oil in a large non-reactive wok or saucepan over medium heat and cook the ginger, garlic, green chile peppers, fennel seeds and fenugreek seeds, stirring, until golden, about 1 minute. Add the cashews and raisins and stir until the raisins expand, about 1 minute.

2. Add the tomatoes, sugar, salt, paprika, and cayenne pepper and cook, over medium-high heat for the first 2 to 3 minutes. Then cover the pan and cook, stirring

occasionally, over medium heat until the tomatoes are very soft, about 10 minutes. Add the vinegar, and simmer, uncovered, until semi-thick, about 15 minutes. (It will continue to thicken as it cools.) Serve immediately or let cool, then store in an airtight container in the refrigerator, about 1 year.

Red Tomato Chutney Preserve with Sesame Seeds

Tamatar-Til ki Chutni

Makes about 2 cups

This bold chutney, with special seasonings from southern India, has a light crunch from the roasted dals *(dried beans, peas, and lentils). Among all the other regular uses, this chutney pairs famously with grilled seafood such as Grilled Sea Bass (page 518).*

1 tablespoon sesame seeds, dry-roasted
    (Dry-Roasting Spices, page 35)
2 tablespoons peanut oil
1 tablespoon black mustard seeds
2 tablespoons minced fresh curry leaves
1 tablespoon dried yellow split chickpeas
    (channa dal), sorted
1 tablespoon dried split pigeon peas (toor dal),
    sorted
1 cup finely chopped onion
2 tablespoons peeled and minced fresh ginger
1 tablespoon minced fresh garlic cloves
1 to 3 fresh green chile peppers, such as serrano,
    minced with seeds
1/4 teaspoon ground turmeric
1 teaspoon salt, or to taste
1/8 teaspoon ground asafoetida
2 large tomatoes, finely chopped
2 tablespoons distilled white vinegar

1. Prepare the sesame seeds. Then, heat the oil in a medium wok or saucepan over medium-high heat and add the mustard seeds; they should splutter upon contact with the hot oil, so lower the heat and cover the pan until the spluttering subsides.

Add the curry leaves and both the dals, and stir until the dals are golden, about 30 seconds. Add the onion and cook, stirring, until golden, about 3 minutes. Add the ginger, garlic, and green chile peppers, stir 1 minute, then mix in the turmeric, salt, and asafoetida.

2. Add the tomatoes and vinegar and cook until most of the juices evaporate and the chutney is semi-thick, 7 to 10 minutes. (It will continue to thicken as it cools.) Transfer to a serving dish, garnish with the sesame seeds, and serve hot or cold, or store in an airtight container in the refrigerator, about 1 year.

Fragrant Mango Chutney Preserve
Aam ki Chutni

Makes about 4 cups

In India, mango chutney (and pickle) is one of those things around which the women in a family will create cherished legacies and fables. The secrets to their recipes are zealously guarded and passed down from one generation to another.

This chutney is made with tart, unripe green mangoes and simmered along with fragrant Indian spices in a sugar syrup until everything turns the color of pure honey. It is easy to make and has tremendous staying power—that is, if it's not gone before you snap your fingers.

Choose the hardest green mangoes you can find. If they give to any pressure, they are too ripe and will not work.

4 large unripe green mangoes, (about 3/4 pound each), washed and wiped dry
2 (3-inch) sticks cinnamon, broken
10 to 12 black cardamom pods, crushed lightly to break the skin
10 to 12 green cardamom pods, crushed lightly to break the skin
1 tablespoon fennel seeds
1 tablespoon black peppercorns
1 tablespoon whole cloves
1 1/2 teaspoons kalonji seeds
1 tablespoon fenugreek seeds
4 cups sugar
1 tablespoon salt, or to taste
3/4 cup distilled white vinegar

1. With a vegetable peeler, peel the mangoes, then cut the fruit around the center seed into thin 1 1/2- to 2-inch long pieces. Place all the spices in a large, heavy, non-reactive saucepan and roast over medium-high heat, stirring and shaking the pan, until heated through, about 1 minute.

2. Add the mangoes, sugar, and salt, and bring to a boil, stirring constantly over medium-high heat until the sugar melts and comes to a boil. Boil 1 minute, then reduce the heat to medium-low, cover the pan and cook, stirring occasionally, about 10 minutes.

3. Uncover the pan, add the vinegar, and cook, stirring occasionally, until the sugar caramelizes and takes on a rich honey-like color and consistency, about 20 minutes. (Do not make the chutney very thick; it will thicken as it cools.)

4. Let cool completely, then put it in sterile jars. This chutney does not need to be refrigerated. It stays fresh about 6 months at room temperature. The color deepens over time, but that does not affect the taste.

Spicy Apricot Chutney Preserve

Aadu ki Chutni

Makes about 4 cups

A must-make summer chutney. Use the very firm apricots, just before they start to ripen. This chutney can also be made with firm peaches, nectarines, or pineapples.

1/4 cup Basic Ginger-Garlic Paste
    (page 47 or store-bought)
3 tablespoons vegetable oil
3 (1-inch) sticks cinnamon
6 to 8 black cardamom pods, crushed lightly
    to break the skin
8 whole cloves
3 small onions, cut in half lengthwise and
    thinly sliced
1 teaspoon kalonji seeds
3/4 teaspoon ground fenugreek seeds
1 tablespoon ground fennel seeds
5 to 7 fresh green chile peppers, such as serrano,
    minced with seeds
2 pounds fresh unripe apricots, pitted and
    cut into wedges
2 tablespoons salt, or to taste
1 1/2 cups sugar
1/4 to 1/3 cup distilled white vinegar

1. Prepare the ginger-garlic paste. Then, heat the oil in a large nonstick wok or saucepan over medium-high heat and cook the cinnamon, cardamom pods, and cloves, stirring, about 1 minute. Add the onions and cook, stirring, until golden, about 7 minutes. Add the kalonji, fenugreek, and fennel seeds, and then mix in the ginger-garlic paste and green chile peppers and sauté about 2 minutes.

2. Add the apricots, sugar, and salt and cook, stirring, over medium heat until the sugar melts, about

3 minutes. Increase the heat to medium-high and cook until the sugar caramelizes into a rich golden color, the apricots are soft, and the chutney is thick, about 15 minutes.

3. Add the vinegar, and boil over high heat about 2 minutes, or until the chutney thickens once again. (Do not make the chutney very thick; it will thicken as it cools.) Let cool completely, and put in sterile jars. This chutney does not need to be refrigerated. It stays fresh about 6 months at room temperature. The color deepens over time, but that does not affect the taste.

Spicy Apple-Ginger Chutney Preserve

Saeb-Adrak ki Chutni

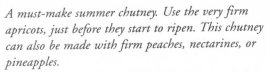

Makes about 4 cups

I generally make this chutney with apples that grow in my yard but never get eaten because they are so tart (even when fully ripe). Instead of leaving them for the squirrels and birds, I make this spicy, sweet, and sour chutney that will make any creative cook proud. Of course, if you don't have apples in your backyard (or don't even have a backyard), farm stand or store-bought tart apples do just fine.

This chutney has a lot of heat from the chile peppers, so adjust to your taste and use it sparingly.

2 tablespoons Basic Ginger-Garlic Paste
    (page 47 or store-bought)
3 tablespoons vegetable oil
20 to 25 dried red chile peppers, such as chile de arbol,
    with stems
4 (1-inch) sticks cinnamon
6 to 8 black cardamom pods, crushed lightly
    to break the skin
10 whole cloves
2 tablespoons fennel seeds

2 teaspoons kalonji seeds

2 medium onions, cut in half lengthwise and thinly sliced

5 to 6 (1-inch) pieces peeled fresh ginger, cut in half lengthwise and thinly sliced

6 fresh garlic cloves, cut in half lengthwise and thinly sliced

2 teaspoons coarsely ground fenugreek seeds

2 to 3 teaspoons cayenne pepper

2 pounds tart apples, such as Pippin or Granny Smith, peeled and cut in 1/2-inch pieces

2 cups sugar

1 1/2 tablespoons salt

1/4 cup distilled white vinegar

1. Prepare the ginger-garlic paste. Then, heat the oil in a large nonstick wok or saucepan over medium-high heat and cook the red chile peppers, cinnamon, cardamom pods, and cloves, stirring, about 1 minute. Add the fennel and kalonji seeds, and stir about 30 seconds, then add the onion, ginger, and garlic and cook, stirring until golden, about 10 minutes.

2. Add the fenugreek seeds and cayenne pepper and stir 1 minute. Then add the apples, sugar, ginger-garlic paste, and salt, and cook over medium heat, stirring, until the sugar melts, about 3 minutes. Increase the heat to medium-high and cook until the sugar caramelizes into a rich golden color, the apples are soft, and the chutney is thick, about 15 minutes.

3. Add the vinegar and boil over high heat about 2 minutes, or until the chutney thickens once again. (Do not make the chutney very thick; it will thicken as it cools.) Let cool completely and put in sterile jars. This chutney does not need to be refrigerated. It stays fresh about 6 months at room temperature. The color deepens over time, but that does not affect the taste.

Cranberry Chutney Preserve
Karonda Chutni

Makes about 4 cups

A little sweet, a little tangy, and so perfect with roasted turkey. This chutney is my invention and one that has become a favorite of family and friends and a crucial part of our annual Thanksgiving menu. It is also great on hot toasted bread, in plain yogurt, or with any rice pullao *(pilaf).*

2 tablespoons Bengali 5-Spices (Panch-Phoran), page 27, coarsely ground

1 tablespoon vegetable oil

2 (1-inch) sticks cinnamon

8 to 10 black cardamom pods, crushed lightly to break the skin

10 to 12 whole cloves

2 tablespoons peeled and minced fresh ginger

2 (12-ounce) packages fresh cranberries, washed

4 cups sugar

4 cups water

1 tablespoon ground ginger

1 1/2 teaspoons salt, or to taste

5 to 7 tablespoons distilled white vinegar

1. Prepare the 5-spices. Then, heat the oil in a large non-reactive wok or saucepan over medium-high heat and cook the cinnamon, cardamom pods, and cloves, stirring, about 30 seconds.

2. Add the fresh ginger and panch-phoran and cook, stirring, about 1 minute. Add the cranberries, sugar, water, ground ginger, and salt, and bring to a boil over high heat. Cover and cook, stirring occasionally, until slightly thickened, about 7 minutes.

3. Reduce the heat to medium, uncover the pan, add the vinegar, and cook until the chutney is quite thick, about 10 minutes. (Do not make the chutney very thick; it will thicken as it cools.) Transfer to a bowl, let cool, and serve at room temperature, or refrigerate at least 2 hours and serve chilled. This chutney stays fresh in the refrigerator about 3 months, or in the freezer about 1 year.

Variation: Mix in 1 tablespoon lemon or orange rind (no white pith) and substitute 1 cup of orange juice for 1 cup of water.

Sonth Chutneys

Sonth (pronounced sawnth) is a savory dark brown, velvety smooth sauce-like chutney with sweet overtones—even though its main ingredient is dried raw mango (pieces or powder) or tamarind, both of which are very sour.

This chutney is often seen in Indian restaurants, where it is generally served with different appetizers, including *tandoor*-grilled foods. In India, however, it is mostly served over special *chaats* (snacks and salads infused with complex sweet, salty, tangy, and spicy flavors), but I find that these chutneys also beautifully complement an array of American appetizers and grilled fare, especially when presented alongside plain whisked yogurt and some Chaat Masala.

The consistency of most *sonths* is like that of a semi-thick batter but some people prefer it watery and others like it thicker. (Note: Dried ginger is also called *sonth* in Hindi, so don't be confused if you see that term used on packages.)

Sonth Chutney with Dried Mango Slices

Amchur ki Sonth

Makes about 4 cups

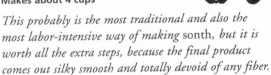

This probably is the most traditional and also the most labor-intensive way of making sonth, *but it is worth all the extra steps, because the final product comes out silky smooth and totally devoid of any fiber.*

We start by boiling dried mango pieces in a pressure cooker (or in a pot) until they are very soft, then pass them through a food mill to make a smooth, fiber-free sauce. (This contrasts versions starting with mango or tamarind powder, where all the natural fiber is also ground and simply cooked with everything together.)

Jaggery (the British English word for gur—*thickened sugar cane juice) is an essential ingredient that gives this chutney its rustic character. It is sold in solid* chunks that have to be grated, ground, or crushed in a mortar and pestle before it can be measured.

Dried mango slices (amchur pieces*), ginger pieces (sund or sonth*)*, and jaggery (gur) are all available in Indian markets.*

1 tablespoon cumin seeds, dry-roasted and
    finely ground (Dry-Roasting Spices, page 35)
1 tablespoon Chaat Masala, or to taste
    (page 20 or store-bought)
4 ounces dried raw mango slices
1 (2-inch) piece dried ginger, coarsely chopped
4 to 6 dried red chile peppers, such as chile de arbol,
    broken
1 cup coarsely grated or crushed jaggery,
    or 1¼ cups dark brown sugar
2 teaspoons salt, or to taste
1 teaspoon ground paprika
1 teaspoon black salt
4 cups water

1. Prepare the cumin seeds and chaat masala. Then place everything (except 1 cup of the water) in a pressure cooker. Secure the lid and cook over high heat until the regulator indicates high pressure, then cook about 1 more minute. Remove pot from the heat and allow to depressurize on its own, 12 to 15 minutes. Carefully remove the lid. (This can also be done in a pan. Put all the ingredients, and an extra ½ to 1 cup water, in a pan and bring to a boil over high heat. Reduce the heat to medium-low, cover the pan, and simmer until the mango pieces are very soft, about 30 minutes.)

2. Pass everything through a food mill into a large bowl to extract a smooth sauce. Bring the reserved one cup of water to a boil in a small saucepan. Pour the boiling hot water over the fibrous remains in the food mill and collect any remaining pulp. Stir the extra pulp into the sauce; it should be like a semi-thick batter. Adjust the seasonings, transfer to a bowl and serve at room temperature, or transfer to an airtight container and refrigerate about 2 months, or freeze about 1 year.

Variation: Substitute 4 ounces seedless tamarind pulp in place of the dried mango slices.

Minty Sonth Chutney with Mango (or Tamarind) Powder and Jaggery

Pudina Sonth

Makes about 4 cups

The use of powdered mango or tamarind makes this recipe easier and faster than others, because you don't have the prep work for the fresh mango or tamarind.

1½ tablespoons cumin seeds, dry-roasted and coarsely ground (Dry-Roasting Spices, page 35)

2 tablespoons Chaat Masala (page 20 or store-bought)

8 quarter-size slices of peeled fresh ginger

1 to 3 fresh green chile peppers, such as serrano, stemmed

20 to 25 large fresh mint leaves

1 cup coarsely grated or crushed jaggery, or 1¼ cup dark brown sugar

3 to 4 cups water

1 cup mango or tamarind powder, sifted to remove any lumps

1 teaspoon ground paprika

½ teaspoon ground ginger

2 teaspoon salt, or to taste

½ teaspoon black salt

1. Prepare the cumin seeds and chaat masala. Then, in a blender, blend together the ginger, chile peppers, mint leaves with about ½ cup of the water to make a smooth paste.

2. In a large non-reactive saucepan, mix together the jaggery and 3 cups of the water (disregard any lumps; they will melt when heated) and bring to a boil, stirring occasionally, until all the lumps dissolve completely, 3 to 4 minutes. Pass through a fine-mesh strainer to remove any impurities. Return the jaggery to the saucepan and add the ginger-mint mixture, mango or tamarind powder, chaat masala, paprika, ground ginger, cumin, salt, and black salt.

3. Bring to a boil over high heat. Reduce the heat to medium-low, and simmer, stirring occasionally, about 5 minutes. The sauce should be like a semi-thick batter. Mix in up to 1 cup of water if the sauce

thickens too quickly. Adjust seasoning, transfer to a bowl, then let cool. Serve at room temperature. Or transfer to an airtight container and refrigerate about 2 months, or freeze about 1 year.

Variation: Try this with applesauce and lemon juice. Use about 4 cups of applesauce and about ¼ cup fresh lemon juice instead of the mango powder and water. Adjust the salt and sugar, as needed.

Sonth Chutney with Fresh and Dried Fruits

Fallon vaali Sonth

Makes about 4 cups

This chutney, with a sweeter flavor (compared to that of the smooth sonth *chutneys), makes for a surprising mouthful when you bite on small pieces of fruit. Use it as a topping over plain, lightly salted yogurt or over special yogurt* raitas, *and serve it with rice* pullaos *(pilafs).*

1 cup finely chopped mixed dried fruits, such as raisins, peaches, apricots, plums, figs, and dates

1½ cups water + 4 cups water, measured separately

2 tablespoons cumin seeds, dry-roasted and ground (Dry-Roasting Spices, page 35)

2 tablespoons Chaat Masala, or to taste (page 20 or store-bought)

1 cup coarsely grated or crushed jaggery, or 1¼ cups dark brown sugar

1 cup mango or tamarind powder, sifted to remove lumps

1 tablespoon peeled and finely minced fresh ginger

2 teaspoons ground ginger

2 teaspoons salt, or to taste

1 teaspoon black salt

1 tablespoon vegetable oil

1 teaspoon cumin seeds

1 teaspoon ground paprika

1 to 2 cups chopped ripe fruits, such as bananas, mangoes, pineapple, and peaches

1. Soak the dried fruits overnight in 1½ cups of the water. Meanwhile, prepare the cumin seeds and chaat masala. When ready, drain the fruits, reserving the water.

2. In a large non-reactive saucepan, mix together the jaggery and 2 cups of the water (disregard any lumps; they will melt when heated), and bring to a boil over high heat, stirring occasionally, until all the lumps dissolve completely, 3 to 4 minutes. Pass through a fine-mesh strainer to remove any impurities. Return to the pan. Mix in the mango or tamarind powder and up to 2 cups water, including the reserved fruit-water in this measurement. Mix well and bring to a boil over high heat.

3. Add the drained dried fruits, fresh and dried ginger, chaat masala, salt, and black salt, reduce the heat to medium-low, and simmer, stirring occasionally and adding more water if the sauce thickens too quickly, until it reaches a semi-thick batter-like consistency, about 10 minutes. Adjust the seasonings and transfer to a serving bowl.

4. Heat the oil in a large nonstick wok or saucepan over medium-high heat and add the cumin seeds; they should sizzle upon contact with the hot oil. Quickly, remove the pan from the heat, add the paprika, and mix into the chutney. Serve at room temperature, or transfer to an airtight container and refrigerate about 2 months, or freeze about 1 year. Just before serving, mix in ripe fruits and serve.

Sweet Sonth Chutney with Dates
Khajjur ki Sonth

Makes about 4 cups

This simple puréed chutney, typically served over bhel-poori *(a savory street salad made with puffed rice, broken flour chips, potatoes, and special chutneys), is sweet enough to counter the fire started by the red and green chile pepper chutneys that are also added to* bhel-poori. *Look for tamarind pulp in Indian or ethnic markets.*

**1¹⁄₂ tablespoons cumin seeds, dry-roasted and
    coarsely ground (Dry-Roasting Spices, page 35)**
2 cups chopped pitted dates
¹⁄₂ cup seedless tamarind pulp
2 cups hot water
¹⁄₂ to ³⁄₄ cup sugar
1 teaspoon salt, or to taste

1. Prepare the cumin seeds. Soak the dates and tamarind pulp in 1 cup hot water, about 1 hour to soften.

2. With clean fingers, mush the pulp to release it from the fibrous parts of the dates and to separate any tamarind seeds that may still be present. Then pass the softened date-tamarind pulp through a fine-mesh strainer or a food mill (I prefer the food mill, especially for large quantities) into a large bowl to extract a smooth paste. Pour the remaining hot water over the fibrous remains in the food mill and collect any remaining pulp and mix into the already extracted paste.

3. Transfer to a small saucepan, add the sugar, cumin, and salt, and bring to a boil over high heat. Reduce the heat to medium-low and simmer about 5 minutes. Mix in up to 1 cup of water if the chutney thickens too quickly. Adjust the seasoning, then let cool. Serve at room temperature, or transfer to an airtight container and refrigerate about 2 months, or freeze about 1 year.

Mango Pickles

Quick Mango Pickle
Aam ka Achaar

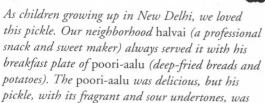

Makes about 2 cups

As children growing up in New Delhi, we loved this pickle. Our neighborhood halvai *(a professional snack and sweet maker) always served it with his breakfast plate of* poori-aalu *(deep-fried breads and potatoes). The* poori-aalu *was delicious, but his pickle, with its fragrant and sour undertones, was always the greater attraction.*

Most authentic mango pickles are made with the mango peel left on, but because here you peel the mangoes, this takes much less time to cure.

2 tablespoons Bengali 5-Spices (Panch-Phoran),
    coarsely ground (page 27)
2 large unripe green mangoes (about 3/4 pound each),
    washed and wiped dry
1 cup mustard or olive oil
3 large cloves fresh garlic, coarsely chopped
1 teaspoon black peppercorns, coarsely ground
1 teaspoon ground turmeric
1/8 teaspoon ground asafoetida
1 tablespoon salt, or to taste

1. Prepare the 5-spices. Then, with a vegetable peeler, peel the mango, then cut the fruit around the center seed into thin ½-inch-by-2-inch pieces. Heat the oil in a large nonstick wok or saucepan over medium-high heat and add the garlic, panch-phoran, peppercorns, turmeric, and asafoetida. They should sizzle upon contact with the hot oil.

2. Quickly add the mangoes and the salt, reduce heat to medium and cook, stirring, until the mangoes absorb all the flavors, 15 to 20 minutes. Let cool and allow to marinate at room temperature at least 2 days before serving. Store in the refrigerator about 1 month. Serve chilled or at room temperature.

Indian Pickles

Pickle-making is an art passed from mother to daughter in India, inspired by the selection of fresh fruits and vegetables available to them. Although the actual process of making pickles is not very time consuming, it always turns out to be a day-long family project, mostly because pickles are always made in large batches and generously distributed among family and friends.

Indian pickles are traditionally placed in glazed earthenware jars, and the mouth of the jar is covered with a piece of muslin and matured in the sun. (The muslin allows any excess moisture to escape and keeps the bugs away.) In America, I generally use glass jars which work fine.

Mama's Punjabi Mango Pickle
Mama ka Punjabi Aam ka Achaar

Makes about 6 cups

All mango pickles are made with unripe green mangoes, and in that respect this pickle is no different. Yet to me it is very special, because this is how it has been made in my family for as long as my mother can remember. To this day, my mother makes it every year and sends it to me in America. In Mama's authentic version, the mangoes are cut through the center seed (by the produce vendors, who use special knives), but for ease and convenience, I discard the seeds when I make this.

No part of this pickle ever gets wasted. All the pieces get eaten, and the leftover masala *spices and the oil find their way into cooked dishes and bread dough, or are added to rice* pullaos *(pilafs),* samosas *(stuffed deep-fried triangular pastries), and* pakoras *(batter-fried fritters). After all the mango pieces are gone, tiny pearl onions are tossed into the pickle jar, and allowed to marinate about 4 days before serving.*

There are a few important steps to keep in mind when making this pickle. Don't skimp on the salt and the oil; they are the only preservatives. The salt should be on the high side and there should be at least half an inch of oil floating on top of the pickle.

4 large unripe green mangoes (about ³/₄ pound each), washed and wiped dry
¹/₂ cup fennel seeds
¹/₄ cup fenugreek seeds
2 tablespoons black peppercorns
2 tablespoons kalonji seeds
¹/₂ cup salt, or to taste
2 teaspoons ground turmeric
2 teaspoons cayenne pepper, or to taste
1 small piece of muslin or 4 layers of cheesecloth (enough to cover the mouth of the jar)
1¹/₂ to 2 cups mustard oil or olive oil

1. Cut each unpeeled mango around the center seed into 1-inch-by-½-inch pieces. Discard the center seeds. In a spice or coffee grinder, very coarsely grind together all the whole spices. Remove to a bowl and mix in the salt, turmeric, and cayenne pepper.

2. Heat the oil in a large nonstick wok or saucepan over medium-high heat until just smoking, and add the spice mixture. It should sizzle upon contact with the hot oil. Remove from the heat and stir, about 30 seconds. Add the mangoes and mix well, making sure all the pieces are well coated with the spices.

3. Let cool and transfer to a large sterile glass jar. There should be at least ½ inch of oil on the surface. (Heat and add more oil, if needed.) Cover the jar with the muslin, securing it with a rubber band, and place in a warm, sunny spot in the kitchen or outside in the sun, shaking the jar once or twice a day until the spices are plump and soft and the mango pieces are crisp-tender, 10 to 12 days. (If the pickle jar is outside in

the sun, bring it inside in the evening.) This pickle stays fresh at room temperature about 2 years.

Mama-in-Law's Mango Pickle with Roasted Spices

Saasu-Ma ka Aam ka Achaar

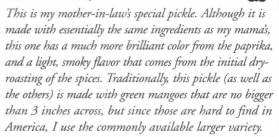

Makes about 6 cups

This is my mother-in-law's special pickle. Although it is made with essentially the same ingredients as my mama's, this one has a much more brilliant color from the paprika, and a light, smoky flavor that comes from the initial dry-roasting of the spices. Traditionally, this pickle (as well as the others) is made with green mangoes that are no bigger than 3 inches across, but since those are hard to find in America, I use the commonly available larger variety.

4 large unripe green mangoes (about ³/₄ pound each), washed and wiped dry
²/₃ cup fennel seeds
¹/₄ cup fenugreek seeds
2 tablespoons kalonji seeds
2 tablespoons black peppercorns
¹/₂ cup salt
2 teaspoons ground turmeric
2 teaspoons ground paprika
2 teaspoons cayenne pepper, or to taste
1¹/₂ cups mustard or olive oil
1 small piece of muslin or 4 layers of cheesecloth (enough to cover the mouth of the jar)

1. Cut each unpeeled mango around the center seed into 1-inch-by-½-inch pieces. Discard the center seeds.

2. Place the fennel, fenugreek, kalonji, and peppercorns in a heavy cast-iron skillet and dry-roast the spices, stirring and shaking the pan over moderate heat, until just a shade darker and fragrant, about 3 minutes. Let cool and transfer to a spice or coffee grinder, and grind them very coarse. Remove to a bowl and mix in the salt, turmeric, paprika, and cayenne pepper.

3. Heat the oil in a medium nonstick wok or saucepan over medium-high heat until just smoking. Let cool until just lukewarm, then add the spice mixture and the mangoes and mix well, making sure all the pieces are well coated with the spices.

4. Transfer to a large sterile glass jar. There should be at least ½ inch of oil on the surface. Cover the jar with the muslin, securing it with a rubber band, and place in a warm, sunny spot in the kitchen or outside in the sun, shaking the jar once or twice a day until the spices are plump and soft and the mango pieces are crisp-tender, 10 to 12 days. (If the pickle jar is outside in the sun, bring it inside in the evening.) This pickle stays fresh at room temperature about 2 years.

Cooked South Indian Mango Pickle
South ka Aam ka Achaar

Makes about 2 cups

This is a classic south Indian mango pickle, made with red chile peppers and asafoetida. It is cooked rather than cured in the sun, so it is typically made and consumed within a short period. Pair it with rice and yogurt, or serve it with pooris *(puffed deep-fried breads) and a side of spicy potatoes.*

2 large unripe green mangoes (about ³/₄ pound each), washed and wiped dry
¹/₂ teaspoon ground turmeric
3 to 5 dried red chile peppers, such as chile de arbol, broken
2 teaspoons fenugreek seeds
¹/₃ cup mustard or peanut oil
2 teaspoons black mustard seeds, coarsely ground
¹/₄ teaspoon ground asafoetida
2 tablespoons salt

1. Cut each unpeeled mango around the center seed into 1-inch-by-½-inch pieces. Discard the center seeds. Place the mango in a bowl, add the turmeric, and toss to mix well.

2. In a small skillet, roast the red chile peppers and fenugreek seeds over medium heat until golden, about 1 minute. Cool and grind in a spice or coffee grinder to make a fine powder.

3. Heat the oil in a large nonstick wok or saucepan over high heat, add the mustard seeds and asafoetida, and stir about 1 minute. Add the mangoes, ground chile-fenugreek mixture, and salt, and cook over high heat, about 1 minute.

4. Reduce the heat to medium-low, cover the pan and cook, stirring occasionally, until the mangoes are soft, about 15 minutes. Let cool and transfer to a large sterile jar. This pickle stays fresh at room temperature about 1 week or about 3 months in the refrigerator. Serve chilled or at room temperature.

Rama's Grated Mango Pickle
Rama ka Aam ka Achaar

Makes about 2 cups

This quick pickle is a favorite in my friend Rama's family in Bangalore. Make more than you need, and serve it with rice and curries, or with sandwiches.

3 large unripe green mangoes (about ³/₄ pound each), washed and wiped dry
1 teaspoon ground fenugreek seeds
¹/₄ teaspoon ground asafoetida
¹/₃ cup peanut oil
5 to 7 dried red chile peppers, such as chile de arbol, broken
1 tablespoon black mustard seeds
1 teaspoon cayenne pepper, or to taste

1. With a vegetable peeler, peel the mangoes, then grate the fruit around the center seed of each mango. Discard the center seeds. Place the fenugreek and asafoetida in a small cast-iron skillet and roast over medium heat, stirring and shaking the pan, until a few shades darker, about 1 minute.

2. Heat the oil in a large nonstick wok or saucepan over medium-high heat, add the red chile peppers and cook, stirring, until a few shades darker, about 1 minute. Add the mustard seeds; they should splutter upon contact with the hot oil, so lower the heat and cover the pan until the spluttering subsides.

3. Add the grated mango and cayenne pepper and cook, stirring, until golden, 5 to 7 minutes. Mix in the roasted fenugreek and asafoetida, stir about 1 minute and remove from the heat. Let cool and transfer to a large sterile jar. This pickle stays fresh about 1 week at room temperature or about 6 months in the refrigerator. Serve chilled or at room temperature.

Lime and Lemon Pickles

Sun-Cured Pickled Lime (or Lemon) Wedges
Nimboo ka Achaar

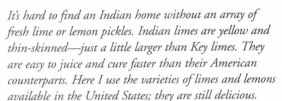

Makes about 4 cups

It's hard to find an Indian home without an array of fresh lime or lemon pickles. Indian limes are yellow and thin-skinned—just a little larger than Key limes. They are easy to juice and cure faster than their American counterparts. Here I use the varieties of limes and lemons available in the United States; they are still delicious.

Pickles are traditionally cured outside in the sun for several weeks, but you can set the jar in a sunny part of your kitchen. The pickle will take an extra 7 to 10 days, unless you move it as the sun rays move.

With indefinite staying power, this pickle actually improves with age as the juices turn darker, thicken, and actually transform into jelly and eventually into fine crystals. At this point, this pickle becomes an age-old Indian home remedy for indigestion, stomach upsets, and nausea.

20 to 24 fresh limes (about 2 pounds)
1/2 cup peeled and minced fresh ginger
1/4 cup salt
2 tablespoons coarsely crushed ajwain seeds
4 cups fresh lime or lemon juice
   (from 20 additional limes)
1 small piece muslin or 4 layers cheesecloth
   (enough to cover the mouth of the jar)

1. Wash and wipe dry the limes. Cut each one into 8 wedges and place in a large sterile glass jar. Mix in the ginger, salt, and ajwain seeds, cover the jar with your palm or the lid, and shake vigorously to mix.

2. Uncover, add the lime juice, and shake the jar again. (The juice should cover the limes by about 1/2 inch; if not, add some more lime juice.) Cover the jar with the muslin, securing it with a rubber band, and place in a warm, sunny spot in the kitchen or

outside in the sun. (If the pickle jar is outside in the sun, bring it inside in the evening.)

3. Shake the jar once or twice each day, until the lime wedges are soft and light buff in color, and the juices are thick, 15 to 20 days. This pickle stays fresh at room temperature almost indefinitely.

Variation: Along with ajwain seeds, add 1 tablespoon each ground cumin and coriander, and 1 teaspoon coarsely ground black pepper.

Sweet and Sour Fresh Lime Pickle
Khatta-Meetha Nimboo ka Achaar

Makes about 4 cups

This sweet, sour, and spicy hot pickle from my husband's cousin, Sanjokta Bhanjii, is authentically cured in the sun, but can be placed in a warm, sunny spot until the juices thicken and the pickle changes color. Sitting on the kitchen counter, the lovely pale yellow pickles with specks of red chile peppers look so inviting that they often get eaten within days of being made. But the real flavors develop after about a month and keep getting better.

20 fresh limes (about 2 pounds)
1 cup sugar
1/4 cup salt
1 1/2 to 2 tablespoons cayenne pepper, or to taste
2 tablespoons ajwain seeds, coarsely ground
4 cups fresh lime or lemon juice
   (from 20 additional limes)
1 small piece muslin or 4 layers cheesecloth
   (enough to cover the mouth of the jar)

1. Wash and wipe dry the limes. Cut each one into 8 wedges, and place in a large sterile glass jar. Mix in the sugar, salt, cayenne pepper, and ajwain seeds, cover the jar with your palm or the lid, and shake vigorously to mix.

2. Uncover, add the lime juice, and shake the jar again. (The juice should cover the limes by about 1/2 inch; if not, add some more lime juice.) Cover the jar with the muslin, securing it with a rubber band, and place in a warm, sunny spot in the kitchen or outside in the sun. (If the pickle jar is outside in the sun, bring it inside in the evening.)

3. Shake the jar once or twice each day, until the lime or lemon wedges are soft and light buff in color, and the juices are thick, 15 to 20 days. This pickle stays fresh at room temperature almost indefinitely.

Variation: Add whole fresh green chile peppers, such as serranos (or halve them lengthwise through the stem or slice them in rounds), and add thinly cut julienne strips of fresh ginger along with the limes.

Crushed Lemon and Fresh Red Chile Pepper Pickle

Pissa Nimboo-Laal Mirch ka Achaar

Makes about 2 cups

So simple and classic, this pickle is an almost instinctive addition to my cooking—every time a dish needs some spunk, my hand reaches right for this jar. Remember to remove any seeds from your lemons or limes, or they will get crushed along with the lemon and impart a bitter aftertaste to this piquant pickle.

All types of fresh green chile peppers (such as serrano, jalapeño, or Thai) and fresh red chile peppers (such as cayenne, or chile de arbol, before they are dried) work well in this recipe.

12 to 15 thin-skinned, seedless lemons or limes (about 1 pound)
12 to 15 fresh red or green chile peppers, stemmed
1 tablespoon ajwain seeds, coarsely ground
1/4 cup salt
1 small piece muslin or 4 layers cheesecloth (enough to cover the mouth of the jar)

1. Wash and wipe dry the lemons or limes, then coarsely chop them, with the rind, and remove any seeds. Transfer to a food processor, along with the chile peppers, and process until minced.

2. Add the ajwain seeds and salt, and process again until smooth. Transfer to a sterile glass jar. Cover the jar with the muslin, securing it with a rubber band, and place in a warm, sunny spot in the kitchen or outside in the sun. (If the pickle jar is outside in the sun, bring it inside in the evening.)

3. Shake the jar once or twice each day, until the pickle is light buff in color and the juices are thick, about 1 week. This pickle stays fresh at room temperature about 1 year.

Lemon-Pickled Fresh Ginger Sticks

Adrak Nimboo

Makes about 2 cups

This is called a pickle, but it is actually just marinated ginger sticks—not unlike the ginger you get with sushi, only the sushi ginger is sweet and this one is savory. Serve it on the side with any meal, or scatter over green salads or grilled meats and chicken, roll it in griddle-fried parantha *breads, or use as a last-minute garnish over chickpea and legume dishes, such as Spicy Chickpeas with Pomegranate Seeds (page 377).*

1/2 pound fresh ginger, peeled and cut into 2-inch matchsticks
1 tablespoon salt
2 teaspoons ajwain seeds, coarsely crushed
1 1/2 cups fresh lemon or lime juice (from 7 to 10 limes)

1. Place the ginger in a large non-reactive bowl. Add the salt and mix well. Set aside about 2 hours at room temperature. (By then the salt will have drawn out the juices from the ginger, and the bowl will have a fair amount of juice.)

2. Add the ajwain seeds and lemon juice and set aside at room temperature until the ginger sticks are pink, 2 to 4 hours. Transfer to a sterile glass jar and store in the refrigerator, about 6 months. Serve chilled or at room temperature.

Minced Ginger-Lime Pickle

Pissa Hua Adrak Nimboo ka Achaar

Makes about 2 cups

This multi-purpose pickle can be used as a relish, as a marinade for fish and paneer cheese, or as a pick-me-up for a variety of cooked meats and vegetables. Which is why it is one of my staple and used in various recipes throughout this book, such as Cauliflower with Minced Ginger-Lime Pickle (page 284) and Marinated Paneer Cheese with Ginger-Lime Pickle (page 322).

1 pound fresh ginger, peeled and cut crosswise into
    thin round slices
15 to 20 fresh green chile peppers, such as serrano,
    coarsely chopped
1½ tablespoons ajwain seeds, coarsely ground
¼ cup salt, or to taste
1 cup fresh lime juice (from 5 to 7 limes)

In a food processor or a blender, process together the ginger and green chile peppers until minced. Transfer to a large sterile jar and add all the remaining ingredients. Cover the jar with your palm or the lid and shake vigorously to mix. Set aside at room temperature about 4 hours. This pickle stays fresh about 6 months in the refrigerator. Served chilled or at room temperature.

Variations: Mix in coarsely ground black pepper or hot red pepper flakes, to taste.

Green Chile Pepper Pickles

Vinegar-Marinated Green Chile Peppers

Sirkae vaali Hari Mirch

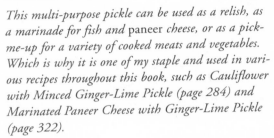

Makes about 1½ cups

The spicy vinegar can be used in salad dressings and in soups. The hot chile peppers are lovely when served with any type of puff pastry appetizers or over rice. Try these only if you know you like spicy, complex seasonings.

1 tablespoon Tamarind Paste (page 54)
15 to 20 fresh green chile peppers, such as serrano,
    thinly sliced
1 tablespoon salt, or to taste
½ cup distilled white vinegar
1 tablespoon sugar
1 tablespoon dried mint leaves

1. Prepare the tamarind paste. Then, place the chile peppers in a small non-reactive bowl. Add the salt and mix well. Set aside about 2 hours at room temperature. (By then the salt will have drawn out the juices from the chile peppers, and the bowl will have a fair amount of juice.)

2. Mix in the vinegar, tamarind paste, sugar, and mint. Refrigerate at least 24 hours before using. Then, transfer to a sterile glass jar and store in the refrigerator about 1 year. Serve chilled or at room temperature.

Pickled Chile Pepper Purée with Tamarind

Hari Mirch aur Imli ka Achaar

Makes about 1¹/₂ cups

This is a purée of fresh chile peppers (with a lot of heat) that I often use as a dip with vegetables. To temper the heat, use milder peppers such as jalapeño, or mix in some green bell peppers. Don't omit the urad dal—the starch released when it is boiled is what gives this pickle its silky smoothness.

¹/₄ cup white urad beans (dhulli urad dal), dry-roasted and coarsely ground (Dry-Roasting Spices, page 35)

1 tablespoon sesame seeds, dry-roasted and coarsely ground (Dry-Roasting Spices, page 35)

¹/₃ cup Tamarind Paste (page 54)

¹/₂ pound fresh green chile peppers, such as serranos, coarsely chopped

1 large clove fresh garlic, chopped

1¹/₄ cups water

2 tablespoons coriander seeds

1 tablespoon cumin seeds

1 tablespoon sugar

1¹/₂ teaspoons salt, or to taste

1. Prepare the dal, sesame seeds, and tamarind paste. Then, place the green chile peppers, dal, garlic, tamarind paste, and water in a nonstick saucepan and bring to a boil over high heat. Reduce the heat to medium-low, cover the pan and cook about 5 minutes. Add the coriander, cumin, sugar, and salt, and continue to cook until the peppers are soft, 7 to 10 minutes.

2. Transfer to a food processor or a blender and process to make a smooth paste. Remove to a serving bowl, lightly mix in the sesame seeds with some of them visible as a garnish, and serve. Or transfer to a sterile glass jar and store in the refrigerator about 6 months. Serve chilled or at room temperature.

Prabha's Green Chile Pepper Pickle

Prabha ka Hari Mirch ka Achaar

Makes about 1¹/₂ cups

This very hot condiment, from my friend Prabha Chauhan in California, will set off fireworks in your mouth, but is too good to resist. It pairs well with griddle-fried parantha *breads or with rice and curry. It is also lovely with grilled foods. Citric acid is available in most supermarkets.*

2 teaspoons fenugreek seeds

1 tablespoon fennel seeds

¹/₂ teaspoon ground turmeric

¹/₂ cup mustard or peanut oil

1 to 2 tablespoons salt

1 pound fresh green chile peppers, such as serrano, cut into ¹/₄-inch diagonal slices

1 tablespoon citric acid or 2 tablespoons distilled white vinegar

1. In a mortar and pestle (or a spice or coffee grinder), coarsely grind together the fenugreek and fennel seeds. Remove to a bowl and mix in the turmeric.

2. Heat the oil in a large nonstick wok or saucepan over medium-high heat. Reduce the heat to low, add the ground spices and salt, and stir a few seconds. Add the green chile peppers and cook until they are crisp-tender, 3 to 5 minutes. Mix in the citric acid (or vinegar) and cook another 2 to 3 minutes. Let cool, then transfer to a sterile glass jar and store in the refrigerator about 1 year. Serve chilled or at room temperature.

Other Vegetable Pickles

Crunchy Cucumber Pickle
Kheerae ka Achaar

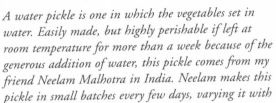

Makes about 2 cups

Crispy texture and bold flavor, with a unique set of spices and flavors—this is India's answer to the word "pickle" as we know it in America.

4 to 5 small seedless cucumbers (about 3/4 pound), diagonally sliced
1 teaspoon salt, or to taste
2 tablespoons peanut oil
3 to 5 dried red chile peppers, such as chiles de arbol, with stems
3 to 5 fresh green chile peppers, such as serrano, halved lengthwise
1 teaspoon black mustard seeds
1/8 teaspoon ground asafoetida
1 tablespoon dried curry leaves
1 medium onion, cut into 1/2-inch pieces
2 large cloves fresh garlic, minced
1/4 cup distilled white vinegar

1. In a bowl, toss the cucumbers with salt and allow to sweat about 1 hour.

2. Heat the oil in a large nonstick wok or saucepan over moderate heat and cook the red chile peppers about 30 seconds. Add the green chile peppers and stir 30 seconds. Add the mustard seeds; they should splutter upon contact with the hot oil, so reduce the heat and cover the pan until the spluttering subsides.

3. Stir in the asafoetida and curry leaves, then add the onion and garlic, and cook, stirring, until barely softened, about 3 minutes. Add the cucumber with all the juices and cook, stirring, about 1 minute.

4. Add the vinegar and boil over high heat about 1 minute. Remove from the heat. Let cool, transfer to a sterile glass jar, and refrigerate at least 2 days before serving. This pickle stays fresh about 6 months in the refrigerator. Serve chilled or at room temperature.

Water Pickle with Crispy Cauliflower and Carrots
Paani Vaala Gobhi-Gajjar ka Achaar

Makes about 2 cups

A water pickle is one in which the vegetables set in water. Easily made, but highly perishable if left at room temperature for more than a week because of the generous addition of water, this pickle comes from my friend Neelam Malhotra in India. Neelam makes this pickle in small batches every few days, varying it with whatever vegetables are in season.

The spices in this pickle may be unusual, but its flavors will be quite familiar because they are somewhat akin to those of the popular cucumber pickle served in America with sandwiches and hamburgers.

1 pound cauliflower, cut into 1 1/2-inch florets, stems discarded
3 to 4 small carrots, peeled and diagonally sliced
2 cups water
8 to 10 fresh green chile peppers, such as serrano, stemmed and halved lengthwise
1 (1-inch) piece fresh ginger, peeled, cut in half lengthwise, and thinly sliced
3 tablespoons distilled white vinegar
2 teaspoons black mustard seeds, ground
1 1/2 teaspoons salt, or to taste
1/4 teaspoon cayenne pepper, or to taste
1/8 teaspoon ground turmeric
1 small piece muslin or 4 layers cheesecloth (enough to cover the mouth of the jar)

1. Place the vegetables and water in a medium saucepan and bring to boil over high heat. Boil 30 seconds, then cover the pan and remove from the heat. Set aside about 1 minute. Transfer to a large sterile glass jar with a wide mouth and mix in all the remaining ingredients.

2. Cover the jar with the muslin, securing it with a rubber band, and place in a warm, sunny spot in the kitchen or outside in the sun. (If the pickle jar is outside in the sun, bring it inside in the evening.) Shake the jar once or twice each day, until the vegetables are sour, 2 to 4 days. This pickle stays fresh at room temperature about 1 week and about 6 months in the refrigerator, getting more and more pungent over time. Serve chilled or at room temperature.

Spicy Cranberry Pickle
Karonda Achaar

Makes about 2 cups

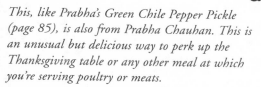

This, like Prabha's Green Chile Pepper Pickle (page 85), is also from Prabha Chauhan. This is an unusual but delicious way to perk up the Thanksgiving table or any other meal at which you're serving poultry or meats.

¼ cup Bengali 5-Spices (Panch-Phoran),
   page 27 or store-bought
½ teaspoon ground turmeric
1 tablespoon salt, or to taste
½ cup mustard oil
1 (12-ounce) package fresh cranberries, washed
1 tablespoon citric acid or 2 tablespoons distilled
   white vinegar

1. In a mortar and pestle, coarsely grind the 5-spices mixture. Mix in the turmeric and salt.

2. Heat the oil in a large nonstick wok or saucepan over medium-high heat until smoking. Reduce the heat to low, add the spices, and stir a few seconds. Add the cranberries and cook until they are crisp-tender, 10 to 12 minutes. Mix in the citric acid (or vinegar) and cook another 2 to 3 minutes. Let cool, transfer to a sterile jar and store in the refrigerator, about 1 year. Serve chilled or at room temperature.

Pearl Onions in Pickling Spices
Pyaz ka Achaar

Makes about 2 cups

This pickle is traditionally a by-product of leftover mango pickle masala (see Mama's Punjabi Mango Pickle, page 79), but there's a loyal following who make them directly. Serve these onions with pan-fried parantha breads or deep-fried poori breads, or present them with any Indian meal.

1 pound pearl onions, peeled
1 tablespoon salt, or to taste
1 tablespoon fenugreek seeds
1 tablespoon fennel seeds
2 teaspoons black peppercorns
1½ teaspoons kalonji seeds
1 teaspoon ground turmeric
1 teaspoon cayenne pepper, or to taste
½ cup mustard or olive oil
1 small piece muslin or 4 layers cheesecloth
   (enough to cover the mouth of the jar)

1. Make a cross-cut at the base of each onion, going three-quarters of the way to the top. Lightly open the cuts and stuff a pinch of salt in each one. Reserve any leftover salt. In a spice or coffee grinder, very coarsely grind together the fenugreek, fennel, peppercorns and kalonji. Remove to a bowl and mix in the turmeric, cayenne pepper, and the reserved salt.

2. Heat the oil in a large nonstick wok or saucepan over medium-high heat and add the spice mixture; it should sizzle upon contact with the hot oil. Add the onions and cook about 5 minutes, making sure all the onions are well coated with the spice mixture.

3. Let cool and transfer to a sterile glass jar. Cover the jar with the muslin, securing it with a rubber band, and place in a warm, sunny spot in the kitchen or outside in the sun. (If the pickle jar is outside in the sun, bring it inside in the evening.) Shake the jar once or twice each day, until the spices are plump and soft and the onions are crisp-tender, 3 to 5 days. The onions will release some juices; that is quite normal. Store about 10 days at room temperature and about 6 months in the refrigerator. The onions keep getting stronger over time.

Pickled Turnips with Black Mustard Seeds

Shalgam ka Achaar

Makes about 4 cups

In the summers, when I was growing up, my aunt would often make a huge jar of these spicy turnips. Sometimes, though, she would set them out in the early sun for one last day, and inevitably, my cousins and I couldn't help but eat it all by day's end.

Blanched until barely tender, then tossed with ground black mustard seeds and salt, here turnips take on a unique flavor, reminiscent of the pungent Korean pickled condiment kimchi.

2 to 3 cups water
1½ pounds turnips, cut into 1-inch pieces
    (peeled or unpeeled)
1 tablespoon black mustard seeds, coarsely ground
1 tablespoon salt
1 teaspoon cayenne pepper, or to taste
1 small piece muslin or 4 layers cheesecloth
    (enough to cover the mouth of the jar)

1. Bring the water to a boil in a large pot. Add the turnips and boil about 1 minute. Drain and transfer the turnips to a tray lined with paper towels and air-dry them about 10 minutes.

2. Transfer to a large sterile glass jar with a wide mouth and add the mustard seeds, salt, and cayenne pepper. Toss well, then cover the jar with the muslin securing it with a rubber band, and set aside at room temperature until the turnips turn sour, 5 to 7 days. To cure faster, place in the sun during the day, bringing the pickle inside in the evening. Shake the jar once or twice a day. This pickle stays fresh at room temperature about 1 week (longer in the refrigerator), getting more and more pungent over time.

Pickled Turnips and Cauliflower

Shalgam Gobhi ka Achaar

Makes about 8 to 10 cups

A yield of 8 to 10 cups may sound like a lot, but it really is not—ask any north Indian. This pickle is more like a tangy side dish, meant to be eaten in moderation because of its spicy strong flavors, yet it is not uncommon to see people devour it, piece after piece, at mealtimes. As children, my brother Rakesh and I would wash off the spices and then eat the vegetables.

When I was growing up, this authentic Punjabi pickle, my mother's age-old recipe, was made every winter (sometimes two or three times), a practice you may eventually follow.

3 to 4 cups water
1¼ pounds small turnips, peeled and
    cut into ¼-inch thick slices
1½ pounds cauliflower, cut into 1½-inch florets,
    stems discarded
3 ounces fresh ginger, peeled and cut into
    thin round slices
2 ounces fresh garlic cloves, peeled
½ cup mustard oil
2 tablespoons garam masala
3 tablespoons salt
½ cup sugar
¼ cup black mustard seeds, coarsely ground
1 teaspoon cayenne pepper, or to taste
2 teaspoons ground paprika
1 cup distilled white vinegar
1 small piece muslin or 4 layers cheesecloth
    (enough to cover the mouth of the jar)

1. Bring the water to a boil in a large pot. Add the turnips and cauliflower and blanch about 1 minute; do not allow them to soften. Drain and transfer to a tray lined with paper towels and air-dry them about 10 minutes. Process the ginger and garlic in a food processor or a blender to make a fine paste.

2. Heat the oil in a large nonstick wok or saucepan over medium-high heat and add the ginger-garlic paste. Cook, stirring, over medium heat until rich golden in color, about 4 minutes. Add the garam masala and stir about 30 seconds.

3. Add the vegetables and salt and cook, stirring, 2 to 3 minutes. Add the sugar and cook, stirring, about 1 minute. Remove from heat and mix in the mustard seeds, cayenne pepper, paprika, and vinegar. Transfer to a large, sterile glass jar with a wide mouth. Cover the jar with the muslin, securing it with a rubber band, and place in a warm, sunny spot in the kitchen or outside in the sun. (If the pickle jar is outside in the sun, bring it inside in the evening.) Shake the jar once or twice each day, until the turnips are sour, 5 to 7 days. (Taste, and if not sour enough, cover and set aside longer.) This pickle stays fresh at room temperature about 3 months, getting more and more pungent over time.

Variations: Use ¹/₂ cup ground or crushed jaggery (gur) instead of sugar for an earthier, more robust flavor. You can also substitute carrot sticks for some of the turnips and cauliflower.

Mixed Vegetable Pickle with Garlic
Lalit ka Sabzi ka Achaar

Makes about 4 cups

This recipe is from Lalit Pant, who has for the last 35 years, managed upscale Indian restaurants all over the world, including in Los Angeles. Lalit always serves this pickle as part of the first course, with paapads *(lentil wafers), Indian appetizers such as* samosas *(savory stuffed and deep-fried triangular pastries), and* pakoras *(chickpea flour batter-fried fritters), but it can be served with just about every Indian meal.*

¹/₂ **cup vegetable oil**
2 **tablespoons fennel seeds**
1 **tablespoon fenugreek seeds**
1 **tablespoon cumin seeds**
2 **teaspoons kalonji seeds**
¹/₂ **teaspoon ground turmeric**
1 **pound carrots, finely chopped**
1 **pound cauliflower, finely chopped**
2 **large heads fresh garlic, peeled and chopped**
5 **to** 7 **fresh green chile peppers, such as serrano, diagonally sliced**
¹/₂ **cup distilled white vinegar**
1 **(15-ounce) can tomato sauce**
1 **tablespoon salt, or to taste**
¹/₂ **teaspoon ground paprika**
¹/₂ **teaspoon cayenne pepper, or to taste**

1. Heat the oil in a large nonstick wok or saucepan over medium-high heat and add the fennel, fenugreek, cumin, and kalonji seeds. They should sizzle upon contact with the hot oil. Quickly add the turmeric, stir about 30 seconds, and add the vegetables, garlic, and green chile peppers. Cook, stirring, until the vegetables are lightly golden, about 5 minutes.

2. Add the vinegar, tomato sauce, salt, paprika, and cayenne pepper, and bring to a boil over high heat. Reduce the heat to medium-low, cover the pan, and simmer until the vegetables are crisp-tender, about 7 minutes. Let cool, transfer to a large sterile jar, and store in the refrigerator about 10 days. Serve chilled or at room temperature.

Eggplant and Malanga Root Pickle

Bharti ka Baingan-Kachaalu ka Achaar

Makes about 4 cups

I tried this pickle at my friend Bharti Dhalwala's home and loved it, so she graciously shared the recipe. It has a smooth, silky texture and a tangy, assertive flavor and is quite simple to make. Present it with any Indian menu, or pair it with mathri *(deep-fried pastry crackers) or any other store-bought crackers.*

Indian eggplants are small and look like purple eggs with a green crown. Malanga root, called kachaalu *in Hindi, is a close relative of taro root (*arbi*), only much larger. It's got a brown and somewhat hairy skin and dense white flesh. Look for both in Indian and Asian markets.*

1 pound small Indian eggplants or Chinese eggplants, cut into 2-inch pieces
2 teaspoons ground turmeric
1 pound malanga root or taro root
2 tablespoons black mustard seeds, coarsely ground
1 tablespoon fennel seeds, coarsely ground
1 tablespoon salt
1 teaspoon cayenne pepper, or to taste
1¹/₂ to 2 cups mustard oil

1. Make a cross-cut at the base of each eggplant, going three-quarters of the way to the top. Place in a saucepan along with 2 cups water and 1 teaspoon turmeric, and bring to a boil over high heat. Reduce the heat to medium-low, cover the pan, and simmer until the eggplants are half cooked (crisp-tender), about 7 minutes. Drain the eggplants over a bowl and reserve about ¾ cup water.

2. In the same saucepan, place the malanga root and about 4 cups of fresh water, and bring to a boil over high heat. Reduce the heat to medium-low, cover the pan, and simmer until the malanga root is soft, adding more water if it evaporates, about 15 minutes. Remove from the water, let cool, then peel and cut into ¾-inch pieces. Discard the water.

3. In a large bowl, mix together the eggplants, malanga root, mustard and fennel seeds, salt, cayenne pepper, the remaining 1 teaspoon turmeric, and mix well, making sure all the vegetables are well coated.

4. Heat the oil in a small saucepan over medium-high heat until smoking. Remove from the heat, add to the bowl with the vegetables, and mix again. Let cool and transfer to a large sterile jar. There should be at least ½ inch of oil on the surface, if not, then heat and add some more. Cover the jar with the muslin, securing it with a rubber band, and place in a warm, sunny spot in the kitchen, or outside in the sun, shaking the jar once or twice a day for 2 days.

5. Mix in the reserved eggplant water and shake the jar again. Place in a warm, sunny spot in the kitchen, or outside in the sun again, shaking the jar once or twice a day until the vegetables are very soft and tangy, 6 to 8 days. This pickle stays fresh at room temperature about 1 month, and in the refrigerator about 6 months. Serve chilled or at room temperature.

Starters and Snacks

Spicy Savories and Trail Mixes 95

Spicy Lentil Wafers

Salt and Pepper Cashews

Spicy Mixed Nuts and Seeds

Spicy Pressed Rice Flakes Mixture

Savory Cereal Mixture with Nuts

Spicy Batter-Fried Peanuts

Crispy Taro Chips with Asafoetida

Pastry Crackers and Puff Pastries (Mathri) 99

Pastry Crackers
with Black Pepper and Ajwain Seeds

Savory Pastry Diamonds

Puff Pastry Twists
with Cumin and Ajwain Seeds

Pastry Swirls with Roasted
Red Bell Peppers and Potatoes

Puff Pastry Rolls
with Asparagus and Scallions

Mushroom Turnovers
with Curry Powder

Curried Chicken or Lamb Turnovers

Stuffed Fried Pastries (Samosae) 103

Traditional Stuffed
Triangular Pastries

Sindhi-Style Stuffed
Triangular Pastries

Stuffed Tortilla Triangles

Stuffed Phyllo Triangles

Spicy 7-Layered Baked Pastries

Stuffed Phyllo Baked Pastry Pouches

Fillings for Samosas 108

Potato Filling

Spicy Mixed Vegetable
Samosa Filling

Yellow Mung Bean and
Spinach Samosa Filling

Green Split Pea Samosa Filling

Sprouted Green Mung Bean
Samosa Filling

Meat Samosa Filling

Mung Bean Puffed Pastries

Fritters (Pakorae or Bhajiae) 112

Basic Batter for Pakora Fritters

Sliced, Chopped, and Stuffed Vegetable Fritters 113

Potato Fritters with Chives

Fresh Green Bean Pakora Fritters
with Ginger

Cauliflower Pakora Fritters
with Cilantro

Bell Pepper Pakora Fritters
with Ajwain Seeds

Pumpkin Pakora Fritters
with Bengali 5-Spices

Garlicky Eggplant Pakora Fritters

Baby Spinach Pakora Fritters

Stuffed Napa Cabbage Roll
Pakora Fritters

Bread Pakora Fritters
Stuffed with Coconut Chutney

 = Vegan   = Pressure-Cooker Quick

Shredded and Minced Vegetable and Flour Mixture Fritters 117

Shredded Cabbage
Pakora Fritters with Yogurt

Chopped Onion Pakora Fritters

Fresh Fenugreek Pakora Fritters
with Pomegranate Seeds

Mixed Vegetable Pakora Fritters

Spicy Green Split Pea Pakora Fritters

Pinched Rice Flour
Pakora Fritters with Papaya

Rice Flour and Cashew
Pakora Fritters

Cheese and Meat Fritters 121

Mama's Paneer Cheese
Pakora Fritters

Crumbled Paneer Cheese
Pakora Fritters with Green Chutney

Cottage Cheese Pakora Fritters
with Red Bell Peppers

Traditional Chicken Pakora Fritters

Marinated Chicken Pakora Fritters

Ground Meat Pakora Fritters

Fish Pakora Fritters

Shrimp Pakora Fritters

Potato Snacks 125

Mashed Batter-Fried Potato Balls

Thrice-Baked Potato Skins
with Petite Peas

Stuffed Potatoes
with Spicy Shredded Chicken

Indian French Fries with Tomatoes

Savory Croquettes and Dumplings (Vadae) 128

Mung Bean Croquettes

Mung Bean Croquettes
with Spinach

Punjabi-Style Fermented
Urad Bean Croquettes

South Indian Croquettes
with Curry Leaves

Rice Croquettes with Cashews

Coconut–Red Chile Croquettes
with Mixed Beans

Spicy Stuffed Croquettes

Steamed Fermented Rice Cakes (Iddli) 133

Traditional Steamed Fermented
Rice Cakes

Instant Steamed Semolina Cakes
with Yogurt

Steamed Spicy Fermented
Rice Cakes

Savory Bean and Rice Cakes (Dhokla) 135

Traditional Steamed
Split Chickpea Cakes

Falguni's Steamed
Chickpea Flour Cakes

Steamed Mung Bean Bites

Gujarati Chickpea Flour Rolls

Gujarati Stuffed
Chickpea Flour Rolls

Spicy Steamed Chickpea
Zucchini Cake

Indian Street Foods 140

Crispy Puffs
with Spicy Tamarind Water

Crispy Puffs with Potatoes
and Spicy Yogurt

Puffed Rice with Onion,
Potatoes, and Spicy Chutneys

Crispy Flour Chips with
Vegetables and Spicy Chutneys

Flour Chips with Yogurt and
Mango Powder Chutney

Potato Patties 143

Basic Mashed Potato Patties

Tofu and Potato Patties

Basic Stuffed Potato Patties

Fillings for Potato Patties

Sourdough Bread and Potato Ovals

Potato and Tapioca Patties

Potato and Cashew Patties

Stuffed Lentil Wafer Rolls

Kabaabs 148

Skewered Minced Lamb Kabaabs
with Saffron

Marinated Lamb Kabaabs

Pan-Fried Lamb Kabaabs

Flattened Lamb Kabaab Skewers
with Cardamom Seeds

Flattened Lamb Kabaab Skewers
with Nuts and Poppy Seeds

Deep-Fried Lamb Kabaab Patties

Pinched Lamb Kabaabs
with Fenugreek Leaves

Silky Skewered Minced Chicken

Grilled Chicken Drumstick Kabaabs

Pan-Roasted Egg-Stuffed Chicken
Drumstick Kabaabs

Pan-Cooked Chicken Liver Kabaabs

Spicy Batter-Coated Fish Kabaabs

Skewered Minced
Paneer Cheese Kabaabs

Chutney-Marinated Broiled
Paneer Cheese Kabaabs

Skewered Paneer and
Vegetable Kabaabs

Paneer Cheese Kabaabs
with Pomegranate Seeds

Black Chickpea Kabaabs

Skewered Vegetable Kabaabs
with Fresh Fenugreek Leaves

Tikka Kabaabs and Marinades 160

Basic Grilled Lamb Tikka Kabaabs

Basic Chicken Tikka Kabaabs

Basic Fish Tikka Kabaabs

Turmeric Lamb Tikka Marinade

Rosemary Lamb Tikka Marinade

Fresh Green Chutney Lamb
Tikka Marinade

Royal Lamb Tikka Marinade

Garlic Chicken Tikka Marinade

Citrus Chicken Tikka Marinade

Mint Chicken Tikka Marinade

Chile Chicken Tikka Marinade

Creamy Chicken Tikka Marinade

Silky Chicken Tikka Marinade

Grilled Fish Tikka Marinade

Sesame Fish Tikka Marinade

Starters and snacks are highly favored in the Indian culture, in which entertaining guests at a moment's notice is a way of life. Family and friends drop by for a visit, often unannounced, and whipping up a welcome in the form of snacks and appetizers is a pleasurable challenge for the host. They provide something tantalizing to the senses for everyone to nibble on while spending time together.

Some of these snacks are also the can't-resist tidbits eaten throughout the day in India—at home or at vendor stands—to tide you over until mealtime.

There are two main categories of snacks in India: the nibbles and munchies that are made in advance and that can be stored almost like pantry staples, and the kind meant to be eaten freshly made and hot.

The first, usually the deep-fried savories and spicy trail-mix-like combinations such as *sev* (savory chick-pea flour noodles), *bhujia* (savory chickpea flour or potato vermicelli), and spiced crackers and pastries (*mathri*), are traditionally made in large batches because they can be stored for long periods. They can also now be found in some Indian and even non-Indian markets all over the world, including the United States.

The second category includes the delicacies patrons have come to know and love from Indian restaurants and mom-and-pop shops—*samosas* (stuffed deep-fried triangular pastries), *pakoras* (fritters), *chaats* (dishes with savory, tangy, and spicy flavors), *kabaabs* (grilled or deep-fried finger food), *tikkas* (grilled boneless meats), and more.

Always served with an assortment of chutneys and attractive garnishes, these specialty snacks are substantial, filling foods that often also serve as brunches and light meals. They are true Indian fast foods.

Spicy Savories and Trail Mixes

Spicy Lentil Wafers
Paapad

Allow 1 to 2 wafers per serving

Light as air, but with enough spice and crunch to whet appetites, lentil wafers (or paapadh *and* paapadum *as they are called in the north and south, respectively), are the everyday snack always present in Indian homes and restaurants.*

Available in a range of flavors, tastes, shapes, and textures, paapads *are among the few traditional Indian snacks that really benefit from mass production. Look for them in Indian grocery stores in the United States in packages—they are round like tortillas, but thinner, and come plain or studded with spices.* Paapads *can then be roasted in a number of ways or deep-fried. The classic way to roast is over an open flame (popular in northern India), or in an oven, toaster oven, toaster (broken in half), or in the microwave. Have the exhaust fan on because smoke will rise, especially when flame-roasting.*

Flame Roasting

Using tongs, hold each *paapad* over the flame and roast it, beginning with the edges and moving toward the center.

Oven or Toaster Oven

Place under the preheated broiler until crisp—no more than 35 seconds—making sure the edges do not burn.

Toaster

Toast as you would a slice of bread, turning the *paapad* to make sure the edges get browned.

Microwave Oven

Cook on high power about 1 minute, watching to make sure the *paapad* doesn't burn or begin to smoke. (This method is so quick and easy that you may find yourself making them this way all the time at home and will start a new trend at the office—if you have a microwave.)

Deep-Frying

Follow the directions for deep-frying (page 38), making sure to drain each *paapad* well. Typically, the oil used for *paapad* frying is not reusable, because it gets gelatinized in the process.

Salt and Pepper Cashews
Namkeen Kaaju

Makes about 2 cups

In a country where deep-frying is a way of life, everything gets fried (including people, in the hot summer sun), and cashews are no different.

You can make this recipe with other nuts, such as peanuts, almonds, and walnuts, and seeds such as shelled sunflower, pumpkin, and melon seeds. If you use nuts of different sizes, fry them separately, or coarsely chop them so that they all cook together evenly.

1/2 cup peanut oil for deep-frying
2 cups raw cashews
1/4 teaspoon salt, or to taste
1/4 teaspoon freshly ground black pepper, or to taste

1. Heat the oil in a medium nonstick wok or saucepan over medium heat and fry, stirring and turning the cashews until golden, about 1 minute. Before removing them from the wok, hold them for a few seconds between the slotted spatula and the sides of the wok to drain out as much oil as possible. (Do not drain on paper towels, or the spices will not adhere to the nuts.)

2. Transfer to a bowl and quickly mix in the salt and pepper and toss well, making sure the cashews are well-coated.

3. Serve them while they are still warm (but not hot, or they will be soft from the oil), or cool to room temperature, transfer to an airtight container and store 2 to 3 weeks at room temperature or about 3 months in the refrigerator.

Spicy Mixed Nuts and Seeds

Masaladaar Maevae

Makes about 2¹/₂ cups

India's version of trail mix, this mixture can be made with one type of nut, or several together. If you use nuts of different sizes fry them separately, or coarsely chop them so that they all cook together evenly. Black salt adds citrusy flavor to the mix but you can leave it out if you don't have it or can't easily find it.

**1 teaspoon cumin seeds, dry-roasted and coarsely
    ground (Dry-Roasting Spices, page 35)**
**1¹/₂ to 2 teaspoons Chaat Masala
    (page 20 or store-bought)**
1/4 teaspoon cayenne pepper, or to taste
1/4 teaspoon black salt (optional)
1/2 cup peanut oil for deep-frying
**2 cups mixed shelled raw nuts, such as almonds,
    cashews, peanuts, pistachios**
**1/2 cup mixed shelled raw seeds, such as sunflower,
    pumpkin, melon**

1. Prepare the cumin seeds and chaat masala. Then, in a small bowl, mix together the cumin seeds, chaat masala, cayenne pepper, and black salt.

2. Heat the oil in a medium-size nonstick wok or saucepan over medium heat and fry the nuts until golden, about 1 minute. Before removing them from the wok, hold them for a few seconds between the slotted spatula and the sides of the wok to drain out as much oil as possible. (Do not drain them on paper towels, or the spices will not adhere.) Transfer them to a medium bowl, quickly add the spice mixture and toss well, making sure that the nuts are well coated.

3. Remove all the oil from the wok, then in whatever oil remains on the wok surface, stir-fry the seeds over medium-low heat until the seeds are fragrant and golden, 1 minute. Add to the spiced nuts and toss together. Taste and adjust seasonings. (Keep in mind that the warm nuts will be soft, but will harden as they cool.) Let cool completely then serve or transfer to an airtight container and store 2 to 3 weeks at room temperature or about 3 months in the refrigerator.

Spicy Pressed Rice Flakes Mixture

Chivda

Makes about 5 cups

This is another Indian pantry staple snack. In some parts of India it is made at home, but it is mostly purchased. Look for it in Indian markets in the United States.

Keep the oil at medium heat at all times. The rice flakes and coconut fry almost instantly, and if the heat is high they will burn. If kopra isn't available, to dry fresh coconut for this recipe, cut it into thin, 1-inch strips, place them on a baking tray, and dry them in a preheated 200°F oven until crispy but still white. (Any browning means that the heat is too high.) Alum (fatkari) is a white rock-candy look-alike that is always ground into a powder before using. It is available in Indian markets.

**1/2 cup dried split yellow chickpeas (channa dal),
    sorted and washed in 3 to 4 changes of water**
1/8 teaspoon ground alum
2 to 3 cups peanut oil for deep-frying
2 cups pressed rice flakes (poha)
1/4 teaspoon ground turmeric
1 teaspoon salt, or to taste
**1 (3-by-1-inch) piece dried coconut (kopra),
    thinly sliced (optional)**
**1 cup shelled raw peanuts, with or without
    the red skin**
**1 to 3 fresh green chile peppers, such as serrano,
    minced with seeds**
**2 tablespoons finely chopped fresh cilantro,
    including soft stems**
1¹/₂ tablespoons finely chopped fresh curry leaves
1 teaspoon citric acid
1 teaspoon ground cumin
1 teaspoon ground coriander
1 teaspoon cayenne pepper, or to taste
1/2 teaspoon ground fenugreek seeds
1 teaspoon sugar

1. Place the dal in water to cover by 1 inch. Mix in the alum and soak overnight. Then, drain and spread the dal on a tray lined with several layers of paper towels or cheesecloth until completely dry, 1 to 2 hours. Stir a few times with your fingers to ensure proper drying. (Otherwise, remaining water will cause spluttering when the dal is deep-fried.)

2. Heat the oil in a large wok or saucepan over medium heat until a few rice flakes dropped into the hot oil bubble and rise to the top immediately. Put the rice flakes in a large fine-mesh metal strainer (in 2 batches, if needed) and place the strainer with the rice flakes in it into the hot oil. Fry, stirring the rice flakes in the strainer until they are crisp and very lightly golden, about 1 minute. Transfer to a bowl lined with paper towels. Add the turmeric and ½ teaspoon salt to the rice flakes, and toss lightly.

3. Similarly, fry the coconut slices (if using), then the dal, and finally, the peanuts. Mix each into the rice flakes. Add the remaining ½ teaspoon salt and toss again.

4. Remove all but 1 tablespoon of the oil from the wok. Heat the oil on medium-low heat and cook the green chile peppers, cilantro, and curry leaves, stirring, until golden and crisp, about 5 minutes.

5. Add the citric acid, cumin, coriander, cayenne pepper, fenugreek seeds, and sugar to the wok, and stir about 1 minute. Then add the fried ingredients and mix lightly until they are well-coated with the spices. Keep uncovered at all times, and cool to room temperature. Store in an airtight container up to 2 months.

Savory Cereal Mixture with Nuts

Milla-Julla Namkeen

Makes about 8 cups

Probably the first of the Indian snacks to be marketed in the United States in Indian stores, this savory mixture (or its many versions) is a perpetual Indian favorite. Eaten as a snack or tossed over yogurt or into a green salad, it lends a spicy crackle and crunch. You can buy it in the Indian market, or make my easy and more healthful version at home—without deep-frying.

Mixed melon seeds, called char-magaz *in Hindi, is a mixture of cantaloupe, watermelon, cucumber, and pumpkin seeds, and can be made (page 12) or bought in Indian markets.*

1½ tablespoons Chaat Masala (page 20 or store-bought), or to taste

3 tablespoons peanut oil

½ cup shelled raw peanuts, with red skins on

½ cup coarsely chopped raw cashews

½ cup mixed melon seeds or shelled raw sunflower seeds

1 teaspoon black mustard seeds

¼ teaspoon ground asafoetida

½ teaspoon cayenne pepper, or to taste

¼ teaspoon ground ginger

½ cup finely chopped fresh cilantro, including soft stems

2 tablespoons dried curry leaves

1½ teaspoons citric acid

3 cups puffed rice cereal

2 cups corn flake cereal

2 cups canned potato sticks

1. Prepare the chaat masala. Heat 1 tablespoon oil in a large wok or skillet and cook the peanuts and cashews over medium heat, stirring as needed, until fragrant and golden, 2 to 4 minutes. Transfer to a bowl. Alternately, roast in the oven at 350°F until fragrant and lightly golden, 10 to 15 minutes.

2. In the same pan, add the melon (or sunflower) seeds to the wok and dry-roast until golden, 1 minute. Transfer to the peanut bowl.

3. Heat the remaining 2 tablespoons oil over medium-high heat and add the mustard seeds and asafoetida. They should splutter upon contact with the hot oil, so cover the pan and lower the heat until the spluttering subsides. Mix in the cayenne pepper and ginger, and then add first the cilantro, then the curry leaves, chaat masala, and citric acid, and stir about 30 seconds.

4. Add the puffed rice cereal, corn flakes, potato sticks, roasted nuts, and seeds. Reduce the heat to low and cook, stirring occasionally, about 5 minutes, making sure everything is well-coated with the spices. Let cool completely. Transfer it to an airtight container and store at room temperature about 2 months.

Spicy Batter-Fried Peanuts
Besan-Tali Moong-Phalli

Makes about 2 cups

Even though they are batter-coated and deep-fried, these peanuts are too small to be called pakora fritters (although that's what they truly are). I invariably make them in large batches, but the challenge is not making them, it's trying not to eat them all at once! Try this with cashews or almonds too.

1/2 cup chickpea flour
1 teaspoon ground ginger
1/2 1 teaspoon salt, or to taste
1/2 to 1 teaspoon cayenne pepper, or to taste
1/8 teaspoon baking soda
1/8 teaspoon ground asafoetida
2 cups shelled raw peanuts, with or without red skin
3 tablespoons fresh lemon juice
1 1/2 to 2 cups peanut oil for deep-frying

1. Put the chickpea flour into a sifter or a fine-mesh strainer and sift the flour into a medium bowl. Mix in the ginger, salt, cayenne pepper, baking soda, and asafoetida. Mix in the peanuts and then add the lemon juice and mix with clean fingers, making sure the peanuts are coated with a thick batter (add 1 tablespoon water, if needed).

2. Heat the oil in a large wok or skillet over medium-high heat until it reaches 325°F to 350°F on a frying thermometer or until a small bit of batter dropped into the hot oil bubbles and rises to the top immediately. Then add the batter-coated peanuts, piece by piece (or by the handful), adding as many as the wok can hold at one time. Separate them quickly with a fork or a slotted spatula and fry, stirring and turning, until crisp and golden, about 1 minute. Repeat with the remaining peanuts. Transfer to paper towels with a slotted spatula to drain. Let cool and serve, or store in an airtight container in the refrigerator up to 15 days.

Crispy Taro Chips with Asafoetida
Tali Arbi kae Lacchae

Makes 4 to 6 servings

A specialty of Trivandrum in the south, these taro chips are fried in coconut oil and are always served hot and crisp. For a change of flavor, fry the taro sticks, then toss with 2 or more teaspoons of chaat masala (page 20 or store-bought) and a squeeze of fresh lime.

1 pound taro root, peeled and cut into thin
    julienne sticks
1 1/2 to 2 cups coconut or peanut oil for deep-frying
1/8 teaspoon ground asafoetida
1/2 teaspoon cayenne pepper, or to taste
1/2 teaspoon salt, or to taste

1. Heat the oil in a large wok over medium-high heat until it reaches 325°F to 350°F on a frying thermometer or when a small piece of taro root dropped into the hot oil rises to the top after 15 to 20 seconds.

2. Add the taro root sticks in 2 or 3 batches, adding as many as the wok can hold at one time. Fry, stirring and turning, until crisp and golden, about 1 minute per batch. Transfer to paper towels with a slotted spatula to drain.

3. Let cool and remove all but 1 teaspoon of oil from the wok. Heat the oil and add the asafoetida, cayenne pepper, and salt. Add the taro root sticks and mix well. Serve hot.

Pastry Crackers and Puff Pastries (Mathri)

Think of a savory, flaky pie crust and you will not be too far from understanding *mathri* or *mathi* crackers. Sometimes bland—made just with a basic flour, *ghee* (or oil), and water dough—sometimes sweetened with a thin layer of melted sugar, and sometimes enhanced with one or more flours, spices and herbs, *mathri* are found all over India. Richer in fat than some of the other Indian pantry snacks, they quickly satiate the munchies.

Store in an airtight container at room temperature about 2 months. Eat them warmed or at room temperature with a cup of hot tea, or serve them with a spicy mango pickle.

Pastry Crackers with Black Pepper and Ajwain Seeds

Ajwaini Mathri

Makes 16 pieces

This recipe, from my friend Rita Bhalla in Los Angeles, is one of the best I've ever tasted. With an oregano-like flavor from the ajwain seeds and a peppery kick, this pastry is delicious by itself or with mango pickle. Also try it with soups, crumble it over salads, or enjoy it with a tall glass of chilled beer.

All mathris *should be fried at low heat so they can cook all the way through and develop a rich golden hue.*

2 cups all-purpose flour
¼ cup semolina
¼ cup canola oil
2 tablespoons melted ghee
1 teaspoon coarsely ground ajwain seeds
½ to 1 teaspoon coarsely ground black pepper + 16 black peppercorns
1 teaspoon salt, or to taste
½ cup warm water
1½ to 2 cups vegetable oil for deep-frying

1. Place the flour, semolina, oil, ghee, ajwain seeds, ground pepper, and salt in a mixing bowl and rub lightly with clean fingers to mix. Then add the water, a little at a time, and mix until the dough gathers into a semi-firm ball that does not stick to your fingers. (Lightly coat your fingers with oil, if needed.)

2. Divide the dough into 16 equal portions and, with a rolling pin, flatten each one into a thin 3- to 4-inch disc that's about ⅛-inch thick. If the dough sticks to the rolling surface, coat very lightly with oil; do not dust with dry flour.

3. With the tip of a knife, poke a few holes or make ¼-inch slits all over in each round. (These will prevent any puffing of the dough, or they will turn into *poori* breads.) Place one peppercorn in the center of each mathri and press it in firmly.

4. Heat the oil in a large wok or skillet over medium heat until it reaches 300°F to 325°F on a frying thermometer, or when a small drop of dough starts to bubble while it is still submerged. (Lower the heat if it rises immediately or browns.) Add the discs, as many as the wok can comfortably hold at one time, and fry, turning as needed, until lightly golden and crisp. Do not brown them and make sure the centers are crisp. Drain on paper towels. Let cool completely, and store in airtight containers at room temperature about 2 months.

Variations: To add more interest to mathris, along with the flour and spices, mix in ½ cup finely chopped onion, 2 tablespoons finely chopped fresh curry leaves, or 2 teaspoons dried fenugreek leaves.

Savory Pastry Diamonds
Namak-Paarae or Nimki

Makes 4 to 6 servings

These diamond-shaped savory pastry bites are a lighter and much smaller version of mathris. *They are made and eaten in much the same way as the* mathris.

1¹/2 cups self-rising flour, plus more for dusting
1 tablespoon cornstarch
3 tablespoons vegetable oil
¹/2 teaspoon coarsely ground ajwain seeds
¹/2 teaspoon salt, or to taste
About ¹/3 cup water
¹/2 to 2 cups peanut oil for deep-frying

1. Place the flour, cornstarch, oil, ajwain seeds, and salt in a food processor and pulse a few times to mix. Then, with the motor running, pour the water in a slow stream and process until the dough gathers into a semi-firm ball that does not stick to the sides of the work bowl. Transfer to a bowl, cover, and set aside 1 to 4 hours. This allows the gluten to develop.

2. Lightly oil your clean hands and gather the dough into a smooth, large ball. Coat it well with the dry flour, flatten it into a disc with your fingertips, and roll it into a large 8- to 9-inch circle (don't worry about the shape) about ¹/8 inch thick. If the dough sticks to the rolling surface, dust with more flour. (The rolling can be done on a lightly floured surface, but this is not a common practice in India.)

3. With a knife, make diagonal cuts through the length of the rolled circle, about ¹/2 inch apart. Then make opposite diagonal cuts, separating the rolled dough into diamond-shaped bits.

4. Heat the oil in a large wok or over medium heat until it reaches 300°F to 325°F on a frying thermometer, or when a small drop of dough starts to bubble while it is still submerged. (Lower the heat if it rises immediately or browns.) Add the dough bits, as many as the wok can comfortably hold at one time, and fry, turning as needed with a slotted spatula until lightly golden and crisp. Do not brown them and make sure that the centers are crisp. (Check by breaking one piece.) Transfer with a slotted spatula to paper towel to drain. Let cool completely, then store in airtight containers at room temperature, up to 2 months.

Puff Pastry Twists with Cumin and Ajwain Seeds
Puff Pastry ki Lumbi Mathri

Makes 30 pieces

These are a popular savory bakery item all over India. No one I know in India makes them at home, but in America, with puff pastry sheets readily available in supermarkets, I find it easy to make them.

¹/2 teaspoon cumin seeds, dry-roasted and coarsely ground (Dry-Roasting Spices, page 35)
Half of 1 (20-ounce) package frozen puff pastry (1 sheet)
1 large egg white
1 tablespoon water
¹/4 to ¹/3 teaspoon coarsely ground ajwain seeds
1 tablespoon all-purpose flour for dusting

1. Prepare the cumin seeds. Preheat the oven to 325°F. Thaw the pastry sheet at room temperature, until it is slightly softened but still cold to the touch, 15 to 20 minutes. Lightly grease a baking sheet. On a lightly floured surface, unfold and gently roll the pastry sheet to make a smooth 14-inch square. Cut in half.

2. In a small bowl, whisk together the egg white and water and brush it lightly over each half sheet. Sprinkle the cumin and ajwain seeds evenly on one half, then place the second half over it, egg wash side down. Dust lightly with flour and roll gently with a rolling pin to make a 14-by-7-inch rectangle (or larger).

3. Cut crosswise into about 30 half-inch strips. Twist and lightly stretch each strip and place, about 1 inch apart, on a lightly greased baking sheet. Brush with the egg wash for a shiny glaze and bake until crispy and golden, 10 to 12 minutes. Serve hot or at room temperature.

Variations: Instead of cumin and ajwain seeds, spread about ¹/4 cup or more of any green chutney (leaving at least a ¹/2–inch border so the chutney doesn't spill out while rolling), and then proceed with the recipe from Step 2. Or, try a layer of grated jalapeño Jack cheese.

Pastry Swirls with Roasted Red Bell Peppers and Potatoes

Shimla Mirch aur Aalu Bhari Puff-Pastry ki Mathri

Makes 48 pieces

A recipe to write home about, just as my daughter Sumi proudly did, to me. Sumi created this recipe to impress her husband, Monti, with her cooking skills. "I can also cook," she told him, "it's not only Mom."

This recipe is somewhat time-consuming, because the bell peppers are roasted and the potatoes boiled and mashed, but it's all quite simple.

1 (20-ounce) package frozen puff pastry sheets (2 sheets)

3 large russet (or any) potatoes

3 red bell peppers

1 tablespoon vegetable oil

1 medium onion, coarsely chopped

2 tablespoons peeled and minced fresh ginger

1 1/2 tablespoons ground coriander

1/2 teaspoon ground cumin

1/2 teaspoon garam masala

1/4 teaspoon salt, or to taste

1. Preheat the broiler and lightly grease a broiler-safe baking sheet. Thaw the pastry sheets at room temperature, until they are slightly softened but still cold to the touch, 15 to 20 minutes Meanwhile, cook the potatoes in lightly salted boiling water to cover until soft, about 20 minutes, then peel and mash them.

2. Cut the bell peppers in half and place them, cut side down, on the baking sheet, place on the top rack of the oven or under the broiler, and broil the peppers until completely charred, about 5 minutes. Remove from the oven, and lower the oven to 325°F. Transfer the peppers to a bowl, then cover with a dish or a seal within a zip-closure plastic bag until cool enough to handle. Then peel off and discard most of the charred skin, leaving some on for flavor. Chop finely.

3. Heat the oil in a large nonstick wok or saucepan over medium-high heat and cook the onion, stirring, until golden, about 2 minutes. Mix in the ginger and cook another minute. Add the mashed potatoes, coriander, cumin, garam masala, and salt, and cook stirring until golden, 2 to 3 minutes. Mix in the roasted bell peppers and stir about 2 minutes to blend the flavors. Let cool to room temperature, then divide into 2 equal parts.

4. On a lightly floured surface, working with each pastry sheet separately, unfold and gently roll the sheet to make it smooth. Placing the shorter side toward you and spread one half of the potato filling evenly over the sheet, leaving about a 3/4-inch border along the edges. Baste the border with water.

5. Starting from the side closest to you, roll tightly like a jelly roll. When you reach the end, press lightly on the basted edge to seal the roll. Lightly roll back and forth to lengthen the filled roll. Keeping the sealed side down, slice into 24 1/2-inch swirls and place them 1 inch apart on a baking sheet. Repeat with the second pastry sheet. Bake until crispy and golden, about 15 to 20 minutes. Serve hot or at room temperature.

Puff Pastry Rolls with Asparagus and Scallions

Asparagus Bharae Puff-Pastry kae Rolls

Makes 24 pieces

Select thick and juicy asparagus spears for this recipe. If using the thinner ones, allow 2 per pastry roll. Make sure about 1 inch of the asparagus tips are visible after you roll the pastry around them.

2 teaspoons Chaat Masala (page 20 or store-bought)

1 (20-ounce) package frozen puff pastry sheets (2 sheets)

2 to 3 scallions, green parts only, minced

1/4 cup finely chopped fresh cilantro, including soft stems

24 thick asparagus spears, each about 6 inches long

1. Prepare the chaat masala. Thaw the pastry sheets at room temperature until they are slightly softened but still cold to the touch, 15 to 20 minutes. Preheat the oven to 350°F and lightly grease a baking sheet.

2. On a lightly floured surface, unfold and sprinkle both the pastry sheets evenly with the chaat masala, scallion, and cilantro and gently, with a rolling pin, roll each sheet, making sure that the scallion and cilantro are pressed well into the pastry. (Dust with dry flour if the dough becomes sticky.) Then cut each sheet into 12 squares. Roll each square to make it slightly larger.

3. Working with each square separately, place one asparagus spear diagonally across the center with about 1 inch of the tip outside the pastry. Fold in half over the asparagus, then make a roll. Baste the corner with water and press to seal. Place, 1-inch apart, on the baking sheet, with the sealed side down. Bake until crispy and golden, 15 to 20 minutes. Transfer to cooling racks. Serve hot or at room temperature.

Mushroom Turnovers with Curry Powder

Khumbi Pattice

Makes 24 pieces

When I was growing up, there were only three fillings for these turnovers (translated, for some reason, as "patties" in English in India and here): vegetable, chicken, and mutton. And they were found only in special bakeries of British influence. Today, various versions of these are found all over, even in rural villages.

This is a convenient recipe to make, with all ingredients found at the supermarket. If you like, substitute for the mushrooms any dry-cooked filling of your choice. Simply fill, baste with egg wash, and bake.

1½ to 2 teaspoons Basic Curry Powder
(page 15 or store-bought)
2 tablespoons vegetable oil
1 large onion, finely chopped
1 teaspoon minced fresh garlic
1 to 3 green chile peppers, such as serrano,
minced with seeds
3 tablespoons all-purpose flour
3 cups finely chopped mushrooms
¼ cup finely chopped fresh cilantro, including soft stems
½ teaspoon salt, or to taste
1 (20-ounce) package frozen puff pastry sheets
(2 sheets)
1 large egg white, beaten lightly with
1 tablespoon water

1. Prepare the curry powder. Heat the oil in a large nonstick wok or saucepan over medium-high heat and cook the onion, stirring, until transparent, 2 to 3 minutes. Add the garlic, green chile peppers, curry powder, and flour, and stir over medium-low heat until the garlic and onion are golden, 2 to 3 minutes. Add the mushrooms, cilantro, and salt and cook until the mixture is completely dry, another 3 to 5 minutes. Let cool before using.

2. Divide the filling into two equal parts, one for each pastry sheet. Thaw the pastry sheets at room temperature, until they are slightly softened but still cold to the touch, 15 to 20 minutes.

3. Preheat the oven to 375°F. Lightly grease a baking sheet. On a lightly floured surface, working with each pastry sheet separately, unfold and gently roll it with a rolling pin to make it smooth. Then cut each sheet into 12 squares. Roll each square to make it slightly larger. Baste the edges with water, place 1 tablespoon of filling in the center of each square and fold one corner over the filling to the diagonal corner to form a triangle. Seal the edges by pressing with the back of a fork.

4. Brush the top of each turnover with the beaten egg and then poke a few holes with a fork so the steam can escape. Place the turnovers on the baking sheet and bake until puffed and golden, about 20 minutes. Transfer to cooling racks. Serve hot or at room temperature.

Curried Chicken or Lamb Turnovers

Murgh Pattice

Makes 24 pieces

If your palate likes spicy hot tastes, add to this filling any chile-pepper chutney such as Vinegar-Marinated Green Chile Peppers (page 84). Then cool off with a glass of iced coffee.

1 pound ground chicken or lamb
1 large onion, finely chopped
1 to 3 fresh green chile peppers, such as serrano, minced with seeds
1/2 cup finely chopped fresh cilantro, including soft stems
1 tablespoon ground coriander
1 teaspoon ground cumin
1 teaspoon dried fenugreek leaves
1/2 teaspoon garam masala
1/4 teaspoon ground turmeric
1/2 teaspoon salt, or to taste
2 tablespoons all-purpose flour
1 (20-ounce) package frozen puff pastry sheets (2 sheets)
1 large egg white, beaten lightly with 1 tablespoon water

1. Place everything (except the flour, puff pastry, and the egg wash) in a large nonstick skillet or saucepan and cook over medium-high heat, stirring and breaking up any lumps in the ground chicken, until golden, about 5 minutes. If using lamb, cook an extra 5 to 7 minutes. Reserve the pan.

2. Let the meat cool until it is safe enough to handle, about 15 minutes, then transfer to a food processor, add the flour, and process to make it as smooth as possible. Return to the pan and cook about 5 minutes to bind the filling and remove the raw taste of the flour.

3. Make the turnovers as per the directions for Mushroom Turnovers with Curry Powder, starting from Step 2.

Variation: Put filling into 6 to 8 small bell peppers or 8 to 10 small tomatoes and bake in a preheated 400°F oven until the peppers (or tomatoes) are soft, about 30 minutes.

Stuffed Fried Pastries (Samosae)

Most every old culture in the world has some form of filled, wrapped, and fried pastry. In India, they are called *Samosas*. These savory stuffed deep-fried triangular pastries are beloved by Indians who serve them as snacks with one or more chutneys. Via Indian restaurants, they have won fans the world over.

Here, I offer traditional recipes, and some shortcuts and variations to make them at home. I have included some recipes using puff-pastry, wonton skins, phyllo sheets, and flour tortillas. Of course, these yield different textures and tastes, but they enable you to make delicious pastries with the least amount of effort.

Samosas can be refrigerated 4 to 5 days and even frozen. Reheat in a preheated 400°F oven for 8 to 10 minutes, or give them a quick second fry. This works best when the first frying is brief and not until the *samosas* are golden and fully cooked.

Traditional Stuffed Triangular Pastries

Samosae

Makes 24 pieces

There are 3 basic steps to making samosas—*making the pastry dough, filling the* samosas, *and deep-frying them. As for the filling you can use just about any dry-cooked vegetable or meat, as long as it is finely chopped or minced and cooked.*

1 recipe any Samosa Filling (pages 108 to 110)
1 1/2 cups self-rising flour
3 tablespoons vegetable oil
1/2 teaspoon coarsely ground ajwain seeds
1/2 teaspoon salt, or to taste
About 1/3 cup water
1 cup all-purpose flour in a medium bowl or a pie dish, for coating and dusting
1 1/2 to 2 cups peanut oil for deep-frying

1. Prepare the filling. Then prepare the dough: Place the self-rising flour, oil, ajwain seeds, and salt in a food processor and pulse a few times to mix. With the motor running, pour the water in a slow stream and process until the flour gathers into a semi-firm ball that does not stick to the sides of the work bowl. Remove to a bowl, cover with plastic wrap or a lid, and let rest at least 1 hour and up to 4 hours. (This allows the gluten to develop.) If keeping for a longer period, refrigerate the dough.

2. **To roll and assemble:** Lightly oil your clean hands (to prevent the dough from sticking to them), then divide into 12 1½-inch balls. Cover with aluminum foil and set aside. Working with each ball separately, flatten it into a disc with your fingertips, coat well with dry flour, then roll with a rolling pin into a 6- to 7-inch circle of uniform ⅛-inch thickness. If the dough sticks to the rolling surface, coat once again with flour.

3. Cut the circle in half and brush with water about ½-inch in, along the straight edge. Pick up the two corners and place one over and around the other along the straight edge, then press along the straight edge to seal, making a cone. Also pinch the point of the cone to seal.

Alternately, fold in half, sealing the straight edge to make a simpler cone.

4. Hold the cone between your thumb and forefinger, with the pointed side down toward the work surface. Fill the mouth of the cone with 2 to 3 tablespoons of filling. Brush the edges of the mouth of the cone with water and press them together to seal. You should end up with a stuffed triangular pastry. Cover with foil and set aside until ready to fry. Repeat with all the other balls of dough.

5. **To fry:** Heat the oil in a wok or skillet over medium-high heat until it reaches 325°F to 350°F on a frying thermometer, or when a small piece of the dough dropped into the hot oil rises to the top after 15 to 20 seconds. Place the samosas in the wok, as many as it can hold at one time without crowding, and fry, turning them a few times with a slotted spatula, until crispy and golden on all sides, 4 to 5 minutes. (If the samosas brown too quickly, it means the heat is too high; lower it.) Transfer to paper towels to drain, then serve.

Variation: For bite-size servings, in Step 2 divide the filling and dough into 48 balls. Roll each ball of dough into a 2-inch circle, stuff with a teaspoon of filling, wrap, then fry according to directions, about 2 minutes or until golden.

Sindhi-Style Stuffed Triangular Pastries
Sindhi Samosae

Makes 24 pieces

The Sindhi people, originally from northwest India (now Pakistan) and now scattered all over India and the world, have a unique way of wrapping their samosas. *With no leavening or oil in the dough and fennel seeds as the main flavor, these* samosas *are considerably different. My friend Moyne Puri graciously showed me how easily and quickly they could be folded.*

1 recipe any Samosa Filling of your choice (pages 108 to 110)
1½ cups self-rising flour
1½ teaspoons fennel seeds, coarsely ground
¼ teaspoon salt, or to taste
About ¾ cup water
1 cup all-purpose flour in a medium bowl or a pie dish, for coating and dusting
2 to 3 cups peanut oil for deep-frying

1. Prepare the filling. Then, in a small bowl, mix together 2 tablespoons of the self-rising flour with about 2 tablespoons water to make a thick paste that will be used as a glue for sealing the pastries.

2. Prepare the dough: Place the remaining self-rising flour, fennel seeds, and salt in a food processor and pulse a few times to mix. With the motor running, pour the water in a slow stream and process until the flour gathers into a pliable ball that does not stick to the sides of the work bowl. (This dough does not need to rest.)

3. To roll and assemble: Divide the dough into 8 balls. Flatten each one into a 3- to 4-inch disc. Working with 4 discs at a time, brush the top surface of each generously with oil then dust each one with about 2 teaspoons flour. Working with the remaining 4 discs one at a time, brush with oil and place on top of one of the floured discs, oil side down, like a sandwich. Then press each "sandwich" together to make 1 larger disc. You will now have four large discs.

4. Working with each of the 4 discs one at a time, dust lightly with the flour and roll with a rolling pin to make 8- to 9-inch circles of uniform ⅛-inch thickness. (If the dough sticks to the rolling surface, dust again with flour.)

5. Heat a griddle or a skillet over medium heat and cook each rolled circle very lightly on both sides until it just starts to firm up but not brown, about 30 seconds per side. (You'll see the edges of the sandwiched circle starting to separate.) Remove it to a cutting board. Carefully pull the two sides apart to separate into two paper-thin circles, and stack them. Repeat with the other three discs. You should end up with a stack of 8 samosa skins. Cut the stack of skins into 3 equal parts, making a total of 24 long strips. Keep covered with foil.

6. Working with each strip separately, lay it lengthwise in front of you on the work surface and place about 1 tablespoon of the filling on the strip near the lower right corner. Then fold the right corner over the filling to the left side to make a triangle. Repeatedly fold the stuffed triangle diagonally from one side to the other until you get to the end of the dough strip. Tuck in any extra dough to seal. In the end you should have a multi-folded triangle. Repeat with all the strips.

7. Heat the oil in a wok or skillet over medium-high heat until it reaches 325°F to 350°F on a frying thermometer or when a small piece of dough dropped into the hot oil rises to the top after 15 to 20 seconds. Add as many samosas as the wok can hold at one time without crowding, and fry, turning them a few times with a slotted spatula, until crispy and golden on all sides, 4 to 5 minutes. (If the samosas brown too quickly, lower the heat.) Transfer to paper towels to drain, then serve.

Variation: An electric tortilla maker does a wonderful job of making samosa skins. Instead of rolling the discs manually in Step 4, place each dough portion in the hot tortilla press and press down the lid. The dough will instantly spread and make a loud hissing sound as the water in the dough steams. Quickly, remove from the press and separate the two layers. Repeat with the remaining discs, then follow the recipe from Step 5.

Stuffed Tortilla Triangles
Tortilla Samosae

Makes 24 pieces

Flour tortillas, so popular in Mexican cuisine, are also a fall-back pantry essential in most Indian kitchens in the Unites States. With a taste and texture not too far removed from Indian pastry, Indians fry them to make crispy mathri *crackers, and* papri-chaat *(a savory snack made with flour chips, potatoes, yogurt, and special sauces), fold and stuff them to make* samosa *pastries, or cook them lightly on a tava-griddle to serve as* chapatis *(whole-wheat griddle breads) or* paranthas *(griddle-fried breads) with Indian meals.*

Choose thin flour tortillas, about 8-inches in diameter, found in the refrigerator section of supermarkets. The thicker ones render doughy samosas. You can also buy rolled-out but uncooked tortillas in some American markets. They are a much better choice.

1 recipe any Samosa Filling of your choice (pages 108 to 110)
1½ to 2 cups peanut oil for deep-frying
12 (8- to 9-inch) flour tortillas

1. Stack and cut the tortillas in half to make 24 semi-circles. Working with each half separately, brush with water about ½-inch in, along all the edges. Then place 1½ to 2 tablespoons of the samosa filling on one side of the semi circle. Fold the other side over the filling to cover it. Press the edges well to seal in the filling. Repeat with the remaining halves.

2. Deep-fry as per directions for Traditional Stuffed Triangular Pastries (page 103), starting from Step 5.

Variation: A similar samosa can be made with little (4-inch) square or round wonton skins. Since the wonton skins are thin and small, do not cut them in half. Each takes only about 1 to 2 teaspoons of the filling and they fry very quickly, in just about 1 minute.

Stuffed Phyllo Triangles

Phyllo kae Samosae

Makes 24 pieces

Crispy and flaky, these Middle Eastern pastry look-alikes pack a hefty dose of Indian flavors.

Phyllo (also called filo) sheets, found in the freezer section of most American and Middle Eastern markets, are thin 17-by-12-inch pastry sheets. They dry out very fast, so you have to work quickly and keep the extra ones covered with a damp cloth at all times. When you brush them with butter or oil, start from the edges and work your way toward the center.

1 recipe any Samosa Filling of your choice (pages 108 to 110)
6 phyllo pastry sheets (about ¼ pound)
1 to 2 tablespoons melted butter or vegetable oil

1. Brush each phyllo sheet with melted butter and stack one on top of the other on a cutting board. With a sharp knife, cut them lengthwise into 4 equal strips, each about 3 inches wide. You should have 24 long strips. Stack again and cover with a damp (not wet) clean cotton kitchen towel.

2. Preheat the oven to 350°F. Lightly grease a baking sheet. Working with each strip separately, place it lengthwise in front of you on the work surface and put about 1 tablespoon of the filling near the lower right corner. Fold the right corner over the filling to the left side to make a triangle. Repeatedly fold the stuffed triangle diagonally from one side to the other until you get to the end of the phyllo. Tuck in any extra to seal. In the end you should have a multi-folded triangle. Repeat with all the strips.

3. Brush the top of all the triangles with the butter, place them on the baking sheet, and bake, turning once midway through baking, until crispy and golden, about 25 minutes. Transfer to cooling racks. Serve hot, warm, or at room temperature.

Spicy 7-Layered Baked Pastries

Satpura Samosae

Makes 16 pieces

Satpura *here means "with 7 layers." The authentic version of these* samosas *are potato-filled, spicy, flaky, crispy stacks of phyllo-like dough, which are folded in half and deep-fried. These* samosas, *a specialty of a small eatery in Old Delhi in northern India, are what my mother often served at her special tea parties for my or my brother's birthdays. (When I was growing up, tea parties were all the rage; it's formal dinners these days.) People served all sorts of fun foods, sometimes homemade goodies, and other times foods made by special* halvais *(professional savory and sweet makers) who came to the house and set up shop there, like caterers.*

1 large russet (or any) potato
1 tablespoon melted ghee or vegetable oil
1 teaspoon cumin seeds
½ teaspoon garam masala
¼ teaspoon cayenne pepper, or to taste
⅛ teaspoon ground asafoetida
¼ teaspoon salt, or to taste
7 phyllo pastry sheets (about ¼ pound)
¼ to ⅓ cup melted unsalted butter or vegetable oil

1. Boil the potato in lightly salted water to cover until tender, about 20 minutes. Drain, let cool, then peel and mash in a small bowl. Heat the oil in a small non-stick wok or saucepan over medium-high heat and add the cumin seeds; they should sizzle upon contact with the hot oil. Quickly add the mashed potato, garam masala, cayenne pepper, asafoetida, and salt, and stir until golden, 5 to 7 minutes. Let cool.

2. Baste each phyllo sheet generously with the melted butter and stack one on top of the other on a cutting board. With a sharp knife, cut lengthwise into 4 equal strips, about 3 inches wide, cutting through all 7 sheets. Cut each strip in half crosswise and then cut each half in half again to make a total of 16 rectangles, each made up of 7 layers. Cover with a damp (not wet) clean cotton kitchen towel.

3. Preheat the oven to 350°F. Lightly grease a baking sheet. With a rolling pin, lightly roll each rectangular stack of 7 layers to make sure the layers adhere to each other properly. Brush the top layer with butter and place 1 teaspoon of the filling in the center. Fold in half to, cover the filling. Press the edges well to seal in the filling. Repeat with the remaining rectangles.

4. Brush the top and bottom layers of the samosas generously with butter once again and place on the baking sheet. Bake until crispy and golden, 15 to 20 minutes. Transfer to cooling racks. Serve.

Variation: Drain out most of the juices from Basic Green Chutney (page 58) and use about 1/2 teaspoon in place of the mashed potato. Or apply a scant layer of the chutney along with the butter on each layer in Step 3 and then bake the samosas.

Stuffed Phyllo Baked Pastry Pouches
Potli-Samosae

Makes 24 pieces

This recipe was inspired by pastries made by my cousin Amita Molloy. Folded phyllo sheets, filled and pinched to seal, are when baked, transformed into crispy little filled pouches—similar to the filled crepe-wrapped snack known as "beggar's purses." Although these pouches can be baked on a tray, I bake them in a mini-muffin pan. They stay contained in their individual compartments and brown well on all sides.

1 recipe any Samosa Filling of your choice
    (pages 108 to 110)
12 phyllo pastry sheets (about 1/2 pound)
1/4 to 1/3 cup melted unsalted butter or vegetable oil

1. Brush each phyllo sheet generously with butter and stack one on top of the other on a cutting board. With a sharp knife, cut the sheets in half, crosswise, to make a total of 24 pieces. Stack once again, and cover with a damp (not wet) clean cotton kitchen towel.

2. Preheat the oven to 350°F. Lightly grease a mini-muffin pan or a baking sheet. Working with each piece separately, fold in half and then in half again to make an approximately 6-by-4-inch rectangle. Place about 1 tablespoon of the filling in the center, then pick up the phyllo by the four corners and pinch them together just above the filling to seal, making a little pouch.

Alternately, tie each one lightly with chives, scallion greens, or thin strips of carrots, or any other greens or vegetables. Repeat with all the pieces.

3. Brush all the pouches with the butter, and place each in one cup of the muffin pan or all of them on a baking sheet and bake until crispy and golden, about 25 minutes. Transfer to cooling racks. Serve hot, warm, or at room temperature.

Fillings for Samosas

Potato Filling
Samosae mein bharnae kae Aalu

Makes about 4 cups

Although any type of dry-cooked vegetable or meat makes for delicious samosa *fillings, there are some traditional ones. Potatoes are tops on the list.*

This samosa filling can also be used to stuff vegetables such as tomatoes, eggplants, bell peppers, and others, and even serve as a side dish. You can use any of the dry-cooked potato dishes in the book to fill your samosas.

4 to 5 medium russet (or any) potatoes
    (about 1¹/₂ pounds)
2 tablespoons peanut oil
2 teaspoons cumin seeds
¹/₂ teaspoon coarsely ground fenugreek seeds
2 tablespoons peeled and minced fresh ginger
1 to 3 fresh green chile peppers, such as serrano,
    minced with seeds
1¹/₂ tablespoons ground coriander
¹/₂ teaspoon salt, or to taste
¹/₂ teaspoon garam masala
¹/₄ cup finely chopped fresh cilantro,
    including soft stems
1 teaspoon mango powder

1. Cook the potatoes in lightly salted boiling water to cover until tender, about 20 minutes. Drain, let cool, then peel and finely chop. Heat the oil in a large nonstick wok or saucepan over medium-high heat and add the cumin seeds; they should sizzle upon contact with the hot oil. Quickly add the fenugreek seeds and mix in the potatoes.

2. Stir about 2 minutes, then add the ginger, green chile peppers, coriander, salt, and garam masala, and stir occasionally until the potatoes are golden, about 10 minutes.

3. Add the cilantro and mango powder and cook another 5 minutes. Remove from heat and let cool before using.

Variation: Mix in ¹/₂ cup thawed frozen peas, 1 cup finely chopped fresh spinach, or ¹/₂ cup soaked red lentils (dhulli masoor dal) along with the potatoes. Adjust the seasonings.

Spicy Mixed Vegetable Samosa Filling
Samosae mein bharnae ki Sabziyan

Makes about 4 cups

Mix at least three vegetables—carrots, beans, mushrooms, potatoes, peas, cauliflower, or any others you fancy. The underlying flavor of this filling comes from the special kadhai masala *blend, which has fenugreek, fennel, and pomegranate seeds. It's named for a blend of spices often used in foods fried in the* kadhai *(Indian wok).*

1¹/₂ to 2 tablespoons Spicy Masala for Wok-Cooked
    Foods (Kadhai Masala), page 26 or store-bought
2 tablespoons vegetable oil
1 medium onion, finely chopped
1 to 3 fresh green chile peppers, such as serrano,
    minced with seeds
1 tablespoon peeled and finely chopped fresh ginger
4 cups finely chopped mixed fresh or frozen vegetables
¹/₂ teaspoon salt, or to taste
Freshly ground black pepper, to taste

1. Prepare the kadaai masala. Heat the oil in a large nonstick wok or saucepan over medium-high heat and add the kadhai masala; it should sizzle upon contact with the hot oil. Quickly add the onion and stir about 2 minutes.

2. Add the green chile peppers, ginger, vegetables, salt, and black pepper, and cook over medium heat the first 2 to 3 minutes, and then over medium-low heat until the vegetables are soft, 5 to 7 minutes more. Remove from the heat and let cool before using.

Yellow Mung Bean and Spinach Samosa Filling

Samosae mein bharnae ki Mung Dal

Makes about 4 cups

This is another popular samosa *filling that also doubles as a side dish. In addition to* samosas, *try it for filling* parantha *(griddle-fried breads) and different vegetables. The mung beans have to be soaked overnight, but otherwise the filling is quick and easy to make.*

$1^{1}/_{4}$ cup dried yellow mung beans (dhulli mung dal), sorted and washed in 3 to 4 changes of water

2 tablespoons vegetable oil

1 teaspoon cumin seeds

$1^{1}/_{2}$ tablespoons peeled and minced fresh ginger

1 fresh green chile pepper, such as serrano, minced with seeds

1 tablespoon ground coriander

1 cup finely chopped fresh spinach

$^{1}/_{4}$ teaspoon ground turmeric

$^{1}/_{2}$ teaspoon salt, or to taste

1 cup water

1. Soak the mung beans overnight in water to cover by 2 inches, then drain. Heat the oil in a large non-stick wok or saucepan over medium-high heat and add the cumin seeds; they should sizzle upon contact with the hot oil. Quickly add the ginger, green chile pepper, and coriander, and stir about 30 seconds.

2. Add the spinach and stir until wilted, about 1 minute. Mix in the mung beans, turmeric, and salt, and stir about 2 minutes. Add the water, lower the heat to medium-low, cover the pan and cook until all the water has been absorbed and the dal is soft, about 10 minutes. Let cool before using.

Green Split Pea Samosa Filling

Samosae mein bharnae ki Muttar Dal

Makes about 4 cups

Another popular samosa *filling, made with green split peas. Use in all types of savory pastries,* paranthas *(griddle-fried breads) and in* pooris *(puffed deep-fried whole-wheat breads).*

$1^{1}/_{4}$ cups green split peas (muttar dal), sorted and washed in 3 to 4 changes of water

2 tablespoons vegetable oil

$1^{1}/_{2}$ teaspoons cumin seeds

1 large onion, finely chopped

2 teaspoons ground coriander

1 teaspoon ground ginger

1 teaspoon ground fennel seeds

$^{1}/_{2}$ teaspoon cayenne pepper, or to taste

$^{1}/_{2}$ teaspoon salt, or to taste

$^{1}/_{8}$ teaspoon ground asafoetida

1 cup water

2 teaspoons mango powder

1. Soak the split peas overnight in water to cover by 2 inches, then drain. Heat the oil in a small nonstick wok or saucepan over medium-high heat and add the cumin seeds; they should sizzle upon contact with the hot oil. Quickly add the onion and cook, stirring, until golden, about 2 minutes.

2. Add the dal, coriander, ginger, fennel seeds, cayenne pepper, salt, and asafoetida, and cook about 1 minute. Add the water, bring to a quick boil over high heat, then reduce the heat to low, cover the pan and cook until the split peas are tender, about 10 minutes. Mix in the mango powder and let cool before using.

Sprouted Green Mung Bean Samosa Filling

Samosae mein bharnae ki Phooti Hui Mung Dal

Makes about 4 cups

Lending a nutritional boost and a delicate crunch to the normally soft-cooked fillings are sprouted small beans and lentils (dals). Use any one type or mix them together, but stick to the smaller dals only (not the larger dried beans). Grated potatoes are the binder to ensure that the filling doesn't fall out as you eat the samosas.

Sprout the dal at home in advance or look for the sprouts in health food stores or farmers' markets.

2 cups sprouted green mung beans (Sprouting Beans, page 39 or store-bought)
6 small russet (or any) potatoes
2 tablespoons peanut oil
2 teaspoons cumin seeds
1 large onion, finely chopped
2 tablespoons ground coriander
1/2 teaspoon ground turmeric
1 to 3 fresh green chile pepper, such as serrano, minced with seeds
1 teaspoon salt, or to taste
2 tablespoons fresh lemon juice
1/2 cup finely chopped fresh cilantro, including soft stems

1. Prepare the mung beans in advance. Cook the potatoes in lightly salted boiling water to cover until tender, about 20 minutes. Drain, let cool, then grate into a medium bowl.

2. Heat the oil in a large nonstick wok or saucepan over medium-high heat and add the cumin seeds; they should sizzle upon contact with the hot oil. Quickly add the onions and cook, stirring, until golden, about 5 minutes.

3. Add the coriander and turmeric, then mix in the green chiles, sprouted dal, and salt, and cook about 3 minutes. Add the grated potatoes, lemon juice, and cilantro, and cook over medium-high heat, stirring, until completely dry, about 5 minutes. Remove from heat and let cool before using.

Meat Samosa Filling

Samosae mein bharnae ka Gosht

Makes about 3 cups

Popular among non-vegetarians, this filling is also very delicious as a stuffing in parantha *(griddle-fried breads) and an array of vegetables.*

1 cup fresh fenugreek leaves
1 cup coarsely chopped fresh cilantro, including soft stems
2 large cloves fresh garlic, peeled
5 to 7 quarter-size slices peeled fresh ginger
1 fresh green chile pepper, such as serrano, coarsely chopped
1 tablespoon garam masala
1/2 teaspoon cayenne pepper, or to taste
1/4 teaspoon ground turmeric
1/4 teaspoon freshly ground nutmeg
1 pound extra lean ground meat (lamb, beef, or chicken)
1 cup frozen peas, thawed
1/2 cup bread crumbs
1/2 teaspoon salt, or to taste

1. In a food processor, process together the fenugreek leaves, cilantro, garlic, ginger, and green chile pepper until minced. Add all the remaining ingredients, except the peas, and process again to mix well.

2. Transfer to a large nonstick wok or skillet, mix in the peas, and cook, stirring, over medium-high heat until the meat is golden and completely dry, 7 to 10 minutes. Let cool before using.

Mung Bean Puffed Pastries

Mung Dal ki Khasta Kachauriyan

Makes about 30 pieces

Belonging to Rajasthan in the northwest and Uttar Pradesh in the north-central part of India, kachauries are another of India's savory pastries. These crispy and flaky 2- to 3-inch puffed-up rounds of pastry dough are always filled with something exciting, whether it is spices, nuts, lentils, or dried peas. Serve them with any sonth *chutney (sweet and sour tamarind) or green chutney of your choice.*

This recipe was given to me by Pushpa Khatod, my daughter's mother-in-law. Her important advice: the pastry for the kachauries is quite thick and should be fried over medium heat for a long time. Do not increase the heat at any time. Also, if any kachauri *falls apart while frying, quickly remove it from the wok or it will disintegrate and spoil the oil.*

³/₄ cup dried yellow mung beans (dhulli mung dal),
    sorted and washed in 3 to 4 changes of water
1¹/₂ tablespoons fennel seeds
1 tablespoon coriander
1 teaspoon cumin seeds
1 teaspoon hot red pepper flakes, or to taste
¹/₂ teaspoon black peppercorns
5 whole cloves
2 black cardamom pods, seeds only
¹/₂ cup vegetable oil
¹/₄ teaspoon ground asafoetida
2 tablespoons chickpea flour
2 teaspoons salt, or to taste
3 cups all-purpose flour
¹/₂ teaspoon ground turmeric
¹/₄ cup lukewarm water, or as needed
2 to 3 cups peanut oil for deep-frying

1. Soak the dal in water to cover by 2 inches, and drain. Then make the filling: In a food processor or a blender, process the dal to make a coarse paste. In a spice or a coffee grinder, coarsely grind together all the whole spices (fennel to cardamom).

2. Heat ¼ cup of the vegetable oil in a large nonstick wok or saucepan over medium-high heat and add the asafoetida, then the ground spices, and stir about 30 seconds. Mix in the chickpea flour and stir another 30 seconds.

3. Add the dal paste and cook over medium heat, stirring and breaking any lumps, about 10 minutes. Add the salt and stir to mix well. Let cool and divide equally into 30 portions (about 1 tablespoon each). Make a ball of each portion and set aside. If the balls seem to fall apart, this means the filling is too dry; moisten it with 1 to 2 tablespoons hot water.

4. Make the dough: In a medium bowl, using clean fingers, rub together the flour, turmeric, and the remaining ¼ cup oil until well mixed. Add enough water to make a soft and pliable dough, adding a little at a time. Place the dough on a cutting board and pound lightly with a meat mallet about 2 minutes. Turn the dough over during the 2 minutes to pound different sections. This makes the dough very elastic. Divide the dough equally into 30 portions.

5. Assemble the kachauries: In a small bowl, make a paste of 2 tablespoons all-purpose flour and 1 tablespoon water and keep ready. Working with one portion of the dough at a time, with your fingers press out a 3-inch patty. Brush the top surface lightly with water and place one portion of the dal filling in the center. Lift the edges over the filling, bring them together and pinch to seal. Then gently push in the pinched edges down to make a slight depression in the center and to flatten the patty to 1-inch thick. Brush the entire kachauri lightly with the flour-water paste and set aside. Finish assembling all the kachauries. Cover with a clean, damp cotton kitchen towel and set aside.

6. Heat the oil in a wok or skillet over medium-high heat until it reaches 300°F to 325°F on a frying thermometer, or when a small piece of the dough dropped into the hot oil rises to the top after 15 to 20 seconds. Reduce the heat to medium and add the kachauries, adding as many as the wok can hold at one time without crowding, and fry slowly, turning only once after the bottom is golden-brown, about 3 to 4 minutes. When the other side is golden-brown, about 3 to 4 minutes more, remove from the wok with a slotted metal spatula and transfer to paper towels to drain. Serve immediately, or let cool and refrigerate up to 15 days.

Variations: Substitute for the yellow mung beans (dhulli mung dal) equal amounts of dried split yellow peas (peeli muttar dal) or green split peas (hari muttar dal), fresh green peas, or a mixture of cashews, almonds, and pistachios.

Fritters
(Pakorae or Bhajiae)

Called *pakoras* (pronounced *pakauradha*) in the north or *bhajias* in the south and west, these are special batter-fried finger foods. Whether they are slices of vegetables, *paneer* cheese, chicken, lamb, or fish cloaked in a thin, crispy, spiced chickpea flour batter, or uneven balls of diced vegetables mixed with chickpea flour, *pakoras* are a unifying culinary phenomenon in India.

Served with any one or an array of puréed green, yogurt-based, or *sonth* (sweet and sour tamarind) chutneys, ideally all *pakoras* are meant to be eaten hot and crisp out of the wok, because most of them become soggy as they cool. The soggy ones, however, have their own following, especially in packed "on-the-go" meals—where the extra moisture can be soaked up when rolled in *chapatis* (whole-wheat griddle breads) or *paranthas* (griddle-fried breads), in pita pockets, in sandwiches, or when simply served over a bed of rice.

The cornerstone of all *pakoras* is chickpea flour, or *besan* as it is called in India. Chickpea flour is heavy and tends to compress under its own weight in a container, so it is crucial to sift it. Sifting gets rid of any lumps and incorporates air into the flour, for a smooth batter.

Make a test *pakora* first and adjust the batter accordingly, adding more chickpea flour or water, as needed. A thick batter will result in heavy and doughy *pakoras;* a thin batter will coat the vegetables poorly, forming a broken shell around them. Also, slap the batter-coated vegetables lightly along the sides of the bowl to remove all the excess batter before frying.

Sometimes *pakoras* are double-fried—if the pieces are large or dense or if they're not being served right away. For making in advance, all *pakoras* can be lightly fried, allowed to cool then refrigerated in an air-tight container or zip-closure bags about 5 days, or frozen up to 2 months. To reheat, bring them to room temperature and refry in hot oil. (Cold,

refrigerated *pakoras* will immediately bring down the oil temperature and consequently make the *pakoras* absorb extra oil, so bringing them to room temperature is important.)

In this section, most recipes start with the basic batter and then are built upon to create different taste variations. For frying, refer to the box "Frying Fritters (Pakorae Talna)" below.

Frying Fritters
(Pakorae Talna)

1. Heat the oil in a wok or skillet until it reaches 350°F to 375°F on a frying thermometer or a small teaspoon of batter dropped into the hot oil bubbles and rises to the top immediately.

2. With clean hands, put the sliced or chopped vegetables (or other items) into the batter (in batches if necessary) and mix lightly with your fingers. Working with each piece separately, shake off the excess batter by tapping it lightly against the sides of the batter bowl, then put it into the hot oil carefully with your fingers (or with tongs) to avoid oil spluttering. Add as many pieces as the wok can hold at one time without crowding, and fry each batch, turning a few times with a slotted spoon, until crispy and golden on all sides, about 1 to 2 minutes for small, thin pieces, 2 to 3 minutes for bigger pieces. Transfer to paper towels to drain. Repeat the process with remaining pieces.

Basic Batter
for Pakora Fritters
Pakorae ka Besan

Makes 40 to 50 fritters

This is the most basic batter for pakora *fritters, to which you can add as many or as few herbs and spices as you wish. With no other additions, this basic recipe forms a light, crisp coating around a large array of foods. More than anything else, it is the consistency of the batter that is really important. Thick, it will be doughy, thin it will not coat properly.*

¹/₂ **cup chickpea flour (besan)**
¹/₃ **teaspoon salt, or to taste**
¹/₈ **teaspoon baking soda**
¹/₃ **to ¹/₂ cup water**

1. Sift the chickpea flour into a medium bowl, add the salt and baking soda and mix well.

2. Add ¹/₃ cup water to make a smooth batter of medium consistency. If the batter is thin, add some more chickpea flour; if it seems too thick, mix in some more water. The batter is now ready.

Sliced, Chopped, and
Stuffed Vegetable Fritters

Potato Fritters with Chives
Aalu kae Pakorae

Makes 25 to 30 fritters

Although there is a tendency among Indians to peel potatoes before cooking, I seldom do. The purists may disagree with me, but the way I see it, why knowingly throw away good vitamins? Just be sure to scrub the potatoes thoroughly before cooking.

¹/₂ **teaspoon Chaat Masala (page 20 or store-bought)**
1 recipe Basic Batter for Pakora Fritters (left)
2 teaspoons ground coriander
1 teaspoon coarsely ground cumin or ajwain seeds
2 tablespoons minced chives
3 to 4 small russet (or any) potatoes, thinly sliced
1¹/₂ to 2 cups oil for deep-frying

Prepare the chaat masala. Prepare the basic batter. Mix in the coriander, cumin (or ajwain), and chives. Add the potato slices in the batter. Heat the oil and fry the potato slices as per directions in the box "Frying Fritters (Pakorae Talna)" on page 112. Transfer all the fried pakoras to a serving platter, sprinkle the chaat masala on top, and serve.

Variation: Substitute for the potatoes any other starchy root vegetables, such as sweet potatoes, yams, yucca, or taro. Unripe green tomatoes also work in this batter.

Fresh Green Bean Pakora Fritters with Ginger

Hari Phalliyon kae Pakorae

Makes 40 to 50 fritters

This is a pakora of my own making and one that wins raves. These delicate and crisp delights are great to begin any meal or to serve with a cup of afternoon tea. Use the non-stringy beans in a variety of colors (green, yellow, and purple). If using any others, remove the strings. Select young and tender 5- to 6-inch-long beans and allow at least 6 to 8 per person. They disappear fast.

1/2 teaspoon Chaat Masala (page 20 or store-bought)
1 recipe Basic Batter for Pakora Fritters (page 113)
1 teaspoon ground coriander
1/2 teaspoon ground cumin
1/2 teaspoon crushed ajwain seeds
1 tablespoon peeled and finely minced or ground fresh ginger
40 to 50 fresh green beans (about 1/2 pound), trimmed from the stem end only
1 1/2 to 2 cups oil for deep-frying

Prepare the chaat masala. Prepare the basic batter. Mix in the coriander, cumin, ajwain seeds, and ginger. Add the beans to the batter. Heat the oil and fry the beans as per directions in the box "Frying Fritters (Pakorae Talna)" on page 112. Transfer all the fried pakoras to a serving platter, sprinkle the chaat masala on top, and serve.

Cauliflower Pakora Fritters with Cilantro

Gobhi kae Pakorae

Makes 20 to 25 pieces

Cauliflower can be cut into all type of pieces—large or small florets or thick or thin stem slices. Just remember that while the thin, small pieces are fine at the first go, the larger, thicker ones will need to be double-fried.

A 1 1/2-pound head of cauliflower becomes less than 1 pound of florets once the stems are removed, so make sure you get a large enough head.

1 teaspoon Chaat Masala (page 20 or store-bought)
1 large head cauliflower (about 1 1/2 pounds), cut into 2-inch florets
1/2 teaspoon salt, or to taste
1/2 teaspoon hot red pepper flakes, or to taste
1 1/2 recipes Basic Batter for Pakora Fritters (page 113)
1 to 2 tablespoons chickpea flour
1/4 cup minced fresh cilantro, including soft stems
1 to 3 fresh green chile peppers, such as serrano, minced with seeds
1/4 teaspoon garam masala
1/2 teaspoon coarsely ground ajwain seeds
1 1/2 to 2 cups peanut oil for deep-frying
1/4 cup mustard oil for deep-frying

1. Prepare the chaat masala. Place the cauliflower florets in a bowl and toss with salt and red pepper flakes. Set aside to let the flavors blend. Prepare the basic batter. Mix in the chickpea flour, cilantro, green chile peppers, garam masala, and ajwain seeds. Add the florets to the batter. Heat the oil and fry the florets as per directions in the box "Frying Fritters (Pakorae Talna)" on page 112.

2. Let cool, then press each fritter between the palms of your hands to flatten. As you do this, the batter coating will break and reveal parts of the florets. Refry the dense florets in hot oil until the pakoras are lightly browned and crisp, 1 to 2 minutes. Drain on paper towels. Transfer all the fried pakoras to a serving platter, sprinkle the chaat masala on top, and serve.

Bell Pepper Pakora Fritters with Ajwain Seeds

Shimla Mirch kae Pakorae

Makes about 30 pieces

Colorful and curvaceous, the red and orange bell peppers, cut crosswise into curly 1/2-inch-thick semi-circle slices, are intriguing pakoras to offer your guests.

1 tablespoon Basic Ginger Paste (page 46
   or store-bought)
1/2 teaspoon Chaat Masala (page 20 or store-bought)
3 to 4 orange or red bell peppers, stemmed and seeded
1 recipe Basic Batter for Pakora Fritters (page 113)
2 teaspoons ground coriander
1/2 teaspoon coarsely ground ajwain seeds
1/2 teaspoon hot red pepper flakes, or to taste
1 1/2 to 2 cups oil for deep-frying

1. Prepare the ginger-garlic paste and chaat masala. Cut each bell pepper lengthwise into 2 halves, then cross-wise into 1/2-inch thick half moons.

2. Prepare the basic batter. Mix in the coriander, ajwain seeds, red pepper flakes, and ginger-garlic paste.

3. Add the bell pepper slices to the batter. Heat the oil and fry the bell pepper slices as per directions in the box "Frying Fritters (Pakorae Talna)" on page 112. Transfer all the fried pakoras to a serving platter, sprinkle the chaat masala on top, and serve.

Pumpkin Pakora Fritters with Bengali 5-Spices
Pethae kae Pakorae

Makes 24 pieces

My mother and grandmother always pushed these fritters toward us, but at the time our fingers always found others. We just did not like pumpkin pakoras. Little did we know! As an adult and a mother, I found history repeating itself. No matter! More for me.

1/2 teaspoon Chaat Masala (page 20 or store-bought)
2 teaspoons Bengali 5-Spices (Panch-Phoran),
   page 27 or store-bought
1 recipe Basic Batter for Pakora Fritters (page 113)
1 teaspoon sugar
1 (2- by 6-inch) piece pumpkin or butternut squash,
   cut into 1/4-inch-thick slices
1 1/2 to 2 cups peanut oil for deep-frying

1. Prepare the chaat masala and the 5-spices. Then prepare the basic batter and mix in the 5-spices and the sugar.

2. Add the pumpkin slices to the batter. Heat the oil and fry the pumpkin slices as per directions in the box "Frying Fritters (Pakorae Talna)" on page 112. Transfer all the fried pakoras to a serving platter, sprinkle the chaat masala on top, and serve.

Garlicky Eggplant Pakora Fritters
Baingan Kae Pakorae

Makes 35 to 40 pieces

A little mushy because of the nature of the vegetable, these pakoras are, nevertheless, authentic. Though traditionally made with thick, round slices of the large globe eggplants dipped in a thicker-than-usual batter, I find that the long, light purple Chinese eggplants yield sweeter and lighter pakoras.

1 teaspoon Chaat Masala (page 20 or store-bought)
1/2 tablespoon Basic Garlic Paste (page 47
   or store-bought)
1 recipe Basic Batter for Pakora Fritters (page 113)
1/4 cup finely chopped fresh cilantro,
   including soft stems
1/2 teaspoon coarsely ground ajwain seeds
1/2 teaspoon hot red pepper flakes, or to taste
1 1/2 to 2 cups peanut oil for deep-frying
1/4 cup mustard oil
2 Chinese eggplants, each 7 to 8 inches long
   and 2-inches in diameter, cut in 1/4-inch-thick
   diagonal slices

1. Prepare the chaat masala and ginger-garlic paste. Then prepare the basic batter. Mix in the cilantro, garlic paste, ajwain seeds, and red pepper flakes. Add the eggplant slices to the batter.

2. Heat the peanut and mustard oils and fry the eggplant slices as per directions in the box "Frying Fritters (Pakorae Talna)" on page 112. Transfer all the fried pakoras to a serving platter, sprinkle the chaat masala on top, and serve.

Variation: Try this batter with 25 to 30 slices of zucchini, opo squash, or any other summer squash.

Baby Spinach Pakora Fritters

Palak kae Pakorae

Makes 50 to 60 pieces

These green and brown pakoras *look enticing and are crunchy at every bite—they may be the first ones to disappear from your appetizer platter. Allow 6 to 8 per person.*

1 teaspoon Basic Garlic Paste (page 47
    or store-bought)
1 teaspoon Chaat Masala (page 20 or store-bought)
1 recipe Basic Batter for Pakora Fritters (page 113)
50 to 60 baby spinach leaves with stems
    (about 1/2 pound)
2 teaspoons ground coriander
1/2 teaspoon coarsely ground ajwain seeds
1/2 teaspoon hot red pepper flakes, or to taste
1/2 to 2 cups peanut oil for deep-frying

1. Prepare the garlic paste and the chaat masala. Prepare the basic batter. Mix in the garlic paste, coriander, ajwain seeds, and red pepper flakes. Add the spinach to the batter.

2. Heat the oil and fry the spinach leaves as per directions in the box "Frying Fritters (Pakorae Talna)" on page 112. Transfer all the fried pakoras to a serving platter, sprinkle the chaat masala on top, and serve.

Stuffed Napa Cabbage Roll Pakora Fritters

Napa Bundh Gobhi kae Pakorae

Makes 12 to 15 pieces

Here, there's another layer to the pakora *classic— the filling is wrapped in Napa cabbage leaves before being coated in the batter and fried. The cabbage lends its distinctive flavor to the traditional fritters, and they look like egg rolls, adding variety to my* pakora *offerings.*

1/2 teaspoon Chaat Masala (page 20 or store-bought)
1 1/2 cup any dry-cooked vegetable or meat filling
    (choose from Fillings for Samosa Pastries,
    pages 108 to 110)
1 recipe Basic Batter for Pakora Fritters (page 113)
12 to 15 outer leaves Napa cabbage
1 1/2 to 2 cups oil for deep-frying
Shredded cabbage to line a platter

1. Prepare the chaat masala and the filling, then prepare the batter. Wash and cut off the leafy top 5 inches of each cabbage leaf. Place in a microwave-safe dish, cover with the lid of the dish, and cook 3 to 4 minutes on high power, to wilt the leaves. (Or wilt over medium heat in a large pan.) Let cool.

2. Place about 2 tablespoons or more of the filling on each leaf, crosswise at the stem end, folding it with the stem end tucked inside, to make a roll. Pinch the edges to seal the roll. Dip each roll in the batter to coat it well.

3. Heat the oil and fry the cabbage rolls as per directions in the box "Frying Fritters (Pakorae Talna)" on page 112. Transfer all the fried pakoras to a serving platter, sprinkle the chaat masala on top, and serve on a bed of shredded cabbage.

Bread Pakora Fritters Stuffed with Coconut Chutney

Double-Roti kae Pakorae

Makes 24 pieces

Use any coconut chutney of your choice—Shahina's Shredded Coconut Chutney (page 62) is one of my favorites. If you wish, replace the coconut chutney with any of the green chutneys.

1/2 teaspoon Chaat Masala (page 20 or store-bought)
1/2 cup or more any Coconut Chutney (pages 61 to 63)
1 recipe Basic Batter for Pakora Fritters (page 113)
1/2 teaspoon coarsely ground black mustard seeds
1/4 teaspoon ground fenugreek seeds
1 tablespoon minced fresh curry leaves
1/4 teaspoon ground asafoetida
12 thin slices packaged white or whole-wheat bread, with or without crusts removed
1 cup peanut oil for deep-frying

1. Prepare the chaat masala and the coconut chutney. Prepare the batter. Place the basic batter in a flat-bottomed dish and mix in the mustard and fenugreek seeds, curry leaves, and asafoetida.

2. Spread the coconut chutney generously on 6 of the bread slices and cover with the remaining 6 slices. Cut each "sandwich" into 4 squares or triangles.

3. Heat the oil in a large skillet (not a wok) until it reaches 350°F to 375°F on a frying thermometer, or a piece of bread dropped into the hot oil bubbles and rises to the top immediately.

4. Carefully, dip each square (or triangle) into the batter and add it to the hot oil, adding as many as the skillet can hold at one time. Fry, turning as needed, until golden on both sides, about 2 minutes.

Drain on paper towels. Transfer to a serving platter. Sprinkle with the chaat masala and serve.

Variation: Cut sourdough bread slices or any type of rolls into 1/2-inch-thick sticks, dip it the batter, and fry until golden.

Shredded and Minced Vegetable and Flour Mixture Fritters

Shredded Cabbage Pakora Fritters with Yogurt

Bundh Gobhi kae Pakorae

Makes 30 to 40 pieces

These pakoras are different—they are not batter-coated as other pakoras, but are crispy nugget-like pieces. No separate batter is made, instead the cabbage, chickpea flour, and spices are all mixed together and the mixture is then fried as balls. Toss a spoon or two of sambar, curry, or any other blended spice powder to vary the flavor every time you make these pakora fritters.

1/2 teaspoon Chaat Masala (page 20 or store-bought)
1 1/2 cups finely shredded or chopped cabbage or Brussels sprouts (or mixed)
1 fresh green chile pepper, such as serrano, minced with seeds
1/4 cup finely chopped fresh cilantro, including soft stems
1 tablespoon peeled and minced fresh ginger
1 tablespoon ground coriander
1 teaspoon dried fenugreek leaves
1/2 teaspoon coarsely ground ajwain seeds
1 teaspoon salt, or to taste
1/4 teaspoon baking soda
1 to 1 1/2 cups chickpea flour (besan)
1/4 to 1/3 cup nonfat plain yogurt, whisked until smooth
1 1/2 to 2 cups mustard or peanut oil for deep-frying

1. Prepare the chaat masala. In a bowl, mix together all the ingredients, except the oil and chaat masala to make a semi-thick mixture, adding more chickpea flour if the mixture seems too soft or some water if it is too firm. Set aside about 15 to 20 minutes.

2. Heat the oil as per directions in the box "Frying Fritters (Pakorae Talna)" on page 112. Carefully, with your fingers or a tablespoon, drop 1-inch uneven balls of the mixture carefully into the hot oil and fry as directed in the box. Transfer all the fried pakoras to a serving platter, sprinkle the chaat masala on top, and serve.

Chopped Onion Pakora Fritters

Kattae Pyaz kae Pakorae

Makes 25 to 30 pieces

Lovely by themselves, but outstanding when simmered in a kadhi *sauce (a special yogurt curry) such as Nani Mama's Yogurt Curry with Onion Fritters (page 426), these* pakoras *are made from seasoned batter itself rather than foods dipped in batter. They are one of the easiest to make.*

¹/₂ teaspoon Chaat Masala (page 20 or store-bought)
¹/₂ cup chickpea flour
1 small onion, finely chopped or minced
1 small russet (or any) potato, peeled and grated
¹/₂ cup finely chopped fresh cilantro,
    including soft stems
1 tablespoon peeled and finely chopped fresh ginger
2 teaspoons coriander, coarsely crushed
    with the back of a spoon
1 teaspoon dried fenugreek leaves
¹/₂ teaspoon ground cumin
¹/₂ teaspoon ground ajwain seeds
¹/₄ teaspoon baking soda
1 teaspoon salt, or to taste
2 to 3 tablespoons water
1¹/₂ to 2 cups peanut oil for deep-frying

1. Prepare the chaat masala. Sift the chickpea flour in a medium bowl and mix in the onion, potato, ginger, coriander, fenugreek, cumin, ajwain seeds, baking soda, and salt. Add the water as needed to make a semi-thick mixture.

2. Heat the oil as per directions in the box "Frying Fritters (Pakorae Talna)" on page 112. Carefully, with your fingers or a tablespoon, drop 1-inch uneven balls of the mixture carefully into the hot oil and fry as directed in the box. Transfer all the fried pakoras to a serving platter, sprinkle the chaat masala on top, and serve.

Fresh Fenugreek Pakora Fritters with Pomegranate Seeds

Hari Methi kae Pakorae

Makes 25 to 30 pieces

From my friend Neelam Malhotra come these spicy pakora *fritters that, good as they are by themselves, are irresistable immersed in* kadhi *(special yogurt curry) dishes such as Fenugreek Yogurt Curry with Fritters (page 428).*

Fenugreek leaves are somewhat bitter. Although I like them that way, Neelam first salts and washes them before starting with the recipe, which you can try if you prefer. Make these pakoras *as leafy as possible, with the chickpea flour acting only as a binder.*

¹/₂ teaspoon Chaat Masala (page 20 or store-bought)
2 cups finely chopped fresh fenugreek leaves,
    including soft stems
¹/₂ cup chickpea flour
1 to 3 fresh green chile peppers, such as serrano,
    minced with seeds
2 tablespoons coarsely ground coriander
1 tablespoon ground pomegranate seeds
1 teaspoon mango powder
¹/₂ teaspoon salt, or to taste
¹/₈ teaspoon baking soda
1¹/₂ to 2 cups peanut oil for deep frying

1. Prepare the chaat masala. Put the chopped fenugreek leaves in a bowl and add all the other ingredients, except the oil and chaat masala and mix well to make a semi-thick mixture, and set aside, about 20 minutes. Do not add any water; the washed leaves will be moist and the salt and spices will cause them to release more.

2. Heat the oil as per directions in the box "Frying Fritters (Pakorae Talna)" on page 112. Carefully, with your fingers or a tablespoon, drop 1-inch uneven balls of the mixture into the hot oil and fry as directed in the box. Transfer all the pakoras to a serving platter, sprinkle the chaat masala on top, and serve.

Mixed Vegetable Pakora Fritters

Milli-Julli Sabziyon kae Pakorae

Makes 25 to 30 pieces

This recipe is made by mixing chickpea flour into grated vegetables. We do not make a batter, as we do for most of the other pakoras mentioned in this chapter. There's enough moisture in the vegetables.

Grate each vegetable by hand or put all of them in the food processor and pulse until minced for smooth textured pakoras.

1 teaspoon Chaat Masala (page 20 or store-bought)
1 cup finely chopped fresh spinach leaves
1/2 cup each: grated carrots, broccoli, potatoes, zucchini
1/2 cup each minced onion, red bell pepper
1/2 cup finely chopped fresh cilantro, including soft stems
1 tablespoon peeled and minced fresh ginger
1 to 3 fresh green chile peppers, such as serrano, minced with seeds
1 teaspoon salt, or to taste
1/2 teaspoon coarsely ground ajwain seeds
1/2 teaspoon coarsely ground black pepper
1/4 teaspoon baking soda
1 cup chickpea flour (besan), or more as needed
1/2 to 2 cups oil for deep-frying

1. Prepare the chaat masala. In a bowl, mix everything except the oil and chaat masala together to make a semi-thick mixture, adding more chickpea flour if the batter seems too soft or some water if firm.

2. Heat the oil as per directions in the box "Frying Fritters (Pakorae Talna)" on page 112. Carefully, using clean fingers or a spoon, drop 1-inch balls of the mixture into the hot oil and fry as directed in the box. Transfer fritters to a platter, sprinkle with the chaat masala, and serve.

Spicy Green Split Pea Pakora Fritters

Muttar Dal kae Pakorae

Makes 20 to 25 pieces

In these pakora *fritters, everything except half the split peas are minced in the food processor. The minced* dal *(legumes) acts as a binding agent, and the remaining half of the peas add a welcome crunch.*

1/2 teaspoon Chaat Masala (page 20 or store-bought)
1/2 cup green split peas (muttar dal), sorted and washed in 3 to 4 changes of water
5 quarter-size slices peeled fresh ginger
1 to 3 fresh green chile peppers, such as serrano, stemmed
1 small green bell pepper, coarsely chopped
1 small onion, coarsely chopped
1 small russet (or any) potato, coarsely chopped
2 small carrots, coarsely chopped
1 cup coarsely chopped cooking greens, your choice, such as radish, spinach, daikon, or mustard
1/2 cup coarsely chopped fresh cilantro, including soft stems
1 1/2 tablespoons ground coriander
1 teaspoon ground dried oregano
1/2 teaspoon coarsely ground ajwain seeds
1/2 teaspoon ground cumin
1/4 teaspoon baking soda
1 teaspoon salt, or to taste
2/3 cup chickpea flour, or more as needed
2 to 3 cups peanut oil for deep-frying

1. Prepare the chaat masala. Soak the split peas in water to cover by 2 inches, about 4 hours, then drain.

2. In a food processor, pulse together the ginger, green chile and bell peppers, onion, potato, carrots, greens, and half the split peas until just minced. (Do not over-process into a purée.) Remove to a bowl, mix in the remaining split peas, all the spices, baking soda, and salt. Then add the chickpea flour and mix well to make a semi-thick mixture. If the mixture seems too soft add more chickpea flour, and if it seems too dry add some water, and mix again.

3. Heat the oil as per directions in the box "Frying Fritters (Pakorae Talna)" on page 112. Carefully, using clean fingers or a spoon, drop 1-inch balls of the mixture into the hot oil and fry as directed in the box. Transfer to a platter, sprinkle with the chaat masala, and serve.

Pinched Rice Flour Pakora Fritters with Papaya

Chaval Atta aur Papitae kae Pakorae

Makes 35 to 40 pieces

The dough-like batter of this pakora *is first formed into long, thin rolls and fried. Then portions of the rolls are pinched off and re-fried to make crunchy and unusual* pakoras. *The surprise flavor in these comes from the unripe papayas.*

4 to 6 quarter-size slices peeled fresh ginger
1 to 3 fresh green chile peppers, such as serrano, stemmed
1 small onion, coarsely chopped
1/2 cup coarsely chopped fresh cilantro, including soft stems
12 to 15 fresh spinach leaves, with stems
2 tablespoons fresh lemon juice
1 1/2 cups peeled and chopped firm unripe papaya
2/3 cup rice flour
1/2 cup chickpea flour
1/2 teaspoon salt, or to taste
1/8 teaspoon baking soda
1 tablespoon vegetable oil
1 teaspoon mustard seeds
1/4 teaspoon ground asafoetida
1 tablespoon coarsely ground dried curry leaves
1 1/2 to 2 cups peanut oil for deep-frying
2 to 3 cups shredded lettuce (any kind)

1. In a food processor, pulse together the ginger, green chile peppers, onion, cilantro, spinach, and lemon juice until just minced. (Do not purée.) Add the papaya and pulse until coarsely chopped (do not mince). Transfer to a bowl. Add the rice and chickpea flours, salt, and baking soda and mix well to make a thick, almost dough-like mixture. Add some more rice or chickpea flour, if needed.

2. Heat 1 tablespoon oil in a small nonstick saucepan over medium-high heat and add the mustard seeds and asafoetida. They should splutter upon contact with the hot oil, so cover the pan and reduce the heat until the spluttering subsides. Quickly add the curry leaves, stir 30 seconds, then mix the spices into the mixture.

3. Heat the peanut oil as per directions in the box "Frying Fritters (Pakorae Talna)" on page 112. Divide the mixture into 12 equal portions and form into rolls or cylinders, each about 1 inch thick and 3 inches long (they don't have to be smooth). Carefully slide them into the hot oil, adding as many as the wok can hold at one time without crowding, and fry, turning and moving them around as needed until golden, 2 to 3 minutes.

4. Transfer with slotted spatula to paper towels to drain. When cool enough to handle, pinch off about 1-inch pieces from each roll and refry in hot oil, drain on paper towels again, then serve on a bed of shredded lettuce.

Rice Flour and Cashew Pakora Fritters

Chaval Atta aur Kaaju kae Pakorae

Makes 15 to 20 pieces

The addition of rice flour brings a welcome lightness, both in taste and texture, to these fragrant cashew nut balls that are often called bhajias *in the southern and western parts of India.*

4 to 6 quarter-size slices of peeled fresh ginger
1 fresh green chile pepper, such as serrano, stemmed
1 small onion, coarsely chopped
1/2 cup coarsely chopped fresh cilantro, including soft stems
8 to 10 fresh spinach leaves, with stems
1 cup raw cashews
1/3 cup rice flour
1/4 cup chickpea flour
1/2 teaspoon salt, or to taste
1/8 teaspoon baking soda
2 to 3 cups shredded lettuce (any kind)
1 1/2 to 2 cups peanut oil for deep frying

1. In a food processor, process together the ginger, green chile pepper, onion, cilantro, and spinach until minced. Add the cashews and pulse until the nuts are coarsely chopped. Remove to a bowl. Mix in the rice and chickpea flours, salt, and baking soda.

2. Heat the oil per directions in the box "Frying Fritters (Pakorae Talna)" on page 112. Carefully, using clean fingers or a spoon, drop 3/4- to 1-inch balls of the mixture into the hot oil and fry as directed in the box. Transfer to paper towels to drain. Then serve on a platter lined with shredded lettuce.

Variation: Substitute peanuts or almonds for the cashews, or mix different nuts together.

Cheese and Meat Fritters

Mama's Paneer Cheese Pakora Fritters

Mama kae Paneer Pakorae

Makes 20 pieces

My mother's trick to making really soft, melt-in-your-mouth paneer *cheese pakoras is in making the cheese—she weights it down only until it just sets and some of the whey remains inside. Or, once the* paneer *cheese is made, she whips it up in a food processor to break all the grain and shapes it into a square or rectangle before cutting it into the desired size pieces.*

8 ounces (1 recipe) Paneer Cheese (page 43 or store-bought)
1 teaspoon Chaat Masala (page 20 or store-bought)
1 recipe Basic Batter for Pakora Fritters (page 113)
1/4 cup minced fresh cilantro, including soft stems
1 to 3 fresh green chile peppers, such as serrano, minced with seeds
1/2 teaspoon coarsely ground ajwain seeds
1 1/2 to 2 cups peanut oil for deep-frying

1. Prepare the paneer cheese, then the chaat masala. Cut the paneer cheese into pieces or place in a food processor and process until it starts to gather into a dough. Transfer it to a cutting board and shape into a large square or rectangle and cut into 20 1/2-by-2-inch rectangles.

2. Prepare the basic fritter batter. To the batter, mix in the cilantro, green chile peppers, and ajwain seeds. Heat the oil as per directions in the box "Frying Fritters (Pakorae Talna)" on page 112. Dip each paneer cheese rectangle into the batter to coat well and fry as directed in the box. Transfer to a platter, sprinkle with the chaat masala, and serve.

Crumbled Paneer Cheese Pakora Fritters with Green Chutney

Paneer aur Hari Chutni kae Pakorae

Makes about 30 pieces

These pakora *fritters can be made with or without the chutney. When making them without the chutney, finely chop and mix in the chutney ingredients.*

And if you find yourself out of paneer *cheese, well-dried firm or extra-firm tofu and fresh mozzarella cheese are good substitutes. Just mix in some more chickpea or rice flour if the mixture seems too soft.*

1 teaspoon Chaat Masala (page 20 or store-bought)
8 ounces (1 recipe) Paneer Cheese (page 43 or store-bought), coarsely crumbled
1/2 cup Basic Green Chutney (page 58)
1 recipe Basic Batter for Pakora Fritters (page 113)
1/4 cup rice flour, or more as needed
1 1/2 to 2 cups peanut oil for deep-frying

1. Prepare the chaat masala, paneer cheese, and the green chutney. In a bowl, toss together the paneer cheese and the chutney and marinate 1 to 2 hours at room temperature.

2. Prepare the pakora batter, mix in the rice flour, then add the marinated paneer cheese (plus the marinade) and 1 tablespoon of the oil to make a semi-thick mixture.

3. Heat the oil as per directions in the box "Frying Fritters (Pakorae Talna)" on page 112. Carefully, with your clean fingers or a spoon, drop 1-inch balls of the mixture into the hot oil and fry as per directions in the box. Transfer to a platter, sprinkle with the chaat masala, and serve.

Cottage Cheese Pakora Fritters with Red Bell Peppers

Paneer aur Laal Shimla Mirch kae Pakorae

Makes 20 to 25 pieces

With the color and crunch of red bell pepper and the smoothness of cottage cheese that melts lightly as it heats up, these double-fried pakoras *are easy and satisfying.*

1/2 teaspoon Chaat Masala (page 20 or store-bought)
1 red bell pepper, minced
1/2 cup large curd cottage cheese
1 small russet (or any) potato, grated
2/3 cup chickpea flour, or more as needed
1/4 cup finely chopped scallions, green parts only
1 tablespoon peeled and minced fresh ginger
1 to 3 fresh green chile peppers, such as serrano, minced with seeds
1 teaspoon ground coriander
1/4 teaspoon salt, or to taste
1 1/2 to 2 cups peanut oil for deep-frying

1. Prepare the chaat masala. In a medium bowl, mix together all the ingredients (except the oil and chaat masala) to make a thick, dough-like batter. (If the batter is too soft, add a little more chickpea flour.) Divide into 20 to 25 uneven balls.

2. Heat the oil as per directions in the box "Frying Fritters (Pakorae Talna)" on page 112, carefully drop the balls into the hot oil and fry as directed in the box.

3. Let cool, then press them lightly between the palms of your hands into small discs with ragged edges. Refry them in hot oil until crisp, 2 to 3 minutes. Drain on paper towels, transfer to a platter, sprinkle with the chaat masala, and serve.

Traditional Chicken Pakora Fritters

Murgh kae Pakorae

Makes 10 to 15 pieces

These were one of my favorite treats when I was little. My brother and I loved volunteering to go to the pakora stands to buy them for the family—not from the goodness of our hearts or to be of help, but so we could eat some right there as we waited for our order.

If you're convinced you know what fried chicken tastes like, just wait till you try this finger-licking-delicious recipe!

2 tablespoons Basic Ginger-Garlic Paste
   (page 47 or store-bought)
1 (2$^1/_2$- to 3-pound) chicken, skinned and cut into
   serving pieces (discard the back and wings)
2 cups water
1 teaspoon garam masala
$^1/_2$ teaspoon salt, or to taste
$^1/_2$ teaspoon Chaat Masala (page 20 or store-bought)
1 teaspoon dry-roasted and coarsely ground cumin
   seeds (Dry-Roasting Spices, page 35)
1 recipe Basic Batter for Pakora Fritters (page 113)
2 tablespoons minced fresh cilantro,
   including soft stems
1 tablespoon ground coriander
1 teaspoon ground cumin seeds
$^1/_2$ teaspoon hot red pepper flakes, or to taste
$^1/_2$ teaspoon coarsely ground ajwain seeds
1$^1/_2$ to 2 cups peanut oil for deep-frying

1. Prepare the ginger-garlic paste. Then place the chicken, water, ginger-garlic paste, garam masala, and salt in a small saucepan and bring to a boil over high heat. Reduce the heat to medium-low, cover the pan and simmer until the chicken is tender and all the water has been absorbed, 15 to 20 minutes. If the chicken cooks before the water dries up, uncover the pan and cook until the chicken is completely dry. Let cool, remove the bones and cut into smaller pieces, if you wish.

2. Meanwhile, prepare the chaat masala and the dry-roasted cumin seeds. Then, prepare the basic batter, and mix in the cilantro, coriander, cumin, red pepper flakes, and ajwain seeds.

3. Add the chicken to the batter. Heat the oil and fry the chicken as per directions in the box "Frying Fritters (Pakorae Talna)" page 112. Transfer to a platter, sprinkle with the roasted cumin and chaat masala.

Marinated Chicken Pakora Fritters

Murgh Pakorae

Makes 20 to 24 pieces

These can be made with any cut of chicken, with or without the bone, but with no skin—drumettes (the drumstick look-alike portion of the wings) and drumsticks are very popular. However, I prefer chicken breast tenders because they are softer, cook faster, and are boneless, which makes them easier to eat.

$^1/_2$ small onion, coarsely chopped
4 quarter-size slices peeled fresh ginger
1 large clove garlic, peeled
1 to 3 fresh green chile peppers, such as serrano,
   stemmed
$^1/_4$ cup nonfat plain yogurt, whisked until smooth
1 tablespoon fresh lime or lemon juice
1 teaspoon garam masala
$^1/_2$ teaspoon salt, or to taste
10 to 12 chicken breast tenders, each cut diagonally
   in half
$^1/_2$ teaspoon Chaat Masala (page 20 or store-bought)
1 recipe Basic Batter for Pakora Fritters (page 113)
1 to 2 tablespoons rice flour
1$^1/_2$ to 2 cups peanut oil for deep frying

1. In a food processor or a blender, process together the onion, ginger, garlic, and chile peppers until minced. Then add the yogurt, lime juice, oil, garam masala, and salt, and process until smooth. Transfer to a medium bowl. Add the chicken and mix until all the pieces are fully coated with the mixture. Cover and marinate at least 4 and up to 24 hours in the refrigerator.

2. Prepare the chaat masala and the basic batter. Bring the chicken to room temperature, then mix it into the pakora batter along with the rice flour.

3. Heat the oil and fry the chicken as per directions in the box "Frying Fritters (Pakorae Talna)" on page

112. You can fry just once, but for the best flavor and texture, let cool, then refry in hot oil until heated through. Transfer to paper towels again. Sprinkle with the chaat masala and serve.

Ground Meat Pakora Fritters

Keema Pakorae

Makes 20 to 25 pieces

Not to be confused with other meat appetizers like kabaabs *(roasted or grilled ground meat and other foods) or* koftas *(deep-fried vegetable or meat balls), these are batter-coated deep-fried fritters featuring ground meat. Petite and light, they are perfect finger food—enough to whet your guests' appetites, but not enough to fill them up.*

Although ground beef is not common in India, it works really well in these fritters.

1/2 teaspoon Chaat Masala (page 20 or store-bought)
3 to 4 slices packaged white or whole-wheat bread (crusts on or not)
1 small onion, coarsely chopped
1/2 cup coarsely chopped fresh cilantro, including soft stems
4 to 6 quarter-size slices peeled fresh ginger
1 large fresh garlic clove, peeled
1 to 3 fresh green chile peppers, such as serrano, stemmed
1 pound extra lean ground meat (beef or lamb)
1 tablespoon dried fenugreek leaves
1 teaspoon garam masala
1/2 teaspoon salt, or to taste
1 recipe Basic Batter for Pakora Fritters (page 113)
2 tablespoons rice flour
1/4 teaspoon ground turmeric
1 1/2 to 2 cups oil for deep-frying

1. Prepare the chaat masala. Soak the bread in water to cover about 1 minute. Then squeeze out all the water and coarsely crumble the bread.

2. In a food processor, process together the crumbled bread, onion, cilantro, ginger, garlic, and green chile peppers until minced. Add the ground meat, fenugreek leaves, garam masala, and salt, and process again to

mix well. Divide into 20 to 25 portions and shape each one into a 2-inch disc.

3. Prepare the basic batter and mix in the rice flour and turmeric. Heat the oil as per directions in the box "Frying Fritters (Pakorae Talna)" on page 112. Dip each disc in the batter to coat well , and fry as explained in the box. Transfer to a platter, sprinkle with the chaat masala, and serve.

Fish Pakora Fritters

Macchi kae Pakorae

Makes 12 to 15 pieces

Use any thick, firm, white fish fillets and cut them into any shapes and sizes, large or small (although I find that the smaller pieces are easier to serve and eat as finger food). The batter for these should be thicker than most pakora batters, *which is why there's some extra flour.*

A trick for authentic flavor is to add about a quarter cup of mustard oil to the wok while deep-frying. It is for used for all commercial pakoras, *but home cooks generally use peanut oil.*

1 teaspoon Chaat Masala (page 20 or store-bought)
1 1/4 pounds halibut, salmon or sea bass fillets, about 1 inch thick, cut into 1 1/2-inch pieces
3 tablespoons distilled white vinegar
2 large cloves garlic, finely ground
1/2 teaspoon hot red pepper flakes, or to taste
1/2 teaspoon ground turmeric
1/2 teaspoon salt, or to taste
1 recipe Basic Batter for Pakora Fritters (page 113)
2 tablespoons chickpea or rice flour
1 teaspoon ground cumin
1/2 teaspoon coarsely ground ajwain seeds
1/8 teaspoon ground asafoetida
2 to 3 scallions, green parts only, minced
1 1/2 to 2 cups oil for deep-frying
2 tablespoons finely chopped fresh cilantro leaves

1. Prepare the chaat masala. Place the fish pieces in a bowl. Add the vinegar, garlic, red pepper flakes, turmeric, and salt, and mix well, making sure all the pieces are well-coated. Cover and marinate at least 1 and up to 3 hours in the refrigerator.

2. Prepare the basic batter, then mix in the flour, cumin, ajwain, asafoetida, and scallion greens. Heat the oil as per directions in the box "Frying Fritters (Pakorae Talna)" on page 112. Dip each fish piece in the batter to coat well and fry as directed in the box. Transfer to a platter, sprinkle with the chaat masala and cilantro, and serve.

Shrimp Pakora Fritters
Jhinga kae Pakorae

Makes 15 to 20 pieces

For the best taste and presentation, choose the tail-on jumbo shrimp.

1 teaspoon Chaat Masala (page 30 or store-bought)
15 to 20 fresh jumbo shrimp (about 1 pound), shelled and deveined, with tails on
2 to 3 tablespoons fresh lime or lemon juice
2 large cloves fresh garlic, peeled and minced
¹/₂ teaspoon ground turmeric
¹/₂ teaspoon hot red pepper flakes, or to taste
¹/₂ teaspoon coarsely ground ajwain seeds
¹/₂ teaspoon salt, or to taste
1 recipe Basic Batter for Pakora Fritters (page 113), made with yogurt instead of water
1 teaspoon coarsely ground cumin seeds
¹/₄ cup finely chopped fresh cilantro, including soft stems
1¹/₂ to 2 cups oil for deep-frying

1. Prepare the chaat masala. Place the shrimp in a bowl. Add the lime juice, garlic, turmeric, red pepper flakes, ajwain, and salt, and mix well, making sure all the pieces well-coated. Cover and marinate at least 1 and up to 3 hours in the refrigerator.

2. Prepare the basic batter, using yogurt instead of water, then mix in the cumin and cilantro. Heat the oil as per directions in the box "Frying Fritters (Pakorae Talna)" on page 112. Dip each shrimp in the batter to coat well and fry as directed in the box. Transfer to a platter, sprinkle with the chaat masala, and serve.

Potato Snacks
Mashed Batter-Fried Potato Balls
Aalu Bhonda

Makes 10 to 12 pieces

These legendary delights from the central and southern parts of India are spicy mashed potatoes cloaked in a chickpea flour batter. Offer them with coconut and other southern Indian chutneys, such as South Indian Cilantro Chutney (page 60).

Bhonda means ball, and these round pakora-*type batter-coated balls are typically made with mashed potatoes that are first cooked with traditional southern seasonings of mustard seeds and curry leaves, then shaped into rounds, dipped in batter and fried. They are traditionally made with peeled white potatoes, but here I use red potatoes in their jackets (just scrub them well).*

1 teaspoon Chaat Masala (page 20 or store-bought)
4 to 5 small red potatoes (about 1 pound), unpeeled but scrubbed well
1 teaspoon vegetable oil
1 teaspoon black mustard seeds
1 tablespoon dried yellow split chickpeas (channa dal), sorted
1 tablespoon dried white urad beans (dhulli urad dal), sorted
1 tablespoon minced fresh curry leaves
¹/₃ cup finely chopped onion
1 to 3 fresh green chile peppers, such as serrano, minced with seeds
1 tablespoon peeled minced fresh ginger
¹/₄ teaspoon ground asafoetida
¹/₂ cup finely chopped fresh cilantro, including soft stems + 3 tablespoons
¹/₂ teaspoon salt, or to taste
1 recipe Basic Batter for Pakora Fritters (page 113)
2 teaspoons rice flour
1¹/₂ to 2 cups peanut oil for deep-frying

1. Prepare the chaat masala. Cook the potatoes in lightly salted boiling water to cover until soft, about 20 minutes. Drain, let cool, then coarsely mash (do not peel).

2. Heat the vegetable oil in a large nonstick wok or saucepan over medium-high heat and add the mustard seeds. They should splutter upon contact with the hot oil, so cover the pan until the spluttering subsides. Quickly add the dals and cook, stirring, until golden, 1 minute.

3. Add the curry leaves and onion and stir until golden, 1 to 2 minutes. Mix in the green chile peppers, ginger, and asafoetida, stir momentarily, and add the potatoes, ½ cup cilantro, and the salt. Cook over medium heat, stirring, until golden, 5 to 7 minutes. Let cool. Using clean hands, shape the mixture into 10 to 12 round balls and set aside.

4. Prepare the basic batter, then mix in the rice flour and the 3 tablespoons cilantro. Dip each potato ball into the batter to coat well.

5. Fry as per directions in the box "Frying Fritters (Pakorae Talna)" on page 112. Transfer to a platter, sprinkle with the chaat masala, and serve.

Thrice-Baked Potato Skins with Petite Peas
Muttar Bharae Baked Aalu

Makes 20 to 24 pieces

This recipe, made with potato skins, is a Western concept with Indian flavors. Serve them as is, or top them with any yogurt-based chutney of your choice (pages 68 to 69).

10 to 12 small russet potatoes (about 2 pounds), unpeeled but scrubbed well
2 tablespoons vegetable oil
1 tablespoon peeled minced fresh ginger
1 small clove fresh garlic, minced
1 small onion, finely chopped
1 medium tomato, finely chopped
¼ cup finely chopped fresh cilantro, including soft stems

1 fresh green chile pepper, such as serrano, minced with seeds
1 tablespoon ground coriander
½ teaspoon ground cumin
⅛ teaspoon ground turmeric
¾ cup frozen petite peas, thawed
½ teaspoon salt, or to taste
¼ cup grated mild cheddar or any other melting cheese

1. Preheat oven to 400°F. Wrap each potato in foil and bake until tender, about 45 minutes. Unwrap and let cool, then cut each potato in half lengthwise. Using a grapefruit (or other) spoon, scoop out the insides of each potato half, leaving a ¼-inch shell. Reserve the insides. Lower oven temperature to 350°F.

2. Brush each shell with oil, inside and out. Place, cut side up, on a baking sheet and bake until crisp and golden, about 20 minutes. When the potatoes are done, raise oven temperature back to 400°F.

3. To prepare the stuffing, heat the oil in a small nonstick wok or saucepan over medium-high heat and cook the ginger, garlic, and onion, stirring, until golden, about 2 minutes. Add the tomato, cilantro, and chile pepper and stir, about 2 minutes. Stir in the coriander, cumin, and turmeric, then add the peas and salt and cook, stirring a few times until the peas are soft, about 5 minutes. Mix in the reserved potatoes and cook another 2 minutes.

4. Divide the stuffing equally among the potato shells and fill each one. Sprinkle the cheddar cheese on top and bake at 400°F until golden, about 5 minutes. Serve.

Variation: Use ¾ cup finely chopped mixed vegetables, such as carrots, zucchini, or green beans, instead of the peas.

Stuffed Potatoes with Spicy Shredded Chicken
Murgh Bharae Aalu

Makes 12 to 15 pieces

Select the long, thin, oval potatoes; they are easier to scoop out and look appealing, especially when garnished with wilted cherry tomatoes and scallion greens. This dish can be served with any dried bean dish, such as Classic Kidney Bean Curry with Onions (page 371), or a vegetable curry.

1 teaspoon Chaat Masala (page 20 or store-bought), or to taste

12 to 15 medium white or purple potatoes

2 tablespoons peanut oil

1 small clove fresh garlic, minced

1 tablespoon peeled minced fresh ginger

1/2 cup finely chopped onion

1 fresh green chile pepper, such as serrano, minced with seeds

1/4 cup finely chopped fresh cilantro, including soft stems

1 cup cooked shredded chicken

1/2 teaspoon garam masala

1/4 teaspoon salt, or to taste

10 to 15 cherry or pear-shaped tomatoes

1 to 2 tablespoons fresh lime or lemon juice

1/4 cup minced scallion greens

1. Prepare the chaat masala. Cook the potatoes in lightly salted boiling water to cover until soft but not broken, about 15 minutes. Peel them if you wish, but it's not necessary. Slice off a 1/4-inch cap from one end of each potato and carefully, with a paring knife and a small spoon, scoop out the insides, leaving a 1/4-inch barrel-shaped shell. Reserve the insides, the shells, and the caps.

2. Heat 1 tablespoon of the oil in a small nonstick wok or saucepan over medium-high heat and cook the garlic, ginger, and onion, stirring until golden, about 2 minutes. Add the green chile pepper, cilantro, and chicken, then mix in the garam masala and salt and cook, stirring, over medium heat until everything is golden, about 5 minutes. Mix in the reserved potatoes and stir, 1 minute. Let cool.

3. Fill each potato shell with the stuffing and fit the caps on. Place in a nonstick skillet and drizzle the remaining 1 tablespoon oil on top. Cook, turning over medium heat until golden on all sides, about 10 minutes. Remove to a serving platter.

4. To the skillet add the cherry tomatoes and cook, shaking the skillet until slightly softened, about 1 minute. Transfer to the potato platter as a garnish. Sprinkle the chaat masala and lime juice over everything, garnish with the scallion greens, and serve.

Indian French Fries with Tomatoes

Tamatar vaalae Aalu kae Chips

Makes 4 to 6 servings

This is my brother, Rakesh Bhatla's, creation—spicy French fries, lightly moistened with tomatoes and topped with a dusting of savory chaat masala. It's almost like a warm chaat salad, and goes really well with a glass of chilled beer.

1 teaspoon Chaat Masala (page 20 or store-bought), or to taste

4 to 5 small russet potatoes, peeled and cut into 1/2-inch fingers

1/2 teaspoon salt, or to taste

11/2 to 2 cups peanut oil for deep-frying

1 large firm tomato, coarsely chopped

1 fresh green chile pepper, such as serrano, minced with seeds

1. Prepare the chaat masala. Then, place the potato fingers in a medium bowl, toss with salt and set aside about 30 minutes. Wash, drain, and dry well on cotton kitchen or paper towels.

2. Heat the oil in a large wok or skillet over medium-high heat until it reaches 325°F to 350°F on a frying thermometer or, until a small piece of the potato dropped into the hot oil takes 15 to 20 seconds to rises to the top. Deep-fry, turning and moving the potato fingers until golden and crispy. Drain on paper towels.

3. Let cool and remove all but 1 teaspoon of oil from the wok. Reheat the oil over medium-high heat and stir-fry the tomatoes and green chile pepper until just tender, about 1 minute. Add the fried potatoes and mix well. Transfer to a serving platter, sprinkle with the chaat masala, and serve.

Savory Croquettes and Dumplings (Vadae)

Pakaudhis (*mungi kae laddu*), *bhallae* (*vadae*, *badae*, or *vadai*), *ammavadai*, and *gujjia* are all different regional names for deep-fried spongy cakes, or croquettes. When these cakes are served in a sauce, they are called dumplings.

Made with an array of different *dals* (legumes) and shaped into balls, circles, doughnuts, and half moons, all the croquettes in this section are variations on the same theme. They have different names and different seasonings in different parts of India, and their distinction lies in the type of *dals* used. When made with yellow mung beans (*dhulli mung dal*) they are *pakaudhis*, with white urad beans (*dhulli urad dal*) they are *bhallae* or *vadae*, with a mixture of *dals* they are *ammavadai*. However, *vadae* are also made with split pigeon peas (*toor dal*) and yellow split chickpeas (*channa dal*), and can be made with other *dals* as well. Making them is time- and labor-intensive, but they store well in the refrigerator and freezer, so you can make a large batch when you have time.

Mung Bean Croquettes
Pakaudhiyan or Mungi kae Laddoo

Makes 18 to 20 pieces

These authentic Punjabi croquettes are sold on every street corner. They are lightly fried for your perusal, then when you make your selection the vendor will instantly refry them, press them between the palms of his hands and serve them to you warm on dried banana leaves with a sonth *(sweet and sour tamarind) chutney and a handful of spicy grated daikon radishes. They are often transformed into a special yogurt dish, Simple Mung Bean Croquette Raita (page 236), and served as a snack or part of a meal.*

1 cup dried yellow mung beans (dhulli mung dal), sorted and washed in 3 to 4 changes of water
3 quarter-size slices peeled fresh ginger
1 fresh green chile pepper, such as serrano, stemmed
1 to 3 tablespoons hot water
$1/2$ teaspoon salt, or to taste
$1/8$ teaspoon baking soda
$1^1/2$ to 2 cups peanut oil for deep-frying

1. Soak the dal overnight in water to cover by 2 inches. Drain. In a food processor, process together the ginger and green chile pepper until minced. Add the drained dal and process, adding the hot water as needed to make a fluffy, semi-thick batter that can be shaped. Mix in the salt and baking soda.

2. Heat the oil in a large wok or a skillet to 350°F to 375°F on a frying thermometer or until a pinch of batter dropped into the hot oil bubbles and immediately rises to the top. Pick up about 2 tablespoons of the batter using clean fingers or a spoon and push it carefully into the hot oil. (Don't worry about the shape when you slide it into the oil.) Add as many croquettes as the wok will hold at one time without crowding, and fry, turning with a slotted spoon, until they are crispy and golden on all sides, 2 to 3 minutes.

3. With a slotted spatula, transfer croquettes to paper towels to drain. Repeat process with the remaining batter. Transfer to a platter and serve hot or at room temperature.

Mung Bean Croquettes with Spinach
Palak ki Pakaudhiyan

Makes 12 to 15 pieces

These croquettes, loaded with nutrition and immensely satisfying, are hugely popular in workplace cafeterias and college campuses throughout India. Eat them with an array of chutneys or pressed between two pieces of bread.

1 teaspoon Chaat Masala (page 20 or store-bought)

1 teaspoon cumin seeds, dry-roasted and coarsely ground (Dry-Roasting Spices, page 35)

1 cup dried yellow mung beans (dhulli mung dal), sorted and washed in 3 to 4 changes of water

1 tablespoon peeled minced fresh ginger

1 large onion, finely chopped

1 tablespoon coriander, coarsely ground

1/2 teaspoon ajwain seeds, coarsely ground

1/2 teaspoon salt, or to taste

1/4 teaspoon baking soda

1/2 small bunch fresh spinach (4 to 5 ounces), trimmed, washed, and finely chopped

1 1/2 to 2 cups peanut oil for deep-frying

1. Soak the dal overnight in water to cover by 2-inches. Meanwhile, prepare the chaat masala and the cumin seeds. When ready, drain and place the dal in a food processor, then process, adding the hot water as needed to make a fluffy, semi-thick batter that can be shaped. Mix in all the remaining ingredients (except the spinach and oil) and process again. Remove to a bowl and mix in the spinach, then allow to rest about 30 minutes.

2. Heat the oil in a large wok or skillet to 350°F to 375°F on a frying thermometer, or until a pinch of batter dropped into the hot oil bubbles and immediately rises to the top. Pick up about 2 tablespoons of the batter with clean fingers or a spoon and push it carefully into the hot oil. (Don't worry about the shape when you slide the croquettes into the oil.) Add as many as the wok will hold at one time without crowding, and fry, turning with a slotted spatula, until they are crisp and golden on all sides, 2 to 3 minutes.

3. With a slotted spatula, transfer croquettes to paper towels to drain. Repeat process with the remaining batter. Transfer to a platter, garnish with chaat masala, and serve.

Variation: To make cabbage vadae, replace the spinach with finely chopped green cabbage and mix in 1/2 cup finely chopped fresh cilantro.

Punjabi-Style Fermented Urad Bean Croquettes
Urad Dal kae Bhallae

Makes 10 to 12 pieces

*This is my mother's Punjabi recipe, which follows the authentic method for shaping the batter into donuts. As kids we really enjoyed watching her as she stretched a moist cloth over the top of a small bowl (*katori*), placed some of the batter on it, went round and round with her finger to make a hole in the center of the dough and then deftly and gently slid it into the hot oil. Moments later a crispy golden doughnut emerged with a lovely hole in the center. Magic!*

If making donut-shaped vadae *seems difficult, drop about 1 tablespoon of the batter into the hot oil with your fingers or a spoon, in the same manner as Mung Bean Croquettes (page 128).*

1 cup dried split white urad beans (dhulli urad dal), sorted and washed in 3 to 4 changes of water

1 tablespoon cumin seeds, dry-roasted and coarsely ground (Dry-Roasting Spices, page 35)

5 to 7 quarter-size slices peeled fresh ginger

1 to 3 fresh green chile peppers, such as serrano, stemmed

1/4 to 1/3 cup hot water

1/4 teaspoon baking soda

1/4 teaspoon ground asafoetida

1 teaspoon salt, or to taste

1 1/2 to 2 cups peanut oil for deep-frying

1 (10-inch-square) piece of muslin or 4 layers of cheesecloth

1 small 3-inch diameter bowl

1. Soak the dal overnight in water to cover by 2 inches. Meanwhile, prepare the cumin. When ready, drain the dal. In a food processor, process together the ginger and green chile peppers until minced. Add the drained dal and process, adding the hot water as needed to make a fluffy, thick batter that can be shaped.

2. Mix in the cumin, baking soda, asafoetida, and salt. Cover and keep in a warm, draft-free place, 8 to 10 hours to ferment. Then, with a whisk or a fork, whisk the batter to incorporate air into it and make it fluffy, about 1 minute.

3. Heat the oil in a large wok or skillet to 350°F to 375°F on a frying thermometer, or until a pinch of batter dropped into the hot oil bubbles and immediately rises to the top.

4. Meanwhile, have ready a small bowl of water. Wet the cheesecloth with water, squeeze it out completely and wrap it tautly over the top of the bowl. There will be some overhang. Holding the overhang securely under the bowl, with a clean hand, place about 2 tablespoons of the batter on the cheesecloth and, with lightly moistened fingers, spread it into a 3-inch disc. With your forefinger, make a ½-inch hole in the center of the disc to make a doughnut. Gently push from one side to slide each doughnut into the hot oil. (Dip your fingers in the bowl of water as you work.) Add as many doughnuts as the wok can hold at one time without crowding and deep-fry, turning occasionally with a slotted spatula until they are crisp and golden on all sides, 2 to 3 minutes. Remove croquettes to paper towels to drain. Repeat the process with the remaining batter. Transfer to a platter and serve hot.

South Indian Croquettes with Curry Leaves

Vadai

Makes 15 to 20 pieces

These are made essentially in the same way as their Punjabi counterparts, but the batter also contains rice and they come with an entirely different set of seasonings.

**1 cup dried white urad beans (dhulli urad dal),
    sorted and washed in 3 to 4 changes of water**
**¼ cup long-grain white rice, sorted and washed
    in 3 to 4 changes of water**
4 quarter-size slices peeled fresh ginger
20 to 25 fresh curry leaves
½ teaspoon ground fenugreek seeds
¼ teaspoon ground asafoetida
1 teaspoon salt, or to taste
¼ to ⅓ cup hot water
½ teaspoon cayenne pepper, or to taste
1 teaspoon coarsely ground black pepper, or to taste
¼ teaspoon baking powder
1½ to 2 cups peanut oil for deep-frying

1. Soak together the dal and rice overnight in water to cover by 2-inches. Drain.

2. In a food processor, process together the ginger and curry leaves until minced. Add the drained dal, rice, fenugreek seeds, asafoetida, and salt, and process, adding hot water as needed to make a fluffy, thick batter that can be shaped. Cover and keep in a warm and draft-free place, 8 to 10 hours to ferment. Mix in the cayenne and black peppers, and the baking powder. Then, with a whisk or a fork, whisk the batter to incorporate air into it and make it fluffy, about 1 minute.

3. Heat the oil in a large wok or skillet to 350°F to 375°F on a frying thermometer or until a pinch of batter dropped into the hot oil bubbles and immediately rises to the top.

4. Meanwhile, have ready a small bowl of water. With lightly moistened clean hands, form 2-inch patties from the batter and add them carefully, one at a time, to the hot oil. Add as many as the wok can hold at one time without crowding, and fry, turning occasionally with tongs or a slotted spoon, until they are crisp and golden on all sides, 2 to 3 minutes. (Dip your fingers in the bowl of water as you work.) Transfer croquettes to paper towels to drain. Transfer to a platter and serve hot.

Rice Croquettes with Cashews

Medhu Vadai

Makes about 20 pieces

Made with a mixture of rice and white urad beans (dhulli urad dal) medhu vadais originated in a small village located on a road between Mysore and Bangalore. At one time, the name was reserved for a specific dumpling, but now it is often used generically for all kinds of vadais. This authentic recipe comes from Raghu Nanjappa, who recently took my husband and me to the restaurant where it all started.

Authentic medhu vadais always have a hole, but if making it seems complicated, you can make them into little rounds or balls.

1 cup long-grain white rice, sorted and washed
    in 3 to 4 changes of water
1/2 cup dried white urad beans (dhulli urad dal),
    sorted and washed in 3 to 4 changes of water
1/4 to 1/2 cup hot water
1/4 teaspoon baking soda
1/2 teaspoon salt, or to taste
1 tablespoon peanut oil
1 teaspoon black mustard seeds
2 tablespoons dried yellow split chickpeas (channa dal)
1 teaspoon coarsely ground fenugreek seeds
1/4 teaspoon ground asafoetida
2 tablespoons minced fresh curry leaves
1/3 cup coarsely chopped cashews
1 1/2 to 2 cups peanut oil for deep-frying
1 small 3-inch diameter bowl
One 10-inch square piece of plastic wrap

1. Setting aside 2 tablespoons of the rice, soak the rice and dal in water to cover by 2 inches, about 4 hours. Drain and transfer to a food processor and process, adding hot water as needed to make a fluffy, semi-thick batter that can be shaped. Add the baking soda and salt, and process again. Remove to a bowl.

2. Heat 1 tablespoon oil in a large cast-iron or non-stick wok or a saucepan, over medium-high heat and add the mustard seeds. They should splutter upon contact with the hot oil, so cover the pan and lower the heat until the spluttering subsides. Quickly add the reserved 2 tablespoons rice, chickpea dal, fenugreek seeds, asafoetida, curry leaves, and cashews, and cook, stirring, until golden, about 1 minute. Mix into the batter. Cover and let rest in a warm, draft-free place about 2 hours.

3. Heat the oil for frying in a large wok or skillet to 350°F to 375°F on a frying thermometer, or until a pinch of batter dropped into the hot oil bubbles and immediately rises to the top.

4. Meanwhile, have ready a small bowl of water. Wrap a small piece of plastic wrap tautly around the 3-inch bowl and brush with a light coating of oil. Place 1 tablespoon of the batter on the wrap and with lightly moistened, clean fingers, spread the batter into a 3-inch disc. With your forefinger, make a 1/2-inch hole in the center of the disc to make a

doughnut shape. Gently slide each doughnut to the side and into the hot oil. (Dip your fingers in a bowl of water as you work.)

5. Deep-fry, adding 3 to 4 croquettes at a time and turning them with tongs 2 to 3 times until puffed and golden, about 3 minutes per batch. Transfer to paper towels to drain. Transfer to a platter and serve hot.

Coconut–Red Chile Croquettes with Mixed Beans
Ammavadai

Makes 20 to 25 pieces

*Using any one or a mixture of split pigeon peas (*toor dal*), yellow split chickpeas (*channa dal*), and white urad beans (*dhulli urad dal*), and rice or rice flour, with grated coconut as the supporting flavor, this mixture is yet another popular* vadai *variation, called* ammavadai. Ammavadai *are generally spiced with dried red chile peppers, along with the standard* vadai *spices.*

1/4 cup each: split pigeon peas (toor dal), yellow split
    chickpeas (channa dal), white urad beans (dhulli
    urad dal), sorted and washed in 3 to 4 changes
    of water
1/2 cup rice flour
1 cup grated fresh or frozen coconut or shredded
    unsweetened dried coconut
1/3 cup nonfat plain yogurt
1/2 to 1 cup finely chopped onions
2 tablespoons peeled minced fresh ginger
1/4 cup finely chopped fresh cilantro,
    including soft stems
2 to 4 dried red chile peppers, such as chile de arbol,
    coarsely ground
1 to 3 fresh green chile peppers, such as serrano,
    minced without seeds
1 teaspoon salt, or to taste
1/4 teaspoon ground asafoetida
1/4 teaspoon baking powder
1/4 to 1/2 cup hot water
1 1/2 to 2 cups peanut oil for deep-frying

1. Soak the dals in water to cover by 1 inch, about 3 hours. Drain and transfer to a food processor. Process until as smooth as possible. Add the rice flour, coconut, and yogurt, and process again until smooth. Remove to a bowl. Add all the remaining ingredients (except the oil for frying) and mix well, adding the hot water as needed to make a fluffy, thick batter that can be shaped.

2. Heat the oil in a large wok or skillet to 350°F to 375°F on a frying thermometer or until a pinch of batter dropped into the hot oil bubbles and immediately rises to the top. Shape, deep-fry, and serve as per directions for South Indian Croquettes with Curry Leaves (page 130), from Step 5.

Spicy Stuffed Croquettes
Namkeen Gujjia

Makes 10 to 12 pieces

A specialty of Uttar Pradesh, a state adjacent to New Delhi in northern India, gujjias *are made with the same batter as for the Punjabi-Style Fermented Urad Bean Croquettes (page 129), but are crescent-shaped, are always stuffed with a nut and raisin filling, and are usually served in a pool of yogurt.*

1 cup dried white urad beans (dhulli urad dal), sorted and washed in 3 to 4 changes of water
5 to 7 quarter-size slices peeled fresh ginger
1 to 3 fresh green chile peppers, such as serrano, stemmed
^{1}/4 to ^{1}/3 cup water
1 teaspoon cumin seeds
^{1}/2 teaspoon ground asafoetida
^{1}/4 teaspoon baking soda
^{1}/2 teaspoon salt, or to taste
3 tablespoons shelled and coarsely ground raw pistachios
2 tablespoons chopped raisins
1 tablespoon shelled and coarsely ground raw almonds
1^1/2 to 2 cups peanut oil for deep-frying
1 (10-inch-square) piece of muslin or 4 layers cheesecloth
1 small 3-inch diameter bowl
1 (10-inch-square) piece of plastic wrap

1. Soak the dal overnight in water to cover by 2-inches. Drain. In a food processor, process the ginger and green chile peppers until minced. Add the drained dal and the water as needed, and process to make as smooth as possible. Mix in the cumin seeds, asafoetida, baking soda, and salt. (The batter should be thick and slightly grainy. If it seems thin, add some chickpea flour. You should actually be able to pick up this batter with your fingers to stuff it and shape it.)

2. Transfer to a bowl, cover, and keep in a warm, draft-free place about 8 to 10 hours to ferment. Then, with a whisk or a fork, whisk the batter to incorporate air into it and make it fluffy, about 3 minutes.

3. In a small bowl, mix together the pistachios, raisins, and almonds. Then, heat the oil in a large wok or skillet to 350°F to 375°F on a frying thermometer, or until a pinch of batter dropped into the hot oil bubbles and immediately rises to the top.

4. Have ready another small bowl of water. Wrap a small piece of plastic wrap tautly around a 3-inch bowl and brush lightly with oil. Place ^{1}/2 tablespoon of the batter on the wrap and, with lightly moistened clean fingers, spread it into a 3-inch semicircle. Place about 1 teaspoon of the nut mixture in the center of the semicircle. Cover the filling with another tablespoon of the batter and lightly press the top batter into the bottom, sealing in the filling, maintaining the shape. With your hands or a slotted spoon, slide the semicircles carefully into the hot oil. If the batter sticks to your fingers, dip your hands in the bowl of water as you go along.

5. Deep-fry, adding as many semi-circles as the wok can hold at one time without crowding, turning occasionally until they are crisp and golden on all sides, 2 to 3 minutes. With a slotted spatula, transfer croquettes to paper towels to drain. Repeat the process with the remaining batter. Transfer to a platter and serve hot.

Steamed Fermented Rice Cakes (*Iddli*)

Iddlis are soft and spongy, 2½-inch discs, made from a fermented rice and lentil batter. They are generally pure white in color and are eaten with a coconut chutney and a *sambar* (soupy split pigeon peas), though some people, like my daughter Supriya, love their mild-tasting *iddlis* straight.

Iddlis are typically made in special molds. Imagine compartmented egg-poaching trays, set one on top of the other, each one about 2 inches apart, fitted onto a central stem (also called a tree) with a base that stands about 1 inch high to allow room for water. Each standard *iddli* compartment is concave-shaped, and about 2½ inches in diameter. There are smaller compartmented trays, as well.

However, you can use ramekins, egg poachers, and even cup cake molds, and steam them in a steamer or in a large pan, resting them on a steamer basket to keep them about ½ inch above the water.

Traditional Steamed Fermented Rice Cakes

Iddli

Makes 16 to 20 pieces

These are the basic iddli *cakes, of which there are many variations. Most of the variations come from the use of different* dals *(legumes), grains, and herbs and spices. The process of making the actual* iddli *cakes remains the same. So essentially, if you can make one type of* iddli, *you can make them all.*

²/₃ cup parboiled (converted) rice, sorted, washed in 3 or 4 changes of water
¹/₂ cup dried white urad beans (dhulli urad dal), sorted, washed in 3 or 4 changes of water
4 tablespoons water
¹/₂ cup semolina
¹/₄ to ¹/₂ cup plain yogurt
1 teaspoon salt, or to taste
¹/₂ teaspoon baking powder

1. Soak the rice and the dal in separate bowls overnight, in water to cover by 2 inches. Drain. In a blender or a food processor, grind the rice, adding about 2 tablespoons water until smooth yet somewhat grainy. Transfer to a bowl and grind the dal with about 2 tablespoons water until as fine as possible.

2. Mix the dal into the rice, along with the semolina, yogurt, and salt. With a whisk or a fork, whip well to incorporate air into the batter and make it fluffy, about 1 minute. Cover the bowl and set it in a warm, dry place about 8 to 10 hours to ferment.

3. Grease the iddli molds (or coat with non-stick spray) and keep them ready. Add the baking powder to the fermented batter and whisk well to make it fluffy. Little bubbles of air should be visible on the sides. Add more water if the batter seems too thick. Then pour ¼ to ⅓ cup batter into each mold and place the iddli trays on the stand.

4. Put about 1 inch of water inside a pressure cooker or large pot, and place the iddli stand in the pot. Cover the pot, leaving the vent open if you're using a pressure cooker or the cover askew if you're using a regular pot, to allow the steam to escape. Cook over high heat until the iddli are soft and spongy, about 10 to 12 minutes. Allow the steam to escape from the sides, but do not remove the lid of the pot for 10 to 12 minutes.

5. Let cool, then remove each iddli from the mold with a spoon or clean fingers. Pry lightly with a knife or a small spatula if they get stuck. Serve.

Instant Steamed Semolina Cakes with Yogurt

Sooji ki Iddli

Makes 16 to 20 pieces

This is one of my Santa Monica friend Bharti Dhalwala's winning recipes. Eno is the brand name of a product marketed as an antacid powder. It's a mixture of baking soda and citric acid and is popularly called a fruit salt (because of the citric acid). Besides its marketed use as an antacid, Eno has, over the last 50 years or more, become a necessity in southern and

western Indian kitchens. *It is used in all the steamed
and baked cakes, but you can use citric acid and baking soda.*

2 cups semolina

2 teaspoons melted butter

4¼ cups (18 ounces) nonfat plain yogurt

8 to 10 fresh curry leaves, chopped

1 teaspoon salt, or to taste

¼ cup water

1½ teaspoons Eno fruit salt or ¾ teaspoon each
    of baking soda and citric acid

1. Place the semolina and butter in a wok or skillet
and roast, stirring over medium heat about 5 minutes. The semolina should not turn golden; if it does,
lower the heat or remove the pan from the heat.
Transfer to a large bowl.

2. In a food processor, process together the yogurt,
curry leaves, and salt. Add to the semolina. With a
whisk or a fork, whip well to incorporate air into the
batter and make it fluffy, about 1 minute. Add about
¼ cup or more water, as needed. Allow to rest about
1 hour.

3. Grease the iddli molds (or coat with non-stick
spray). Mix the fruit salt into the batter; it will
bubble immediately. Quickly, before it subsides,
pour ¼ to ⅓ cup of the batter into each mold and
place each tray on the stand.

4. Put about 1 inch of water inside a pressure cooker
or large pot, then place the iddli stand in the pot.
Cover the pot, leaving the vent open if you're using a
pressure cooker pot or the cover askew if you're using
a regular pot, to allow the steam to escape. Cook over
high heat until the iddli are soft and spongy, about
10 to 12 minutes. Allow the steam to escape from
the sides, but do not remove the lid of the pot 10 to
12 minutes.

5. Let cool and remove each iddli from the mold
with a spoon or with clean fingers. Pry lightly with a
knife or a small spatula if they get stuck. Serve.

Steamed Spicy Fermented Rice Cakes

Masala Iddli

Makes 16 to 20 pieces

*These cakes are a category all their own, although
they are basically made in the same manner as other
iddlis. The difference is that herbs and spices are
mixed into the batter before the iddlis are steamed
and, once done, they are topped with a fragrant tarka
(sizzling flavor topping).*

1 recipe batter for Traditional Steamed Fermented
    Rice Cakes (page 133) or Instant Steamed
    Semolina Cakes with Yogurt (page 133)

½ cup finely chopped onion

1 tablespoon peeled minced fresh ginger

1 to 3 fresh green chile peppers, such as serrano,
    minced with seeds

¼ cup finely chopped fresh cilantro,
    including soft stems

½ teaspoon ground asafoetida

2 tablespoons peanut oil

2 to 4 dried red chile peppers, such as chile de arbol,
    whole or broken

1 teaspoon black mustard seeds

1 tablespoon finely chopped fresh curry leaves

1. Prepare either of the iddli batters. When the fermented batter is ready (through step 2 in either
recipe), mix in the onion, ginger, green chile peppers,
cilantro, and half (¼ teaspoon) the asafoetida. Then
continue with Step 3 of the recipe.

2. When the iddlis are steamed, transfer them to a
serving plate. Heat the oil in a small nonstick wok or
saucepan over medium-high heat and add the red
chile peppers and mustard seeds. They should splutter
upon contact with the hot oil, so cover the pan until
the spluttering subsides. Quickly add the remaining
asafoetida and curry leaves, and stir about 30 seconds.
Add to the iddlis and toss lightly to mix. Serve.

Variation: In Step 1, mix in 1 to 2 cups finely chopped
steamed vegetables and ¼ teaspoon salt, or 1 tablespoon
masala from any mango pickle, or be creative and mix in some
sun-dried tomatoes and fresh basil.

Savory Bean and Rice Cakes (Dhokla)

Dhoklas—a signature Gujarati snack, are spongy, bite-size (or large) savory, cake-like pieces of steamed *dals* (legumes), rice, chickpea flour, or semolina. There are two basic *dhokla* recipes: One is the time-consuming soak-grind-ferment-and-steam recipe, and the other is the instant mix-and-steam recipe; both yield excellent results.

Dhoklas are typically steamed in flat round trays that have straight, 1-inch-high raised edges (*thalis*). The authentic *dhokla* mold is a 3- to 4-tier tree-like stand with a base that stands at least 1 inch high to keep all the trays well above the water line. But 8-inch or 9-inch metal cake pans, pie dishes, and other similar containers all work well. Just rest them on metal bowls (or thoroughly washed tuna cans) placed in a large pot of water into which the pan can fit. (I like using a pressure cooker.) Make sure the batter is well above the water level, then steam them.

Traditional Steamed Split Chickpea Cakes
Khaman Dhokla

Makes 4 to 6 servings

*Made the traditional way by soaking yellow split chickpeas (*channa dal*), these routinely made, spicy dhoklas are as delicious with a hot cup of tea as they are when served as appetizers with a glass of chilled beer or wine.*

Prepare the batter in advance; the dal soaks overnight and the batter has to sit 12 hours. The batter should be semi-thick, with the tiniest bit of a grain. If the batter is thin, add 1 to 2 teaspoons semolina.

1 cup dried yellow split chickpeas (channa dal), sorted and washed in 3 to 4 changes of water
1/2 cup nonfat plain yogurt, whisked until smooth
1/2 cup water, or more as needed
1/4 cup peanut oil
1/4 teaspoon ground asafoetida
1 teaspoon salt, or to taste
1/2 teaspoon baking soda
1/2 teaspoon citric acid
4 to 6 dried red chile peppers, such as chile de arbol, with stems
1 teaspoon black mustard seeds
1 to 3 fresh green chile peppers, such as serrano, whole or split in half lengthwise
2 tablespoons finely chopped fresh curry leaves
2 to 3 tablespoons finely chopped fresh cilantro, including soft stems
1 tablespoon fresh or frozen grated coconut

1. Soak the dal overnight in water to cover by 2 inches. Drain and process in a food processor, adding the yogurt and the water to make a smooth semi-thick batter, yet with a soft grain. Transfer to a bowl and set in a warm, dry place at least 12 hours to ferment.

2. Mix in 2 tablespoons oil, asafoetida, and salt, and with a whisk or a fork, whip well to incorporate air into the batter, about 1 minute.

3. Put about a 1-inch layer of water in a pressure cooker or a large pot to be used for steaming the dhokla. Grease well the dhokla tray or trays, or a metal pie pan with raised edges. Mix the baking soda and citric acid into the batter, which will make it foam immediately. Working quickly, transfer to the dhokla tray or pie pan and place the tray in the steaming pot, making sure it sits about 1 inch above the water level. Cover the pot, leaving the vent open if you're using a pressure cooker, or leaving the cover a little askew if you're using a regular pot, to allow the steam to escape. Cook over high heat about 15 to 20 minutes, or until a toothpick inserted in the center of the cake comes out clean. Remove trays from the pot.

4. Heat the remaining 2 tablespoons oil in a small nonstick wok or saucepan over medium-high heat, and add the red chile peppers and mustard seeds. They should splutter upon contact with the hot oil, so lower the heat and cover the pan until the spluttering subsides. Quickly add the green chile peppers, curry leaves, cilantro, and coconut, and cook, stirring, about 1 minute. Spread the mixture evenly over the dhokla cake. Let cool, cut into the desired size squares, rectangles or other shapes, place them on a serving platter and serve.

Falguni's Steamed Chickpea Flour Cakes
Falguni ka Khaman Dhokla

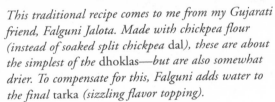

Makes 4 to 6 servings

This traditional recipe comes to me from my Gujarati friend, Falguni Jalota. Made with chickpea flour (instead of soaked split chickpea dal*), these are about the simplest of the* dhoklas—*but are also somewhat drier. To compensate for this, Falguni adds water to the final* tarka *(sizzling flavor topping).*

1 tablespoon Basic Ginger and Green Chile Pepper Paste (page 48)
1 cup chickpea flour (besan)
1/2 cup water
1/2 teaspoon salt, or to taste
4 tablespoons vegetable oil
1/2 teaspoon citric acid
1/2 teaspoon baking soda
1 teaspoon black mustard seeds
1 teaspoon white sesame seeds
2 fresh green chile peppers, such as serrano, quartered lengthwise
10 to 15 fresh curry leaves
1 teaspoon sugar, dissolved in 1/3 cup water
1/2 cup chopped fresh cilantro, including soft stems
1/2 cup fresh or frozen grated coconut

1. Prepare the ginger-green chile paste. Then, in a bowl, mix together the chickpea flour and water and, using a whisk or a fork, whip well to incorporate air and make a semi-thick batter, about 1 minute. Add the ginger-green chile paste, salt, 2 tablespoons oil, and mix well.

2. Put about 1 inch of water in a pressure cooker or in a large pot that will be used for steaming the dhokla. Grease well 1 large or 2 small dhokla trays or metal pie pans with raised edges.

3. Mix the citric acid and baking soda into the batter, which will make it foam immediately. Working quickly, transfer the batter to the trays and place the tray in the pot, making sure it sits about 1 inch above the water level. Cover the pot, leaving the vent open if you're using a pressure cooker or leaving the cover a little askew if you're using a regular pot, to allow the steam to escape. Cook over high heat about 15 to 20 minutes, or until a toothpick inserted in the center of the dhokla comes out clean. Remove from the pot.

4. Heat the remaining 2 tablespoons oil in a small nonstick wok or saucepan over medium-high heat and add the mustard seeds. They should splutter upon contact with the hot oil, so lower the heat and cover the pan until the spluttering subsides. Add the sesame seeds, green chile peppers, and curry leaves, and cook about 30 seconds. Mix in the sugar-water and pour evenly over the dhokla cake. Let cool and cut into the desired size squares, rectangles, or other shapes, and place them on a serving platter. Garnish with the cilantro and coconut, and serve.

Variation: To make white dhokla, use semolina instead of chickpea flour.

Steamed Mung Bean Bites

Dhokla-Iddli

Makes 4 to 6 servings

In this recipe, for which I have 2 versions—from my friend Falguni's mother and my fried Jaywanti Thakar of Mumbai (Bombay)—yellow mung beans (dhulli mung dal) and yellow split chickpeas (channa dal) are used for the batter, then the dhoklas are made in special small molds that are traditionally used to make the South Indian rice cakes called iddli (page 133). You end up with little 1-inch discs. Topped with colorful chutneys and other things, these delicate bite-sized rounds make for a spicy first course.

Sev are thin, crispy-fried vermicelli-like chickpea flour noodles sold in packages in Indian markets.

1/2 cup each: dried yellow mung beans (dhulli mung dal), and dried yellow split chickpeas (channa dal), sorted and washed in 3 to 4 changes of water

2 tablespoons Basic Ginger and Green Chile Pepper Paste (page 48)

1/4 cup any green chutney, such as Cilantro-Lime Chutney (page 59)

2 tablespoons Garlic and Fresh Red Chile Pepper Chutney (page 65)

3/4 to 1 cup water

2 to 3 tablespoons peanut oil

1/4 teaspoon ground asafoetida

1 teaspoon salt, or to taste

1/2 teaspoon citric acid

1/2 teaspoon baking soda

1 cup sev noodles

1/2 cup finely chopped onions

1/4 cup finely chopped fresh cilantro, including soft stems

1. In separate bowls, soak both the dals overnight in water to cover by at least 2 inches. Prepare the ginger-green chile paste and the chutneys. When ready, drain and process each dal separately in a food processor, adding up to 1/2 cup of water each, to make a paste as smooth as possible.

2. Transfer both the dals to a bowl and mix together well. Add the oil, ginger-green chile paste, asafoetida, and salt, and whip well with a whisk or a fork to incorporate air and make a batter, about 1 minute. The batter should be semi-thick, with the tiniest bit of a grain. If batter is thin, add 1 to 2 teaspoons of semolina.

3. Grease the iddli molds (or coat with non-stick spray). Mix the citric acid and baking soda into the batter; it will bubble immediately. Working quickly, before the bubbling subsides, pour 2 tablespoons of the batter into each mold and place each tray on the stand.

4. Put about 1 inch of water in a pressure cooker or large pot then place the iddli stand in the pot. Cover the pot, leaving the vent open if you're using a pressure cooker or leaving the cover a little askew if you're using a regular pot, to allow the steam to escape. Cook over high heat until the cakes are soft and spongy, about 10 to 12 minutes. Allow the steam to escape from the sides, but do not remove the lid from the pot for 10 to 12 minutes. Let cool. Using a spoon or clean fingers, remove each dhokla-iddli from the mold. Pry lightly with a knife or a small spatula if they stick.

5. Line a serving platter with a mixture of the sev noodles, onion, and cilantro, and place the small dhoklas over the mixture. Top each dhokla with a layer of green chutney, place a dollop of garlic chutney on top, and serve.

Gujarati Chickpea Flour Rolls
Khandvi

Makes 4 to 6 servings

Another Gujarati specialty, khandvi *rolls are delicate little things—yellow cakes dotted with blackened mustard seeds, flecks of green cilantro, and white coconut. You will almost be sorry to destroy these silky smooth rolls by eating them, but then, they're too good not to! Allow 3 to 4 per person.*

1 cup chickpea flour
1 fresh green chile pepper, such as serrano, stemmed
5 to 6 quarter-size slices peeled fresh ginger
1 tablespoon fresh lemon juice
2 cups nonfat plain yogurt, whisked until smooth
³/4 teaspoon salt, or to taste
¹/4 teaspoon ground turmeric
2 cups water
¹/4 cup fresh or frozen grated coconut
¹/4 cup finely chopped fresh cilantro, including soft stems
2 tablespoons peanut oil
2 fresh green chile peppers, such as as serrano, quartered lengthwise, with or without seeds
4 to 6 dried red chile peppers, such as chile de arbol, with stems
1 tablespoon black mustard seeds
¹/8 teaspoon ground asafoetida
2 tablespoons finely chopped fresh curry leaves
¹/8 teaspoon ground paprika

1. Sift the chickpea flour through a fine-mesh strainer to remove any lumps. Grease or lightly spray two 12-by-18-inch baking trays and set aside.

2. In a blender (not a food processor) blend together the whole green chile pepper, ginger, lemon juice, and 1 cup of the yogurt until smooth. Then add the remaining 1 cup yogurt, chickpea flour, salt, and turmeric, and blend again until smooth.

3. Transfer to a large nonstick wok or saucepan, mix in the water, and cook, stirring constantly and scraping the sides to prevent any lumping, over medium-high heat, 2 to 3 minutes, then over medium-low heat until it starts to splutter and turns into a very thick batter, 3 to 5 minutes.

4. Pour the batter into the 2 trays and, with a scraper or a spatula, spread it evenly and as thinly as you can. Set aside to cool, about 30 minutes. With a knife or pizza cutter, cut each sheet of batter into 6-by-2-inch strips and roll each strip tightly like a jellyroll. Transfer the rolls to a serving platter and sprinkle the coconut and cilantro on top.

5. Heat the oil in a small saucepan over medium-high heat and add the green and red chile peppers. Stir a few minutes, then add the mustard seeds; they will splutter upon contact with the hot oil, so reduce the heat and cover the pan until the spluttering subsides. Add the asafoetida and curry leaves. When they sizzle, add the paprika and immediately pour over the khandvi rolls. Serve warm or refrigerate up to 2 hours and serve cold.

Gujarati Stuffed Chickpea Flour Rolls
Bharvan Khandvi

Makes 4 to 6 servings

This is a stuffed khandvi *roll. The first and the last part of the cooking method is the same as for Gujarati Chickpea Flour Rolls (left). But before making the rolls the sheet of batter is covered with a topping, which becomes the filling.*

1 recipe Gujarati Chickpea Flour Rolls (left)
1 small or half large seedless cucumber, coarsely chopped
1 small red bell pepper, coarsely chopped
¹/4 cup finely chopped fresh cilantro, including soft stems + 2 tablespoons
2 tablespoons peanut oil
2 fresh green chile peppers, such as serrano, quartered lengthwise, with or without seeds
4 to 6 whole dried red chile peppers, such as chile de arbol,
1 tablespoon black mustard seeds
¹/8 teaspoon ground asafoetida
2 tablespoons finely chopped fresh curry leaves
¹/8 teaspoon ground paprika
2 tablespoons fresh or frozen grated coconut

1. Prepare the chickpea flour roll recipe through Step 4—up to spreading the cooked batter on the trays.

2. In a food processor, process together the cucumber, red bell pepper, and cilantro until minced. Transfer them to a medium nonstick skillet and cook over medium heat until the vegetables first release their juices and then until the juices dry up, 2 to 4 minutes. Sprinkle over the batter in the trays and let cool, about 30 minutes.

3. With a knife or pizza cutter, cut each sheet of batter into 6-by-2-inch strips then roll each strip tightly like a jellyroll. (Push seeping filling back in with your fingers.) Transfer the rolls to a serving platter and sprinkle the coconut and cilantro on top.

4. Heat the oil in a small saucepan over medium-high heat and add the green and red chile peppers. Stir a few minutes, then add the mustard seeds; they will splutter upon contact with the hot oil, so reduce the heat and cover the pan until the spluttering subsides. Add the asafoetida and the curry leaves. When they sizzle, add the paprika, then immediately pour over the khandvi rolls. Serve warm or refrigerate at least 2 hours and serve cold.

Variation: Try a thin layer of Cilantro-Lime Chutney (page 59) or Fresh Coconut Chutney with Cilantro (page 61) instead of this filling.

Spicy Steamed Chickpea Zucchini Cake

Handwa

Makes 4 to 6 servings

Falling somewhere between dhokla *(steamed yellow split chickpea cakes) and* iddli *(steamed, fermented rice cakes) is another popular snack called* handwa *(pronounced* haandva*).*

Handwa *is made with a fermented rice and chickpea flour batter and a summer squash (mostly opo squash, though I like to use zucchini). It is more like a spicy bread and is baked in an oven.*

2 tablespoons Basic Ginger and Green Chile Pepper Paste (page 48)
1 cup rice flour
1/2 cup chickpea flour
2/3 cup buttermilk
About 2/3 cup water
1 tablespoon ground coriander
1 teaspoon garam masala
1/2 teaspoon ground turmeric
1 teaspoon salt, or to taste
1/2 cup grated zucchini
3 tablespoons vegetable oil
1 teaspoon black mustard seeds
1/4 teaspoon ground asafoetida
2 tablespoons finely chopped fresh curry leaves
2 to 3 tablespoons Basic Green Chutney (page 58)

1. Prepare the ginger-green chile pepper paste. In a bowl, mix together the rice and chickpea flours, then add the buttermilk, plus water as needed to make a batter that will pour easily. Mix in the ginger-chile paste, coriander, garam masala, turmeric, and salt, and using a whisk or a fork, whip well to incorporate air into the batter and make it fluffy, about 1 minute. Mix in the zucchini.

2. Heat the oil in a small saucepan over medium-high heat and add the mustard seeds; they should splutter upon contact with the hot oil, so cover the pan until the spluttering subsides. Add the asafoetida and curry leaves, and mix the spices into the batter. Cover and place in a warm, draft-free place 8 to 10 hours to ferment.

3. Preheat oven to 400°F. Grease a flat, ovenproof dish with raised edges (such as a shallow metal cake pan or pie pan). Pour the batter into the dish and bake about 45 minutes, or until a knife inserted into the cake comes out clean.

4. Meanwhile, prepare the chutney. Cut the cake into pieces, top each one with a drop of chutney, and serve warm.

Indian Street Foods

Crispy Puffs with Spicy Tamarind Water
Paani Poori

Makes 4 to 6 servings

Called gol-guppas in northern India and paani-poories elsewhere, the golf ball–size, crispy, hollow, puffed balls used in this dish are extremely fragile and break very easily. They are made with whole-wheat or semolina and are available ready-made at Indian markets. Making them at home, though possible, is very labor-intensive and no one really does it anymore.

To eat them the traditional way—with "the works"—poke a hole in each, fill it with a little spicy potato and chickpea mixture, top it with sonth (sweet and sour mango and tamarind) chutney, then pour in 1 to 2 tablespoons of the spicy mint and tamarind water and pop it into your mouth, whole, filled with all the goodies. Allow 4 to 6 per person.

1 large russet (or any) potato
1/2 cup Minty Sonth Chutney with Mango (or Tamarind) Powder and Jaggery (page 77)
1/2 gallon Spicy Tamarind Water with Mint and Roasted Cumin (page 658)
1 teaspoon New Delhi Street Food Masala (Papri Masala), page 20, or Chaat Masala (page 20 or store-bought)
1/4 cup finely chopped fresh cilantro, including soft stems
1/2 cup canned chickpeas, drained and coarsely mashed
1/2 cup sprouted green mung beans (saabut mung dal) (optional)
25 to 30 paani-poori puffs, store-bought

1. Cook the potato in lightly salted boiling water to cover until tender, about 20 minutes. Meanwhile, prepare the chutney, tamarind water, and masala.

2. Drain the potatoes, let cool, then peel and finely chop or mash them. In a large bowl, mix together the potato, cilantro, chickpeas, sprouted dal (if using), and masala.

3. With a clean thumb or forefinger, gently make a big hole on the thin side of the paani-poori puff and fill with up to 2 teaspoons of the potato mixture. Dunk each filled puff into a bowl full of tamarind water and eat immediately. Or, at large gatherings, set out the paani-poori puffs, the chutney, and the tamarind water like a salad bar and let everyone help themselves.

Crispy Puffs with Potatoes and Spicy Yogurt
Batata Poori Chaat

Makes 4 to 6 servings

Batata means potatoes and batata poori chaat is made with the same crispy, puffy 1-inch balls that are used in paani-poori, but the presentation is very different. This time the stuffed poori balls are topped with spicy yogurt and a sonth chutney, with no spicy water served alongside. Oftentimes, softened bhallas (deep-fried, fermented lentil dumplings) and gujjiyas (stuffed, deep-fried, fermented lentil dumplings) are also mixed into the chaat (savory-tangy-spicy snack) or stuffed into the paani-pooris.

1 large russet (or any) potato
1/4 cup Minty Sonth Chutney with Mango (or Tamarind) Powder and Jaggery (page 77)
1/4 cup Cilantro-Lime Chutney (page 59 or store-bought)
1 tablespoon New Delhi Street Food Masala (Papri Masala), page 20, or Chaat Masala (page 20 or store-bought)
1 cup canned chickpeas, drained and coarsely mashed
1/4 cup finely chopped fresh cilantro, including soft stems
1 to 3 fresh green chile peppers, such as serrano, minced with seeds
1 tablespoon peeled minced fresh ginger
20 to 24 paani-poori puffs, store-bought
2 cups nonfat plain yogurt, whisked until smooth
1 teaspoon cumin seeds, dry-roasted and coarsely ground (Dry-Roasting Spices, page 35)
1/2 teaspoon salt, or to taste
1/2 teaspoon cayenne pepper, or to taste

1. Cook the potato in lightly salted boiling water to cover until tender, about 15 minutes. Drain the potato, let cool, then peel and mash it. Meanwhile prepare both chutneys and the masala.

2. In a medium bowl, mix together the mashed potato, chickpeas, cilantro, green chile peppers, ginger, and masala.

3. With a clean thumb or forefinger, gently make a big hole on the thin side of each puffed poori and fill with about 1 tablespoon of the potato mixture. Place on a serving platter, and scatter whatever potato mixture is leftover on top of the poories.

4. Into the yogurt, mix in the cumin, salt, and cayenne pepper, and pour it over the stuffed poories. Drizzle the chutneys on top and serve.

Puffed Rice with Onion, Potatoes, and Spicy Chutneys

Bhel Poori

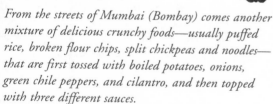

Makes 4 to 6 servings

From the streets of Mumbai (Bombay) comes another mixture of delicious crunchy foods—usually puffed rice, broken flour chips, split chickpeas and noodles—that are first tossed with boiled potatoes, onions, green chile peppers, and cilantro, and then topped with three different sauces.

The vendors have all this ready for your asking and make it fresh for each customer. Making the dry ingredients for this specialty at home is quite a task, so most of us simply visit the Indian markets and buy it, apportioned and ready mixed, all set to be tossed with other wonderful flavors.

Mix it together just before eating, or better still, set everything out on the table like a salad bar and let people help themselves.

2 to 4 tablespoons Sweet Sonth Chutney with Dates (page 78)
1 to 3 tablespoons Garlic and Fresh Red Chile Pepper Chutney (page 65)
1 to 3 tablespoons Roasted Dal and Fresh Green Chile Pepper Chutney (page 66)
1 large russet (or any) potato
4 cups bhel-poori mix, store-bought
1 medium onion, finely chopped
1 cup finely chopped fresh cilantro, including soft stems
1/2 cup shelled, chopped roasted peanuts

1. Prepare the chutneys. Cook the potato in lightly salted boiling water to cover until tender, about 20 minutes, then peel and finely chop.

2. In a large bowl, mix together the bhel-poori mix, mashed potato, onion, and cilantro. Add all the chutneys and toss to mix well. Scatter the peanuts on top and serve immediately or the mixture will get soggy.

Crispy Flour Chips with Vegetables and Spicy Chutneys

Sev-Poori

Makes 4 to 6 servings

Sev-poori *are crispy pastry chips topped with a spicy mixture of potatoes, onions, and crispy chickpea noodles (sev), supported by yogurt and different chutneys—the idea is to be able to eat each chip whole, with everything on it, and see who can be the least messy.*

Made from all-purpose flour, the poori *chips (called* papri *chips in the north) are quite easy to make at home. You can make them from scratch (see Flour Chips with Yogurt and Mango Powder Chutney, page 142). or cut thin flour tortillas into 1½- to 2-inch rounds or squares and deep-fry them until golden. Tortilla chips are almost like authentic* poori *chips.*

Many varieties of sev are available in Indian markets. Buy tiny, thin ones that look like curly bits of angel hair or vermicelli pasta. Allow 2 to 4 topped sev-poori *chips per person.*

1/4 cup Basic Green Chutney (page 58)

1/4 cup Minty Sonth Chutney with Mango
(or Tamarind) Powder and Jaggery (page 77)

1 to 3 tablespoons Garlic and Fresh Red Chile Pepper
Chutney (page 65)

1 large russet (or any) potato

20 to 24 flour chips, store-bought or homemade

1 medium onion, finely chopped

1/2 cup sprouted green mung beans (saabut mung dal),
(optional)

1 cup finely chopped fresh cilantro,
including soft stems

1/2 cup plain yogurt, whisked until smooth

1/2 cup crispy sev noodles

1. Prepare the chutneys. Boil the potato in lightly salted boiling water to cover until tender, about 20 minutes. Drain, let cool, then peel and chop finely. Lay out the poori chips on a serving platter.

2. Mix together the potato, onion, sprouted beans (if using), and cilantro, and place about 1 tablespoon on each chip, then place 2 teaspoons yogurt on top of that. Drizzle from 1 to 2 teaspoons of each of the chutneys over the yogurt and top with a sprinkling of sev. Serve immediately or they will get soggy.

Flour Chips with Yogurt and Mango Powder Chutney

Papri Chaat

Makes 4 to 6 servings

Made with the same chips as those for sev-poories *(page 141),* papri chaat *is a very north Indian thing, and is not quite as popular in the rest of the country. With a lot of chips, topped with coarsely mashed potatoes and chickpeas, yogurt,* sonth *chutney, and spices, this street food is just as easy to make for one person as it is for large gatherings. Once the ingredients are ready, the final assembly takes only a few minutes.*

Present it buffet-style, if you wish. Buy the papri *chips from an Indian market, or make them the easy way, as in this recipe.*

1/2 cup or more Sonth Chutney with Dried Mango
Slices (page 76)

2 teaspoons New Delhi Street Food Masala (Papri Masala),
page 20, or Chaat Masala (page 20 or store-bought)

1 large russet (or any) potato

12 (8-inch) thin flour tortillas, preferably vegetarian style

2 to 3 cups peanut oil for deep-frying

1 cup canned chickpeas, drained, rinsed,
and coarsely mashed

1 1/2 to 2 cups plain nonfat yogurt,
whisked until smooth

1/2 teaspoon cayenne pepper, or to taste

1 to 3 fresh green chile peppers, such as serrano,
minced with seeds

1/4 cup finely chopped fresh cilantro,
including soft stems

1. Prepare the chutney and the masala. Boil the potato in lightly salted boiling water until tender, about 20 minutes. Drain, let cool, then peel and coarsely mash. Cut the flour tortillas into 1-inch pieces.

2. Heat the oil in a wok or skillet over high heat until it reaches 350°F to 375°F on a frying thermometer or until a tiny piece of the tortilla dropped into the hot oil bubbles and immediately rises to the top. Deep-fry the tortilla pieces in 3 or 4 batches, turning them with a slotted spatula, until golden, about 2 minutes per batch.

3. Using a slotted spatula transfer to paper towels to drain. Let cool and use immediately, or store in airtight containers about 1 month.

4. To serve, spread the chips on a serving platter, then one at a time, top with the potato and chickpea mixture, pour the yogurt evenly on the top and sides, making sure that most of the chips are covered (with some peeking through), then drizzle the sonth chutney over the yogurt. Sprinkle the masala and cayenne pepper, then the green chile peppers and cilantro. Serve immediately or it will get soggy.

Potato Patties

Tikki patties are round, crusty, pan- or deep-fried potato patties—another one of India's favorite street foods. *Tikkis* are generally made with mashed potatoes and come plain or filled with a wide variety of vegetables, legumes, cheeses, and meats. They are traditionally fried in a pool of oil that collects in the center of a large, over-size, cast-iron, concave *tava* griddle. As they start to turn a rich golden hue, they are gently pushed toward the sloped outer edges of the *tava*, where they sit until all the excess oil drains out and the mild heat gently crisps and darkens the flat under-sides. They are turned once to crisp the other side.

Tikki patties are customarily served whole with an assortment of saucy chutneys, or open-faced and topped with yogurt, special *masalas* (spice blends) and fresh herbs. *Tikkis* can be presented as you would hamburger patties, sandwiched between two pieces of bread with all kinds of fixings—even ketchup.

Home cooks often deep-fry the *tikkis* until just golden and then crisp them on a *tava* griddle. All *tikki* patties can be made 4 to 5 days in advance then cooled completely and stored in the refrigerator. Reheat in a skillet or a preheated 400°F oven, about 10 minutes.

Basic Mashed Potato Patties
Aalu ki Tikkiyan

Makes 8 to 10 pieces

When professional cooks make their tikkis, *they generally mix some bread with the mashed potatoes because bread helps the patties maintain their shape and texture. Once they are put together and patties are made, the cooking procedure for all the* tikkis *is essentially the same. When preparing these for a large gathering, make bite-size (about 1¼-inch) rounds. They will be easier to eat and you'll get many more.*

4 medium russet (or any) potatoes (about 1 pound)
2 to 3 slices white bread, crusts removed
¹/₂ teaspoon salt, or to taste
¹/₄ cup peanut or vegetable oil

1. Cook the potatoes in lightly salted boiling water to cover until tender, about 20 minutes. Drain, let cool, then peel and mash or grate. Soak the bread in water to cover, about 2 minutes. Then squeeze out all the water, tear the slices into tiny pieces, and place them in a large bowl. Add the potatoes and salt, and with clean hands gently mix everything together. (Don't use a food processor; overmixing will result in glutinous potatoes.)

2. With lightly greased hands, divide the potatoes into 8 to 10 portions and shape each one into a smooth 1½- to 2-inch patty.

3. Heat 3 tablespoons of the oil in a large, heavy, nonstick skillet over medium-high heat. Place the patties in the skillet in a single layer, in batches if needed. Press on them lightly with a spatula, making sure all the edges are in contact with the skillet. Let cook undisturbed about 1 minute, reduce the heat to medium-low and continue to cook, watching carefully until the bottom side is golden, about 5 minutes.

4. Carefully turn each tikki over with the spatula. Add 1 to 2 tablespoons more oil (if needed) and increase the heat to high about a minute. Then reduce the heat to medium-low once again and cook until the second side is golden, about 4 to 5 minutes. Lower the heat and push the patties to the sides of the pan until they are well browned and a have a thick, crispy crust. Turn a few times, as needed.

Alternately, deep-fry the patties in hot oil and then finish cooking them on a tava-griddle. (If, when you deep-fry, the patties seem to open up or disintegrate, make a paste with ¼ cup all-purpose flour and ¼ cup water and coat remaining patties in it before deep-frying.) Serve hot.

Tofu and Potato Patties

Tofu-Aalu ki Tikkiyan

Makes 8 to 10 pieces

Tofu, truly a versatile food, combines well with potatoes and takes on the flavor of the spices and herbs while lending a lovely smoothness and a nutrition boost to the snack. This recipe is an inspiration from Lalit Pant, a friend and poker partner.

1 large russet (or any) potato
1 fresh green chile pepper, such as serrano, stemmed
2 quarter-size slices peeled fresh ginger
1 (10¹/₂-ounce) package firm tofu, crumbled and
    dried well on paper towels
¹/₄ teaspoon salt, or to taste
Freshly ground black pepper, to taste
¹/₄ cup peanut or vegetable oil

1. Cook the potato in lightly salted boiling water to cover until tender, about 15 minutes. Drain, let cool, peel, place in a medium bowl, and mash.

2. In a food processor, process together the chile pepper and ginger until minced, then add the tofu and pulse a few times until smooth. Add the tofu mixture to the potatoes, along with salt and black pepper and, with clean hands, gently mix everything together. (Don't use the food processor for this; over-mixing will result in glutinous potatoes.)

3. With lightly greased hands, divide the mixture into 8 to 10 portions and shape each one into a smooth 1½- to 2-inch patty and cook as you would Basic Mashed Potato Patties (page 143), starting from Step 3.

Variations: For more flavor, along with the tofu, mix in 2 teaspoons ground coriander, 1 teaspoon dried mint leaves, and ¹/₄ teaspoon ground cumin. You can also mix in about ¹/₂ cup minced fresh spinach leaves.

Basic Stuffed Potato Patties

Bhari hui Aalu ki Tikkiyan

Makes 8 to 10 pieces

These delights are the beginning of an entire genre of beloved tikki *patties. You bite into them expecting just potatoes. Instead, you are rewarded with a colorful, tasty surprise tucked into their centers.*

2 large russet (or any) potatoes (about 1 pound)
2 slices white bread, crusts removed
¹/₂ teaspoon salt, or to taste
1 recipe Tikki Filling (page 145)
1¹/₂ to 2 cups peanut oil for deep-frying

1. Cook the potatoes in lightly salted boiling water to cover until tender, about 20 minutes. Drain, let cool, then peel and mash or grate. Soak the bread in water to cover, about 2 minutes. Squeeze out all the water from the bread, tear it into tiny pieces and place them in a large bowl. Add the potatoes and salt, and with clean hands, gently mix everything together. (Don't use a food processor; over-mixing will result in glutinous potatoes.)

2. With lightly greased hands, divide the potatoes into 8 to 10 equal portions and do the same with the tikki filling. Working with each portion separately, flatten the potatoes into a 4-inch round. Place one portion of the tikki filling in the center of the potato round. Bring the edges together and pinch to seal, then press down the pinched top to form a smooth round or oval.

3. Cook as you would the Basic Mashed Potato Patties (page 143), starting from Step 3.

Variation: For a more formal presentation, dip each patty in beaten egg whites, coat well with plain or seasoned bread crumbs, and deep-fry.

Fillings for Potato Patties

*Tikkiyon Mein Bharnae
ki Cheezain*

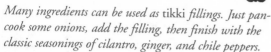

Makes filling for 8 to 10 pieces

Many ingredients can be used as tikki *fillings. Just pan-cook some onions, add the filling, then finish with the classic seasonings of cilantro, ginger, and chile peppers.*

1 tablespoon olive oil

²/₃ cup finely chopped onion

Any of the following: ²/₃ cup Paneer Cheese (page 43 or store-bought), grated; ²/₃ cup soaked and drained dried yellow mung beans (dhulli mung dal) or red lentils (dhulli masoor dal); ²/₃ cup frozen petite peas, thawed; 1 cup minced carrots, green beans, zucchini, or cauliflower; ²/₃ cup minced chicken tenders, cooked until opaque inside

¹/₄ cup finely chopped fresh cilantro, including soft stems

¹/₄ teaspoon salt, or to taste

Freshly ground black pepper to taste

1 tablespoon peeled minced fresh ginger

1 to 3 fresh green chile peppers, such as serrano, minced with seeds

Heat the oil in a small nonstick skillet over medium-high heat and cook the onion, stirring, until golden, about 3 minutes. Add the paneer cheese or other filling, cilantro, salt, and black pepper, and cook, stirring, until golden, about 2 minutes. Mix in the ginger and chile peppers and set aside to cool. The stuffing is ready to use.

Sourdough Bread and Potato Ovals

Aalu Double-Roti ki Tikki

Makes 15 to 20 pieces

Made with crusty sourdough bread rolls instead of white bread and fresh seasonings, these tikkis *have an entirely different texture and taste. Serve them with any puréed green chutney or yogurt chutney.*

2 large russet (or any) potatoes (about 1 pound)

1 fresh 4-ounce sourdough roll, cut into ¹/₂-inch dice

¹/₂ cup nonfat plain yogurt

¹/₂ cup milk, heated in a pot or microwave

¹/₄ cup finely chopped fresh cilantro, including soft stems

2 tablespoons peeled minced fresh ginger

2 to 3 fresh green chile peppers, such as serrano, minced with seeds

¹/₂ teaspoon salt, or to taste

1 to 2 tablespoons plain dried bread crumbs, if needed

¹/₂ cup rice flour or all-purpose flour

1¹/₂ to 2 cups peanut oil for deep-frying

1. Cook the potatoes in lightly salted boiling water to cover until tender, about 20 minutes. Drain, let cool, then peel and mash. Meanwhile, in a medium bowl, mix together the bread, yogurt, and hot milk. When the bread soaks up all the liquids, add the mashed potatoes, cilantro, ginger, green chile peppers, and salt and, with clean hands, gently mix everything together. (Don't use a food processor; over-mixing will result in glutinous potatoes.) If the mixture seems too soft, mix in 1 to 2 tablespoons bread crumbs.

2. Put the rice (or all-purpose) flour in a flat bowl. Divide the potato mixture into 15 to 20 portions, shape each one into a smooth 2-inch oval or round, and coat with the flour in the bowl.

3. Heat the oil in a large wok or skillet until it reaches 350°F to 375°F on a frying thermometer or until a small piece of the potato mixture dropped into the hot oil bubbles and immediately rises to the top. Add the potato ovals into the hot oil carefully with your fingers or a spoon to avoid spluttering. Add as many as the wok can hold at one time without crowding and fry each batch, turning a few times with a slotted spatula, until crispy and golden on all sides, about 1 to 2 minutes.

4. Transfer to paper towels to drain. Repeat the process with the remaining ovals. Transfer to a serving platter and serve hot.

Potato and Tapioca Patties

Aalu-Sabudana ki Tikki

Makes 15 to 20 pieces

These are not true tikkis; *they are much lighter in texture because of the tapioca. They are, however, a revelation, being delicately and unexpectedly light on the inside and crisp on the outside.*

1/3 cup tapioca pearls
2 large russet (or any) potatoes (about 1 pound)
1/2 cup boiling water
1 tablespoon peeled minced fresh ginger
4 to 6 scallions, white parts only, minced
1/4 cup minced fresh spinach leaves
1 tablespoon ground coriander
1/2 teaspoon ground cumin
1/2 teaspoon garam masala
1 to 2 tablespoons plain dried bread crumbs, if needed
1 1/2 to 2 cups peanut oil for frying

1. In a small pan, soak 1 tablespoon of the tapioca in the boiling water about 30 minutes. Meanwhile, cook the potatoes in lightly salted boiling water to cover until tender, about 20 minutes. Drain, let cool, then peel and mash.

2. In a small pan, cook the soaked tapioca over medium heat until it turns glutinous, about 5 minutes. (You will still see the grain.) Let cool. Coarsely grind the remaining tapioca in a coffee or spice grinder. Transfer to a flat dish and set aside for coating the patties.

3. In a bowl, add the mashed potatoes, ginger, scallions, spinach, coriander, cumin, garam masala, and the cooked tapioca. With clean hands, gently mix everything together. (Don't use a food processor; over-mixing will result in glutinous potatoes.) If the mixture seems too soft, mix in 1 to 2 tablespoons of bread crumbs.

4. With lightly greased hands, divide the potato mixture into 20 portions and shape each one into a round ball, then flatten lightly to make a smooth disc or oval. Coat each disc with the ground tapioca, then press between the palms of your hands to ensure that the tapioca adheres nicely.

5. Heat the oil in a large wok or skillet until it reaches 350°F to 375°F on a frying thermometer or until a small piece of the potato mixture dropped into the hot oil bubbles and immediately rises to the top. Add the discs and deep-fry according to the directions for Sourdough Bread and Potato Ovals (page 145), starting from Step 3. Drain on paper towels. Serve.

Potato and Cashew Patties

Aalu aur Kaaju ki Tikki

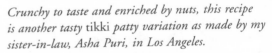

Makes 20 pieces

Crunchy to taste and enriched by nuts, this recipe is another tasty tikki *patty variation as made by my sister-in-law, Asha Puri, in Los Angeles.*

1 teaspoon Chaat Masala (page 20 or store-bought)
2 large russet (or any) potatoes (about 1 pound)
1 tablespoon peeled minced fresh ginger
1 teaspoon fresh green chile pepper, such as serrano, minced with seeds
1 tablespoon ground coriander
1 teaspoon dried fenugreek leaves
1/4 teaspoon coarsely ground ajwain seeds
1/4 teaspoon cayenne pepper, or to taste
1/2 teaspoon salt, or to taste
2 large eggs, lightly beaten
1/2 cup coarsely chopped raw cashews
1 1/2 to 2 cups peanut oil for deep-frying

1. Prepare the chaat masala. Cook the potatoes in lightly salted boiling water to cover until tender, about 20 minutes. Cool, then peel and mash. In a large bowl, add the mashed potatoes, ginger, green chile pepper, coriander, fenugreek, ajwain, cayenne pepper, and salt. With clean hands, gently mix everything together. (Don't use a food processor; overmixing will result in glutinous potatoes.)

2. With lightly greased hands, divide the mixture into 20 portions and shape each one into a round ball, then flatten lightly to make a smooth patty or an oval.

3. Heat the oil in a large wok or skillet until it reaches 350°F to 375°F on a frying thermometer or until a small piece of the mixture dropped into the hot oil bubbles and immediately rises to the top. Dip each patty in the beaten egg, then coat well with the cashews and deep-fry according to the directions for Sourdough Bread and Potato Ovals (page 145), starting from Step 3, until crisp and golden. Drain on paper towels, garnish with the chaat masala, and serve.

Stuffed Lentil Wafer Rolls
Paapad Rolls

Makes 25 to 30 pieces

I first ate these at the home of a family friend, Lalit Pant in Los Angeles, and since then I have become an ardent fan. These spicy rolls are very addictive; allow 3 to 5 per person.

1 recipe Cumin Potatoes (page 251)
8 sundried spicy lentil wafers (paapad), store-bought
Warm water in a flat bowl to dip the wafers
2 tablespoons all-purpose flour mixed with
**   2 tablespoons water**
1¹/₂ to 2 cups peanut oil for deep frying

1. Prepare the potatoes, then coarsely mash them. Divide into 8 portions.

2. Working with each paapad separately, place in the water until soft, about 10 seconds. Shake off any excess water and transfer to a large plate.

3. Place one portion of the potato mixture in the center of each wafer. Fold the paapad over the filling to make a semi-circle. Then make a lengthwise roll, starting from the straight edge, rolling toward the rounded edges, securing the filling inside. Before reaching the end, seal the exposed edge with the flour-water paste and place seam side down on a cutting board until all the rolls are made. Cut each roll into 3 to 4 pieces.

4. Heat the oil in a large wok or skillet until it reaches 350°F to 375°F on a frying thermometer or until a small piece of the mixture dropped into the hot oil bubbles and immediately rises to the top. Place the rolls into the hot oil, adding as many as the wok can hold at one time without crowding, and fry until golden (almost instantly). Drain on paper towels and serve.

Kabaabs

Kabaabs (also written *kabaabs* or *kebabs*) were bequeathed to us by the Mughal emperors who ruled India from the 16th to the mid-18th century. There are numerous *kabaab* variations but generally they are grilled or deep-fried meats (bone-in or boneless), *paneer* cheese, or vegetables. The pieces are sometimes marinated, and may be used whole, or ground and cooked on skewers or as patties (similar to hamburgers).

Within the *kabaab* category are the smaller *tikkas*—2- to 2½-inch pieces of boneless meats, *paneer* cheese, or chunks of vegetables that are marinated before being cooked.

Both the *kabaabs* and *tikkas* can be a first or the main course. Often, *kabaabs* and *tikkas* are rolled up in bread wraps, topped with chopped salads and fresh chutneys, and served as quick fixes. These rolled and wrapped delights are a major part of India's street food.

Leftover *kabaabs* and *tikkas* can be shredded and added to everyday salads, sandwiches, pita pockets, and Mexican-style tacos. They can also be simmered with *masalas* (spice blends) and sauces to make special entrées such as Grilled Chicken in Spicy Sauce (page 462).

Skewered Minced Lamb Kabaabs with Saffron
Seekh Kabaabs

Makes 4 to 6 servings

Seekh is the Hindi word for skewers and seekh kabaabs are skewer-grilled minced meat, paneer *cheese, or vegetable rolls. The spicy hot minced mixture is pressed on metal skewers and grilled in the* tandoor. *The end product may look like hot dogs, but tastes a lot different!*

1 teaspoon Kashmiri Garam Masala (page 19)
    or garam masala
½ teaspoon Chaat Masala (page 20 or store-bought)
½ cup Basic Onion Paste (page 48)
½ teaspoon saffron threads
1 tablespoon milk
1½ pounds extra lean ground lamb
1 teaspoon salt, or to taste
1 to 3 tablespoons semolina or chickpea flour, if needed
12 to 15 metal or bamboo skewers, soaked in water
    at least 30 minutes
2 cups shredded lettuce, such as green or red leaf,
    to line a platter

1. Prepare the garam masala, chaat masala, and the onion paste. Roast the saffron in a small skillet, about 1 minute, then grind it with the back of a spoon and soak it in the milk about 30 minutes.

2. Place the lamb in a large mixing bowl and mix in the onion and ginger-garlic pastes, garam masala, salt, and saffron milk. Cover and marinate in the refrigerator about 4 hours.

3. Preheat the grill to 375°F to 400°F, or the broiler. Moisten your clean fingers with water and divide the meat into 12 to 15 equal parts. Work each portion into a long, thin shape, similar to a hot dog. If the mixture seems too soft to work with, mix in the semolina (or chickpea flour), using as much as needed to make a soft dough that holds its shape.

4. Thread onto the skewers and grill at medium-high or broil on the top rack (about 6 inches away from the heating element), turning frequently until crispy yet still moist. Transfer to a platter lined with lettuce, dust lightly with the chaat masala, and serve.

Marinated Lamb Kabaabs
Boti Kabaabs

Makes 4 to 6 servings

Boti is a piece of bone-in meat. The authentic version of these kabaabs *calls for bone-in pieces, although over the years this has changed and* boti kabaabs *all over*

India are now made with boneless meat. My recipe here uses boneless leg of lamb.

For a true and authentic version, ask your butcher to trim and cut lamb shanks into 1½-inch pieces.

- ¼ cup Basic Ginger-Garlic Paste (page 47 or store-bought)
- 1½ to 2 pounds boneless leg of lamb, all visible fat trimmed, cut into 1½-inch pieces
- ½ cup nonfat plain yogurt, whisked until smooth
- ¼ cup fresh lemon or lime juice
- 1 tablespoon vegetable oil
- 1 tablespoon ground coriander
- 1 tablespoon ground cumin
- 2 teaspoon garam masala
- 1 teaspoon cayenne pepper, or to taste
- 1½ teaspoons salt, or to taste
- 6 metal or bamboo skewers, soaked in water at least 30 minutes
- 1 tablespoon melted unsalted butter
- 2 tablespoons finely chopped fresh cilantro, including soft stems

1. Prepare the chaat masala. With a fork, prick each piece of lamb all over and place in a large non-reactive bowl. In another bowl, mix together the yogurt, ginger-garlic paste, lemon juice, oil, coriander, cumin, garam masala, cayenne pepper, and salt. Add the yogurt mixture to the lamb pieces. Mix well, making sure that all the pieces are coated with the marinade. Cover and marinate in the refrigerator about 24 hours.

2. Thread the marinated pieces of chicken on metal or bamboo skewers (4 to 5 pieces per skewer) and discard the marinade. (If you absolutely must, immediately boil the marinade about 5 minutes and use it in sauces. Boiling kills any bacteria.)

3. Preheat a grill on medium-high heat (375°F to 400°F) and grill, turning the skewered pieces over until they are lightly charred and very tender, about 20 minutes. During the last minute or so, baste with the melted butter. Remove to a serving platter, garnish with the cilantro and serve.

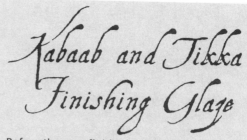

Kabaab and Tikka Finishing Glaze

Before they are finished, all *tandoor*-cooked *kabaabs* and *tikkas* are basted with a special finishing glaze that is made with seasoned *ghee*, butter, or oil and, occasionally, lemon juice. Brushed on the foods during the last few minutes, while the meat is still in the *tandoor* (or on your grill), this glaze really jazzes up the flavors and gives the food a brilliant shine.

Start with:

- 1 to 2 tablespoons melted butter or any vegetable oil, mixed with ½ teaspoon Asian sesame oil or ghee

Add:

- 2 tablespoons fresh lemon or lime juice, or vinegar
- ½ teaspoon dried fenugreek leaves
- ¼ teaspoon ground black salt, or to taste

Then mix in any one of the following:

- ½ to 1 teaspoon dry-roasted and coarsely ground cumin or black peppercorns (Dry-Roasting Spices, page 35)
- 1 teaspoon Chaat Masala (page 20 or store-bought)

Pan-Fried Lamb Kabaabs

Bhunnae Boti Kabaab

Makes 4 to 6 servings

Made with boneless leg of lamb, these kabaabs are first softened in a spicy water bath, then coated with eggs and spices and pan-fried until they develop a rich golden crust. Serve them with Yogurt Chutney with Puréed Greens (page 68).

1 (2-foot-long) piece of cheesecloth
4 bay leaves
1 tablespoon black peppercorns
10 cloves
2 (1-inch) sticks cinnamon, broken into 2 to 3 pieces
4 black cardamom pods, crushed lightly
    to break the skin
6 to 8 green cardamom pods
3 tablespoons Basic Ginger-Garlic Paste
    (page 47 or store-bought)
1¹/₂ to 2 pounds boneless leg of lamb, all visible fat
    trimmed, cut into 1-inch pieces
5 to 6 cups water
1 teaspoon salt, or to taste
2 large eggs, lightly beaten
¹/₂ teaspoon cayenne pepper, or to taste
¹/₂ teaspoon garam masala
³/₄ to 1 cup bread crumbs
¹/₂ cup finely chopped fresh cilantro,
    including soft stems
¹/₂ cup vegetable oil for pan-frying

1. Fold the cheesecloth twice, so you have a 5- to 6-inch square with 4 layers. Place the bay leaves, peppercorns, cloves, cinnamon, and both kinds of cardamom pods on top. Tie the seasoning pouch closed with kitchen string. Crush the contents lightly with a pestle or meat pounder to coarsely break all the spices.

2. Prepare the ginger-garlic paste, and place in a large nonstick pan along with the lamb, seasoning pouch, water, and salt. Bring to a boil, and boil over high heat about 5 minutes. Reduce the heat to low, cover the pan and cook until all the water has been absorbed and the meat is very tender, 50 to 60 minutes. (If the meat is not tender, add up to 1 cup more

water and continue cooking.) Watch carefully that the pan doesn't boil over.

3. Let cool, then add the eggs, cayenne pepper, garam masala, ³/₄ cup bread crumbs, and cilantro, and mix well. The meat should be completely dry. If not, mix in another ¹/₄ cup bread crumbs.

4. Heat the oil in a large skillet over medium-high heat and fry the lamb pieces, adding as many as the skillet can hold at one time, turning a few times with a slotted spatula, until golden and crisp, about 5 minutes. Drain on paper towels and serve hot.

Flattened Lamb Kabaab Skewers with Cardamom Seeds

Pasindae Illaichi

Makes 4 to 6 servings

Here, boneless strips of flattened lamb (called pasinda *or* pasanda*) are marinated and grilled. Because they are thin, they marinate and cook quickly, though flattening them is quite a job.*

2 tablespoons Basic Ginger-Garlic Paste
    (page 47 or store-bought)
1¹/₂ pounds boneless leg of lamb, all visible fat
    trimmed
1 teaspoon garam masala
1 teaspoon salt, or to taste
¹/₂ cup nonfat plain yogurt, whisked until smooth
2 tablespoons fresh lemon or lime juice
1 tablespoon ground unsweetened dried coconut
1 teaspoon ground paprika
1 teaspoon ground green cardamom seeds
¹/₂ teaspoon ground black cardamom seeds
6 to 8 metal or bamboo skewers, soaked in water
    at least 30 minutes
Chopped cilantro, lemon wedges, and scallion whites

1. Prepare the ginger-garlic paste. Cut the lamb into thin 1-by-1¹/₂-inch pieces. Place the pieces on a cutting board, cover with plastic wrap and, with the flat side of a meat mallet, pound them until they are at least 2 inches long and about ¼-inch thick. (These are the pasindas.)

2. In a small non-reactive bowl, combine the ginger-garlic paste, garam masala and salt, and rub it well into the lamb pieces. Cover with plastic wrap and marinate in the refrigerator about 2 hours.

3. In another small bowl, mix together the yogurt, lime juice, coconut, paprika, and both the cardamom seeds, and add them to the lamb. Mix well, cover with plastic wrap and marinate at least 4 more hours in the refrigerator.

4. To skewer, fold each pasinda in half and poke the skewer through the center. Then pull both the sides away from one another to make a small curve.

5. Preheat a grill to high heat (400°F to 425°F) and grill, turning the skewered lamb pieces until they are seared on all sides, 1 to 2 minutes. Then move the skewers to the sides where the heat is slightly lower and continue to grill, turning, until the lamb is golden brown and very tender, about 10 minutes. Transfer to a serving platter, garnish with chopped cilantro, lemon wedges, and scallion whites, and serve.

Variation: Grill in a preheated broiler 10 to 12 inches from the source of heat. Baste and turn the skewers over a few times. If placed closer, the thin pieces will burn.

Flattened Lamb Kabaab Skewers with Nuts and Poppy Seeds
Maeva-Khaskhas Pasindae

Makes 4 to 6 servings

This is a variation of the Flattened Lamb Kabaab Skewers with Cardamom Seeds (page 150). The preparation and cooking are the same—only the marinade is different.

2 tablespoons Basic Ginger-Garlic Paste (page 47 or store-bought)
1½ pounds boneless leg of lamb, all visible fat trimmed
1 tablespoon chickpea flour (besan), dry-roasted (page 35)
2 tablespoons coarsely chopped cashews
2 tablespoons blanched raw almonds
1 tablespoon poppy seeds
½ teaspoon garam masala
½ teaspoon cayenne pepper, or to taste
1 small onion, coarsely chopped
½ cup nonfat plain yogurt, whisked until smooth
2 tablespoons fresh lime juice

1. Prepare the ginger-garlic paste. Cut the lamb into thin 1-by-1½-inch pieces. Place the pieces on a cutting board, cover with plastic wrap and, with the flat side of a meat mallet, pound them until they are at least 2 inches long and about ¼-inch thick. (These are the pasindas.)

2. Dry-roast the chickpea flour. Then, in a food processor, process together the cashews, almonds, poppy seeds, chickpea flour, garam masala, and cayenne pepper until finely ground. Add the onion, yogurt, and lime juice, and process again to make a smooth paste.

3. Place the pasindas in a large non-reactive bowl, add the marinade and mix well. Cover with plastic wrap or the lid of the bowl and marinate in the refrigerator at least 4 and up to 24 hours.

4. Skewer, grill, and serve according to the directions for Flattened Lamb Kabaab Skewers with Cardamom Seeds (page 150), starting from Step 4.

Deep-Fried Lamb Kabaab Patties

Shaami Kabaabs

Makes 4 to 6 servings

Made with boneless pieces of lamb that are simmered with yellow split chickpeas (channa dal) and spices (a pressure cooker does this quickly), ground until they are really fine, then shaped into round patties, and fried. They may look like unpretentious patties, but shaami kabaabs *are a culinary tour de force.*

Make sure that the kabaab *mixture is completely dry or the* kabaabs *will disintegrate in the oil while frying. If that happens, add 1 to 2 tablespoons chickpea or all-purpose flour to the unused mixture. The flour will absorb the excess moisture.*

Serve the kabaabs *with a side of Lemon-Marinated Red Onion Rings (page 204).*

1 pound boneless leg of lamb, all visible fat trimmed, cut into small pieces
¹/₂ cup dried yellow split chickpeas (channa dal), sorted and washed in 3 to 4 changes of water
6 to 8 quarter-size slices peeled fresh ginger
2 large cloves fresh garlic, peeled
1 small onion, coarsely chopped
6 green cardamom pods, crushed lightly to break the skin
4 black cardamom pods, crushed lightly to break the skin
2 (1-inch) sticks cinnamon
8 whole cloves
1¹/₂ cups water
1 to 3 fresh green chile peppers, such as serrano, stemmed
1 large egg, lightly beaten
1 tablespoon ground coriander
Freshly ground black pepper, to taste
1¹/₂ to 2 cups peanut oil for deep-frying

1. Place the lamb, dal, ginger, garlic, onion, both cardamoms, cinnamon, cloves, and water in a pressure cooker. Secure the lid and cook over high heat until the regulator indicates high pressure, then cook about 1 minute more. Reduce the heat to low and continue to cook another 3 minutes. Then remove from the heat and allow the pot to depressurize on its own, 12 to 15 minutes.

2. Carefully remove the lid and cook over medium-high heat, stirring, until the lamb is completely dry, about 7 to 10 minutes. Let cool and remove all the whole spices.

3. In a food processor, process the green chile peppers until minced. Mix in the cooked lamb, egg, coriander, and black pepper, and process to make a soft dough that can hold its shape, about 15 seconds. Shape into 16 to 20 2-inch patties and set aside.

4. Heat the oil in a large wok or skillet until it reaches 350°F to 375°F on a frying thermometer or until a small piece of the mixture dropped into the hot oil bubbles and immediately rises to the top. Fry the kabaabs, as many as the wok can hold at one time without crowding, turning a few times with a slotted spatula until golden and crispy on all sides, about 5 minutes. Drain on paper towels. Transfer to a platter and serve hot.

Variation: Instead of a pressure cooker, place all the ingredients in a large pot with an extra ¹/₂ cup of water and cook over medium-high heat the first 3 minutes and then over medium-low heat until the lamb and dal are soft and completely dry, about 45 minutes. Let cool, remove the whole spices, and continue from Step 3.

Pinched Lamb Kabaabs with Fenugreek Leaves

Gosht kae Methi Kabaab

Makes 4 to 6 servings

With the addition of bread and the fragrance of fenugreek leaves, these knobby kabaabs *take on a completely new identity. They are also an easier version to make, because you don't have to shape these* kabaabs *as precisely as you do most others.*

2 tablespoons Basic Ginger-Garlic Paste
    (page 47 or store-bought)
3 slices white bread, crusts removed
1 pound minced leg of lamb
1 to 3 fresh green chile peppers, such as serrano,
    coarsely chopped
1 tablespoon ground coriander
2 teaspoons dried fenugreek leaves
1 teaspoon garam masala
1/2 teaspoon ground cumin
1/2 teaspoon ground paprika
1/4 teaspoon ground turmeric
1 teaspoon salt, or to taste
1 large egg, lightly beaten
1 1/2 to 2 cups peanut oil for deep-frying

1. Prepare the ginger-garlic paste. Soak the bread slices in water to cover until soft, about 1 minute. Drain, squeeze out all excess water, and crumble finely. In a bowl, mix together everything except the oil. Cover and marinate in the refrigerator about 1 hour.

3. Heat the oil in a large wok or skillet over medium-high heat until it reaches 325°F to 350°F on a frying thermometer or until a small piece of the mixture dropped into the hot oil takes 15 to 20 seconds to rise to the top.

4. Using clean hands, pinch about 1 tablespoon of the mixture, flatten lightly by pressing it between your fingers and thumb to make irregular-shaped patties, and carefully add it to the oil. Add as many kabaabs as the wok can hold at one time without crowding, and fry, turning them a few times with a slotted spatula, until golden and crispy on all sides, about 5 minutes. Drain on paper towels. Transfer to a platter and serve.

Silky Skewered Minced Chicken

Murgh Reshmi Seekh Kabaabs

Makes 4 to 6 servings

Characterized by a silky smoothness (raesham means silk), these long hot-dog-shaped kabaabs have a lovely pale hue that comes from the cashews and egg whites.

Part of the Mughlai heritage, these kabaabs are delicious with tandoori naan (grilled leavened breads).

Black salt is a grayish-pink rock salt that imparts a unique fragrance to foods. It is an essential ingredient in chaat masala and is often added to cold beverages such as Sparkling Savory Mint-Lime Cooler (page 657). Look for it in Indian markets.

1/2 cup Basic Green Chutney (page 58)
1 tablespoon fresh lime juice
1 tablespoon melted unsalted butter
1/4 teaspoon ground black salt or Chaat Masala
    (page 20 or store-bought)
1 1/2 to 2 pounds boneless skinless chicken breasts,
    cut in small pieces
1/2 small onion, coarsely chopped
1/2 cup coarsely chopped cashews
3 to 4 large cloves fresh garlic, peeled
8 quarter-size slices peeled fresh ginger
1 to 3 fresh green chile peppers, such as serrano,
    coarsely chopped
2 large egg whites, lightly beaten
1 tablespoon ground coriander
1 teaspoon garam masala
1/2 teaspoon ground white pepper
1/4 teaspoon freshly ground nutmeg
1/4 cup all-purpose flour, as needed
12 to 15 metal or bamboo skewers, soaked in water
    at least 30 minutes
1 tablespoon vegetable oil
1 small onion, cut in half lengthwise and thinly sliced
1/2 cup finely chopped fresh cilantro, including soft stems

1. Prepare the chutney. Then, in a small bowl, mix together the lime juice, butter, and black salt (or chaat masala), and reserve.

2. In a blender or a food processor, process together the chicken, onion, cashews, garlic, ginger, chile peppers, egg whites, and all the spices until as smooth as possible. Cover and marinate in the refrigerator about 4 hours.

3. Preheat a grill to 375°F to 400°F, or preheat the broiler. Moisten your clean fingers with water, divide the meat into 12 to 16 equal parts, and make each portion into a long, thin shape, similar to a hot dog. If the mixture seems too soft to work with, mix in the

all-purpose flour, using as much as needed to make a soft dough that holds its shape. Thread the chicken onto the skewers, brush with the lime-butter mixture and grill over medium-high heat coals, or broil on the top rack (about 6-inches away from the heating element), turning frequently, until firm and lightly charred on all sides, about 10 minutes. Transfer to a platter.

4. Heat the oil in a small nonstick skillet over medium-high heat and cook the sliced onion until golden, about 3 minutes. Add the cilantro and stir about 1 minute, then scatter over kabaabs. Dot with some of the chutney and serve the remaining chutney on the side.

Grilled Chicken Drumstick Kabaabs

Tangdhi Kabaabs

Makes 4 to 6 servings

Taang *means leg,* tangdhi *is a little leg, and* tangdhi kabaabs *are kabaabs made with little chicken drumsticks.*

Although you can essentially use any marinade, the true and authentic version of these kabaabs uses a relatively dry one without any yogurt, according to Sunil Vora, a prominent Indian restaurateur and an ardent chef in the Los Angeles area.

2 tablespoons Basic Ginger-Garlic Paste
    (page 47 or store-bought)
1 teaspoon cumin seeds, dry-roasted, coarsely
    ground (Dry-Roasting Spices, page 35)
12 skinless chicken drumsticks
2 tablespoons vegetable oil
2 tablespoons fresh lime juice
1 tablespoon ground coriander
1 teaspoon ground cumin
1 teaspoon garam masala
1 teaspoon dried fenugreek leaves
1/2 teaspoon cayenne pepper, or to taste
1/4 teaspoon ground turmeric
1/4 teaspoon freshly ground nutmeg
1 tablespoon melted ghee
Lemon wedges, onion slivers, and split fresh
    green chile peppers, for garnish

1. Prepare the ginger-garlic paste and the cumin seeds. Then, with a sharp knife, make 2 to 3 deep cuts crosswise on each drumstick and place in a large non-reactive bowl.

2. In a bowl, mix together all the remaining ingredients (except the ghee, roasted cumin, and the garnishes) and add to the drumsticks. Mix well, making sure that some of the marinade reaches inside the gashes and all the pieces are well-coated. Cover and marinate in the refrigerator at least 8 and up to 12 hours.

3. Preheat a grill to 375°F to 400°F, or preheat the broiler. Wrap the bone side of each drumstick with a piece of foil, and grill over medium-high heat or broil on the top rack (about 6-inches away from the heating element), turning frequently, until firm and lightly charred on all sides, about 20 minutes.

4. During the last 2 to 3 minutes, heat the ghee in a small saucepan over medium-high heat, mix in the roasted cumin seeds, and baste over the drumsticks. Transfer to a serving platter, garnish with the lemon wedges, onion, and green chile peppers, and serve.

Pan-Roasted Egg-Stuffed Chicken Drumstick Kabaabs

Anda-Bharae Tangdhi Kabaabs

Makes 4 to 6 servings

Fragrantly spiced boneless chicken drumsticks stuffed with a delicate hard-boiled-egg filling are another popular and much regarded kabaab in northern India. Here I stuff them with boiled eggs, but in place of the eggs you could essentially fill them with any dry-cooked dish; paneer *cheese is very popular.*

Remove the bone from the drumsticks yourself, or just have the butcher do it for you.

2 to 3 tablespoons Basic Ginger-Garlic Paste
   (page 47 or store-bought)
2 large eggs
1/4 cup grated cheddar or Monterey Jack cheese
1/2 cup finely chopped fresh cilantro,
   including soft stems
1 fresh green chile pepper, such as serrano,
   minced with seeds
Salt and freshly ground black pepper, to taste
12 skinless and boneless chicken drumsticks
2 tablespoons fresh lime juice
2 tablespoons minced fresh mint leaves
1 tablespoon ground coriander
1 teaspoon garam masala
1 teaspoon dried fenugreek leaves
1/2 teaspoon ground paprika
2 tablespoons vegetable oil
1 small onion, cut into half lengthwise
   and thinly sliced

1. Prepare the ginger-garlic paste. In a medium sauce-pan, place the eggs in water to cover by 2 inches and bring to a boil over high heat. Reduce the heat to medium, cover the pan and simmer until hard-boiled, 10 to 12 minutes. Let cool or plunge into cold water, shell them, then mince them. Mix with the cheese, 1/4 cup of the cilantro, and chile pepper, and season lightly with salt and black pepper if you wish. Divide into 12 portions.

2. With a thin sharp knife, make several cuts in the drumstick meat. Butterfly (open up like a book) each boned drumstick and place one portion of the egg filling in the center of each drumstick. Close it like a book, then secure with toothpicks along the opening and place in a non-reactive pan. Repeat with all the drumsticks.

3. In a small bowl, mix together the ginger-garlic paste, lime juice, mint, coriander, garam masala, fenugreek leaves, and paprika, and add to the drum-sticks. Mix well, making sure that some of it reaches inside the cuts in the meat and that all pieces are well-coated. Cover and marinate in the refrigerator at least 8 and up to 12 hours.

4. Heat the oil in a large nonstick skillet over medium-high heat and cook the onion, stirring, until golden, about 4 minutes. Add the marinated drumsticks, plus

the marinade, and cook, turning as needed, until golden on all sides, about 10 minutes. Add the remaining 1/4 cup of the cilantro, cook about 2 min-utes, then transfer to a serving platter and serve hot.

Pan-Cooked Chicken Liver Kabaabs
Kalaeji Kabaabs

Makes 4 to 6 servings

When I was growing up, my aunt would often serve these kabaabs *as a breakfast or brunch item when we visited, with spicy* paranthas *(griddle-fried breads) and a glass of* lussi *(yogurt cooler).*

2 tablespoons Basic Ginger-Garlic Paste
   (page 47 or store-bought)
1 pound chicken livers, cut into 1-inch pieces
1/2 cup canned tomato sauce
1/4 cup nonfat plain yogurt, whisked until smooth
1 large onion, finely chopped
2 tablespoons fresh lime juice
1 to 2 tablespoons vegetable oil
1 tablespoon ground coriander
1 tablespoon dried fenugreek leaves
1 teaspoon ground cumin
1 teaspoon garam masala
12 to 15 metal or bamboo skewers, soaked in water
   at least 30 minutes

1. Place the liver pieces in a non-reactive bowl and mix in all the remaining ingredients. Cover with plastic wrap and marinate in the refrigerator at least 4 and up to 24 hours.

2. Transfer the liver and all the marinade to a non-stick skillet and bring to a boil over high heat. Reduce the heat to medium-low, cover the pan and simmer until the liver is tender and the sauce has almost evaporated, about 15 minutes. Let cool.

3. Preheat a grill to 375°F to 400°F or preheat the broiler. Thread the meat onto the skewers and grill, or broil on the top rack (about 6 inches from the heating element), turning frequently, until lightly charred on all sides, about 10 minutes. Transfer to a platter and serve hot.

Spicy Batter-Coated Fish Kabaabs

Macchi Kabaabs

Makes 4 to 6 servings

Served with Indian French Fries with Tomatoes (page 127), this fish kabaab, dipped in a spicy rice flour batter then dredged in corn meal and deep-fried, is an Indian fish and chips meal.

1¹/₂ pounds any firm white fish fillets, such as sea bass or cod, about 1-inch thick, cut into 3-inch pieces
1 teaspoon salt, or to taste
¹/₄ teaspoon ground turmeric
¹/₂ cup rice flour
2 teaspoons hot red pepper flakes, or to taste
1 teaspoon ground cumin seeds
¹/₂ teaspoon ground fenugreek seeds
¹/₈ teaspoon ground asafoetida
¹/₄ to ¹/₃ cup water
1¹/₂ to 2 cups peanut oil for deep-frying
¹/₂ cup cornmeal
1 tablespoon fresh lemon juice
1 to 2 tablespoons finely chopped fresh cilantro, including soft stems
Lemon wedges

1. Place the fish pieces in a large non-reactive bowl, add the salt and turmeric, and mix well. Cover and marinate in the refrigerator 1 to 2 hours.

2. In a medium bowl, mix together the rice flour, red pepper flakes, cumin, fenugreek, asafoetida, and just enough water to form a thick paste.

3. Heat the oil in a wok or large skillet over high heat until it registers 350°F to 375°F on a frying thermometer or until a small piece of fish dropped into the hot oil bubbles and immediately rises to the top.

4. Smear each piece of fish with the rice flour paste, dredge it in the corn meal and carefully add to the hot oil, adding as many pieces as the wok can hold at one time. Fry, turning as needed, until they are golden and crisp, 2 to 3 minutes. Transfer to paper towels to drain. Transfer to a serving dish, garnish with lemon wedges and cilantro, and serve.

Skewered Minced Paneer Cheese Kabaabs

Paneer Seekh Kabaabs

Makes 4 to 6 servings

Lightly grilled and very delicate, these kabaabs *are perfect for vegetarians who want* kabaab *flavor without the meat.*

1 teaspoon Chaat Masala (page 20 or store-bought) + ¹/₄ teaspoon
¹/₂ cup chopped cashews, soaked in water to cover about 1 hour, then drained
1 to 3 fresh green chile peppers, such as serrano, coarsely chopped
4 quarter-size slices peeled fresh ginger
¹/₂ small onion, coarsely chopped
¹/₂ cup coarsely chopped fresh cilantro, including soft stems
8 ounces (1 recipe) Paneer Cheese (page 43 or store-bought), crumbled
1 tablespoon ground coriander
1 teaspoon ground cumin
1 teaspoon mango powder
1 teaspoon salt, or to taste
2 to 4 tablespoons all-purpose flour, as needed
12 to 15 metal or bamboo skewers, soaked in water at least 30 minutes
1 tablespoon melted unsalted butter
2 cups shredded lettuce, such as green or red leaf, or romaine

1. Prepare the chaat masala and the paneer cheese. Then, in a food processor, process together the cashews, green chile peppers, ginger, onion, and cilantro until fine. Then add the paneer cheese and all the remaining ingredients (except the flour, butter, chaat masala, and lettuce) and process until everything is well mixed and starts to gather together, about 1 minute.

2. Preheat a grill to 375°F to 400°F or preheat the broiler. Moisten your clean fingers with water, and divide the mixture into 12 to 15 equal parts, making long, thin shapes, similar to hot dogs. If the mixture seems too soft to work with, mix in some all-purpose flour, using as much as needed to make a soft dough that holds its shape.

3. Thread onto the skewers and grill or broil on the top rack (about 6 inches from the heating element), turning frequently, until firm and lightly golden. (Do not overcook, or they will become tough.)

4. Heat the butter in a small saucepan over medium-high heat, mix in 1 teaspoon chaat masala and lightly baste the kabaabs just before removing them from the heat. Transfer to a platter lined with the lettuce, sprinkle the ¼ teaspoon chaat masala on top, and serve.

Chutney-Marinated Broiled Paneer Cheese Kabaabs

Hari Chutney Paneer Kabaabs

Makes 4 to 6 servings

This is very delicate and easy to make, especially if you have the chutney in your freezer. (If not, and you can't make it fresh, a store-bought version will work in a pinch.)

Substitute pesto for the green chutney and you'll end up with a surprising yet familiar dish that will remind you of pesto-coated mozzarella cheese, because paneer and fresh mozzarella are actually quite similar.

8-ounces (1 recipe) Paneer Cheese (page 43 or store-bought), cut into 1-by-1½-inch pieces
½ cup Basic Green Chutney (page 58 or store-bought)
½ cup nonfat plain yogurt or nonfat sour cream, whisked until smooth
¼ teaspoon salt, or to taste
1 tablespoon vegetable oil
2 to 3 scallions, green parts only, minced
¼ teaspoon garam masala

1. Prepare the paneer and the green chutney. Place the paneer pieces in a large non-reactive bowl. In a small bowl, mix together the yogurt (or sour cream), green chutney, and salt. Add to the paneer cheese pieces and mix well, making sure all the pieces are well-coated. Cover and marinate in the refrigerator overnight.

2. Preheat the broiler. Oil or coat with foil a large broiler-safe tray and place the paneer cheese pieces on it in a single layer. Place the tray on the top rack, about 4 to 5 inches from the heating element, and broil until the pieces are barely golden, about 5 minutes. (Do not overcook; they will toughen.)

3. Turn off the broiler and turn on the oven to 500°F. Place the tray on the bottom rack bake until the pieces are just golden on the bottom, about 5 minutes. Alternately, leave the tray in the broiler, turn the paneer over with a spatula, and broil about 3 minutes more until golden. Transfer to a serving platter, garnish with scallion greens and garam masala, and serve.

Skewered Paneer and Vegetable Kabaabs

Paneer Shaslik Kabaabs

Makes 4 to 6 servings

The Indian version of shish kabaabs, made with paneer instead of meat, and a popular item on most typical Indian restaurant menus, these familiar skewered kabaabs have a chickpea flour marinade. The flour soaks up the juices and forms a thin, almost invisible shell around the individual pieces.

For your vegetable selection, choose those that cook fast, because paneer cheese toughens very quickly. Good choices are bell peppers of different colors, small mushrooms, thinly sliced Japanese eggplant or squash, pearl or quartered onions, and cherry tomatoes. You can also use fruit such as pieces of apple, pineapple, peach, nectarine, and kumquat.

8 ounces (1 recipe) Paneer Cheese (page 43), cut into 16 equal pieces
2 tablespoons Basic Ginger-Garlic Paste (page 47 or store-bought)
About 1½ pounds mixed fresh vegetables of your choice, cut into 1½-inch pieces
1 cup nonfat plain yogurt, whisked until smooth
2 tablespoons fresh lemon juice
2 tablespoons peanut oil
2 tablespoons chickpea flour
1 teaspoon garam masala
½ teaspoon cayenne pepper, or to taste
¼ teaspoon ground turmeric
1 teaspoon salt, or to taste
4 to 6 metal or bamboo skewers, soaked in orange juice or water at least 30 minutes
Shredded lettuce (optional)

1. Prepare the paneer cheese. Prepare the ginger-garlic paste. Place the paneer cheese and vegetables in a large non-reactive bowl. In a small bowl mix together the paneer, lemon juice, oil, chickpea flour, ginger-garlic paste, garam masala, cayenne pepper, turmeric, and salt. Add to the paneer cheese pieces and vegetables and mix well, making sure that all the pieces are well-coated. Cover and marinate in the refrigerator at least 8 hours or up to 12.

2. Preheat a grill to 375°F to 400°F or preheat the broiler. Thread the vegetables and paneer cheese onto the skewers and grill over medium-high heart coals, or broil on the top rack (about 4 to 5 inches from the heating element), turning frequently, until lightly golden, 5 to 7 minutes. (Don't overcook, as paneer cheese will toughen.) Baste occasionally with the marinade. Transfer to a serving platter and serve the shaslik on skewers, or slide the pieces off onto a bed of shredded lettuce, if using.

Paneer Cheese Kabaabs with Pomegranate Seeds
Anardana Paneer Kabaabs

Makes 4 to 6 servings

My daughter Sumi's sister-in-law, Anu Khatod, has a great hand in the kitchen, as we can see from this sumptuous dish that she fed dozens and dozens of people at a July 4th party. Influenced by her Punjabi upbringing in America, Anu uses sour cream with her Indian spices.

Do not discard the marinade left in the bowl after the paneer *cheese pieces are removed; use it in curries, rice, or soups.*

1/2 teaspoon dry-roasted and coarsely ground cumin seeds (Dry-Roasting Spices, page 35)
8 ounces (1 recipe) Paneer Cheese (page 43 or store-bought), cut into 1-inch or larger pieces, each about 1/3-inch thick
1 cup sour cream, any kind
2 to 3 large cloves fresh garlic, minced
2 tablespoons peeled minced fresh ginger
2 teaspoons ground dried pomegranate seeds
1 1/2 teaspoons garam masala
1 1/2 teaspoons ground paprika
1 teaspoon salt, or to taste

1. Prepare the cumin seeds and paneer cheese. Then, place the paneer cheese in a flat dish. In a medium bowl, mix together the sour cream, garlic, ginger, pomegranate seeds, garam masala, paprika, and salt. Add to the paneer cheese, making sure that all the pieces are well-coated. Cover and marinate in the refrigerator at least 8 hours or up to 12.

2. Preheat the broiler. Grease a broiler-safe tray or cover with foil. Leaving all the marinade behind, transfer the paneer cheese, piece by piece, to the broiling tray and broil on the top rack (4 to 5 inches from the heating element) until the top side is golden, about 5 minutes. Turn once and broil the other side until golden, about 3 minutes. (Do not overcook; the paneer will toughen.) Transfer to a serving platter, sprinkle the roasted cumin on top, and serve.

Black Chickpea Kabaabs
Kaala Channa Kabaabs

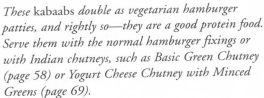

Makes 4 to 6 servings

These kabaabs double as vegetarian hamburger patties, and rightly so—they are a good protein food. Serve them with the normal hamburger fixings or with Indian chutneys, such as Basic Green Chutney (page 58) or Yogurt Cheese Chutney with Minced Greens (page 69).

1 cup dried black chickpeas (kaalae channae), sorted and washed in 3 to 4 changes of water
2 to 3 cups water
1 teaspoon garam masala
1 teaspoon salt, or to taste
2 large cloves fresh garlic, peeled
5 to 6 quarter-size slices peeled fresh ginger
1 to 3 fresh green chile peppers, such as serrano, coarsely chopped
1/2 cup coarsely chopped fresh cilantro, including soft stems
3/4 to 1 cup chickpea flour
1 to 1 1/2 cups peanut oil for deep-frying

1. Soak the dal overnight in water to cover by 2 inches. Then drain and place the dal, water, garam masala, and salt in a pressure cooker. Secure the lid and cook over high heat until the regulator indicates high pressure, then cook about 1 minute more. Reduce the heat to low and continue to cook another 1 minute. Remove the pot from the heat and allow to depressurize on its own, 12 to 15 minutes. Then, carefully open the lid and check to see if the chickpeas are very soft, with some of them broken; if not, cover, bring up to pressure, and cook under pressure another minute.

Alternately, place the dal, spices and water in a large pot, cover and boil until the chickpeas are soft and all the water has evaporated, about 30 minutes.

2. Let cool, then transfer to a food processor along with garlic, ginger, chile peppers, and cilantro, and process until smooth. Add half the chickpea flour and process once again, adding more flour until everything starts to gather, almost like soft dough that can be shaped. Divide into 25 portions and shape into smooth patties or rolls.

3. Heat the oil in a wok or skillet over high heat until it registers 350°F to 375°F on a frying thermometer or until a small piece of the mixture dropped into the hot oil bubbles and immediately rises to the top. Fry the kabaabs, as many as the wok can hold at one time without crowding, turning them with a slotted spatula a few times until golden and crispy on all sides, about 3 minutes per batch. Drain on paper towels. Transfer to a platter and serve hot.

Skewered Vegetable Kabaabs with Fresh Fenugreek Leaves

Sabzi-Seekh Kabaabs

Makes 4 to 6 servings

Lots of vegetables, some starchy and some otherwise, paneer cheese, nuts, herbs, and spices, all come together harmoniously to give you a vibrant, healthful dish.

1 teaspoon Chaat Masala (page 20 or store-bought)
1 large russet (or any) potato
1 small orange-fleshed yam
1/4 cup coarsely chopped cashews
1/4 cup coarsely chopped almonds
6 quarter-size slices of peeled fresh ginger
2 large cloves fresh garlic, peeled
1 to 3 fresh green chile peppers, such as serrano, coarsely chopped
1 cup Paneer Cheese (page 43 or store-bought), coarsely crumbled
1 cup finely chopped fresh fenugreek leaves
3 cups coarsely chopped mixed fresh vegetables, such as cauliflower, broccoli, carrots, green beans
2 to 3 tablespoons bread crumbs
1/2 teaspoon ajwain seeds
1/2 teaspoon cayenne pepper, or to taste
1 teaspoon salt, or to taste
16 to 20 metal or bamboo skewers, soaked in water at least 30 minutes
1 to 2 tablespoons melted unsalted butter
About 2 cups shredded green or red leaf lettuce

1. Prepare the chaat masala. Cook the potato and the yam in lightly salted boiling water to cover until tender, about 20 minutes. Drain, let cool, then peel. Transfer to a medium bowl and mash together.

2. In a food processor, process together the cashews, almonds, ginger, garlic, and green chile peppers, until minced. Add the paneer cheese and fenugreek leaves and process again until minced. Transfer to a large bowl.

3. Place the vegetables in the food processor and process until minced. Add to the processed nut mixture. Then add the bread crumbs, mashed potato and yam, ajwain seeds, cayenne pepper, and salt, and mix well.

4. Divide into 16 to 20 portions, then shape and cook as per directions for Skewered Minced Paneer Cheese Kabaabs (page 156), starting from Step 2. Baste with the butter before cooking the kabaabs. Transfer to a platter lined with lettuce, dust lightly with the chaat masala, and serve.

Variation: Shape the mixture into patties and deep-fry as per directions for Deep-Fried Lamb Kabaab Patties (page 152), starting with Step 4.

Tikka Kabaabs and Marinades

Basic Grilled Lamb Tikka Kabaabs

Gosht Tikka

Makes 4 to 6 servings

Tikkas are boneless, skinless pieces of meat that are first marinated and then grilled. Since lamb is a tough and gamy meat to start with, lamb tikkas require robust marinades, stronger spices, more intense flavors, and a longer marinating period than chicken and fish.

Select any one of the tikka marinades listed on pages 162 to 166, mix in some more ginger, garlic, and spices if you wish, then follow the directions in this recipe.

1 recipe Tikka Marinade of your choice
   (pages 162 to 166)
1¹/₂ to 2 pounds boneless leg of lamb, all visible fat
   trimmed, cut into 1¹/₂-inch pieces
1 recipe Kabaab and Tikka Finishing Glaze
   (see box, page 149)
8 to 10 metal or bamboo skewers soaked,
   in water at least 30 minutes
Lemon and tomato wedges
1 to 2 fresh green chile peppers, such as serrano,
   stemmed, seeded, and thinly sliced

1. Prepare the marinade. Then, place the lamb in a large non-reactive bowl. Add the marinade (saving about ¼ cup to use for basting as you grill) and mix well, making sure all the pieces are well-coated. Cover the bowl and marinate the lamb in the refrigerator at least 12 and up to 36 hours. (To prevent potential salmonella contamination, never marinate poultry, meats, or seafood at room temperature.)

2. When ready to cook, prepare the finishing glaze. Then, thread the lamb pieces on skewers (4 to 5 per skewer), and discard the used marinade. (If you prefer, immediately boil the marinade about 5 minutes and use it as a sauce. Boiling kills any bacteria.)

3. Preheat a grill over high heat to 400°F to 425°F and grill the lamb skewers, turning and rotating as needed, until they are seared on all sides, about 5 minutes. Then move the skewers to the sides where the heat is lower and continue to grill until the lamb is tender, 20 to 25 minutes. Baste occasionally with the reserved marinade. During the last minute or so, baste with the finishing glaze and transfer to a serving platter lined with lemon and tomato wedges. Top with green chile peppers and serve.

Variation: Place the skewered pieces in a broiler tray and grill about 8 inches from the heating element, until charred all over. Then heat the oven to 450°F, cover the skewers with foil, and bake until the lamb is soft and tender, about 25 minutes.

Basic Chicken Tikka Kabaabs

Murgh Tikka

Makes 4 to 6 servings

Skinless, boneless pieces of tandoor-grilled chicken, flavored with one of the countless Indian marinades, are popular items on restaurant menus and are quite easy to enjoy at home, as well. Granted, we don't have a tandoor, but we do have grilling options, an oven, and, if all else fails, a saucepan.

1 recipe Tikka Marinade of your choice
   (pages 162 to 166)
2 pounds skinless boneless chicken breasts,
   cut into 1¹/₂-inch pieces
1 recipe Kabaab and Tikka Finishing Glaze
   (see box, page 149)
8 to 10 metal or bamboo skewers, soaked in water
   at least 30 minutes
2 cups shredded greens, such as romaine or
   green leaf lettuce
Lemon and tomato wedges
Scallions, thinly sliced
1 to 2 fresh green chile peppers, such as serrano,
   stemmed, seeded, and thinly sliced

1. Prepare the marinade. Then place the chicken in a large non-reactive bowl, add the marinade (saving about ¼ cup to use for basting as you grill), and mix well, making sure all the pieces are well-coated. Cover the bowl and marinate the chicken in the refrigerator, at least 6 and up to 24 hours. (To prevent potential salmonella contamination, never marinate poultry, meat, or seafood at room temperature.)

2. When ready to cook, prepare the finishing glaze and set aside. Then, thread the marinated pieces of chicken on skewers (4 to 5 pieces per skewer) and discard the used marinade. (If you prefer, immediately boil the marinade about 5 minutes and then use it as a sauce. Boiling kills any bacteria.)

3. Preheat a grill over medium-high heat to 375°F to 400°F and grill, turning and rotating the chicken until lightly charred on all sides and tender, about 20 minutes. Baste occasionally with the reserved marinade. During the last minute or so, baste with the finishing glaze. Transfer to a platter lined shredded greens. Garnish with lemon and tomato wedges, sliced scallions, and green chile peppers, and serve.

Variation: Place the skewered pieces in a broiler tray and grill about 8 inches from the heating element, until charred all over. Then heat the oven to 450°F, cover the skewers with foil, and bake until the chicken is soft and tender, about 25 minutes.

Basic Fish Tikka Kabaabs
Macchi Tikka

Makes 4 to 6 servings

Fish tikkas are very soft and delicate. They fall apart easily and should be handled with care at all times—before they are placed on the grill, while cooking, and after they are cooked.

1 recipe Tikka Marinade of your choice (pages 162 to 166)
1½ to 2 pounds firm white fish fillets, such as sea bass, halibut, or orange roughy, about ¾ to 1 inch thick, cut into 1½-inch pieces
8 to 10 metal or bamboo skewers, soaked in water at least 30 minutes
1 tablespoon melted butter
Salad greens, lime or lemon, and tomato wedges, scallion whites, thinly sliced
1 to 2 fresh green chile peppers, such as serrano, stemmed, seeded, and thinly sliced

1. Prepare the marinade. Then place the fish pieces in a large non-reactive bowl, add the marinade (saving about ¼ cup to use for basting as you grill), and mix well, making sure all the pieces are well-coated. Cover and marinate in the refrigerator, about 2 hours. (To prevent potential salmonella contamination, never marinate any poultry, meat, or seafood at room temperature.)

2. Thread fish pieces on skewers (4 to 5 pieces per skewer) and discard the used marinade. (If you absolutely must, immediately boil the marinade about 5 minutes and then use it in sauces. Boiling kills any bacteria.)

3. Preheat a grill over medium-high heat to 375°F to 400°F and grill, turning and rotating the skewers, until lightly charred and tender, about 10 minutes. Baste occasionally with the reserved marinade. During the last minute or so, baste with the melted butter. Transfer to a platter lined with salad greens. Garnish with fresh lime or lemon and tomato wedges, scallion whites, and green chile peppers. Serve.

Variation: Place the skewered pieces in a broiler tray and grill about 10 inches from the heating element, turning the skewers once or twice, until the pieces are flaky and lightly charred on all sides, about 10 minutes.

Turmeric Lamb
Tikka Marinade
Gosht Tikka—Haldi

Makes 4 to 6 servings

3 tablespoons Basic Ginger-Garlic Paste
(page 47 or store-bought)
3/4 cup nonfat plain yogurt, whisked until smooth
2 to 3 tablespoons fresh lime juice
2 teaspoons garam masala
1 teaspoon ground cumin
1 teaspoon salt, or to taste
1 tablespoon peanut oil
1 teaspoon ground turmeric
1/2 teaspoon cayenne pepper, or to taste

1. Prepare the ginger-garlic paste. In a large non-reactive bowl, mix together the yogurt, ginger-garlic paste, lime juice, garam masala, cumin, and salt.

2. Heat the oil in a small saucepan over medium-high heat and add the turmeric and cayenne pepper; they should sizzle upon contact with the hot oil. Quickly, before they burn, mix everything into the yogurt.

Rosemary Lamb
Tikka Marinade
Gosht Tikka—Rosemary

Makes 4 to 6 servings

2 to 3 tablespoons Basic Ginger-Garlic Paste
(page 47 or store-bought)
1/2 cup nonfat plain yogurt, whisked until smooth
2 tablespoons distilled white vinegar
1/2 cup coarsely chopped fresh cilantro,
including soft stems
1 tablespoon minced fresh rosemary leaves
1 teaspoon garam masala
1 teaspoon salt, or to taste
1 tablespoon peanut oil
1 teaspoon ground paprika
1/2 teaspoon cayenne pepper, or to taste

Grilling Marinades

Indians have a special set of flavors and marinades reserved for grilled foods, especially *tikka kabaabs*. Here, I offer some of my favorite marinades, from a seemingly limitless collection. Although most of the marinades in this book can be used interchangeably, I have arranged them by types of meats, so the strength of the marinade will be self-explanatory. If you wish to use the lamb marinade for poultry or fish, keep in mind that poultry and fish tend to be lighter and less intense, so you should use less of the marinade or simply decrease its potency, and vice versa.

For marinating time, lamb usually needs at least 24 hours, chicken at least 12 hours, and fish at least 2 hours.

Every recipe is enough to marinate about 2 pounds of *tikka kabaabs*.

1. Prepare the ginger-garlic paste. In a large non-reactive bowl, mix together the yogurt, ginger-garlic paste, vinegar, cilantro, rosemary, garam masala, and salt.

2. Heat the oil in a small saucepan over medium-high heat and add the paprika and cayenne pepper; they should sizzle upon contact with the hot oil. Quickly, before they burn, mix everything into the yogurt.

Fresh Green Chutney Lamb Tikka Marinade

Gosht Tikka—Hari Chutni

Makes 4 to 6 servings

This marinade has two steps: first marinate the lamb with the ginger-garlic paste, then mix in the remaining flavorings.

1/4 cup Basic Green Chutney (page 58)
3 tablespoons Basic Ginger-Garlic Paste
    (page 47 or store-bought)
1 teaspoon Chaat Masala (page 20 or store-bought)
3/4 teaspoon salt, or to taste
1 1/2 to 2 pounds boneless leg of lamb, all visible fat
    trimmed, cut into 1 1/2-inch pieces
1/2 cup nonfat plain yogurt, whisked until smooth
1 teaspoon garam masala
1 tablespoon peanut oil
1 teaspoon Asian sesame oil
1 teaspoon ground paprika

1. Prepare the chutney, ginger-garlic paste, and chaat masala. In a large non-reactive bowl, mix together the ginger-garlic paste, salt, and the lamb, and refrigerate about 2 hours.

2. Add the yogurt, green chutney, garam masala, and chaat masala to the lamb, and mix well. Then, heat both the oils in a small nonstick saucepan over medium-high heat, add the paprika, quickly pour into the bowl with the lamb, and mix well.

Royal Lamb Tikka Marinade

Gosht Tikka—Shahi

Makes 4 to 6 servings

Replete with cream, cheese, and ground nuts, this recipe lends some truly exotic tastes to the foods.

2 tablespoons Basic Cashew Paste (page 53)
2 tablespoons Almond and Poppy Seed Paste
    (page 52)
3 tablespoons Basic Ginger-Garlic Paste
    (page 47 or store-bought)
1 to 3 fresh green chile peppers, such as serrano,
    minced with seeds
1/4 cup heavy cream
1/4 cup grated Monterrey Jack cheese
2 tablespoons vegetable oil
2 tablespoons lemon juice
Green chile peppers, such as serrano,
    minced with seeds
1 tablespoon white poppy seeds
2 teaspoons ground black cumin seeds
1 teaspoon ground green cardamom seeds
1/2 teaspoon ground mace
1 teaspoon salt, or to taste
1 teaspoon freshly ground black pepper, or to taste

Prepare all the pastes, then mix all the ingredients together in a large bowl.

Garlic Chicken Tikka Marinade

Murgh Tikka—Lussan

Makes 4 to 6 servings

1 tablespoon Basic Garlic Paste (page 47 or store-bought)
3 to 4 tablespoons fresh lemon juice
1 tablespoon olive oil
1 tablespoon ground coriander
1 teaspoon ground cumin
1 teaspoon garam masala
1/2 teaspoon black freshly ground black pepper
1 teaspoon salt, or to taste
1/2 teaspoon ground green cardamom seeds

Prepare the garlic paste. Then, mix everything together, in a large, non-reactive bowl.

Citrus Chicken Tikka Marinade

Murgh Tikka—Phal-Rus

Makes 4 to 6 servings

Very fresh tasting and different from the standard Indian marinades, this marinade can easily double as a salad dressing. Make more than you need and reserve for another day.

3 to 4 tablespoons fresh lime juice
2 tablespoons frozen orange juice pulp
1 tablespoon olive oil
1/4 cup nonfat plain yogurt, whisked until smooth
2 tablespoons peeled minced fresh ginger
1 large clove fresh garlic, minced
1 1/2 teaspoons garam masala
1/2 teaspoon grounds cumin
1/2 teaspoon ground dried oregano
1/4 teaspoon cayenne pepper, or to taste
1 teaspoon salt, or to taste

Mix everything together in a large non-reactive bowl.

Mint Chicken Tikka Marinade

Murgh Tikka—Pudina

Makes 4 to 6 servings

1 medium onion, coarsely chopped
1 small green bell pepper, coarsely chopped
1 to 3 fresh green chile peppers, such as serrano, stemmed
3 large cloves fresh garlic, peeled
6 to 8 quarter-size slices peeled fresh ginger
1 cup lightly packed fresh mint leaves
1/2 cup nonfat plain yogurt
1 to 2 tablespoons fresh lime juice
1 teaspoon garam masala
1 teaspoon salt, or to taste

1. In a food processor or blender, process together the onion, bell pepper, green chile peppers, garlic, ginger, and mint until minced.

2. Add the yogurt, lime juice, garam masala, and salt, and process again until smooth. Transfer to a large non-reactive bowl to marinate.

Chile Chicken Tikka Marinade

Murgh Tikka—Laal Mirchi

Makes 4 to 6 servings

1 tablespoon peanut oil
4 to 6 dried red chile peppers, such as chile de arbol, broken
1/2 teaspoon black peppercorns
6 to 8 quarter-size slices peeled fresh ginger
2 large cloves fresh garlic, peeled
1 cup coarsely chopped fresh cilantro, including soft stems
2 tablespoons distilled white vinegar
1 teaspoon salt, or to taste

1. Heat the oil in a small nonstick saucepan over medium-high heat and cook the red chile peppers, peppercorns, ginger, and garlic, stirring until golden, about 1 minute.

2. Transfer to a small food processor or a blender, mix in the cilantro, vinegar, and salt, and process until smooth.

Creamy Chicken Tikka Marinade
Murgh Tikka—Malai

Makes 4 to 6 servings

Malai is clotted cream. Since it is not readily available, I use heavy cream instead. No matter what you use, the end result is a marinade that yields pale-white, smooth and delicate tikka kabaabs.

2 tablespoons Hyderabadi Ginger-Garlic Paste
    (page 48)
1 teaspoon freshly ground white pepper
1 teaspoon salt, or to taste
1/4 cup heavy cream
1/4 cup grated pepper-Jack cheese
1 large egg (or 2 egg whites), lightly beaten
2 fresh green chile peppers, such as serrano,
    coarsely chopped
1 tablespoon cornstarch
1/8 teaspoon ground mace
1/8 teaspoon ground nutmeg

1. Prepare the ginger-garlic paste. In a large non-reactive bowl, combine the paste, white pepper, and salt, rub the chicken pieces with this mixture, and set aside 30 to 40 minutes.

2. In a blender, blend together the cream, cheese, egg, chile peppers, cornstarch, mace, and nutmeg, and blend until smooth. Add to the chicken and mix well.

Silky Chicken Tikka Marinade
Murgh Tikka—Raeshmi

Makes 4 to 6 servings

Raesham, the Hindi word for silk, is the perfect adjective for the soft-cooked chicken pieces in this dish, characterized by a lovely smoothness, thanks to the cream and egg whites in this marinade.

1/2 cup coarsely chopped cashew nuts or
    blanched almonds
3 scallions, white parts only, coarsely chopped
2 fresh green serrano or jalapeño peppers
4 large cloves garlic, peeled
6 to 8 quarter-size slices peeled fresh ginger
3 tablespoons fresh lime or lemon juice
1 tablespoon heavy cream
1 large egg, white only
1 teaspoon garam masala
1/2 teaspoon finely ground green cardamom seeds
1 teaspoon salt, or to taste

1. Soak the cashews (or almonds) in water to cover about 1 hour. Drain. In a blender or a small food processor, process together the cashews, scallions, peppers, garlic, and ginger until minced.

2. Add the lime juice, cream, egg white, garam masala, cardamom seeds, and salt, and process until smooth.

Grilled Fish Tikka Marinade

Macchi Tikka—Tandoori

Makes 4 to 6 servings

This is a standard tandoori marinade, except it comes with the addition of ajwain seeds, which, in India, are almost always added to fish dishes. Use this marinade with lighter and more delicate fish like halibut, sea bass, and grouper. It is also lovely with shrimp and lobster meat.

3 tablespoons Basic Ginger-Garlic Paste (page 47 or store-bought)
1/4 cup nonfat plain yogurt, whisked until smooth
2 to 3 tablespoons fresh lemon juice or distilled white vinegar
2 teaspoons garam masala
2 teaspoons ground cumin
1 teaspoon cayenne pepper, or to taste
1 teaspoon salt, or to taste
1/2 teaspoon coarsely ground ajwain seeds
1/4 teaspoon ground turmeric

Prepare the ginger-garlic paste. Mix all the ingredients well in a large non-reactive bowl.

Sesame Fish Tikka Marinade

Macchi Tikkae—Til

Makes 4 to 6 servings

Use this full-bodied marinade with the stronger and more robust fish, like salmon, tuna, and mahi-mahi.

1 teaspoon Chaat Masala (page 20 or store-bought)
1 teaspoon sesame seeds, dry-roasted (page 35)
2 tablespoons Basic Ginger-Garlic Paste (page 47 or store-bought)
2 tablespoons Tamarind Paste (page 54)
1/4 cup nonfat plain yogurt, whisked until smooth
1/2 teaspoon Asian sesame oil
2 teaspoons garam masala
1 teaspoon salt, or to taste
1/2 teaspoon cayenne pepper, or to taste
1/4 teaspoon ground asafoetida

1. Prepare the chaat masala, sesame seeds, ginger-garlic paste, and the tamarind paste.

2. In a large non-reactive bowl, mix together all the ingredients, except the chaat masala and sesame seeds. Sprinkle the chaat masala and sesame seeds as a garnish, just before serving.

Variation: Try this recipe adding Indian Grilling Masala (page 25) instead of garam masala.

Soups

Basic Broths 169

Vegetarian Broth

Spicy Chicken Broth

Spicy Lamb Broth

Tomato Soups 171

Creamy Tomato Soup

Tomato Soup
with Fresh Curry Leaves

Tomato Soup
with Sautéed Vegetables

Tomato Soup
with Yellow Mung Beans

South Indian Soups (Rasam) 173

Traditional South Indian
Split Pigeon Pea Soup

Classic South Indian Ginger Soup

South Indian Tamarind Soup

South Indian Lemon Soup
with Mung Beans

South Indian Buttermilk Soup

Mysore Coconut Soup

Chunky South Indian Tomato Soup

Spicy South Indian
Vegetable Soup with Tamarind

Mulligatawny Soup

Bean and Lentil Soups 180

Yellow Mung Bean and Spinach
Soup with Sizzling Cumin Oil

Quick Sindhi Split Pigeon Pea Soup
with Tamarind

Quick Lentil, Barley,
and Vegetable Soup

Fast Black Bean Soup, Indian Style

Chilled Chickpea Soup

Chickpea Soup with Chicken Broth

Quick Black Chickpea Soup
with Cumin Seeds

Vegetable Soups 185

Goan Caldo-Verde Soup
with Cauliflower

Cabbage Soup with Vegetables

Quick Puréed Root Vegetable Soup

Chilled Potato Soup

Carrot-Ginger Soup

Curried Green Pea Soup

Puréed Pumpkin Soup

Puréed Spinach Soup

Yogurt Soups 189

Fragrant Yogurt Soup

Creamy Almond–Poppy Seed Soup

Yogurt Soup
with Flame-Roasted Eggplant

Puréed Mushroom Soup
with Yogurt

Spinach Yogurt Soup

Vegetable Soup
with Yogurt and Coconut

Chilled Roasted Vegetable Soup

Fish and Chicken Soups 193

Goan Shrimp Soup

Spicy Shrimp Soup
with Coconut Milk and Tomato

Chicken Soup
with Ginger and Coconut Milk

Cashew Corn Soup
in Chicken Broth

Chicken Soup with Cream-Style
Corn and Green Chile Peppers

Chicken Soup
with Chayote Squash

 = Vegan = Pressure-Cooker Quick

My first week in America 30 years ago, brought me the surprising sight at my local supermarket of rows of colorful cans featuring pictures of steaming soup. Until just a week before, I had known only homemade soups, prepared from scratch just moments before they were served.

Of course, in years to come, with two American-born and -raised children—whose lives were filled with school and camping activities—I came to realize the convenience of canned soup. But to me, soup is best when it's the result of imagining a blending of flavors, buying fresh seasonal vegetables and other ingredients (or making use of leftover refrigerated produce), combining them and spicing them the way my taste buds direct me that day. Serving and eating canned soup just doesn't give me the same satisfaction.

Soups, in fact, are one of the easiest things to make, because once you put all the ingredients in the pot, they pretty much cook themselves. They showcase the cook's skill in preparing comforting foods, are easy to make for company, and are generally filling. Because Indian soups are often vegetable-based, they can be ideal foods for health-conscious people, who can first fill up on healthful soup and then easily eat less of the meats, breads, and fried foods featured as main courses.

Most of my soup recipes are vegetarian, as is representative of Indian cuisine. Meat broths are just not common in India. You could, for flavoring, substitute all or part of the water in a soup with a meat or chicken broth—just make sure the quantity of liquid remains the same.

Indian soups are generally served steaming hot. Chilled soups, though not an age-old concept, are gaining popularity in the urban areas, so I've included a few.

Basic Broths

Vegetarian Broth
Akhni

Makes about 3 cups

Made by simmering together some of India's most popular seasonings and aromatics, this basic broth has an intense concentration of intoxicating flavors. Add it to soups, dals *(legume dishes), rice* pullaos *(pilafs), and curries.*

1 tablespoon vegetable oil
3 dried red chile peppers, such as chile de arbol, broken into pieces
1 teaspoon cumin seeds
1 teaspoon black peppercorns
2 large cloves fresh garlic, chopped
4 quarter-size slices peeled fresh ginger
4 black cardamom pods, crushed lightly to break the skin
5 green cardamom pods, crushed lightly to break the skin
1 (1-inch) stick cinnamon
10 whole cloves
1 teaspoon fennel seeds
1/4 teaspoon ajwain seeds
1 large onion, chopped
1 green bell pepper, chopped
5 cups water

1. Heat the oil in a large saucepan over medium-high heat and cook the red chile peppers, cumin and black peppercorns, stirring, about 30 seconds. Then add the garlic, ginger, black and green cardamom pods, cinnamon, cloves, fennel, and ajwain seeds, and stir about 1 minute.

2. Add the onion and bell pepper, reduce the heat to medium, cover the pan and cook until softened, about 5 minutes.

3. Add the water and bring to a boil over high heat. Reduce the heat to medium-low, cover the pan, and simmer until the broth is reduced by about half,

about 1 hour. Simmer longer for a more concentrated broth.

4. Strain and discard the spices. Or pass everything through a food mill to obtain a stronger essence of flavors.

Variation: In step 1, along with all of the above, mix in about 1/2 cup each of any one or all of the following: fresh mint, cilantro stems, lemon leaves or lemongrass, fresh fenugreek leaves. Then add an extra cup of water in Step 3.

Spicy Chicken Broth
Murgh Yakhni

Makes about 3 cups

This delicately flavored broth is an almost clear soup that mothers serve when someone is under the weather. If you wish, use it cup for cup in any of the tomato soups or in rice pullaos, *in place of the water called for in the recipe.*

1 (2 1/2- to 3-pound) chicken, skin removed
5 to 6 cups water
3 large cloves fresh garlic, peeled
8 quarter-size slices peeled fresh ginger
8 to 10 fresh lemon or lime leaves or 1 tablespoon of fresh lemon or lime juice
3 (2-inch) sticks cinnamon, broken in pieces
10 cloves, crushed lightly
4 black cardamom pods, crushed lightly to break the skin
6 green cardamom pods, crushed lightly to break the skin
2 bay leaves
1 teaspoon black peppercorns, crushed lightly
1 teaspoon salt, or to taste

1. Rinse and place the whole chicken in a large saucepan. Add the water and all the remaining ingredients and bring to a boil over high heat. Reduce the heat to medium-low, cover the pan and simmer until the meat is very tender, about 45 minutes.

2. With large tongs or a large slotted spoon, transfer the chicken to a bowl. When cool enough to handle, separate the meat from the bones and reserve meat for another recipe. Return the bones to the pan and continue to simmer until the broth is reduced by at least half, about 1 hour. Simmer longer for a more concentrated broth.

3. Let cool. Then secure a piece of muslin or 4 layers of cheesecloth over a large bowl and pour the broth through to collect a clear broth. Discard the muslin or cheesecloth and chill the broth in the refrigerator, at least 2 hours. With a spoon, remove and discard the layer of fat that solidifies on the top. Reheat to serve as a soup or use as a flavored broth in other recipes.

Spicy Lamb Broth
Gosht Yakhni

Makes about 3 cups

True yakhni *is made with lamb's trotters (foot bones, called* paayae*) that are cut into 2-inch pieces and then boiled and slow-simmered with herbs and aromatics. An easier way is to use bone-in lamb pieces.*

A common practice in India, and one often followed by Indians in America, is to first boil the meat in generous amounts of water, then drain and discard the water and wash the meat in fresh water to get rid of the frothy scum that surfaces and any gamey smell usually associated with lamb. The lamb is then boiled once again to make the actual yakhni.

This broth is strong. Enjoy it as a thin soup with a side of salad and garlic bread, use it as a flavor boost in pullaos *(pilafs) and curries, or mix some into any of the vegetable or lentil soups, cup for cup, in place of water, for added protein and flavor.*

2 pounds leg of lamb with bone, all visible fat trimmed
1 large onion, finely chopped
2 small carrots, finely chopped
2 small turnips, finely chopped
1 green bell pepper, finely chopped
3 large cloves fresh garlic, peeled
8 quarter-size slices peeled fresh ginger
1 to 3 fresh green chile peppers, such as serrano, chopped
8 to 10 fresh lemon or lime leaves or 2 lemongrass stalks (bottom 4 inches only), sliced (optional)
1 cup coarsely chopped fresh cilantro, including soft stems
3 (2-inch) sticks cinnamon, broken
10 cloves, crushed lightly
4 black cardamom pods, crushed lightly to break the skin
2 bay leaves
2 tablespoons coriander seeds
1 teaspoon black peppercorns, crushed lightly with the back of a spoon to break
1 teaspoon salt, or to taste
6 to 7 cups water

1. Rinse the lamb and place it in a large saucepan. Cover generously with water and boil over high heat about 3 minutes. Drain and discard the water and wash the meat in cold water. Then, separate the bones from the meat, then cut the meat with a sharp knife into 1-inch pieces.

2. Place the meat and the bones, along with all the remaining ingredients, in a large saucepan and bring to a boil over high heat. Reduce the heat to medium-low, cover the pan and simmer until the meat is very tender, about 1 hour.

3. Remove the meat pieces and reserve for another recipe. Keep the bones in the pan and continue to simmer until the broth is reduced by at least half, about 1 hour. Simmer longer for a more concentrated broth.

4. Let cool. Secure a piece of muslin or 4 layers of cheesecloth around a large bowl and pour the broth through the cloth into the bowl. Discard the cloth. Chill the clear broth in the refrigerator, at least 2 hours. With a spoon, remove and discard the layer of fat that solidifies on the top. Reheat to serve.

Tomato Soups

Creamy Tomato Soup
Tamatar ka Soop

Makes 6 to 8 servings

Smooth, rich, and comforting, this is the soup I associate with cold New Delhi winters. With potato cutlets or slices of grilled bread on the side, we used to pretend we were eating a very "European" meal.

1 teaspoon cumin seeds, dry-roasted and coarsely ground (Dry-Roasting Spices, page 35)
1 small red onion, coarsely chopped
2 quarter-size slices peeled fresh ginger
1 medium carrot, unpeeled, coarsely chopped
1 small russet (or any) potato, unpeeled, coarsely chopped
1 tablespoon vegetable oil
1 1/2 pounds ripe tomatoes, coarsely chopped
4 cups water
1 teaspoon salt
1 teaspoon sugar
1 tablespoon cornstarch
1 cup milk, any kind
1/4 teaspoon nutmeg (freshly grated preferred)
1/2 cup plain whole-milk or low-fat yogurt, whisked until smooth
2 tablespoons finely chopped fresh cilantro
Freshly ground black pepper, to taste

1. Prepare the cumin seeds. Then, place the onion and ginger in a food processor and pulse until minced. Transfer to a bowl. Then add the carrot and potato and pulse until minced. Transfer to another bowl. Add the tomatoes and pulse until coarsely chopped. Leave in the food processor.

2. Heat the oil in a large nonstick saucepan over medium heat and cook the onion and ginger, stirring, until translucent, about 1 minute. Add the minced carrot and potato and cook, stirring, 1 minute. Mix in the tomatoes, increase the heat to high and cook, stirring, 2 to 3 minutes. Add the water, salt, and

sugar, cover the pan and bring to a boil. Reduce the heat to medium and cook about 15 minutes.

3. Let cool, then if desired, pass the soup through a food mill or a fine-mesh strainer into a heatproof bowl. (If you prefer a chunky soup, do not strain.) Return to the pan and boil once again.

4. Dissolve the cornstarch in the milk and stir it into the boiling soup. Season with the cumin and nutmeg. Transfer to a serving bowl, swirl in the yogurt, garnish with the cilantro and black pepper, and serve.

Tomato Soup with Fresh Curry Leaves
Kari Pattae vaala Tamatar ka Soop

Makes 6 to 8 servings

Indians are big on tomato soups, making them with every flavor imaginable. When juicy, delicious, vine-ripened tomatoes are available, they may well be the only main ingredient. Other times, selected vegetables are added to give the soup more body, as I do in this recipe. Look for curry leaves and ground asafoetida in Indian markets or specialty food stores.

1 teaspoon vegetable oil
15 to 20 fresh curry leaves
4 to 5 quarter-size slices peeled fresh ginger
1 small onion, coarsely chopped
1/8 teaspoon ground asafoetida
1 to 3 fresh green chile peppers, such as serrano, coarsely chopped
1 1/2 pounds ripe tomatoes, coarsely chopped
2 small carrots, unpeeled, coarsely chopped
1 large round white (or any kind) potato, unpeeled, coarsely chopped
1 cup coarsely chopped fresh cilantro, including soft stems
1/2 cup coarsely chopped broccoli or cauliflower stems (optional)
3 to 5 cups water
1 teaspoon salt, or to taste
Freshly ground black pepper, to taste
1 tablespoon heavy or light cream

1. Heat the oil in a large saucepan over medium-high heat and cook the curry leaves, ginger, and onion, stirring until golden, 1 to 2 minutes.

2. Stir in first the asafoetida and then all the vegetables and 3 cups water, and bring to a boil over high heat. Reduce the heat to medium-low, cover the pan, and simmer until the vegetables are very soft, about 30 minutes.

3. Let cool off the heat, then pass the soup through a food mill or blend in a blender until smooth. If using a blender, pour through a fine-mesh strainer into a bowl, if you prefer a smoother consistency.

4. Return the soup to the saucepan, add the salt and black pepper and more water as necessary for the consistency you like. Boil over high heat about 2 minutes, or longer if you wish. Transfer to a serving bowl, swirl in the cream and serve. Or present in cups, with each cup of soup topped with a few drops of cream.

Tomato Soup with Sautéed Vegetables
Sabziyon vaala Tamatar ka Soop

Makes 6 to 8 servings

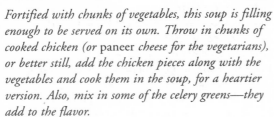

Fortified with chunks of vegetables, this soup is filling enough to be served on its own. Throw in chunks of cooked chicken (or paneer *cheese for the vegetarians), or better still, add the chicken pieces along with the vegetables and cook them in the soup, for a heartier version. Also, mix in some of the celery greens—they add to the flavor.*

1 tablespoon olive oil
1 bay leaf
2 teaspoons cumin seeds
3 to 4 leeks, white parts only, cleaned and chopped
1 large clove fresh garlic, minced
1 tablespoon peeled minced fresh ginger
1 cup finely chopped celery stems
1 tablespoon ground coriander
¹/₂ teaspoon ground paprika

3 cups mixed fresh or frozen vegetables, cut into ³/₄-inch or smaller pieces, such as green beans, carrots, mixed bell peppers, broccoli, potatoes, peas
1¹/₂ pounds ripe tomatoes, coarsely chopped
1 cup coarsely chopped fresh cilantro, including soft stems + more for garnish
1 teaspoon salt, or to taste
1 teaspoon freshly ground black pepper, or to taste
2 to 3 cups water

1. Heat the oil in a large nonstick pan over medium-high heat. Add the bay leaf and cumin seeds; they should sizzle upon contact with the hot oil. Quickly add the leeks and cook, stirring, until they start to turn golden, 3 to 4 minutes.

2. Add the garlic, ginger, and celery, and cook, stirring, about 2 minutes, then mix in the coriander and paprika. Add the vegetables and cook, stirring, until crisp-tender, 7 to 10 minutes. Transfer to a bowl.

3. In a food processor or a blender, process together the tomatoes and cilantro to make a fine purée and transfer to the pan in which the vegetables were cooked. Mix in the salt and black pepper and bring to a boil over high heat. Reduce the heat to medium-low, add the water, cover the pan, and simmer about 10 minutes.

4. Mix in the reserved vegetables and bring to a rolling boil, then simmer about 5 more minutes, or a little longer if you prefer your vegetables to be soft. Transfer to a serving bowl, garnish with cilantro, and serve.

Tomato Soup with Yellow Mung Beans
Dhulli Moong aur Tamatar ka Soop

Makes 4 to 6 servings

This is the standard home tomato soup that my mother fed the family at least three times a week. It can be made with many types of dal *(legumes), but my mom and I use yellow mung beans because they take about the same time as the tomatoes to cook and give the soup a flavor and protein boost.*

Yellow mung beans come in clear, 1- or 2-pound packages (larger in Indian markets) and are available in the Asian section of most supermarkets, as well as in most ethnic markets.

1¹/₂ pounds vine-ripened tomatoes, coarsely chopped
1 small russet (or any) potato, unpeeled,
    coarsely chopped
1 small onion, quartered
2 small carrots, coarsely chopped
12 to 15 green beans, ends removed,
    coarsely chopped
¹/₂ cup dried split yellow mung bean (dhulli mung dal),
    sorted and washed in 3 to 4 changes of water
4 to 5 quarter-size slices peeled fresh ginger
1 large clove garlic, peeled
¹/₂ cup coarsely chopped fresh cilantro,
    including soft stems
4 to 6 cups water
1 teaspoon salt, or to taste
1 teaspoon freshly ground black pepper, or to taste
1 tablespoon peanut oil
1 tablespoon coriander seeds, coarsely ground
1 teaspoon cumin seeds, coarsely ground
Minced scallions, green parts only, or chives

1. Place everything except the oil, coriander and cumin seeds, and scallion greens in a large saucepan and bring to a boil over high heat. Reduce the heat to medium-low and cook, uncovered, until the dal and the green beans are tender, about 35 minutes.

2. Let cool, then pour contents into a blender and blend until smooth. If you prefer a smoother texture, pass soup through a food mill or a fine-mesh strainer into a bowl.

3. Return the soup to the pan and bring to a boil over high heat, adding more water if you prefer a thinner soup. Reduce the heat to medium-low, cover the pan and simmer 7 to 10 minutes to blend the flavors. Transfer to a serving bowl, cover and keep warm.

4. Heat the oil in a small saucepan over medium-high heat and add the coriander and cumin seeds; they should sizzle upon contact with the hot oil. Quickly transfer them to the soup and stir lightly. Garnish with scallion greens and serve.

South Indian Soups (Rasam)

Traditional South Indian Split Pigeon Pea Soup
Toor Dal Rasam

Makes 4 to 6 servings

Toor dal, also called split pigeon peas or red gram, are yellow-gold split discs similar to yellow split peas. This dal *(legume) is popular all over India, but especially in the southern parts and along the west coast, where it is a pantry staple. In the United States, it is found in Indian markets.*

Enjoy this thick soup as a first course or serve it with steamed white rice. For a simpler version, add about 2 tablespoons rasam *powder (South Indian Soup Powder, page 29) and some tamarind paste to cooked* dal.

¹/₄ cup dried split pigeon peas (toor dal),
    sorted and washed in 3 to 4 changes of water
3 tablespoons Tamarind Paste (page 54 or
    store-bought)
5 to 6 cups water
1 tablespoon minced peeled fresh ginger
1 fresh green chile pepper, such as serrano,
    minced with seeds
¹/₄ teaspoon ground turmeric
¹/₂ teaspoon salt, or to taste
1 large tomato, finely chopped
¹/₈ teaspoon ground asafoetida
2 teaspoons peanut oil or melted ghee
2 whole dried red chile peppers,
    such as chile de arbol
1 teaspoon black mustard seeds
¹/₂ teaspoon cumin seeds
1 tablespoon minced fresh curry leaves
¹/₄ cup finely chopped fresh cilantro,
    including soft stems

1. Soak the dal in 1 cup water until it absorbs the water and softens slightly, about 30 minutes. Meanwhile, prepare the tamarind paste. Then, transfer the dal to a medium saucepan, add the ginger, green chile pepper, turmeric, salt and another cup of water, and bring to a boil over high heat. Reduce the heat to medium-low and simmer, watching carefully and stirring, until the dal is very soft, about 30 minutes.

2. In another saucepan, mix together the tomatoes, tamarind, asafoetida, and the remaining water and bring to a boil over high heat. Reduce the heat to medium-low, cover the pan and simmer until the tomatoes are soft, about 5 minutes. Add the cooked dal mixture, adding more water if you prefer a thinner soup, and bring to a boil once again. Transfer to a serving bowl.

3. Heat the oil (or ghee) in a small saucepan over medium-high heat and add the red chile peppers and the mustard and cumin seeds; they should splutter upon contact with the hot oil, so cover the pan until the spluttering subsides. Add the curry leaves and cilantro and stir 1 minute. Transfer to the soup. Mix well and serve.

Classic South Indian Ginger Soup
Adrak (Inji) Rasam

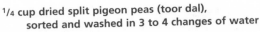

Makes 4 to 6 servings

With no tamarind or lemon juice, this rasam *has the pure intensity of ginger as its main flavor. This version is particularly popular to settle an upset stomach. Mix in about 1 tablespoon of jaggery (*gur*) or brown sugar, if you wish.*

Serve alone as a soup with Spicy Lentil Wafers (page 95) or during a meal with steamed white rice and a bowl of Tomato and Cucumber Pachadi with Asafoetida (page 240).

¹/₄ cup dried split pigeon peas (toor dal),
    sorted and washed in 3 to 4 changes of water
1 teaspoon cumin seeds
1 teaspoon black peppercorns
1 to 3 fresh green chile peppers, such as serrano,
    stemmed
5 quarter-size slices peeled fresh ginger
4 to 5 cups water
¹/₂ teaspoon salt, or to taste
1 teaspoon peanut oil or melted ghee
1 teaspoon mustard seeds
¹/₄ teaspoon ground asafoetida
1 whole dried red chile pepper, such as chile de arbol
5 to 6 fresh green curry leaves
¹/₄ cup finely chopped fresh cilantro,
    including soft stems

1. Soak the dal 30 minutes in ¹/₂ cup water. Then, in a blender, grind together the dal and water, cumin seeds, black peppercorns, green chile peppers, and ginger to make as smooth a paste as possible.

2. Transfer to a medium saucepan. Mix in the water and salt and bring to a boil over high heat. Reduce the heat to medium-low and simmer, about 5 minutes. Transfer to a bowl, cover, and keep warm.

3. Heat the oil (or ghee) in a small saucepan over medium-high heat and add the mustard seeds; they should splutter upon contact with the hot oil, so cover the pan and lower the heat until the spluttering subsides. Quickly add the asafoetida, red chile pepper, and curry leaves. Stir about 30 seconds and mix well into the soup. Garnish with the cilantro and serve.

South Indian Tamarind Soup
Dakshini Imli (Puli) Rasam

Makes 4 to 6 servings

The simplest of its kind, this rasam *is made with fresh tamarind extract and a generous helping of pre-mixed spicy* rasam *powder, and balanced with a tiny amount of jaggery (*gur*).*

Tamarind pulp, with or without seeds, comes cellophane-wrapped, in 7- to 8-ounce packages, and dried split chickpeas (channa dal) come in clear, 1- or 2-pound packages, or larger in Indian markets. Both are available in Indian and Asian markets.

$1/3$ cup seedless tamarind pulp

4 to 5 cups water

2 tablespoons dried split chickpeas (channa dal), sorted and washed in 3 to 4 changes of water

2 to 3 tablespoons South Indian Soup Powder (Rasam Podi), page 29 or store-bought

1 tablespoon peanut oil or melted ghee

3 whole dried red chile peppers, such as chile de arbol

$1/2$ teaspoon black mustard seeds

$1/2$ teaspoon cumin seeds

1 tablespoon minced fresh curry leaves

$1/8$ teaspoon ground asafoetida

$1/4$ teaspoon ground turmeric

1 teaspoon salt, or to taste

1 tablespoon grated jaggery (gur), or brown sugar

1. Soak the tamarind in 1 cup water about 2 hours. Mash with clean fingers or a wooden spoon and pass through a fine-mesh strainer into a bowl to extract the pulp. Add another ½ cup water to the leftover pulp, mash and pass through the strainer again to extract more pulp. Discard the residue.

2. Soak the dal in about ½ cup water about 30 minutes, then drain. Meanwhile, prepare the soup powder.

3. Heat the oil (or ghee) in a large saucepan and add the red chile peppers, mustard and cumin seeds; they should splutter upon contact with the hot oil, so lower the heat and cover the pan until the spluttering subsides. Mix in the soaked dal and curry leaves and cook, stirring, about 3 minutes. Then add the asafoetida, turmeric, and salt, and stir about 30 seconds.

4. Mix in the tamarind extract, jaggery, soup powder, and the remaining water, and bring to a boil over high heat. Reduce the heat to medium-low, cover the pan and simmer until the dal is soft, about 15 minutes. Taste, adjust the seasonings, and serve.

Rasams

Rasams are tangy, highly spiced, thin and watery south Indian *dal* (legume) soups. Ranging in taste from mild to fiery hot, *rasams* are almost a year-round staple in most southern homes. Served piping hot and with all their bold flavors, *rasams* are considered potent antidotes for congestion, fevers, colds, and a gamut of similar ailments (perfect for cold-weather months in the United States). Paradoxically, *rasams* are also popular in the summer (and it gets pretty hot in southern India), because they cause the body to sweat and eventually cool down.

Rasam soups are served with other foods, rather than as a first course. The chunkier *rasams* are traditionally eaten over steamed rice and the watery ones are drunk. Often, *rasams* are served as a snack with *iddli* (Steamed Fermented Rice Cakes, page 133) or *vadai* (Deep-Fried Fermented Lentil Croquettes, page 128) floated in the soup.

With all these possibilities, it really speeds preparation if you keep a supply of *rasam* powder in your pantry. You can make the blend at home, as explained on page 29, or buy it from an Indian market. The store-bought *rasam* powder is always very spicy hot, so exercise caution when using it.

South Indian Lemon Soup with Mung Beans

Dakshini Nimboo aur Mung Dal Rasam

Makes 4 to 6 servings

Made with easy-to-cook split yellow mung beans and lemon juice instead of tamarind, this rasam offers a more delicate and a lighter flavor. For variation, purée 1 large tomato with the ginger and green chile peppers in Step 3.

Try it over steamed white rice or serve it with Long-Grain Rice with Roasted Peanuts (page 540) and a bowl of plain yogurt.

¹/₂ cup dried split yellow mung beans (dhulli mung dal), sorted and washed in 3 to 4 changes of water
6 cups water
¹/₄ teaspoon ground turmeric
¹/₂ teaspoon salt, or to taste
4 quarter-size slices peeled fresh ginger
1 to 3 fresh green chile peppers, such as serrano, stemmed
2 teaspoons peanut oil or melted ghee
2 whole dried red chile peppers, such as chile de arbol
¹/₂ teaspoon black mustard seeds
¹/₂ teaspoon cumin seeds
¹/₂ teaspoon freshly ground black pepper, or to taste
¹/₈ teaspoon ground asafoetida
6 to 10 fresh curry leaves
1 to 2 tablespoons fresh lemon juice
¹/₂ cup finely chopped fresh cilantro, including soft stems

1. Soak the dal in 1 cup water until it absorbs the water and softens slightly, about 30 minutes. Then transfer to a large saucepan, add the turmeric, salt, and 2 cups water and bring to a boil over high heat. Reduce the heat to medium-low and simmer, watching carefully and stirring, until the dal is very soft, 20 to 30 minutes.

2. With a hand-held beater or immersion blender, whip the dal in the pan, or stir it vigorously to make it as smooth as possible.

3. In a blender, blend together the ginger and green chile peppers, adding some water until smooth, about 30 seconds. Transfer to the dal and add more water to make about 4 cups of soup. Bring to a boil over high heat. Reduce the heat to medium-low, cover the pan, and simmer about 5 minutes.

4. Heat the oil (or ghee) in a small saucepan over medium-high heat and add the red chile peppers, and mustard and cumin seeds; they should splutter upon contact with the hot oil, so cover the pan and reduce the heat until the spluttering subsides. Add the black pepper, asafoetida, and curry leaves, stir about 30 seconds, and mix well into the dal. Add the lemon juice and cilantro, bring to a boil once again, and serve.

South Indian Buttermilk Soup

Dakshini Lussi (Mor) Rasam

Makes 4 to 6 servings

Pale in color thanks to the buttermilk, this is a popular creamy rasam variation. To prevent the soup from curdling, add the buttermilk slowly and keep stirring until it comes to a rapid boil. Serve the soup with steamed white rice and a side of Spicy South Indian Potatoes (page 252).

1 tablespoon peanut oil or melted ghee
2 to 3 whole dried red chile peppers, such as chile de arbol
1 tablespoon dried yellow split chickpeas (channa dal), sorted and washed in 3 to 4 changes of water
1 tablespoon coriander
¹/₂ teaspoon fenugreek seeds
¹/₂ teaspoon black peppercorns
¹/₈ teaspoon ground asafoetida
¹/₄ cup dried split pigeon peas (toor dal), sorted and washed in 3 to 4 changes of water
3 to 4 cups water
1 large tomato, coarsely chopped
¹/₂ teaspoon salt, or to taste
¹/₂ cup finely chopped fresh cilantro, including soft stems

1 teaspoon mustard seeds
1 teaspoon cumin seeds
5 to 6 fresh green curry leaves
1¹/₂ cups buttermilk
3 to 4 scallions, green parts only, finely chopped

1. In a small saucepan, heat 2 teaspoons oil (or ghee) over medium heat, add the whole red chile peppers and stir until golden, about 30 seconds, then add the channa dal, coriander, fenugreek, peppercorns, and asafoetida, and cook, stirring, until the channa dal is golden, about 1 minute. Let cool, then transfer to a blender and blend, adding about ¼ cup water to make a smooth paste.

2. In a medium saucepan, add toor dal, 3 cups water, tomato, and salt. Bring to a boil over high heat. Reduce the heat to medium-low, cover the pan, and simmer until the toor dal is soft, about 30 minutes. Mix in the cilantro and the spice paste and simmer until another 5 minutes to blend the flavors.

3. In a small saucepan, heat the remaining 1 teaspoon of the ghee over medium heat and add the mustard and cumin seeds and the curry leaves; they should splutter upon contact with the hot oil, so cover the pan and reduce the heat until the spluttering subsides. Add the spiced oil to the soup. Then add the buttermilk and scallions and stir well to mix. Serve.

Mysore Coconut Soup
Mysore Nariyal (Thengu) Rasam

Makes 4 to 6 servings

Thicker than most other rasam soups, this lovely variation comes from Mysore, a city in the southern Indian state of Karnatka. In addition to rich flavor from coconut milk, this soup also has a little crunch from the grated coconut. Fresh or frozen coconut (found in Indian markets) works best here. Dried coconut can substitute, but some flavor will be lost.

1 cup dried split pigeon peas (toor dal),
      sorted and washed in 3 to 4 changes of water
5 to 6 cups water
¼ teaspoon ground turmeric
¹/₂ teaspoon salt, or to taste
¼ cup Tamarind Paste (page 54 or store-bought)
¹/₂ cup fresh or canned Coconut Milk
      (page 44 or store-bought)
1 tablespoon peanut oil or melted ghee
2 whole dried red chile peppers, such as chile de arbol
1 teaspoon black mustard seeds
1 teaspoon cumin seeds
¹/₂ teaspoon coarsely ground black pepper, or to taste
¼ teaspoon ground asafoetida
6 to 10 fresh curry leaves
2 tablespoons fresh or frozen grated coconut
1 large tomato, finely chopped
¹/₂ cup finely chopped fresh cilantro, including soft stems

1. Soak the dal in 2 cups water until it absorbs the water and softens slightly, about 30 minutes. Then transfer to a large saucepan, add the turmeric, salt and another cup of water and bring to a boil over high heat. Reduce the heat to medium-low and simmer, watching carefully and stirring, until the dal is very soft, about 30 minutes. Meanwhile, prepare the tamarind paste and coconut milk.

2. When soft, whip the dal in the saucepan with a hand-held beater or immersion blender, or stir it vigorously to make it as smooth as possible.

3. Heat the oil (or ghee) in a large saucepan over medium-high heat and add the mustard and cumin seeds; they should splutter upon contact with the hot oil, so cover the pan and reduce the heat until the spluttering subsides. Add the black pepper, asafoetida, curry leaves, and grated coconut, and stir about 1 minute. Add the tomato and cook, stirring, another 2 minutes.

4. Mix in the tamarind paste and the remaining water and bring to a boil over high heat. Reduce the heat to medium-low, cover the pan, and simmer until the tomato is very soft, about 10 minutes.

5. Mix in the dal and simmer about 5 minutes to blend the flavors. Then stir in the coconut milk and cilantro, cook another 2 minutes, and serve.

Chunky South Indian Tomato Soup

Tamatar Rasam

Makes 4 to 6 servings

With chunks of tomato lending texture to a naturally smooth rasam, *this soup is a little more substantial than most rasams. Eat it for lunch with steamed white rice or toss in some* vadai *(South Indian Croquettes with Curry Leaves, page 130) and serve it as an anytime snack. I love this* rasam *with a tuna or a chicken sandwich, too.*

1 tablespoon South Indian Soup Powder (Rasam Podi), page 29 or store-bought
1 teaspoon cumin seeds
1 teaspoon black peppercorns
4 large tomatoes (about 2 pounds), coarsely chopped
5 to 6 cups water
1/2 teaspoon salt, or to taste
2 teaspoons peanut oil or melted ghee
1 teaspoon black mustard seeds
1/8 teaspoon ground asafoetida
1 tablespoon minced fresh curry leaves
1/4 cup finely chopped fresh cilantro, including soft stems

1. Prepare the soup powder. Then, in a small skillet, roast the cumin seeds and peppercorns over medium heat until fragrant and a few shades darker, about 2 minutes. Transfer them to a cutting board and grind them coarsely with the back of a large spoon.

2. Blend half the tomatoes in a blender until smooth. Transfer to a medium saucepan. Mix in the remaining chopped tomatoes, and then add about 5 cups water, roasted cumin and black pepper, salt, and rasam powder, and bring to a boil over high heat. Reduce the heat to medium-low, cover the pan, and simmer until the chopped tomatoes are soft, 5 to 7 minutes. (Add more water for a thinner rasam.)

3. Heat the oil (or ghee) in a small nonstick saucepan over medium-high heat and add the mustard seeds; they should splutter upon contact with the hot oil, so cover the pan and reduce the heat until the

spluttering subsides. Add the asafoetida, curry leaves, and cilantro and stir about 30 seconds. Mix into the rasam. Bring to a boil again, then serve hot.

Spicy South Indian Vegetable Soup with Tamarind

Tarkari Rasam

Makes 4 to 6 servings

Rasam *soups are generally simple thin broths, but sometimes health-conscious mothers sneak in fresh vegetables. These hearty* rasams *make a great meal with rice and a coconut chutney (pages 61 to 63). Try them also with* dosas *(rice and* dal *crepes) or with* iddli *(steamed fermented rice cakes).*

Drumsticks, called muringakkai *in Tamil are green, fibrous, foot-long beans, 1/4- to 1/3-inch in diameter, and are favored in the southern state of Tamilnadu. You may find fresh ones in Indian markets here, but you can use cut canned beans, too.*

1/2 cup dried split pigeon peas (toor dal), sorted and washed in 3 to 4 changes of water
5 to 6 cups water
1 tablespoon Basic Ginger-Garlic Paste (page 47 or store-bought)
1/4 cup Tamarind Paste (page 54 or store-bought)
1 to 2 tablespoons South Indian Soup Powder (Rasam Podi), page 29 or store-bought
1 tablespoon peanut oil or melted ghee
1 teaspoon black mustard seeds
1 teaspoon cumin seeds
1/8 teaspoon ground asafoetida
1 small onion, finely chopped
3 cups coarsely chopped fresh or frozen mixed vegetables, such as eggplant, okra, carrots, drumsticks, and green beans
1 teaspoon salt, or to taste
1 tablespoon minced fresh curry leaves
1/2 cup finely chopped fresh cilantro, including soft stems

1. Soak the dal in 1 cup water until it absorbs the water and softens slightly, about 30 minutes. Meanwhile prepare the ginger-garlic paste and the tamarind paste.

2. When soft, transfer the dal to a medium saucepan, add another cup of water, and bring to a boil over high heat. Reduce the heat to medium-low and simmer, watching carefully and stirring, until the dal is very soft, 20 to 30 minutes. Meanwhile, prepare the soup powder.

3. Heat the oil (or ghee) in a large nonstick saucepan over medium-high heat and add the mustard and cumin seeds and the asafoetida; they should splutter upon contact with the hot oil, so cover the pan and reduce the heat until the spluttering subsides. Quickly add the onion and stir about 1 minute.

4. Add vegetables, the soup powder, and salt and cook, stirring, about 5 minutes. Then add the cooked dal, the remaining water, tamarind paste, ginger-garlic paste, curry leaves, and cilantro, and bring to a boil over high heat. Reduce the heat to medium-low, cover the pan, and simmer until the vegetables are tender, 10 to 12 minutes. (Add more water if you prefer a thinner soup.) Serve hot.

Mulligatawny Soup
Millagu-Tanni

Makes 4 to 6 servings

The Anglicized term mulligatawny *comes from the Tamil words* millagu-tanni, *meaning pepper-water (*millagu *is black pepper and* tanni *is water). Mulligatawny belongs to the* rasam *family of spicy soups. Today, chicken and lamb are often added to this soup, but they are not traditional additions—just something people have come to enjoy. My recipe here is the authentic vegetarian version.*

For a non-vegetarian soup, pan-cook about a cup of ½-inch cubes of chicken or lamb, along with the onion and garlic and substitute chicken or lamb stock for part or all the water.

¼ cup Tamarind Paste (page 54 or store-bought)
1 tablespoon coriander seeds
1 teaspoon cumin seeds
1 teaspoon black peppercorns
½ teaspoon dried fenugreek seeds
4 to 5 cups water
1 large tomato, coarsely chopped
1 teaspoon salt, or to taste
1 tablespoon peanut oil
3 dried red chile peppers, such as chile de arbol, whole or broken
1 teaspoon black mustard seeds
½ teaspoon cumin seeds
1 small onion, finely chopped
1 to 2 fresh green chile peppers, such as serrano, sliced diagonally, with seeds
1 large clove fresh garlic, minced
¼ teaspoon ground turmeric
¼ teaspoon ground asafoetida

1. Prepare the tamarind paste. Then, heat a small skillet and dry-roast together the coriander and cumin seeds, peppercorns, and fenugreek over medium heat until they are a few shades darker, about 3 minutes. Let cool, then grind them finely.

2. Stir together the water, tamarind paste, and tomato in a large saucepan, bring to a boil over medium-high heat, and boil about 5 minutes. Mix in the roasted spices and the salt, and boil another 5 minutes.

3. Heat the oil in a small saucepan over medium-high heat and add the red chile peppers, and the mustard and cumin seeds; they should splutter upon contact with the hot oil, so lower the heat and cover the pan until the spluttering subsides. Add the onion and green chile peppers and cook, stirring, until lightly browned and soft, about 3 minutes. Add the garlic, turmeric, and asafoetida and stir another minute.

4. Mix these seasonings into the tomato soup base and simmer over low heat about 10 minutes to blend the flavors. Adjust seasonings, if needed, and serve.

Variation: Instead of dry-roasting the spices in step 1, use 2 tablespoons South Indian Soup Powder (Rasam Podi), page 29 or store-bought.

Bean and Lentil Soups

Yellow Mung Bean and Spinach Soup with Sizzling Cumin Oil

Mung Dal aur Palak ka Soop

Makes 4 to 6 servings

*This is probably one of the most popular soup recipes from northern India. Since split mung beans (*mung dal*) are a staple in most home pantries, this delicate soup can be prepared at a moment's notice and is easy on the stomach. You may need to make a trip to the Indian grocery store for the* mung dal *and other ingredients, but this soup uses many commonly found ingredients and cooks quickly.*

For a more filling dish, toss in about 1 cup cooked rice and about half a cup thawed frozen corn along with the spinach, if you wish.

1 tablespoon Basic Ginger-Garlic Paste
    (page 47 or store-bought)
1 cup dried split yellow mung beans (dhulli mung dal),
    sorted and washed in 3 to 4 changes of water
1 medium russet (or any) potato, peeled and
    cut into small pieces
5 to 6 cups water
1/4 teaspoon ground turmeric
1/4 teaspoon hot red pepper flakes, or to taste
3/4 teaspoon salt, or to taste
2 cups firmly packed finely chopped fresh spinach
    (from 1 small bunch)
1 cup finely chopped fresh cilantro, including soft stems
2 tablespoons peanut oil
1 teaspoon melted ghee (optional)
1 teaspoon cumin seeds
1 tablespoon ground coriander
1/4 teaspoon ground paprika
Freshly ground black pepper, to taste

1. Prepare the ginger-garlic paste. Place the dal and potato with 5 cups water, the ginger-garlic paste, turmeric, red pepper flakes, and salt in a medium saucepan and boil over high heat about 5 minutes. Reduce the heat to medium-low and cook until the dal is soft and creamy, about 40 minutes. For a thinner soup, add another cup of water and boil again.

2. Add the spinach and cilantro during the last 5 to 10 minutes. Transfer to a serving bowl.

3. Heat the oil (and ghee, if using) in a small saucepan over medium-medium-high heat and add the cumin seeds; they should sizzle upon contact with the hot oil. Quickly add the coriander. Remove the pan from the heat stir in the paprika, then mix the spiced oil into the hot dal. Sprinkle the black pepper on top and serve.

Quick Sindhi Split Pigeon Pea Soup with Tamarind

Sindhi Toor Dal ka Soop

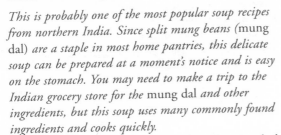

Makes 4 to 6 servings

This quick-cooking soup is made in a pressure cooker. Indians have been using pressure cookers for the last 40 years or so. Even traditionalists like my mother got one and used it often, sometimes two or three times a day. As a result, I grew up learning to cook with them, so I know their worth in the kitchen. In America, I still use them at every opportunity.

This soup is my aunt's special recipe. Based on a Sindhi kadhi—*a special yogurt or* dal *(legume) curry—this soup can be made thin or thick.*

2 to 3 tablespoons Tamarind Paste (page 54)
    or lemon juice
1 cup dried yellow split pigeon peas (toor dal),
    sorted and washed in 3 to 4 changes of water
1 tablespoon peeled minced fresh ginger
1 to 3 fresh green chile peppers, such as serrano,
    coarsely chopped
1 large tomato, coarsely chopped
1/4 teaspoon ground turmeric
1/2 teaspoon salt, or to taste
5 cups water, or more as needed
1 tablespoon vegetable oil
1 teaspoon cumin seeds
1 teaspoon mustard seeds

12 to 15 fresh curry leaves
2 tablespoons chickpea flour
1/2 teaspoon ground paprika
1/8 teaspoon ground asafoetida

1. Prepare the tamarind paste. Then, place the dal, ginger, green chile peppers, tomato, turmeric, salt, and water in a pressure cooker. Secure the lid and cook over high heat until the regulator indicates high pressure, then cook about 30 seconds more. Remove from the heat and allow to depressurize on its own, 12 to 15 minutes. Carefully remove the lid, let cool, then pass everything through a food mill or a fine-mesh strainer and place in a bowl.

2. Heat the oil in a large nonstick wok or saucepan over medium-high heat and add the cumin and mustard seeds; they should splutter upon contact with the hot oil, so cover the pan and reduce the heat until the spluttering subsides. Quickly add the curry leaves, stir a few seconds, then add the chickpea flour, paprika, and asafoetida and stir until the chickpea flour is fragrant and golden, 1 to 2 minutes.

3. Mix in the dal soup, the tamarind, and more water if you want, bring to a boil, and continue to boil, over medium-high heat the first 2 to 3 minutes and then over medium heat, 5 to 7 minutes, to blend the flavors. Transfer to a serving bowl and serve hot.

Quick Lentil, Barley, and Vegetable Soup
Dal, Jau aur Sabziyon ka Soop

Makes 4 to 6 servings

Pearl barley adds a silky smoothness to this satisfying soup. Serve it with naan *(leavened oven-baked bread) or* parantha *(unleavened, flaky pan-fried bread) and a glass of chilled Indian beer.*

1/2 cup dried lentils (masoor dal), sorted and washed in 3 to 4 changes of water
1/4 cup pearl barley
1 tablespoon vegetable oil
1 tablespoon melted ghee
2 bay leaves

1 teaspoon cumin seeds
1/8 teaspoon ground asafoetida
1 cup finely chopped onion
1 tablespoon peeled minced fresh ginger
2 teaspoons minced garlic
1 to 3 fresh green chile peppers, such as serrano, minced with seeds
3 cups finely chopped fresh or frozen mixed vegetables, such as bell peppers, green beans, carrots, celery, peas, corn and others
4 to 5 cups water
1 (15-ounce) can tomato sauce
1 teaspoon salt, or to taste
1/2 teaspoon freshly ground black pepper
2 to 3 tablespoons fresh lime juice
1 teaspoon dried fenugreek leaves
1/2 teaspoon garam masala

1. Soak the lentils and barley in a medium bowl of water to cover until they absorb some water and soften slightly, about 1 hour. Then pour through a fine-mesh strainer over another bowl, saving the water to use as part of the soup.

2. Heat the oil and ghee in a pressure cooker over medium-high heat and add the bay leaves and cumin seeds; they should sizzle upon contact with the hot oil. Quickly add the asafoetida and onions and cook, stirring, until the onions are golden, about 5 minutes. Mix in the ginger, garlic, and green chile peppers and stir momentarily, then add the lentils and barley. Cook, stirring, over medium-high heat about 5 minutes. Add the vegetables and cook another 5 minutes.

3. Mix in the water, tomato sauce, salt, and black pepper. Secure the lid of the pressure cooker and cook over high heat until the regulator indicates high pressure, then cook 1 minute more. Remove from the heat and allow to depressurize on its own, 12 to 15 minutes. Carefully remove the lid and check to see if the lentils are tender. If not, reseal the lid, bring back up to high pressure and cook another 30 seconds, or cover with another lid and cook until tender.

4. Carefully open the pressure cooker, add the lime juice and fenugreek leaves, and bring to a boil over high heat. Adjust seasonings and remove the bay leaves, if needed, then transfer to a serving bowl, mix in the garam masala, and serve.

Fast Black Bean Soup, Indian Style

Kaalae Rajma ka Soop

Makes 4 to 6 servings

*Once you know how to cook one type of dried beans
in a pressure cooker, you can cook all dried beans,
and black beans, more commonly associated with
Mexican cooking, are no different. In fact, I find they
cook faster than some other beans and legumes (such
as black chickpeas) that are part of the traditional
Indian pantry—and they are a great source of protein, calcium, and iron. Although this soup strays
from the Mexican tradition, even a Mexican friend
was astonished at its delicious flavor.*

1 cup dried black beans, sorted and washed
    in 3 to 4 changes of water

4 cups water

1 to 3 fresh green chile peppers, such as serrano,
    minced with seeds

1 teaspoon salt, or to taste

1 tablespoon peanut oil

1 teaspoon cumin seeds

1/2 cup finely chopped onion

1 tablespoon peeled minced fresh ginger

1 large clove fresh garlic, minced

1 large tomato, finely chopped

1 tablespoon ground coriander

1 teaspoon ground cumin

1/4 teaspoon ground turmeric

1/8 teaspoon ground asafoetida

1/2 cup nonfat plain yogurt, whisked until smooth

1/2 cup finely chopped fresh cilantro,
    including soft stems

1 (15-ounce) can tomato sauce

1/2 teaspoon garam masala

1. Place the beans in a pressure cooker along with the
water, chile peppers, and salt. Secure the lid and cook
over high heat until the regulator indicates high pressure, then cook about 1½ minutes more. Remove
from the heat and allow to depressurize on its own,
12 to 15 minutes. Carefully remove the lid and check
if the beans are soft. If not, secure lid, bring back up
to high pressure and cook another 30 seconds, or
cover with another lid and cook over medium heat
until tender.

2. Heat the oil in a medium nonstick wok or saucepan over medium-high heat and add the cumin
seeds; they should sizzle upon contact with the hot
oil. Quickly add the onion and cook, stirring, until
golden, about 3 minutes. Add the ginger, garlic, and
tomato, and cook until all the juices evaporate, 5 to
7 minutes.

3. Add the coriander, cumin, turmeric, and asafoetida,
stir and cook 30 seconds, then stir in the yogurt,
a little at a time, to prevent it from curdling. Cook
about 1 minute, then mix into the beans. Add the
cilantro, tomato sauce, and more water if the soup
seems thick, and cook another 5 minutes. Transfer to a serving bowl, garnish with garam masala,
and serve.

Chilled Chickpea Soup

Channae ka Thanda Soop

Makes 4 to 6 servings

*Indians don't typically serve their soups chilled. But I
got creative with this creamy chickpea soup, which is
truly Indian in every other way, except temperature. It is
great for warmer weather not only because it's chilled,
but because this quick dish uses canned chickpeas,
meaning you spend almost no time in a hot kitchen.*

4 quarter-size slices peeled fresh ginger

1 large clove fresh garlic, peeled

1 fresh green chile pepper, such as serrano, stemmed

2 (15½-ounce) cans chickpeas, drained and rinsed

1/2 cup coarsely chopped fresh cilantro,
    including soft stems

3 cups nonfat plain yogurt

1/4 teaspoon salt, or to taste

1/2 teaspoon freshly ground black pepper

1 tablespoon peanut oil

2 to 3 dried red chile peppers, such as chile de arbol,
    with stems

1 teaspoon cumin seeds, coarsely ground

1/2 teaspoon ajwain seeds, coarsely ground

1. In a food processor or a blender, process together the ginger, garlic, green chile pepper, chickpeas, and ¼ cup cilantro until smooth. Then mix in the yogurt, salt, and black pepper and process again until smooth. Transfer to a serving bowl.

2. Heat the oil in a small nonstick saucepan over medium-high heat and cook the red chile peppers, stirring until softened, about 30 seconds. Then add the cumin and ajwain seeds; they should sizzle upon contact with the hot oil. Quickly add the other ¼ cup cilantro and stir until wilted, about 1 minute. Transfer to the soup and swirl lightly to mix, with parts of the spiced oil visible as a garnish.

Chickpea Soup with Chicken Broth

Murgh Yakhni aur Channae ka Soop

Makes 4 to 6 servings

The broth adds a rich layer of flavor and the chickpeas make this simple soup hearty.

3 quarter-size slices peeled fresh ginger
1 (15½-ounce) can chickpeas, drained and rinsed
3 cups canned reduced-fat low-sodium chicken broth or 1 recipe Spicy Chicken Broth (page 169)
2 tablespoons unsalted butter
2 tablespoons all-purpose flour
1 cup lowfat milk, at room temperature
½ teaspoon salt, or to taste
½ teaspoon freshly ground black pepper
1 to 2 tablespoons fresh lime juice
¼ to ½ cup whipping cream (optional)
1 tablespoon peanut oil
1 to 3 fresh green chile peppers, such as serrano, stemmed, seeded, and cut into thin diagonal slices
1 teaspoon black mustard seeds
¼ teaspoon ground asafoetida

1. In a food processor or a blender, process together ginger, chickpeas, and broth until smooth.

2. Melt the butter in a large nonstick saucepan over medium-low heat, add the flour and cook, stirring and watching, until golden and fragrant, about 2 minutes. Increase the heat to medium-high and add the milk in a thin stream, stirring constantly to prevent the formation of any lumps, until the sauce is smooth, about 2 minutes.

3. Mix in the processed chickpea blend, then the salt, black pepper, and lime juice. Bring to a boil over high heat. Reduce the heat to medium-low, cover the pan, and simmer about 5 minutes to blend the flavors, adding more broth or water if you prefer a thinner soup. Mix in the cream (if using) and boil again. Transfer to a serving bowl.

4. Heat the oil in a small nonstick saucepan over medium-high heat and cook the red chile peppers, stirring until softened, about 30 seconds. Add the mustard seeds and asafoetida; they should splutter upon contact with the hot oil, so cover the pan and reduce the heat until the spluttering subsides. Quickly add the spiced oil to the soup and swirl lightly to mix, with parts of it visible as a garnish. Serve hot or let soup cool. Refrigerate for at least 2 hours and serve chilled.

Quick Black Chickpea Soup with Cumin Seeds

Kaalae Channae ka Soop

Makes 4 to 6 servings

This soup is a potent potion—in flavor and nutrients. Black chickpeas outdo most other dried beans in nutrition as they are richer in protein, calcium, and minerals. Black chickpeas are a little firm even when fully cooked, and they have a nutty, earthy flavor beautifully balanced when cooked with Indian seasonings. This flavor is enhanced if you cook them in a cast-iron pan.

Black chickpeas (more brown than black, really) are available in Indian markets. If you can't find them, use regular dried yellow chickpeas or even black beans.

1 tablespoon Basic Ginger-Garlic Paste (page 47) or store-bought
1 cup dried black chickpeas (kaalae channae), sorted and washed in 3 to 4 changes of water
6 to 7 cups water
2 (1-inch) sticks cinnamon
4 black cardamom pods, crushed lightly to break the skin
1/2 teaspoon salt, or to taste
1 (15-ounce) can tomato sauce
2 tablespoons vegetable oil
1 teaspoon melted ghee (optional)
1 (1-inch) piece peeled fresh ginger, cut into thin matchsticks
1 teaspoon cumin seeds
1 tablespoon ground coriander
1/4 teaspoon ground turmeric
1 large tomato, finely chopped
1/4 cup finely chopped fresh cilantro, including soft stems

1. Prepare the ginger-garlic paste. Then, soak the chickpeas overnight in water to cover by 2 inches, then drain. Place the chickpeas, water, cinnamon, cardamom pods, ginger-garlic paste, and salt in a pressure cooker, secure the lid, cook over high heat until the regulator indicates high pressure, then cook 3 more minutes. Remove from the heat and allow the pressure to depressurize on its own, 15 to 20 minutes. Open the lid carefully and check the chickpeas; they should be soft and watery. If not, reseal the lid, bring back up to high pressure, and cook 1 more minute.

2. Transfer to a large cast-iron wok (preferably) or skillet, mix in the tomato sauce and cook over high heat, stirring occasionally, about 5 minutes, then over medium-low heat about 1 hour. In the end you should have at least 4 cups of soup. If needed, add more water and bring to a boil.

3. Heat the oil and the ghee in a large nonstick wok or saucepan over medium-high heat and cook the ginger sticks, stirring frequently, until golden, about 1 minute. Add the cumin seeds; they should sizzle upon contact with the hot oil. Quickly add the coriander and turmeric, stir about 30 seconds, then mix in the chopped tomato and cilantro and cook until the tomatoes are slightly soft. Mix everything into the soup.

4. Transfer the soup to a serving bowl, leaving the chickpeas in the pan. Remove about ½ cup of the chickpeas, coarsely mash them, and add them to the soup. Reserve the rest for another purpose. (Eat them as is, or toss into salads or over rice *pullaos*.)

Vegetable Soups

Goan Caldo-Verde Soup with Cauliflower
Goa ka Gobhi Soop

Makes 4 to 6 servings

Goa, a small state on the western coast of India, was under Portuguese rule from 1510 to 1961. Their stay of more 450 years led to an intermingling of the Indian and the Portuguese cultures—so much so that today Goan food is a delicious fusion of the two cuisines.

Caldo-verde literally translates to "hot and green" in Portuguese, and this popular cauliflower and potato soup traditionally gets its color from the cauliflower greens. You can substitute any greens from vegetables in the cruciferous family, such as kohlrabi and Brussels sprouts.

1 pound russet (or any) potatoes, peeled and chopped
1 medium onion, coarsely chopped
2 cups cauliflower florets (from about a 1-pound head)
1 large clove fresh garlic, peeled
7 to 8 cups water
2 teaspoons olive oil
2 cups shredded cauliflower leaves or any other greens
1 teaspoon salt, or to taste
1 tablespoon grated pepper Jack cheese

1. Place the potatoes, onion, cauliflower, garlic, and 6 cups water in a large saucepan and bring to a boil over high heat. Reduce the heat to medium-low, cover the pan and simmer until the vegetables are soft, about 30 minutes.

2. Let the vegetables cool, then purée in a blender or a food processor until smooth. Return to the saucepan. Add the remaining water, olive oil, cauliflower leaves, and salt. Cover and simmer over medium heat, stirring as necessary, until the greens are soft, about 20 minutes. Transfer to a serving bowl, garnish with the cheese, and serve.

Cabbage Soup with Vegetables
Bandh Gobhi aur Sabziyon ka Soop

Makes 8 to 10 servings

Loaded with vegetables, this is a satisfying soup I make very often. It is not something I grew up with, but it's inspired by the foods I love. Make it with your favorite vegetables or whatever vegetables you have on hand. Once you're done chopping, this soup is a cinch to make. This recipe makes a lot of soup and stays fresh in the refrigerator about a week. Make it in advance to serve at large gatherings or serve it with different meals for your family.

1 tablespoon vegetable oil
1 small onion, thinly sliced
1 to 3 fresh green chile peppers, such as serrano, stemmed
2 large round white (or any) potatoes, finely chopped
4 to 5 cups finely chopped fresh vegetables, such as celery, beets, green beans, cauliflower, carrots, bell peppers, and any others
1 small head green cabbage, shredded
2 cups finely chopped greens, such as spinach, mustard, turnip, or beet greens, or any others
2 large tomatoes, coarsely chopped
4 to 5 cups water
1 cup finely chopped fresh cilantro, including soft stems
$^1/_2$ cup finely chopped fresh curry leaves
3 tablespoons fresh lemon juice
1 teaspoon salt, or to taste
$^1/_2$ teaspoon freshly ground black peppercorns, or to taste
2 teaspoons dried mint leaves
1 teaspoon garam masala

1. Heat the oil in a large stockpot or saucepan over medium heat and cook the onions and green chile peppers about 5 minutes. Add the potatoes, chopped vegetables, cabbage, greens, and tomatoes and cook, stirring, another 5 minutes.

2. Add the water and bring to a boil over high heat. Then, cover the pan and cook until the vegetables are tender, about 15 minutes. Mix in all the remaining ingredients and cook until everything is nice and soft, about 15 minutes more, then serve.

Variation: Add about a cup of skinless, boneless chicken or fish pieces with the vegetables in step 1, for added flavor and protein.

Quick Puréed Root Vegetable Soup
Jadhi Sabziyon ka Soop

Makes 4 to 6 servings

This easy and colorful soup comes to me courtesy of my mother. I usually use beets for the soup, even if I mix in other root vegetables. I made it for years here in the United States before I realized why some of my Eastern European neighbors enjoyed it so much: it reminded them of their red beet borscht.

4 to 5 cups coarsely chopped root vegetables, such as beets, kohlrabi, potatoes, turnips, and carrots

1 small onion, coarsely chopped

1 large tomato, coarsely chopped

1 to 3 fresh green chile peppers, such as serrano, stemmed

5 quarter-size slices peeled fresh ginger

1 cup coarsely chopped fresh cilantro, including soft stems

4 to 5 cups water

1 teaspoon salt, or to taste

1/2 teaspoon freshly ground black pepper

1 to 2 tablespoons fresh lime or lemon juice

1 tablespoon peanut oil

1 teaspoon cumin seeds

1/2 teaspoon ajwain seeds, coarsely crushed

1 tablespoon ground coriander

1/2 teaspoon garam masala

Snipped chives

1. Place the all the root vegetables in a pressure cooker. Add the onion, tomato, green chile peppers, ginger, cilantro, and 3 cups water. Secure the lid of the pressure cooker and cook over high heat until the regulator indicates high pressure, then cook 1 minute.

Remove from the heat and allow to depressurize on its own, 12 to 15 minutes. Carefully remove the lid.

2. Let cool, then blend everything in a blender in 2 to 3 batches until smooth. For a very smooth texture, pass the blended soup through a food mill, adding the remaining water as necessary for desired consistency.

3. Return the soup to the pressure cooker, mix in the salt, black pepper, and lemon juice and bring to a boil over high heat. Reduce the heat to medium-low and simmer another 5 minutes to blend the flavors. Transfer to a serving bowl.

4. Heat the oil in a small saucepan over medium-high heat and add the cumin and ajwain seeds; they should sizzle upon contact with the hot oil. Quickly add the coriander and garam masala and transfer the seasoned oil to the soup. Swirl lightly to mix, with parts of it visible as a garnish. Sprinkle the chives on top and serve.

Chilled Potato Soup
Aalu ka Thanda Soop

Makes 4 to 6 servings

We've all had our share of potato soups, but this creamy, soothing one, loaded with flavors from the southern part of India, may surprise you. It's traditionally eaten chilled, but to eat it warm, gently heat the soup over medium heat about 3 minutes. Do not boil; the yogurt may curdle.

1 pound russet (or any) potatoes

2 tablespoons peanut oil

1 teaspoon mustard seeds

1 large onion, finely chopped

1/4 teaspoon ground asafoetida

1 tablespoon peeled minced fresh ginger

1 tablespoon minced fresh curry leaves

1 teaspoon minced fresh mint

1/4 cup coarsely chopped fresh cilantro, including soft stems

1 tablespoon ground coriander

1 teaspoon salt, or to taste

2 cups water

2 cups nonfat plain yogurt or 1 cup light cream and 1 cup yogurt

1/2 teaspoon freshly ground black pepper

1. Boil the potatoes in lightly salted water to cover until tender, then peel and coarsely chop them. Heat the oil in a large saucepan over medium heat and add the mustard seeds; they should splutter upon contact with the hot oil, so cover the pan and reduce the heat until the spluttering subsides. Quickly add the onion and cook, stirring until golden, about 5 minutes.

2. Add the asafoetida, ginger, curry leaves, mint, and cilantro, and stir 1 minute. Add the coriander, salt, and potatoes, and cook, stirring, until the potatoes are golden, 7 to 10 minutes. Add the water and bring to a boil over high heat. Reduce the heat to medium-low, cover the pan and simmer until the potatoes start to break, about 5 minutes.

3. Let cool, then transfer to a blender or food processor and process until smooth. Transfer to a serving bowl, mix in the yogurt (or cream and yogurt), adjust the seasoning, and refrigerate at least 2 hours or until ready to serve. Garnish with the black pepper and serve.

Carrot-Ginger Soup
Gajjar-Adrak ka Soop

Makes 4 to 6 servings

The intermingling of the naturally sweet carrots and generous helpings of fresh ginger leaves a lingering play of flavors in the mouth; it's hard to put the spoon down. This is a recipe I often make for formal dinners, and I serve it with wedges of parantha *(griddle-fried flat breads). Minced Chicken Chaat Salad with Lentil Paapad Wafers (page 217) is another lovely accompaniment.*

1 teaspoon dry-roasted and coarsely ground
    black pepper (Dry-Roasting Spices, page 35)
2 tablespoons vegetable oil
2 bay leaves
1 teaspoon cumin seeds
1 cup finely chopped onion
8 to 10 quarter-size slices peeled fresh ginger
1 pound carrots, unpeeled, coarsely chopped

1 cup coarsely chopped fresh cilantro,
    including soft stems
5 to 6 cups water
1 teaspoon salt, or to taste
1 cup light cream or plain yogurt (any kind),
    whisked until smooth
1 to 2 tablespoons fresh lemon juice

1. Prepare the black pepper. Then, heat the oil in a large nonstick wok or saucepan over medium-high heat and cook the bay leaves and cumin seeds, stirring frequently; they should sizzle upon contact with the hot oil. Quickly add the onion and cook, stirring, until golden, about 5 minutes. Add the ginger and cook another minute.

2. Add the carrots and cilantro and cook, stirring, until the carrots are golden, about 7 minutes. Add 5 cups water and the salt and bring to a boil over high heat. Reduce the heat to medium-low, cover the pan and simmer until the carrots are soft, about 10 minutes.

3. Let cool, remove the bay leaves, then purée the carrots with all the juices in a blender until smooth. Return to the pan and boil until the soup is reduced by about one quarter (For a thinner soup, add the remaining 1 cup water and boil again.) Mix in the cream or yogurt and bring to a quick boil. Transfer to a serving bowl, mix in the lemon juice, garnish with black pepper, and serve.

Variation: Instead of the carrots, make this soup with orange-flesh yams, white-flesh sweet potatoes, or any of the summer or winter squashes.

Curried Green Pea Soup
Muttar ka Soop

Makes 4 to 6 servings

With no curry powder added but made with traditional curry technique, this soup can also be a curry sauce served with any of the deep-fried vegetable, paneer cheese, or meat kofta balls, such as Spinach Balls in Green Curry (page 418). To make it into a sauce, add less water or simply cook longer, uncovered, to reduce the liquid.

2½ cups fresh or thawed frozen green peas
6 to 7 cups water
1 cup plain yogurt, any kind
1 teaspoon cornstarch
1 small coarsely chopped onion
1 to 2 fresh green chile peppers, such as serrano, stemmed
4 quarter-size slices peeled fresh ginger
1 large clove fresh garlic, peeled
1 to 2 tablespoons peanut oil
1 tablespoon ground coriander
1 teaspoon ground cumin
1 teaspoon salt, or to taste
¼ teaspoon freshly ground black pepper

1. Place the peas and 2 cups water in a medium saucepan and bring to a boil over high heat. Reduce the heat to medium-low, cover the pan, and simmer until the peas are tender, about 20 minutes. Let cool, then transfer along with the water to a blender or food processor and process until smooth. Transfer to a bowl.

2. In the same blender, blend together the yogurt, cornstarch and another cup of water. Transfer to a bowl and set aside. Then process together the onion, green chile peppers, ginger, and garlic until smooth.

3. Heat the oil in a large nonstick wok or saucepan over medium heat, add the processed onion-garlic mixture and cook, stirring, until golden, about 5 minutes. Add the coriander and cumin, then add the puréed peas, salt, and the remaining 3 cups water and bring to a boil over high heat. Reduce the heat to medium-low, cover the pan, and simmer about 10 minutes.

4. Mix in the puréed yogurt, raise the heat to medium-high, and boil until the soup is smooth, about 3 minutes. Transfer to a serving bowl, garnish with the black pepper, and serve.

Puréed Pumpkin Soup
Pethae ka Soop

Makes 4 to 6 servings

Flavored with some of the most fragrant Indian seasonings, this pumpkin soup can be served at a Thanksgiving feast or an autumn harvest meal. Most of the ingredients can be found in the supermarket. The flavor burst the spices add makes it worth a quick trip to the Indian market.

½ pound pumpkin, peeled, seeded, and coarsely chopped, or 1 (15-ounce) can pumpkin (not pumpkin pie filling)
½ pound round white (or any) potatoes, coarsely chopped
1 large onion, coarsely chopped
4 to 6 quarter-size slices peeled fresh ginger
1 large clove fresh garlic, peeled
1 to 3 fresh green chile peppers, such as serrano, stemmed
¼ teaspoon ground turmeric
½ teaspoon salt, or to taste
5 to 6 cups water
1 teaspoon fresh lime or lemon juice
1 tablespoon vegetable oil
1 teaspoon cumin seeds
1 teaspoon fennel seeds, coarsely ground
½ teaspoon fenugreek seeds, coarsely ground
¼ teaspoon kalonji seeds

1. Place the pumpkin (if using fresh), potatoes, onion, ginger, garlic, green chile peppers, turmeric, salt, and 4 cups water in a large saucepan and bring to a boil over high heat. Reduce the heat to medium-low, cover the pan and simmer, until the vegetables are soft, about 30 minutes. (If using canned pumpkin, mix it into the soup in step 2, after it has been passed through the food mill or processed.)

2. Let cool, and pass soup through a food mill into a bowl or process in a food processor. Return to the pan and mix in the lime juice. Mix in 1 to 2 cups water and boil over high heat about 2 minutes. Adjust the seasonings.

3. Heat the oil in a small nonstick wok or saucepan over medium-high heat and add all the seeds; they should sizzle upon contact with the hot oil. Quickly mix the spiced oil into the soup and simmer about 5 minutes to blend the flavors. Serve.

Puréed Spinach Soup
Palak ka Soop

Makes 4 to 6 servings

If you or people in your family don't already love spinach, this delicious, simple soup could make you a convert. It may even have people wondering, "Is it really spinach?"

1 small (8- to 10-ounce) bunch fresh spinach, trimmed, washed, and coarsely chopped
1 cup coarsely chopped fresh cilantro, including soft stems
2 tablespoons coarsely chopped fresh mint
1 medium onion, coarsely chopped
4 quarter-size slices peeled fresh ginger
1 large clove fresh garlic, peeled
4 cups water
2 tablespoons vegetable oil
1 tablespoon all-purpose flour
1 cup milk (any kind)
1 teaspoon garam masala
1/2 cup plain yogurt (any kind), whisked until smooth

1. Place the spinach, cilantro, mint, onion, ginger, and garlic in a large saucepan. Add the water and bring to a boil over high heat. Reduce the heat to medium-low, cover the pan and simmer, until the onions are soft, about 10 minutes. Let cool, then purée in a blender or food processor until smooth.

2. Heat the oil in separate large nonstick wok or saucepan over medium-high heat, add the flour and cook, stirring, until golden and very fragrant, about 1 minute. Add the milk in a thin stream, stirring constantly to ensure no lumps form. Slowly, while stirring constantly, add the puréed spinach and the garam masala, and mix well. Transfer soup to a serving bowl, add the yogurt, swirl lightly to mix with parts of it visible as a garnish, and serve.

Yogurt Soups

Fragrant Yogurt Soup
Dahi ka Soop

Makes 4 to 6 servings

The fragrance of ginger, asafoetida, and fresh curry leaves enhances this thick, creamy soup, transforming it into a delicious mouthful. Serve it as a starter course with whole-wheat crackers, or as a curry with rice, or with slices of sourdough bread and a spicy potato salad such as the Red Potato Chaat Salad (page 212).

3 tablespoons long grain white rice
1 tablespoon dried yellow urad beans (dhulli urad dal), sorted and washed in 3 to 4 changes of water
1 tablespoon dried split yellow mung beans (dhulli mung dal), sorted and washed in 3 to 4 changes of water
1 teaspoon ground cumin
3 cups plain yogurt (any kind), whisked until smooth
1 1/2 cups water
1 to 3 fresh green chile peppers, such as serrano, stemmed
3 quarter-size slices peeled fresh ginger
1 large clove fresh garlic, peeled
1/4 teaspoon ground turmeric
1/2 teaspoon salt, or to taste
1 tablespoon peanut oil
1 teaspoon black mustard seeds
6 to 8 fresh curry leaves
1/4 teaspoon ground asafoetida
2 tablespoons finely chopped fresh cilantro, including soft stems

1. In a small nonstick or cast-iron skillet over medium heat, dry-roast together the rice, both the dals, and the cumin seeds, stirring and shaking the skillet until the mixture is fragrant and golden, about 3 minutes. Transfer to a spice or a coffee grinder and grind to make it as fine as possible.

2. In a blender or food processor, blend together the yogurt, water, green chile peppers, ginger, and garlic until smooth. Mix in the turmeric, salt, and the ground rice-dal mixture, and blend again until as smooth as possible.

3. Heat the oil in a large nonstick wok or saucepan over medium-high heat and add the mustard seeds and curry leaves; they should splutter upon contact with the hot oil, so cover the pan and reduce the heat until the spluttering subsides.

4. Add the asafoetida and the yogurt mixture and bring to a boil, stirring constantly, over high heat. Reduce the heat to medium-low and simmer about 10 minutes. Transfer to a serving dish, mix in the cilantro, and serve.

Creamy Almond–Poppy Seed Soup
Badaam aur Khas-khas ka Soop

Makes 4 to 6 servings

Being rich in vitamins and minerals, almonds are believed to rejuvenate and energize the brain cells, and are often called brain food in India. Mineral-rich poppy seeds are also considered very powerful, and both of these are routinely used, separately or together—in drinks, such as Hot Milk with Pistachios and Poppy Seeds (page 656) and in curries like Chicken in Fried Masala Curry (page 458), so why not in a soup?

1/2 cup Almond and Poppy Seed Paste (page 52)
2 tablespoons vegetable oil
1 (1-inch) stick cinnamon
6 whole cloves
3 black cardamom pods, crushed lightly
 to break the skin
2 bay leaves
1 cup finely chopped onion
1 teaspoon freshly ground black pepper
1 teaspoon garam masala
1 cup water
2 cups lowfat milk
1/4 cup dry-roasted almonds (page 35 or store-bought)
1 cup nonfat plain yogurt, whisked until smooth
1/2 teaspoon salt, or to taste

1. Prepare the nut-seed paste. Then heat the oil in a large nonstick wok or saucepan over medium-high heat and cook the cinnamon, cloves, cardamom pods, and bay leaves, stirring frequently, for 1 minute. Add the onion and continue to cook until browned, about 7 minutes. Add the almond and poppy seed paste, black pepper, and garam masala, and cook, stirring, until golden, about 5 minutes.

2. Add the water and bring to a boil over high heat. Reduce the heat to medium-low, add the milk and simmer, stirring, until the soup is thick, about 10 minutes. Meanwhile roast the almonds.

3. Let cool, remove the bay leaves, then mix in the yogurt and salt. Transfer to a serving bowl, refrigerate at least 2 hours or up to 2 days before serving. Garnish with the roasted almonds and serve.

Yogurt Soup with Flame-Roasted Eggplant
Bhunae Baigan aur Dahi ka Soop

Makes 4 to 6 servings

The smoky, sweet flavor of roasted eggplant dramatically dresses up plain yogurt in this simple soup. All you need is a bit of toasted cumin to give it some more pizzazz. This almost fat-free chunky soup is delicious served with grilled chicken and fish. Try some chilled, as a salad dressing over a bowl of baby greens. Use thin eggplants in this recipe if you can—their flavor, when roasted, is more pronounced.

1 pound small thin eggplants
3 cups nonfat plain yogurt, whisked until smooth
1/2 cup lowfat milk
1/2 teaspoon salt, or to taste
1 1/2 teaspoons cumin seeds
1 teaspoon sesame seeds

1. Roast and mash the eggplants as described in Roasting and Grilling Vegetables (page 36). Then, place the roasted eggplant pulp in a blender or a food processor, add the yogurt, milk, and salt, and blend until smooth. Transfer to a serving bowl.

2. Place the cumin seeds in a small nonstick skillet and dry-roast, stirring over medium heat until fragrant and a few shades darker, about 2 minutes. Let cool, then grind coarsely with the back of a large spoon. Mix into the yogurt.

3. Similarly, place the sesame seeds in the skillet and dry-roast them until golden, about 1 minute. Sprinkle them over the soup as a garnish. Serve hot, or refrigerate at least 2 hours and serve chilled.

Puréed Mushroom Soup with Yogurt
Khumbi Soop

Makes 4 to 6 servings

An unusual Indian twist to mushroom soup, this creamy chilled concoction, which requires little cooking, goes well with hot buttered bread.

1 teaspoon dry-roasted and coarsely ground cumin seeds (Dry-Roasting Spices, page 35)
1/2 teaspoon dry-roasted and coarsely ground black peppercorns (page 35)
2 tablespoons vegetable oil
3 to 4 medium leeks, white parts only, rinsed and finely chopped
1 to 3 fresh green chile peppers, such as serrano, minced with seeds
1 pound white or brown mushrooms, quartered
1 large clove fresh garlic, minced
2 cups nonfat plain yogurt, whisked until smooth
1 cup lowfat milk
1 to 2 tablespoons fresh lemon juice
1 teaspoon salt, or to taste
3 to 4 scallions, green parts only, minced

1. Prepare the cumin seeds and peppercorns. Then heat the oil in a large nonstick wok or saucepan over medium-high heat and cook the leeks and green chile peppers, stirring, until golden, about 5 minutes. Add the mushrooms and garlic, and cook, stirring, until golden, about 7 minutes. (The mushrooms will first release their juices and then dry out.) Let cool, transfer to a food processor or a blender, and process until smooth.

2. Place the yogurt in a large serving bowl and mix in the milk, mushrooms, lemon juice, the prepared cumin and black pepper, and the salt. Store, covered, in the refrigerator at least 2 hours or until ready to serve. Garnish with scallion greens and serve.

Spinach Yogurt Soup
Palak aur Dahi ka Soop

Makes 4 to 6 servings

Here is a nearly effortless spinach soup to make, once you wash the spinach. With much more yogurt, this is also creamier and more tart than Puréed Spinach Soup (page 189).

1 small (8- to 10-ounce) bunch fresh spinach, trimmed, washed, and coarsely chopped
1/2 cup water
1 to 3 fresh green chile peppers, such as serrano, stemmed
3 cups nonfat plain yogurt, whisked until smooth
1/2 cup milk (any kind)
1/2 teaspoon salt, or to taste
1 tablespoon peanut oil
1/2 teaspoon cumin seeds
1/2 teaspoon black mustard seeds
1 teaspoon dried mint leaves
1/2 teaspoon dried ground fenugreek leaves

1. In a saucepan, cover and cook the spinach with the water until wilted, about 5 minutes. Transfer to a food processor and process until smooth. With the spinach still in the food processor, add the green chile peppers, yogurt, milk, and salt, and process again until blended and smooth. Transfer to a serving bowl.

2. Heat the oil in a small nonstick wok or saucepan over medium-high heat and cook the cumin and mustard seeds; they should splutter upon contact with the hot oil, so cover the pan and reduce the heat until the spluttering subsides. Quickly add the mint and fenugreek leaves and transfer the seasoned oil to the soup. Swirl lightly to mix, with parts of it visible as a garnish, and serve.

Vegetable Soup with Yogurt and Coconut

Avial

Makes 4 to 6 servings

This specialty from southern India is studded with chunks of meltingly soft vegetables floating in a thick golden soup. Avial is generally made very spicy hot and is often served over cooked rice.

Look for fresh coconut in Indian, Asian, and Mexican markets, and some well-stocked supermarkets.

4 to 5 cups coarsely chopped fresh vegetables, such as eggplant, bell peppers, carrots, zucchini, potatoes, onions, cauliflower, pumpkin, kohlrabi

3 cups water

1/2 teaspoon ground turmeric

1/2 teaspoon salt, or to taste

1 (4-inch) piece of fresh coconut, shelled, peeled, and coarsely chopped, or 1/2 cup canned coconut milk

1 to 3 fresh green chile peppers, such as serrano, stemmed

1 1/2 cups plain yogurt (any kind)

1/4 cup finely chopped fresh cilantro, including soft stems + 2 tablespoons for garnish

1 tablespoon peanut oil

1 teaspoon black mustard seeds

1 tablespoon fresh curry leaves

1/4 teaspoon ground asafoetida

1. Place the vegetables, water, turmeric, and salt in a large nonstick saucepan. Cover and bring to a boil over high heat. Reduce the heat to medium and simmer until the vegetables are crisp-tender, 20 to 25 minutes.

2. In a food processor or a blender, process together the coconut (or coconut milk), chile peppers, and yogurt until smooth, and then mix it into the vegetable soup, along with the cilantro. Cover the pan and simmer about 10 minutes to blend the flavors. Transfer to a serving bowl.

3. Heat the oil in a small nonstick saucepan over medium-high heat and add the mustard seeds; they should splutter upon contact with the hot oil, so cover the pan and reduce the heat until the spluttering subsides. Add the curry leaves and asafoetida, stir

a few seconds, then mix the spiced oil into the soup. Garnish with chopped cilantro and serve.

Chilled Roasted Vegetable Soup

Bhuni Sabziyon ka Thanda Soop

Makes 4 to 6 servings

I love roasted vegetables, even those I wasn't used to in India. Here I mix them with nonfat yogurt and add Indian seasonings to make an unusual soup. My children love it with hamburgers and French fries, and I with Stuffed Potato Paranthas (page 586), and other paranthas (griddle-fried flatbreads).

1 teaspoon cumin seeds, dry-roasted and coarsely ground (Dry-Roasting Spices, page 35)

3 large red bell peppers, stemmed, halved lengthwise, and seeded

4 small Chinese or Japanese eggplants, halved lengthwise

2 large tomatoes, halved

1 large red onion, thinly sliced

5 quarter-size slices peeled fresh ginger

2 large cloves fresh garlic, peeled

1/2 cup coarsely chopped fresh cilantro, including soft stems

3 cups nonfat plain yogurt, whisked until smooth

1/2 teaspoon freshly ground black pepper

1. Prepare the cumin seeds. Preheat the broiler. Place the bell pepper halves, eggplants, tomatoes, onion, ginger, and garlic on a baking tray and roast on the center rack of the oven broiler, turning occasionally until the peppers and tomatoes are charred and the onion, ginger, and garlic are golden, about 5 minutes. Remove the pieces as they turn golden.

2. Transfer everything to a blender, including accumulated juices. (Deglaze the baking tray with 1/2 cup water, taking care to dissolve the browned juices, then add to the blender also.) Add the cilantro and blend until smooth. Transfer to a large serving bowl.

3. Mix in the yogurt, garnish with the roasted cumin and black pepper, refrigerate for at least 1 hour and up to 12 hours, and serve chilled.

Fish and Chicken Soups

Goan Shrimp Soup
Goa ka Jhinga Soop

Makes 4 to 6 servings

Shrimp and seafood abound in the southwestern coastal waters of Goa, so it's no wonder that the Goans eat them in a number of different ways. This shrimp soup makes a lovely starter course. To intensify the flavor, you can boil the shrimp shells in the water for half an hour, then strain and add the liquid to the soup.

1 pound medium (about 30) fresh or thawed frozen
    shrimp, shell on, rinsed
5 to 6 cups water
1/4 teaspoon ground turmeric
1 tablespoon minced fresh garlic
2 tablespoons olive oil
1 large onion, finely chopped
1 large tomato, finely chopped
2 to 3 fresh green chile peppers, such as serrano,
    halved lengthwise
1/2 teaspoon salt, or to taste
1/2 teaspoon freshly ground black pepper
1/4 cup finely chopped fresh cilantro,
    including soft stems

1. Wash shrimp well and place them and the water, ground turmeric, and garlic in a large saucepan over high heat. Bring to a boil, then reduce the heat to medium-low, cover the pan, and simmer until the shrimp are pink and opaque, 5 to 7 minutes. Leaving the water in the pan, remove the shrimp with a slotted spoon to a bowl. Let cool, then shell and devein each shrimp and set aside until the soup is ready.

2. Heat the oil in a small nonstick wok or saucepan over medium-high heat and cook the onion, stirring, until golden. Add the tomatoes and cook until softened, about 5 minutes. Transfer to the pan with the shrimp-cooking water, add the green chile peppers, and simmer about 5 minutes to blend flavors.

3. Return shrimp to the pan, season with salt and black pepper, garnish with cilantro, and serve.

Spicy Shrimp Soup with Coconut Milk and Tomato
Jhinga, Nariyal Doodh, aur Tamatar ka Soop

Makes 4 to 6 servings

Shrimp, or prawns (the variety most often found in India), are very popular among Indians, especially along the coastal regions where there is also an abundance of coconut palms. Here is a delicious soup from the western state of Kerala that uses both shrimp and coconut. Serve it with steamed long-grain white rice and Stuffed Lentil Wafer Rolls (page 147).

1 pound large (about 20) fresh or thawed frozen
    shrimp, shell on, rinsed
5 to 6 cups water
2 large cloves fresh garlic, minced
1/2 teaspoon salt, or to taste
1 large onion, coarsely chopped
1 large tomato, coarsely chopped
1 cup coarsely chopped fresh cilantro,
    including soft stems
1 tablespoon vegetable oil
1 tablespoon ground coriander
1/4 teaspoon ground turmeric
1 to 3 fresh green chile peppers, such as serrano,
    sliced diagonally or split in half lengthwise
    and seeded
1 tablespoon tamarind powder or 1 to 2 tablespoons
    fresh lemon juice
1 cup canned coconut milk
2 tablespoons finely chopped scallion greens, chives,
    or cilantro

1. Place the shrimp, 5 cups water, garlic, and salt in a large saucepan and bring to a boil over high heat. Reduce the heat to medium-low, cover the pan, and simmer until the shrimp are pink and opaque, about 3 minutes. Remove the shrimp from the soup with a slotted spoon, let them cool, then shell and devein them, leaving the tails intact on half (reserve the tailed shrimp for garnish).

2. In a food processor or a blender, process the onion to make a smooth paste. Transfer to a bowl. Process the tomato and cilantro to make a smooth purée and transfer to a separate bowl. Then add the shrimps without the tails to the work bowl and pulse a few times until they are minced. Mix the shrimp pieces into the soup.

3. Heat the oil in a small nonstick saucepan over medium-high heat and cook the onion paste, stirring, until golden, about 5 minutes. Add the coriander and turmeric and stir another minute. Then mix in the puréed tomato and cilantro and the green chile peppers and cook, stirring, until most of the juices evaporate, about 5 minutes.

4. Transfer to the soup. Add the tamarind powder and coconut milk and bring to a boil over high heat. Reduce the heat to medium-low and simmer about 5 minutes. Transfer to a serving bowl, mix in the reserved tails-on shrimp, garnish with your choice of greens, and serve.

Chicken Soup with Ginger and Coconut Milk
Adrak aur Nariyal vala Murgh Soup

Makes 4 to 6 servings

This coconut-flavored chicken soup with sour undertones is a take on one I had in a resort in the southwestern coastal state of Kerala. That soup had a lot more coconut milk; here I replace some with yogurt.

Chickens in India are almost never cooked with the skin on, so if you don't want to remove the skin yourself, buy your chicken at a butcher and have it skinned. If not making the broth from scratch, use about 4 cups of reduced-fat, low-sodium canned chicken broth; reduce the salt you add to the soup.

Try this over rice, or for a special presentation, form ¾-inch balls of cooled cooked rice and place them in individual bowls. Then pour this soup over them and serve.

1 (2½- to 3-pound) chicken, skinned
4 to 5 cups water
1 teaspoon salt, or to taste
1 cup Coconut Milk (page 44 or store-bought)
½ cup coarsely chopped fresh cilantro, including soft stems
1 fresh green chile pepper, such as serrano, stemmed
6 quarter-size slices peeled fresh ginger
20 fresh curry leaves + 10 for final seasoning
1 tablespoon ground coriander
1 teaspoon ground cumin
1 cup plain yogurt (any kind), whisked until smooth
2 cups water
2 tablespoons vegetable oil
1 teaspoon cumin seeds
4 dried red chile peppers, such as chile de arbol, with stems
2 teaspoons peeled minced fresh ginger
⅛ teaspoon ground asafoetida

1. Rinse the chicken, then place it in a large saucepan. Add 4 cups water and salt and bring to a boil over high heat. Reduce the heat to medium-low, cover the pan, and simmer until the meat is very tender, about 45 minutes. Meanwhile, prepare the coconut milk.

2. With a slotted spoon, remove the chicken to a bowl. When cool enough to handle, cut the breast meat into ½-inch pieces and reserve for the soup. (Use the remaining chicken for another recipe.) With a slotted spoon, remove any scum from the broth.

3. In a food processor or a blender, process together the cilantro, green chile pepper, ginger, 20 curry leaves, coriander, and cumin to make a smooth paste. Add the yogurt and process again until smooth. Stir the mixture into broth and bring to a boil over high heat. Reduce the heat to medium-low, cover the pan, and simmer about 10 minutes to blend the flavors.

4. Mix in the reserved chicken pieces and the coconut milk and simmer over medium-low heat about 5 minutes. Transfer to a serving bowl, cover, and keep warm.

5. Heat the oil in a small nonstick wok or saucepan over medium-high heat and add the cumin seeds; they should sizzle upon contact with the hot oil. Quickly add the red chile peppers, 10 curry leaves, and asafoetida, and add the seasoning to the soup. Swirl lightly to mix, with parts of it visible as a garnish. Serve.

Cashew Corn Soup in Chicken Broth

Kaaju-Makki Soop

Makes 4 to 6 servings

This is another soup of my own creation. My American friends love it with a slice of fragrant focaccia bread. Made with chicken broth, this soup has a rich, comforting chowder-like quality. If you prefer a smoother soup, pass it through a food mill.

1 cup coarsely chopped raw cashews

1 cup lowfat milk

1 tablespoon peanut oil

10 to 12 scallions, white and light green parts, minced (to make 1 cup)

1 large clove fresh garlic, minced

3 cups reduced-fat low-sodium chicken broth, or 1 recipe Spicy Chicken Broth (page 169)

1 cup frozen corn kernels, thawed

1 cup water

2 to 3 tablespoons fresh lemon juice

1 teaspoon coarsely ground black pepper

$1/2$ teaspoon garam masala

$1/4$ teaspoon ground ginger

$1/4$ teaspoon salt, or to taste

$1/4$ cup finely chopped fresh cilantro, including soft stems

1. Place the cashews and milk in a microwave-safe bowl and cook on high 3 minutes. Remove from the microwave and set aside to soak and soften, 10 minutes.

2. Heat the oil in a large saucepan over medium-high heat, add the scallions and garlic and cook, stirring, until barely golden, about 2 minutes. Add the broth and simmer, about 5 minutes.

3. In a food processor, process together the cashews, milk, and corn to make a coarse purée. Transfer to the pan with the broth. Rinse the processor with the 1 cup water and add to the soup. Mix in the rest of the ingredients (except the cilantro) and simmer another 10 minutes to blend the flavors. Transfer to a serving bowl, garnish with the cilantro, and serve.

Chicken Soup with Cream-Style Corn and Green Chile Peppers

Murgh aur Makki ka Soop

Makes 4 to 6 servings

I enjoyed this soup throughout my childhood in India, but my mother didn't make it; it was a family favorite that we enjoyed in Chinese restaurants. Today, this soup is as Indian and as commonly made in Indian homes as tomato soup.

In place of the homemade broth, you can use about 4 cups of reduced-fat, low-sodium canned chicken broth and reduce the amount of added salt.

1 ($2^1/2$- to 3-pound) chicken, skinned

4 to 5 cups water

1 teaspoon salt, or to taste

1 ($15^1/2$-ounce) can cream-style corn

$1/3$ cup cornstarch

2 large egg whites, lightly beaten

2 to 4 tablespoons distilled white vinegar

1 to 3 fresh green chile peppers, such as serrano, diagonally sliced or split in half lengthwise and seeded (optional)

$1/4$ teaspoon freshly ground black pepper, or to taste

1. Rinse and place the chicken in a large saucepan. Add the water and salt and bring to a boil over high heat. Reduce the heat to medium-low, cover the pan, and simmer until the meat is very tender, about 45 minutes.

2. With large tongs or a slotted spoon transfer the chicken to a bowl. When cool enough to handle, shred about 1 cup of the meat and reserve for the soup. (Cover and refrigerate the remaining chicken for another use.) With a slotted spoon, remove any scum from the broth, then mix in the corn and bring to a boil over high heat. Reduce the heat to medium-low and simmer about 5 minutes.

3. Dissolve the cornstarch in about $1/3$ cup water and add it to the soup, stirring constantly to prevent the formation of lumps. Continue to stir until the soup thickens, about 2 minutes.

4. Mix the egg whites with 2 to 3 tablespoons water and stir them into the soup slowly. Keep stirring as you add the egg, or it will coagulate into big lumps. Mix in the vinegar and the green chile peppers, if using, sprinkle the black pepper on top and serve hot.

Chicken Soup with Chayote Squash
Murgh aur Chow-Chow ka Soop

Makes 4 to 6 servings

This is an Indian twist on an American "good-for-the-soul" soup classic. My friend Sohini Baliga, a native of Bangalore (in the southern state of Karnataka), shared the recipe, which, when served with crusty whole-wheat bread, is a complete, nutritious meal.

This recipe uses chayote squashes, which are called chow-chow *in southern India. The pear-shaped squash with a center seed has a ridged, pale green skin. Use it like other summer squash, although it is firmer, and requires a little longer cooking time. Choose fresh-looking, firm, unblemished squash. Peeling them, though preferred, is not essential.*

1 tablespoon olive oil
1 tablespoon melted butter
2 to 3 tablespoons peeled minced fresh ginger
2 tablespoons cumin seeds
2 bay leaves

1/2 teaspoon freshly ground black pepper, or to taste
1 to 3 fresh green chile peppers, such as serrano, minced with seeds
1 large onion, halved lengthwise and thinly sliced
4 to 5 small tomatoes (about 1 pound), coarsely chopped
2 medium chayote squash, peeled or unpeeled, coarsely chopped
4 small russet (or any) potatoes, peeled or unpeeled, quartered
1 pound skinless, boneless chicken thighs
1 teaspoon salt, or to taste
5 to 6 cups water
1 tablespoon fresh lemon juice
1 teaspoon garam masala
1/2 cup finely chopped fresh cilantro, including soft stems
1/2 cup thinly sliced scallions, green parts only

1. Heat the oil and butter in a large nonstick wok or saucepan over medium-high heat and add the ginger, cumin seeds, bay leaves, black pepper, and green chile peppers. Cook, stirring, about 1 minute.

2. Add the onion, tomatoes, squash, potatoes, chicken, salt, and water, and bring to a boil over high heat. Reduce the heat to medium-low, cover the pan, and simmer until the chicken is opaque and fork-tender, 30 to 40 minutes.

3. Remove the bay leaves. Mash some of the potatoes and squash pieces against the inside of the pot to thicken the soup. Add the lemon juice and garam masala and cook another few minutes. Transfer to a serving bowl, mix in the cilantro and scallion greens, and serve.

Variation: Substitute turnips, rutabagas, carrots, or any other firm squash for the chayote.

Salads

Fresh Chopped Salads (Cachumbar) 199

Gingered Yellow Tomato and
Armenian Cucumber Salad

Armenian Cucumber and Peanut
Salad with Sizzling Mustard Seeds

Pickling Cucumber
and Red Lentil Salad

Daikon, Sprouted Mung Bean,
and Roasted Peanut Salad

Tomato Salads 201

Tomato and Scallion Salad
with Crispy Sev Noodles

Multi-Colored Warm Tomato Salad

Pan-Fried Green Tomato Salad

Cabbage Salads 202

Kerala Cabbage and
Red Onion Salad

Yogurt Coleslaw

Cabbage and Broccoli Salad
with Roasted Peppercorns

Lemony Cabbage Salad
with Mustard Seeds

Marinated Salads 204

Lemon-Marinated Red Onion Rings

Zucchini Salad with Pineapple Bits

Carrot and Cashew Salad

Marinated Peanut Salad

Okra and Radish Salad

Bean and Legume Salads 207

Sprouted Green Mung Bean
and Cabbage Salad

Mixed Sprouted Bean Salad
with Potato Vermicelli

Parsi-Style Sprouted Bean Salad

Spicy Dew Bean Salad

Red Bean Salad with Tamarind

Black-Eyed Pea Salad

Soybean and Tomato Salad

Chickpea Chaat Salad
with Fresh Pomegranate Seeds

Potato and Root Vegetable Salads 211

Potato Salad with Yogurt

Red Potato Chaat Salad

Potato, Sweet Potato, and Pea Salad

Taro Root Salad with Ajwain Seeds

Sweet Potato Salad with Tamarind

Green Salads 214

Mixed Greens
with Pan-Roasted Tomatoes

Spinach Salad
with Roasted Cumin Seeds

Paneer Cheese Salad
with Baby Greens

Fruit Salads 215

Spicy Mixed Berry Salad

Savory Summer Fruit Salad

Non-Vegetarian Salads 216

Indian Egg Salad

Tandoori Chicken Salad

Minced Chicken Chaat Salad
with Spicy Lentil Wafers

Gingered Shrimp Salad

 = Vegan   = Pressure-Cooker Quick

Salads have universal appeal—they tempt with their colors, textures, and tastes, and with the allure of eating refreshing and satisfying foods. Indian salads fulfill that promise in delicous and sometimes surprising ways. They feature the vibrant greens of herbs and lettuces, the luscious reds of tomatoes and bell peppers, and the cool whites of potatoes and *paneer* cheese. They are sometimes crunchy and crisp, other times warm and wilted, and can be made with fresh seasonal vegetables or everyday produce and pantry items. Of course, they are always creatively seasoned with tangy and hot seasonings.

The most basic Indian salad is the classic chopped salad served with most meals—chopped tomatoes, cucumbers, daikon radishes, and onions spiked with salt, cayenne powder, and lemon juice. There are other kinds of chopped salad and other kinds of salads popular throughout the country.

One important realm of Indian salads are the *chaats. Chaats* are defined less by specific ingredients than by textures and flavors; they are a complex mix of savory, sweet, salty, tangy, and spicy foods and seasonings. The Hindi word *chaat* means "to lick the plate clean." Once you've tried the tantalizing, lip-smacking flavors of *chaats*, you'll know how the dishes got their name.

Because *chaat* salads can be made with different ingredients, you'll find them in different subsections of this chapter. They can be made with vegetables (Potato, Sweet Potato, and Pea Salad, page 212), fruits (Savory Summer Fruit Salad, page 216), dried beans (Mixed Sprouted Bean Salad with Potato Vermicelli, page 207), or chicken and other meats (Tandoori Chicken Salad, page 217). *Chaat* snacks reflect similar multiple layers of flavor but resemble composed dishes more than salads. Look for them in the Starters and Snacks chapter.

Here are some popular Indian salads. Enjoy them as part of buffet, as a first course, or as a small meal with a cup of soup and *paranthas* (griddle-fried breads).

Fresh Chopped Salads (Cachumbar)

Fresh chopped salads—or, as I call them, chop-chop salads—are known in India as *cachumbar* or *cachumar* salads. They feature lots of raw salad vegetables in a kaleidoscope of colors that have been finely chopped and tossed with spices and fresh lemon juice.

A basic *cachumbar* salad has no formal recipe. Simply mix in a bowl finely diced tomatoes, cucumbers, daikon radishes, scallions, cilantro, and a few mint leaves. Then add salt, pepper, *chaat masala*, and fresh lime or lemon juice, to taste. And if you love the heat of chile peppers, throw in some minced green chiles, such as serrano.

Gingered Yellow Tomato and Armenian Cucumber Salad

Adrak vaala Tamatar-Kheerae ka Salaad

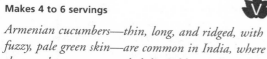

Makes 4 to 6 servings

Armenian cucumbers—thin, long, and ridged, with fuzzy, pale green skin—are common in India, where they are known as tar or kakdi. Sold mainly in the hot summer months, they are said to be cooling to the body. They are primarily available in Indian and Middle-Eastern markets, although some American supermarkets carry them. If you can't find them, use Japanese cucumbers or any other seedless variety.

1¹/₂ teaspoons Chaat Masala (page 20 or store-bought), or more to taste

1 pound yellow tomatoes, finely chopped

¹/₂ pound Armenian or any seedless cucumbers, finely chopped

2 cups finely chopped romaine lettuce or fresh spinach leaves

¹/₄ cup finely chopped fresh cilantro, including soft stems

1 fresh green chile pepper, minced with seeds

1 to 2 tablespoons peeled minced fresh ginger

¹/₄ teaspoon ground ajwain seeds

1 to 2 tablespoon fresh lime or lemon juice

Prepare the chaat masala. Then mix everything in a large bowl. Adjust the seasonings and serve. If you wish to serve the salad chilled, mix all the ingredients except the chaat masala and ajwain seeds, and chill up to 24 hours. Add the spices just before serving, or the salt in the chaat masala will draw out the juices from the ingredients and make the salad too liquidy.

Armenian Cucumber and Peanut Salad with Sizzling Mustard Seeds

Kakri ki Koshumbir

Makes 4 to 6 servings

My friend Promilla Rawal makes this salad whenever she craves the flavors of her native state, Maharashta, located in the central western part of India. This salad, with the delicate fragrances of coconut and sesame, is lovely when served with a yellow mung bean dish (pages 342 to 346) and steamed rice.

2 teaspoons Marathi Curry Powder with Coconut and Sesame Seeds (page 17 or store-bought)

1 pound Armenian or any seedless cucumbers, finely chopped

¹/₂ cup roasted and lightly salted peanuts, coarsely chopped

¹/₂ cup finely chopped fresh cilantro, including soft stems

1 fresh green chile pepper, such as serrano, minced with seeds

¹/₄ teaspoon salt, or to taste

1 tablespoon peanut oil

1 teaspoon black mustard seeds

¹/₈ teaspoon ground asafoetida

1 tablespoon minced fresh curry leaves

1. Prepare the curry powder. In a serving bowl, mix the cucumbers, peanuts, cilantro, green chile pepper and salt.

2. Heat the oil in a small nonstick saucepan over medium-high heat and add the mustard seeds; they should splutter upon contact with the hot oil, so cover the pan and reduce the heat until the spluttering subsides.

3. Quickly add the curry powder, asafoetida, and curry leaves, and stir for a few seconds. Transfer to the salad. Mix well and serve. If you wish to serve the salad chilled, mix only the cucumbers, peanuts, cilantro, and green chile pepper, and chill up to 24 hours. Add the spices just before serving, or the salt will draw out the juices from the ingredients and make the salad too liquid.

Pickling Cucumber and Red Lentil Salad
Kheera aur Laal Dal ra Salaad

Makes 4 to 6 servings

Cucumbers grown in India are much closer in size, shape, and taste to the pickling variety available in America. With a soft skin that does not need peeling, and almost no seeds, these cucumbers are my first choice in this salad. You may use the English, Japanese, or any other seedless variety, if you wish.

$1/2$ **cup red lentils (dhulli masoor dal), sorted, washed and soaked in water to cover about 2 hours, then drained**
$1^{1}/4$ **pounds pickling or seedless cucumbers, finely chopped**
4 scallions, white and light green parts only, finely chopped
2 tablespoons finely chopped fresh cilantro, with soft stems
1 tablespoon vegetable oil
$1/2$ **teaspoon black mustard seeds**
$1/2$ **teaspoon cumin seeds**
$1/2$ **teaspoon coarsely ground black pepper**
1 teaspoon peeled minced fresh ginger
1 to 2 tablespoons fresh lemon juice
$1/2$ **teaspoon salt, or to taste**

1. In a serving bowl, mix the dal, cucumbers, scallions, and cilantro.

2. Heat the oil in a small nonstick saucepan over medium-high heat and add all the spices; they should sizzle upon contact with the hot oil. Quickly add the ginger, stir for a few seconds, then add the lemon juice and salt. Transfer to the salad, mix well and serve.

Daikon, Sprouted Mung Bean, and Roasted Peanut Salad
Mooli, Phooti Mung Dal aur Moong-Phalli ka Salaad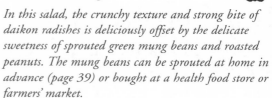

Makes 4 to 6 servings

In this salad, the crunchy texture and strong bite of daikon radishes is deliciously offset by the delicate sweetness of sprouted green mung beans and roasted peanuts. The mung beans can be sprouted at home in advance (page 39) or bought at a health food store or farmers' market.

$1^{1}/2$ **teaspoons Chaat Masala (page 20 or store-bought), or more to taste**
$1/2$ **cup raw shelled peanuts, red skin on**
1 cup finely chopped daikon radishes
1 cup finely chopped daikon or red radish leaves
$1^{1}/2$ **cups sprouted green mung beans (saabut mung dal), page 39 or store-bought**
8 to 10 scallions, white parts only, thinly sliced
1 fresh green chile pepper, such as serrano, minced with seeds or to taste
1 tablespoon fresh lime or lemon juice

1. Prepare the chaat masala. Then, in a small cast-iron or nonstick skillet, roast the peanuts, stirring and shaking the pan, over medium heat until they are golden. Let cool, then grind coarsely with a mortar and pestle or a spice grinder.

2. In a serving bowl, mix the radishes, radish leaves, mung dal, scallions, chile pepper, and ground peanuts. Add the chaat masala and lime juice and toss to mix. Serve, preferably at room temperature.

Tomato Salads

Tomato and Scallion Salad with Crispy Sev Noodles

Tamatar, Harae Pyaz, aur Sev ka Salaad

Makes 4 to 6 servings

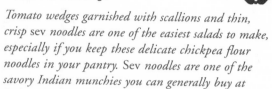

Tomato wedges garnished with scallions and thin, crisp sev noodles are one of the easiest salads to make, especially if you keep these delicate chickpea flour noodles in your pantry. Sev noodles are one of the savory Indian munchies you can generally buy at Indian markets.

6 to 8 small, firm, vine-ripened tomatoes, cut into thin wedges
10 to 12 scallions, white and light green parts only, thinly sliced
1 small lime
1/4 teaspoon salt, or to taste
Coarsely ground black pepper, to taste
2 tablespoons minced fresh cilantro leaves
1 tablespoon minced fresh mint leaves
1/4 cup packaged fine sev noodles

1. Place the tomato wedges on a large serving platter and scatter the scallions over them.

2. Cut the lime in half and microwave on high about 30 seconds. Squeeze 1 or both the halves over the tomatoes. Top with salt, black pepper, cilantro, mint, and sev noodles, and serve.

Multi-Colored Warm Tomato Salad

Rang-Birangae Tamatar ka Salaad

Makes 4 to 6 servings

As pretty as a picture and with a taste that fully complements its appearance, this salad is quite a party pleaser. Make it in the summer months when tomatoes are in season—oozing with natural flavor and vine-ripened goodness. Use as many colors, sizes, and varieties of tomatoes as you can lay your hands on—even unripe green ones, which have a bracingly tart taste.

2 to 3 cups mixed baby lettuce, mesclun, or other mixed greens
1 tablespoon olive oil
1 teaspoon cumin seeds
1 teaspoon black mustard seeds
1 fresh green chile pepper, such as serrano, minced with seeds
2 tablespoons minced fresh curry leaves
1/8 teaspoon ground asafoetida
2 tablespoons fresh lemon juice
1 1/2 pounds firm vine-ripened tomatoes of mixed colors, coarsely chopped
5 to 7 cherry or pear-shaped tomatoes of mixed colors

1. Line a serving platter with the lettuce. Keeping a large nonstick wok or saucepan tilted to one side, heat the oil and add the cumin and mustard seeds; they should sizzle immediately upon contact with the hot oil. Lay the pan flat, and quickly add the green chile pepper, curry leaves, asafoetida and lemon juice and cook 1 minute.

2. Add the tomatoes and stir gently until heated through, but still firm, 1 to 2 minutes. Transfer to the lettuce-lined platter and serve.

Pan-Fried Green Tomato Salad

Bhunnae Harae Tamatar ka Salaad

Makes 4 to 6 servings

Fried green tomatoes, though primarily known in the United States as a southern specialty, are fairly common in India and make for a delicious, light, and crisp salad that often doubles as a side dish.

1/2 teaspoon Chaat Masala (page 20 or store-bought)
3 to 4 large unripe green tomatoes (about 1 1/2 pounds), each cut into 8 wedges
1 tablespoon peanut oil
1 tablespoon ground coriander
1/2 teaspoon salt, or to taste
1 tablespoon fresh lemon juice
1/4 cup finely chopped fresh cilantro, with soft stems

1. Prepare the chaat masala. Then, lay the tomato wedges in a single layer in a large nonstick skillet. Drizzle the oil over them and cook over medium-high heat until the bottoms are golden, about 4 minutes.

2. Turn each piece over, sprinkle the coriander and salt over them, and cook until the other side is golden, about 2 minutes.

3. Add the lemon juice and cilantro, very carefully mix everything together, and cook about 30 seconds. Transfer to a serving dish, sprinkle with the chaat masala, and serve.

Cabbage Salads

Kerala Cabbage and Red Onion Salad

Kerala ka Bundh Gobhi aur Laal Pyaz ka Salaad

Makes 4 to 6 servings

This salad, a typical lunchtime favorite from the southwestern state of Kerala, is strongly flavored with coconut oil and sesame seeds. The coconut gives the salad an authentic flavor, because in one form or another coconut is almost always used in Kerala cuisine. If you use peanut oil, add a tablespoon or two of grated fresh or frozen coconut or shredded unsweetened dried coconut to compensate for the change of flavor.

1 tablespoon sesame seeds, dry-roasted (page 35)
1 small red onion, cut in half lengthwise and thinly sliced
2 cups shredded green cabbage
1 green bell pepper, cut into thin matchsticks
4 small tomatoes, cut into thin wedges
1 tablespoon coconut or peanut oil
1 teaspoon mustard seeds
4 whole dried red chile peppers, such as chile de arbol
10 to 12 fresh curry leaves
1 tablespoon distilled white vinegar
1/4 teaspoon salt, or to taste

1. Roast the sesame seeds. Then in a large serving bowl, mix the onion, cabbage, bell pepper, and tomatoes.

2. Heat the oil in a small nonstick wok or saucepan over medium-high heat and add the mustard seeds; they should splutter upon contact with the hot oil, so cover the pan and reduce the heat until the spluttering subsides. Quickly add the red chile peppers and curry leaves and cook, stirring, about 30 seconds. Add the vinegar and salt and transfer the mixture to the salad. Toss well, and garnish with sesame seeds. Refrigerate up to 2 hours, and serve chilled.

Yogurt Coleslaw
Dahi-Bundh Gobhi ka Salaad

Makes 4 to 6 servings

This slaw is a bit different from any you've tasted before. Not only is it made with yogurt instead of mayonnaise, but it's hotter and tangier, thanks to the combination of serrano pepper, ginger, lime juice, and chaat masala. *Serve as a mid-day meal or add another cup or two of yogurt to turn it into a crunchy* raita.

¹/₄ cup almond slivers, dry-roasted (page 35)
1 teaspoon Chaat Masala (page 20 or store-bought)
1 cup plain yogurt (any kind), whisked until smooth
1 tablespoon fresh lime or lemon juice
1 fresh serrano pepper, minced, with seeds
1 tablespoon peeled minced fresh ginger
¹/₂ teaspoon freshly ground black pepper, or to taste
¹/₂ teaspoon salt, or to taste
2 cups finely shredded green cabbage
2 cups finely shredded purple cabbage
1 cup finely diced bell peppers of mixed colors
2 pickling cucumbers, grated
10 to 12 scallions, white and light green parts only, minced
¹/₂ cup finely chopped fresh cilantro, including soft stems
1 tablespoon minced fresh mint leaves
Ground paprika

1. Prepare the almonds and the chaat masala. In a medium bowl, mix the yogurt, lime juice, serrano pepper, ginger, chaat masala, black pepper, and salt.

2. Place the green and purple cabbage, bell pepper, cucumbers, scallions, cilantro, and mint in a large bowl. Add the yogurt dressing and toss to mix well. Transfer to a wide serving bowl, garnish with the paprika and almonds, and serve.

Variation: To make a quick and crunchy hot side dish, lightly pan-cook the mixed vegetables and greens in 1 tablespoon vegetable oil and season with salt and pepper.

Cabbage and Broccoli Salad with Roasted Peppercorns
Bundh Gobhi aur Kaali Mirch ka Salaad

Makes 4 to 6 servings

Lettuce, popularly called salaad-patta *in India, has never been readily available, so cabbage leaves often substitute. Since the peppercorns give this salad its personality, make sure your peppermill grindings are quite coarse so you'll get a burst of peppercorn flavor with every mouthful.*

2 cups finely shredded green cabbage
1 cup finely shredded romaine lettuce
1 cup ¹/₂- to 1-inch broccoli florets
8 to 10 small cherry or pear-shaped tomatoes, halved
¹/₂ cup grated daikon radish
¹/₄ cup finely chopped fresh cilantro, with soft stems
¹/₂ cup nonfat plain yogurt, whisked until smooth
1 tablespoon peeled minced fresh ginger
1 teaspoon fresh lime juice
¹/₂ teaspoon salt, or to taste
1¹/₂ teaspoons multi-colored peppercorns, dry-roasted, coarsely ground + more for garnish (page 35)

In a large serving bowl, mix the cabbage, lettuce, broccoli, tomatoes, daikon radish, and cilantro. In a small bowl, mix the yogurt, ginger, lime juice, salt, and pepper, and add to the salad. Roast the peppercorns. Toss the salad well then garnish with a few coarse grindings from the peppermill. Serve.

Lemony Cabbage Salad with Mustard Seeds

Dakshini Bundh Gobhi Salaad

Makes 4 to 6 servings

This southern Indian variation of cabbage salad can be served any time of the day, either at room temperature or chilled. Be careful not to overcook the cabbage—keep it crisp, cooking it only to blend the flavors. For added flavor, mix in ¼ cup grated fresh or frozen coconut along with the cabbage.

1 tablespoon peanut oil
¹/₂ teaspoon black mustard seeds
¹/₂ teaspoon cumin seeds
2 whole dried red chili peppers, such as chile de arbol
5 fresh curry leaves
2 cups finely shredded green cabbage
2 tablespoons fresh lemon juice
¹/₂ teaspoon salt, or to taste

Heat the oil in a large nonstick wok or skillet over medium heat and add the mustard and cumin seeds; they should sizzle upon contact with the hot oil. Quickly add the red chili peppers and the fresh curry leaves and stir a few seconds, then, add the cabbage and cook briefly—no more than 10 to 15 seconds. If you see the cabbage wilting, transfer it to a large bowl immediately. Add the lemon juice and salt. Toss and serve immediately, or refrigerate 1 to 2 hours to serve chilled.

Marinated Salads

Lemon-Marinated Red Onion Rings

Nimboo vaalae Pyaz

Makes 4 to 6 servings

Almost like a relish, this salad offers a tangy crunch and is indispensable with tandoori *and other grilled fare. My mother always made it with very small red onions (about 1 inch in diameter); the rings not only looked very pretty, but were easy to eat. Use the smallest red onions you can find. This salad is also lovely when made with thinly sliced sweet white onions, such as Vidalia or Maui.*

1 teaspoon Basic Ginger Paste
    (page 46 or store-bought)
4 to 6 small red onions, cut into rings
2 teaspoons salt, or to taste
¹/₄ to ¹/₂ cup finely chopped fresh cilantro,
    including soft stems
2 tablespoons fresh lemon or lime juice
¹/₂ teaspoon hot red pepper flakes, or to taste

1. Prepare the ginger paste. Then, in a non-reactive bowl, place the onions, add the salt, and toss well. Cover and let marinate about 2 hours at room temperature. Then pour into a fine-mesh strainer and drain all the juices and salt (or wash under running water and then drain).

2. Transfer to a serving bowl and mix in the cilantro, lemon juice, ginger paste, and red pepper flakes. Cover and refrigerate about 2 hours in the refrigerator to marinate. Serve chilled.

Variation: This recipe can be made using distilled white vinegar and 2 to 3 teaspoons sugar instead of lemon juice.

Zucchini Salad with Pineapple Bits

Zucchini aur Annanas ka Salaad

Makes 4 to 6 servings

I first had this salad at a wedding in Jodhpur, a city in the northwestern state of Rajasthan. I would not have expected a nontraditional dish like this to be served as part of the menu, but was pleasantly surprised by its most unusual ingredients and flavors. Later, I learned that the young bride herself had given the caterer this recipe.

To keep the salad brilliantly colorful and lightly crunchy cook the squash only briefly, just until the color intensifies.

4 to 6 zucchini, cut into $1/2$-inch pieces
2 cups canned pineapple pieces, plus $1/4$ cup juice
1 to 3 fresh green chile peppers, such as serrano, minced with seeds
$1/2$ cup nonfat plain yogurt, whisked until smooth
$1/2$ teaspoon salt, or to taste
1 teaspoon coarsely ground black pepper, or to taste
1 tablespoon vegetable oil
1 teaspoon cumin seeds
$1/4$ teaspoon ajwain seeds
1 tablespoon peeled minced fresh ginger
$1/8$ teaspoon ground asafoetida
2 tablespoons fresh lemon juice

1. Place the zucchini in a microwave-safe bowl. Cover and cook in the microwave on high power about 2 minutes. Let cool, then drain and transfer to a serving bowl. Add the pineapple and juice, green chile peppers, yogurt, salt, and black pepper, and mix well.

2. Heat the oil in a small saucepan over medium-high heat and add the cumin and ajwain seeds; they should sizzle upon contact with the hot oil. Quickly add the ginger and asafoetida, cook another 30 seconds, and add the lemon juice. Transfer to the zucchini, stirring gently to mix. Serve at room temperature or refrigerate at least 2 hours to serve chilled.

Carrot and Cashew Salad

Gajjar aur Kajju ka Salaad

Makes 4 to 6 servings

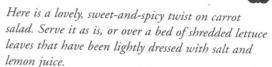

Here is a lovely, sweet-and-spicy twist on carrot salad. Serve it as is, or over a bed of shredded lettuce leaves that have been lightly dressed with salt and lemon juice.

$3/4$ to 1 pound carrots, peeled and grated
$1/4$ cup grated fresh or frozen coconut or
    2 tablespoons shredded unsweetened dried coconut
15 to 20 raw cashews, coarsely chopped
$1/2$ cup finely chopped fresh cilantro, including soft stems
$1/2$ teaspoon salt, or to taste
1 to 2 tablespoons fresh lemon juice
1 teaspoon peanut oil
1 teaspoon black mustard seeds
1 teaspoon cumin seeds
1 tablespoon finely chopped fresh curry leaves
$1/8$ teaspoon ground asafoetida
2 fresh green chile peppers, such as serrano, halved lengthwise

1. In a large serving bowl, mix the carrots, coconut, cashews, cilantro, salt, and lemon juice.

2. In a small saucepan, heat the oil over medium heat and add the mustard and cumin seeds; they should splutter upon contact with the hot oil, so cover the pan until the spluttering subsides.

3. Add the curry leaves, asafoetida, and green chile peppers and cook, stirring, 1 minute. Transfer to the carrots, stirring gently to mix. Serve at room temperature or refrigerate at least 2 hours to serve chilled.

Marinated Peanut Salad
Moong-phalli ka Salaad

Makes 4 to 6 servings

This is a delightfully different presentation of peanuts. I first ate this dish at a club in Coorg, a tiny district in the southwestern corner of Karnatka. Coorg is a lush, mountainous area with acres of land devoted to growing coffee, black pepper, cardamom, oranges, and rice. The rest of Coorg is a natural habitat for wildlife and sandalwood.

After that first taste, this appetizer salad has become a regular in my home. (You can also make it with blanched almonds or halved cashews in place of the peanuts.) Serve it with red wine (such as Merlot) or Indian beer.

2 teaspoons Chaat Masala (page 20 or store-bought)
1/2 cup orange juice
1 teaspoon ground dried mint leaves
1/4 teaspoon salt, or to taste
2 cups raw peanuts, red skins removed
1 cup finely chopped, firm tomato
3 to 4 scallions, finely chopped
1/2 cup finely chopped fresh cilantro,
    including soft stems
2 tablespoons fresh lemon juice

1. Prepare the chaat masala. Then, in a medium bowl mix the orange juice, 1 teaspoon chaat masala, mint, salt, and peanuts. Cover and marinate in the refrigerator, 2 to 4 hours.

2. Transfer the peanuts to a large nonstick skillet and cook over medium-high heat, stirring, 2 to 3 minutes, then reduce the heat to medium and cook until most of the liquid evaporates. Transfer to a serving bowl and let cool. Then mix in the tomato, scallions, cilantro, and lemon juice. Sprinkle the remaining chaat masala on top and serve.

Okra and Radish Salad
Bhindi aur Mooli ka Salaad

Makes 4 to 6 servings

This is a very attractive green, white, and red salad, delicately crunchy yet also slightly chewy because of the okra.

Select young okra, which should be no more than 3 inches long with a tiny bit of soft fuzz—it's a good indication that the okra are tender. If you can only find larger okra, which are older and tend to be more fibrous, test one before buying: If the tip snaps off, the okra is all right to use; if it bends but does not break, it is too fibrous and should not be purchased.

1/2 teaspoon Chaat Masala (page 20 or store-bought)
1 pound fresh tender okra, rinsed and patted dry
10 to 12 small red radishes, thinly sliced
1/2 small onion, coarsely chopped
1 small tomato, coarsely chopped
1 quarter-sized slice peeled fresh ginger
1 clove fresh garlic, peeled
1 tablespoon fresh lime juice
1 fresh green chili pepper, such as serrano, stemmed
1/4 cup finely chopped fresh cilantro,
    including soft stems
1/4 teaspoon salt, or to taste
1/2 teaspoon freshly ground black pepper, or to taste

1. Prepare the chaat masala. Then, cut a thin slice off the stem end of a piece of okra. Then, working from the stem down, make a partial slit into the okra, stopping 1/2 inch from the tip. (This forms a pocket for the marinade to penetrate but keeps the okra intact.) Repeat with all the okra.

2. Bring a medium pot of water to a boil over high heat and add the okra. Cover the pan and turn off the heat. Remove the okra after 1 minute, drain well and lay flat on a kitchen towel to air-dry for a few minutes. Transfer to a work bowl, toss in the radishes, and set aside.

3. In a food processor or a blender, pulse together the onion, tomato, ginger, garlic, lime juice, and chile pepper until minced. (Do not purée.) Add to the okra, add the salt and black pepper, and mix well. Cover and let the okra marinate in the refrigerator, 2 to 4 hours. Transfer to a serving platter, sprinkle with the chaat masala and serve.

Bean and Legume Salads

Sprouted Green Mung Bean and Cabbage Salad

Phooti Mung Dal aur Bundh Gobhi ka Salaad

Makes 4 to 6 servings

This substantial salad can be served as a side dish or enjoyed as a work-day lunch—low on carbohydrates but high in nutrition, it'll fill you up but won't leave you sleepy at your desk. Sprout the beans in advance or buy them at a health food store or Indian market.

**2 cups sprouted green mung beans
    (page 39 or store-bought)**
1 tablespoon sesame seeds, dry-roasted (page 35)
1 teaspoon Chaat Masala (page 20 or store-bought)
1 cup thinly shredded green cabbage
1 cup thinly shredded red cabbage
1 cup finely chopped onion
**1/2 cup finely chopped fresh cilantro,
    including soft stems**
1 tablespoon peeled minced fresh ginger
**1 fresh green chile pepper, such as serrano,
    minced with seeds**
4 small tomatoes, each cut into 6 to 8 wedges
1/4 cup fresh orange juice
2 tablespoons fresh lime juice
1/2 teaspoon salt, or to taste
Freshly ground black pepper, to taste
2 cups mixed baby greens, or any other lettuce
1/4 cup coarsely chopped roasted peanuts

1. Prepare the sprouted beans in advance. Prepare the sesame seeds and the chaat masala. Then, in a bowl, mix everything except the sesame seeds, baby greens, and peanuts. Cover and marinate at least 2 hours in the refrigerator.

2. Mound the mixture over a bed of baby greens, scatter the sesame seeds and peanuts on top, and serve.

Mixed Sprouted Bean Salad with Potato Vermicelli

Phooti Mung Dal aur Aalu Bhujia ki Chaat

Makes 4 to 6 servings

Made with a mixture of sprouted dals *(legumes) and grains, this nutritious salad tastes so good that you'll want to serve it often. The* dals *are delicious, but the real flavor punch comes from the spicy potato vermicelli, called* aalu-bhujia.

Aalu-bhujia *(sometimes spelled on packages as* aloo-bhujia*) are thin, wispy 1/2-inch bits of deep-fried batter made from potato and chickpea flours. Look for them in the savory section of Indian markets under the Haldiram brand.*

**3 cups sprouted mixed dals and grains,
    such as green mung beans, green and red
    lentils, and whole-wheat kernels**
**1 teaspoon New Delhi Street Food Masala
    (page 20), or store-bought Chaat Masala**
**1 cup packaged potato vermicelli (aalu bhujia),
    store-bought**
**1/4 cup finely chopped fresh cilantro,
    including soft stems**
**1 fresh green chile pepper, such as serrano,
    minced with seeds**
1 to 2 tablespoons fresh lime juice

Prepare the sprouted dals and grains in advance. Prepare the masala. Then, mix everything in a large serving bowl and serve immediately, before the vermicelli gets soggy.

Parsi-Style Sprouted Bean Salad

Parsi Phooti Dal ka Salaad

Makes 4 to 6 servings

Indians generally cook sprouted beans. Some people, like my grandmother, cooked them until they were completely soft, whereas others prefer them crisp-tender. However you like them cooked, sprouted beans are a healthful, tasty addition to any meal.

Here is a traditional recipe from my Parsi sister-in-law, Khushnoor, who lightly cooks the sprouted beans and then flavors them with her special, star anise–rich garam masala.

3 to 4 cups sprouted mixed dals, such as mung beans
    and green lentils (page 39 or store-bought)
1 tablespoon Parsi Garam Masala with Star Anise
    (page 19) or store-bought garam masala
1 tablespoon sprouted fenugreek seeds (page 10)
2 tablespoons peanut oil
1 small onion, finely chopped
1 fresh green chile pepper, such as serrano,
    minced with seeds
1/2 cup finely chopped fresh cilantro,
    including soft stems
1 teaspoon salt or to taste
2 tablespoons water
1 to 2 tablespoons fresh lime juice
1 tomato, cut into wedges

1. Prepare the sprouted beans in advance. Then prepare the masala and the fenugreek seeds. Then, heat the oil in a medium nonstick wok or saucepan over medium-high heat and cook the onion, stirring, until golden, about 5 minutes. Add the garam masala, green chile pepper, and cilantro, and cook, stirring, about 1 minute.

2. Add the sprouted dals, fenugreek seeds, salt, and water, and reduce the heat to medium-low. Cover the pan and cook from 3 to 10 minutes, depending on the desired softness. Mix in the lime juice. Transfer to a serving platter, garnish with tomato wedges and serve warm or at room temperature.

Spicy Dew Bean Salad

Moth Dal ki Chaat

Makes 4 to 6 servings

Dried dew beans, called muth *(pronounced* moath*)* dal, *are smaller and duller in color than green mung beans. Cook them as you would Spicy Dry-Cooked Split Green Mung Beans (page 346), or transform them into this delicious street salad, often called a* chaat *in India.*

This salad, though rarely made at home, is consumed all the time and is typically peddled by mobile vendors. Generally, these vendors have a big basket of boiled, salted muth dal, *out of which they dole servings to eager customers, who choose toppings from a selection of mouth-watering seasonings and garnishes.*

1/4 cup any sonth chutney of your choice
    (pages 76 to 78 or store-bought)
1 1/2 teaspoons Chaat Masala (page 20 or store-bought),
    or to taste1 cup dried dew beans (muth dal),
    sorted and washed in 3 to 4 changes of water
1/2 cup dried split yellow chickpeas (channa dal),
    sorted and washed in 3 to 4 changes of water
1/3 teaspoon ground turmeric
1/2 teaspoon cayenne pepper, or to taste
1/2 teaspoon salt, or to taste
3 to 4 cups water
2 tablespoons peeled minced fresh ginger
1 medium tomato, finely chopped
4 to 5 scallions, finely chopped
2 to 3 tablespoons fresh lime juice
1/3 cup finely chopped fresh cilantro,
    including soft stems

1. Prepare the sonth chutney and the chaat masala. Then place both dals, the turmeric, cayenne pepper, salt, and water in a medium saucepan and bring to a boil over high heat. Reduce the heat to medium-low, cover the pan, and simmer until all the water has evaporated, about 25 minutes, leaving behind a soft-cooked, dry dal. Mix in the ginger and let cool.

2. When cool, mix in the tomato, scallions, lime juice, cilantro, and chaat masala. Transfer to a serving dish, drizzle with sonth chutney, and serve, preferably at room temperature.

Red Bean Salad with Tamarind

Chotae Rajma ka Salaad

Makes 4 to 6 servings

Every time my mother cooked chotae rajma *(small kidney beans similar to red beans) in preparation for making a curry, my brother and I would ask her to set aside a bowl for us. We loved to eat them as is, but very often my mother would make them into this spicy salad, which we loved even more.*

1/2 teaspoon cumin seeds, dry-roasted and
    coarsely ground (page 35)
2 tablespoons Tamarind Paste (page 54)
    or 1 tablespoon tamarind powder
1 teaspoon Chaat Masala (page 20 or store-bought)
1 cup dried red (chotae rajma) or pinto beans, sorted,
    washed and soaked overnight in 2 cups water
1 large clove fresh garlic, minced
2 black cardamom pods, pounded lightly
    to break the skin
1 (1-inch) stick cinnamon, broken lengthwise
1 teaspoon salt, or to taste
1/4 cup nonfat plain yogurt, whisked until smooth
2 tablespoons peeled minced fresh ginger
1 fresh green chile pepper, such as serrano,
    minced with seeds
1/4 cup finely chopped fresh cilantro,
    including soft stems
1 tablespoon minced fresh mint leaves

1. Prepare the cumin seeds, tamarind paste, and chaat masala. Then place the dal and the soaking water, garlic, cardamom pods, cinnamon, and salt in a medium nonstick saucepan and bring to a boil over high heat. Reduce the heat to medium-low, cover the pan, and simmer until all the water evaporates, leaving behind beans that are soft and tender but not broken, about 1 hour. (Add more water during cooking, if necessary.) Transfer to a serving bowl.
2. In a small bowl, mix the cumin seeds, yogurt, tamarind, ginger, green chile pepper, and chaat masala. Add to the cooked beans and mix well, adjusting the

seasonings, if necessary. Transfer to a serving dish, mix in the cilantro and mint leaves, and serve, preferably at room temperature.

Black-Eyed Pea Salad

Lobia ka Salaad

Makes 4 to 6 servings

Black-eyed peas—called lobia, ravaan, *or* raungi— *are often used in saucy curries, but they also make great snack salads, called* chaat. *In India, you'll often find this salad served in disposable, biodegradable bowls made of dried coconut leaves. In America, I serve them in one of Mother Nature's edible cups— the outer leaves of radicchio or butter lettuce.*

1/2 teaspoon Chaat Masala (page 20 or store-bought)
1 cup black-eyed peas (lobia), sorted, washed,
    and soaked overnight in 2 cups water
1/4 teaspoon ground turmeric
1 teaspoon salt, or to taste
1 large firm tomato, finely chopped
4 to 5 scallions, white parts only, minced
1 tablespoon peeled minced fresh ginger
1 tablespoon minced fresh mint leaves
1 fresh green chile pepper, such as serrano,
    minced with seeds
1 to 2 tablespoons fresh lime juice
1/2 cup plain yogurt (any kind), whisked until smooth
1 tablespoon peanut oil
1 teaspoon cumin seeds
1 tablespoon ground coriander
1/2 teaspoon ground cumin
1/4 teaspoon ground black salt (optional)
1/2 teaspoon ground paprika
Several outer leaves of radicchio or butter lettuce,
    or about 3 cups shredded greens

1. Prepare the chaat masala. Then, place the black-eyed peas and soaking water, turmeric, and salt in a medium nonstick saucepan and bring to a boil over high heat. Reduce the heat to medium-low, cover the pan, and simmer until all the water evaporates, leaving behind beans that are soft and tender but not broken, about 1 hour. (Add more water during cooking, if necessary.)

2. Transfer to a bowl and mix in the tomato, scallions, ginger, mint, green chile pepper, and lime juice. Let cool, then mix in the yogurt.

3. Heat the oil in a small nonstick saucepan over medium-high heat and add the cumin seeds; they should sizzle upon contact with the hot oil. Quickly add the coriander, ground cumin, black salt, and paprika, stir 30 seconds, and transfer to the black-eyed peas. Mix well. Present the salad in radicchio or butter lettuce cups, or mounded over a bed of shredded greens. Garnish with chaat masala, and serve at room temperature or chilled.

Soybean and Tomato Salad
Soyabean aur Tamatar ka Salaad

Makes 4 to 6 servings

Although made with a bean that is not commonly used in India, this salad comes loaded with Indian flavors and the numerous health benefits of soy.

Frozen soybeans are available in most upscale produce markets and health food stores; be sure to look for shelled soybeans.

1 teaspoon Chaat Masala (page 20 or store-bought)
1¹/2 cups frozen shelled soybeans, thawed
¹/2 cup water
2 cups finely chopped dark green lettuce, such as romaine, green leaf or red leaf
1 large, firm tomato, finely chopped
4 scallions, white and light green parts only, minced
1 tablespoon peanut oil
1 (1-inch) piece fresh ginger, cut into thin matchsticks
1 teaspoon cumin seeds
1 large clove fresh garlic, minced
1 tablespoon ground coriander
¹/4 teaspoon coarsely ground black pepper, or to taste
¹/2 teaspoon salt, or to taste
1 to 2 tablespoons fresh lemon juice

1. Prepare the chaat masala. Then, place the soybeans and water in a microwave-safe dish. Cook in the microwave on high power 5 to 6 minutes, or until the beans are very soft to the touch. Place the lettuce, tomato, and scallion in a large serving bowl.

2. Heat the oil in a medium nonstick saucepan over medium-high heat and add the ginger and cumin seeds; they should sizzle upon contact with the hot oil. Quickly add first the garlic, coriander, and black pepper, then the soybeans, any remaining cooking water, and salt. Cover and cook, stirring and shaking the pan, until the soybeans are well-coated, about 5 minutes.

3. Transfer to the bowl with the lettuce, tomato and scallion, and add the lemon juice and chaat masala. Toss and serve warm or at room temperature.

Chickpea Chaat Salad with Fresh Pomegranate Seeds
Channa Chaat—Anardana

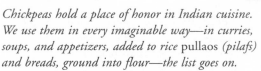

Makes 4 to 6 servings

Chickpeas hold a place of honor in Indian cuisine. We use them in every imaginable way—in curries, soups, and appetizers, added to rice pullaos *(pilafs) and breads, ground into flour—the list goes on.*

This dish—a chaat salad—is one of India's prized recipes, for both its complex flavors and versatility. Serve it as a starter course, a side dish, or just as a snack. Or make it in large quantities for potlucks, picnics, or brunches, and serve it with bhatura *(leavened and deep-fried bread),* kulcha *(baked leavened bread), pita bread, or sourdough rolls.*

2 teaspoons Chaat Masala (page 20 or store-bought)
1¹/2 tablespoons Tamarind Paste (page 54)
1 large, firm vine-ripened tomato, finely chopped
1 small seedless cucumber, such as Armenian or Japanese, finely chopped
4 to 5 scallions, white parts only, thinly sliced
¹/2 cup finely chopped fresh cilantro, including soft stems

2 tablespoons peanut oil
1 teaspoon minced fresh garlic
1 tablespoon peeled minced fresh ginger
1 fresh green chile pepper, such as serrano, minced with seeds
1½ tablespoons ground coriander
2 (15½-ounce) cans chickpeas, rinsed and drained well
¼ cup water
½ cup fresh pomegranate seeds

1. Prepare the chaat masal and tamarind paste. Then, in a medium bowl, mix the tomato, cucumber, scallions, ¼ cup of the cilantro and ½ teaspoon of the chaat masala.

2. Heat the oil in a large nonstick skillet over medium-high heat then cook the garlic, ginger, and green chile pepper, stirring, until golden, about 1 minute. Add the ground coriander, the remaining chaat masala, and the remaining cilantro, and stir about 30 seconds.

3. Add the chickpeas, water, and tamarind, and cook, stirring as necessary, until the chickpeas are tender and all the juices evaporate, about 4 minutes.

4. Transfer to a serving platter. Lightly mix in the tomato mixture and scatter the pomegranate seeds on top. Serve at room temperature or chilled.

Potato and Root Vegetable Salads

Potato Salad with Yogurt
Aalu aur Dahi ka Salaad

Makes 4 to 6 servings

This salad is so tasty, it may replace the potato salad you normally make. Low in fat and calories, it also comes with a boost of calcium, protein, and some friendly lactobacillus, found in yogurt with active cultures.

1½ teaspoons cumin seeds, dry-roasted and coarsely ground (page 35)
1½ pounds russet, red, or Yukon gold potatoes, peeled or unpeeled
1 cup nonfat plain yogurt, whisked until smooth
¼ teaspoon salt, or to taste
¼ teaspoon freshly ground black pepper, or to taste
6 to 8 scallions, white parts only, finely chopped
2 tablespoons peanut oil
1 tablespoon peeled minced fresh ginger
1 to 2 fresh green chile peppers, such as serrano, minced with seeds
¼ cup finely chopped fresh cilantro, including soft stems
½ teaspoon salt, or to taste

1. Prepare the cumin seeds. Then, in a medium pan, cover the potatoes with water, bring to a boil, and cook until tender, about 15 minutes. Drain, Let cool, then cut into ¾-inch pieces. Prepare the cumin seeds. In a medium bowl, mix the yogurt, salt, black pepper, and scallions.

2. Heat the oil in a large skillet over medium-high heat and lightly cook the potatoes, stirring, about 3 minutes. Add the ginger, green chile peppers, cilantro, and salt, and cook, turning as needed, until the potatoes are golden on all sides, about 5 minutes.

3. Transfer to a serving dish and drizzle the yogurt sauce and half the roasted cumin over the potatoes. Mix lightly. Garnish with the remaining cumin and serve.

Red Potato Chaat Salad

Laal Aalu ki Chaat

Makes 4 to 6 servings

Lemon juice is often used in India, and is delicious in potato salads. Here I also add lemon peel, unheard of as an ingredient in India, to enhance the refreshing lemon flavor. Use a citrus zester or a grater, or be sure to remove the bitter white pith from the back of the peel.

This salad can also serve as a side dish to accompany chicken and meat curries.

1¹/₂ to 2 teaspoons Chaat Masala
    (page 20 or store-bought)
1¹/₂ pounds small red potatoes, unpeeled
2 tablespoons olive oil
1 teaspoon cumin seeds
1¹/₂ teaspoons grated lemon peel (zest)
1 tablespoon minced fresh mint leaves
1 fresh green chile pepper, such as serrano,
    minced with seeds
¹/₂ teaspoon salt, or to taste
¹/₂ cup finely chopped fresh cilantro,
    including soft stems
2 to 3 tablespoons fresh lemon juice

1. Prepare the chaat masala. In a medium pot, cover the potatoes with water, bring to a boil, and cook until tender, about 15 minutes. Drain, let cool, then cut into ½-inch pieces. (Do not remove the skin.)

2. In a large skillet, heat the oil over medium-high heat and add first the cumin seeds, then the lemon peel, mint, and green chile pepper. Cook, shaking the skillet, about 30 seconds. Add the potatoes and salt and cook, turning the potatoes as needed, until golden on all sides, about 7 minutes. Reduce the heat if they start to brown too quickly.

3. Add the cilantro and lemon juice, cook another minute, then mix in half the chaat masala. Transfer to a serving dish. Sprinkle with the remaining chaat masala and serve warm or at room temperature.

Potato, Sweet Potato, and Pea Salad

Aalu, Shakkar-kandi, aur Muttar ki Chaat

Makes 4 to 6 servings

Belonging in the chaat *category, this is a fresh-tasting, spicy-and-tart salad. It is made by sautéeing white potatoes and sweet potatoes (*shakkar-kandi*), and then topping them with savory, mouth-watering spices. Make it as part of a holiday brunch or serve with barbecued foods.*

3 to 4 tablespoons Tamarind Paste (page 54)
¹/₂ to 1 teaspoon Chaat Masala
    (page 20 or store-bought)
1 pound small white potatoes
¹/₂ pound small, pale-fleshed sweet potatoes
2 to 3 tablespoons peanut oil
1 cup frozen peas, thawed
¹/₂ teaspoon salt, or to taste
¹/₂ teaspoon cayenne pepper, or to taste
¹/₂ cup finely chopped fresh cilantro,
    including soft stems
¹/₂ cup finely chopped sweet onion or
    white parts of scallions

1. Prepare the tamarind paste and chaat masala. Then, in separate pots, cover the white potatoes and sweet potatoes in lightly salted water, bring to a boil, and cook until tender, about 15 minutes for the potatoes and 15 to 20 minutes for the sweet potatoes (depending on their thickness). Drain and let cool, then peel all the potatoes. Cut each white potato in half lengthwise, and cut the sweet potatoes into thick rounds.

2. In a large cast-iron or nonstick skillet, heat the oil over medium-high heat and cook the white potatoes and sweet potatoes until golden-brown on both sides, about 7 minutes, turning as needed. As you cook them, press each piece with the back of the spatula to flatten it as much as possible. Transfer to a plate, and when they are cool enough to handle, use clean fingers to coarsely break each piece into 2 or 3 smaller pieces.

3. Add the peas to the same skillet and cook over medium-high heat, stirring, until barely golden, about 4 minutes.

4. Mix the potatoes and sweet potatoes into the peas. Then add the tamarind paste, salt, cayenne pepper, chaat masala, and cilantro and cook, turning a few times as needed, about 2 minutes. Adjust seasonings, adding more salt, chaat masala, or tamarind, if needed. Transfer to a serving platter, top with the chopped onions, and serve.

Taro Root Salad with Ajwain Seeds
Arbi ki Chaat

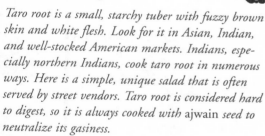

Makes 4 to 6 servings

Taro root is a small, starchy tuber with fuzzy brown skin and white flesh. Look for it in Asian, Indian, and well-stocked American markets. Indians, especially northern Indians, cook taro root in numerous ways. Here is a simple, unique salad that is often served by street vendors. Taro root is considered hard to digest, so it is always cooked with ajwain *seed to neutralize its gasiness.*

1/2 teaspoon Chaat Masala (page 20 or store-bought), or to taste
6 to 8 small taro roots (about 1 pound)
2 to 3 tablespoon finely chopped fresh cilantro, including soft stems
1 tablespoon minced fresh mint leaves
1 fresh green chile pepper, such as serrano, minced with seeds
1/2 teaspoon ajwain seeds, coarsely ground
1/4 teaspoon salt, or to taste
1 to 1 1/2 tablespoons fresh lime juice

Prepare the chaat masala. Then, in a medium pot, cover the taro root with water, bring to boil, and cook until tender, about 15 minutes. Let cool slightly, then peel and cut into 1/2-inch pieces. Place in a serving bowl and mix in all the remaining ingredients. Serve warm or at room temperature.

Sweet Potato Salad with Tamarind
Shakkar-kandi ki Chaat

Makes 4 to 6 servings

This dish could be part of your next Thanksgiving banquet or a frequent addition to autumn meals. It is healthful, with no added fat, and has a flavor that will add sparkle to any evening's menu.

For a more authentic flavor, cook the sweet potatoes (called shakkar-kandi*) on a grill until tender instead of boiling. Then peel and proceed with the recipe.*

1 teaspoon cumin seeds, dry-roasted and coarsely ground (page 35)
2 tablespoons Tamarind Paste (page 54)
4 small sweet potatoes (about 1 pound)
1 tablespoon peeled minced fresh ginger
1 tablespoon brown sugar
1/2 teaspoon salt, or to taste
1/4 cup finely chopped fresh cilantro, including soft stems
1 fresh green chile pepper, such as serrano, minced with seeds

Prepare the cumin seeds and tamarind paste. In a large pot, cover the sweet potatoes with water, bring to a boil, and cook until tender, about 15 minutes. Let cool, then peel and cut into 3/4-inch pieces. Place in a serving bowl and mix in all the remaining ingredients. Cover and refrigerate about 1 hour to serve chilled.

Green Salads

Indian cuisine is full of greens but not green salads. Lettuce, a mainstay of American salads, has traditionally been unavailable in India. The small amount of lettuce that could be purchased was tough, and therefore was used primarily for garnish. Furthermore, Indians have traditionally not eaten greens raw, believing them to be hard to digest, so greens are almost always cooked before being served. This, however, has changed over recent years, and Indians are now buying and eating more fresh lettuce.

While traditional recipes may not feature lettuce or other greens, I have created many green salads in my kitchen in Santa Monica, inspired by the flavors, seasonings, and vegetables of India, but using lettuce and fresh greens, and presented in a way Americans can appreciate.

Mixed Greens with Pan-Roasted Tomatoes

Bhunae Tamatar vaala Hara Salaad

Makes 4 to 6 servings

This salad features salad greens topped with pan-roasted chunks of vine-ripened tomatoes, meltingly soft and full of tangy juices. Complementing them is a spicy buttermilk and chaat masala *dressing.*

1¹/₂ teaspoons Chaat Masala (page 20 or store-bought)
4 to 5 cups coarsely broken mixed sweet and bitter greens, such as iceberg, romaine, green oak, endive, and arugula, rinsed and drained
1 tablespoon peanut oil
4 to 6 small firm vine-ripened tomatoes, coarsely chopped
1 tablespoon peeled minced fresh ginger
¹/₄ teaspoon salt, or to taste
¹/₂ cup buttermilk
Freshly ground black pepper, to taste

1. Prepare the chaat masala. Place the lettuce in a large salad bowl. Heat the oil in a large nonstick skillet over medium-high heat, add the tomatoes, ginger and salt, and cook, shaking the skillet and turning the tomato pieces once or twice, until they are soft but retain their shape, about 3 minutes. Sprinkle half the chaat masala on top and transfer to the lettuce bowl. Do not mix.

2. Add the buttermilk and the remaining chaat masala to the skillet and stir, being sure to scrape the bottom of the skillet to incorporate any tomato bits and juices into the buttermilk. Bring to a boil over high heat. Let cool, then add it to the salad and toss to mix. Top with freshly ground black pepper and serve.

Spinach Salad with Roasted Cumin Seeds

Palak ka Salaad

Makes 4 to 6 servings

A quick salad, this recipe calls for baby spinach bathed in a honey-yogurt dressing and topped with dry-roasted cumin seeds.

2 teaspoons cumin seeds, dry-roasted and coarsely ground (page 35)
5 cups firmly packed baby spinach leaves, trimmed, washed well and spin-dried
1 teaspoon peanut oil
¹/₂ teaspoon ground ginger
1 tablespoon fresh lemon juice
1 tablespoon melted honey
1 cup nonfat plain yogurt, whisked until smooth
¹/₂ teaspoon salt, or to taste
Freshly ground black pepper, to taste

1. Prepare the cumin seeds. Then place the spinach leaves in a salad bowl.

2. Heat the oil in a small saucepan and add first the ginger, then the lemon juice and honey, and stir to mix. Remove from the heat and let cool. Mix in the yogurt, 1 teaspoon cumin seeds, salt, and black pepper. Add to the spinach and toss lightly to mix. Sprinkle the remaining cumin seeds on top and serve.

Paneer Cheese Salad with Baby Greens

Paneer vaala Hara Salaad

Makes 4 to 6 servings

Here, the cheese is fried—to delicious effect. But the real surprise comes from the amazing flavor the baby greens take on after being tossed with the sonth *chutney and spices.*

8 ounces (1 recipe) Paneer Cheese (page 43 or store-bought), cut into 1/2-by-3-inch pieces
1/2 cup any sonth chutney of your choice (pages 76 to 78)
2 teaspoons Chaat Masala (page 20 or store-bought)
1 cup peanut oil for deep-frying
1/2 cup nonfat plain yogurt, whisked until smooth
4 cups mixed baby greens

1. Prepare the paneer, sonth chutney, and chaat masala. Heat the oil in a large nonstick skillet over medium-high heat until it reaches 325°F to 350°F on a frying thermometer or a small piece of paneer cheese dropped into the hot oil rises to the top in 15 to 20 seconds. Add the paneer cheese, 2 to 4 pieces at a time, and fry until barely golden, 30 to 40 seconds.

2. Transfer to a plate, let cool, then when cool enough to handle, coarsely break them into 1/2-inch pieces. Mix the pieces with 1/4 cup sonth chutney and 1 teaspoon chaat masala. Cover and keep warm.

3. In a small bowl, mix together the yogurt and the remaining sonth chutney. Toss the baby greens with this mixture and spread them on a serving platter. Place the paneer cheese over the greens, garnish with the remaining chaat masala, and serve.

Fruit Salads

Spicy Mixed Berry Salad

Berriyon ki Chaat

Makes 4 to 6 servings

There are several Indian berries that are unknown in the United States: falsa, *a small, round berry with a deep red color, similar to blueberries;* jamun, *a dark purple, oval fruit with a long center seed; and* baer, *similar to dates, ranging in color from pale green to brown, also featuring a long center seed. Typically,* falsas *and* jamuns *are put into small terra cotta or metal containers along with special spice blends. The mouth of the container is covered with a dried leaf or a piece of paper and shaken vigorously until the berries become very soft and thoroughly covered with spices.*

I've often thought about preparing the berries I find in America this way, but because they are already soft, this treatment is sure to turn them into mush. So instead, I gently toss them with chaat masala.

2 to 3 cups fresh mixed berries, such as raspberries, blackberries, and boysenberries
1 teaspoon Chaat Masala (page 20 or store-bought), or more to taste
Finely chopped fresh mint leaves

Rinse and drain the berries, blot with paper towels, then place on a towel and allow to air-dry until as dry as possible. Meanwhile, prepare the chaat masala. Transfer to a serving bowl, add the chaat masala, and toss lightly. Garnish with mint leaves and serve.

Savory Summer Fruit Salad

Phallon ki Chaat

Almost like a Mexican fruit salsa, this sweet and savory salad can be served as a snack or as part of an Indian meal or Western-style cook-out.

1 to 2 teaspoons Chaat Masala (page 20 or store-bought)
2 pounds mixed fruits, such as peaches, nectarines, and apricots, pitted and coarsely chopped
1 large mango, peeled and coarsely chopped
1 cup cherries, pitted and halved
1 cup strawberries, coarsely chopped
1 tablespoon peeled minced fresh ginger
1/2 cup finely chopped fresh cilantro, including soft stems
1 tablespoon minced fresh mint leaves
1 fresh green chile pepper, such as serrano, minced with seeds
1 to 2 tablespoons fresh lime or lemon juice

1. Prepare the chaat masala. Then, in a large serving bowl, mix together the peaches, nectarines, apricots, and mango. Remove about 1 cup of the mixed fruits, mash coarsely, and return to the bowl.

2. Mix in the cherries and strawberries, then add the ginger, cilantro, mint, chili pepper, lime juice, and chaat masala. Mix well and serve.

Variation: Vary the fruit depending upon what is on hand or in season. Exotic fruits, like the tart star fruit (*kamrak*), can be an attractive addition.

Non-Vegetarian Salads

Indian Egg Salad

India ka Andae ka Salaad

Makes 4 to 6 servings

Try this mayonnaise-free egg salad on sandwiches, or use as a stuffing for hollowed-out cherry tomatoes or small bell peppers. It can also be simply presented over a bed of greens. You can use store-bought curry powders, but they don't compare to homemade.

1/2 cup plain Yogurt Cheese (page 42)
1 teaspoon dry-roasted and coarsely ground cumin seeds (page 35)
1 tablespoon dry-roasted sesame seeds (page 35)
1 teaspoon Basic Curry Powder (page 15 or store-bought)
4 large eggs
1/4 cup finely chopped fresh cilantro, including soft stems
1 tablespoon peeled minced fresh ginger
1 to 2 fresh green chile peppers, such as serrano, minced with seeds
1/4 teaspoon salt, or to taste

1. Prepare the yogurt cheese. Then prepare the cumin, the sesame seeds, and the curry powder. In a medium saucepan, place the eggs in water to cover by 2 inches and bring to a boil over high heat. Reduce the heat to medium, cover the pan and simmer until hard-boiled, 10 to 12 minutes. Let cool or plunge into cold water, shell them, then chop finely.

2. Place the eggs in a large serving bowl, mix in all the remaining ingredients and serve.

Tandoori Chicken Salad
Tandoori Murgh ki Chaat

Makes 4 to 6 servings

Although smoky, tender tandoori *chicken generally disappears fast, if there's any left over, it can be used to make other dishes. Here I transform it into a spicy and delicate* chaat *salad that gets its flavor boost from a sizzling ginger-mint* tarka *(sizzling flavor topping).*

If you want to make this salad in a hurry, buy the tandoori *chicken from an Indian restaurant already cooked, or make it with any type of grilled chicken.*

1 (2- to 2¹/₂-pound) (1 recipe) Grilled Tandoori Chicken (page 445)
1 teaspoon cumin seeds, dry-roasted and coarsely ground (page 35)
1 teaspoon Chaat Masala (page 20 or store-bought), or to taste
1 large tomato, cut into ¹/₂-inch pieces
2 to 3 small seedless cucumbers, such as Armenian or Japanese, cut into ¹/₂-inch pieces
6 to 8 scallions, white parts only, thinly sliced
¹/₄ cup finely chopped fresh cilantro, including soft stems
1¹/₂ tablespoons vegetable oil
1 (1-inch) piece peeled fresh ginger, cut into thin matchsticks
1 to 2 fresh green chile peppers, such as serrano, minced with seeds
2 tablespoons minced fresh mint leaves
2 to 3 tablespoons fresh lemon or lime juice

1. Prepare the tandoori chicken, then pull the meat off the bone and shred it. Prepare the cumin seeds and the chaat masala. In a serving bowl, mix the shredded chicken, tomato, cucumbers, scallions, and cilantro.

2. Heat the oil in a small nonstick saucepan over medium-high heat and cook the ginger, stirring, until golden, about 3 minutes. Mix in the green chile peppers and mint and stir about 1 minute. Then add the lemon juice and chaat masala and stir a few seconds. Add to the chicken and mix well. Taste and adjust the seasonings. Sprinkle with the roasted cumin and serve.

Minced Chicken Chaat Salad with Spicy Lentil Wafers
Murgh Keema aur Paapad ki Chaat

Makes 4 to 6 servings

As you cook the chicken, do not break up all the chunks. They add lovely texture to the salad. Paapad wafers are sun-dried, paper-thin rounds of lentil flour dough. They are available at Indian markets, and come both plain and lightly spiced.

1 large russet potato, unpeeled
2 tablespoons vegetable oil
1 pound boneless, skinless chicken breasts, minced
1 large onion, finely chopped
1 tablespoon peeled minced fresh ginger
1 large clove fresh garlic, minced
1 fresh green chile pepper, such as serrano, minced with seeds
1 teaspoon garam masala
1 teaspoon dried fenugreek leaves
1 teaspoon salt, or to taste
¹/₂ cup nonfat plain yogurt, whisked until smooth
1 to 2 tablespoons fresh lime juice
1 red bell pepper, finely chopped
¹/₂ cup finely chopped fresh cilantro, including soft stems
4 to 6 Spicy Lentil Wafers, microwaved for 1 minute each (page 95)

1. In a small pan, cover the potato with water, bring to a boil, and cook until tender, about 10 minutes. Let cool, then peel, finely chop, and set aside. In a nonstick saucepan, heat the oil over medium-high heat and cook the chicken, onion, ginger, garlic, green chile pepper, garam masala, fenugreek leaves, and salt, stirring to break most of the lumps, until the chicken is golden, about 5 minutes.

2. Add all the yogurt at once, and cook until most of the liquid has evaporated and the yogurt is absorbed, about 5 minutes.

3. Mix in the lime juice, red bell pepper, potato, and cilantro, and cook another 3 minutes. Let cool. Meanwhile, prepare the paapads.

4. Transfer the chicken and vegetables to a serving platter. Break the paapads into small pieces and place them around the chicken. Serve.

Variation: Mix some shredded lettuce into the chicken mixture, then break the paapads into bits, scatter them all over, and serve.

Gingered Shrimp Salad
Adrak-Jhinga ka Salaad

Makes 4 to 6 servings

The sheer visual appeal of this salad is surpassed only by its tantalizing flavors.

1 teaspoon Chaat Masala (page 20 or store-bought)
1 pound extra-large shrimp (about 20),
    shelled and deveined, with tails left on
1 (1-inch) piece fresh ginger, peeled and
    cut into thin matchsticks
1 large clove fresh garlic, minced
2 tablespoons fresh lime or lemon juice
1 teaspoon coarsely ground ajwain seeds
1/2 teaspoon salt, or to taste
1/4 teaspoon cayenne pepper, or to taste
1/2 teaspoon freshly ground black pepper, or to taste
2 tablespoons vegetable oil
2 tablespoons minced fresh mint leaves
2 cups mixed baby greens
1 each of red and yellow bell peppers,
    cut into thin 1 1/2-inch matchsticks
1 small seedless cucumber, such as Armenian or
    Japanese, cut into thin 1 1/2-inch matchsticks
3 to 4 scallions, white parts only, thinly sliced

1. Prepare the chaat masala. Place the shrimp in a large non-reactive bowl. Add the ginger, garlic, lime juice, ajwain seeds, salt, cayenne and black peppers and mix well, making sure all the shrimp are well-coated with the marinade. Refrigerate about 2 hours.

2. Heat the oil in a large nonstick wok or saucepan over medium-high heat and cook the mint leaves, stirring, about 30 seconds. Add the shrimp and the marinade and cook until the shrimp are pink, about 3 minutes.

3. In a large bowl, mix the greens, bell peppers, and cucumber, and toss with the chaat masala. Transfer to a serving platter. Scatter the cooked shrimp over the greens, top with the scallions, and serve.

Yogurt Raitas and Pachadis

Basic Raitas 222

Simple Salt and Pepper Raita

Summer Iced Raita

Ginger and Scallion Raita

Crushed Lemon Pickle Raita

Vegetable Raitas 223

Potato Raita with Roasted Cumin
and Black Peppercorns

Potato Raita with Puréed Greens

Potato and Beet Raita

Beet and Scallion Raita

Tomato Raita
with Fresh Mint Leaves

Cucumber and Radish Raita

Mustard Seed Raita

Sprouted Beans and Vegetable Raita

Kashmiri Morel Mushroom Raita

Raitas with Herbs and Greens 227

Fresh Spinach Raita
with Ginger-Lime Pickle

Frozen Spinach Raita

Sautéed Spinach Raita

Spicy Raita with Lamb's Quarters

Puréed Watercress Raita

Crumbled Tofu and
Mint Chutney Raita

Creamy Tofu Raita
with Fresh Greens

Grilled or Roasted Vegetable Raitas 230

Roasted Bell Pepper Raita

Traditional Grilled Eggplant Raita

Garlicky Roasted
Chinese Eggplant Raita

Pan-Roasted Eggplant Raita
with Sesame Seeds

Grilled Zucchini
and Pearl Onion Raita

Fresh and Dried Fruit Raitas 232

Dried Fruit Raita

Mango Raita with Fresh Ginger

Mango Chutney Raita

Banana Raita

Mandarin Orange Raita

V = Vegan   **P** = Pressure-Cooker Quick

*I*ndians have been eating and drinking yogurt for centuries. On the surface yogurt plays a vital, easily recognized roll as a fire-quencher—soothing the palate when the spicy hot foods of Indian or any cuisine are just a bit too much. But yogurt is also one of those multi-faceted foods, also believed to improve health and longevity. Rich in protein, calcium, phosphorus, and the B vitamins, yogurt is an almost-perfect food and unlike milk, it is easy to digest, even with people who have lactose intolerance.

When yogurt is eaten with a meal, it is believed to promote the overall digestion and assimilation of most nutrients present in the meal. It helps maintain a proper balance of the good and bad bacteria in the system, especially after the use of antibiotics. (Antibiotics destroy the good bacteria along with the bad ones, and yogurt replenishes the good bacteria in the body.)

With all the therapeutic benefits—some proved and others still-popular beliefs— it is no surprise that Indians have made yogurt a crucial part of their daily diets. Whether it is served plain and unadorned, or transformed into a *raita* or a *pachadi*, yogurt is considered a necessity, and not merely an accompaniment to a meal.

Yogurt becomes a *raita* when it is enriched with something as simple as salt and pepper or with anything you can think of, including cooked meats. A similar flavored yogurt in the southern part of India is called a *pachadi*. The main difference between a *raita* and a *pachadi* is that while the yogurt in the *raitas* is generally whisked until smooth, in the *pachadis* it is mostly (not always) incorporated in its thick and lumpy form. If the *pachadi* yogurt is smooth, usually some of the other ingredients give it some texture, such as pressed rice flakes or soft-cooked vegetables.

The spice selections and their treatments also differ from north to south. While the north Indian *raitas* generally call for straight or dry-roasted spices such as cumin seeds, the south Indian *pachadis* are customarily dressed with a sizzling *tarka* (a hot, seasoned oil topping) that is stirred lightly into the flavored yogurt just before it is served.

All *raitas* are served chilled—almost immediately after they are made, but they can be made a few hours ahead of time and kept in the refrigerator. *Pachadis*, traditionally served at room temperature, may also be served chilled.

Basic Raitas

Simple Salt and Pepper Raita
Namak aur Rangeen Mirchon ka Raita

Makes 4 to 6 servings

Eat your everyday yogurt plain and pure, or season it with salt and a few coarse grindings from your pepper-mill and instantly create a delicious mealtime accompaniment. Try it on a baked potato instead of sour cream.

3 cups nonfat plain yogurt, whisked until smooth
¹/₃ teaspoon salt, or to taste
Freshly ground mixed peppercorns, such as red, black, green, and white, to taste

In a serving bowl, mix together the yogurt, salt, and half the mixed peppercorns. Sprinkle the remaining pepper on top as a garnish, and refrigerate until ready to serve.

Summer Iced Raita
Mattha

Makes 4 to 6 servings

This raita, with a light, icy crunch, is made by adding some crushed ice, salt, and black pepper to plain yogurt. This dish reminds Indians of those lazy (and scorching) summer afternoons when grand-mother would insist that we eat this raita to combat the summer heat. It gets hot in America too, and grandmother was right. Eat it by itself or serve it as part of a light summer brunch.

3 cups nonfat plain yogurt, whisked until smooth
1 cup crushed ice (kept chilled)
¹/₄ teaspoon salt, or to taste
Freshly ground black pepper, to taste

Mix everything together in a large bowl and serve immediately.

Ginger and Scallion Raita
Adrak aur Harae Pyaz ka Raita

Makes 4 to 6 servings

With strong flavors that offset the mild-tasting yogurt, this dish can be served as an accompaniment to any meal. But it isn't uncommon for some people to eat it alone, as a snack, on a hot summer afternoon. This raita pairs perfectly with lamb curries and biryanis (layered rice dishes).

3 cups nonfat plain yogurt, whisked until smooth
1¹/₂ tablespoons peeled minced fresh ginger
5 to 6 scallions, white and light green parts, minced
1 fresh green chile pepper, such as serrano, minced with seeds
1 teaspoon sugar
¹/₃ teaspoon salt, or to taste
¹/₂ teaspoon ground paprika
1 to 2 tablespoons minced fresh mint leaves

In a serving bowl, mix together the yogurt, ginger, scallions, sugar, and salt. Garnish with paprika and mint, and serve.

Crushed Lemon Pickle Raita
Nimboo Achaar ka Raita

Makes 4 to 6 servings

With the essence of sun-cured lemon peel and chile pep-pers tingling in your mouth, this spunky raita can be eaten by the bowlful, almost like a soup—which it can be if you serve it as the first course. Also try it over sal-ads or as a dip. The pickle has to be made in advance.

1 tablespoon Crushed Lemon and Fresh Red Chile Pepper Pickle (page 83)
3 cups nonfat plain yogurt, whisked until smooth
2 to 3 tablespoons snipped chives

1. Prepare the pickle. Then place the yogurt in a serving bowl and mix in the lemon pickle. Add salt and pepper, if needed.

2. Add the chives and swirl lightly to mix, with some of them visible as a garnish.

Vegetable Raitas

Potato Raita with Roasted Cumin and Black Peppercorns

Jeerae vaalae Aalu ka Raita

Makes 4 to 6 servings

Although any type of potatoes can be used for this recipe, the softness of russet potatoes really complements the smoothness of the yogurt. This is an everyday home raita *that goes well with all meals, even a simple rice* pullao *(pilaf).*

1 large russet potato
1¹/₄ teaspoons cumin seeds
¹/₂ teaspoon black peppercorns, or to taste
2¹/₂ cups nonfat plain yogurt, whisked until smooth
¹/₃ teaspoon salt, or to taste
¹/₂ cup minced chives or scallion greens
¹/₂ red bell pepper, finely chopped

1. Boil the potato in lightly salted water to cover until tender, then peel it, and chop it finely. Then, place the cumin and black peppercorns in a small nonstick saucepan and dry-roast over medium-high heat until they are fragrant and a few shades darker, about 2 minutes. Let cool, then grind coarsely in a mortar and pestle or a spice grinder.

2. Place the yogurt in a serving bowl, mix in the potato, salt, and half the ground cumin-pepper mixture.

3. Add the chives and swirl lightly to mix, with a few of them visible as a garnish. Top with the remaining cumin-pepper mixture, scatter the red bell pepper over everything, and serve.

Potato Raita with Puréed Greens

Aalu aur Saag ka Raita

Makes 4 to 6 servings

This inviting, traditional raita, *with a greens twist, looks good and seems cooling even before you dig into it. To make it into a salad, add extra potatoes.*

1 large russet potato
1 teaspoon cumin seeds
2 cups nonfat plain yogurt, whisked until smooth
1 cup coarsely chopped fresh spinach leaves
1 cup coarsely chopped fresh cilantro,
     including soft stems
3 to 4 scallions, coarsely chopped
¹/₄ teaspoon salt, or to taste
1 teaspoon ground pomegranate seeds

1. Boil the potato in lightly salted water to cover until tender, then peel it, and chop it finely. Then, place the cumin in a small nonstick saucepan and dry-roast over medium-high heat until they are fragrant and a few shades darker, about 2 minutes. Let cool, then grind coarsely in a mortar and pestle or a spice grinder. Then, place the yogurt in a large serving bowl; mix in the potato.

2. In a food processor a blender, process together the spinach, cilantro, and scallions until puréed. Transfer to the yogurt. Add the salt, pomegranate seeds, and half the cumin and mix well. Sprinkle the remaining cumin on top and swirl lightly with a fork, with most of it visible as a garnish. Serve.

Potato and Beet Raita
Aalu aur Chukandar ka Raita

Makes 4 to 6 servings

Potato raita *takes on a new character with the simple addition of beets and sesame seeds. When you fold in the beets, make sure some of them are peeking through the white yogurt, showing off their burgundy beauty.*

3 small russet potatoes
2 small beets
1 tablespoon sesame seeds
1 teaspoon cumin seeds
2 cups nonfat plain yogurt, whisked until smooth
1 to 2 tablespoons fresh lemon juice
1 tablespoon peeled minced fresh ginger
1 teaspoon sugar
1/3 teaspoon salt, or to taste

1. Place the potatoes and beets in a small saucepan with water to cover and bring to a boil over high heat. Reduce the heat to medium-low, cover the pan, and simmer until tender, about 15 minutes. Remove from the heat, let cool, then peel and chop them finely.

2. While the beets and potatoes are cooking, place the sesame and cumin seeds in a small nonstick saucepan and dry-roast over medium-high heat until they are fragrant and a few shades darker, about 2 minutes. Let cool, then grind coarsely in a mortar and pestle or a spice grinder.

3. Place the yogurt in a large serving bowl. Mix in the lemon juice, ginger, sugar, salt, and half the sesame seeds. Mix in the potatoes and fold in the beets. Sprinkle the remaining sesame seeds and the cumin seeds on top and serve.

Beet and Scallion Raita
Chukandar aur Harae Pyaz ka Raita

Makes 4 to 6 servings

Your guests are in for a surprise. This pink yogurt dish looks like a sweet berry yogurt—but the spicy, savory impact of the first bite refutes that perception immediately.

3 medium beets
2 cups nonfat plain yogurt, whisked until smooth
4 to 5 scallions, minced
1 teaspoon minced fresh garlic
1 fresh green chile pepper, such as serrano, minced with seeds
1/2 teaspoon salt, or to taste
1/2 teaspoon freshly ground black pepper, or to taste
2 tablespoons finely chopped cilantro

1. Place the beets in a small pan with water to cover by 2 inches and bring to a boil over high heat. Reduce the heat to medium-low, cover the pan, and simmer until tender, about 15 minutes. Remove from the heat, let cool, then peel and chop finely. Set aside about 1 tablespoon for garnish.

2. Place the yogurt in a serving dish and mix in the beets, scallions, garlic, green chile pepper, salt, and black pepper. Garnish with the reserved beets and the cilantro, and serve.

Tomato Raita with Fresh Mint Leaves
Tamatar aur Pudinae ka Raita

Makes 4 to 6 servings

This refreshing raita *makes the best of summer's flavors. Serve it on the side as a dip with cut up vegetables, or increase the quantity of the mint leaves and chile peppers and present it as a chutney with appetizers.*

1/2 teaspoon cumin seeds

2 cups nonfat plain yogurt, whisked until smooth

1/4 cup finely chopped fresh mint leaves

1 large tomato, finely chopped

3 to 4 scallions, green parts only, thinly sliced

1 teaspoon minced fresh garlic

1/2 teaspoon salt, or to taste

1/4 teaspoon coarsely ground black pepper

1. Place the sesame and cumin seeds in a small non-stick saucepan and dry-roast over medium-high heat until they are fragrant and a few shades darker, about 2 minutes. Let cool, then grind coarsely in a mortar and pestle or a spice grinder.

2. Place the yogurt in a serving dish and stir in the mint, tomato, scallions, garlic, and salt. Sprinkle black pepper and cumin on top and swirl lightly to mix, with parts of them visible as a garnish. Serve.

Cucumber and Radish Raita

Kheera aur Mooli ka Raita

Makes 4 to 6 servings

Almost like a salad, this has lots of colorful vegetables, adding a light crunch to the otherwise smooth yogurt. After grating and chopping, you should have about 3 cups of the vegetables, but the proportions don't have to be precise.

1 teaspoon Chaat Masala (page 20 or store-bought)

2 cups nonfat plain yogurt, whisked until smooth

2 to 4 seedless cucumbers, grated (peeled or unpeeled)

12 to 15 red radishes, grated and squeezed

1 large firm tomato, finely chopped

1 fresh green chile pepper, such as serrano, minced with seeds

1/2 teaspoon salt, or to taste

1/2 teaspoon freshly ground black pepper, or to taste

1/2 teaspoon ground paprika

Cilantro or mint leaves

Prepare the chaat masala. Place the yogurt in a serving bowl. Add the cucumbers, radishes, tomato, green chile pepper, chaat masala, salt, and pepper and stir to mix well. Garnish with the paprika and cilantro or mint leaves, and serve.

Mustard Seed Raita

Raayi ka Raita

Makes 4 to 6 servings

This is not your traditional soothing raita. Strong and forceful, this Bengali specialty comes with the pungent bite of mustard seeds, giving it a very mustardy personality, similar to Dijon mustard. A little bit goes far. You may prefer it more as a dip or a chutney, and you can even use it as a sandwich spread or a marinade rather than a raita.

1 tablespoon black mustard seeds

1 tablespoon yellow or brown mustard seeds

4 cups nonfat plain yogurt, whisked until smooth

1/2 teaspoon salt, or to taste

3 to 4 pickling cucumbers, peeled and finely chopped

1 small red onion, finely chopped

1 to 2 teaspoons mustard oil or peanut oil

1/4 cup finely chopped fresh cilantro

1. In a mortar and pestle or a spice grinder, coarsely grind all the mustard seeds. Remove to a small non-reactive bowl and mix in about 1/2 cup yogurt and the salt. Set aside to ferment at least 4 and up to 12 hours at room temperature.

2. Place the yogurt in a large serving bowl and mix in the fermented mustard seed mixture. Mix in the cucumbers and onions. Swirl in the mustard oil, garnish with the cilantro, and serve.

Sprouted Beans
and Vegetable Raita

Phooti Dalon aur Sabziyon Ka Raita

Makes 4 to 6 servings

This salad-like raita, loaded with sprouted dals (legumes) and chopped vegetables, makes a perfect working person's lunch with, maybe, a bowl of soup and garlic bread. It is nutritious, lowfat, filling, and delicious.

You should be able to find sprouted beans and lentils in health food stores, specialty produce stores, and Indian markets, or you can try sprouting them in advance.

1/2 cup sprouted split mung beans (mung dal) (page 39 or store-bought)
1 cup sprouted red lentils (page 39 or store-bought)
1 teaspoon dry-roasted sesame seeds (page 35)
1 teaspoon Chaat Masala (page 20 or store-bought)
2 cups nonfat plain yogurt, whisked until smooth
1 small tomato, finely chopped
1 to 4 seedless cucumbers, grated (peeled or unpeeled)
1/4 cup finely chopped fresh cilantro, including soft stems
1 fresh green chile pepper, such as serrano, minced with seeds
1/2 teaspoon salt, or to taste
1/2 teaspoon freshly ground black pepper, or to taste

1. Prepare the beans and lentils in advance. Prepare the sesame seeds and chaat masala.

2. Place the yogurt in a large serving bowl. Mix in everything except 2 tablespoons of the red lentils, the sesame seeds, and the chaat masala. Sprinkle the reserved red lentils and sesame seeds on top, top with the chaat masala, and serve.

Kashmiri Morel
Mushroom Raita

Kashmiri Gucchiyon ka Raita

Makes 4 to 6 servings

Indian morel mushrooms are grown in Kashmir, and from there they make their way to the rest of the country. Rings of these prized morel mushrooms adorn this raita, which mushroom fans might enjoy all on its own. Use other mushroom varieties, such as white button, oyster, or shiitake, if morels are not available.

1 medium russet potato
2 1/2 teaspoons Kashmiri Raita Masala (page 24)
3 cups nonfat plain yogurt, whisked until smooth
Salt, to taste
1 tablespoon vegetable oil
1 medium onion, cut in half lengthwise and thinly sliced
8 to 10 large fresh or dried reconstituted morel mushrooms, thinly sliced
1/4 cup finely chopped fresh cilantro

1. Boil the potato in lightly salted water to cover until tender, then peel it and finely chop it. While it's cooking, prepare the raita masala. Then place the yogurt in a large serving bowl and mix in 2 teaspoons raita masala. Add salt, if needed (there is already some in the masala).

2. Heat the oil in a small nonstick skillet over medium-high heat and cook the onion, stirring, until golden, 2 to 3 minutes. Add the potato and cook, stirring, about 1 minute, then add the morel mushrooms and cilantro and cook another minute. Transfer to the yogurt, and mix well. Garnish with the remaining 1/2 teaspoon raita masala and serve.

Variation: You can substitute other vegetables by replacing the morel mushrooms with 1 cup grated daikon or red radishes, or with 2 cups thinly sliced, golden fried fresh okra.

Raitas with Herbs and Greens

Fresh Spinach Raita with Ginger-Lime Pickle
Palak ka Khatta Raita

Makes 4 to 6 servings

For those who want their raitas to serve as a salad or a vegetable on the side, this dish fits the bill.

1 tablespoon Minced Ginger-Lime Pickle (page 84)
1 teaspoon dry-roasted and coarsely ground cumin seeds (page 35)
2½ cups nonfat plain yogurt, whisked until smooth
1 small bunch (8 to 10 ounces) fresh spinach, trimmed of roots only, washed and finely chopped
⅓ teaspoon salt, or to taste
⅓ teaspoon freshly ground black pepper, or to taste

Prepare the ginger-lime pickle in advance. Prepare the cumin seeds. Then place the yogurt in a serving bowl. Add the spinach, ginger-lime pickle, salt, and black pepper, and stir to mix. Lightly swirl in the cumin seeds, with parts of them visible as a garnish, and serve.

Frozen Spinach Raita
Manju Bansal ka Palak Raita

Makes 4 to 6 servings

My friend Manju Bansal is from Kanpur, a city in the heart of northern India. The spices in this recipe reflect her city's heritage, and the frozen spinach, her American practicality.

¼ teaspoon whole cumin seeds + 1 teaspoon dry-roasted and coarsely ground cumin seeds (page 35)
3 cups nonfat plain yogurt, whisked until smooth
¼ teaspoon salt, or to taste
¼ teaspoon ground black salt (optional)

1 teaspoon olive oil
¼ teaspoon black mustard seeds
A scant pinch ground asafoetida
1 small onion, finely chopped
1 teaspoon peeled minced fresh ginger
1 (10-ounce) package thawed frozen spinach (reserve all juices)

1. Prepare the roasted cumin seeds. Then place the yogurt in a serving bowl. Mix in the salt and black salt.
2. Heat the oil in a small saucepan over medium-high heat. Add the mustard seeds and ¼ teaspoon whole cumin seeds; they should sizzle upon contact with the hot oil. Quickly stir in the asafoetida, then the onion and ginger, and cook, stirring, until golden, about 3 minutes.
3. Add the spinach plus all the juices and cook until most of the juices evaporate, about 4 minutes. Let cool, then stir well into the yogurt. Mix half the roasted cumin into the yogurt, sprinkle the remaining on top, and serve.

Sautéed Spinach Raita
Bhuni Palak ka Raita

Makes 4 to 6 servings

Spinach raitas are generally made with puréed, steamed, or boiled spinach. However, I find that a quick sauté brings more flavor to this raita, which is then made even tastier with a sprinkling of dry-roasted sesame seeds and coarsely chopped peanuts.

1 teaspoon dry-roasted and coarsely ground cumin seeds (Dry-Roasting Spices, page 35)
1 teaspoon sesame seeds, dry-roasted (Dry-Roasting Spices, page 35)
1 tablespoon vegetable oil
1 tablespoon peeled minced fresh ginger
1 teaspoon minced fresh garlic
1 small bunch fresh spinach (8 to 10 ounces), trimmed of roots only, washed and finely chopped,
3 cups nonfat plain yogurt, whisked until smooth
½ teaspoon salt, or to tasteFreshly ground black pepper, to taste
¼ cup roasted peanuts, coarsely chopped

1. Prepare the cumin and sesame seeds. Then heat the oil in a large nonstick wok or saucepan over medium-high heat and cook the ginger and garlic, stirring, until golden, about 1 minute. Add the spinach and cook, stirring, until completely wilted and slightly golden, 3 to 5 minutes. Set aside to cool.

2. Place the yogurt in a serving bowl. Add the salt, then mix in the cooled spinach, plus any juices that may have accumulated.

3. Lightly swirl in the cumin and sesame seeds, and the black pepper, with parts of them visible as a garnish. Sprinkle the peanuts on top and serve.

Spicy Raita with Lamb's Quarters
Bathuae ka Raita

Makes 4 to 6 servings

Belonging to the "goosefoot" greens family, along with spinach, beets, and Swiss chard, lamb's quarters (bathua *in Hindi*) *are a naturalized weed in America, but are relatively unknown as cooking greens. In India however, they are very commonly used.*

The soft leaves resemble the foot of a goose and have a delicate, spinach-like flavor. They are naturally starchy, and are often mixed with spinach, mustard, and other greens, to lend a dish the much-desired smoothness.

Here, I steam them to make a popular north Indian raita. *Look for them in farmers' markets or in specialty produce stores. Buy more than you need; they freeze very well—raw as well as steamed.*

2 cups finely chopped lamb's quarters leaves
2 cups nonfat plain yogurt, whisked until smooth
3 to 4 scallions, green parts only, finely chopped
1/4 teaspoon salt, or to taste
Freshly ground black pepper, to taste
1 to 2 teaspoons olive oil
1 fresh green chile pepper, such as serrano, minced with seeds
1 teaspoon cumin seeds

1. Place the leaves in a large saucepan of water to cover over high heat and bring to a boil. Boil until soft, 4 to 5 minutes. Alternately, cover and cook in a microwave-safe dish on high, 2 to 3 minutes.

2. Let cool. Transfer to a food processor and pulse until coarsely chopped, or chop by hand.

3. Place the yogurt in a serving dish and gently mix in the greens. Add the scallions, salt, and black pepper, and mix again.

4. Heat the oil in a small saucepan over medium-high heat and add the chile pepper and cumin seeds; they should sizzle upon contact with the hot oil. Quickly add them to the yogurt, swirl lightly, and serve.

Puréed Watercress Raita
Hara Raita

Makes 4 to 6 servings

Watercress is not found in India, but in America I use it interchangeably with spinach. It has a sharp, mustard-like flavor, and when puréed with scallions, chile pepper, and cilantro, these leaves become part of a uniform chutney. And when we mix this chutney with yogurt, we instantly have a lovely raita.

For a change of flavors, substitute other strong greens, such as daikon, mustard, or turnip greens, for the watercress, or, of course, spinach.

1 teaspoon dry-roasted and coarsely ground cumin seeds (page 35)
3 large scallions, coarsely chopped
1 fresh green chile pepper, such as serrano, stemmed
1/2 cup coarsely chopped fresh cilantro, including soft stems
1 cup firmly packed fresh watercress leaves
2 to 3 cups nonfat plain yogurt, whisked until smooth
1/2 teaspoon salt, or to taste
1 cup finely chopped yellow and red tomatoes
Freshly ground black pepper, to taste

1. Prepare the cumin seeds. Then, in a food processor or a blender, process together the scallions, green chile pepper, cilantro, and watercress to make a smooth purée.

2. Place the yogurt in a serving bowl and mix in the puréed greens and salt. Pile up the tomatoes in the center. (Do not mix them into the raita.) Sprinkle the roasted cumin and black pepper on top, and serve.

Crumbled Tofu and Mint Chutney Raita

Tofu aur Pudina Chutni ka Raita

Makes 4 to 6 servings

This raita, *traditionally made just with yogurt and mint chutney, takes on a new character and healthful benefits with the simple addition of tofu. You can serve it as a substantial side dish or as a dip with snacks and finger foods.*

2 tablespoons Mint Chutney with Pomegranate Seeds (page 58)

1 teaspoon Chaat Masala (page 20 or store-bought)

1¹/₂ cups nonfat plain yogurt, whisked until smooth

¹/₂ teaspoon salt, or to taste

1 (10¹/₂-ounce) package firm tofu, towel-dried and coarsely crumbled

1 large red bell pepper, stemmed, seeded, and finely chopped

Prepare the chutney and the chaat masala. Then place the yogurt in a large serving bowl and mix in the chutney, chaat masala, and salt. Add the tofu and mix again. Garnish with the red bell pepper and serve.

Creamy Tofu Raita with Fresh Greens

Tofu ka Hara Raita

Makes 4 to 6 servings

Though tofu isn't an Indian food, I include it in my recipes because it is a healthful, versatile ingredient. This dish reflects parental creativity: its similarity to a basic raita *in color, texture, and taste allows us to sneak in nutrients without detection by children. Serve it to accompany a meal, or try it as a sauce at your next barbecue.*

¹/₂ teaspoon Roasted Cumin-Pepper Masala (page 23)

1 (10¹/₂-ounce) package firm tofu, towel-dried and coarsely crumbled

1 cup coarsely chopped fresh dry spinach leaves, rinsed and blotted

¹/₂ cup coarsely chopped fresh cilantro, including soft stems

1¹/₂ cups nonfat plain yogurt, whisked until smooth

1 tablespoon peeled minced fresh ginger

4 to 6 scallions, white parts only, minced

1 fresh green chile pepper, such as serrano, minced with seeds

¹/₄ teaspoon salt, or to taste

Prepare the masala. Then, in a food processor or blender, process together the tofu, spinach, and cilantro until smooth. Transfer to a serving bowl, mix in the yogurt, ginger, scallions, chile pepper, and salt. Garnish with the cumin-pepper masala and serve.

Grilled or Roasted Vegetable Raitas

Roasted Bell Pepper Raita
Bhuni Shimla Mirch ka Raita

Makes 4 to 6 servings

This is not a traditional raita, because roasting bell peppers is not a common practice in India. It is something I make in my home in America, and my family loves it.

3 to 4 bell peppers of different colors, stemmed, seeded, and cut into ³/₄-inch pieces
1 teaspoon olive oil
1 teaspoon minced fresh garlic
¹/₂ teaspoon ajwain seeds, coarsely ground
2 cups nonfat plain yogurt, whisked until smooth
¹/₂ teaspoon salt, or to taste
Freshly ground black pepper, to taste
Fresh mint leaves

1. Preheat the oven to 500°F. Put the bell peppers in a bowl and toss with the oil, garlic, and ajwain seeds. Transfer to a broiler tray and roast on the center rack until browned on the underside, 5 to 7 minutes. Leaving the tray on the same rack, switch the oven to broiler heat (and transfer the tray to the broiler, if needed). Broil until the tops of the vegetables are soft and lightly charred, 3 to 5 minutes.

2. Place the yogurt in a large serving bowl, stir in the salt and black pepper, then add the roasted bell peppers. Garnish with mint and serve.

Traditional Grilled Eggplant Raita
Bhunae Baigan ka Raita

Makes 4 to 6 servings

Indians have long taken advantage of the smoky flavor that eggplants develop when grilled or roasted. That flavor really shines through in this traditional raita. The smaller and thinner the eggplants, the more pronounced the flavor, because more of the outside surface and, consequently, the insides get roasted and absorb the flavor.

2 teaspoons dry-roasted and coarsely ground cumin seeds (Dry-Roasting Spices, page 35)
1 tablespoon dry-roasted sesame seeds (Dry-Roasting Spices, page 35)
2 to 3 (1¹/₄ pounds) small eggplants, roasted, any method, peeled, and mashed (Roasting and Grilling Vegetables, page 36)
2 cups nonfat plain yogurt, whisked until smooth
1 teaspoon minced fresh garlic
¹/₄ cup finely chopped fresh cilantro, with soft stems
¹/₂ teaspoon ground cayenne pepper
¹/₂ teaspoon salt, or to taste
¹/₂ teaspoon freshly ground black pepper, or to taste

1. Prepare the cumin and sesame seeds. Prepare the eggplants.

2. Place the yogurt in a serving bowl and mix in the mashed eggplant. Add the garlic, cilantro, cumin, cayenne pepper, salt, and black pepper. Garnish with the sesame seeds and serve.

Variation: Make an easier version by mixing the mashed grilled eggplant into the yogurt and seasoning it only with salt, black pepper, and dry-roasted cumin.

Garlicky Roasted Chinese Eggplant Raita

Lambae Baigan-Lussan ka Raita

Makes 4 to 6 servings

This non-traditional raita *with familiar flavors is not one people in India would make, but one Indians in America would certainly appreciate. I use what are called Chinese eggplants here in America, because they are similar to the small eggplants found in India.*

¹/₂ teaspoon dry-roasted and coarsely ground cumin seeds (Dry-Roasting Spices, page 35)

1 pound long, thin Chinese eggplants, cut into ¹/₄-inch diagonal slices

1 teaspoon olive oil

¹/₂ teaspoon cayenne pepper, or to taste

1 teaspoon minced fresh garlic

2 cups nonfat plain yogurt, whisked until smooth

¹/₂ teaspoon salt, or to taste

¹/₂ teaspoon freshly ground black pepper, to taste

¹/₄ cup finely chopped fresh cilantro, including soft stems

¹/₄ teaspoon ground paprika

1. Prepare the cumin seeds. Then preheat the oven to 500°F. Put the eggplant in a bowl and toss with the oil, garlic, and cayenne pepper. Transfer to a broiler tray and roast on the center rack until browned on the underside, 5 to 7 minutes. Leaving the tray on the same rack, switch to the broiler heat (or raise the heat to broil and transfer the tray to the broiler, if needed). Broil until the tops of the vegetables are soft and lightly charred, 3 to 5 minutes. Let cool.

2. Place the yogurt in a large serving bowl and mix in the salt and black pepper. Add the roasted eggplant and cilantro, and mix well. Garnish with the roasted cumin and paprika, and serve.

Pan-Roasted Eggplant Raita with Sesame Seeds

Baigun-Til ka Raita

Makes 4 to 6 servings

Reminiscent of the flavors of the Far East, this sesame-roasted eggplant raita *will surely find itself welcome in many homes. The cooked eggplant can be enjoyed without the yogurt, as well.*

1 tablespoon dry-roasted sesame seeds (page 35)

1 tablespoon vegetable oil

3 to 4 drops sesame oil

1 teaspoon minced fresh garlic

1 teaspoon coarsely crushed ajwain seeds

1 small oval eggplant, cut into 1-inch pieces

3 cups nonfat plain yogurt, whisked until smooth

¹/₂ teaspoon salt, or to taste

1. Prepare the sesame seeds. Then heat both the oils in a large nonstick wok or saucepan over medium-high heat and cook the garlic and ajwain seeds, stirring, until golden, about 30 seconds. Add the eggplant and cook, stirring, until golden brown, 5 to 7 minutes. Cover the pan and cook over low heat until the eggplant pieces are very soft, 7 to 10 minutes. Let cool.

2. Place the yogurt in a serving bowl. Add the salt, then mix in the cooled eggplant, plus any juices that may have accumulated. Mix in the sesame seeds, with some of them visible as a garnish. Serve.

Grilled Zucchini and Pearl Onion Raita

Bhuna Ghia aur Chotae Pyaz ka Raita

Makes 4 to 6 servings

This is my adaptation of a similar raita *routinely made by my mother. I use zucchini, which is rarely seen in India, while my mother used pale green opo squash. Pearl onions, generally reserved for pickles, salads, and* sambars *(a soupy south Indian lentil dish), lend a delightful crunch to this smooth* raita.

1 tablespoon Roasted Cumin-Pepper Masala (page 23)
3 small zucchini
20 pearl onions, peeled
2 cups nonfat plain yogurt, whisked until smooth
1/2 cup finely chopped fresh cilantro, including soft stems
1/2 teaspoon salt, or to taste

1. Prepare the cumin-pepper masala. Then, preheat a grill over medium-high heat, and grill the zucchini and onions according to Roasting and Grilling Vegetables directions on page 36. Set aside the onions. Let the zucchini cool, then lightly remove the charred skin (leave some of the charred bits on for flavor), and mash the zucchini.

2. Place the yogurt in a large serving bowl and mix in the zucchini pulp, onions, cilantro, salt, and half the cumin-pepper masala. Lightly swirl in the remaining masala, with some of it visible as a garnish. Serve.

Fresh and Dried Fruit Raitas

Dried Fruit Raita

Sookhae Phallon ka Raita

Makes 4 to 6 servings

When I was growing up, this dessert-like raita, *studded with dried fruits, was served at festive occasions and weddings—mainly because dried fruits were expensive, not so easy to come by, and therefore reserved for when you had guests. In America, dried fruit is easy to find, so you can make this delicious dish any time. Serve it with elaborate* biryanis *(baked layered rice dishes), such as Hyderabadi Layered Rice with Cooked Chicken (page 560), or over a bowl of chopped fresh soft fruits, like bananas, mangoes, peaches, and pineapples.*

1/4 cup any sonth chutney of your choice (pages 76 to 78)
1 teaspoon Chaat Masala (page 20 or store-bought)
1/2 cup lowfat milk
1 cup finely chopped mixed dried fruit, such as peaches, plums, apricots, and raisins
2 cups nonfat plain yogurt, whisked until smooth
1/2 teaspoon salt, or to taste
1/2 teaspoon freshly ground black pepper
1/2 cup finely chopped fresh cilantro, including soft stems

1. Prepare the chutney and the masala. Then place the milk and the dried fruits in a microwave-safe bowl and cook on high, about 1 minute. Cover the bowl and allow the dried fruits to soften, about 1 hour. Let cool, then transfer them, with the liquid, to a serving bowl.

2. Add the yogurt, salt, pepper, and cilantro, and mix well. Lightly swirl in the sonth chutney, with parts of it visible as a garnish. Sprinkle the chaat masala on top and serve.

Mango Raita with Fresh Ginger

Aam-Adrak ka Raita

Makes 4 to 6 servings

Reserve this for the summer, when mangoes are at their peak. When served as a raita, *this dish is lovely with grilled and* tandoori *fare. On its own, it is a sweet and spicy snack or a savory dessert that is surprisingly welcome after a summer afternoon brunch.*

2 large soft ripe mangoes
2 cups nonfat plain yogurt, whisked until smooth
1 tablespoon peeled minced fresh ginger
1 tablespoon fresh lemon juice
1 fresh green chile pepper, such as serrano, minced with seeds
$^1/_2$ teaspoon salt, or to taste
$^1/_2$ teaspoon freshly ground black pepper, or to taste

1. Cut or peel off the skin of the mangoes, then cut around the seed to make 2 cheeks of the flesh. Cut this fruit and the other fruit left near the seed into $^1/_2$-inch pieces. Place three-quarters of the pieces in a shallow serving dish. Coarsely mash the remaining quarter with a fork to make a textured, chunky sauce, and set the sauce aside.

2. To the mango chunks, add the yogurt, ginger, lemon juice, green chile pepper, salt, and black pepper, and mix gently. Drizzle the mango sauce on top and serve.

Mango Chutney Raita

Aam ki Chutni ka Raita

Makes 4 to 6 servings

A lot of people add sugar to yogurt to sweeten it. But my father always added mango and other fruit chutneys to his bowl of yogurt, and ate it as a last course. That was his dessert and his yogurt of the day.

$^1/_2$ cup Fragrant Mango Chutney Preserve (page 73)
2 tablespoons Dessert Masala (page 32)
2 cups nonfat plain yogurt, whisked until smooth

1. Prepare the mango chutney and the dessert masala. Then, in a food processor or blender, process together the chutney and 1 cup yogurt until smooth.

2. Remove to a serving bowl and mix in the remaining yogurt. Add the dessert masala and stir lightly to mix, with parts of it visible as a garnish.

Banana Raita

Kaelae ka Raita

Makes 4 to 6 servings

Sweet and savory, this raita *adds a welcome sweet touch to any meal. Serve it over spicy* biryanis *(baked layered rice dishes) and rice* pullaos *(pilafs), or with chile-fried curries to mellow their heat.*

$^1/_4$ cup any sonth chutney of your choice (pages 76 to 78)
$^1/_2$ teaspoon dry-roasted and coarsely ground cumin seeds (Dry-Roasting Spices, page 35)
2 cups nonfat plain yogurt, whisked until smooth
1 tablespoon sugar
$^1/_4$ teaspoon salt, or to taste
$^1/_2$ teaspoon freshly ground black pepper, or to taste
$^1/_4$ cup sliced raw almonds
2 small ripe bananas, peeled and sliced diagonally

1. Prepare the chutney and the cumin seeds. Then place the yogurt in a bowl and mix in the sugar, salt, black pepper, and half the almonds.

2. Gently mix in the bananas. Then swirl in the sonth chutney, sprinkle the cumin seeds and the remaining almonds on top, and serve.

Mandarin Orange Raita

Suntarae ka Raita

Makes 4 to 6 servings

Mandarin oranges, or santras *as they are called in India, are customarily added to thickened yogurt cheese and to whipped cream to make quick desserts. Here, I make a savory and spicy-hot* raita *that can easily be a dressing for salads or a sauce with grilled meats.*

**2 teaspoons Chile Pepper Paste (page 53),
    or to taste**
1 teaspoon Chaat Masala (page 20 or store-bought)
2 cups nonfat plain yogurt, whisked until smooth
1/4 teaspoon salt, or to taste
**1 cup canned mandarin orange segments,
    drained well**
1 tablespoon peeled minced fresh ginger
2 tablespoons finely chopped fresh mint leaves
**1/4 cup shelled and coarsely chopped raw peanuts,
    without the red skin**

1. Prepare the chile paste and the chaat masala. Then place the yogurt in a serving bowl and mix in the chile paste, chaat masala, and salt. Fold in the mandarin segments, ginger, and mint leaves.

2. Place the peanuts in a small skillet and roast over medium heat until fragrant and golden, about 2 minutes. Scatter over the yogurt mixture and serve.

Dumpling Raitas

Traditional Raita with Softened Chickpea Batter Drops

Bheegi Boondi ka Raita

Makes 4 to 6 servings

Here is a traditional boondi *raita, made by briefly soaking freshly made chickpea batter drops in boiling water and then draining and squeeze-drying them before adding them to yogurt. Hot water not only softens the* boondi, *but, more importantly, pulls out the oil, making it a healthier dish.*

**2 1/2 cups Crispy Chickpea Batter Drops (Boondi),
    page 45 or store-bought**
**1 teaspoon dry-roasted and coarsely ground cumin
    seeds (Dry-Roasting Spices, page 35)**
2 cups nonfat plain yogurt, whisked until smooth
1/4 cup lowfat milk
3 cups boiling water for soaking the boondi
1/2 teaspoon salt, or to taste
1/2 teaspoon freshly ground black pepper
1/2 teaspoon ground paprika
1 tablespoon fresh cilantro
**1 tablespoon finely chopped scallion,
    green parts only**

1. Prepare the boondi drops and cumin. Then, in a serving bowl, whisk together the yogurt and milk until smooth.

2. Soak the boondi in boiling water, about 1 minute, then transfer to a fine-mesh strainer and drain. Press lightly on the boondi to squeeze out all the excess water.

3. Add the boondi to the yogurt, then mix in the salt, black pepper, and half the cumin. Garnish with the remaining cumin, paprika, cilantro, and scallions, and serve.

Boondi

Tiny droplets of chickpea flour batter, deep-fried until golden and crisp, are called *boondi*. Many Indian home cooks rely on them, sometimes as a main ingredient to make special *raitas* (in this chapter) or curries, such as Punjabi Chickpea Drops Curry (page 423), or to add a crispy crunch or a soft texture (when they are soaked and softened) and an extra flavor to *chaats* (savory salads and snacks that come smothered in one or many sauces) such as Flour Chips with Yogurt and Mango Powder Chutney (page 142).

They are very easy to make at home and have a long refrigerator life. (You'll find complete instructions on page 45.) You can also buy them in Indian markets in different flavors. One brand to look for is Haldiram.

Raita with Crispy Chickpea Batter Drops
Sookhi Boondi ka Raita

Makes 4 to 6 servings

More and more, the trend in India the last few years has been toward adding dry, crispy boondi *(chickpea batter drops) instead of soaked* boondi, *to yogurt, just before serving. Although a dish made this way is less healthy than one with soaked* boondi, *it makes for a pleasantly crunchy dish, and is a lot quicker and easier to prepare. Flavored and plain* boondi *drops are available in Indian markets all over the country, or try making them yourself—it's simple.*

2 cups savory Crispy Chickpea Batter Drops
    (Boondi), page 45 or store-bought
1 teaspoon dry-roasted and coarsely ground
    cumin seeds (page 35)
2 cups nonfat plain yogurt, whisked until smooth
1/4 teaspoon salt, or to taste
1/2 teaspoon freshly ground black pepper, or to taste
1/2 teaspoon ground paprika for garnish
1/4 cup finely chopped fresh cilantro,
    including soft stems

1. Prepare the boondi and the cumin. Then place the yogurt in a serving bowl and mix in the salt, black pepper, cumin, and paprika.

2. Lightly mix in the boondi with some of them visible as garnish (or just mound them all on top). Sprinkle the cilantro on top and serve immediately (or the boondi will get soggy).

Raita with Chickpea Flour Pancakes
Doiyon ka Raita

Makes 4 to 6 servings

With time on their hands and faced with transportation difficulties and lack of refrigeration, Indian home cooks in olden days found numerous ways to use the same ingredients, most of them staples in the kitchen, like chickpea flour. Make these pancakes when no one is home, or half will disappear right from the skillet and you won't have enough for the raita.

2 teaspoons Punjabi Raita and Buttermilk Masala
    (page 23)
1/4 cup chickpea flour
1/8 teaspoon baking soda
1/8 teaspoon salt, or to taste
2 tablespoons minced scallions, white parts only
1 tablespoon finely chopped fresh cilantro,
    including soft stems
1 fresh green chile pepper, such as serrano,
    minced with seeds
1/4 cup water
1 to 2 tablespoons peanut oil
2 cups nonfat plain yogurt, whisked until smooth
1 tablespoon minced fresh mint leaves

1. Prepare the masala. Then, in a small bowl, mix together the chickpea flour, baking soda, salt, scallions, cilantro, and green chile pepper. Add the water to make a semi-thin batter. Set aside about 30 minutes to rest.

2. Heat 1 teaspoon of the oil in a medium nonstick skillet over medium heat. Add about 2 tablespoons of the batter and spread it with a spatula to make a 3-inch pancake. When the bottom turns golden, about 1 minute, turn it over and slide it toward the side of the pan, making room for others. Make similar pancakes with the remaining batter, starting in the center and moving out the side after the first side turns golden. Add more oil, as necessary.

3. When the bottoms of the pancakes at the side of the pan brown, about 1 minute, turn them over and let the other side brown, about 30 seconds, then remove to a plate. Break each pancake into ½ -inch pieces and set aside.

4. In a serving bowl, mix together the yogurt, raita masala, and the pancake pieces. Garnish with the mint and serve.

Simple Mung Bean Croquettes Raita

Pakaudhiyon ka Raita

Makes 4 to 6 servings

Pakaudhi *dumplings, also called* mungi ke laddoo, *are deep-fried balls of yellow mung beans. They are a Punjabi specialty served in a pool of savory yogurt and topped with* sonth *(a smooth brown chutney) and mint chutneys, chile peppers, and tangy spices. This is the simple version of the Punjabi* raita, *with fewer spices and without the chutneys.*

**2 teaspoons dry-roasted and coarsely ground
    cumin seeds (Dry-Roasting Spices, page 35)**
16 to 20 (1 recipe) Mung Bean Croquettes (page 128)
3 to 4 cups nonfat plain yogurt, whisked until smooth
½ teaspoon salt, or to taste
½ teaspoon freshly ground pepper, or to taste

3 cups water for soaking the croquettes
**1 fresh green chile pepper, such as serrano,
    minced with seeds**
**2 tablespoons finely chopped fresh cilantro,
    with soft stems**

1. Prepare the cumin seeds and the croquettes. Then place the yogurt in a large serving bowl, mix in the salt, black pepper, and 1 teaspoon cumin seeds, and refrigerate until needed.

2. An hour before serving, put the water in a large saucepan, bring to a boil, then remove from the heat and soak the croquettes until they absorb the water and become soft, 2 to 3 minutes. Press lightly to see if the center is soft; if not, add more water (if necessary) and bring to a boil again over high heat. When the croquettes are soft, remove them from water; let cool. When cool enough to handle, press each croquette between the palms of your hands to squeeze out all the excess water.

3. Add the croquettes to the yogurt and mix gently until all croquettes are well-coated with the yogurt. Garnish with the remaining 1 teaspoon cumin, green chile pepper, and cilantro, and serve.

Spicy Mung Bean Croquettes Raita with Sonth Chutney

Pakaudhiyon ki Chaat

Makes 4 to 6 servings

This is a dressed-up version of Simple Mung Bean Croquette Raita (left). Loaded with different chutneys and spices, this one falls in the street food category, and is eaten more as a substantial snack or even a quick lunch when you are out shopping. If your chutneys and spices are prepared ahead of time, this raita *is basically an assembly job. To enjoy it as the locals all over north India do, serve and eat it as spicy-hot as you can tolerate, then cool down with any of the chilled Indian beverages, such as Sweet Mango-Yogurt Cooler (page 653).*

1 teaspoon dry-roasted and coarsely ground cumin seeds (Dry-Roasting Spices, page 35)

2 teaspoons New Delhi Street Food Masala (page 20)

1/4 cup any sonth chutney of your choice, such as Minty Sonth Chutney with Mango Powder and Jaggery (page 77)

2 to 3 tablespoons Mint Chutney with Pomegranate Seeds (page 58)

16 to 20 (1 recipe) Mung Bean Croquettes (page 128)

3 to 4 cups nonfat plain yogurt, whisked until smooth

1/2 teaspoon salt, or to taste

1/2 teaspoon freshly ground black pepper, or to taste

1 tablespoon peeled minced fresh ginger

2 tablespoons finely chopped fresh mint leaves

3 cups water for soaking the croquettes

1 to 3 fresh green chile peppers, such as serrano, minced with seeds

1 tablespoon finely chopped fresh cilantro

1/2 teaspoon ground paprika or cayenne pepper

1. Prepare the cumin and the masala, the sonth and mint chutneys, and the croquettes—in advance, if possible.

2. Place the yogurt in a bowl, mix in the salt, black pepper, cumin, ginger, and mint leaves, and refrigerate until needed.

3. An hour before serving, put the water in a large saucepan, bring to a boil, then remove from the heat and soak the croquettes until they absorb the water and become soft, 2 to 3 minutes. Press lightly to see if the center is soft; if not, add more water (if necessary) and bring to a boil again over high heat. When the croquettes are soft, remove them from water; let cool. When cool enough to handle, press each croquette between the palms of your hands to squeeze out all the excess water.

4. Place croquettes in a large flat serving dish and carefully pour the yogurt over the croquettes until they are well-coated. Add more yogurt than you think is necessary, because the croquettes will absorb some of it. Drizzle the sonth chutney over the yogurt, then scatter the mint chutney on top. Garnish with the chile peppers, cilantro, chaat masala, and paprika or cayenne pepper, and serve.

Traditional Urad Dal Croquettes Raita
Dahi-Vadae

Makes 4 to 6 servings

This raita is made with dumplings alternately called vadae, badae, *or* bhallae *in different parts of India, and made and presented much like the Simple Mung Bean Croquettes Raita (page 236). Vadae are made with fermented white urad* dal, *while mung bean croquettes (*pakaudhi*) are made with yellow mung beans. The different legumes yield different croquettes—the urad* dal *ones, here, are a little heavier and more textured. Vadae are served at celebrations, which, in Indian families, could be once a week.*

10 to 12 (1 recipe) Punjabi-Style Fermented Urad Bean Croquettes (page 129)

1/4 cup any sonth chutney of your choice, such as Minty Sonth Chutney with Mango Powder and Jaggery (page 77)

1 tablespoon ground cumin

1/2 teaspoon cayenne pepper, or to taste

1/2 teaspoon ground black salt

1/8 teaspoon ground asafoetida

4 quarter-size slices peeled fresh ginger

1 to 3 fresh green chile peppers, such as serrano, stemmed +1 fresh green chile pepper, minced with seeds

3 to 4 cups nonfat plain yogurt, whisked until smooth

1/2 cup lowfat milk

3 cups water to soak croquettes

1 teaspoon ground paprika

1/4 cup finely chopped fresh cilantro

1. Prepare the croquettes and the sonth chutney. Then, in a small skillet, dry-roast together the cumin, cayenne pepper, black salt, and asafoetida over medium heat, stirring and shaking the pan until fragrant and a few shades darker, about 2 minutes. Let cool.

2. In a small food processor or blender, process together the ginger and stemmed green chile peppers with 1 to 2 tablespoons of the yogurt to make a smooth paste.

3. In a medium bowl, whisk together the remaining yogurt and milk until smooth. Mix in the ginger-chile pepper mixture and most of the roasted cumin-cayenne pepper mixture (save some for garnish), and refrigerate.

4. An hour before serving, put the water in a large saucepan, bring to a boil, then remove from the heat and soak the croquettes until they absorb the water and become soft, 2 to 3 minutes. Press lightly to see if the center is soft; if not, add more water (if necessary) and bring to a boil again over high heat. When the croquettes are soft, remove them from water; let cool. When cool enough to handle, press each croquette between the palms of your hands to squeeze out all the excess water.

5. Place the croquettes in a serving dish and pour the yogurt on top, ensuring that each croquette is well-coated with yogurt. Add more yogurt than you think is necessary, because the croquettes will absorb some of it. Drizzle the sonth chutney over the yogurt, then sprinkle the reserved cumin-cayenne pepper mixture, paprika, minced green chile pepper, and cilantro on top and serve.

Crispy Urad Dal Croquettes in Yogurt
Sookhae Dahi Bhallae

Makes 4 to 6 servings

Traditionally, the urad dal *croquettes are soaked before being added to the yogurt. However, occasionally I simply add them to the yogurt, so they retain their crunch. If you do want to soak the croquettes, follow the directions in Step 2 of Simple Mung Bean Croquettes Raita (page 236).*

5 to 6 (1/2 recipe) Mung Bean Croquettes (page 128)

1 teaspoon cumin seeds, dry-roasted and coarsely ground (Dry-Roasting Spices, page 35)

2 teaspoons New Delhi Street Food Masala (Papri Masala), page 20, or to taste

1/4 cup any sonth chutney of your choice, such as Minty Sonth Chutney with Mango Powder and Jaggery (page 77)

1/2 to 1 cup Fresh Coconut Chutney with Cilantro (page 61)

3 cups nonfat plain yogurt, whisked until smooth

1/2 cup lowfat milk

1/4 teaspoon salt, or to taste

1/2 teaspoon freshly ground black pepper, or to taste

1/2 teaspoon cayenne pepper, or to taste

1 to 2 fresh green chile peppers, such as serrano, minced with seeds

1 tablespoon minced fresh green mint leaves

1 tablespoon minced fresh cilantro, including soft stems

1. Prepare the croquettes, cumin, masala, and chutneys in advance, if possible. Place the yogurt in a large serving dish, mix in the coconut chutney, milk, salt, black pepper, cayenne pepper, and roasted cumin, and refrigerate until needed.

2. An hour before serving, cut each croquette in half across the width and add to the yogurt. Mix gently until all of the croquettes are well-coated with yogurt. Drizzle the sonth chutney on top. Garnish with the masala, green chile peppers, mint, and cilantro, and serve.

Meat Raitas

Shredded Chicken Raita
Murgh ka Raita

Makes 4 to 6 servings

What makes this raita *stand out is the addition of delicious spicy chicken. Truly a rare addition to creamy yogurt, and one that purists may scoff at, but in my opinion, most soft-cooked chicken, such as leftover tandoori or grilled chicken, tastes divine in this recipe.*

2 to 3 tablespoons Crushed Lemon and Fresh Red Chile Pepper Pickle (page 83)
1/2 recipe Pan-Cooked Chile-Chicken Thighs (page 448)
2 cups nonfat plain yogurt, whisked until smooth
2 to 3 tablespoons snipped chives

1. Prepare the pickle in advance. Prepare the chicken. Shred the chicken pieces by hand or simply mince them in a food processor and set aside.

2. Place the yogurt in a large serving bowl and mix in the lemon pickle. Add the chicken and mix well. Add the chives and swirl lightly to mix, with some of them visible as a garnish. Serve.

Ground Lamb Raita
Gosht ka Raita

Makes 4 to 6 servings

Kashmir lies on the northern tip of India, with the Himalayan mountain ranges dominating the landscape and the growing season limited to the short summer months, so the Kashmiri people tend to eat a lot more meat-based meals. They are one of the few communities in India that make non-vegetarian raitas. This one can be served as a side dish or as a cool entrée in the summer.

1/4 cup dried yellow split chickpeas (channa dal), sorted and washed in 3 to 4 changes of water
2 teaspoons Kashmiri Raita Masala (page 24)
4 cups nonfat plain yogurt, whisked until smooth
1 cup trimmed and ground leg of lamb
1 cup finely chopped onion
1 large clove fresh garlic, minced
1/2 cup finely chopped fresh cilantro, including soft stems
1 tablespoon peeled minced fresh ginger
1 fresh green chile pepper, such as serrano, minced with seeds
2 teaspoons ground coriander
1/4 teaspoon salt, or to taste

1. Soak the dal in water to cover, 1 hour. Meanwhile, prepare the raita masala. Then, place 3 cups of the yogurt in a large serving bowl. Mix in 1½ teaspoons of the raita masala. Reserve.

2. Drain the dal, then place it and the lamb, onion, garlic, cilantro, ginger, green chile pepper, coriander, and salt in a small nonstick skillet and cook, stirring, over medium-high heat until the lamb and onions brown, about 5 minutes. Add the remaining 1 cup yogurt and cook, stirring until the lamb and dal are tender, about 20 minutes.

3. Let cool, transfer to the bowl with the yogurt and masala, and mix well. Garnish with the remaining ½ teaspoon raita masala and serve.

South Indian Pachadis

Basic Cucumber Pachadi

Sohini ki Kheera Pachadi

Makes 4 to 6 servings

Most pachadis *follow the seasoning technique of this dish—the most basic* pachadi *(the recipe is from my friend Sohini Baliga). You'll notice that in some of the* pachadis, *the yogurt is not whisked smooth, and for the most part, a slightly chunky quality is their charm.*

All pachadis *come with the typical south Indian seasoning of mustard seeds and curry leaves, and though they are popular with southern curries such as South Indian Pumpkin Curry with Split Pigeon Peas (page 397), they can be eaten with just about any meal.*

3 small seedless cucumbers, peeled and grated
1/2 cup finely chopped fresh cilantro,
    including soft stems
1/4 teaspoon salt, or to taste
2 cups nonfat plain yogurt (do not whisk)
1 to 2 teaspoons peanut oil
1/2 teaspoon cumin seeds
1/2 teaspoon black mustard seeds
8 fresh green curry leaves
2 to 3 fresh green chile peppers, such as serrano,
    cut in half lengthwise and seeded

1. Place the cucumbers, cilantro, and salt in a serving bowl, and fold in the yogurt until just incorporated.
2. Heat the oil in a small nonstick saucepan over medium-high heat and add the cumin and mustard seeds; they should splutter upon contact with the hot oil, so cover the pan and lower the heat until the spluttering subsides. Add 5 of the curry leaves and the green chile peppers and stir about 1 minute. Transfer the seasonings to the yogurt bowl and fold in gently. Lightly crumble the remaining 3 curry leaves to release their aroma, and add them to the pachadi as a garnish. Serve.

Tomato and Cucumber Pachadi with Asafoetida

Tamatar aur Kheera Pachadi

Makes 4 to 6 servings

This pachadi *has no onions, for those who don't eat them. Onions and garlic are associated with base desires, and are not favored by a number of religious Hindus. (If you like onions, see the next recipe.)*

One teaspoon of oil may seem really ineffectual, but you want to use as little as possible for pachadis—*the idea is to have just enough to cook the spices, and therefore season the dish. Purists will tell you that you shouldn't be able to see the oil after it's mixed into the dish; it would be a sure sign of an over-generous, some would say sloppy, hand with the oil.*

The tomatoes and the cucumbers are chopped instead of grated making this pachadi *similar to a salad. Serve it with an Indian meal or with grilled meats or hamburgers.*

4 to 5 small seedless cucumbers, peeled and
    finely chopped
1 large tomato, finely chopped
1/2 cup finely chopped fresh cilantro,
    including soft stems
1/4 teaspoon salt, or to taste
2 cups nonfat plain yogurt (do not whisk)
1 teaspoon peanut oil
1 teaspoon black mustard seeds
1 teaspoon dried yellow split chickpeas (channa dal)
1/2 teaspoon cumin seeds
2 tablespoons minced fresh curry leaves
A scant pinch ground asafoetida
2 to 3 fresh green chile peppers, such as serrano,
    cut in half lengthwise and seeded
A few fresh cilantro leaves

1. Place the cucumbers, tomato, cilantro, and salt in a serving bowl and fold in the yogurt until just incorporated.
2. Heat the oil in a small nonstick saucepan over medium-high heat and add the mustard seeds; they should splutter upon contact with the hot oil, so cover the pan and lower the heat until the spluttering subsides. Quickly add the dal and stir until golden, about 30 seconds, then add the cumin seeds, curry

leaves, and asafoetida and stir another 30 seconds. Transfer the seasonings into the yogurt bowl and fold in gently. Garnish with the green chile peppers and cilantro leaves, and serve.

Tomato, Cucumber, and Onion Yogurt

Tamatar, Kheera, aur Pyaz ki Pachadi

Makes 4 to 6 servings

This chunky yogurt dish is for people who like tomato and cucumber, plus onions and a lot more. You can find the dals *(legumes) and all the spices at an Indian market.*

4 to 5 small seedless cucumbers, peeled and finely chopped
1 large tomato, finely chopped
1 small white onion, cut in half lengthwise and thinly sliced
1/2 cup finely chopped fresh cilantro, including soft stems + extra for garnish
1/2 teaspoon salt, or to taste
1 1/2 cups nonfat plain yogurt (do not whisk)
1 teaspoon peanut oil
2 dried red chile peppers, such as chile de arbol, coarsely broken
1 tablespoon peeled minced fresh ginger
1 teaspoon cumin seeds
1 teaspoon black mustard seeds
1 teaspoon dried yellow split chickpeas (channa dal)
1 teaspoon dried yellow split pigeon peas (toor dal)
1 tablespoon minced fresh curry leaves
2 fresh green chile peppers, such as serrano, diagonally sliced thin 1/2 teaspoon ground fenugreek seeds
2 tablespoons finely chopped fresh cilantro, including soft stems

1. Place the cucumbers, tomato, onion, cilantro, and salt in a serving bowl and fold in the yogurt until just incorporated.

2. Heat the oil in a small nonstick saucepan over medium-high heat and add the red chile peppers and ginger, stir a few seconds, then add the cumin and mustard seeds; they should splutter upon contact with the hot oil, so cover the pan and lower the heat until the spluttering subsides. Quickly add both dals,

curry leaves, green chile peppers, and fenugreek, and stir until golden, about 1 minute. Transfer seasoning into the yogurt bowl and fold it in gently. Garnish with the cilantro leaves and serve.

Yogurt with Sautéed Tomatoes and Coconut

Bhunae Tamatar aur Nariyal ki Pachadi

Makes 4 to 6 servings

This is an easily made pachadi, *but be sure not to over-mix the yogurt and coconut milk, and refrigerate any leftovers immediately.*

1/2 cup Coconut Milk (page 44 or store-bought)
2 cups nonfat plain yogurt (do not whisk)
1 tablespoon peeled minced fresh ginger
1/4 cup finely chopped fresh cilantro, including soft stems
1 to 3 fresh green chile peppers, such as serrano, minced with seeds
1/4 cup fresh or frozen grated coconut or unsweetened shredded coconut
1/2 teaspoon salt, or to taste
1 tablespoon peanut or coconut oil
3 dried red chile peppers, such as chile de arbol, with stems
1 teaspoon dried yellow split chickpeas (channa dal)
1 teaspoon black mustard seeds
1 teaspoon cumin seeds
8 to 10 fresh curry leaves
2 large tomatoes, coarsely chopped

1. Prepare the coconut milk. Then, in a serving bowl, lightly mix together the yogurt, coconut milk, ginger, cilantro, green chile peppers, coconut, and salt. (It should not be smooth.)

2. Heat the oil in a small nonstick saucepan over medium-high heat and add the red chile peppers, dal, mustard and cumin seeds; they should splutter upon contact with the hot oil, so cover the pan and lower the heat until the spluttering subsides. Quickly add the curry leaves and stir 30 seconds. Add the tomatoes and cook, stirring, until softened, about 2 minutes, then fold everything into the yogurt. Serve.

Yogurt with Fried Green Tomato Chutney

Harae-Tamatar ki Chutni ki Pachadi

Makes 4 to 6 servings

This American pachadi *variation, was inspired by the green tomatoes that grow in my backyard. The fruity sourness of green tomatoes marries well with the standard south Indian seasonings of mustard seeds and curry leaves. Try making this* pachadi *with unripe peaches or tart apples (such as pippin or Granny Smith). Or you can use very firm, unripe red tomatoes.*

2 tablespoons Tamarind Paste (page 54
   or store-bought)
1 teaspoon South Indian Sambar Powder
   (page 28 or store-bought)
1 tablespoon peanut oil
1 tablespoon black mustard seeds
1 to 3 fresh green chile peppers, such as serrano,
   coarsely chopped with seeds
2 large firm green tomatoes, coarsely chopped
1 small onion, coarsely chopped
8 to 10 fresh curry leaves
1 teaspoon salt, or to taste
2 cups nonfat plain yogurt (do not whisk)

1. Prepare the tamarind paste and sambar powder. Then heat the oil in a large nonstick wok or saucepan over medium-high heat and add the mustard seeds; they should splutter upon contact with the hot oil, so cover the pan and lower the heat until the spluttering subsides. Quickly add the green chile peppers, tomatoes, and onion, and cook, stirring, until the tomatoes are golden, about 3 minutes. Remove from the heat and let cool.

2. Transfer to a food processor or blender, add the tamarind, curry leaves, and salt, and process to make a smooth chutney.

3. Place the yogurt in a serving bowl and fold in the chutney, with parts of it visible as a garnish. Top with the sambar powder and serve.

Yogurt with Mashed Potato and Fresh Cilantro

Masslae Aalu aur Dhaniyae ki Pachadi

Makes 4 to 6 servings

If you are looking for new ways to flavor mashed potatoes, here is a recipe for you. Lots of buttery soft potatoes moistened with creamy yogurt virtually transform this pachadi *into a spicy mashed potato casserole. Serve it as part of a summer brunch menu or in place of potato salad at your next barbecue.*

1 pound russet (or boiling) potatoes
1 tablespoon peanut oil
1 teaspoon cumin seeds
$1/2$ teaspoon fenugreek seeds, coarsely ground
$1/2$ teaspoon coarsely ground black pepper
$1/8$ teaspoon ground asafoetida
1 fresh green chile pepper, such as serrano,
   minced with seeds
$1/4$ teaspoon ground turmeric
1 teaspoon salt, or to taste
1 cup nonfat plain yogurt (do not whisk)
$1/2$ cup finely chopped fresh cilantro,
   including soft stems
3 dried red chile peppers, such as chile de arbol,
   with stems
1 teaspoon black mustard seeds
1 teaspoon dried yellow split chickpeas (channa dal)
5 to 7 fresh curry leaves

1. Boil the potatoes in lightly salted water to cover until soft, about 20 minutes. Let cool, then peel and mash them coarsely with a fork.

2. Heat 1 teaspoon oil in a medium nonstick wok or saucepan over medium-high heat and add the cumin, fenugreek, black pepper, and asafoetida. Stir about 30 seconds. Add the mashed potatoes, green chile pepper, turmeric, and salt, and cook, stirring, over medium-high heat until heated through, about 2 minutes. Reduce the heat to low, cover the pan, and cook, stirring occasionally, about 10 minutes.

3. Let cool to room temperature. Transfer to a serving bowl and fold in the yogurt until just incorporated. Lightly mix in the cilantro.

4. Heat the remaining oil in a small nonstick saucepan over medium-high heat and add the red chile peppers and mustard seeds; they should splutter upon contact with the hot oil, so cover the pan and lower the heat until the spluttering subsides. Quickly add the dal and curry leaves and stir until golden, about 30 seconds. Transfer to the yogurt bowl and stir lightly to mix, leaving most of it visible as a garnish. Serve.

Chopped Salad with Yogurt
Cachumbar Pachadi

Makes 4 to 6 servings

Indian chopped salads are made with finely chopped fresh vegetables topped with fresh herbs and spices. But here, I mix the salad with yogurt. I use some traditional Indian vegetables, such as fresh tomatoes, daikon radishes, and cucumbers, and some untraditional ones, such as jicama and zucchini.

3 cups finely chopped mixed fresh vegetables, such as tomato, red and daikon radishes, cucumber, scallion, jicama, and zucchini
1/2 cup finely chopped fresh cilantro, including soft stems
1 tablespoon peeled minced fresh ginger
1 tablespoon grated fresh coconut or shredded unsweetened dried coconut
1 fresh green chile pepper, such as serrano, minced with seeds
1 teaspoon salt, or to taste
2 cups nonfat plain yogurt (do not whisk)
2 teaspoons peanut oil
1 teaspoon cumin seeds
1 teaspoon black mustard seeds
1 teaspoon dried white urad beans (dhulli urad dal)
1 teaspoon dried yellow split chickpeas (channa dal)
A scant pinch ground asafoetida
2 tablespoons minced fresh curry leaves

1. Place the chopped vegetables in a flat serving dish and mix in the cilantro, ginger, coconut, green chile pepper, and salt. Then lightly fold in the yogurt.

2. Heat the oil in a small nonstick saucepan over medium-high heat and add the cumin and mustard seeds; they should splatter upon contact with the hot oil, so cover the pan and lower the heat until the spluttering subsides. Quickly add both the dals, the asafoetida, and the curry leaves, and stir until the dals are golden, about 1 minute. Transfer the seasonings to the yogurt and swirl lightly to mix, leaving most of it visible as a garnish. Serve.

Yogurt with Pumpkin and Tamarind
Imli-Petha ki Pachadi

Makes 4 to 6 servings

Cubes of tamarind-flavored pumpkin (called parangikkai *in Tamil, the language of Tamilnadu in the south) add a delightfully sweet and sour touch to this spicy* pachadi. *The yogurt in this* pachadi *is whisked until smooth, but the delicate chunkiness comes from the perfectly cooked pumpkin.*

The cooked pumpkin without the yogurt also tastes superb. Serve it as a side dish with a potato or a chicken curry, or present it as part of a winter holiday menu.

1 tablespoon peanut oil
1 teaspoon fenugreek seeds, coarsely ground
1/2 teaspoon black peppercorns, coarsely ground
1/8 teaspoon ground asafoetida
1 pound pumpkin or any other orange squash, peeled and cut into 1/2-inch pieces
1 fresh green chile pepper, such as serrano, minced with seeds
1 teaspoon salt, or to taste
2 teaspoons dried tamarind powder
1 teaspoon dried coconut powder
1/2 cup finely chopped fresh cilantro, including soft stems
1 cup nonfat plain yogurt, whisked until smooth
1 teaspoon melted ghee
3 whole dried red chile peppers, such as chile de arbol
1 teaspoon black mustard seeds

1. Heat the oil in a medium nonstick saucepan over medium-high heat then add the fenugreek, black peppercorns, and asafoetida; stir 30 seconds. Mix in the pumpkin, green chile pepper, and salt, and cook, stirring, over medium-high heat until heated through, about 2 minutes. Reduce the heat to low, cover the pan and cook, stirring occasionally, until the pumpkin is soft, 20 to 30 minutes.

2. Add the tamarind and coconut during the last 5 minutes of cooking. When completely cooked, mix in the cilantro and let cool to room temperature. Transfer to a serving bowl and fold in the yogurt until just incorporated.

3. Heat the ghee in a small nonstick saucepan over medium-high heat and add the red chile peppers and mustard seeds; they should splutter upon contact with the hot oil, so cover the pan and lower the heat until the spluttering subsides. Quickly transfer to the yogurt bowl, mix lightly, and serve.

Yogurt with Pressed Rice Flakes
Poha Pachadi

Makes 4 to 6 servings

Pressed rice flakes, called poha, *are roller-pressed, flattened rice flakes with ragged edges. They soak up the yogurt and lend a delightful texture to this* pachadi. *They are available in Indian markets. Use the thin variety; the thicker ones can also be used, but are a little too dense.*

This pachadi *features smooth yogurt but gets a delicate, somewhat chunky texture from the rice flakes.*

1 cup pressed rice flakes (poha), sorted
1 tablespoon grated fresh or frozen coconut
     or shredded unsweetened dried coconut
1/4 cup finely chopped fresh cilantro,
     including soft stems
1 fresh green chile pepper, such as serrano,
     minced with seeds
2 cups nonfat plain yogurt, whisked until smooth
1/4 teaspoon salt, or to taste
1 teaspoon coconut or peanut oil
6 to 8 fresh curry leaves
1/2 teaspoon black mustard seeds
1/4 teaspoon ground paprika
1/8 teaspoon ground asafoetida

1. In a skillet, dry-roast the rice flakes, coconut, cilantro, and green chile pepper over medium heat until fragrant and golden, about 2 minutes. Place the yogurt in a serving bowl and mix in the roasted rice flakes mixture and salt.

2. Heat the oil in a small saucepan over medium-high heat and add the curry leaves and mustard seeds; they should splutter upon contact with the hot oil, so lower the heat and cover the pan until the spluttering subsides. Stir in the paprika and asafoetida, then immediately transfer the seasonings to the yogurt and swirl lightly to mix, with parts of it visible as a garnish. Serve.

Spicy Yogurt with Mango and Coconut

Aam aur Nariyal ki Pachadi

Makes 4 to 6 servings

The mango-coconut blend delivers tropical flair, but it isn't sweet. Tart and spicy seasonings offer a twist that may not be familiar, but still will intrigue and please your taste buds.

Peel the mango with a vegetable peeler or a knife, then cut the fruit into small pieces. Avoid the rough flesh near the large center seed.

**1 large semi-ripe mango, peeled and cut into
   ¹/₂-inch pieces**
**1 tablespoon dried coconut powder (kopra)
   or unsweetened shredded dried coconut**
1 tablespoon peeled minced fresh ginger
**1 fresh green chile pepper, such as serrano,
   minced with seeds**
¹/₂ teaspoon salt, or to taste
1¹/₂ cups nonfat plain yogurt (do not whisk)
1 teaspoon peanut oil
**2 dried red chile peppers, such as chile de arbol,
   broken**
1 teaspoon black mustard seeds
A scant pinch ground asafoetida
5 to 7 fresh curry leaves

1. Place the mango pieces in a serving bowl and carefully mix in the coconut powder (or dried coconut), ginger, green chile pepper, and salt. Then fold in the yogurt.

2. Heat the oil in a small nonstick saucepan over medium-high heat and add the red chile peppers and mustard seeds; they should splutter upon contact with the hot oil, so cover the pan and lower the heat until the spluttering subsides. Quickly add the asafoetida and curry leaves and stir about 30 seconds. Transfer to the yogurt and stir lightly to mix, leaving most of it visible on top as a garnish. Serve.

Yogurt with Sautéed Ripe Banana

Bhunae Kaelae ki Pachadi

Makes 4 to 6 servings

Cooking bananas is a very south Indian thing. While northerners add ripe bananas and other fruits to raitas *and chutneys, in the south they sauté them with a bunch of aromatic spices before making their* pachadis. *This one is served chilled, so it's great for summer menus, but enjoy it any time on the side of curries and other vegetable dishes. This recipe can also be made with pineapples, mangoes, peaches, or nectarines.*

3 cups nonfat plain yogurt, whisked until smooth
¹/₄ cup grated fresh or frozen coconut
¹/₄ teaspoon + ¹/₂ teaspoon salt, or to taste
¹/₂ teaspoon freshly ground black pepper, or to taste
1 teaspoon black mustard seeds
1 teaspoon cumin seeds
¹/₂ teaspoon fenugreek seeds
¹/₈ teaspoon ground asafoetida
1 tablespoon dried curry leaves
1 teaspoon hot red pepper flakes, or to taste
1 tablespoon peanut oil
**2 medium firm ripe bananas, peeled and
   cut into ¹/₄-inch pieces**
2 to 3 tablespoons fresh lemon juice

1. In a serving bowl, mix together the yogurt, coconut, ¹/₄ teaspoon salt, and black pepper. In a spice or a coffee grinder, grind together the mustard, cumin, and fenugreek seeds, and the asafoetida, curry leaves, and red pepper flakes until fine.

2. Heat the oil in a large nonstick wok or saucepan over medium-high heat and add the ground spice mixture; it should sizzle immediately. Quickly add the bananas and ¹/₂ teaspoon salt and cook, turning the pieces carefully, until golden on both sides, about 3 minutes.

3. Mix in the lemon juice and cook another minute. Transfer the seasoned bananas to the yogurt and swirl lightly to mix, with parts of them visible as a garnish. Refrigerate at least 2 hours to chill, then serve.

Yogurt with Green Papaya and Coconut

Hara Papita aur Nariyal Pachadi

Makes 4 to 6 servings

Papayas grow widely in the southern states of India, so it is no surprise that they show up extensively in everyday dishes. Here is one example. If you don't have fresh coconut in your markets, look for frozen coconut in the Indian and Asian markets.

$^1/_2$ cup grated fresh or frozen coconut

$^1/_2$ cup coarsely chopped fresh cilantro, including soft stems

2 quarter-size slices peeled fresh ginger

1 to 3 fresh green chile peppers, such as serrano, coarsely chopped

1 teaspoon sugar

$^1/_2$ teaspoon salt, or to taste

$^1/_4$ teaspoon ground black mustard seeds

2 cups nonfat plain yogurt (do not whisk)

1 small unripe green papaya, peeled and grated to make 1 cup

1 small seedless cucumber, grated

2 small carrots, grated

1 teaspoon peanut oil

1 to 2 dried red chile peppers, such as chile de arbol, coarsely broken

1 teaspoon black mustard seeds

$^1/_8$ teaspoon ground asafoetida

$^1/_8$ teaspoon ground paprika

1. In a small food processor, process together the coconut, cilantro, ginger, green chile peppers, sugar, salt, and ground mustard seeds, adding about ¼ cup of the yogurt to make a smooth paste.

2. Place the yogurt in a serving dish and very lightly mix in first the coconut paste, then the papaya, cucumber, and carrots, leaving a few vegetables showing their color through the yogurt.

3. Heat the oil in a small saucepan over medium-high heat and cook the red chile peppers and mustard seeds; they should splutter upon contact with the hot oil, so lower the heat and cover the pan until the spluttering subsides. Add the asafoetida and paprika, then transfer the seasonings to the pachadi and stir it in, leaving some visible as a garnish. Serve.

Vegetables on the Side

Potatoes and Other Roots 251

Cumin Potatoes

Spicy Potatoes
with Onions and Tomatoes

Spicy South Indian Potatoes

Spicy Smashed Potatoes
with Chaat Masala

Rajasthani Potatoes
with Cashews and Raisins

Bengali Hot Potatoes
with Dry-Roasted Spices

Pomegranate Potatoes

Potatoes with Bell Pepper Confetti

Russet Potatoes
with Fresh Fenugreek Greens

Crispy Fork-Mashed Potatoes
with Roasted Peanuts

Mashed Potatoes with Peas
and Sesame Seed Powder

Ginger Mashed Potatoes
with Yogurt

Spicy Potato Balls

Tangy Sweet Potatoes

Fragrant Baby Turnip Halves

Grated Turnips with Turmeric

Chopped Turnips with
Apples and Green Tomatoes

Crispy Taro Root Fingers
with Ajwain Seeds

Taro Root Rounds with Tomatoes

Ginger-Baked Taro Roots
with Chaat Masala

Tangy Lotus Roots

Quick Pan-Cooked Lotus Roots

Eggplant 263

Mashed Fire-Roasted Eggplant

Creamy Mashed Eggplant with Peas

Mashed Eggplant
with Mustard Seeds

Easy Mashed Spicy Eggplant
and Potatoes

Roasted Eggplant with Mustard Oil

Lowfat Stir-Fried Chinese Eggplant
with Sesame Seeds

Indian Eggplant
with Garlic and Tamarind

Spice-Stuffed Indian Eggplant

Potato-Stuffed Oval Eggplant

Eggplant with Red Potatoes

Sweet and Sour Eggplant
with Jaggery

Kerala Coconut Eggplant

Quick Garlic and
Chile Pepper Eggplant

Quick Japanese or Chinese
Eggplant with Cilantro

 = Vegan   = Pressure-Cooker Quick

Spinach and Other Greens 295

Chopped Spinach
with Red Potatoes

Cooked Spinach
with Sliced Almonds

Braised Beet Greens

Carrots, Peas, and Other Basic Vegetables 297

Dry-Cooked Carrots, Peas,
and Potatoes

Carrots with Fresh Spinach
Ribbons

Spicy Chopped Carrots
with Fresh Coconut

Smoked Sugar-Snap Peas

Petite Peas and Potatoes

Spicy Green Peas
with Onion and Ginger

Mixed Bell Peppers with Peas

Spicy Mushrooms and Bell Peppers

Oven-Roasted Bell Peppers,
Indian Style

Spicy Chopped Tomatoes

Fire-Roasted Corn-on-the-Cob

Fragrant Spiced Corn

Zesty Everyday Green Beans

Mixed Green and Yellow Beans
with Fresh Pomegranate Seeds

Spicy Yard-Long Beans

Asparagus with Purple Potatoes

Pan-Grilled Asparagus Tips

Tangy Asparagus
with Onions and Tomatoes

Mixed Vegetables 306

Mixed Cauliflower, Carrots,
and Green Beans in a Wok

North Indian–Style Mixed
Cauliflower, Carrots,
and Green Beans

South Indian–Style
Mixed Vegetables

Mixed Pumpkin, Squash, and
Eggplant with Bengali 5-Spices

Marinated Mixed Vegetables
in Tomato Butter-Cream Sauce

Savory Fruit Dishes 309

Tart Apples with Cooked Onions

Tart Apples with Cumin Seeds

Spicy Star Fruit

Green Mangoes in Coconut Milk

Spicy Mashed Fresh Peaches

Sweet and Sour Ripe Bananas

Spicy Green Plantains

Watermelon Whites with Ginger

When I first came to the United States in the 1970s, curious friends asked me, "If your mother doesn't eat meat, what does she live on?" Astonished, I would reply, "Vegetables and *dals*, of course." It took me years to realize that the love of— even dependence on—eating meat and, at the time, the disinterest in vegetables and grains in the United States meant my answer didn't make sense to them.

Not only did Americans have access to fewer fresh vegetables before and during the 1970s, but popular culture also equated vegetarianism with rather dull and uninteresting meals and almost no substantial nutrition. The fact that vegetables and greens had minerals and vitamins was not completely lost, but even well-meaning mothers and cooks did little else besides open cans of vegetables or steam or overcook the frozen ones, raising entire generations of children who associated veggies with unpalatable tastes and textures.

In India, however, people have always enjoyed vegetables. With our religious beliefs promoting vegetarianism, vegetables have played a crucial role in our lives. That is why, even today, no matter where in India you go, you will see vegetables being served. Popular dishes like Cauliflower with Potato Wedges and Peas (page 284), Mashed Fire-Roasted Eggplant (page 263), and Stuffed Whole Okra with Spices (page 291) are served day after day, and can be here in America as well, because they are simple to make and delicious.

Cooking vegetables, like any cooking, is about understanding the basic flavors and then adding seasonings in the form of spices and herbs, and even the intermixing of various vegetables to make new dishes. That explains why over my years in the United States, I've come to enjoy preparing vegetables that don't grow in India—zucchini, certain squashes, white asparagus, broccoli, you name it, and include them in this book.

I've been happy to see that in the United States, the increasing awareness of vegetable varieties in supermarkets and produce stores, and the emphasis on their nutritional benefits, has led many people to seek out flavorful ways to add vegetables to their diets. For you, and the many Indians who do love vegetables, you'll find many here to add to your meals. Start with Cumin Potatoes (page 251) and make your way to okra (yes, okra—they can be delicious) via the eggplants and squashes, and don't miss out on the spinach, green peas, and beans. Try the dishes with northern spices (coriander and cumin) or the southern way, with mustard seeds and curry leaves and make them spicy hot or mild, to your taste.

Potatoes and Other Roots

Cumin Potatoes

Jeera-Aalu

Makes 4 to 6 servings

This is an easy from-the-pantry dish almost universal in appeal. Served in place of home fries with steak or hamburgers, it always hits the spot. The potatoes taste best when freshly made, and the aroma from these potatoes will surely lead everyone immediately to the table.

5 medium russet potatoes (about 1¹/₂ pounds)
3 tablespoons peanut oil
2 teaspoons cumin seeds
1¹/₂ tablespoons ground coriander
1 teaspoon ground cumin
³/₄ teaspoon salt, or to taste
¹/₂ teaspoon ground paprika
1 teaspoon mango powder or 1 to 2 tablespoons
    fresh lemon juice
¹/₂ cup finely chopped fresh cilantro,
    including soft stems
¹/₂ teaspoon freshly ground black pepper, or to taste
Sprigs of fresh cilantro

1. Boil the potatoes in water to cover until tender, about 20 minutes. Drain, let cool, then peel and cut into ¹/₂-inch pieces.

2. Heat the oil in a large nonstick skillet over medium-high heat. Add the cumin seeds; they should sizzle upon contact with the hot oil. Quickly add the potatoes and then the coriander, ground cumin, salt, and paprika. Add the potatoes and cook, stirring carefully to avoid mashing them, until golden, about 10 minutes.

3. Add the mango powder and cilantro and cook, stirring, another 5 to 7 minutes. Transfer to a serving platter, garnish with freshly ground black pepper and cilantro sprigs, and serve.

Variation: Instead of cutting the potatoes, very coarsely mash them with a fork and then proceed with the recipe. Or, instead of the cilantro, mix in ¹/₂ cup Basic Green Chutney (page 58) and finish cooking.

Spicy Potatoes with Onions and Tomatoes

Aalu, Pyaz aur Tamatar

Makes 4 to 6 servings

A workhorse dish, this recipe is the daily side dish that is as good as gourmet food when you are hungry. Which is probably why my mother—who could make it in her sleep—made it often, packing it inside a parantha (griddle-fried bread) for our school lunches.

She always made hers with fresh homemade ghee. I use vegetable oil for most of it, but sometimes I can't help but sneak in some ghee for flavoring, even when I make a healthier version. It really does something special to these potatoes.

4 medium russet potatoes (about 1¹/₄ pounds)
2 tablespoons vegetable oil
2 teaspoons melted ghee (optional)
1 large onion, finely chopped
1 to 3 fresh green chile peppers, such as serrano,
    minced with seeds
1 large tomato, finely chopped
1 tablespoon ground coriander
¹/₂ teaspoon ground cumin
¹/₄ teaspoon ground turmeric
¹/₄ teaspoon ground paprika
³/₄ teaspoon salt, or to taste
¹/₂ cup finely chopped fresh cilantro,
    including soft stems
¹/₄ teaspoon garam masala

1. Boil the potatoes in water to cover until tender, about 20 minutes. Drain, let cool, then peel and cut into ¹/₂-inch pieces.

2. Heat the oil (and ghee, if using) in a large nonstick wok over medium-high heat and cook the onion, stirring frequently, until golden, 5 to 7 minutes. Add the green chile peppers and tomato and cook until most of the juices evaporate, 3 to 4 minutes.

3. Add all the spices and salt. Cook, stirring, about 1 minute, then add the potatoes and cilantro and cook over high heat until heated through. Reduce the heat to medium-low and cook until the potatoes are well mixed with the onions and tomatoes, and the oil separates to the sides, about 10 minutes. Transfer to a serving dish, sprinkle the garam masala on top, and serve.

Spicy South Indian Potatoes

Dakshini Aalu

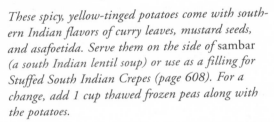

Makes 4 to 6 servings

These spicy, yellow-tinged potatoes come with southern Indian flavors of curry leaves, mustard seeds, and asafoetida. Serve them on the side of sambar (a south Indian lentil soup) or use as a filling for Stuffed South Indian Crepes (page 608). For a change, add 1 cup thawed frozen peas along with the potatoes.

5 medium russet potatoes (about 1¹/₂ pounds)

3 tablespoons peanut oil

1 teaspoon black mustard seeds

¹/₂ teaspoon fenugreek seeds, coarsely ground

1 tablespoon dried white urad beans (urad dal), sorted

1 tablespoon dried yellow split chickpeas (channa dal), sorted

1 medium onion, cut in half lengthwise and thinly sliced

1 tablespoon ground coriander

¹/₄ teaspoon hot red pepper flakes, or to taste

¹/₄ teaspoon ground turmeric

¹/₈ teaspoon ground asafoetida

1¹/₂ to 2 tablespoons minced fresh curry leaves

1 to 3 fresh green chile peppers, such as serrano, minced with seeds

³/₄ teaspoon salt, or to taste

¹/₂ cup finely chopped cilantro, including soft stems

2 tablespoons fresh lemon juice

1. Boil the potatoes in water to cover until tender, about 20 minutes. Drain, let cool, then peel and cut them into ³/₄-inch pieces or coarsely mashed.

2. Heat the oil in a large nonstick wok or skillet over medium-high heat and add the mustard and fenugreek seeds and both the dals; they should splutter upon contact with the hot oil, so cover the pan and reduce the heat until the spluttering subsides.

3. Quickly add the onion and cook, stirring, until golden, about 5 minutes. Then mix in the coriander, pepper flakes, turmeric, asafoetida, curry leaves, and green chile peppers. Cook 1 minute, then add the potatoes, salt, and cilantro. Cover and cook, stirring occasionally and mashing a few of the pieces, over medium-low heat until the potatoes are golden, 5 to 7 minutes. Transfer to a serving dish, mix in the lemon juice, and serve.

Spicy Smashed Potatoes with Chaat Masala

Masaladar Aalu kae Tukrae

Makes 4 to 6 servings

This is another wonderful Indian equivalent to spicy home fries. Boiled potatoes are pan-fried with coriander and tangy dried pomegranate to give this dish a lovely taste and visual appeal. Present it with a dal (legume dish) or a meat or paneer cheese curry, or drizzle on some Yogurt Chutney with Puréed Greens (page 68) and serve it as a snack.

1 teaspoon Chaat Masala (page 20 or store-bought)

5 medium russet potatoes (about 1¹/₂ pounds)

3 tablespoons peanut oil

1 teaspoon cumin seeds

¹/₂ teaspoon hot red pepper flakes, or to taste

1¹/₂ tablespoons ground coriander

¹/₂ teaspoon salt, or to taste

2 tablespoons peeled minced fresh ginger

3 to 5 fresh green chile peppers, such as serrano, split lengthwise

1 tablespoon ground dried pomegranate seeds

1 tablespoon minced fresh mint leaves

1. Prepare the chaat masala. Then, boil the potatoes in water to cover until tender, about 20 minutes. Drain, let cool slightly, then peel and cut in half lengthwise. Press each potato half between the palms of clean hand, to flatten it. (The edges will become ragged.)

2. Heat the oil over medium-high heat and add the cumin seeds and red pepper flakes; they should sizzle upon contact with the hot oil. Quickly add the potatoes, coriander, chaat masala, and salt, and cook, turning the potatoes a few times, until golden, 5 to 7 minutes.

3. Reduce the heat to medium-low, add the ginger, green chile peppers, and pomegranate seeds, and cook until the potatoes are rich brown in color and somewhat crusty, 10 to 15 minutes. Transfer to a serving dish, top with the mint leaves, and serve.

Rajasthani Potatoes with Cashews and Raisins

Rajasthani Aalu

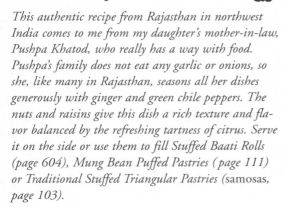

Makes 4 to 6 servings

This authentic recipe from Rajasthan in northwest India comes to me from my daughter's mother-in-law, Pushpa Khatod, who really has a way with food. Pushpa's family does not eat any garlic or onions, so she, like many in Rajasthan, seasons all her dishes generously with ginger and green chile peppers. The nuts and raisins give this dish a rich texture and flavor balanced by the refreshing tartness of citrus. Serve it on the side or use them to fill Stuffed Baati Rolls (page 604), Mung Bean Puffed Pastries (page 111) or Traditional Stuffed Triangular Pastries (samosas, page 103).

5 medium russet potatoes (about 1¹/₂ pounds)
2¹/₂ tablespoons Basic Ginger and Green Chile Pepper Paste (page 48)
2 tablespoons peanut oil
2 tablespoons chopped raw cashews
2 tablespoons golden raisins
1 tablespoon fennel seeds
1¹/₂ teaspoons cumin seeds
¹/₄ teaspoon ground turmeric
¹/₈ teaspoon ground asafoetida
¹/₂ cup frozen peas, thawed
1 teaspoon salt, or to taste
¹/₂ teaspoon garam masala
1 to 2 tablespoons fresh lemon juice
1 teaspoon ground dried pomegranate seeds
¹/₄ cup finely chopped fresh cilantro, including soft stems

1. Boil the potatoes in water to cover until tender, about 20 minutes. Drain, let cool, then peel and coarsely mash them. Meanwhile, prepare the ginger-green chile paste.

2. Heat 1 tablespoon oil in a large nonstick wok or saucepan over medium-high heat and cook the cashews and raisins, stirring, until golden, about 1 minute. With a slotted spoon, drain well and transfer to a bowl.

3. Add the remaining oil to the pan and cook the fennel and cumin seeds, stirring frequently; they should sizzle upon contact with the hot oil. Quickly add the turmeric and asafoetida, then add the potatoes and cook over medium heat, about 5 minutes.

4. Add the peas and cook about 5 minutes. Mix in the ginger-green chile paste, salt, and garam masala and cook another 5 to 7 minutes over medium-low heat. Mix in the lemon juice, pomegranate seeds, and cilantro, and serve.

Bengali Hot Potatoes with Dry-Roasted Spices
Bengali Mirchi Aalu

Makes 4 to 6 servings

This delicacy, from Bengal in the east, offers yet another flavor to everyday potatoes. The potatoes in this dish are traditionally deep-fried, but I just boil and pan-cook them.

5 medium russet potatoes (about 1¹/₂ pounds)
1 teaspoon kalonji seeds
1 to 3 dried red chile peppers, such as chile de arbol, broken
1 to 3 fresh green chile peppers, such as serrano, coarsely chopped
2 tablespoons white poppy seeds
¹/₂ teaspoon coarsely ground fenugreek seeds
2 tablespoons peanut oil
1 teaspoon mustard oil
¹/₂ teaspoon sugar
1 teaspoon salt, or to taste

1. Boil the potatoes in water to cover until tender, about 20 minutes. Drain, let cool, then peel and cut them into ¾-inch pieces.

2. Place the kalonji seeds in a small skillet and dry-roast them, stirring and shaking the pan over medium heat until they are fragrant, about 1 minute. Transfer to a bowl and reserve for garnish. Similarly, dry-roast the red and green chile peppers and the poppy and fenugreek seeds until fragrant, about 2 minutes. Let cool and grind them in a spice or coffee grinder until fine.

3. Heat both the oils in a large nonstick wok or skillet over medium-high heat and cook the potatoes until golden, 5 to 7 minutes. Add the ground spices, sugar, and salt, and cook, stirring and turning carefully, about 10 minutes. Transfer to a serving dish, sprinkle the roasted kalonji seeds on top, and serve.

Pomegranate Potatoes
Aalu Anardana

Makes 4 to 6 servings

Roasted dried pomegranate seeds add a distinctive sourness and a dark brown color to dishes. When combined with dry-roasted cumin seeds, the dish takes on incredible visual appeal and piquant flavor.

12 to 15 baby white or red potatoes (about 1¹/₄ pounds)
3 tablespoons vegetable oil
3 tablespoons ground dried pomegranate seeds
3 tablespoons ground coriander seeds
1 teaspoon salt, or to taste
¹/₂ cup finely chopped fresh cilantro, including soft stems
1 to 2 fresh green chile peppers, such as serrano, minced with seeds
2 teaspoons cumin seeds, dry-roasted and coarsely ground (page 35)
¹/₄ cup fresh pomegranate seeds or tomato wedges

1. Boil the potatoes in water to cover until tender, about 20 minutes. Drain, let cool, then peel and cut in half lengthwise.

2. Heat the oil in a cast-iron or nonstick wok or saucepan over medium-high heat. Add the pomegranate and coriander seeds and stir until darkened, about 1 minute. Mix in the potatoes and salt and cook, stirring over medium heat, 5 to 7 minutes. Add the cilantro, green chile peppers, and cumin seeds, and cook 3 to 5 minutes to blend the flavors. Transfer to a serving dish, garnish with fresh pomegranate seeds or tomato wedges, and serve.

Potatoes with Bell Pepper Confetti

Aalu-Shimla Mirch

Makes 4 to 6 servings

Colorful and delicious, these potatoes make a great party dish. Although any kind of potatoes will do in this dish, I love it with russet potatoes, which come out soft and crumbly.

4 medium russet potatoes (about 1¼ pounds)
2 tablespoons vegetable oil
1 teaspoon melted ghee
1 teaspoon cumin seeds
½ teaspoon coarsely ground black pepper
1 tablespoon ground coriander
½ teaspoon dried fenugreek leaves
1 teaspoon salt, or to taste
½ teaspoon mango powder
½ cup finely chopped fresh cilantro,
    including soft stems
3 to 4 small bell peppers of mixed colors,
    finely chopped
¼ teaspoon garam masala

1. Boil the potatoes in water to cover until tender, about 20 minutes. Drain, let cool, then peel and cut them into ¾-inch pieces.

2. Heat the oil and ghee in a large nonstick wok or skillet over medium-high heat and add the cumin seeds and black pepper; they should sizzle immediately on contact with the hot oil. Quickly add the remaining spices and salt, then mix in the potatoes. Cook, turning as needed, until golden, 3 to 5 minutes.

3. Reduce the heat to medium, add the cilantro and bell peppers, cover, and cook, stirring occasionally, 3 to 5 minutes. Transfer to a serving dish, sprinkle the garam masala on top, and serve.

Russet Potatoes with Fresh Fenugreek Greens

Methi-Aalu

Makes 4 to 6 servings

This highly fragrant dish has a very loyal following among the Punjabi people in northern India. For an authentic Punjabi version, cook this dish in a cast-iron wok called a kadhai.

Fresh fenugreek greens can be found in Indian, Middle Eastern, and some farmers' markets. Buy more than you need, wash and spin-dry the leaves and soft stems, then chop and freeze them in freezer bags. Or dry them at home—place them on cloth or paper towels and air-dry them outdoors in the shade until they are crisp and moisture-free. Dried fenugreek leaves, called kasoori methi, *a popular Indian herb, are also available in Indian markets.*

If needed, substitute spinach or watercress leaves for the fresh fenugreek greens and about 2 tablespoons of dried fenugreek leaves.

3 to 4 bunches fresh fenugreek greens
    (about 1 pound)
3 tablespoons peanut oil
1 fresh green chile pepper, such as serrano,
    minced with seeds
4 medium russet potatoes (about 1¼ pounds),
    peeled and cut into ½-inch pieces
½ teaspoon salt, or to taste
¼ teaspoon ground turmeric
½ cup water

1. Pick out the leaves and the softest stems of the fenugreek greens, discarding the hard and fibrous parts, and wash them well. Then chop them finely in the food processor or by hand.

2. Heat the oil in a large cast-iron or nonstick wok or a saucepan over medium-high heat and cook the fenugreek greens and the green chile pepper, stirring and scraping the sides of the wok, about 3 minutes. Then reduce the heat to medium low and cook until the leaves are completely dry and deep green in color, 10 to 15 minutes.

3. Add the potatoes, salt, and turmeric, and stir about 2 minutes. Then add the water, cover the pan and cook, over medium-high heat until heated through, and then over medium-low heat until the potatoes are very soft, 20 to 30 minutes. Stir and scrape the pan as needed, making sure the potatoes don't stick to the bottom. Serve.

Variation: To make this dish with dried fenugreek leaves instead of fresh, soak 1½ cups of the dried leaves in water to cover about 2 hours. Drain and save any water (use it in place of the water in the recipe). Then proceed with the recipe from Step 2.

Crispy Fork-Mashed Potatoes with Roasted Peanuts

Bhunae Aalu aur Moong-Phalli

Makes 4 to 6 servings

This is my special recipe—perfect to serve during the Navratrae *fasts (*nav *is nine and* ratrae *is nights), when eating grains is forbidden. Celebrated twice a year—once in the beginning of summer (April-May) and once in winter (September-October)—when the climatic, solar, and other cosmic changes are believed to influence peoples' minds and bodies,* Navratrae *is a time for fasting and worshiping.*

4 medium russet (or any) potatoes
    (about 1¼ pounds)
2 tablespoons vegetable oil
1 tablespoon melted ghee
¼ cup coarsely chopped raw peanuts,
    without red skin
1 tablespoon peeled minced fresh ginger
1 to 3 fresh green chile peppers, such as serrano,
    minced with seeds
½ teaspoon salt, or to taste
⅓ cup finely chopped fresh cilantro,
    including soft stems
1 tablespoon fresh lemon juice
½ teaspoon coarsely ground black pepper

1. Boil the potatoes in water to cover until tender, about 20 minutes, then peel and coarsely mash them with a fork, leaving a few large (about ¾-inch) pieces.

2. Heat the oil and ghee in a large nonstick wok or skillet over medium-high heat, add the peanuts, ginger, and green chile peppers, and cook, stirring, until golden, 1 minute.

3. Add the potatoes and salt and cook, stirring occasionally until golden, about 5 minutes. Mix in the cilantro and lemon juice, reduce the heat to medium-low and cook without stirring until the potatoes develop a delicate golden crust on the bottoms, about 10 minutes.

4. Turn once and cook another 5 to 7 minutes or until crusty once more. Transfer to a serving dish, sprinkle the black pepper on top, and serve.

Mashed Potatoes with Peas and Sesame Seed Powder

Muttar aur Til kae Masslae Aalu

Makes 4 to 6 servings

Sesame seed powder, made with asafoetida and fenugreek seeds, adds more fragrance to a dish than you can ever imagine. If you love potatoes every which way, you'll love this exotically spiced but simple dish.

4 medium russet (or any) potatoes
    (about 1¼ pounds)
¼ cup South Indian Sesame Seed Powder (page 31)
1 tablespoon peanut oil
1 tablespoon peeled minced fresh ginger
1 to 2 fresh green chile peppers, such as serrano,
    minced with seeds
¼ teaspoon ground turmeric
1 cup frozen peas, thawed
1 teaspoon salt, or to taste
½ cup finely chopped fresh cilantro,
    including soft stems
1 tablespoon fresh lemon juice

1. Boil the potatoes in water to cover until tender, about 20 minutes. Drain, let cool, then peel and coarsely mash them with a fork. Meanwhile, prepare the sesame seed powder.

2. Heat the oil in a large nonstick wok or skillet over medium-high heat, add the ginger, green chile peppers, and turmeric, and stir about 30 seconds. Quickly add the potatoes, peas, sesame seed powder, and salt, and cook, turning as needed, over high heat for the first 2 to 4 minutes and then over medium-low heat until the potatoes are well-coated with the spices and slightly golden, 7 to 10 minutes. Mix in the cilantro and lemon juice, transfer to a serving dish, and serve.

Ginger Mashed Potatoes with Yogurt
Dahi-Adrak ke Masslae Aalu

Makes 4 to 6 servings

If you're bored of the same plain mashed potatoes and love the refreshing flavors of ginger and yogurt, this spicy Indian version is for you.

**5 medium russet (or any) potatoes
    (about 1¹/₂ pounds)**
1 cup nonfat plain yogurt, whisked until smooth
¹/₄ cup minced scallions, white parts only
**¹/₄ cup finely chopped fresh cilantro,
    including soft stems**
1 tablespoon finely chopped fresh mint
**1 to 3 fresh green chile peppers, such as serrano,
    minced with seeds**
1 teaspoon salt, or to taste
2 tablespoons vegetable oil
**2 black cardamom pods, crushed lightly
    to break the skin**
1 (1-inch) stick cinnamon, broken into small pieces
1 teaspoon cumin seeds
1 teaspoon coarsely ground black pepper
2 tablespoons peeled minced fresh ginger
¹/₄ teaspoon ground paprika
2 tablespoons finely chopped chives

1. Boil the potatoes in water to cover until tender, about 20 minutes. Drain. Then, while still warm, peel and coarsely mashed or grate them. With a fork,

lightly mix in the yogurt, scallions, cilantro, mint, green chile peppers, and salt. Transfer to a serving dish.

2. Heat the oil in a small nonstick saucepan over medium-high heat and add the cardamom pods, cinnamon, cumin, and black pepper. Stir 1 minute, add the ginger, and stir until golden, about 1 minute.

3. Remove from the heat, stir in the paprika, and immediately pour the cooked spices over the mashed potatoes and swirl lightly to mix, with parts of it visible as a garnish. Scatter the chives on top and serve.

Spicy Potato Balls
Masaladar Aalu kae Koftae

Makes 4 to 6 servings

This recipe is close to my friend Neelam Malhotra's heart. She first ate these croquettes in Ooty, a resort near Bangalore in the south, then she made them at home, and passed the recipe on to me. Make your own potato balls as suggested in this recipe, or in a pinch, simply use thawed frozen potato croquettes, available in most supermarkets.

**4 medium russet (or any) potatoes
    (about 1¹/₄ pounds)**
**1 tablespoon Basic Ginger-Garlic Paste
    (page 47 or store-bought)**
1 tablespoon peeled minced fresh ginger
3 tablespoons peanut oil
**1 to 3 fresh green chile peppers, such as serrano,
    stemmed minced with seeds**
1 cup canned tomato sauce
1 tablespoon distilled white vinegar
2 teaspoons sugar
¹/₄ teaspoon salt, or to taste
5 to 6 scallions, finely chopped

1. Boil the potatoes in water to cover until tender, about 20 minutes. Meanwhile, prepare the ginger-garlic paste. Then, drain the potatoes, let cool, then peel and mash or grate them. In a large bowl, mix together the potatoes and fresh ginger and, with clean hands, shape into 20 to 25 small balls or finger shapes. Transfer to a plate.

2. Heat 2 tablespoons oil in a large nonstick skillet over medium-high heat and cook the potato balls, gently shaking the skillet until they are golden all around, about 5 minutes. Turn each one carefully with a spatula if necessary; do not stir them, or they will break. Transfer to a bowl.

3. Heat the remaining 1 tablespoon oil in the skillet, add the ginger-garlic paste and green chile peppers, and stir 1 minute. Add the tomato sauce, cook 1 minute, then add the vinegar, sugar, and salt.

4. Mix in the potato balls and cook, shaking the skillet carefully until they are well-coated with the sauce. Cook, shaking the skillet until most of the sauce evaporates, about 5 minutes. Add the scallions and cook until they are limp, about 3 minutes. Serve.

Tangy Sweet Potatoes
Khatti Shakkar-Kandi

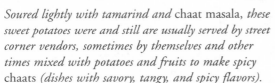

Makes 4 to 6 servings

Soured lightly with tamarind and chaat masala, *these sweet potatoes were and still are usually served by street corner vendors, sometimes by themselves and other times mixed with potatoes and fruits to make spicy* chaats *(dishes with savory, tangy, and spicy flavors).*

1¹/₂ to 2 tablespoons Tamarind Paste (page 54)

1 teaspoon Chaat Masala (page 20 or store-bought), or to taste

3 to 4 small pale-fleshed sweet potatoes (shakkar-kandi, about 1¹/₂ pounds), peeled and cut in ³/₄-inch pieces

1 to 1¹/₂ cups water

¹/₄ teaspoon salt, or to taste

¹/₄ cup finely chopped cilantro, including soft stems

1. Prepare the tamarind paste and the chaat masala. Then, place the sweet potatoes, water, and salt in a large nonstick wok or skillet. Cover and bring to a boil, over medium-high heat for the first 1 to 2 minutes, then over medium-low heat until tender, about 5 more minutes.

2. Add the tamarind and chaat masala and cook, turning the pieces once or twice, until all the water evaporates and the tamarind appears as a glaze on the pieces, 2 to 3 minutes. Mix in the cilantro and cook another 2 minutes. Transfer to a platter and serve hot, at room temperature, or cold.

Fragrant Baby Turnip Halves
Bhunae Chotae Shalgam

Makes 4 to 6 servings

This simple dish is best made with the farmers' market variety of small, 1-inch white turnips that have a naturally sweet and delicate flavor. If you can't find them, use the larger purple-tinged ones, but first peel and cut them into 1-inch pieces. It's a good winter dish to serve with a dal *(legume dish) or a curry. I also like it with Pan-Fried Fish Fillets with Ajwain Seeds (page 520).*

1 tablespoon Basic Ginger-Garlic Paste (page 47 or store-bought)

2 tablespoons vegetable oil

1 teaspoon cumin seeds

1¹/₂ pounds small white turnips, halved

1 to 2 fresh green chile peppers, such as serrano, minced with seeds

1 teaspoon salt, or to taste

2 teaspoons sugar, or to taste

1 to 2 tablespoons fresh lemon juice

¹/₄ cup finely chopped fresh cilantro, including soft stems

1. Prepare the ginger-garlic paste. Then heat the oil in a large nonstick wok or saucepan over medium-high heat and add the cumin seeds; they should sizzle upon contact with the hot oil. Quickly add the turnips and cook, stirring, until lightly golden, 3 to 5 minutes.

2. Add the ginger-garlic paste, green chile peppers, salt, and sugar, cover the pan, and cook over medium-low heat until the turnips are crisp-tender, 5 to 7 minutes. Mix in the lemon juice and cilantro, transfer to a serving dish, and serve.

Grated Turnips with Turmeric

Kutrae Shalgam ki Sabzi

Makes 4 to 6 servings

Turmeric and ginger are the two primary flavors in this simple lunchtime favorite. The ginger is chopped coarsely to add a burst of flavor every time you bite a piece of turnip, but you can mince it if you prefer it that way. Serve this dish with freshly made chapati *(whole-wheat flatbreads).*

Baby turnips, the size and shape of large red radishes, are about 1 inch in diameter. They have a sweet and mild flavor and a soft, smooth skin that does not need to be removed. If you use larger turnips, make sure they are not fibrous and peel them before cooking.

2 tablespoons vegetable oil
1 (1¹/₂-inch) piece peeled fresh ginger,
    coarsely chopped
1 teaspoon cumin seeds
1 to 3 fresh green chile peppers, such as serrano,
    minced with seeds
1 large onion, finely chopped
1 pound baby turnips, trimmed and grated
¹/₄ teaspoon ground turmeric
¹/₄ teaspoon hot red pepper flakes, or to taste
³/₄ teaspoon salt, or to taste
1 teaspoon sugar, or to taste
¹/₄ cup finely chopped fresh cilantro,
    including soft stems
¹/₂ teaspoon garam masala

1. Heat the oil in a large nonstick wok or saucepan over medium-high heat, and cook the ginger, stirring, until golden, 1 minute. Add the cumin seeds; they should sizzle upon contact with the hot oil. Quickly add the green chile peppers and onion and cook, stirring, until golden, 2 to 4 minutes.

2. Add the turnips, turmeric, red pepper flakes, and salt, and cook, stirring, about 4 minutes. Then add the sugar, cover the pan, reduce the heat to medium-low and cook 5 to 7 minutes. Mix in the cilantro and cook another 2 minutes. Transfer to a serving dish, sprinkle the garam masala on top, and serve.

Chopped Turnips with Apples and Green Tomatoes

Shalgam, Saeb aur Harae Tamatar ki Sabzi

Makes 4 to 6 servings

Turnips cooked with tart apples, green tomatoes, and cauliflower florets are not a dish any Indian would think of making, but it tastes very good. I came about this recipe quite by accident. One day when I was cooking turnips, my glance fell on the green apples and tomatoes in my fruit basket and, on the spur of the moment, I added some to the dish. The results were spectacular, and even my mother-in-law, who was visiting from India, said she would make her turnips this way. And she has.

The final cooking time is up to you, depending on how soft you like your vegetables. I prefer them crisp-tender, so I cook the vegetables the final time about 10 minutes.

1 tablespoon vegetable oil
1 pound small turnips, finely chopped
1 small tart apple, finely chopped
1 cup finely chopped cauliflower florets
1 large firm green tomato, finely chopped
1 large red tomato, finely chopped
1 to 2 fresh green chile peppers, such as serrano,
    minced with seeds
¹/₂ teaspoon hot red pepper flakes, or to taste
¹/₂ teaspoon salt, or to taste
¹/₄ teaspoon ground turmeric
1 cup finely chopped fresh spinach

1. Heat the oil in a large nonstick wok or saucepan over medium heat and cook the turnips, apple, and cauliflower, stirring, until fragrant and golden, 7 to 10 minutes.

2. Mix in all the remaining ingredients (except the spinach) and cook, over high heat for the first 3 to 4 minutes and then over low heat until the vegetables are as soft as you desire, 10 to 20 minutes. Mix in the spinach during the last 2 minutes. Transfer to a serving dish and serve.

Crispy Taro Root Fingers with Ajwain Seeds

Ajwaini Arbi

Makes 4 to 6 servings

Taro roots (arbi or arvi), *the small (1½- to 3-inch) starchy tubers with fuzzy brown skin and white flesh, are a popular north Indian vegetable. Look for them in Indian, Asian, and some gourmet produce markets in the United States.*

In this recipe, we first boil the taro roots and then pan-cook them. Both steps are essential. Boiling tenderizes the roots, making them starchy (and a little gummy—that is the nature of this vegetable), and pan-cooking dramatically alters that by making them beautifully crispy on the outside.

This dish tastes divine with Garlicky Yellow Mung Beans with Zucchini Wheels (page 343) and chapati breads. You could pair it with a vegetable, chicken, or a meat curry, or serve it as a snack with a glass of wine.

10 to 12 small taro roots (about 1½ pounds)
3 tablespoons vegetable oil
½ teaspoon coarsely ground ajwain seeds
1 tablespoon ground coriander
1 teaspoon ground cumin
¼ teaspoon ground turmeric
½ teaspoon mango powder
½ teaspoon salt, or to taste
½ cup finely chopped cilantro, including soft stems

1. Boil the taro roots in water to cover until tender, about 20 minutes. Drain, let cool, then peel and slice them lengthwise into four quarters.

2. Heat the oil in a large nonstick skillet over medium-high heat and place the taro roots in it in a single layer, in 2 batches if needed. Cook, shaking the skillet and moving the pieces around, until the undersides are golden, 5 to 7 minutes. Turn each piece over and cook until golden on the second side, about 5 minutes.

3. Sprinkle the ajwain seeds, coriander, cumin, turmeric, mango powder, and salt into the pan, and cook another 2 minutes. Add the cilantro and cook until it wilts and clings to the pieces, about 2 minutes. Serve.

Taro Root Rounds with Tomatoes

Tamatar vaali Arbi

Makes 4 to 6 servings

In this recipe, the taro roots are boiled and pan-cooked, but here we further cook them with tomatoes and spices to make my mother's special side dish that pairs famously with Nani Mama's Yogurt Curry with Onion Fritters (page 426) and a rice pullao *(pilaf).*

My recipe is a little different from the way my mother makes it. She deep-fries the boiled taro root pieces and I pan-cook them.

10 to 12 small taro roots (about 1½ pounds)
1 teaspoon cumin seeds, dry-roasted and ground
    (Dry-Roasting Spices, page 35)
½ teaspoon Chaat Masala (page 20 or store-bought)
2 tablespoons olive or canola oil
1 teaspoon ajwain seeds, coarsely ground
1 teaspoon cumin seeds
1 tablespoon peeled minced fresh ginger
½ teaspoon salt, or to taste
2 large tomatoes, finely chopped
½ cup finely chopped fresh cilantro,
    including soft stems
1 large fresh garlic clove, minced

1. Boil the taro roots in water to cover until tender, about 20 minutes. Meanwhile, prepare the cumin and chaat masala. Drain the taro roots, let cool, then peel and slice into ¼-inch rounds.

2. Heat the oil in a large nonstick skillet over medium-high heat, and add the ajwain and unroasted cumin seeds and ginger; they should sizzle upon contact with the hot oil. Quickly add the taro roots and salt and cook, turning once or twice, until golden, about 10 minutes. Transfer to a bowl.

3. To the same pan, add the tomatoes, cilantro, and garlic, and cook, stirring as needed, until most of the juices evaporate, 5 to 7 minutes. Add the dry-roasted cumin and continue to cook, turning carefully a few times until the taro roots are well-coated with the tomato mixture, 3 to 5 minutes. Transfer to a serving dish, sprinkle the chaat masala on top, and serve.

Ginger-Baked Taro Roots with Chaat Masala
Adrak-Chaat Masala Arbi

Makes 4 to 6 servings

For a twist to your next breakfast or brunch, present these flavorful, quickly cooked taro roots (cylindrical brown-skinned tubers) in place of potatoes. Or offer them as finger foods with a glass wine.

10 to 12 small taro roots (about 1½ pounds)
1 teaspoon Chaat Masala (page 20 or store-bought)
2 tablespoons peanut oil
2 tablespoons fresh lemon or lime juice
2 tablespoons peeled and minced fresh ginger
1 fresh green chile pepper, such as serrano, minced with seeds
½ cup finely chopped fresh cilantro, including soft stems
½ teaspoon ajwain seeds, coarsely ground
¾ teaspoon salt, or to taste

1. In a large saucepan, boil the taro roots in water to cover until tender, about 20 minutes. Meanwhile, prepare the chaat masala. Then peel and cut the taro roots into ¼-inch rounds and place them in a large, flat oven-proof safe pan. Add the oil, lemon juice, ginger, green chile pepper, cilantro, ajwain seeds, and salt and mix well with your clean fingers or a spoon.

2. Preheat the oven to 425°F. Bake until the taro pieces turn crispy and golden, 20 to 25 minutes. Turn a few times. Transfer to a serving platter, sprinkle the chaat masala on top, and serve.

Tangy Lotus Roots
Kamal-Kakdi ki Sabzi

Makes 4 to 6 servings

Lotus roots (kamal-kakdi or bhain) are the buff-colored, tube-like roots of the lotus plant (also called the water lily). They have 10 holes that run the length of the whole root, and when you slice them,

these holes give it a very attractive, naturally lacy appearance (somewhat like pasta wheels) that is dramatically different from any other sliced vegetable. Serve this dish with any curry or dal (legume dish).

Fresh lotus roots are available at Asian and Indian markets. Choose the clean-looking roots with smooth, blemish-free skin. If fresh roots are not available, try the canned ones, drained; they are quite good.

1 tablespoon Basic Ginger-Garlic Paste (page 47 or store-bought)
1 pound fresh lotus roots
2 tablespoons peanut oil
1 medium onion, cut in half lengthwise and thinly sliced
1 large tomato, coarsely chopped
1 fresh green chile pepper, such as serrano, minced with seeds
1 tablespoon ground coriander
¼ teaspoon ground turmeric
1 teaspoon salt, or to taste
1 cup water
¼ cup finely chopped fresh cilantro, including soft stems
1 teaspoon mango powder
¼ teaspoon garam masala

1. Prepare the ginger-garlic paste. Then, wash the lotus roots well outside and inside by allowing running water to flow through the length of the root. Then peel and slice them on the diagonal into thin rounds.

2. Heat the oil in a large nonstick wok or saucepan over medium-high heat and cook the onion until golden, stirring, 5 to 7 minutes. Add the ginger-garlic paste, tomato, and green chile pepper and cook about 1 minute.

3. Add the coriander, turmeric, and salt, then the lotus roots and water, cover the pan, and bring to a boil. Reduce the heat to medium-low and simmer, stirring occasionally, until the lotus roots are crisp-tender, 5 to 7 minutes. (Cook longer for a softer texture.) Mix in the cilantro and mango powder, transfer to a serving dish, sprinkle the garam masala on top, and serve.

Quick Pan-Cooked Lotus Roots

Kamal-Kakdi ki Sabzi

Makes 4 to 6 servings

Because fresh lotus roots require a special trip to an Asian or Indian market, I often use canned ones, which I store in my pantry. Here is an easy recipe to serve with paranthas *(griddle-fried breads).*

1 tablespoon Basic Ginger-Garlic Paste (page 47 or store-bought)
2 tablespoons peanut oil
1 medium potato (any kind), peeled and cut into ¹/₂-inch pieces
1 (14-ounce) can lotus roots, drained and roots cut into thin slices
1 teaspoon cumin seeds
1 fresh green chile pepper, such as serrano, minced with seeds
1 tablespoon ground coriander
¹/₄ teaspoon ground paprika
1 teaspoon salt, or to taste
¹/₂ cup water
¹/₄ cup finely chopped fresh cilantro, including soft stems
1 teaspoon mango powder
¹/₄ teaspoon garam masala

1. Prepare the ginger-garlic paste. Then in a medium nonstick wok or saucepan, heat 1 tablespoon of the oil over medium-high heat and cook the potatoes and lotus roots, stirring until golden, 5 to 7 minutes.

2. Push everything to one side of the skillet. Add the remaining 1 tablespoon oil and tilt the skillet to pool all the oil in the corner opposite the vegetables. When the oil is hot, add the cumin seeds; they should sizzle upon contact with the oil. Quickly add the ginger-garlic paste and green chile pepper and cook, about 30 seconds.

3. Mix in the coriander, paprika, and salt and stir about 2 minutes. Add the water and bring to a boil over high heat. Reduce the heat to medium-low, cover the pan, and simmer, stirring occasionally, until the potatoes are soft and the lotus roots are crisp-tender, 5 to 7 minutes. (Cook longer for a softer texture.)

4. Mix in the cilantro and mango powder, transfer to a serving dish, sprinkle the garam masala on top, and serve.

Eggplant

Native to India and grown all over the world, eggplants come in a variety of shapes, sizes, and colors such as egg-shaped dark-purple Indian eggplants, larger oval eggplants, and thin light-purple Chinese eggplants. I have used different eggplant varieties in my dishes, so you will see how they each can be used. Use what is available in your market, but before cooking, estimate how the cooking time or result might differ so you can adapt the recipe as needed. When selecting your eggplants, regardless of variety, choose eggplants that are shiny and seem light for their size. They will have fewer seeds.

Mashed Fire-Roasted Eggplant

Baingan ka Bhartha

Makes 4 to 6 servings

Seasoned just with salt, this authentic home-style specialty is a textured eggplant mash with lots of natural flavor. It has no resemblance to the heavily creamed and spiced bhartha *(mashed eggplant) dishes that you find in Indian restaurants. My family loves its smoky aroma and taste, so we often quickly devour it at mealtimes. I also often present it as a dip for fresh vegetables and in sandwiches in place of grilled eggplants.*

2 medium oval-shaped eggplants
    (about ³/₄-pound each)
3 tablespoons vegetable oil
5 to 7 fresh green chile peppers, such as serrano,
    whole (puncture skin to prevent bursting),
    or mince 1 pepper
1 large onion, finely chopped
2 large tomatoes, finely chopped
1¹/₂ cups finely chopped fresh cilantro,
    including soft stems
1 teaspoon salt, or to taste

1. Flame-char or roast the eggplants, then peel and mash, as per Roasting and Grilling Vegetables on page 36.

2. Heat the oil in a large wok or saucepan over medium-high heat, add the green chile peppers and onion, and cook, stirring, until golden, about 7 minutes. Add the tomatoes and 1 cup cilantro and cook, stirring occasionally, until the tomato juices evaporate, about 5 minutes.

3. Mix in the eggplant pulp and salt. Reduce the heat to medium-low and cook, stirring occasionally, about 15 minutes. Mix in the remaining ¹/₂ cup chopped cilantro during the last 5 minutes. Transfer to a serving dish, dig out the chile peppers and place on top as a garnish (and a warning), and serve.

Creamy Mashed Eggplant with Peas

Baingan ka Shahi Bhartha

Makes 4 to 6 servings

This dish is often called shahi bhartha *because the addition of cream and spices gives it a richer status, normally associated with the* rajas *and* maharajas *(kings and emperors). Save it for special occasions, and serve it as part of a larger menu with Grilled Tandoori Chicken (page 445), Split Urad Beans and Yellow Split Chickpeas with Spinach (page 368), a yogurt* raita *and oven-grilled* naan *or other flatbreads.*

1 large oval-shaped eggplant (about 1 pound)
2 tablespoons melted ghee or vegetable oil
1 large onion, finely chopped
1 large clove fresh garlic, minced
1 to 3 fresh green chile peppers, such as serrano,
    minced with seeds
1 tablespoon ground coriander
1 teaspoon ground cumin
¹/₂ teaspoon garam masala
¹/₂ teaspoon cayenne pepper, or to taste
¹/₂ teaspoon ground paprika
1 teaspoon salt, or to taste
1 large tomato, finely chopped
1 cup finely chopped fresh cilantro,
    including soft stems
1 cup frozen peas, thawed
¹/₄ cup heavy or light cream
2 tablespoons finely chopped fresh cilantro

1. Flame-char or roast the eggplant, then peel and mash, as per Roasting and Grilling Vegetables on page 36.

2. Heat the ghee or oil in a large nonstick wok or saucepan over medium-high heat and cook the onion, stirring occasionally, until golden, about 5 minutes. Add the garlic and green chile peppers, mix in the coriander, cumin, garam masala, cayenne pepper, paprika and salt, and stir about 1 minute.

3. Add the tomato and cilantro and cook, stirring, until all the tomato juices evaporate, 5 to 7 minutes. Mix in the mashed eggplant and the peas. Reduce the heat to medium-low and cook, stirring occasionally, about 15 minutes. Mix in the cream and cook 1 minute. Transfer to a serving dish, garnish with the chopped cilantro, and serve.

Mashed Eggplant with Mustard Seeds
Raayi vaala Bhartha

Makes 4 to 6 servings, about 4 cups

This classic from Southern India comes with the typical southern tarka *(sizzling flavor topping) of mustard seeds, asafoetida, and fresh curry leaves. Serve this eggplant dish with any soupy split pigeon pea* (toor dal) *dish, called* sambar *(pages 353 to 356), and rice, or serve it as a dip with chopped vegetables or wedges of pita bread.*

2 medium oval eggplants (about ³/4-pound each)
¹/4 cup finely chopped fresh cilantro, including soft stems
1 to 3 fresh green chile peppers, such as serrano, minced with seeds
1 teaspoon salt, or to taste
2 tablespoons fresh lime or lemon juice
1 tablespoon peanut oil
1 teaspoon dried white urad beans (dhulli urad dal)
1 teaspoon black mustard seeds
¹/8 teaspoon ground asafoetida
1 tablespoon chopped dried curry leaves

1. Flame-char or roast the eggplants, then peel and mash, as per Roasting and Grilling Vegetables on

page 36. Place in a serving bowl and mix in the cilantro, green chile peppers, salt, and lime juice.

2. Heat the oil in a small nonstick saucepan over medium-high heat and cook the dal, stirring, about 30 seconds. Add the mustard seeds, asafoetida, and curry leaves; they should splutter upon contact with the hot oil, so lower the heat and cover the pan until the spluttering subsides.

3. Transfer to the eggplant and swirl lightly to mix, with some of the seasonings visible as a garnish, and serve.

Easy Mashed Spicy Eggplant and Potatoes
Baingan-Aalu ka Bhartha

Makes 4 to 6 servings

This is a convenient bhartha *(mashed eggplant) variation. Made with potatoes and eggplants that are first cooked in the microwave oven, the taste is quite different from any traditional* bhartha.

2 to 3 small oval eggplants (about 1 pound total)
2 tablespoons peanut oil
1¹/2 teaspoons cumin seeds
2 tablespoons peeled minced fresh ginger
1¹/2 tablespoons ground coriander
1 teaspoon ground cumin
2 medium-large russet potatoes (about ³/4 pound), peeled and finely chopped
1 large tomato, finely chopped
1 cup finely chopped fresh cilantro, including soft stems
1 to 2 fresh green chile peppers, such as serrano, minced with seeds
1 teaspoon salt, or to taste
1 teaspoon melted ghee (optional)
Chopped cilantro

1. Peel and coarsely chop the eggplants. Then place them in a microwave-safe dish. Cover and cook on high 5 to 6 minutes, or until quite soft. Let cool, then coarsely mash.

2. Heat the oil in a small nonstick wok or skillet and add the cumin seeds; they should sizzle upon contact with the hot oil. Quickly add the ginger, coriander, and cumin, then mix in the potatoes, tomato, cilantro, green chile peppers, and salt. Cover the pan and cook, stirring occasionally, over medium-high heat, about 5 minutes.

3. Mix in the mashed eggplant, reduce the heat to low and continue to cook until the potatoes are soft, 15 to 20 minutes. Add the ghee (if using) and mash some of the potatoes during the last 5 minutes of cooking. Transfer to a serving dish, garnish with the cilantro, and serve.

Roasted Eggplant with Mustard Oil

Baingan ka Chokha

Makes 4 to 6 servings, about 3 cups

Our dear friend, Apurva Chandra, who is from the northeastern state of Bihar, gave me this unusual recipe—a favorite in his family's kitchen in India. Called chokha, *this same dish can be made with coarsely mashed potatoes or roasted zucchini.*

The bold flavors come with a sinus-cleansing guarantee. Serve it over rice, or with parantha *(griddle-fried breads) and a yogurt* raita *on the side. Its intense fresh flavors are lovely in sandwiches; use it as a spread, just as you would a strong Dijon-style mustard.*

2 to 3 small oval eggplants (about 1 pound total)
2 tablespoons mustard oil
1 cup finely chopped onions
1 to 3 fresh green chile peppers, such as serrano, minced with seeds
2 large cloves fresh garlic, minced
1 tablespoon peeled minced fresh ginger

1. Flame-char or roast the eggplants, then peel and mash, as per Roasting and Grilling Vegetables on page 36.

2. Place the mashed eggplants in a serving bowl, mix in all the remaining ingredients, and serve.

Lowfat Stir-Fried Chinese Eggplant with Sesame Seeds

Til vaalae Lambae Baingan

Makes 4 to 6 servings

The thin, long, light-purple eggplants, known in America as Chinese eggplants, are also a popular vegetable all over India. When compared to the other varieties, these eggplants have a thin skin and a distinct, sweetish flavor that shines through despite the presence of sour mango powder in this dish. Most other eggplants can be used here, but these or the darker-colored Japanese eggplants work best in this recipe.

Eggplant absorbs oil like blotting paper, but if you first cook it in a nonstick pan without any oil, you can successfully make a lowfat and heart-healthy recipe.

1 tablespoon sesame seeds, dry-roasted (Dry-Roasting Spices, page 35)
6 to 8 small Chinese eggplants (about 1¹/₂ pounds), cut in ¹/₄-inch slices
¹/₂ teaspoon salt, or to taste
1 tablespoon olive oil
1 teaspoon cumin seeds
1 large clove garlic, minced
1 to 3 fresh green chile peppers, such as serrano, minced with seeds
¹/₂ cup finely chopped fresh cilantro, including soft stems
¹/₂ teaspoon mango powder
¹/₂ teaspoon garam masala

1. Roast the sesame seeds. Then place the eggplants in a medium nonstick wok or skillet and sprinkle with salt. Cover and cook over medium heat, turning once or twice, until golden, 5 to 7 minutes. Transfer to a bowl, cover and keep warm. (The salt draws out the eggplant juices, adding moisture for the eggplants to cook in.)

2. Heat the oil in the same pan over medium-high heat and add the cumin seeds; they should sizzle upon contact with the hot oil. Quickly add the garlic, green chile peppers, and cilantro followed by the eggplant and mango powder and stir carefully to mix. Cook over medium heat about 5 minutes. Transfer to a serving platter, sprinkle the garam masala and sesame seeds on top, and serve.

Indian Eggplant with Garlic and Tamarind

Imli vaalae Chottae Baingan

Makes 4 to 6 servings

Indian eggplants look like dark-purple eggs with a green crown; they resemble young full-size oval eggplants, but the Indian variety is actually already fully grown, just much smaller. (They're 1½ to 2 inches long ovals.) They taste like regular eggplants and can easily be used in their place. And best of all, they are great conversation starters. (Look for them in Indian and Middle Eastern markets.)

1 teaspoon Chaat Masala (page 20 or store-bought)
2 to 3 tablespoons Tamarind Paste (page 54)
1 to 1¼ pounds Indian eggplants (about 18)
    or the equivalent weight of larger eggplants
1 to 1½ tablespoons olive oil
1 teaspoon minced garlic
1 tablespoon ground coriander
¼ teaspoon salt, or to taste
½ cup finely chopped fresh cilantro,
    including soft stems,
2 to 3 scallions, green parts only, minced

1. Prepare the chaat masala and tamarind paste. Wash well and wipe dry the eggplants, then cut each one in half lengthwise through the stem (both halves should have a stem). If using other eggplants, cut them into 1½- to 2-inch pieces. Place the eggplants in a large nonstick wok, cover, and cook over medium-high heat, turning occasionally, until they just begin to brown, 3 to 5 minutes.

2. Drizzle the oil over the eggplants and then mix in the garlic, coriander, chaat masala, and salt. Reduce the heat to medium, cover the wok and cook, turning occasionally, until the eggplants are soft, 10 to 15 minutes.

3. Add the cilantro and tamarind paste and cook, turning carefully, about 5 minutes to blend the flavors. Transfer to a serving dish, garnish with scallion greens, and serve.

Spice-Stuffed Indian Eggplant

Masala Bharae Chottae Baingan

Makes 4 to 6 servings

Here is a recipe that delivers a zesty mouthful in every bite. It is made with really small oval eggplants, each not more than 2 inches long. Instead of pan-cooking the eggplants, baste lightly with oil and grill on a stovetop or outdoor grill. Serve this dish with freshly made paranthas (griddle-fried breads) as part of a party buffet menu.

1 tablespoon Basic Ginger-Garlic Paste
    (page 47 or store-bought)
1 to 1¼ pounds small Indian eggplants (about 18)
    or small Japanese eggplants
2 tablespoons ground coriander
1 teaspoon ground fennel seeds
1 teaspoon ground cumin
¼ teaspoon ground fenugreek seeds
1 tablespoon ground pomegranate seeds
1 teaspoon mango powder
½ teaspoon cayenne pepper, or to taste
¼ teaspoon ground turmeric
½ teaspoon salt, or to taste
3 tablespoons mustard or olive oil
¼ cup finely chopped fresh cilantro,
    including soft stems

1. Prepare the ginger-garlic paste. Then cut the eggplants: Starting at the bottom, make a deep cross-cut toward the stem, stopping about ¼-inch from the stem. Keep the stem intact. (You should be able to pick up each eggplant by the stem.)

2. In a small bowl, mix together the coriander, fennel, cumin, fenugreek, pomegranate seeds, mango powder, cayenne pepper, turmeric, and salt. Fill each eggplant with about ½ teaspoon of the spice mixture, making sure that all the cut surfaces are covered. Save leftover spices.

3. Heat the oil in a large wok, preferably cast-iron, or a nonstick skillet over medium heat, add the eggplants, and cook, turning a few times, about 5 minutes. Then reduce the heat to low, cover the pan, and cook, turning occasionally, until the eggplants are almost black and crispy on the outsides and meltingly soft inside, about 1 hour. Add the leftover spice mixture during the last 10 minutes. Mix in the cilantro, transfer to a serving dish, and serve.

Potato-Stuffed Oval Eggplant

Aalu Bharae Baingan

Makes 4 to 6 servings

The idea for this recipe comes from my friend Shammi Puri in Los Angeles. Shammi uses many different stuffings, and once the eggplants are stuffed and ready to go, she deep-fries them as is traditionally done with stuffed vegetables all over India. My recipe, however, is lighter. I simply pan-fry the stuffed eggplants. Try this recipe with Italian oval eggplants— they are sweet and very delicious. It also works well with scooped out zucchinis and small bell peppers.

2 small oval eggplants (8 to 10 ounces each), preferably Italian, cut in half lengthwise, through the stem

3 tablespoons peanut oil

1 teaspoon cumin seeds

2 tablespoons peeled minced fresh ginger

1¹/2 tablespoons ground coriander

1 teaspoon ground cumin

2 medium-large potatoes (³/4 to 1 pound), peeled and finely chopped

1 large tomato, finely chopped

¹/2 cup finely chopped fresh cilantro, including soft stems + 2 tablespoons

1 to 3 fresh green chile peppers, such as serrano, minced with seeds

1 teaspoon salt, or to taste

2 tablespoons all-purpose flour

2 tablespoons water

1. Place the eggplant halves, cut side up, in a microwave-safe dish. Cover and cook on high 5 minutes, or until quite soft. Let cool and lightly scrape out the pulp, leaving behind a ¼-inch of flesh along the inside of the shell. In a separate bowl, mash the pulp.

2. Heat 1 tablespoon oil in a small nonstick wok or skillet and add the cumin seeds; they should sizzle upon contact with the hot oil. Quickly add the ginger, coriander, and ground cumin, then mix in the potatoes, tomato, cilantro, green chile peppers, and salt. Cover the pan and cook over medium-high heat, stirring occasionally, about 3 minutes. Add the mashed eggplant, reduce the heat to low and cook until the potatoes are soft, 15 to 20 minutes.

3. Meanwhile, in a small bowl, mix together the flour and water to make a paste. Fill each eggplant half with the potato mixture and spread a layer of the flour paste over the potatoes, making sure the top and sides are well covered by the paste. (For color contrast and visual presentation, this paste should encase only the potatoes inside the eggplants. The paste forms a shell, ensuring that the potatoes remain contained inside the eggplants when we pan-fry them.) Sprinkle the 2 tablespoons chopped cilantro on top of the paste.

4. Heat the remaining 2 tablespoons oil in a large skillet over medium-high heat and place the eggplants in it, stuffing side down. Pan-fry, watching carefully and reducing the heat, until golden, 3 to 4 minutes. Turn over and pan-fry the skin side until crisp, 2 to 3 minutes. Transfer to a serving platter and serve whole, or make 1-inch cuts all the way through the eggplant shell before serving.

Eggplant with Red Potatoes

Baingan aur Laal Aalu

Makes 4 to 6 servings

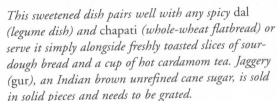

My daughter Supriya loves this dish wrapped within freshly made paranthas *(griddle-fried breads). And no wonder. It's delicious and substantial and needs only light accompaniments. It also makes a good snack. This recipe works well with all types of eggplants.*

3 tablespoons peanut oil or melted ghee (page 41)

2 teaspoons cumin seeds

2 tablespoons ground coriander

1/4 teaspoon ground turmeric

1 teaspoon salt, or to taste

1 large oval eggplant (about 1 pound), cut into 3/4-inch pieces

2 large red potatoes (or any kind), cut into 1/2-inch pieces

1 to 3 fresh green chile peppers, such as serrano, minced with seeds

1 teaspoon mango powder

1/2 cup finely chopped fresh cilantro, including soft stems

1/2 teaspoon garam masala

1. Heat the oil in a large cast iron or nonstick wok or saucepan over medium-high heat and add the cumin seeds; they should sizzle upon contact with the hot oil. Quickly add the coriander, turmeric, and salt, then add the eggplant, potatoes, and green chile peppers. Cover the pan and cook over high heat, stirring, until heated through, 2 to 3 minutes.

2. Reduce the heat to medium-low and continue to cook, stirring occasionally, until the potatoes are tender and the eggplant is very soft, 20 to 25 minutes. Stir every 3 to 4 minutes.

3. Add the mango powder and cilantro during the last 5 minutes of cooking. Transfer to a serving dish, sprinkle the garam masala on top, and serve.

Sweet and Sour Eggplant with Jaggery

Khattae-Meethae Baingan

Makes 4 to 6 servings

This sweetened dish pairs well with any spicy dal *(legume dish) and* chapati *(whole-wheat flatbread) or serve it simply alongside freshly toasted slices of sourdough bread and a cup of hot cardamom tea. Jaggery (gur), an Indian brown unrefined cane sugar, is sold in solid pieces and needs to be grated.*

1 tablespoon Tamarind Paste (page 54)

2 tablespoons peanut oil

1 (1-inch) stick cinnamon

1 teaspoon cumin seeds

1 large onion, cut in half lengthwise and thinly sliced

1 large clove garlic, minced

1 to 3 fresh green chile peppers, such as serrano, minced with seeds

5 to 7 Chinese or Japanese eggplants (about 1 1/4 pounds), cut diagonally into long 1/3-inch-thick slices

1 tablespoon ground coriander

1/2 teaspoon ground cumin

1 teaspoon salt, or to taste

2 tablespoons grated jaggery (gur), or dark brown sugar

1/2 cup finely chopped fresh cilantro, including soft stems

1/4 teaspoon garam masala

1. Prepare tamarind paste. Then, heat the oil in a large nonstick wok or saucepan over medium-high heat and add the cinnamon and cumin seeds; they should sizzle upon contact with the hot oil. Quickly add the onion and cook, stirring, over medium heat until golden, 5 to 7 minutes. Add the garlic and green chile pepper and stir about 30 seconds. Transfer to a bowl and set aside.

2. To the same pan add the eggplants and cook over high heat until heated through. Reduce the heat to medium, cover the pan and cook, stirring occasionally, until they soften slightly, 7 to 10 minutes.

3. Mix in the onion and spice mixture, then add the coriander, cumin, and salt. Cover and cook, stirring occasionally, until the eggplants are soft, 7 to 10 minutes.

4. Add the tamarind and jaggery, stir for a minute, then mix in the cilantro and cook another 2 to 3 minutes to blend the flavors. Transfer to a serving dish, sprinkle the garam masala on top, and serve.

Kerala Coconut Eggplant
Kerala ka Nariyal-Baingan

Makes 4 to 6 servings

Typical of Kerala, this dish is at once hot, slightly sweet, and refreshing. You can make it with just about any kind of eggplant. Serve it with South Indian Mustard and Asafoetida Pilaf (page 539) or Yogurt with Mashed Potato and Fresh Cilantro (page 242).

1/2 cup Coconut Milk (page 44 or store-bought)
1 tablespoon shredded unsweetened dried coconut or 1 (3-inch) piece fresh coconut, grated
1 to 3 dried red chile peppers, such as chile de arbol, broken into pieces
1 to 3 fresh green chile peppers, such as serrano, chopped
4 to 5 quarter-size slices peeled fresh ginger
1 large clove fresh garlic, peeled
1 small onion, coarsely chopped
2 teaspoons ground coriander
1 teaspoon garam masala + 1/4 teaspoon for garnish
1/2 teaspoon ground turmeric
3 tablespoons peanut oil
3 to 4 Chinese eggplants (about 11/4 pounds), cut into 3/4-inch pieces
1 teaspoon salt, or to taste
1 tablespoon fresh lemon juice
1/2 cup finely chopped fresh cilantro, including soft stems
1 tablespoon finely chopped fresh mint leaves

1. Prepare the coconut milk. Reserve. Then, put the coconut, red and green chile peppers, ginger, garlic, and onion in a blender or a food processor and process until smooth. Mix in the coriander, garam masala, and turmeric and process again to make a smooth paste.

2. Heat the oil in a large nonstick saucepan over medium-high heat and cook the coconut-onion paste, stirring as needed, until golden, 3 to 5 minutes.

3. Add the eggplants, coconut milk, and salt, and cook over high heat about 4 minutes. Then reduce the heat to medium, cover the pan and cook, stirring occasionally, until the eggplants are soft, 20 to 25 minutes. Mix in the lemon juice, cilantro, and mint, and cook another 2 to 4 minutes. Transfer to a serving dish, sprinkle the garam masala on top, and serve.

Quick Garlic and Chile Pepper Eggplant
Lussun aur Mirch vaalae Baingan

Makes 4 to 6 servings

Indians typically deep-fry the chopped eggplant first for this dish and then cook it with the spices. My recipe is a more user-friendly version, in which I microwave the chopped eggplants before sautéing them. The result is a quick, less messy, lowfat dish.

11/4 pounds eggplant (any kind), cut into 1/2-inch pieces
2 tablespoons vegetable oil
1 teaspoon cumin seeds
1/2 teaspoon coarsely ground black pepper, or to taste
1 small onion, finely chopped
2 medium fresh garlic cloves, minced
1 to 3 fresh green chile peppers, such as serrano, minced
1 large tomato, coarsely chopped
1 tablespoon ground coriander
1/2 teaspoon ground turmeric
1 teaspoon salt, or to taste
1/2 cup finely chopped fresh cilantro, including soft stems
1/4 teaspoon garam masala

1. Place the eggplant in a microwave-safe dish. Cover and microwave on high until soft, about 4 minutes.

Heat the oil in a large nonstick wok or saucepan over medium-high heat and add the cumin seeds and black pepper; they should sizzle upon contact with the hot oil. Quickly mix in the onion, garlic, and chile peppers and cook, stirring, until golden, 3 to 5 minutes.

2. Add the tomato, coriander, turmeric, and salt, and cook 1 minute. Then mix in the eggplant and cilantro and cook, stirring as needed, over medium heat until the eggplant is soft, 5 to 7 minutes. Transfer to a serving dish, sprinkle the garam masala on top, and serve.

Quick Japanese or Chinese Eggplant with Cilantro

Dhania vaalae Lambae Baingan

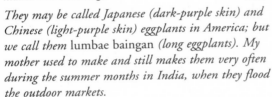

Makes 4 to 6 servings

They may be called Japanese (dark-purple skin) and Chinese (light-purple skin) eggplants in America; but we call them lumbae baingan *(long eggplants). My mother used to make and still makes them very often during the summer months in India, when they flood the outdoor markets.*

These eggplants have a thin skin, a sweeter taste and a silky texture when compared to the others, including the Indian eggplants. They cook fast and take well to Indian spices. To speed up preparation time, soften the eggplants in the microwave for a few minutes, before you cook them, as in this recipe.

1¼ pounds Japanese or Chinese eggplants, cut diagonally into ¾-inch slices
2 tablespoons peanut oil
1 teaspoon cumin seeds
½ teaspoon black mustard seeds
¼ teaspoon coarsely ground fenugreek seeds
1 large clove fresh garlic, minced
1 to 3 fresh green chile peppers, such as serrano, minced with seeds
1 tablespoon dried curry leaves
1 tablespoon ground coriander
1 teaspoon dried mint leaves
¼ teaspoon ground turmeric
½ teaspoon salt, or to taste
½ cup finely chopped fresh cilantro, including soft stems
½ teaspoon mango powder

1. Place the eggplants in a microwave-safe dish. Cover and cook on high about 4 minutes. Heat the oil in a large nonstick skillet over medium-high heat and add the cumin, mustard and fenugreek seeds, garlic, and green chile peppers; they should sizzle upon contact with the hot oil.

2. Quickly add the curry leaves, coriander, mint, and turmeric, stir about 30 seconds, then add the eggplant and salt and cook about 2 minutes. Add the cilantro, cover the skillet, reduce the heat to medium and cook, stirring as needed, until the eggplant is soft, 5 to 7 minutes. Mix in the mango powder and serve.

Squashes and Gourds

Spicy Pumpkin Purée

Pethae ki Sabzi

Makes 4 to 6 servings

Called kaddu *or* petha *in Hindi, pumpkins in India are frequently cooked in side dishes, soups, and desserts. The skin of the pumpkin and other winter squashes is thick and hard, and difficult to peel. To peel, using a sharp knife, very carefully cut the squash into long pieces, then slice off the skin. Try it with White Urad Beans with Fresh Lemon Juice (page 357) and whole-wheat* chapati *(griddle breads) or even whole-wheat tortillas.*

3 tablespoons vegetable oil
1/2 teaspoon fennel seeds
1/2 teaspoon coarsely crushed fenugreek seeds
1/4 teaspoon kalonji seeds
1 medium red onion, cut in half lengthwise and thinly sliced
1 tablespoon peeled minced fresh ginger
1 to 3 fresh green chile peppers, such as serrano, thinly sliced
1 1/2 pounds pumpkin (or any orange or yellow winter squash), peeled and cut into 1/2-inch pieces
1 tablespoon ground coriander
1/4 teaspoon ground turmeric
1 teaspoon salt, or to taste
1/4 cup water, or more as needed
1/4 cup finely chopped fresh cilantro, including soft stems

1. Heat the oil in a medium-large, nonstick wok or saucepan over medium-high heat and add the fennel, fenugreek, and kalonji seeds; they should sizzle upon contact with the hot oil. Quickly add the onion and cook, stirring, until golden, 5 to 6 minutes.

2. Stir in the ginger and green chile peppers, then add the pumpkin. Cook, stirring, 5 to 7 minutes. Mix in the coriander, turmeric, and salt, then add the water. Cover the pan and cook, over high heat about 2 minutes, then over low heat until the pumpkin is very soft, about 20 minutes. With a ladle, stir vigorously to mash the softened pumpkin. Transfer to a serving dish, garnish with chopped cilantro, and serve.

Haridwar Pumpkin Purée with Dried Pomegranate Seeds

Haridwar ka Anardana Petha

Makes 4 to 6 servings

Haridwar is one of India's holy cities—Hari is another name for Lord Rama (of Ramayana *fame) and* dwar *means door in Hindi, so the city's name means "the home of God." Located on the banks of the holy Ganges River, this city has long been the place where people go to worship and to find inner peace. To my friend Neelam, who was born there, there are many nostalgic memories of her home, including eating this dish along with hot and spicy Haridwar Potato Curry (page 405) and* poori *(puffed deep-fried breads). I also love it with potato* paranthas *(griddle-fried breads).*

2 tablespoons vegetable oil
2 teaspoons cumin seeds
1 teaspoon coarsely ground fenugreek seeds
1 tablespoon ground coriander seeds
1/8 teaspoon ground asafoetida
1 to 3 fresh green chile peppers, such as serrano, minced with seeds
1 1/2 pounds pumpkin, peeled and finely chopped
1/2 teaspoon ground turmeric
1/2 teaspoon salt, or to taste
1/4 cup water, or more as needed
1 teaspoon sugar
2 teaspoons ground dried pomegranate seeds
1 tablespoon ground dried mint leaves

1. Heat the oil in a large nonstick wok or saucepan over medium-high heat, then add the cumin and fenugreek seeds; they should sizzle upon contact with the hot oil. Quickly add the coriander and asafoetida and stir about 30 seconds.

2. Add the green chile peppers, pumpkin, turmeric, and salt, and cook, stirring, over medium-high heat until golden, 7 to 10 minutes. Add the water cover the pan, reduce the heat to low, and cook, stirring, until the pumpkin is very soft, about 20 minutes.

3. Remove the pan from the heat, mix in the sugar, pomegranate seeds, and mint, cover the pan, and set aside 30 to 40 minutes, allowing the flavors to permeate the pumpkin. Reheat and transfer to a serving dish, garnish with the fresh mint leaves, and serve.

Quick Pumpkin and Carrot Purée

Pethae aur Gaajar ki Sabzi

Makes 4 to 6 servings

This recipe comes from my husband's cousin, Sanjokta Bhanji. Made with ginger and garlic as the main flavors, this dish is a perfect example of simple home cooking. All the vegetables are chopped and put in a pressure cooker. Only the ginger is grated, because it does not dissolve into the dish like all the other vegetables do. Because this is a salt-free dish, the natural sweetness of the vegetables really shines through.

1 (1 1/2-pound) pumpkin, acorn, or butternut squash
    (peeled or unpeeled), cut into 1/2-inch pieces
1 small onion, coarsely chopped
2 small carrots, coarsely chopped
1 small red bell pepper, coarsely chopped
1 tablespoon peeled and grated fresh ginger
3 small cloves fresh garlic, peeled
1 to 3 fresh green chile peppers, such as serrano,
    with stems
1 tablespoon vegetable oil
1 tablespoon ground coriander
1 teaspoon ground cumin
1/2 teaspoon fenugreek seeds
1/4 teaspoon ground turmeric
1/4 teaspoon hot red pepper flakes, or to taste
1/2 cup water, or more as needed
1/2 cup finely chopped fresh cilantro,
    including soft stems
Freshly ground black pepper

1. Put everything except the cilantro and black pepper into a pressure cooker. Secure the lid and cook over high heat until the regulator indicates high pressure, then cook about 10 seconds more. Remove pot

from the heat and allow to depressurize on its own, 12 to 15 minutes.

2. Open the lid carefully, and remove the green chile peppers, if you wish, to minimize the heat. The contents should be very soft. Stir with a spoon, then mix in the cilantro and coarsely mash everything with a masher or wooden spoon into a textured purée. Transfer to a serving dish, sprinkle the black pepper on top and serve.

Butternut Squash with Fenugreek Seeds

Methi vaala Petha

Makes 4 to 6 servings

This winter squash, a close cousin to the popular orange pumpkin, is another Western vegetable that doesn't grow in India, but lends itself very well to Indian food. It comes with a soft, edible skin that can be eaten after it's cooked, so all the beta-carotene and vitamins stay in the dish. Butternut squash actually also works well in all my pumpkin recipes.

1 tablespoon Basic Ginger-Garlic Paste
    (page 47 or store-bought)
2 tablespoons vegetable oil
1 small onion, cut in half lengthwise and thinly sliced
1 to 3 fresh green chile peppers, such as serrano,
    minced with seeds or thinly sliced
1 teaspoon fenugreek seeds, coarsely ground
1 tablespoon ground coriander
1/4 teaspoon ground turmeric
1 teaspoon salt, or to taste
1 small butternut squash (1 1/2 to 2 pounds),
    cut into 1/2-inch pieces
1/4 cup nonfat plain yogurt, whisked until smooth
1/2 cup finely chopped fresh cilantro,
    including soft stems
1/4 cup water, or more as needed

1. Prepare the ginger-garlic paste. Then, heat the oil in a medium-large, nonstick wok or saucepan over medium-high heat and cook the onion and green chile peppers, stirring until golden, 4 to 5 minutes.

2. Add the fenugreek seeds; they should sizzle upon contact with the hot oil. Quickly add the coriander, turmeric, and salt, then mix in the butternut squash and the ginger-garlic paste. Cook, stirring, over high heat until fragrant, 5 to 7 minutes.

3. Mix in the yogurt, reduce the heat to low, cover the pan and cook, stirring occasionally, 15 to 20 minutes. Add the cilantro (save some for garnish) and water, and continue to cook over low heat, stirring and mashing some of the squash, until tender, 10 to 15 minutes. Transfer to a serving dish, garnish with the reserved cilantro, and serve.

Banana Squash with Spicy Lentil Nuggets
Vadi vaala Petha

Makes 4 to 6 servings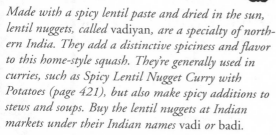

Made with a spicy lentil paste and dried in the sun, lentil nuggets, called vadiyan, *are a specialty of northern India. They add a distinctive spiciness and flavor to this home-style squash. They're generally used in curries, such as Spicy Lentil Nugget Curry with Potatoes (page 421), but also make spicy additions to stews and soups. Buy the lentil nuggets at Indian markets under their Indian names* vadi *or* badi.

2 tablespoons vegetable oil
1 large lentil nugget, broken into ¹/₂-inch pieces
¹/₂ teaspoon mustard seeds
¹/₂ teaspoon cumin seeds
¹/₄ teaspoon fenugreek seeds
¹/₄ teaspoon kalonji seeds
¹/₈ teaspoon ground asafoetida
¹/₄ teaspoon ground turmeric
1 tablespoon peeled minced fresh ginger
1 cup finely chopped tomato
1 pound banana or any other orange squash, peeled and cut into ¹/₂-inch pieces
¹/₂ teaspoon salt, or to taste
³/₄ cup water
1 teaspoon ground dried pomegranate seeds
1 teaspoon sugar
¹/₄ teaspoon garam masala

1. Heat the oil in a large nonstick wok or saucepan over medium-high heat, add the lentil nugget pieces and cook until golden brown. Leaving the oil behind, with a slotted spoon transfer the nuggets to paper towels to drain.

2. To the oil add the mustard, cumin, fenugreek, kalonji, and cumin seeds; they should sizzle upon contact with the hot oil. Quickly add the asafoetida and turmeric, then add the ginger, tomato, squash, salt, and the fried nuggets.

3. Add the water, cover the pan and cook, over medium-high heat for the first 2 to 3 minutes and then over medium heat until the squash is very soft, about 25 minutes.

4. Mix in the pomegranate seeds and sugar, and cook another 2 to 3 minutes. Transfer to a serving dish, sprinkle the garam masala on top, and serve.

Roasted Baby Zucchini Rounds
Bhunni hui Choti Zucchini

Makes 4 to 6 servings

Zucchini does not grow in India, but I have adapted it for many Indian dishes because it works so well. For this dish, I use the farmers' market variety of baby zucchini—ones that are 4 to 5 inches long and no more than ³/₄-inch in diameter. The larger ones can be used, but will not be as tender nor cook as quickly as the baby ones.

1 tablespoon canola oil
1 teaspoon cumin seeds
¹/₂ teaspoon coarsely ground black pepper, or to taste
15 to 20 baby green zucchini or yellow squash (about 1¹/₂ pounds), cut in ¹/₂-inch rounds
1 large clove fresh garlic, minced
2 teaspoons ground coriander
¹/₂ teaspoon ground cumin
¹/₂ teaspoon salt, or to taste
¹/₂ cup finely chopped fresh cilantro, including soft stems
1 fresh green chile pepper, such as serrano, minced with seeds
4 medium tomatoes, cut into wedges
¹/₄ teaspoon garam masala

1. Heat the oil in a nonstick wok or saucepan over medium-high heat and add the cumin seeds and black pepper; they should sizzle upon contact with the hot oil. Quickly add the zucchini, garlic, coriander, cumin, salt, ¼ cup cilantro, and green chile pepper, and cook, stirring occasionally, until they are marked all over with brown spots, 3 to 5 minutes. Transfer to a serving dish.

2. To the same wok, add the tomatoes and stir over high heat until slightly softened, 2 to 3 minutes. Add to the zucchini as a garnish. Sprinkle the garam masala and the remaining ¼ cup cilantro on top, and serve.

Variation: This recipe also works well with baby crook-neck, patty pan, and Mexican pale green squash.

Spice-Stuffed Baby Zucchini

Masala Bhari Choti Zucchini

Makes 4 to 6 servings

With each zucchini a spicy mouthful, this side dish pairs well with Spinach with Paneer Cheese (page 328) or Kerala Egg and Potato Curry with Coconut Milk (page 443), along with rice or chapatis (whole-wheat flatbreads), and is also perfect as an appetizer. Any leftovers can be used in sandwiches.

¼ cup store-bought shelled dry-roasted peanuts

1 tablespoon ground coriander

1 teaspoon ground cumin

1 teaspoon mango powder

¼ teaspoon cayenne pepper, or to taste

¼ teaspoon ground turmeric

½ teaspoon garam masala

½ teaspoon salt, or to taste

15 to 20 mixed baby green zucchini and yellow squash (about 1½ pounds)

2 tablespoons vegetable oil

1 tablespoon peeled minced fresh ginger

1 large clove fresh garlic, minced

¼ cup finely chopped fresh cilantro, including soft stems

1. Put the peanuts in food processor and process until ground. In a small bowl, mix together the coriander, cumin, mango powder, cayenne pepper, turmeric, ¼ teaspoon garam masala, and salt.

2. Wash and wipe dry the zucchinis. With a sharp knife, make a long slit along the length of one side of each zucchini, starting at the bottom tip and stopping about ½ inch from the stem, leaving the stem intact. (Do not cut them into 2 pieces; just make a pocket for the stuffing.) Stuff about ½ teaspoon of the spice mixture into each zucchini pocket. Reserve any leftovers.

3. Heat the oil in a large nonstick skillet over medium-high heat and cook the zucchini (in two batches, if needed), turning each one with kitchen tongs, until golden on all sides. Add the ginger and garlic to the pan and cook about 1 minute. Add the reserved spice mixture, ground peanuts, and cilantro and cook another 2 minutes. Transfer to a serving dish, sprinkle remaining ¼ teaspoon garam masala on top, and serve.

Baby Yellow Patty Pan Squash with Chopped Tomatoes

Tamatar vaalae Chotae Patty Pan Ghiae

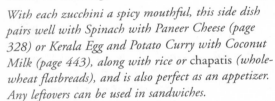

Makes 4 to 6 servings

Here is a simple squash side dish with mild flavor (unless you decide to fire it up with more than 1 chile pepper, as I often do). I use Roma tomatoes in this recipe because they have more pulp and less juice than other varieties. Present it with a curry, pile it atop Simple Cumin Basmati Rice (page 535) or other rice, or serve it with a side of Shredded Chicken Raita (page 239).

15 to 20 baby yellow patty pan squash (about 1½ pounds)

6 to 8 Roma tomatoes (about 1 pound), coarsely chopped

1 fresh green chile pepper, such as serrano, minced with seeds

1 tablespoon olive oil

1 tablespoon peeled minced fresh ginger

1 tablespoon ground coriander

½ teaspoon ground cumin

½ teaspoon salt, or to taste

¼ cup finely chopped fresh cilantro, including soft stems

1. Cut a thin slice off the stem and bottoms of each squash. Then, starting at the top, make a deep cross-cut toward the bottom, stopping about ¼-inch from the bottom. Do not cut all the way; the squash bottom should remain intact.

2. Place all the squash (without any oil) in a nonstick skillet. Cover and cook, turning occasionally, over medium-high heat until they are marked all over with browned spots, 3 to 5 minutes.

3. Add all the remaining ingredients (except cilantro), cover the skillet, and cook, stirring, until the squash is tender and most of the juices evaporate, 5 to 7 minutes. Mix in the cilantro, transfer to a serving dish, and serve.

Spicy Garlic-Flavored Patty Pan Squash

Masaladar Chotae Patty Pan Ghiae

Makes 4 to 6 servings

These convex, disk-shaped squashes with scalloped edges come in light green, dark green, and yellow. All of them can be used interchangeably (by weight) with any of the other summer squashes. But the ones I use in this recipe are the cup-shaped, baby ones (often called scallopini), not more than 1-inch in diameter. They cook in minutes and are little morsels of pure flavor.

1½ teaspoons Basic Garlic Paste (page 47)
15 to 20 baby patty pan squash of mixed colors with stems (about 1½ pounds)
1 tablespoon ground coriander
1 teaspoon ground cumin
1 teaspoon mango powder
1 teaspoon dried mint leaves
½ teaspoon ground paprika
¼ teaspoon cayenne pepper, or to taste
1 teaspoon salt, or to taste
2 tablespoons vegetable oil
10 to 12 cherry tomatoes, halved
½ cup finely chopped fresh cilantro, including soft stems

1. Prepare the garlic paste. Then prepare the squash: Starting at the bottom make a deep cross-cut, toward the stem, stopping about ¼-inch from the stem. Keep the stem intact. (You should be able to pick up each squash by the stem.)

2. In a small bowl, mix together the coriander, cumin, mango powder, mint, paprika, cayenne pepper, and salt.

3. Heat the oil in a large nonstick skillet over medium-high heat, add the squash and garlic paste, and cook, stirring, until golden about 10 minutes. Reduce the heat to medium, add ¾ of the spice mixture and cook, stirring and shaking the pan, about 2 minutes. Transfer to a bowl.

4. Add the tomatoes to the pan and stir until soft, about 2 minutes, then mix in the squash. Add the cilantro and the reserved spice mixture and cook another minute, transfer to a serving dish, and serve.

Grilled Mashed Zucchini with Onions and Tomatoes

Zucchini ka Bhartha

Makes 4 to 6 servings

My mother made this dish with grated and steamed opo squash (marrow or lauki*). But, I think grilling brings out a lot more flavor. Use large, overgrown zucchinis from your own or your neighbor's yard.*

1 to 2 large zucchinis (1¼ pounds total)
3 tablespoons vegetable oil
1 medium onion, finely chopped
1 fresh green chile pepper, such as serrano, minced with seeds
1 large clove fresh garlic, minced
2 teaspoons ground coriander
¼ teaspoon ground turmeric
1 teaspoon salt, or to taste
2 medium tomatoes, finely chopped
½ cup finely chopped fresh cilantro, including soft stems

1. Flame-char or roast the zucchini, then peel and mash, as per Roasting and Grilling Vegetables, page 36.

2. Heat the oil in a large wok or saucepan over medium-high heat and cook the onion, stirring, until golden, 5 to 7 minutes. Add the green chile peppers and garlic, and cook another minute. Then mix in the coriander, turmeric, and salt.

3. Add the tomatoes and cilantro (save some for garnish) and cook, stirring occasionally, until most of the juices evaporate, 5 to 7 minutes. Add the zucchini pulp. Reduce the heat to medium-low and cook, stirring occasionally, another 10 to 15 minutes. Transfer to a serving dish, mix in the chopped cilantro, and serve.

Zucchini with Coconut Milk
Naariyal Doodh ki Zucchini

Makes 4 to 6 servings

Coconut milk adds its sweet, creamy richness to this south Indian specialty that is generally made with eggplant or pumpkin. Serve it on the side with sambar *(south Indian lentil soup) and rice or pair it with a chicken or meat curry.*

1 cup Coconut Milk (page 44 or store-bought)
5 quarter-size slices peeled fresh ginger
1 large clove garlic, peeled
1 fresh green chile pepper, such as serrano, stemmed
1/2 cup coarsely chopped fresh curry leaves
1/2 cup coarsely chopped fresh cilantro, including soft stems
1 tablespoon grated fresh or frozen coconut, or shredded unsweetened dried
2 tablespoons vegetable oil
1 tablespoon ground coriander seeds
1/4 teaspoon ground turmeric
1 teaspoon salt, or to taste
6 to 8 small zucchinis (each 6 to 7 inches long), cut into 1-inch rounds

1. Prepare the coconut milk. In a food processor or a blender, process together the ginger, garlic, green chile pepper, curry leaves, cilantro (save some for garnish), and coconut to make a smooth paste, adding a spoonful or two of water, if needed.

2. Heat the oil in a large nonstick wok or saucepan over medium heat, add the ginger-cilantro paste and cook, stirring, until golden, about 5 minutes.

3. Add the coriander, turmeric, and salt, then mix in the zucchinis. Cook, stirring, 2 to 3 minutes, then add the coconut milk, cover the pan, reduce the heat and cook, stirring occasionally, until the zucchinis are soft, 5 to 7 minutes. Transfer to a serving dish, garnish with chopped cilantro, and serve.

Manju's Stuffed Zucchini Boats
Manju ki Paneer Bhari Zucchini

Makes 4 to 6 servings

Stuffed vegetables are always fun—a bit of work perhaps, but beautiful to look at and, if your flavors are right, a delight to the palate. Here is one such recipe from my friend Manju Bansal. Make it with the small yellow squash or green zucchini. They are easy to pick up and eat, so they make great finger foods. Serve this over a bed of wilted greens—such as spinach, mustard greens, or arugula—seasoned with chaat masala.

1 cup mashed Paneer Cheese (page 43 or store-bought) or ricotta cheese
1 teaspoon Mughlai Garam Masala with Nutmeg and Mace (page 18)
8 to 10 small zucchini, each cut in half lengthwise
2 tablespoons vegetable oil
1/2 cup coarsely chopped fresh cilantro, including soft stems
1 tablespoon ground coriander
1/2 teaspoon ground fennel seeds
1 teaspoon mango powder
1/2 teaspoon cayenne pepper, or to taste
1/4 teaspoon ground turmeric
1/8 teaspoon ground asafoetida
1 teaspoon salt, or to taste
1 teaspoon cumin seeds
1 large tomato, coarsely chopped

1. Prepare the paneer in advance. Prepare the masala. Scoop out the white flesh from each zucchini half, leaving a ¼-inch thick shell. Place the shells in a large skillet, cut side down. Drizzle 1 tablespoon oil over them and cook over medium-high heat until the edges are golden, 4 to 5 minutes. Turn each zucchini over and lightly cook the other side. Transfer to a serving platter and keep warm.

2. In a food processor, process together the zucchini pulp, paneer (or ricotta) cheese, cilantro, coriander, fennel seeds, mango powder, cayenne pepper, garam masala, turmeric, asafoetida, and salt until smooth.

3. Heat the remaining 1 tablespoon oil in a small nonstick wok or saucepan over medium-high heat and add the cumin seeds; they should sizzle upon contact with the hot oil. Quickly add the processed zucchini-cheese mixture and stir about 5 minutes. Use it to stuff each zucchini boat.

4. In the same pan, add the tomato and cook over medium heat stirring until softened and coated with any remains in the pan. Transfer to the zucchini as a garnish and serve.

Quick Spicy Opo Squash
Lauki ki Sabzi

Makes 4 to 6 servings

This flavorful dish, moist with natural juices, is a summertime favorite that shows up very often in north Indian homes. Commonly called marrow, ghia, doodhi, or lauki in India, opo squash cooks into a delicate and light dish that, like other summer squashes, is easy on the stomach—a fact that makes it popular with older members of the family.

It cooks up fast in the pressure cooker and can be served with a mung or any other dal (dried legume) dish and whole-wheat griddle flatbreads. This dish is somewhat juicy, so you can also pair it with a dry-cooked vegetable or a paneer cheese dish such as Basic Paneer Cheese Scramble (page 320).

2 teaspoons vegetable oil
1 teaspoon cumin seeds
1 fresh green chile pepper, such as serrano, minced with seeds
1/4 teaspoon ground turmeric
1 large onion, cut in half lengthwise and thinly sliced
2 large tomatoes, finely chopped
1/2 cup finely chopped fresh cilantro, including soft stems

1¼ pounds opo squash, cut into 3/4-inch pieces (peeled or unpeeled)
1 teaspoon salt, or to taste
Freshly ground black pepper, to taste

1. Heat the oil in a pressure cooker over medium-high heat and add the cumin seeds, green chile pepper, and turmeric; they should sizzle upon contact with the hot oil.

2. Quickly add the onion and cook about 3 minutes. Add the tomatoes, cilantro, opo squash, and salt. Secure the lid and cook over high heat until the regulator indicates high pressure, then cook about 30 seconds more. Remove from the heat and allow the pot to depressurize on its own, 12 to 15 minutes. Open the lid carefully, transfer the contents to a serving dish, sprinkle the black pepper on top, and serve.

Variation: To make in a saucepan, cook the onion in the oil, add the remaining ingredients, cover, and cook over low heat until the squash is soft, about 40 minutes, adding about 1/4 cup water as needed.

Chayote Squash, Indian Style
Chow-Chow ki Sabzi

Makes 4 to 6 servings

Known as chow-chow in India, the pale green, pear-shaped chayote squash, popular in the southern parts of the United States, is also a popular south Indian vegetable. That's why my friend Sohini Baliga, who was born in Kerala, relies on it for a quick addition to any meal.

1 tablespoon peanut oil
1 teaspoon black mustard seeds
1/2 teaspoon cumin seeds
3 dried red chile peppers, such as chile de arbol, broken
2 tablespoons minced fresh curry leaves, or dried
4 fresh green chayote squashes (about 8 ounces each), peeled and chopped or quartered
1/4 teaspoon ground turmeric
1/8 teaspoon ground asafoetida
1 teaspoon salt, or to taste
1 1/2 cups water
1/4 cup finely chopped fresh cilantro, including soft stems

1. Heat the oil in a medium nonstick wok or saucepan over medium-high heat and add the mustard and cumin seeds; they should splutter upon contact with the hot oil, so cover the pan and lower the heat until the spluttering subsides.

2. Add the red chile peppers, curry leaves, chayote, turmeric, and asafoetida, and cook, stirring, about 2 minutes. Then add the salt and water, cover the pan, and bring to a boil over high heat. Reduce the heat to medium-low, cover the pan, and simmer until the chayote is soft, 15 to 20 minutes. Transfer to a serving dish, mix in the cilantro, and serve.

Variation: Cook 1 large, thinly sliced onion until golden or lightly cook halved cherry tomatoes and add to the dish as a garnish.

Mixed Summer Squashes with Fresh Ginger
Garmiyon ki Milli-Julli Ghia-Tori

Makes 4 to 6 servings

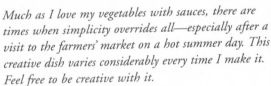

Much as I love my vegetables with sauces, there are times when simplicity overrides all—especially after a visit to the farmers' market on a hot summer day. This creative dish varies considerably every time I make it. Feel free to be creative with it.

1 large russet (or any kind) potato
1 tablespoon olive oil
1 teaspoon black mustard seeds
1 teaspoon cumin seeds
1/2 teaspoon coarsely ground fenugreek seeds
1/2 teaspoon kalonji seeds
2 tablespoons peeled minced fresh ginger
1 large clove fresh garlic, minced
1 fresh green chile pepper, such as serrano, minced with seeds
1 tablespoon ground coriander
1/4 teaspoon ground turmeric
10 to 12 pearl onions, halved

2 pounds mixed summer squashes, such as zucchini, yellow squash, yellow crook-neck, and patty pan, cut into 3/4-inch pieces
1 large tomato, coarsely chopped
1 tablespoon minced fresh mint leaves
1 teaspoon salt, or to taste
Freshly ground black pepper, to taste

1. Boil the potato in water to cover until tender, about 15 minutes. Drain, let cool, then peel and cut it into 3/4-inch pieces.

2. Heat the oil in a large nonstick wok or skillet over medium-high heat and add the mustard, cumin, fenugreek, and kalonji seeds; they should sizzle upon contact with the hot oil. Quickly add the ginger, garlic, green chile pepper, coriander, and turmeric, and cook, stirring, about 30 seconds.

3. Add the onions and potato and cook, stirring, until golden, about 3 minutes. Transfer to a bowl.

4. Add the squashes to the cooking pan and cook about 5 minutes. Then add the tomato, mint, and salt, cover the pan, and cook, over medium-high heat for the first 1 to 2 minutes, then over medium-low heat until the vegetables are crisp-tender, 7 to 10 minutes. Mix in the reserved onions and potatoes and cook another 5 minutes to blend the flavors. Transfer to a serving dish, sprinkle the black pepper on top, and serve.

Simple Pan-Cooked Gherkins
Tindora ki Sabzi

Makes 4 to 6 servings

Gherkins, called tindora *in India, are small, tender cucumbers (usually used in the United States for pickles), with a smooth variegated green skin. They are 1 to 1½ inches long and ½ to ¾ inch in diameter. Although technically cucumbers, they look like and are cooked like squash. They have a distinct, almost sweet taste when raw. Look for them in Indian markets or specialty produce stores in the summer months.*

- 2 tablespoons peanut oil
- 2 teaspoons black mustard seeds
- 3 dried red chile peppers, such as chile de arbol, broken
- 1 pound gherkins (tindora), halved or quartered lengthwise
- 1/2 teaspoon salt, or to taste
- 1 large tomato, finely chopped

1. Heat the oil in a large skillet over medium-high heat and add the mustard seeds; they should splutter upon contact with the hot oil, so cover the pan and lower the heat until the spluttering subsides.

2. Add the red chile peppers, gherkins, and salt, and cook, stirring, until golden, about 4 minutes. Add the tomato, reduce the heat to low, cover the pan and cook until the vegetables are crisp-tender and the juices completely evaporated, 3 to 5 minutes. Serve.

Stuffed Indian Round Squash with Spicy Onion and Tomatoes

Masala Bharae Tindae

Makes 4 to 6 servings

There is a variety of squash found in northern India called tinda. *Tinda squashes are round, green, with a smooth skin that is lightly fuzzy when the squashes are fresh. Ranging anywhere from 1 to 1½ inches in diameter, these squashes can be found in Indian markets only in the summer months. Choose the smaller, blemish-free, firm ones—they will be less seedy.*

If you can't find tinda *squash, make this recipe using green patty pan squashes or the small round zucchinis that can be found in the farmers' and specialty produce markets. Failing that, use the large zucchinis (about 1¼ to 1½ inches in diameter), cut them into 1½-inch pieces and proceed with the recipe, keeping in mind that the zucchinis will cook much faster.*

- 1½ teaspoons Basic Ginger-Garlic Paste (page 47 or store-bought)
- 8 to 10 round squashes (tinda)
- 1½ tablespoons ground coriander
- 1 teaspoon mango powder
- 1/2 teaspoon ground cumin
- 1/4 teaspoon ground turmeric
- 1/4 teaspoon cayenne pepper, or to taste
- 1 teaspoon salt, or to taste
- 2 tablespoons vegetable oil
- 1 small onion, finely chopped
- 1 large tomato, finely chopped
- 1/4 cup finely chopped fresh cilantro, including soft stems
- 1 fresh green chile pepper, such as serrano, minced with seeds
- 1/4 teaspoon garam masala

1. Prepare the ginger-garlic paste. Then prepare the squash: Leaving the bottom part intact, make a deep cross-cut in the top of each squash, making sure they still remain whole. Then, in a small bowl, mix together the coriander, mango powder, cumin, turmeric, cayenne pepper, and salt.

2. Fill each squash with about ½ teaspoon of the spice mixture, making sure that all the cut surfaces are covered. Save the leftover spices.

3. Heat the oil in a large nonstick skillet over medium-high heat and cook the onion, stirring until golden, about 5 minutes. Add the squashes and the ginger-garlic paste and cook, stirring, until the squashes are golden, about 5 minutes.

4. Reduce the heat to medium-low, add the tomato, cilantro, and green chile pepper, cover the pan and cook until the squashes are tender, about 15 minutes. Add the reserved spice mixture and cook another 2 to 3 minutes. Transfer to a serving dish, sprinkle the garam masala on top, and serve.

Baked Bitter Melon with Baby Red Potatoes

Karelae-Aalu ki Sabzi

Makes 4 to 6 servings

This eponymous vegetable, also called bitter gourd, is an acquired taste. But, balanced with rich potatoes and delicious spices, it is worth trying. You'll be surprised how good it is.

Bitter melons are long ovals with pointed ends and a naturally uneven, ridged, and bumpy skin. The smaller they are, the younger and less seedy. In Indian or Asian markets, look for a deep green color; yellowing is a sign of age, increased bitterness, and seeds. But, just in case you end up with the seedy ones, simply scrape off the white pith and seeds before you start cooking.

As a rule, bitter melons are first peeled, then salted and allowed to sweat, then washed to drain out all the bitter juices. I skip this step because the salting doesn't make it drastically sweeter and I prefer to retain the nutrients in the vegetable that would be lost. Also, I bake the bitter melons, as opposed to the customary deep-frying.

4 small baby red potatoes
8 to 10 small bitter melons (about 1¹/₄ pounds total)
3 tablespoons mustard or vegetable oil
¹/₄ teaspoon ground turmeric
1 teaspoon cumin seeds
1 teaspoon fennel seeds
2 small onions, cut in half lengthwise and thinly sliced
1 large clove fresh garlic, minced
1 tablespoon ground coriander
1 teaspoon mango powder
¹/₂ teaspoon ground cumin
¹/₄ teaspoon cayenne pepper, or to taste
1 teaspoon salt, or to taste
2 small tomatoes, cut into wedges
¹/₄ cup finely chopped fresh cilantro

1. Boil the potatoes in water to cover until tender, about 15 minutes. Drain, let cool, then cut into thin wedges. Preheat the oven to 500°F. Lightly grease a baking tray. Wash the bitter melons and cut them into ¹/₃-inch-thick round slices. Add 1 teaspoon oil and the turmeric and toss with the bitter melon slices to mix well. Place on the baking tray in a single layer and bake until golden, 15 to 20 minutes. Turn over and reposition the slices on the tray for even cooking, and remove the pieces as they turn golden, after about 5 minutes.

2. Heat the remaining oil in a large nonstick wok or skillet over medium-high heat and add the cumin and fennel seeds; they should sizzle upon contact with the hot oil. Quickly add the onion and cook, stirring, until medium brown, about 7 minutes. Transfer to a bowl.

3. To the pan, add the potatoes and garlic and cook, stirring occasionally, about 5 minutes. Mix in the baked bitter melons and the cooked onions, then add all the remaining spices and the salt. Cook over medium heat, turning gently, about 10 minutes. Transfer to a serving platter.

4. To the pan, add the tomato wedges and chopped cilantro and stir about 2 minutes. Add to the bitter melon platter as a garnish and serve.

Bitter Melon Stuffed with Mashed Potatoes

Aalu Bharae Karelae

Makes 4 to 6 servings

Here's another take on bitter melons with potatoes. We often cook them together because the natural sweetness and starchiness of potatoes helps to balance the bitterness of the squash.

Bitter or not, bitter melons are considered healthful and quite a delicacy, because bitter melons are highly regarded in Ayurvedic *medicine. They are believed to help purify the blood and alleviate gout and rheumatism, and to be beneficial to diabetic patients because they contain a plant insulin, which helps lower the blood sugar.*

Stuffed bitter melons are traditionally deep-fried, but pan-frying them gets them crispy and brown with a lot less oil. Save the scraped skin to make Bitter Melon Skins with Onions and Potatoes (page 282).

8 to 10 small bitter melons (about 1¼ pounds)

4 small russet (or any) potatoes (about 1 pound)

1 to 3 fresh green chile peppers, such as serrano, minced with seeds

1 tablespoon peeled minced fresh ginger

¼ cup finely chopped fresh cilantro, including soft stems + 2 tablespoons for garnish

1 teaspoon mango powder

½ teaspoon salt, or to taste

3 to 4 tablespoons mustard or vegetable oil

1 teaspoon black mustard seeds

½ teaspoon coarsely ground fenugreek seeds

1 tablespoon ground coriander

¼ teaspoon hot red pepper flakes, or to taste

⅛ teaspoon ground asafoetida

1. Wash and dry the bitter melons. With a vegetable peeler, lightly scrape off the ridged skin. Leaving about ½-inch intact at both ends, make a long, deep lengthwise slit on one side, from the top down, to make a pocket. With a grapefruit or any other spoon, scoop out the white pulp and seeds. (If you'd like to reduce some of the bitterness, sprinkle the cut melons, inside and out, generously with salt. Set aside about 1 hour to marinate and sweat. Then wash out all the salt and wipe each one dry.)

2. Boil the potatoes in water to cover until tender, about 15 minutes. Drain, let cool, then peel and coarsely mash them. Then add green chile peppers, ginger, cilantro, mango powder, and salt, and mix.

3. Heat 1 tablespoon oil in a small saucepan over medium-high heat and add the mustard and fenugreek seeds; they should splutter upon contact with the hot oil, so lower the heat and cover the pan until the spluttering subsides. Quickly add the coriander, red pepper flakes, and asafoetida, transfer to the potatoes, and mix well.

4. Divide the potatoes into the same number of portions as you have bitter melons. Fill each bitter melon pocket with the potatoes. Bring the two cut sides together and tie each bitter melon with clean cotton (kitchen) string to ensure the filling does not fall out during cooking.

5. Place in a nonstick skillet and drizzle the remaining oil over them. Cook, turning as needed, over medium-high heat about 5 minutes and then over medium-low, until they are crispy and brown on all sides, 20 to 25 minutes. Transfer to a serving platter. Cut off the threads or leave them for each guest to unravel. (This is fun when the setting is informal.) Garnish with cilantro and serve.

Variation: Instead of potatoes, stuff the melons with Punjabi Dry-Cooked Yellow Mung Beans (page 345) or Basic Paneer Cheese Scramble (page 320).

Bitter Melon Rounds with Coconut
Nariyal vaalae Karelae

Makes 4 to 6 servings

This is a typical south Indian treatment of bitter melons. The bitter melons are boiled in water before they are spiced up with the standard southern seasonings of coconut, mustard seeds, and asafoetida. The coconut lends a delicate sweetness, helping to balance their bitterness.

8 to 10 small bitter melons (about 1¼ pounds), trimmed and cut into ¼-inch rounds

¼ teaspoon ground turmeric

1 cup water

1 small onion, coarsely chopped

1 large clove fresh garlic, peeled

1 to 3 fresh green chile peppers, such as serrano, stemmed

15 to 20 fresh curry leaves

1 cup grated fresh or shredded unsweetened dried coconut

3 tablespoons vegetable oil

½ teaspoon salt, or to taste

2 to 4 whole dried red chile peppers, such as chile de arbol

1 teaspoon dried white urad beans (dhulli urad dal) or yellow split chickpeas (channa dal)

1 teaspoon black mustard seeds

½ teaspoon coarsely ground fenugreek seeds

⅛ teaspoon ground asafoetida

¼ teaspoon garam masala

1. Place the bitter melon slices, turmeric, and water in a saucepan and bring to a boil over high heat. Reduce the heat to medium-low, cover the pan, and simmer until tender, about 5 minutes. Drain, reserving the water for another use.

2. In a food processor or a blender, process together the onion, garlic, green chile peppers, and curry leaves until smooth. Add the coconut and process again, adding 1 to 2 tablespoons of the reserved water, if needed, to make a smooth paste.

3. Heat half the oil in a large nonstick wok or saucepan over medium-high heat and cook the coconut paste, stirring, until golden, about 5 minutes. Add the bitter melon and salt and cook, stirring about 5 minutes.

4. Heat the remaining oil in a small saucepan over medium-high heat and add the red chile peppers, dal, mustard seeds, and fenugreek seeds; they should splutter upon contact with the hot oil, so cover the pan and lower the heat until the spluttering subsides. Quickly add the asafoetida and transfer the spice mix to the bitter melon. Cook over low heat about 5 minutes to blend the flavors. Transfer to a serving dish, sprinkle the garam masala on top, and serve.

Variation: To make a simpler dish, boil the bitter melons, then make the *tarka* seasoning as explained in step 4, and cook the boiled bitter melons in with the *tarka* until golden, about 5 to 7 minutes.

Bitter Melon Skins with Onions and Potatoes
Karelae kae Chilkae ki Sabzi

Makes 2 to 4 servings

Even though I don't like to peel bitter melons, I will, on occasion, do so, which then allows me to make this delicious side dish, which my mother served to us with paranthas *(griddle-fried breads) for breakfast.*

1 large russet (or any) potato
2 tablespoons vegetable oil
1/4 teaspoon coarsely ground fenugreek seeds
1/4 teaspoon fennel seeds
1/4 teaspoon kalonji seeds
1 medium onion, finely chopped
**1/3 to 1/2 cup bitter melon skin
  (from 6 to 8 bitter melons)**
**1 fresh green chile pepper, such as serrano,
  minced with seeds**
1 large tomato, finely chopped
**1/4 cup finely chopped fresh cilantro,
  including soft stems**
2 teaspoons ground coriander
1/2 teaspoon mango powder
1/2 teaspoon salt, or to taste
1/4 teaspoon garam masala

1. Boil the potato in lightly salted water to cover until tender, about 15 minutes. Drain, let cool, then peel and cut in 1/4-inch pieces.

2. Heat the oil in a large nonstick wok or saucepan over medium-high heat and add the fenugreek, fennel, and kalonji seeds; they should sizzle upon contact with the hot oil. Quickly add the onion and cook, stirring, until golden, about 3 minutes.

3. Add the bitter melon skins and green chile peppers and cook, stirring, until they are dark brown, about 5 minutes. Then add the tomato, potatoes, and cilantro, and stir, about 5 minutes. Mix in the coriander, mango powder, and salt, and stir, another 5 minutes. By now, the ingredients should be dark brown and completely dry. Transfer to a serving dish, sprinkle the garam masala on top, and serve.

Cauliflower, Cabbage, and Other Crucifers

Fried Cauliflower Florets with Red Chili Flakes
Laal-Mirch vaali Tali Gobhi

Makes 4 to 6 servings

Simply deep-fried and sprinkled with salt and red pepper flakes, this is a quick and delicious preparation that brings back memories of my childhood—when watching fat content was not such an important part of life. I don't eat it as frequently now, but I love this dish just the same. This dish can also be made with eggplant, zucchini, or potatoes.

1 cup peanut oil for deep frying
1 small head (about 1 pound) cauliflower, trimmed and cut into 2-inch florets
1/2 teaspoon salt, or to taste
1/2 teaspoon hot red pepper flakes, or to taste

Heat the oil in a large nonstick wok or skillet over medium-high heat then fry the cauliflower florets, a few at a time, removing them to paper towels as each batch turns golden, 1 to 2 minutes per batch. Transfer to a serving dish, sprinkle with the salt and red pepper, and serve hot.

Simple Pan-Cooked Cauliflower
Bhunni Gobhi

Makes 4 to 6 servings

This home-style dish is typically made with ghee or mustard oil in a cast-iron wok, with just salt, cayenne

pepper, and turmeric and the cauliflower and potatoes are cooked until they are quite mushy. This is a common way to cook them, because well-cooked vegetables are easier to digest.

With its delightful, soft texture this is a perfect side dish with the firmer vegetable and meat curries, although in Indian homes it is mostly served with dal (legume) *entrées, such as Yellow Mung Beans with Sautéed Onion and Ginger (page 342).*

2 tablespoons vegetable oil
2 medium russet potatoes, peeled and cut into 1/2-inch pieces
1 small head cauliflower, trimmed and cut into 1-inch florets, soft stems cut into 1/2-inch pieces
1 tablespoon peeled minced fresh ginger
1/2 teaspoon ground turmeric
1/2 teaspoon cayenne pepper, or to taste
1 teaspoon salt, or to taste
1/2 cup finely chopped fresh cilantro, including soft stems
1/2 teaspoon garam masala

1. Heat half of the oil in a large nonstick wok or saucepan over medium heat and cook the potatoes, stirring, until golden, about 5 minutes. Transfer to a bowl, leaving behind as much oil as possible.

2. Add the remaining oil and the cauliflower to the pan and cook, stirring, until golden, about 5 minutes. Mix in the potatoes.

3. Add the ginger, turmeric, cayenne pepper, and salt. Cover the pan, reduce the heat to low and cook, stirring as needed, until the cauliflower and potatoes are very soft (almost mushy), 20 to 30 minutes. Add 1 to 2 tablespoons water, if needed. Add the cilantro during the last 5 minutes of cooking. Transfer to a serving dish, sprinkle the garam masala on top, and serve.

Variation: To make this dish more eye-catching, cut the potatoes and cauliflower into tiny 1/4-inch pieces. Or, add 1 small finely chopped red bell pepper with the cilantro.

Cauliflower with Potato Wedges and Peas

Gobhi, Aalu, Muttar ki Sabzi

Makes 4 to 6 servings

This is another simple and common cauliflower dish in India, where no part of a cauliflower is thrown away. The hard and fibrous stem is saved to make a separate dish (Spicy Cauliflower Stems, page 285) or peeled so the soft insides can be added to this dish.

2 tablespoons peanut oil
5 fresh green chile peppers, such as serrano (puncture skin to prevent bursting)
1 teaspoon cumin seeds
1 tablespoon peeled minced fresh ginger
1 tablespoon ground coriander
1 teaspoon ground cumin
$1/4$ teaspoon ground turmeric
$1/2$ teaspoon salt, or to taste
2 small red, white, or Yukon gold potatoes, cut into wedges
1 small head cauliflower, trimmed and cut into 1-inch florets, soft stems cut into $1/2$-inch pieces
1 cup shelled fresh peas or frozen peas, thawed
2 to 4 tablespoons water
1 large red bell pepper, finely chopped
$1/4$ cup finely chopped fresh cilantro, including soft stems
$1/2$ teaspoon mango powder
$1/4$ teaspoon garam masala

1. Heat the oil in a large nonstick wok or saucepan over medium-high heat and cook the green chile peppers, stirring, about 30 seconds. Add the cumin and ginger; they should sizzle upon contact with the hot oil.

2. Quickly add the coriander, cumin, and turmeric, then mix in the potatoes, cauliflower, peas, and 2 tablespoons water. Cover the pan and cook, over high heat the first 2 to 3 minutes, and then over medium-low heat, stirring occasionally, until the potatoes are soft, 20 to 25 minutes. Stir carefully, and add more water, if needed.

3. During the last 5 minutes, mix in the red bell pepper, cilantro, and mango powder. Transfer to a serving dish, sprinkle the garam masala on top, and serve.

Cauliflower with Minced Ginger-Lime Pickle

Adrak-Nimbbo kae Achaar vaali Gobhi

Makes 4 to 6 servings

Here is a dish with a difference—lots of flavor, and only 1 tablespoon of oil. It has a refreshingly different taste, it's easy to make, and it's healthy. How can you go wrong?

2 tablespoons Minced Ginger-Lime Pickle (page 84)
1 small cauliflower, trimmed and cut into 1-inch florets, soft stems cut into $1/2$-inch pieces
1 large potato (any kind), peeled and chopped
1 tablespoon canola oil
$1^1/2$ teaspoons cumin seeds
1 tablespoon ground coriander
$1/4$ teaspoon ground turmeric
1 small tomato, coarsely chopped
$1/2$ cup finely chopped fresh cilantro, including soft stems
Freshly ground black pepper, to taste

1. Prepare the ginger pickle in advance. Then, place the cauliflower and potato in a large bowl and toss well with the ginger pickle. Cover and marinate in the refrigerator, 1 to 2 hours.

2. Heat the oil in a large nonstick wok or skillet over medium-high heat and add the cumin seeds; they should sizzle upon contact with the hot oil. Quickly add the marinated cauliflower, plus the pickle and potatoes and cook, stirring, until golden, 5 to 7 minutes.

3. Add the coriander, turmeric, tomato, and cilantro, cover the pan, and cook over medium heat until the potato pieces are tender, 7 to 10 minutes. (Add 2 to 3 tablespoons water, if needed.) Transfer to a serving dish, sprinkle the black pepper on top, and serve.

Grilled Yogurt-Marinated Cauliflower

Tandoori Phool

Makes 4 to 6 servings

This authentic tandoor-grilled Mughlai cauliflower is traditionally made with a whole head. I make mine with large florets, which almost look like baby cauliflowers.

1 teaspoon Chaat Masala (page 20 or store-bought)
1 cup nonfat plain yogurt, whisked until smooth
1/4 cup chickpea flour
1/2 cup coarsely chopped fresh cilantro, including soft stems
2 large cloves garlic, peeled
6 quarter-size slices peeled fresh ginger
2 fresh green chile peppers, such as serrano, stemmed
1 teaspoon garam masala
1 teaspoon salt, or to taste
2 tablespoons peanut oil
1/2 teaspoon coarsely ground fenugreek seeds
1 teaspoon ground paprika
1 medium head cauliflower (about 1 1/4 pounds)
4 to 6 metal or bamboo skewers soaked in water at least 30 minutes
1 to 2 tablespoons melted butter, for basting
Scallions and lemon wedges

1. Prepare the chaat masala. Then, in a food processor or a blender, process together the yogurt, chickpea flour, cilantro, garlic, ginger, green chile peppers, garam masala, and salt until smooth. Heat the oil in a small saucepan over medium-high heat until hot but not smoking, about 1 minute. Remove from the heat and add the fenugreek and paprika, then immediately mix into the yogurt mixture.

2. Place the cauliflower stem side up on a cutting board. Cut off the thick main stem as close to the florets as possible before it separates into branches. Then cut the head into 3- to 4-inch florets and place with their heads down, into a large, flat, microwave-safe dish; cover and cook in the microwave on high until crisp-tender, 3 to 4 minutes. Let cool.

3. Pour half the yogurt mixture over the florets, then turn each one over and pour the remaining yogurt over them, making sure that all the heads are well-coated with the marinade. Cover and marinate in the refrigerator 6 to 24 hours.

4. Preheat a grill to medium-high heat (about 375°F). Skewer the florets from the stem to the head and place on the grill, turning as needed, until the florets are soft and charred in a few places, 10 to 12 minutes. Baste with the melted butter and grill another 3 to 5 minutes. Transfer to a serving platter. Sprinkle the chaat masala on top, garnish with the scallions and lemon wedges, and serve.

Spicy Cauliflower Stems

Dandal ki Sabzi

Makes 4 to 6 servings

Called dandal, *the main stem of the cauliflower is usually discarded by most cooks, but not by Indians. We know that inside the hard fibrous covering of this stem lies a delicately soft vegetable—a vegetable that cooks into a delicious side dish.*

1 tablespoon Bengali 5-Spices (Panch-Phoran), page 27 or store-bought
6-inch stems from 3 cauliflowers (or 3-inch stems from 6 cauliflowers)
2 tablespoons mustard or peanut oil
1 large onion, cut in half lengthwise and thinly sliced
2 tablespoons peeled minced fresh ginger
1 to 3 fresh green chile peppers, such as serrano, minced with seeds
1 tablespoon coriander seeds, coarsely ground
1 teaspoon ground cumin
1/2 teaspoon ground paprika
1/4 teaspoon ground turmeric
1 teaspoon cayenne pepper, or to taste
1 teaspoon salt, or to taste
1 large tomato, finely chopped
1/2 cup finely chopped fresh cilantro, including soft stems
1 teaspoon mango powder
1/2 teaspoon garam masala

1. Prepare the 5-spice mixture. Then wash the cauliflower stems well. Cut each inch stem in half crosswise and then into halves or quarters lengthwise, depending on their thickness.

2. Heat the oil in a medium cast-iron or nonstick wok or skillet over medium-high heat and add the 5-spice mixture; they should sizzle upon contact with the hot oil. Quickly add the cauliflower stems and cook, stirring, until golden, 4 to 5 minutes.

3. Add the onion, ginger, and green chile peppers, and stir until golden, 3 to 5 minutes. Mix in the coriander, cumin, paprika, turmeric, cayenne pepper, and salt, and stir about 1 minute. Add the tomato and cilantro and cook, stirring, until all the juices dry up and the spices cling to the pieces, 3 to 5 minutes. Mix in the mango powder. Transfer to a serving dish, sprinkle the garam masala on top, and serve.

Cauliflower Stems with Pomegranate Seeds
Dandal Anardana

Makes 4 to 6 servings

This lesser-used vegetable has always been a favorite among Punjabis, who cook it into this peppery hot and spicy dish with tart undertones. Although it is generally served on the side, I think it is fun to present these stems as a part of the finger-food menu. Each piece is easy to pick up by hand and its taste will tickle the taste buds.

6-inch stems from 3 to 4 cauliflowers (or 3-inch stems from 6 cauliflowers)

1 tablespoon mustard or peanut oil

2 tablespoons peeled minced fresh ginger

1 fresh green chile pepper, such as serrano, minced with seeds

2 tablespoons ground coriander

¼ teaspoon ground turmeric

1 teaspoon salt, or to taste

2 tablespoons nonfat plain yogurt, whisked until smooth

1 tablespoon ground dried pomegranate seeds

¼ cup finely chopped fresh cilantro, including soft stems

1. Wash the cauliflower stems well. Cut each stem in half crosswise and then into halves or quarters lengthwise, depending on their thickness.

2. Heat the oil in a cast-iron or nonstick wok or skillet over medium-high heat and cook the cauliflower stems, stirring, over medium-high heat the first 2 to 3 minutes and then over medium heat until golden brown, 5 to 7 minutes.

3. Add all the remaining ingredients (except the pomegranate seeds and cilantro), cover the pan and cook, stirring as needed, until all the juices evaporate and the stems are soft, 15 to 20 minutes.

4. In the meantime, place the pomegranate seeds in a small nonstick skillet and roast over medium heat, stirring and shaking the skillet, until dark brown, about 2 minutes—keeping in mind that the seeds will continue to darken even after they are removed from the heat. Add the pomegranate seeds to the cauliflower stems during the last 5 minutes of cooking. Mix in the cilantro, transfer to a serving dish, and serve.

Green Cabbage with Yellow Mung Beans
Bundh Gobhi aur Mung Dal

Makes 4 to 6 servings

As it cooks, the yellow mung beans absorb all the juices from the cabbage and add body to this vegetable that normally turns limp when it is cooked. Made with a south Indian spin, this typically Punjabi side dish can be served with any meal and any staple, be it bread or rice.

2 to 3 tablespoons peanut oil

1¼ teaspoons mustard seeds

½ teaspoon coarsely ground fenugreek seeds

⅛ teaspoon ground asafoetida

1 tablespoon ground coriander

2 to 3 tablespoons dried curry leaves

2 to 3 tablespoons peeled minced fresh ginger

1 to 3 fresh green chile peppers, such as serrano, minced with seeds

1 small head green cabbage (about 1¼ pounds), finely shredded

½ cup dried yellow mung beans (dhulli mung dal), sorted and washed in 3 to 4 changes of water

1 teaspoon salt, or to taste

½ cup finely chopped fresh cilantro, including soft stems

¼ teaspoon garam masala

1. Heat the oil in a large nonstick wok or saucepan over medium-high heat and add the mustard and fenugreek seeds, asafoetida, coriander, and curry leaves; they should sizzle upon contact with the hot oil. Quickly add the ginger and green chile peppers and cook, stirring, about 2 minutes.

2. Add the cabbage, dal, and salt, cover the pan and cook, stirring as needed, over medium-high heat the first 2 to 3 minutes and then over medium-low heat until the dal is tender, 15 to 20 minutes. Mix in the cilantro during the last 5 minutes of cooking. Transfer to a serving bowl, sprinkle the garam masala on top, and serve.

Stir-Fried Cabbage with Spinach and Red Potatoes

Bundh Gobhi, Palak aur Laal Aalu

Makes 4 to 6 servings

A crunchy and colorful side dish, this is quick to cook and delicious enough to be enjoyed as a warm salad. Be aware that, like any other stir-fried vegetable, the cabbage will lose its crunch if allowed to sit for a long time and is then reheated.

4 small red (or any) potatoes

3 tablespoons vegetable oil

1½ teaspoons cumin seeds

1 fresh green chile pepper, such as serrano, minced with seeds

1 tablespoon ground coriander

½ teaspoon ground cumin

¼ teaspoon ground fenugreek seeds

¼ teaspoon ground turmeric

1 small head green cabbage (about 1¼ pounds), finely shredded

1 small bunch fresh spinach (8 to 10 ounces), trimmed, washed and finely chopped,

1 cup finely chopped fresh cilantro, including soft stems

1 teaspoon salt, or to taste

8 to 10 cherry tomatoes, halved

1. Boil the potatoes in lightly salted water to cover until tender, about 20 minutes. Drain, let cool, then cut into ½-inch pieces. Do not peel. Meanwhile, prepare the chaat masala.

2. Heat the oil in a large nonstick wok or saucepan over medium-high heat and add the cumin seeds and green chili pepper; they should sizzle upon contact with the hot oil. Quickly add the coriander, cumin, fenugreek, and turmeric, then add the cabbage, spinach, cilantro, and salt. Cook over medium-high heat, stirring, until lightly golden, about 5 minutes. Transfer to a serving dish.

3. Add the potatoes and the remaining 1 tablespoon of the oil to the wok and cook about 2 minutes. Add the tomatoes and cook, stirring, until slightly softened, about 2 minutes.

4. Add the tomatoes to the cabbage and lightly mix them in. Sprinkle the chaat masala on top and serve.

Cooked Brussels Sprouts with Ginger and Garlic

Adrak—Lussan kae Brussels Sprouts

Makes 4 to 6 servings

Brussels sprouts are not Indian, and even today a lot of my Indian friends will not eat them. To me, they don't know what they're missing—including anti-oxidants and cancer-fighting nutrients. I cook them with Indian spices and they are delicious.

1 tablespoon Hyderabadi Ginger-Garlic Paste (page 48)
1 pound (about 20) baby Brussels sprouts
2 tablespoons fresh lime juice
1/2 teaspoon coarsely ground ajwain seeds
1/2 teaspoon freshly ground black pepper, or to taste
1/4 teaspoon salt, or to taste
2 tablespoons vegetable oil
1 large onion, cut in half lengthwise and thinly sliced
1 large tomato, finely chopped
1/2 cup nonfat plain yogurt, whisked until smooth

1. Prepare the ginger-garlic paste. Then trim and make a deep cross cut in the stem of each Brussels sprout. Transfer to a bowl and add the lime juice, ginger-garlic paste, ajwain seeds, black pepper, and salt. Toss to mix well.

2. Heat the oil in a large nonstick wok or saucepan over medium-high heat and cook the onion until golden. Leaving as much oil as possible in the pan, remove the onions to a bowl.

3. Add the Brussels sprouts to the pan and cook, stirring, until golden, 5 to 7 minutes. Add the tomato and cook until most of the juices evaporate, about 3 minutes. Add the yogurt, a little at a time, stirring constantly to prevent it from curdling, until all of it is absorbed, leaving behind a delicate glaze on the Brussels sprouts. Transfer to serving dish, scatter the cooked onion on top, and serve.

Punjabi Kohlrabi

Punjabi Ganth Gobhi ki Sabzi

Makes 4 to 6 servings

Called ganth-gobi, *which means "knotted cabbage," kohlrabi, with the texture of turnips and the taste of cabbage, is juicy, easily prepared, and is often cooked this way in India. Be sure to choose small ones—they will be sweeter—and peel the vegetable first, as it can be fibrous.*

2 tablespoons mustard oil or ghee
1 tablespoon peeled minced fresh ginger
1 large clove fresh garlic, minced
1 fresh green chile pepper, such as serrano, minced with seeds
1 tablespoon ground coriander
1/2 teaspoon ground cumin
1/4 teaspoon ground turmeric
1 teaspoon salt, or to taste
4 to 6 small kohlrabi with greens (about 1 pound), peeled and cut into 3/4-inch pieces, and the leaves finely chopped
1/2 cup water, or as needed
1/4 teaspoon garam masala

1. Heat the oil in a large nonstick wok or saucepan over medium-high heat. Add the ginger, garlic, and chili pepper, and stir about 30 seconds. Add the coriander, cumin, turmeric, and salt, then mix in the kohlrabi and leaves. Cook about 5 minutes over medium heat.

2. Add the water, cover the pan, and bring to a boil over high heat. Then reduce the heat to low and cook until the kohlrabi is tender and most of the water has evaporated, stirring occasionally, 20 to 25 minutes. Transfer to a serving dish, sprinkle the garam masala on top, and serve.

Kashmiri Kohlrabi
Kashmiri Ganth Gobhi

Makes 4 to 6 servings

Because of their geographical location (Kashmir is on the mountainous northern tip of India in the Himalayas), Kashmiris are known to add warming spices such as dried ginger and asafoetida to even the simplest preparations to ward off the chill. This dish is a typical example.

1/2 teaspoon Kashmiri Garam Masala (page 19)
2 to 3 tablespoons vegetable oil
1 teaspoon cumin seeds
1/2 teaspoon coarsely ground fenugreek seeds
4 whole cloves
1/8 teaspoon ground asafoetida
4 to 6 small kohlrabi with greens (about 1 pound), peeled and cut into 3/4-inch pieces, and the leaves finely chopped
1 teaspoon ground coriander
1/2 teaspoon ground ginger
1/2 teaspoon ground turmeric
1 teaspoon salt, or to taste
1 to 3 fresh green chile peppers, such as serrano, minced with seeds
1/2 cup finely chopped fresh cilantro, including soft stems
1/2 cup water, or as needed
Freshly ground black pepper, to taste

1. Prepare the garam masala. Then heat the oil in a large nonstick wok or saucepan over medium-high heat. Add the cumin and fenugreek seeds, cloves, and asafoetida; they should sizzle upon contact with the hot oil. Quickly add the kohlrabi and leaves and cook, stirring, 5 to 7 minutes over medium heat. Mix in all the remaining ingredients (except the water and black pepper) and continue to cook, stirring, 2 to 3 minutes.

2. Add the water, cover the pan, and bring to a boil over high heat. Reduce the heat to low and cook, stirring occasionally, until the kohlrabi is tender and most of the water has evaporated, 20 to 25 minutes. Transfer to a serving dish, sprinkle the black pepper on top, and serve.

Okra

Called lady-fingers or *bhindi* in Hindi, okra is a summer vegetable and grows all over India. In America it can be found in Indian, Asian, Middle Eastern, and well-stocked produce and farmers' markets. Select young, tender okra that are not more than 3 inches long and still retain a tiny bit of the soft fuzz—it's an indication of how young and tender the okra is. The larger ones tend to be fibrous. If you can locate only the larger ones, try snapping the tip off of one with your fingers. If the tip snaps and breaks off, the okra is fine; but if it just bends and does not break, the okra is too fibrous.

Crispy Baked Okra Bits
Oven Mein Bhunni Bhindi

Makes 4 to 6 servings

If you are not yet an okra fan (and especially if you are), keep reading! Okra does not have to be slimy; Indians make wonderful dishes that keep okra dry. Although it's often fried, in a continuing effort to make my home dishes lowfat and heart-healthy, I often bake okra. Once cooked, I just toss it with some salt or chaat masala *and serve it as a side dish, in sandwiches, or over salads. Or I cook it with other vegetables, as in Okra with Potatoes and Pear Tomatoes (page 290). Baked okra also freezes very well.*

1 1/2 pounds fresh tender okra, rinsed and patted dry
1 tablespoon peanut oil
1/2 teaspoon salt, or to taste

1. Cut off the very end of the stem and discard. Then cut the okra into 1/2-inch diagonal (or straight) slices. (Discard the tips of the okra only if they look too brown.) Toss with the oil and salt, and spread evenly on a baking sheet or broiler pan.

2. Preheat the broiler and broil the okra 4 to 5 inches from the source of heat until the tops are browned, 3 to 5 minutes.

3. Turn off the broiler and heat the oven to 450°F. Place the sheet with the okra on the lowest rack in the oven and bake until the bottom is golden, 3 to 5 minutes. Transfer to a bowl and set aside. (With the okra subjected to heat once from the top and then from the bottom, there is no need to stir.) Serve hot.

Variation: To broil the okra whole, cut a thin slice from the stem end and discard. Then, starting at the stem end and stopping about 3/4-inch from the tip, split each okra in half lengthwise most of the way through. (Do not cut the okra into 2 pieces; both cut sides should remain attached at the tip.) Then toss with the oil and salt and cook as explained above.

Chopped Okra with Onions
Cutti Bhindi aur Pyaz

Makes 4 to 6 servings

Before you plan to cook this dish, rinse and thoroughly dry the okra. Make sure your hands, the cutting board, and the knife are dry, and don't stir too much—stirring will break the pieces, making them gummy.

1¼ pounds fresh tender okra, rinsed and patted dry
2 tablespoons peanut oil
2 small onions, cut in half lengthwise and thinly sliced
1 fresh green chile pepper, such as serrano, minced with seeds
1 tablespoon ground coriander
1 teaspoon ground cumin
1 teaspoon mango powder
¼ teaspoon ground turmeric
¾ teaspoon salt, or to taste
½ cup finely chopped fresh cilantro including soft stems
¼ teaspoon garam masala

1. Cut off the very end of the okra stem and discard. Cut each okra into ½-inch pieces. (Discard the tips of the okra only if they look too brown.) Then place in a large cast-iron or nonstick wok or skillet and cook (with no oil) over medium to low heat, turning the pieces a few times very carefully with a spatula until golden brown, 7 to 10 minutes. Transfer to a bowl.

2. Add the oil to the same pan and cook the onion over medium-high heat, stirring, until golden, 5 to 7 minutes. Mix in the green chile pepper and the okra

and cook over medium-low heat, turning occasionally, 2 to 3 minutes.

3. Add the coriander, cumin, mango powder, turmeric, and salt, cook about 5 minutes, then mix in the cilantro and cook another 3 minutes. Transfer to a serving dish, sprinkle the garam masala on top, and serve.

Okra with Potatoes and Pear Tomatoes
Bhindi, Aalu aur Tamatar

Makes 4 to 6 servings

Here, okra pieces are first browned in the oven, then embellished with small, orange pear-shaped tomatoes, potatoes, and onions—all of which lend a softness and color contrast to the green-brown okra pieces. If you can't find orange pear-shaped tomatoes, use red, or just use chopped firm Roma tomatoes.

2 cups (1 recipe) Crispy Baked Okra Bits (page 289)
1 large russet (or any) potato
1 tablespoon Basic Ginger-Garlic Paste (page 47 or store-bought)
2 tablespoons peanut oil
1 small onion, coarsely chopped
1 to 3 fresh green chile peppers, such as serrano, minced with seeds
½ cup finely chopped fresh cilantro, including soft stems
1 tablespoon ground coriander
1 teaspoon ground cumin
1 teaspoon mango powder
¼ teaspoon ground turmeric
½ teaspoon salt, or to taste
15 to 18 small orange or red pear tomatoes
¼ teaspoon garam masala

1. Cook the okra. Meanwhile, boil the potato in lightly salted water to cover, until tender, 15 to 20 minutes. Drain, let cool, then peel and cut the potato into ¾-inch pieces. Prepare the ginger-garlic paste.

2. Heat 1 tablespoon oil in a large cast-iron or nonstick wok or skillet over medium heat and cook the onion until golden, stirring frequently, about 5 minutes. Transfer to a bowl.

3. Add the remaining oil to the same pan and cook the potatoes, stirring, over medium-high heat until golden, about 3 minutes. Mix in the ginger-garlic paste, green chile peppers, cilantro, onion, and okra, and cook over medium-low heat, turning occasionally, about 5 minutes. Add the coriander, cumin, mango powder, turmeric, and salt, and cook, stirring, another 5 to 7 minutes. Transfer to a serving dish and keep warm.

4. Add the pear tomatoes to the pan and cook, shaking the pan, until they are slightly soft and glazed with the spices remaining in the skillet, about 2 minutes. Then add them to the okra as a garnish. Top with the garam masala and serve.

Stuffed Whole Okra with Spices
Masala Bhari Bhindi

Makes 4 to 6 servings

This is a great party dish because it offers an intriguing presentation and is one that involves some labor, so I save it for special occasions. Each piece of okra is first slit lengthwise to make a pocket, then is stuffed with a special mixture of spices before it is cooked. Serve it with Nine-Jewel Paneer Cheese Curry (page 336) or with Punjabi Red Beans with Mango Pickle Masala (page 372), a yogurt raita *and rice, and/or* parantha *(griddle-fried breads).*

1 tablespoon ground coriander
1 teaspoon ground cumin
1 teaspoon mango powder
1 teaspoon ground fennel seeds
1/2 teaspoon ground fenugreek seeds
1/2 teaspoon ground turmeric
1/2 teaspoon garam masala + 1/4 teaspoon for garnish
1/4 teaspoon ground paprika
1/4 teaspoon cayenne pepper, or to taste

1 teaspoon salt, or to taste
1 1/2 pounds fresh tender okra, rinsed and patted dry
3 tablespoons peanut oil
1 1/2 teaspoons cumin seeds
1/8 teaspoon ground asafoetida
1 large onion, cut in half lengthwise and thinly sliced
1 large tomato, coarsely chopped
2 tablespoons minced scallions, white parts only

1. In a small bowl, mix together the first nine spices, from coriander to cayenne pepper, and the salt.

2. For each okra, cut off the very end of the stem and discard. Then make a long slit on one side from the stem down, stopping 3/4-inch from the tip. (This forms a pocket for the stuffing, but keeps the okra intact.) Stuff 1/4 to 1/2 teaspoon of the spice mixture into each okra pocket. Reserve any leftover spice mixture.

3. Heat 2 tablespoons oil in a large cast-iron or non-stick skillet and add the cumin seeds and asafoetida; they should sizzle upon contact with the hot oil. Quickly add the onion and cook, stirring, over medium-high heat until golden, about 5 minutes. With a slotted spatula, transfer to a bowl, leaving behind any oil.

4. Lay all the stuffed okras in the skillet in a single layer. Drizzle the remaining 1 tablespoon oil on top and cook over medium-low heat, turning the pieces very carefully, until golden brown, about 10 minutes.

5. Scatter the cooked onions over the okra and then add any leftover spices. Mix carefully and cook over medium-low heat, turning occasionally, about 5 minutes. Transfer to a serving dish.

6. Add the tomatoes to the skillet and cook over high heat until wilted and coated with any spices left in the skillet, about 2 minutes. Transfer to the okra platter, scatter the scallions and garam masala on top, and serve.

Variation: Do not stuff the okras. Instead, cook them until golden, about 10 minutes, then add the spices on top and finish cooking.

Spicy Broiled Whole Okra

Masaladar Oven-Bhunni Saabut Bhindi

Makes 4 to 6 servings

One of the easiest ways to prepare okra is to toss them with oil and spices, then broil them. This is a technique I learned in the United States, applied to a vegetable favored in India but not here. Perhaps this dish will inspire more people to be okra-lovers. If you wish, toss in some cherry tomatoes, pearl onions, or cut-up red or yellow bell peppers along with the okra, and broil everything together. Then serve this dish with a dal *(legume) dish or with any curry.*

1¹/₂ tablespoons Basic Ginger-Garlic Paste
    (page 47 or store-bought)
1 teaspoon Chaat Masala (page 20 or store-bought)
1¹/₂ pounds fresh tender okra, rinsed and patted dry
2 tablespoons peanut oil
1 tablespoon fresh lemon or lime juice
1 tablespoon ground coriander
1 teaspoon ground cumin
¹/₄ teaspoon cayenne pepper, or to taste
¹/₂ teaspoon salt, or to taste
2 tablespoons finely chopped fresh cilantro

1. Prepare ginger-garlic paste and chaat masala. For each okra, cut off the very end of the stem and discard. Then make a long slit on one side from the stem down, stopping ¾-inch from the tip. (Do not cut the okra into 2 pieces; both sides should remain attached at the tip.) Transfer to a bowl.

2. In a small bowl, mix together the oil, ginger-garlic paste, lemon juice, coriander, cumin, cayenne pepper, and salt and add to the okra. Toss to mix, then spread evenly on a baking sheet or broiler pan.

3. Preheat the oven to broil or preheat the broiler, then cook the okra 4 to 5 inches from the heat source until the tops are brown, 3 to 5 minutes.

4. Turn off the broiler and preheat the oven to 450°F. Place the okra on the lowest rack in the oven and bake until the bottoms of the okra are golden, 3 to 5 minutes. Transfer to a bowl and set aside. (With the

okra subjected to heat once from the top and once from the bottom, there is no need to stir.) Transfer to a serving dish, sprinkle the cilantro and chaat masala on top, and serve.

Whole Okra with Tomato Sauce

Tamatar vaali Saabut Bhindi

Makes 4 to 6 servings

Crispy baked okras drizzled with a thick and smooth red sauce, makes for another attractive dinner or party dish. Pair it with Cashew and Poppy Seed Chicken Curry (page 460) or with any other chicken or lamb curry, or a dal *(legume) dish and a rice* pullao *(pilaf).*

1 tablespoon Basic Ginger-Garlic Paste
    (page 47 or store-bought)
1¹/₂ pounds fresh tender okra, rinsed and patted dry
3 tablespoons peanut oil
1 teaspoon salt, or to taste
1 teaspoon cumin seeds
1 tablespoon ground coriander
¹/₂ teaspoon garam masala + ¹/₄ teaspoon for garnish
¹/₄ teaspoon ground turmeric
2 large tomatoes, finely chopped
1 fresh green chile pepper, such as serrano,
    minced with seeds
¹/₂ cup finely chopped fresh cilantro,
    including soft stems
¹/₄ cup nonfat plain yogurt, whisked until smooth
1 cup water

1. Prepare the ginger-garlic paste. To prepare the okra, cut a thin slice from the stem end and discard. Then, starting at the stem end and stopping about ¾-inch from the tip, split each okra in half lengthwise most of the way through. (Do not cut the okra into 2 pieces; both cut sides should remain attached at the tip.) Then toss with 1 tablespoon oil and ½ teaspoon salt, and spread evenly on a baking sheet or broiler pan.

2. Preheat the broiler and broil the okra 4 to 5 inches from the heat source until the tops are browned, 3 to 5 minutes. Turn off the broiler and heat the oven to 450°F. Place the sheet with the okra on the lowest rack in the oven and bake until the bottom is golden, 3 to 5 minutes. Transfer to a bowl and set aside. (With the okra subjected to heat once from the top and then from the bottom, there is no need to stir.)

3. Meanwhile, heat the remaining 2 tablespoons oil in a large nonstick wok or saucepan over medium-high heat and add the cumin seeds; they should sizzle upon contact with the hot oil. Quickly add the coriander, garam masala, turmeric, and the remaining ½ teaspoon salt. Then add the tomatoes, ginger-garlic paste, green chile pepper, and cilantro (reserving some for garnish), and cook, stirring until most of the juices evaporate and the sauce is thick, about 7 minutes.

5. Mix in the yogurt, a little at a time, stirring constantly to prevent it from curdling, then add the water and bring to a boil over high heat. Reduce the heat to medium-low, cover the pan, and simmer until the sauce is thick and smooth, about 10 minutes.

6. Place the okra on a serving platter and drizzle the sauce on top as a garnish, making sure that parts of the okra are visible through the sauce. Top with cilantro and garam masala, and serve.

Egg-Fried Okra Fingers
Undae vaali Tali-Bhindi

Makes 4 to 6 servings

This is a crispy okra dish from the Parsi people of Goa. The Parsis, who have roots in Iran, generally combine their vegetables with some non-vegetarian fare—in this case, eggs. Serve this dish on the side with a saucy curry or a dal (legume) dish, or as part of the appetizer platter.

¹/₂ teaspoon Chaat Masala (page 20 or store-bought)
1¹/₄ pounds fresh tender okra, rinsed and patted dry
2 large eggs, whisked until smooth
¹/₄ cup all-purpose flour
1 teaspoon salt, or to taste
¹/₂ teaspoon freshly ground black pepper, or to taste
1¹/₂ to 2 cups peanut oil for deep-frying
¹/₂ cup bread crumbs
¹/₄ teaspoon cayenne pepper, or to taste

1. Prepare the masala. To prepare the okra, cut a thin slice from the stem end and discard. Then, starting at the stem end and stopping about ¾-inch from the tip, split each okra in half lengthwise most of the way through. (Do not cut the okra into 2 pieces; both cut sides should remain attached at the tip.) Transfer to a large bowl.

2. In a small bowl, mix together the eggs, flour, salt, and black pepper, pour into the bowl with the okra, and mix carefully with your clean fingers or a spoon, making sure all the pieces are well-coated with the egg mixture. (If needed, add one more egg.)

3. Heat the oil in a large wok until it registers 350°F to 375°F on a frying thermometer, or until a small piece of okra dropped into the hot oil quickly rises to the surface and browns. Roll each okra in the bread crumbs or add the bread crumbs to the okra bowl and toss to mix. Then add the okra to the hot oil, 1 at a time to avoid clumping together. Adding as many as the wok can hold with a little space between each, and fry until crisp and golden, 2 to 3 minutes per batch. With a slotted spoon, remove to paper towels to drain. Transfer to a serving platter, sprinkle the chaat masala and cayenne pepper on top, and serve.

Rajasthani Batter-Fried Okra

Rajastani Besan-Tali Bhindi

Makes 4 to 6 servings

This special recipe from the northwestern state of Rajasthan always lures people back for seconds. The okra is quartered lengthwise, coated with a spicy fennel-flavored chickpea flour batter, and deep-fried. It's rich, so drain it well on paper towels, and serve with lowfat entrées such as Rajasthani Mixed Lentils and Beans (page 367) and whole-wheat chapatis (griddle breads).

1 teaspoon Chaat Masala (page 20 or store-bought)
1¼ pounds fresh tender okra, rinsed and patted dry
⅓ cup chickpea flour, sifted
1 tablespoon ground coriander
1 teaspoon ground fennel seeds
½ teaspoon ajwain seeds, coarsely ground
½ teaspoon ground cumin
½ teaspoon cayenne pepper, or to taste
½ teaspoon salt, or to taste
⅛ teaspoon ground asafoetida
¼ cup nonfat plain yogurt, whisked until smooth
1½ to 2 cups peanut oil for deep frying

1. Prepare the masala. To prepare okra: Cut off a thin slice from the very end of the stem end of each okra and discard. Then quarter each one lengthwise.

2. In a large bowl, mix together the chickpea flour, coriander, fennel and ajwain seeds, cumin, ¼ teaspoon cayenne pepper, salt, asafoetida, and yogurt to make a thick, smooth batter. (Add a spoonful of water if the batter is too thick.) Add in the okra pieces and mix carefully with your clean fingers or a spoon, making sure all the pieces are well-coated with the batter.

3. Heat the oil in a large wok until it registers 350°F to 375°F on a frying thermometer, or until a small piece of okra dropped into the hot oil quickly rises to the surface and browns. Then add the okra to the hot oil, 1 at a time to avoid clumping together. Adding as many as the wok can hold with a little space between each, and fry until crisp and golden, 2 to 3 minutes per batch. With a slotted spoon, remove to paper towels to drain. Transfer to a serving platter, sprinkle the chaat masala and the remaining ¼ teaspoon cayenne pepper on top, and serve.

Kerala Okra with Sizzling Coconut Oil

Vendaka-Roast

Makes 4 to 6 servings

Called vendaka-roast, *this is a typical Kerala-style okra preparation. In Kerala they typically make the whole dish in coconut oil, but to me that is too overpowering, so I use peanut oil for cooking the dish and add the coconut oil in the final seasoning.*

2 tablespoons peanut oil
1½ pounds fresh young okra, rinsed, patted dry, and cut into 1-inch pieces
1 large onion, coarsely chopped
1 large tomato, finely chopped
1 teaspoon salt, or to taste
¼ teaspoon ground turmeric
1 teaspoon tamarind powder
1 tablespoon coconut oil
1 teaspoon black mustard seeds
1 teaspoon hot red pepper flakes, or to taste
8 to 10 fresh curry leaves, crumpled
⅛ teaspoon ground asafoetida

1. Heat 1 tablespoon peanut oil in a large nonstick wok or saucepan over medium-high heat and cook the okra, stirring, until barely golden, 7 to 10 minutes. With a slotted spoon, transfer to a bowl.

2. Add the remaining 1 tablespoon peanut oil and cook the onion until barely golden, about 5 minutes. Transfer to the bowl of okra.

3. To the pan, add the tomato, salt, and turmeric, and cook until the tomatoes are barely soft, 2 to 3 minutes. Return the okra and onions to the pan, add the tamarind, and mix well. Cook 2 to 3 minutes and transfer to a serving bowl.

4. Heat the coconut oil in a small nonstick wok or saucepan over medium-high heat and add the mustard seeds; they should splutter upon contact with the hot oil, so cover the pan and lower the heat until the spluttering subsides. Quickly add the hot red pepper flakes, curry leaves, and asafoetida. Add to the okra, mix well, and serve.

Spinach and Other Greens

Chopped Spinach with Red Potatoes

Palak aur Laal Aalu

Makes 4 to 6 servings

With flavor accents from garam masala, ginger, and garlic, this simple home-style preparation is perfect for a casual supper with chapatis *(griddle breads). To give it a protein boost, mix in a cup of extra-firm tofu or cooked chicken along with the tomatoes in Step 3.*

2 small bunches fresh spinach (about 1 pound), trimmed of roots only, washed well and coarsely chopped
4 small red potatoes (about 1 pound), cut into wedges
1 cup water
³/4 teaspoon salt, or to taste
2 to 3 tablespoons peanut oil
1 teaspoon cumin seeds
1 large onion, finely chopped
1 tablespoon peeled minced fresh ginger
1 large clove fresh garlic, minced
1 to 3 fresh green chile peppers, such as serrano, minced with seeds
1 large tomato, finely chopped
1 tablespoon ground coriander
1¹/2 teaspoons garam masala
¹/4 teaspoon ground turmeric

1. Place the spinach, potatoes, water, and salt in a large nonstick saucepan and bring to a boil over high heat. Reduce the heat to medium-low, cover the pan, and simmer until the potatoes are soft, most of the water has evaporated, and the dish is just moist, 15 to 20 minutes. Stir vigorously and break some of the potatoes to give the dish a somewhat creamy texture. Set aside.

2. Heat the oil in a medium nonstick saucepan over medium-high heat and add the cumin seeds; they should sizzle upon contact with the hot oil. Quickly add the onion and cook, stirring, until golden, about 5 minutes. Add the ginger, garlic, and green chile peppers, and stir until golden. Then add the tomato and cook, stirring, until most of the juices evaporate, 5 to 7 minutes.

3. Add the coriander, 1 teaspoon garam masala, and turmeric, cook about 1 minute, and transfer to the spinach and potato mixture. Mix well, cover the pan and simmer over medium-low heat, 5 to 7 minutes, to blend flavors. Transfer to a serving dish, sprinkle the remaining ¹/2 teaspoon garam masala on top, and serve.

Cooked Spinach with Sliced Almonds

Badaam vaali Palak

Makes 4 to 6 servings

A quick cooking with garlic, ginger, and a touch of Bengali 5-Spices turns fresh spinach into a lovely side dish. Instead of the almonds, you may substitute pistachios, cashews, or pine nuts, but remember to add the nuts just before serving or they will absorb the moisture from the spinach and become soggy.

1 tablespoon Bengali 5-Spices (Panch-Phoran),
    page 27 or store-bought
2 tablespoons sliced almonds, dry-roasted
    (Dry-Roasting Spices, Nuts, Flours, page 35)
1 tablespoon olive oil
1 tablespoon peeled minced fresh ginger
1 large clove fresh garlic, minced
1 to 3 fresh green chile peppers, such as serrano,
    minced with seeds
1/8 teaspoon ground asafoetida
2 small bunches fresh spinach (about 1 pound),
    trimmed of roots only, washed well and
    coarsely chopped
1 1/2 teaspoons salt, or to taste
1 red bell pepper, finely chopped
1/4 teaspoon garam masala

1. Prepare the 5-spice powder and roast the almonds. Then, heat the oil in a medium cast-iron or nonstick wok over medium-high heat and add the 5-spices; they should sizzle upon contact with the hot oil. Then add the ginger, garlic, and green chile peppers, and stir about 30 seconds.

2. Add the asafoetida, spinach, and salt, and stir over high heat 2 to 3 minutes. Cover the pan, reduce the heat to medium-low, and cook until the spinach is well glazed with the spices. Uncover the pan, increase the heat to high, and dry any juices that may have accumulated. Transfer to a serving dish and keep warm.

3. To the same pan, add the bell pepper and cook, stirring, until crisp-tender, 1 to 2 minutes. Scatter over the spinach. Sprinkle the roasted almonds and garam masala on top and serve.

Braised Beet Greens

Chukandar kae Patton ki Sabzi

Makes 4 to 6 servings

These mildly sweet greens, belonging to the chard family, are full of fiber and vitamins, and can be added to salads or cooked, as in this recipe. The same holds true for red or green chard, mustard, daikon, turnip, and other lesser-known greens. All can be used interchangeably. Serve this dish on the side with a vegetable or meat curry, or mix it into Steamed Turmeric and Red Peppercorn Basmati Rice (page 534) and present it with a yogurt raita.

2 to 3 tablespoons vegetable oil
1 teaspoon cumin seeds
1 large onion, finely chopped
1 tablespoon peeled minced fresh ginger
1 large clove fresh garlic, minced
1 tablespoon ground coriander
1 teaspoon ground cumin
1/4 teaspoon salt, or to taste
4 to 5 cups finely chopped beet greens,
    including stems
1 cup water or low-sodium canned chicken broth
1/4 teaspoon garam masala

1. Heat 2 tablespoons oil in a large nonstick skillet over medium-high heat and add the cumin seeds; they should sizzle upon contact with the hot oil. Quickly add the onion and cook, stirring until golden, about 7 minutes. Add the ginger and garlic and stir about 1 minute.

2. Add the coriander, cumin, and salt, stir 1 minute, then mix in the beet greens and water (or broth). Cover the skillet, reduce the heat to medium, and cook, stirring a few times, until the greens are soft and most of the water has evaporated, about 15 minutes.

3. Increase the heat to medium-high, add the remaining 1 tablespoon oil and cook the greens, stirring frequently, until they are very soft, 5 to 7 minutes. Transfer to a serving dish, sprinkle the garam masala on top, and serve.

Carrots, Peas, and Other Basic Vegetables

Dry-Cooked Carrots, Peas, and Potatoes

Sookhae Gaajar, Muttar, aur Aalu

Makes 4 to 6 servings

The natural sweetness of seasonal baby carrots makes for a mildly flavored home-cooking dish, perfect to serve with a dal (legume) dish and chapatis (griddle breads).

Baby carrots are sold in bundles (with greens attached); the small carrot nibs sold in sealed packages don't have the same freshness and flavor. If you can't find baby carrots, use fresh larger carrots (sold with greens).

2 tablespoons vegetable oil
1 teaspoon cumin seeds
1 tablespoon peeled and finely chopped fresh ginger
1 to 3 fresh green chile peppers, such as serrano, minced with seeds
1 tablespoon ground coriander
1/2 teaspoon ground cumin
1/4 teaspoon ground turmeric
1/2 teaspoon salt, or to taste
1 pound baby carrots, cut into 1/2-inch pieces
1/2 pound baby white (or any) potatoes, cut into 1/2-inch pieces
1 cup fresh or thawed frozen peas
1/4 cup water
1/4 cup finely chopped fresh cilantro, including soft stems
1/2 teaspoon mango powder
1/4 teaspoon freshly ground black pepper

1. Heat the oil in a large nonstick wok or saucepan over medium-high heat and add the cumin seeds; they should sizzle upon contact with the hot oil. Quickly add the ginger and green chile peppers, and stir until golden, about 1 minute.

2. Add the coriander, cumin, turmeric, and salt, then mix in the carrots, potatoes, and peas. Cover the pan and cook over high heat until heated through. Reduce the heat to medium-low, add the water, and cook, stirring occasionally, until the potatoes are tender, about 15 minutes. Add the cilantro during the last 5 minutes of cooking. Carefully mix in the mango powder. Transfer to a serving dish, sprinkle the black pepper on top, and serve.

Carrots with Fresh Spinach Ribbons

Gaajar aur Palak ki Sabzi

Makes 4 to 6 servings

Brightly colored and full of beta carotene, this dish was a weekly feature in meals my mother made (and still makes), and now I serve it too. She cooks hers until the carrots are really soft, but I cook just until the carrots are crisp-tender. Cook to your preference.

If your carrots are young (baby carrots) and naturally tender, there is no need to peel them. Simply wash and scrub them well.

2 tablespoons vegetable oil or melted ghee
1 teaspoon cumin seeds
1 tablespoon peeled minced fresh ginger
1 to 3 fresh green chile peppers, such as serrano, minced
1 pound baby carrots, scrubbed well and cut diagonally into thin slices (or peeled larger carrots)
1 tablespoon ground coriander
1/4 teaspoon ground turmeric
1 teaspoon salt, or to taste
1 large tomato, finely chopped
1 1/2 cups fresh spinach, cut into thin ribbon-like strips
1/4 teaspoon garam masala

1. Heat the oil (or ghee) in a medium nonstick wok or saucepan over medium-high heat and add the cumin seeds; they should sizzle immediately. Then add the ginger and green chile peppers and stir until golden, about 1 minute.

2. Mix in the carrots, then add the coriander, turmeric, and salt. Stir about 1 minute, add the tomato, then cover the pan and cook until the carrots are crisp-tender, 5 to 7 minutes.

3. Mix in the spinach, cover again, and cook until the spinach is just wilted or until the carrots are soft, 5 to 7 minutes. Transfer to a serving dish, sprinkle the garam masala on top, and serve.

Spicy Chopped Carrots with Fresh Coconut

Masaladar Nariyal vaali Gaajar

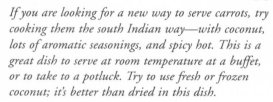

Makes 4 to 6 servings

If you are looking for a new way to serve carrots, try cooking them the south Indian way—with coconut, lots of aromatic seasonings, and spicy hot. This is a great dish to serve at room temperature at a buffet, or to take to a potluck. Try to use fresh or frozen coconut; it's better than dried in this dish.

2 tablespoons vegetable oil
2 to 4 dried red chile peppers, such as chile de arbol, broken
1 teaspoon black mustard seeds
1/2 teaspoon cumin seeds
1 tablespoon dried yellow split chickpeas (channa dal)
1 teaspoon ground coriander
1/8 teaspoon ground asafoetida
1/2 teaspoon salt, or to taste
1 pound young carrots, cut into 1/2-inch pieces or thin 2-inch long sticks
1/2 pound potatoes (any kind), peeled and cut into 1/2-inch pieces
2 to 3 tablespoons water
1 tablespoon fresh lemon juice
1/4 cup finely grated fresh or frozen coconut
1 fresh green chile pepper, such as serrano, minced with or without seeds

1. Heat the oil in a large nonstick wok or saucepan over medium-high heat and add the red chile peppers, mustard seeds, cumin, and dal; they should splutter upon contact with the hot oil, so lower the heat and cover the pan until the spluttering subsides.

2. Quickly add the coriander, asafoetida, and salt, then mix in the carrots, potatoes, and water. Cook over high heat, stirring, 3 to 4 minutes. Reduce the heat to medium-low, cover the pan and cook, stirring occasionally, until the potatoes are tender, about 15 minutes. Transfer to a serving dish, mix in the lemon juice, coconut, and green chile pepper, and serve.

Smoked Sugar-Snap Peas

Dhuandar Saabut Muttar

Makes 4 to 6 servings

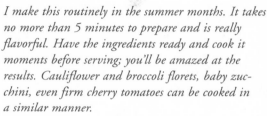

I make this routinely in the summer months. It takes no more than 5 minutes to prepare and is really flavorful. Have the ingredients ready and cook it moments before serving; you'll be amazed at the results. Cauliflower and broccoli florets, baby zucchini, even firm cherry tomatoes can be cooked in a similar manner.

The sugar-snaps here are not truly smoked in a smoker, but they are quickly stir-fried in a smoking hot pan. As soon as you add the oil and the black pepper, an intense smoke arises and, within minutes, penetrates the peas, making them very flavorful. Do not overcook the peas; they should retain their delicate crunch. Serve them with grilled foods, over green salads, pasta, or rice, or keep them on the kitchen counter for people to snack on as they go in and out of the kitchen.

1/2 to 1 teaspoon dry-roasted coarsely ground black peppercorns (Dry-Roasting Spices, page 35)
1 pound sugar-snap peas
1 tablespoon canola oil
1/4 teaspoon salt, or to taste

1. Place the sugar-snap peas in a nonstick wok or saucepan and cook them over high heat about 1 minute.

2. Add the oil, salt, and black pepper and cook, stirring, until smoke starts to arise, about 1 minute. Cover the pan and continue to cook, shaking the pan, about 1 minute. Then reduce the heat to low and cook until the peas are crisp-tender and shiny, about 2 minutes. Serve.

Petite Peas and Potatoes
Sookhae Muttar-Aalu

Makes 4 to 6 servings

Peas are appealing to just about everyone. They look lovely, cook easily and quickly, and taste delicious in so many dishes. Indians are used to shelling fresh peas from the pod as a normal part of their cooking, but it is a tedious job. If you don't mind shelling, do cook the fresh ones—they have a firmer texture and a brighter taste. Because it's harder to find fresh peas in a pod, and cooks don't always have time to shell, here is a recipe using frozen peas.

2 to 3 large red potatoes
2 tablespoons vegetable oil
1 teaspoon black mustard seeds
1 teaspoon cumin seeds
1/8 teaspoon ground asafoetida
**1/4 cup finely chopped fresh cilantro,
    including soft stems**
**1 (1-pound) package frozen petite peas (2 cups),
    thawed**
1 tablespoon ground coriander
1 tablespoon dried curry leaves
1 teaspoon salt, or to taste
1 large tomato, coarsely chopped
Freshly ground black pepper

1. Boil the potatoes in water to cover until tender, about 15 minutes. Drain, let cool, then cut them into ½-inch pieces.

2. Heat the oil in a nonstick wok or saucepan over medium-high heat and add the mustard seeds, cumin seeds, and asafoetida; they should splutter upon contact with the hot oil, so lower the heat and cover the pan until the spluttering subsides. Quickly add the potatoes and cilantro and cook, stirring lightly, until golden, 2 to 3 minutes.

3. Add the peas, coriander, curry leaves, and salt, and cook until the peas are golden, 3 to 5 minutes. Transfer to a serving dish and keep warm.

4. Add the tomatoes to the same pan and cook until softened, 1 to 2 minutes. Mix them into the peas as a garnish. Sprinkle the black pepper on top and serve.

Spicy Green Peas with Onion and Ginger
Muttar-Pyaz Masala

Makes 4 to 6 servings

The sweetness of green peas is pleasantly offset by the pungent ginger, green chile peppers, and other spicy additions in this side dish. Served warm, it is a traditional side dish—a perfect companion to all vegetarian and meat curries and whole-wheat flat breads. Chilled, it can be served as a salad with a hot soup, such as Creamy Tomato Soup (page 171), and toasted sourdough rolls.

2 tablespoons peanut oil
2 tablespoons peeled minced fresh ginger
**1 to 3 fresh green chile peppers, such as serrano,
    minced with seeds**
1 teaspoon cumin seeds
1 large onion, cut in half lengthwise and thinly sliced
1 teaspoon ground coriander
1/2 teaspoon ground cumin
1/4 teaspoon cayenne pepper, or to taste
1/4 teaspoon ground turmeric
1 teaspoon salt, or to taste
1 (1-pound) package frozen peas, thawed
1 teaspoon mango powder
1 tablespoon fresh lemon juice
1/2 teaspoon garam masala

1. Heat the oil in a large cast-iron or nonstick wok or skillet over medium-high heat and add the ginger, green chile peppers, and cumin seeds; they should sizzle upon contact with the hot oil. Quickly add the onion and cook until golden, about 5 minutes.

2. Add the coriander, cumin, cayenne pepper, turmeric, and salt, then mix in the peas and cook, stirring until all the juices evaporate and the spices cling to the peas, 10 to 12 minutes. Mix in the mango powder and lemon juice, sprinkle the garam masala on top, and serve.

Mixed Bell Peppers with Peas

Shimla Mirch aur Muttar

Makes 4 to 6 servings

This somewhat saucy side dish can easily be served as a spicy chutney, a spread on sandwiches, or a topping for rice or couscous. It is especially lovely when scooped up with fresh parantha *breads.*

2 tablespoons peanut oil
1 teaspoon cumin seeds
1 tablespoon finely chopped fresh curry leaves
1 large onion, cut in half lengthwise and thinly sliced
2 large tomatoes, coarsely chopped
3 large bell peppers (red, orange, or yellow), cut into 1-inch pieces
1 cup frozen peas, thawed
1 to 3 fresh green chile peppers, such as serrano, minced with seeds
1 teaspoon salt, or to taste
1 tablespoon ground coriander
1/2 teaspoon mango powder
1/4 teaspoon ground turmeric
1/2 cup finely chopped fresh cilantro, including soft stems
1/4 teaspoon garam masala

1. Heat the oil in a large nonstick wok or skillet over medium-high heat and add the cumin seeds; they should sizzle upon contact with the hot oil. Quickly add the curry leaves and onion and cook, stirring, until golden, 3 to 5 minutes.

2. Add the tomatoes, bell peppers, peas, green chile peppers, and salt, and cook until most of the juices evaporate, about 5 minutes. Mix in the coriander, mango powder, turmeric, and cilantro and cook about 5 minutes over medium heat to blend the flavors. Transfer to a serving dish, sprinkle the garam masala on top, and serve.

Variation: Boil 1 large potato in lightly salted water to cover until tender. Then peel, chop, and add it to the dish along with the bell peppers.

Spicy Mushrooms and Bell Peppers

Masala Khumb aur Shimla Mirch

Makes 4 to 6 servings

Make sure most of the juices in this dish evaporate, leaving behind only a delicate sheen on the vegetables. Then serve on the side or present as a topping on open-faced sandwiches or over cooked rice.

2 tablespoons vegetable oil
1 teaspoon cumin seeds
2 small red onions, cut in half lengthwise and thinly sliced
1 1/2 pounds small mushrooms (or quartered large mushrooms)
1 large tomato, finely chopped
2 large yellow or green bell peppers, cut into 1/2-inch pieces
1 tablespoon peeled minced fresh ginger
1 large clove fresh garlic, minced
1 to 3 fresh green chile peppers, such as serrano, minced with seeds
2 teaspoons ground coriander
1/2 teaspoon ground cumin
1/2 teaspoon salt, or to taste
1/4 teaspoon garam masala

1. Heat the oil in a nonstick skillet over medium-high heat. Add the cumin seeds; they should sizzle upon contact with the hot oil. Quickly add the onions and cook until golden, about 5 minutes. Transfer to a bowl.

2. To the same pan, add the mushrooms and cook, stirring, over medium-high heat until they release their juices and then turn golden as the juices evaporate, 3 to 5 minutes. Add to the bowl with the onions.

3. To the same pan, add the tomato, bell peppers, ginger, garlic, and green chile peppers and cook, stirring, until most of the juices evaporate, about 5 minutes.

4. Add the coriander, cumin, and salt, then mix in the onions and mushrooms. Stir over medium-high heat about 3 minutes. Transfer to a serving dish, sprinkle the garam masala on top, and serve.

Oven-Roasted Bell Peppers, Indian Style

Bhunni Shimla Mirch

Makes 4 to 6 servings

This is a California-inspired dish. The peppers are flavored with Indian spices and are different from any you've tasted before. Serve them as a side dish with grilled meat or chicken, toss them in salads, mix them in cooked rice dishes or even in plain yogurt to make a raita.

Instead of roasting them in the oven, you can also grill them over hot coals until charred, then peel only the heavily charred portions and proceed with the recipe from Step 3.

8 small to medium bell peppers of mixed colors
    (about 2 pounds), quartered lengthwise,
    seeded and stemmed
1/4 teaspoon salt, or to taste
1 tablespoon olive oil
1 large clove fresh garlic, minced
1 to 3 fresh green chile peppers, such as serrano,
    minced with seeds
1/2 teaspoon coarsely ground ajwain seeds
2 tablespoons minced fresh basil leaves
1 tablespoon minced fresh mint leaves

1. Preheat the broiler. Place the bell peppers on a lightly greased baking sheet, skin side up, and broil in the oven, about 8 inches from the heating element, until the skin is charred, about 5 minutes. Let cool, then peel off any black skin you wish to, leaving most of the lightly charred skin on the peppers. Transfer to a bowl and mix in the salt.

2. Heat the oil in a small saucepan over medium-high heat and cook the garlic, green chile peppers, and ajwain seeds about 1 minute, then add the basil and mint and cook another minute. Transfer to the grilled peppers and mix well. Serve immediately or refrigerate up to 10 days.

Spicy Chopped Tomatoes

Tamatar ki Sabzi

Makes 4 to 6 servings

This is a delicious soft-cooked tomato dish that people from the northern parts of India are partial to. Quick-cooking, light, and incredibly flavorful, this dish is a delight with paranthas *(griddle-fried breads) and over rice.*

2 tablespoons vegetable oil
1 (1-inch) piece peeled fresh ginger,
    cut into thin matchsticks
1 medium onion, cut in half lengthwise and
    thinly sliced
1 teaspoon cumin seeds
1 tablespoon ground coriander
3 large tomatoes (about 1 1/2 pounds),
    cut into large pieces
1 to 3 fresh green chile peppers, such as serrano,
    minced with seeds
1/2 teaspoon salt, or to taste
1/2 cup finely chopped fresh cilantro,
    including soft stems
Freshly ground black pepper, to taste

1. Heat the oil in a large nonstick wok or saucepan over medium-high heat and cook the ginger and onion, stirring, until golden, about 5 minutes.

2. Add the cumin seeds; they should sizzle upon contact with the hot oil. Quickly add the coriander and then mix in the tomatoes, green chile peppers, and salt. Cook, stirring, until mushy, about 5 minutes. Add the cilantro and cook about 2 minutes. Transfer to a serving dish, sprinkle the black pepper on top, and serve.

Fire-Roasted Corn-on-the-Cob

Bhunna hua Bhutta

Makes 2 to 4 servings

Starting in the early summer and well into the rainy monsoon season in India, there is an enticing aroma in the air. The smoky fragrance of spiced roasting corn wafts down the streets, drawing large crowds of people. Try this easy recipe for your next summer cookout.

1 teaspoon Chaat Masala (page 20 or store-bought)
4 ears fresh corn
1 lime, cut in half or wedges

1. Preheat a grill. While it's heating prepare the masala. Then, remove the husks from the corn and place each ear directly over medium-hot heat. Grill, turning as each side gets brown spots, until the whole ear is marked with black and brown spots, about 5 minutes.

2. Put the chaat masala in a small salad plate. Press the cut side of the lime over the chaat masala, making sure the spices stick to the lime. Then, rub the spicy lime all over the corn, squeezing very gently as you go along until the whole ear is glazed with the spices and lime juice. Serve with additional chaat masala.

Fragrant Spiced Corn

Makki ki Sabzi

Makes 4 to 6 servings

Here is one of my favorite backup dishes. I generally serve it on the side of dals (legumes) and griddle-fried breads, but if I need an appetizer salad, I present it over lettuce leaves with a glass of chilled Indian beer.

2 tablespoons Tamarind Paste, or to taste (page 54)
2 teaspoons cumin seeds
1/2 teaspoon fenugreek seeds
1/2 teaspoon red pepper flakes
1 (1-pound) package frozen corn, thawed
2 tablespoons corn oil
1 small onion, finely chopped
3/4 teaspoon salt, or to taste
1 red bell pepper, finely chopped
3 tablespoons finely chopped fresh cilantro, including soft stems
Freshly ground black pepper, to taste

1. Prepare the tamarind paste. Then in a small non-stick skillet, dry-roast together the cumin, fenugreek, and red pepper flakes over medium heat, stirring and shaking the skillet until the spices are highly fragrant and a few shades darker, about 2 minutes. Transfer to a bowl, let cool, and grind finely in a mortar and pestle or in a spice or coffee grinder.

2. Place the corn in a nonstick skillet, and stir over medium-high heat until any clinging water evaporates. Transfer to a bowl.

3. In the same skillet, heat the oil over medium-high heat and cook the onion, stirring, until golden, 3 to 5 minutes. Add the corn, roasted spices, and salt, and cook until the corn is golden, 2 to 3 minutes.

4. Mix in the tamarind paste and cook until it evaporates and glazes the corn. Add the red bell pepper and cilantro, and cook about 2 minutes. Transfer to a serving dish, sprinkle the black pepper on top, and serve.

Zesty Everyday Green Beans

Har Roz ki Hari Phalliyan

Makes 4 to 6 servings

Ordinary everyday green beans take on a brand new look and flavor when they are cooked the Indian way, with fragrant spices. Here is a simple recipe that can be made with one trip to the supermarket. The only ingredient you will not find there is mango powder, but you can use fresh lemon juice in its place if you don't already have it. Either adds a sour element to the dish that balances the spicy and starchy elements.

1 pound green beans, strings removed
2 tablespoons peanut oil
1 teaspoon cumin seeds
1 fresh green chile pepper, such as serrano, minced with seeds
1 tablespoon peeled minced fresh ginger
2 small red or white potatoes, cut into wedges
1 tablespoon ground coriander
1/2 teaspoon ground cumin
1/4 teaspoon ground turmeric
1 teaspoon salt, or to taste
1 large tomato, coarsely chopped
1/2 teaspoon mango powder or 1 tablespoon fresh lemon juice
1/4 teaspoon garam masala

1. To prepare the beans, trim only the stem ends and then cut into 1/2-inch diagonal slices, or chop coarsely.

2. Heat the oil in a large nonstick wok or saucepan over medium-high heat. Add the cumin seeds, green chile pepper, and ginger, and stir about 30 seconds. Add the beans and the potatoes, then mix in the coriander, cumin, turmeric, and salt, and stir 2 to 3 minutes over high heat.

3. Add the tomato, reduce the heat to medium, and cook, stirring occasionally, until the potatoes are tender and all the juices have evaporated, 12 to 15 minutes. Mix in the mango powder. Transfer to a serving dish, sprinkle the garam masala on top, and serve.

Mixed Green and Yellow Beans with Fresh Pomegranate Seeds

Anardana vaali Hari aur Peeli Phalliyan

Makes 4 to 6 servings

This green bean dish has great color and flavor provided by the mixed beans, the almonds, and vibrant, pungent dried pomegranate seeds.

1/2 cup sliced almonds, dry-roasted (Dry-Roasting Spices, Nuts, Flours, page 35)
1 pound mixed green beans and yellow beans, strings removed
2 tablespoons peanut oil
2 dried red chile peppers, such as chile de arbol, broken
1/2 teaspoon cumin seeds
1/2 teaspoon black mustard seeds
2 small purple, russet or white potatoes, cut into 1/2-inch pieces
4 small carrots, cut into 1/2-inch pieces
1 tablespoon peeled minced fresh ginger
1 tablespoon ground coriander
1/4 teaspoon ground turmeric
1 teaspoon salt, or to taste
1 large tomato, coarsely chopped
1 teaspoon ground dried pomegranate seeds
1/4 cup fresh pomegranate seeds
1/4 teaspoon garam masala

1. Roast the almonds. Trim only the stem ends of the beans and then cut them into 1/2-inch diagonal slices.

2. Heat the oil in a large nonstick wok or saucepan over medium-high heat and add the red chile peppers, cumin, and mustard seeds; they should splutter upon contact with the hot oil, so lower the heat and cover the pan until the spluttering subsides.

3. Add the potatoes, beans, carrots, ginger, coriander, turmeric, and salt, and cook about 3 minutes over high heat. Add the tomato, reduce the heat to medium-low, cover the pan, and cook, stirring occasionally, until the potatoes are soft, 10 to 12 minutes.

4. Mix in the dried pomegranate seeds. Transfer to a serving dish, garnish with sliced almonds, fresh pomegranate seeds, and garam masala, and serve.

Spicy Yard-Long Beans
Masaladar Lobia ki Phalliyan

Makes 4 to 6 servings

I love the light tangy taste and earthy flavor of these beans, which are a close relative of black-eyed peas and are called lobia ki phalli *in the north (*lobia *is the Hindi name for black-eyed peas). The Indian variety is about 9 to 12 inches long, and the ones I find in America are actually about 18 inches long, but they both taste very similar. Look for them in Indian and Asian stores, and in farmers' markets and well-stocked produce markets.*

2 tablespoons peanut oil
1 teaspoon cumin seeds
1 large clove fresh garlic, minced
2 tablespoons peeled minced fresh ginger
1 fresh green chile pepper, such as serrano, minced with seeds
1 tablespoon ground coriander
1 teaspoon dried curry leaves
1/2 teaspoon ground cumin
1/4 teaspoon ground turmeric
1 large tomato, coarsely chopped
1 pound yard-long beans, cut into 1/2-inch pieces
1 teaspoon salt, or to taste
1 medium white potato, boiled until tender, peeled, and cut into 1/2-inch pieces
1/4 cup finely chopped fresh cilantro, including soft stems
1/4 teaspoon garam masala

1. Heat the oil in a large nonstick wok or saucepan over medium-high heat, add the cumin seeds, garlic, ginger, and green chile pepper, and stir about 1 minute.

2. Add coriander, curry leaves, cumin, and turmeric, followed by the tomato, beans, and salt. Cover the pan, reduce the heat to medium-low, and cook until the beans are partially cooked, about 6 minutes.

3. Add the boiled potato and cilantro, and cook until the beans are tender and all the juices have evaporated, about 10 minutes. Transfer to a serving dish, sprinkle the garam masala on top, and serve.

Asparagus with Purple Potatoes
Shatwar aur Kashni Aalu

Makes 4 to 6 servings

Although asparagus is not an everyday Indian vegetable, my mother still remembers eating it as a child. Here is my take on my grandmother's recipe.

For this dish, snap off the fibrous asparagus stems and discard, or use them to make broth or soup.

1 to 2 tablespoons vegetable oil
1 teaspoon cumin seeds
1 tablespoon peeled minced fresh ginger
1 to 3 fresh green chile peppers, such as serrano, minced with seeds
2 medium purple potatoes (or any kind), cut into 1/2-inch pieces
1 teaspoon ground coriander
1/4 teaspoon ground turmeric
1/2 teaspoon salt, or to taste
1 1/4 pound asparagus, trimmed and cut diagonally into 3/4-inch pieces
Freshly ground black pepper, to taste

1. Heat the oil in a medium nonstick wok or saucepan over medium-high heat and add the cumin seeds; they should sizzle upon contact with the hot oil. Quickly add the ginger and green chile peppers, then mix in the potatoes, coriander, turmeric, and salt. Stir about 1 minute, then cover the pan and cook over medium heat about 7 minutes.

2. Add the asparagus and cook, over high heat about 3 minutes and then over medium-low heat until the potatoes are soft and no juices remain in the pan, 5 to 7 minutes. Transfer to a serving dish, sprinkle the black pepper on top, and serve.

Variation: Pan-cook 1 cup finely chopped onion and 1 cup chopped firm tomatoes, and lightly mix them into the asparagus just before serving.

Pan-Grilled Asparagus Tips

Bhunnae huae Shatwar

Makes 4 to 6 servings

Cooked in a ridged griddle (or skillet) these asparagus tips look like they were cooked on the grill, with flavors to match.

2 tablespoons Basic Ginger-Garlic Paste
(page 47 or store-bought)
1 pound asparagus tips (top 4 to 5 inches only)
2 tablespoons nonfat plain yogurt, whisked until smooth
1 tablespoon peanut oil
1/2 teaspoon salt, or to taste
15 to 20 cherry or pear tomatoes
Freshly ground black pepper, to taste

1. Prepare the ginger-garlic paste. Place the asparagus tips in a flat dish. Mix together the yogurt, ginger-garlic paste, oil, and salt, and add to the asparagus. Mix well, making sure all the pieces are well-coated with the marinade. Cover and marinate 1 hour in the refrigerator.

2. Heat a ridged nonstick skillet or griddle over high heat and add the asparagus tips in one or two batches, making sure that each one lies flat on the skillet. Cook, turning the tips, until they are marked with golden lines, 5 to 7 minutes. Transfer to a serving platter and keep warm.

3. Add the tomatoes to the same skillet, add any leftover marinade and cook, shaking the pan, until the tomatoes are marked with golden lines, 2 to 3 minutes. Add them to the asparagus, garnish with the black pepper, and serve.

Tangy Asparagus with Onions and Tomatoes

Khattae Shatwar, Pyaz aur Tamatar

Makes 4 to 6 servings

Here is a zesty quick-cooking asparagus dish. To preserve the rich green color of the asparagus, I often cook it in the microwave before adding it to the pan.

2 to 3 tablespoons vegetable oil
1/2 teaspoon cumin seeds
1/2 teaspoon ajwain seeds
2 small onions, cut in half lengthwise and thinly sliced
1 tablespoon peeled minced fresh ginger
1 large clove fresh garlic, minced
1 to 3 fresh green chile peppers, such as serrano,
minced with seeds
1 tablespoon ground coriander
1/2 teaspoon ground cumin
1/2 teaspoon salt, or to taste
1/4 cup nonfat plain yogurt, whisked until smooth
1 large tomato, coarsely chopped
1 pound asparagus, trimmed and cut diagonally
into 3/4-inch pieces
1/4 teaspoon garam masala

1. Heat the oil in a medium nonstick wok or saucepan over medium-high heat, then add the cumin and ajwain seeds; they should sizzle upon contact with the hot oil. Quickly add the onions and cook, stirring, until golden-brown, about 5 minutes. Remove from the pan.

2. To the pan add the ginger, garlic, and green chile peppers and stir about 1 minute, then add the coriander, cumin, and salt and stir a few seconds. Add the yogurt, a little at a time, stirring constantly to prevent it from curdling, about 3 minutes. Add the tomato and cook until slightly soft, about 1 minute.

3. Meanwhile, place the asparagus in a microwave-safe dish, cover with plastic wrap, and cook at high power 3 minutes. Add to the pan after the tomato has cooked. Mix in the reserved onions and stir about 2 minutes to blend the flavors. Transfer to a serving dish, sprinkle the garam masala on top, and serve.

Mixed Vegetables

Mixed Cauliflower, Carrots, and Green Beans in a Wok

Milli-Julli Kadhai Sabzian

Makes 4 to 6 servings

Kadhai is the Indian term for a round-bottomed wok, and this dish, authentically made in a kadhai, *is a north Indian dish generally associated with the flavors of bell peppers and dried fenugreek leaves.*

Kadhai vegetables are almost a one-pot meal when served with griddle-fried parantha *breads or with a rice* pullao *(pilaf) and a yogurt* raita. *They also work well with* dals *(legumes), chicken and meat curries, and even dry-cooked paneer cheese scrambles (pages 320 to 321).*

1¹/₂ to 2 tablespoons Spicy Masala for Wok-Cooked Foods (page 26 or store-bought)
2 large cloves fresh garlic, peeled
6 to 8 quarter-size slices peeled fresh ginger
1 to 3 fresh green chile peppers, such as serrano, stemmed
1 tablespoon ground coriander
1 teaspoon ground cumin
¹/₂ teaspoon cayenne pepper, or to taste
¹/₄ teaspoon ground turmeric
3 tablespoons peanut oil
2 small onions, cut in half lengthwise and thinly sliced
3 to 4 cups mixed fresh vegetables, such as cauliflower, potatoes, carrots, green beans, and peas, cut into ¹/₂-inch pieces
1 teaspoon salt, or to taste
1 large tomato, coarsely chopped
2 cups mixed yellow, red, green, and orange bell peppers, cut into ¹/₂-inch pieces
¹/₂ cup finely chopped fresh cilantro, including soft stems
¹/₂ teaspoon chaat masala

1. Prepare the kadhai masala. Then, in a food processor or a blender, process together the garlic, ginger, and green chile peppers until fine. Add the coriander, cumin, cayenne pepper, and turmeric, and process

again to make a smooth paste, adding 1 to 2 tablespoons water, if needed.

2. Heat the oil in a large nonstick wok or saucepan over medium-high heat, add the onions and cook, stirring, about 3 minutes. Add the garlic and spice paste, and cook about 2 minutes.

3. Add all the vegetables (except the bell peppers and tomato) and the salt, and cook, stirring, until the vegetables start to turn golden, 4 to 6 minutes. Add the tomato, stir 1 minute, and add the bell peppers and the kadhai masala. Cover the pan, reduce the heat to medium, and cook until the vegetables are tender, 5 to 7 minutes. Mix in the cilantro, transfer to a serving dish, sprinkle the chaat masala on top, and serve.

Variation: As a shortcut, use mixed frozen vegetables. The tomatoes and bell peppers (if included) should still be added after the other vegetables.

North Indian–Style Mixed Cauliflower, Carrots, and Green Beans

Uttar ki Jhalfrezi

Makes 4 to 6 servings

Many of my family's lunches were made with this dish—lots of mildly spiced vegetables supported with fresh tomatoes that just melted in your mouth, along with tandoori *chicken and* naan *breads.*

Like kadhai *dishes (described in the previous recipe),* jhalfrezi *dishes are about flavors. Whether you make them with vegetables, chicken, meat, seafood, or* paneer *cheese, they all have lots of vegetables, tomatoes, and vinegar (or lemon juice), and are mostly served in Indian restaurants but are easy enough to be made at home. Variation of this dish are made all over India, with coriander and turmeric in the north, curry leaves and coconut in the south.*

2 tablespoons Basic Ginger-Garlic Paste (page 47 or store-bought)
3 tablespoons peanut oil
1 teaspoon cumin seeds
¹/₄ teaspoon coarsely ground ajwain seeds

2 small onions, cut into 3/4-inch pieces

1 (1-inch) piece fresh ginger, peeled and cut into thin matchsticks

1 to 3 fresh green chile peppers, such as serrano, minced with seeds

1 tablespoon ground coriander

1/2 teaspoon cayenne pepper, or to taste

1/4 teaspoon ground turmeric

3 to 4 cups mixed vegetables, such as cauliflower, potatoes, carrots, green beans, green bell peppers, and peas, cut into 3/4- to 1-inch pieces

1 teaspoon salt, or to taste

4 small tomatoes, cut into 6 wedges each

1 to 2 tablespoons distilled white vinegar

1/2 cup finely chopped fresh cilantro, including soft stems

1/2 teaspoon garam masala

1. Prepare the ginger-garlic paste. Then, heat the oil in a large nonstick wok or saucepan over medium-high heat and add the cumin and ajwain seeds; they should sizzle upon contact with the hot oil. Quickly add the onions and ginger, and cook about 1 minute. Add the ginger-garlic paste and cook another minute.

2. Mix in the coriander, cayenne pepper, and turmeric, then add the vegetables and salt and cook, stirring, until golden, about 5 minutes.

3. Add the tomato wedges, stir 1 minute, then cover the pan, reduce the heat to medium, and cook until the vegetables are crisp-tender, about 5 minutes. Add the vinegar and cilantro, stir 1 minute, then transfer to a serving dish, mix in the garam masala, and serve.

South Indian–Style Mixed Vegetables
Dakshini Jhalfraezi

Makes 4 to 6 servings

As we go southward, vegetable jhalfraezi *takes on a new shape and flavor. This one is not quite as saucy and is flavored with curry leaves and garam masala— which is a blend of cinnamon, black pepper, cloves, and cardamom, all locally grown spices.*

3 small white potatoes

4 small carrots

12 to 15 green beans

2 small green bell peppers

2 tablespoons coconut or vegetable oil

2 small onions, cut in half lengthwise and thinly sliced

2 tablespoons minced fresh curry leaves

2 tablespoons grated fresh or frozen coconut or shredded unsweetened dried

2 large cloves fresh garlic, minced

1/8 teaspoon ground asafoetida

1 teaspoon garam masala

1/2 teaspoon salt, or to taste

1 large tomato, finely chopped

1 to 2 tablespoons fresh lemon juice

2 tablespoon finely chopped fresh cilantro

1. Cut all the vegetables into 3-inch matchsticks. Then heat the oil in a large nonstick wok or saucepan over medium-high heat and cook the onion and curry leaves, stirring, until golden, about 5 minutes. Add the coconut, garlic, and asafoetida and stir 30 seconds, then add the vegetables, garam masala, and salt and cook about 5 minutes.

2. Add the tomatoes and cook until all the juices evaporate, about 5 minutes. Transfer to a serving dish, mix in the lemon juice, garnish with the cilantro, and serve.

Mixed Pumpkin, Squash, and Eggplant with Bengali 5-Spices
Bengali Milli-Julli Sabzian

Makes 4 to 6 servings

Bengali 5-Spices—a mixture of mustard, cumin, kalonji, fenugreek, and fennel seeds—adds a remarkable pickle-like fragrance and taste to these vegetables. Serve them with a similar flavored dal *(legume) dish, such as Red Lentils with Bengali 5-Spices (page 349), and steamed rice, or with any fish curry.*

1 tablespoon coarsely ground Bengali 5-Spices
(Panch-Phoran), page 27 or store-bought

2 tablespoons mustard or peanut oil

2 dried red chile peppers, such as chile de arbol, broken

2 tablespoons minced fresh curry leaves

4 to 6 cups mixed vegetables, such as pumpkin, opo
or any other squash, eggplants, potatoes, yams,
and peas (fresh or frozen), cut into 3/4-inch pieces

1/2 teaspoon ground paprika

1 teaspoon salt, or to taste

1 teaspoon sugar

1/2 cup finely chopped fresh cilantro,
including soft stems

1. Prepare the 5-spices powder. Heat the oil in a large nonstick wok or saucepan over medium-high heat and cook the red chile peppers until golden, 30 seconds. Add the 5-spices powder; they should sizzle upon contact with the hot oil. Quickly add the curry leaves and vegetables and cook until golden, about 7 minutes.

2. Add the paprika, salt, and sugar, reduce the heat to medium-low, cover the pan and cook, stirring occasionally, until the vegetables are soft, 10 to 12 minutes. (If all the juices evaporate before the vegetables are done, add 1/4 cup water and finish cooking them.) Transfer to a serving dish, mix in the cilantro, and serve.

Marinated Mixed Vegetables in Tomato Butter-Cream Sauce

Makhani Sabzian

Makes 4 to 6 servings

Makhani *means made in butter, and in Indian cuisine, this term is also almost synonymous with a creamy tomato sauce that is popularly served with* tandoori *chicken or* paneer *cheese. It is also delicious with a harvest of vegetables.*

This dish is rich in calories, so I reserve it for special occasions. Pair it with Smoked Black Urad Beans (page 361), or Basic Grilled Lamb Tikka Kabaabs (page 160), and tandoori naan *breads.*

2 cups (1/2 recipe) Butter-Cream Sauce with
Fresh Tomatoes (page 389)

2 tablespoons Basic Ginger-Garlic Paste
(page 47 or store-bought)

3 small potatoes

2 small onions, quartered

10 to 12 cauliflower florets (2-inches each)

6 to 8 baby patty pan squash, halved

1 green bell pepper, cut in half lengthwise and
thinly sliced into 3/4-inch pieces

1/2 cup nonfat plain yogurt, whisked until smooth

2 tablespoons fresh lime or lemon juice

1 tablespoon peanut oil

1 teaspoon garam masala

1 teaspoon dried fenugreek leaves

1/2 teaspoon ground cumin

1 teaspoon ground paprika

1/2 teaspoon salt, or to taste

1. Prepare the butter-cream sauce. Prepare the ginger-garlic paste. Boil the potatoes in water to cover until tender, about 15 minutes. Drain, let cool, then peel and cut them into 3/4-inch pieces.

2. Place the onions and vegetables in a large non-reactive bowl. In a small bowl, mix together the yogurt, lime juice, oil, ginger-garlic paste, garam masala, fenugreek leaves, cumin, paprika, and salt, and add to the vegetables. Mix well, making sure the vegetables are well-coated with the marinade. Marinate in the refrigerator at least 2 and up to 24 hours.

3. Place the vegetables on a baking tray and broil, turning them once or twice, under the broiler, 4 to 5 inches from the source of heat, until they are lightly charred.

Alternately, grill over medium-high heat or pan-cook until golden. Transfer to a serving platter.

4. While the vegetables are cooking, prepare the sauce. Then cook it further over high heat [If you've already prepared the sauce, why do we need to refer again to cook it over high heat to reduce it further.] until most of the juices evaporate and the sauce is very thick, about 10 minutes. Drizzle over the vegetables and serve. (Or, cook the vegetables in the sauce about 5 minutes and then serve.)

Variation: Cut paneer cheese or tofu into 1/2-inch pieces and cook in the sauce about 5 minutes, before the sauce is mixed with the vegetables.

Savory Fruit Dishes

Tart Apples with Cooked Onions

Pyaz vaalae Khattae Saeb

Makes 4 to 6 servings

Inspired by the tree in my backyard, which sheds tart apples by the bucketful, this recipe consistently remains a big hit, year after year. You could also try this recipe using unripe tart peaches, nectarines, or mangoes in place of the apples. Serve as a side dish with Grilled Chicken in Spicy Sauce (page 462), Potato Salad with Yogurt (page 211) and a rice or Indian flatbread.

1¹/₂ tablespoons Basic Ginger-Garlic Paste
    (page 47 or store-bought)
2 tablespoons olive oil
1 large finely chopped onion
1 fresh green chile pepper, such as serrano,
    minced with seeds
1 pound tart apples, such as the Granny Smith or
    pippin, cut into ¹/₂-inch pieces
¹/₂ teaspoon salt, or to taste
¹/₂ teaspoon coarsely ground black pepper
¹/₄ cup finely chopped fresh cilantro,
    including soft stems

1. Prepare the ginger-garlic paste. Heat the oil in a nonstick wok or saucepan over medium-high heat and cook the onion until golden, 2 to 4 minutes.

2. Add the green chile pepper and the ginger-garlic paste and cook, stirring, over low heat about 1 minute.

3. Add the apples, salt, and pepper, and cook, stirring, another 2 to 4 minutes. Mix in the cilantro and cook another 2 minutes. Transfer to a serving dish and serve.

Variation: Mix the finished dish into a bowlful of nonfat plain yogurt, add some dry-roasted cumin and cayenne pepper (page 35) and serve as a raita (yogurt side dish) with grilled fare.

Tart Apples with Cumin Seeds

Khattae Saebon ki Sabzi

Makes 4 to 6 servings

While the sweeter apples disappear fast from the fruit basket, the sour ones get left behind to be used in pies and desserts. But how many desserts can one make or eat? Here is a delicious alternative—and one that does full justice to tart apples.

1 tablespoon peanut oil
1 teaspoon cumin seeds
1 fresh green chile pepper, such as serrano,
    minced with seeds
1 tablespoon ground coriander
1 pound tart apples, such as Granny Smith or pippin,
    cut into ¹/₂-inch pieces
¹/₂ teaspoon salt, or to taste
¹/₂ cup finely chopped red bell pepper
¹/₄ cup finely chopped fresh cilantro,
    including soft stems
1 to 2 teaspoons sugar, if needed
Freshly ground black pepper, to taste

1. Heat the oil in a large nonstick wok or saucepan over medium-high heat and add the cumin seeds; they should sizzle upon contact with the hot oil. Quickly add the green chile pepper and coriander, then add the apples, salt, bell pepper, and cilantro. Cook, stirring, over medium heat for the first 2 to 3 minutes, then cover the pan and cook over medium-low heat until the apples are soft, 5 to 7 minutes.

2. Taste and adjust the seasonings, adding 1 to 2 teaspoons of sugar if the apples are overly tart. Transfer to a serving dish, top with black pepper, and serve.

Spicy Star Fruit

Kamrak ki Sabzi

Makes 4 to 6 servings

Anu Khatod, my daughter's sister-in-law, makes this unusual side dish with star fruit. Serve it with Cochin Coconut Shrimp with Tomatoes (page 511) and Basic Oven-Grilled Leavened Bread (tandoori naan, page 594).

Also called carambola *in English, star fruit has translucent yellow-green flesh. When you cut it cross-wise, each piece comes out looking like a star, hence its name. Star fruit is deliciously sour and tastes superb with a sprinkling of* chaat masala. *(Which is why it often shows up in special fruit* chaat *salads.)*

1/2 teaspoon Chaat Masala (page 20 or store-bought)
1 tablespoon vegetable oil
1/4 teaspoon fennel seeds
1/4 teaspoon cumin seeds
1/4 teaspoon mustard seeds
1/4 teaspoon fenugreek seeds
1/4 teaspoon kalonji seeds
2 teaspoons ground coriander
1/2 teaspoon sugar
1/4 teaspoon cayenne pepper, or to taste
1/8 teaspoon ground turmeric
1/8 teaspoon ground asafoetida
3 star fruits (2 1/2 to 3 inches each),
      thinly sliced or chopped

1. Prepare the chaat masala. Then, heat the oil in a small nonstick wok or saucepan over medium-high heat and add the fennel, cumin, mustard, fenugreek, and kalonji seeds; they should sizzle upon contact with the hot oil.

2. Quickly add the coriander, sugar, cayenne pepper, turmeric, and asafoetida and stir a few seconds. Add the star fruit and cook, stirring, until golden, 3 to 5 minutes. Transfer to a serving dish, top with the chaat masala, and serve.

Green Mangoes in Coconut Milk

Harae Aam ki Sabzi

Makes 4 to 6 servings

Although sweetened with coconut milk, this south Indian dish is also spicy and refreshing. It is delicious served over rice. In India they use the really small green mangoes, but since those are harder to come by in America, I generally use the commonly available large ones.

1/2 cup Coconut Milk (page 44 or store-bought)
1 large green unripe mango (about 3/4 pound)
1/2 cup nonfat plain yogurt, whisked until smooth
2 teaspoons ground cumin
1/2 teaspoon salt, or to taste
1 tablespoon peanut oil
4 whole dried red chile peppers, such as chile de arbol
1/2 teaspoon black mustard seeds
8 to 10 fresh curry leaves

1. Prepare coconut milk. Then, with a vegetable peeler, peel the mango, then cut the fruit around the center seed into 1/2-inch pieces. Place the mango, yogurt, cumin, and salt in a medium nonstick saucepan and cook over medium heat, stirring as needed, until the mango is very soft, 7 to 10 minutes. Add the coconut milk and bring to a quick boil. Transfer to a serving dish.

2. Heat the oil in a small nonstick saucepan over medium-high heat and add the red chile peppers and mustard seeds; they should splutter upon contact with the hot oil, so lower the heat and cover the pan until the spluttering subsides. Quickly add the curry leaves, stir a few seconds, and transfer to the dish with the mango. Stir lightly to mix, and serve.

Spicy Mashed Fresh Peaches
Aadhoo ka Bhartha

Makes 4 to 6 servings

Bhartha is a mashed vegetable dish that is popularly made with eggplant or opo squash. Here, I make it with coarsely puréed fresh, ripe peaches from my own garden. My inventive summer dish goes as well with grilled chicken, meat, and seafood as it does on the side with Spinach with Paneer Cheese (page 328) and whole-wheat chapati flatbreads.

2 tablespoons peanut oil
2 medium onions, cut in half lengthwise and
    thinly sliced
1¹/₂ teaspoons cumin seeds
1 large tomato, finely chopped
1 large clove fresh garlic, minced
1 tablespoon peeled minced fresh ginger
1 fresh green chile pepper, such as serrano,
    minced with seeds
¹/₄ teaspoon coarsely ground ajwain seeds
¹/₂ teaspoon coarsely ground black pepper
¹/₂ teaspoon salt, or to taste
1 teaspoon fresh lime juice
2 cups coarsely mashed ripe peaches
    (about 1¹/₂ pounds), peeled or unpeeled
¹/₂ cup finely chopped fresh cilantro,
    including soft stems

1. Heat the oil in a large nonstick wok or saucepan over medium-high heat and cook the onions until golden brown, 5 to 7 minutes.

2. Tilt the pan to collect all the oil in one spot, then add the cumin seeds; they should sizzle upon contact with the hot oil. Quickly add the tomato, garlic, ginger, and green chile pepper, and cook until all the juices evaporate, 3 to 5 minutes.

3. Add the ajwain seeds, black pepper, salt, and lime juice, stir a few seconds, then add the peaches, and cilantro (save some cilantro for garnish) and cook over medium heat until all the juices evaporate, the bhartha is very thick and traces of oil are visible on the sides, 7 to 10 minutes. Transfer to a serving dish, garnish with the reserved cilantro, and serve.

Sweet and Sour Ripe Bananas
Khatti-Meethi Kaelae ki Sabzi

Makes 4 to 6 servings

Cooking with bananas is a very southern Indian concept. They use bananas at all stages of ripeness; in fact, they also use the banana skins and the banana stems to make side dishes. The leaves, of course, are used as disposable plates. When done, this dish is almost a textured mash. Cut the bananas into larger pieces if you wish.

Jaggery is a brown, unrefined cane sugar sold in solid blocks. It's a British term; in Hindi it's called gur. Look for it in Indian markets.

1¹/₂ teaspoons black mustard seeds
1 teaspoon cumin seeds
¹/₂ teaspoon fenugreek seeds
¹/₈ teaspoon ground asafoetida
1¹/₂ tablespoons dried curry leaves
1 teaspoon hot red pepper flakes, or to taste
2 tablespoons peanut oil
3 large, firm, ripe bananas, peeled and
    cut into ¹/₄-inch pieces
¹/₃ teaspoon salt, or to taste
3 to 4 tablespoons fresh lemon juice
3 tablespoons grated jaggery (gur) or brown sugar

1. In a mortar and pestle or spice grinder, grind together the mustard, cumin, and fenugreek seeds, asafoetida, curry leaves, and red pepper flakes to make them as fine as possible.

2. Heat the oil in a large nonstick wok or saucepan over medium-high heat and add the ground spice mixture; it should sizzle immediately. Quickly add the bananas and salt, and cook, turning carefully, until golden on both sides.

3. Sprinkle the lemon juice over the bananas, and then the jaggery, and cook, stirring, another minute. Transfer to a serving dish and serve.

Spicy Green Plantains
Harae Kaelae ki Sabzi

Makes 4 to 6 servings

The green starchy bananas called plantains that are now found increasingly in American markets may be intimidating to cooks who have no idea how to use them. But they are routinely consumed all over the southern parts of India. Because the peel is tough, cut the banana into slices and then remove the peel.

1 tablespoon peanut oil or melted ghee
2 dried red chile peppers, such as chile de arbol, broken
1/2 teaspoon cumin seeds
1 teaspoon black mustard seeds
1/8 teaspoon ground asafoetida
1/4 teaspoon ground turmeric
2 large green plantains (about 1 pound), cut into 1/2-inch pieces and peeled
1/2 teaspoon salt, or to taste
1 to 1 1/2 cups water, or as needed
2 tablespoons chopped cilantro

1. Heat the oil (or ghee) in a large nonstick wok or saucepan over medium-high heat. Add the red chile peppers, cumin, and mustard seeds; they should splutter upon contact with the hot oil, so lower the heat and cover the pan until the spluttering subsides. Quickly add, first the asafoetida and turmeric, then the plantains and salt, and cook about 2 minutes.

2. Add the water, about 1/2 cup at a time, and cook, uncovered, until the plantain pieces are tender but not mushy. If, after the plantains are soft, you have too much liquid left in the pan, increase the heat to high and cook until it evaporates. Transfer to a serving dish, sprinkle the cilantro on top, and serve.

Variation: For a creamy dish, during the last 5 minutes add about 1/4 cup coconut milk (page 44 or store-bought) and adjust the seasonings.

Watermelon Whites with Ginger
Tarbooz ki Sabzi

Makes 4 to 6 servings

Indians make use of almost every part of a vegetable or fruit. This dish is made with the white rind and flesh of the watermelon. It cooks like zucchini, but the pieces maintain their shape and texture. After you cut out the red watermelon, peel off the green skin from the thick white rind, and use all the white and whatever red is left behind for this dish.

2 tablespoons vegetable oil
1 teaspoon cumin seeds
1 large onion, cut in half lengthwise and thinly sliced
1 (1-inch) piece fresh ginger, peeled and cut into thin matchsticks
1 large potato (any kind), peeled and cut into 1/2-inch pieces
1 large clove fresh garlic, minced
1 fresh green chile pepper, such as serrano, minced with seeds
1 tablespoon ground coriander
1/4 teaspoon ground cumin
1/4 teaspoon ground turmeric
1/4 teaspoon ground paprika
1/2 teaspoon salt, or to taste
4 to 5 cups peeled and chopped watermelon rind
1 pound Roma tomatoes, finely chopped
1/2 cup finely chopped fresh cilantro, including soft stems
1/4 teaspoon garam masala

1. Heat the oil in a large nonstick wok or saucepan over medium-high heat and add the cumin seeds; they should sizzle upon contact with the hot oil. Quickly add the onion, ginger, and potato, and cook until golden, about 5 minutes.

2. Add the garlic and green chile pepper, and then add the coriander, cumin, turmeric, paprika, and salt and stir about 30 seconds.

3. Add the watermelon rind and tomatoes and cook over high heat, about 2 minutes. Then reduce the heat to medium-low, cover the pan, and cook until the watermelon and potatoes are very soft, about 10 minutes. Mix in the cilantro during the last 2 minutes of cooking. Transfer to a serving dish, sprinkle the garam masala on top, and serve.

Paneer Cheese

Paneer Cheese Appetizers 315

Spicy Peppered Paneer Cheese

Crunchy Paneer Cheese Pâté

Seared Paneer Cheese
in Lemon Cream

Seared Paneer Cheese
with Caper Sauce

Marinated Paneer Cheese
with Saffron Yogurt Sauce

Paneer Cheese Wedges
with Chickpea Flour

Paneer Cheese Balls

Paneer Cheese Wraps

Paneer Cheese Scrambles and Side Dishes 320

Basic Paneer Cheese Scramble

Paneer Cheese Scramble
with Soybeans

Paneer Cheese Scramble
with Morel Mushrooms

Paneer Cheese Scramble
with Apple-Ginger Chutney

Grated Paneer Cheese
with Minced Cauliflower

Marinated Paneer Cheese
with Ginger-Lime Pickle

Sautéed Paneer Cheese
with Green Chutney

Spicy Diced Paneer Cheese
with Ajwain Seeds

Paneer Cheese with Cauliflower
and Broccoli

Oven-Baked Paneer Cheese
with Puréed Cilantro

Paneer Cheese Bites
with Sun-Dried Tomatoes

Paneer Cheese Glazed
with Puréed Tomatoes

Paneer Cheese Chile-Fry
with Crispy Ginger

Quick Spinach with
Crumbled Paneer Cheese

Paneer Cheese Main Dishes and Curries 327

Paneer Cheese with Baby Spinach
and Fresh Fenugreek Leaves

Spinach with Paneer Cheese

Paneer Cheese with
Coconut and Corn

Griddle-Fried Paneer Cheese

Silky Paneer Cheese Curry
with Red Chile Peppers

Stir-Fried Paneer Cheese
with Onions and Bell Peppers

Curried Paneer Cheese and Potatoes

Curried Paneer Cheese
with Peas and Potatoes

Paneer Cheese Curry
with Two Onions

Royal Paneer Cheese Curry

Stuffed Paneer Cheese Balls
in Creamy Tomato Sauce

Paneer Cheese Curry
with Coconut Milk

Nine-Jewel Paneer Cheese Curry

India's prized cheese is called *paneer*. In India, it is made with milk from the water buffalo (but here it is made with cow's milk).

Paneer is generally made at home, fresh, whenever the meal calls for it—which, in certain families in India, may mean twice a week. Luckily, *paneer* is also readily available at the neighborhood shops that sell Indian sweets and savories) and from special *paneer* stands all over India.

Paneer is simply a chunk of curdled milk solids that have been separated from the liquid whey. The curdling or breaking down of the milk is done with the help of a sour agent such as yogurt, lemon juice, vinegar, or citric acid. Once the milk is broken down into curds and whey, it is passed through a piece of muslin or layers of cheesecloth. The curds (*paneer*) remain in the muslin, while the whey simply drains out.

Spongy and mildly sweet, *paneer* cheese has always been a source of inspiration to Indian cooks. It doesn't melt, it easily reflects other flavors, and lends elegant smoothness to every dish. And, best of all, it

can be quite low in fat if you make it with reduced-fat milk. It is still cheese, of course, which is high in cholesterol, but, when cooked the Indian way—with a number of other ingredients—it is distributed among multiple servings. Also, if you, like the majority of people in India, do not eat any meats or eggs, cheese is a vital source of protein.

Paneer cheese is very easy to make; simply follow the directions on page 43. The *paneer* recipes in this and other chapters always call for freshly made *paneer* as the first choice, but now that it is beginning to be available in some Indian markets, you can substitute store-bought *paneer* for convenience.

In this chapter, there are starters or party appetizers such as Seared Paneer Cheese in Lemon Cream (page 316), great anytime dishes such as Oven-Baked Paneer Cheese with Puréed Cilantro (page 324), main courses such as the classic Spinach with Paneer Cheese (page 328), and specialty dishes such as Royal Paneer Cheese Curry (page 334). (See the Desserts chapter for sweet *paneer* recipes.)

Paneer Cheese Appetizers

Spicy Peppered Paneer Cheese

Kaali Mirch vaala Paneer

Makes 6 to 8 servings

Coated with roasted black pepper and fresh ginger, this smooth cheese is lovely when presented alongside others as part of a platter. It is also incredible in sandwiches and bagels. Look for muslin in fabric stores, or just fold readily available cheesecloth in 4 layers to hold the cheese.

1/2 gallon milk

1/2 teaspoon salt, or to taste

2 cups plain yogurt, whisked until smooth,
   or 3 to 4 tablespoons fresh lime or lemon juice

1 (2-foot-square) piece fine muslin or 8-foot-piece
   cheesecloth folded in 4 layers

1 tablespoon peanut oil

2 tablespoons peeled minced fresh ginger

1 tablespoon black peppercorns, dry-roasted and
   coarsely ground (Dry-Roasting Spices, page 35)

2 tablespoons fine plain bread crumbs

1 (8-ounce) package cream cheese, at room temperature

1 to 3 fresh green chile peppers, such as serrano,
   stemmed

1. Place the milk and salt in a large, heavy pan and bring to a boil over high heat, stirring gently. Just before the milk boils and the bubbles spill over, mix in the yogurt or the lemon juice and stir gently, until the milk curdles and separates into curds and whey (whey is translucent green in color), 1 to 2 minutes. Remove pan from the heat.

2. Drape the muslin or cheesecloth over a large pan and pour the curdled milk into it. As you do this, the whey will drain through the muslin into the pan, and the curds will remain in the muslin. Once all the curds are in the muslin, pick up the muslin by all 4 corners and tie the 4 ends into a knot over the kitchen faucet. Let drain, 3 to 5 minutes.

3. While the cheese is draining, heat the oil in a small saucepan over medium heat and cook, the ginger,

stirring, until golden, about 1 minute. Add the black pepper and bread crumbs and stir until the seasonings are dry but not scorched. Remove from the heat and spread the mixture evenly on a plate.

4. Transfer the paneer curds from the muslin to a food processor, then add the cream cheese and chile peppers and process until well mixed.

5. With lightly buttered clean hands, or using a piece of waxed paper, shape the cheese mixture into a ball, then roll the ball evenly in the bread crumb mixture, making sure it is well-coated. Keep it as a ball or press lightly with your hands to flatten it into a patty, an oval, a rectangle, or a log. Serve as you would any other cheese balls or spreads, such as with an assortment of crackers or with crudités.

Crunchy Paneer Cheese Pâté

Pyaz vaala Paneer ka Gol Tukra

Makes 6 to 8 servings; about 8 ounces

This smooth paneer cheese, with the light crunch of onions and red bell peppers, can be molded into a log, a ball, or any shape you choose. Serve it on your cheese-and-crackers platter, or offer it with an array of parantha *(griddle-fried breads) or* naan *(grilled leavened breads)* wedges.

1/2 to 1 teaspoon Chaat Masala (page 20
   or store-bought)

8 ounces (1 recipe) Paneer Cheese (page 43
   or store-bought)

2 tablespoons vegetable oil

1 teaspoon cumin seeds

1/2 teaspoon coarsely ground black pepper

1 small onion, finely chopped

1 tablespoon peeled minced fresh ginger

1 to 3 fresh green chile peppers, such as serrano,
   minced with seeds

1/2 cup minced red bell pepper

1/4 teaspoon salt

1. Prepare the masala. Prepare the paneer cheese. Then crumble the cheese coarsely, place it in a food processor and pulse a few times until smooth. Transfer to a large bowl.

2. Heat the oil in a small nonstick wok or saucepan over medium-high heat and add the cumin seeds and black pepper; they should sizzle upon contact with the hot oil. Quickly add the onion and cook, stirring, until golden, about 3 minutes. Add the ginger, green chile peppers, red bell pepper, and salt, and stir about 2 minutes. Let cool.

3. Add the vegetables to the paneer cheese and mix well with clean fingers or a spoon. Then shape into a ball (or any shape you prefer), garnish with chaat masala, and serve.

Paneer Substitutes

Ricotta cheese, a soft-curd cow's milk cheese, is almost like *paneer*. Once drained, it can be used similarly. Lay some muslin or cheesecloth in a large bowl, put the ricotta in the cloth, then tie the ends together. Weigh down the cheese with a large pot full of water to drain out the whey, and you will be left with a soft, cake-like chunk of cheese. Use it interchangeably in all the *paneer* cheese scramble dishes. If the recipe calls for large pieces, be aware that even though ricotta cheese can be cut into pieces, the pieces will disintegrate easily, so use a very light touch while stirring.

Tofu, a soft cheese made from soy milk instead of cow's milk, can also be used in place of *paneer* cheese to make appetizers, side dishes, and entrées. The texture and flavor of dishes made with tofu will be smoother and lighter, but, though different, they will be a delicious and healthier substitute—with some people actually preferring tofu to *paneer* cheese.

You can either buy firm tofu or make it at home. Simply buy plain soy milk and follow the directions for making *paneer* cheese on page 43.

Seared Paneer Cheese in Lemon Cream
Halka-Bhoona Khatta Paneer

Makes 4 to 6 servings

Lemon butter, made by adding lemon juice to simmering butter, adds a flavor boost to plain foods, and when you mix in some ginger, chaat masala, *and a touch of cream, it takes on a delicate smoothness that complements the foods even more. Here I use it over lightly seared* paneer *cheese. Serve on a platter with crackers or with wedges of pan-fried* parantha *breads. This dish can also be served on the side with a* dal *(legume dish), such as Yellow Mung Beans with Sautéed Onion and Ginger (page 342), and rice.*

1 teaspoon Chaat Masala (page 20 or store-bought), or to taste
8 ounces (1 recipe) Paneer Cheese (page 43 or store-bought)
1/4 cup minced chives
1/2 teaspoon salt, or to taste
1/2 teaspoon coarsely ground black pepper
1 tablespoon vegetable oil
1 tablespoon unsalted butter
1 1/2 tablespoons peeled minced fresh ginger
1 fresh green chile pepper, such as serrano, minced with seeds
2 tablespoons fresh lemon juice
1/4 cup heavy cream or plain yogurt, whisked until smooth

1. Prepare the masala. Prepare the paneer cheese then cut it into 4 long flat pieces, each about 1/4-inch thick. Season lightly with chives, salt, and black pepper.

2. Heat the oil in a large nonstick skillet or griddle over medium-high heat and quickly sear the paneer cheese pieces until lightly golden, about 15 to 20 seconds per side. Transfer to a serving dish, cover, and keep warm.

3. Heat the butter in a small saucepan over medium heat until it just starts to bubble. Add the ginger and green chile pepper and cook, stirring, until golden, about 1 minute. Add the lemon juice and chaat masala and bring to a quick boil.

4. Add the cream (or yogurt) and stir until just heated through. (If you're using yogurt, don't heat for a long period or the yogurt will separate.) Drizzle over the paneer cheese and serve.

Seared Paneer Cheese with Caper Sauce
Ek-Minut Bhoona Kair vaala Paneer

Makes 4 to 6 servings

You may not think of capers as an Indian seasoning, but capers (or a close relative) do grow in the northwestern state of Rajasthan, where they are generally sold as dried berries called kair. *The Rajasthanis routinely make a caper curry and even deep-fry the capers, which is considered quite a delicacy. Brine-packed capers are definitely not Indian, but that is the form I find them in here; they are lovely in this dish.*

^{1}/$_2$ teaspoon Chaat Masala (page 20 or store-bought), or to taste

8 ounces (1 recipe) Paneer Cheese (page 43 or store-bought)

^{1}/$_2$ teaspoon salt, or to taste

^{1}/$_2$ teaspoon coarsely ground black pepper

1 tablespoon vegetable oil

1^1/$_2$ tablespoons unsalted butter

^{1}/$_4$ cup drained brine-packed capers (with 1 tablespoon brine reserved)

^{1}/$_4$ cup minced red or orange bell pepper

1 tablespoon peeled minced fresh ginger

1 to 3 fresh green chile peppers, such as serrano, minced with seeds

1. Prepare the masala. Prepare the paneer cheese then cut it into 10 to 12 large pieces, each about ½-inch thick. Season lightly with salt and black pepper.

2. Heat the oil in a large nonstick skillet or griddle over medium-high heat and quickly sear the paneer cheese pieces until golden, about 1 minute per side. Transfer to a serving dish, cover, and keep warm.

3. Heat the butter in a small saucepan over medium heat until it starts bubbling. Add the capers, bell pepper, ginger, and green chile peppers and cook,

stirring, about 2 minutes. Add the reserved brine and bring to a quick boil. Then drizzle everything over the paneer pieces, garnish with chaat masala, and serve.

Marinated Paneer Cheese with Saffron Yogurt Sauce
Kesari Paneer

Makes 4 to 6 servings

This is an elegant paneer *dish, serve it as a special hors d'oeuvre or if with a meal, do as you would with a meat dish—serve it as a separate course with vegetables on the side. Drizzle some of the saffron sauce over the vegetables, too.*

2 tablespoons Basic Ginger-Garlic Paste (page 47 or store-bought)

^{1}/$_4$ teaspoon saffron, dry-roasted and ground (Dry-Roasting Spices, page 35)

8 ounces (1 recipe) Paneer Cheese (page 43 or store-bought)

^{1}/$_2$ cup plain yogurt (any kind), whisked until smooth

1 teaspoon garam masala

^{1}/$_2$ teaspoon ajwain seeds

^{1}/$_4$ teaspoon cayenne pepper, or to taste

^{1}/$_4$ teaspoon ground paprika

1 teaspoon salt, or to taste

3 tablespoons vegetable oil

1 cup water

2 teaspoons cornstarch

1 teaspoon cumin seeds

1 tablespoon ground coriander

^{1}/$_4$ teaspoon ground green cardamom seeds

^{1}/$_4$ cup finely chopped fresh cilantro

1. Prepare the ginger-garlic paste and the saffron. Prepare the paneer cheese, then cut it into triangles about ½ inch thick. In a large bowl, mix together the yogurt and saffron and allow to steep at least 30 minutes. Then add in the ginger-garlic paste, garam masala, ajwain seeds, cayenne pepper, paprika, and salt. Add the paneer cheese pieces and mix well. Cover and marinate at least 4 and up to 8 hours in the refrigerator.

2. Heat 2 tablespoons oil in a large nonstick skillet over medium-high heat. Fry the paneer pieces until lightly golden, 15 to 20 seconds per side. Transfer to a serving platter and keep warm.

3. Mix together the water and cornstarch and stir it into the marinade left sticking to the pan.

4. In a small nonstick wok or skillet, heat the remaining 1 tablespoon oil over medium-high heat then add the cumin seeds; they should sizzle upon contact with the hot oil. Quickly mix in the coriander and the cornstarch mixture and bring to a quick boil over high heat. The sauce should thicken immediately. Mix in the cardamom seeds. Drizzle the sauce over the paneer cheese, garnish with the cilantro, and serve.

Paneer Cheese Wedges with Chickpea Flour

Besan Paneer

Makes 4 to 6 servings

Here is an exotic and quick-cooking delicacy from my friend Neelam Malhotra, who's New-Delhi born but now lives in Bangalore, the capital of the southern state of Karnatka. Neelam sprinkles some chickpea flour over the paneer pieces after they are lightly cooked. This forms a delicate shell around the pieces and seals all the flavors inside.

8 ounces (1 recipe) Paneer Cheese (page 43 or store-bought)
2 tablespoons peanut oil
1 teaspoon cumin seeds
1 tablespoon peeled minced fresh ginger
1 teaspoon ground cumin
1/2 teaspoon hot red pepper flakes, or to taste
1/2 teaspoon ground turmeric
2 tablespoons dried fenugreek leaves
1 teaspoon mango powder
1 teaspoon salt, or to taste
2 to 3 tablespoons chickpea flour
1/4 cup finely chopped fresh cilantro

1. Prepare the paneer cheese then cut it into 1-inch wedges or rectangles. Heat the oil in a large nonstick

wok or saucepan over medium heat and add the cumin seeds; they should sizzle upon contact with the hot oil.

2. Quickly add the ginger, stir 30 seconds, then mix in the cumin, red pepper flakes, and turmeric. Add the fenugreek leaves, mango powder, and salt, then mix in the paneer cheese pieces. Cook, turning, until lightly browned, 15 to 20 seconds per side.

3. Sprinkle the chickpea flour evenly over the paneer cheese, and cook, turning the pieces, about 2 minutes. The chickpea flour will roast and form a fragrant coating over the pieces. Transfer to a serving dish, sprinkle the cilantro on top, and serve.

Paneer Cheese Balls

Paneer Koftas

Makes 4 to 6 servings

Like most other koftas *(meat or vegetable balls), the ones made with* paneer *cheese make great finger food. Serve these with an herb-based or yogurt-based chutney, or simmer in one of the many curry sauces, such as Classic Spicy Curry Sauce (page 388) and serve as an entrée. Allow 3 to 4 paneer balls per person.*

1 teaspoon Chaat Masala (page 20 or store-bought)
8 ounces (1 recipe) Paneer Cheese (page 43 or store-bought)
1 small potato (any kind), boiled in water to cover until tender, then peeled and grated
1/4 cup finely chopped fresh cilantro, including soft stems
1 tablespoon peeled minced fresh ginger
1 to 3 fresh green chile peppers, such as serrano, minced with seeds
1/2 teaspoon ajwain seeds, coarsely ground
1/2 teaspoon garam masala
3/4 teaspoon salt, or to taste
1 to 1 1/2 cups peanut oil for deep-frying

1. Prepare the chaat masala. Prepare the paneer, then grate the cheese by hand or briefly in a food processor. Transfer to a bowl, then add the potato, cilantro, ginger, chile peppers, ajwain seeds, garam masala, and salt. Combine until the mixture resembles a soft dough.

2. Divide the cheese dough into 15 to 20 portions, each about 1¼-inches, and shape each portion into a smooth ball.

3. Line a tray or cookie sheet with paper towels. Heat the oil in a wok until it reaches 325°F to 350°F on a frying thermometer, or until a small piece of dough dropped into the hot oil rises to the top in 15 to 20 seconds. Put the paneer balls into the hot oil carefully, to avoid splattering, adding as many as the wok can hold at one time without crowding. Fry, turning once or twice, until golden on all sides, 2 to 3 minutes. With a slotted spoon, transfer to the lined tray to drain. Place on a serving platter, sprinkle the chaat masala on top and serve.

Paneer Cheese Wraps
Paneer Kaathi Kabaab

Makes 10 to 12 rolls

Kaathi *wraps (or rolls) are the Indian equivalent of burritos. They are generally made with Malhotra lamb or chicken, but my friend Neelam Malhotra, who is a vegetarian, makes them with* paneer *cheese. This is her creative recipe. Preparing a wrap entails making the separate elements, then assembling the wrap. If making the potato* rotis *(flatbreads) poses a problem, use whole-wheat or flour tortillas. Be sure not to overcook the* paneer, *as it tastes better when slightly underdone.*

8 ounces (1 recipe) Paneer Cheese (page 43 or store-bought)
1 recipe Griddle-Cooked Flour and Potato Bread for Spicy Wraps (page 600)
¹/₂ cup (¹/₄ recipe) Yogurt Cheese (page 42), whisked until smooth

3 tablespoons Basic Ginger-Garlic Paste (page 47 or store-bought)
1 teaspoon Chaat Masala (page 20 or store-bought)
2 to 3 teaspoons mustard or peanut oil
1 tablespoon ground cumin
1 teaspoon cayenne pepper, or to taste
1 teaspoon salt, or to taste
1 large white onion, cut in half lengthwise and thinly sliced
1 to 3 fresh green chile peppers, such as serrano, minced with seeds
¹/₂ cup finely chopped fresh cilantro, including soft stems
2 tablespoons fresh lemon juice

1. Prepare the paneer cheese, potato bread wraps, yogurt cheese, ginger-garlic paste, and chaat masala. Then cut the paneer into ¹/₂-inch pieces.

2. In a large non-reactive bowl, mix together the yogurt cheese, oil, ginger-garlic paste, cumin, cayenne pepper, and salt. Add the paneer pieces and mix well. Cover and marinate at least 2 hours at room temperature or up to 24 hours in the refrigerator.

3. Preheat the oven to 400°F and lightly grease a baking sheet. Remove the paneer cheese pieces from the marinade and place them in a single layer on the baking sheet. (Discard mayonnaise.) Bake, turning the pieces once or twice, until barely golden, 5 to 7 minutes. (Do not overbake, or the pieces will toughen.) Transfer to a bowl, cover, and keep warm.

4. In another bowl, mix together the onion, green chile peppers, cilantro, lemon juice, and chaat masala. Adjust seasoning, adding salt if you wish.

5. To assemble, lay out all the potato rotis. Place the paneer cheese pieces along the center length of each roti, top with the onion-chile pepper mixture and roll tightly. Serve immediately or wrap each one in foil and refrigerate up to 2 days.

Paneer Cheese Scrambles and Side Dishes

Basic Paneer Cheese Scramble
Paneer ki Bhurji

Makes 4 to 6 servings

With innumerable variations, this is by far the most popular dry-cooked paneer *side dish. It looks like scrambled eggs with onion and tomato, but tastes a lot different. Enhance it even more by mixing in a cup of boiled peas or corn along with the* paneer *cheese in Step 4.*

8 ounces (1 recipe) Paneer Cheese (page 43 or store-bought)
2 tablespoons vegetable oil
2 cups finely chopped onions
2 large tomatoes, finely chopped
1 to 3 fresh green chile peppers, such as serrano, minced with seeds
2 teaspoons ground coriander
1/2 teaspoon ground cumin
1/4 teaspoon ground turmeric
1 teaspoon salt, or to taste
1/2 cup finely chopped fresh cilantro, including soft stems
Freshly ground black pepper, to taste

1. Prepare the paneer cheese and coarsely crumble. Heat the oil in a medium nonstick wok or skillet over medium-high heat, add the onions and cook, stirring, until golden, 3 to 5 minutes.

2. Add the tomatoes and green chile peppers and cook, stirring as needed, until most of the juices evaporate, about 7 minutes. Add all the spices and the salt, then mix in the paneer cheese. Cook, stirring, over medium-high heat for the first 3 to 4 minutes and then over medium heat until golden, about 10 minutes. Mix in the cilantro. Transfer to a serving dish, sprinkle the black pepper on top, and serve.

Paneer Cheese Scramble with Soybeans
Soyabeans vaali Paneer Bhurji

Makes 4 to 6 servings

The addition of shelled, pre-cooked soy beans along with a few other herbs and spices makes for a more substantial paneer *scramble. They add a delicate crunch to the generally soft* paneer *cheese. This recipe can also be doubled easily to make an entrée, when served with vegetables and Indian breads. Look for shelled soybeans in the frozen vegetable section of your supermarket or in Asian markets.*

8 ounces (1 recipe) Paneer Cheese (page 43 or store-bought)
1 cup shelled frozen soybeans, thawed
2 tablespoons vegetable oil
1 teaspoon cumin seeds
1/2 teaspoon fenugreek seeds, coarsely ground
1 large onion, finely chopped
1 large tomato, finely chopped
1 to 3 fresh green chile peppers, such as serrano, minced with seeds
1 1/2 tablespoons ground coriander
1/2 teaspoon ground cumin
1/4 teaspoon ground turmeric
1/4 teaspoon hot red pepper flakes, or to taste
1 teaspoon salt, or to taste
1/2 cup finely chopped fresh cilantro, including soft stems
1 tablespoon minced fresh mint leaves
1/4 teaspoon garam masala

1. Prepare the paneer cheese and crumble it coarsely. Put the soybeans in a microwave-safe dish. Cover and cook in the microwave on high power 3 to 4 minutes or until the soybeans are very soft.

Alternately, put them in a saucepan in water to cover and boil until tender.

2. Heat the oil in a medium nonstick wok or skillet over medium-high heat and add the cumin and fenugreek seeds; they should sizzle upon contact with the hot oil. Quickly add the onion and cook, stirring, until golden, about 10 minutes. Add the tomato and green chile peppers and cook, stirring as needed, until most of the juices evaporate, about 7 minutes.

3. Add all the coriander, cumin, turmeric, red pepper flakes, and salt to the pan, then mix in the soy beans and stir about 5 minutes. Add the paneer cheese and cook, stirring, over medium-high heat the first 2 to 3 minutes and then over medium heat until golden, 10 minutes. Mix in the cilantro and mint. Transfer to a serving dish, garnish with garam masala, and serve.

Paneer Cheese Scramble with Morel Mushrooms
Sookha Gucchi Paneer

Makes 4 to 6 servings

Morel mushrooms, called gucchiyan *in Hindi, are grown in Kashmir and are popular all over northern India. They have a delicate smoky fragrance and an earthy flavor. When sliced into thin rounds, these mushrooms look like stars and, along with the red bell pepper, they add a luxurious elegance to this dish. You can also use other mushrooms like white button, porcini, or chanterelle.*

8 ounces (1 recipe) Paneer Cheese (page 43 or store-bought)

3 tablespoons vegetable oil

1 large onion, finely chopped

1 to 3 fresh green chile peppers, such as serrano, minced with seeds

1 red bell pepper, cut into 1/4-inch pieces

1 cup (about 15 medium) fresh or reconstituted dried morel mushrooms, sliced crosswise into thin rounds

1 teaspoon cumin seeds

1 teaspoon black mustard seeds

1/4 teaspoon salt, or to taste

1/4 cup finely chopped fresh cilantro, including soft stems

1/4 teaspoon garam masala

1. Prepare the paneer and cut into 1/2-inch pieces. Heat 2 tablespoons oil in a medium nonstick wok or

skillet over medium-high heat and cook the onion and green chile peppers, stirring, until lightly browned and soft, about 10 minutes. Transfer to a bowl.

2. Add the red bell pepper and mushrooms to the pan and cook about 1 minute. Transfer to the bowl with the onion and green chile peppers.

3. Heat the remaining 1 tablespoon oil in the pan and add the cumin and mustard seeds; they should splatter upon contact with the hot oil, so lower the heat and cover the pan until the splattering subsides. Quickly add the paneer cheese and salt and cook, stirring lightly, until golden. Mix in the mushroom mixture and cook over medium heat, stirring, about 5 minutes to blend the flavors. Mix in the cilantro. Transfer to a serving dish, sprinkle the garam masala on top, and serve.

Paneer Cheese Scramble with Apple-Ginger Chutney
Saeb aur Adrak Chutni vaala Paneer

Makes 4 to 6 servings

This innovative dish keeps guests guessing where its delicate flavor comes from. Try it for brunch.

8 ounces (1 recipe) Paneer Cheese (page 43 or store-bought)

1 cup (1/2 recipe) Tart Apple-Ginger Chutney with Green Tomatoes (page 71)

2 tablespoons vegetable oil

1 small onion, finely chopped

2 teaspoons ground coriander

1/2 teaspoon salt, or to taste

1/2 cup finely chopped, fresh cilantro, including soft stems

Freshly ground black pepper, to taste

1. Prepare the paneer cheese and crumble it coarsely. Prepare the chutney. Heat the oil in a medium non-stick wok or skillet over medium-high heat and cook the onion, stirring, until lightly brown, about 10 minutes. Add the paneer cheese and cook, stirring, about

2 minutes. Then mix in the chutney and cook, stirring occasionally, about 5 minutes.

2. Add the coriander and salt, reduce the heat to medium, and cook until the paneer is barely golden, about 7 minutes. Mix in the cilantro, transfer to a serving dish, season with black pepper, and serve.

Variation: Add finely diced or grated tart apples along with some minced ginger and lemon juice instead of the chutney in step 3. Unripe peaches, plums, and nectarines also work well.

Grated Paneer Cheese with Minced Cauliflower
Sookha Gobhi Paneer

Makes 4 to 6 servings

Here is a simple side dish that can also be served as a salad. For a light crunch, mince the cauliflower by hand so the pieces will not be as fine as they are if chopped in a food processor.

8 ounces (1 recipe) Paneer Cheese (page 43
 or store-bought)
2 tablespoons vegetable oil
1 small head cauliflower, minced to make 2 cups
1/2 cup finely chopped fresh cilantro
1 teaspoon cumin seeds
1 tablespoon peeled minced fresh ginger
1 to 3 fresh green chile peppers, such as serrano,
 minced with seeds
1/4 teaspoon ground turmeric
1/2 teaspoon hot red pepper flakes, or to taste
1 teaspoon salt, or to taste
1 teaspoon ground cumin
1 small tomato, finely chopped
Tomato wedges

1. Prepare the paneer cheese and grate it, preferably by hand. Heat 1 tablespoon oil in a large nonstick wok or skillet over medium-high heat and stir-fry the cauliflower and cilantro until the cauliflower is golden, about 3 minutes. Transfer to a bowl.

2. Heat the remaining 1 tablespoon oil over high heat. Add the cumin seeds; they should sizzle upon

contact with the hot oil. Quickly add the ginger and green chile peppers, cook 1 minute, then mix in the turmeric, red pepper flakes, salt, and cumin.

3. Add the chopped tomato and grated paneer cheese and cook, stirring, until heated through, about 2 minutes. Transfer to a serving dish and spoon in the cauliflower. Garnish with tomato wedges and serve.

Marinated Paneer Cheese with Ginger-Lime Pickle
Adrak-Nimboo vaala Paneer

Makes 4 to 6 servings

Ginger-lime pickle, with its citrusy hot flavors, gives this dish its distinctive zip. Serve it as a side dish or crumble it into salads. With its tremendous staying power, ginger-lime pickle is a ready marinade and flavor booster you may want to have on hand all the time.

1 to 1 1/2 tablespoons Minced Ginger-Lime Pickle
 (page 84)
8 ounces (1 recipe) Paneer Cheese (page 43
 or store-bought)
1 tablespoon vegetable oil
1/2 cup finely chopped fresh cilantro,
 including soft stems
Freshly ground black pepper, to taste

1. Prepare the ginger-lime pickle in advance. Prepare the paneer cheese then cut it into 1/2-inch pieces.

2. Place the paneer cheese in a medium non-reactive bowl. Mix in the ginger-lime pickle, cover and marinate at room temperature or in the refrigerator, 1 to 4 hours.

3. Heat the oil in a medium nonstick wok or skillet over medium-high heat and add the marinated paneer cheese. Cook, stirring lightly, until heated through, 1 to 2 minutes. Add the cilantro and cook, turning as needed, until the paneer is golden, 2 to 3 minutes. Transfer to a serving dish, garnish with black pepper, and serve.

Sautéed Paneer Cheese with Green Chutney

Paneer Hari Chutni

Makes 4 to 6 servings

With lip-smacking flavors and just a few easy steps, this is a dish you will enjoy making and eating. It's versatile; serve it as a salad, snack, side dish, or entrée.

1 to 1½ teaspoons Chaat Masala (page 20 or store-bought)
¾ teaspoon cumin seeds, dry-roasted and coarsely ground (Dry-Roasting Spices, page 35)
8 ounces (1 recipe) Paneer Cheese (page 43 or store-bought)
1 cup coarsely chopped fresh cilantro, including soft stems
2 tablespoons fresh lemon juice
1½ tablespoons ground coriander
1½ teaspoons ground cumin
1 teaspoon salt, or to taste
2 to 3 tablespoons peanut oil
1 large tomato, cut into ½-inch pieces

1. Prepare the chaat masala and the cumin. Prepare the paneer cheese and cut it into 1½-by-½-inch pieces. In a food processor or blender, process together the cilantro, lemon juice, coriander, cumin, and salt to make a smooth chutney.

2. Place the paneer cheese in a flat dish and carefully mix in the chutney, making sure that all the pieces are well-coated. Cover and marinate in the refrigerator, 1 to 4 hours.

3. Heat the oil in a large nonstick wok or skillet over medium-high heat and cook the paneer pieces (in 2 batches, if necessary), stirring, until just heated through, 1 to 2 minutes per batch. Transfer to a serving platter, cover, and keep warm.

4. Add any remaining marinade to the skillet along with the tomato and cook, stirring, until the tomato is soft, about 1 minute. Transfer to the paneer platter. Garnish with the chaat masala and cumin seeds and serve.

Variation: To grill the marinated paneer, drain the pieces, then thread them onto metal or pre-soaked wooden skewers and grill over medium heat until very lightly charred. Serve with or without the tomato.

Spicy Diced Paneer Cheese with Ajwain Seeds

Paneer Ajwaini

Makes 4 to 6 servings

With the thyme and pepper-like flavor of ajwain seeds and the fresh ginger shining through, this is a refreshing and elegant yet easy paneer cheese dish.

¾ teaspoon black peppercorns, dry-roasted and coarsely ground (Dry-Roasting Spices, page 35)
8 ounces (1 recipe) Paneer Cheese (page 43 or store-bought)
2 tablespoons peanut oil
2 small onions, cut in half lengthwise and thinly sliced
1 to 3 fresh green chile peppers, such as serrano, sliced diagonally
2 tablespoons peeled minced fresh ginger
¼ teaspoon ajwain seeds, coarsely ground
½ teaspoon salt, or to taste
2 tablespoons fresh lemon juice
½ cup finely chopped fresh cilantro, including soft stems
¼ teaspoon garam masala

1. Prepare the peppercorns. Prepare the paneer cheese then cut it into ½-inch pieces.

2. Heat the oil in a large nonstick wok or saucepan over medium-high heat and cook the onions, stirring, until golden, about 10 minutes. Add the green chile peppers and cook another 1 minute.

3. Add the paneer cheese, ginger, ajwain seeds, salt, and black pepper, and cook, turning the pieces very carefully, until barely golden, about 5 minutes. Mix in the lemon juice and cilantro and cook another 2 minutes. Transfer to a serving dish, garnish with the garam masala, and serve.

Paneer Cheese with Cauliflower and Broccoli

Gobhi aur Hari Gobhi ka Paneer

Makes 4 to 6 servings

The brilliant green broccoli florets stand out like gems against the golden paneer *and cauliflower, adding visual appeal plus texture, flavor, and nutrients to an easy everyday dish. To make sure everything cooks evenly, cut the cauliflower and broccoli into tiny ½-inch florets, similar in size to the* paneer *cheese pieces. Cut the bell peppers into ¼-inch pieces.*

1/2 teaspoon dry-roasted and coarsely ground
  black pepper (Dry-Roasting Spices, page 35),
  or to taste
8 ounces (1 recipe) Paneer Cheese (page 43
  or store-bought)
5 to 7 quarter-size slices peeled fresh ginger
1 to 3 fresh green chile peppers, such as serrano,
  stemmed
2 to 3 tablespoons vegetable oil
1½ tablespoons ground coriander
1/2 teaspoon ground cumin
1/2 teaspoon salt, or to taste
1/4 cup finely chopped fresh cilantro, including
  soft stems (reserve some for garnish)
2 cups fresh broccoli florets
1 cup fresh cauliflower florets
1 cup finely chopped mixed red and yellow
  bell peppers

1. Prepare the pepper. Prepare the paneer cheese then cut it into ½-inch pieces.

2. In a small food processor, process together the ginger and green chile peppers until minced, about 30 seconds. Heat the oil in a large nonstick wok or saucepan, then add the ginger and green chile peppers and cook over medium-high heat, stirring, until golden, 1 to 2 minutes.

3. Add the paneer cheese, coriander, cumin, and ¼ teaspoon salt and cook, turning carefully, until golden, about 5 minutes. Add the cilantro and cook another 2 minutes. Transfer to a serving dish.

4. To the same pan, add the cauliflower and broccoli florets, bell peppers, and the remaining ¼ teaspoon salt and stir until crisp-tender, about 5 minutes. Transfer to the serving dish and mix lightly with the paneer. Garnish with cilantro, sprinkle the black pepper on top, and serve.

Oven-Baked Paneer Cheese with Puréed Cilantro

Dhania-Paneer Bake

Makes 4 to 6 servings

Marinated and baked in the oven until barely golden, this side dish is lovely with a dal *(legume) dish or Cucumber and Radish Raita (page 225) and Simple Cumin Basmati Rice (page 535).*

1 teaspoon Chaat Masala (page 20 or store-bought)
8 ounces (1 recipe) Paneer Cheese (page 43
  or store-bought)
6 quarter-size slices peeled fresh ginger
2 large cloves fresh garlic, peeled
1 to 3 fresh green chile peppers, such as serrano,
  stemmed
1 tablespoon fresh lemon juice
1 cup coarsely chopped fresh cilantro,
  including soft stems
1/2 cup plain yogurt, whisked until smooth
2 to 3 teaspoons mustard or peanut oil
1 teaspoon salt, or to taste

1. Prepare the masala. Prepare the paneer cheese then cut into ½-inch pieces. In a food processor or a blender, process together the ginger, garlic, green chile peppers, lemon juice, and cilantro to make a smooth purée.

2. Transfer to an ungreased flat ovenproof dish and mix in the yogurt, oil, and salt. Add the paneer cheese pieces and marinate at least 2 hours at room temperature or up to 24 hours in the refrigerator.

3. Preheat the oven to 450°F. Bake the paneer cheese, turning the pieces once or twice, until barely golden, about 10 minutes. (Do not overcook or the paneer will become tough.) Sprinkle the chaat masala on top and serve.

Paneer Cheese Bites with Sun-Dried Tomatoes

Dhoop mein Sookhae Tamatar ka Paneer

Makes 4 to 6 servings

I made it for my niece Jyoti's pre-wedding music evening—an event when people sing Indian folksongs and make fun of the new in-laws. This breaks the ice and brings the two families closer amidst a lot of laughter. Food is also a big part of the evening.

Sun-dried tomatoes are not Indian, but they work in this dish. I use oil-packed sun-dried tomatoes in this recipe and even use some of the oil from the bottle to make the dish.

8 ounces (1 recipe) Paneer Cheese (page 43 or store-bought)

1 cup chopped drained oil-packed sun-dried tomatoes (with 3 tablespoons olive oil reserved)

1½ teaspoons cumin seeds

½ teaspoon coarsely ground black peppercorns

1 large onion, cut in half lengthwise and thinly sliced

1 fresh green chile pepper, such as serrano, minced with seeds

1½ tablespoons ground coriander

½ teaspoon dried fenugreek leaves

½ teaspoon salt, or to taste

1 small bunch snipped chives

1. Prepare the paneer cheese and cut it into ½-inch pieces. Heat the oil in a large nonstick wok or saucepan over medium-high heat and add the cumin seeds and peppercorns; they should sizzle upon contact with the hot oil. Quickly add the onion and cook, stirring, until golden, about 5 minutes.

2. Add the paneer cheese, green chile pepper, coriander, fenugreek leaves, and salt, and cook, stirring and turning carefully until golden, about 5 minutes. Add the sun-dried tomatoes and continue to cook, turning a few times, about 5 minutes. Transfer to a serving dish, sprinkle the snipped chives on top, and serve.

Paneer Cheese Glazed with Puréed Tomatoes

Tamatar vaala Sookha Paneer

Makes 4 to 6 servings

With a fragrant glaze of puréed tomatoes clinging to the paneer *and a refreshing thyme-like aroma from the ajwain seeds, this dish is a classic north Indian masterpiece. For variation, mix in about 1 cup of thawed frozen peas during the last 5 minutes.*

1 tablespoon cumin seeds, dry-roasted and coarsely ground (Dry-Roasting Spices, page 35)

8 ounces (1 recipe) Paneer Cheese (page 43 or store-bought)

1 large onion, coarsely chopped

1 large clove fresh garlic, peeled

3 quarter-size slices peeled fresh ginger

1 fresh green chile pepper, such as serrano, minced with seeds

1 large tomato, coarsely chopped

1 cup coarsely chopped fresh cilantro, including soft stems

2 to 3 tablespoons vegetable oil

¾ cup coarsely ground mixed nuts, such as cashews, almonds, or peanuts

1 teaspoon salt, or to taste

½ teaspoon freshly ground black pepper

½ teaspoon ajwain seeds, coarsely crushed

¼ teaspoon garam masala

A few sprigs fresh cilantro

1. Prepare the cumin. Prepare the paneer cheese then cut it into 1-by-2-inch pieces. Put the onion, garlic, ginger, and green chile pepper in a food processor and pulse a few times until just minced. (Do not overprocess or the onion will become watery.) Transfer to a bowl, then process the tomato and cilantro until puréed.

2. Heat the oil in a large nonstick wok or saucepan over medium-high heat and cook the onion mixture, stirring, over medium-high heat the first 2 to 3 minutes and then over medium heat until the onions are a nicely browned, about 10 minutes. Add ½ cup nuts and stir about 2 minutes. (Reserve the remaining nuts for garnish.)

3. Add the paneer cheese, cumin, salt, pepper, and ajwain seeds and cook, stirring carefully, about 5 minutes. Add the puréed tomatoes and cook, stirring as needed, until all the juices evaporate and cling to the paneer cheese, about 10 minutes. Transfer to a serving dish, sprinkle the reserved nuts and garam masala on top, garnish with the cilantro sprigs, and serve.

Paneer Cheese Chile-Fry with Crispy Ginger

Mirchi Paneer aur Tala Adrak

Makes 4 to 6 servings

Even though the name says "chile-fry," the paneer *is actually sautéed and then simmered in a juice. It's called a fry because the red chiles are fried before* paneer *is added to the pan. This refreshing dish combines some great flavors—the heat of dried red and fresh green chile peppers blends with a piquant citrus sauce and the sweetness of finely diced red bell peppers.*

¹/₂ teaspoon black peppercorns, dry-roasted and coarsely crushed (Dry-Roasting Spices, page 35)

¹/₂ teaspoon Chaat Masala (page 20 or store-bought)

8 ounces (1 recipe) Paneer Cheese (page 43 or store-bought)

¹/₂ cup Crispy Fried Fresh Ginger (page 45)

2 to 3 tablespoons peanut oil

4 to 6 dried red chile peppers, such as chile de arbol, with stems

1 large clove fresh garlic, minced

5 to 6 scallions, white parts only, thinly sliced

1 to 3 fresh green chile peppers, such as serrano, minced with seeds

³/₄ teaspoon salt, or to taste

¹/₂ cup finely chopped fresh cilantro, including soft stems

¹/₄ cup fresh orange juice

2 to 3 tablespoons distilled white vinegar

1 cup finely chopped red bell pepper

1. Prepare the peppercorns and the masala. Prepare the paneer cheese and cut into 1-inch squares. Prepare the fried ginger and save for garnish (reserve the oil).

2. Heat (or reheat) the oil (used for frying the ginger) in a large nonstick skillet over medium-high heat and cook the red chile peppers, stirring, about 1 minute. Add the paneer cheese pieces and cook (in 2 to 3 batches, if needed), turning them once, until barely golden on both sides, about 1 to 2 minutes per batch.

3. Add the garlic, scallions, green chile peppers, black pepper, and salt and cook about 2 minutes. Add the cilantro, orange juice, and vinegar and cook until most of the juices are absorbed by the paneer cheese, about 5 minutes.

4. Add the red bell pepper and cook about 2 minutes, then reduce the heat to low, cover the pan, and cook another 5 minutes to blend the flavors. Transfer to a serving dish, garnish with the fried ginger and chaat masala, and serve.

Quick Spinach with Crumbled Paneer Cheese
Jaldi ka Saag Paneer

Makes 4 to 6 servings

This dish is a quick and easy alternative to traditional saag paneer *dishes. I always have some* paneer *cheese in my freezer, but if you don't, buy some at your local Indian market, or substitute extra-firm* tofu *instead.*

8 ounces (1 recipe) Paneer Cheese (page 43
   or store-bought) or tofu
2 tablespoons olive or vegetable oil
1 teaspoon cumin seeds
$1/2$ teaspoon black mustard seeds
$1/4$ teaspoon coarsely ground fenugreek seeds
1 large tomato, coarsely chopped
1 large clove fresh garlic, minced
1 fresh green chile pepper, such as serrano,
   minced with seeds
2 small bunches fresh spinach (about 1 pound),
   trimmed of roots only, washed well,
   and coarsely chopped
2 teaspoons ground coriander
$3/4$ teaspoon garam masala
$3/4$ teaspoon salt, or to taste
Freshly ground black pepper, to taste

1. Prepare the paneer cheese and crumble it coarsely. Heat the oil in a large nonstick wok or saucepan over medium-high heat and add the cumin, mustard seeds, and fenugreek; they should sizzle upon contact with the hot oil. Quickly add the tomato, garlic, and chile pepper and cook, stirring, about 1 minute.

2. Add the spinach. Cover the pan and cook, stirring once or twice until wilted, about 3 minutes. Add the paneer cheese, coriander, garam masala, and salt and cook over medium heat, uncovered, stirring as needed, until all the juices evaporate and the dish is quite dry, about 5 minutes. Transfer to a serving dish, garnish with freshly ground black pepper, and serve.

Paneer Cheese Main Dishes and Curries

Paneer Cheese with Baby Spinach and Fresh Fenugreek Leaves
Palak aur Methi Paneer

Makes 6 to 8 servings

Best made in a cast-iron wok, this dish traditionally turns black-green and becomes almost dry. It has the heady fragrance and pleasant bitterness of fresh fenugreek leaves, offset by the delicate paneer *cheese.*

The authentic recipe calls for deep-frying the paneer *cheese pieces, a step I do without. If you wish to, lightly fry the* paneer *pieces until just golden, then add about $1/2$ cup water along with the yogurt and cook until most of it evaporates.*

8 ounces (1 recipe) Paneer Cheese (page 43
   or store-bought)
$1/4$ cup Crispy Fried Fresh Ginger (page 45)
4 cups packed (2 small bunches) fresh baby spinach
2 cups packed fresh fenugreek leaves (or $1/4$ cup dried)
4 quarter-size slices peeled fresh ginger
1 large clove fresh garlic, peeled
1 to 3 fresh green chile peppers, such as serrano,
   stemmed
2 tablespoons peanut oil
1 tablespoon melted ghee
1 teaspoon salt, or to taste
$1/4$ teaspoon ground turmeric
$1/2$ cup plain yogurt, whisked until smooth

1. Prepare the paneer cheese and cut it into thick $3/4$-inch pieces. Prepare the crispy fried ginger.

2. Trim and wash the spinach. If using fresh fenugreek, pick out the leaves and the softest stems and discard the hard and fibrous parts. Wash well. Transfer the spinach, prepared fresh or dried fenugreek, fresh ginger, garlic, and green chile peppers to a food processor and process until minced, about 1 minute.

3. Heat the oil and ghee in a large cast-iron or non-stick wok or a saucepan over medium-high heat and cook the greens, stirring and scraping the sides of the wok, over medium-high heat the first 2 to 3 minutes and then over medium heat until well-roasted and deep green in color, 15 to 20 minutes.

4. Mix in the paneer cheese, salt, and turmeric and cook, stirring, 2 to 3 minutes. Add the yogurt, a little at a time, stirring constantly to prevent it from curdling, and continue to cook until all the juices evaporate and paneer pieces are soft, 3 to 5 minutes. Transfer to a serving dish, garnish with the fried ginger, and serve.

Spinach with Paneer Cheese
Saag Paneer

Makes 4 to 6 servings

The proportion of spinach to paneer *cheese varies according to the cook's taste. Generally, there is a lot more spinach and less* paneer *in the dish, but I prefer more* paneer. *Also, the authentic recipe calls for the* paneer *pieces to be deep-fried, another step I avoid. If you wish, lightly fry the* paneer *pieces until they are just golden. This firms up the pieces, so you don't have to be as careful when stirring.*

8 ounces (1 recipe) Paneer Cheese (page 43 or store-bought)
2 small bunches (about 1 pound) fresh spinach, trimmed of roots only, washed well and coarsely chopped
1 large onion, coarsely chopped
4 quarter-size slices peeled fresh ginger + 1 (1-inch) piece peeled and cut into thin matchsticks
3 large cloves fresh garlic, peeled + 1 clove minced
¹/₄ cup water
2 tablespoons vegetable oil
1 tablespoon melted ghee

2 (1-inch) sticks cinnamon
5 green cardamom pods, crushed lightly to break the skin
1 tablespoon ground coriander
1 teaspoon garam masala
1 teaspoon dried fenugreek leaves
¹/₂ teaspoon salt, or to taste
¹/₄ cup plain yogurt (any kind), whisked until smooth
1 to 2 tablespoons unsalted butter, at room temperature
4 whole dried red chile peppers, such as chile de arbol
¹/₂ teaspoon ground paprika

1. Prepare the paneer cheese and cut it into 1-by-¹/₂-inch squares.

2. Place the spinach, onion, ginger slices, whole garlic, and water in a large nonstick saucepan. Cover and bring to a boil over high heat. Reduce the heat to medium-low, cover the pan, and simmer until the spinach is wilted and the onion tender, about 10 minutes. Let cool, then pulse lightly in a food processor until just minced (do not make a smooth purée). Return to the pan.

3. Heat the oil and ghee in a small saucepan over medium-high heat and cook the cinnamon, cardamom pods, and ginger matchsticks, stirring, until the ginger is golden, 1 to 2 minutes. Add the minced garlic, coriander, garam masala, fenugreek leaves, and salt and stir a few seconds. Then add the yogurt, a little at a time, stirring constantly to prevent curdling. Immediately transfer to the spinach, cover, and simmer over medium heat, 10 to 15 minutes.

4. Add the paneer cheese to the pan and stir gently to mix, trying not to break the pieces. Cover and simmer, stirring occasionally, about 10 minutes to blend the flavors. Transfer to a serving dish.

5. Heat the butter in a small saucepan, add the dried chile peppers, and cook, stirring, until golden, about 30 seconds. Remove the pan from the heat, add the paprika, then immediately add to the spinach dish and swirl lightly to mix, with parts of the chile peppers visible as a garnish. Serve hot.

Paneer Cheese with Coconut and Corn

Nariyal aur Makki ka Paneer

Makes 4 to 6 servings

Paneer cheese cooked in a fresh coconut masala (a paste made by grinding together coconut, onion, and other fresh ingredients) with the southern flavors of mustard seeds and curry leaves is an unusual addition to the predominantly north Indian paneer repertoire.

The deep-green Mexican pasilla peppers are a variety that falls between jalapeño and green bell peppers in heat (although some can be really hot) and work well in this dish.

¼ cup Coconut Milk (page 44 or store-bought)
8 ounces (1 recipe) Paneer Cheese (page 43 or store-bought)
4 to 6 quarter-size slices peeled fresh ginger
1 (3-inch-piece) fresh coconut, peeled and coarsely chopped, or 1 tablespoon unsweetened shredded dried coconut
1 pasilla pepper or green bell pepper, coarsely chopped
1 large onion, coarsely chopped
15 to 20 fresh curry leaves (or 1 teaspoon dried)
2 tablespoons vegetable oil
1 teaspoon cumin seeds
1 teaspoon black mustard seeds
⅛ teaspoon ground asafoetida
1 tablespoon ground coriander
¾ teaspoon salt, or to taste
1½ cups frozen corn (unthawed)
½ teaspoon freshly ground black pepper, or to taste
½ cup finely chopped fresh cilantro, including soft stems

1. Prepare the coconut milk. Prepare the paneer cheese then cut into thin 1-inch pieces. In a food processor or a blender, process together the ginger, coconut, and pasilla pepper until minced. Add the onion and curry leaves and pulse a few times, until just minced. (Do not overprocess or the onion will become watery.)

2. Heat the oil in a large nonstick wok or saucepan over medium-high heat and add the cumin and mustard seeds; they should splatter upon contact with the hot oil, so cover the pan and lower the heat until the splattering subsides. Quickly add the ginger-onion mixture and cook, stirring, until browned, about 10 minutes.

3. Add the asafoetida, coriander, and salt, then add the paneer cheese and coconut milk, and cook over medium heat, turning the pieces carefully, until lightly golden, 5 to 7 minutes.

4. Add the frozen corn, cover the wok, and cook, stirring carefully, over medium-low heat, until the corn is tender and all the moisture is absorbed into the paneer, about 10 minutes. Mix in the black pepper and cilantro, transfer to a serving dish, and serve.

Griddle-Fried Paneer Cheese

Tava-Paneer

Makes 4 to 6 servings

Indian cuisine has several showcase dishes that are cooked on a large (sometimes up to 2 feet in diameter), concave cast-iron griddle right in front of guests. This griddle, called a tava or tawa, is much larger than the small, almost indispensable tava used for everyday flatbreads.

As the tava sits on the hot stove, its center shimmers with a thin layer of sizzling oil. Along the periphery lies a variety of marinated or partially cooked vegetables, paneer cheese, and meats that receive final touches at the hands of the chef—who quickly stir-fries them with one or more of the many tomato-based sauces and spice blends that lie close at hand. The sauces coat the pieces and then are absorbed or evaporate, dyeing the paneer an exotic reddish hue. This is my home version, made in a skillet.

1/2 teaspoon Chaat Masala (page 20 or store-bought)

8 ounces (1 recipe) Paneer Cheese (page 43 or store-bought)

1/2 cup canned tomato sauce

1/4 cup heavy cream

1 teaspoon garam masala

3 tablespoons melted ghee or vegetable oil

1 teaspoon cumin seeds

1 teaspoon ajwain seeds, coarsely crushed

2 small onions, cut in half lengthwise and thinly sliced

1 (1-inch) piece peeled fresh ginger, cut into thin matchsticks + 1 tablespoon peeled and minced ginger

1 to 3 fresh green chile peppers, such as serrano, minced with seeds

1 tablespoon ground coriander

1/2 teaspoon salt, or to taste

1/4 cup finely chopped fresh cilantro, including soft stems

1. Prepare the chaat masala. Prepare the paneer cheese then cut it into ¾-inch pieces. In a bowl, mix together the tomato sauce, cream, and garam masala.

2. Heat the ghee or oil on a large tava griddle or a skillet over medium-high heat and add the cumin and ajwain seeds; they should sizzle upon contact with the hot oil. Quickly add the onion and ginger matchsticks and cook, stirring, until golden, 5 to 7 minutes.

3. Add the minced ginger, green chile peppers, and coriander, stir about 30 seconds, then add the paneer cheese pieces and salt. Cook, carefully turning the pieces, until lightly golden, about 2 minutes.

4. Add the tomato-cream mixture and cook, stirring and turning the pieces carefully, until the liquid evaporates completely, leaving behind a lovely red glaze, 2 to 3 minutes. Mix in the cilantro and stir another minute. Sprinkle the chaat masala on top and serve straight from the tava or transfer to a serving dish.

Variation: For a variety of flavors, mix in finely chopped bell peppers, zucchini, broccoli, or other vegetables and use any of the sauces in the Vegetarian Curries chapter instead of the tomato-cream sauce.

Silky Paneer Cheese Curry with Red Chile Peppers

Paneer, Laal Mirchi

Makes 4 to 6 servings

My India-born friend Rita Bhalla, who now lives in Los Angeles, calls this her "red chile" paneer because the main flavor and heat comes from whole and ground red chile peppers. Whipping cream lends this dish its signature silky-creamy texture and a lovely yellow-white color.

1 tablespoon Basic Ginger-Garlic Paste (page 47 or store-bought)

8 ounces (1 recipe) Paneer Cheese (page 43 or store-bought)

2 tablespoons vegetable oil

4 to 6 whole dried red chile peppers, such as chile de arbol

1 teaspoon cumin seeds

2 medium tomatoes, finely chopped

1/4 to 1/2 cup heavy cream

1 tablespoon ground coriander

1/2 teaspoon hot red pepper flakes, or to taste

1/4 teaspoon ground turmeric

1 teaspoon salt, or to taste

1/2 cup finely chopped fresh cilantro, including soft stems

1/4 teaspoon garam masala

1. Prepare the ginger-garlic paste. Prepare the paneer cheese and cut it into 1-inch-by-½-inch pieces. Heat the oil in a large nonstick wok or saucepan over medium-high heat and cook the red chile peppers, stirring, until golden brown, about 1 minute. Add the cumin seeds; they should sizzle upon contact with the hot oil. Quickly add the ginger-garlic paste and cook, stirring, about 1 minute. Then add the tomatoes and cook until the juices evaporate, about 5 minutes.

2. Add the cream and cook, stirring, over medium heat until it is well incorporated into the sauce, about 5 minutes. Mix in the coriander, red pepper flakes, turmeric, and salt, then add the paneer cheese and cook, stirring carefully, about 5 minutes. Mix in the cilantro and cook about 2 minutes. Transfer to a serving dish, sprinkle the garam masala on top, and serve.

Stir-Fried Paneer Cheese with Onions and Bell Peppers
Kadhai Paneer

Makes 4 to 6 servings

A kadhai is an Indian wok used to make a lot of different dishes. However, only dishes with the flavors that emerge when fresh onions, bell peppers, ginger, and garlic are cooked with selected Indian spices such as fenugreek, fennel, and dried pomegranate seeds, are considered kadhai foods. So, it is the flavor, not the pan, that describes kadhai dishes.

Instead of the paneer cheese in this kadhai, you can use boiled potatoes, mixed vegetables, chicken, lamb, or seafood. Cook the vegetables in the dish until they are very soft and mushy—an Indian preference—or stop cooking when they are crisp-tender.

4 ounces (1/2 recipe) Paneer Cheese (page 43 or store-bought)

3 tablespoons peanut oil

1 (1-inch) piece peeled fresh ginger, cut into thin matchsticks

2 large cloves garlic, thinly sliced

2 small onions, cut in half lengthwise and thinly sliced

1^1/$_2$ tablespoons ground coriander

2 teaspoons ground dried fenugreek leaves

1 teaspoon ground cumin

^{1}/$_2$ teaspoon ground anise or fennel seeds

1 teaspoon ground dried pomegranate seeds

^{1}/$_2$ teaspoon ground black cardamom seeds

^{1}/$_2$ teaspoon hot red pepper flakes, or to taste

^{1}/$_2$ teaspoon salt, or to taste

^{1}/$_4$ teaspoon ground black salt

4 small tomatoes, cut into wedges

4 to 5 small bell peppers of assorted colors, cut into thin matchsticks

^{1}/$_4$ cup finely chopped fresh cilantro, including soft stems

Coarsely ground black pepper, to taste

1. Prepare the paneer cheese and cut it into thick 1½-by-½-inch rectangles.

2. Heat the oil in a large nonstick wok or skillet over medium-high heat, add the ginger and garlic, and cook, stirring, until golden, about 1 minute. Add the onions and cook, stirring, until barely golden, 2 to 3 minutes. With a slotted spoon, transfer the mixture to a bowl, leaving all the oil behind.

3. In the wok, add the coriander, fenugreek, cumin, anise or fennel, pomegranate and cardamom seeds, red pepper flakes, salt, and black salt, and stir over medium heat about 2 minutes. Add the tomatoes and bell peppers, cover the wok, and cook until slightly softened, about 5 minutes. Carefully mix in the paneer cheese, cover the wok, and continue to cook, turning once or twice, until the pieces are soft and the dish is somewhat saucy, about 5 minutes.

4. Add the reserved onions and the cilantro and cook over medium-high heat, uncovered, about 5 minutes. Transfer to a serving platter (or serve straight from the wok), top with black pepper, and serve.

Variation: For a quicker version, make this dish with Spicy Masala for Wok-Cooked Foods (page 26). Cook 1 to 1½ tablespoons of the masala in hot oil, add the vegetables and ½-inch cubes of paneer cheese, and finish cooking the dish.

Curried Paneer Cheese and Potatoes

Paneer Muttar ki Kari

Makes 4 to 6 servings

This is a curry made without any onions or garlic, but still with plenty of flavor. I love its simplicity and the fact that it is delicious, healthy, and cooks very quickly.

8 ounces (1 recipe) Paneer Cheese (page 43 or store-bought)
2 tablespoons melted ghee or vegetable oil
5 to 7 fresh green chile peppers, such as serrano, skin punctured to prevent bursting
1 teaspoon cumin seeds
1 tablespoon peeled and chopped fresh ginger
1/8 teaspoon ground asafoetida
1 tablespoon ground coriander
1/2 teaspoon dried fenugreek leaves
1/4 teaspoon ground paprika
1/4 teaspoon ground turmeric
1/4 teaspoon hot red pepper flakes
1 teaspoon salt, or to taste
3 to 4 medium tomatoes, finely chopped
1/2 cup finely chopped fresh cilantro, including soft stems
1 large russet potato, peeled and cut into 3/4-inch pieces
3 to 4 cups water
1 tablespoon minced fresh mint
1/4 teaspoon garam masala

1. Prepare the paneer cheese and cut it into 1-inch or larger pieces.

2. Heat the ghee (or oil) in a large nonstick saucepan over medium-high heat and add the green chile peppers, cumin seeds, and ginger; they should sizzle upon contact with the hot oil. Quickly add the asafoetida, coriander, fenugreek leaves, paprika, turmeric, red pepper flakes, and salt, and stir about 30 seconds.

3. Add the tomatoes and cilantro and cook until most of the liquid tomatoes evaporates, about 10 minutes. Add the potato and cook, stirring, about 5 minutes. Add the water, cover the pan, and cook over medium-high heat the first 2 to 3 minutes and then over medium heat until the potatoes are tender, 20 to 25 minutes. Stir

occasionally. When the potatoes are soft, using the back of a ladle or a wooden spoon, mash a few of them against the sides of the pan to thicken the gravy.

4. Add the paneer cheese, cover the pan and simmer, stirring occasionally, about 5 minutes. (Add another 1/2 cup water if the sauce gets too thick.) Transfer to a serving dish, lightly mix in the mint and garam masala, and serve.

Curried Paneer Cheese with Peas and Potatoes

Paneer, Mutter aur Aalu ki Kari

Makes 6 to 8 servings

This is a rich dish, but consider that it can feed 6 to 8 people, with some left over. If you are concerned about health, drain the paneer *cheese well after deep-frying and omit the cream.*

8 ounces (1 recipe) Paneer Cheese (page 43 or store-bought)
3/4 cup (1/2 recipe) Boiled Onion Paste (page 49)
1 to 1 1/2 cups peanut oil for deep-frying
3 to 5 fresh green chile peppers, such as serrano, skin punctured to prevent bursting
1 (1-inch) stick cinnamon
3 black cardamom pods, crushed lightly to break the skin
1 1/2 teaspoons cumin seeds
1 tablespoon ground coriander
1/4 teaspoon ground turmeric
1/4 teaspoon cayenne pepper, or to taste
1/4 teaspoon ground paprika
1/8 teaspoon ground nutmeg
1 large tomato, finely chopped
1/4 cup nonfat plain yogurt, whisked until smooth
4 small russet potatoes (or any kind), peeled and cut into 4 wedges each
4 cups water
3/4 teaspoon salt, or to taste
1 cup frozen peas, thawed
1/4 cup heavy cream (optional)
1 teaspoon dried fenugreek leaves
1/4 cup finely chopped fresh cilantro, including soft stems
1/4 teaspoon garam masala

1. Prepare the paneer cheese then cut into 1-inch pieces. Prepare the onion paste.

2. Line a tray with paper towels. Heat the oil in a large wok until it reaches 325°F to 350°F on a frying thermometer, or until a small piece of paneer cheese dropped into the hot oil bubbles and rises to the top immediately. Standing far from the wok (because the paneer cheese will splatter from the moisture), carefully add the paneer cheese pieces, one at a time, adding as many as the wok will hold without crowding. Fry the paneer, turning once or twice, until just golden on both sides, about 30 seconds. (This happens very quickly, so work fast.) With a slotted spoon, transfer to paper towels to drain.

3. Remove all but 2 tablespoons of the oil from the wok and heat it over medium-high heat. Add the green chile peppers, cinnamon, cardamom pods, and cumin seeds; they should sizzle upon contact with the hot oil. Quickly add the coriander, turmeric, cayenne pepper, paprika, and nutmeg, and stir about 30 seconds. Add the tomato and cook, stirring, until all the juices evaporate, about 5 minutes. Add the yogurt, a little at a time, stirring constantly to prevent it from curdling.

4. Add the potatoes and cook, stirring, about 5 minutes. Then add the water and salt and bring to a boil over high heat. Reduce the heat to medium-low, cover the pan, and simmer until the potatoes tender, about 20 minutes. Mix in the peas and paneer cheese, cover the pan, and simmer until the peas and paneer cheese pieces are soft and the sauce is thick, about 10 minutes. Add the cream (if using) and fenugreek leaves and simmer about 5 minutes to blend the flavors. Transfer to a serving dish. Mix in the cilantro and garam masala and serve.

Paneer Cheese Curry with Two Onions

Do-Pyaza Paneer

Makes 4 to 6 servings

Although some people refer to all the do-pyaza *dishes as special curries,* do-pyaza *literally means "with 2 onions." In this case, it does not mean 2 whole onions, but onions prepared 2 ways and added at different stages of cooking. You can also use 2 different types of onions, as I do in this recipe.*

8 ounces (1 recipe) Paneer Cheese (page 43 or store-bought)

2 tablespoons vegetable oil

1 (1-inch) stick cinnamon

3 green cardamom pods, crushed lightly to break the skin

2 black cardamom pods, crushed lightly to break the skin

1½ teaspoons cumin seeds

1 cup finely chopped white or yellow onions

1 teaspoon fresh garlic, minced

½ teaspoon hot red pepper flakes, or to taste

¼ teaspoon ground turmeric

3 to 4 small red onions, quartered (cut the larger ones into eighths)

1 tablespoon ground coriander

3 to 4 small tomatoes, quartered

¼ cup finely chopped fresh cilantro, including soft stems

½ teaspoon garam masala

1. Prepare the paneer cheese and cut into 1¼-inch pieces.

2. Heat the oil in a large nonstick wok or saucepan over medium-high heat and add the cinnamon, green and black cardamom pods, and cumin seeds; they should sizzle upon contact with the hot oil. Quickly add the chopped onion and cook, stirring, until golden, about 5 minutes.

3. Mix in the garlic, red pepper flakes, and turmeric, then add the quartered red onions and the coriander and cook, stirring, over medium-low heat until lightly browned, about 5 minutes. Add the tomatoes and paneer cheese pieces and cook, stirring and turning carefully, until the paneer cheese is very soft, 5 to 7 minutes. Add the cilantro during the last 2 minutes of cooking. Transfer to a serving dish, lightly mix in the garam masala, and serve.

Royal Paneer Cheese Curry

Shahi Paneer

Makes 4 to 6 servings

Shahi, *meaning "fit for an emperor" in Hindi, amply describes this exotic Mughlai nut-adorned paneer dish that comes in a rich and sinful creamy tomato sauce.*

8 ounces (1 recipe) Paneer Cheese (page 43 or store-bought)
4 cups (1 recipe) Butter-Cream Sauce with Fresh Tomatoes (page 389)
1¹/₂ tablespoons melted ghee
1 (1-inch) piece peeled fresh ginger, cut into thin matchsticks
1 to 3 fresh green chile peppers, such as serrano, each split lengthwise in half, with or without seeds
1 teaspoon cumin seeds
¹/₂ cup golden raisins
¹/₄ cup coarsely chopped shelled raw pistachios
¹/₄ cup raw almond slivers
1 teaspoon ground dried fenugreek leaves
2 tablespoons heavy cream

1. Prepare the paneer cheese then cut into thick 1½-inch squares. Prepare the cream sauce.

2. Heat 1 tablespoon ghee in a large nonstick wok or saucepan over medium-high heat and cook the ginger and green chile peppers, stirring, until golden, about 2 minutes. Add the cumin seeds; they should sizzle upon contact with the hot oil. Quickly add the raisins, pistachios, and almond slivers and stir until the raisins start to expand, about 1 minute. Remove everything to a bowl and reserve.

3. Add the remaining ½ tablespoon ghee to the pan and cook the paneer cheese pieces, stirring, about 2 minutes. Add the cream sauce and fenugreek leaves and simmer about 10 minutes to blend the flavors. Transfer to a serving dish, swirl in the heavy cream, garnish with the raisin-nut mixture, and serve.

Variation: For a different presentation, cut the chunk of paneer cheese into 2 parts horizontally to make 2 large slabs. Simmer the slabs in the sauce about 10 minutes. Garnish with the raisin-nut mixture and serve.

Stuffed Paneer Cheese Balls in Creamy Tomato Sauce

Malai Kofta Curry

Makes 6 to 8 servings

Stuffed with pistachios, almonds, and raisins, these paneer kofta *balls are an impressive addition to any formal table. When presented in a creamy tomato-enriched sauce such as this one, they become a delightful main course.*

As appetizers, paneer *cheese balls can be served with any of the fresh green or yogurt chutneys, such as Cilantro-Lime Chutney (page 59) or Yogurt-Almond Chutney (page 69) They are rich, for sure, and when served as an entrée they truly are a guilty indulgence, so keep the rest of the meal simple. Good accompaniments are Zesty Everyday Green Beans (page 303), Ginger and Scallion Raita (page 222), and a side of fresh breads.*

8 ounces (1 recipe) Paneer Cheese (page 43 or store-bought)
4 cups (1 recipe) Butter-Cream Sauce with Fresh Tomatoes (page 389)
1 medium russet potato (or any kind)
¹/₂ cup coarsely chopped cashews
5 to 6 quarter-size slices peeled fresh ginger
8 scallions, white parts only, coarsely chopped
¹/₂ teaspoon freshly ground black pepper, or to taste
1 teaspoon salt, or to taste
1 tablespoon melted ghee or unsalted butter
¹/₂ cup finely chopped onion
2 tablespoons coarsely chopped raw pistachios
2 tablespoons coarsely chopped raw almonds
2 tablespoons chopped raisins
1¹/₂ to 2 cups peanut oil for deep-frying
¹/₄ cup finely chopped fresh cilantro, including soft stems

1. Prepare the paneer cheese and crumble it coarsely. Prepare the cream sauce and keep it ready. While you're making either the cheese or the sauce, also boil the potato in water to cover until tender, then peel and grate it.

2. In a food processor, process together the cashews, ginger, and scallions until minced. Add the paneer cheese, black pepper, and salt, and process until it starts to gather like a dough, about 30 seconds. Transfer to a bowl, add the potato, then mix with clean hands to make a soft dough. Cover and reserve.

3. for the filling. Heat the ghee in a small saucepan over medium-high heat and cook the onion, stirring, until golden, about 2 minutes. Add the pistachios, almonds, and raisins and stir another 2 minutes. Let cool.

4. Divide the paneer dough and the raisin-nut filling each into 15 to 20 portions. Working with each paneer portion separately, flatten into a disk, place the nuts in the center, then close the disk around the filling and shape into 1½-inch smooth balls.

5. Heat the oil in a large wok over medium-high heat until it reaches 325°F to 350°F on a frying thermometer, or a small bit of the dough dropped into the hot oil bubbles and rises to the top immediately. Fry the paneer balls, as many as the wok can hold at one time without crowding, turning them a few times until golden and crispy on all sides, about 5 minutes. With a slotted spoon, transfer to paper towels to drain.

6. Preheat the oven to 400°F. Transfer the paneer balls an oven-proof baking dish and pour in the prepared cream sauce. Cover and bake about 20 minutes. Do not stir at any time. Remove from the oven, spoon the sauce over the paneer balls if they seem dry, garnish with the cilantro, and serve.

Variation: In place of the Butter-Cream Sauce with Fresh Tomatoes, use any of the other curry sauces you find in the Vegetarian Curries chapter.

Paneer Cheese Curry with Coconut Milk

Paneer Korma

Makes 4 to 6 servings

Here, paneer *is braised in coconut milk with many whole spices. Because this is a rich entrée, you may want to reserve it for special occasions. But then again, it's so satisfying and delicious, you may not.*

1 cup Coconut Milk (page 44 or store-bought)
8 ounces (1 recipe) Paneer Cheese (page 43 or store-bought)
¼ cup Dessert Masala (page 32)
1 small onion, coarsely chopped
2 to 3 large cloves fresh garlic, peeled
5 to 6 quarter-size slices peeled fresh ginger
1 to 3 fresh green chile peppers, such as serrano, stemmed
10 raw cashews, coarsely chopped
1 large tomato, coarsely chopped
2 tablespoons vegetable oil
2 bay leaves
1 teaspoon cumin seeds
1 (1-inch) stick cinnamon
4 green cardamom pods, pounded lightly to break the skin
4 cloves
⅛ teaspoon ground nutmeg
⅛ teaspoon ground mace
1 teaspoon ground coriander
1 teaspoon garam masala
1 cup frozen peas, thawed
1 teaspoon salt, or to taste
Freshly ground black pepper, for garnish

1. Prepare the coconut milk. Prepare the paneer cheese then cut into 1½-by-½-inch thick rectangles. Prepare the dessert masala.

2. In a food processor or a blender, process together the onion, garlic, ginger, green chile peppers, and cashews about 1 minute to make a smooth paste. Transfer to a bowl, add the tomato to the food processor, and process until puréed.

3. Heat the oil in a large nonstick wok or saucepan over medium-high heat and cook the bay leaves, cumin, cinnamon, cardamom pods, and cloves, stirring, until fragrant, about 1 minute. Reduce the heat to medium and add, the nutmeg and mace, then the coriander and garam masala. Stir about 30 seconds, then add the onion paste and cook, stirring, until well browned, about 10 minutes.

4. Add the puréed tomato and cook, stirring constantly, until the juices evaporate, about 3 minutes. Add the paneer cheese, peas, salt, and coconut milk. Cover the pan, lower the heat, and simmer until the paneer pieces are soft and the sauce is thick, 10 to 15 minutes. Transfer to a serving dish, garnish with black pepper, and serve.

Nine-Jewel Paneer Cheese Curry
Navrattan Korma

Makes 6 to 8 servings

This dish is a treasure loaded with nine culinary jewels (nav is nine and rattan is jewels) in the guise of paneer cheese, vegetables, and nuts. It is a rich classic of Mughlai cuisine served on special occasions.

1 cup fresh or canned Coconut Milk
    (page 44 or store-bought)
8 ounces (1 recipe) Paneer Cheese (page 43
    or store-bought)
1 cup plain yogurt, whisked until smooth
1¹/₂ cups water
1 teaspoon salt, or to taste
3 tablespoons vegetable oil
¹/₄ cup coarsely chopped raw cashews
¹/₄ cup coarsely chopped raw almonds
¹/₄ cup raisins
3 cups finely chopped mixed fresh or (thawed)
    frozen vegetables, such as carrots, potatoes,
    cauliflower, beans, and peas
2 bay leaves
5 black cardamom pods, pounded lightly
    to break the skin
2 (1-inch) sticks cinnamon
4 whole cloves
1 large onion, finely chopped
1 tablespoon peeled minced fresh ginger
2 teaspoons fresh garlic, minced
1 to 3 fresh green chile peppers, such as serrano,
    minced with seeds
1 tablespoon ground coriander
1 teaspoon ground cumin
1 teaspoon garam masala + more for garnish
¹/₂ cup finely chopped fresh cilantro,
    including soft stems

1. Prepare the coconut milk. Prepare the paneer cheese then cut into ¾-inch thick pieces. In a blender, blend together the yogurt, coconut milk, water, and salt until smooth.

2. Heat 1 tablespoon oil in a large nonstick saucepan over medium-high heat and cook the cashews, almonds, and raisins, stirring, until the raisins expand, about 1 minute. Transfer to a bowl. Add 1 more tablespoon oil to the same pan and cook the vegetables, stirring, until golden, about 10 minutes. Transfer to a different bowl.

3. Add the remaining 1 tablespoon oil to the same pan and cook the bay leaves, cardamom pods, cinnamon, and cloves, stirring, about 1 minute. Add the onion and cook, stirring, until well browned, 10 minutes. Add the ginger, garlic, and green chile peppers and stir about 1 minute. Then add the coriander, cumin, and 1 teaspoon garam masala and stir another minute.

4. Add the yogurt-coconut milk mixture and cook, stirring about 5 minutes. Mix in the paneer cheese pieces and the cooked vegetables, cover the pan, reduce the heat to medium-low, and simmer until the vegetables are tender and the sauce is very thick, about 15 minutes. Mix in the cilantro during the last 5 minutes of cooking. Transfer to a serving dish, garnish with the nut-raisin mixture, sprinkle on some garam masala, and serve.

Variation: If you want the vegetables to retain their color, don't sauté them as described in Step 4, but cover and cook them in the microwave on High power 4 minutes. Then add them to the dish along with the paneer cheese in Step 8.

Dried Beans, Lentils, and Peas

Mung Beans
(Mung Dal) 342

Yellow Mung Beans
with Sautéed Onion and Ginger

Garlicky Yellow Mung Beans
with Zucchini Wheels

Yellow Mung Beans
with Fresh Curry Leaves

Roasted Yellow Mung Beans
and Potatoes

Punjabi Dry-Cooked
Yellow Mung Beans

Sindhi Dry-Cooked
Yellow Mung Beans

Spicy Dry-Cooked
Split Green Mung Beans

Gujarati Green Mung Beans
with Green Masala Paste

Punjabi Green Mung Beans
with Sizzling Ginger

Lentils
(Masoor Dal) 348

Dry-Cooked Red Lentils
with Cumin Seeds

Red Lentils with Bengali 5-Spices

Green Lentils with Sautéed Onion

Roasted Green Lentils
with Tomatoes

Split Pigeon Peas
(Toor Dal) 351

Punjabi-Style Split Pigeon Peas

Falguni's Gujarati Split Pigeon Peas

Crispy Split Pigeon Pea Cake

Basic South Indian Soupy
Split Pigeon Peas

Hazram's Soupy Pigeon Peas

Madras-Style Pigeon Peas
with Vegetables

Split Pigeon Peas
with Coconut and Vegetables

Soupy Split Pigeon Peas
with Jaggery

Urad Beans
(Urad Dal) 357

White Urad Beans
with Fresh Lemon Juice

White Urad Beans
with Roasted Fenugreek Leaves

Spicy Split Black Urad Beans
with Split Chickpeas

Stir-Fried Black Urad Beans

Kashmiri Fennel-Flavored
Black Urad Beans with Yogurt

Punjabi Black Urad Beans

Smoked Black Urad Beans

Black Urad Beans in a Slow Cooker

Split Chickpeas and Split Peas (*Channa Dal* and *Muttar Dal*) 363

Yellow Split Chickpeas
with Spinach

Yellow Split Chickpeas
with Opo Squash

Dry-Cooked Green Split Peas

Garlicky Dried Green Peas Curry

Spicy Dried Yellow Peas

Mixed Beans and Lentils 366

Spicy Mixed 5 Beans and Lentils

Rajasthani Mixed 5 Beans
and Lentils

Parsi Mixed Lentils, Beans,
and Vegetables

Split Urad Beans and Yellow Split
Chickpeas with Spinach

Whole Dried Bean Dishes 369

Spicy Adzuki Beans

Mustard-Roasted Adzuki Beans

Classic No-Onion
Kidney Bean Curry

Classic Kidney Bean Curry
with Onions

Kashmiri Small Red Beans

Punjabi Red Beans
with Mango Pickle Masala

Black Beans
in Traditional Curry Sauce

Curried Black-Eyed Peas

Black-Eyed Peas in Yogurt Curry

Small White Beans
with Indian Spices

Spicy Soybeans in Yogurt Sauce

Whole Chickpea Dishes 377

Chickpeas with Ginger,
Garlic, and Chaat Masala

Spicy Chickpeas
with Pomegranate Seeds

Pickle-Flavored Chickpeas

Chickpeas with Spinach
and Potato Wedges

Chickpeas in
Traditional Curry Sauce

Chutney Chickpeas with Tamarind

Canister Chickpeas
(or Dried Yellow Peas)

Fresh Green Chickpeas
with Lentil Nuggets

Black Chickpeas with Sizzling
Ginger and Cumin Seeds

Black Chickpeas
with Chickpea Masala

Dried beans, lentils, and peas (the legumes collectively called *dal*) are always a major part of the Indian meal. They are nutritious, filling, and so versatile—there are literally thousands of ways to prepare them. To Indians, they are integral to our very existence and delicious—they are our staples and our comfort foods. They are served year-round and some families even cook them twice a day.

Varying in size from a few millimeters to that of a dime, *dals* are life-giving powerhouses of dietary fiber, carbohydrates, protein, minerals, and vitamins, and are quite low in fat. However, their protein lacks some of the essential amino acids. For a complete protein, they must be combined or served alongside other protein-rich whole grains, meats, eggs, breads, nuts, yogurt or other milk products—a fact that Indians discovered centuries ago because in India, *dals* are always served with some form of flatbread, such as *chapatis* (whole-wheat griddle breads), *paranthas* (griddle-fried breads), or *poories* (puffed deep-fried breads), or with rice.

Dal dishes come in many forms—thin and soupy, like the everyday *sambar* (Basic South Indian Soupy Split Pigeon Peas, page 353), thick and creamy like Punjabi Black Urad Beans (page 360), or dry-cooked like rice pilafs such as Sindhi Dry-Cooked Yellow Mung Beans (page 346). *Dals* can be hearty, rich, and complex centerpiece entrées, or just comforting, humble affairs, meant to keep body and soul together until the next meal.

Indian home cooks generally begin making a meal with *dal*, and everything else simply follows.

The importance of *dals* and whole beans in the cuisine, however, also stems from the mind-boggling variety of them found in India. All dried beans, lentils, and peas fall under the *dal* umbrella in India, but classification depends on the size: all the smaller varieties of whole legumes are called *dal*; larger legume varieties generally go by their individual Indian names, such as kidney beans, chickpeas, or dried peas. When the larger ones are milled and split into smaller pieces, they then also classify as a *dal*—for example split chickpea *dal* and split pea *dal*.

Different parts of the country favor some over others—the north favoring mung beans (*mung dal*), black urad beans (*urad dal*) and chickpeas (*channa dal*), and the south, pigeon peas (*toor dal*) and red lentils (*masoor dal*). As even Indian cooks do these days, I use a pressure cooker to speed preparing these dishes, as you'll see in the recipes. This makes it easy to incorporate *dals* into everyday meals.

Types of Beans, Peas, and Lentils

There are many forms of *dals* (legumes) used in India—whole, split, split with skin, skinned—you name it. Each variety and sub-variety is matched to specific preparations.

Most *dals* keep well for a long time if stored in air-tight containers in a cool, dark place—just be very sure to keep out all moisture. Don't use a damp or moist cup or hands to remove any *dal* from the container. For best long-term care, you can throw a bay leaf or cinnamon stick into your *dal* container; it will add flavor and keep bugs away. If you stick to these rules, your *dals* may well keep indefinitely. That's why Indian cooks always have many different kinds of *dals* in their pantry. That way they are all available, whether to make an entrée focusing on one *dal*, or to just use a tablespoon to enrich a dish.

Here is an introduction to the various Indian *dals* and beans I use. I list first all the smaller *dals* and then the larger whole beans, from the most common to the less common. I refer first to the Indian name, then the English name. For each *dal* form, I then describe it in English and provide the Indian and the English-Indian hybrid names you may see. All *dals* are available in Indian and some ethnic markets.

Mung Dal

Mung beans or green gram. This *dal* is one of the most basic in northern India. Small, kidney-shaped, and with a green skin, this *dal* is available as whole green mung beans with skin on (*saabut mung* or green mung *dal*), green split mung beans with skin on (*chilkae vaali mung*), and yellow skinned and split mung beans (*dhulli mung* or yellow mung *dal*). All these are considered easy to digest, especially the skinless yellow variety.

The yellow skinned and split mung beans (dhulli mung) are often ground into a flour that is used to make a variety of savory dishes, treats, and snacks.

Masoor, Malika Massoor, or Massar Dal

Lentils. These familiar green-brown discs come in two sizes, with the common American variety being larger then the Indian ones. Both can be used interchangeably. This *dal* is available as green-brown whole lentils with the skin on (*saabut masoor*), red whole lentils without the skin, or red skinned and split lentils (*dhulli masoor* or red masoor *dal*). Like mung *dal*, they cook fast and digest easily. In fact, yellow mung and red lentils are often cooked together, because they cook in the same amount of time.

Toor, Tuar, Arhar Dal

Pigeon peas or red gram. These pale green whole beans are available more commonly as yellow-gold discs split and without the skin. They are very popular all over India, especially in the southern parts and along the west coast, where they lend themselves to a variety of preparations. Sold primarily in Indian markets as plain or oiled (to prevent infestation, which is more prevalent for this bean than others), both are essentially the same and can be used interchangeably. Like the mung and masoor *dals*, they are easy to cook and easy on the stomach.

Channa, Chola Dal

Yellow split chickpeas or split Bengal gram. This *dal* is very similar in appearance to yellow split peas, but is actually made from black chickpeas. Considered somewhat harder to digest, this *dal* is always cooked with something carminative (gas-reducing)—ginger, garlic, ground asafoetida, or ajwain seeds.

Urad, Maas, Maanh Dal

Urad beans or black gram. These small, dull-black beans resemble green mung *dal* in appearance. They are available as black whole urad beans (*saabut urad* or black urad dal), as black split urad beans with skin on (*chilkae vaali urad* or split black urad dal) and as white skinned and split urad beans (*dhulli urad* or white urad dal). Considered hardest to digest among the *dals*, this *dal* takes a long time to soften and to digest and because of its dense nature, and often calls for a lot of spices and flavorings.

Like yellow split and skinned mung beans, skinless white urad beans (*urad dal*) are often ground into a flour and used to make a variety of savories, treats, and snacks.

Moth, Muth Dal

Dew beans. These are a duller and much smaller version of whole green mung beans (*saabut mung*). They are available primarily in Indian stores. Sold whole and with skin, this *dal* is popularly used to prepare *chaats* (snack dishes with savory, tangy, and spicy flavors) and salads, such as Spicy Dew Bean Salad (page 208), or crunchy savory munchies like *dal-muth* (pronounced *moath*), which are hot and spicy chip-like munchies found packaged at Indian markets.

Sookhae Muttar and Muttar Ki Dal

Dried peas and green and yellow split peas. Mutter *dal* is available whole or split without the skin. The whole ones are simply called dried green peas or *sookhae muttar*, and are cooked like black-eyed peas (lobia). When split, they are treated more like a *dal*. Yellow split peas are made from mature green peas (the vegetable) that turn yellow before they are dried and made into a *dal*.

All these varieties are relatively easy to digest and lend themselves to an array of preparations, but are mostly prepared as *chaats* (snack dishes with savory, tangy, and spicy flavors), salads, and savory munchies.

Chori Dal

Adzuki beans. These reddish-brown beans, slightly bigger than mung beans, are available in Indian and Asian stores, whole with skin on. Often prepared simply with a few spices, this *dal* cooks similarly to green whole mung beans and is quite easily digested.

Lobia

Black-eyed peas or cow peas. Not quite as easily digested, *lobia* must be cooked well and for a long time with carminative (gas-reducing) spices—ginger, garlic, ground asafoetida, or ajwain seeds.

Raajma

Kidney or red beans. These are available everywhere in supermarkets and Indian markets. There is also another variety called *chitree vaalae raajma,* which is similar to pinto beans. I also include red beans and Mexican black beans in this category because they cook and taste like *raajma,* and take on Indian flavors very well. All these beans can be used interchangeably.

Channae, Cholae

Chickpeas, garbanzo beans, or Bengal gram. These come as small or large tan heart-shaped beans or black heart-shaped beans. The tan chickpeas are easily available everywhere—both dried and pre-cooked and canned. The black variety are usually only sold in Indian markets. They are harder to digest than most other beans, but the black variety is considered to be far more nutritious than its tan counterpart. I frequently use canned chickpeas because they are so convenient.

Soyabeans Bhatmas

Soy beans. These beans are pale yellow and look like dried yellow peas, although they are not perfectly round. They are commonly grown in the United States, but Americans don't eat them much. They are only gaining in popularity as it becomes more apparent that soy is beneficial to health. Look for them in Indian markets and health food stores, and cook them as you would chickpeas and kidney beans.

To Cook Dried Beans, Lentils, and Peas

Before you start to cook, place the *dals* (of any variety or form) in a large bowl and wash them in 3 to 4 changes of water. All the husks and hollow grains float to the top and can be poured out with the water. This does not happen if you wash them in a fine-mesh strainer under running water.

Then cook them in a pressure cooker or saucepan. The smaller ones (such as mung beans and lentils) can be cooked in a saucepan, but for the larger beans (such as chickpeas or kidney beans), it's best to use a pressure cooker. Of course, these beans can be made without a pressure cooker, but the cooking time is greatly reduced with one. The newer models of pressure cookers, with their built-in safety features, are quite safe to use. (Read your instruction booklet; it will tell you how yours works.)

If you want to cook them in a saucepan, you can boil them continuously in 3 to 7 times the water until tender; start with 3 times the water and keep adding more as needed. The larger beans (such as chickpeas) will need more water than the smaller skinless *dals* (such as yellow mung beans), or you can soak them overnight in water to cover, then boil them until tender.

One other cooking method is to bring to a boil over high heat, turn off the heat and allow the beans to soak 1 to 2 hours. Then simmer over medium heat until the beans are soft.

All cooked beans stay fresh in the refrigerator about 5 days. Reheat with additional water in the microwave or over medium heat. For maximum flavor, reheat any previously cooked or leftover *dal* and then add a fresh *tarka* (sizzling flavor topping), which was used in the main recipe, just before serving.

A note about using *dals* as seasonings: *Dals* are also used as seasonings or to add texture to a dish. They are often processed with herbs and spices, or are simply dry-roasted before being added to a dish. They do not need to be soaked before being used in this way.

Mung Beans (Mung Dal)

Yellow Mung Beans with Sautéed Onion and Ginger
Dhulli Mungi ki Dal

Makes 4 to 6 servings

Yellow mung dal *is a hands-down favorite in northern India. Considered light and easy to digest, this quick-cooking* dal *is comfort food par excellence. It marries well with whole-wheat* chapatis *(whole-wheat griddle breads) and with rice—the two food staples of India.*

1 cup yellow mung beans (dhulli mung dal),
    sorted and washed in 3 to 4 changes of water
3$^{1}/_{2}$ to 4 cups water
3 to 5 whole fresh green chile peppers,
    such as serrano
$^{1}/_{4}$ teaspoon ground turmeric
$^{3}/_{4}$ teaspoon salt, or to taste
$^{1}/_{4}$ cup finely chopped fresh cilantro,
    including soft stems
2 tablespoons peanut or canola oil
1 teaspoon melted ghee (optional)
1 teaspoon cumin seeds
$^{1}/_{2}$ small onion, finely chopped
1 tablespoon peeled minced fresh ginger
1 tablespoon ground coriander
$^{1}/_{2}$ teaspoon ground cumin
$^{1}/_{4}$ teaspoon ground paprika
Freshly ground black pepper

1. Place the dal, 3½ cups water, green chile peppers, turmeric, and salt in a medium saucepan and bring to a boil over high heat. Reduce the heat to medium and cook the dal, uncovered, stirring occasionally and watching carefully that it doesn't boil over, about 10 minutes. Reduce the heat to low, add the remaining water, if needed, and simmer until the dal is soft and creamy, about 15 minutes. Mix in the cilantro during the last 5 minutes of cooking. Transfer to a serving bowl, cover, and keep warm.

2. Heat the oil (and the ghee, if using) in a small saucepan over medium-high heat and add the cumin seeds; they should sizzle upon contact with the hot oil. Quickly add the onion and cook, stirring, until golden, about 1 minute. Add the ginger and cook another minute. Then add the coriander and cumin and stir about 30 seconds. Remove the pan from the heat and add the paprika. Immediately pour the tarka over the warm dal and swirl lightly to mix, with parts of it visible as a garnish. Top with black pepper and serve.

Garlicky Yellow Mung Beans with Zucchini Wheels

Zucchini vaali Dhulli Mung Dal

Makes 4 to 6 servings

I generally make my yellow mung dal in a pan and not in a pressure cooker. But here is a pressure cooker recipe for those who want to speed up cooking.

It is quite customary to toss a vegetable or two into the dal as it cooks. Here, I add mild-tasting zucchini, which, along with mung dal, is considered light and easy to digest. On occasion, I've added white watermelon rind (used in India) or radishes, and they also worked very well.

1 tablespoon Basic Ginger-Garlic Paste (page 47 or store-bought)
1 cup yellow mung beans (dhulli mung dal), sorted and washed in 3 to 4 changes of water
3 to 3¹/₂ cups water

3 to 4 small zucchini, cut into ³/₄-inch slices
1 fresh green chile pepper, such as serrano, minced with seeds
2 black cardamom pods, crushed lightly to break the skin
1 (1-inch) stick cinnamon
¹/₄ teaspoon ground turmeric
³/₄ teaspoon salt, or to taste
1 tablespoon fresh lime juice
2 tablespoons peanut oil
1 teaspoon cumin seeds
1 small onion, cut in half lengthwise and thinly sliced
1 tablespoon peeled minced fresh ginger
1 tablespoon ground coriander
¹/₂ teaspoon ground cumin
¹/₄ teaspoon ground paprika
2 tablespoons finely chopped cilantro
¹/₄ teaspoon garam masala

1. Prepare the ginger-garlic paste. Then, place the dal, water, zucchini, ginger-garlic paste, green chile pepper, cardamom pods, cinnamon, turmeric, and salt in a pressure cooker. Secure the lid and cook the over high heat until the regulator to indicates high pressure, then cook about 30 seconds. Remove from the heat and allow the pot to depressurize on its own, 12 to 15 minutes. Carefully remove the lid, mix in the lime juice, and transfer to a serving bowl. Cover the bowl and keep warm.

2. To make the tarka, heat the oil in a small saucepan over medium-high heat and add the cumin seeds; they should sizzle upon contact with the hot oil. Quickly add the onion and cook, stirring, until golden, about 2 minutes. Then add the minced ginger, stir a few seconds and add the coriander and cumin and stir about 30 seconds.

3. Remove the pan from the heat, add the paprika, and immediately pour over the hot dal and swirl lightly to mix, with parts of it visible as a garnish. Sprinkle the cilantro and garam masala on top and serve.

Yellow Mung Beans with Fresh Curry Leaves

South ki Mung Dal

Makes 4 to 6 servings

Yellow mung dal takes on an intriguing change of taste and flavor when we give it a tarka *(a sizzling flavor topping) of mustard seeds, asafoetida, and fresh curry leaves—the classic south Indian seasonings. With a little more water than other mung bean dishes, this is a soupier* dal—*good for serving with rice, the favored south Indian staple grain. (The northerners prefer whole-wheat.)*

1 cup yellow mung beans (dhulli mung dal),
    sorted and washed in 3 to 4 changes of water

3¹/₂ to 4 cups water

¹/₄ teaspoon ground turmeric

³/₄ teaspoon salt, or to taste

¹/₄ cup finely chopped fresh cilantro,
    including soft stems

2 tablespoons peanut or canola oil

1 teaspoon ghee (optional)

4 to 6 whole dried red chile peppers,
    such as chile de arbol

1 teaspoon black mustard seeds

¹/₂ teaspoon cumin seeds

2 tablespoons minced fresh curry leaves

¹/₂ teaspoon ground fenugreek seeds

¹/₈ teaspoon ground asafoetida

¹/₄ teaspoon ground paprika

1. Place the dal, 3½ cups water, turmeric, and salt in a medium saucepan and bring to a boil over high heat. Reduce the heat to medium and cook the dal, uncovered, stirring occasionally and watching carefully that it doesn't boil over, about 10 minutes. Reduce the heat to low, add the remaining ½ cup water, and simmer until the dal is soft and creamy, about 15 minutes. Mix in the cilantro during the last 5 minutes of cooking. Remove to a serving bowl, cover, and keep warm.

2. Heat the oil (and the ghee, if using) in a small nonstick saucepan over medium heat and cook the red chile peppers, stirring, about 30 seconds (stand

back in case they burst). Add the mustard and cumin seeds; they should splutter upon contact with the hot oil, so lower the heat and cover the pan until the spluttering subsides. Add the curry leaves, fenugreek seeds, and asafoetida, and cook about 1 minute. Remove from heat, add the paprika and immediately pour the tarka over the warm dal. Swirl lightly to mix, with parts of it visible as a garnish. Serve.

Roasted Yellow Mung Beans and Potatoes

Bhuni Mung Dal aur Aalu

Makes 4 to 6 servings

Flavored strongly with mustard oil and kalonji seeds, this typical Bengali-style soupy dal *with potatoes is perfect over steamed short-grain rice.*

1 tablespoon mustard oil

1 cup yellow mung beans (dhulli mung dal),
    sorted and washed in 3 to 4 changes of water

1 large russet potato (or any kind), peeled and
    cut into ¹/₂-inch pieces

4 to 4¹/₂ cups water

1 teaspoon salt, or to taste

¹/₄ teaspoon cayenne pepper, or to taste

¹/₄ teaspoon ground turmeric

1 to 3 teaspoons sugar

1 to 2 tablespoons fresh lemon juice

¹/₄ cup finely chopped fresh cilantro,
    including soft stems

1 tablespoon vegetable oil

1 teaspoon cumin seeds

¹/₂ teaspoon kalonji seeds

1 large clove fresh garlic, minced

¹/₈ teaspoon ground asafoetida

1. Heat the mustard oil in a large nonstick wok or saucepan over medium-high heat and roast the dal and potato, stirring and shaking the pan, until the dal is golden, about 3 minutes.

2. Add 4 cups water, salt, cayenne pepper, and turmeric and bring to a boil over high heat. Reduce the heat to medium and cook the dal, stirring occasionally and watching carefully that it doesn't boil over, about 10 minutes. Reduce the heat to low, add the remaining ½ cup water, and simmer until the dal is soft and creamy, about 15 minutes. Mix in the sugar, lemon juice, and cilantro, and transfer to a serving dish. Cover and keep warm.

3. Heat the vegetable oil in a small nonstick saucepan over medium-high heat and add the cumin and kalonji seeds; they should sizzle upon contact with the hot oil. Quickly add the garlic and asafoetida, stir a few seconds, and add to the dal. Swirl lightly to mix, with parts of it visible as a garnish. Serve.

Punjabi Dry-Cooked Yellow Mung Beans

Sookhi Dhulli Mung Dal

Makes 4 to 6 servings

This typical Punjabi dry-cooked dal—similar to a rice pilaf, with each grain soft and fluffy, yet separate— can be presented as a warm salad, especially if you fold in some finely chopped ripe, firm tomatoes, and seedless cucumbers.

Try this dal as a stuffing for samosas (deep-fried triangular pastries), paranthas (griddle-fried breads), and hollowed-out vegetables such as bell peppers, tomatoes, bitter melons, and zucchinis.

1 cup yellow mung beans (dhulli mung dal), sorted and washed in 3 to 4 changes of water
2 cups water
¼ teaspoon ground turmeric
½ teaspoon salt, or to taste
¼ cup finely chopped cilantro, including soft stems
½ teaspoon mango powder
2 tablespoons canola oil or melted ghee
1 teaspoon cumin seeds
1 small onion, cut in half lengthwise and thinly sliced
1 tablespoon peeled minced fresh ginger
1 fresh green chile pepper, such as serrano, minced with seeds
1 small tomato, coarsely chopped
1 tablespoon ground coriander
½ teaspoon ground paprika
¼ teaspoon garam masala

1. Soak the dal in water to cover by 2 inches, about 2 hours. Drain and transfer to a medium saucepan. Add the water, turmeric, and salt and bring to a boil over high heat. Reduce the heat to medium-low and cook, stirring once or twice, until the dal is soft and all the water has been absorbed, 10 to 12 minutes. Very gently, trying not to break the dal, mix in the cilantro and mango powder. Transfer to a serving dish, cover, and keep warm.

2. To make the tarka, heat the oil (or ghee) over medium-high heat and add the cumin seeds; they should sizzle upon contact with the hot ghee. Quickly add the onion and cook, stirring, until golden, 2 to 3 minutes. Add the ginger and green chile pepper, then add the tomato and cook, stirring, until the tomato is slightly soft, about 1 minute. Add the coriander and paprika and stir about 30 seconds. Transfer to the dal and swirl lightly to mix, with parts of it visible as a garnish, sprinkle the garam masala on top, and serve.

Sindhi Dry-Cooked Yellow Mung Beans

Sindhi Sookhi Mung Dal

Makes 4 to 6 servings

Here is a dal dish I remember eating at my Sindhi friend's home in New Delhi. The Sindhi people generally add a lot of tomatoes and onions to their dishes—both cooked and raw, as in this dish, which also has fresh green chile peppers. Serve it as a salad, or top it with any green chutney and chaat masala and call it a chaat (a snack with layers of tangy, spicy flavors).

1 cup yellow mung beans (dhulli mung dal),
    sorted and washed in 3 to 4 changes of water
2 cups water
1/4 teaspoon ground turmeric
1/2 teaspoon salt, or to taste
1/2 teaspoon mango powder
3 tablespoons finely chopped cilantro,
    including soft stems
1 large tomato, finely chopped
1/2 small onion, finely chopped
1 fresh green chile pepper, such as serrano,
    minced with seeds
2 tablespoons vegetable oil or melted ghee
1 teaspoon cumin seeds
1 tablespoon ground coriander
1/4 teaspoon cayenne pepper, or ground paprika

1. Soak the dal in water to cover by 2 inches, about 2 hours. Drain and transfer to a medium saucepan. Add the water, turmeric, and salt and cook over medium-high heat, stirring once or twice, until the dal is soft and all the water has been absorbed, 10 to 12 minutes.

2. Very carefully, trying not to break the dal, mix in the mango powder and cilantro, then transfer to a serving dish. Scatter the tomato, onion, and green chile pepper over the dal and mix lightly with a fork.

3. Heat the oil (or ghee) over medium-high heat and add the cumin seeds; they should sizzle upon contact with the hot oil. Quickly add the coriander and cayenne pepper (or paprika), pour over the dal, and serve.

Spicy Dry-Cooked Split Green Mung Beans

Chilkae vaali Mung Dal

Makes 4 to 6 servings

Split mung dal with its green skin on, makes a delicious fiber-rich entrée with a side of okra, cauliflower, or eggplant, and a yogurt raita, and also works well as a stuffing for snacks and vegetables, especially hollowed out cherry tomatoes.

    This dal, with its green skin, is a little harder than the skinless yellow mung dal, so I first soak it in water to tenderize it and then cook it in a saucepan. (If using a pressure cooker, the dal needs no soaking.)

1 1/2 cups split green mung beans (chilkae vaali mung
    dal), sorted and washed in 3 to 4 changes of water
2 tablespoons vegetable oil
1 1/2 teaspoons cumin seeds
1 (1-inch) stick cinnamon
3 black cardamom pods, crushed lightly
    to break the skin
2 tablespoons peeled and finely chopped fresh ginger
1 to 3 fresh green chile peppers, such as serrano,
    minced with seeds
2 large tomatoes, finely chopped
1 tablespoon ground coriander
1 teaspoon dried fenugreek leaves
1/2 teaspoon ground cumin
1/4 teaspoon ground turmeric
1/8 teaspoon ground asafoetida
3/4 teaspoon salt, or to taste
3 1/2 to 4 cups water
Fresh lime juice, to taste
1/2 cup finely chopped fresh cilantro,
    including soft stems
1/4 cup finely chopped scallions, white parts only
1/4 teaspoon garam masala

1. Soak the dal in water to cover by 2 inches, about 2 hours. Drain. Heat the oil in a medium saucepan over medium-high heat. Add the cumin seeds, cinnamon, and cardamom pods; they should sizzle upon contact with the hot oil. Quickly add the ginger, green chile peppers, and tomatoes and stir about 1 minute.

2. Add the coriander, fenugreek leaves, cumin, turmeric, asafoetida, and salt, then add the dal plus all the water. Bring to a boil over high heat, then reduce the heat to medium-low, cover the pan, and cook until all the water has been absorbed and the dal is tender, about 30 minutes. Add extra water, if needed. Mix in the lime juice, cilantro, and scallions, transfer to a serving dish, sprinkle the garam masala on top, and serve.

Gujarati Green Mung Beans with Green Masala Paste
Gujarati Hara Masala Saabut Mung Dal

Makes 4 to 6 servings

Hara masala—*a green spice paste made of finely ground ginger, garlic, and green chile peppers*—*is almost indispensable to my Gujarati friend Naina Kapadia's cooking, and this* dal *preparation is no exception.*

Whole mung beans with their green skin on take over an hour if cooked in an ordinary pan, so to speed up the process Indian cooks routinely make this dal *(and most others, with or without the skin) in a pressure cooker.*

1½ teaspoons Gujarati Green Paste (page 48)
1¼ cups green mung beans (saabut mung dal), sorted and washed in 3 to 4 changes of water
4½ to 5 cups water
½ teaspoon ground turmeric
1 teaspoon salt, or to taste
2 tablespoons peanut oil
4 to 6 dried red chile peppers, such as chile de arbol, broken
⅛ teaspoon ground asafoetida
¼ teaspoon garam masala
2 tablespoons finely chopped fresh cilantro

1. Prepare the masala paste. Then, place the dal, water, masala paste, turmeric, and salt in a pressure cooker. Secure the lid of the pressure cooker and cook it over high heat until the regulator indicates high pressure, then cook about 30 seconds more. Remove the pot from the heat and allow to depressurize on its own, 12 to 15 minutes. Carefully open the lid and

check to see if the dal is very soft and creamy; if not, cover and simmer until soft, about 10 minutes. Transfer to a serving dish, cover, and keep warm.

2. Heat the oil in a small nonstick saucepan over medium-high heat, add the red chile peppers and cook, stirring, until they are a few shades darker. (If using the chiles whole, stand back from the pan in case they burst.) Remove from the heat, add the asafoetida, then lightly mix into the dal, with parts of it visible as a garnish. Sprinkle the garam masala and cilantro on top and serve.

Punjabi Green Mung Beans with Sizzling Ginger
Punjabi Saabut Mung Dal

Makes 4 to 6 servings

Indians, especially the Punjabis, love the sharp bite of fresh ginger. They add it to dishes on the spur-of-the-moment dictates of their palate—raw or cooked, in large chunks or in smaller pieces, cut long and thin, minced or ground, and sometimes a little of each. If you like ginger, this is your dish.

1 cup green mung beans (saabut mung dal), sorted and washed in 3 to 4 changes of water
4½ to 5 cups water
2 nickel-size slices peeled fresh ginger
1 tablespoon peeled and minced (or ground) fresh ginger
1 to 3 fresh green chile peppers, such as serrano, minced with seeds
1 teaspoon salt, or to taste
¼ teaspoon ground turmeric
¼ teaspoon hot red pepper flakes, or to taste
2 tablespoons peanut oil
1 (1-inch) piece fresh ginger, peeled and cut into thin matchsticks
1 teaspoon cumin seeds
1 small onion, finely chopped
1 large tomato, coarsely chopped
1 tablespoon ground coriander
½ teaspoon ground cumin
¼ teaspoon paprika
¼ teaspoon garam masala

1. Place the dal, water, ginger slices, minced or ground ginger, green chile peppers, salt, turmeric, and red pepper flakes in a pressure cooker. Secure the lid and cook over high heat until the regulator indicates high pressure, then cook 30 seconds more. Remove from the heat and allow the pot to depressurize on its own, 12 to 15 minutes. Carefully open the lid and stir the dal; it should be very soft and creamy. If not, simmer over medium heat until done. Remove to a serving dish, cover, and keep warm.

2. Heat the oil in a small nonstick saucepan over medium heat and cook the ginger matchsticks until golden, about 2 minutes. Add the cumin seeds; they should sizzle upon contact with the hot oil. Quickly add the onion and cook, stirring, until golden, about 2 minutes. Add the tomato and cook until soft, about 2 minutes.

3. Stir in the coriander, cumin, and paprika, then transfer to the dal and swirl lightly, with bits of it visible as a garnish. Sprinkle the garam masala on top and serve.

Lentils (Masoor Dal)

Dry-Cooked Red Lentils with Cumin Seeds
Sookhi Dhulli Masoor Dal

Makes 4 to 6 servings

This lentil dish, more like a rice pilaf than a soup, is made with pre-soaked whole red lentils (split red ones are fine, too). For a vivid color presentation, I throw in some beets, but avoid turmeric (which is usually a must in dal dishes), because it colors everything yellow.

Serve with a soft-cooked vegetable side dish, such as a bhartha (a mashed eggplant dish, pages 263 to 264), or a squash, such as Quick Spicy Opo Squash (page 277), or present it atop lettuce leaves as a salad.

1 cup red lentils (dhulli masoor dal), sorted and
    washed in 3 to 4 changes of water
2 cups water
1/4 cup cooked and minced fresh or drained canned beets
2 tablespoons vegetable oil
3 to 5 dried red chile peppers, such as chile de arbol
1 1/2 teaspoons cumin seeds
1 tablespoon peeled minced fresh ginger
2 teaspoons ground coriander
1/2 teaspoon ground cumin
1/2 teaspoon garam masala
1/2 teaspoon salt, or to taste
1/4 cup finely chopped cilantro, including soft stems
1 tablespoon fresh lime or lemon juice
4 scallions, finely sliced

1. Place the dal, water, and beets in a bowl and allow to soak about 2 hours or longer.

2. Heat the oil in a medium nonstick saucepan over medium-high heat and cook the red chile peppers until golden, about 1 minute. (Stand away from the pan, in case they burst.) Add the cumin seeds; they should sizzle upon contact with the hot oil. Quickly add the ginger and stir, about 1 minute.

3. Add the coriander, cumin, garam masala, and then mix in the dal plus all the water, and the salt, and cook over high heat until the water evaporates and the dal is

tender, about 5 minutes. Stir a few times with a fork just to fluff it, taking care not to break the dal.

4. With a fork, gently mix in the cilantro and lime juice, cover the pan, and set over low heat about 2 minutes to blend the flavors. Transfer to a serving dish, lightly mix in the scallions, and serve.

Red Lentils with Bengali 5-Spices
Bengali Dhulli Masoor Dal

Makes 4 to 6 servings

Bengali 5-Spices (Panch-Phoran), is a blend of 5 seeds—black mustard, cumin, fenugreek, kalonji, and fennel. They are sizzled in hot oil so the seeds release their true flavors and make the foods very fragrant. This is the standard Bengali seasoning. Make the blend (page 27) or buy it from an Indian market.

1 tablespoon Basic Ginger-Garlic Paste
    (page 47 or store-bought)
2 teaspoons Bengali 5-Spices (Panch-Phoran),
    page 27 or store-bought
1 cup red lentils (dhulli masoor dal), sorted and
    washed in 3 to 4 changes of water
4¹/₂ cups water
¹/₄ teaspoon ground turmeric
³/₄ teaspoon salt, or to taste
1 small onion, finely chopped
1 fresh green chile pepper, such as serrano,
    minced with seeds
1 tablespoon ground coriander
¹/₂ teaspoon ground cumin
¹/₄ teaspoon ground paprika or cayenne pepper
1 to 2 teaspoon sugar
2 tablespoons mustard or peanut oil
4 to 6 whole dried red chile peppers,
    such as chile de arbol

1. Prepare the ginger-garlic paste and the 5-spices mixture. Then, place the dal, water, turmeric, and salt in a medium saucepan and bring to a boil over high heat. Reduce the heat to medium and cook the dal, stirring occasionally and watching carefully that it doesn't boil over, about 10 minutes.

2. Add the onion, ginger-garlic paste, green chile pepper, coriander, cumin, paprika (or cayenne pepper),

and sugar, reduce the heat to low, and simmer until the dal is soft and creamy, about 15 minutes. Remove to a serving dish, cover, and keep warm.

3. Heat the oil in a small saucepan over medium-high heat and cook the red chile peppers, stirring, about 30 seconds (stand back in case they burst). Then add the panch-phoran; they should sizzle upon contact with the hot oil. Immediately, pour over the hot dal and swirl lightly to mix, with parts of it visible as a garnish, and serve.

Green Lentils with Sautéed Onion
Saabut Masoor Dal

Makes 4 to 6 servings

Even to the most fussy and unadventurous palates, the introduction of Indian spices opens up a whole new range of tastes that are subsequently difficult to ignore. This particular recipe—similar to the lentil soup of many cultures, is the perfect way to introduce a novice to Indian food. Westerners will notice the absence of flavor from the ham-bone (unthinkable in India, except to a small minority of Christians), yet will be pleasantly surprised by new, complex, and delicious flavors.

1¹/₄ cups green lentils (saabut masoor dal),
    sorted and washed in 3 to 4 changes of water
4 to 4¹/₂ cups water
1 (1-inch) stick cinnamon
2 black or 4 green cardamom pods, crushed lightly
    to break the skin
1 large clove fresh garlic, coarsely chopped
¹/₄ teaspoon ground turmeric
¹/₄ teaspoon cayenne pepper, or to taste
1 teaspoon salt, or to taste
2 tablespoons peanut oil
1 teaspoon cumin seeds
1 medium onion, finely chopped
1¹/₂ tablespoons peeled minced fresh ginger
1 fresh green chile pepper, such as serrano,
    minced with seeds
1¹/₂ tablespoons ground coriander
¹/₂ teaspoon ground cumin
¹/₂ teaspoon ground paprika
¹/₄ teaspoon garam masala

1. Place the dal, water, cinnamon, cardamom pods, garlic, turmeric, cayenne pepper, and salt in a pressure cooker. Secure the lid and cook over high heat until the regulator indicates high pressure, then cook 30 seconds more. Remove from the heat and allow the pot to depressurize on its own, 12 to 15 minutes. Carefully open the lid and check to see if the beans are very soft and some of them are broken; if not, cover, bring up to high pressure again, and cook another 30 seconds. Or cover and boil until soft, about 30 minutes more. Remove to a serving dish, cover, and keep warm.

2. Heat the oil in a small nonstick saucepan over medium-high heat and add the cumin seeds; they should sizzle upon contact with the hot oil. Quickly add the onion and cook, stirring, until golden, about 3 minutes. Add the ginger and green chile pepper and cook about 1 minute, then add the coriander, cumin, and paprika and stir a few seconds. Transfer to the dal and swirl lightly to mix, with parts of it visible as a garnish. Sprinkle the garam masala on top and serve.

Variation: For a different flavor, try this recipe using green mung dal instead of the lentils. (Both these dals are interchangeable in most recipes.)

Roasted Green Lentils with Tomatoes
Bhunni Saabut Masoor Dal

Makes 4 to 6 servings

With just one tablespoon of oil and a whole lot of flavor, this dish is an excellent choice for those who are watching their fat intake. For an authentic presentation, use the small-grained Indian or French varieties of green lentils. However, even the regular brown lentils sold in supermarkets, as well as green mung dal, work well in this recipe.

1¼ cups green lentils (saabut masoor dal), sorted and washed in 3 to 4 changes of water
1 tablespoon mustard oil
4 whole dried red chile peppers, such as chile de arbol
½ teaspoon garam masala
¼ teaspoon ground fenugreek seeds
⅛ teaspoon ground asafoetida
2 tablespoons peeled minced fresh ginger
1½ teaspoons minced garlic
1 fresh green chile peppers, such as serrano, minced with seeds
1 tablespoon ground coriander
½ teaspoon ground paprika
4½ to 5 cups water
¾ teaspoon salt, or to taste
2 medium tomatoes, coarsely chopped
¼ cup finely chopped fresh cilantro, including soft stems

1. Place the dal in a large nonstick saucepan and stir over medium heat until dry. Add the oil, red chile peppers, garam masala, fenugreek, and asafoetida and cook, stirring, until the dal is golden, about 3 minutes. Reduce the heat if too much smoke arises. Add the ginger, garlic, green chile pepper, coriander, and paprika and stir another 5 minutes.

2. Add the water and salt and bring to a boil over high heat. Reduce the heat to low, cover the pan, and cook, stirring occasionally, until the dal is soft and creamy, about 1 hour, adding more water if it dries too quickly. Mix in the tomatoes and cook until they are quite soft, about 5 minutes. Transfer to a serving dish, mix in the cilantro, and serve.

Split Pigeon Peas (Toor Dal)

Punjabi-Style Split Pigeon Peas
Punjabi Toor Dal

Makes 4 to 6 servings

The Punjabis make their toor dal just as they would their yellow mung dal, with a tarka (a sizzling flavor topping) of cumin and coriander. The curry leaves, though not a common addition in the north, do add a lot of flavor, and nowadays more and more Punjabi families use them.

1¹/₂ cups split pigeon peas (toor dal), sorted and washed in 3 to 4 changes of water
4 to 4¹/₂ cups water
1 teaspoon salt
¹/₄ teaspoon ground turmeric
1 to 2 tablespoon fresh lime or lemon juice, or to taste
2 tablespoons vegetable oil
1 small onion, finely chopped
1 to 2 tablespoons minced fresh curry leaves
1 fresh green chile pepper, such as serrano, minced with seeds
1 teaspoon cumin seeds
1 tablespoon peeled minced fresh ginger
1 tablespoon ground coriander
¹/₂ teaspoon ground cumin
¹/₂ teaspoon ground paprika
Finely chopped fresh cilantro

1. Place the dal in a large saucepan and add water, salt, and turmeric. Bring to a boil over high heat. Reduce the heat to low, cover the saucepan (partially at first, then completely), and cook, stirring occasionally, until the dal is creamy, 35 to 40 minutes. As the dal cooks, some of it may foam and rise to the top. Stir the foam back into the dal. Mix in the lime juice and transfer to a serving dish. Cover and keep warm.

2. Heat the oil in a small saucepan and cook the onion, curry leaves and green chile pepper, stirring, until golden, about 2 minutes. Add the cumin seeds and

ginger and stir about 1 minute. Add the coriander, ground cumin, and paprika and stir about 1 minute, then transfer to the dal and swirl lightly to mix, with parts of it visible as a garnish. Top with the cilantro and serve.

Falguni's Gujarati Split Pigeon Peas
Falguni Ki Toor Dal

Makes 4 to 6 servings

Rarely is a Gujarati wedding or formal occasion complete without this traditional thin and soupy, yet captivating dal. It is flavored with sweet jaggery, known as gur (thickened sugar cane juice), tangy kokum (dried sour fruit of the magosteen-oil tree), and dried red chile peppers.

Jaggery and kokum, are available in Indian markets. My friend Falguni Jalota, who gave me this recipe, adds the asafoetida at 2 separate stages of cooking: first raw into the dal, and then after sizzling it in hot oil. Serve this dish with steamed rice or drink it as a soup.

1 cup split pigeon peas (toor dal), sorted and washed in 3 to 4 changes of water
6 cups water
4 pieces dried kokum halves, washed
2 tablespoons ground jaggery
1 tablespoon ground coriander
1 teaspoon ground cumin
¹/₂ teaspoon ground turmeric
¹/₄ teaspoon cayenne pepper, or to taste
¹/₄ teaspoon ground asafoetida
1 teaspoon salt, or to taste
3 large tomatoes, coarsely chopped
1 to 3 fresh green chile peppers, such as serrano, stemmed
6 to 8 quarter-size slices peeled fresh ginger
10 to 15 fresh curry leaves
¹/₄ cup finely chopped fresh cilantro
2 tablespoons vegetable oil
1 (1-inch) stick cinnamon
4 whole cloves
5 to 7 whole dried red chile peppers, such as chile de arbol
1 teaspoon black mustard seeds
1 teaspoon cumin seeds

1. Place the dal with 3 cups water in a large saucepan (not nonstick) and boil over high heat about 5 minutes. Reduce the heat to medium, cover the pan, and cook until the dal is very soft and broken, about 30 minutes. Let cool, then with an electric hand-held mixer, beat it on medium speed to make a smooth purée, about 1 minute. Mix in the remaining 3 cups water, kokum, jaggery, coriander, cumin, turmeric, cayenne pepper, half the asafetida, and salt.

2. In a food processor, process together the tomatoes, green chile peppers, ginger, and curry leaves to make a smooth purée, about 30 seconds, and add it to the dal.

3. Boil the soupy dal over high heat about 5 minutes, then reduce the heat to medium-low, cover the pan, and simmer the dal about 20 minutes. Transfer to a serving dish, mix in the cilantro, cover, and keep warm.

4. Heat the oil in a small saucepan over medium-high heat and cook the cinnamon, cloves, and red chile peppers about 30 seconds. Then add the mustard and cumin seeds, and the remaining ⅛ teaspoon asafetida; they should splutter upon contact with the hot oil, so lower the heat and cover the pan until the spluttering subsides. Transfer to the dal and swirl lightly to mix, with parts of it visible as a garnish. Serve.

Crispy Split Pigeon Pea Cake
Sookhi Toor Dal

Makes 4 to 6 servings

This toor dal dish, in the form of a savory upside down cake, is a specialty of my friend Sohini's family in south India. This dish uses very little water—just enough to cook the dal and then disappear—forming a thin crust at the bottom. Garnished with the southern Indian seasonings of mustard seeds, curry leaves, and asafoetida, this is a spectacular variation from an everyday dal dish.

1 cup split pigeon peas (toor dal), sorted and washed in 3 to 4 changes of water
1³/₄ cups water
¹/₂ teaspoon salt, or to taste
¹/₄ teaspoon ground turmeric
3 tablespoons peanut oil
2 dried red chile peppers, such as chile de arbol, broken
1 teaspoon black mustard seeds
¹/₈ teaspoon ground asafoetida
1 tablespoon dried curry leaves

1. Soak the dal in the water about 1 hour or longer. Transfer the dal and water to a small, nonstick saucepan, add the salt and turmeric, and bring to a boil over high heat. Reduce the heat to medium-low, cover the pan, and simmer until all water is absorbed.

2. Reduce the heat further and drizzle 2 tablespoons oil into the dal along the circumference of the pan. Cover and allow the dal to develop a thin crust at the bottom (do not stir), 30 to 40 minutes. With a rubber spatula lightly dislodge the edges, then invert the cake onto a serving platter.

3. Heat the remaining 1 tablespoon oil in a small nonstick saucepan. Add the red chile peppers and mustard seeds; they should splutter upon contact with the hot oil, so cover the pan and reduce the heat until the spluttering subsides. Add the asafoetida and curry leaves, stir a few seconds, then pour everything over the dal as a garnish. Serve.

Variation: For added flavor, mix finely chopped ginger, garlic, or cilantro into the dal in Step 1, while it cooks.

Basic South Indian
Soupy Split Pigeon Peas

Sambar

Makes 4 to 6 servings

Made in a pressure cooker, this is the most basic and popular sambar *recipe—just the* dal *with spices. It is certainly how northerners bring southern flavor to their tables.*

2 to 3 tablespoons Tamarind Paste (page 54)
2 tablespoons South Indian Sambar Powder
    (page 28 or store-bought)
1 cup split pigeon peas (toor dal), sorted and washed
    in 3 to 4 changes of water
4$^1/_2$ to 5 cups water
5 to 7 fresh green chile peppers, such as serrano
1 tablespoon minced fresh curry leaves
$^1/_4$ teaspoon ground turmeric
1 teaspoon salt, or to taste
$^1/_2$ cup finely chopped fresh cilantro,
    including soft stems
2 to 3 tablespoons peanut oil
8 to 10 whole dried red chile peppers,
    such as chile de arbol
1 small onion, finely chopped
1 tablespoon peeled minced fresh ginger
$^1/_4$ teaspoon ground asafoetida
1 teaspoon black mustard seeds
2 tablespoons finely chopped cilantro

1. Prepare the tamarind paste and the sambar powder. Then, place the dal, water, green chile peppers, curry leaves, turmeric, and salt in a pressure cooker. Secure the lid and cook over high heat until the regulator indicates high pressure, then cook 1 minute more. Remove from the heat and allow the pot to depressurize on its own, 12 to 15 minutes. Carefully open the lid and mix in the tamarind and cilantro. Stir vigorously to mash the dal, then transfer to a serving bowl, cover, and keep warm.

2. Heat the oil in a small nonstick saucepan over medium heat. Add the red chile peppers, stirring about 30 seconds (stand back in case they burst), then the onion, and cook, stirring, until lightly browned, about 5 minutes. Add the ginger, fry a few seconds, then add the asafoetida and mustard seeds; they should splutter upon contact with the hot oil, so lower the heat and cover the pan until the spluttering subsides. Add the sambar powder and cook, about 30 seconds. Transfer to the dal and swirl lightly to mix, with parts of it visible as a garnish. Top with the cilantro and serve.

South Indian Sambar

Made authentically with split pigeon peas *(toor dal)*, *sambar* (pronounced *saambar*) is to most south Indians what *mung dal* preparations are to the north Indians—frequently made, light, easily digested staples. Served mostly as a complement to rice and other south Indian specialties, such as *iddlis* (steamed fermented rice cakes) and *dosas* (griddle-fried, fermented rice and lentil crepes), *sambars* are meant to be soupy, spicy hot, tangy soups—with different communities adding their unique subtleties.

You begin *sambars* by first cooking the pigeon peas until they are very soft. Then a core blend of seasonings is added, including South Indian Sambar Powder (page 28), which includes red chile peppers, coconut, coriander, and fenugreek seeds, plus tamarind, and a *tarka* (a sizzling flavor topping) of black mustard seeds, asafoetida, and fresh curry leaves.

Hazram's Soupy Pigeon Peas
Hazram ka Sambar

Makes 4 to 6 servings

Hazram, the lady in charge of all cooking in my friend Neelam Malhotra's home in the southern city of Bangalore, is from a small village nearby. And her sambar*, made in a very simple manner with just the very basic spices, is a favorite with my husband and me. She indulges us by making it every time we visit.*

Although there are 4 steps to making it, the recipe is quite easy and fast using the pressure cooker, and the sambar *is really delicious.*

2 to 3 tablespoons Tamarind Paste (page 54)
2 tablespoons South Indian Sambar Powder
    (page 28 or store-bought)
1 cup split pigeon peas (toor dal), sorted and
    washed in 3 to 4 changes of water
5 cups water
1^1/$_2$ teaspoons black mustard seeds
^{1}/$_8$ teaspoon ground asafoetida
1 to 3 fresh green chile peppers, such as serrano,
    minced with seeds
^{1}/$_4$ cup finely chopped fresh curry leaves,
    or 1 tablespoon dried
2 tablespoons ground coriander
1 teaspoon ground dried fenugreek leaves
^{1}/$_4$ teaspoon ground turmeric
1 teaspoon salt, or to taste
2 to 3 tablespoons peanut oil
5 to 7 dried red chile peppers, such as chile de arbol,
    with stems
1 small onion, cut in half lengthwise and thinly sliced
1 large tomato, coarsely chopped
^{1}/$_2$ cup finely chopped fresh cilantro

1. Prepare the tamarind paste and the sambar powder. Then place the dal and water in a pressure cooker, secure the lid, and cook over high heat until the regulator indicates high pressure, then cook 30 seconds more. Remove from the heat and allow the pot to depressurize on its own, 12 to 15 minutes. Carefully open the lid and stir vigorously to mash the dal. Keep over low heat while you proceed with the next step.

2. In a small bowl, combine the mustard seeds, asafoetida, green chile peppers, and curry leaves. In another bowl combine the coriander, sambar powder, fenugreek leaves, turmeric, and salt.

3. Heat the oil in a large, nonstick wok or saucepan over moderate heat and cook the red chile peppers and onion until golden brown, about 4 minutes. Add the mustard seeds-curry leaves mixture and cook, stirring, about 1 minute. Add the tomato and cook until all the juices evaporate, about 2 minutes.

4. Add the coriander-sambar powder mixture, stir about a minute, then add the tamarind paste and cook about 3 minutes. Mix in the dal and bring to a boil over high heat. Reduce the heat to low, add the cilantro, and simmer about 10 minutes to blend the flavors. Transfer to a bowl and serve.

Madras-Style Pigeon Peas with Vegetables
Madras ka Sabzi Sambar

Makes 4 to 6 servings

This unique Madras-style soupy dish comes flavored with sesame oil and fresh coconut, yet it is without any sweetness; it also comes loaded with soft-cooked vegetables. In India they make this sambar *in pure sesame oil (which in India is called* gingelly *oil), but I find that a tiny bit of Asian sesame oil, with its toasted aroma, combined with peanut oil, lends a special magic to the taste.*

^{1}/$_4$ cup Tamarind Paste (page 54)
1 cup split pigeon peas (toor dal), sorted and
    washed in 3 to 4 changes of water
6 cups water
^{1}/$_4$ teaspoon ground turmeric
^{1}/$_2$ teaspoon Asian sesame oil
3 tablespoons peanut oil
4 to 6 whole dried red chile peppers,
    such as chile de arbol
1 teaspoon black mustard seeds
^{1}/$_2$ teaspoon ground fenugreek seeds
^{1}/$_4$ cup ground fresh coconut

1/8 teaspoon ground asafoetida

1 to 3 fresh green chile peppers, such as serrano, split lengthwise into 2 pieces

2 tablespoons minced fresh curry leaves

1 tablespoon peeled minced fresh ginger

1 large clove fresh garlic, minced

1 1/2 teaspoons salt, or to taste

3 cups mixed fresh vegetables, such as onions, eggplant, green beans, okra, and summer squash, cut into 1-inch pieces

1/4 cup finely chopped fresh cilantro, including soft stems

1. Prepare the tamarind paste. Then, soak the dal in water to cover by 2 inches, about 2 hours. Drain and place in a large saucepan along with the water, turmeric, and sesame oil, and bring to a boil over high heat. Reduce the heat to low, cover the saucepan, partially at first and then completely, and cook, stirring occasionally, until creamy, 25 to 30 minutes. (As the dal cooks, some of it may foam and rise to the top. Mix the foam back into the dal.) Stir vigorously to mash the dal. Keep over low heat while you proceed with the next steps.

2. Heat 2 tablespoons peanut oil in a medium non-stick saucepan over medium-high heat and add the red chile peppers, mustard seeds, fenugreek, coconut, and asafoetida. Cover and cook, shaking the pan, about 1 minute. Add the green chile peppers and curry leaves, cook about 1 minute, then add the ginger and garlic and cook about 2 minutes. Mix into the dal.

3. To the same pan, add the remaining 1 tablespoon oil, vegetables, and salt and cook, stirring, over medium-high heat until golden, about 5 minutes. Add the tamarind paste, cover the pan, and cook until the vegetables are tender, about 5 minutes. Transfer to the dal and cook, stirring occasionally, about 10 minutes to blend the flavors. (Add more water if you desire a soupier sambar.) Transfer to a serving bowl, mix in the cilantro, and serve.

Split Pigeon Peas with Coconut and Vegetables

Sabzi aur Nariyal Sambar

Makes 4 to 6 servings

Coconuts grow in abundance in Kerala in the south, and this creamy sambar, made with grated coconut and coconut milk, captures every bit of their freshness. The paste, made with pan-roasted spices and dals, *also adds a smooth thickness to this quick pressure-cooked version.*

1/4 cup Tamarind Paste (page 54)

1/2 cup Coconut Milk (page 44 or store-bought)

3/4 to 1 cup split pigeon peas (toor dal), sorted and washed in 3 to 4 changes of water

4 to 4 1/2 cups water

1 teaspoon salt, or to taste

1/2 teaspoon ground turmeric

4 cups fresh vegetables, such as tomatoes, okra, potatoes, zucchini, eggplant, cauliflower, carrots, and bell peppers, cut into 1-inch pieces

2 tablespoons peanut oil

3 to 5 whole dried red chile peppers, such as chile de arbol

1/4 cup grated fresh coconut or unsweetened dried shredded coconut

1 teaspoon black mustard seeds

1 teaspoon cumin seeds

1 teaspoon fenugreek seeds

1 tablespoon coriander seeds

1 tablespoon yellow split chickpeas (channa dal), sorted

1 tablespoon white urad beans (dhulli urad dal), sorted

1/4 teaspoon cayenne pepper, or to taste

1/8 teaspoon ground asafoetida

2 tablespoons minced fresh curry leaves

1/2 cup finely chopped fresh cilantro, including soft stems

1. Prepare the tamarind paste and coconut milk. Then, place the dal, water, salt, turmeric, and vegetables in a pressure cooker. Secure the lid and cook over high heat until the regulator indicates high pressure, then cook 1 minute more. Remove from the heat and allow the pot to depressurize on its own, 12 to 15 minutes. Carefully open the lid and stir lightly.

2. Heat the oil in a small nonstick saucepan over medium-high heat and cook the red chile peppers and coconut until the coconut is golden, about 1 minute. Add the mustard, cumin, fenugreek, and coriander seeds and the channa and urad dals and cook until golden, about 1 minute. Add the cayenne pepper, asafoetida, and curry leaves and stir another 1 minute.

3. Let cool, transfer the spice mixture to a blender or a food processor, and process to make a paste, adding up to 3 tablespoons water, as needed. Mix the paste into the dal, then add the tamarind and coconut milk and bring to a boil over high heat. Reduce the heat to medium and simmer about 10 minutes. Transfer to a serving bowl, mix in the cilantro, and serve.

Soupy Split Pigeon Peas with Jaggery
Gur vaali Toor Dal

Makes 4 to 6 servings

This pressure-cooked recipe is my friend Naina Kapadia's Gujarati nod to sambar—*not what purists would recognize as a* sambar, *but delicious to me. Almost a soup, because Naina uses a blender, it goes well with steamed* basmati *rice.*

1¹/₂ tablespoons Gujarati Curry Powder with Coriander and Cumin (dhana-jeera masala, page 16)
1 cup split pigeon peas (toor dal), sorted and washed in 3 to 4 changes of water
6 cups water
10 to 12 fresh curry leaves
¹/₂ teaspoon ground turmeric
¹/₂ teaspoon cayenne pepper, or to taste
1 teaspoon salt, or to taste
2 tablespoons fresh lime or lemon juice
¹/₄ cup grated jaggery (gur)
2 tablespoons peanut oil
1 teaspoon black mustard seeds
1 teaspoon cumin seeds
¹/₂ teaspoon fenugreek seeds
¹/₈ teaspoon ground asafoetida
¹/₄ cup finely chopped fresh cilantro, including soft stems

1. Prepare the masala, then place the dal, water, and curry leaves in a pressure cooker. Secure the lid and cook over high heat until the regulator indicates high pressure, then cook 30 seconds more. Remove from the heat and allow the pot to depressurize on its own, 12 to 15 minutes. Carefully open the lid. Let cool, then blend in the pot with a hand-held immersion mixer or transfer to a blender and purée, then return it to the pressure cooker.

2. In a small bowl, combine the curry powder, turmeric, cayenne pepper, and salt. Reserve 1 teaspoon of the mixture and add the rest to the processed dal. Mix in the lime juice and jaggery.

3. To make the tarka, heat the oil in a small saucepan over medium-high heat and add the mustard, cumin, and fenugreek seeds; they should sizzle upon contact with the hot oil. Remove the pan from the heat and add the reserved 1 teaspoon curry powder mixture and the asafoetida. Immediately add the tarka to the dal and mix well. Transfer to a serving bowl, mix in the cilantro, and serve.

Urad Beans (Urad Dal)

White Urad Beans with Fresh Lemon Juice
Dhulli Urad Dal

Makes 4 to 6 servings

This is another skinless dal that I cook without a pressure cooker, but I do soak it before cooking. The dal absorbs the water, then cooks much faster.

Lying somewhere between soupy and dry-cooked dals, this dish has a silky smoothness that is different from any other. Do not over-cook it or stir excessively—this will cause the beans to disintegrate and become starchy. Use a light hand when stirring, especially during the actual cooking. A common practice is to simply swirl the pan contents and lightly stir the dal with the round bottom of a ladle.

- 1¼ cups white urad beans (dhulli urad dal), sorted and washed in 3 to 4 changes of water
- 3½ to 4 cups water
- ¼ teaspoon ground turmeric
- 1 teaspoon salt, or to taste
- 1½ tablespoons fresh lemon juice, or more to taste
- ½ cup finely chopped fresh cilantro, including soft stems
- 2 tablespoons vegetable oil
- 1 teaspoon ghee (optional)
- 1½ teaspoons cumin seeds
- 1 small onion, finely chopped
- 2 tablespoons peeled minced fresh ginger
- 1 fresh green chile pepper, such as serrano, minced with seeds
- 1 tablespoon minced red bell pepper
- 1 tablespoon ground coriander
- ½ teaspoon ground cumin
- ½ teaspoon ground paprika

1. Soak the dal in water to cover by 2 inches, about 2 hours. Then place the dal, 3½ cups water, turmeric, and salt in a medium saucepan and bring to a boil over high heat. Reduce the heat to medium and cook the dal, stirring occasionally and watching carefully that it doesn't boil over, about 10 minutes. Reduce the heat to low, add the remaining water, if needed, and simmer until each bean is soft but not broken and very little water remains in the pan, about 15 minutes. Carefully, mix in the lemon juice and cilantro and transfer to a serving bowl. Cover and keep warm.

2. Heat the oil (and ghee, if using) in a small saucepan over medium-high heat and add the cumin seeds; they should sizzle upon contact with the hot oil. Quickly add the onion, reduce the heat to medium, and cook until golden, about 4 minutes.

3. Add the ginger, green chile pepper, and bell pepper and stir about 1 minute. Add the coriander, cumin, and paprika, stir a few seconds, and add to the dal. Swirl lightly to mix, with parts of it visible as a garnish. Serve.

White Urad Beans with Roasted Fenugreek Leaves
Bhuni Methi vaali Dhulli Urad Dal

Makes 4 to 6 servings

Urad dal takes on a brand new identity when we mix in some roasted fenugreek leaves. If you can't find them, use 1 small bunch of fresh spinach and mix in 1 tablespoon of dried fenugreek leaves.

- 1¼ cups dried white urad beans (dhulli urad dal), sorted and washed in 3 to 4 changes of water
- 3½ to 4 cups water
- ¼ teaspoon ground turmeric
- 1 teaspoon salt, or to taste
- 1 small bunch fresh fenugreek leaves (about ¼ pound)
- 2 tablespoons peanut oil
- 1½ teaspoons cumin seeds
- 2 tablespoons peeled minced fresh ginger
- 1 fresh green chile pepper, such as serrano, minced with seeds
- 1 tablespoon ground coriander
- ½ teaspoon ground cumin
- ½ teaspoon ground paprika

1. Place the dal, 3½ cups water, turmeric, and salt in a medium saucepan and bring to a boil over high heat. Reduce the heat to medium and cook the dal, stirring occasionally but watching carefully that it doesn't boil over, about 10 minutes. Reduce the heat to low, add the remaining ½ cup water, if needed, and simmer until each bean is soft but not broken and very little water remains in the pan, about 15 minutes. Cover and keep warm.

2. Meanwhile, discard the hard and fibrous part of the fenugreek greens, pick out the leaves and the softest stems, and wash them well. Chop finely in the food processor or by hand.

3. Heat 1 tablespoon oil in a medium cast-iron or nonstick wok or a saucepan and cook the fenugreek greens over medium-high heat, stirring and scraping the sides of the wok, about 3 minutes. Reduce the heat to medium low and cook until the leaves are completely dry and deep green, 10 to 15 minutes. Mix lightly into the dal.

4. Heat the remaining 2 tablespoons oil in a small saucepan over medium-high heat and add the cumin seeds; they should sizzle upon contact with the hot oil. Quickly add the ginger and green chile pepper and stir about 1 minute. Add the coriander, cumin, and paprika, stir a few seconds, then add the seasonings to the dal. Swirl lightly to mix, with parts of it visible as a garnish. Serve.

Spicy Split Black Urad Beans with Split Chickpeas
Urad-Channae ki Dal

Makes 4 to 6 servings

Called maanh-cholaeyan di dal *in Punjabi, this dish is a true family favorite all over the north, especially at* dhabas *(family-owned-and-operated roadside eateries all over north India, and a favorite among interstate bus and truck drivers).*

This dish is commonly made in a pressure cooker, as I make it here. Serve it with paranthas *(griddle-fried breads) and mango pickle for brunch, or with a*

side of vegetables, yogurt *raita, a seasoned rice dish, and/or Indian flatbreads.*

1 cup split black urad beans (chilkae vaali urad dal), sorted and washed in 3 to 4 changes of water
⅓ cup yellow split chickpeas (channa dal), sorted and washed in 3 to 4 changes of water
1 tablespoon peeled minced fresh ginger
1 to 2 fresh green chile peppers, such as serrano, minced with seeds
4 black cardamom pods, crushed lightly to break the skin
1 (1-inch) stick cinnamon, broken lengthwise
½ teaspoon ground turmeric
1 teaspoon salt, or to taste
4½ to 5 cups water
2 tablespoons vegetable oil
1 small onion, finely chopped
1 (1-inch) piece fresh ginger, peeled and cut into thin matchsticks
1 tablespoon ground coriander
1 teaspoon ground cumin
½ teaspoon ground paprika
½ teaspoon garam masala
½ cup finely chopped fresh cilantro, including soft stems

1. Place the dals, minced ginger, green chile peppers, cardamom pods, cinnamon, turmeric, salt, and 4½ cups water in a pressure cooker. Secure the lid and cook over high heat until the regulator indicates high pressure, then cook 1 minute more. Remove from the heat and allow the pot to depressurize on its own, 12 to 15 minutes. Carefully open the lid and check to see if the beans are very soft, with some of them broken; if not, cover, bring up to pressure, and cook under pressure another 15 to 20 seconds. Or, cover and boil until soft, about 30 minutes, adding water if needed. Transfer to a serving dish, cover, and keep warm.

2. Heat the oil in a small saucepan over medium-high heat and cook the onion and ginger matchsticks until golden, 3 to 5 minutes. Add the coriander and cumin, stir a few seconds, then remove from the heat and add the paprika. Lightly swirl everything into the dal, with parts of it visible as a garnish. Sprinkle the garam masala and cilantro on top, and serve.

Stir-Fried Black Urad Beans

Bhuni Saabut Urad Dal

Makes 4 to 6 servings

Most recipes call for cooking the dal *until soft and creamy, but in this recipe the* dal *is cooked until each bean is tender and soft, yet remains separate. We then combine it with a spicy* masala *to make a salad-like dish that is spectacular over a bed of wilted greens.*

1¼ cups black urad beans (saabut urad dal),
    sorted and washed in 3 to 4 changes of water

5 to 6 cups water

½ teaspoon salt, or to taste

⅛ teaspoon ground turmeric

1 tablespoon olive oil

½ teaspoon cumin seeds

¼ teaspoon black cumin seeds

1 tablespoon peeled minced fresh ginger

1 large clove fresh garlic, minced

1 fresh green chile pepper, such as serrano,
    minced with seeds

⅛ teaspoon ground asafoetida

1 tablespoon ground coriander

1 cup finely chopped tomato

1 tablespoon fresh lemon juice

½ cup finely chopped scallions

¼ cup finely chopped cilantro

1. Soak the beans overnight in water to cover by 2 inches. Drain and place them in a large saucepan. Add 5 cups of water, salt, and turmeric, cover the pan, and boil over high heat, about 5 minutes. Reduce the heat to medium-low and continue to cook until the dal is very soft, each bean bursts open to reveal its white interior, and most of the water has evaporated, about 1½ hours. (Add more water if the dal dries out sooner.)

2. Heat the oil in a large nonstick wok or skillet over medium-high heat and add the cumin seeds; they should sizzle upon contact with the hot oil. Quickly add the ginger, garlic, and green chile pepper and cook about 1 minute. Add the asafoetida and coriander and stir a few seconds.

3. Add the tomato and stir until most of the juices evaporate, about 2 minutes. Then add the dal and lemon juice, cover the pan, reduce the heat, and simmer over low heat about 5 minutes to blend the flavors. Transfer to a serving dish, lightly mix in the scallions and cilantro, and serve.

Kashmiri Fennel-Flavored Black Urad Beans with Yogurt

Kashmiri Saabut Urad Dal

Makes 4 to 6 servings

Whenever my friend Sunil Vora makes this, his special-occasions-only dal, *he reminisces about his childhood in Kashmir—the snow-clad Himalayas, the countryside full of flowers in spring, and his mother's cooking.*

Yogurt plays an important part in Kashmiri foods, as we see in this dal *dish. The* dal *is first cooked in salted water until tender, then combined with yogurt, ground ginger, and fennel seeds—the two must-have spices in Kashmiri cuisine.*

¼ teaspoon Kashmiri Garam Masala (page 19)
    or garam masala

1¼ cups black urad beans (saabut urad dal),
    sorted and washed in 3 to 4 changes of water

5 to 6 cups water

1 teaspoon salt, or to taste

1 tablespoon unsalted butter, at room temperature

1 cup nonfat plain yogurt, whisked until smooth

1 tablespoon ground fennel seeds

1 teaspoon ground ginger

¼ teaspoon ground turmeric

1. Soak the dal overnight in water to cover by 2 inches. Meanwhile prepare the kashmiri garam masala. When ready, drain and place the dal in a large saucepan. Add 5 cups water and salt, cover the pan, and boil over high heat about 5 minutes. Reduce the heat to medium-low and continue to cook until the dal is soft and very little water remains in the pan, about 1½ hours. If the dal softens sooner, uncover and cook over high heat until most of the water evaporates. Add more water if the dal dries out sooner.

2. Add the butter, yogurt, fennel seeds, ginger, and turmeric and bring to a boil over high heat, stirring constantly to prevent the yogurt from curdling. Reduce the heat to medium-low, cover the pan, and simmer until each bean bursts open to reveal its white interior and starts to break apart, 25 to 30 minutes. Transfer to a serving dish, sprinkle the garam masala on top, and serve.

Punjabi Black Urad Beans

Dhaba ki Saabut Urad Dal

Makes 4 to 6 servings

This filling and powerfully flavored dal, *served at roadside eateries called* dhabas, *has satisfied millions of hungry travelers who pass along the interstate highways of the Punjab in northwestern India. It is a time-honored and simple way of cooking black urad beans. Serve it with slices of raw or marinated onions, a side of fresh okra, cauliflower, or eggplant, and fresh* paranthas *(griddle-fried breads).*

To cook it faster, put all the ingredients in a pressure cooker, then follow the pressure cooker directions in the next recipe (Smoked Black Urad Beans).

1 cup black urad beans (saabut urad dal), sorted and washed in 3 to 4 changes of water
1/4 cup yellow split chickpeas (channa dal), sorted and washed in 3 to 4 changes of water
1/4 cup red or pinto beans, sorted and washed in 3 to 4 changes of water
8 cups water or more, as needed
1 large red onion, coarsely chopped
1 to 3 fresh green chile peppers, such as serrano, minced with seeds
2 (1-inch) pieces peeled fresh ginger, cut into thin matchsticks
2 large cloves fresh garlic, minced
6 black cardamom pods, crushed lightly to break the skin
2 (1-inch) sticks cinnamon, broken lengthwise
1 teaspoon cayenne pepper, or to taste
1/2 teaspoon ground turmeric
1 teaspoon salt, or to taste
1 tablespoon dried mint leaves
2 tablespoons unsalted butter, at room temperature
1/4 teaspoon garam masala

1. Soak the dals and beans overnight, in water to cover by at least 2 inches. Drain and place in a large cast-iron or other heavy saucepan. Add 6 cups water and all the remaining ingredients (except the mint, butter, and garam masala), cover the pan and boil over high heat, about 10 minutes. Reduce the heat to medium and cook, stirring occasionally, about 1 hour.

2. Reduce the heat to medium-low and continue to cook until the dal is very soft, thick, and creamy, about 3 to 4 hours, adding 2 cups or more water as needed. Add the mint leaves and the butter and cook another 30 minutes. Transfer to a serving dish, sprinkle the garam masala on top, and serve.

Smoked Black Urad Beans

Dhuandar Urad Saabut

Makes 4 to 6 servings

When I was growing up in New Delhi, this dal *was cooked over a pail-shaped coal-burning stove, called* angeethi *or* sigri, *for hours and hours until it became soft and creamy. As it simmered, sometimes covered and other times uncovered, the smoke from the coals lent a lovely aroma to it. This aroma was further enhanced by the addition of fragrant herbs and spices.*

In America, I cook this dal *in a pressure cooker for convenience, and although it doesn't provide the same flavor as the smoky coals, I add a few drops of liquid smoke (found in supermarkets and in specialty food stores).*

1 cup black urad beans (saabut urad dal),
    sorted and washed in 3 to 4 changes of water

1/4 cup yellow split chickpeas (channa dal),
    sorted and washed in 3 to 4 changes of water

2 tablespoons kidney beans, sorted and washed
    in 3 to 4 changes of water

1 tablespoon peanut oil

4 to 6 fresh green chile peppers, such as serrano,
    skin punctured to prevent bursting

5 whole dried red chile peppers, such as chile de arbol

1 tablespoon peeled minced fresh ginger

1 large clove fresh garlic, minced

1 tablespoon ground coriander

1/2 teaspoon ground cumin

1/2 teaspoon ground oregano leaves

1/4 teaspoon ground fenugreek seeds

1/4 teaspoon ground turmeric

1/8 teaspoon ground asafoetida

1 teaspoon salt, or to taste

1/4 teaspoon liquid hickory smoke

7 to 8 cups water

1 (15-ounce) can tomato sauce

1/2 cup finely chopped fresh cilantro,
    including soft stems

1 teaspoon dried fenugreek leaves

1/4 cup nonfat plain yogurt, whisked with 1/2 cup water

1/4 teaspoon garam masala

1. In a bowl, mix together the dals and the kidney beans. Then heat the oil in a medium cast-iron or nonstick saucepan over medium-high heat and cook the green and red chile peppers, stirring, until golden, about 1 minute. (Stand back from the pan in case they burst.) Add the ginger and garlic, then the coriander, cumin, oregano, fenugreek seeds, turmeric, asafoetida, salt, and liquid smoke. Stir about 30 seconds.

2. Add the dals and beans and stir constantly over medium-low heat until fragrant and well roasted, about 5 minutes. Transfer to a pressure cooker, add 6 cups water, secure the lid and cook over high heat until the regulator indicates high pressure, then cook 1 minute more. Reduce the heat to low and continue to cook another 3 minutes. Remove from the heat and allow the pot to depressurize on its own, 12 to 15 minutes. Carefully open the lid and check to see if the beans are very soft with some of them broken; if not, add remaining 2 cups water, cover, bring back up to high pressure, and cook under pressure another 1 minute. Or cover and boil until soft, about 30 minutes.

3. Mix in the tomato sauce, cilantro, fenugreek leaves, and yogurt-water, and cook, stirring occasionally, over low heat until the dal is thick and creamy, 45 to 60 minutes. Transfer to a serving dish, sprinkle the garam masala on top, and serve.

Black Urad Beans in a Slow Cooker

Slow-Cooker Mein Saabut Urad Dal

Makes 4 to 6 servings

On the other end of the spectrum of convenience products from speedy pressure cookers are the slow cookers that cook dried beans long and slow, but with little effort.

Here is my recipe for black urad beans from my daughter, Sumi. Sumi gives the process a jump-start by boiling the dal *in a pan before placing it in the cooker. Then, once the* dal *is cooked, she adds a* tarka *(sizzling seasoning topping) that dramatically perks up its flavor and aroma.*

1¼ cups black urad beans (saabut urad dal),
    sorted and washed in 3 to 4 changes of water
¼ cup red or kidney beans, sorted and washed
    in 3 to 4 changes of water
1 to 3 fresh green chile peppers, such as serrano,
    minced with seeds
1 tablespoon peeled minced fresh ginger
1 large clove fresh garlic, minced
1 medium onion, finely chopped
5 black cardamom pods, crushed lightly
    to break the skin
2 (1-inch) sticks cinnamon, broken
2 bay leaves
¼ teaspoon ground turmeric
1 teaspoon salt, or to taste
7 to 8 cups water
1 (15-ounce) can tomato sauce
¼ cup nonfat plain yogurt, whisked until smooth
1½ tablespoons olive oil, melted butter, or ghee
1 (1½-inch) piece fresh ginger, peeled and
    cut into thin matchsticks
3 to 5 whole dried red chile peppers,
    such as chile de arbol
1½ teaspoons cumin seeds
1 teaspoon dried fenugreek leaves
¼ teaspoon ground paprika
⅛ teaspoon ground asafoetida

1. Place the dal, beans, green chile peppers, minced ginger, garlic, onion, cardamom pods, cinnamon, bay leaves, turmeric, salt, and 5 cups water in a large saucepan and boil over high heat about 5 minutes.

2. Transfer to a slow cooker. Choose the highest setting and cook the dal until soft and creamy, 10 to 12 hours. Stir every once in awhile. Once most of the water has been absorbed by the dal, boil the remaining water and add it to the pot. Mix in the tomato sauce during the last hour of cooking. Transfer to a serving dish, swirl in the yogurt, and keep warm.

3. Heat the oil in a small nonstick saucepan over medium-high heat and cook the ginger matchsticks and red chile peppers until golden, about 1 minute. (Stand back from the pan just in case the peppers burst.) Add the cumin seeds; they should sizzle upon contact with the hot oil. Quickly add the fenugreek leaves, then remove from the heat, add the paprika and asafoetida, and immediately add the tarka to the dal. Swirl lightly to mix, with parts of it visible as a garnish. Serve.

Split Chickpeas and Split Peas (Channa Dal and Muttar Dal)

Yellow Split Chickpeas with Spinach

Channa Dal Sai-Bhaji

Makes 4 to 6 servings

My niece, Mini, who grew up in Mumbai (Bombay), makes this dish and shared it with me. A specialty of the Sindhi community settled in Bombay (they were originally from northwest India, an area that is now in Pakistan), this dish (sai-bhaji) is almost a one-pot meal, traditionally served with steamed rice.

It is very simple with the pressure cooker, and although this recipe calls for frozen spinach, it turns out all the more delicious when you use fresh.

2 tablespoons olive oil
1 teaspoon cumin seeds
1 medium onion, finely chopped
1 large clove fresh garlic, minced
1 tablespoon peeled minced fresh ginger
1/2 cup yellow split chickpeas (channa dal),
    sorted and washed in 3 to 4 changes of water
1 large tomato, finely chopped, or 1/2 cup canned
    tomato sauce
1 teaspoon salt, or to taste
1/2 teaspoon cayenne pepper, or to taste
1 (8-ounce) package frozen spinach, thawed
1/2 bunch (/14 cup) fresh dill, finely chopped
1 small russet potato (or any kind), peeled and
    finely chopped
1 small carrot, peeled and finely chopped
1 cup water
1 tablespoon fresh lime or lemon juice
Finely chopped fresh cilantro

1. Heat the oil in a large pressure cooker over medium-high heat and add the cumin seeds; they should sizzle upon contact with the hot oil. Quickly add the onion, garlic, and ginger and cook, stirring, until golden, about 5 minutes. Add the dal and cook, stirring, about 5 minutes. Then add the tomato (or tomato sauce), salt, and cayenne pepper, and stir about 2 minutes.

2. Add the spinach, dill, potato, and carrot, stir about 5 minutes then add the water. Secure the lid and cook over high heat until the regulator indicates high pressure, then cook 30 seconds more. Remove from the heat and allow the pot to depressurize on its own, 12 to 15 minutes. Carefully open the lid, add the lemon juice, and stir well, mashing some of the dal and vegetables with a ladle or a spatula. Transfer to a serving dish, garnish with the cilantro, and serve.

Yellow Split Chickpeas with Opo Squash

Channa Dal aur Lavki

Makes 4 to 6 servings

This is one of my favorite dals *to make in the pressure cooker. It has a mild chickpea-like taste, but it cooks much faster and is much lighter on the stomach than dishes made with whole chickpeas. The mild-flavored, pale green bottle-shaped opo squash, besides adding interest, further lightens the* dal *and increases its digestibility.*

1 cup yellow split chickpeas (channa dal),
    sorted and washed in 3 to 4 changes of water
4 1/2 cups water
1/4 teaspoon ground turmeric
1 teaspoon salt, or to taste
1 fresh green chile pepper, such as serrano,
    minced with seeds
1 small opo squash (about 3/4 pound), peeled and
    cut into 1-inch pieces
2 large cloves fresh garlic, chopped
2 tablespoons vegetable oil
1 teaspoon cumin seeds
1/4 teaspoon ajwain seeds
1 small onion, finely chopped
1 medium tomato, finely chopped
1/2 teaspoon ground paprika
1/4 cup finely chopped fresh cilantro,
    including soft stems
1/4 teaspoon garam masala

1. Place the dal, water, turmeric, salt, green chile pepper, squash, and garlic in a pressure cooker. Secure the lid and cook over high heat until the regulator indicates high pressure, then cook 30 seconds more. Remove from the heat and allow the pot to depressurize on its own, 12 to 15 minutes. Carefully open the lid; the dal should be thick and creamy and the squash should be soft. Transfer to a serving dish, cover, and keep warm.

2. Heat the oil in a small saucepan over medium-high heat and add the cumin and ajwain seeds; they should sizzle upon contact with the hot oil. Quickly add the onion and cook until golden, about 5 minutes. Add the tomato and paprika and cook until most of the juices evaporate, 2 to 4 minutes. Transfer everything to the dal and swirl lightly to mix, with parts of it visible as a garnish. Mix in the cilantro, sprinkle the garam masala on top, and serve.

Dry-Cooked Green Split Peas

Sookhi Muttar Dal

Makes 4 to 6 servings

This dry-cooked dal is a really versatile dish. Serve it on its own with a cup of afternoon tea, spoon it atop green salads, or use it to fill paranthas *(griddle-fried breads),* poories *(puffed deep-fried breads),* samosas *(deep-fried triangular pastries) and even baked stuffed vegetables (bell peppers, tomatoes, and more).*

1¼ cups green split peas (muttar dal), sorted and washed in 3 to 4 changes of water

2 tablespoons vegetable oil

1½ teaspoons black mustard seeds

½ teaspoon ground fenugreek seeds

⅛ teaspoon ground asafoetida

1½ tablespoons dried curry leaves

1 tablespoon peeled minced fresh ginger

1 fresh green chile peppers, such as serrano, minced with seeds

3 to 3½ cups water

¾ teaspoon salt, or to taste

1 small tomato, finely chopped

1 to 2 tablespoons fresh lemon juice

¼ teaspoon garam masala

1. Soak the dal in water to cover by 2 inches, about 2 hours, then drain. Heat the oil in a large nonstick wok or saucepan over medium-high heat and add the mustard seeds; they should splutter upon contact with the hot oil, so cover the pan until the spluttering subsides. Add the fenugreek seeds and asafoetida, then mix in the curry leaves and stir about 1 minute. Add the ginger and green chile peppers, stir about 1 minute, then mix in the dal, 2 cups water, and salt, and bring to a boil over high heat.

2. Reduce the heat to medium-low, cover the pan, and simmer, stirring as needed, until the dal is tender, about 7 minutes. Add ½ cup more water if the dal sticks to the pan. Mix in the tomato and lemon juice, cover, and cook over low heat, about 5 minutes. Remove to a serving dish, sprinkle the garam masala on top, and serve.

Garlicky Dried Green Peas Curry

Rassadar Sookhae Muttar

Makes 4 to 6 servings

When they're short on time, a lot of busy south Indian wives and mothers find themselves making this simple dish and serving it with steamed rice.

¼ cup dried whole green peas (sookhae harae muttar), sorted and washed in 3 to 4 changes of water

2 tablespoons peanut oil

1 teaspoon cumin seeds

1 teaspoon black mustard seeds

3 dried red chile peppers, such as chile de arbol, broken or whole with stems 2 large cloves fresh garlic, minced

2 large tomatoes, finely chopped

1 medium onion, finely chopped

⅛ teaspoon ground asafoetida

¼ teaspoon ground turmeric

1 teaspoon salt, or to taste

4 to 5 cups water

1 teaspoon melted coconut oil, melted ghee, or vegetable oil

1. Soak the peas overnight in water to cover by 2 inches, then drain. Heat the oil in a large nonstick wok or saucepan over medium-high heat and add the cumin and mustard seeds; they should splutter upon contact with the hot oil, so lower the heat and cover the pan until the spluttering subsides. Quickly add the red chile peppers, garlic, tomatoes, onion, asafoetida, and turmeric, and cook, stirring, until most of the juices evaporate, about 15 minutes.

2. Add the drained peas, salt, and 4 cups water, and bring to a boil over high heat. Reduce the heat to medium-low, cover the pan, and simmer until the peas are tender and the sauce thick, about 1 hour, adding the remaining 1 cup water as needed. Transfer to a serving bowl, mix in the coconut oil (or ghee or vegetable oil), and serve.

Spicy Dried Yellow Peas

Masaladar Sookhae Peelae Muttar

Makes 4 to 6 servings

I cook these pearly yellow peas in a pressure cooker to make a delicious entrée which pairs well with dishes like Mixed Cauliflower, Carrots, and Green Beans in a Wok (page 306) or Butternut Squash with Fenugreek Seeds (page 272). Serve with a yogurt raita and any homemade or store-bought Indian breads.

1/4 cup dried whole yellow peas (sookhae peelae muttar), sorted and washed in 3 to 4 changes of water

1 teaspoon cumin seeds, dry-roasted and coarsely ground (Dry-Roasting Spices, page 35)

4 to 5 cups water

1/2 teaspoon salt, or to taste

4 black cardamom pods, crushed lightly to break the skin

1 (1-inch) stick cinnamon, broken lengthwise

1 large tomato, coarsely chopped

1 small onion, coarsely chopped

6 quarter-size slices peeled fresh ginger

1 large clove fresh garlic, peeled

1 fresh green chile pepper, such as serrano, minced with seeds

12 to 15 fresh mint leaves

1 tablespoon ground coriander

1 teaspoon ground cumin

1/4 teaspoon ground turmeric

1/8 teaspoon ground asafoetida

1/2 cup finely chopped fresh cilantro, including soft stems

2 to 3 tablespoons fresh lemon or lime juice

2 tablespoons vegetable oil

1/4 teaspoon ajwain seeds, coarsely ground

1/4 teaspoon ground black salt

1. Soak the peas overnight in water to cover by 2 inches. Meanwhile, prepare the cumin seeds. Drain the dried peas and place them in a pressure cooker, along with 4 cups water, salt, cardamom pods, and cinnamon. Secure the lid and cook over high heat until the regulator indicates high pressure, then cook 1 minute more. Remove from the heat and allow the pot to depressurize on its own, 12 to 15 minutes. Carefully open the lid and check to see if the peas are soft; if not, add the remaining water, cover, bring up to high pressure, and cook under pressure about 30 seconds. Or, cover and boil until soft, about 30 minutes.

2. In a food processor, process together the tomato, onion, ginger, garlic, green chile pepper, and mint leaves until smooth. Add the coriander, ground cumin, turmeric, and asafoetida, and process again to mix well. Transfer to the cooked peas and cook, stirring as needed until most of the juices are absorbed and the sauce is thick, about 20 minutes. Mix in the cilantro and lemon juice.

3. Heat the oil in a small saucepan over medium-high heat and add the ajwain seeds and black salt; they should sizzle upon contact with the hot oil. Quickly add to the peas and cook another 5 minutes. Transfer to a serving dish, sprinkle the roasted cumin seeds on top, and serve.

Mixed Beans and Lentils

Spicy Mixed 5 Beans and Lentils

Panchrattani Dal

Makes 4 to 6 servings

Panch means the number 5 and rattan means jewels, and this lovely mixture of 5 different legumes lives up to its name. It's richly flavorful, delivers a lot of fiber and nutrition, and is quick to make in a pressure cooker.

¼ cup each: black split urad beans (chilkae vaali urad dal), green mung beans (saabut mung dal), green lentils (saabut masoor dal), split pigeon peas (toor dal) and yellow split chickpeas (channa dal), sorted and washed in 3 to 4 changes of water

1 small onion, finely chopped

2 tablespoons peeled minced fresh ginger

1 teaspoon minced fresh garlic

1 tablespoon ground coriander

2 teaspoon ground cumin

½ teaspoon garam masala

½ teaspoon ground turmeric

⅛ teaspoon ground asafoetida

1 teaspoon salt, or to taste

4 to 5 cups water

1 tablespoon vegetable oil or melted ghee

1 to 3 fresh green chile peppers, such as serrano, split lengthwise, with or without seeds

1 teaspoon cumin seeds

½ teaspoon ground paprika

1. Heat the oil in a medium cast-iron or nonstick saucepan over medium-high heat, add the dals and onion, and stir constantly over medium-low heat until fragrant and well roasted, about 5 minutes. Mix in the ginger and garlic, then the coriander, cumin, garam masala, turmeric, asafoetida, and salt, and stir about 30 seconds.

2. Transfer to a pressure cooker, add 4 cups water. Secure the lid and cook over high heat until the regulator indicates high pressure, then cook 1 minute more. Remove from the heat and allow the pot to depressurize on its own, 12 to 15 minutes. Carefully open the lid and check to see if the dal is very soft and creamy; if not, add the remaining 1 cup water, cover, bring up to pressure, and cook under high pressure about 30 seconds. Or cover and boil until soft, about 30 minutes.

3. Uncover and simmer over medium-low heat about 10 minutes, then remove to a serving dish, cover, and keep warm.

4. Heat the oil (or ghee) in a small saucepan and cook the green chile peppers about 30 seconds. Add the cumin seeds; they should sizzle upon contact with the hot oil. Remove from the heat, add the paprika, and add the tarka to the cooked dal. Swirl lightly to mix, with parts of it visible as a garnish, and serve.

Rajasthani Mixed 5 Beans and Lentils

Panch Bheli Dal

Makes 4 to 6 servings

This is Pushpa Khatod's (my daughter's mother-in-law) authentic regional dal. It reflects the Rajasthani preference for foods containing no garlic or onion. It features ginger, green chile peppers, and asafoetida as the main flavors, and remains an evergreen favorite, served with baati (Basic Rajasthani Rolls, page 603).

2 tablespoons Basic Ginger and Green Chile Pepper Paste (page 48)

1/3 cup yellow mung beans (dhulli mung dal), sorted and washed in 3 to 4 changes of water

1/4 cup white urad beans (dhulli urad dal), sorted and washed in 3 to 4 changes of water

2 tablespoons split green mung beans (chilkae vaali mung dal), sorted and washed in 3 to 4 changes of water

2 tablespoons split pigeon peas (toor dal), sorted and washed in 3 to 4 changes of water

2 tablespoons yellow split chickpeas (channa dal), sorted and washed in 3 to 4 changes of water

1/4 teaspoon salt, or to taste

1/4 teaspoon ground turmeric

4 whole cloves

4 to 4 1/2 cups water

2 to 3 tablespoons vegetable oil or melted ghee

2 green cardamom pods, crushed lightly to break the skin

2 whole dried red chile peppers, such as chile de arbol

1 (1-inch) stick cinnamon, broken lengthwise

1 bay leaf

1 teaspoon cumin seeds

1 tablespoon dried curry leaves

1/8 teaspoon ground asafoetida

1/4 teaspoon ground paprika

2 tablespoons finely chopped fresh cilantro

1. Prepare the ginger-chile paste. Place the dals in a pressure cooker, along with the salt, turmeric, 2 cloves, and water. Secure the lid and cook over high heat until the regulator indicates high pressure, then cook 1 minute more. Remove from the heat and allow the pot to depressurize on its own, 12 to 15 minutes. Carefully open the lid and check to see if the dal is soft and creamy; if not, cover and boil until soft, about 10 minutes. Transfer to a serving dish, cover, and keep warm.

2. Heat the oil (or ghee) in a large nonstick wok or saucepan over medium-high heat and cook the cardamom pods, the remaining 2 cloves, red chile peppers, cinnamon, and bay leaf about 30 seconds. Add the cumin seeds and asafoetida; they should sizzle upon contact with the hot ghee. Quickly add the curry leaves and then mix in the ginger-chile paste and stir about 1 minute.

3. Add the paprika and immediately mix in about 1/4 cup water and bring to a boil over high heat. Transfer to the dal and swirl lightly to mix, with parts of it visible as a garnish. Garnish with the cilantro and serve.

Parsi Mixed Lentils, Beans, and Vegetables

Dhansak Dal

Makes 4 to 6 servings

In the Gujarati language, dhan *means dal (legumes) and* sak *means vegetables;* dhansak *is a famous Parsi dish made with a mixture of different* dals *and vegetables. (The Parsi are of Iranian descent, now settled in Western India.)*

This recipe, from my sister-in-law, Khushnoor, is scrumptious when served with chapatis *(whole-wheat flatbreads) or rice.* Dhansak *has a multitude of ingredients and flavors that harmonize brilliantly with one another, and also, cook well in a pressure cooker.*

2 to 3 tablespoons Tamarind Paste (page 54)

1/4 cup each, red lentils (dhulli masoor dal), and split pigeon peas (toor dal), sorted and washed in 3 to 4 changes of water

2 tablespoons each, yellow mung beans (dhulli mung dal), yellow split chickpeas (channa dal), and white urad beans (dhulli urad dal), sorted and washed in 3 to 4 changes of water

1 medium russet (or any) potato, chopped (peeled or unpeeled)

1 large tomato, chopped

1 (3-inch) piece pumpkin, finely chopped

1 small Chinese or Japanese eggplant, finely chopped

2 small onions, 1 coarsely chopped and 1 cut in half lengthwise and thinly sliced

1 cup coarsely chopped fresh fenugreek leaves, or 1/4 cup dried

1/4 cup coarsely chopped fresh cilantro, including soft stems, + more for garnish

1 tablespoon chopped fresh mint leaves

3 to 5 fresh green chile peppers, such as serrano, minced with seeds

1/4 teaspoon ground turmeric

1 teaspoon salt, or to taste

3 cups water

1 tablespoon Basic Ginger-Garlic Paste (page 47 or store-bought)

2 tablespoons Gujarati Lentil Masala (Dhansak Masala), page 26 or store-bought

1 1/2 tablespoons ground coriander

2 teaspoons ground cumin

1 teaspoon cayenne pepper, or to taste

2 teaspoons garam masala

3 tablespoons vegetable oil

1 to 2 tablespoons ground jaggery (gur)

1. Prepare the tamarind paste. Then, place all the dals in a pressure cooker along with the potato, tomato, pumpkin, eggplant, chopped onion, fenugreek leaves, cilantro, mint, green chile peppers, turmeric, salt, and water. Secure the lid and cook over high heat until the regulator indicates high

pressure, then cook 30 seconds more. Remove from the heat and allow the pot to depressurize on its own, 12 to 15 minutes. Carefully open the lid, let cool, then blend in the pot with a hand-held immersion mixer or transfer to a food processor or blender, process to make a thick and smooth purée, then return to the pot.

2. Meanwhile, prepare the ginger-garlic paste and lentil masala. Then, in a small bowl mix together the ginger-garlic paste, coriander, cumin, cayenne pepper and garam masala with 1 to 2 tablespoons water to make a thick paste.

3. Heat the oil in a large nonstick wok or saucepan over medium-high heat and cook the sliced onions, stirring, until golden, 5 to 7 minutes. Add the spice paste and Gujarati masala and stir until fragrant, 1 to 2 minutes. Mix into the dal along with the tamarind and jaggery, and simmer over low heat, 5 to 7 minutes. (Add some water if the dal seems too thick.) Transfer to a serving dish, garnish with the cilantro, and serve.

Split Urad Beans and Yellow Split Chickpeas with Spinach
Urad Channae ki Dal aur Palak

Makes 4 to 6 servings

This is another dal (legume) dish close to my heart, one that I cook and write about frequently. Laden with tomatoes, spinach, many herbs and spices, you could eat it on its own or thin it down with some water or yogurt and serve it as a chunky soup with a sandwich. As an entrée I love this pressure-cooked dal with a side of Baked Bitter Melon with Baby Red Potatoes (page 280) or Traditional Grilled Eggplant Raita (page 230), and whole-wheat chapati flatbreads.

3/4 cup split urad beans (chilkae vaali urad dal), sorted and washed in 3 to 4 changes of water

1/2 cup yellow split chickpeas (channa dal), sorted and washed in 3 to 4 changes of water

4 to 5 cups water

1/4 teaspoon ground turmeric

1/4 teaspoon cayenne pepper, or to taste

1 teaspoon salt, or to taste

1 large bunch fresh spinach (about 1 pound), trimmed of roots only, washed, and finely chopped

1 cup finely chopped fresh cilantro, including soft stems

2 tablespoons peeled minced fresh ginger

3 tablespoons vegetable oil

1 1/2 teaspoons cumin seeds

1 small onion, finely chopped

1 large clove fresh garlic, minced

1 large tomato, finely chopped

1 to 3 fresh green chile peppers, such as serrano, minced with seeds

1 tablespoon ground coriander

1 teaspoon ground cumin

1 teaspoon ground dried fenugreek seeds

1/2 teaspoon ground paprika

1/2 teaspoon garam masala

1. Place the dals, 4 cups water, turmeric, cayenne pepper, and salt in a pressure cooker. Secure the lid and cook over high heat until the regulator indicates high pressure, then cook 1 minute more. Remove from the heat and allow the pot to depressurize on its own, 12 to 15 minutes. Carefully open the lid, stir the dal, and simmer over medium-low heat, about 10 minutes, adding more water, if needed.

2. Add the spinach, cilantro, and ginger and continue to simmer until the spinach is wilted and the dal is creamy, about 15 minutes. Transfer to a serving dish, cover, and keep warm.

3. Heat the oil in a small saucepan over medium-high heat and add the cumin seeds; they should sizzle upon contact with the hot oil. Quickly add the onion and cook, stirring, until golden, about 3 minutes. Add the garlic, tomato, and green chile peppers, stir 1 minute, then add the coriander, cumin, fenugreek, and paprika. Transfer to the dal and swirl lightly to mix, with parts of it visible as a garnish. Sprinkle the garam masala on top and serve.

Whole Dried Bean Dishes

Spicy Adzuki Beans
Laal Chori Dal

Makes 4 to 6 servings

Called adzuki beans, these deep red-brown oval beans are a little larger than green mung beans. They are quite easy to cook, and when cooked in a pressure cooker they don't require endless time in the kitchen.

Start with 5 cups of water and add more if you prefer a thinner dish. And keep in mind that all dals (legumes) thicken as they cool, so if you cook this ahead of time, keep it somewhat thin, or simply add some water and bring to a boil again before serving.

1 1/4 cups dried adzuki beans (laal chori dal), sorted and washed in 3 to 4 changes of water

5 to 6 cups water

1 large tomato, finely chopped

1 tablespoon minced peeled fresh ginger

1 to 3 fresh green chile peppers, such as serrano, minced with seeds

1 teaspoon salt, or to taste

1/2 teaspoon ground turmeric

1/4 cup finely chopped fresh cilantro

2 tablespoons peanut oil

1 teaspoon cumin seeds

1 tablespoon ground coriander

1/2 teaspoon ground cumin

1/2 teaspoon ground paprika

1/4 teaspoon garam masala

1. Place the dal, 4 cups water, tomato, ginger, green chile peppers, salt, and turmeric in a pressure cooker. Secure the lid and cook over high heat until the regulator indicates high pressure, then cook 1 minute more. Remove from the heat and allow the pot to depressurize on its own, 12 to 15 minutes. Carefully open the lid and check to see if the beans are very soft, with some of them broken; if not, add more water as needed, cover, bring up to pressure, and cook under high pressure about 30 seconds. Or cover and boil until the dal is soft and creamy, about 30 minutes.

2. Heat the oil in a small nonstick saucepan over medium-high heat and add the cumin seeds; they should sizzle upon contact with the hot oil. Quickly add the coriander and cumin, cook 5 to 10 seconds, and remove from the heat. Mix in the paprika and then lightly swirl everything into the dal, with parts of it visible as a garnish. Sprinkle the garam masala on top and serve.

Mustard-Roasted Adzuki Beans
Bhuni Laal Chori Dal

Makes 4 to 6 servings

Made without a formal tarka *(a sizzling flavor topping), as would be customary for most dal dishes, this dish gets its unique smoky flavor from the initial gentle roasting of the beans in mustard oil, mustard seeds, and other spices. Once it is roasted, this dal can be cooked in a pressure cooker as in Spicy Adzuki Beans (page 369), or in a pan.*

  This recipe requires cooking the beans for about 1 hour, but if you have the time, cook it as long as 2 hours. The longer you cook it, the more flavor it has. Just keep the heat low and watch the water, adding about ¼ cup at a time as it dries up.

1 tablespoon mustard oil
1 teaspoon black mustard seeds
1 cup dried adzuki beans (red chori dal),
    sorted and washed in 3 to 4 changes of water
1 large tomato, finely chopped
12 to 15 fresh curry leaves
¹⁄₈ teaspoon ground asafoetida
1 tablespoon peeled minced fresh ginger
1 large clove fresh garlic, peeled
1 tablespoon ground coriander
¹⁄₂ teaspoon ground cumin
1 teaspoon salt, or to taste
5 to 6 cups water
¹⁄₄ cup finely chopped fresh cilantro, including soft stems
¹⁄₂ cup nonfat plain yogurt, whisked until smooth

1. Heat the oil in a large nonstick wok or saucepan over medium-high heat and add the mustard seeds; they should splutter upon contact with the hot oil, so cover the pan and reduce the heat until the spluttering subsides.

2. Add everything except the water, cilantro, and yogurt, and stir to roast the dal until it is fragrant and lightly golden, about 10 minutes. Add about 4 cups water and bring to a boil over high heat. Reduce the heat to medium-low, cover the pan, and simmer until the dal is soft and creamy, about 1 hour. Stir occasionally and add more water as needed. Transfer to a serving dish, mix in the cilantro, then swirl in the yogurt with parts of it visible as a garnish. Serve.

Classic No-Onion Kidney Bean Curry
Bina Pyaz kae Rassae vaalae Rajma

Makes 4 to 6 servings

There are two basic ways of making kidney bean curry: one is with onion and the other without, and though the end result of both is visually quite similar, the taste is remarkably different. You will find regional differences in the way this dish is prepared, as people from different parts of India use different spices (mustard seeds and curry leaves in the south, and black cardamom and fenugreek leaves in the north), but the basic procedure is the same.

  This is the lighter, no-onion north-Indian version, made with generous helpings of tomatoes and yogurt.

1¹⁄₄ cups dried kidney beans, sorted and washed
    in 3 to 4 changes of water
4 black cardamom pods, crushed lightly
    to break the skin
1 (2-inch) stick cinnamon, broken lengthwise
¹⁄₄ teaspoon ground turmeric
1 teaspoon salt, or to taste
4 to 5 cups water
2 tablespoons vegetable oil
1 tablespoon melted ghee

1 teaspoon cumin seeds
1 tablespoon peeled minced fresh ginger
1 large clove fresh garlic, minced
2 large tomatoes, finely chopped
1/2 cup finely chopped fresh cilantro,
    including soft stems
1/4 cup nonfat plain yogurt, whisked until smooth
1 tablespoon ground coriander
1 teaspoon dried fenugreek leaves
1/2 teaspoon ground cumin
1/2 teaspoon garam masala + more for garnish

1. Soak the beans overnight in water to cover by 2 inches. Then drain and place them in a pressure cooker, along with the cardamom pods, cinnamon, turmeric, salt, and 4 cups water. Secure the lid of the pressure cooker, place over high heat, and cook until the gauge indicates high pressure, then cook about 1 minute more. Reduce the heat to low and continue to cook another 3 minutes. Then remove from the heat and allow pot to depressurize on its own, 15 to 20 minutes. Carefully open the lid and check to see if the beans are very soft, with some of them broken; if not, cover, bring up to pressure again, and cook under pressure another minute. Or cover and boil until soft, about 1/2 hour.

2. Meanwhile, prepare the sauce. Heat the oil and ghee in a small saucepan over medium-high heat and add the cumin seeds, they should sizzle upon contact with the hot oil. Quickly, add the ginger and garlic and stir a few seconds. Add the tomatoes and cilantro (reserve some for garnish) and cook, stirring occasionally, until the juices evaporate, 8 to 10 minutes.

3. Mix in the yogurt, a little at a time, stirring constantly to prevent it from curdling. Add the coriander, fenugreek leaves, cumin, and garam masala, and stir about 1 minute. Transfer to the pot with the kidney beans and simmer, stirring occasionally, over low heat, another 15 to 20 minutes. Add up to 1 cup more water if you prefer a thinner dish. Transfer to a serving dish, sprinkle the garam masala and cilantro on top, and serve.

Classic Kidney Bean Curry with Onions

Pyaz Masalae kae Rassae vaalae Rajma

Makes 4 to 6 servings

This classic recipe is made with a base of ground onions and other curry ingredients like ginger, garlic, and tomatoes. The first part of the recipe remains the same as Classic No-Onion Kidney Bean Curry (page 370), but the sauces are considerably different in taste and flavor, because of the onions. This one also doesn't contain yogurt.

1 1/4 cups dried kidney beans, sorted and washed
    in 3 to 4 changes of water
4 black cardamom pods, crushed lightly
    to break the skin
1 (2-inch) stick cinnamon, broken lengthwise
1/4 teaspoon ground turmeric
1 teaspoon salt, or to taste
4 to 5 cups water
1/2 cup (1 recipe) Basic Curry Paste with Onion
    (page 50)
1 tablespoon ground coriander
1 teaspoon dried fenugreek leaves
1/2 teaspoon ground cumin
1/2 teaspoon garam masala + more for garnish
1/4 cup finely chopped fresh cilantro,
    including soft stems + more for garnish

1. Soak and cook the kidney beans along with the cardamom pods, cinnamon, turmeric, salt, and 4 cups water, until they are tender, as per Step 1 of Classic No-Onion Kidney Bean Curry (page 370).

2. Meanwhile, prepare the onion paste and then mix in the coriander, fenugreek leaves, cumin, and garam masala and stir, about 2 minutes. Transfer to the cooked kidney beans, add the cilantro, and simmer over low heat, stirring occasionally, 15 to 20 minutes. Add up to 1 1/2 cups more water as it cooks if you prefer a thinner, saucier dish. Transfer to a serving dish, sprinkle the garam masala and cilantro on top, and serve.

Kashmiri Small Red Beans

Kashmiri Chottae Raajma

Makes 4 to 6 servings

No visit to Kashmir is complete unless bags of small red raajma beans (and saffron) are purchased to be brought back to the rest of the family. These beans are a smaller version of kidney beans. Since the authentic ones are not available in America, I routinely use small red beans and cook them in the pressure cooker.

1 teaspoon vegetable oil
1¼ cups dried small red beans, sorted and washed
    in 3 to 4 changes of water
2 bay leaves
5 black cardamom pods, crushed lightly
    to break the skin
1 tablespoon peeled minced fresh ginger
1 teaspoon minced fresh garlic cloves
1 teaspoon ground fennel seeds
½ teaspoon hot red pepper flakes, or to taste
½ teaspoon ground dried ginger
¼ teaspoon ground turmeric
⅛ teaspoon ground asafoetida
½ teaspoon salt, or to taste
5 cups water
1 cup nonfat plain yogurt, whisked until smooth
½ cup finely chopped fresh cilantro,
    including soft stems
½ teaspoon garam masala

1. Heat the oil in a pressure cooker over medium-low heat. Add the beans, bay leaves, cardamom pods, ginger, garlic, fennel seeds, red pepper, dried ginger, turmeric, asafoetida, and salt, and stir constantly until fragrant and well roasted, about 5 minutes.

2. Carefully, standing far from the pan, add 4 cups water. (The heated metal pan causes the water to sizzle and steam upon contact.) Or let the pan cool down before adding the water. Secure the lid and cook over high heat until the regulator indicates high pressure, then cook 1 minute more. Reduce the heat to low and continue to cook another 3 minutes. Remove from the heat and allow the pot to depressurize on its own, 12 to 15 minutes.

3. Carefully open the lid and check to see if the beans are very soft with some of them broken; if not, then cover, bring up to pressure, and cook under high pressure another minute. Or cover and boil until the dal is soft and creamy, about 45 minutes.

4. Meanwhile, in a blender or a food processor, process together the yogurt, the remaining 1 cup water and the cilantro, and add to the beans. Cook over medium-high heat until the sauce is thick, about 10 minutes. Transfer to a serving dish, sprinkle the garam masala on top, and serve.

Punjabi Red Beans with Mango Pickle Masala

Punjab kae Achaari Raajma

Makes 4 to 6 servings

With their pantry well stocked with a variety of mango pickles, the Punjabi people often add some to their dishes. Here is one such dish that my mother cooks in her pressure cooker. If you don't have any mango pickle and don't have time to make one (pages 79 to 81), buy some from an Indian market and use only the spices (generally called masala) in the pickle, not the pieces. If you do choose to mix in the pieces, chop them finely and make sure the seeds are discarded.

1¼ cups dried red or kidney beans, sorted and
    washed in 3 to 4 changes of water
4½ cups hot water
2 to 3 teaspoons any mango pickle
    (pages 79 to 81, or store-bought)
½ teaspoon salt, or to taste
1 small onion, coarsely chopped
5 quarter-size slices peeled fresh ginger
1 large clove fresh garlic, peeled
3 to 4 small tomatoes, coarsely chopped
½ cup coarsely chopped fresh cilantro,
    including soft stems + more for garnish
1 fresh green chile pepper, such as serrano, stemmed
¾ cup nonfat plain yogurt, whisked until smooth
½ cup water
2 to 3 tablespoons peanut oil

1 tablespoon ground coriander
$^1/_2$ teaspoon ground cumin
$^1/_4$ teaspoon ground turmeric
$^1/_4$ teaspoon ground paprika
1 teaspoon ground dried fenugreek leaves
$^1/_4$ teaspoon garam masala

1. In a pressure cooker, soak the red beans, mango pickle masala, and salt in the hot water about 6 hours, or until the beans swell up and become much lighter in color. Secure the lid and cook over high heat until the regulator indicates high pressure, then cook 30 seconds more. Remove from the heat and allow the pot to depressurize on its own, 12 to 15 minutes. Carefully open the lid and check to see if the beans are very soft with some of them broken; if not, cover, bring up to pressure, and cook under high pressure another minute. Or cover and boil until the dal is soft and creamy, about 30 minutes.

2. Meanwhile, prepare the sauce. In a food processor, process together the onion, ginger, and garlic to make a fine paste. Remove to a bowl and process the tomatoes, cilantro, and green chile pepper until puréed. Remove to a separate bowl, then process the yogurt and water until smooth.

3. Heat the oil in a medium nonstick wok or saucepan over medium heat and cook the onion-garlic paste, stirring, until well browned, about 10 minutes. Add the puréed tomato mixture and stir until all the juices evaporate and traces of oil are visible on the sides, about 5 minutes. Mix in the coriander, cumin, turmeric, paprika and fenugreek leaves, and stir about 30 seconds. Add the yogurt-water and cook, stirring continuously, until it is completely incorporated into the dish and the mixture is dry, about 2 minutes.

4. Transfer everything to the softened beans and simmer over medium heat, about 15 minutes, to blend the flavors. Add more water if you prefer a thinner sauce, or cook longer if you favor thicker sauce. (The beans will thicken as the dish cools, so add your water accordingly.) Transfer to a serving dish, garnish with garam masala and cilantro, and serve.

Black Beans in Traditional Curry Sauce
Rassadar Kaalae Rajma

Makes 4 to 6 servings

Black beans, though not Indian by origin, have a remarkable affinity for the traditional bold and robust Indian flavors. Like red beans, they cook quickly in a pressure cooker, are nutritious like black chickpeas, and taste incredible with whole-wheat breads such as chapatis *or* paranthas, *or with* basmati *rice.*

$1^1/_2$ cups black beans, sorted and washed
    in 3 to 4 changes of water
4 to $4^1/_4$ cups water
$^1/_4$ teaspoon ground turmeric
1 teaspoon salt, or to taste
1 (15-ounce) can tomato sauce
2 tablespoons peanut oil
1 teaspoon ghee
2 teaspoons cumin seeds
1 small onion, finely chopped
1 tablespoon peeled minced fresh ginger
1 large clove fresh garlic, minced
$1^1/_2$ tablespoons ground coriander
1 tablespoon ground fenugreek leaves
1 teaspoon ground cumin
1 teaspoon garam masala + $^1/_4$ teaspoon for garnish
$^1/_2$ teaspoon ground turmeric
$^1/_4$ teaspoon cayenne pepper, or to taste
$^1/_4$ cup finely chopped fresh cilantro,
    including soft stems

1. Soak the beans overnight in water to cover by 2 inches. Then drain and place them in a pressure cooker along with the water, turmeric, and salt. Secure the lid and cook over high heat until the regulator indicates high pressure, then cook 30 seconds more. Remove from the heat and allow the pot to depressurize on its own, 12 to 15 minutes. Carefully open the lid and check to see if the beans are very soft with some of them broken; if not, cover, bring up to pressure, and cook under high pressure another minute. Or cover and boil until the dal is soft and creamy, about 30 minutes. Add the tomato sauce and simmer over medium-low heat about 15 minutes.

2. Heat the oil and ghee in a small saucepan over medium-high heat and add the cumin seeds; they should sizzle upon contact with the hot oil. Quickly add the onion and stir until golden, about 5 minutes. Then add the ginger and garlic and stir about 1 minute.

3. Add the coriander, fenugreek leaves, ground cumin, garam masala, turmeric, and cayenne pepper, stir about 30 seconds, and transfer to the cooked beans. Mix in the cilantro and simmer about 10 minutes. Transfer to a serving dish, sprinkle the garam masala on top, and serve.

Curried Black-Eyed Peas
Rassaedar Lobia

Makes 4 to 6 servings

Here is a standard everyday curry, made easy with the pressure cooker, and enlivened with green chile peppers, garam masala, and yogurt.

1¼ cups dried black-eyed peas (lobia), sorted and washed in 3 to 4 changes of water

3 to 3½ cups water

1 teaspoon salt, or to taste

2 tablespoons peanut oil

1 teaspoon cumin seeds

1 tablespoon peeled minced fresh ginger

1 small clove fresh garlic, minced

1 fresh green chile pepper, such as serrano, minced with seeds

1 large tomato, finely chopped

½ cup finely chopped fresh cilantro, including soft stems + more for garnish

1 tablespoon ground coriander

1 teaspoon ground dried fenugreek leaves

½ teaspoon ground cumin

¼ teaspoon ground turmeric

½ cup nonfat plain yogurt, whisked until smooth

¼ teaspoon garam masala

1. Soak the black-eyed peas overnight in water to cover by 2 inches. Then place them in a pressure cooker along with the water and salt. Secure the lid and cook over high heat until the regulator indicates high pressure, then cook 1 minute more. Remove from the heat and allow the pot to depressurize on its own, 12 to 15 minutes. Carefully open the lid and check to see if the beans are very soft with some of them broken; if not, cover, bring up to pressure, and cook under high pressure another minute. Or cover and boil until the dal is soft and creamy, about 30 minutes.

2. Meanwhile, prepare the sauce. Heat the oil in a medium nonstick wok or saucepan over medium-high heat. Add the cumin seeds; they should sizzle upon contact with the hot oil. Quickly add the ginger, garlic, and green chile pepper and stir until golden, 30 seconds.

3. Add the tomato and cilantro and cook, stirring, until all the juices evaporate and the mixture is completely dry, 3 to 5 minutes. Mix in the coriander, fenugreek leaves, ground cumin, and turmeric and stir about 30 seconds.

4. Add the yogurt, a little at a time, stirring constantly to prevent it from curdling. Then transfer everything to the black-eyed peas and simmer over medium heat about 15 minutes to blend the flavors. Add more water if you prefer a thinner sauce, or cook longer if you favor a thicker sauce. Transfer to a serving dish, garnish with garam masala and cilantro, and serve.

Black-Eyed Peas in Yogurt Curry
Dahi ka Lobia

Makes 4 to 6 servings

Another pressure-cooked dish, I first cooked black-eyed peas this way on a day when I was completely out of tomatoes. Now I find myself torn every time I make black-eyed peas, because both alternatives are equally delicious.

1 tablespoon Basic Ginger-Garlic Paste
    (page 47 or store-bought)

1 cup dried black-eyed peas (lobia), sorted and
    washed in 3 to 4 changes of water

3 cups water

2 black cardamom pods, crushed lightly
    to break the skin

1 (1-inch) stick cinnamon, broken lengthwise

1 teaspoon salt, or to taste

3 tablespoons vegetable oil

1 teaspoon cumin seeds

1/2 teaspoon coarsely ground fenugreek seeds

1 small onion, cut in half lengthwise and thinly sliced

1 to 3 fresh green chile peppers, such as serrano,
    minced with seeds

1 tablespoon ground coriander

1/2 teaspoon ground cumin

1/4 teaspoon ground turmeric

1 cup nonfat plain yogurt, whisked until smooth

1/2 teaspoon ground green cardamom seeds

1/4 cup finely chopped fresh cilantro,
    including soft stems + more for garnish

1/4 teaspoon garam masala

1. Soak the black-eyed peas overnight in water to cover by 2 inches. Meanwhile, prepare the ginger-garlic paste. When ready, place the peas in a pressure cooker along with the water, cardamom pods, cinnamon, and salt. Secure the lid and cook over high heat until the regulator indicates high pressure, then cook 1 minute more. Remove from the heat and allow the pot to depressurize on its own, 12 to 15 minutes. Carefully open the lid and check to see if the beans are very soft with some of them broken; if not, cover, bring up to pressure, and cook under high pressure another minute. Or cover and boil until the dal is soft and creamy, about 30 minutes.

2. Meanwhile, prepare the sauce. In a medium non-stick saucepan, heat the oil over medium heat and add the cumin and fenugreek seeds; they should sizzle upon contact with the hot oil. Quickly add the onion and cook, stirring, until golden, about 3 minutes, then mix in the green chile peppers and the ginger-garlic paste and stir about 30 seconds. Add the coriander, ground cumin, and turmeric and stir another minute.

3. Add the yogurt, a little at a time, stirring constantly to prevent it from curdling. Transfer everything to the black-eyed peas, mix in the ground cardamom seeds and cilantro, cover, and bring to a boil over high heat (no need to secure the lid). Reduce the heat to low and simmer about 15 minutes, adding more water, if necessary. Transfer to a serving dish, sprinkle the garam masala and cilantro on top, and serve.

Small White Beans with Indian Spices
Sufaid Rajma

Makes 4 to 6 servings

These beans aren't found in India, but I enjoy cooking them here with an Indian twist. They cook just like kidney beans, easily in the pressure cooker, and taste wonderful.

1 cup white beans, washed

4 to 4 1/2 cups water

1 teaspoon salt, or to taste

2 bay leaves

2 black cardamom pods, crushed lightly
    to break the skin

1 (1-inch) stick cinnamon

3 tablespoons vegetable oil

1 large clove fresh garlic, minced

1 1/2 teaspoon cumin seeds

2 large tomatoes, finely chopped

1 to 3 fresh green chile peppers, such as serrano,
    minced with seeds

1 1/2 tablespoons peeled minced fresh ginger

2 tablespoons ground coriander

1 teaspoon ground cumin

1/2 teaspoon ground turmeric

1/2 cup nonfat plain yogurt, whisked until smooth

1/2 teaspoon ground, dried fenugreek leaves

1/2 cup finely chopped fresh cilantro,
    including soft stems

1/4 teaspoon garam masala

1. Soak the beans in water to cover by 2 inches at least 4 hours. Drain, then place them in a pressure cooker along with 4 cups water, salt, bay leaves, cardamom pods, and cinnamon. Secure the lid and cook over high heat until the regulator indicates high pressure, then cook 1 minute more. Reduce the heat to low and continue to cook another minute. Remove from the heat and allow the pot to depressurize on its own, 12 to 15 minutes. Carefully open the lid and check to see if the beans are very soft with some of them broken; if not, cover, bring up to pressure, and cook under high pressure another minute. Or cover and boil until the dal is soft and creamy, about 30 minutes.

2. Meanwhile, heat the oil in a medium nonstick saucepan, and cook the garlic until barely golden, about 30 seconds. Add the cumin seeds; they should sizzle upon contact with the hot oil. Quickly add the tomatoes, green chile peppers, and ginger and cook, stirring as needed, initially over high and then over medium heat until all the juices evaporate, about 10 minutes.

3. Add the coriander, ground cumin, and turmeric and cook, stirring, about 1 minute. Then add the yogurt, a little at a time, stirring constantly to prevent it from curdling, until it is absorbed. Mix in the fenugreek leaves and cilantro, and simmer another 5 minutes. Transfer to the pressure cooker. Stir well and bring to a boil over high heat. Reduce the heat to low and simmer about 15 minutes, uncovered, adding more water, if necessary. Transfer to a serving dish, sprinkle the garam masala on top, and serve.

Spicy Soybeans in Yogurt Sauce

Dahi vaalae Soyabeans

Makes 4 to 6 servings

Soybeans (pronounced soyabeans *in Hindi), are grown in India. But despite their numerous nutrition benefits, for some reason they have not made it into mainstream home cooking. They cook just like other beans—the dried ones cook quickly in the pressure cooker and the frozen ones easily in a pan.*

They taste delicious and take famously to Indian seasonings.

In this recipe I use shelled frozen soybeans (now popularly called edamame—*the Japanese name), which can be bought at Asian markets and in upscale produce and health-food stores.*

2 large tomatoes, coarsely chopped
1 to 3 fresh green chile peppers, such as serrano, stemmed
1/2 cup coarsely chopped fresh cilantro, including soft stems
3/4 cup nonfat plain yogurt
2 cups water
2 tablespoons vegetable oil
1 teaspoon cumin seeds
1/2 teaspoon coarsely ground fenugreek seeds
1 small onion, finely chopped
1 tablespoon peeled minced fresh ginger
1 large clove fresh garlic, minced
1 tablespoon ground coriander
1/4 teaspoon ground turmeric
1 teaspoon salt, or to taste
1 (16-ounce) package frozen shelled soybeans (edamame), thawed
1/4 teaspoon garam masala

1. In a food processor or a blender, process together the tomatoes, green chile peppers, and cilantro. Remove to a bowl and process the yogurt and water until smooth.

2. Heat the oil in a large saucepan over medium-high heat and add the cumin and fenugreek seeds; they should sizzle upon contact with the hot oil. Quickly add the onion, ginger, and garlic and cook until golden, about 4 minutes. Add the coriander, turmeric, and salt, then mix in the processed tomatoes and cook until most of the juices evaporate, about 5 minutes.

3. Add the soybeans and stir about 5 minutes. Mix in the yogurt-water mixture, and bring to a boil over high heat. Reduce the heat to medium-low, cover the pan, and simmer until the beans are soft and the sauce is thick, about 30 minutes. Transfer to a serving bowl, sprinkle garam masala on top, and serve.

Whole Chickpea Dishes

Chickpeas with Ginger, Garlic, and Chaat Masala
Channa–Chaat Masala

Makes 4 to 6 servings

Almost a salad, this user-friendly dish cooks quickly and easily because it is made with canned chickpeas. Just remember to rinse the canned chickpeas well to wash off the preservatives.

1 teaspoon Chaat Masala (page 20 or store-bought), or more to taste

2 tablespoons peanut oil

5 to 7 fresh green chile peppers, such as serrano, skin punctured to prevent bursting

2 teaspoons cumin seeds

2 tablespoons peeled minced fresh ginger

1 large clove fresh garlic, minced

1 1/2 tablespoons ground coriander

1/2 teaspoon ground cumin

1/2 teaspoon dried fenugreek leaves

4 (15 1/2-ounce) cans chickpeas, drained and rinsed well

1/3 cup water

1 to 2 tablespoons fresh lime or lemon juice

1/2 cup finely chopped fresh cilantro, including soft stems

Tomato wedges, sliced scallions, and chopped cilantro, for garnish

1. Prepare the chaat masala. Then, heat the oil in a large nonstick wok or skillet over medium-high heat and cook the green chile peppers, stirring gently, about 30 seconds (stand back in case they burst). Add the cumin seeds; they should sizzle upon contact with the hot oil. Quickly add the ginger and garlic and stir about 30 seconds.

2. Add the coriander, cumin, and fenugreek leaves, stir momentarily, then mix in the chickpeas and water. Cover and cook over medium heat until the

chickpeas are soft, about 4 minutes. Add the lime juice, chaat masala, and cilantro and cook, stirring, another 5 minutes. Transfer to a serving dish, mix in the tomato wedges, scallions, and cilantro, and serve.

Spicy Chickpeas with Pomegranate Seeds
Pindi Channae—Anardana

Makes 4 to 6 servings

This soft-cooked, almost blackened chickpea dish is India's answer to fast food. (The color comes from a special dry-roasted mixture of spices.) This dish is served throughout India with freshly made bhaturas *(deep-fried leavened flatbreads) or* kulchas *(baked leavened flatbreads).*

1 teaspoon Chaat Masala (page 20 or store-bought)

1 tablespoon ground dried pomegranate seeds

1 1/2 teaspoons ground cumin

1 teaspoon mango powder

1/2 teaspoon garam masala

1/2 teaspoon cayenne pepper or ground paprika

6 quarter-size slices peeled fresh ginger

1 large clove garlic, peeled

1 to 3 fresh green chile peppers, such as serrano, stemmed

2 tablespoons peanut oil

1 tablespoon ground coriander

1/4 teaspoon ground black salt

4 (15 1/2-ounce) cans chickpeas, drained and rinsed well

1/2 cup water

1 tablespoon vegetable oil or melted ghee

1 teaspoon cumin seeds

1 (1-inch) piece peeled fresh ginger, cut into thin matchsticks

1/2 cup finely chopped fresh cilantro, including soft stems

1/2 cup finely chopped scallions

2 to 3 small tomatoes, cut into wedges

1. Prepare the chaat masala. Place the pomegranate seeds, cumin, mango powder, garam masala, and cayenne pepper (or paprika) in a small skillet and roast, stirring and shaking the skillet, over medium heat until the spices are fragrant and dark brown (almost like the color of instant coffee), about 3 minutes. Transfer to a bowl. In a food processor or a blender, process together the ginger slices, garlic, and green chile peppers until minced.

2. Heat the oil (or ghee, if using) in a large nonstick skillet over medium-high heat and cook the ginger-garlic mixture, stirring, until golden, about 1 minute. Add the coriander, chaat masala, and black salt, then mix in the chickpeas and water and cook, stirring as needed until tender and almost dry, about 5 minutes. Add the roasted spices, reduce the heat to medium and cook another 5 minutes to blend the flavors. Transfer to a serving dish and keep warm.

3. Heat the ghee in a small saucepan over medium-high heat and add the cumin seeds; they should sizzle upon contact with the hot oil. Quickly add the ginger matchsticks and cook until golden, about 3 minutes. Add the cilantro and stir 1 minute, then add the scallions and tomato wedges. Stir about 1 minute and add to the chickpeas. Mix lightly, with parts of it visible as a garnish, and serve.

Pickle-Flavored Chickpeas
Achaari Channae

Makes 4 to 6 servings

This is another creatively flavored entrée made with chickpeas. Its main flavor-giving seeds are from a Bengali mix, but they are also very much a part of the north Indian kitchen. This dish can also be served as part of an Indian afternoon high-tea menu with samosas (savory triangular pastries) and Simple Carrot Halva (page 621).

1 large russet (or any) potato
1 to 2 tablespoons Tamarind Paste (page 54)
1 tablespoon Bengali 5-Spices (Panch-Phoran), page 27 or store-bought
1 tablespoon peanut oil

1 tablespoon mustard oil
2 tablespoons peeled minced fresh ginger
1 large clove fresh garlic, minced
1 fresh green chile pepper, such as serrano, minced with seeds
1 tablespoon ground coriander
1/4 teaspoon ground turmeric
1/8 teaspoon ground asafoetida
3 (15 1/2-ounce) cans chickpeas, drained and rinsed well
1/2 cup water
1/2 cup finely chopped fresh cilantro, including soft stems
1/4 teaspoon garam masala

1. Boil the potato in lightly salted water to cover until tender, about 20 minutes. Meanwhile, prepare the tamarind paste, then in a mortar and pestle, or with the back of a large spoon, coarsely grind the panch-phoran seeds. When the potato is cooked, let cool, then peel and finely chop it.

2. Heat both the oils in a large nonstick skillet over medium-high heat and add the panch-phoran; they should sizzle upon contact with the hot oil. Quickly add the ginger, garlic, and green chile pepper, then add the coriander, turmeric, and asafoetida.

3. Mix in the chickpeas, potato, and water and cook, stirring carefully, until they are tender and most of the liquid evaporates, about 5 minutes. Add the tamarind paste and cilantro and cook another 2 minutes. Transfer to a large platter, sprinkle the garam masala on top, and serve.

Chickpeas with Spinach and Potato Wedges
Sookhae Channae, Palak, aur Aalu

Makes 4 to 6 servings

Indians cook chickpeas in a many ways, and with the convenience of canned chickpeas, it's easy to make them often. Here is one uncommon recipe with familiar flavors.

2 tablespoons Tamarind Paste (page 54)

1 tablespoon Chickpea Masala with Pomegranate Seeds (page 24 or store-bought)

1 tablespoon Basic Ginger-Garlic Paste (page 47 or store-bought)

3 to 4 small (about 1 pound) unpeeled red or Yukon gold potatoes

3 tablespoons peanut oil

3 to 5 dried red chile peppers, such as chile de arbol, broken

1 1/2 teaspoons cumin seeds

1 teaspoon fenugreek seeds, coarsely ground

1/4 teaspoon ground turmeric

1 tablespoon chickpea flour

1 large bunch (12 to 14 ounces) fresh spinach, trimmed, washed and finely chopped

2 (15 1/2-ounce) cans chickpeas, drained and rinsed well

1 1/2 cups water

1/2 cup finely chopped fresh cilantro, including soft stems

1 tablespoon ground coriander

1/4 teaspoon garam masala

2 small tomatoes, cut into 6 wedges each

1. Prepare the tamarind paste, the chickpea masala, and the ginger-garlic paste. Boil the potatoes in lightly salted water to cover until soft, about 20 minutes. Let cook, then cut into wedges. Heat the oil in a large nonstick wok or skillet over medium-high heat and add the red chile peppers, cumin, and fenugreek seeds; they should sizzle upon contact with the hot oil. Quickly add the turmeric and chickpea flour and stir over medium heat until fragrant, about 1 minute.

2. Add the ginger-garlic paste and stir 1 minute. Then add the spinach and cook, stirring, until wilted, about 3 minutes. Add the potatoes, chickpeas, water, tamarind paste, and cilantro, and bring to a boil over high heat. Cover the pan, reduce the heat to medium, and cook until the chickpeas are soft, about 7 minutes. Mix in the coriander, chickpea masala, and garam masala during the last 5 minutes of cooking. Transfer to a serving dish, garnish with the tomato wedges, and serve.

Chickpeas in Traditional Curry Sauce

Rassaedar Channae

Makes 4 to 6 servings

Made the traditional way with dried chickpeas, this dish is a Saturday ritual in my mother's home in New Delhi. It has a thin, soupy sauce into which my mother loves dipping chapatis (whole-wheat griddle breads), not rice, as one normally would with soupy entrées. A big time-saver is the pressure cooker, or for even faster results, use four 15½-ounce cans of chickpeas (drained and rinsed well) instead of the dried ones and begin with Step 2.

1 1/4 cups dried chickpeas, sorted and washed in 3 to 4 changes of water

4 to 4 1/2 cups water

1/4 teaspoon baking soda

1 teaspoon salt or to taste

1 small onion, coarsely chopped

1 to 3 fresh green chile peppers, such as serrano, stemmed

1 large clove fresh garlic, peeled

5 quarter-size slices peeled fresh ginger

2 large tomatoes, coarsely chopped

2 tablespoons peanut oil

1 teaspoon cumin seeds

1 teaspoon ground coriander

1/2 teaspoon garam masala + 1/4 teaspoon for garnish

1/4 teaspoon ground turmeric

1/4 teaspoon ground paprika

1 tablespoon fresh lime juice

1/4 cup plain nonfat yogurt, whisked until smooth

1/4 cup finely chopped fresh cilantro, including soft stems

1. Soak the chickpeas overnight in water to cover by 2 inches. Then drain and place them in a pressure cooker along with the water, baking soda, and salt. Secure the lid and cook over high heat until the regulator indicates high pressure, then cook 1 minute more. Reduce the heat to low and continue to cook another 3 minutes. Remove from the heat and allow the pot to depressurize on its own, 12 to 15 minutes.

Carefully open the lid and check to see if the beans are very soft with some of them broken; if not, cover, bring up to pressure, and cook under high pressure another minute. Or cover and boil until the chickpeas are soft and creamy, about 30 minutes.

2. Meanwhile, in a food processor or a blender, process together the onion, green chile peppers, garlic, and ginger to make a paste. Remove to a bowl, then purée the tomatoes.

3. Heat the oil in a small nonstick saucepan over medium-high heat and add the cumin seeds; they should sizzle upon contact with the hot oil. Quickly add the onion-garlic paste and cook, stirring, over medium heat until browned, about 5 minutes. Add the tomatoes and cook until the juices evaporate, about 7 minutes.

4. Add the coriander, garam masala, turmeric, paprika, and lime juice, then add the yogurt a little at a time, stirring constantly to prevent it from curdling. Mix into the chickpeas and simmer about 15 minutes to blend the flavors. Add more water for a thinner curry. Transfer to a serving dish, mix in the cilantro and garam masala, and serve.

Chutney Chickpeas with Tamarind

Imli-Channae

Makes 6 to 8 servings

What separates one chickpea dish from another, besides the method of preparation, is the spices. This dish, made with naturally sour tamarind, is as much an entrée as it is a chutney when paired with samosas, *sandwiches, and grilled fare.*

This dish was originally made popular by vendors who traversed the streets of northern India with a cannister of chickpeas strapped to their bicycle, and set up shop wherever there was a crowd or whenever they were stopped by hungry customers.

1³/₄ cups dried chickpeas, sorted and washed in 3 to 4 changes of water

¹/₄ cup Tamarind Paste (page 54)

1¹/₂ tablespoons Basic Ginger-Garlic Paste (page 47 or store-bought)

5 to 6 cups water

¹/₄ teaspoon baking soda

1 teaspoon salt, or to taste

3 to 5 black cardamom pods, crushed lightly to break the skin

1 (1-inch) stick cinnamon

2 bay leaves

3 tablespoons peanut oil

1 teaspoon cumin seeds

¹/₂ teaspoon ajwain seeds

1 large onion, finely chopped

1¹/₂ cups finely chopped tomatoes

1 tablespoon ground coriander

1 teaspoon ground cumin

¹/₂ teaspoon garam masala

¹/₄ teaspoon ground turmeric

¹/₄ teaspoon ground black salt

1 to 3 fresh green chile peppers, such as serrano, split lengthwise in half

¹/₂ cup finely chopped fresh cilantro, including soft stems

2 tablespoons minced fresh mint leaves

1. Soak the chickpeas overnight in water to cover by 2 inches. Meanwhile, prepare the tamarind paste and the ginger-garlic paste. When ready, drain the chickpeas and place them in a pressure cooker along with 5 cups water, baking soda, salt, cardamom pods, cinnamon, and bay leaves. Secure the lid and cook over high heat until the regulator indicates high pressure, then cook 2 minutes. Remove from the heat and allow the pot to depressurize on its own, 12 to 15 minutes.

2. Carefully open the lid and check to see if the beans are very soft with some of them broken; if not, add more water as needed, cover, bring up to pressure, and cook under high pressure another minute. Or, cover and boil until the chickpeas are soft and creamy, about 45 minutes.

3. Heat the oil in a small nonstick saucepan over medium-high heat and add the cumin and ajwain seeds; they should sizzle upon contact with the hot oil. Quickly add the onion and cook, stirring, until golden, about 5 minutes. Add the ginger-garlic paste and stir about 1 minute. Add the tomatoes and continue to cook until the tomatoes are soft and all the juices evaporate, about 5 minutes.

4. Add the coriander, ground cumin, garam masala, turmeric, and black salt, then add the tamarind paste and bring to a quick boil. Mix into the chickpeas along with the green chile peppers, cilantro, and mint, and simmer until the sauce is very thick, about 15 minutes. Stir vigorously and smash some of the chickpeas to further thicken the dish. Serve.

Canister Chickpeas (or Dried Yellow Peas)

Peepae vaalae Chholae

Makes 4 to 6 servings

Made interchangeably with a special variety of small chickpeas, or with dried yellow peas, this is basically a one-step preparation. All the ingredients (except the tamarind and any garnishes) are cooked together until the chickpeas are meltingly soft and so flavorful.

Popularly called canister chickpeas or peepae vaalae chholae, *this was another dish originally prepared and stored in large metal canisters that were strapped onto bicycles, then sold from door to door by vendors. Considered contraband by parents because they were not prepared or served under hygienic conditions, of course they were therefore devoured as a snack any time we kids could get them, along with* kulcha *(baked leavened flatbreads).*

You don't have to wait for anyone to come knocking; it cooks up in under an hour with a pressure cooker.

1¼ cups dried chickpeas (or yellow peas), sorted and washed in 3 to 4 changes of water
¼ cup Tamarind Paste (page 54)
1½ tablespoons Basic Ginger-Garlic Paste (page 47 or store-bought)
1 large russet (or any) potato, peeled and cut into ¾-inch pieces
1 (1-inch) piece fresh ginger, cut into thin matchsticks
4 to 5 cups water
1 tablespoon vegetable oil or melted ghee
¼ teaspoon baking soda
1 teaspoon salt, or to taste
3 to 5 black cardamom pods, crushed lightly to break the skin
5 to 7 green cardamom pods, crushed lightly to break the skin
5 to 7 whole cloves
1 (1-inch) stick cinnamon
2 bay leaves
1 small onion, chopped
1 fresh green chile pepper, such as serrano, minced with seeds
2 large tomatoes, finely chopped
1 tablespoon ground coriander
1 teaspoon ground cumin
½ teaspoon garam masala
½ teaspoon cayenne pepper
¼ teaspoon ground turmeric
½ cup finely chopped fresh cilantro, including soft stems
8 scallions, white parts only, halved lengthwise
1 to 3 fresh green chile peppers, such as serrano, split in half lengthwise

1. Soak the chickpeas overnight in water to cover by 2 inches. Meanwhile, prepare the tamarind paste and ginger-garlic paste, then drain and place the chickpeas in a pressure cooker along with all the other ingredients (except the tamarind paste, cilantro, scallions, and green chile peppers). Secure the lid and cook over high heat until the regulator indicates high pressure, then cook 1 minute more. Reduce the heat to low and continue to cook another 2 minutes. Remove from the heat and allow the pot to depressurize on its own, 12 to 15 minutes.

2. Carefully open the lid and check to see if the beans are very soft with some of them broken; if not, add more water, as needed, cover, bring up to pressure, and cook under high pressure another minute. Or cover and boil until the chickpeas are soft and creamy, about 45 minutes.

3. Mix in the tamarind paste and cilantro. With a ladle, mash some of the chickpeas and simmer another 15 minutes. Transfer to a serving dish, garnish with the scallions and green chile peppers, and serve.

Fresh Green Chickpeas with Lentil Nuggets
Rassaedar Vadi-Chholia

Makes 4 to 6 servings

Green chickpeas, called hara chholia, *are rarely seen here but grab them if you see them at farmers' markets or Indian stores. They are a common sight during the Indian summers, which is when the Punjabis take advantage and cook them almost every other day, freezing some for later use—such as for Punjabi Green Chickpeas Pilaf (page 552).*

Like all other beans when fresh, young chickpeas come encased in pods. Each pod contains one or two divine tasting green chickpeas, which are transformed into curries, salads, pullaos *(rice pilafs), and side dishes.*

Crispy dried lentil nuggets, called badiyan *or* vadiyan, *are generally very spicy hot and impart a unique fragrance. Buy them at an Indian market.*

1 large lentil nugget (badiyan)
3 tablespoons peanut oil
1 cup finely chopped onion
1 tablespoon peeled minced fresh ginger
1 to 3 fresh green chile peppers, such as serrano, minced with seeds
1 cup finely chopped tomatoes
1 tablespoon ground coriander
1 teaspoon ground cumin
¼ teaspoon ground turmeric
¼ teaspoon hot red pepper flakes, or to taste
2 cups shelled fresh green chickpeas
1 large potato, peeled and cut into ½-inch pieces
½ cup nonfat plain yogurt, whisked until smooth
2 to 3 cups water
Chopped cilantro and garam masala

1. With a rolling pin or the back of a small saucepan, break the lentil nugget into half-inch pieces. (The nugget is very soft and easy to break; if it breaks into smaller piece, that's fine.) Heat 1½ tablespoons oil in a medium nonstick saucepan over medium heat and fry the nugget pieces in 2 to 3 batches, frying similar-size pieces at one time and removing them as they brown, which happens very quickly.

2. To the same pan, add remaining 1½ tablespoons oil and the onion, and cook, stirring, until golden, about 5 minutes. Add the ginger and green chile peppers and cook, stirring, another 2 minutes. Then mix in the tomatoes and cook, stirring, until all the juices evaporate, about 5 minutes.

3. Add the coriander, ground cumin, turmeric, and red pepper flakes, stir briefly, then add the green chickpeas and the fried nuggets. Cook, stirring, over medium heat about 5 minutes to roast them. Add the yogurt a little at a time, stirring constantly to prevent it from curdling, until absorbed. Add the water and bring to a boil over high heat. Reduce the heat to medium-low, cover the pan and cook until the chickpeas are tender, about 30 minutes. Transfer to a serving dish, garnish with cilantro and garam masala, and serve.

Variation: This dish can also be made with shelled frozen fresh soybeans, available in Asian and health-food markets. (Green chickpeas and frozen soybeans cook in the same amount of time.)

Black Chickpeas with Sizzling Ginger and Cumin Seeds

Adrak-Jeera vaalae Kaalae Channae

Makes 4 to 6 servings

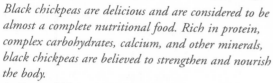

Black chickpeas are delicious and are considered to be almost a complete nutritional food. Rich in protein, complex carbohydrates, calcium, and other minerals, black chickpeas are believed to strengthen and nourish the body.

Because black chickpeas are only available in the United States in their dried form (not canned), they have to be soaked and boiled before they are recipe ready. Indians routinely boil them in a pressure cooker (to speed up softening). Once softened, they are further cooked in a cast-iron wok, which deepens their natural color, adds a lovely glaze, and fortifies them with iron and other trace minerals, making these already super beans into a powerhouse of nutrition.

1½ cups dried black chickpeas, sorted and washed
    in 3 to 4 changes of water
5 cups water
1 tablespoon Basic Ginger-Garlic Paste
    (page 47 or store-bought)
2 (1-inch) sticks cinnamon
2 black cardamom pods, crushed lightly
    to break the skin
1 fresh green chile pepper, such as serrano,
    minced with seeds
½ teaspoon salt, or to taste
¼ teaspoon ground black salt
2 tablespoons vegetable oil
1 teaspoon melted ghee (optional)
1 (1-inch) piece peeled fresh ginger,
    cut into thin matchsticks
1 teaspoon cumin seeds
1 tablespoon ground coriander
½ teaspoon ground paprika
¼ cup finely chopped fresh cilantro

1. Soak the chickpeas overnight in water to cover by 2 inches. Meanwhile, prepare the ginger-garlic paste. When ready, drain the chickpeas then place them in a pressure cooker, along with 4½ cups water, the cinnamon, cardamom podes, green chile pepper, ginger-garlic paste, salt, and black salt. Secure the lid and cook over high heat until the regulator indicates high pressure, then cook 1 minute more. Reduce the heat to low and continue to cook another 3 minutes. Remove from the heat and allow the pot to depressurize on its own, 12 to 15 minutes.

2. Carefully open the lid and check to see if the beans are very soft with some of them broken; unlike other beans, black chickpeas do not become soft to the point of disintegrating. If not sufficiently cooked, cover, bring up to pressure, and cook under high pressure another minute. Or cover and boil until soft, about 30 minutes.

3. Transfer to a large cast-iron wok or skillet and cook over high heat about 5 minutes, then over medium-low heat until all the water evaporates and the chickpeas are glazed with a dark brown coating, about 40 minutes. Stir occasionally.

4. Heat the oil (and the ghee, if using) in a large non-stick wok or saucepan over medium-high heat and cook the ginger matchsticks, stirring, until golden, about 1 minute. Add the cumin seeds; they should sizzle upon contact with the hot oil. Quickly add the coriander and paprika, stir about 30 seconds, then mix into the chickpeas. Transfer to a serving dish, mix in the cilantro, and serve.

Black Chickpeas with Chickpea Masala

Masaladar Kaalae Channae

Makes 4 to 6 servings

This is a common way you'll find chickpeas sold by Indian street vendors. Strongly flavored and chile-hot, this pressure-cooked, roadside specialty is generally topped with a minty green chutney, making it even more spicy, and is served as a snack with bhaturas *(deep-fried leavened flatbreads) or* kulchas *(baked leavened flatbreads).*

1½ cups dried black chickpeas, sorted and washed in 3 to 4 changes of water

5 cups water

3 to 4 tablespoons Chickpea Masala with Pomegranate Seeds (Channa Masala), page 24 or store-bought

¾ teaspoon salt, or to taste

½ cup finely chopped tomatoes

4 scallions, white parts only, finely chopped

¼ cup finely chopped fresh cilantro, including soft stems

2 tablespoons peanut oil

1 teaspoon melted ghee (optional)

1 teaspoon cumin seeds

1 tablespoon peeled minced fresh ginger

1 to 3 fresh green chile peppers, such as serrano, split lengthwise in half or minced

1 tablespoon ground coriander

½ teaspoon ground paprika

1. Soak the chickpeas overnight in water to cover by 2 inches. Meanwhile, prepare the channa masala. When ready, drain the chickpeas, then place them in a pressure cooker, along with 4½ cups water and salt. Secure the lid and cook over high heat until the regulator indicates high pressure, then cook 1 minute more. Reduce the heat to low and continue to cook another 3 minutes. Remove from the heat and allow the pot to depressurize on its own, 12 to 15 minutes. Carefully open the lid and check to see if the beans are very soft with some of them broken; unlike other beans, black chickpeas do not become soft to the point of disintegrating. If not sufficiently cooked, add more water, cover, bring up to pressure, and cook under high pressure another minute. Or cover and boil until soft, about 45 minutes.

2. Transfer the softened chickpeas to a cast-iron wok or saucepan and cook over medium-high heat about 5 minutes, then over medium-low heat until all the water evaporates and the chickpeas are glazed with a dark brown coating, about 40 minutes. Stir occasionally. Mix in half the chickpea masala, then add the tomatoes, scallions, and cilantro and cook, stirring gently, about 2 minutes. Transfer to a serving dish and sprinkle the remaining chickpea masala evenly on top.

3. Heat the oil (and ghee, if using) in a small saucepan over medium-high heat and add the cumin seeds; they should sizzle upon contact with the hot oil. Quickly add the ginger and green chile peppers and cook until golden, about 1 minute. Mix in the coriander and paprika and immediately pour everything over the chickpeas. Stir lightly to mix and serve.

Vegetarian Curries

Curry Sauces 388

Classic Spicy Curry Sauce

Butter-Cream Sauce
with Fresh Tomatoes

Yogurt-Cream Sauce with Nuts

Minty Green Curry Sauce

Classic Vegetable Curries 391

Curried Fresh Peas or Corn
and Potatoes

Whole Cauliflower
in Traditional Curry Sauce

Spicy Okra Curry

Crispy Fried Okra in Yogurt Sauce

Eggplant Curry
with Sambar Powder

Curried Eggplants
with Hot and Spicy Lentil Nuggets

Bitter Melon Curry

Simple Turnip Curry

Curried Baby White Turnips
with Turnip Greens

South Indian Pumpkin Curry
with Split Pigeon Peas

Kerala Cucumber Curry

Mushrooms in Almond
and Poppy Seed Sauce

Anaheim Peppers
in Spicy Tamarind Sauce

Hyderabadi Tomatoes
in Spicy Tamarind Sauce

Hyderabadi Spicy Eggplants with
Roasted Peanut and Sesame Sauce

Stuffed Bell Peppers
in Tomato-Cream Sauce

Onion Wedges in Curry Sauce

Potato Curries 403

Rajasthani Potato Curry

Pot-Roasted Fried Whole Potatoes
in Yogurt Curry

Minty Pot-Roasted Potato Curry

Haridwar Potato Curry

Curried Almond and
Poppy Seed Potatoes

Yogurt and Potato Curry

Diced Potato Curry
with Pickling Spices

Quick Potatoes and Peas Curry
with Tomato Sauce

Greens Entrées 408

Spicy Puréed Spinach Greens

Spinach, Fenugreek Greens,
and Broccoli

Punjabi Mustard Greens

Mustard Greens
with Cauliflower Florets

Savory Fruit Curries 411

Green Mango Curry

Mango Curry with Split Pigeon Peas

Watermelon Whites
in Tomato and Onion Sauce

Peach Halves
in Savory Ginger-Peach Sauce

Curried Jackfruit

A more misunderstood culinary term than "curry" would be hard to find. In Indian languages, curry means "a dish with a sauce," not any dish that has a teaspoon or two of a store-bought commercial blend of spices called curry powder in it—a blend that was probably originally put together by the British to recreate Indian flavors in their own kitchens.

The word curry is believed to be an English pronunciation (or should I say, mispronunciation) of the south Indian Tamil (the language of Tamilnadu, formerly Madras) word *kari*, which simply means a sauce, and was probably coined sometime during the British Raj, or rule, in India (1858 to 1947). Today, curry has become almost synonomous with Indian cuisine.

Because a curry is a saucy dish, this term includes all dishes with a sauce—whether the sauce is thick or thin or simply clings to the foods. A true curry, as understood by Indians, is a dish that results from the long, slow simmering of special *masala* pastes (see the Kitchen Basics chapter), dried herbs, and spices with different foods, where all the juices and flavors intermingle and develop as the foods cook in them. This meaning of curry also holds true in other parts of the world, such as Sri Lanka, Thailand, and Myanmar (Burma)—other countries where curries are part of the cuisine.

Curries can be enjoyed any time of the day with any meal; they add necessary moisture to the meal. Sometimes full-bodied and spicy, made with onions and garlic or without, with tomatoes and cream or nuts and yogurt, the far-reaching culinary category of curries—similar to, say, salads or soups—can be simple or complex.

Most cooks who make curries regularly don't measure or follow recipes. They add handfuls of whatever appeals to them and is on hand at the moment—much to the frustration of someone trying to learn or recreate a particular taste from a past meal (as I know from experience). Once you are familiar with the art of curry making and understand how certain spices and foods work together, making a curry will seem quite simple—which is why Indian cooks around the world rely on them as staples.

At the base of most curries lies a wet *masala*, also called *masala* paste, such as Spicy Yellow Curry Paste (page 52) or Basic Curry Paste without Onion (page 51). The paste is made with any one or more aromatic and elemental flavor ingredients, such as tomatoes, ginger, garlic, and onions, which are sweated and cooked until they slowly break down and their flavors become concentrated. As each ingredient evolves, it blends with the others to form a distinctive sauce. Fortifying and enriching the wet ingredients are a selection of dry *masalas* in the form of spices and herbs. Then there are some volume-adding liquids, such as buttermilk, yogurt, cream, water, and broth. From all these essential flavor components come the true character and final flavor of each curry.

One unique kind of curry, called *kadhi,* deserves special mention. Each community has its own versions, each flavorful and worthy of culinary exploration. At the base of most *kadhis* is a yogurt and a thickener, such as chickpea flour or *dal* (beans, lentils, or peas). These yellow or white saucy dishes, with a variety of greens, vegetables, or batter dumplings in them, are satisfying, soothing, and delicious. *Kadhis* are mild and delicate enough to be soothing, yet can be tangy and spicy enough to be addicting and memorable.

Keeping Western food trends and eating habits in mind, where many baked, roasted, or grilled foods are served with gravy created separately from the dish, this chapter begins with a few classic stand-alone curry sauces that are the backbone of Indian cuisine. You can make them separately and add them to your dishes. However, in Indian cuisine, these sauces are usually further simmered with other foods, such as steamed vegetables, *koftas* (fried vegetable or meat balls), or *tikkas* (grilled boneless meats, paneer cheese, or chunks of vegetables).

In this chapter I offer Indian vegetarian classics and some new recipes from my kitchen, after years of experimenting with foods available in the United States. (Non-vegetarian curries made with meat, chicken, or fish, are in the Non-Vegetarian Fare chapter, dried bean curries are in the Beans, Lentils, and Peas chapter, and *paneer* cheese curries are in the Paneer Cheese chapter.)

Curry Sauces

Classic Spicy Curry Sauce
Har-roz ki Kari

Makes about 4 cups

This is about as authentic as you can get when making a home-style curry sauce. Although robust and substantial, this stalwart of Indian cuisine is also as low in fat as it can possibly be.

Don't be misled by the term "spicy" in the title. In Indian cuisine, it doesn't automatically mean spicy hot. A curry can be spiced with bold flavors and it need not be hot at all. In fact, it can be completely devoid of any chile peppers, if that is what you prefer.

A curry sauce requires proper bhunna, *or roasting and browning of the wet* masala *(chopped or ground tomatoes, ginger, garlic, and onions, or other ingredients). This should be done slowly, over medium heat. You can tell the* masala *is well-roasted and has developed its flavor when traces of oil appear on the surface and sides of the browned* masala. *This oil separation is very pronounced if you add a lot of oil to your dishes; mine use very little oil, so all you'll see is tiny glistening drops of oil.*

To use, make the sauce and then add cooked or steamed vegetables, vegetable koftas *(meats or vegetable balls),* tikkas *(grilled meats or vegetables), or* pakoras *(batter-fried fritters) to the sauce and simmer a few minutes. Or pour some over cooked rice dishes to give them a new character. This sauce (and all other stand-alone sauces) can also be served on the side with grilled, roasted, and other dry-cooked foods.*

2 large cloves fresh garlic, peeled
4 to 6 quarter-size slices peeled fresh ginger
1 to 3 fresh green chile peppers, such as serrano, stemmed
1 large onion, coarsely chopped
1 large tomato, coarsely chopped
3 tablespoons peanut oil
1 tablespoon ground coriander
1 teaspoon ground cumin
1 teaspoon dried fenugreek leaves
1/2 teaspoon ground paprika
1/4 teaspoon ground turmeric
1/2 teaspoon salt, or to taste
1/2 cup nonfat plain yogurt, whisked until smooth
About 5 cups water
1/4 teaspoon garam masala
3 tablespoons finely chopped fresh cilantro

1. In a food processor or blender, process together the garlic, ginger, green chile peppers, and onion to make a smooth paste. Transfer to a small bowl. Process the tomato until smooth and transfer to another bowl.

2. Heat the oil in a large nonstick wok or saucepan over medium-high heat and cook the onion mixture, stirring, over medium-high heat the first 2 to 3 minutes and then over low heat until well browned, 8 to 10 minutes.

3. Add the processed tomato, increase the heat to medium-high, and cook, stirring occasionally, until all the juices evaporate and drops of oil appear on the top and sides, 8 to 10 minutes.

4. Add the coriander, cumin, fenugreek, paprika, turmeric, and salt, and cook, stirring, 2 to 3 minutes. Then mix in the yogurt a little at a time, stirring constantly to prevent it from curdling.

5. Add the water and bring to a boil over high heat. Reduce the heat to medium-low, cover the pan, and simmer until the sauce is reduced to about 4 cups, 12 to 15 minutes. Add more water for a thinner sauce, or cook longer for a thicker curry. If using as a stand-alone sauce, transfer to a serving bowl, garnish with the garam masala and cilantro; serve hot.

Butter-Cream Sauce with Fresh Tomatoes
Tamatar ki Makhani Kari

Makes about 4 cups

As a building block of many vegetarian and also non-vegetarian recipes, this sauce, often called makhani gravy, ranks high in the hierarchy of Indian sauces. It's a popular favorite in Indian restaurants around the world—with its familiar tomato flavor, it instantly appeals to foreign palates.

Serve this sauce on the side with grilled or broiled foods, or simmer any vegetables or paneer cheese in it to make outstanding entrées such as Royal Paneer Cheese Curry (page 334) or Stuffed Bell Peppers in Tomato-Cream Sauce (page 401).

2 tablespoons melted ghee or unsalted butter
1 (1-inch) stick cinnamon
2 bay leaves
2 black cardamom pods, crushed lightly
　　to break the skin
5 to 7 green cardamom pods, crushed lightly
　　to break the skin
10 whole cloves
3 to 4 cloves fresh garlic, coarsely chopped
6 to 8 quarter-size slices peeled fresh ginger
1 to 3 fresh green chile peppers, such as serrano,
　　coarsely chopped
5 large tomatoes (about 2¹/₂ pounds),
　　coarsely chopped
1 teaspoon ground paprika
¹/₂ teaspoon ground nutmeg
2¹/₂ cups water
1 teaspoon salt, or to taste
1 teaspoon ground dried fenugreek leaves
¹/₂ to 1 cup heavy cream

1. Heat the ghee (or butter) in a large nonstick wok or saucepan over medium heat and cook the cinnamon, bay leaves, black and green cardamom pods, cloves, garlic, ginger, and green chile peppers, stirring, until lightly browned, about 2 minutes.

2. Add the tomatoes, paprika, nutmeg, and water and bring to a boil over high heat. Reduce the heat to medium-low, cover the pan, and simmer, stirring occasionally, until the tomatoes are very soft and the volume reduces by about half, 20 to 25 minutes.

3. Let cool and pass through a food mill or fine-mesh strainer and discard the fibers. (Add an additional ¹/₂ cup water to extract maximum pulp.) Return to the pan, add the salt and fenugreek, and cook, stirring as needed, over medium-high heat about 10 minutes. If there is too much spluttering, cover the pan, reduce the heat, and cook an extra 5 to 7 minutes.

4. Add the cream and simmer over low heat another 5 minutes to blend the flavors. If using as a stand-alone sauce, transfer to a serving bowl; serve hot.

Variation: A quicker, easier version of this sauce can also be made using 2 15-ounce cans of tomato sauce instead of the fresh tomatoes.

Yogurt-Cream Sauce with Nuts
Korma Kari

Makes about 4 cups

Lots of powdered nuts (there are many in the masala), supported with fragrant cardamom seeds, cinnamon, and other spices, make for a creamy and smooth sauce that gets its delicious brown color from the long, slow cooking of sliced onions.

Serve on the side with sautéed vegetables, especially mushrooms, or with grilled meats, chicken, and seafood. Or, simmer the foods in the sauces a few minutes before serving.

²/₃ cup Fragrant Masala with Nuts (page 25)
2 cups nonfat plain yogurt
2 cups water
¹/₂ cup heavy cream
2 tablespoons melted ghee or vegetable oil
1 large onion, cut in half lengthwise and thinly sliced
1 teaspoon minced garlic
¹/₄ teaspoon salt, or to taste
2 tablespoons finely chopped fresh cilantro

1. Prepare the masala. Then, in a blender, blend together the yogurt, water, and cream until smooth. Heat the ghee (or oil) in a large nonstick wok or saucepan over medium-high heat and cook the onion, stirring, over high heat the first 2 to 3 minutes and then over medium-low heat until it's well browned and crisp, 10 to 12 minutes. Add the garlic and cook, stirring, about 1 minute, then add the masala and salt and cook, stirring, another minute.

2. Increase the heat to high and add the blended yogurt, a little at a time, stirring constantly to prevent it from curdling. Bring to a boil over high heat. Reduce the heat to medium-low, cover the pan, and simmer, stirring occasionally, until the sauce is thick and smooth and traces of oil are visible on the sides, 15 to 20 minutes. If using as a stand-alone sauce, transfer to a serving bowl, garnish with the cilantro and serve hot.

Minty Green Curry Sauce
Pudinae ki Hari Kari

Makes about 4 cups

Serve this green-brown sauce as is on the side, or mix into it some grilled or roasted lamb, chicken, seafood, paneer cheese, or steamed vegetables, then simmer for a few minutes before presenting it as a main dish. Also try this sauce with any of the koftas *(vegetable or meat balls), such as Spinach Balls in Green Curry (page 418).*

2 large cloves fresh garlic, peeled
6 quarter-size slices peeled fresh ginger
1 fresh green chile pepper, minced with seeds
3 to 5 scallions, green parts only, coarsely chopped
1 small onion, coarsely chopped
1/2 cup coarsely chopped fresh cilantro,
     including soft stems
1/4 cup coarsely chopped fresh mint leaves
1 tablespoon fresh lime juice
1 teaspoon garam masala
2 to 3 tablespoons peanut oil
1 tablespoon ground coriander
1 teaspoon ground cumin
1/2 teaspoon salt, or to taste
1/2 cup nonfat plain yogurt, whisked until smooth
4 cups water

1. In a food processor, process together the garlic, ginger, green chile pepper, scallions, and onion, until minced. Add the cilantro, mint, and lime juice and process to make a smooth paste. Add the garam masala and process again.

2. Heat the oil in a large nonstick wok or saucepan over medium-high heat. Add the paste and cook, stirring, over medium-high heat the first 2 to 3 minutes and then over medium-low heat until traces of oil are visible on the sides, 10 to 12 minutes.

3. Add the coriander, cumin and salt, then add the yogurt, a little at a time, stirring constantly to prevent it from curdling.

4. Add the water and bring to a boil over high heat. Reduce the heat to medium-low, cover the pan, and simmer until the sauce is thick and traces of oil are visible on the sides, 10 to 12 minutes. If using as a stand-alone sauce, transfer to a serving bowl; serve hot.

Variation: To make a more substantial sauce, purée a cup or two of fresh spinach or other greens along with the cilantro and mint. Adjust the water in Step 4, adding more as needed.

Classic Vegetable Curries

Curried Fresh Peas or Corn and Potatoes
Rassa Kae Muttar Aalu ya Makki Aalu

Makes 4 to 6 servings

Make this dish with corn or with peas; it's good both ways. If you decide on peas, for an authentic taste, shell fresh peas from the pod. (To get 1½ cups of shelled peas, you need about 1½ pounds of fresh pea pods.) The frozen ones, though a modern convenience, tend to make the dish rather sweet. Frozen corn however, works well.

1 tablespoon peanut oil
1 teaspoon cumin seeds
1 tablespoon ground coriander
1 teaspoon ground cumin
1 teaspoon ground dried fenugreek leaves
2 large tomatoes, finely chopped
½ recipe Spicy Yellow Curry Paste (page 52)
1 pound russet potatoes, peeled and
    cut in 1-inch cubes
1½ cups shelled fresh peas, or fresh corn
    (from 3 to 4 small ears) or frozen corn kernels
3 cups water
¼ cup finely chopped fresh cilantro,
    including soft stems
¼ teaspoon garam masala

1. Heat the oil in a large nonstick wok or saucepan over medium-high heat and add the cumin seeds; they should sizzle upon contact with the hot oil. Quickly add the coriander, ground cumin, and fenugreek leaves, then add the tomatoes and cook, stirring, until most of the juices evaporate, 4 to 6 minutes.

2. Mix in the curry paste and stir about 3 minutes, then add the potatoes and peas or corn, and stir-fry about 5 minutes. Add the water, cover the pan and cook, stirring as needed, over medium-high heat the first 2 to 3 minutes and then over medium-low heat until the potatoes are soft, 7 to 10 minutes. Adjust the salt, and add more water if you prefer a thinner sauce.

3. Mix in the cilantro, cook 1 minute, then transfer to a serving dish, sprinkle the garam masala on top, and serve.

Whole Cauliflower in Traditional Curry Sauce
Saabut Gobhi Masala

Makes 4 to 6 servings

In this recipe, a whole head of cauliflower, smothered in a fragrant curry sauce, makes for a dinner party dish par excellence. I simplify the cooking by microwaving the cauliflower first, but you can also steam it, and then pan-cook it for a fresher, lighter taste and a healthier dish. (Traditionally it is deep fried.)

1 (1½-pound) cauliflower, washed
3 tablespoons vegetable oil
¼ teaspoon salt, or to taste + ½ teaspoon
1 medium onion, coarsely chopped
8 quarter-size slices peeled fresh ginger
2 large cloves fresh garlic, peeled
1 to 3 fresh green chile peppers, such as serrano,
    stemmed
2 large tomatoes, coarsely chopped
½ cup nonfat plain yogurt, whisked until smooth
1 cup water
¼ teaspoon ground nutmeg
1½ teaspoons ground coriander
1 teaspoon ground cumin
½ teaspoon garam masala + ¼ teaspoon for garnish
¼ teaspoon ground turmeric
½ cup finely chopped fresh cilantro,
    including soft stems

1. Trim off the cauliflower leaves and cut off as much of the center stalk as possible, creating a cavity where you cut the head from the stalk (so the sauce will later add flavor inside the head). Remove the fibrous outer covering of the stalk with a knife, then chop the stalk coarsely and place it in a food processor bowl.

2. Place the cauliflower head in a microwave-safe dish. Brush the head on both sides with about 1 tablespoon oil and sprinkle lightly with ¼ teaspoon salt. Cover and microwave on high power until lightly softened, about 3 minutes.

3. Transfer to a large nonstick wok or saucepan (large enough to hold the cauliflower) and cook over medium-low heat until golden on all sides. Use kitchen tongs to turn the head as needed, making sure that most parts are covered with browned spots.

4. To the food processor with the chopped cauliflower stalk, add the onion, ginger, garlic, and green chile peppers and process to make a smooth paste. Transfer to a bowl. Process the tomatoes until puréed and transfer to another bowl. Then process together the yogurt, water, and nutmeg until smooth.

5. Heat the remaining oil over medium heat in the large nonstick wok or saucepan you used to cook the cauliflower, and cook the onion-ginger paste until browned, about 10 minutes. Add the puréed tomatoes and cook, stirring, until most of the juices evaporate, about 10 minutes.

6. Add the coriander, cumin, garam masala, turmeric, and ½ teaspoon salt and cook about 2 minutes. Add the yogurt-water mixture and half the cilantro and bring to a boil over high heat. Reduce the heat to medium-low, place the cauliflower, head up, in the sauce, spoon some of the sauce over the head, cover the pan, and simmer about 10 minutes. Turn the cauliflower over, spoon some of the sauce inside the center cavity, cover again, and simmer until the cauliflower is tender, about 20 minutes. (Test by inserting a sharp knife in the center.)

7. Using tongs, gently transfer the cauliflower to a serving dish, cover, and keep warm. Add the remaining cilantro to the sauce and cook over high heat, stirring, until the sauce is very thick, about 5 minutes. Spoon it over the cauliflower. Sprinkle the garam masala on top and serve.

Variation: This dish can be made with light green broccoflower, large eggplant halves, and even with oversize zucchinis. For a different flavor, use Butter-Cream Sauce with Fresh Tomatoes (page 389).

Spicy Okra Curry
Bhindi Kari

Makes 4 to 6 servings

Okra becomes slippery when cooked directly in liquid sauces. To prevent this, I pan-cook the okra to seal the surface before adding it to this delicious sauce. This prevents it from softening completely. Select small, young okra that are not more than 3 inches long and still retain a tiny bit of the soft fuzz.

¹/₂ cup Coconut Milk (page 44 or store-bought)
2 tablespoons Tamarind Paste (page 54)
1¹/₂ pounds small, fresh, tender okra, rinsed and patted dry
4 to 5 quarter-size slices peeled fresh ginger
1 large clove fresh garlic, peeled
1 to 3 fresh green chile peppers, such as serrano, stemmed
1 large tomato, coarsely chopped
1 tablespoon ground coriander
1 teaspoon ground cumin
2 tablespoons peanut oil
¹/₄ teaspoon ground turmeric
1 teaspoon salt, or to taste
1 large potato (any kind), peeled or unpeeled, cut into ¹/₂-inch pieces
¹/₄ cup finely chopped cilantro

1. Prepare the coconut milk and tamarind paste. Prepare the okra: cut off a thin slice of the stem end of each okra and discard, then cut the okra into ½-inch diagonal slices. (Cut off and discard the tips only if they look too brown.) Then place the okra in a large cast-iron or nonstick wok or skillet and cook (with 2 teaspoons of the peanut oil if the okra sticks to the bottom, as it may in the cast-iron pan) over medium-low heat, turning the pieces only when browned, until all sides are golden brown, 7 to 10 minutes. Transfer to a bowl.

2. In a food processor or a blender, process together the ginger, garlic, and green chile peppers until minced. Add the tomato, coconut milk, tamarind, coriander, and cumin, and process again to make a smooth paste.

3. Heat the peanut oil in a large nonstick wok or saucepan over medium-high heat, add the processed paste, and cook over medium-high heat the first 2 to 3 minutes, then over medium heat until golden brown, 5 to 7 minutes. Add the turmeric and salt, then add the potato and cook, stirring, until golden, about 5 minutes.

4. Add the water and bring to a boil over high heat. Reduce the heat to medium-low, cover the pan, and simmer until the potato is tender and the gravy thick, 5 to 7 minutes. Mix in the okra and cook another 5 minutes to blend the flavors. Mix in the cilantro and serve.

Crispy Fried Okra in Yogurt Sauce
Dahi Rassae Mein Tali Bhindi

Makes 4 to 6 servings

This dish is from the Parsi people (of Iranian descent) now settled in western India. It's not as smooth as one would expect a saucy okra dish to be. Instead, each piece of crispy fried okra stands on its own in a delicately smooth yogurt sauce. Try it with a simple rice pullao (pilaf).

2 teaspoons Basic Ginger-Garlic Paste (page 47 or store-bought)
1¼ pounds small fresh, tender okra, rinsed and patted dry
1 cup peanut oil for deep-frying
2 teaspoons ground cumin
¼ teaspoon ground turmeric
¼ teaspoon cayenne pepper
1½ cups nonfat plain yogurt, whisked with 1 tablespoon cornstarch until smooth
1 teaspoon salt, or to taste
¼ teaspoon garam masala

1. Prepare the ginger-garlic paste. Prepare the okra: cut off a thin slice of the stem end of each okra and discard, then cut the okra into ⅓-inch slices. (Cut off and discard the tips only if they look too brown.)

2. Heat the oil in a wok until it registers 350°F to 375°F on a frying thermometer or a small piece of okra dropped into the hot oil bubbles and rises to the top immediately. Add the okra (in 2 batches, if needed) and fry until crisp and lightly browned, 2 to 3 minutes. Transfer to a bowl and mix well with the ginger-garlic paste.

3. Discard all except 1 tablespoon oil from the wok (use this oil for other cooking, if you like). Heat the oil and add the cumin, turmeric, and cayenne pepper, Mix in the yogurt-cornstarch mixture, a little at a time, stirring constantly to prevent it from curdling. Cook, stirring, until most of the yogurt evaporates and the sauce becomes thick, 3 to 5 minutes.

4. Mix in the fried okra and salt, and cook about 5 minutes, until the flavors are blended. Transfer to a serving dish, top with the garam masala, and serve.

Variation: A similar curry can be made using 1 cup canned tomato sauce and ½ cup coconut milk instead of the yogurt.

Eggplant Curry with Sambar Powder
South kae Baingan

Makes 4 to 6 servings

Eggplant is an evergreen Indian favorite. It is used all over the country and there are many special eggplant dishes. Here is one from southern India.

1 tablespoon South Indian Sambar Powder (page 28 or store-bought) or South Indian Soup Powder (page 29 or store-bought)
1 cup nonfat plain yogurt
½ cup water
1 fresh green chile pepper, such as serrano, stemmed
10 to 12 fresh curry leaves
1 teaspoon rice flour
1 teaspoon salt, or to taste
2 tablespoons vegetable oil
1 teaspoon coarsely ground fenugreek seeds
¼ teaspoon hot red pepper flakes
2 small oval eggplants (about ½ pound each), quartered lengthwise through the stem
2 tablespoons finely chopped fresh cilantro

1. Prepare the sambar powder or soup powder. Then, in a blender or a food processor, process together the yogurt, water, green chile pepper, curry leaves, sambar or soup powder, rice flour, and salt until smooth.

2. Heat the oil in a large nonstick skillet over medium-high heat and add the fenugreek seeds and red pepper flakes, then quickly add the eggplants and cook, stirring, until lightly browned, 3 to 4 minutes. Transfer to a bowl.

3. Add the processed yogurt mixture to the skillet and cook, stirring constantly, over high heat until it comes to a boil. Return the eggplants to the skillet, reduce the heat to medium-low, cover the skillet and cook until the eggplants are soft and the sauce thick, 5 to 7 minutes. Transfer to a serving dish, sprinkle the cilantro on top, and serve.

Curried Eggplants with Hot and Spicy Lentil Nuggets

Baingan Vadiyan

Makes 4 to 6 servings

The Indian name for spicy, sun-dried lentil nuggets is vadiyan *or* badiyan. *On a heat scale of 1 to 10, the authentic version of this curry is probably a 9, but I tempered this recipe. It still packs a hefty punch, though, and is best served with steamed* basmati *rice and a soothing yogurt* raita. *A pressure cooker simplifies this curry, cooking it in a fraction of the traditional time.*

1 large clove fresh garlic, peeled
4 to 6 quarter-size slices peeled fresh ginger
1 small onion, coarsely chopped
2 large tomatoes, coarsely chopped
¹/₂ cup coarsely chopped fresh cilantro,
   including soft stems
¹/₄ cup vegetable oil
1 large lentil nugget, broken coarsely into
   1-inch pieces

1 tablespoon ground coriander
¹/₂ teaspoon ground cumin
¹/₄ teaspoon ground turmeric
¹/₂ teaspoon garam masala + ¹/₄ teaspoon for garnish
¹/₂ teaspoon salt, or to taste
2 to 3 medium russet potatoes, peeled and
   cut into 1-inch pieces
2 small oval eggplants (about ¹/₂ pound each),
   cut into 1¹/₂-inch pieces
2 cups water
¹/₄ cup minced fresh cilantro leaves

1. In a food processor, process together the garlic, ginger, and onion to make a paste. Transfer to a bowl and process the tomatoes and cilantro until smooth.

2. Heat the oil in a small nonstick wok or saucepan over medium-high heat and fry the lentil nugget, turning the pieces until browned, about 30 seconds. With a slotted spoon, transfer the nugget pieces to a dish, leaving as much oil in the pan as possible.

3. Add the garlic-ginger-onion paste to the pan and cook, stirring, over medium heat until well browned, 12 to 15 minutes. (Do not cook quickly over high heat—the onions will burn and will not develop a rich flavor.)

4. Transfer the cooked paste to a pressure cooker, add the puréed tomatoes and cilantro, and cook, stirring, over medium-high heat until all the juices evaporate, 3 to 5 minutes. Mix in all the spices and salt, then add the potatoes, eggplants, fried nuggets, and water. Secure the lid and cook over high heat until the pressure regulator indicates high pressure, then cook about 30 seconds more. Remove from the heat and allow the pot to depressurize on its own, 12 to 15 minutes.

5. Carefully open the lid and check to see if the potatoes and nugget pieces are soft and the sauce is thick; if not, cover and boil until soft, about 10 minutes. (For a saucier dish, add more water and bring to a boil over high heat.) Transfer to a serving dish, mix in the minced cilantro leaves and garam masala, and serve.

Bitter Melon Curry

Rassadar Karaelae

Makes 4 to 6 servings

Bitter melons are used throughout India, although they are not a common main ingredient for curry. But for those who like bitter melons—such as my friend Neelam Malhotra, who lives in the southern city of Bangalore and gave me this recipe, and for me—this is a delicious way to eat them. The bitterness is somewhat tempered by the potatoes and the intoxicating fragrance of the Bengali 5-Spices (panch-phoran) as they sizzle in the hot oil.

Look for bitter melons in Indian, Asian, and well-stocked produce markets. I generally do not peel bitter melons. If you prefer to do so, reserve the peel and try making a side dish, such as Bitter Melon Skins with Onions and Potatoes (page 282).

1 large russet (or any) potato
1 pound (3 large) bitter melons
2 to 3 tablespoons vegetable oil
1¹/₂ teaspoons Bengali 5-Spices (Panch-Phoran), page 27 or store-bought
2 tablespoons peeled minced fresh ginger
2 cups finely chopped tomatoes
1 to 3 fresh green chile peppers, such as serrano, minced with seeds
¹/₄ teaspoon ground turmeric
¹/₈ teaspoon ground asafoetida
1 teaspoon salt, or to taste
¹/₃ cup nonfat plain yogurt, whisked until smooth
¹/₂ cup finely chopped fresh cilantro, including soft stems
1 to 1¹/₂ cups water

1. Boil the potato in lightly salted water to cover until tender, 15 to 20 minutes. Meanwhile prepare the 5-spices. Then, drain the potato, let cool, then peel and cut into ½-inch pieces.

2. Make a long, 1-inch deep cut into one side of each bitter melon but don't split into 2 pieces. (The cut allows the flavors to penetrate inside.) Then cut each bitter melon into 2-inch pieces.

3. Heat the oil in a large nonstick skillet over medium heat and add the 5-spices; they should sizzle upon contact with the hot oil. Quickly add the bitter melon pieces and cook, stirring, until golden brown on all sides, 10 minutes. Push the bitter melon pieces to one side of the pan, add the potato, and cook, stirring, until golden, about 4 minutes.

4. Transfer the bitter melon and potato to a bowl. In the same cooking pan, add the ginger, tomatoes, green chile peppers, turmeric, asafoetida, and salt. Cook until most of the tomato juices evaporate, 2 to 3 minutes. Mix in the yogurt, a little at a time, stirring constantly to prevent it from curdling. Then add the water and bring to a boil over high heat.

5. Add the bitter melon and potato, cover the pan, and bring to a boil again. Then reduce the heat to low, mix in the cilantro, and simmer, covered, about 10 minutes to blend the flavors. Transfer to a serving dish and serve hot.

Simple Turnip Curry

Rassae kae Shalgam

Makes 4 to 6 servings

Turnips cooked in a thin-sauced curry, without any onions or garlic, have a very mild taste, although this dish does have flavorful ingredients. This age-old lunch-time favorite among the older members of my family in India is a comfort food today, because it brings with it a whole lifetime of memories.

2 tablespoons peanut oil
1 teaspoon cumin seeds
1¹/₂ pounds small turnips, cut into thin half-moons
1¹/₂ tablespoons peeled minced fresh ginger
1 large tomato, finely chopped
¹/₂ teaspoon cayenne pepper, or to taste
¹/₄ teaspoon ground turmeric
¹/₂ teaspoon salt, or to taste
¹/₄ cup nonfat plain yogurt, whisked until smooth
2¹/₂ cups water
2 teaspoons sugar
¹/₄ teaspoon garam masala

1. Heat the oil in a large nonstick wok or saucepan over medium-high heat and add the cumin seeds; they should sizzle upon contact with the hot oil. Quickly add the turnips and ginger, reduce the heat to medium-low, and cook, stirring, until golden, about 5 minutes.

2. Add the tomato, cayenne pepper, turmeric, and salt, and cook until all the juices evaporate, about 3 minutes. Mix in the yogurt, stirring constantly to prevent it from curdling.

3. Add the water and bring to a boil over high heat, then reduce the heat to medium, cover the pan, and cook until the turnips are very soft, about 10 minutes. Mix in the sugar, transfer to a serving dish, sprinkle the garam masala on top, and serve hot.

Curried Baby White Turnips with Turnip Greens

Chottae Shalgam ki Kari

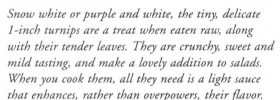

Makes 4 to 6 servings

Snow white or purple and white, the tiny, delicate 1-inch turnips are a treat when eaten raw, along with their tender leaves. They are crunchy, sweet and mild tasting, and make a lovely addition to salads. When you cook them, all they need is a light sauce that enhances, rather than overpowers, their flavor.

If baby turnips aren't available, select the smallest turnips you can find and cut them into 1-inch pieces. I add turnip greens to the sauce, but if your turnips come without them, throw in some spinach or mustard greens.

2 to 3 tablespoons vegetable oil
1 teaspoon cumin seeds
1/2 teaspoon ajwain seeds
1 small sweet onion, such as Vidalia or Maui, finely chopped
1 tablespoon peeled minced fresh ginger
1 cup finely chopped turnip greens (or any other greens)
1/4 cup finely chopped fresh curry leaves
1 fresh green chile pepper, such as serrano, minced with seeds
1 large tomato, finely chopped
1 tablespoon ground coriander
1/2 teaspoon ground turmeric
1/2 teaspoon salt, or to taste
20 to 25 baby turnips (about 1 pound), stems and roots trimmed
1 cup water
1/4 cup finely chopped fresh cilantro, including soft stems
1/4 teaspoon garam masala

1. Heat the oil in a large nonstick pan over medium-high heat and add the cumin and ajwain seeds; they should sizzle upon contact with the hot oil. Quickly add the onion and cook, stirring, over medium heat until browned, about 7 minutes.

2. Add the ginger, turnip greens, curry leaves, and green chile pepper, and stir about 1 minute. Then add the tomato and cook until all the juices evaporate, about 5 minutes. Add the coriander, turmeric, and salt, then add the turnips and cook, stirring, another 5 minutes.

3. Add the water, cover the pan, increase the heat to high, and bring to a boil. Reduce the heat to medium and simmer until the turnips are fork-tender and the sauce is medium-thick, 10 to 15 minutes. Transfer to a serving dish, mix in the cilantro, sprinkle the garam masala on top, and serve.

South Indian Pumpkin Curry with Split Pigeon Peas
Kaddu (Parangikkai) Kootu

Makes 4 to 6 servings

Kootu is a dal (legume) and vegetable curry. My friend Rama, who lives in Bangalore, gave me this typical southern Indian recipe, which can be made with orange pumpkin or, if you find it, with white pumpkin and yams.

1½ **pounds pumpkin or butternut squash, peeled and cut into** ½-**inch pieces**
½ **cup dried split pigeon peas (toor dal), sorted and washed in 3 to 4 changes of water**
¼ **teaspoon ground turmeric**
½ **teaspoon salt, or to taste**
2 **cups water**
½ **cup grated fresh or frozen coconut, or shredded unsweetened dried coconut**
1 **teaspoon ground cumin**
1 **tablespoon coconut or peanut oil**
2 **dried red chile peppers, such as chile de arbol, with stems**
1 **teaspoon dried white urad beans (dhulli urad dal), sorted**
1 **teaspoon black mustard seeds**
1 **tablespoon minced fresh curry leaves**

1. Place the pumpkin, pigeon peas, turmeric, salt, and water in a large nonstick saucepan and bring to a boil over high heat. Reduce the heat to medium-low, cover the pan, and simmer until the pumpkin and dal are crisp-tender, 10 to 15 minutes.

2. Add the coconut and cumin and continue to simmer until the pumpkin and dal are very soft and most of the water has evaporated, 10 to 12 minutes. Transfer to a serving dish.

3. Heat the oil in a large nonstick wok or saucepan over medium-high heat and cook the red chile peppers and urad beans, stirring, until lightly browned, about 30 seconds. Add the mustard seeds; they should splutter upon contact with the hot oil, so cover the pan and lower the heat until the spluttering subsides. Quickly add the curry leaves and add to the pumpkin. Swirl lightly to mix, with parts of it visible as a garnish. Serve hot.

Kerala Cucumber Curry
Kheera (Olan) Kari

Makes 4 to 6 servings

I got this curry from the chef of a resort in the Kerala backwaters of coastal southwestern India. The cucumbers of choice in this recipe are a small, firm, seedless variety, such as Armenian cucumbers. If you can't find those, any firm seedless variety will do.

½ **cup Coconut Milk (page 44 or store-bought)**
½ **cup dried split pigeon peas (toor dal), sorted and washed in 3 to 4 changes of water**
2 **cups water**
1 **fresh green chile pepper, such as serrano, minced with seeds**
1 **tablespoon peeled minced fresh ginger**
10 **to 12 fresh whole curry leaves**
1 **pound small seedless cucumbers, peeled and cut into 1-inch pieces**
2 **teaspoons coconut oil**
1 **teaspoon black mustard seeds**
2 **dried red chile peppers, such as chile de arbol, with stems**
1 **tablespoon minced fresh curry leaves**

1. Prepare the coconut milk. Then, place the dal, water, green chile pepper, ginger, and whole curry leaves in a large nonstick saucepan and bring to a boil over high heat. Reduce the heat to medium-low, cover the pan, and simmer until the dal is soft and creamy, 20 to 25 minutes.

2. Add the cucumber and continue to cook until the pieces are soft, 5 to 7 minutes. Add the coconut milk and bring to a gentle simmer, about 5 minutes. Transfer to a serving bowl.

3. Heat the oil in a small nonstick wok or saucepan over medium-high heat and add the mustard seeds; they should splutter upon contact with the hot oil, so cover the pan and reduce the heat until the spluttering subsides. Quickly add the red chile peppers and minced curry leaves, cook about 30 seconds, then swirl into the cooked cucumber and serve.

Mushrooms in Almond and Poppy Seed Sauce
Badaam-Khumb Masala

Makes 4 to 6 servings

Here is a fragrant and creamy brown curry sauce that deliciously showcases mushrooms at their best. Although white button mushrooms are commonly used and work well, also try this recipe with morel, chanterelle, shiitake, or portobello mushrooms.

1 small onion, coarsely chopped
5 quarter-size slices peeled fresh ginger
2 large cloves fresh garlic, peeled
1 to 3 fresh green chile peppers, such as serrano, stemmed
1/2 cup (about 50) coarsely chopped raw almonds
1 tablespoon white poppy seeds
1 teaspoon garam masala
2 to 3 tablespoons olive oil
1 (1-inch) stick cinnamon
3 black cardamom pods, crushed lightly
      to break the skin
1 tablespoon ground coriander
1/4 teaspoon freshly ground nutmeg
1 teaspoon salt, or to taste
1/2 cup nonfat plain yogurt, whisked until smooth
1 1/2 pounds medium mushrooms, cleaned and trimmed
1 cup water
1/4 cup finely chopped fresh cilantro,
      including soft stems
1/2 teaspoon freshly ground black pepper, to taste

1. In a food processor, process together the onion, ginger, garlic, green chile peppers, almonds, poppy seeds, and garam masala to make a smooth paste.

2. Heat the oil in a large nonstick saucepan over medium-high heat, add the cinnamon and cardamom pods, and cook, stirring, the a few seconds. Add the processed onion paste and cook, stirring occasionally, until medium to well browned, 8 to 10 minutes. Add the coriander, nutmeg, and salt, and stir a few seconds.

3. Add the yogurt, a little at a time, stirring constantly to prevent it from curdling, then mix in the mushrooms and stir until they release their juices,

3 to 5 minutes. Add the water and bring to a boil over high heat. Reduce the heat to medium and simmer until the sauce becomes thick and creamy, about 10 minutes. (Add more water, if needed.) Mix in the cilantro and cook until wilted, about 2 minutes. Transfer to a serving, dish, sprinkle the black pepper on top, and serve.

Anaheim Peppers in Spicy Tamarind Sauce
Mirchi ka Saalan

Makes 4 to 6 servings

This is based on one of my friend Yasmin AliKhan's savory, pickle-like Hyderabadi recipes. It is traditionally hot and rather high in fat because it is made with deep-fried Anaheim and green chile peppers. Here, I have modified both heat and fat. If you still find it too hot, reduce (or omit) the serrano peppers, as well as the cayenne pepper. Traditionally, the spices are each roasted and ground separately, but I do everything at once.

Yasmin advises that this saalan should not be re-heated. Serve it hot or at room temperature, or straight out of the refrigerator.

1/2 cup Tamarind Paste (page 54)
1 tablespoon shelled raw peanuts, red skin removed
1 tablespoon grated fresh or frozen coconut or
      shredded unsweetened dried coconut
1 tablespoon coriander seeds
1 teaspoon sesame seeds
1 teaspoon white poppy seeds
2 1/2 teaspoons black cumin seeds
1/2 teaspoon cayenne pepper
1/4 teaspoon ground turmeric
4 fresh Anaheim peppers, split in half, then seeded
      and cut into 3 to 4 pieces each
2 to 6 fresh serrano peppers, coarsely chopped
1 1/2 teaspoons salt
1/2 cup peanut oil
1/2 teaspoon black mustard seeds
1/4 teaspoon fenugreek seeds
1/4 teaspoon kalonji seeds
1 large onion, cut in half lengthwise and thinly sliced
1 cup water
7 to 10 fresh curry leaves

1. Prepare the tamarind paste. Put the peanuts in a small nonstick skillet and roast them over medium heat until a few shades darker, about 2 minutes. Transfer to a bowl. Then roast together the coconut, coriander, sesame, and poppy seeds, and 2 teaspoons black cumin seeds until a few shades darker, about 2 minutes. (Or roast each separately, following tradition.) Transfer to the peanut bowl. Let cool, then grind everything in a spice grinder or food processor, together or in batches, to make them as fine as possible. Mix in the cayenne pepper and turmeric, and reserve.

2. Place the Anaheim and serrano peppers in a bowl and toss with the salt. Set aside about 30 minutes, then wash, drain, and dry them on a towel. (Drying is essential, or the oil will splutter when you fry them.)

3. Heat the oil in a large nonstick wok or saucepan over medium-high heat and add the reserved ½ teaspoon cumin seeds and the mustard, fenugreek, and kalonji seeds, then the towel-dried peppers and fry (in 2 batches, if needed) until they are barely browned, 1 to 2 minutes. Leaving the oil behind, drain well and transfer everything to a bowl.

4. In the same oil, fry the onion over medium-high heat until golden, 5 to 7 minutes. Leaving the onion in the skillet, remove most of the oil and discard or reserve for another purpose. To the onions, add the tamarind paste, water, curry leaves, roasted spice mixture and 1 teaspoon salt and cook over medium heat until the sauce is very thick and the oil separates to the side, about 20 minutes. Mix in the fried peppers and cook another 10 to 12 minutes to blend the flavors. Serve.

Hyderabadi Tomatoes in Spicy Tamarind Sauce

Tamatar ka Saalan

Makes 4 to 6 servings

This is a spicy, lip-smacking, soft-cooked tomato dish that comes from my friend Yasmin AliKhan's kitchen in Los Angeles. True to her Hyderabadi heritage, Yasmin makes this (and all her other saalans, *or tamarind-flavored vegetable curries) with strong, bold flavors, starting with fresh vine-ripe tomatoes, and simmering them with a bunch of freshly roasted spices until they almost disintegrate in a pickle-like, buff-colored sauce.*

This curried dish stays fresh for about 2 weeks and tastes lovely in open-face sandwiches.

½ cup Tamarind Paste (page 54)

3 to 4 tablespoons Hyderabadi Ginger-Garlic Paste (page 48)

¼ cup chopped shelled raw peanuts, red skin removed

2 tablespoons grated fresh or frozen coconut or shredded unsweetened dried coconut

2 tablespoons coriander seeds

2½ teaspoons black cumin seeds

2 teaspoons white poppy seeds

2 teaspoons sesame seeds

1 teaspoon hot red pepper flakes, or to taste

¼ teaspoon ground turmeric

3 tablespoons peanut oil

3 whole dried red chile peppers, such as chile de arbol

1 teaspoon black mustard seeds

1 teaspoon kalonji seeds

8 to 10 small firm tomatoes (about 2 pounds), each cut into 8 wedges

2 small onions, cut in half lengthwise and thinly sliced

1½ teaspoons salt, or to taste

1. Prepare the tamarind paste and the ginger-garlic paste. Then place the peanuts in a small nonstick skillet and roast over medium heat, stirring and shaking the skillet, until a few shades darker, about 2 minutes. Transfer to a bowl. In the same manner, roast together the coconut, coriander, 2 teaspoons cumin seeds, poppy seeds, sesame seeds, and red pepper flakes, until a few shades darker, about 2 minutes. (Or roast each separately, following tradition.) Transfer to the peanut bowl. Let cool, then grind the peanut mixture in a spice grinder or food processor (in batches, if necessary) until as fine as possible. Mix in the turmeric and grind again.

2. Heat the oil in a large nonstick wok or saucepan over medium-high heat and add the red chile peppers, mustard seeds, kalonji, and the remaining ½ teaspoon cumin seeds; they should sizzle upon contact with the hot oil.

3. Quickly add the tomatoes, onions, ginger-garlic paste, and salt, then mix in the roasted spices and cook, stirring occasionally, over high heat for the first 3 to 5 minutes, then over medium-low heat until the tomatoes are very soft, about 10 minutes. Add the tamarind paste, and cook over low heat, stirring only once or twice, until the oil separates to the sides, about 30 minutes. Serve hot or at room temperature.

Hyderabadi Spicy Eggplants with Roasted Peanut and Sesame Sauce

Bhagarae-Baingan

Makes 4 to 6 servings

This calorie-rich dish from Hyderabad comes to me from a native—my friend Shahina Bhalla. The recipe has several steps, but once you start cooking, it's actually quite easy. Making the spice mixture requires the most time, but it can be made once (in bulk) and refrigerated up to 6 months.

I simplified the recipe technique and made this a healthier dish. In the authentic version, the onion and garlic are usually charred over a direct flame and the eggplants are usually deep-fried, but I prefer to broil all these ingredients. They still develop smoky and sweet flavors that blend well with the seasonings.

¼ cup Tamarind Paste (page 54)
1 pound small Indian or Chinese eggplants
2 to 3 tablespoons peanut oil
2 medium onions, cut in half (unpeeled)
1 small head fresh garlic, separated into cloves (unpeeled)
¼ cup raw peanuts, red skin removed
¼ cup shredded unsweetened dried coconut
3 to 5 dried red chile peppers, such as chile de arbol, broken
¼ cup sesame seeds
3 teaspoons cumin seeds
½ teaspoon fenugreek seeds
2½ to 3 cups water
1½ teaspoons mustard seeds
15 to 20 fresh curry leaves
¼ cup finely chopped fresh cilantro, including soft stems

1. Prepare the tamarind paste. Then, preheat the broiler. Keeping the stems intact, make a long slit in each eggplant. (If using Chinese eggplants, make a slit along the length and then cut them into 2-inch pieces cross-wise around the middle.) Toss with 1 teaspoon oil, then place on a baking or broiler tray and broil 4 to 5 inches from the heating element, turning once or twice until crisp-tender, about 10 minutes. Set aside and leave the broiler on.

2. Place the onions and garlic on a broiling tray and broil 4 to 5 inches from the heating element, turning once or twice until completely charred, about 10 minutes. Let cool, peel off most of the charred skin from the onions and garlic, and process in a blender or a food processor until smooth. Leave in the processor.

3. Meanwhile, in a small nonstick skillet over medium heat, dry-roast the peanuts until golden and transfer to a heat-proof bowl. Then dry-roast the coconut until golden and transfer to the same bowl. Then dry-roast the red chile peppers, sesame seeds, 1½ teaspoons cumin seeds, and fenugreek seeds until a few shades darker, and transfer to the same bowl. Let cool and grind everything together in a spice or a coffee grinder until fine. Add to the processed onion mixture, then add about ½ cup water and process again to make a smooth paste.

4. Heat the remaining oil in a large nonstick wok or saucepan over medium-high heat and add the remaining 1½ teaspoons cumin seeds and the mustard seeds; they should splutter upon contact with the hot oil, so cover the pan and lower the heat until the spluttering subsides. Quickly add the curry leaves, stir 1 minute, and add the processed onion and spice paste. Cook, stirring, over medium-high heat until golden, 3 to 5 minutes. Add the remaining 2 cups water and bring to a boil. Reduce the heat to medium-low, cover the pan, and simmer until the oil separates and floats to the top and sides, 20 to 30 minutes.

5. Mix in the tamarind paste and the eggplants, cover the pan, and simmer until the eggplants are very soft, 15 to 20 minutes. Add more water if needed; this dish should have a soft, thick sauce—more sauce than vegetables. Transfer to a serving dish, mix in the cilantro, and serve.

Variation: To make a simpler version, do not roast the vegetables; buy roasted, unsalted peanuts and dry-roast the spices, then grind the peanuts and the spices together.

Stuffed Bell Peppers in Tomato-Cream Sauce

Tamatar ki Kari Mein Bharvaan Shimla Mirch

Makes 6 to 8 servings

This dish is a knockout if you use fresh colorful baby bell peppers—the kind you can find at farmers' markets or in your own garden. Otherwise, use the smallest ones you can find. Also, make sure each bell pepper comes with its stem intact. The cheese used for this dish in India is not available here, but cheddar or Monterey Jack work well.

1 recipe Butter-Cream Sauce with Fresh Tomatoes (page 389)
3 to 4 small russet (or any kind) potatoes
12 to 15 baby bell peppers, in assorted colors
1 cup part-skim ricotta cheese
¼ cup grated mild cheddar or Monterey Jack cheese

2 tablespoons minced scallions, white and light green parts only
2 tablespoons finely chopped fresh cilantro, including soft stems + more for garnish
1 tablespoon peeled minced fresh ginger
1 fresh green chile pepper, minced with seeds
1 tablespoon ground coriander
1 teaspoon ground dried pomegranate seeds
½ teaspoon salt, or to taste
2 tablespoons vegetable oil
1 teaspoon cumin seeds
¼ teaspoon garam masala

1. Prepare the butter-cream sauce. Then, boil the potatoes in lightly salted water to cover until tender, about 20 minutes. Let cool, then peel and coarsely mash them.

2. Cut a small circle around the stem of each bell pepper and carefully remove the top, to make a cap. Remove the membranes and the seeds from inside each pepper and discard. In a medium bowl, mix together the mashed potato, ricotta and cheddar cheese, scallions, cilantro, ginger, green chile pepper, coriander, pomegranate seeds, and salt.

3. Heat the oil in a large nonstick skillet over medium-high heat and add the cumin seeds; they should sizzle upon contact with the hot oil. Quickly add the potato mixture and cook, stirring, until golden, about 5 minutes.

4. Divide the potato mixture equally among the bell peppers and fill each one. Place the cap on top of each pepper. Transfer the bell peppers, cap side up, to a large saucepan or skillet (or 2 small ones if the peppers don't fit in 1) and pour the butter-cream sauce on top and around each one. Cover and bring to a quick boil over high heat. Then reduce the heat to medium-low and simmer, spooning the sauce over the peppers a few times, until the bell peppers are soft and shriveled, about 20 minutes. Transfer to a serving dish, garnish with the cilantro and garam masala, and serve.

Variation: Make this recipe by stuffing small tomatoes, scooped-out small eggplants, or zucchini halves instead of bell peppers.

Onion Wedges in Curry Sauce

Rassadar Pyaz

Makes 4 to 6 servings

The fact that it is a curry classifies this dish as an entrée, yet it is not a substantial dish. Serve it with any one or more dry-cooked protein-rich dishes, such as Chutney-Marinated Broiled Paneer Cheese Kabaabs (page 157) or Black Chickpea Kabaabs (page 158), or with grilled meats.

When you cut the onions into wedges, leave them attached to their base. As the onions cook, the layers open up but stay intact.

7 to 8 small onions (about 2 pounds)
2 tablespoons vegetable oil
1 teaspoon cumin seeds
2 large tomatoes, finely chopped
$^3/_4$ teaspoon salt, or to taste
$^1/_2$ teaspoon cayenne pepper
$^1/_4$ teaspoon ground turmeric
2$^1/_2$ cups water
1 cup nonfat plain yogurt, whisked until smooth
1 cup finely chopped fresh cilantro,
  including soft stems
Freshly ground black pepper, to taste

1. Cut 3 onions into 6 wedges each, leaving each wedge attached at its base. Finely chop the remaining ones to make 1½ cups chopped onion.

2. Heat the oil in a large nonstick wok or saucepan over medium-high heat and add the cumin seeds; they should sizzle upon contact with the hot oil. Quickly add the chopped onion and cook, stirring, until golden-brown, 5 to 7 minutes. Add the tomatoes, onion wedges, salt, cayenne pepper, and turmeric and cook, stirring, until the tomatoes are soft and most of the juices evaporate, 5 to 7 minutes.

3. Add the water and bring to a boil over high heat. Reduce the heat to low, cover the pan, and simmer, 5 to 7 minutes. Increase the heat to high and mix in the yogurt, a little at a time, stirring constantly to prevent it from curdling. Continue to boil until the sauce is as thick as you desire, about 10 minutes. Add the cilantro and cook until wilted but still green in color, about 3 minutes. Transfer to a serving dish, top with the black pepper, and serve.

Potato Curries

Rajasthani Potato Curry
Rajasthani Rassadar Aalu

Makes 4 to 6 servings

Made without any garlic or onions and with spices that are not fully ground, this Rajasthani dish goes well with all types of poories *(deep-fried puffed breads). The potatoes in this dish are traditionally deep-fried, but here, again, I prefer to pan-cook them for rich color and flavor but less fat.*

1¼ pounds small potatoes, each not more than
     1¼-inch across
¼ teaspoon ground turmeric
3 tablespoons vegetable oil
1 (1-inch) stick cinnamon
5 green cardamom pods, crushed lightly
     to break the skin
2 teaspoons coriander seeds, coarsely ground
1 teaspoon cumin seeds, coarsely ground
½ teaspoon fenugreek seeds, coarsely ground
1 tablespoon peeled minced fresh ginger
1 fresh green chile pepper, such as serrano,
     minced with seeds
⅛ teaspoon ground asafoetida
½ teaspoon salt, or to taste
½ cup nonfat plain yogurt, whisked until smooth
1 to 2 cups water
¼ cup finely chopped fresh cilantro,
     including soft stems
Freshly ground black pepper, to taste

1. Boil the potatoes in lightly salted water to cover until tender, about 20 minutes. Drain, let cool, then peel them, put them in a bowl, and toss well with the turmeric. (If the potatoes are large, cut each one in half.) Heat about 1 tablespoon oil in a large nonstick wok or saucepan over medium-high heat and cook the potatoes, stirring, until golden, 3 to 5 minutes. Transfer to a bowl.

2. Add the remaining oil to the pan and cook the cinnamon and cardamom pods, stirring, a few seconds. Add the coriander, cumin, and fenugreek seeds, then add the ginger, green chile pepper, and asafoetida and stir about 1 minute. Return the potatoes to the pan, add the salt, and cook everything together about 2 minutes. Add the yogurt, a little at a time, stirring constantly to prevent it from curdling.

3. Add the water and bring to a boil over high heat. Reduce the heat to medium-low, cover the pan, and simmer until the potatoes are very soft and almost breaking, 5 to 7 minutes. Mix in the cilantro. Transfer to a serving dish, sprinkle the black pepper on top, and serve.

Pot-Roasted Fried Whole Potatoes in Yogurt Curry
Pahaadi Dum-Aalu

Makes 4 to 6 servings

From the mountains (pahaad) *surrounding the Valley of Kashmir comes this dish, which is traditionally made with a special variety of potatoes called* pahaadi-aalu. *These thin-skinned potatoes are similar to the white and red varieties found in America, and are known to maintain their shape even after prolonged cooking.*

This is the traditional deep-fried version. You could also brown the potatoes in 2 to 3 tablespoons of oil or, if you wish, completely skip the deep-frying or browning in Step 2 and go straight to Step 3.

1½ pounds small white or red potatoes,
     each not more than 1¼-inch across
1 cup nonfat plain yogurt
1½ cups water
1½ cups peanut oil for deep-frying
2 teaspoons cumin seeds
2 black cardamom pods, crushed lightly
     to break the skin
1 (1-inch) stick cinnamon, broken
3 whole cloves
1 tablespoon ground fennel seeds
1 tablespoon ground coriander
½ teaspoon ground ginger
½ teaspoon cayenne pepper, or to taste
⅛ teaspoon ground asafoetida
1 teaspoon salt, or to taste
½ teaspoon garam masala

1. Boil the potatoes in lightly salted water to cover until crisp-tender, about 10 minutes. Drain, let cool, then prick each potato all over with a fork. (So the spices penetrate the insides.) Meanwhile, in a blender, blend together the yogurt and water until smooth.

2. Heat the oil in a large wok over medium-high heat until it reaches 325°F to 350°F on a frying thermometer, or until a small piece of potato dropped into the hot oil rises to the top in 15 to 20 seconds. Add the potatoes to the hot oil, adding as many as the wok can hold at one time without crowding, and fry, turning them carefully with a slotted spatula, until they are golden, 2 to 3 minutes. Drain on paper towels.

3. Remove all but 2 tablespoons oil from the wok and discard or reserve for another use. Heat the oil in a large nonstick wok or saucepan over medium-high heat and add the cumin seeds, cardamom pods, cinnamon, and cloves; they should sizzle upon contact with the hot oil. Quickly add the potatoes, fennel seeds, coriander, ginger, cayenne pepper, asafoetida, and salt, and stir carefully until the spices cling to the potatoes, about 3 minutes.

4. Add the yogurt-water and bring to a boil, stirring constantly, over high heat. Reduce the heat to low, cover the pan and simmer until most of the water has been absorbed, leaving behind a medium-thick sauce, about 10 minutes. Transfer to a serving dish, sprinkle the garam masala on top, and serve.

Minty Pot-Roasted Potato Curry

Pudina Dum-Aalu

Makes 4 to 6 servings

With fresh mint leaves as the predominant flavor, this lighter, north Indian version of dum-aalu *(pot-roasted potatoes) calls for pan-cooking the potatoes instead of the traditional deep-frying, as is done in*

the previous recipe, Pot-Roasted Fried Whole Potatoes in Yogurt Curry.

10 to 12 small new potatoes (about 1¼ pounds)
1 medium onion, coarsely chopped
5 to 6 quarter-size slices peeled fresh ginger
1 large clove fresh garlic, peeled
¼ cup coarsely chopped fresh mint leaves
1 tablespoon shredded unsweetened dried coconut
1 tablespoon ground coriander
½ teaspoon ground paprika
¼ teaspoon ground turmeric
3 to 4 tablespoons peanut oil
3 to 5 fresh green chile peppers, such as serrano, split lengthwise in half
1 teaspoon cumin seeds
½ teaspoon salt, or to taste
2 to 3 cups water
1 teaspoon ground dried mint leaves
½ teaspoon garam masala

1. Boil the potatoes in lightly salted water to cover until tender, about 20 minutes. Drain, let cool, then peel them.

2. In a food processor or a blender, process together the onion, ginger, garlic, fresh mint leaves, and coconut until smooth. Add the coriander, paprika and turmeric and process again to make a smooth paste.

3. Heat 2 tablespoons oil in a large nonstick wok or saucepan over medium-high heat and add the green chile peppers and cumin seeds; they should sizzle upon contact with the hot oil. Quickly add the potatoes and cook, stirring, until golden, 3 to 5 minutes. Transfer to a bowl.

4. Add the remaining oil to the pan, then add the onion-mint paste and cook over medium heat, stirring, until golden, 7 to 10 minutes. Mix in the potatoes, salt, and water, cover the pan, and simmer until the sauce is thick and the potatoes are very soft and fragrant, 5 to 7 minutes. Transfer to a serving dish, top with dried mint leaves and garam masala, and serve.

Haridwar Potato Curry

Haridwar kae Aalu

Makes 4 to 6 servings

Haridwar is one of India's many holy cities on the banks of the Ganges River. It also is a source of a delicious local cusine. Here is one such dish shared by my friend Neelam Malhotra. It is served at roadside eateries with deep-fried poori *breads and spicy pumpkin purées.*

4 medium russet potatoes (about 1¼ pounds)

3 tablespoons vegetable oil

3 to 5 dried red chile peppers, such as chile de arbol, with stems

1 tablespoon coarsely ground coriander seeds

2 teaspoons cumin seeds

¾ teaspoon coarsely ground fenugreek seeds

¼ teaspoon ground turmeric

½ teaspoon cayenne pepper, or to taste

⅛ teaspoon ground asafoetida

2 large red tomatoes, coarsely chopped

½ cup nonfat plain yogurt, whisked until smooth

1 teaspoon salt, or to taste

2½ to 3 cups water

2 small green (or unripe red) tomatoes, cut into wedges

½ cup finely chopped fresh cilantro, including soft stems

2 fresh green chile peppers, such as serranos, split in half lengthwise

1 teaspoon ground dried pomegranate seeds

1 teaspoon dried mint leaves

1 teaspoon dried fenugreek leaves

1. Boil the potatoes in lightly salted water to cover until tender, about 20 minutes. Drain, let cool, then peel and coarsely break them with a fork.

2. Heat the oil in a large nonstick wok or saucepan over medium-high heat and add the red chile peppers, coriander, cumin, and fenugreek seeds; they should sizzle upon contact with the hot oil. Quickly add the turmeric, cayenne pepper, and asafoetida, then mix in the chopped red tomatoes and cook until all the juices evaporate, about 10 minutes.

3. Add the potatoes and salt and cook over medium heat, turning gently, about 5 minutes. Add the

yogurt, a little at a time, stirring constantly to prevent it from curdling, and cook 2 to 3 minutes until completely incorporated. Then add the water and bring to a boil over high heat. Reduce the heat to low, cover the pan, and cook until the sauce is reduced by ⅓, 8 to 10 minutes.

4. Add the green tomato wedges and cilantro and cook another 5 minutes. Transfer to a serving dish, and add the pomegranate seeds, mint, and fenugreek leaves. Swirl lightly to mix, with some of them visible as a garnish. Serve.

Curried Almond and Poppy Seed Potatoes

Badaam aur Khus-Khus kae Aalu

Makes 4 to 6 servings

With the richness of poppy seeds, cashews, and heavy cream, these potatoes take on an incredible fragrance and a silky, smooth appearance that makes for a great party dish.

4 quarter-size slices peeled fresh ginger

2 large cloves fresh garlic, peeled

¼ cup coarsely chopped raw cashews

1½ teaspoons white poppy seeds

1 teaspoon garam masala

2 tablespoons vegetable oil

1 teaspoon cumin seeds

3 to 5 dried red chile peppers, such as chile de arbol, with stems

¼ teaspoon turmeric

8 to 10 small potatoes (about 1¼ pounds), cut into 4 to 6 wedges each

½ teaspoon salt, or to taste

½ cup nonfat plain yogurt, whisked until smooth

1 cup water

¼ cup heavy cream or coconut milk (optional)

½ teaspoon coarsely ground green cardamom seeds

1. In a small food processor, process together the ginger, garlic, cashews, and poppy seeds, adding about 2 tablespoons water to make a paste. Mix in the garam masala and transfer to a bowl.

2. Heat the oil in a large nonstick wok or saucepan over medium-high heat and add the cumin seeds and red chile peppers; they should sizzle upon contact with the hot oil. Quickly add the potatoes, turmeric, and salt and stir until golden, 5 to 7 minutes.

3. Add the ginger-poppy seed paste and continue to stir over medium-low heat until traces of oil are visible on the sides, 7 to 10 minutes. Add the yogurt, a little at a time, stirring constantly to prevent it from curdling.

4. Add the water, cover the pan, and cook over medium heat until the potatoes are soft and the sauce is thick, about 10 minutes. Add the cream or coconut milk, if using, and simmer another 3 minutes. Transfer to a serving dish, lightly stir in the cardamom seeds, and serve.

Yogurt and Potato Curry
Dahi-kae-Aalu

Makes 4 to 6 servings

A specialty of Uttar-Pradesh, a state just adjacent to New Delhi in the north, this home-style potato dish is often part of a brunch menu with poories (puffed deep-fried breads) and hot chai tea. This dish is also great with a side of okra or cauliflower and parathas (griddle-fried breads) and a glass of Sweet Mango-Yogurt Cooler (page 653).

8 to 10 small thin-skinned white or red potatoes (about 1¼ pounds), cut into 4 to 6 wedges each

1 cup nonfat plain yogurt, whisked until smooth

1 large tomato, coarsely chopped

2 to 3 tablespoons vegetable oil

1 tablespoon peeled minced fresh ginger

1 to 3 fresh green chile peppers, such as serrano, minced with seeds

1 teaspoon cumin seeds

¼ teaspoon ground turmeric

¼ teaspoon hot red pepper flakes, or to taste

⅛ teaspoon ground asafoetida

½ teaspoon salt, or to taste

¼ cup finely chopped fresh cilantro, including soft stems

1. Boil the potatoes in lightly salted water to cover until tender, about 20 minutes. Drain, let cool, peel them if you wish to, then break up coarsely with your fingers into 1-inch pieces. Reserve. In a blender, blend together the yogurt and tomato until smooth.

2. Heat the oil in a large nonstick wok or saucepan over medium-high heat and add the ginger, green chile peppers, and cumin seeds; they should sizzle upon contact with the hot oil. Quickly add the turmeric, red pepper flakes, asafoetida, and salt, then add the blended yogurt-tomato mixture and bring to a boil over high heat. Reduce the heat to medium-low, cover the pan, and simmer about 5 minutes.

3. Add the potatoes and simmer 7 to 10 minutes to blend the flavors. Transfer to a serving dish, garnish with the cilantro, and serve.

Diced Potato Curry with Pickling Spices
Achaari Aalu

Makes 4 to 6 servings

This is one of the most popular Punjabi potato dishes. It is another breakfast or brunch specialty, customarily served with freshly made poories (puffed deep-fried breads). I use the Bengali 5-Spices mixture of seeds to simplify the recipe. The Punjabis generally add the same spices, one by one. This is a great recipe for the pressure cooker, because it shaves off at least 20 minutes of stirring and watching.

2 tablespoons vegetable oil

1 tablespoon Bengali 5-Spices (Panch-Phoran), page 27 or store-bought

1½ tablespoons ground coriander

½ teaspoon ground cumin

½ teaspoon ground paprika

½ teaspoon salt, or to taste

3 cups finely chopped tomatoes

1 to 3 fresh green chile peppers, such as serrano, minced with seeds

¾ cup finely chopped fresh cilantro, including soft stems

**5 medium russet potatoes (about 1¹/2 pounds),
peeled and cut in ¹/2-inch pieces**
4 cups water
¹/4 teaspoon garam masala

1. Heat the oil in a pressure cooker over medium-high heat and add the panch-phoran; they should sizzle upon contact with the hot oil. Quickly add the coriander, cumin, paprika, and salt and then mix in the tomatoes, green chile peppers, and half of the cilantro. Cook, stirring occasionally, until all the juices evaporate, 10 to 12 minutes. Reduce the heat to low, add the potatoes, and cook, stirring occasionally, about 5 minutes.

2. Add the water and secure the lid. Cook over high heat until the pressure regulator indicates high pressure, then cook about 1 minute more. Remove from the heat and allow the pot to depressurize on its own, 12 to 15 minutes. Carefully open the lid and check to see if the potatoes are soft and the sauce thick, mashing a few as you stir; if not, cover and boil until soft, about 10 minutes.

3. Mix in the remaining cilantro and cook another 5 minutes over low heat, stirring occasionally. Transfer to serving dish, sprinkle the garam masala on top, and serve.

Variation: To add more substance and make the dish go further, mix in about 1 cup paneer cheese, diced into ¹/2-inch cubes, and/or 1 cup thawed frozen peas with the cilantro in Step 3, and simmer about 10 minutes. Adjust the seasoning.

Quick Potatoes and Peas Curry with Tomato Sauce
Jaldi Banae Muttar-Aalu

Makes 4 to 6 servings

I make this easy main dish with canned tomato sauce—not an authentic Indian ingredient, but one that I occasionally use, especially when I run out of fresh tomatoes or I'm in a hurry. For extra protein,

add about 1 cup cubed, store-bought paneer *cheese or tofu. Serve it with a side of Spicy Broiled Whole Okra (page 292) and a* basmati *rice pilaf.*

4 medium russet (or any) potatoes (about 1¹/4 pounds)
2 tablespoons vegetable oil
1 teaspoon cumin seeds
¹/2 teaspoon kalonji seeds (optional)
1¹/2 tablespoons ground coriander
¹/2 teaspoon ground cumin
¹/2 teaspoon ground paprika
¹/2 teaspoon salt, or to taste
1 (15-ounce) can tomato sauce
1 to 3 fresh green chile peppers, such as serrano, minced with seeds
³/4 cup finely chopped fresh cilantro, including soft stems
1¹/2 cups frozen peas, thawed
1¹/2 to 2 cups water
1 teaspoon dried fenugreek leaves
¹/4 teaspoon garam masala

1. In a medium saucepan, boil the potatoes in water to cover until tender, about 20 minutes. Drain, let cool, then peel and cut into ¹/2-inch pieces.

2. Heat the oil in a medium nonstick saucepan over medium-high heat and add the cumin and kalonji seeds (if using); they should sizzle upon contact with the hot oil. Quickly add the coriander, cumin, paprika, and salt, then mix in the tomato sauce, green chile peppers, and half the cilantro, and cook, stirring occasionally, until it thickens considerably, 10 to 12 minutes.

3. Reduce the heat to low, add the potatoes and peas, and cook, stirring occasionally, about 5 minutes. Add the water and bring to a boil over high heat. Reduce the heat to medium-low, cover the pan, and simmer until the sauce is thick, about 5 minutes.

4. Mix in the remaining cilantro and fenugreek leaves, and cook 5 more minutes over low heat, stirring occasionally. Transfer to serving dish, sprinkle the garam masala on top, and serve.

Greens Entrées

Spicy Puréed Spinach Greens
Palak ka Saag

Makes 4 to 6 servings

Enjoy this quick-cooking and nutritious green purée by the bowlful with chapatis *(whole-wheat griddle breads) or* paranthas *(griddle-fried breads), or make substantial entrées with it, similar to Spinach with Paneer Cheese (page 328) or Traditional Indian Chicken with Spinach (page 453), by simmering it further with a cup or two of chopped vegetables,* paneer *cheese, or grilled meats, to blend the flavors.*

5 quarter-size slices peeled fresh ginger
2 large cloves fresh garlic, peeled
1 to 2 green chile peppers, such as serrano, stemmed
2 (1-pound) packages frozen chopped spinach, thawed
2 tablespoons melted ghee or vegetable oil
1 teaspoon cumin seeds
1 medium onion, finely chopped
1 tablespoon ground coriander
1 tablespoon dried fenugreek leaves
1 teaspoon garam masala + 1/4 teaspoon for garnish
1/2 teaspoon ground paprika
1 (15-ounce) can tomato sauce
2 tablespoons cornmeal or whole-wheat flour, dissolved in 1/4 cup water
1 tablespoon unsalted butter, cream, or plain yogurt

1. In a food processor or a blender, process together the ginger, garlic, and green chile peppers until minced. Then add the spinach and process again to make a coarse purée.

2. Heat the ghee (or oil) in a small nonstick wok or saucepan over medium-high heat and add the cumin seeds; they should sizzle upon contact with the hot oil. Quickly add the onion and cook, stirring, until golden, about 3 minutes. Mix in the coriander, fenugreek leaves, garam masala, and paprika, then add the tomato sauce and cook, stirring, about 2 minutes.

3. Mix in the puréed spinach and cook, stirring, until it comes to a boil, about 2 minutes. Add the cornmeal (or whole-wheat) mixture and simmer over medium heat about 10 minutes to blend the flavors. (For a thinner dish, add up to 1/2 cup water and bring to a boil over high heat.) Reduce the heat to medium-low, cover the pan, and simmer again, about 5 minutes. Transfer to a serving dish, add the butter (cream or yogurt) and swirl lightly to mix, with parts of it visible as a garnish, sprinkle the garam masala on top, and serve.

Spinach, Fenugreek Greens, and Broccoli
Palak aur Methi ka Saag

Makes 4 to 6 servings

Fenugreek leaves, along with the other aromatic ingredients, add a refreshing spark to this customary Indian treatment of cooking greens.

2 small bunches fresh spinach (about 1 pound total), trimmed of roots only, washed, and coarsely chopped
2 cups coarsely chopped fresh fenugreek leaves
1 1/2 cups coarsely chopped fresh cilantro, including soft stems
1/2 pound broccoli, chopped
1 small onion, coarsely chopped
6 quarter-size slices peeled fresh ginger
2 large cloves fresh garlic, peeled
1 to 2 fresh green chile peppers, such as serrano, stemmed
2 (1-inch) sticks cinnamon
3 black cardamom pods, crushed lightly to break the skin
1/2 cup water
1/2 teaspoon salt, or to taste
2 tablespoons melted ghee or vegetable oil
1 teaspoon cumin seeds
1 teaspoon dried fenugreek leaves
1/4 teaspoon hot red pepper flakes, or to taste
2 small tomatoes, each cut into 6 wedges

1. Place the spinach, fenugreek leaves, cilantro, broccoli, onion, ginger, green chile peppers, cinnamon, cardamom pods, and water in a large nonstick wok or saucepan. Cover and cook over medium-high heat the first 2 to 3 minutes, then over medium heat until the broccoli is soft and the greens are wilted, 5 to 7 minutes.

2. Let cool, remove the cinnamon and cardamom pods, transfer to a food processor and pulse until coarsely puréed. Return to the pan, add the salt, and cook over medium heat about 20 minutes, adding up to ½ cup water if the dish seems dry. Transfer to a serving dish and keep warm.

3. Heat the ghee (or oil) in a small nonstick saucepan and add the cumin seeds; they should sizzle upon contact with the hot oil. Quickly add the dried fenugreek leaves and red pepper flakes, then add the tomatoes, and cook until they are slightly soft, about 3 minutes. Add to the spinach, and mix lightly with parts of it visible as a garnish. Serve.

Variation: Pan-cook, then mix in 1 small head chopped cauliflower, or 1½ to 2 cups diced tofu, paneer cheese, or boiled potatoes during the last 10 minutes of cooking in Step 2. You can also add the same amount of cooked chicken or fish.

Punjabi Mustard Greens
Sarson ka Saag

Makes 6 to 8 servings

Most Hindus who lived in the parts of the Punjab that became Pakistan during the 1947 partition of India and Pakistan moved to New Delhi in India. My parents were married in Lahore (in Pakistan) in 1947 then moved to New Delhi within months of their marriage. I was born in New Delhi, but the cooking style of my grandmother and mother remained Punjabi.

My grandmother, an exceptional cook, was the official saag *(greens) cooker in our family. She would painstakingly trim each leaf and stem just so, then chop and vigilantly simmer the greens for hours over low heat until they were practically puréed. This all amounted to hours of work for my grandmother. The*

result was served with a dollop of butter and hearty corn flatbreads. The greens melted on your tongue, with the most exquisite feel and flavor.

Today, I use many modern conveniences, which allow me to make this still-delicious recipe without laboring all day.

1 large bunch mustard greens (about 1 pound), trimmed and coarsely chopped

1 small bunch fresh spinach (about 8 ounces), trimmed and coarsely chopped

1 small bunch lambs quarters (about 4 ounces), trimmed and coarsely chopped (optional)

1 small bunch fresh fenugreek leaves (about 4 ounces), trimmed and coarsely chopped

1 cup fresh dill leaves, trimmed and coarsely chopped

3 to 4 small turnips, with any greens, chopped

1 teaspoon salt, or to taste

1 to 2 cups water

2 to 3 tablespoons corn meal

2 tablespoons corn oil

1 tablespoon melted ghee

1 large onion, finely chopped

1 (1-inch) piece fresh ginger, peeled and cut into thin matchsticks

1 tablespoon peeled minced fresh ginger

2 large cloves fresh garlic, minced

1 fresh green chile pepper, such as serrano, minced with seeds

1 large tomato, finely chopped

1 tablespoon ground coriander

2 teaspoons dried fenugreek leaves

1 teaspoon garam masala

½ cup nonfat plain yogurt, whisked until smooth

1 tablespoon melted unsalted butter

1½ teaspoons cumin seeds

½ teaspoon ground paprika

¼ teaspoon ground black salt (optional)

1. Place all the greens, turnips, salt, and 1 cup water in a large nonstick saucepan and cook over medium-high heat until the greens are wilted, about 5 minutes. Remove from the heat, let cool, then transfer to a food processor and pulse until coarsely puréed. (Do not overprocess.)

2. Return to the pan, cover, and simmer over medium heat until the greens are very smooth, about 30 minutes, adding up to ½ cup more water, if needed. During the last 10 minutes, add the corn meal, a little at a time, until all of it is incorporated.

3. Heat the oil and ghee in a medium saucepan over medium-high heat, add the onion and ginger matchsticks, and cook, stirring, until golden, about 10 minutes. Add the minced ginger and garlic, stir about 1 minute, then add the green chile pepper and tomato and cook until the juices evaporate, about 5 minutes.

4. Add the coriander, fenugreek leaves, and garam masala and transfer everything into the mustard greens. Mix well and simmer another 20 to 30 minutes. Transfer to a serving dish and swirl in the yogurt, with parts of it visible as a garnish.

5. In a small pan, heat the butter over medium heat and add the cumin seeds; they should sizzle upon contact with the hot oil. Quickly add the paprika and black salt (if using), and drizzle over the greens as a garnish. Serve.

Mustard Greens with Cauliflower Florets
Gobhi Sarson

Makes 4 to 6 servings

Here is another way of preparing this wintertime favorite. To enjoy it the traditional way, serve it as Punjabis do—with lots of whipped butter (though I tend to use just the bare minimum or use the American adaptation of nonfat sour cream).

2 large bunches mustard greens (about 1½ pounds), trimmed and coarsely chopped
1 small bunch spinach (about 8 ounces), trimmed and coarsely chopped
1 to 1½ cups water
1 large onion, coarsely chopped
6 to 8 quarter-size slices peeled fresh ginger
2 large cloves fresh garlic, peeled

1 fresh green chile pepper, such as serrano, stemmed
1 large tomato, coarsely chopped
2 tablespoons corn meal
2 tablespoons corn or mustard oil, or melted ghee
1 teaspoon cumin seeds
1 tablespoon coarsely ground coriander
1 teaspoon dried fenugreek leaves
1 teaspoon garam masala
¼ teaspoon ground turmeric
1 teaspoon salt, or to taste
1 small head cauliflower (about 1 pound), cut into 1½-inch florets
½ cup nonfat plain yogurt, whisked until smooth
1 tablespoon whipped unsalted butter or nonfat sour cream

1. Place the mustard greens and spinach in a large nonstick wok or saucepan and add 1 cup water. Cook over medium-high heat until wilted, about 5 minutes. Let cool, then coarsely process in the food processor.

2. In the same work bowl, process together the onion, ginger, garlic, and green chile pepper until minced. Transfer to a bowl. Then purée the tomato and corn meal.

3. In a separate large nonstick saucepan, heat the oil (or ghee) over medium-high heat and add the cumin seeds; they should sizzle upon contact with the hot oil. Quickly add the onion-ginger mixture and stir until golden, about 5 minutes. Add the puréed tomato and cook, stirring, until most of the juices evaporate, about 3 minutes. Stir in the coriander, fenugreek leaves, garam masala, turmeric, and salt, then add the cauliflower florets and cook, stirring, over medium heat, about 5 minutes.

4. Add the yogurt, a little at a time, stirring constantly to prevent it from curdling. Cover the pan and cook, stirring occasionally, until the florets are crisp-tender, 7 to 10 minutes. Add the puréed greens and continue to simmer until the florets are soft and the greens are smooth and creamy, adding up to ½ cup more water, if needed, 15 to 20 minutes. Transfer to a serving dish, swirl in the butter (or sour cream), and serve.

Savory Fruit Curries

Green Mango Curry
Manga Kari

Makes 4 to 6 servings

This sweet-and-sour dish is a Kerala favorite, meant to be served over rice or with chapatis *(whole-wheat griddle breads) and* paapads *(spicy lentil wafers). In Kerala, they use the small, green, unripe mangoes (*kairi*) with the peel and all, and cut them in large pieces, through the center seed. (This is generally done by the vendors, who use special knives, though some families do it themselves at home.) But these days more and more people simply cut around the center seed. They may or may not peel the mangoes. I generally peel mangoes with a vegetable peeler.*

1 tablespoon South Indian Sambar Powder
    (page 28 or store-bought)
2 large unripe green mangoes, cut into 1¹⁄₂-inch pieces
    (peeled or unpeeled)
1 tablespoon peeled minced fresh ginger
1 tablespoon minced fresh curry leaves
1 to 3 fresh green chile peppers, such as serrano,
    minced with seeds
¹⁄₄ teaspoon ground turmeric
1 teaspoon salt, or to taste
2¹⁄₂ cups water
1 tablespoon coconut or peanut oil
¹⁄₈ teaspoon ground asafoetida
¹⁄₄ cup grated jaggery (gur)
¹⁄₄ cup finely chopped fresh cilantro,
    including soft stems
¹⁄₄ teaspoon garam masala

1. Prepare the sambar powder. Then, in a large non-reactive saucepan, add the mangoes, ginger, curry leaves, green chile peppers, turmeric, salt, and 2 cups water, and bring to a boil over high heat. Reduce the heat to medium-low, cover the pan, and simmer until the mango pieces are soft, 10 to 12 minutes.

2. Heat the oil in a small nonstick wok or saucepan over medium-high heat and add the sambar powder and asafoetida, stir a few seconds, then mix into the mango.

3. Dissolve the jaggery in ¹⁄₂ cup water, then strain and discard any residue. Add to the mango pieces. Mix in the cilantro and cook about 2 minutes. Transfer to a serving dish, sprinkle the garam masala on top, and serve.

Mango Curry with Split Pigeon Peas
Manga-Toor Dal Kootu

Makes 4 to 6 servings

Kootu *is a south Indian soft-cooked combination curry, typically made with one or a mixture of vegetables or fruits, and split pigeon peas (*toor dal*), yellow split chickpeas (*channa dal*), or yellow mung beans (*dhulli mung dal*). This often-made summer dish is somewhat sweet from the mangoes and the coconut milk, but the yogurt and chile peppers, as well as the fragrant spices, more than balance the sweetness. Serve it over rice with a side of Spicy South Indian Potatoes (page 252).*

¹⁄₂ cup Coconut Milk (page 44 or store-bought)
¹⁄₂ cup dried split pigeon peas (toor dal),
    sorted and washed in 3 to 4 changes of water
¹⁄₂ teaspoon salt, or to taste
¹⁄₄ teaspoon ground turmeric
3 cups water
2 medium firm ripe mangoes, peeled and
    cut into 1-inch pieces
¹⁄₂ cup nonfat plain yogurt, whisked until smooth
2 tablespoons peanut oil
3 to 4 whole dried red chile peppers,
    such as chile de arbol
1 teaspoon black mustard seeds
1 teaspoon cumin seeds
¹⁄₈ teaspoon ground asafoetida
¹⁄₂ teaspoon coarsely ground fenugreek seeds
1 tablespoon dried curry leaves
¹⁄₄ cup finely chopped fresh cilantro,
    including soft stems

1. Prepare the coconut milk. Then, in a large saucepan, cook the dal, salt, and turmeric with 2 cups water, over medium-high heat for the first 2 to 3 minutes and then over medium heat until soft, 15 to 20 minutes.

2. Add the mango and the remaining 1 cup water and cook, 5 to 7 minutes. Add the coconut milk and yogurt and simmer, 3 to 5 minutes. Transfer to a serving dish.

3. Heat the oil in a large nonstick wok or saucepan over medium-high heat and add the chile peppers, then the mustard and cumin seeds; they should splutter upon contact with the hot oil, so cover the pan and reduce the heat until the spluttering subsides. Quickly add the asafoetida, fenugreek, and curry leaves. Transfer the spices to the mango curry and mix well. Then mix in the cilantro and serve.

Watermelon Whites in Tomato and Onion Sauce

Rassadar Tarbooz

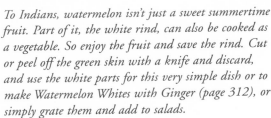

Makes 4 to 6 servings

To Indians, watermelon isn't just a sweet summertime fruit. Part of it, the white rind, can also be cooked as a vegetable. So enjoy the fruit and save the rind. Cut or peel off the green skin with a knife and discard, and use the white parts for this very simple dish or to make Watermelon Whites with Ginger (page 312), or simply grate them and add to salads.

1 tablespoon vegetable oil
2 to 3 small onions, cut in half lengthwise and thinly sliced
2 large tomatoes, finely chopped
1¹/₂ pounds peeled watermelon rinds (whites), cut into 1-inch pieces
1 cup finely chopped fresh cilantro, including soft stems
1 teaspoon salt, or to taste

1. Heat the oil in a large nonstick wok or saucepan over medium-high heat and cook the onions, stirring, until golden, about 10 minutes.

2. Add the tomatoes, watermelon whites, half the cilantro, and the salt and cook over high heat for 3 to 5 minutes. Cover the pan, reduce the heat to medium-low, and cook until the watermelon and tomatoes release all their juices (there is a lot of juice in this dish). Continue to cook, stirring occasionally, until the watermelon pieces are tender, about 30 minutes. Mix in the remaining cilantro during the last 5 minutes of cooking and serve.

Peach Halves in Savory Ginger-Peach Sauce

Aadhoo ki Sabzi

Makes 4 to 6 servings

This dish is my creation, inspired by the peach tree in my backyard in Santa Monica. It is one of the many peach dishes that I've created over the years.

Serve it alongside Spicy Mushrooms and Bell Peppers (page 300), or with grilled meat, chicken, or seafood and paranthas *(griddle-fried breads), and a rice* pullao *(pilaf).*

10 to 12 large ripe fresh peaches
3 tablespoons peanut oil
1 teaspoon cumin seeds
1 large onion, finely chopped
2 tablespoons peeled minced fresh ginger
1 to 3 fresh green chile peppers, such as serrano, minced with seeds
1 tablespoon ground coriander
1 teaspoon garam masala
¹/₂ teaspoon ground cumin
1 teaspoon salt, or to taste
¹/₂ cup finely chopped fresh cilantro, including soft stems
¹/₄ cup fresh lemon juice
¹/₂ teaspoon freshly ground black pepper, or to taste

1. Peel and cut each peach lengthwise in half and discard the center seeds. In a food processor, purée half the peaches and reserve the remaining ones.

2. Heat the oil in a large nonstick skillet over medium-high heat and add the cumin seeds; they should sizzle upon contact with the hot oil. Quickly add the onion and cook, stirring, until golden, 5 to 7 minutes. Add the ginger and green chile peppers, stir a few seconds, then add the coriander, garam masala, cumin, and salt.

3. Add the puréed peaches and cook, stirring occasionally, over medium-high heat the first 5 to 7 minutes and then over medium-low heat until the most of the juices evaporate and the sauce becomes thick, 10 to 12 minutes.

4. Add the reserved peach halves, cilantro, and lemon juice, cover the pan, and cook until the peaches soften in the sauce, about 10 minutes. Transfer to a serving dish, sprinkle the black pepper on top, and serve.

Curried Jackfruit
Kathal ki Kari

Makes 4 to 6 servings

Oval-shaped, weighing up to 100 pounds, and ranging in size from 8 inches to 2 feet long and 6- to 18-inches in diameter, jackfruits are the largest of tree-grown fruits. These ridged and spiky-skinned fruits are believed to have originated in western India; today, jackfruits are popular in most of the tropical areas of southeast Asia, and throughout India, where they are eaten as a vegetable when unripe and as a fruit when ripe.

The unripe jackfruits are green-brown in color, with a white and odorless fruit. As they ripen, the exterior changes to yellow-green and they emit an unpleasant aroma. However, when cut, the fruit has a pleasant pineapple-banana-like fragrance. The ripe fruit can be eaten on its own or transformed into ice creams and puddings.

Canned jackfruit pieces are available in Indian markets and make this dish easy to make. In some Asian markets in America, the unripe jackfruit is sold cut into 1- to 2-pound pieces. At home, these are cut into smaller pieces and deep-fried before they are added to curries or other dishes. (I prefer to pan-fry the pieces instead.) The texture and taste of cooked jackfruit is very similar to chicken and in India it is often referred to as the "vegetarian's meat."

1½ tablespoons Bengali 5-Spices (Panch-Phoran), page 27 or store-bought
2 teaspoons ground coriander seeds
1 small onion, coarsely chopped
4 to 5 quarter-size slices of peeled fresh ginger
1 large clove fresh garlic, peeled
2 medium tomatoes, coarsely chopped
½ cup coarsely chopped fresh cilantro, including soft stems + 2 tablespoons for garnish
½ cup nonfat plain yogurt, whisked until smooth
1 (20-ounce) can jackfruit, drained or 1½ pounds fresh, peeled and cut into 1-inch pieces
4 tablespoons vegetable oil
2 to 2½ cups water
¼ teaspoon garam masala

1. In a spice or coffee grinder, grind the Bengali 5-spices to make a fine powder. Remove to a small bowl and mix in the coriander.

2. In a food processor or blender, process together the onion, ginger, and garlic to make a smooth paste. Remove to a bowl and then process together the tomatoes, cilantro, and yogurt until smooth.

3. Place the jackfruit pieces in a medium nonstick wok and cook, stirring, over medium-high heat until dry, about 2 minutes. Add 2 tablespoons of the oil and cook, stirring, until the pieces are golden brown, about 5 minutes. Transfer to a bowl.

4. Heat the remaining oil in the pan and cook, stirring the onion paste over medium heat until browned, about 7 minutes. Add the ground spices and stir about 2 minutes, then add the puréed tomato-yogurt mixture and cook, stirring, until most of the juices evaporate, about 3 minutes.

5. Add the jackfruit pieces, stir about 2 minutes, then add the water and bring to a boil over high heat. Reduce the heat to medium-low, cover the pan and simmer, until the jackfruit pieces are soft and the sauce is thick, about 10 minutes. Transfer to a serving dish, sprinkle the garam masala and cilantro on top and serve.

Variation: For a vegan alternative, omit the yogurt and add an extra tomato in Step 2.

Mixed Vegetable Curries

Kerala Mixed Vegetable Curry
Kerala ki Tarkari

Makes 4 to 6 servings

With coconut as the predominant flavor, this simple curry is a perfect example of Kerala cuisine, which is heavily coconut-based because coconut palms grow abundantly along the coastal areas. This dish can be made with any vegetables, such as carrots, eggplant, cauliflower, zucchini, pumpkin, yams, and peas. You can even use frozen vegetables, if you like.

1/2 cup Coconut Milk (page 44 or store-bought)
1 tablespoon coconut oil
2 (1-inch) sticks cinnamon
8 green cardamom pods, crushed lightly
    to break the skin
6 whole cloves
1 large onion, cut in half lengthwise and thinly sliced
1 to 3 fresh green chile peppers, such as serrano,
    minced with seeds
2 tablespoons peeled minced fresh ginger
5 to 6 cups mixed fresh or thawed frozen vegetables,
    cut into 1-inch pieces
1 cup water
1 teaspoon salt, or to taste
1/4 cup chopped fresh cilantro, including soft stems
1 tablespoon peanut oil
1 teaspoon black mustard seeds
2 tablespoons finely chopped fresh curry leaves
1/8 teaspoon ground asafoetida
1/4 teaspoon garam masala

1. Prepare the coconut milk. Then, heat the coconut oil in a large nonstick wok or saucepan over medium-high heat, add the cinnamon, cardamom, and cloves, and cook, stirring, until fragrant, 1 minute. Add the onion, green chile peppers, and ginger and cook until the onion is golden, 5 to 7 minutes.

2. Mix in the vegetables, water, and salt, and bring to a boil over high heat. Reduce the heat to medium-low, cover the pan, and simmer until the vegetables are soft, 7 to 10 minutes. Add the coconut milk and cilantro and bring to a gentle boil, then simmer over low heat about 5 minutes.

3. Heat the peanut oil in a small saucepan over medium-high heat and add the mustard seeds; they should splutter upon contact with the hot oil, so cover the pan until the spluttering subsides. Quickly add the curry leaves and asafoetida and mix into the vegetables. Transfer to a serving dish, sprinkle the garam masala on top, and serve.

Mixed Vegetables in Tomato-Cream Sauce
Tamatar Kari mein Milli Julli Sabziyan

Makes 4 to 6 servings

Don't let the chile peppers in the ingredients list fool you, because peppers or not, this delicately flavored dish tastes quite familiar—reminiscent of Italian cuisine. The tomatoes and the cream balance the heat of the chile peppers and the cream adds a silky smoothness.

I first cook the vegetables in the microwave for convenience, but you can steam or boil them until crisp-tender. Serve it with paranthas *(griddle-fried breads) and grilled meats, or present it with cooked pasta.*

5 to 6 cups mixed vegetables, such as carrots, cauliflower, potatoes, green beans, Chinese eggplants, and peas cut into ³/₄-inch pieces

3 to 4 quarter-size slices peeled fresh ginger

2 large cloves fresh garlic, peeled

1 to 3 fresh green chile peppers, such as serrano, stemmed

2 tablespoons melted ghee or unsalted butter

1 tablespoon fresh lime juice

1 cup nonfat plain yogurt, whisked until smooth

¹/₂ teaspoon cayenne pepper, or to taste

1 teaspoon garam masala

¹/₂ teaspoon salt, or to taste

1 cup water or vegetable broth

1 (15-ounce) can tomato sauce

2 tablespoons heavy cream

¹/₄ teaspoon freshly ground black pepper

1. Place the vegetables in a microwave-safe dish, cover, and cook on high power until crisp-tender, 3 to 4 minutes.

2. In a blender, blend together the ginger, garlic, green chile peppers, ghee, lime juice, yogurt, cayenne pepper, garam masala, and salt until smooth. Transfer to a large nonstick wok or saucepan and cook, stirring, over medium-high heat until most of the juices evaporate and traces of the ghee appear on the sides, 5 to 7 minutes.

3. Add the water and bring to a boil over high heat. Add the vegetables, plus any juices, reduce the heat to medium-low, cover the pan, and simmer 7 to 10 minutes.

4. Mix in the tomato sauce and cream and simmer another 5 minutes to blend the flavors. Transfer to a serving dish, garnish with the black pepper, and serve.

Hot and Tangy Goan Mixed Vegetables
Sabzi Vindaloo

Makes 4 to 6 servings

Vindaloo *means "with vinegar" and this Portuguese-influenced specialty has today become one of Goa's trademark curries. Had the Portuguese not introduced vinegar to India during their rule of Goa from 1510 to 1961, this dish could very well be just another curry.*

This dish also contains red chile peppers that make it very hot, and today the name vindaloo *signifies a very spicy and tangy dish, from the red chile peppers and vinegar. It works best with sweeter or starchy vegetables and steamed rice to balance some of the flavor. This dish can be made using potatoes in place of the mixed vegetables.*

1 recipe Goan Vindaloo Paste (page 54)

4 to 5 cups mixed fresh vegetables, such as carrots, kohlrabi, potatoes, and green beans cut into 1-inch pieces

3 to 4 cups water

¹/₄ cup finely chopped fresh cilantro

1. Prepare the vindaloo paste. To the paste add the vegetables and cook, stirring, over medium heat, 7 to 10 minutes.

2. Add the water and bring to a boil over high heat. Reduce the heat to medium-low, cover the pan, and simmer until the vegetables are tender and the sauce thick, 10 to 15 minutes. Transfer to a serving dish, mix in the cilantro, and serve.

Sindhi Mixed Vegetables with Split Pigeon Peas

Sindhi Sabzi Kari

Makes 4 to 6 servings

A soupy specialty from the Sindhi community (originally from northwest India, an area now in Pakistan), this dish is traditionally served with steamed or lightly spiced basmati *rice. The number of ingredients in this dish might seem daunting, but there are just 3 relatively easy cooking steps and the pressure cooker helps shorten the cooking time.*

Cluster beans (guar ki phalli) *are thin, like* haricot vert *green beans, and about 5 inches long. These native Indian beans have an assertive taste and are used just like regular green beans to make all sorts of dishes. Kokum is the sour, sun-dried fruit of the mangosteen-oil tree, and is popularly used in the western and southern parts of India as a souring agent in foods. Cluster beans and kokum are available in Indian markets.*

**3/4 cup dried split pigeon peas (toor dal),
    sorted and washed in 3 to 4 changes of water**

6 cups water

3 tablespoons vegetable oil or melted ghee

**2 to 4 whole dried red chile peppers,
    such as chile de arbol**

**2 to 4 whole fresh green chile peppers, such as serrano,
    skin punctured to prevent bursting**

1 teaspoon cumin seeds

1/2 teaspoon coarsely ground fenugreek seeds

1/8 teaspoon ground asafoetida

3 tablespoons chickpea flour

**1/2 pound small okra, stem end trimmed,
    then split lengthwise**

**1/2 pound cluster beans (guar ki phalli),
    or any other green beans, cut in half**

1 medium potato (any kind), cut into 1/2-inch pieces

**2 pieces dried kokum halves, washed and finely
    chopped, or 2 tablespoons Tamarind Paste
    (page 54)**

1 tablespoon peeled minced fresh ginger

2 tablespoons finely chopped curry leaves

1 tablespoon ground coriander

1 1/2 teaspoons salt, or to taste

1/2 teaspoon ground turmeric

**1/2 cup finely chopped fresh cilantro,
    including soft stems**

1. Soak the dal in 2 cups water 30 to 40 minutes. Transfer to a pressure cooker and secure the lid. Cook over high heat until the regulator indicates high pressure, then cook about 30 seconds more. Remove from the heat and allow the pot to depressurize on its own, 12 to 15 minutes. Carefully open the lid, let cool, then pass the dal through a food mill, or blend (or whisk) to make a smooth purée.

2. Heat the oil (or ghee (or oil) in a large nonstick wok or saucepan over medium-high heat and add the red and green chile peppers, cumin, fenugreek seeds, and asafoetida; they should sizzle upon contact with the hot oil. Quickly add the chickpea flour and roast, stirring, over medium heat until fragrant and golden, about 2 minutes.

3. Add the puréed dal, the remaining 4 cups water, all the vegetables, kokum pieces, ginger, curry leaves, coriander, salt, and turmeric and bring to a boil over high heat. Reduce the heat to medium-low, cover the pan, and cook, stirring occasionally, until the vegetables are tender, 30 to 40 minutes. Transfer to a serving bowl, mix in the cilantro, and serve.

Vegetable Ball (Kofta) Curries

Zucchini Balls in Creamy Tomato Sauce
Zucchini Koftae ki Kari

Makes 4 to 6 servings

Koftas are vegetable or meat balls or rolls. They are made with grated vegetables, ground meats, or mashed paneer *cheese and are mostly deep-fried—although some meat versions served in curries are sometimes just cooked in the sauce itself, such as in Kashmiri Hand-Pressed Meat Rolls in Curry Sauce (page 497). The koftas in this dish are made with zucchini.*

1 pound zucchini, grated and squeezed
1 large russet (or any) potato, peeled and grated
**1/2 cup finely chopped fresh cilantro,
    including soft stems**
**1 fresh green chile pepper, such as serrano,
    minced with seeds**
1/2 teaspoon salt, or to taste
2 teaspoons ground coriander
1/2 teaspoon ajwain seeds, coarsely ground
1/4 teaspoon baking soda
2/3 cup chickpea flour (besan), or more as needed
1 1/2 to 2 cups oil for deep-frying
**4 cups (1 recipe) Butter-Cream Sauce with
    Fresh Tomatoes (page 389)**
1/4 teaspoon garam masala

1. In a large bowl, mix together everything (except the butter-cream sauce and the garam masala) to make a thick, soft dough, adding more chickpea flour if needed. Divide into 12 to 15 portions and shape each portion into smooth round balls.

2. Heat the oil in a large wok over medium-high heat until it reaches 325°F to 350°F on a frying thermometer or until a small drop of dough put into the hot oil rises to the top in 15 to 20 seconds. Add the zucchini balls into the hot oil, adding as many as the

wok can hold at one time without crowding, and deep-fry, turning them around with a slotted spatula, until they are firm and golden, about 3 minutes. Drain and transfer to an ovenproof serving dish.

3. Prepare the butter-cream sauce. Preheat the oven to 400°F. Pour the sauce over the koftas. Cover with foil and bake at least 15 minutes, or until the koftas absorb the juices and become soft. Sprinkle the garam masala on top and serve.

Stuffed Potato Balls in Tomato and Coconut Chutney Curry
Chutni Bharae Aalu Koftae ki Kari

Makes 4 to 6 servings

Here, mashed potato balls, stuffed with a tangy coconut chutney, are baked in a luscious tomato and coconut milk sauce. Delicious!

1 3/4 cups Coconut Milk (page 44 or store-bought)
**1/2 cup Fresh Coconut Chutney with Cilantro
    (page 61)**
**1 1/2 tablespoons Basic Ginger and Green Chile Pepper
    Paste (page 48)**
4 medium russet (or any) potatoes (about 1 1/4 pounds)
**1/2 cup finely chopped fresh cilantro,
    including soft stems**
1 tablespoon ground coriander
1/2 teaspoon salt, or to taste
1/8 teaspoon baking soda
1/2 cup chickpea flour
1 1/2 to 2 cups peanut oil for deep frying
1 teaspoon cumin seeds
1 teaspoon black mustard seeds
1 large onion, finely chopped
1 tablespoon ground coriander
1/2 teaspoon ground fenugreek seeds
1 large tomato, coarsely chopped
1 1/2 cups water
1/4 teaspoon garam masala

1. Prepare the coconut milk, the chutney, and the ginger-chile paste. Then boil the potatoes in lightly salted water to cover until tender, about 20 minutes. Drain, let cool, then peel and grate them into a large bowl.

2. Into the potatoes mix in the cilantro, ginger-chile pepper paste, coriander, salt, baking soda, and chickpea flour, and mix well. Divide into 15 to 20 portions. Working with each portion separately, using clean hands, flatten each into a patty and place about ¼ teaspoon of the chutney in the center. Then shape the patty into a smooth, round ball, with the chutney inside. Repeat with the remaining portions.

3. Heat the oil in a large wok over medium-high heat until it reaches 325°F to 350°F on a frying thermometer or until a small bit of the dough dropped into the hot oil rises to the top in 15 to 20 seconds. Add the potato balls to the hot oil, adding as many as the wok can hold at one time without crowding, and fry, turning them around with a slotted spatula, until they are firm and golden, about 3 minutes. Transfer to an oven-safe serving dish.

4. To make the sauce: Heat 2 tablespoons of the oil (in which the koftas were fried) in a large nonstick wok or saucepan over medium-high heat and add the cumin and mustard seeds; they should splutter upon contact with the hot oil, so cover the pan and lower the heat until the spluttering subsides. Quickly add the onion and cook, stirring, until golden, 5 to 7 minutes. Add any remaining coconut chutney and cook, stirring, until lightly golden, about 5 minutes.

5. Stir in the coriander and fenugreek seeds, then add the tomato and cook until it is soft, about 3 minutes. Add the water and bring to a boil over high heat. Reduce the heat to medium-low, cover the pan, and simmer about 10 minutes. Add the coconut milk and simmer 3 to 5 minutes to blend the flavors.

6. Preheat the oven to 400°F. Pour the sauce over the kofta balls and mix lightly. Cover with foil and bake at least 15 minutes, or until the koftas absorb the juices and become soft. Sprinkle the garam masala on top and serve.

Spinach Balls in Green Curry
Harae Rassae mein Palak Koftae

Makes 4 to 6 servings

Fried balls of spinach and chickpea flour floating in a creamy cilantro sauce make for a substantial, flavorful entrée. Serve it with rice or paranthas *(griddle-fried breads).*

1 large russet (or any) potato
1 small bunch fresh spinach (8 to 10 ounces), trimmed and washed (do not pat dry)
1 large clove fresh garlic, peeled
1 fresh green chile pepper, such as serrano, stemmed
½ cup minced onion
1 tablespoon ground dried pomegranate seeds
1 teaspoon dried fenugreek leaves
½ teaspoon ajwain seeds
½ teaspoon salt, or to taste
⅛ teaspoon baking soda
½ cup chickpea flour
1 to 1½ cups peanut oil for deep-frying
4 cups (1 recipe) Minty Green Curry Sauce (page 390)
½ cup nonfat plain yogurt, whisked until smooth
1 large bunch fresh cilantro, including soft stems
¼ cup heavy cream

1. Boil the potato in lightly salted water to cover until tender, 15 to 20 minutes. Drain, let cool, then peel and grate. Reserve. In a food processor, process together the spinach, garlic, and green chile pepper until minced. Transfer to a large bowl.

2. Add the potato, onion, pomegranate seeds, fenugreek leaves, ajwain seeds, salt, and baking soda, and mix well. Let sit about 30 minutes, then add enough chickpea flour to make a soft dough. Divide the dough into 20 to 25 portions and, using clean hands, shape into smooth balls.

3. Heat the oil in a large wok over medium-high heat until it reaches 325°F to 350°F on a frying thermometer or until a small bit of dough dropped into

the hot oil rises to the top in 15 to 20 seconds. Add the spinach balls to the hot oil, adding as many as the wok can hold at one time without crowding, and deep-fry, turning them around with a slotted spatula until they are firm and golden, about 3 minutes. Drain and set aside.

4. Prepare the minty green curry sauce and leave in the pan. In a blender, process together the yogurt, cilantro, and cream until smooth, then mix it into the curry sauce and bring to a boil over high heat. Reduce the heat to medium-low, cover the pan, and simmer about 10 minutes.

5. Add the koftas to the pan and cook over medium heat until they absorb the juices and become soft, 10 to 15 minutes. Once the koftas have absorbed the sauce they are very fragile, so handle them with care. Serve hot.

Lotus Root Balls in Classic Curry Sauce

Kamal-Kakdi Koftae ki Kari

Makes 4 to 6 servings

Lotus roots (kamal-kakdi or bhain) are the pale, buff-colored, tube-like roots of the lotus plant (also called the water lily). The root has 10 holes that run its whole length, and when you slice it, these holes give it a naturally lacy appearance. It is essential to thinly slice the lotus roots before mincing them in a food processor, because lotus roots have hair-like threads along their length, and if they are not cut, they interfere with the texture of the dish.

2 medium russet (or any) potatoes
2 small lotus roots (5 to 6 ounces each)
4 quarter-size slices peeled fresh ginger
1 large clove fresh garlic, peeled
1 to 2 fresh green chile peppers, such as serrano, stemmed

1/2 cup finely chopped fresh cilantro, including soft stems
1 tablespoon ground coriander
1 tablespoon ground dried pomegranate seeds
1/2 teaspoon ground cumin
1/2 teaspoon salt, or to taste
1/4 teaspoon baking soda
1/2 cup chickpea flour
1 1/2 to 2 cups peanut oil for deep frying
4 cups (1 recipe) Classic Spicy Curry Sauce (page 388)
1/4 teaspoon garam masala

1. Boil the potatoes in lightly salted water to cover until tender, about 20 minutes. Drain, let cool, then peel and mash them in a bowl. Peel and thinly slice the lotus roots. Then transfer them to a food processor along with the ginger, garlic, and green chile peppers and process until minced. Transfer to the bowl with the potatoes.

2. Add the cilantro, coriander, pomegranate seeds, cumin, salt, and baking soda, and mix well. Then add the chickpea flour to make a soft dough. Divide the dough into 20 to 25 portions and, using clean hands, shape into smooth balls.

3. Heat the oil in a large wok over medium-high heat until it reaches 325°F to 350°F on a frying thermometer or until a small bit of the dough dropped into the hot oil rises to the top in 15 to 20 seconds. Add the lotus-root balls into the hot oil, adding as many as the wok can hold at one time without crowding, and deep-fry, turning them around with a slotted spatula until they are firm and golden, about 3 minutes. Drain and transfer to an ovenproof serving dish.

4. Prepare the curry sauce. Preheat the oven to 400°F. Pour the sauce over the kofta balls and mix lightly. Cover with foil and bake at least 15 minutes, or until the koftas absorb the juices and become soft. Sprinkle the garam masala on top and serve.

Nugget and Chickpea Flour Curries

Curried Soybean Nuggets
Rassadar Soya ki Badiyan

Makes 4 to 6 servings

Soybean nuggets (badiyan) have always been considered a vegetarian's "meat" in India. Their protein-rich chewy texture, shape, and size, is even reminiscent of boneless cubes of meat. When cooked, they live up to their reputation. Here is a sumptuous recipe from my friend Bharti Dhalwala.

1¹/₂ cups soybean nuggets
1 small onion, coarsely chopped
2 large cloves fresh garlic, peeled
6 quarter-size slices peeled fresh ginger
¹/₂ cup nonfat plain yogurt, whisked until smooth
¹/₂ teaspoon salt, or to taste
2 tablespoons vegetable oil
1 (1-inch) stick cinnamon
2 black cardamom pods, crushed lightly
    to break the skin
4 green cardamom pods, crushed lightly
    to break the skin
2 bay leaves
4 cloves
1 teaspoon cumin seeds
1 large tomato, finely chopped
1 fresh green chile pepper, such as serrano,
    minced with seeds
¹/₄ teaspoon ground turmeric
1¹/₂ to 2 cups water
¹/₄ cup finely chopped fresh cilantro,
    including soft stems
¹/₄ teaspoon garam masala

1. Soak the nuggets in lightly salted water to cover, about 1 hour. Drain and squeeze out all the water from the nuggets and place them in a non-reactive bowl. Meanwhile, in a food processor, process together the onion, garlic, ginger, yogurt, and salt

until smooth. Mix in the salt and transfer to the bowl with the nuggets. Mix, making sure all the nuggets are well-coated with the marinade.

2. Heat the oil in a large nonstick wok or saucepan over medium-high heat and add the cinnamon, black and green cardamom pods, bay leaves, cloves, and cumin seeds, and stir about 30 seconds. Add the marinated nuggets and cook over high heat, stirring, until they are completely dry, about 5 minutes.

3. Add the tomato, green chile pepper, and turmeric, and stir until the tomato is soft, about 5 minutes. Add the water and bring to a boil over high heat. Reduce the heat to medium-low, cover the pan, and simmer until the nuggets are tender, 15 to 20 minutes. Mix in the cilantro during the last 5 minutes of cooking. Transfer to a serving dish, sprinkle the garam masala on top, and serve.

Soybean Nugget Curry with Red Bell Peppers
Rassadar Soya ki Badiyan aur Shimla Mirch

Makes 4 to 6 servings

This delicious entrée comes with protein-rich, soft, chewy soybean nuggets (badiyan) and naturally sweet red bell peppers floating in a tomato-yogurt sauce.
It is popular among India's vegetarians, who serve it with a side of dry-cooked vegetables and chapatis (whole-wheat griddle breads) or paranthas (griddle-fried breads) or with a basmati rice pullao (pilaf).

1¹/₂ cups soybean nuggets
2 tablespoons vegetable oil
2 small onions, cut in half lengthwise and thinly sliced
1 teaspoon cumin seeds
1 large clove fresh garlic, minced
2 tablespoons peeled minced fresh ginger
1 tablespoon ground coriander
¹/₄ teaspoon ground turmeric
2 large tomatoes, finely chopped
1¹/₂ to 2 cups water
¹/₂ teaspoon salt, or to taste

1/2 cup nonfat plain yogurt, whisked until smooth
1/2 cup finely chopped fresh cilantro,
    including soft stems
1 large red bell pepper, cut into 1/2-by-1-inch pieces
1/4 teaspoon garam masala

1. Soak the nuggets in lightly salted water to cover, about 1 hour. Then drain and squeeze out all the water from the nuggets.

2. Meanwhile, heat the oil in a large nonstick wok or saucepan over medium-high heat and cook the onions, stirring, until golden, about 5 minutes. Add the cumin seeds; they should sizzle upon contact with the hot oil. Quickly add the garlic and ginger and stir until golden, about 1 minute.

3. Add the coriander and turmeric, stir about 30 seconds, then add the tomatoes and cook until the juices evaporate, about 10 minutes. Mix in the drained nuggets and cook, stirring, until the nuggets are well-coated with the sauce, about 10 minutes.

4. Add the water and salt and bring to a boil over high heat. Reduce the heat to medium, cover the pan, and simmer about 5 minutes. Add the yogurt, a little at a time, stirring constantly to prevent it from curdling, and simmer until the nuggets absorb the juices and the sauce is thick and smooth, about 20 minutes. Mix in the cilantro and bell pepper during the last 10 minutes of cooking. Transfer to a serving dish, sprinkle the garam masala on top, and serve.

Spicy Lentil Nugget Curry with Potatoes

Vadiyan-Aalu

Makes 4 to 6 servings

Lentil nuggets, called vadiyan *or* badiyan, *can be made at home, but most of us generally buy them from Indian markets. A specialty of Amritsar, a city in Punjab,* vadiyan *are generally very hot and spicy, and are meant to be added by the piece to flavor a dish, not used whole. This flavor remains close to all Punjabi hearts, in India and abroad.*

5 medium russet potatoes (about 1 1/2 pounds)
1 large clove fresh garlic, peeled
4 to 6 quarter-size slices peeled fresh ginger
1 small onion, coarsely chopped
1/4 cup vegetable oil
2 large lentil nuggets, broken coarsely into
    1-inch pieces
1 1/2 cups canned tomato sauce
1 tablespoon ground coriander
1/2 teaspoon ground cumin
1/4 teaspoon ground turmeric
1/2 teaspoon salt, or to taste
1/2 teaspoon garam masala
4 to 5 cups water
1/4 cup finely chopped fresh cilantro,
    including soft stems

1. Boil the potatoes in lightly salted water to cover until tender, about 20 minutes. Let cool, then peel and cut them into 1-inch pieces. Reserve. In a food processor, process together the garlic, ginger, and onion to make a paste. Transfer to a bowl.

2. Heat the oil in a large nonstick wok or saucepan over medium-high heat and fry the nugget pieces in one or two batches, turning them until browned, 1 to 2 minutes. (If using a saucepan, tilt it to pool the oil in one place.) With a slotted spoon, remove the nugget pieces, leaving as much oil in the pan as possible.

3. Add the garlic-ginger-onion paste to the pan and cook, stirring, over medium heat until well browned, 12 to 15 minutes. (Do not cook quickly over high heat—the onions will burn and will not develop a rich flavor.)

4. Add the tomato sauce and cook, stirring over medium-high heat, about 2 minutes. Mix in the coriander, cumin, turmeric, salt, and 1/4 teaspoon garam masala, then add the fried nuggets and water and bring to a boil oven high heat. Cover the pan, reduce the heat to medium, and cook until the nuggets are fork tender, about 30 minutes.

5. Add the potatoes and cilantro, cover the pan, and simmer another 10 minutes to blend the flavors. Transfer to a serving dish, sprinkle the remaining 1/4 teaspoon garam masala on top, and serve.

Chickpea Pancakes in Curry Sauce

Rassadar Doiyan

Makes 4 to 6 servings

A specialty of Punjab, doiyan *are tiny chickpea flour pancakes. This dish, made with the pancakes floating in a fragrant curry sauce, are a favorite on my mother's side of the family.*

To make more pancakes than you need to feed hungry mouths before you can add them to the sauce or to use them for another dish, such as Raita with Chickpea Flour Pancakes (page 235), just double the ingredients for the pancakes (not the curry sauce).

1 recipe Classic Spicy Curry Sauce (page 388)
¼ cup chickpea flour (besan)
1 fresh green chile pepper, such as serrano, minced with seeds
⅛ teaspoon salt, or to taste
⅛ teaspoon baking soda
¼ cup water
2 to 3 tablespoons peanut oil
2 tablespoons finely chopped fresh cilantro, including soft stems
¼ teaspoon garam masala

1. Prepare the curry sauce and leave it in the pan. In a small bowl, mix together the chickpea flour, green chile pepper, salt, and baking soda, then add the water to make a semi-thin batter. Set aside 15 to 20 minutes.

2. Heat 1 tablespoon oil in a medium skillet over medium heat. Add about 1 tablespoon the batter and spread it with a spoon to make a 1½-inch pancake. As it firms up, push to one side of the skillet and make similar pancakes with the remaining batter, adding more oil as needed.

3. Turn over each pancake that is on the side of the pan as the bottom browns, about 30 seconds. Allow the second side to brown, about 30 seconds, then transfer the pancake to a plate. Continue until all the batter has been used.

4. Add the pancakes to the curry sauce and bring to a boil over high heat. Reduce the heat to medium-low, cover the pan, and simmer until the pancakes absorb the juices from the sauce, 5 to 7 minutes. Transfer to a serving dish, garnish with the cilantro and garam masala, and serve.

Spicy Curried Chickpea Drops

Boondi Ki Sabzi

Makes 4 to 6 servings

Chickpea drops, called boondi, *are crispy, deep-fried ¼-inch drops of chickpea flour batter. Used in a multitude of recipes, some savory and others sweet, they are a blessing in the kitchen. This village-style curry—a lunchtime favorite—is one that Indian grandmothers turn to when the vegetable vendor fails to show up at their doorsteps. In this recipe from my friend Bharti Dhalwala, I call for* boondi *purchased from the Indian markets, which, in most cases, is already salted, so make the necessary adjustments. Or try making your own* boondi *(page 45).*

1 tablespoon vegetable oil
1 teaspoon cumin seeds
1 small onion, minced
1 large tomato, finely chopped
1 small onion, cut in half lengthwise and thinly sliced
½ teaspoon salt, or to taste (if needed)
½ teaspoon cayenne pepper, or to taste
¼ teaspoon ground turmeric
4 cups water
1 cup nonfat plain yogurt, whisked until smooth
2 cups packaged boondi drops
¼ cup finely chopped fresh cilantro, including soft stems

1. Heat the oil in a large nonstick wok or saucepan over medium-high heat and add the cumin seeds; they should sizzle upon contact with the hot oil. Quickly add the minced onion and cook, stirring, until golden, about 5 minutes.

2. Add the tomato, sliced onion, salt (if needed) cayenne pepper, and turmeric and cook, stirring, until the tomato is soft and most of the juices evaporate, 5 to 7 minutes.

3. Add the water and bring to a boil over high heat. Reduce the heat to low, cover the pan, and simmer 5 to 7 minutes. Increase the heat to high and mix in the yogurt, a little at a time, stirring constantly to prevent it from curdling, and continue to boil until the sauce is somewhat thick, 3 to 5 minutes.

4. Mix in the boondi drops and boil, stirring, 2 to 3 minutes. Transfer to a serving dish, mix in the cilantro, and serve.

Punjabi Chickpea Drops Curry

Punjabi Rassadar Boondi

Makes 4 to 6 servings

This is an unpretentious soupy curry, with drops of delicately fried chickpea batter called boondi *that soften in the sauce almost to the point of becoming a part of it.*

1 small onion, coarsely chopped
4 quarter-size slices peeled fresh ginger
1 fresh green chile pepper, such as serrano, stemmed
2 tablespoons vegetable oil
1 large tomato, finely chopped
1 tablespoon ground coriander
1/2 teaspoon hot red pepper flakes, or to taste
1/4 teaspoon ground turmeric
1/2 teaspoon salt, or to taste
1/4 cup nonfat plain yogurt, whisked until smooth
4 cups water
2 cups purchased boondi drops
1/4 cup chopped fresh cilantro, including soft stems

1. In a blender or a food processor, process together the onion, ginger, and green chile pepper until smooth.

2. Heat the oil in a large nonstick wok or saucepan over medium-high heat, add the onion-ginger paste and cook, stirring, until golden, 3 to 5 minutes.

3. Add the tomato and cook until most of the juices evaporate, about 5 minutes. Add the coriander, red pepper flakes, turmeric, and salt, and stir 30 seconds. Then mix in the yogurt, a little at a time, stirring constantly to prevent it from curdling, until all of it is incorporated, about 1 minute.

4. Add the water and bring to a boil over high heat. Reduce the heat to low, cover the pan, and simmer 5 to 7 minutes. Mix in the boondi and cook 2 to 3 minutes. Transfer to a serving dish, garnish with cilantro, and serve.

Rajasthani Chickpea Flour Bits in Yogurt Sauce

Rajasthani Gattae ki Kari

Makes 4 to 6 servings

Gattae are little ½-inch pieces of boiled chickpea flour dough, and this curry is very different from any of the previously mentioned chickpea flour curries. Although also made in other communities, gattae ki kari *remains a specialty of Rajasthan and comes to me from a native—Pushpa Khatod, my daughter's mother-in-law.*

There are 2 steps to this recipe: making the gattae *bits and making the sauce for them.*

The gattae *are versatile: You can serve them in a sauce, add them to rice, or simply cut them into thin slices and pan-cook them in 1 to 2 tablespoons of oil and serve as appetizers.*

To make the gattae:
1 tablespoon Basic Ginger and Green Chile Pepper
    Paste (page 48)
1 cup chickpea flour
¹/₄ teaspoon ground coriander
¹/₄ teaspoon ajwain seeds
¹/₄ teaspoon ground fennel seeds
¹/₄ teaspoon cayenne pepper
¹/₄ teaspoon salt, or to taste
¹/₈ teaspoon ground turmeric
1¹/₂ tablespoons peanut oil
2 to 4 tablespoons nonfat plain yogurt,
    whisked until smooth

To make the sauce:
2 tablespoons peanut oil
1 teaspoon cumin seeds
¹/₂ teaspoon ajwain seeds
¹/₈ teaspoon ground asafoetida
2 tablespoons Basic Ginger and Green Chile Pepper
    Paste (page 48)
¹/₄ teaspoon cayenne pepper dissolved in ¹/₄ cup water
2 cups nonfat plain yogurt, whisked well with
    1 cup water until smooth
¹/₄ teaspoon ground turmeric

1 tablespoon ground coriander
1 teaspoon salt
3 to 4 cups water
Chopped cilantro

1. Prepare the ginger-chile paste. To make the gattae: In a small bowl, mix together the chickpea flour, coriander, fennel, cayenne pepper, salt, and turmeric. Then rub in the ginger-chile paste and oil. Add 2 tablespoons yogurt, and more as needed, to make a semi-stiff dough. If the dough sticks to your fingers, scrape it off, coat your fingers with some water or oil, and continue.

2. Using clean hands, divide the dough into 6 parts and roll each part into a ½-inch thick and 6- to 7-inch long roll. Place all the rolls in a large saucepan, add water to cover by at least 1 inch and boil over medium-high heat, 2 to 3 minutes. Then reduce the heat to medium-low and simmer until the rolls firm up and turn much lighter in color, 20 to 25 minutes. Drain, saving the water for cooking the sauce. Cut the rolls into ½-inch pieces (gattae).

3. To make the sauce: Heat the oil in a large nonstick wok or saucepan over medium-high heat and add the cumin, ajwain, and asafoetida; they should sizzle upon contact with the hot oil. Quickly add the ginger-chile paste and the cayenne pepper dissolved in water, and stir about 1 minute.

4. Add the whisked yogurt-water, turmeric, coriander, and salt, stirring constantly, and boil over high heat about 3 minutes. Add the gattae and boil another 2 minutes.

5. Add 3 cups water (measure in the reserved water from Step 2) and bring to a boil over high heat. Reduce the heat to medium-low, cover the pan, and simmer until the gattae are soft and the sauce is thick, about 15 minutes. (Add more water and cook another minute for a thinner sauce.) Transfer to a serving dish, garnish with the cilantro, and serve.

Variation: For heartier gattae, mix about 2 cups chopped fresh spinach into the dough in Step 1 and then proceed with the recipe.

Punjabi Chickpea Flour Bits in Curry Sauce

Punjabi Gattae ki Kari

Makes 4 to 6 servings

This Punjabi version of chickpea flour bits (gattae), as made by my mother, comes in a traditional curry sauce and tastes very different from the previous recipe, Rajasthani Chickpea Flour Bits in Yogurt Sauce.

1 cup chickpea flour

1 teaspoon garam masala

1/2 teaspoon ajwain seeds

1/3 teaspoon salt, or to taste

3 to 4 tablespoons vegetable oil

1/4 cup water + more to boil the gattae rolls

1 small onion, coarsely chopped

6 quarter-size slices peeled fresh ginger

1 small clove fresh garlic, peeled

3 tablespoons vegetable oil

3 to 5 fresh green chile peppers, such as serrano, skin punctured to prevent bursting

1 tablespoon ground coriander

1/4 teaspoon ground turmeric

1/4 teaspoon cayenne pepper, or to taste

1/2 teaspoon salt, or to taste

2 small tomatoes, coarsely chopped

3 cups water

1/4 cup finely chopped cilantro

1. To make the gattae: In a bowl, mix together the chickpea flour, garam masala, ajwain seeds, salt, and 1 tablespoon oil. Then make the gattae as in Steps 1 and 2 of Rajasthani Chickpea Flour Bits in Yogurt Sauce (page 424), using up to 1/4 cup water instead of the yogurt.

2. In a food processor or blender, process together the onion, ginger, and garlic to make a smooth paste.

3. Heat 2 to 3 tablespoons oil in a large nonstick wok or saucepan over medium heat and cook the chile peppers and onion paste, stirring, until golden, about 5 minutes. Add the coriander, turmeric, cayenne pepper, and salt, then add the tomatoes and stir until soft, about 3 minutes.

4. Add the gattae and stir about 5 minutes, then add the water, measuring the water in which the gattae were cooked as part of the 3 cups needed for the sauce. Bring to a boil over high heat. Reduce the heat to medium-low, cover the pan, and simmer 10 to 12 minutes to allow the gattae to absorb the flavors of the sauce. Transfer to a serving dish, mix in the cilantro, and serve.

Special Yogurt Curries

Quick Punjabi Yogurt Curry
Punjabi Kadhi

Makes 4 to 6 servings

If you are familiar with Indian spices and stock them in your pantry, this kadhi *literally takes only 5 minutes to put together and another 15 to 20 minutes to cook.*

If you like pakoras *(batter-fried fritters) in your* kadhi, *have 12 to 15 mixed-vegetable* pakoras *ready before you start cooking. You can also add a handful or two of chopped bell peppers or greens during the last 5 minutes of cooking.*

All kadhis *are typically served with steamed bas-mati rice. In fact, the* kadhi-chaval *(yogurt curry and rice) combination is as popular in India as rice and beans are in Mexican cuisine. But I still love my* kadhi *with* chapatis *(whole-wheat griddle breads).*

1/4 cup chickpea flour
3 to 5 quarter-size slices peeled fresh ginger
1 large clove fresh garlic, peeled
2 fresh green chile peppers, such as serrano, coarsely chopped
3 cups nonfat plain yogurt
3 cups water
2 tablespoons vegetable oil
1 teaspoon cumin seeds
1 teaspoon black mustard seeds
1/2 teaspoon coarsely ground fenugreek seeds
1/8 teaspoon ground asafoetida
1 tablespoon dried ground curry leaves
1 tablespoon ground coriander
1/2 teaspoon dried fenugreek leaves
1/4 teaspoon ground turmeric
1 teaspoon salt, or to taste
1/2 cup finely chopped fresh cilantro, including soft stems

1. Put the chickpea flour, ginger, garlic, green chile peppers, yogurt, and water in a blender and blend until smooth.

2. Heat the oil in a large nonstick wok or a saucepan over medium-high heat and add the cumin and mustard seeds; they should splutter upon contact with the hot oil, so lower the heat and cover the pan until the spluttering subsides. Then add the fenugreek, asafoetida, curry leaves, coriander, fenugreek leaves, turmeric, and salt. Stir momentarily over high heat. Then slowly add the yogurt mixture, stirring constantly, and continue to stir until it comes to a boil, 2 to 4 minutes. Watch carefully and reduce the heat if the sauce starts to boil over.

3. Continue to cook over high heat, stirring and watching carefully, until the kadhi looks smooth and silky, 10 to 12 minutes. Or reduce the heat to medium-low and simmer until the kadhi is done. Add the cilantro during the last 5 minutes of cooking. Transfer to a serving dish and serve.

Nani Mama's Yogurt Curry with Onion Fritters
Pakora Kadhi

Makes 4 to 6 servings

Nani Mama is what my children call my mother, their grandmother. And this is her version of Punjabi kadhi *(yogurt curry), which my children continue to prefer—over mine, that is.*

When I was growing up, she never used curry leaves in her kadhi. *It is an adaptation she has added over the years. Her* kadhi *is as outstanding now as it was then.*

15 to 20 Chopped Onion Pakora Fritters (page 118)
3 cups nonfat plain yogurt
3 cups water
1/4 cup chickpea flour
10 to 15 fresh curry leaves
1 1/2 tablespoons ground coriander
1/4 teaspoon fenugreek seeds, coarsely ground
1/8 teaspoon ground asafoetida
1/4 teaspoon ground turmeric
3/4 teaspoon salt, or to taste
3 tablespoons vegetable oil
1/4 cup minced onion

2 tablespoons peeled minced fresh ginger

1½ tablespoons coriander seeds, coarsely crushed
    with the back of a spoon

1 teaspoon dried fenugreek leaves

Chopped cilantro

4 to 6 whole dried red chile peppers,
    such as chile de arbol

1 teaspoon cumin seeds

¼ teaspoon ground paprika

1. Prepare the pakoras. Then, in a blender, blend together the yogurt, water, chickpea flour, and curry leaves until smooth. (Blend well, or the yogurt will curdle while cooking.) Transfer to a bowl and mix in the coriander, turmeric, and salt.

2. Heat 1½ tablespoons oil in a large nonstick wok or a saucepan over medium-high heat and cook the onion and ginger, stirring, until golden, about 1 minute. Add the coriander and fenugreek seeds and the asafoetida, and stir momentarily. Then slowly add the yogurt mixture, stirring constantly, and continue to stir until it comes to a boil, 2 to 4 minutes. Watch carefully and reduce the heat if the sauce starts to boil over.

3. Reduce the heat to medium-low and simmer, uncovered, stirring occasionally and watching carefully, until the sauce looks smooth and silky and traces of oil are visible on the top surface and the sides, 30 to 35 minutes. (At this point, the sauce should be somewhat soupy; it will thicken after the pakoras are added.)

4. Add the fenugreek leaves and the pakoras and simmer another 3 to 5 minutes, allowing the pakoras to soften as they absorb the sauce. Transfer to a serving dish, garnish with chopped cilantro, cover, and keep warm.

5. Heat the remaining 1½ tablespoons n a small nonstick saucepan over medium-high heat and cook the red chile peppers until they start to brown, about 1 minute. Remove the pan from the heat and add the cumin seeds; they should sizzle upon contact with the hot oil. Quickly add the paprika and pour over the kadhi. With a fork, lightly mix the tarka into the kadhi, with parts of it showing on top as a garnish. Serve.

Spicy Yogurt Curry with Spinach Ribbons
Palak vaali Kadhi

Makes 4 to 6 servings

This yogurt sauce is basically made the same way as that of Nani Mama's Yogurt Curry with Onion Fritters (page 426)—after all, it is a kadhi—but this recipe is a lighter version, full of greens, which Indians routinely make as a healthier version or when they don't want to make the pakora *fritters.*

3 cups nonfat plain yogurt

3 cups water

¼ cup chickpea flour

1 to 3 fresh green chile peppers, such as serrano,
    minced with seeds

1 large clove fresh garlic, peeled + 1 clove minced

1½ tablespoons ground coriander

¼ teaspoon ground turmeric

¾ teaspoon salt, or to taste

3 tablespoons vegetable oil

1 small onion, cut in half lengthwise and
    thinly sliced

1 tablespoon peeled minced fresh ginger

1 tablespoon coriander seeds, coarsely crushed
    with the back of a spoon

½ teaspoon ground fenugreek seeds

¼ teaspoon ground asafoetida

1 large bunch fresh spinach (12 to 14 ounces),
    trimmed, washed, and cut into thin ribbons

1 teaspoon dried fenugreek leaves

1 tablespoon melted ghee

4 to 6 whole dried red chile peppers,
    such as chile de arbol

½ teaspoon cumin seeds

1 teaspoon black mustard seeds

¼ teaspoon ground paprika

1. In a blender (not a food processor), blend together the yogurt, water, chickpea flour, green chile peppers, and the whole garlic clove until smooth. (Blend well, or the yogurt will curdle while cooking.) Transfer to a bowl and mix in the coriander, turmeric, and salt.

2. Heat the oil in a large nonstick wok or a saucepan over medium-high heat and cook the onion, stirring, until golden, about 5 minutes. Add the ginger and minced garlic and cook, stirring, another minutes. Add the coriander, fenugreek, and asafoetida, stir about 30 seconds. Then slowly add the yogurt mixture, stirring constantly, and continue to stir until it comes to a boil, 2 to 4 minutes. Watch carefully and reduce the heat if the sauce starts to boil over.

3. Once the sauce comes to a boil, reduce the heat to medium-low and simmer, uncovered, stirring occasionally and watching carefully, until it looks smooth and silky and traces of oil are visible on the top surface and the sides, 30 to 35 minutes. Mix in the spinach and fenugreek leaves during the last 5 minutes of cooking. Transfer to a serving dish, cover, and keep warm.

4. Heat the ghee in a small saucepan over medium-high heat and add the red chile peppers, cumin, and mustard seeds; they should splutter upon contact with the hot oil, so lower the heat and cover the pan until the spluttering subsides. Remove from the heat, mix in the paprika, then add to the kadhi and swirl lightly with a fork to mix , with parts of it visible on top as a garnish. Serve.

Fenugreek Yogurt Curry with Fritters
Methi-Kadhi

Makes 4 to 6 servings

This recipe, shared by my friend Neelam Malhotra, is made in mustard oil and is full of fragrant fenugreek pakoras (fritters), which adds yet another dimension to the everyday kadhi (yogurt curry).

12 to 15 Fresh Fenugreek Pakora Fritters
    with Pomegranate Seeds (page 118)
3 cups nonfat plain yogurt
3 cups water
1/4 cup chickpea flour
1 to 3 fresh green chile peppers, such as serrano,
    stemmed
3 tablespoons mustard oil
2 tablespoons peeled minced fresh ginger
1 teaspoon minced garlic
2 tablespoons coriander seeds, coarsely crushed
    with the back of a spoon
1 teaspoon coarsely ground fenugreek seeds
12 to 15 fresh curry leaves
1/2 cup finely chopped daikon radishes
1/8 teaspoon ground asafoetida
1 teaspoon ground cumin
1/4 teaspoon ground turmeric
1 teaspoon dried fenugreek leaves
2 tablespoons finely chopped fresh cilantro

1. Prepare the pakoras. Then, in a blender, blend together the yogurt, water, chickpea flour, and green chile peppers until smooth. (Blend well, or the yogurt will curdle while cooking.) Transfer to a bowl and set aside.

2. Heat the oil in a large nonstick wok or a saucepan over medium-high heat and cook the ginger and garlic, stirring, until golden, about 1 minute. Add the coriander, fenugreek seeds, curry leaves, daikon radishes, asafoetida, cumin, and turmeric. Stir momentarily. Then slowly add the yogurt mixture, stirring constantly, and continue to stir until it comes to a boil, 2 to 4 minutes. Watch carefully and reduce the heat if the sauce starts to boil over.

3. Reduce the heat to medium-low and simmer, uncovered, stirring occasionally and watching carefully, until the kadhi is smooth and silky and traces of oil are visible on the top surface and the sides, 30 to 35 minutes. (The sauce, at this point should be somewhat soupy; it will thicken after the pakoras are added.)

4. Add the fenugreek leaves and the pakoras and simmer 3 to 5 minutes, allowing the pakoras to soften as they absorb the sauce. Transfer to a serving dish, garnish with cilantro, and serve.

Soupy Gujarati Curry
Gujarati Kadhi

Makes 4 to 6 servings

The people from Gujarat in northwestern India tend to add sugar to most of their dishes. This is their unique touch, which not only distinguishes their dishes, but also gives them a lovely balance. This kadhi is very soupy and I love it that way. Serve it as a soup or pair it with rice and vegetables and present it as an entrée, just the way my friend Falguni Jalota normally does.

4 cups nonfat plain yogurt
2 tablespoons chickpea flour
4 cups water
1 to 3 fresh green chile peppers, such as serrano, minced with seeds
2 tablespoons peeled minced fresh ginger
1/2 teaspoon salt, or to taste
1 tablespoon sugar
1/2 tablespoon ghee or vegetable oil
1 (1-inch) stick cinnamon
3 cloves
1 teaspoon black mustard seeds
1 teaspoon cumin seeds
3 to 4 whole dried red chile peppers, such as chile de arbol
1/4 teaspoon ground asafoetida
4 to 5 fresh curry leaves
1/2 cup finely chopped fresh cilantro, including soft stems

1. In a blender or food processor, blend together the yogurt, chickpea flour, and water until smooth. Transfer to a medium saucepan and mix in the green chile peppers, ginger, salt, and sugar. Bring to a boil over medium-high heat, stirring constantly. When it comes to a boil, reduce heat and simmer about 20 minutes.

2. Heat the ghee (or oil) in a small nonstick wok or saucepan over medium-high heat and add the cinnamon, cloves, and mustard seeds; they should splutter upon contact with the hot oil, so lower the heat and cover the pan until the spluttering subsides. Quickly add the cumin, red chile peppers, asafoetida, and curry leaves, and stir about 30 seconds.

3. Add the spices to the yogurt mixture, along with the cilantro, and simmer about 5 minutes. Transfer to a serving dish and serve hot.

Sindhi Tamarind Curry with Vegetables
Sindhi Kadhi

Makes 4 to 6 servings

Although this dish is called a kadhi, it is not a true kadhi in the strictest sense of the word because it has no yogurt. But it does have chickpea flour, which is another important ingredient of traditional kadhis.

Given to me by my Sindhi friend, Kanta Kaytee, who makes this dish at every opportunity, this kadhi contains no garlic and comes full of many soft-cooked vegetables that are delicious over steamed rice.

3 tablespoons peanut oil
1 teaspoon cumin seeds
1/4 teaspoon fenugreek seeds
1 tablespoon peeled minced fresh ginger
1 to 3 fresh green chile peppers, such as serrano, minced with seeds
2 tablespoons chickpea flour
4 cups water
1/4 teaspoon ground turmeric
1/2 teaspoon cayenne pepper
1 teaspoon salt, or to taste
2 to 3 small Japanese eggplants, cut into 1-inch pieces
1 small opo squash (1/2 to 2/3 pound), peeled and cut into 1-inch pieces
8 to 10 small okras, cut into 1-inch pieces
4 to 6 small potatoes (about 1 pound), unpeeled, cut into 1-inch pieces
2 tablespoons Tamarind Paste (page 54)
1/2 cup water
1/4 cup finely chopped fresh cilantro, including soft stems

1. Heat the oil in a large nonstick wok or saucepan over medium-high heat and add the cumin and fenugreek seeds; they should sizzle upon contact with the hot oil. Quickly add the ginger, green chile peppers, and chickpea flour, and stir over low heat until the chickpea flour is golden and very fragrant, about 5 minutes.

2. Add the water and bring to a boil, stirring constantly, over high heat. Reduce the heat to medium-low and simmer until the water is reduced by about ⅓, about 10 minutes. Add the turmeric, cayenne pepper, and salt and boil another 2 to 3 minutes.

3. Add all the vegetables and cook over low heat until the vegetables are soft and the kadhi is thick, about 45 minutes. Meanwhile, prepare the tamarind paste, then dissolve it in the water.

4. Mix in the tamarind-water mixture and simmer another 3 to 5 minutes. Transfer to a serving dish, mix in the cilantro, and serve.

Buttermilk and Cucumber Creamy Curry
Chaach aur Kheerae ki Kadhi

Makes 4 to 6 servings

This authentic recipe, from Sushi Mysoor of Karnatka in the south, is a quick-cooking saucy dish that goes well with and adds a richness to plain steamed rice. Fresh coconut really makes a difference in this recipe, but you could use frozen coconut, available at Indian markets, or unsweetened dried coconut.

1 tablespoon peanut oil
3 to 5 whole dried red chile peppers,
    such as chile de arbol
7 to 10 fresh curry leaves
1 teaspoon cumin seeds
1 teaspoon black mustard seeds
¼ cup grated fresh coconut
1 to 3 fresh green chile peppers, such as serrano,
    minced with seeds
2 teaspoons peeled minced fresh ginger
¼ cup fresh cilantro, including soft stems
3 large seedless cucumbers, such as English cucumbers,
    peeled and cut into 1-inch pieces
½ teaspoon salt, or to taste
¼ teaspoon ground paprika
3 cups nonfat plain yogurt, whisked until smooth
2 cups buttermilk

1. Heat the oil in a large nonstick wok or saucepan over medium-high heat and add the red chile peppers, curry leaves, cumin, and mustard seeds; they should splutter upon contact with the hot oil, so lower the heat and cover the pan until the spluttering subsides.

2. Quickly add the coconut, green chile peppers, ginger, and cilantro, and cook over medium heat until the coconut is golden, about 5 minutes. Add the cucumber, salt, and paprika, and cook until the pieces soften, about 10 minutes.

3. In a blender, blend together the yogurt and the buttermilk and add to the pan. Simmer over medium heat until hot, about 5 minutes. (Do not boil, or the kadhi will curdle.) Transfer to a serving dish and serve hot.

South Indian Yogurt Curry
South ki Dahi-Kadhi

Makes 4 to 6 servings

Although this dish belongs in the kadhi *category, it contains no chickpea flour, as is normal for most* kadhis. *Instead, it is thickened and flavored with roasted* dals *(legumes), coconut, and spices.*

2 tablespoons vegetable oil
5 quarter-size slices peeled fresh ginger
2 dried red chile peppers, such as chile de arbol,
    with stems
12 to 15 fresh curry leaves
1 teaspoon fenugreek seeds
1 tablespoon coriander seeds
1 tablespoon dried white urad beans (dhulli urad dal),
    sorted
1 tablespoon dried split pigeon peas (toor dal), sorted
1 tablespoon dried yellow split chickpeas (channa dal),
    sorted
¼ cup grated fresh or frozen coconut or shredded
    unsweetened dried coconut
⅛ teaspoon ground asafoetida
3 cups nonfat plain yogurt, whisked until smooth
¼ teaspoon ground turmeric
1 teaspoon salt, or to taste
1 teaspoon mustard seeds
1 teaspoon cumin seeds
¼ teaspoon ground paprika

1. Heat 1 tablespoon oil in a small nonstick saucepan over medium-high heat and add the ginger, red chile peppers, and curry leaves. Cook, stirring, until golden, about 1 minute. Add the fenugreek and coriander seeds, all the dals, coconut, and asafoetida, and cook, stirring, about 1 minute. Let cool, transfer to a blender, and blend, adding some of the yogurt to facilitate blending, until smooth. Then add the rest of the yogurt, turmeric, and salt, and blend again until smooth.

2. Transfer to a large nonstick wok or saucepan and cook, stirring constantly, over medium-high heat until it comes to a boil. Then reduce the heat to medium and cook, stirring, until the curry thickens a little and is smooth, about 5 minutes. Transfer to a serving dish.

3. Heat the remaining 1 tablespoon of the oil in the saucepan you used in Step 1, and add the mustard and cumin seeds; they should sizzle upon contact with the hot oil. Remove from the heat, quickly add the paprika, and transfer to the kadhi. Swirl lightly to mix, with parts of it visible as a garnish, and serve.

South Indian Yogurt and Coconut Milk Curry with Vegetables
South ki Nariyal Doodh ki Kadhi

Makes 4 to 6 servings

The south Indians generally make their dishes very hot and spicy, as seen in this soupy kadhi *(yogurt curry), whose heat goes straight to all your senses—so beware! Adjust the chile peppers to suit your palate, if you like, and serve it with steamed rice to tone down the heat.*

¹/₄ cup dried split pigeon peas (toor dal),
    sorted and washed in 3 to 4 changes of water
1 tablespoon dried yellow split chickpeas (channa dal),
    sorted and washed in 3 to 4 changes of water
2¹/₂ cups water
1 cup Coconut Milk (page 44 or store-bought)
6 to 8 quarter-size slices peeled fresh ginger

2 to 5 fresh green chile peppers, such as serrano,
    stemmed
15 to 20 fresh curry leaves
2 tablespoons ground coriander
1 teaspoon ground cumin
1 teaspoon salt, or to taste
2 cups nonfat plain yogurt, whisked until smooth
1 tablespoon vegetable oil
4 whole dried red chile peppers, such as chile de arbol,
    skins pierced to prevent bursting
1 teaspoon cumin seeds
1 teaspoon mustard seeds
1 teaspoon ground fenugreek seeds
¹/₈ teaspoon ground asafoetida
2 to 3 small Chinese or Japanese eggplants,
    cut into 1-inch pieces
1 large green bell pepper, cut into 1-inch pieces
1 large tomato, cut into ¹/₂-inch pieces
¹/₄ cup finely chopped fresh cilantro,
    including soft stems

1. Soak the dals in the water 1 hour or longer. Meanwhile, prepare the coconut milk. Then, drain the dals, reserving the water. Place the drained dals, ginger, green chile peppers, and curry leaves in a blender and blend, adding some of the water to facilitate the blending, until smooth, about 30 seconds. Add 1 tablespoon coriander, the cumin, and salt, and blend again. Then add the yogurt and blend once again until smooth.

2. Heat the oil in a large nonstick wok or saucepan and fry the red chile peppers until golden, 1 minute, then add the cumin and mustard seeds; they should splutter upon contact with the hot oil, so cover the pan until the spluttering subsides. Quickly add the remaining 1 tablespoon coriander, fenugreek seeds, and asafoetida, stir 30 seconds, and add the eggplant, bell pepper, and tomato. Cook, stirring, 1 minute.

3. Add the yogurt mixture, a little at a time, stirring constantly to prevent it from curdling, until it comes to a boil. Rinse the blender with the remaining water, add it to the kadhi, and boil again. Reduce the heat to medium and cook, stirring, 5 to 7 minutes, then add the coconut milk and cilantro and simmer until the vegetables are soft and the kadhi is thick and smooth, 5 to 7 minutes. Serve hot.

Non-Vegetarian Fare

Eggs 436

Scrambled Eggs 436

Scrambled Eggs with Onions

Scrambled Eggs
with Crumbled Paneer Cheese

Parsi Scrambled Eggs with Corn

Omelets 438

Parsi Omelet with Tamarind

Spicy Omelet with Ground Masala

Mashed Potato Omelet

Stuffed Omelets

Spicy Green Chutney Omelet Filling

Tomato and Paneer Cheese
Omelet Filling

Oven-Roasted Vegetable
Omelet Filling

Ground Meat Omelet Filling

French Toast 441

Savory Indian-Style French Toast

Stuffed Green Chutney French Toast

Egg Curries 442

Spicy North Indian Egg Curry

Kerala Egg and Potato Curry
with Coconut Milk

Goan Egg-Drop Curry
with Coconut and Tamarind

Chicken 444

Grilled and Dry-Cooked
Chicken and Turkey Dishes 445

Grilled Tandoori Chicken

Griddle-Fried Chicken Skewers
with Mango-Ginger Sauce

Oven-Roasted
Yogurt-Marinated Chicken

Pan-Cooked Onion Chicken

Mint-Cilantro Chicken

Pan-Cooked Chile-Chicken Thighs

Tamarind Chicken

Ginger Chicken with Citrus Juices

Peach and Tomato Chicken

Coriander and Apple Chicken

Diced Chicken
with Cumin and Red Bell Peppers

Chickpea Masala Chicken

Roasted Turkey with Indian Flavors

Chicken Dishes with Greens 453

Spicy Green Masala Chicken

Traditional Indian Chicken
with Spinach

Chicken Tenders with Sautéed Spinach

Hyderabadi Fenugreek Chicken

Punjabi Fenugreek Chicken

Cilantro Chicken Drumsticks
in a Wok

Chicken Curries 456

Basic Chicken Curry

Chicken Curry with Chopped
Onions and Tomatoes

Chicken Curry
with Dry-Roasted Spices

Chicken in Fried Masala Curry

Saffron Chicken Curry
with Dry-Roasted Almonds

Cashew and Poppy Seed
Chicken Curry

South Indian Coconut Chicken Curry

Almond Chicken
in Coconut Milk Sauce

Grilled Chicken in Spicy Sauce

Butter Chicken Curry

Chicken and Cracked-Wheat Curry

Goan-Style Spicy Chicken Curry

Yogurt Chicken Curries 464

Yogurt Chicken Curry
with Caramelized Onions

Fragrant Chicken Curry
with Coconut and Sesame Seeds

Hyderabadi Chicken Curry

Baked Yogurt-Mint Chicken Curry

Chicken Tenders
in Creamy White Sauce

Parsi Peanut Chicken

Nirmala's Sindhi Chicken Curry

 = Vegan    = Pressure-Cooker Quick

Ground Chicken Curries 469

Soft-Cooked Ground Chicken
with Cardamom Seeds

Diced Chicken
with Pomegranate Seeds

Chicken Kofta Balls
in Kashmiri Cashew-Saffron Sauce

Meat 471

Classic Lamb Curries 472

Basic Pan-Roasted Lamb Curry

Classic Marinated Lamb Curry

Curried Lamb with Whole Spices

Lamb Curry with Pickling Spices

Marinated Lamb Shanks Curry
with Potatoes

Rita's Mutton Curry

Mughlai Lamb Curry
with Cashews and Coconut Milk

Mughlai Pot-Roasted Lamb
with Almonds and Poppy Seeds

Sunil's Kashmiri Pot-Roasted Lamb
with Dried Ginger

Lamb and Grain Curries 478

Parsi Lamb Curry

Punjabi Split Chickpeas
and Lamb Curry

Hyderabadi Mashed Lamb
and Cracked-Wheat

Hyderabadi Lamb
with Mixed Legumes

Lamb Chop and Cutlet Dishes 481

Fragrant Lamb Chops
in Yogurt Curry

Mughlai Lamb Chop Curry
with Almond and Poppy Seeds

Parsi Lamb Chops Curry

Milk-Simmered Rib Chops

Milk-Simmered, Batter-Fried
Lamb Rib Chops

Citrus-Glazed Lamb Loin Chops

Pan-Sautéed Lamb Chops
with Rosemary

Sautéed Lamb Cutlets with Fenugreek

Whole Leg of Lamb and Rack of Lamb 487

Pot-Roasted Leg of Lamb

Hyderabadi Spicy Leg of Lamb
Raan with Screwpine Essence

Spinach-Stuffed Honey-Roasted
Boneless Leg of Lamb

Grilled Butterflied Leg of Lamb

Spicy Rack of Baby Lamb

My California-Style
Rack of Baby Lamb

Ground Meat and Meat Balls (Keema and Kofta) 492

Ground Meat
with Potato Wedges

Ground Meat with Red Lentils

Ground Meat with Spinach
and Coconut Milk

Ground Meat with Nuts and Raisins

Spicy Meat Balls

Stuffed Meat Balls
in Yogurt-Cream Sauce

Egg-Stuffed Meat Balls
in Yogurt-Cream Sauce

Kashmiri Hand-Pressed Meat Rolls
in Curry Sauce

Ground Meat Rolls
in Spicy Buttermilk Sauce

Kashmiri Meat Balls
in Red Paprika Sauce

Yogurt-Braised Meat Balls

*A*lthough a predominantly vegetarian country, India enjoys a wealth of delicious non-vegetarian dishes, including specialties such as Parsi Scrambled Eggs with Corn (page 437), Grilled Tandoori Chicken (page 445), Hyderabadi Chicken Curry (page 466), Kashmiri Slow-Cooked Spicy Lamb Curry (page 505), and Spicy Goan Shrimp Curry (page 515).

There are various degrees of vegetarianism in India, inspired mostly by religious and spiritual beliefs. There are sects who do not eat any non-vegetarian foods. There are vegetarians who won't eat meat, poultry, or fish but will eat eggs. There are some who won't eat meat or poultry, but will eat fish, believing it to be a harvest of the waters and even call it *jal-tori,* meaning water-squash. The Muslims will not eat pork and the Hindus stay away from beef.

An interesting point: Most Indian vegetarians consider dairy products acceptable for their diets because they believe milk does not destroy life, but sustains it—and throughout the country, milk is used in many dishes in various forms of yogurt, *paneer* cheese, milk, and cream.

Some Indians, however, will eat all types of non-vegetarian foods and this chapter offers a selection of main dishes featuring eggs, chicken, meat, and fish—some classic recipes known throughout the world, others popular within India, and yet others that are favorites in the United States. There are also some non-vegetarian recipes in other chapters—Starters and Snacks, Soups, and Salads—where they are grouped in subcategories identifying them as non-vegetarian.

Eggs

There are some families in India in which even the word "egg" is a taboo, but in most cases, eggs are very much a part of the everyday kitchen.

Certain communities, such as the Zoroastrian community of Parsis—descendants of Persians from Iran who fled Alexander the Great's invasion and settled in the Mumbai (Bombay) area; the Christians of Kerala on the southern tip of India; the Goans on the western coast, with their Portuguese heritage; and the Muslims all over the country, are particularly fond of eggs. Dishes range from simple scrambles and omelets to elaborate *kofta* (vegetable or meat balls), curries, and *biryani* (layered rice dishes).

Scrambled Eggs

Called *bhurji* in the north and *akoori* in the west, Indian scrambled eggs are usually spicy, and are often deliciously enriched with greens, vegetables, and crumbled *paneer* cheese.

Indian scrambled eggs are very versatile. Serve the simple ones with *paranthas* (griddle-fried breads) and a glass of sweet *lussi* (yogurt cooler), or mix in some greens, colorful vegetables, any leftover cooked and shredded chicken, or ground meat, and offer them as a quick, last-minute side dish with a *dal* (legume), or a vegetable curry.

Indians cook their scrambles and omelets until well-done and lightly browned, so if you prefer scrambled eggs runnier and omelets lighter, adjust the cooking time to your taste.

Scrambled Eggs with Onions
Undae ki Bhurji

Makes 2 to 4 servings

Whisked eggs cooked with golden fried onions. With a little cilantro, this is as simple as you can get with Indian egg scrambles.

6 large eggs, lightly beaten
1/4 teaspoon salt, or to taste
1/4 teaspoon freshly ground black pepper, or to taste
2 tablespoons vegetable oil
2 medium onions, finely chopped
1/4 cup finely chopped fresh cilantro,
   including soft stems
1 to 2 fresh green chile peppers, such as serrano,
   minced with seeds

1. In a medium bowl, whisk together the eggs, salt, and black pepper.

2. Heat the oil in a large nonstick wok or saucepan over medium-high heat and cook the onion, stirring, until golden, about 5 minutes.

3. Add the eggs and cook, stirring occasionally, over medium heat until just firm, about 3 minutes, or to desired doneness. Add the cilantro and the green chile pepper and cook until lightly browned, another 2 minutes. Serve.

Variation: Wilt 2 cups finely chopped fresh spinach in the microwave, or cook 8 to 10 mushrooms (finely chopped) in a nonstick skillet until golden, then add the vegetables to the eggs along with the cilantro. Adjust the seasonings.

Scrambled Eggs with Crumbled Paneer Cheese
Undae aur Paneer ki Bhurji

Makes 4 to 6 servings

This is the hearty Indian version of scrambled eggs and cheese. Paneer is the delicate homemade curdled milk cheese that is a daily staple in India. This dish is one you'll want to cook quickly so if you don't have paneer pre-made, look for it in the refrigerator section of Indian markets.

1 cup Paneer Cheese (page 43 or store-bought), coarsely crumbled
2 tablespoons peanut oil
1 small onion, finely chopped
1 large tomato, finely chopped
1 to 2 fresh green chile peppers, such as serrano, minced with seeds
1¹/₂ tablespoons peeled minced fresh ginger
1 teaspoon fresh lemon juice
¹/₈ teaspoon coarsely ground ajwain seeds
¹/₂ teaspoon salt, or to taste
6 large eggs, lightly beaten
¹/₄ cup finely chopped fresh cilantro, including soft stems
Freshly ground black pepper

1. Prepare the paneer cheese. Then, heat the oil in a large nonstick wok or saucepan over medium-high heat and cook the onion, tomato, and green chile peppers, stirring, until most of the tomato juices are dry, about 5 minutes. Mix in the paneer cheese, ginger, lemon juice, ajwain seeds, and salt, and stir about 1 minute. Transfer to a bowl.

2. To the same pan, add the eggs and cook over medium heat, stirring once or twice, until firm, about 2 minutes, or to desired doneness. Mix in the paneer cheese and cilantro. Transfer to a serving dish, sprinkle some black pepper on top, and serve.

Variations: For a smoother scramble, blend together the eggs and paneer cheese in a food processor about 30 seconds, then make the dish.

Parsi Scrambled Eggs with Corn
Makki Akoori

Makes 4 to 6 servings

Corn akoori, a typically Parsi dish, incorporates corn into an egg scramble—something not usually done in the rest of India, or for that matter, the world, although it is tasty.

2 tablespoons vegetable oil
1 small onion, finely chopped
1 large tomato, finely chopped
¹/₄ cup finely chopped fresh cilantro, including soft stems
1¹/₄ cups fresh or (thawed) frozen corn kernels
6 large eggs, lightly beaten
¹/₂ teaspoon salt, or to taste
¹/₄ teaspoon freshly ground black pepper, or to taste
1 to 2 fresh green chile peppers, minced with seeds

1. Heat the oil in a large nonstick wok or saucepan over medium-high heat and cook the onion, stirring, until golden, about 3 minutes. Add the tomato, cover, and cook about 3 minutes. Mix in the cilantro and corn and cook, stirring, about 5 minutes.

2. Add the eggs, salt, and black pepper and cook over medium heat, stirring once or twice, until they firm up and turn golden, about 4 minutes, or to desired doneness. Transfer to a serving dish. Sprinkle the green chile peppers on top, and serve.

Parsi Omelet
with Tamarind

Parsi Imli Aamlate

Makes 4 to 6 servings

The Parsis in Mumbai (formerly Bombay) often add tamarind to their omelets—something that not many of us would think of doing—but it sure tastes good.

Indians make omelets in the Italian frittata or Spanish frittada style—cooked on one side until lightly browned, then flipped and cooked on the other side—serve them open-faced or folded in.

1 tablespoon Tamarind Paste (page 54)
6 large eggs, lightly beaten
6 scallions, white and light green parts only, minced
1/4 cup finely chopped fresh cilantro, including soft stems
1/4 cup minced red bell pepper
1 fresh green chile pepper, such as serrano, minced with seeds
1 teaspoon peeled minced fresh ginger
1 small clove fresh garlic, minced
1/2 teaspoon salt, or to taste
1/2 teaspoon freshly ground black pepper
1 teaspoon sugar
2 tablespoons vegetable oil
1 small onion, finely chopped onion

1. Prepare the tamarind paste. Then, in a medium bowl, whisk the eggs and then mix in all the ingredients (except the oil and onion).

2. Heat the oil in a large cast-iron or nonstick skillet over medium-high heat and cook the onion, stirring, until golden, about 3 minutes. Add the egg mixture (in 2 batches, if necessary), cover, and cook over medium heat until the bottom is golden and the top is somewhat firm, about 4 minutes.

3. Slide the omelet onto a large plate. Holding a large spatula over the omelet, invert the plate, flipping the omelet over. Slide the omelet back into the skillet with the uncooked side down. Cook until the second side is golden, about 3 minutes. Transfer to a serving platter, cut into wedges, and serve.

Spicy Omelet with
Ground Masala

Pissa Masala Aamlate

Makes 4 to 6 servings

If you like your eggs smooth, this is the dish for you. The omelet is flavored with blended seasonings (masala) that are then folded into the beaten eggs so the flavor enriches the whole omelet.

6 large eggs, lightly beaten
1 teaspoon salt, or to taste
1/2 teaspoon freshly ground black pepper
1 small coarsely chopped onion
1/4 cup coarsely chopped fresh cilantro, including soft stems
1 fresh green chile pepper, coarsely chopped
1 medium clove fresh garlic, peeled
2 quarter-size slices peeled fresh ginger
1 to 2 tablespoons vegetable oil

1. In a bowl, whisk the eggs, salt, and black pepper. In a food processor, process together the onion, cilantro, green chile pepper, garlic, and ginger until puréed. Fold into the eggs and mix well.

2. Heat the oil in a large nonstick skillet over medium-high heat and add the egg mixture (in 2 to 3 batches, if necessary), cover, and cook over medium heat until the bottom is golden and the top is somewhat firm, about 3 minutes.

3. Slide the omelet onto a large plate. Holding a large spatula over the omelet, invert the plate, flipping the omelet over. Slide the omelet back into the skillet with the uncooked side down. Cook until the other side is golden, about 2 minutes. Transfer to a serving platter, cut into wedges, and serve.

Mashed Potato Omelet

Undae aur Aalu ka Aamlate

Makes 4 to 6 servings

I love potato and egg combinations. Here I mix mashed potatoes to beaten eggs to make an unusual but irresistible omelet.

1 medium russet (or any) potato
6 large eggs, lightly beaten
1/2 cup onion, finely chopped
1/2 cup finely chopped fresh cilantro, including soft stems
1 tablespoon peeled minced fresh ginger (optional)
1 to 2 fresh green chile peppers, such as serrano, minced with seeds
1/4 teaspoon salt, or to taste
1/4 teaspoon freshly ground black pepper, or to taste
2 tablespoons peanut oil

1. Cook the potato in lightly salted boiling water to cover until tender, about 20 minutes. Drain, let cool, then peel, transfer to a medium bowl and mash. Add the eggs, onion, ¼ cup cilantro, ginger, green chile pepper, salt, and black pepper and mix well.

2. Heat the oil in a large nonstick skillet over medium-high heat and add the egg mixture (in 2 to 3 batches, if necessary), cover, and cook over medium heat until the bottom is golden and the top is somewhat firm, about 3 minutes. Sprinkle the remaining ¼ cup cilantro on top and, with a spatula, lightly press it into the omelet.

3. Slide the omelet onto a large plate. Holding a large spatula over the omelet, invert the plate, flipping the omelet over. Slide the omelet back into the skillet with the uncooked side down. Cook until the other side is golden, about 2 minutes. Fold in half (cilantro side out) or cut into wedges (with the cilantro side on top) and serve.

Stuffed Omelets

Bharae Huae Aamlate

Makes 4 2-egg omelets

Stuffed omelets are popular all over the world and Indians enjoy their own spicy combinations. Make the fillings first(choices follow the main recipe), then fill the omelet as in Step 4. For each 2-egg omelet, use:

¼ cup any stuffing (pages 440 to 441)
2 large eggs, separated
1 tablespoon finely chopped fresh cilantro, including soft stems
A pinch of salt and freshly ground black pepper
1 to 2 teaspoons vegetable oil

1. Prepare the stuffing. Then, with an electric mixer on medium setting (or a whisk or a fork), whip the egg whites until they reach the soft peak stage. Mix in the yolks and whisk a few seconds more until they are incorporated. Then add the cilantro, salt, and black pepper and mix well.

2. Heat the oil in a large nonstick skillet over medium-high heat and add the egg mixture, cover, and cook over medium heat until the bottom is just golden and the top is somewhat firm, about 1 minute.

3. Slide the omelet onto a large plate. Holding a large spatula over the omelet, invert the plate, flipping the omelet over. Slide the omelet back into the skillet with the uncooked side down. Cook 30 seconds.

4. Place the filling along the diameter of the omelet and fold the omelet in half. Cook, turning once, until golden on both sides. Serve.

Spicy Green Chutney Omelet Filling

Hari Chutney Bharae Aamlate

Makes about 1 cup, enough for 4 2-egg omelets

Green chutney, a tangy and sharp purée of scallions and herbs, is a perennial Indian accompaniment with snacks and meals. Here, I mix it with sautéed spinach and then use it as a filling for omelets.

1/2 cup Basic Green Chutney (page 58 or store-bought)
1 tablespoon vegetable oil
1 small onion, finely chopped
1/2 small bunch fresh spinach (4 to 5 ounces), trimmed, washed, and finely chopped
Salt, to taste

1. Prepare the chutney. Then, place it in a fine-mesh strainer set over a bowl to drain out most of the juices. (Press on it slightly just before using.)

2. Heat the oil in a small nonstick wok or saucepan over medium heat and cook the onion, stirring, until golden, about 5 minutes. Add the spinach and cook, stirring, until it wilts, about 1 minute. Remove from the heat and mix in the chutney. Add salt, if needed. It is now ready to use.

Tomato and Paneer Cheese Omelet Filling

Tamatar aur Paneer Bharae Aamlate

Makes about 1 cup, enough for 4 2-egg omelets

Cooked paneer *cheese and tomatoes make a delicious filling for omelets. This filling can also be used in samosas (stuffed deep-fried triangular pastries), open-faced sandwiches, and on the side of* paranthas *(griddle-fried breads). Instead of the* paneer *cheese, you can also use ricotta cheese, firm tofu, or cooked and shredded chicken.*

1 cup Paneer Cheese (page 43 or store-bought), finely crumbled
1 tablespoon vegetable oil
1 medium onion, finely chopped
1 large tomato, finely chopped
1/4 cup finely chopped fresh cilantro, including soft stems
1 fresh green chile pepper, such as serrano, minced with seeds
1 tablespoon peeled minced fresh ginger
1/2 teaspoon salt, or to taste
Freshly ground black pepper, to taste
1/4 teaspoon garam masala

1. Prepare the paneer cheese. Then, heat the oil in a medium nonstick wok or saucepan over medium-high heat and cook the onion, stirring, until golden, about 3 minutes. Add the tomato, cilantro, and green chile pepper and cook, stirring, until most of the juices evaporate, about 2 minutes.

2. Add the paneer cheese, ginger, salt, and black pepper and continue to cook until everything is completely dry, about 5 minutes. Mix in the garam masala. It is now ready to use.

Oven-Roasted Vegetable Omelet Filling

Bhunni Sabzi Bharae Aamlate

Makes about 1 cup, enough for 4 2-egg omelets

As the vegetables start to roast in the oven, they will release a fair amount of juices. If, by the time the vegetables are done, the juices don't dry up, transfer everything to a skillet and cook briefly over high heat until the juices evaporate.

2 red or yellow bell peppers, finely chopped
1 small Chinese eggplant, finely chopped
1 small zucchini, finely chopped
1 small tomato, finely chopped
6 to 8 medium mushrooms, thinly sliced
1 small onion, thinly sliced
1/4 cup finely chopped fresh cilantro, including soft stems
1 large clove fresh garlic, minced
1 tablespoon vegetable oil
1/4 teaspoon salt, or to taste

Preheat the oven to broil or preheat the broiler. In a medium bowl, toss all the ingredients together, then spread evenly on a flat, broiler-safe dish. Broil on the top rack of the oven or in the broiler, 4 to 5 inches from the heat source, until the vegetables are soft and lightly charred, about 7 minutes. (Stir them a few times as they cook.) They are now ready to use.

Ground Meat Omelet Filling
Keema Bharae Aamlate

Makes about 1 cup, enough for 4 2-egg omelets

*Some Indians use ground meat (*keema*) as a stuffing for many vegetables and snacks—as do people in other parts of the world. Here, I use it to add interest to omelets. Serve the omelets as part of a holiday brunch with* paranthas *(griddle-fried breads) or with slices of toasted bread and hot cardamom tea.*

1/3 pound ground meat (any kind) or chicken
1 large tomato, finely chopped
1/4 cup nonfat plain yogurt
1/4 cup finely chopped fresh cilantro,
    including soft stems
1 large clove fresh garlic, minced
1 tablespoon ground coriander
1/2 teaspoon ground ginger
1/2 teaspoon garam masala
1/4 teaspoon salt, or to taste

Place all the ingredients in a medium wok or saucepan and cook, stirring occasionally, until the meat is soft and most of the juices have evaporated, about 20 minutes. It is now ready to use.

French Toast

Savory Indian-Style French Toast
Indian ke French Toas

Makes 4 servings

The Indian style of French toast is a savory version of the fried egg-dipped bread classic. It is salted and, more often than not, cooked with spices and herbs. It is then eaten with chutneys and sauces, and even with ketchup. The toasts are great for school lunches.

1/2 teaspoon Chaat Masala (page 20 or store-bought)
3 large eggs, lightly beaten
4 tablespoons nonfat plain yogurt,
    whisked until smooth
2 tablespoons finely chopped fresh cilantro,
    including soft stems
1/4 teaspoon salt, or to taste
1/4 teaspoon cayenne pepper, or to taste
2 tablespoons peanut oil
6 to 8 slices white or whole-wheat bread

1. Prepare the chaat masala. In a flat dish, whisk together the eggs, yogurt, cilantro, salt, and cayenne pepper until smooth.

2. Heat the oil in a medium nonstick skillet over medium heat. With tongs, lay each slice of bread (one at a time) in the egg mixture, press lightly until well-coated on the bottom, then turn over and coat the other side.

3. Carefully place in the skillet and cook, turning once, until golden on both sides, about 1 minute per side. Repeat with the remaining slices. Transfer to serving platter, cut in half on the diagonal if you wish, sprinkle the chaat masala, on top, and serve.

Variations: To the basic egg mixture in Step 1, you can add 1 to 2 teaspoons Basic Ginger-Garlic Paste (page 47 or store-bought), 1 to 2 ground green chile peppers, 1/4 cup ground or minced onion, chopped chives, or scallions, 1/4 cup pepper-Jack cheese, or 1/4 cup puréed semi-firm tofu.

Stuffed Green Chutney French Toast

Hari Chutney French Toas

Makes 4 servings

Spicy and colorful, these lovely sandwiches are great for lunch snacks, or as finger foods.

1/2 cup Basic Green Chutney (page 58),
    + 2 tablespoons
1 teaspoon melted butter
8 slices white or whole-wheat bread
3 large eggs, lightly beaten
3 tablespoons nonfat plain yogurt,
    whisked until smooth
1/4 cup minced red bell pepper
1/4 teaspoon salt, or to taste
2 tablespoons peanut oil
1/4 cup finely chopped fresh cilantro,
    including soft stems

1. Prepare the chutney. Mix the butter into 1/2 cup chutney, then spread generously on 4 of the bread slices. Cover each with the remaining 4 slices to make sandwiches.

2. In a flat dish, whisk together the eggs, yogurt, 2 tablespoons chutney, red bell pepper, and salt.

3. Heat 1 tablespoon of the oil in a medium nonstick skillet over moderate heat. With tongs, lay each sandwich (one at a time) in the egg mixture, press lightly to coat the bottom, then turn over and coat the other side.

4. Carefully, place in the skillet and cook, turning once, until golden on both sides, about 1 minute per side. Scatter about 1 tablespoon cilantro on top, turn over once more, and cook momentarily to seal in the cilantro. Repeat with the remaining sandwiches. Transfer to serving platter, cut into 3 long pieces or 4 small triangles, and serve with the cilantro side up.

Variations: Try this with different chutneys or dry-cooked vegetable or ground meat stuffings.

Egg Curries

Spicy North Indian Egg Curry

Undae ki Kari

Makes 4 to 6 servings

Making the curry sauce, though time consuming, is really quite simple. Once the sauce is made and the eggs boiled, consider the dish done. Serve for lunch or a light dinner.

4 cups (1 recipe) Classic Spicy Curry Sauce (page 388)
6 large eggs
2 teaspoons vegetable oil
3 to 5 dried red chile peppers, such as chile de arbol,
    with stems
1 teaspoon cumin seeds
1 tablespoon coarsely ground raw almonds
    (from about 10 almonds)
1/4 cup finely chopped fresh cilantro,
    including soft stems
1/4 teaspoon garam masala

1. Prepare the curry sauce. Meanwhile, in a medium saucepan, place the eggs in water to cover by 2 inches and bring to a boil over high heat. Reduce the heat to medium, cover the pan and simmer until the eggs are hard-boiled, about 10 to 12 minutes. Let cool or plunge into cold water, shell them, then cut them in half. Place the eggs in the curry sauce and simmer over medium heat about 10 minutes.

2. Heat the oil in a small nonstick wok or saucepan over medium-high heat and cook the red chile peppers 30 seconds. Add the cumin seeds; they should sizzle upon contact with the hot oil. Quickly add the ground almonds and stir about 1 minute.

3. Mix everything into the egg curry and simmer another 5 minutes to blend the flavors. Transfer to a serving dish, mix in the cilantro, sprinkle the garam masala on top and serve.

Variation: For a richer finish, mix in 2 to 3 tablespoons heavy cream or sour cream during the last 2 to 3 minutes of cooking.

Kerala Egg and Potato Curry with Coconut Milk
Kerala ki Unda aur Aalu Kari

Makes 4 to 6 servings

The southern, Kerala-style onion paste, with a fragrance of golden-fried onion and curry leaves, makes for a substantial curry with robust flavors and a thick sauce. Add a few boiled eggs and you have a delicious entrée. Serve it over rice or present it with paranthas *(griddle-fried breads) and a cup of green cardamom tea.*

¹/₂ cup Kerala Fried Onion Paste (page 50)
¹/₂ cup Coconut Milk (page 44 or store-bought)
6 large eggs
2 tablespoons vegetable oil
1 teaspoon cumin seeds
1 tablespoon ground coriander
¹/₂ teaspoon garam masala
¹/₂ teaspoon ground cumin
¹/₂ teaspoon ground paprika
¹/₄ teaspoon ground turmeric
1 teaspoon salt, or to taste
3 small russet potatoes, peeled and cut into
    6 wedges each
1¹/₂ to 2 cups water
1 teaspoon dried fenugreek leaves
¹/₄ cup finely chopped fresh cilantro, including soft stems
Freshly ground black pepper

1. Prepare the onion paste and coconut milk. Then place the eggs in a medium saucepan and bring to a boil over high heat. Reduce the heat to medium, cover the pan and cook until hard-boiled, about 10 to 12 minutes. Let cool or plunge into cold water, then shell them and cut in half lengthwise.

2. Heat the oil in a large nonstick wok or saucepan over medium-high heat and add the cumin seeds; they should sizzle upon contact with the hot oil. Quickly add the coriander, garam masala, cumin, paprika, turmeric, and salt and stir about 30 seconds. Then add the onion paste and the potatoes and cook over medium heat, stirring to roast the potatoes, about 5 minutes.

3. Add the coconut milk and cook about 5 more minutes. Then mix in 1¹/₂ cups water and bring to a boil over high heat. Reduce the heat to medium-low and simmer, covered, until the potatoes are tender and the sauce thick, 10 to 15 minutes. (Add the remaining ¹/₂ cup water if the sauce is too thick before the potatoes are done.)

4. Mix in the fenugreek leaves and cilantro, then carefully add the halved eggs and simmer about 5 minutes. Transfer to a serving dish, sprinkle the black pepper on top, and serve.

Goan Egg-Drop Curry with Coconut and Tamarind
Goa ki Unda Kari

Makes 4 to 6 servings

Lots of coconut, a little bit of tamarind, and fragrant spices are the flavor elements of this traditional egg curry from Goa, in the west. Use fresh coconut for the best and most delicate flavor.

1 to 2 tablespoons Tamarind Paste (page 54)
¹/₂ cup + 2 tablespoons Coconut Milk
    (page 44 or store-bought)
8 large eggs
¹/₂ cup grated fresh or frozen coconut or
    shredded unsweetened dried coconut
1 large clove fresh garlic, peeled
1 tablespoon ground coriander
1 teaspoon ground mustard seeds
¹/₂ teaspoon ground cumin
¹/₄ teaspoon ground turmeric
¹/₈ teaspoon ground cinnamon
¹/₈ teaspoon ground cloves
¹/₂ piece star anise, finely ground
2 tablespoons vegetable oil
1 medium onion, finely chopped
1 fresh green chile pepper, such as serrano,
    minced with seeds
2 to 3 cups water
1 teaspoon salt, or to taste

1. Prepare the tamarind paste and coconut milk. Then, in a medium saucepan, place 6 eggs in water to cover by 2 inches and bring to a boil over high heat. Reduce the heat to medium, cover the pan and simmer until the eggs are hard-boiled, about 10 to 12 minutes. Let cool or plunge into cold water, shell them, then cut them in half lengthwise.

2. In a food processor or a blender, process together the coconut, garlic, coriander, mustard seeds, cumin, turmeric, cinnamon, cloves, and star anise to make it as smooth as possible.

3. Heat the oil in a large nonstick wok or saucepan over medium-high heat and cook the onion, stirring, until golden, about 5 minutes. Add the green chile pepper and the coconut-spice mixture and stir another 5 minutes. Add the water, tamarind paste, and salt and bring to a boil over high heat. Reduce the heat to medium-low, cover the pan, and simmer until the sauce is smooth, about 15 minutes. Then add ½ cup coconut milk and bring to a boil over medium heat.

4. In a small bowl, lightly beat the 2 tablespoons coconut milk and the 2 remaining eggs (discard the yolks, if you wish to). Pour this mixture into the curry and stir lightly to mix, until the eggs are firm, about 2 minutes.

5. Then add the hard-boiled eggs and simmer over medium-low heat about 5 minutes to blend the flavors. Serve hot.

Chicken

Chicken these days often signals humdrum meals in America. Because it is easy to find, relatively affordable, and usually cooks quickly, families eat it a lot, often preparing it in the same simple ways.

Indians, however, continue to think of chicken as more than a dinner fallback; instead, Indian chicken recipes are refreshingly unique, with imaginative flavoring. To name just a few: Tandoori Chicken, which is authentically grilled in a clay oven; the special *kormas* (rich yogurt, cream, and nut-based curries), such as Hyderabadi Chicken Curry (page 466); and the super-hot *vindaloo* Goan-Style Spicy Chicken Curry (page 463).

Some information to know: Indian chicken is always trimmed of skin and excess fat. The concept of eating the skin simply isn't understood in India. And today, given what we know about the fat content of poultry skin, this is a smart practice. Even though chicken may lose some moisture and flavor without the skin and fat, Indian cooks resolve this by marinating or pan-cooking the chicken with *masalas* (spice blends) and seasonings and by monitoring the temperature and cooking times.

Most authentic Indian chicken preparations call for bone-in pieces, because as they cook, the bones add to the flavor of the chicken, as well as to the fun of eating chicken—right off the bone. However, for convenience, and aesthetics, it is fine to make the dishes with boneless pieces, as well. Most of the time, that is my preference.

For variety, keep in mind that most of the chicken recipes also work well with turkey. Cut the pieces into the sizes specified in the recipes before cooking. If the pieces are larger, adjust the cooking time accordingly.

Grilled and Dry-Cooked
Chicken and Turkey Dishes

Grilled Tandoori Chicken
Tandoori Murgh

Makes 4 to 6 servings

Whenever the words "tandoori chicken" are mentioned, a dramatically red chicken may flash before your eyes. This arresting red color, however, is purely for visual appeal. The chicken's real flavor comes from the marinade, and its smoky richness from the juices and marinades as they drip onto hot coals. (For best flavor, marinate the chicken the day before cooking or leave enough time for the two marinating steps.)

Authentically, this chicken should be roasted whole in a tandoor, *but the best alternatives are an outdoor grill, a smoker, a rotisserie, and, failing all those, the oven or broiler. This recipe offers directions for grilling, broiling, and roasting. For the outdoor grill and the oven, you can either roast a whole chicken or, for ease and convenience, use serving-size pieces.*

**2 tablespoons Basic Ginger-Garlic Paste
 (page 47 or store-bought)**
1 (2¹/₂- to 3-pound) whole chicken, skinned
2 tablespoons fresh lime or lemon juice
¹/₂ teaspoon salt, or to taste
¹/₃ cup nonfat plain yogurt, whisked until smooth
2 tablespoons heavy cream
1 tablespoon peanut oil
1 teaspoon garam masala
1 teaspoon ground dried fenugreek leaves
¹/₂ teaspoon ground cumin
1 teaspoon ground paprika
¹/₄ teaspoon cayenne pepper, or to taste
¹/₈ teaspoon ground turmeric
1 tablespoon melted butter for basting
Scallion whites and lemon wedges

1. Leaving the chicken whole, with a sharp knife make deep, 1½-inch cuts all over the chicken—3 on each breast, 3 on each thigh and 2 on each drumstick—then place in a non-reactive dish. In a small bowl, mix together the lime juice and salt and rub it over the chicken, making sure to reach inside the cuts. Cover with plastic wrap and marinate in the refrigerator about 2 hours. Meanwhile, prepare the ginger-garlic paste.

2. After the chicken has marinated, in another small bowl, mix together the yogurt, cream, oil, ginger-garlic paste, garam masala, fenugreek leaves, and cumin.

3. Heat the oil in a small nonstick saucepan over medium-high heat until hot but not smoking. Remove from the heat and add the paprika, cayenne pepper, and turmeric. Mix the spiced oil into the yogurt mixture. Rub the yogurt well over and inside the chicken. Cover with plastic wrap and marinate in the refrigerator, at least 8 and up to 24 hours.

4. To grill: Preheat the grill to medium-high (about 375°F to 400°F). Grill, turning the chicken as needed, until the meat is soft and charred in a few places and opaque inside, 20 to 25 minutes. Baste with the melted butter and grill, turning, another 3 to 5 minutes.

To broil: Preheat the broiler. Place the marinated chicken (whole or cut up into serving pieces) on a roasting or broiler pan with a tray underneath to catch the dripping juices and broil in the lower center section of the oven or broiler (about 10-inches from heat source) until the chicken is opaque inside when tested with a knife, 25 to 30 minutes. Turn a few times and watch the heat. If the chicken browns too quickly, cover with foil.

To bake (with a gas oven): Preheat the oven to 375°F. Cut the chicken into serving pieces and place on a roasting rack with a tray underneath to catch the juices. Bake, covered with aluminum foil, in the center section of the oven until the chicken is lightly browned and the meat is soft and opaque inside when tested with a knife, 30 to 35 minutes. Turn and baste the pieces with the butter a few times while they're cooking.

5. Transfer to a serving platter, garnish with the scallions and lemon wedges, and serve whole or quartered.

Griddle-Fried Chicken Skewers with Mango-Ginger Sauce

Tava Murgh Kabaab aur Aam ki Chutni

Makes 4 to 6 servings

Inspired by the abundance of fruit readily available in California, and guided by Indian cooking traditions, I created this dish. The sweetness of ripe mangoes, offset by tangy lime juice and mildly hot ginger, all come together to give these griddle-cooked chicken strips an incredible flavor. Grill the chicken, if you wish.

1½ cups (1 recipe) Puréed Fresh Mango-Ginger Chutney (page 70)
8 to 10 quarter-size slices peeled fresh ginger
1 to 3 fresh green chile peppers, such as serrano, stemmed
2 tablespoons fresh lime or lemon juice
1 tablespoon ground coriander
1 teaspoon garam masala
½ teaspoon salt, or to taste
Freshly ground black pepper, to taste
16 to 20 strips chicken tenders
8 to 16 metal skewers or wooden skewers soaked in water 30 minutes
1 tablespoon canola oil
2 cups shredded lettuce (any kind)

1. Prepare the mango chutney. Then, in a small food processor or a blender, process together the ginger, chile peppers, cilantro, lime juice, coriander, garam masala, salt, and black pepper.

2. Place the chicken in a large non-reactive bowl, add the marinade and mix well, making sure all the pieces are well-coated. Cover with plastic wrap or foil and marinate in the refrigerator up to 24 hours.

3. Thread on skewers by pushing the skewer through the length of the tenderloin. Put 1 or 2 tenders per skewer. Using ¼ cup of the mango chutney, brush it on each skewered piece of chicken.

4. Heat a large cast-iron tava or a nonstick griddle or skillet over medium-high heat and coat lightly with the oil. Place the chicken skewers on the griddle and cook, turning them over once or twice, until they are golden on both sides, about 2 minutes on each side. Transfer to a platter lined with shredded lettuce, drizzle some of the mango chutney on top, and serve the remaining chutney on the side.

Oven-Roasted Yogurt-Marinated Chicken

Oven ka Dahi-Murgh

Makes 4 to 6 servings

This is an easy spicy and tender chicken dish. Once it's marinated, you just cook it in the oven. It's that simple!

1½ tablespoons Basic Ginger-Garlic Paste (page 47 or store-bought)
1 (2½- to 3-pound) whole chicken
1 cup nonfat plain yogurt, whisked until smooth
2 tablespoons vegetable oil
¼ cup finely chopped fresh cilantro, including soft stems
1½ tablespoons ground coriander
1 teaspoon freshly ground black pepper, or to taste
1 teaspoon ground cumin
1 teaspoon ground fennel seeds
1 teaspoon green cardamom seeds
1 teaspoon cayenne pepper
⅛ teaspoon ground asafoetida
½ teaspoon salt, or to taste
3 cloves
2 (1-inch) sticks cinnamon, broken lengthwise
2 tablespoons minced fresh mint leaves
¼ cup Crispy Fried Onions (page 44)

1. Prepare the ginger-garlic paste. Leaving the chicken whole, remove all the skin and make deep, 1½-inch cuts all over the chicken—3 on each breast, 3 on each thigh, and 2 on each drumstick.

2. In a large non-reactive bowl, mix together the yogurt, oil, cilantro, ginger-garlic paste, all the ground spices, and salt. Add the chicken and mix well, making sure the marinade reaches inside the cavity and the cuts. Cover and marinate at least 2 and up to 24 hours in the refrigerator.

3. Preheat the oven to 400°F. Place the chicken, breast side down, in a roasting pan (or a heavy metal tray or a casserole dish) and pour any marinade over the chicken. Toss in the cloves, cinnamon, and mint.

4. With heavy-duty foil, make a tent over the chicken and place on the center rack of the oven. Roast about 40 minutes, or until golden. Reduce the heat to 375°F, turn the bird over (breast side up), and roast, basting occasionally with the pan juices, until the breast side is well-browned, 20 to 25 minutes.

5. While the chicken is cooking, prepare the fried onions. Remove the chicken from the oven and allow to stand about 5 minutes. Transfer to a serving platter, garnish with fried onions, and serve.

Pan-Cooked Onion Chicken
Pyaz Murgh

Makes 4 to 6 servings

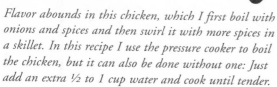

Flavor abounds in this chicken, which I first boil with onions and spices and then swirl it with more spices in a skillet. In this recipe I use the pressure cooker to boil the chicken, but it can also be done without one: Just add an extra ½ to 1 cup water and cook until tender.

1 teaspoon Chaat Masala (page 20 or store-bought)
½ cup Basic Onion Paste (page 48)
½ cup Crispy Fried Onions (page 44)
1 (2½- to 3-pound) chicken, skinned and cut into 1½-inch pieces through the bones, drumsticks left whole (discard the back and wings)
1½ cups water
12 to 15 fresh curry leaves
2 (1-inch) sticks cinnamon
2 black cardamom pods, crushed lightly to break the skin
1 teaspoon salt, or to taste
⅛ teaspoon ground asafoetida
2 tablespoons peanut oil
1 tablespoon ground coriander
1 teaspoon ground cumin

1. Prepare the chaat masala. Prepare the onion paste and fried onions and reserve separately. Then place the chicken, water, onion paste, curry leaves, cinnamon, cardamom pods, salt, and asafoetida in a pressure cooker. Secure the lid of the pressure cooker and cook over high heat until the regulator indicates high

pressure, then cook about 30 seconds more. Remove from the heat and allow the pot to depressurize on its own, 12 to 15 minutes.

2. Carefully open the lid and, with a slotted spoon, transfer the chicken pieces to a large nonstick skillet. Strain the liquid from the pot into a bowl, leaving the whole spices in the strainer. Pour the liquid over the chicken and cook over medium-high heat until completely dry, about 5 minutes.

3. Drizzle the oil over the chicken, then top with the coriander and cumin and cook, stirring, until the pieces are golden, about 5 minutes. Transfer to a serving dish, garnish with the chaat masala, scatter the crispy fried onions on top, and serve.

Mint-Cilantro Chicken
Murgh Dhania-Pudina

Makes 4 to 6 servings

This simple dish, full of fresh herb flavor, is a delicate preparation with a minimum of seasonings. A variation of this chicken is made throughout India; this is my interpretation. Make it with a cut-up whole chicken or any parts of your choice. Just remove the skin but keep the bone in.

2 tablespoons Basic Ginger-Garlic Paste (page 47 or store-bought)
3 tablespoons peanut oil
1 large onion, cut in half lengthwise and thinly sliced
1 (2½-to 3-pound) chicken, skinned and cut into serving pieces (discard the back and wings)
1 teaspoon salt, or to taste
½ teaspoon coarsely ground black pepper, or to taste, + more for garnish
½ teaspoon ground turmeric
1 cup finely chopped fresh cilantro, including soft stems
¼ cup finely chopped fresh mint leaves
1 fresh green chile pepper, such as serrano, minced with seeds
2 to 3 tablespoons fresh lemon juice

1. Prepare the ginger-garlic paste. Then, heat the oil in a large nonstick wok or saucepan over medium-high heat and cook the onion, stirring, until golden, about 7 minutes.

2. Mix in the ginger-garlic paste, then add the chicken, salt, black pepper, and turmeric, and cook, stirring as needed, over medium heat for the first 2 to 3 minutes and then over medium heat until the chicken is almost cooked, about 15 minutes.

3. Add the cilantro, mint, green chile pepper, and lemon juice and continue to cook until the chicken is tender and all the oil separates to the sides, about 20 minutes. Remove chicken pieces to a serving dish, garnish with black pepper, and serve.

Pan-Cooked Chile-Chicken Thighs
Bhuna Mirchi Murgh

Makes 4 to 6 servings

Called "chile-fry" in southern India, this dish is generally made with a whole chicken. Mine is an easy-to-cook and easy-to-eat version made with cut-up chicken pieces.

2 tablespoons peanut oil
1 teaspoon Asian sesame oil
5 to 7 dried red chile peppers, such as chile de arbol, with stems
2 (1-inch) pieces peeled fresh ginger, cut into thin matchsticks
2 medium onions, finely chopped
1 large clove fresh garlic, minced
1/2 teaspoon ground paprika
2 to 2 1/2 pounds skinless chicken thighs, cut in half through the bone
1 cup finely chopped fresh cilantro, including soft stems
1/4 cup distilled white vinegar
1/2 cup water
1 teaspoon salt, or to taste
1/2 teaspoon freshly ground black pepper, or to taste

1. Heat the oils together in a large nonstick pan over medium heat and cook the red chile peppers and ginger, stirring, until lightly browned, about 2 minutes.

2. Add the onions and cook until well-browned, about 10 minutes. Add the garlic, paprika, and chicken and cook, stirring, about 5 minutes.

3. Add the cilantro, vinegar, water, salt, and black pepper. Cook over high heat until it comes to a boil and then over medium heat until the chicken pieces are tender and most of the liquid has evaporated, and the oil separates to the sides, about 20 minutes. Transfer to a serving plate and serve hot.

Tamarind Chicken
Imli Murgh

Makes 4 to 6 servings

From the formerly Portuguese-ruled coastal state of Goa comes this celebrated tart chicken dish, featuring tamarind and vinegar.

3 to 4 tablespoons Tamarind Paste (page 54)
3 tablespoons peanut oil
1 (1-inch) stick cinnamon, broken lengthwise
2 black cardamom pods, lightly crushed to break the skin
1 teaspoon cumin seeds
1 large onion, cut in half lengthwise and thinly sliced
1 tablespoon peeled minced fresh ginger
1 large clove fresh garlic, peeled
1 1/2 to 2 pounds skinless, boneless chicken thighs or breasts, cut into bite-size pieces
1 tablespoon ground coriander
1/4 teaspoon ground turmeric
1 1/4 teaspoons salt, or to taste
3 to 5 fresh green chile peppers, such as serrano, whole with skin punctured or split lengthwise in half
1 tablespoon distilled white vinegar
1 tablespoon brown sugar
2 tablespoons chopped cilantro

1. Prepare the tamarind paste. Then, heat the oil in a large nonstick saucepan over medium-high heat and add the cinnamon, cardamom pods, and cumin seeds; they should sizzle upon contact with the hot oil.

2. Quickly add the onion and cook over medium heat until browned, about 10 minutes. Mix in the ginger and garlic, then add the chicken, coriander, turmeric, and salt, and cook, stirring and turning the pieces, until golden, 5 to 7 minutes.

3. Add the tamarind paste, green chile peppers, vinegar, and brown sugar and cook until the chicken is soft and the thick sauce clings to the pieces, 7 to 10 minutes. Transfer to a serving dish, garnish with chopped cilantro, and serve.

Ginger Chicken with Citrus Juices
Phal-Rus mein Adrak Mursh

Makes 4 to 6 servings

Lusciously sauced with citrus juices, this spiced-up everyday chicken dish comes packed with flavor. At once sweet and tart, it tastes good both hot and cold, and leftovers are a natural choice for sandwiches, salads, and even pizza.

2 to 3 tablespoons vegetable oil
2 medium onions, finely chopped
1 to 3 fresh green chile peppers, such as serrano, minced with seeds
2 tablespoons peeled minced fresh ginger
1 cup finely chopped fresh cilantro, including soft stems
1$^1/_2$ to 2 pounds skinless boneless chicken breasts, cut into 1$^1/_2$-inch pieces
$^1/_3$ cup canned pineapple juice
$^1/_3$ cup fresh orange juice
$^1/_3$ cup fresh lemon juice
1 teaspoon salt, or to taste
$^1/_2$ teaspoon freshly ground black pepper, or to taste
1 large red bell pepper, finely chopped
$^1/_4$ teaspoon garam masala

1. Heat the oil in a large nonstick saucepan over medium-high heat and cook the onions, stirring, until well-browned (almost caramel color), about 12 minutes.

2. Add the green chile peppers, ginger, and ½ cup cilantro, then mix in the chicken, all the fruit juices, and the salt and black pepper. Cover the pan and bring to a boil over high heat. Uncover and cook, stirring as needed, until all the juices evaporate and the chicken is soft, about 30 minutes. Add the bell

pepper and the remaining ½ cup cilantro during the last 5 minutes of cooking. Transfer to a serving dish, sprinkle the garam masala on top, and serve.

Peach and Tomato Chicken
Aadhoo aur Tamatar ka Mursh

Makes 4 to 6 servings

Here is an exciting dish inspired by the peach tree in my backyard. It may seem like an odd pairing, but the tangy tomato and lemon juice, the sweet ripe peaches, the onions, and the hot green chile peppers all balance out, and the spices weave their own special magic in the dish.

6 to 8 quarter-size slices peeled fresh ginger
2 large cloves fresh garlic, peeled
1 to 3 fresh green chile peppers, such as serrano, stemmed
6 large ripe peaches, peeled, pitted, and coarsely chopped
1 large tomato, coarsely chopped
3 tablespoons peanut oil
2 large onions, finely chopped
1 tablespoon ground coriander
1 teaspoon ground cumin
$^1/_2$ teaspoon garam masala + $^1/_4$ teaspoon for garnish
$^1/_2$ teaspoon coarsely ground black pepper
1 teaspoon salt, or to taste
1 (2$^1/_2$- to 3-pound) chicken, skinned and cut into serving pieces (discard the back and wings)
2 tablespoons fresh lime juice
$^1/_2$ cup finely chopped fresh cilantro, including soft stems

1. In a food processor, process together the ginger, garlic, and green chile peppers until minced. Then add the peaches and tomato and process until puréed.

2. Heat the oil in a large nonstick wok or saucepan over medium-high heat and cook the onions until browned, about 10 minutes. Add the coriander, cumin, ½ teaspoon garam masala, black pepper, and salt.

3. Add the chicken, mix in the puréed peaches and tomato, and cook over high heat the first 5 to 7 minutes, then over medium-low heat until the chicken is tender and most of the juices evaporate and a thick sauce clings to the chicken.

4. Add the lime juice and ¼ cup cilantro during the last 5 minutes of cooking. Transfer to a serving dish, garnish with the garam masala, and serve.

Coriander and Apple Chicken

Saeb-Dhania Murgh

Makes 4 to 6 servings

This dish is flavored both with the fresh leaves (cilantro) and the dried seeds of the coriander plant, and supported by tart apples and classic Indian seasonings. Serve it with a side of Potato-Stuffed Oval Eggplant (page 267), a raita *(seasoned yogurt dish), and store-bought* chapatis *(whole-wheat griddle breads) or whole-wheat tortillas.*

1 (2¹/₂- to 3-pound) chicken, skinned and cut into
    serving pieces (discard the back and wings)
2 tablespoons peeled minced fresh ginger
2 large cloves fresh garlic, minced
2 tablespoons fresh lemon juice
¹/₄ cup nonfat plain yogurt, whisked until smooth
1 teaspoon salt, or to taste
2 tablespoons peanut oil
1 teaspoon cumin seeds
2 tablespoons ground coriander
12 to 15 fresh curry leaves
1 large onion, finely chopped
1 fresh green chile pepper, such as serrano,
    minced with seeds
¹/₂ teaspoon ground paprika
¹/₄ teaspoon ground turmeric
1¹/₂ cups coarsely chopped fresh cilantro,
    including soft stems
1 tart apple, such as Granny Smith or pippin,
    coarsely chopped (with or without peel)
¹/₂ teaspoon garam masala
Freshly ground black pepper, to taste

1. Place the chicken in a non-reactive bowl. Add the ginger, garlic, lemon juice, yogurt, and salt and mix well, making sure all the pieces are well-coated with the marinade. Cover with plastic wrap and marinate in the refrigerator, at least 4 and up to 24 hours.

2. Heat the oil in a large nonstick wok or saucepan over medium-high heat and add the cumin seeds; they should sizzle upon contact with the hot oil. Quickly add the coriander and curry leaves and stir 1 minute.

3. Add the onion, green chile pepper, paprika, and turmeric and stir about 1 minute. Mix in the chicken, plus all the marinade, and cook, stirring as needed, 5 to 7 minutes.

4. In a food processor, process together the cilantro and apple until fine, and add it to the chicken. Reduce the heat to medium and continue to cook, turning as needed, until the chicken is tender, about 30 minutes. Add the garam masala during the last 5 minutes of cooking. Transfer to a serving dish, garnish with black pepper, and serve.

Diced Chicken with Cumin and Red Bell Peppers

Jeera aur Laal Shimla Mirch ka Murgh

Makes 4 to 6 servings

For the cook in a hurry, here is a spicy-hot chicken dish that can be cooked right away, or marinated the day before and then quickly pan-fried. And it makes a good presentation, too, with the tiny pieces of onion and red bell peppers lending color and a delicate crunch.

1¹/₂ tablespoons Basic Ginger-Garlic Paste
    (page 47 or store-bought)
1 teaspoon ground cumin, dry-roasted (page 35)
1¹/₂ pounds boneless skinless chicken thighs or tenders
    with tendons removed, cut into 1-inch pieces
2 tablespoons distilled white vinegar
1 teaspoon coarsely ground black pepper, or to taste
¹/₂ teaspoon salt, or to taste
2 tablespoons peanut oil
1 teaspoon cumin seeds
¹/₂ cup nonfat plain yogurt, whisked until smooth
1 large onion, finely chopped
1 large red bell pepper, finely chopped
¹/₂ cup finely chopped fresh cilantro,
    including soft stems
¹/₂ teaspoon garam masala

1. Prepare the ginger-garlic paste. Prepare the cumin. Place the chicken in a large non-reactive bowl. Add the ginger-garlic paste, vinegar, black pepper, and salt and mix, making sure all the pieces are well-covered with the marinade. Cover with plastic wrap and marinate in the refrigerator at least 4 and up to 24 hours.

2. Heat the oil in a medium, nonstick wok or skillet and add the cumin seeds; they should sizzle upon contact with the hot oil. Quickly add the chicken with all the marinade and cook, turning as needed, until lightly golden on all sides, about 7 minutes. (The moisture from the chicken may cause some splattering, so cover the pan for a few seconds until the splattering subsides.)

3. Add the yogurt, a little at a time, stirring constantly to prevent it from curdling, then mix in the onion and bell pepper and cook until all the juices evaporate and the chicken is rich golden in color and very soft, about 5 minutes. Mix in the cilantro and dry-roasted cumin and stir 1 minute. Transfer to a serving platter, sprinkle the garam masala on top, and serve.

Chickpea Masala Chicken
Channa Masala Murgh

Makes 4 to 6 servings

Channa or chickpea masala, a very north Indian blend that includes pomegranate seeds and fenugreek leaves and is typically reserved for chickpea preparations, is remarkable in other dishes as well. Every addition adds not only flavor, but a smoky, roasted aroma and a rich brown color. Try it in this mouthwatering chicken dish.

1/4 cup Chickpea Masala with Pomegranate Seeds (page 24)

2 tablespoons Basic Ginger-Garlic Paste (page 47 or store-bought)

1 (2 1/2- to 3-pound) chicken, skinned and cut into serving pieces (discard the back and wings)

1 cup nonfat plain yogurt, whisked until smooth

1 teaspoon garam masala + 1/4 teaspoon for garnish

1/2 teaspoon ground paprika

1 teaspoon salt, or to taste

2 tablespoons peanut oil

3 to 5 dried red chile peppers, such as chile de arbol, with stems

1 teaspoon cumin seeds

2 tablespoons finely chopped fresh curry leaves

1/4 cup finely chopped fresh cilantro, including soft stems

1. Prepare the chickpea masala and ginger-garlic paste. Then, place the chicken in a large non-reactive bowl and add the yogurt, ginger-garlic paste, 1 teaspoon garam masala, paprika, and salt. Mix well, making sure the chicken pieces are well coated with the marinade. Cover with plastic wrap and refrigerate at least 4 and up to 24 hours.

2. Heat the oil in a large nonstick wok or saucepan over medium-high heat and add the red chile peppers, and cumin seeds; they should sizzle upon contact with the hot oil. Quickly add the curry leaves and stir about 1 minute.

3. Add the chicken plus all the marinade and cook over medium-high heat for the first 3 to 5 minutes and then over medium heat until the chicken is golden, about 10 minutes.

4. Add the cilantro and cook about 5 minutes. Then add the chickpea masala and cook until the chicken is tender and the gravy thick, about 20 minutes. Transfer to a serving dish, sprinkle the 1/4 teaspoon garam masala on top, and serve.

Roasted Turkey with Indian Flavors
India ki Turkey

Makes 10 to 12 servings

Nobody in India makes turkey. Yet in America, Thanksgiving turkey has become a yearly ritual for most Indian families. Over the years, my husband Pradeep and I have tried different recipes until one year, we made a turkey with tandoori *flavors and served it with my cranberry chutney. There's been no turning back.*

As a standard rule for roasting a turkey without stuffing, allow 15 minutes per pound; for a stuffed turkey, increase the cooking time to 18 minutes per pound.

1 (14- to 16-pound) fresh turkey, washed and patted dry
20 to 25 raw cashews
12 quarter-size slices peeled fresh ginger
10 large cloves fresh garlic, peeled
3 to 5 fresh green chile peppers, such as serrano, stemmed
1 cup coarsely chopped fresh cilantro, including soft stems
$1/2$ cup fresh mint leaves
$1^1/4$ cups nonfat plain yogurt, whisked until smooth
$1/3$ cup heavy cream
$1/3$ cup fresh lemon or lime juice
$1^1/2$ teaspoons salt, or to taste
2 to 3 tablespoons vegetable oil
1 tablespoon ground dried fenugreek leaves
1 tablespoon garam masala
1 tablespoon ground paprika
$1/2$ teaspoon freshly ground nutmeg
$1/4$ teaspoon freshly ground mace
3 to 4 cups canned chicken broth, reduced fat, low-sodium preferred
3 tablespoons all-purpose flour
Salt and ground black pepper, to taste

1. Remove the neck and giblets from the turkey. Making sure the skin does not tear, run your fingers gently between the skin and the flesh of the turkey, starting at the neck cavity and moving towards the breast, tail and drumsticks. The idea is to loosen the skin and create a pocket.

2. In a food processor, process together the cashews, ginger, garlic, green chile peppers, cilantro, and mint leaves until minced. Add the yogurt, cream, lemon juice, and salt, and process to make a smooth paste. Transfer to a bowl.

3. Heat the oil in a small saucepan over medium-high heat and cook the fenugreek leaves, garam masala, paprika, nutmeg, and mace, stirring, about 30 seconds, then mix the spices and oil into the bowl with the yogurt mixture.

4. Remove ¼ cup of the marinade to a bowl and cover and refrigerate for the gravy. Divide the remaining marinade into 3 portions. Rub one portion under the loosened turkey skin and rub the second portion over the skin and inside the cavity. Reserve the remaining portion in the refrigerator for basting the turkey as it cooks. Fold the wings across the back and tie them together with heavy kitchen string, then tie the ends of the drumsticks together and insert an instant-read meat thermometer into the thickest part of the thigh, making sure it does not touch the bone. Cover the turkey securely with plastic wrap and refrigerate at least 12 and up to 36 hours.

5. Preheat the oven to 325°F. Place the turkey, breast side up, in a large roasting pan. Baste once with the reserved marinade and roast, uncovered, basting every 35 to 45 minutes until the turkey is well-browned and a meat thermometer reads 180°F, 4½ to 5 hours. (If the skin browns too fast, cover it with a piece of oil-basted muslin or tent loosely with heavy-duty aluminum foil.) Remove from the oven and allow the turkey to stand about 15 minutes before carving.

6. Meanwhile, make the gravy. Pour the pan juices through a fine-mesh strainer into a medium bowl and then, with a spoon, skim off all the extra fat that floats to the top. Put about 2 tablespoons of the fat into a medium nonstick saucepan.

7. Add about 1 cup chicken broth to the roasting pan and bring to a gentle simmer over low heat, stirring and scraping any browned bits. Pass through a fine-mesh strainer into the bowl with the pan juices.

8. Mix the flour into the reserved turkey fat and cook, stirring, over medium heat until very fragrant and golden, about 3 minutes. Mix in the reserved marinade and cook until it is completely incorporated, about 1 minute. Add the remaining broth and bring to a boil over high heat. Reduce the heat to medium-low and simmer until the gravy is thick, about 5 minutes. Add salt and black pepper to taste. Transfer to a bowl and serve with the turkey.

Chicken Dishes with Greens

Spicy Green Masala Chicken
Hara Masala Mursh

Makes 4 to 6 servings

Made with my Los Angeles friend Naina Kapadia's recipe for fresh Gujarati hara masala *paste (a paste made with ginger, garlic, and green chile peppers), and with lots of cilantro and mint, this intensely spicy chicken is best served with steamed* basmati *rice and a tall glass of chilled beer to soothe a fiery palate.*

3 tablespoons Gujarati Green Paste (page 48)

2 tablespoons olive oil

2 small onions, cut in half lengthwise and thinly sliced

1 cup finely chopped fresh cilantro, including soft stems

2 tablespoons minced fresh mint leaves

1 tablespoon ground coriander

1 teaspoon ground oregano

1/2 teaspoon garam masala

1/4 teaspoon ground turmeric

1 teaspoon salt, or to taste

2 to 2 1/2 pounds skinless chicken thighs, drumsticks, or quartered breasts

1 cup nonfat plain yogurt, whisked until smooth

Freshly ground black pepper

2 tablespoons chopped cilantro

1. Prepare the hara masala paste. Heat the oil in a large nonstick wok or saucepan over medium-high heat and cook the onions until barely golden, about 3 minutes. Add the hara masala paste and cook another minute.

2. Mix in the cilantro, mint, coriander, oregano, garam masala, turmeric, and salt, and cook 1 minute. Remove from the heat, add the chicken and yogurt, and stir well to mix. Cover with plastic wrap and marinate in the refrigerator at least 4 to and up to 24 hours.

3. Return to the heat and cook, stirring, over high heat the first 5 to 7 minutes and then over medium heat until the chicken is tender and the sauce thick, turn the pieces occasionally, about 30 minutes. Transfer to a serving dish, garnish with black pepper and cilantro, and serve.

Traditional Indian Chicken with Spinach
Saag-Mursh

Makes 4 to 6 servings

Saag-murgh, *a dish popular in Indian restaurants, is generally made with small pieces of chicken that often get lost in a smooth purée of creamy spinach. This traditional home version, on the other hand, made with large pieces of bone-in chicken and chopped spinach, has more texture, is lower in fat, higher in nutrition, and really delicious.*

3 tablespoons Basic Ginger-Garlic Paste (page 47 or store-bought)

1 (2 1/2- to 3-pound) chicken, skinned and cut into 2-inch pieces (discard the back and wings)

1 cup nonfat plain yogurt, whisked until smooth

2 tablespoons minced fresh mint leaves

1 tablespoon ground dried fenugreek leaves

1 1/2 teaspoons garam masala

1/2 teaspoon ground paprika

1/4 teaspoon hot red pepper flakes, or to taste

1/4 teaspoon freshly ground nutmeg

1 teaspoon salt, or to taste

3 tablespoons peanut oil

1 large onion, finely chopped

2 large bunches fresh spinach (12 to 14-ounces each), trimmed, washed, and coarsely chopped

1/4 cup milk, preferably lowfat

1/4 teaspoon garam masala

1. Prepare the ginger-garlic paste. Then, place the chicken pieces in a large non-reactive bowl. Add the yogurt, ginger-garlic paste, mint, fenugreek leaves, garam masala, paprika, red pepper flakes, nutmeg, salt, and 1 tablespoon oil and mix well, making sure all the pieces are well-coated with the marinade. Cover with plastic wrap and marinate in the refrigerator at least 4 and up to 24 hours.

2. Heat the remaining 2 tablespoons oil in a large nonstick wok or saucepan over medium heat and cook the onion, stirring, until well-browned, 10 to 12 minutes. Add the spinach, cover the pan and cook, stirring once or twice, until it wilts, about 5 minutes.

3. Add the chicken and all the marinade and cook, stirring, over high heat the first 2 to 3 minutes and then over medium-low heat until the chicken is tender and the spinach clings to each piece, about 30 minutes. Add the milk and simmer another 2 minutes. Transfer to a serving dish, sprinkle the garam masala on top, and serve.

Chicken Tenders with Sautéed Spinach
Jaldi ka Saag-Murgh

Makes 4 to 6 servings

This marinated chicken dish, enhanced with garlicky chopped spinach, is not the standard restaurant-style, long-cooked saag-murgh. Instead, it is a quick and easy dish, for when you want flavors you love but don't have time to cook the old-fashioned way.

1¹/₂ pounds skinless boneless chicken tenders, tendons removed

5 to 7 quarter-size slices peeled fresh ginger

4 large cloves fresh garlic, peeled

¹/₂ cup fresh cilantro, including soft stems

3 to 4 tablespoons fresh lime or lemon juice

1 tablespoon ground coriander

1 teaspoon ground cumin

1 teaspoon garam masala, + ¹/₄ teaspoon

1 teaspoon salt, or to taste

2 tablespoons olive oil

1 large bunch fresh spinach (12 to 14 ounces), tough stems removed, washed, and finely chopped

1 teaspoon minced garlic

2 small tomatoes, cut into wedges

1. Place the chicken in a non-reactive bowl. In a food processor or blender, process together the ginger, whole garlic cloves, and cilantro until minced. Add the lime juice, coriander, cumin, 1 teaspoon garam masala, and salt, and process again until smooth. Transfer to the bowl with the chicken and mix well,

making sure all the pieces are well-coated with the mixture. Cover and marinate in the refrigerator at least 2 and up to 24 hours.

2. Heat 1 tablespoon oil in a large nonstick skillet over medium-high heat and cook the spinach, stirring, until wilted, about 3 minutes. Add the minced garlic and stir another 3 minutes. Remove to a bowl.

3. In the same skillet, heat the remaining 1 tablespoon oil over medium-high heat and add the marinated chicken tenders, piece by piece (in 2 batches if necessary), making sure that each one lies flat and isn't crowded in the skillet. Cook until the bottoms are golden, about 4 minutes. Turn each piece over and cook until the other side is golden, about 3 minutes.

4. Carefully mix in the spinach and any juices that may have accumulated in the bowl, and stir until all the juice evaporates, about 5 minutes. Transfer to a serving platter and keep warm.

5. Add the tomato wedges to the skillet and cook, shaking the skillet, until tomatoes are slightly softened, about 2 minutes. Transfer to the chicken platter as a garnish. Sprinkle the ¹/₄ teaspoon garam masala on top and serve.

Hyderabadi Fenugreek Chicken
Hyderabad ka Methi Murgh

Makes 4 to 6 servings

You can make this simple dish, from my friend Yasmin AliKhan, with dried fenugreek leaves, but fresh ones make all the difference. When Yasmin told me I could use dried methi (fenugreek leaves), her purist mother loudly differed saying, "Neelam, use only fresh. Nothing else is good enough." So here it is—fresh fenugreek chicken. Fresh fenugreek leaves are available in Indian, Middle Eastern, and farmers' markets. (If you can't find fresh leaves, use ¹/₄ cup dried.)

2 tablespoons Hyderabadi Ginger-Garlic Paste
   (page 48)
3 tablespoons peanut oil
1 large onion, cut in half lengthwise and thinly sliced
1 (2 1/2- to 3-pound) chicken, skinned and cut into
   serving pieces (discard the back and wings)
1 to 3 fresh green chile peppers, such as serrano,
   coarsely chopped
1 teaspoon salt, or more to taste
1/2 teaspoon cayenne pepper
1/2 teaspoon freshly ground black pepper
1/4 teaspoon ground turmeric
2 cups packed fresh washed fenugreek leaves,
   minced by hand or food processor
1 tablespoon finely chopped fresh cilantro,
   including soft stems

1. Prepare the ginger-garlic paste. Then heat the oil in a large nonstick wok or saucepan over medium-high heat and cook the onion, stirring, until browned, about 10 minutes.

2. Mix in the ginger-garlic paste, then add the chicken, green chile peppers, salt, cayenne pepper, black pepper, and turmeric and cook, stirring as needed, over high heat the first 3 to 5 minutes and then over medium-low heat until the chicken is browned but still firm, about 15 minutes.

3. Add the fenugreek leaves and continue to cook until the chicken is very tender and all the oil separates to the sides, about 20 minutes. With a slotted spoon, transfer to a serving dish, garnish with chopped cilantro, and serve.

Punjabi Fenugreek Chicken
Punjab ka Methi Murgh

Makes 4 to 6 servings

Made with pan-roasted fresh fenugreek leaves, this is the home version of a popular restaurant-style dish from northern India. It looks superb, keeps well, and tastes even better the next day.

2 cups packed fresh washed fenugreek leaves
1 1/2 cups nonfat plain yogurt, whisked until smooth
1/2 cup water
3 tablespoons peanut oil
2 medium onions, finely chopped
2 tablespoons peeled minced fresh ginger
2 teaspoons minced fresh garlic
1 fresh green chile pepper, such as serrano,
   minced with seeds
1 1/2 pounds boneless skinless chicken breasts,
   cut into thin 2-by-1-inch pieces
1 tablespoon ground coriander
1 1/4 teaspoons garam masala
1/2 teaspoon ground paprika
1/4 teaspoon ground turmeric
1 teaspoon salt, or to taste

1. In a food processor, process the fenugreek leaves until minced. Transfer to a cast-iron or nonstick wok or saucepan. In the same food processor, process together the yogurt and water until smooth.

2. Place the wok with the fenugreek leaves over medium-high heat and cook, stirring, until all the moisture dries up (there is always some water clinging to the leaves after they are washed). Reduce the heat to medium-low, add 1 tablespoon oil and roast, stirring the leaves, until they are fragrant and much darker in color, 15 to 20 minutes. Remove to a bowl.

3. Add the remaining oil to the same wok and cook the onions over medium-high heat, stirring, until golden, about 5 minutes. Add the ginger, garlic, and green chile pepper, stir 1 minute, then mix in the chicken, coriander, 1 teaspoon garam masala, paprika, turmeric, and salt. Cook the chicken, stirring as needed, until it is golden on all sides, about 7 minutes.

4. Mix in the cooked fenugreek leaves and the yogurt-water mixture and bring to a boil over high heat. Cover the pan, reduce the heat to medium, and cook, stirring as needed, until the chicken is very tender, the sauce thick, and the oil separates to the sides, about 20 minutes. Transfer to a serving dish, garnish with the 1/4 teaspoon garam masala, and serve.

Cilantro Chicken Drumsticks in a Wok

Kadhai mein Dhania Tangdi-Mursh

Makes 4 to 6 servings

This dish, commonly cooked in kadhai *woks at dhabas (roadside restaurants), is customarily made with a cut-up whole chicken. I use only chicken drumsticks, so my recipe is faster and easier. Along with onions and bell peppers, this dish gets its trademark flavors from the unique* kadhai masala, *which is a blend of coriander, fenugreek, mint, and many other spices.*

2 tablespoons Spicy Masala for Wok-Cooked Foods (kadhai masala), page 26 or store-bought

2 large tomatoes, coarsely chopped

3 cups coarsely chopped fresh cilantro, including soft stems + 2 tablespoons finely chopped

3 tablespoons peanut oil

2 (1-inch) pieces peeled fresh ginger, cut into thin matchsticks

2 small onions, cut in half lengthwise and thickly sliced

2 large cloves fresh garlic, minced

10 to 12 skinless chicken drumsticks

$1/2$ teaspoon salt, or to taste

2 green, red, or yellow bell peppers, cut into $1^1/2$-by-$1/2$-inch strips

$1/2$ teaspoon garam masala

1. Prepare the kadhai masala. Then, in a food processor, process together the tomatoes and cilantro to make as smooth as possible.

2. Heat the oil in a large nonstick wok or saucepan over medium-high heat and cook the ginger and onion, stirring, until golden, about 5 minutes.

3. Add the garlic and kadhai masala and stir about 1 minute. Add the drumsticks and salt and cook, stirring, until golden, about 7 minutes.

4. Add the bell peppers, tomatoes and cilantro mixture, and cook until the chicken is tender and the sauce thick, about 20 minutes. Serve in the wok, or transfer to a serving dish, garnish with finely chopped cilantro and garam masala, and serve.

Chicken Curries

Basic Chicken Curry

Har-Roz ki Mursh Kari

Makes 4 to 6 servings

Perfect when served with rice or bread and easy enough to cook every day, this traditional chicken curry is usually the first one taught to all novice Indian cooks. Once you understand the basic procedure, you can vary it as you like.

3 large cloves fresh garlic, peeled

6 quarter-size slices peeled fresh ginger

1 large onion, coarsely chopped

2 large tomatoes, coarsely chopped

$1/2$ cup coarsely chopped fresh cilantro, including soft stems

1 to 3 fresh green chile peppers, stemmed

3 tablespoons vegetable oil

2 bay leaves

5 green cardamom pods, crushed lightly to break the skin

2 (1-inch) sticks cinnamon

$1^1/2$ tablespoons ground coriander

1 teaspoon ground cumin

1 teaspoon garam masala + $1/4$ teaspoon for garnish

$1/2$ teaspoon ground turmeric

1 teaspoon salt, or to taste

$1/4$ teaspoon freshly ground black pepper, or to taste

$1/2$ cup nonfat plain yogurt, whisked until smooth

1 ($2^1/2$- to 3-pound) chicken, skinned and cut into serving pieces (discard the back and wings)

1 cup water, or more as required

Cilantro sprigs

1. In a food processor, process together the garlic, ginger, and onion until minced. Remove to a bowl. Then process together the tomatoes, cilantro, and green chile peppers until smooth. Remove to another bowl and set aside.

2. Heat the oil in a large pan over medium-high heat and cook the bay leaves, cardamom pods, and cinnamon, stirring, about 30 seconds. Add the onion-garlic mixture and cook until browned, about 7 minutes. Add the tomato-cilantro mixture and continue to cook, stirring, until all the juices evaporate and the oil separates to the sides, about 7 minutes.

3. Add the coriander, cumin, 1 teaspoon garam masala, turmeric, salt, and black pepper, then mix in the yogurt, stirring constantly to prevent it from curdling, and cook, stirring, until it is incorporated into the sauce.

4. Add the chicken pieces and stir about 5 minutes to brown them. Then add 1 cup water, cover the pan, and cook over high heat, about 5 minutes. Reduce heat to moderate and cook until the chicken is tender and the sauce thick, about 30 minutes, turning the pieces over a few times and adding more water if you prefer a thinner sauce. Transfer to a serving dish, garnish with garam masala and cilantro, and serve.

Chicken Curry with Chopped Onions and Tomatoes

Kattae Pyaz aur Tamatar ki Murgh Kari

Makes 4 to 6 servings

Here is an easy chicken curry for anyone who doesn't have the time to grind the masala *ingredients, as in the previous recipe. Simply chop the ginger, garlic, onion, and tomato and proceed. Be aware however, that the sauce, though very good, will not be as smooth as one made with the ground* masalas.

3 tablespoons vegetable oil
6 green cardamom pods, crushed lightly to break the skin
1 (2-inch) stick cinnamon, broken lengthwise
5 fresh green chile peppers, such as serrano, skin punctured to prevent bursting
1 teaspoon minced fresh garlic
1 tablespoon peeled minced fresh ginger
1 1/2 cups finely chopped tomatoes
1/2 cup finely chopped fresh cilantro, including soft stems (reserve some for garnish)
1 tablespoon ground coriander
1 teaspoon ground cumin
1 teaspoon garam masala + 1/4 teaspoon for garnish
1 teaspoon dried fenugreek leaves
1/4 teaspoon ground turmeric
1/4 teaspoon ground paprika
1 teaspoon salt, or to taste
1/2 cup nonfat plain yogurt, whisked until smooth
1 (2 1/2- to 3-pound) chicken, skinned and cut into serving pieces (discard the back and wings)
1 cup water, or more as required

1. Heat the oil in a large saucepan over medium-high heat and cook the cardamom pods, cinnamon, and green chile peppers about 1 minute.

2. Add the onion and cook over medium heat until well-browned, about 7 minutes. Then add the garlic, ginger, tomatoes, and cilantro, and cook until all the juices evaporate, about 5 minutes.

3. Mix in the coriander, cumin, 1 teaspoon garam masala, fenugreek leaves, turmeric, paprika, and salt. Then add the yogurt, a little at a time, stirring constantly to prevent it from curdling, until it is absorbed in the sauce, about 1 minute.

4. Add the chicken and water, cover the pan, and cook over high heat about 5 minutes. Reduce heat to moderate and cook, turning the pieces over a few times, until the chicken is tender and the sauce thick, about 30 minutes. Add more water if you prefer a thinner sauce. Transfer to a serving dish, garnish with garam masala and cilantro, and serve.

Chicken Curry with Dry-Roasted Spices

Bhuna-Masala Murgh

Makes 4 to 6 servings

Dry-roasted spices, with their rich dark color and highly fragrant aroma, added at two different stages of cooking, lend a smoky richness to this authentic curry. Roast more spices than you need—use some now and store the rest in an airtight bottle for later use.

1 1/2 tablespoons Basic Ginger-Garlic Paste
    (page 47 or store-bought)
2 teaspoons ground cumin
1 teaspoon garam masala + 1/4 teaspoon for garnish
1 teaspoon white poppy seeds
1 teaspoon ground ginger
1 teaspoon ground green cardamom seeds
1 teaspoon ground dried pomegranate seeds
3 tablespoons vegetable oil
1 1/2 cups finely chopped onion
2 to 2 1/2 pounds skinless chicken thighs, drumsticks,
    or quartered breasts
1 1/2 tablespoons ground coriander
1 teaspoon salt, or to taste
1 cup nonfat plain yogurt, whisked until smooth
2 tablespoons chopped cilantro

1. Prepare the ginger-garlic paste. Then, place the cumin, 1 teaspoon garam masala, poppy seeds, ginger, cardamom, and pomegranate seeds in a small nonstick skillet and roast over medium-low heat until well-browned and fragrant, 1 to 2 minutes. Remove to a bowl.

2. Heat the oil in a large nonstick skillet over medium-high heat and cook the onion until well-browned, about 7 minutes. Add the ginger-garlic paste, then add the chicken, coriander, and salt. Cook, turning the pieces once or twice, until golden on both sides, about 7 minutes.

3. Add the yogurt, a little at a time, stirring constantly to prevent it from curdling, until all of it is used up. Mix in the roasted spices and cook over medium heat until all the liquid evaporates and the chicken is coated with a thick, creamy sauce, about 15 minutes. Transfer to a serving dish, garnish with garam masala and chopped cilantro, and serve.

Chicken in Fried Masala Curry

Talae Masalae ka Murgh

Makes 4 to 6 servings

This quintessential favorite—loaded with luxuriously rich nuts and seeds and moistened with coconut milk—is deliciously decadent. It's an excellent dish for special occasions.

3/4 cup Coconut Milk (page 44 or store-bought)
1/4 cup vegetable oil
1 small onion, coarsely chopped
2 black cardamom pods, crushed lightly
    to break the skin
1 (1-inch) stick cinnamon, broken
4 cloves
2 bay leaves
6 quarter-size slices peeled fresh ginger
2 large cloves fresh garlic, peeled
1/4 cup chopped raw almonds
1/4 cup chopped raw cashews
1/4 cup chopped raw peanuts
1 tablespoon coriander seeds
1 tablespoon white poppy seeds
1 teaspoon cumin seeds
1 teaspoon white sesame seeds
1/4 teaspoon nutmeg
2 to 2 1/2 pounds skinless chicken thighs, drumsticks,
    or quartered breasts
1 teaspoon salt, or to taste
1 cup water, or more as needed
2 to 3 tablespoons finely chopped fresh cilantro

1. Prepare the coconut milk. Then, make the masala paste, heat 3 tablespoons oil in a large nonstick wok or saucepan over moderate heat and fry together the onion, cardamom pods, cinnamon, cloves, bay leaves, ginger, garlic, almonds, cashews, and peanuts until golden, about 7 minutes. Drain and remove to a bowl.

2. To the oil, add the coriander, poppy, cumin, and sesame seeds, and the nutmeg, and cook, stirring, until golden, about 1 minute. Drain and mix with the fried ingredients. When everything is cool, discard the bay leaves and shell the cardamom pods; add the cardamom seeds to the mixture and discard the shells. Then transfer the fried mixture to a food processor, add 1/2 cup coconut milk and process to make the paste as smooth as possible.

3. To the same oil pan, add the chicken, the remaining 1 tablespoon oil, and salt and cook, stirring the pieces, until well-browned, about 15 minutes.

4. Add half the masala paste and cook about 5 minute. Then add the water, cover the pan, and cook over high heat the first 2 to 3 minutes, then over medium-low heat until the chicken pieces are tender and the sauce thick, about 20 minutes. (Add up to 1 cup more water if you prefer a thinner sauce.)

5. Mix in the remaining half of the masala paste and the coconut milk, cover the pan and simmer another 10 minutes. Transfer to a serving dish, sprinkle the cilantro on top, and serve.

Saffron Chicken Curry with Dry-Roasted Almonds
Kesari Murgh Kari

Makes 4 to 6 servings

Saffron and black cumin seeds offer yet another unique flavor to the familiar chicken curry. Black cumin seeds (shah-jeera) are very fragrant and have an assertive flavor. They are much thinner than the regular cumin seeds. If you can't find them, use regular cumin seeds.

1/2 cup Yogurt Cheese (page 42)
1/2 cup nonfat plain yogurt, whisked until smooth
1 tablespoon vegetable oil
1/2 cup minced red onion
1 to 3 fresh green chile peppers, such as serrano, minced with seeds
1/4 cup ground raw almonds
1 teaspoon ground black cumin seeds
1 teaspoon garam masala
1/2 teaspoon ground ginger
1/2 teaspoon ground green cardamom seeds
1 teaspoon salt, or to taste
1 1/2 pounds skinless boneless chicken breasts, cut into 1 1/2-inch pieces
1 teaspoon saffron threads
2 tablespoons lowfat milk
1 tablespoon finely chopped fresh mint leaves
1/4 teaspoon freshly ground black pepper or to taste
1/4 cup dry-roasted sliced almonds (page 35)

1. Prepare the yogurt cheese. Then, in a large bowl, mix together the cheese, yogurt, oil, onion, green chile pepper, raw almonds, cumin, garam masala, ginger, cardamom, and salt. Add the chicken and mix well, making sure all the pieces are well-coated with the marinade. Cover and marinate at least 4 and up to 24 hours in the refrigerator.

2. When ready to cook, in a small bowl, mix the saffron and milk and set aside about 30 minutes. Place the chicken and all the marinade in a medium non-stick skillet or saucepan, cover, and cook, stirring once or twice, over medium-high heat, about 5 minutes. Uncover the pan, reduce the heat to medium, and continue to cook, stirring as needed, until the chicken is tender, about 20 minutes. Meanwhile, prepare the almonds.

3. Reduce the heat to low, add the saffron-milk and the mint leaves. Cover the pan again and cook another 5 minutes to blend the flavors. Remove to a serving dish, sprinkle the black pepper on top, garnish with the roasted almonds, and serve.

Cashew and Poppy Seed Chicken Curry

Kaaju aur Khus-Khus ka Murgh

Makes 4 to 6 servings

A rich and highly flavorful curry (especially if you add the cream), this preparation is made on special occasions, when its aroma makes a statement. Good on its own, it is also outstanding with naans *(leavened oven-baked breads), to soak up the luscious sauce.*

1/2 cup coarsely chopped raw cashews

2 teaspoons white poppy seeds

1/2 cup hot water

Seeds from 10 green cardamom pods

2 large cloves garlic

6 quarter-size slices peeled fresh ginger

3 scallions, coarsely chopped

1 cup coarsely chopped fresh cilantro, including soft stems

1 to 2 fresh green chile peppers, such as serrano, stemmed

1 cup nonfat plain yogurt, whisked until smooth

2 tablespoons olive oil

1 1/2 teaspoons cumin seeds

1/2 teaspoon coarsely ground fenugreek seeds

1/2 teaspoon coarsely ground black peppers

1 tablespoon ground coriander

1 teaspoon garam masala

1 teaspoon salt, or to taste

1 1/2 pounds chicken tenders, cut into 1-inch pieces

1/4 cup heavy cream or water

1/4 cup dry-roasted cashew halves (page 35)

1. Soak the cashews and poppy seeds in hot water, about 1 hour. Transfer to a blender, add the cardamom seeds, garlic, ginger, scallions, cilantro, green chile peppers, and yogurt, and blend to make as smooth as possible, about 1 minute.

2. Heat the oil in a large, nonstick skillet over medium-high heat and add the cumin, fenugreek, and black pepper; they should sizzle upon contact with the hot oil. Quickly add the coriander, garam masala, salt, and chicken. Cook, stirring, until the chicken is golden, about 5 minutes. Remove to a bowl and keep warm.

3. To the same pan, add the cashew-yogurt mixture and cook over high heat, stirring as needed, until most of the juices evaporate and the mixture becomes highly fragrant, about 10 minutes. Meanwhile, roast the cashew halves.

4. Add the chicken to the pan, reduce the heat to medium, cover the pan, and cook about 10 minutes to blend the flavors. Adjust salt, if you wish. Add the cream (or water) and boil a few minutes. Transfer to a serving dish, garnish with the roasted cashew halves, and serve.

South Indian Coconut Chicken Curry

South ka Nariyal Murgh

Makes 4 to 6 servings

With a mild and delicate sauce, this basic coconut chicken curry from southern India is served with simple steamed basmati *rice.*

1 cup Coconut Milk (page 44 or store-bought)

2 tablespoons peanut oil

4 whole dried red chile peppers, such as chile de arbol

1 large onion, cut in half lengthwise and thinly sliced

10 to 12 fresh curry leaves, minced

2 tablespoons peeled minced fresh ginger

2 large cloves fresh garlic, minced

1 to 3 fresh green chile peppers, such as serrano, minced with seeds

1/4 cup grated fresh or 2 tablespoons dried shredded unsweetened coconut

1 1/2 to 2 pounds skinless boneless chicken breasts, cut into 2-inch pieces

1/2 teaspoon ground turmeric

1/8 teaspoon ground asafoetida

1 teaspoon salt, or to taste

Chopped cilantro

Freshly ground black pepper

1. Prepare the coconut milk. Then, heat the oil in a large nonstick wok or saucepan over medium-high heat, and cook the red chile peppers and onion, stirring, until well-browned, about 5 minutes.

2. Add the curry leaves, ginger, garlic, green chile peppers, and coconut and stir about 1 minute. Add the chicken, turmeric, asafoetida, and salt and cook, stirring and turning the pieces, until golden brown, about 5 minutes.

3. Add the coconut milk, cover the pan, reduce the heat to medium and simmer until the chicken absorbs all the flavors and is tender, about 20 minutes. Transfer to a serving dish, top with cilantro and black pepper, and serve.

Almond Chicken in Coconut Milk Sauce

Badaam-Nariyal Doodh ka Murgh

Makes 4 to 6 servings

Here is a recipe from my cousin Sunita Chopra's southern California kitchen. Sunita does something very interesting: She mixes chickpea flour, almonds, and coconut milk—a very unusual marinade combination, but certainly one that makes delicious chicken. Try it with chapatis *(whole-wheat griddle breads) or over a* basmati rice *pullao* (pilaf).

1 cup Coconut Milk (page 44 or store-bought)
1 large onion, coarsely chopped
1 tablespoon chickpea flour
1/4 teaspoon ground cinnamon
1/4 teaspoon ground cloves
6 quarter-size slices peeled fresh ginger
2 large cloves fresh garlic, peeled
1 to 3 fresh green chile peppers, such as serrano, stemmed

20 to 25 shelled raw almonds, coarsely chopped
3 tablespoons vegetable oil
1 teaspoon salt, or to taste
1 (2 1/2- to 3-pound) chicken, skinned and cut into serving pieces (discard the back and wings)
1/4 cup sliced raw almonds
2 tablespoons small raisins
1 cup nonfat plain yogurt, whisked until smooth
1 to 2 tablespoons minced fresh mint leaves

1. Prepare the coconut milk. Then, in a small food processor, process together the onion, chickpea flour, cinnamon, and cloves until smooth. Remove to a bowl, then process together the ginger, garlic, green chile peppers, chopped almonds, 1 tablespoon oil, and salt to make a smooth paste.

2. Place the chicken in a large non-reactive bowl. Add the ginger-garlic-almond paste and mix well, making sure all the pieces are well-coated with the marinade. Cover with plastic wrap and marinate at least 4 and up to 24 hours in the refrigerator.

3. Heat the remaining 2 tablespoons oil in a large nonstick wok or saucepan over medium heat and cook the sliced almonds and raisins, stirring, until the almonds are golden, about 1 minute. Drain well and remove to a bowl.

4. To the same oil, add the marinated chicken and cook, stirring occasionally, until lightly browned, about 10 minutes. Add the onion paste, then add the yogurt, a little at a time, stirring constantly to prevent it from curdling. Cover the pan, reduce the heat, and cook, stirring once or twice, until the yogurt is absorbed, about 15 minutes.

5. Add the coconut milk, cover the pan again, and continue to simmer until the chicken is tender, about 20 minutes. Transfer to a serving dish, scatter the fried almonds and raisins and the mint leaves on top, and serve.

Grilled Chicken in Spicy Sauce
Murgh Tikka Masala

Makes 4 to 6 servings

This dish, called murgh tikka masala, *has multiple levels of delectable flavor. It is made with grilled boneless cubes of chicken* (tikkas) *simmered in a full-bodied and spicy curry sauce. I generally make the tikkas a day ahead—serve some with chilled beer or wine, then make this curry the next day. You can also make this recipe with any leftover grilled chicken, meat, or fish. If you're using fish, add it just minutes before serving or it will disintegrate in the sauce.*

½ recipe Basic Chicken Tikka Kabaabs (page 160), made with Mint Chicken Tikka Marinade (page 164) or Creamy Chicken Tikka Marinade (page 165)

½ cup (½ recipe) Fried Onion Paste (page 49)

2 large tomatoes, coarsely chopped

½ cup coarsely chopped fresh cilantro, including soft stems, + more for garnish

1 tablespoon coriander

1 teaspoon ground cumin

2 teaspoons dried fenugreek leaves

1 teaspoon ground paprika

1 teaspoon garam masala

1 teaspoon salt, or to taste

1 cup water

½ cup heavy cream

1. Make the tikka kabaabs and cut them into smaller pieces if you wish. Then make the fried onion paste (reserving the ghee).

2. In a food processor, process together the tomatoes and cilantro until puréed.

3. Place the onion paste, along with 1 tablespoon of the ghee in which the onion paste was fried. Add the puréed tomatoes and cook, stirring, over medium-high heat until all the juices evaporate, about 7 minutes.

4. Add the coriander, cumin, fenugreek leaves, paprika, garam masala, and salt and stir about 1 minute. Then add the water and the grilled chicken kabaab pieces and simmer about 5 minutes. Add the cream and simmer another 5 minutes to blend the flavors. Transfer to a serving dish, garnish with some chopped cilantro, and serve.

Variation: Substitute any of the *tikkas* in "Starters and Snacks" with different meats, paneer cheese, or vegetables, to create a new dish every time.

Butter Chicken Curry
Murgh Makhani

Makes 4 to 6 servings

Makhani *means with butter added, and as much as the (clarified) butter is important, the real trademark of this dish lies with tomatoes, green chile peppers, and whole garam masala spices, that are delicately balanced with the smooth sweetness of heavy cream and the smoky flavored chicken.*

1 recipe Grilled Tandoori Chicken (page 445)

4 cups (1 recipe) Butter-Cream Sauce with Fresh Tomatoes (page 389)

1 tablespoon peanut oil

1 (1-inch) piece peeled fresh ginger, cut into thin matchsticks

2 to 4 fresh green chile peppers, such as serrano, split in half lengthwise

1. Make the tandoori chicken, then cool and remove the meat in very coarse pieces from the bones.

2. Make the butter-cream sauce and add the chicken pieces into it while it is still in the pan. Cover and simmer about 10 minutes to blend the flavors. Transfer to a serving dish.

3. Heat the oil in a small saucepan over medium-high heat and cook the ginger and green chile peppers, stirring, until golden, about 3 minutes. Transfer to the chicken and swirl lightly to mix, with parts of it visible as a garnish. Serve hot.

Chicken and Cracked-Wheat Curry

Haleem-Murgh

Makes 6 to 8 servings

This authentic Hyderabadi dish comes to me from my friend Bharti Mahendra, a native of Hyderabad. Her mother makes this dish with bone-in chicken pieces, and once they are tender, she shreds the meat off the bones and then proceeds with the recipe. Bharti makes hers with small pieces of boneless chicken. For more flavor, add part or all chicken broth in place of the water.

1¹/₂ tablespoons Basic Ginger-Garlic Paste
    (page 47 or store-bought)
1 cup cracked whole-wheat
1 pound boneless skinless chicken breasts,
    cut into 1-inch pieces
3 to 4 cups water
2 to 3 tablespoons fresh lime or lemon juice
¹/₂ cup nonfat plain yogurt, whisked until smooth
1 tablespoon chickpea flour
3 tablespoons peanut oil or ghee
1 medium-large onion, cut in half lengthwise and
    thinly sliced
1 teaspoon cayenne pepper, or to taste
1 teaspoon salt, or to taste
1 to 3 fresh green chile peppers, such as serrano,
    sliced diagonally
¹/₂ cup finely chopped fresh cilantro, including soft
    stems (reserve some for garnish)
¹/₄ cup finely chopped fresh mint leaves
    (reserve some for garnish)

1. Prepare the ginger-garlic paste. Then, place the cracked wheat, half the chicken, and the water in a large saucepan and bring to boil over high heat. Boil about 5 minutes, reduce the heat to medium-low, cover the pan, and cook until the chicken softens and starts to fall apart, about 1 hour.

2. Let cool, mix in the lime juice, then blend everything in a blender or a food processor to make a smooth purée. Remove to a bowl and, in the same blender, blend together the yogurt and chickpea flour and keep separate.

3. Heat the oil in a large nonstick wok or saucepan over medium heat and cook the onion, stirring, until browned, about 7 minutes. Add the remaining chicken, and the ginger-garlic paste, cayenne pepper, and salt and cook, stirring, until the chicken is soft and browned, about 7 minutes.

4. Add the blended yogurt and cook, stirring, until it the liquid evaporates, about 2 minutes. Then mix in the puréed cracked wheat and chicken mixture and bring to a boil over high heat. Reduce the heat to medium-low, cover the pan, and simmer about 10 minutes to blend the flavors.

5. Mix together the green chile peppers, cilantro, and mint leaves, and mix the remaining into the dish during the last 2 to 3 minutes of cooking. Transfer to a serving dish, garnish with the reserved cilantro and mint, and serve.

Goan-Style Spicy Chicken Curry

Murgh Vindaloo

Makes 4 to 6 servings

This unique vinegar-added chicken curry is a super-hot Goan specialty that, on first bite, sends "danger" signals through your taste buds. For those who want less of a challenge, go easy on the chile peppers and serve this dish with steamed basmati *rice, soothing* yogurt *raita, and chilled lemonade.*

1 tablespoon Goan Vindaloo Powder (page 28)
3 dried red chile peppers, broken (optional)
4 large cloves fresh garlic, peeled
6 quarter-size slices peeled fresh ginger
1 large onion, coarsely chopped
¹/₄ cup distilled white vinegar
1 teaspoon garam masala + ¹/₄ teaspoon for garnish
1 teaspoon salt, or to taste
¹/₄ teaspoon ground turmeric
2 large tomatoes, coarsely chopped
15 to 20 fresh curry leaves
1 (2¹/₂- to 3-pound) chicken, skinned and cut into
    serving pieces (discard the back and wings)
2 tablespoons peanut oil
¹/₄ cup finely chopped cilantro

1. Prepare the vindaloo powder. Then, in a food processor or a blender, process together the red chile peppers (if using), garlic, ginger, onion, and vinegar until smooth. Add the vindaloo and garam masalas, salt, and turmeric, and process to make a smooth paste. Remove to a bowl and then process the tomatoes and curry leaves until puréed.

2. Place the chicken in a large non-reactive bowl. Add the chile pepper-onion-vinegar paste and mix well, making sure all the chicken pieces are well-coated. Cover and marinate in the refrigerator at least 4 and up to 24 hours.

3. Heat the oil in a large nonstick saucepan over medium-high heat and add the marinated chicken, plus all the marinade. Cook, stirring, until golden, about 10 minutes.

4. Add the puréed tomatoes and cook, stirring as needed, until the chicken is tender and the sauce thick, about 10 minutes. (Add up to ½ cup water for a thinner sauce.) Transfer to a serving dish, garnish with chopped cilantro and garam masala, and serve.

Variation: To make a dry vindaloo, when you reach Step 3, cook the chicken until tender and completely dry, about 30 minutes. Do not add tomatoes.

Yogurt Chicken Curry with Caramelized Onions
Bhunnae Pyaz ka Dahi-Mursh

Makes 4 to 6 servings

This dish gets its rich brown color from slowly caramelized onions. Caramelizing onions is an exacting task, but they are worth the work, so don't skimp on cooking time or try to speed it up by increasing the heat. The flavor they impart to the dish is its own reward.

3 tablespoons peanut oil
5 black cardamom pods, crushed lightly
    to break the skin
2 (1-inch) sticks cinnamon
2 medium onions, finely chopped
1 teaspoon sugar
2 pounds skinless chicken thighs, each cut in half
    through the bone
2 tablespoons peeled minced fresh ginger
1 large clove fresh garlic, minced
1 to 3 fresh green chile peppers, such as serrano,
    minced with seeds
1½ tablespoons ground coriander
¼ teaspoon ground cloves
¼ teaspoon freshly ground black pepper
1 teaspoon salt, or to taste
1½ cups nonfat plain yogurt, processed in
    a food processor or blender until smooth
¼ teaspoon garam masala
Finely chopped scallions, green parts only

1. Heat the oil in a large saucepan over medium-high heat and cook the cardamom pods and cinnamon until fragrant, about 1 minute. Add the onions and cook, stirring, until golden, about 5 minutes. Reduce the heat to medium-low, sprinkle the sugar on the onions, and continue to cook, stirring, until well-browned, about 10 minutes.

2. Add the chicken, ginger, garlic, green chile peppers, coriander, cloves, black pepper, and salt, and stir over high heat until the chicken firms up, about 4 minutes.

3. Add the yogurt, a little at a time, stirring constantly to prevent it from curdling. Keep stirring until it comes to a boil. Reduce the heat to medium, cover the pan, and cook, turning the pieces a few times, until the chicken is tender and the sauce is thick, about 25 minutes. (If the chicken becomes tender and the sauce seems thin, uncover the pan and cook over high heat until the sauce thickens.) Transfer to a serving platter, garnish with garam masala and scallions, and serve.

Fragrant Chicken Curry with Coconut and Sesame Seeds

Khushbudar Murgh Korma

Makes 4 to 6 servings

This is a unique dish from my friend Yasmin AliKhan's kitchen in Los Angeles. Ever the traditionalists—her mother and grandmother, and to some extent, Yasmin herself, insist on preparing each nut and spice individually—I have simplified the recipe somewhat by roasting and grinding them all at once.

1 tablespoon Hyderabadi Ginger-Garlic Paste (page 48)
15 shelled raw almonds, coarsely chopped (or store-bought roasted almonds)
1/4 cup shredded unsweetened dried coconut
1 tablespoon white poppy seeds
1 tablespoon sesame seeds
1 tablespoon coriander seeds
1 teaspoon black cumin seeds
3 tablespoons peanut oil
2 (1-inch) sticks cinnamon
7 to 10 green cardamom pods, crushed lightly to break the skin

2 medium onions, finely chopped
1 (2 1/2- to 3-pound) chicken, skinned and cut into serving pieces (discard the back and wings)
1 teaspoon salt, or to taste
1 cup nonfat plain yogurt, whisked until smooth
2 tablespoons fresh lemon or lime juice
1/2 teaspoon ground green cardamom seeds
1/2 teaspoon freshly ground black pepper, or to taste
2 tablespoons minced fresh mint leaves

1. Prepare the ginger-garlic paste. Put the almonds in a small nonstick skillet and roast, stirring and shaking the skillet over medium heat, until fragrant and golden, about 2 minutes. Remove to a bowl. Add the coconut, poppy, sesame, coriander, and cumin seeds and roast until golden, about 2 minutes. Add to the bowl with the nuts. Let cool, then transfer everything to a spice or a coffee grinder and grind to make a fine powder.

2. Heat the oil in a large nonstick wok or saucepan over medium heat, and cook the cinnamon and cardamom pods, stirring, until fragrant, about 1 minute. Add the onions and cook over medium-high heat until golden, about 7 minutes. Add the roasted spices and stir another minute. Add the chicken, ginger-garlic paste, and salt, and cook, turning the pieces, until they are a rich golden color, about 15 minutes.

3. Add the yogurt, a little at a time, stirring constantly to prevent it from curdling, and cook over high heat until most of it dries up and the chicken is very tender, about 15 to 20 minutes. Mix in the lemon juice.

4. Sprinkle the ground cardamom seeds and black pepper on top, cover the pan, reduce the heat to low, and simmer 15 to 20 minutes to blend the flavors. Do not uncover the pan or stir.

Alternatively, preheat the oven to 200°F. Transfer everything to an oven-safe serving dish, cover and roast in the oven 15 to 20 minutes to blend the flavors. Garnish with the mint leaves and serve.

Hyderabadi Chicken Curry
Hyderabadi Mursh Korma

Makes 4 to 6 servings

Time-intensive though it might be, this is a perfect dinner party dish, given to me by my friend Yasmin AliKhan. It is an incredibly flavorful crowning achievement for the table. Your guests will remember its captivating flavors, and you will quickly forget the time spent in preparation. This chicken dish also forms the basis of Hyderabadi Layered Rice with Mixed Vegetables, an elaborate biryani *(page 559).*

1 tablespoon Hyderabadi Ginger-Garlic Paste
    (page 48)
1/4 cup vegetable oil
1 large onion, cut in half lengthwise and
    then into thin slivers
1/4 teaspoon ground turmeric
1/2 teaspoon cayenne pepper
1 teaspoon salt, or to taste
1 (1-inch) stick cinnamon
3 black cardamom pods, crushed lightly
    to break the skin
5 to 7 green cardamom pods, crushed lightly
    to break the skin
3 whole cloves
3/4 teaspoon black cumin seeds
2 tablespoons slivered almonds
1 cup nonfat plain yogurt, whisked until smooth
1/2 cup coarsely chopped fresh cilantro, including
    soft stems (reserve some for garnish)
1 to 3 fresh green chile peppers, such as serrano,
    minced with seeds
1 tablespoon coarsely chopped fresh mint leaves
1 (2 1/2- to 3-pound) chicken, skinned and cut into
    serving pieces (discard the back and wings)

1. Prepare the ginger-garlic paste. Heat the oil in a large nonstick saucepan over medium heat and do not increase the heat at any stage of cooking. Cook the onion, stirring, until well-browned, about 10 minutes. Add the ginger-garlic paste, then the turmeric, cayenne pepper, and salt, and stir about 1 minute.

2. Add the cinnamon, black and green cardamom pods, cloves, cumin, and almonds, and stir another

minute. Then add the yogurt, a little at a time, stirring constantly to prevent it from curdling, and cook until the oil separates to the sides, about 7 minutes. Mix in the cilantro, green chile peppers, and mint, and cook another minute.

3. Add the chicken and cook, turning the pieces, until they are soft, the sauce is very thick, and the oil separates to the sides, about 30 minutes. Transfer to a serving dish, garnish with the reserved cilantro, and serve.

Baked Yogurt-Mint Chicken Curry
Dum Mursh Dahi-Pudina

Makes 4 to 6 servings

There are many yogurt and mint chicken dishes in Indian cuisine, each a little different. In this recipe, I add the same set of ingredients in two stages: once to marinate the chicken and once to make the sauce. Each adds a different flavor.

This saucy dish is an intriguing accompaniment to rice, and can also be layered with cooked rice and baked to make an exotic biryani.

3 1/2 tablespoons Basic Ginger-Garlic Paste
    (page 47 or store-bought)
2 tablespoons dried mint leaves
2 teaspoons dried fenugreek leaves
2 teaspoons garam masala
1 teaspoon salt, or to taste
2 pounds skinless boneless chicken breasts or thighs,
    cut into 1 1/2-inch pieces
2 cups nonfat plain yogurt, whisked until smooth
3 tablespoons peanut oil
1 large onion, finely chopped
1 to 3 fresh green chile peppers, such as serrano,
    minced with seeds
1/2 teaspoon ground green cardamom seeds
2 tablespoons minced fresh mint leaves

1. Prepare the ginger-garlic paste. Then, in a small bowl, mix together the dried mint and fenugreek leaves, garam masala, and salt. Place the chicken in a large non-reactive bowl. Add 2 tablespoons ginger-garlic paste, half the spice mixture, and 1 cup yogurt.

Mix well, making sure all the chicken pieces are well-coated with the marinade. Cover with plastic wrap and marinate in the refrigerator at least 4 and up to 24 hours.

2. Heat the oil in an ovenproof saucepan over medium heat and cook the onion, stirring, until well-browned, about 10 minutes. Add the green chile peppers, the remaining ginger-garlic paste and the remaining spice mixture. Stir 1 minute, then add the remaining 1 cup yogurt, a little at a time, stirring constantly to prevent it from curdling, and cook until it comes to a vigorous boil.

3. Preheat the oven to 350°F. Mix in the chicken, plus the marinade, and cook, stirring, about 5 minutes. Remove from the heat and cover, first with aluminum foil and then with the pan cover, to seal the pan.

4. Place the pan on the center rack of the oven and bake about 50 minutes, or until the chicken is tender and the sauce smooth. Lightly swirl in the ground cardamom seeds and mint leaves, with parts of them visible as a garnish, and serve.

Chicken Tenders in Creamy White Sauce
Murgh Sufaed-Saas

Makes 4 to 6 servings

From the British legacy comes this rich childhood favorite. It's a dish with a little chicken and a lot of mildly fragrant cream sauce, which is divine to dunk into with fresh naan *(leavened oven-baked) and* parantha *(griddle-fried) breads.*

1/2 cup Basic Onion Paste (page 48 or store-bought)
4 to 5 cups fresh or canned chicken broth
5 to 7 quarter-size slices peeled fresh ginger
4 large cloves fresh garlic, coarsely chopped
3 bay leaves
6 cloves
1 teaspoon garam masala + 1/4 teaspoon for garnish
1/2 teaspoon salt, or to taste
1 1/2 pounds skinless boneless chicken tenders, tendons removed

2 tablespoons vegetable oil
1/4 cup cornstarch
1 tablespoon ground coriander
1 teaspoon ground paprika
1/4 teaspoon ground nutmeg
1/4 teaspoon ground mace
1 cup milk
1 cup heavy cream
5 to 7 large cherry tomatoes, cut into wedges
1/2 cup finely chopped fresh cilantro

1. Prepare the onion paste. Place the broth, ginger, garlic, bay leaves, cloves, 1 teaspoon garam masala, and salt in a large pan and bring to a boil over high heat. Reduce the heat to medium-low, cover the pan, and simmer about 10 minutes.

2. Add the chicken, increase the heat to medium-high, cover the pan, and cook until the chicken pieces are tender, about 15 minutes. Remove the chicken to a bowl. Pass the broth through a strainer and save for the sauce. (You should have at least 3 cups. If not, add some more chicken broth.)

3. Heat the oil in a large nonstick wok or saucepan over medium heat and cook the onion paste, stirring, until transparent, about 5 minutes. (Do not increase the heat.) Add the cornstarch and continue to cook, stirring, until golden and fragrant, about 5 minutes.

4. Add the coriander, paprika, nutmeg, and mace, then mix in the reserved chicken broth and milk, a little at a time, stirring constantly to prevent lumps from forming. Bring to a boil over high heat, then reduce the heat to medium-low, cover the pan, and simmer about 5 minutes. (If the sauce seems thin, dissolve 1 to 2 more tablespoons cornstarch in about 1/2 cup of milk and stir it in.)

5. Mix in the reserved chicken pieces and the cream and simmer, stirring as needed, until the sauce is almost like a thick custard and the oil separates to the sides, about 20 minutes. Add the tomatoes and cilantro and cook another 5 minutes. Transfer to a serving dish, garnish with the garam masala, and serve.

Parsi Peanut Chicken

Parsi Moong-Phalli Murgh

Makes 4 to 6 servings

The Parsis (of Iranian origin, now living in western India) make a special chicken curry flavored with tamarind, peanuts, and coconut. When made with a thick sauce, it tastes delicious with rice or perfect with any homemade or purchased Indian flatbread.

1/4 cup Meat Masala with Cumin and Peanuts
    (page 27)
2 small onions, coarsely chopped
1/4 cup grated fresh or frozen coconut or
    shredded unsweetened dried coconut
2 large cloves fresh garlic, peeled
7 quarter-size slices peeled fresh ginger
2 tablespoons tamarind powder
1/2 teaspoon ground turmeric
1 large tomato, coarsely chopped
20 to 25 fresh curry leaves
2 tablespoons peanut oil
2 pounds skinless chicken thighs, cut in half
    through the bone
1 teaspoon salt, or to taste
1/2 cup finely chopped fresh cilantro,
    including soft stems
1/2 to 1 1/2 cups water
1/4 cup peanuts, dry-roasted and coarsely chopped
    (page 35)

1. Prepare the meat masala. Then, in a food processor or a blender, process together the onions, coconut, garlic, ginger, tamarind, and turmeric to make smooth paste. Transfer to a bowl and process the tomato and curry leaves until smooth.

2. Place the onion-tamarind paste in a large nonstick wok or saucepan over medium-high heat and cook, stirring, until most of the juices evaporate, about 1 minute. Then add the oil and cook, stirring, until fragrant, 2 minutes.

3. Add the chicken and salt and cook about 5 minutes, then mix in the processed tomato and bring to a boil over high heat. Reduce the heat to low, cover the pans and cook until most of the juices evaporate and the chicken is tender, about 10 minutes.

4. Add the meat masala and cilantro and cook, stirring, about 5 minutes. Add the cups water, with the amount based on how thick or thin you want the sauce to be, and bring to a boil over high heat. Reduce the heat to low and simmer about 15 minutes, or until the sauce is as thick as you desire. Meanwhile, prepare the peanuts. Then, transfer the chicken to a serving dish, sprinkle the peanuts on top, and serve.

Nirmala's Sindhi Chicken Curry

Nirmala ka Sehal Murgh

Makes 4 to 6 servings

Sehal is a Sindhi word meaning "cooked with tomatoes and onion." Sindhis, originally from northwest India (now Pakistan), are settled in the Mumbai (formerly Bombay) area and elsewhere in the world.

    This is a garlicky dish from my friend Nirmala Bhamani—typical of Sindhi cooking—and is very easy to make, since you basically throw everything in the pot and forget about it. This dish can also be made with boneless lamb pieces, but increase the cooking time, because lamb is a tougher meat.

1 tablespoon peanut oil
1 1/2 pounds boneless skinless chicken breasts,
    cut into thin 2-inch pieces
1 tablespoon ground coriander
2 teaspoons ground cumin
1/2 teaspoon ground turmeric
1/2 teaspoon cayenne pepper, or to taste
1 teaspoon salt, or to taste

3 to 5 green cardamom pods, crushed lightly
    to break the skin
2 tablespoons peeled minced fresh ginger
6 to 8 large cloves fresh garlic, finely chopped
12 to 15 scallions, white and light green parts only,
    finely chopped
2 large onions, finely chopped
4 large tomatoes, finely chopped
1 cup finely chopped fresh cilantro, including
    soft stems (reserve some for garnish)
1 to 3 fresh green chile peppers, such as serrano,
    minced with seeds
1 cup nonfat plain yogurt, whisked until smooth

1. Heat the oil in a large nonstick wok or saucepan
over medium-high heat and cook the chicken, stirring, about 5 minutes.

2. Add the coriander, cumin, turmeric, cayenne pepper, salt, and cardamom pods, and stir to coat the
chicken. Then add the ginger, garlic, scallions,
onions, tomatoes, cilantro, and green chile peppers,
and stir about 5 minutes.

3. Add the yogurt, a little at a time, stirring constantly to prevent it from curdling, and cook over
medium-high heat the first 2 to 3 minutes, then over
medium-low heat until the chicken pieces are tender,
about 30 minutes, Stir occasionally. Transfer to a
serving dish, garnish with the reserved cilantro,
and serve.

Soft-Cooked Ground Chicken with Cardamom Seeds

Illaichi Keema

Makes 4 to 6 servings

*Fragrant with cardamom seeds, this quick-to-make dish is
made without any oil. Each of the cardamom seeds have
a different flavor—the green ones are stronger with a
eucalyptus-like aroma, and the black ones have a woody-
smoky aroma with just a hint of eucalyptus. If the flavor
is too strong, reduce the green ones by half, if you wish.*

1¹/₂ pounds ground chicken
1 teaspoon ground green cardamom seeds
1 teaspoon ground black cardamom seeds
¹/₂ teaspoon ground cloves
¹/₂ teaspoon ground cinnamon
1¹/₂ teaspoons salt, or to taste
2 medium onions, finely chopped
2 large tomatoes, finely chopped
2 large cloves fresh garlic, minced
1 tablespoon peeled minced fresh ginger
¹/₂ cup nonfat plain yogurt, whisked until smooth
1 fresh green chile pepper, such as serrano,
    minced with seeds
¹/₄ teaspoon garam masala

1. In a medium non-reactive bowl, mix together the
chicken, cardamom seeds, cloves, cinnamon, and salt.

2. Place the onion and tomatoes in a large nonstick wok
or saucepan and cook, stirring, over medium-high
heat until heated through. Reduce the heat to medium-
low, cover the pan, and cook about 5 minutes.

3. Add the chicken with spices, garlic, and ginger and
cook, stirring, over medium-high heat until all the juices
are dry and the chicken is golden, about 20 minutes.

4. Add the yogurt, a little at a time, stirring constantly
to prevent it from curdling, and simmer over low heat
about 5 minutes. Transfer to a serving dish, sprinkle the
green chile pepper and garam masala on top, and serve.

Diced Chicken with Pomegranate Seeds
Bareek Kattae Murgh ka Keema

Makes 4 to 6 servings

Keema essentially means minced meat, so this dish made with diced chicken is not a true keema. *But the pieces are so small that it almost looks like one. Make sure the pomegranate seeds are well ground, or they may get stuck in your teeth.*

1 tablespoon Basic Ginger-Garlic Paste
    (page 47 or store-bought)
1 pound chicken tenders, tendons removed,
    cut into 1/4-inch pieces
3/4 pound potatoes (any kind), peeled and
    cut into 1/4-inch pieces
1/4 cup canned tomato sauce
1/2 cup finely chopped fresh cilantro,
    including soft stems
1 teaspoon salt, or to taste
1/2 teaspoon cayenne pepper, or to taste
2 tablespoons peanut oil
1 (1-inch) piece peeled fresh ginger,
    cut into thin matchsticks
2 (1-inch) sticks cinnamon
1 large onion, finely chopped
2 tablespoons ground dried pomegranate seeds
1 tablespoon ground coriander
1 teaspoon garam masala
1/4 cup fresh pomegranate seeds or finely chopped
    red bell pepper

1. Prepare the ginger-garlic paste. Place the chicken and potatoes in a non-reactive bowl. Add the tomato sauce, ginger-garlic paste, cilantro, salt, and cayenne pepper, and mix well, making sure all the pieces are well-coated with the marinade. Cover with plastic wrap and marinate about 2 hours in the refrigerator.

2. Heat the oil in a large nonstick wok or saucepan over medium-high heat and cook the ginger until golden, about 2 minutes. Remove to a bowl and reserve for garnish.

3. Add the cinnamon and onion and cook until browned, about 7 minutes. Add the marinated chicken and stir until the chicken is golden and all the juices have evaporated, about 15 minutes.

4. Add the ground pomegranate seeds, coriander, and garam masala and stir another 5 minutes. Transfer to a serving dish, lightly mix in the fresh pomegranate seeds (or bell pepper), scatter the fried ginger on top, and serve.

Chicken Kofta Balls in Kashmiri Cashew-Saffron Sauce
Kashmiri Murgh Kofta Kari

Makes 4 to 6 servings

As in other kofta *preparations, there are three distinct steps to making this classic recipe from Kashmir: making the* koftas *(vegetable or meat balls), making the sauce, then simmering the two together until the meat balls soak up the fragrant sauce and become soft and packed with flavor. The cashew-and-saffron-enriched sauce, in turn, takes on the flavors of the chicken and turns into a luxuriant, delicately sweet purée that is delicious dippings for bread.*

20 to 25 raw almonds, coarsely chopped
6 quarter-size slices peeled fresh ginger
1/2 cup coarsely chopped fresh cilantro,
    including soft stems
2 teaspoons fennel seeds
2 teaspoons garam masala + 1/4 teaspoon for garnish
1/2 teaspoon coarsely ground black pepper
1/4 teaspoon ground green cardamom seeds
1 pound skinless boneless chicken thighs,
    cut into small pieces
1 teaspoon salt, or to taste
1 large egg
3/4 cup raw cashews
8 quarter-size slices peeled fresh ginger
3 large cloves fresh garlic, peeled
1 to 3 fresh green chile peppers, such as serrano,
    stemmed
1/2 teaspoon saffron threads
1/2 cup milk

2 tablespoons vegetable oil

2 bay leaves

1 (1-inch) stick cinnamon, broken lengthwise

2 cups finely chopped tomatoes

3 cups water

2 to 3 tablespoons fresh lemon or lime juice

1/4 cup finely chopped fresh cilantro, including
soft stems (reserve some for garnish)

1 teaspoon ground fennel

1. To make the kofta balls: Place the almonds, ginger, cilantro, fennel seeds, 1 teaspoon garam masala, black pepper, and cardamom seeds in a medium skillet and dry-roast, stirring and shaking the skillet, over moderate heat until fragrant, about 2 minutes. Let cool, transfer to a food processor, and process until finely ground.

2. Add the chicken and ½ teaspoon salt and process until minced. Add the egg and process once again. Remove to a bowl and divide the mixture into 25 equal but unevenly shaped balls. Refrigerate at least 30 minutes and up to 2 hours.

3. To make the sauce: In a clean food processor, process together the cashews, ginger, garlic, green chile peppers, 1 teaspoon garam masala, and saffron until minced. Add the milk and process again to make a smooth paste.

4. Heat the oil in a large nonstick wok or saucepan over medium heat and cook the bay leaves and cinnamon about 30 seconds. Add the cashew paste and cook over medium heat, stirring, until golden, about 5 minutes.

5. Add the tomatoes, increase the heat to medium-high, and cook, stirring, until all the juices evaporate and traces of oil are visible on the sides, about 7 minutes. Add the water and the remaining ½ teaspoon salt, and cook, stirring, over high heat until the sauce comes to a boil. Reduce the heat to medium-low and simmer about 10 minutes.

6. Add the chicken kofta balls and simmer about 20 minutes, adding the lemon juice, cilantro, and ground fennel during the last 5 minutes of cooking. Transfer to a serving dish, garnish with the reserved cilantro and garam masala, and serve.

Meat

A lot of Indians don't eat meat, yet it is a crucial part of the cuisine. Specialties include the *korma* (yogurt-braised) curries of Hyderabad, the coconut curries of Kerala in the south, the roasted *masala* curries of Punjab in the north, the *koftas* (meat balls) of Kashmir in the north, the super-spicy *vindaloo* curries of Goa on the southwestern coast, marinated whole leg or rack of lamb, and much more.

In India, the word "meat" loosely translates to mutton or goat meat. (Mutton is an English word and usually means an older lamb, but in India, traditionally, it refers to goat meat.) Finding goat meat in America is not easy, and even though some butchers can get it for you, for the most part it still remains just a possibility. With that in mind, almost all of the recipes in this chapter call for lamb, and even in the few in which I call for mutton, you can use lamb or beef. Beef, pork, and other red meats popular in the rest of the world are not universally accepted in India, but they are eaten in some parts of the country and because they are popular meats in the United States, I include recipes for them.

A few things apply uniformly to how most meat dishes are prepared in India. First, in most instances, all or a major part of the visible fat is trimmed off before the meat is cooked. Second, the meat is mostly cooked with the bone in, and even when the recipe calls for boneless meats, a few bone-in pieces are often left in the dish because bones enhance flavor and nutrients. (Even though I don't actively call for bones to be added, it's a good practice to follow.)

I tend to gravitate toward certain cuts: the leg of lamb, or the rib or loin chops for special dishes. I find that the meat from the leg, especially the upper butt or the thigh portion, is the best—it's easy to trim off the fat, the flavor is good, and you get a lot of boneless meat that is easy to cook and to serve family or buffet-style. Beef or pork can be used interchangeably with lamb; just cut the pieces in similar sizes, and proceed with the recipe. There is no change in cooking time.

Basic Pan-Roasted Lamb Curry

Bhunnae Gosht ki Kari

Makes 4 to 6 servings

In this basic curry, the meat is stirred and roasted until well-browned. In India, this dish is customarily made with bone-in pieces, but because I noticed people fishing for the boneless ones in the thick curry pool, I make this recipe with boneless pieces. Of course, the addition of a few bone-in pieces (such as lamb shanks or chops), will add more flavor to this curry.

3 tablespoons vegetable oil
1 large onion, finely chopped
1 tablespoon peeled and minced fresh ginger
2 large cloves fresh garlic, minced
2 large tomatoes, finely chopped
2 tablespoons ground coriander
2 teaspoons garam masala
1 teaspoon ground cumin
$^{1}/_{4}$ teaspoon ground turmeric
$^{1}/_{2}$ teaspoon dried cayenne pepper, or to taste
1 teaspoon salt, or to taste
2 pounds boneless leg of lamb (see box page 473), or beef (rump, brisket, or sirloin), all visible fat trimmed and the meat cut into 1$^{1}/_{2}$-inch pieces
1 teaspoon salt, or to taste
1$^{1}/_{2}$ cups nonfat plain yogurt, whisked until smooth
3 to 4 cups water
1 teaspoon dried fenugreek leaves
3 to 4 cups water
$^{1}/_{4}$ cup chopped cilantro

1. Heat the oil in a large nonstick wok or saucepan and cook the onions, stirring as needed, initially over high heat for the first 3 to 5 minutes and then over medium-low heat until well-browned, about 12 minutes.

2. Add the ginger and garlic, stir about 1 minute, then add the tomatoes and cook, until most of the juices evaporate, about 5 minutes.

3. Add the coriander, garam masala (save $^{1}/_{4}$ teaspoon for garnish), cumin, turmeric, and chile powder cayenne pepper and stir about 30 seconds. Mix in the lamb and salt, and stir, initially over high heat the first 3 to 5 minutes, and then over medium-low heat until the lamb is well-browned and fragrant, 15 to 20 minutes.

4. Add the yogurt, a little at a time, while stirring constantly to prevent it from curdling, and cook until it is completely absorbed, about 5 minutes. Add the water, cover the pan, and cook until the lamb is fork-tender (adding more water, if necessary), and the sauce is as thick or as soupy as desired, 50 to 60 minutes. Add the fenugreek leaves during the last 5 minutes of cooking.

5. Transfer to a serving dish, lightly mix in the cilantro, sprinkle the garam masala on top, and serve hot.

Variation: If you're in a hurry, after Step 3, transfer everything (just before you add the yogurt) to a pressure cooker and cook over high heat until the regulator indicates high pressure, then cook about 2 minutes more. Allow the pot to depressurize, 12 to 15 minutes. Carefully open the lid, add the yogurt, and stir until it is absorbed. Add the fenugreek leaves and continue with Step 5.

Classic Marinated Lamb Curry

Dahi Mein Bhigae Gosht ki Kari

Makes 4 to 6 servings

This is another popular way of making an everyday lamb curry. With the meat cleaned and marinated a day ahead, the actual cooking time is reduced, or so it seems, because half the work has already been done.

1 recipe Basic Curry Paste with Onion (page 50)
2 pounds boneless leg of lamb (see box, right)
    or beef (rump, brisket, or sirloin), all visible fat
    trimmed, cut into 1¹/₂-inch pieces
¹/₂ cup nonfat plain yogurt, whisked until smooth
2 teaspoons garam masala
¹/₂ teaspoon ground turmeric
1 teaspoon salt, or to taste
1 tablespoon peanut oil
5 green cardamom pods, crushed lightly
    to break the skin
1 (1-inch) stick cinnamon, broken lengthwise
1 teaspoon cumin seeds
1 tablespoon ground coriander
4 fresh green chile peppers, such as serrano,
    skin punctured to prevent bursting
2 teaspoons ground dried fenugreek leaves
2 to 3 cups water
¹/₄ cup finely chopped fresh cilantro

1. Prepare the curry paste. Then, place the lamb in a large non-reactive bowl. Add the yogurt, curry paste, garam masala (save ¼ teaspoon for garnish), turmeric, and salt and mix well, making sure all the pieces are well-coated with the marinade. Cover with plastic wrap and marinate in the refrigerator, at least 4 and up to 24 hours.

2. Heat the oil in a large nonstick wok or saucepan over medium-high heat, add the cardamom pods, cinnamon, and cumin seeds; they should sizzle upon contact with the hot oil. Quickly add the coriander, then mix in the marinated lamb with the marinade and cook over high heat, stirring, until it comes to a boil. Reduce the heat to medium-low, cover the pan,

and cook until most of the juices are dry, 20 to 25 minutes.

3. Uncover the pan, add the green chile peppers and fenugreek leaves, increase the heat to medium-high and cook, stirring, until the pieces are well-browned and are coated with the sauce, 10 to 12 minutes.

4. Add the water and bring to a boil over high heat. Reduce the heat to medium-low, cover the pan, and simmer until the lamb is fork-tender and the sauce thick. Transfer to a serving dish, mix in half the cilantro, garnish with reserved garam masala and the remaining cilantro, and serve hot.

Variation: To make a saucy dish, add some more whisked yogurt, buttermilk, or water in Step 4 and cook until you have your desired sauce. Adjust the seasonings and serve.

Buying Leg of Lamb

Leg of lamb has two parts to it: the upper butt or thigh portion, which is the part generally sold as leg of lamb; and the bottom part, which is mostly bone with muscles attached and is called lamb shanks. Leg of lamb is sold in the meat section of most supermarkets. You can buy boneless leg of lamb, but if your market does not have it, ask the butcher to debone and trim the fat from the bone-in leg and cut it into pieces.

An average leg of lamb is 5 to 7 pounds. When boned and trimmed of fat, it will have 3 to 4 pounds of meat. Use what is needed and freeze the rest for another recipe. Or cook it all at once and freeze leftovers.

Curried Lamb with Whole Spices
Khada Masala Gosht

Makes 4 to 6 servings

This dish is called khada *or* sabut masala gosht, *which literally translates as meat with "standing" (*khada*) or "whole" (*sabut*) spices. The whole spices are not discarded, as one does a bouquet-garni or a seasoning pouch, but are very much a part of the dish, offering visual appeal and bursts of flavor for the daring. (Those who don't dare can push the spices to the side of their dish.)*

1/2 cup plain yogurt, whisked until smooth

1/4 teaspoon saffron threads

2 tablespoons vegetable oil

4 to 6 dried red chile peppers, such as chile de arbol, stems punctured to prevent bursting

2 (1-inch) sticks cinnamon, broken

1 teaspoon black peppercorns

6 green cardamom pods, crushed lightly to break the skin

4 black cardamom pods, crushed lightly to break the skin

3 bay leaves

6 cloves

1 1/2 teaspoons cumin seeds

1 large onion, cut in half lengthwise and thinly sliced

2 tablespoons Basic Ginger-Garlic Paste (page 47 or store-bought)

2 pounds boneless leg of lamb (see box, page 473) or beef (rump, brisket, or sirloin), all visible fat trimmed, cut into 1 1/2-inch pieces

1 tablespoon ground coriander

1 teaspoon salt, or to taste

5 to 6 cups water

1/2 teaspoon garam masala

1/8 teaspoon ground mace

1/8 teaspoon ground nutmeg

1 fresh green chile pepper, such as serrano, minced with seeds

1/4 cup finely chopped fresh cilantro

1. In a small bowl, mix together the yogurt and saffron and allow to steep until needed. Then, heat the oil in a large nonstick wok or saucepan over medium heat and stir-fry the red chile peppers, cinnamon, black peppercorns, green and black cardamom pods, bay leaves, cloves, and cumin seeds until fragrant, about 2 minutes. Add the onion and cook, stirring, until browned, 10 to 12 minutes.

2. Meanwhile, prepare the ginger-garlic paste. Then add the paste to the wok or pan, along with the lamb, coriander, and salt, and cook, stirring until golden, about 10 minutes.

3. Add the water and cook over high heat the first 5 minutes, then cover the pan, reduce the heat, and cook, stirring occasionally, until the lamb chops are tender and the sauce almost clings to the them, about 40 minutes.

4. Mix in the garam masala, mace, and nutmeg, and cook about 5 minutes to blend the flavors. Transfer to a serving dish, add the saffron-yogurt, and swirl lightly to mix, with parts of it visible as a garnish. Sprinkle the green chile pepper and cilantro on top and serve.

Lamb Curry with Pickling Spices
Achaari Gosht

Makes 4 to 6 servings

Achaar is the Hindi word for pickles signaling the flavors in every mouthful of this intoxicating North Indian curry. Serve with a rice dish and Indian breads.

2 tablespoons Basic Ginger-Garlic Paste (page 47 or store-bought)

1 tablespoon Bengali 5-Spices (page 27 or store-bought)

2 pounds boneless leg of lamb (see box, page 473) or beef (rump, brisket, or sirloin), all visible fat trimmed, cut into 1 1/2-inch pieces

2 to 3 tablespoons fresh lime juice

1 teaspoon ground fennel seeds

1 teaspoon ground fenugreek seeds

1 teaspoon ground black cardamom seeds

1/4 teaspoon ground turmeric

1 teaspoon salt, or to taste

2 tablespoons mustard oil or vegetable oil (or 1 tablespoon each)

2 large onions, finely chopped

1/8 teaspoon ground asafoetida

2 large tomatoes, finely chopped

1/2 cup nonfat plain yogurt, whisked until smooth

3 to 4 cups water

1/2 teaspoon garam masala

2 tablespoons finely chopped fresh cilantro, including soft stems

1. Prepare the ginger-garlic paste and the 5-spice mix. Place the lamb pieces in a large non-reactive bowl. Add the lime juice, ginger-garlic paste, fennel, fenugreek, cardamom seeds, turmeric, and salt and mix well, making sure all the pieces are well-coated with the marinade. Cover and marinate in the refrigerator at least 2 and up to 24 hours.

2. Heat the oil in a large nonstick wok or saucepan over medium-high heat and add the panch-phoran; they should sizzle on contact with the hot oil. Quickly add the onions and asafoetida, then add the lamb and stir until golden, about 10 minutes. Add the tomatoes and cook, stirring, until most of the juices evaporate, about 7 minutes.

3. Mix in the yogurt, a little at a time, stirring constantly to prevent it from curdling, until it is fully absorbed, about 5 minutes. Add the water and bring to a boil over high heat. Reduce the heat to low, cover the pan, and cook until the lamb is fork-tender and the thick sauce clings to the pieces, about 40 minutes. Transfer to a serving dish, sprinkle the garam masala and cilantro on top, and serve.

Marinated Lamb Shanks Curry with Potatoes
Gosht-Aalu ki Kari

Makes 4 to 6 servings

Possibly India's answer to "meat and potatoes," this is another popular way in which lamb is prepared in north India. Growing up, we had this spicy dish frequently for Saturday lunches, only my mother used goat meat. I use baby lamb shanks because they are tender to start with, and smaller in size.

This dish has a somewhat thin sauce that goes well with rice pullaos (pilafs). Cook longer to reduce it, if you prefer a thicker sauce.

1/4 cup Basic Ginger-Garlic Paste (page 47 or store-bought)

2 to 2 1/2 pounds baby lamb shanks (4 to 6 ounces each), all visible fat trimmed

4 to 5 small russet potatoes (about 1 pound), peeled and halved

2 cups nonfat plain yogurt, whisked until smooth

2 teaspoons garam masala + 1/4 teaspoon for garnish

1/2 teaspoon ground turmeric

1 1/2 teaspoons salt, or to taste

3 tablespoons vegetable oil

1 large onion, finely chopped

2 large tomatoes, finely chopped

1 to 3 fresh green chile peppers, such as serrano, minced with seeds

1 tablespoon ground coriander

1 teaspoon ground cumin

1/2 teaspoon ground paprika or cayenne pepper

2 teaspoons dried fenugreek leaves

2 tablespoons finely chopped fresh mint leaves

1. Prepare the ginger-garlic paste. Then, place the lamb shanks and potatoes in a large non-reactive bowl. Add the yogurt, ginger-garlic paste, 2 teaspoons garam masala, turmeric, and salt and mix well, making sure all the pieces are well-coated with the marinade. Cover with plastic wrap and marinate in the refrigerator, at least 4 and up to 24 hours.

2. Heat the oil in a large nonstick wok or saucepan over medium heat and cook the onion until well-browned, 10 to 12 minutes. Add the tomatoes and green chile peppers and cook, stirring, until most of juices evaporate, about 7 minutes.

3. Add the coriander, cumin, and paprika (or cayenne pepper), stir 1 minute then mix in the marinated meat and potatoes, plus all the marinade, and bring to a boil over high heat. Reduce the heat to medium-low, cover the pan, and cook, stirring occasionally, until the lamb is tender and the sauce is as thin or thick as you desire, about 40 minutes, adding 1/2 to 1 cup of water, if needed.

4. Mix in the fenugreek leaves during the last 5 minutes of cooking. Transfer to a serving dish, sprinkle the garam masala and mint leaves on top, and serve hot.

Rita's Mutton Curry

Rita ki Gosht Kari

Makes 4 to 6 servings

My sister-in-law Rita Sawhney's prized mutton curry is a favorite in our family. It's got equal amounts of onion and meat (by weight), and lots of tomatoes and spices. The pieces of meat are first roasted in the masala, *then braised in yogurt until they are meltingly soft and the sauce is incredibly flavorful. If you've never eaten mutton (goat meat in India), this is the recipe to start with.*

You can buy mutton at special Indian or Middle Eastern meat shops, or ask your butcher to order it. If you have difficulty finding it, by all means, use lamb or even beef.

2 tablespoons Basic Ginger-Garlic Paste (page 47 or store-bought)
1 tablespoon Mughlai Garam Masala with Nutmeg and Mace (page 18) or Kashmiri Garam Masala (page 19)
3 to 4 tablespoons peanut oil
4 large onions (about 2 pounds), finely chopped
3 large tomatoes (about 1½ pounds), finely chopped
1 tablespoon ground coriander
1 teaspoon ground paprika
½ teaspoon cayenne pepper, or to taste
½ teaspoon ground turmeric
1 teaspoon salt, or to taste
1 pound leg of goat or lamb (see box, page 473) or beef (rump, brisket, or sirloin), all visible fat trimmed, cut into 1½-inch pieces
1 pound mutton rib chops, all visible fat trimmed
½ cup nonfat plain yogurt, whisked until smooth
1 tablespoon ground dried fenugreek leaves
½ teaspoon garam masala
¼ cup finely chopped fresh cilantro

1. Prepare the ginger-garlic paste and the Mughlai or Kashmiri garam masala. Heat the oil in a large non-stick wok or saucepan over medium heat and cook the onions until well-browned, about 20 minutes. Add the ginger-garlic paste, stir about 1 minute, then add the tomatoes and cook until most of the juices evaporate, about 15 minutes.

2. Add the coriander, Mughlai or Kashmiri garam masala, paprika, cayenne pepper, turmeric, and salt and cook, stirring, about 2 minutes. Add the meat and cook, stirring, until it is well-browned and almost soft, 25 to 30 minutes.

3. Add the yogurt, a little at a time, stirring constantly to prevent it from curdling, then add the fenugreek leaves and continue to cook until the meat is fork-tender and the sauce thick, about 20 minutes. (If the meat is not soft, add up to 1 cup water, ½ cup at a time, and cook.) Transfer to a serving dish, sprinkle the garam masala and cilantro on top, and serve.

Mughlai Lamb Curry with Cashews and Coconut Milk

Kaaju Korma Gosht

Makes 4 to 6 servings

A curry is a korma *(sometimes spelled with a Q) when whatever liquids that are used in cooking are cooked off completely and the foods remain smothered in a thick, paste-like sauce with traces of oil floating on the sides and the top. Most* korma *curries are enriched with a nut paste—in this case, cashews.*

½ cup Basic Cashew Paste (page 53)
2 teaspoons cumin seeds, dry-roasted and coarsely ground (page 35)
1 cup Coconut Milk (page 44 or store-bought)
3 tablespoons peanut oil
2 bay leaves
4 whole dried red chile peppers, such as chile de arbol
1½ teaspoons cumin seeds
1 large onion, finely chopped
1½ to 2 pounds boneless leg of lamb (see box, page 473) or beef (rump, brisket, or sirloin), all visible fat trimmed, cut into 1½-inch pieces
2 tablespoons peeled minced fresh ginger
2 large cloves fresh garlic, minced
1 tablespoon ground coriander
1½ teaspoons garam masala, some reserved for garnish
¼ teaspoon ground nutmeg
⅛ teaspoon ground mace
1 teaspoon salt, or to taste
1 teaspoon ground green cardamom seeds
3 cups water

1. Prepare the cashew paste, cumin seeds, and coconut milk. Then, heat the oil in a large nonstick wok or saucepan over medium-high heat and cook the bay leaves and red chile peppers, stirring, about 1 minute. Add the cumin seeds, they should sizzle upon contact with the hot oil. Quickly, add the onion and cook over medium heat until well-browned, about 10 minutes.

2. Add the meat, ginger, garlic, coriander, dry-roasted cumin, garam masala nutmeg, mace, and salt, and cook the meat, stirring, over medium-high heat the first 2 to 3 minutes and then over medium heat until browned, about 10 minutes.

3. Mix in the cashew paste and cardamom seeds and stir another 5 minutes. Then add half the coconut milk and the water and simmer until the meat is fork-tender, the sauce is thick and the oil separates to the sides, 50 to 60 minutes. Mix in the remaining ½ cup coconut milk during the last 10 minutes of cooking. Transfer to a serving dish, sprinkle the reserved garam masala on top, and serve.

Mughlai Pot-Roasted Lamb with Almonds and Poppy Seeds

Gosht Dum-Pukht

Makes 4 to 6 servings

Dum-pukht *is a popular cooking procedure in India. Authentic* dum-pukht *dishes are cooked in a* pateela, *a deep, tin-plated copper or brass saucepan with a ½-inch lip all around.*

Once all the ingredients are added to the pan, the lip is sealed with a firm whole-wheat flour dough and the pan is then placed over low heat with a piece of hot charcoal on the lid, so the food inside cooks from the top and bottom simultaneously (almost like baking). The food simmers over low heat until the

dough ring hardens and cracks—a sign that the dish is ready. No moisture escapes, so the spicy aromas stay contained, and the foods absorb all possible flavors. In my recipe, I seal in the flavors with aluminum foil and then cook the dish, long and slow.

2 tablespoons Basic Ginger-Garlic Paste
   (page 47 or store-bought)
¼ cup Almond and Poppy Seed Paste (page 52)
1½ teaspoons Mughlai Garam Masala with Nutmeg
   and Mace (page 18)
2 pounds lamb loin chops, all visible fat trimmed
¼ cup coarsely chopped raw cashews
¼ cup raisins
1½ cups nonfat plain yogurt, whisked until smooth
1 to 3 fresh green chile peppers, such as serrano,
   minced
1 teaspoon salt, or to taste
½ teaspoon saffron threads soaked in
   ¼ cup heavy cream about 30 minutes
½ teaspoon ground green cardamom seeds
¼ cup sliced raw almonds

1. Prepare the 2 pastes and the masala. Then, place the lamb in a large nonstick saucepan with a tight-fitting lid and mix in all the ingredients except the saffron, cardamom seeds, and almonds. Marinate at room temperature about 30 minutes.

2. Cover the pan first with aluminum foil and then with the lid (no steam should be allowed to escape). Place over medium-high heat and bring to a boil. Reduce heat to low and simmer, about 1 hour. Do not uncover or stir at any time. Pick up the pan with pot holders and shake it a few times, but do not stir.

3. After about an hour, check to see if the meat is tender; if not, cook another 10 minutes, or longer, until meat is tender. Mix in the saffron-cream and cardamom seeds and cook about 5 minutes to blend the flavors.

4. Transfer to a serving dish, dry-roast the almonds by stirring over medium heat until golden, scatter them over the lamb, and serve.

Sunil's Kashmiri Pot-Roasted Lamb with Dried Ginger

Sunil ka Dum-Pukht Gosht

Makes 4 to 6 servings

My friend Sunil Vora grew up with this dish made with equal proportions of meat and onion, and he loves it to this day. It is flavored with fennel seeds, ground ginger, and asafoetida, the standard Kashmiri seasonings, rather than the Mughlai lavishness of nuts and cream.

1 teaspoon Kashmiri Garam Masala (page 19)

2 pounds boneless leg of lamb (see box, page 473) or beef (rump, brisket, or sirloin), all visible fat trimmed, cut into 1-inch pieces

6 to 8 small red onions (about 2 pounds), cut in half lengthwise and thinly sliced

1 cup nonfat plain yogurt

1 tablespoon ground coriander

1 tablespoon ground fennel seeds

1 teaspoon ground ginger

1 teaspoon ground paprika

1/2 teaspoon cayenne pepper, or to taste

1/8 teaspoon ground asafoetida

1 teaspoon salt, or to taste

1/4 cup finely chopped fresh cilantro, including soft stems

1. Prepare the garam masala. Then, place everything except the garam masala and cilantro in a large saucepan with a tight-fitting lid. Cover the pan first with aluminum foil and then with the lid. (No steam should be allowed to escape.)

2. Cook over low heat about 1 hour. Do not uncover or stir at any time. Pick up the pan with pot holders and shake it a few times, but do not stir. Check to see if the meat is tender; if not, cook another 10 minutes, or longer, until the meat is soft. Transfer to a serving dish, mix in the garam masala, garnish with cilantro, and serve.

Lamb and Grain Curries

Parsi Lamb Curry

Gosht Dhansak

Makes 40 6 servings

Dhansak (meaning dal or legumes, and vegetables), is an authentic Parsi dish from the Mumbai (formerly Bombay) area. It can be cooked vegetarian-style, as in Parsi Mixed Lentils, Beans, and Vegetables (page 367), or it may contain some lamb, beef, pork, or chicken, as in this recipe from my Parsi sister-in law, Khushnoor Chugh, in India. Precise chopping of the greens and vegetables is not crucial, because eventually, all will be puréed to make a smooth sauce.

2 tablespoons Gujarati Lentil Masala (dhansak masala), page 26 or store-bought

1 pound boneless leg of lamb (see box, page 473) or beef (rump, brisket, or sirloin), all visible fat trimmed, cut into 1 1/2-inch pieces

1 1/2 cups dried split pigeon peas (toor dal), sorted and washed in 3 to 4 changes of water

2 medium russet potatoes, chopped (peeled or unpeeled)

1 small Chinese eggplant, chopped

1 (4-inch) piece pumpkin, peeled and chopped

1 (4-inch) piece opo squash or zucchini, chopped

1 small onion, chopped

1 large tomato, chopped

1 cup coarsely chopped fresh fenugreek leaves, or about 3 tablespoons dried

1/2 cup coarsely chopped fresh cilantro, including soft stems

10 to 15 fresh mint leaves

4 to 6 quarter-size slices peeled fresh ginger

1/2 teaspoon ground turmeric

1 teaspoon salt, or to taste

4 cups water

2 tablespoons distilled white vinegar

1 tablespoon grated jaggery (gur) or brown sugar

3 tablespoons peanut oil

1 large onion, finely chopped

1 to 3 fresh green chile peppers, such as serrano, minced with seeds

1 teaspoon cumin seeds

1 large clove fresh garlic, minced

1 tablespoon ground coriander

1/2 teaspoon paprika

1/4 cup finely chopped fresh cilantro,
   including soft stems

1. Prepare the lentil masala. Then, place the lamb, dal, potatoes, eggplant, pumpkin, squash, onion, tomato, fenugreek leaves, cilantro, mint, ginger, turmeric, salt, and water in a pressure cooker. Secure the lid of the pressure cooker and cook over high heat until the regulator indicates high pressure, then cook about 1 minute more. Reduce the heat to low and continue to cook another 3 minutes. Then remove from the heat and allow the pot to depressurize on its own, 12 to 15 minutes.

2. Carefully open the lid and check to see if the lamb is tender; if not, cover, bring up to pressure, and cook under pressure another 1 minute. Or cover and boil until soft, about 1/2 hour.

3. Remove the meat pieces to a bowl and process all the remaining ingredients in a blender to make a thick and smooth purée. Put the purée back into the pressure cooker, mix in the meat, vinegar, and jaggery, and simmer, uncovered, over medium heat until the meat is fork-tender, about 15 minutes.

4. Meanwhile, heat the oil in a small nonstick wok or saucepan over medium-high heat and cook the onion and green chile peppers, stirring, until golden, about 5 minutes. Add the cumin seeds; they should sizzle upon contact with the hot oil. Quickly add the garlic, masala, coriander, and paprika, stir 1 minute, and mix into the pot with the meat. Transfer to a serving dish, lightly mix in the cilantro with some of it visible as a garnish, and serve.

Punjabi Split Chickpeas and Lamb Curry
Punjabi Channa Dal Meat

Makes 4 to 6 servings

Made with yellow split chickpeas (found in Indian markets), this is a popular home-style Punjabi dal-meat curry.

1/2 cup dried yellow split chickpeas (channa dal),
   sorted and washed in 3 to 4 changes of water

2 tablespoons vegetable oil

4 black cardamom pods, crushed lightly
   to break the skin

1 (1-inch) stick cinnamon

1 large onion, finely chopped

1 tablespoon peeled minced fresh ginger

1 teaspoon minced fresh garlic

1 to 3 fresh green chile peppers, such as serrano,
   minced with seeds

1 tablespoon ground coriander

1 teaspoon garam masala + 1/4 teaspoon
   for garnish

1/4 teaspoon ground turmeric

1 teaspoon salt, or to taste

1 pound boneless leg of lamb (see box, page 473)
   or beef (rump, brisket, or sirloin), all visible fat
   trimmed, cut into 1-inch pieces

3 to 4 cups water

2 medium tomatoes, coarsely chopped

2 tablespoons fresh lemon juice

1/2 cup finely chopped fresh cilantro,
   including soft stems

1 tablespoon minced fresh mint leaves

1. Soak the dal in water to cover by 2 inches about 1 hour, then drain. Heat the oil in a large nonstick wok or saucepan over medium-high heat and cook the cardamom pods and cinnamon about 30 seconds. Add the onion and cook, stirring, until golden, about 5 minutes. Add the ginger, garlic, and green chile peppers, then add the coriander, 1 teaspoon garam masala, turmeric, and salt.

2. Add the lamb and cook, stirring, until browned, about 20 minutes. Add the dal and cook another 5 minutes. Then add the water and cook until the meat is tender and the dal creamy, about 30 minutes.

3. Add the tomatoes, lemon juice, cilantro, and mint and cook about 10 minutes to blend the flavors. Transfer to a serving dish, sprinkle the garam masala on top, and serve.

Hyderabadi Mashed Lamb and Cracked-Wheat

Haleem-Gosht

Makes 4 to 6 servings

This is a traditional Muslim dish from the southern state of Hyderabad, where the pieces of lamb are cooked with cracked wheat and a variety of dals (legumes) until they disintegrate. Any remaining larger pieces are deliberately mashed to make this into a creamy, porridge-like dish that is generally eaten during Ramzan (Ramadan)—the month of fasting. During this month, the Muslims fast from dawn until sunset, and eat nourishing foods only after that.

The traditional dish also calls for adding about 2 tablespoons of sizzling hot ghee before serving, a step I omit, but try it if you prefer authentic flavors.

1 cup Crispy Fried Onions (page 44)

2 tablespoons Basic Ginger-Garlic Paste (page 47 or store-bought)

1 cup cracked wheat, sorted and washed in 3 to 4 changes of water, or ²/3 cup whole wheat and ¹/3 cup rolled oats

¹/4 cup each of the following: dried yellow mung beans (dhulli mung dal), ¹/4 cup dried red lentils (dhulli masoor dal), and ¹/4 cup dried yellow split chickpeas (channa dal), each sorted and washed in 3 to 4 changes of water

2 tablespoons ghee or vegetable oil

4 black cardamom pods, crushed lightly to break the skin

2 (1-inch) sticks cinnamon, broken

3 cloves

1 pound boneless leg of lamb (see box, page 473) or beef (rump, brisket, or sirloin), all visible fat trimmed, cut into 1-inch pieces

1 tablespoon ground coriander

1 teaspoon ground cumin

¹/2 teaspoon ground turmeric

¹/4 teaspoon cayenne pepper, or to taste

1 teaspoon salt, or to taste

4 to 5 cups water

2 tablespoons minced fresh mint leaves

1. Prepare the onions and the ginger-garlic paste. Then, in a large bowl, mix together the cracked wheat and all the dals and soak in water to cover by 3 inches, about 1 hour.

2. Meanwhile, heat the ghee in a large nonstick wok or saucepan over medium-high heat and cook the cardamom pods, cinnamon, and cloves, stirring, about 1 minute. Add the lamb, ginger-garlic paste, coriander, cumin, turmeric, cayenne pepper, and salt and cook, stirring, until the lamb is well-browned, about 20 minutes.

3. Drain the soaking wheat and the dals, add them to the lamb and cook, stirring, about 5 minutes. Add the water and bring to a boil over high heat. Reduce the heat to medium-low, cover the pan, and simmer until the lamb is very soft, about 1 hour. Add more water, if necessary, or cook uncovered, until quite dry.

4. With a large fork or a spatula, mash everything until it is porridge-like in consistency. Transfer to a serving dish, mix in the fried onions, garnish with the mint leaves, and serve.

Hyderabadi Lamb with Mixed Legumes

Khichda

Makes 6 to 8 servings

Another porridge-like lamb dish, this one seems like a variation of Hyderabadi Mashed Lamb and Cracked-Wheat (above), but to the people of Hyderabad and to my friend Bharti Mahendra, whose recipe this is, it is an entirely separate dish and a great cold weather comfort food. Khichda does have subtle differences in flavor because, besides dals (legumes) with their skin on, this one also has rice.

2 tablespoons Basic Ginger-Garlic Paste (page 47 or store-bought)

1 pound boneless leg of lamb (see box, page 43) or beef (rump, brisket, or sirloin), all visible fat trimmed, cut into 1¹/2-inch pieces

3 tablespoons melted ghee or vegetable oil

³/4 pound small onions, each cut in half lengthwise and thinly sliced

6 black cardamom pods, crushed lightly
    to break the skin

2 (1-inch) sticks cinnamon

4 cloves

1/2 cup cracked wheat (bulgur)

1/2 cup long-grain white rice

2 tablespoons dried split pigeon peas (toor dal),
    sorted and washed in 3 to 4 changes of water

2 tablespoons dried split green mung beans
    (chilkae vaali mung dal), sorted and
    washed in 3 to 4 changes of water

2 tablespoons dried green lentils (saabut masoor dal),
    sorted and washed in 3 to 4 changes of water

2 tablespoons dried yellow split chickpeas (channa dal),
    sorted and washed in 3 to 4 changes of water

1/2 teaspoon cayenne pepper

1 1/2 teaspoons salt, or to taste

4 to 5 cups water

1 cup finely chopped fresh cilantro,
    including soft stems

2 tablespoons finely chopped mint leaves

1 to 2 tablespoons fresh lemon juice

1. Prepare the ginger-garlic paste. Then, in a bowl, soak the lamb in lightly salted hot water to cover about 1 hour. Drain.

2. Heat the ghee (or oil) in a large nonstick wok or saucepan over medium-high heat and cook the onions, stirring, until browned, about 20 minutes. Transfer to a bowl and reserve for garnish.

3. To the pan, add the lamb, ginger-garlic paste, cardamom pods, cinnamon, and cloves, and cook, stirring, until the lamb is well-browned, about 10 minutes. Mix in the cracked wheat, rice, dals, cayenne pepper, and salt, and stir to roast, about 5 minutes.

4. Add the water and bring to a boil over high heat. Reduce the heat to medium-low, cover the pan, and simmer until the lamb is very soft, about 1 hour. Add more water, if necessary, or cook uncovered until the dish is quite dry.

5. Mix in the cilantro, mint, and lemon juice, then, with a large fork or a spatula, mash everything until it is porridge-like in consistency. Transfer to a serving dish, sprinkle the reserved fried onions on top, and serve.

Lamb Chop and Cutlet Dishes

Fragrant Lamb Chops in Yogurt Curry
Dahi ki Yakhni Chaampein

Makes 4 to 6 servings

Here is yet another recipe from my friend Sunil Vora, a master chef and the owner of a respected Indian restaurant, The Clay Pit in Los Angeles, that defies the standard definitions of culinary terms in India—in this case, yakhni. *This is neither a saucy dish, nor does it contain any* yakhni *(meat broth), but it is still called a* yakhni. *I really can't explain why. All I can say is that its flavoring, from nutmeg, mace, asafoetida, and fennel seeds, among the many others, makes it very special. It presents beautifully on the table as an entrée. It can also be served as a first course.*

2 tablespoons vegetable oil

1/8 teaspoon ground asafoetida

1/4 teaspoon freshly ground nutmeg

1/4 teaspoon freshly ground mace

1 (1-inch) stick cinnamon, broken lengthwise

4 black cardamom pods, crushed lightly
    to break the skin

6 cloves

1/2 teaspoon black peppercorns

8 to 10 lamb rib chops (about 2 pounds),
    all visible fat trimmed

1 cup nonfat plain yogurt, whisked until smooth

2 tablespoons peeled minced fresh ginger

1 teaspoon salt, or to taste

2 teaspoons ground fennel seeds

1 teaspoon ground ginger

1/2 teaspoon garam masala

2 fresh green chile peppers, such as serrano,
    minced or cut lengthwise into thin strips

1/4 cup finely chopped fresh cilantro,
    including soft stems

1. Heat the oil in a large nonstick wok or saucepan over medium-low heat and add the asafoetida, nutmeg, and mace, then quickly add the cinnamon, cardamom pods, cloves, and black peppercorns and cook, stirring, about 1 minute.

2. Add the meat, then add the yogurt, 1 tablespoon at a time, stirring constantly until it is completely absorbed. Cook until the meat is well-browned and fork-tender, about 50 minutes. Halfway through the cooking, mix in the fresh ginger and salt.

3. When the meat is cooked, mix in the fennel seeds, ground ginger, and garam masala and cook another 10 minutes. Transfer to a serving dish, garnish with the green chile peppers and cilantro, and serve.

Mughlai Lamb Chop Curry with Almond and Poppy Seeds
Mughlai Chaamp Kari

Makes 4 to 6 servings

From the north Indian Mughlai kitchen emerges this rich and creamy dish that makes an appearance on most special occasions. I have made it somewhat lighter by using more yogurt and less cream, though traditionally it is just the opposite.

¹/₂ cup Almond and Poppy Seed Paste (page 52)
1 to 2 tablespoons Basic Ginger-Garlic Paste (page 47 or store-bought)
¹/₂ teaspoon Kashmiri Garam Masala (page 19) or garam masala
1 cup nonfat plain yogurt, whisked until smooth
¹/₄ cup heavy cream
3 tablespoons vegetable oil or ghee
4 cloves
1 (1-inch) stick cinnamon, broken
1 tablespoon ground fennel seeds
1 teaspoon cayenne pepper, or to taste
¹/₂ teaspoon ground ginger
¹/₄ teaspoon ground asafoetida
8 to 10 lamb loin chops (about 2 pounds), all visible fat trimmed
1 teaspoon salt, or to taste
1 to 1¹/₂ cups water

1. Prepare the almond-poppy seed paste, the ginger-garlic paste, and the garam masala. Then, in a small bowl, whisk together the yogurt, cream, and almond-poppy seed paste.

2. Heat the oil in a large nonstick wok or saucepan over medium-high heat and add the cloves, cinnamon, fennel, cayenne pepper, ginger, and asafoetida and stir 1 minute. Add the lamb, ginger-garlic paste, and salt and cook, stirring, over medium-high heat until the meat is browned, 10 to 12 minutes.

3. Reduce the heat to medium-low and continue to cook, adding a tablespoon of water every time the meat sticks to the bottom of the pan, until the meat is well-browned, 15 to 20 minutes.

4. Add the rest of the water and cook, stirring, over medium-high heat until the meat is fork-tender, the sauce is thick and almost clinging to the pieces, and all the oil has separated to the sides, about 20 minutes. (If the meat is not tender, add another 1 cup water, cover the pan, and simmer on low heat until soft.)

5. Mix in the whisked yogurt-cream mixture and cook over medium heat, stirring constantly, until everything is incorporated into the dish, leaving behind a thick and smooth sauce, about 5 minutes. Transfer to a serving dish, sprinkle the garam masala on top, and serve.

Parsi Lamb Chops Curry
Parsi Chaamp Kari

Makes 4 to 6 servings

This is a classic example of how different communities in India prepare the same dish. This lamb curry from the Parsi community in Mumbai (formerly Bombay) uses what's available to them—tamarind and coconuts.

1 cup Coconut Milk (page 44 or store-bought)
2 to 4 tablespoons Tamarind Paste (page 54)
¹/₂ cup coarsely chopped raw almonds
3 dried red chile peppers, such as chile de arbol, broken into pieces
1 tablespoon cumin seeds
1 tablespoon coriander seeds

1 tablespoon white poppy seeds
8 quarter-size slices peeled fresh ginger
3 large cloves garlic, coarsely chopped
8 to 10 lamb loin chops (about 2 pounds),
    all visible fat trimmed
1 large onion, coarsely chopped
1 tablespoon black peppercorns
1 (1-inch) stick cinnamon
4 whole cloves
1 to 3 fresh green chile peppers, such as serrano,
    coarsely chopped
1 teaspoon salt, or to taste
5 cups water
2 tablespoons vegetable oil
1/2 teaspoon garam masala

1. Prepare the coconut milk and tamarind paste. Then, in a spice or a coffee grinder, grind together the almonds, red chile peppers, cumin, coriander, and poppy seeds to make a fine powder. Then, in a small food processor or a blender, process together the ginger and garlic until minced. Mix in the almond-spice mixture plus up to 1/4 cup water to make a smooth paste.

2. Place the lamb in a large saucepan. Add the onion, peppercorns, cinnamon, cloves, green chile peppers, salt, and water and bring to a boil over high heat. Reduce the heat to low, cover the pan, and cook until the lamb is fork-tender, adding more water and continuing to cook, if needed, about 40 minutes. With tongs, transfer the meat to a bowl, then strain the broth into another bowl, discarding the spices.

3. In a separate large, nonstick wok or saucepan, heat the oil over medium heat and cook the ginger-almond-spice paste, stirring, until golden, about 5 minutes. Add the coconut milk and the reserved broth (if there is no broth, add about 1/2 cup water), and simmer to make a smooth sauce, about 5 minutes.

4. Mix in the lamb and the tamarind and simmer another 5 minutes to blend the flavors. Transfer to a serving dish, sprinkle the garam masala on top, and serve hot.

Milk-Simmered Rib Chops
Tabakhnat or Tabaknar

Makes 4 to 6 servings

Truly an indulgence, this unusual Kashmiri dish calls for meat to be cooked in milk. Further, it is garnished with pure silver leaves, an old tradition that is alive to this day. (These can be bought in Indian grocery stores.) As if this wasn't enough, "Try cooking it at least once in ghee, the authentic way," says Promella Dhar, who gave me this recipe. Alas, I cook it in oil— for a little less luxury but better health.

12 to 15 lamb rib chops (about 2 pounds),
    all visible fat trimmed
1 to 1 1/2 cups milk
4 whole cloves
1 (1-inch) stick cinnamon
3 black cardamom pods, lightly crushed
    to break the skin
1 tablespoon ground fennel seeds
1 teaspoon ground ginger
1/2 teaspoon salt, or to taste
1/2 cup melted ghee, mustard oil, or vegetable oil
    for pan-frying
4 to 6 silver leaves (optional)

1. Place the chops, milk, cloves, cinnamon, cardamom pods, fennel seeds, ginger, and salt in a heavy wok or saucepan (not nonstick), and bring to a boil over high heat. Reduce the heat to low, cover the pan, and cook until all the milk has been completely absorbed, the lamb is fork-tender, and all the spices cling to the chops, 20 to 25 minutes. Cool at least 1 hour.

2. Heat the ghee or oil in a large wok or skillet over medium-high heat until it registers 325°F to 350°F on a frying thermometer or until a small piece of meat dropped into the hot oil takes 15 to 20 seconds to rise to the top.

3. Standing far from the wok (to avoid splattering), use tongs to add the chops, piece by piece, adding as many as the wok will hold at a time without crowding. Pan-fry, turning them around with a slotted spatula, until they are crispy and golden.

4. Transfer to a tray lined with paper towels to drain, then transfer to a serving platter. Garnish with silver leaves and serve.

Non-Vegetarian Fare   483

Milk-Simmered, Batter-Fried Lamb Rib Chops

Kabargah

Makes 4 to 6 servings

Here is yet another rich authentic lamb rib chops recipe from Promella Dhar's Kashmiri kitchen. The chops are first cooked in a mixture of spices and milk, then dipped in a yogurt and chickpea flour mixture, then deep-fried. Coating the ribs with yogurt cheese before deep frying lends a silky smoothness to these chops.

1/2 cup Yogurt Cheese (page 42) or sour cream
1 (6- to 8-inch) piece muslin or 4 layers of cheesecloth (about 2 feet)
8 whole cloves
2 (1-inch) sticks cinnamon, broken
4 bay leaves
4 black cardamom pods, crushed lightly to break the skin
6 green cardamom pods, crushed lightly to break the skin
1 teaspoon fennel seeds
1/2 teaspoon black peppercorns
1 1/4-inch piece nutmeg
12 to 15 lamb rib chops (about 2 pounds), all visible fat trimmed
1 to 1 1/2 cups milk
1 teaspoon salt, or to taste
1/2 cup chickpea flour
1/4 cup rice flour
1 large egg white
1/2 teaspoon ground ginger
1/4 to 1/3 cup water
1 cup melted ghee, mustard oil or vegetable oil

1. Prepare the yogurt cheese. Then, in a small piece of muslin or 4 layers of folded cheesecloth, loosely tie together the cloves, cinnamon, bay leaves, black and green cardamom pods, fennel seeds, black peppercorns, and nutmeg to make a seasoning pouch.

2. Place in a heavy wok or saucepan (not nonstick) along with the rib chops, milk, and 1/2 teaspoon salt.

Bring to a boil over high heat, then reduce the heat to low, cover the pan, and cook until all the milk has been completely absorbed and the lamb is fragrant and fork-tender, 20 to 25 minutes. Cool at least 1 hour.

3. Meanwhile, in a medium mixing bowl, mix together the chickpea and rice flours, egg white, ground ginger, and the remaining 1/2 teaspoon salt, then add the water and whisk to make a smooth, semi-thick batter.

4. Heat the oil in a large wok or skillet over medium-high heat until it registers 325°F to 350°F on a frying thermometer or until a small piece of meat dropped into the hot oil takes 15 to 20 seconds to rise to the top.

5. Mix the yogurt cheese (or sour cream) with the cooked ribs to coat them, then dip each one into the batter. Using tongs, add the rib chops to the hot oil, piece by piece, standing back from the wok and adding as many as the wok will hold at a time without crowding. Deep-fry, turning them with a slotted spatula or tongs until they are crispy and golden. Transfer to a tray lined with paper towels to drain, then transfer to a serving platter and serve hot.

Citrus-Glazed Lamb Loin Chops

Phal-Ras ki Chaampein

Makes 4 to 6 servings

This is a nod to California cuisine. I've experimented with this recipe over the years and have finally come up with one that I love. Served as an entrée or as finger food, these chops are international in flavor.

2 tablespoons Basic Ginger-Garlic Paste (page 47 or store-bought)
8 to 10 lamb loin chops (about 2 1/2 pounds), all visible fat trimmed
1/4 cup fresh orange juice
3 tablespoons pineapple juice
2 tablespoons fresh lemon juice
1 teaspoon garam masala

1 teaspoon salt, or to taste

3 tablespoons peanut oil

1 teaspoon cumin seeds

$^1/_2$ teaspoon coarsely ground black pepper

2 medium onions, finely chopped

$^1/_2$ cup finely chopped fresh cilantro

1 tablespoon ground dried mint leaves

3 to 5 fresh green chile peppers, such as serrano, halved lengthwise with or without seeds

1. Prepare the ginger-garlic paste and the garam masala. Then, place the lamb chops in a large non-reactive bowl. Add the orange, pineapple and lemon juices, ginger-garlic paste, garam masala, and salt and mix well, making sure all the pieces are well-coated with the marinade. Cover with plastic wrap and marinate in the refrigerator at least 2 and up to 24 hours.

2. Heat the oil in a large nonstick skillet over medium-high heat and add the cumin seeds and black pepper; they should sizzle upon contact with the hot oil. Quickly add the onions and cook, stirring, until golden, about 7 minutes. Remove to a bowl.

3. Leaving as much of the marinade behind as you can, add the lamb chops to the skillet in a single layer and cook until well-browned on both sides, 10 to 15 minutes.

4. Add the onions and the marinade, lower the heat, cover the skillet, and simmer until the chops are tender and well-glazed with the reduced marinade, 15 to 20 minutes. Mix in the cilantro during the last 5 minutes of cooking. Transfer to a serving dish, top with the mint and green chile peppers, and serve hot.

Pan-Sautéed Lamb Chops with Rosemary

Rosemary ki Chaampein

Makes 4 to 6 servings

Rosemary is not an Indian herb. But my years in California often prompt me to sneak some into my Indian preparations, especially since it marries well with the usual Indian flavors.

1 cup Yogurt Cheese (page 42) or sour cream

2 tablespoons Basic Ginger-Garlic Paste (page 47 or store-bought)

20 to 25 black peppercorns

20 to 25 cloves

5 to 7 green cardamom pods

3 black cardamom pods, seeds only

1 tablespoon ground coriander

1 teaspoon ground cumin

$^1/_2$ teaspoon ground cinnamon

$^1/_4$ teaspoon ground nutmeg

$^1/_2$ teaspoon salt, or to taste

$^1/_4$ cup finely chopped fresh rosemary

2 tablespoons vegetable oil

8 to 10 lamb loin chops with bone (about 2$^1/_2$ pounds), trimmed of all visible fat

1 cup water

$^1/_4$ cup minced scallions, green parts only

2 to 3 sprigs of rosemary

1. Prepare the yogurt cheese and the ginger-garlic paste. Then, in a spice or coffee grinder, grind together the peppercorns, cloves, green cardamom pods, and black cardamom seeds. Remove to a small nonstick skillet and mix in the ground coriander, cumin, cinnamon, nutmeg, and salt. Roast, stirring and shaking the skillet, over medium heat until the spices are a few shades darker and fragrant, about 2 minutes.

2. In a bowl, mix together the yogurt cheese (or sour cream), ginger-garlic paste, rosemary, roasted spices, and oil.

3. Place the lamb chops in a non-reactive bowl. Add the yogurt mixture and mix well, making sure all the pieces are well-coated with the marinade. Cover with plastic wrap and marinate in the refrigerator at least 4 and up to 24 hours.

4. Leaving the marinade behind, transfer the chops to a large nonstick skillet and cook, turning once or twice over medium-high heat, until completely dry and well-browned, about 10 minutes.

5. Mix about 1 cup water to the reserved marinade and add it to the skillet. Cover and cook over medium heat until the chops are very tender with a thick sauce clinging to them, about 30 minutes. Transfer to a serving dish, garnish with scallion greens and rosemary sprigs, and serve.

Sautéed Lamb Cutlets with Fenugreek

Methi Chaampein

Makes 4 to 6 servings

Added at different stages during cooking, fenugreek—both as seeds and as leaves—lends its characteristic aroma to this dish. In this recipe I use thin leg cutlets, which cook quickly.

1/2 cup Yogurt Cheese (page 42) or sour cream
6 to 8 quarter-size slices peeled fresh ginger
2 large cloves fresh garlic, peeled
1 to 3 fresh green chile peppers, such as serrano, stemmed
2 tablespoons distilled white vinegar
2 teaspoons garam masala
1 teaspoon ground fenugreek seeds
1 teaspoon salt, or to taste
12 to 15 thin-cut lamb cutlets (about 2 pounds), all visible fat trimmed
1 tablespoon peanut oil
2 tablespoons ground dried fenugreek leaves
1 teaspoon ground paprika
1 to 2 tablespoons fresh lemon or lime juice
2 medium onions, cut in half lengthwise and thinly sliced
1/4 cup finely chopped fresh cilantro, including soft stems

1. Prepare the yogurt cheese. Then, in a food processor or a blender, process together the ginger, garlic, green chile peppers, yogurt cheese, and vinegar until smooth. Add the garam masala, ground fenugreek seeds, and salt and process again until blended.

2. Place the lamb cutlets in a large non-reactive bowl. Add the processed marinade and mix well, making sure all the lamb pieces are well-coated. Cover with plastic wrap and marinate in the refrigerator at least 4 and up to 24 hours.

3. Place the lamb and oil in a large nonstick skillet in a single layer (in 2 batches, if necessary) and cook over medium heat, about 5 minutes per side, turning once, until well-browned on both sides.

4. Sprinkle the fenugreek leaves, paprika, and lemon juice over them and cook another 2 to 3 minutes, turning once. Transfer to a bowl and keep warm.

5. Add the onions to the same skillet and cook over medium heat, stirring, until the onions are slightly wilted and completely coated with whatever spices remain in the skillet, about 3 minutes. Spread evenly on a serving platter and place the lamb cutlets over them. Garnish with cilantro and serve.

Pot-Roasted Leg of Lamb
Raan—Dum-Pukht

Makes 4 to 6 servings

Raan, *a term often used for a whole leg of goat or lamb, actually refers only to the upper thigh portion of the leg. Most people simply use the whole leg and call it a* raan, *but my friend Sunil Vora, owner of The Clay Pit restaurant in Los Angeles, insists that an authentic* raan *should be made only with the thigh portion.*

Here are other crucial raan *facts: The meat should come from baby lamb, not more than 3 months old. It should be poked, pricked, or cut thoroughly to the bone, all the fibers pounded and broken, and the meat well-loosened around the bone. These steps are of utmost importance because, once cooked, you should be able to spoon the soft-cooked meat off the bone. All this translates to a labor of love and slow roasting.*

¹/₂ cup Almond and Poppy Seed Paste, made with coconut milk (page 52)
1 recipe Basic Onion Paste (page 48)
1¹/₂ teaspoons garam masala
¹/₄ cup Crispy Fried Fresh Ginger (page 45), optional
1 (4- to 5-pound) leg of baby lamb (see box, page 473), all visible fat trimmed
1¹/₂ teaspoons garam masala
¹/₂ teaspoon ground nutmeg
¹/₂ teaspoon ground mace
¹/₂ teaspoon cayenne pepper
1¹/₂ teaspoons salt, or to taste
¹/₃ to ¹/₂ cup ghee or vegetable oil
2 (1-inch) sticks cinnamon
4 bay leaves
2 tablespoons fennel seeds
¹/₄ teaspoon ground asafoetida mixed with ¹/₂ cup water
Tomato wedges, thinly sliced scallions, fresh green chile peppers, toasted sliced almonds (optional)

1. Prepare the almond-poppy seed and the onion pastes. Prepare the fried ginger, if using. Carefully trim off the white membrane from the surface of the meat and, with a long-pronged barbecue fork or a thin knife with a pointed tip, prick it thoroughly all around to the bone, until all the fibers are broken.

2. In a bowl, mix together the onion and almond pastes, garam masala, nutmeg, mace, cayenne pepper, and salt and smear well over the surface of the meat. Then prick again to ensure that the paste penetrates inside the meat. Save any leftover seasoning mixture. Tie the meat with a string if it seems to befalling apart. Place in a large bowl, cover with plastic wrap, and marinate in the refrigerator at least 4 and up to 48 hours.

3. Place the marinated lamb in a large, heavy saucepan. In another small saucepan heat the ghee, cinnamon, bay leaves, and fennel seeds until sizzling, then pour slowly over the lamb, making sure the spices oil covers the entire surface well before settling to the bottom of the pan.

4. Cover the lamb and cook over medium heat until all the juices evaporate, about 30 minutes. Reduce the heat to low, turn the lamb over, add the reserved marinade plus ¹/₄ cup of the asafoetida-water and scrape to mix in any spices that stick to bottom of the pan.

5. Reduce the heat to low, cover the pan, and cook about 1 hour until the lamb starts to soften, adding the remaining asafoetida-water as the juices dry up.

6. Continue to cook in this manner, turning the lamb to cook each side, scraping the pan, and adding 2 to 3 tablespoons water whenever the juices dry up, until the lamb takes on a rich, well-browned color all around and becomes fork-tender, 60 to 90 minutes. (Start testing after an hour, then check every 10 minutes until the meat is soft.)

7. Transfer to a serving platter, top with the crispy fried ginger and all the other garnishes (if using), and serve.

Variation: Alternately, starting from Step 4, place the lamb in an ovenproof dish along with all the juices and scrapings (add some water to the pan to loosen the scrapings) and roast at 300°F until spoon-soft, about 2 hours.

Hyderabadi Spicy Leg of Lamb Raan with Screwpine Essence

Kevda Raan

Makes 4 to 6 servings

This fragrant leg of lamb with bold flavors often comes to the table on special occasions, garnished with silver leaves and nuts. Its royal elegance is quite striking and the desire to dig in is irresistible. Serve it family-style with any black urad bean (saabut urad dal) *dish, such as Black Urad Beans in a Slow Cooker (page 362), and naan* (oven-baked) *or* parantha *(griddle-fried) breads.*

Screwpine essence, called ruh-kewra, *has a characteristic pine tree aroma. It may be an acquired taste for those new to it, but it is a special Indian flavor. You can find it, the silver leaves, and other flavoring items for this recipe at an Indian market.*

1 (4- to 5-pound) leg of lamb (see box, page 473), trimmed of all fat
10 quarter-size slices peeled fresh ginger
6 large cloves fresh garlic, peeled
2 tablespoons fresh lemon juice
1 cup nonfat plain yogurt, whisked until smooth
1 tablespoon garam masala
1 1/2 teaspoons salt, or to taste
3 large onions, cut in half lengthwise and thinly sliced
1 tablespoon sugar
1/2 cup melted ghee or peanut oil
6 to 8 whole dried red chile peppers, such as chile de arbol
1/4 cup shelled raw almonds
3 bay leaves
1 teaspoon black cumin seeds
2 cups water
1/2 teaspoon saffron threads, soaked in 1/2 cup milk about 30 minutes
2 to 3 drops screwpine essence (ruh kewra)
1/4 cup finely chopped fresh cilantro, including soft stems
4 to 6 silver leaves
1/4 cup sliced mixed almonds and pistachios

1. Carefully trim off the white membrane from the surface of the meat and, with a long-pronged barbecue fork or a thin knife with a pointed tip, prick it all over. Then make 2-inch long deep cuts, each about 2 inches apart, over the entire surface of the lamb and place in a non-reactive pan.

2. In a food processor, process together 6 slices ginger and 4 cloves garlic until minced. Add the lemon juice, yogurt, garam masala, and salt and process again until smooth. Transfer to the lamb and rub well over the surface of the meat, making sure that it enters the cuts. Cover with plastic wrap and marinate in the refrigerator at least 4 and up to 48 hours.

3. Toss the onions with the sugar. Heat the ghee in a large nonstick wok over medium-high heat and cook the sugar-coated onions (in 2 batches if necessary), stirring, until crispy and golden, about 12 minutes per batch. With a slotted spatula, transfer to paper towels to drain. Then cook the red chile peppers, stirring, until crispy and browned, about 1 minute. Transfer to paper towels. Remove all but 1 tablespoon of the ghee from the wok.

4. In a food processor, process together half the fried onions (save the rest for garnish), the remaining 4 pieces of ginger and 2 cloves garlic, and the almonds and red chile peppers to make a smooth paste.

5. Heat the 1 tablespoon ghee that's left in the wok, stir in the bay leaves and cumin seeds, and cook about 30 seconds. Add the onion-almond paste and cook over medium heat, stirring, until the ghee separates to the sides, about 5 minutes.

6. Add the marinated lamb, leaving the marinade behind, and cook, turning as needed, until well-browned on all sides, about 1 hour. Add the marinade and the water, and bring to a boil over high heat. Reduce the heat to medium-low, cover the pan, and simmer until the lamb is soft-tender, 1 1/2 to 2 hours. (Check after 1 1/2 hours, and then every 10 minutes until it is soft.)

7. Mix in the saffron milk, screwpine essence, and cilantro, and continue to simmer until the sauce is thick and fragrant, about 20 minutes.

8. Transfer to a serving platter, garnish with the silver leaves, the reserved fried onions, and the almonds and pistachios, and serve hot.

Spinach-Stuffed Honey-Roasted Boneless Leg of Lamb

Palak Bhara Raan

Makes 6 to 8 servings

A spectacular party dish, this lamb presents beautifully because before it is served, it is cut into slices that show cross-section swirls of the greens and meat. Garnish it with a handful of roasted cherry tomatoes. Have the butcher prepare the lamb for you: Ask for the leg bone to be removed but wrapped up for you. (Save it for making soup.)

1 cup (1 recipe) Basic Onion Paste (page 48)

1 cup Yogurt Cheese (page 42), whisked until smooth, or sour cream

1 (8-ounce) package frozen spinach, thawed, with juices reserved

1/2 cup coarsely chopped mixed raw nuts, such as cashews, almonds, and pistachios

1/4 cup raisins

1 cup coarsely chopped fresh cilantro, including soft stems

31/2- to 4-pounds boned leg of lamb (about 6 pounds with bone), all visible fat trimmed, bone removed (but not discarded), and the meat butterflied (see box, page 473)

1/4 cup fresh lemon juice

2 tablespoons melted ghee or vegetable oil

11/2 teaspoons salt, or to taste

1 teaspoon ground paprika

2 tablespoons melted honey

1 teaspoon Asian sesame oil

1 tablespoon ground coriander

1 teaspoon ground cumin

1 teaspoon garam masala

1/2 teaspoon cayenne pepper

1 cup water

1. Prepare the onion paste, and yogurt cheese. Then, in a food processor, process together the spinach with all the juices, nuts, raisins, and cilantro to make a thick purée.

2. Place the lamb in a flat non-reactive baking dish. With a long-pronged barbecue fork or the pointed tip of a thin knife, prick it all over. Then make 2-inch long, deep cuts, each about 2 inches apart, over the entire outside surface of the lamb.

3. In a bowl, mix together the lemon juice, ghee, salt, and paprika and rub well over both sides of the meat, making sure you work it into all the cut sections. Spread the puréed spinach on the entire inside surface. Then roll the lamb into a log, and, with cotton kitchen string, tie the roll crosswise and lengthwise to secure it.

4. Mix together the yogurt cheese (or sour cream), onion paste, honey, sesame oil, coriander, cumin, garam masala, and cayenne pepper and rub well over the outside surface of the meat. Save any leftovers in a covered bowl in the refrigerator. Cover with plastic wrap and marinate in the refrigerator at least 12 and up to 48 hours, turning a few times.

5. Preheat the oven to 450°F. Transfer the lamb to an ovenproof dish, along with its marinade, place the reserved bone alongside it, pour the water into the pan, and roast 1 hour.

6. Reduce the heat to 300°F, baste with the reserved refrigerated marinade and roast until most of the juices evaporate, the lamb is well-browned, and becomes soft, about 1 hour.

7. Cut off and discard the string from the roast, slice the lamb into 1/2- to 1-inch slices, place on the serving platter, cover with foil, and keep warm.

8. Add about 1 cup hot water to the pan and scrape off any browned bits sticking to the pan and on the bone. Transfer the liquid to a small saucepan and bring to a quick boil over high heat. Pour some of the gravy over the lamb and the rest into a serving bowl and serve alongside. Serve hot.

Grilled Butterflied Leg of Lamb

Bhuna Raan

Makes 6 to 8 servings

This is a recipe from chef Sunil Vora in Los Angeles. Sunil sneaks in some rosemary along with the standard Indian seasonings to make this outstanding piece of meat. It is so easy to make, especially if you have your butcher remove the bone, trim the fat, and butterfly the leg of lamb. I provide grilling and broiling instructions, so you can cook it either way.

6 large cloves fresh garlic, peeled

6 to 8 quarter-size slices peeled fresh ginger

1 to 3 fresh green chile peppers, such as serrano, stemmed

1/4 cup fresh rosemary leaves

2 tablespoons fresh mint leaves

2 tablespoons fresh lemon juice

2 tablespoons melted honey

1 tablespoon garam masala

2 teaspoons ground cumin

1 teaspoon salt, or to taste

2 tablespoons peanut oil

3 1/2 to 4 pounds boned leg of lamb (about 6 pounds with bone), all visible fat trimmed, bone removed, and the meat butterflied (see box, page 473)

1 tablespoon melted unsalted butter

1 teaspoon dried mint leaves

1/2 teaspoon coarsely ground black pepper

1/2 teaspoon paprika

2 cups shredded green lettuce (any kind)

2 small tomatoes, cut in wedges

1. In a food processor, process together the garlic, ginger, green chile peppers, rosemary, and mint leaves until minced. Add the lemon juice, honey, garam masala, cumin, salt, and oil, and process again to make a smooth paste.

2. Place the lamb in a flat non-reactive baking dish. With a long-pronged barbecue fork or the pointed tip of a thin knife, prick it all over. Then make 2-inch long, deep cuts, each about 2 inches apart, over the entire outside surface of the lamb.

3. Smear the paste well over both sides of the meat, making sure to work it into the cut sections. Cover with plastic wrap and marinate in the refrigerator at least 12 and up to 48 hours, turning a few times.

4. *To grill:* Preheat the grill to medium-high (375°F to 400°F). Place the marinated lamb on the grill, open-faced with the cut (bone) side down, and cook until the bottom is browned, 15 to 20 minutes. Turn over and grill until the second side is browned, 12 to 15 minutes.

5. Fold a large sheet of aluminum foil into 3 layers, large enough to cover the lamb. Place the lamb in the foil and wrap loosely. Continue to grill, turning twice or three times, until the meat is tender and the juices run clear, about 20 to 30 minutes. (Open the wrapped lamb to check after 20 minutes, and every few minutes after that until it is done.)

To broil: Preheat the broiler. Place the marinated lamb on a roasting griddle or broiler pan with a tray underneath to catch the juices and broil, by positioning the pan in the lower-center section of the oven or broiler. Turning two or three times and baste with any juices until the meat is well-browned and tender, 40 to 50 minutes.

6. Heat the butter in a small saucepan over medium heat and add the mint and black pepper; they should sizzle upon contact with the hot oil. Remove from heat and mix in the paprika. Baste the lamb with this mixture and grill or broil another 5 minutes. Line a serving platter with chopped lettuce and tomato wedges, place the lamb on top, and serve.

Spicy Rack of Baby Lamb
Chaamp Masala

Makes 4 to 6 servings

Spicy and elegant, succulent lamb rib chops are a treat every time. And, once marinated, they're ready to eat in less time than it takes to set the table. Rack of lamb is the rib end of the loin, and each rack has about six chops. Present each rack as an individual serving, or separate into dainty chops and set them over a bed of sizzling onions and fresh green chile peppers.

1/2 cup Yogurt Cheese (page 42) or sour cream
15 to 20 raw cashews
10 to 12 green cardamom pods
2 teaspoons fenugreek seeds
2 teaspoons cumin seeds
4 large cloves garlic, peeled
8 to 10 quarter-size slices peeled fresh ginger
1 to 3 fresh green chile peppers, such as serrano, stemmed
1/2 cup fresh mint leaves
1/4 cup fresh lime or lemon juice
1 tablespoon melted ghee or vegetable oil
2 teaspoons garam masala
1 teaspoon salt, or to taste
4 to 6 racks of baby lamb (8 to 10 ounces each)
Fresh mint sprigs

1. Prepare the yogurt cheese. Then, in a spice or a coffee grinder, grind together the cashews, cardamom pods, fenugreek, and cumin seeds to make a fine powder.

2. In a food processor, process together the garlic, ginger, green chile peppers, and mint until minced. Add the yogurt cheese, lemon juice, ghee (or oil), cashew-spice mixture, garam masala, and salt and process again until smooth.

3. Place the racks of lamb in a large non-reactive dish and, with your clean fingers, coat both sides of each rack with the marinade. Cover with plastic wrap and marinate in the refrigerator at least 12 and up to 24 hours.

4. Preheat the oven to 500°F. Place the marinated racks on a heavy baking sheet and roast on the lowest shelf in the oven until the tips of the bones turn golden brown, about 10 minutes.

5. Change the oven setting to "broil." Then, reposition the racks to ensure proper cooking: With oven mitts on your hands, carefully remove the baking sheet from the bottom shelf and place it 8 to 10 inches from the broiler heating element. Broil until the lamb is very fragrant and golden-brown, about 10 minutes. Transfer to a platter, or cut the ribs apart, garnish with mint sprigs, and serve.

My California-Style Rack of Baby Lamb
Meri California ki Chaampein

Makes 4 to 6 servings

Brimming with the powerful flavors of rosemary and mellowed balsamic vinegar, along with popular Indian seasonings, this is a traditional lamb recipe with an element of surprise. Serve it with a tossed green salad and wedges of fresh naan (oven-baked bread).

1/4 cup Yogurt Cheese (page 42) or sour cream
4 large cloves garlic, peeled
6 quarter-size slices peeled fresh ginger
1 to 3 fresh green chile peppers, such as serrano, stemmed
1/4 cup fresh rosemary leaves
1/2 cup balsamic vinegar
2 tablespoons olive oil
1 tablespoon garam masala + 1/4 teaspoon for garnish
1 teaspoon ground dried fenugreek leaves
1 teaspoon salt, or to taste
4 to 6 racks of baby lamb (8 to 10 ounces each)
1/4 teaspoon garam masala
Fresh rosemary sprigs

1. Prepare the yogurt cheese. Then, in a food processor, process together everything except the lamb, ¼ teaspoon garam masala and rosemary sprigs, to make a smooth paste.

2. Place the racks of lamb in a large non-reactive dish and, with your clean fingers, coat both sides of each rack with the marinade. Cover with plastic wrap and marinate in the refrigerator at least 12 and up to 24 hours.

3. Preheat the oven to 500°F. Place the marinated racks on a heavy baking sheet and bake on the lowest shelf in the oven until the tips of the bones turn golden brown, about 10 minutes.

4. Change the oven setting to "broil." Then, reposition the racks to ensure proper cooking: Wearing oven mitts, carefully remove the baking sheet from the bottom shelf and place it 8 to 10 inches from the broiler heating element. Broil until the racks of lamb are very fragrant and golden-brown, about 10 minutes.

5. Transfer to a platter, separate the individual chops by slicing through the meaty part with a sharp knife, sprinkle the garam masala over them, garnish with rosemary sprigs, and serve.

Ground Meat and Meat Balls (Keema and Kofta)

Ground Meat with Potato Wedges
Keema-Aalu

Makes 4 to 6 servings

This soft-cooked keema *(ground meat) curry with potatoes is made throughout India, with each community adding its own unique set of flavors and spices. Serve over rice or with* chapati *(whole-wheat griddle breads). This particular recipe comes with flavors of the north.*

1 tablespoon peanut oil
3 black cardamom pods, lightly crushed to break the skin
1 (1-inch) stick cinnamon, broken lengthwise
2 bay leaves
1 teaspoon cumin seeds
2 to 3 small russet potatoes, peeled and cut into wedges
1¼ pounds ground or minced leg of lamb or top sirloin beef
1 large tomato, finely chopped
½ cup finely chopped fresh cilantro
1 tablespoon peeled minced fresh ginger
1 large clove fresh garlic, minced
1 to 3 fresh green chile peppers, such as serrano, minced with seeds
1 tablespoon ground coriander
1 teaspoon garam masala
1 teaspoon ground fenugreek seeds
¼ teaspoon ground turmeric
1 teaspoon salt, or to taste
1 cup nonfat plain yogurt, whisked until smooth
½ teaspoon ground green cardamom seeds

1. Heat the oil in a large nonstick wok or saucepan over medium-high heat and add the cardamom pods, cinnamon, bay leaves, and cumin seeds; they should sizzle upon contact with the hot oil. Quickly

add the potatoes, meat, tomato, cilantro, ginger, garlic, and green chile peppers, and stir to cook, about 10 minutes.

2. Mix in the coriander, garam masala, fenugreek seeds, turmeric, and salt and cook, stirring and breaking any lumps, over medium heat until the meat is well-browned, 10 to 15 minutes.

3. Add the yogurt, cover the pan, and cook, stirring as needed, until the potatoes are soft and the dish is well-moistened and thick, about 10 minutes. Transfer to a serving dish, mix in the cardamom seeds, and serve.

Variation: Toss in 2 to 3 cups of finely chopped fresh spinach, 1 cup thawed frozen peas, 1 cup small cauliflower florets, or any other vegetable of your choice along with the yogurt in Step 3, and cook until the vegetables are soft, another 5 to 7 minutes.

Ground Meat with Red Lentils
Keema-Dal

Makes 4 to 6 servings

This could very well be the south Indian version of chili—here, ground or minced meat gets an entirely different, somewhat starchy texture with the addition of a dal (beans, lentils, or peas). Try making it with any of the other dals, such as yellow split chickpeas or yellow and green split peas.

1/4 to 1/2 cup Coconut Milk (page 44 or store-bought)
1 cup dried red lentils (dhulli masoor dal) or split pigeon peas (toor dal), sorted and washed in 3 to 4 changes of water
1 tablespoon ground coriander
1 teaspoon garam masala + 1/4 teaspoon for garnish
1 teaspoon dried tamarind powder
1/4 teaspoon ground turmeric
1/8 teaspoon ground asafoetida
1 teaspoon salt, or to taste

2 tablespoons vegetable oil
4 to 6 dried red chile peppers, such as chile de arbol, with stems
1 teaspoon cumin seeds
1 teaspoon black mustard seeds
1/2 teaspoon fenugreek seeds
1 large onion, finely chopped
1/2 cup fresh or frozen grated coconut, or shredded unsweetened dried coconut
1 tablespoon peeled minced fresh ginger
1 large clove fresh garlic, minced
2 tablespoons minced fresh curry leaves or 1 tablespoon dried curry leaves
1 pound lean ground or minced lamb or beef
1 to 1 1/2 cups water
1/2 cup finely chopped fresh cilantro, including soft stems

1. Prepare the coconut milk. Then, in a bowl, soak the dal in water to cover by 2 inches, about 1 hour, then drain. In another bowl, mix together the coriander, 1 teaspoon garam masala, tamarind powder, turmeric, asafoetida, and salt with about 1/2 cup water to make a smooth paste.

2. Heat the oil in a large nonstick wok or saucepan over medium-high heat and cook the red chile peppers, stirring, about 30 seconds. Add the cumin, mustard seeds, and fenugreek seeds; they should splatter upon contact with the hot oil, so lower the heat and cover the pan until the splattering subsides.

3. Add the onion and cook, stirring, until softened, about 2 minutes, then mix in the coconut, ginger, garlic, and curry leaves and stir until the mixture is golden, about 5 minutes. Add the spice paste, meat, and dal and cook, stirring, until the meat is golden, about 10 minutes.

4. Add the water and bring to a boil over high heat. Reduce the heat to medium-low, cover the pan, and simmer until the dal is soft and the sauce is thick, about 10 minutes. Add the coconut milk and cilantro and simmer another 5 minutes. Transfer to a serving dish, mix in the garam masala, and serve hot.

Ground Meat with Spinach and Coconut Milk

Palak-Nariyal Doodh ka Keema

Makes 4 to 6 servings

Saag-gosht (greens and lamb) is one of the most popular combination dishes in Indian cuisine. Here, I make it with ground meat instead of the customary boneless or bone-in piece of lamb.

1/2 cup Coconut Milk (page 44 or store-bought)
1 tablespoon vegetable oil
3 black cardamom pods, lightly crushed
    to break the skin
1 (1-inch) stick cinnamon, broken lengthwise
1 teaspoon cumin seeds
1 1/4 pounds ground leg of lamb or top sirloin beef
2 medium onions, finely chopped
2 large cloves fresh garlic, minced
1 tablespoon peeled minced fresh ginger
1 to 3 fresh green chile peppers, such as serrano,
    minced with seeds
2 tablespoons finely chopped fresh curry leaves
1 tablespoon ground coriander
1 teaspoon garam masala + 1/4 teaspoon for garnish
1 teaspoon ground fenugreek seeds
1 teaspoon salt, or to taste
1 small bunch fresh spinach (8 to 10 ounces),
    trimmed, washed, and finely chopped
1/2 cup finely chopped fresh cilantro

1. Prepare the coconut milk. Then, heat the oil in a large nonstick wok or saucepan over medium-high heat and add the cardamom pods, cinnamon, and cumin seeds; they should sizzle upon contact with the hot oil. Quickly add the lamb, onions, garlic, ginger, green chile peppers, curry leaves, coriander, garam masala, fenugreek seeds, and salt and cook over medium heat, stirring and breaking up any lumps, until the meat is well-browned, 10 to 15 minutes.

2. Add the spinach and cilantro and cook, stirring, until the spinach wilts, about 3 minutes. Add the coconut milk, cover the pan, and cook, stirring as needed, until everything is well moistened and the sauce is thick, about 10 minutes. Transfer to a serving dish, sprinkle the garam masala on top, and serve.

Ground Meat with Nuts and Raisins

Maevae aur Kishmish vaala Keema

Makes 4 to 6 servings

Because cashews, pistachios, and raisins have long been considered expensive foods, this keema *dish could be considered a slightly more sophisticated ground meat dish. Certainly, it looks very elegant, but if you want even more richness and drama, swirl in a tablespoon or 2 of heavy cream or yogurt as a garnish just before serving.*

1 1/2 tablespoons Basic Ginger-Garlic Paste
    (page 47 or store-bought)
2 tablespoons peanut oil
2 (1-inch) sticks cinnamon
4 black cardamom pods, crushed lightly
    to break the skin
1/2 cup coarsely chopped raw cashews
1/2 cup shelled raw pistachios
1/2 cup nonfat plain yogurt, whisked until smooth
1/2 cup golden raisins
1 teaspoon garam masala
1/4 teaspoon freshly ground nutmeg
1 1/4 pounds ground extra lean lamb or beef
1/2 teaspoon salt, or to taste
Freshly ground black pepper, to taste
1 (15-ounce) can tomato sauce
1/2 teaspoon ground green cardamom seeds

1. Prepare the ginger-garlic paste. Then, heat the oil in a large nonstick wok or saucepan over moderate heat and cook the cinnamon, black cardamom, ginger-garlic paste, cashews, and pistachios, stirring, until golden, about 5 minutes. Add the yogurt, a little at a time, stirring constantly to prevent it from curdling, and stir until most of it is absorbed and the oil separates to the sides.

2. Add the raisins, garam masala, nutmeg, meat, salt, and black pepper and cook, stirring, about 5 minutes. Then add the tomato sauce and cook over medium-heat the first 2 to 3 minutes, then over medium heat until most of it is absorbed and the lamb is tender, about 20 minutes. Transfer to a serving dish, sprinkle the cardamom seeds on top, and serve hot.

Spicy Meat Balls
Gosht kae Kofta

Makes 4 to 6 servings

Koftas are meat or vegetable balls. This recipe, using ground meat, is about as simple as koftas can be. The meat is mixed with spices, made into balls, then the balls are deep-fried. You could make a lighter version by pan-frying them in 1 to 2 tablespoons of oil. Or, if you plan to add them to a curry sauce, cook them only in the sauce itself. Present the deep-fried and pan-fried ones as finger foods with an array of chutneys.

1 teaspoon Chaat Masala (page 20 or store-bought)
1½ pounds ground extra lean lamb or beef
1 medium onion, coarsely chopped
½ cup coarsely chopped fresh cilantro,
    including soft stems
1 to 2 dried red chile peppers such as chile de arbol,
    or fresh green chile peppers, such as serrano,
    broken
4 quarter-size slices peeled fresh ginger
1 large clove fresh garlic, peeled
1 teaspoon garam masala
½ teaspoon black peppercorns
1 teaspoon salt, or to taste
2 large egg whites
1½ to 2 cups peanut oil for deep frying

1. Prepare the chaat masala. Then, in a large nonstick pan, cook together the meat, onion, cilantro, red or green chile peppers, ginger, garlic, garam masala, black peppercorns, and salt, stirring, until all the juices evaporate, about 7 minutes.

2. Cool and transfer to a food processor, add the egg whites, and process until smooth and somewhat sticky. Keep a small bowl of water nearby. With lightly moistened clean fingers, divide the mixture into 20 to 25 portions and shape into round balls, each about 1¼-inches in diameter.

3. Heat the oil in a large wok or skillet over medium-high heat until it registers 325°F to 350°F on a frying thermometer or until a small piece of meat dropped into the hot oil takes 15 to 20 seconds to rise to the top. Place the meat balls into the hot oil,

adding as many as the wok can hold at one time without crowding, and deep-fry, turning them around with a slotted spatula until they are firm and golden, about 3 minutes.

4. Transfer to a tray lined with paper towels to drain, then transfer to a serving platter, sprinkle the chaat masala on top, and serve.

Variation: To serve as an entrée, simmer the kofta balls, either uncooked or deep-fried, in Classic Spicy Curry Sauce (page 388) until they absorb the juices and soften, about 15 minutes.

Stuffed Meat Balls in Yogurt-Cream Sauce
Gosht Kofta Korma

Makes 4 to 6 servings

Here is my lighter version of one of India's prized offerings, koftas (meat or vegetable balls), floating in a thick and fragrant nut-based yogurt sauce. To make the dish even lighter, omit the cream from the sauce.

12 to 15 blanched raw almonds (page 35)
2 tablespoons Basic Ginger-Garlic Paste
    (page 47 or store-bought)
1 teaspoon garam masala + ½ teaspoon for garnish
1 recipe Yogurt-Cream Sauce with Nuts (page 389)
2 tablespoons raisins
1 quarter-size slice peeled fresh ginger
1 fresh green chile pepper, such as serrano, stemmed
1 to 2 tablespoons fresh lemon juice
¼ teaspoon coarsely ground black pepper
1½ pounds ground extra lean lamb or beef
1 small onion, minced
1 teaspoon salt, or to taste
½ teaspoon ground green cardamom seeds
½ cup finely chopped fresh cilantro,
    including soft stems

1. Soak the almonds overnight in water to cover by 2 inches to soften them, then drain. Meanwhile, prepare the ginger-garlic paste and the garam masala. Prepare the yogurt-cream sauce the day before and refrigerate, or prepare just before cooking the koftas and leave in the pan.

2. In a small food processor, process together the almonds, raisins, ginger, green chile pepper, and lemon juice to make a coarse purée. Remove to a bowl and mix in the black pepper (and ¼ teaspoon salt, if you wish).

3. In a large bowl, mix together the meat, onion, ginger-garlic paste, 1 teaspoon garam masala, and salt. Keep a small bowl of water nearby. With lightly moistened clean fingers, divide the almond-raisin mixture into 20 to 25 portions and the meat mixture into 20 to 25 portions. Working with each portion of the meat mixture separately, flatten it to make a large patty and place one portion of the almond-raisin in the center of the patty. Then bring the edges of the patty together to enclose the stuffing, and shape into a round ball or an elongated roll. Transfer to a tray. Repeat with the remaining portions. Refrigerate until firm, about 30 minutes.

4. Preheat the oven to 400°F. Place the koftas in a single layer in a flat, ovenproof serving dish. Sprinkle the ground cardamom seeds on top, cover the dish, and bake until firm, about 20 minutes.

5. Pour the yogurt-cream sauce over the koftas, cover again, and continue to bake 20 minutes more.

Alternatively, add the koftas to the sauce in the pan and simmer about 20 minutes.

6. Remove from the oven or pan, sprinkle the garam masala and chopped cilantro on top, and serve hot.

Egg-Stuffed Meat Balls in Yogurt-Cream Sauce
Nargisi Kofta

Makes 4 to 6 servings

From the Mughlai kitchen, known for its rich and often elaborate dishes, comes this special recipe that contributes to India's reputation for a complex cuisine. This is an authentic Indian showcase of enticing aromas and contrasting colors, featuring hard-boiled eggs cloaked in a super-fragrant minced meat shell, then cut in half to reveal their vivid yellow and white

interiors against the browned meat. They look like the narcissus flower and are popularly called by their Indian name, nargis, *hence nargisi koftas.*

Serve these masterpiece koftas as you would any other meat balls: as appetizers with a green or a yogurt chutney, or float them in any curry sauce of your choice.

1 recipe Yogurt-Cream Sauce with Nuts (page 389) or Butter-Cream Sauce with Fresh Tomatoes (page 389)

1 teaspoon Basic Curry Powder (page 15 or store-bought)

9 large eggs

1 pound extra-lean ground lamb or mutton (goat)

½ cup finely chopped onion

1 large clove fresh garlic, minced

1 tablespoon peeled minced fresh ginger

1 to 3 fresh green chile peppers, minced

½ teaspoon cayenne pepper

¼ teaspoon salt, or to taste

1½ cups water

3 to 4 tablespoons dry-roasted chickpea flour (page 35)

1½ to 2 cups peanut oil for deep-frying

½ cup finely chopped fresh cilantro, including soft stems

½ teaspoon garam masala

1. Prepare the yogurt-cream sauce and the curry powder. Then, place 8 eggs in a saucepan with water to cover by 2 inches and bring to a boil over high heat. Reduce the heat to medium, cover the pan, and simmer until hard-boiled, 10 to 12 minutes. Let cool or plunge into cold water, then shell them.

2. To make the koftas: Place the lamb, onion, garlic, ginger, green chile peppers, curry powder, cayenne pepper, salt, and water in a medium saucepan and bring to a boil over high heat. Reduce the heat to medium-low, cover the pan, and simmer until the meat is tender and almost dry, about 10 minutes. Roast the chickpea flour. Then mix it into the meat and cook another 5 minutes.

3. Lightly beat the remaining egg. Transfer the cooked meat to a food processor, mix in the beaten egg, and

process to make a smooth, dough-like mixture. Keep a small bowl of water nearby. Then, with lightly moistened fingers, divide the mixture into 8 portions and flatten each one into a 4- to 5-inch round.

4. Working with 1 hard-boiled egg at a time, dip the egg in water and place in the center of the meat round. Then wrap the meat around the egg to encase the egg completely, making sure that the kofta is smooth and there are no gaps.

5. Heat the oil in a large wok or skillet over medium-high heat until it registers 325°F to 350°F on a frying thermometer or until a small piece of meat ball dropped into the hot oil takes 15 to 20 seconds to rise to the top. Add the meat balls into the hot oil, adding as many as the wok can hold at one time without crowding, and fry, turning them around with a slotted spatula, until they are firm and golden, about 3 minutes.

6. Transfer to a tray lined with paper towels to drain. Let cool. With a sharp knife dipped in hot water, carefully cut each kofta in half lengthwise and place in an ovenproof dish with the cut sides up.

7. Preheat the oven to 350°F. Transfer the sauce to the dish with the eggs, lightly mix in the cilantro, sprinkle the garam masala on top, cover the dish, and bake about 10 to 15 minutes to blend the flavors. Do not stir. Serve hot.

Kashmiri Hand-Pressed Meat Rolls in Curry Sauce
Kashmiri Lambae Koftae ki Kari

Makes 4 to 6 servings

A specialty of Kashmir, these spicy, palm-sized keema rolls, offset by the fragrant bite of shahi-jeera (black cumin), are almost an everyday fare in my friend Promella Dhar's home in New Delhi. She advises that to retain the shape of the rolls, refrigerate them about 30 minutes before adding them to the sauce.

1½ pounds ground extra lean lamb or beef
2 tablespoons mustard oil or any vegetable oil
1½ teaspoons garam masala + ¼ teaspoon for garnish
1 teaspoon cayenne pepper
1 teaspoon salt, or to taste
2½ cups water
2 black cardamom pods, crushed lightly to break the skin
1 (1-inch) stick cinnamon
3 cloves
2 teaspoons ground fennel seeds
½ teaspoon ground ginger
1½ teaspoon black cumin seeds
½ cup nonfat plain yogurt, whisked until smooth

1. Place the meat in a large bowl and mix in 1 tablespoon oil, ¾ teaspoon garam masala, ½ teaspoon cayenne pepper, and ½ teaspoon salt. Cover with plastic wrap and marinate about 1 hour.

2. Keep a small bowl of water nearby. With lightly moistened clean fingers, divide the meat mixture into 16 portions and lightly press each portion in the palm of your hand to make ragged rolls, each about 1 inch thick and 2½ inches long. Refrigerate until ready to use, at least 30 minutes.

3. In a large nonstick skillet, boil 1½ cups water, along with the cardamom pods, cinnamon, cloves, fennel seeds, and ginger, about 2 minutes. Remove from the heat and add the kofta rolls in a single layer, making sure they do not touch or overlap. Boil again, shaking the pan, until all the water evaporates and the kofta rolls are golden on all sides, 10 to 12 minutes.

4. Heat 1 tablespoon oil in a small nonstick saucepan over medium-high heat and add the cumin seeds; they should sizzle upon contact with the hot oil. Quickly transfer to the kofta pan along with the remaining ¾ teaspoon garam masala, ½ teaspoon cayenne pepper, and ½ teaspoon salt. Then stir in the yogurt, a little at a time, stirring constantly to prevent it from curdling and cook, 2 to 4 minutes.

5. Add the remaining 1 cup water and simmer until the koftas are very soft and the sauce is thick, about 10 minutes. Transfer to a serving dish, garnish with garam masala, and serve.

Ground Meat Rolls in Spicy Buttermilk Sauce

Dahi-Ras Mein Kashmiri Koftae

Makes 4 to 6 servings

Hand-pressed and flavored with an exceptional set of spices, these buttermilk-simmered kofta rolls showcase yet another example of Indian creativity. The sauce here is textured, but if you prefer it smoother, purée the browned and spiced onions in a food processor, and then proceed with the recipe.

1¹/₂ pounds extra lean ground lamb or beef
1 tablespoon ground coriander
1 teaspoon ground cumin
1 teaspoon ground ginger
1 teaspoon garam masala + ¹/₄ teaspoon for garnish
1 teaspoon cayenne pepper
¹/₂ cup finely chopped fresh cilantro,
    including soft stems
1 tablespoon peeled minced fresh ginger
1 tablespoon mustard oil or any vegetable oil
1 cup nonfat plain yogurt
2 cups water
4 quarter-size slices peeled fresh ginger
1 large clove fresh garlic, peeled
1 to 3 fresh green chile peppers, such as serrano,
    stemmed
¹/₄ teaspoon ground cloves
¹/₄ teaspoon ground cinnamon
¹/₈ teaspoon ground asafoetida
1 teaspoon salt, or to taste
2 tablespoons melted ghee
1 large onion, cut in half lengthwise and thinly sliced
1 teaspoon black cumin seeds
1 teaspoon white poppy seeds
1 tablespoon ground unsweetened dried coconut
1 teaspoon ground fennel seeds

1. Place the meat in a large bowl and mix in the coriander, cumin, ground ginger, 1 teaspoon garam masala, cayenne pepper, cilantro, minced fresh ginger, oil, and ¹/₂ cup yogurt. Cover and marinate about 1 hour.

2. With lightly moistened clean fingers, divide the meat mixture into 16 portions and lightly press each portion in the palm of your hand to make ragged rolls, each about 1 inch thick and 2¹/₂ inches long. Refrigerate until ready to use, at least 30 minutes.

3. In a blender, blend together the remaining ¹/₂ cup yogurt, water, sliced fresh ginger, garlic, green chile peppers, cloves, cinnamon, asafoetida, and salt to make a spicy buttermilk.

4. Heat the ghee in a large nonstick skillet over medium-high heat and cook the onion, stirring, until browned, about 7 minutes. Add the cumin and poppy seeds; they should sizzle upon contact with the hot oil. Quickly add the coconut and fennel seeds and stir until fragrant, about 2 minutes.

5. Add the spicy buttermilk and bring to a quick boil over high heat. Remove from the heat and add the kofta rolls in a single layer, making sure that they do not touch or overlap. Boil again, shaking the pan, until the buttermilk is absorbed, the kofta rolls are well-browned, and the sauce is very thick, 15 to 20 minutes. Transfer to a serving dish, sprinkle the garam masala on top, and serve.

Kashmiri Meat Balls in Red Paprika Sauce

Rishta Kari

Makes 4 to 6 servings

Smooth and plump, these koftas *are another favorite from the Kashmiri kitchen in northern India. The brilliant paprika-red sauce is generally very hot, but can be made milder to suit your taste.*

1 tablespoon ground ginger
1 tablespoon ground fennel seeds
1 teaspoon garam masala + 1/4 teaspoon for garnish
1 teaspoon ground cumin
1/2 teaspoon cayenne pepper
1/2 teaspoon ground black cardamom seeds
1 teaspoon salt, or to taste
1 1/2 pounds extra lean ground lamb or beef
4 quarter-size slices peeled fresh ginger
4 cups water
1 (1-inch) stick cinnamon
4 cloves
6 green cardamom pods, crushed lightly
    to break the skin
4 black cardamom pods, crushed lightly
    to break the skin
3 tablespoons vegetable oil
1 large onion, cut in half lengthwise and thinly sliced
1/8 teaspoon ground asafoetida
1 teaspoon ground paprika

1. In a small bowl, mix together the ground ginger, fennel seeds, 1 teaspoon garam masala, cumin, cayenne pepper, cardamom seeds, and salt.

2. In a food processor, process together the lamb, fresh ginger, and 1 tablespoon of the spice mixture until smooth. Have a small bowl of water nearby. With lightly moistened clean fingers, divide and shape the meat mixture into 16 balls, each about 1 1/4 inches in diameter. Refrigerate until ready to use, at least 30 minutes.

3. In a large wok or a saucepan, bring the water, cinnamon, cloves, and green and black cardamom pods to a boil over high heat. Reduce the heat to medium, add the meat balls, and simmer until firm, about 10 minutes. Remove the meat balls to a bowl and reserve the broth with the whole spices.

4. Heat the oil in another large nonstick wok or saucepan over medium-high heat and cook the onion until well-browned, about 10 minutes. Remove to a small food processor and process with about 1/4 cup of the broth to make a smooth paste.

5. To the wok, add the asafoetida and paprika, then mix in the meat balls and the remaining spice mixture and cook, stirring, until the meat balls are lightly browned, about 10 minutes.

6. Mix in the onion paste and all the remaining broth (plus the whole spices) and bring to a boil over high heat. Reduce the heat to medium-low, cover the pan, and simmer until the meat balls are very tender and the sauce is thick, about 20 minutes. Transfer to a serving dish, sprinkle the garam masala on top, and serve.

Yogurt-Braised Meat Balls

Gushtaaba Kari

Makes 4 to 6 servings

Gushtaaba *are really large, silky-smooth meat balls that are braised in a delicate yogurt sauce. Authentic* gushtaaba *balls are made by pounding the meat on a stone slab reserved for cooking until all the fibers are completely broken and the meat is reduced to a soft, creamy pulp. With ground ginger, fennel and black cardamom seeds as the main flavorings, this dish is really special.*

1 tablespoon ground ginger
1 tablespoon ground fennel seeds
1 teaspoon ground black cardamom seeds
1 teaspoon salt, or to taste
1½ pounds extra lean ground lamb or beef
4 cups water
3 tablespoons ghee or vegetable oil
1 small onion, cut in half lengthwise and thinly sliced
2 cups nonfat plain yogurt, whisked until smooth
2 tablespoons finely chopped fresh mint leaves

1. In a small bowl, mix together the ground ginger, fennel, cardamom seeds, and salt.

2. In a food processor, process together the lamb and 1 tablespoon of the spice mixture until smooth. Have a small bowl of water nearby. With lightly moistened clean fingers, divide the meat mixture into 8 to 10 portions and shape each portion into a round ball, about 2 inches in diameter. Refrigerate until ready to use, at least 30 minutes.

3. Place the meat balls in a large saucepan with the water and bring to a boil over high heat. Reduce the heat to medium-low, cover the pan, and simmer, turning the meat balls a few times, until firm, about 20 minutes.

4. Heat the ghee in a large nonstick wok or saucepan over medium-high heat and cook the onion, stirring, until browned, about 7 minutes.

5. Transfer the onion to a blender, add the yogurt and the remaining spice mixture, and blend until smooth. Return the yogurt mixtures to the wok and bring to a boil over high heat, stirring constantly to prevent curdling. Reduce the heat to medium-low and cook, stirring, until the sauce browns, about 10 minutes.

6. Add the meat balls and any broth from the pan and cook, turning occasionally, until the meat balls have absorbed the sauce and are very soft, and the sauce is thick, about 15 minutes. Transfer to a serving dish and lightly mix in the mint, with parts of it visible as a garnish. Serve hot.

Regional Meat Specialties

These are dishes that feature lamb, goat, pork, and beef that are enjoyed mostly in the regions they were developed, and not as well known in the rest of India.

Kerala Lamb Chile-Fry with Vinegar
Kerals Gosht Chilly-Fry

Makes 4 to 6 servings

A "chile-fry" is a savory, sour, chile-fired Kerala specialty. It is often cooked in coconut oil, but I find that a spoonful of Asian sesame oil mixed with peanut oil yields a far superior flavor, not to mention less saturated fat.

2 tablespoons peanut oil
1 teaspoon Asian sesame oil
7 to 10 dried red chile peppers, such as chile de arbol, with stems
3 small onions, cut in half lengthwise and thinly sliced
2 (1-inch) pieces of fresh ginger, peeled and cut into thin matchsticks
2 pounds boneless leg of lamb (see box, page 473) or beef (rump, brisket, or sirloin), all visible fat trimmed, cut into 1½-inch pieces
¼ cup minced fresh curry leaves
1 teaspoon minced fresh garlic
½ teaspoon freshly ground black pepper, or to taste
1 cup finely chopped fresh cilantro, including soft stems
¼ cup distilled white vinegar
1 cup water
1 teaspoon salt, or to taste
1 tablespoon sesame seeds, dry-roasted (page 35)

1. Heat both the oils in a large nonstick pan over medium heat cook the red chile peppers until golden, about 1 minute.

2. Add the onions and ginger and cook, stirring, until browned, about 10 minutes. Add the lamb, curry leaves, garlic, and black pepper and cook, stirring, until golden, about 10 minutes.

3. Mix in the cilantro (save some for garnish), vinegar, water, and salt. Cook over high heat until it comes to a boil, then over medium-low heat until the lamb pieces are tender, all the liquid evaporates, and the oil separates to the sides. Meanwhile, roast the sesame seeds. When the lamb is done, transfer it to a serving dish, sprinkle the sesame seeds and reserved cilantro on top, and serve hot.

Kerala Lamb Curry with Coconut Milk
Kerala Gosht-Nariyal Doodh

Makes 4 to 6 servings

A profusion of spicy-hot and delectable flavors, with asafoetida, curry leaves, and coconut milk adding their unique punch, is why this Kerala-style lamb curry is a popular favorite.

1/2 cup Coconut Milk (page 44 or store-bought)
1 large onion, coarsely chopped
2 to 3 large cloves fresh garlic, peeled
5 quarter-size slices peeled fresh ginger
1/2 cup coarsely chopped fresh cilantro,
    including soft stems
1/4 cup coarsely chopped fresh curry leaves
1 to 3 fresh green chile peppers, such as serrano,
    stemmed
1 large tomato, coarsely chopped
1 teaspoon garam masala + 1/4 teaspoon for garnish
1/2 teaspoon cayenne pepper
1/4 teaspoon ground turmeric
1 teaspoon salt, or to taste
1/8 teaspoon ground asafoetida
2 tablespoons peanut oil
5 to 7 whole dried red chile peppers,
    such as chile de arbol
6 green cardamom pods, crushed lightly
    to break the skin
1 teaspoon black peppercorns (optional)
1 teaspoon cumin seeds
1 teaspoon black mustard seeds
2 pounds boneless leg of lamb (see box, page 473)
    or beef (rump, brisket, or sirloin), all visible fat
    trimmed, cut into 1 1/2-inch pieces
3 to 4 cups water
1/4 cup finely chopped fresh cilantro,
    including soft stems

1. Prepare the coconut milk. Then, in a food processor, process together the onion, ginger, garlic, cilantro, curry leaves, and green chile peppers until minced. Add the tomato, 1 teaspoon garam masala, cayenne pepper, turmeric, salt, and asafoetida, and process again to make a smooth paste.

2. Heat the oil in a large nonstick wok or saucepan over medium-high heat and cook the red chile peppers, cardamom pods, and black peppercorns, if using, about 1 minute. Add the cumin and mustard seeds; they should splatter upon contact with the hot oil, so lower the heat and cover the pan until the splattering subsides.

3. Add the lamb and cook, turning, until browned, about 15 minutes. Add the processed paste and continue to cook, over moderately heat for the first 3 to 5 minutes and then over medium-low heat until the pieces are well-browned and traces of oil are visible on the sides of the pan, about 15 minutes.

4. Add the water, cover the pan, and simmer until the lamb is tender and the sauce is as thick or thin as you desire, 30 seconds to 40 minutes. When the lamb is tender, add the coconut milk and simmer about 5 minutes to blend the flavors. Transfer to a serving dish, garnish with the cilantro and garam masala, and serve.

Coorgi Pork Curry
Pandi Curry

Makes 4 to 6 servings

This recipe was given to me by Raghu Nanjappa, who was born in Coorg, India by birth, but is American by choice. He returns home several times a year, to visit his family, but also for the food. Coorg, a lush green and picturesque district in southwest India, is the home of Indian coffee plantations, sandalwood, wildlife sanctuaries, and spices, including black peppercorns and green cardamom.

Pork, a meat not eaten in most parts of India, is very popular in Coorg (and in Goa), where no celebration is complete without a dish like this.

½ cup Coconut Milk (page 44 or store-bought)

¼ cup Tamarind Paste (page 54)

2 dried red chile peppers, such as chile de arbol, broken into pieces

¼ cup coriander seeds

1 tablespoon cumin seeds

2 teaspoons black mustard seeds

1 teaspoon black peppercorns

½ teaspoon ground turmeric

¼ teaspoon cinnamon

¼ teaspoon ground nutmeg

1 teaspoon salt, or to taste

1 small onion, coarsely chopped

6 quarter-size slices peeled fresh ginger

3 large cloves fresh garlic, peeled

1 fresh green chile pepper, such as serrano, stemmed

2 tablespoons peanut oil

1 large onion, finely chopped

1½ pounds boneless pork, such as fresh ham, all visible fat trimmed and cut into 1-inch pieces

1 to 2 cups water

2 tablespoons finely chopped cilantro

1. Prepare the coconut milk and tamarind paste. Then, place the red chile peppers, coriander, cumin, mustard seeds, and black peppercorns in a small, preferably cast-iron, skillet and roast, stirring and shaking the pan, over medium heat until the seeds are a few shades darker, about 2 minutes. Let cool, then grind in a spice or a coffee grinder to make a fine powder. Mix in the turmeric, cinnamon, nutmeg, and salt.

2. In a food processor or a blender, process together the small onion, ginger, garlic, green chile pepper, coconut milk, and tamarind paste until smooth. Mix in the roasted spice mixture and process again, adding up to ¼ cup water, if necessary, to make a smooth paste.

3. Heat the oil in a large nonstick wok or saucepan over moderately heat and cook the large chopped onion, stirring, until browned, about 10 minutes. Add the onion–coconut milk paste and cook, stirring, until golden, about 10 minutes.

4. Add the pork and cook, stirring, until browned, about 15 minutes. Add the water and bring to a boil

over high heat. Reduce the heat to medium-low, cover the pan, and simmer until the pork is fork-tender and the sauce is very thick, about 30 minutes. Transfer to a serving dish, sprinkle the cilantro on top, and serve.

Spicy Goa-Style Lamb Curry
Vindaloo Gosht

Makes 4 to 6 servings

Vindaloo, *meaning "with vinegar," is a savory sauce special to Goa, on the west coast. Vindaloo curries are always very hot; you couldn't possibly make them mild because it all starts by soaking dried red chile peppers in vinegar and then grinding them with other ingredients. So warn your guests!*

6 to 8 dried red chile peppers, such as chile de arbol, broken into pieces

¼ cup distilled white vinegar

3 large cloves garlic, peeled

6 to 8 quarter-size slices peeled fresh ginger

1 large onion, coarsely chopped

1 tablespoon ground cumin

2 teaspoons ground mustard seeds

2 teaspoons garam masala + ½ teaspoon for garnish

1 teaspoon salt, or to taste

½ teaspoon ground turmeric

2 pounds boneless lamb, all visible fat trimmed, and cut into 2-inch pieces

2 to 3 tablespoons peanut oil

30 to 40 finely chopped fresh curry leaves (optional)

1 (15½-ounce) can tomato sauce

2 to 3 cups water

1. Soak the red chile peppers in the vinegar, 1 to 2 hours. Then, in a food processor or a blender, process together the chile peppers plus the vinegar, garlic, ginger, and onion until fine. Mix in the cumin, mustard, 2 teaspoons garam masala, salt, and turmeric, and process again to make a smooth paste.

2. Place the lamb pieces in a large non-reactive bowl. Add the chili-onion-spice paste and mix well, making sure all the pieces are well-coated with the marinade. Cover with plastic wrap and marinate in the refrigerator at least 4 and up to 24 hours.

3. Heat the oil in a large nonstick saucepan over medium-high heat, add the curry leaves and the lamb, plus all the marinade, and cook, stirring, over high heat the first 3 to 5 minutes and then over medium-low heat until the pieces are well-browned, 10 to 12 minutes.

4. Add the tomato sauce and water and cook until the lamb is tender and the sauce thick, about 40 minutes. Transfer to a serving dish, garnish with garam masala, and serve.

Variation: To mellow the peppery heat and to increase the quantity of the dish, add 2 to 3 peeled and diced potatoes along with the lamb in Step 3, then proceed with the recipe.

Spicy Goa-Style Pork Curry
Pork Vindaloo

Makes 6 to 8 servings

This spicy hot dish comes to mind when our thoughts drift to the coastal town of Goa. Of course, there are many other Goan specialties, but this one seems to be an all-time stand-out. Made with malt vinegar (available in specialty food stores and well-stocked supermarkets), dry-roasted red chile peppers, and a touch of sugar, this dish truly says "Goa."

2 pounds boneless leg of pork, all visible fat trimmed, cut into 1-inch pieces
$^1/_2$ cup distilled white vinegar, mixed in 1$^1/_2$ cups hot water
2 tablespoons Basic Ginger-Garlic Paste (page 47 or store-bought)
$^1/_2$ cup malt vinegar
1 tablespoon ground black mustard seeds
1$^1/_2$ tablespoons ground coriander
1 teaspoon ground cumin
1 teaspoon garam masala
$^1/_2$ teaspoon cinnamon
$^1/_2$ to 1 teaspoon cayenne pepper, or to taste
$^1/_2$ teaspoon ground turmeric
1 teaspoon sugar
1 teaspoon salt, or to taste
2 tablespoons mustard or peanut oil
5 dried red chile peppers, such as chile de arbol, with stems
1 large onion, cut in half lengthwise and thinly sliced
1 (1-inch) piece fresh ginger, peeled and cut into thin matchsticks
1 large clove fresh garlic, minced
4 to 5 cups water
2 tablespoons finely chopped fresh cilantro
Freshly ground black pepper, to taste

1. Soak the pork in the vinegar-water solution about 10 minutes. Drain well and place in a large non-reactive bowl. Discard the vinegar-water.

2. Prepare the ginger-garlic paste. Then, in a small bowl, mix together the malt vinegar, ginger-garlic paste, mustard seeds, coriander, cumin, garam masala, cinnamon, cayenne pepper, turmeric, sugar, and salt. Add to the pork and mix well, making sure all the pieces are well covered with the marinade. Cover with plastic wrap and marinate in the refrigerator at least 4 and up to 24 hours.

3. Heat the oil in a large nonstick wok or saucepan over medium-high heat and add the red chile peppers, then the onion, ginger, and garlic, and cook, stirring, until browned, about 7 minutes. Add the marinated pork, plus all the marinade, and cook, stirring, until traces of oil are visible on the sides of the pan, about 30 minutes.

4. Add the water and bring to boil over high heat. Cover the pan and cook over medium-low heat until the pork is fork-tender and the sauce thick, 1½ hours. (Add more water, if necessary.) Transfer to a serving dish, garnish with cilantro and black pepper, and serve.

Variation: To balance the chile pepper heat, mix in 1 large peeled and diced potato during the last 30 minutes of cooking.

Rosita's Goan Pork Curry

Pork Buffat

Makes 4 to 6 servings

This recipe was given to me by Rosita Da Costa Dighe, a Goan by birth and today a resident of Los Angeles. According to her husband, Ajit, Rosita is the best Goan home cook in town. Here's just one of her specialties. The addition of wine to the recipe comes from Goa's Portuguese heritage.

6 to 8 dried red chile peppers, such as chile de arbol, broken into pieces

1 (1-inch) stick cinnamon, crushed to break into small pieces

10 to 12 black peppercorns

1 1/2 teaspoons black mustard seeds

1 teaspoon coriander seeds

1 teaspoon cumin seeds

2 pounds boneless pork, such as fresh ham, all visible fat trimmed and cut in half 1/2-inch pieces

2 cups water

2 medium onions, finely chopped

1 to 3 fresh green chile peppers, such as serrano, minced with seeds

1 tablespoon peeled minced fresh ginger

3 large cloves fresh garlic, minced

1 1/2 teaspoons ground turmeric

1 teaspoon salt, or to taste

1 tablespoon red wine vinegar

2 tablespoons dry red wine (any kind)

1/4 cup finely chopped fresh cilantro, including soft stems

1. In a spice or a coffee grinder, grind together the red chile peppers, cinnamon, black peppercorns, mustard seeds, coriander, and cumin to make as fine a powder as possible.

2. Place everything except the vinegar, red wine, and cilantro in a large saucepan and bring to a boil over high heat. Reduce the heat to low, cover the pan, and simmer, stirring occasionally, until the meat is fork-tender, about 1 hour. (If the meat isn't tender, add up to 1 cup more water and cook until the meat is fork-tender.)

3. Mix in the vinegar and wine and simmer another 10 to 15 minutes to blend the flavors. Transfer to a serving dish, garnish with the cilantro, and serve.

Variation: For a richer dish, mix in 1/2 to 1 cup Coconut Milk (page 44 or store-bought) during the last 10 minutes of cooking.

Goan Beef Curry

Beef Shakuti

Makes 4 to 6 servings

To this day, after living in Los Angeles for more than 20 years, my friend Rosita Da Costa Dighe is still nostalgic for her mother's beef shakuti. *Her long search for any* shakuti masala *blend that remotely resembled the one she grew up eating led her to only one conclusion: She just had to make her own. This is her best reproduction. Try it with lamb, mutton, pork, or chicken, if you like.*

2 tablespoons Basic Garlic Paste (page 47 or store-bought)

1 teaspoon Basic Ginger Paste (page 46 or store-bought)

1 1/2 pounds boneless top sirloin steak, all visible fat trimmed and cut into 1 1/2-inch pieces

1 teaspoon salt, or to taste

1 1/2 cups grated fresh or frozen coconut

1/2 cup Coconut Milk (page 44 or store-bought)

6 dried red chile peppers, such as chile de arbol, broken into pieces

8 whole cloves

4 to 6 pieces star anise, crushed to break into small pieces

2 (1-inch) sticks cinnamon, crushed to break into small pieces

8 to 10 black peppercorns

1 tablespoon coriander seeds

1 1/2 teaspoons white poppy seeds

1 1/2 teaspoons cumin seeds

2 tablespoons peanut oil

3 cups water

2 tablespoons red wine vinegar

2 tablespoons red wine (any kind)

Freshly ground black pepper, to taste

1. Prepare the garlic and the ginger pastes. Then, place the meat in a medium non-reactive dish. Add the garlic and ginger pastes and salt, and mix well, making sure all the pieces are well-coated with the marinade. Cover with plastic wrap and marinate in the refrigerator at least 4 and up to 24 hours.

2. Prepare the coconut milk. In a nonstick skillet, dry-roast the coconut over medium heat, stirring and shaking the skillet, until just golden, 2 to 3 minutes. Transfer to a spice or coffee grinder and grind (in 2 batches, if needed) to make it as fine as possible. Transfer to a bowl.

3. To the same skillet, add the red chile peppers, cloves, star anise, cinnamon, black peppercorns, and coriander, white poppy, and cumin seeds, and dry-roast over medium heat until fragrant, about 2 minutes. Transfer to a spice or coffee grinder and grind to make them as fine as possible. Mix into the coconut.

4. Heat the oil in a large nonstick wok or saucepan over medium-high heat and cook the coconut-spice mixture, stirring, about 3 minutes, then add the beef pieces and continue to stir until the beef pieces are golden, about 15 minutes.

5. Add the water and bring to a boil over high heat. Reduce the heat to medium-low, cover the pan, and simmer until the pieces are tender and the sauce is thick, 30 to 35 minutes.

6. Mix in the coconut milk, vinegar, and wine and simmer another 10 to 15 minutes to blend the flavors. Transfer to a serving dish, sprinkle the black pepper on top, and serve.

Kashmiri Slow-Cooked Spicy Lamb Curry

Rogan-Josh

Makes 6 to 8 servings

Unique to the famed northern valleys of Kashmir and now popular all over the world via Indian restaurants, this outstanding lamb curry comes from

a native Kashmiri, my friend Promella Dhar. Rogan means "paint with" and josh *is "anger," a word normally associated with the color red, which, in this recipe, comes from the cayenne pepper, as well as the prolonged roasting that is a must in all* rogan-josh *recipes. This recipe is spicy-hot. For a milder dish, use part or all paprika in place of the cayenne pepper.*

8 to 10 lamb chops (about 2¹/₂ pounds), all visible fat trimmed
¹/₂ cup nonfat plain yogurt, whisked until smooth
2 teaspoons cayenne pepper, or to taste
1 teaspoon salt, or to taste
¹/₂ teaspoon Kashmiri Garam Masala (page 19)
3 tablespoons mustard or vegetable oil
2 teaspoons black cumin seeds
3 whole cloves
2 black cardamom pods, crushed lightly to break the skin
1 (1-inch) stick cinnamon
1 tablespoon ground fennel seeds
¹/₂ teaspoon ground ginger
1 teaspoon sugar
1 to 1¹/₂ cups water

1. Place the lamb in a large non-reactive bowl. Add the yogurt, 1 teaspoon cayenne pepper, and salt and mix well, making sure all the pieces are well-coated with the marinade. Cover and marinate in the refrigerator at least 4 and up to 24 hours. Meanwhile, prepare the garam masala.

2. Heat the oil in a large nonstick wok or saucepan over medium-high heat and cook the cumin, cloves, cardamom pods, and cinnamon about 1 minute. Add the marinated lamb, plus all the marinade, and cook, stirring, over high heat the first 5 minutes, then over medium-low heat until the meat is well-browned and the yogurt completely absorbed, 25 to 30 minutes.

3. Add the remaining 1 teaspoon cayenne pepper, ground fennel, ginger, and sugar, and continue to cook, adding a tablespoon of water every time the meat sticks to the bottom of the pan, 10 to 15 minutes.

4. Add the water, cover the pan, and cook over medium-high heat, stirring occasionally, until the meat is tender, the sauce is thick and almost clinging to the pieces, and all the oil has separated to the sides, about 20 minutes. (If the meat is not tender, add about ½ cup more water, cover the pan, and simmer on low heat until soft.) Meanwhile, prepare the garam masala. Then spoon out all excess oil from the pan, transfer the meat and curry to a serving dish, garnish with the garam masala, and serve.

Kashmiri Lamb Curry with Saffron
Kashmiri Zaffrani Gosht

Makes 4 to 6 servings

This simple curry with Kashmiri flavors also comes from my friend Promella Dhar. This one does not call for any marinating. Instead, the meat is slow-cooked until tender.

Its true flavors come from the last-minute addition of saffron-cream and the mustard oil, but if you can't find mustard oil, use vegetable oil (minus 2 teaspoons) and mix in about 2 teaspoons of melted ghee. The flavor will be different, but equally good.

¼ to ½ teaspoon saffron threads
¼ cup heavy cream
3 tablespoons mustard oil
3 whole cloves
1 (1-inch) stick cinnamon
¼ teaspoon ground asafoetida
2 pounds boneless lamb loin chops, all visible fat trimmed and cut into 1½-inch pieces
1 tablespoon ground fennel seeds
1 teaspoon cayenne pepper
½ teaspoon ground ginger
1 teaspoon salt, or to taste
1 cup nonfat plain yogurt, whisked until smooth
1 to 1½ cups water
¼ teaspoon garam masala

1. In a small bowl, soak the saffron threads in the cream about 30 minutes, or until needed.

2. Heat the oil in a large nonstick wok or saucepan over medium-high heat and add the cloves, cinnamon, and asafoetida, then add the lamb, fennel, cayenne pepper, ginger, and salt. Add the yogurt, a little at a time, stirring constantly to prevent it from curdling, and cook over medium-high heat, stirring, until all the yogurt is absorbed and the meat starts to brown, 15 to 20 minutes.

3. Reduce the heat to medium and continue to cook, adding a tablespoon of water every time the meat gets sticks to the bottom of the pan, until the meat is well-browned, about 20 minutes.

4. Add the water and cook over medium-high heat, stirring, until the meat is fork-tender, the sauce is thick and almost clinging to the pieces, and all the oil has separated to the sides, 10 to 15 minutes. (If the meat is not tender, add about ½ cup more water, cover the pan, and simmer on low heat until soft.) Spoon out all the excess oil, transfer to a serving dish, add the saffron-cream, and swirl lightly to mix, with parts of it visible as a garnish. Sprinkle the garam masala on top and serve.

Kashmiri Lamb Curry with Turnips
Shabdegh

Makes 6 to 8 servings

Shab *means night, and* degh *is short for* degchi *or* pan, *and this authentic dish, called* shabdegh *in Hindi, is supposed to be simmered all night in a pan over the dying embers of a coal-burning stove (*chulha *or* angeethi). *Today, this translates to: for optimum flavor, this dish should be cooked long and slow over very low heat.*

Along with the slow cooking and maturing of spicy flavors, it is turnips—whole baby turnips or quartered larger ones—that are the indispensable ingredient in this dish.

3 tablespoons melted ghee or vegetable oil

1 small onion, cut in half lengthwise and thinly sliced

2½ pounds mixed lamb rib chops and boneless leg of lamb (see box, page 473) or beef (rump, brisket, or sirloin), all visible fat trimmed, cut into 1½-inch pieces

1 large onion, finely chopped

⅛ teaspoon ground asafoetida

1 teaspoon garam masala

½ to 1 teaspoon cayenne pepper

½ teaspoon ground turmeric

1 teaspoon salt, or to taste

2 tablespoons peeled minced fresh ginger

1 tablespoon ground fennel seeds

1 tablespoon ground coriander

1 teaspoon dried mango powder

1 teaspoon sugar

1½ cups nonfat plain yogurt, whisked until smooth

3 to 4 cups water

1 pound baby turnips, trimmed and left whole or halved lengthwise

¼ cup finely chopped fresh cilantro, including soft stems

½ teaspoon saffron mixed in 2 tablespoons milk

1. Heat the ghee in a large nonstick saucepan over medium-high heat and cook the sliced onion, stirring, until golden, about 5 minutes. Remove from the pan and reserve for garnish.

2. To the pan add the lamb, chopped onion, asafoetida, garam masala, cayenne pepper, turmeric, and salt and cook, stirring, over low heat until the lamb is well-browned, about 25 minutes.

3. Add the ginger, fennel seeds, coriander, mango powder, and sugar and stir another 7 to 10 minutes, adding 1 to 2 tablespoons of water if the meat sticks to the pan. Add the yogurt, a few tablespoons at a time, stirring constantly and letting the first bit dry before adding more, until all of it is absorbed, about 30 minutes.

4. Mix in the water, cover the pan, and simmer about 1½ hours over low heat until the meat is fork-tender and the sauce is thick. Add the turnips during the last 20 to 30 minutes of cooking, to give them enough time to soften.

5. When the turnips are soft, scatter the reserved fried onions, cilantro, and saffron milk on top. Cover and cook over low heat about 15 minutes to blend the flavors. Serve.

Flattened Lamb Strips in Fragrant Yogurt Curry
Dahi-Pasindae

Makes 4 to 6 servings

Pasindae, *or pasandae as they are often called, are strips of boneless mutton (goat) or lamb that are pounded with a meat mallet to break the fibers and flatten them to an even thickness. As a result, they present differently and cook much faster than the customary large pieces of meat. This recipe, from my friend Sunil Vora, is a Mughlai piece de resistance.*

2 pounds boneless leg of lamb (see box, page 473) or beef (rump, brisket, or sirloin), all visible fat trimmed

1½ cups nonfat plain yogurt, whisked until smooth

2 tablespoons ghee or vegetable oil

8 tablespoons peeled minced fresh ginger

2 (1-inch) sticks cinnamon

4 black cardamom pods, crushed lightly to break the skin

2 teaspoons ground fennel seeds

1 teaspoon salt, or to taste

⅛ teaspoon ground asafoetida mixed in 2 tablespoons water

1 tablespoon ground coriander

1 teaspoon ground cumin

1 teaspoon garam masala

½ teaspoon freshly ground black pepper, or to taste

1. On a cutting board, cut the lamb into 4-by-2-inch strips, each about ¼-inch thick. Cover the strips with plastic wrap, then, with the flat side of the meat mallet, pound each strip until they are about 6-by-3-inches and an even ⅛-inch thickness. Transfer to a large nonstick saucepan.

2. In a medium bowl, mix together the yogurt, ghee (or oil), ginger, cinnamon, cardamom pods, fennel

seeds, and salt and add to the pan with the meat. Mix well, making sure all the pieces are well-coated with the mixture. Cover and allow to marinate at room temperature about 30 minutes, but not more than 1 hour. (If keeping for a longer period, refrigerate the meat.)

3. Place the pan over high heat and cook, stirring, until it comes to a boil. Reduce the heat to medium, cover the pan, and cook until the juices evaporate and the meat is quite tender, 20 to 25 minutes.

4. Add the asafoetida-water a little at a time, and cook, stirring, over medium heat until the meat is well-browned and very soft, 15 to 20 minutes.

5. Add the coriander, cumin, and garam masala and stir about 5 minutes to blend the flavors. Transfer to a serving dish, sprinkle the black pepper on top, and serve.

Stuffed Rolled Lamb Strips in Spicy Cream Sauce

Bharvaan Pasindae Masalaedar

Makes 4 to 6 servings

For this dish, flattened lamb pieces (pasindae) *serve as wrappers. They are filled with a spicy meat and hard-boiled egg mixture, then rolled and cooked in a fragrant yogurt sauce. For a silky smoothness in the stuffing, use cream as I do in this recipe, but, if you are watching your fat intake, use yogurt. Purists also call for cream in the sauce, but I don't think it's necessary.*

1/2 teaspoon Kashmiri Garam Masala (page 19)
1/4 cup heavy cream, or nonfat plain yogurt, whisked until smooth
1/4 cup chopped raw cashews
1/4 cup shelled chopped raw almonds
1 large clove fresh garlic, peeled
1 tablespoon peeled minced fresh ginger
1/4 cup finely chopped fresh cilantro, including soft stems

1 fresh green chile pepper, such as serrano, minced
2 teaspoons ground dried pomegranate seeds
1/2 teaspoon garam masala
2 large eggs
2 pounds boneless leg of lamb (see box, page 473) or beef (rump, brisket, or sirloin), all visible fat trimmed
2 tablespoons peanut oil
1 cup nonfat plain yogurt, whisked until smooth
1 cup water
2 teaspoons dry-roasted and coarsely ground cumin seeds (page 35)
1/8 teaspoon ground asafoetida
1 teaspoon salt, or to taste
1 to 2 tablespoons fresh lemon juice
1/4 cup grated cheddar cheese

1. Prepare the Kashmiri garam masala. In a bowl, mix together the cream (or yogurt), cashews, almonds, garlic, ginger, cilantro, green chile pepper, pomegranate seeds, and garam masala and set aside at least 30 minutes to allow the nuts to soften.

2. Meanwhile, in a small saucepan, place the eggs in water to cover by 2 inches and bring to a boil over high heat. Reduce the heat to medium, cover the pan and simmer until hard-boiled, 10 to 12 minutes. Let cool or plunge into cold water, shell them, then mash the eggs with a fork.

3. Cut the lamb into 4-by-2-inch strips, each about 1/4-inch thick. Cover the strips with plastic wrap, then, with the flat side of the meat mallet, pound each strip until they are about 6-by-3-inches and an even 1/8-inch thickness. Trim the edges to make them into rectangles, then mince all trimmed meat (about 1/4 cup) in a food processor or chop finely with a knife.

4. Transfer the cream-nut mixture to a food processor and process to make a smooth paste. Place all the meat trimmings and the cream-nut paste in a small skillet and cook over medium heat, stirring, until golden, about 5 minutes. Remove from the heat and mix in the mashed eggs.

5. Divide the mixture into as many portions as there are meat pieces. Working with each flattened piece of

meat separately, place the filling evenly along the length of it, leaving a ½ inch at both ends. Then roll tightly and tie the roll with cotton kitchen string to secure.

6. Place the rolls in a single layer in a large nonstick skillet (in two batches if necessary). Drizzle the oil over them and cook over medium heat, turning, until well-browned, about 10 minutes.

7. In a bowl, whisk together the yogurt, water, cumin, asafoetida, and salt and add to the skillet. Bring to a boil over high heat. Reduce the heat to medium-low, cover the pan, and simmer until the rolls are fork-tender and the sauce is clinging to the rolls, about 20 minutes.

8. Sprinkle the lemon juice and Kashmiri garam masala on top, and cook, gently shaking the pan but not stirring, about 5 minutes. Transfer to a serving platter, cut into smaller pieces if you wish, top with the cheese, and serve.

Meat Broth Lamb Curry
Gosht Yakhni Kari

Makes 4 to 6 servings

The word yakhni *means "meat broth." However, there is also a signature Kashmiri dish called* yakhni, *not because it is soupy or cooked in meat broth, but because a broth is created—the lamb is first boiled in water until tender and then cooked.*

This particular dish is white, with no onion, garlic, tomatoes, or turmeric—the classic additions to any meat recipe elsewhere in India. Yet it abounds in flavor.

Traditionally, no fat is trimmed off the meat—something that makes sense in northern Kashmir's cold climate. I prefer this healthier alternative from my friend Promella Dhar.

2½ pounds leg of lamb (see box, page 473), or beef (rump, brisket, or sirloin), all visible fat trimmed, the bone separated (but saved) and the meat cut into 2-inch pieces
6 cups water
2 tablespoons ground fennel seeds
1½ teaspoons ground ginger
10 cloves
1 (1-inch) stick cinnamon, broken lengthwise
4 black cardamom pods, crushed lightly
 to break the skin
1 teaspoon salt, or to taste
1 cup nonfat plain yogurt, whisked until smooth
1 tablespoon mustard or vegetable oil
1 teaspoon black cumin seeds
1 teaspoon cumin seeds
1 teaspoon garam masala
2 tablespoons finely chopped fresh cilantro

1. Place the lamb and the bone, water, fennel seeds, ginger, cloves, cinnamon, cardamom pods, and salt in a large nonstick pan and bring to a boil over high heat. Reduce the heat to low, cover the pan, and cook until all the water has been absorbed and the meat is very tender, 50 to 60 minutes. (If the meat is not tender, add up to 1 cup more water and cook until soft.)

2. Mix in the yogurt, a little at a time, stirring constantly to prevent it from curdling, until it is absorbed. Remove the pan from the heat.

3. Heat the oil in a small nonstick saucepan over medium-high heat and add both kinds of cumin seeds; they should sizzle upon contact with the hot oil. Quickly add the garam masala, then mix the spices and oil into the meat and cook, stirring, over medium heat, about 10 minutes to blend the flavors. Transfer to a serving dish, garnish with the cilantro, and serve.

Fish and Shellfish

Geographically, one half of India is a peninsula, with an entire ocean (the Indian Ocean) and a bay (the Bay of Bengal) named after it. The major water link for the other half of the country is the Ganges, a behemoth of a river system that keeps most of the northern and eastern parts of India well-watered. Most of the remaining country is also well-traversed by rivers and streams, and is dotted with small lakes. It's no wonder, then, that the harvest from these waters plays an important role in the lives and the cuisine of India's people.

Despite all this, India has never been known for its seafood. However, of late I've noticed the rising popularity of Indian or Indian-inspired seafood dishes—in upscale restaurants in America and elsewhere, in Indian restaurants, and in the kitchens of adventurous home cooks.

Although there are different fish and shellfish found in Indian waters than in the rest of the world, most of the fish in American fish markets are comparable to Indian varieties, and most take well to Indian flavors. All the recipes in this chapter are made with varieties of fish that are easy to find, such as shrimp, sea bass, halibut, and salmon. You can make northern-Indian favorites such as Pan-Fried Fish Fillets with Ajwain Seeds (page 520), the western-style Spicy Goan Shrimp Curry (page 515); Fish with Bengali 5-Spices from the east (page 523); and Cochin Coconut Shrimp with Tomatoes from the south (page 511).

A few things to remember about preparing fish: Do not overcook, use a gentle hand if stirring or, if possible, don't stir at all or the delicate fish flesh might fall apart. When making fish curries, simply shake or swirl the pan to mix everything. When pan-frying, carefully pick up the pieces with a spatula to turn them over but not more than twice.

Shrimp Dishes

Pan-Fried Shrimp
Bhunni Jhinga

Makes 4 to 6 servings

Quick cooking and really tasty, these shrimp make lovely finger foods or can be presented with a meal.

2 tablespoons Basic Ginger-Garlic Paste (page 47 or store-bought)
16 to 20 fresh or frozen (thawed) jumbo shrimp (11 to 15 per pound), shelled and deveined, with tails intact
$1/2$ teaspoon coarsely ground ajwain seeds
$1/2$ teaspoon cayenne pepper, or to taste
$1/4$ teaspoon coarsely ground black pepper, or to taste
$1/2$ teaspoon salt, or to taste
2 tablespoons fresh lime juice
1 tablespoon vegetable oil
2 cups shredded lettuce, such as green or red leaf
Lime wedges

1. Prepare the ginger-garlic paste. Then place the shrimp in a large non-reactive bowl. Add all the remaining ingredients (except the lettuce and lime wedges) and mix well, making sure all the shrimp are well-coated with the marinade. Cover with plastic wrap and marinate in the refrigerator 1 to 4 hours.

2. Heat a nonstick skillet over medium high heat. Transfer the shrimp, one by one, to the skillet and cook, turning as needed, until pink and opaque, 6 to 8 minutes.

3. Line a platter with shredded lettuce, transfer the shrimp to the platter, and serve with lime wedges on the side.

Variation: Instead of pan-cooking, thread the shrimp on skewers and grill over medium-high (375°F to 400°F) heat until lightly charred and opaque, about 4 minutes.

Spicy Grilled Shrimp

Bhunni Jhinga Masala

Makes 4 to 6 servings

Marinated in a simple fresh purée of oil, ginger, garlic, and green chile peppers, shrimp cooked this way are almost universally appealing. Serve the shrimp right away so they don't get tough and rubbery as they cool.

2 tablespoons Gujarati Green Paste (page 48)

16 to 20 fresh jumbo shrimp (11 to 15 per pound), shelled and deveined, with tails intact

2 tablespoons fresh lemon juice

$^1/_2$ teaspoon salt, or to taste

4 to 5 metal skewers or wooden skewers soaked in water 30 minutes

2 cups shredded lettuce, such as green or red leaf

1. Prepare the masala paste. Then put the shrimp in a large non-reactive bowl. Add the masala paste, lemon juice, and salt and mix until all the shrimp are well-coated with the marinade. Cover and marinate at least 2 and up to 24 hours in the refrigerator.

2. Preheat the grill to medium-high (375°F to 400°F). Line a serving platter with the lettuce. Thread the shrimp on the skewers and grill 3 to 4 minutes per side, turning once, until lightly charred and opaque. Transfer to the serving platter. Serve hot.

Cochin Coconut Shrimp with Tomatoes

Jhinga Nariyal-Tamatar

Makes 4 to 6 servings

This delicately flavored dish was prepared for me by the chef at a restaurant in the city of Cochin. Located along the southwestern coast of India, where seafood and coconut palms abound, the city is well known, understandably, for shrimp and coconut dishes.

$^1/_2$ cup Coconut Milk (page 44 or store-bought)

2 medium tomatoes, coarsely chopped

4 quarter-size slices peeled fresh ginger

2 large cloves fresh garlic, peeled

2 bay leaves

$^1/_2$ teaspoon garam masala

$^1/_2$ cup water

1 small onion, coarsely chopped

1 to 2 fresh green chile peppers, such as serrano, stemmed

2 tablespoons any vegetable oil

1 tablespoon ground fresh or frozen or unsweetened dried coconut

16 to 20 fresh jumbo shrimp (11 to 15 per pound), shelled and deveined, with tails intact

1 tablespoon ground coriander

$^1/_2$ cup nonfat plain yogurt blended with $^1/_2$ cup water

1 teaspoon salt, or to taste

$^1/_4$ cup finely chopped fresh cilantro, including soft stems

1. Place the tomatoes, ginger, 1 clove garlic, bay leaves, garam masala, and water in a medium saucepan, cover, and bring to a boil over high heat. Reduce the heat to medium-low and cook until the tomatoes are soft and very mushy, about 7 minutes. Let cool, then discard the bay leaves and pass through a food mill, or process everything in a food processor or blender until smooth.

2. In the clean work bowl of a food processor or a blender, process together the onion, the remaining 1 clove garlic, and the green chile peppers until minced. Transfer to a large nonstick wok or saucepan and cook over medium heat, stirring, until most of the juices evaporate, about 2 minutes.

3. Add the oil and the ground coconut, reduce the heat to medium-low, and continue to cook, stirring and turning the onion mixture, until well-browned, about 10 minutes. (Do not cook quickly on high heat; the onion will burn and will not develop a rich flavor.)

4. Add the shrimp and coriander, stir about 2 minutes, then mix in the coconut milk, yogurt-water mixture, and salt and bring to a quick boil over high heat. Reduce the heat to low and simmer until the shrimp are pink and opaque and the sauce is thick and creamy, about 7 minutes. Mix in the cilantro during the last 2 minutes of cooking and serve hot.

Marinated Shrimp with Green Mangoes and Bell Peppers

Jhinga Kairi-Shimla Mirch

Makes 4 to 6 servings

Green—unripe, tart—mangoes add their fruity piquancy, and bell peppers their sweetness resulting in a lovely refreshing and balanced dish.

1 large green mango, peeled and cut into
　　1/2-inch pieces
1 small onion, coarsely chopped
4 quarter-size slices peeled fresh ginger
2 large cloves fresh garlic, peeled
1 cup coarsely chopped fresh cilantro,
　　including soft stems
16 to 20 fresh jumbo shrimp (11 to 15 per pound),
　　shelled and deveined, with tails intact
1/2 teaspoon ajwain seeds
1/4 teaspoon cayenne pepper, or to taste
1 teaspoon salt, or to taste
3 tablespoons vegetable oil
2 small onions, cut in half lengthwise and thinly sliced
2 small bell peppers (1 red, 1 yellow), finely chopped
1 tablespoon ground coriander
1 teaspoon dried fenugreek leaves
1 cup canned tomato sauce
1/4 teaspoon garam masala

1. In a food processor or blender, process together ¼ cup mango, onion, ginger, garlic, and ½ cup cilantro to make a smooth paste. Add the ajwain seeds, cayenne pepper, and ¼ teaspoon salt and process again.

2. Place the shrimp in a non-reactive bowl. Add the processed paste and mix well, making sure all the pieces are well-coated with the marinade. Cover with plastic wrap and marinate in the refrigerator at least 1 and up to 24 hours.

3. Meanwhile, heat 2 tablespoons oil in a large non-stick wok or saucepan and cook the onions, stirring, until golden, about 5 minutes. Add the bell peppers and the remaining mango and stir about 3 minutes.

4. Add the coriander, fenugreek leaves, and the remaining salt, mix in the canned tomato sauce and cook, stirring, about 2 minutes. Remove from the heat.

5. Heat the remaining 1 tablespoon oil in a large nonstick skillet over medium-high heat and cook the shrimp plus the marinade, stirring, until the shrimp are pink and opaque and almost dry, about 7 minutes. Mix into the sauce, add the remaining ½ cup cilantro, and cook another 2 minutes to blend the flavors. Transfer to a serving dish, sprinkle the garam masala on top, and serve hot.

Kerala Shrimp Chile-Fry

Kerala ki Jhinga Masala

Makes 4 to 6 servings

I had a version of this dish at a wonderful restaurant in Cochin, in the southwestern state of Kerala. Made to order, it could be hot or mild, with bell pepper and tomato, with tamarind or vinegar, with a touch of cream or with coconut milk. My group tried some of each—because it was all so fresh and delicious, we were all craving more.

　　This recipe is one of the variations we tried. It's a simple dish full of fresh flavors. Up the chiles, if you like it hot.

2 tablespoons Basic Ginger-Garlic Paste
　　(page 47 or store-bought)
16 to 20 fresh jumbo shrimp (11 to 15 per pound),
　　shelled and deveined, with tails intact
1/2 teaspoon hot red pepper flakes, or to taste
1 1/2 tablespoons ground coriander
1/4 teaspoon ground turmeric
2 tablespoons minced fresh curry leaves
2 tablespoons coconut or peanut oil
1 large onion, finely chopped
1 to 3 fresh green chile peppers, such as serrano,
　　minced with seeds
1/2 teaspoon garam masala
1 teaspoon ground cumin
1 large tomato, finely chopped
1 small green bell pepper, cut into 1/2-inch pieces
2 tablespoons fresh lime juice, or more to taste
2 tablespoons finely chopped fresh cilantro

1. Prepare the ginger-garlic paste. Place the shrimp in a medium non-reactive bowl, add 1 tablespoon ginger-garlic paste, the hot pepper flakes, coriander, turmeric, and 1 tablespoon curry leaves and mix well. Cover with plastic wrap and marinate the shrimp at least 1 and up to 24 hours in the refrigerator.

2. Heat the oil in a large nonstick wok or saucepan over medium-high heat and cook the onion, stirring, until golden, about 5 minutes. Mix in the remaining ginger-garlic paste, the green chile peppers, and the remaining curry leaves and cook, continuing to stir, about 1 minute.

3. Add the garam masala and cumin, then mix in the tomato and bell pepper and cook until all the juices evaporate and the bell pepper is soft, about 5 minutes.

4. Add the marinated shrimp plus the marinade, and cook, stirring, until the shrimp are pink and opaque, about 7 minutes. Mix in the lemon juice and cilantro. Transfer to a serving dish and serve hot.

Butterflied Sesame Shrimp
Til Jhinga

Makes 4 to 6 servings

As in much of the world, when Indians say "prawns," they often mean shrimp, especially jumbo shrimp, which is what I use in this recipe. You can also use the same number of fresh tiger prawns, which look like a cross between shrimp and lobster.

2 teaspoons white sesame seeds, dry-roasted
    (page 35)
1 tablespoon Basic Ginger-Garlic Paste
    (page 47 or store-bought)
16 to 20 fresh jumbo shrimp (11 to 15 per pound),
    shelled and deveined, with tails intact
3 tablespoons nonfat plain yogurt,
    whisked until smooth
1 tablespoon Asian sesame oil
1 tablespoon fresh lemon juice
1 tablespoon white sesame seeds, coarsely ground
1 teaspoon garam masala
1 teaspoon ground dried fenugreek leaves
1/4 teaspoon coarsely ground ajwain seeds
1/2 teaspoon salt, or to taste

2 small firm tomatoes, cut into 6 wedges each
1 to 2 fresh green chile peppers, such as serrano,
    thinly sliced on the diagonal
2 to 3 scallions, green parts only, finely chopped

1. Roast the sesame seeds and prepare the ginger-garlic paste. In each shrimp, make a slit by running the tip of a knife along the back curve, then opening them a bit, taking care that you do not cut right through.

2. In a large non-reactive bowl, mix together the yogurt, sesame oil, lemon juice, ginger-garlic paste, sesame seeds, garam masala, fenugreek leaves, ajwain seeds, and salt. Add the shrimp and mix well, making sure all the shrimp are well-coated with the mixture. Cover with plastic wrap and marinate the shrimp at least 1 and up to 24 hours in the refrigerator.

3. Heat a large nonstick skillet over medium-high heat. Then, with a slotted spoon, transfer each shrimp to the skillet, leaving behind the marinade, and cook, pressing gently with a spatula to flatten them. Turn as needed until the shrimp are golden on both sides and opaque, 3 to 5 minutes. Alternately, thread on metal skewers (or wood skewers soaked in water 30 minutes) and grill on a medium-hot (375°F to 400°F) grill until golden. Transfer to a serving platter.

4. In the same skillet, lightly cook the tomatoes, stirring lightly and shaking the pan, until just softened, about 30 seconds. Add the green chile peppers and scallions and stir about 1 minute. Scatter over the shrimp as a garnish. Top with the dry-roasted sesame seeds and serve hot.

Tangy Shrimp with Fresh Mint Leaves
Jhinga Kokum-Pudina

Makes 4 to 6 servings

The surprise smoky and tart flavor in this dish comes from the kokum *(a dried sour fruit of the mangosteen-oil tree). If you can't find* kokum *(available in Indian markets) or prefer not to use it, use Tamarind Paste (page 54) instead.*

1 tablespoon Basic Ginger-Garlic Paste
(page 47 or store-bought)

1 cup Coconut Milk (page 44 or store-bought)

3 pieces dried kokum halves or about 2 tablespoons
Tamarind Paste (page 54)

2 tablespoons coconut or vegetable oil

1 (1-inch) piece peeled fresh ginger,
cut into thin matchsticks

10 to 15 fresh curry leaves

1 to 3 fresh green chile peppers, such as serrano,
minced with seeds

1 large tomato, finely chopped

1 tablespoon ground coriander

1/4 teaspoon ground turmeric

1/4 cup minced fresh curry leaves

1/4 teaspoon salt, or to taste

16 to 20 fresh jumbo shrimp (11 to 15 per pound),
shelled and deveined, with tails intact

2 tablespoons minced fresh mint leaves

1. Prepare the ginger-garlic paste and the coconut milk. Wash the kokum halves well, chop finely and soak the pieces in 1 cup hot water about 30 minutes. Drain and reserve the water. Or, mix the tamarind paste with 1 cup water.

2. Heat the oil in a large nonstick wok or saucepan over medium-high heat and cook the ginger matchsticks until golden, about 1 minute. Mix in the ginger-garlic paste, curry leaves, and green chile peppers and cook over medium-low heat, stirring, about 1 minute.

3. Mix in the tomato, coriander, turmeric, soaked kokum pieces (or tamarind mixture), curry leaves, and salt, and stir about 5 minutes. Add the shrimp and cook, turning once or twice, about 1 minute, then add the reserved kokum water (if not using tamarind), and bring to a boil over high heat. Reduce the heat to medium-low, cover the pan, and simmer until the shrimp are pink and opaque and the juices are almost dry, about 7 minutes.

4. Mix in the coconut milk and cook about 2 minutes. Transfer to a serving dish, mix in the mint leaves, and serve.

Coconut Chutney Shrimp

Jhinga Nariyal Chutni

Makes 4 to 6 servings

This is a saucy shrimp dish that comes with a complex set of flavors. Serve it with rice or Indian breads. To serve as part of a finger-foods buffet, don't add any water and make a thick sauce that clings to each shrimp.

1/2 cup Hazram's Coconut-Tamarind Chutney
with Mint (page 61)

1 tablespoon Tamarind Paste (page 54)

1/4 cup Coconut Milk (page 44 or store-bought)

2 tablespoons vegetable oil

1 (1-inch) stick cinnamon

4 black cardamom pods, crushed lightly
to break the skin

1 medium onion, finely chopped

1 large tomato, finely chopped

1 tablespoon ground coriander

1/2 cup nonfat plain yogurt, whisked until smooth

1 to 1 1/2 cups water

16 to 20 fresh jumbo shrimp (11 to 15 per pound),
shelled and deveined, with tails intact

1/4 cup finely chopped fresh cilantro

1. Prepare the coconut chutney, tamarind paste, and coconut milk. Then heat the oil in a large nonstick wok or saucepan over medium-high heat and cook the cinnamon and cardamom pods, stirring, until fragrant, 1 minute. Add the onion and cook, stirring again, until lightly browned, about 5 minutes.

2. Add the coconut chutney, tomato, and tamarind paste and stir until fragrant, about 5 minutes. Add the coriander, stir 1 minute, then add the yogurt, a little at a time, stirring constantly to prevent it from curdling. Cook until most of the yogurt is absorbed into the sauce, about 5 minutes.

3. Add the coconut milk and water, cover the pan, and simmer, about 2 minutes. Add the shrimp and cook until they are pink and opaque and the sauce is thick, about 7 minutes. Transfer to a serving dish, mix in the cilantro, and serve.

Spicy Goan Shrimp Curry

Jhinga Vindaloo

Makes 4 to 6 servings

Keep your taste buds tingling with this spicy curry from Goa. The Goans serve this dish with steamed basmati *rice, which mellows the heat somewhat, but people in the North eat it with* chapatis *(whole-wheat griddle breads) and a side of a* raita *(seasoned yogurt).*

5 to 7 large cloves fresh garlic, peeled
6 quarter-size slices peeled fresh ginger
25 to 30 fresh curry leaves
2 teaspoons ground cumin
1^1/$_2$ teaspoon hot red pepper flakes, or to taste
1^1/$_2$ teaspoons ground black mustard seeds
1^1/$_2$ teaspoons garam masala + ^{1}/$_2$ teaspoon for garnish
1 teaspoon salt, or to taste
1 teaspoon sugar
^{3}/$_4$ teaspoon ground turmeric
^{1}/$_4$ cup distilled white vinegar
2 large tomatoes, coarsely chopped
2 to 3 tablespoons peanut oil
2 (1-inch) sticks cinnamon
2 bay leaves
1 large onion, cut in half lengthwise and thinly sliced
25 to 30 fresh extra-large shrimp (16 to 20 per pound), shelled and deveined, with tails removed
2 tablespoons finely chopped fresh cilantro

1. In a food processor or a blender, process together the garlic, ginger, curry leaves, cumin, red pepper flakes, mustard seeds, garam masala, salt, sugar, and turmeric with the vinegar to make a fine paste. Transfer to a bowl. Then process the tomatoes until puréed.

2. Heat the oil in a large nonstick saucepan over medium-high heat and cook the cinnamon and bay leaves, stirring, about 30 seconds. Add the onion and cook until browned, about 7 minutes. Mix in the spicy vinegar paste and cook, stirring, over low heat until the masala is browned and the oil separates to the sides, about 10 minutes.

3. Add the puréed tomatoes and cook until most of the juices evaporate and the sauce becomes thick, about 10 minutes. Add the shrimp to the pan and cook until they are pink and opaque, about 7 minutes. Mix in the cilantro during the last 2 minutes of cooking. Transfer to a serving bowl, sprinkle the garam masala on top, and serve.

Variation: For a saucy dish, mix in about 1 cup water during the last 5 minutes of cooking and bring to a boil over high heat. Reduce the heat to medium-low, cover the pan, and simmer a few minutes before serving. Or add about ^{1}/$_2$ cup red wine, as my friend Rosita Dighe from Goa does.

Shrimp Curry with Chayote

Jhinga-Chow-Chow Kari

Makes 4 to 6 servings

This classic saucy dish is a perennial favorite with rice. It can also be watchfully stir-fried over high heat to make a crisp and dry shrimp dish (without much water added), and served with an array of Indian breads.

Chayote (also called mirliton in the southern United States) are small, pear-shaped squash. Substitute any summer squash if you like.

2 tablespoons vegetable oil
1 teaspoon black mustard seeds
3 chayote, peeled and cut into 1-inch pieces
^{1}/$_4$ teaspoon ground turmeric
^{1}/$_2$ teaspoon salt, or to taste
^{1}/$_2$ to 1 cup water
25 to 30 fresh large shrimp (21 to 30 per pound), shelled and deveined, with tails removed
8 to 10 fresh curry leaves (or 1 teaspoon dried)
1 teaspoon cayenne pepper, or to taste
^{1}/$_8$ teaspoon ground asafoetida
^{1}/$_4$ cup finely chopped fresh cilantro, including soft stems

1. Heat the oil in a large nonstick saucepan over medium-high heat, and add the mustard seeds; they should splatter upon contact with the hot oil, so cover the pan until the splattering subsides.

Non-Vegetarian Fare   515

2. Quickly add the chayote, turmeric, salt, and ½ cup water, cover the skillet, and cook, stirring as needed, until the chayote is tender but not mushy, 7 to 10 minutes.

3. Add the shrimp, curry leaves, cayenne pepper, and asafoetida and cook, stirring, until the shrimp are pink and opaque, about 7 minutes. Press some of the chayote along the sides of the pan. For a saucier dish, add the remaining water and simmer about 2 minutes. Transfer to a serving dish, mix in the cilantro, and serve.

Naina's Crab Curry
Naina ki Kekda Kari

Makes 4 to 6 servings

My friend Naina Kapadia makes this curry for her family and a small group of selected friends for special occasions only, because, she says, "It's too much work." Work it is, but most of it is in the cleaning. The crabs themselves cook in less than 15 minutes.

The curry is made with whole crabs, cut up. If you can get them, start with live crabs, have them cleaned and cut before you bring them home, and cook them within hours of buying. Otherwise, use frozen crabs. The recipe calls for a lot of chile peppers, so reduce the number if you prefer a milder dish.

4 Dungeness crabs, about 1¼ pounds each
1½ pounds Roma tomatoes, coarsely chopped
6 to 8 large cloves fresh garlic, peeled
6 to 10 fresh green chile peppers, such as serrano, stemmed
1½ cups coarsely chopped fresh cilantro, including soft stems
3 to 4 tablespoons vegetable oil
2 tablespoons chickpea flour
1 tablespoon ground cumin
1 teaspoon freshly ground black pepper, or to taste
½ teaspoon ground turmeric
1 teaspoon salt, or to taste

1. If not already cleaned, clean the crabs well, taking care to reach every hidden joint with a small steel brush. Then separate the legs from the body and cut the body into 2- to 3-inch pieces.

2. In a blender or a food processor, process together the tomatoes, garlic, green chile peppers, and cilantro until as smooth as possible.

3. Heat the oil in a large saucepan over medium-high heat and cook the chickpea flour, stirring, until golden, about 1 minute. Then add the cumin, black pepper, and turmeric and stir about 1 minute.

4. Add the processed tomato mixture, the crab pieces, and the salt and bring to a boil over high heat. Reduce the heat to medium-low, cover the pan, and simmer until the sauce is medium-thick (like a stew) and the oil floats to the top, about 15 minutes. Transfer to a serving bowl and serve hot.

Fried, Grilled, and Baked Fish

Sohini's Fast and Easy Indian Tuna

Tuna Masala

Makes 2 servings

When canned tuna was on sale and the grad student stipend hadn't arrived yet, this is what got my Santa Monica friend Sohini Baliga through college. Sohini says she often ate this tuna straight out of the pan, standing over the stove, pondering life.

Sohini made it for me to try, and I must admit, it was good. I'm sure even a grad student's finicky mother would not fault it.

1 teaspoon oil
1 teaspoon black mustard seeds
1 tablespoon peeled minced fresh ginger
5 to 7 fresh green curry leaves
1 can white chunk tuna packed in water, drained
1/2 teaspoon salt, or to taste
1 tablespoon finely chopped fresh cilantro,
    including soft stems

1. Heat the oil in small nonstick skillet over medium-high heat and add the mustard seeds; they should splatter upon contact with the hot oil, so cover the pan until the splattering subsides.

2. Quickly add the ginger and curry leaves, cook 1 minute, then add the tuna and salt and cook, stirring, another minute. Transfer to a serving dish, garnish with the cilantro, and serve.

Vinegar-Poached Fish with Fresh Curry Leaves

Khatti Macchi

Makes 4 to 6 servings

Cloaked with lightly crushed fresh curry leaves, then poached in a spicy vinegar broth, and served on a bed of fresh tomatoes, this is a complex but intriguing dish. The curry leaves in this dish are meant only to add flavor; take most of the dull green leaves out before serving.

This unusual recipe has been with me for a long time. As a kid, I used to see my friend's mother make this, and because it was so different, the idea stayed with me.

2 tablespoons vegetable oil
1 1/2 teaspoons ground black mustard seeds
1 large onion, cut in half lengthwise and thinly sliced
1 large tomato, finely chopped
1 to 3 fresh green chile peppers, such as serrano,
    minced with seeds
1 1/2 to 2 pounds any firm white fish fillets,
    such as sea bass, halibut, cod, or swordfish,
    about 3/4-inch thick, cut into 2-inch pieces
1/4 teaspoon coarsely ground ajwain seeds
1/2 teaspoon salt, or to taste
1/2 cup fresh curry leaves, coarsely crumpled
1 cup water
2 tablespoons distilled white vinegar
1/2 teaspoon garam masala

1. Heat the oil in a large nonstick wok or saucepan over medium-high heat and add the mustard seeds; they should sizzle upon contact with the hot oil. Quickly add the onion and cook, stirring, 2 minutes.

2. Add the tomato and the green chile peppers. In a bowl, toss the fish pieces with ajwain seeds and salt, then place them over the tomatoes. Cover the fish well with the curry leaves. Then add the water and vinegar, cover the pan, and cook over medium-high heat the first 2 to 3 minutes and then over medium heat until the fish is flaky and opaque inside, 7 to 10 minutes.

3. Remove most of the curry leaves and discard. Transfer the fish to a serving dish, sprinkle the garam masala on top, and serve.

Grilled Sea Bass

Bhunni Sea-Bass Macchi

Makes 4 to 6 servings

One of the few varieties of fish that withstand the extreme heat of the tandoor *is sea bass. It has begun to appear more and more frequently in Indian restaurants. Cooking fish this way can be recreated at home on the grill. Make sure the fillets you choose are ¾ to 1 inch thick or they will fall apart when cooked.*

2 tablespoons Coconut Milk (page 44 or store-bought)
1½ tablespoons Basic Ginger-Garlic Paste (page 47 or store-bought)
1 teaspoon Chaat Masala (page 20 or store-bought)
3 tablespoons fresh lime or lemon juice
2 teaspoons ground cumin
1 teaspoon coarsely crushed ajwain seeds
1 teaspoon ground paprika
1 teaspoon salt, or to taste
1 tablespoon melted butter of vegetable oil
2 pounds Chilean or Pacific sea bass fillets, about 1 inch thick, cut into 2½-inch pieces
2 cups mixed baby greens
Lime wedges

1. Prepare the coconut milk, ginger-garlic paste, and chaat masala. Then, in a large non-reactive bowl, mix together all the ingredients, except the fish, greens, chaat masala, and lime wedges.

2. Add the fish and mix, making sure all the pieces are well-coated. Cover with plastic wrap and marinate in the refrigerator, at least 4 and up to 12 hours.

3. Preheat the grill to medium-high (375°F to 400°F) or place a grill pan over high heat. Baste the grill or grill pan with oil to prevent the fish from sticking to the grill. Then place the marinated pieces on the grill or in the grill pan (or use a grilling basket) and cook, turning once or twice, until the fish pieces are opaque and just flaky inside and lightly charred on the outside, 5 to 7 minutes.

4. Line a platter with baby greens, and transfer the fish to rest on the greens. Sprinkle the chaat masala on top, and serve hot with lime wedges on the side.

Broiled Indian Swordfish Steaks

Oven ki Masala Macchi

Makes 4 to 6 servings

I love swordfish; it is thick and firm and takes well to Indian flavors. Broiling is not a common procedure in India, because even today not many people have ovens, but in America, it makes cooking swordfish easy. So here, Indian flavoring meets American convenience for a great fish dish.

6 (1-inch-thick) swordfish steaks or fillets (6 to 8 ounces each)
1 teaspoon ground turmeric
½ teaspoon salt, or to taste
4 quarter-size slices peeled fresh ginger
2 large clove fresh garlic, peeled
1 fresh green chile pepper, such as serrano, stemmed
2 tablespoons mustard oil or peanut oil
2 tablespoons heavy cream
1 tablespoon fresh lime or lemon juice
1 tablespoon black mustard seeds, coarsely ground
½ teaspoon ground ajwain seeds
2 tablespoons finely chopped fresh cilantro

1. Place the fish in a large non-reactive bowl, add the turmeric and salt, and mix well. Cover with plastic wrap and marinate at least 1 and up to 24 hours in the refrigerator.

2. In a small food processor or a blender, process together the ginger, garlic, and green chile pepper until minced. Add the oil, cream, lemon juice, mustard seeds, and ajwain seeds and process again to make a smooth paste. Mix into the fish, making sure all steaks are well-coated with the mixture. Cover and refrigerate about 1 hour.

3. Preheat the broiler. Place the fish in a lightly oiled broiler-safe baking dish and broil 4 to 5 inches from the heating element until the top is lightly browned, about 5 minutes. Turn the pieces over and broil until the other side is lightly browned, about 4 to 5 minutes, or until the thickest part of the fish is opaque when checked with a knife. Transfer to plates, sprinkle the cilantro on top, and serve.

Basic Southern Indian Fried Fish

South Ki Tali-Macchi

Makes 4 to 6 servings

One of the most popular fish-cooking methods in southern India is to dredge it in dry ingredients, then pan-fry it until crispy. Have a fishmonger clean and cut your fish for you. Cook the fish with the skin on one side—it adds to the flavor and visual appeal. Your guests can leave it behind, if they choose.

1½ to 2 pounds any small firm fish, such as trout, cut on both sides of the center bone, bone discarded, and cut into 3-inch pieces
1 teaspoon salt, or to taste
⅓ cup rice flour
2 teaspoons cayenne pepper, or to taste
⅛ teaspoon ground turmeric
⅛ teaspoon ground asafoetida
1 cup coconut oil or peanut oil for deep-frying
1 tablespoon fresh lemon juice
4 to 6 lemon wedges

1. Place the fish pieces on a large platter, skin side down. Sprinkle with the salt and marinate about 30 minutes in the refrigerator.

2. In a flat dish, mix together the rice flour, cayenne pepper, turmeric, and asafoetida. With a paper towel, dry each piece of fish, then dredge it in the rice flour mixture.

3. Heat the oil in a large nonstick skillet over medium-high heat until it reaches 325°F to 350°F on a frying thermometer or until a small piece of fish dropped into the hot oil takes 15 to 20 seconds before it rises to the top.

3. Standing far from the wok (to avoid splattering), add the fish, one piece at a time, adding as many as the wok will hold at one time without crowding, and fry, turning the pieces around with a slotted spatula, until they are crispy and golden, 3 to 5 minutes per batch.

4. Transfer to a tray lined with paper towels to drain, then transfer to a serving platter. Sprinkle the lemon juice on top, garnish with lemon wedges, and serve.

Pan-Fried Whole Fish with Tomatoes and Kokum

Tamatar-Kokum ki Macchi

Makes 4 to 6 servings

The natural Indian choice of fish in this recipe is pomfret or mackerel, but it can also be made with trout or cat-fish. Be sure to use a firm fish that will hold its shape and won't fall apart when you turn it in the pan.

Kokum is a dried sour fruit of the mangosteen-oil tree and is very popular in the western and southern parts of India. If you can't find it, use Tamarind Paste (page 54) instead. Look for kokum in Indian markets.

1 medium whole firm fish, such as pomfret, mackerel, trout, or catfish, cleaned, with head and tail intact, washed well and patted dry
1 small onion, coarsely chopped
2 large cloves fresh garlic, peeled
5 quarter-size slices peeled fresh ginger
1 to 3 fresh green chile peppers, such as serrano, stemmed
1 piece dried kokum, coarsely chopped
1 tablespoon ground coriander
1 teaspoon ground fenugreek seeds
1 teaspoon ground cumin
½ teaspoon salt, or to taste
¼ teaspoon ground turmeric
⅛ teaspoon ground asafoetida
¼ cup vegetable oil
4 small firm tomatoes, cut into 6 wedges each
½ cup finely chopped fresh cilantro, including soft stems

1. With a knife, make long and deep diagonal cuts, 1½ inches apart, on both sides of the fish.

2. In a blender or a food processor, process together the onion, garlic, ginger, green chile peppers, and kokum until smooth. Add the coriander, fenugreek, cumin, salt, turmeric, and asafoetida and process again to make a smooth paste.

3. Spread the paste generously on the fish, making sure to stuff some into the cuts. Save any leftover paste. Cover and marinate the fish in the refrigerator, at least 2 and up to 4 hours.

4. Heat the oil in a large nonstick skillet over medium-high heat and very carefully (there will be some splattering, so keep the lid handy) add the fish. Fry, turning once, until golden and flaky, about 5 minutes per side. Transfer to a serving platter. Drain most of the oil, leaving about 1 teaspoon oil in the skillet.

5. Add any remaining onion paste to the skillet and cook, stirring, 1 minute. Add the tomatoes and cilantro and cook until the tomatoes are slightly soft, about 1 minute. Use to garnish the fish, and serve hot.

Pan-Fried Fish Fillets with Ajwain Seeds
Ajwaini Macchi

Makes 4 to 6 servings

A whiff of thyme greets you with this twice-marinated pan-fried delicacy, which is sold in roadside eateries of New Delhi.

1¹/₂ pounds any firm white fish fillets, such as
    sea bass, halibut, cod, or swordfish,
    about 1 inch thick, cut into 3-inch pieces
1 teaspoon salt, or to taste
2 tablespoons fresh lime juice
¹/₄ cup chickpea flour
1 tablespoon Basic Ginger-Garlic Paste
    (page 47 or store-bought)
³/₄ teaspoon ajwain seeds
1 teaspoon ground paprika
¹/₈ teaspoon ground asafoetida
2 tablespoons peanut oil
1 tablespoon mustard oil
5 to 6 scallions, cut into 1-inch diagonal pieces
1 teaspoon Chaat Masala (page 20 or store-bought)
Lemon wedges

1. Place the fish in a large non-reactive bowl, add the salt and lime juice, and toss gently to mix. Cover and marinate in the refrigerator 30 to 60 minutes. Drain well.

2. To the fish, add the chickpea flour, ginger-garlic paste, ajwain seeds, paprika, and asafoetida, and mix, making sure all the pieces are well-coated with the marinade. Cover and marinate at least 2 and up to 4 hours in the refrigerator.

3. Heat both the oils in a large nonstick skillet over medium-high heat and add the fish pieces very carefully (the oil may splatter). Cook, turning once, until both sides are golden and the fish is just flaky and opaque inside, about 4 minutes per side. Transfer to a platter, sprinkle the scallions and chaat masala on top, garnish with the lemon wedges, and serve.

Pan-Fried Sea Bass with Cilantro-Yogurt Sauce
Bhuni Sea-Bass aur Dahi-Dhania Chutni

Makes 4 to 6 servings

Cilantro adds a delicate citrusy fragrance to this lovely dry-cooked fish, which comes to the table garnished with a spicy yogurt sauce. If you can't find sea bass without skin, remove the skin before proceeding with the recipe, or use any other white fish. Salmon works, too.

1 teaspoon Chaat Masala (page 20 or store-bought)
1¹/₂ to 2 pounds sea bass, halibut, or any firm white
    fish fillets, about ³/₄ inch thick, cut into 1-inch
    pieces
2 tablespoons vegetable oil
1 tablespoon ground black mustard seeds
¹/₄ teaspoon ground turmeric
1 cup nonfat plain yogurt, whisked until smooth
2 large bunches fresh cilantro (about 5 ounces each),
    coarsely chopped
2 to 3 tablespoons fresh lemon juice
8 quarter-size slices peeled fresh ginger
1 to 3 fresh green chile peppers, such as serrano,
    stemmed
¹/₂ teaspoon ground paprika
1 teaspoon salt, or to taste
A few cilantro sprigs

1. Prepare the chaat masala. Place the fish pieces in a bowl and gently mix in the oil, mustard seeds, and turmeric. Place the yogurt in a separate serving bowl.

2. Put the cilantro in a food processor or a blender, add the lemon juice, ginger, green chile peppers, paprika, and salt, and process to make a fine purée. Divide the purée into 2 portions. Mix 1 portion into the fish. Cover with plastic wrap and marinate at least 2 and up to 24 hours in the refrigerator. Mix the second portion into the yogurt, along with the chaat masala, to make a saucy chutney. Cover and refrigerate until needed.

3. Heat a large nonstick skillet over medium-high heat, and cook the fish, turning once or twice, until just flaky and opaque inside and golden outside, about 3 to 4 minutes. Transfer to a serving dish, drizzle about ½ cup yogurt sauce on the fish, garnish with the cilantro sprigs, and serve hot with the remaining yogurt sauce on the side.

Blackened Garam Masala Fish

Macchi Garam Masala

Makes 4 to 6 servings

Cajun and Indian cuisines have well-spiced foods in common. This blends the two cuisines. If you can make this one on an outdoor grill, do, because as it cooks, the spices emit a lot of smoke. If you're cooking inside, have the exhaust fan on and the windows open.

1 tablespoon Basic Garlic Paste (page 47 or store-bought)
1 tablespoon Tamarind Paste (page 54)
1¹/₂ to 2 pounds firm white fish fillets, such as halibut, cod, or catfish, about ¹/₂ inch thick, cut into 3-inch pieces
1 tablespoon ground paprika
¹/₂ teaspoon ground ajwain seeds
¹/₂ teaspoon garam masala
¹/₄ teaspoon freshly ground black pepper
¹/₄ teaspoon cayenne pepper, or to taste
¹/₂ teaspoon salt, or to taste
3 tablespoons mustard oil or peanut oil
2 tablespoons fresh lemon or lime juice

1. Prepare the garlic and tamarind pastes. Place the fish in a large, flat dish. Mix together the garlic paste, all the spices and salt, and rub well over the fillets, making sure each one is well-coated. Cover and marinate in the refrigerator at least 1 and up to 4 hours.

2. Heat 1½ tablespoons oil in a large nonstick skillet over high heat until smoking, about 2 minutes. Carefully place the fillets in the pan in a single layer and cook until blackened on the bottom, about 5 minutes.

3. Drizzle the remaining oil on top of the fish fillets and turn them over. Cook, pressing the top blackened side gently with the back of a spatula to flatten, and cook until the other side is well-browned and the inside just flaky and opaque, about 4 minutes. Transfer to a serving dish, drizzle the lemon juice on top, and serve hot.

Basic Fish Curry
Macchi Kari

Makes 4 to 6 servings

This is like many other Indian curries, except that it is made with fish and the fish cooks really fast, so cook the curry ingredients well before adding the fish pieces. For best results, use thick fish steaks or fillets of any firm fish and cut them into 1- to 2-inch pieces. While the curry is being made, mash one of the fish pieces into the sauce to give it more body.

1/2 recipe Fried Onion Paste (page 49)
1 1/2 to 2 pounds any firm fish fillets, such as
    sea bass, halibut, cod, or swordfish,
    about 3/4 inch thick, cut into 2-inch pieces
1/2 teaspoon ground turmeric
1/4 teaspoon cayenne pepper, or to taste
1 tablespoon ground coriander
1 teaspoon ground cumin
1/4 teaspoon ground paprika
1/2 cup nonfat plain yogurt, whisked until smooth
2 large tomatoes, finely chopped
1/2 teaspoon salt, or to taste
1 cup water
1/4 cup finely chopped fresh cilantro,
    including soft stems
1/4 teaspoon garam masala

1. Prepare the onion paste. Place the fish in a bowl and coat well with the turmeric and cayenne pepper. Cover with plastic wrap and marinate at least 1 and up to 24 hours in the refrigerator.

2. Prepare the fried onion paste. Put the paste in a large nonstick wok or saucepan over medium-high heat, add the coriander, cumin, and paprika, and stir about 1 minute. Add the yogurt, a little at a time, stirring constantly, to prevent it from curdling, and cook until it is well incorporated into the sauce, about 3 minutes.

3. Add the tomatoes and cook until they start to soften, about 2 minutes. Add the fish pieces and salt and cook, stirring, until the fish is firm, about 5 minutes.

4. Add the water and bring to a boil over high heat. Reduce the heat to medium-low, cover the pan, and simmer until the fish pieces are just flaky and opaque inside and the sauce is thick, about 5 minutes. Transfer to a serving dish, mix in the cilantro and garam masala, and serve.

Variation: To increase the quantity of the dish, boil, peel and coarsely smash 2 small potatoes and add along with the fish pieces. Or mix in 1 cup of thawed frozen peas when you add the fish pieces. Adjust the seasonings.

Pan-Fried Halibut in Yogurt-Cashew Curry
Dahi-Kaaju Kari Mein Halibut Macchi

Makes 4 to 6 servings

This is about as close as one can get to a do-ahead fish curry. Make the sauce, lightly fry the fish, and assemble them together (through Step 4), then finish cooking just prior to serving. If you're preparing this dish more than an hour ahead of time, refrigerate the fish.

1 1/2 pounds halibut fillets, about 1 inch thick,
    cut into 3-inch pieces
1/4 cup chickpea flour
1 tablespoon minced fresh garlic
1/4 teaspoon ground turmeric
1/4 teaspoon ground paprika or cayenne pepper,
    or to taste
1/4 teaspoon ground green cardamom seeds
1/4 teaspoon salt, or to taste
3 tablespoons ground raw cashews
2 large cloves fresh garlic, peeled
6 quarter-size slices peeled fresh ginger
1 to 3 fresh green chile peppers, such as serrano,
    stemmed
1 cup nonfat plain yogurt, whisked until smooth
1 cup water
3 tablespoons peanut oil
1 large onion, finely chopped
1/2 teaspoon garam masala

1. Prepare the garam masala. Place the fish in a bowl. Mix together the chickpea flour, minced garlic, turmeric, paprika (or cayenne pepper), cardamom seeds, and salt and add to the fish. Toss gently to mix, making sure each piece is well-coated with this mixture. Cover with plastic wrap and marinate in the refrigerator at least 1 and up to 24 hours.

2. Meanwhile, make the curry. In a food processor or a blender, process together the ground cashews, garlic cloves, ginger, green chile peppers, and ½ cup yogurt until smooth. Remove to a bowl. Then process the remaining ½ cup yogurt with 1 cup water until smooth.

3. Heat 2 tablespoons oil in a large nonstick skillet over high heat and cook the onion, stirring, until browned, about 10 minutes. Add the yogurt-cashew paste and continue to cook until all the juices evaporate, about 5 minutes.

4. Add the yogurt-water mixture and bring to a boil over high heat. Reduce the heat to medium-low, cover the pan, and simmer until the sauce is thick and smooth, about 10 minutes. Transfer to an oven-proof dish.

5. Preheat the oven 400°F. To the pan add the remaining 1 tablespoon oil and the fish pieces (in 2 batches, if needed) and fry, turning gently, until the fish is golden on all sides, about 5 minutes per batch. Add to the sauce and mix gently. Sprinkle the garam masala on top, cover the dish, and bake about 10 minutes to blend the flavors. Serve hot.

Fish with Bengali 5-Spices
Macher-Jhol

Makes 4 to 6 servings

There is a pungent mustard flavor in this classic Bengali fish curry. If you can find it, add all or at least 1 teaspoon of mustard oil in this dish. It makes all the difference.

1 tablespoon Bengali 5-Spices (Panch-Phoran), page 27 or store-bought
1¹/₂ to 2 pounds any firm fish fillets, such as halibut or swordfish, about ³/₄ inch thick, cut into 1¹/₂-inch pieces
³/₄ teaspoon ground turmeric
¹/₂ teaspoon salt, or to taste
2 tablespoons mustard oil or vegetable oil
1 teaspoon cayenne pepper, or to taste
¹/₄ cup water
2 cups finely chopped tomatoes
2 tablespoons finely chopped fresh cilantro

1. Prepare the 5-spice mixture. Place the fish pieces in a large non-reactive bowl. Add the ¼ teaspoon turmeric and salt and mix well, making sure all the pieces are well-coated. Cover with plastic wrap and marinate in the refrigerator at least 1 and up to 4 hours.

2. Heat 1 tablespoon oil in a large nonstick skillet over medium heat and fry the fish pieces (leave any juices in the bowl), in 2 or 3 batches if necessary, until golden, about 2 minutes per side. Remove to a bowl.

3. To the bowl with the fish juices, add the remaining ½ teaspoon turmeric, cayenne pepper, and water and mix well to make a paste.

4. Heat the remaining 1 tablespoon oil in the same skillet and add the panch-phoran; they should splatter upon contact with the hot oil, so cover the pan until the splattering subsides. Quickly add the turmeric paste, stir about 1 minute, then add the tomatoes and cook until most of the juices evaporate, about 5 minutes.

5. Mix in the fish, plus any juices that may have accumulated, and cook over medium heat 2 to 3 minutes to blend the flavors. Transfer to a serving dish, sprinkle the cilantro on top, and serve.

Fish with Ground Mustard Seeds

Sarsoon Ki Macchi

Makes 4 to 6 servings

A strong-tasting dish by any standards, this is another Bengali fish specialty. For a milder flavor, use vegetable oil instead of mustard oil.

2 pounds any firm fish fillet, such as halibut
    or swordfish, about 3/4 inch thick, cut into
    2-inch pieces
1/4 teaspoon ground turmeric
1/2 teaspoon salt, or to taste
1/4 cup coarsely ground black mustard seeds
2 tablespoons mustard oil or vegetable oil
1 1/2 cups water
1 to 3 fresh green chile peppers, such as serrano,
    sliced lengthwise
5 to 7 fresh curry leaves
A few sprigs fresh cilantro

1. Place the fish pieces in a large non-reactive bowl, add the turmeric and salt, and mix well, making sure all the pieces are well-coated. Cover with plastic wrap and marinate in the refrigerator at least 1 hour and up to 24 hours.

2. In a small bowl, mix together the mustard seeds and oil, then add about 1/4 cup water to make a paste. Transfer to a large nonstick wok or saucepan and stir over medium heat, adding a sprinkling of water every now and then, until the paste is well-cooked, about 10 minutes.

3. Add the remaining water and bring to a boil over high heat. Add the fish and any juices that might have collected in the bowl, and boil again.

4. Add the green chile peppers and curry leaves. Reduce the heat to medium-low and simmer, turning once, until the fish is just flaky and opaque inside, 3 to 5 minutes per side. Transfer to a serving dish, garnish with the cilantro sprigs, and serve.

Cochin Masala Fish with Pearl Onions

Cochin Meen Kari

Makes 4 to 6 servings

This recipe is generally made with mackerel, but I find that almost any firm fish works well—even salmon and tuna. With its thick and spicy gravy, this dish is a perfect accompaniment to fresh chapati *(whole-wheat griddle breads). The cumin and corian-der seeds are meant to remain coarsely ground in the masala* paste. *They add to the flavor.*

1/2 cup Coconut Milk (page 44 or store-bought)
3 large cloves fresh garlic, peeled
20 fresh curry leaves
1 to 3 fresh green chile peppers, such as serrano,
    stemmed
1 tablespoon cumin seeds
1 tablespoon coriander seeds
1/4 teaspoon ground turmeric
1/8 teaspoon ground asafoetida
1/2 teaspoon salt, or to taste
1 tablespoon coconut oil or peanut oil
15 to 20 pearl onions, peeled
1 1/2 pounds firm white fish fillets, such as
    sea bass or halibut, about 3/4 inch thick,
    cut into 2-inch pieces
1/2 cup finely chopped fresh cilantro,
    including soft stems
1 to 2 cups water
1 cup coarsely chopped tomatoes

1. Prepare the coconut milk. In a blender or a food processor, blend together the garlic, curry leaves, green chile peppers, cumin, coriander, turmeric, asafoetida, salt, and 1/4 cup coconut milk to make a smooth paste.

2. Heat the oil in a large nonstick wok or saucepan over medium-high heat and cook the pearl onions, stirring, until golden, about 4 minutes. Add the garlic-coconut milk paste and cook over medium heat until fragrant and golden, 5 minutes.

3. Add the fish and cook, turning once, about 2 minutes per side, then add the remaining ¼ cup coconut milk and the cilantro and cook until the oil separates to the sides, about 2 minutes.

4. Add the water and bring to a boil over high heat. Reduce the heat to medium-low, cover the pan, and simmer until the sauce is thick and the fish is tender but not breaking apart, about 5 minutes.

5. Transfer to a serving dish, cover with another dish, and keep warm. To the same pan, add the tomatoes and cook, stirring, until softened, about 2 minutes. Spread evenly over the cooked fish as a garnish. Serve hot.

Sohini's Fish Curry with Dried Coconut

Kopra-Macchi Kari

Makes 4 to 6 servings

Sohini Baliga, my friend from Santa Monica, calls this her 5-C's fish curry because it is made with cumin, coriander, chile powder, coconut, and curry leaves. The coconut she uses is the dried variety called kopra, *which is available at Indian markets.*

Choose a strongly flavored fish, such as thresher, shark, tuna, or salmon, so that the flavor of the fish shines through the spices.

2 pounds any firm fish fillets, such as salmon, thresher, shark, or tuna, about ³/4 inch thick, cut into 2-inch pieces

¹/2 teaspoon salt, or to taste

2 tablespoons ground coriander

1 tablespoon ground cumin

¹/4 cup finely chopped dried coconut (kopra) or 1 tablespoon finely ground unsweetened dried coconut

1 teaspoon cayenne pepper, or to taste

2 cups of water

7 to 8 fresh curry leaves

1. Place the fish in a large non-reactive bowl and, with clean fingers, gently mix in the salt and set aside about 30 minutes.

2. In a small bowl, mix together the coriander, cumin, coconut, cayenne pepper, and 1 cup water to make a smooth paste. Transfer to a large nonstick saucepan and bring to a quick boil over high heat.

3. Add the fish and another cup water, and bring to a boil again. Reduce the heat to low, cover the pan, and cook until the fish is just flaky and opaque inside, 7 to 10 minutes. During the last 2 minutes of cooking, lightly crumple the curry leaves and add them to the pan. Do not stir the fish at all. To mix at all, swirl the pan a little on the burner. Transfer to a serving dish and serve hot.

Malabar Fish Curry with Kokum and Coconut Milk

Malabar Meen Kari

Makes 4 to 6 servings

The shriveled up, almost black, prune-like pieces of the kokum *fruit, indigenous to India, impart a smoky-sour flavor and simultaneously darken the food. The mild coconut milk, in turn, balances the sourness. Look for* kokum *in Indian markets.*

¹/4 to ¹/3 cup Coconut Milk (page 44 or store-bought)

2 pounds any firm fish fillets, such as salmon, catfish, or swordfish, about ³/4 inch thick, cut into 2-inch pieces

¹/4 teaspoon ground turmeric

¹/2 teaspoon salt, or to taste

4 coarsely chopped kokum halves

¹/4 cup hot water

1 to 3 fresh green chile peppers, such as serrano, stemmed

1 to 3 dried red chile peppers, such as chile de arbol, broken into pieces

4 quarter-size slices peeled fresh ginger

3 to 4 large cloves fresh garlic, peeled

1 teaspoon ground black mustard seeds

2 tablespoons coconut oil

1 teaspoon black mustard seeds

1 large onion, finely chopped

1¹/2 to 2 cups of water

7 to 8 fresh green curry leaves, lightly crumpled

1. Prepare the coconut milk. Place the fish in a bowl, add the turmeric and salt, and mix well, making sure all the fish pieces are well-coated. Cover and marinate in the refrigerator about 1 hour. Meanwhile, soak the chopped kokum in the hot water about 30 minutes.

2. In a blender or a food processor, process together the kokum, plus the water they were soaking in, the green and red chile peppers, ginger, garlic, and ground mustard seeds to make a smooth paste.

3. Heat the oil in large nonstick skillet over medium-high heat and add the whole mustard seeds; they should splatter on contact with the hot oil, so cover the pan until the splattering subsides. Quickly add the onion, reduce heat to medium-low, cover the pan, and cook until the onion is soft but not golden, 7 to 10 minutes.

4. Add the kokum,-ginger-garlic paste and cook over medium heat, stirring, 3 to 5 minutes. Add the fish and 1½ cups water, and bring to a boil over high heat. Reduce the heat to low, cover the pan, and cook about 5 minutes.

5. Add the coconut milk and curry leaves and simmer until the sauce is thick and the fish is tender, just flaky and opaque inside, about 5 minutes, adding more water if you want a thinner sauce. Do not stir the fish at all. To mix, swirl the pan a little on the burner. Transfer to a serving dish and serve hot.

Spicy Fish Curry with Coconut Sauce
Masaladar Nariyal-Macchi Kari

Makes 4 to 6 servings

The red chile peppers in the marinade make the dish very hot. The coconut milk does a good job of tempering the heat, but if you prefer a milder dish, reduce the quantity of chile peppers and discard all the seeds, then serve with steamed basmati *rice or Asian sticky rice.*

½ cup Coconut Milk (page 44 or store-bought)
4 to 6 dried red chile peppers, such as chiles de arbol, broken into pieces into pieces
1 tablespoon coriander seeds
1 teaspoon black mustard seeds
1 teaspoon black peppercorns
1 small onion, coarsely chopped
2 large cloves fresh garlic, peeled
¼ teaspoon ground turmeric
½ teaspoon salt, or to taste
1½ pounds any firm fish fillets, such as halibut, salmon, or swordfish, cut into 1½-inch pieces
3 tablespoons peanut oil
1 large onion, cut in half lengthwise and thinly sliced
1 (1-inch) piece peeled ginger, cut into thin and long matchsticks
1 tablespoon distilled white vinegar
¼ cup chopped fresh cilantro, including soft stems

1. Prepare the coconut milk. Then, in a small spice or coffee grinder, coarsely grind together the red chile peppers, coriander, mustard seeds, and the peppercorns. In a food processor or a blender, process together the chopped onion and garlic until smooth. Add the ground spice mixture, the turmeric, and the salt and process once again to make a smooth paste.

2. Place the fish pieces in a large non-reactive bowl, add the marinade, and mix well, making sure that all the pieces are well-coated. Cover with plastic wrap and marinate in the refrigerator at least 1 and up to 4 hours.

3. Heat half of the oil in a large nonstick skillet over medium heat and cook the sliced onion and ginger, stirring, until browned, about 7 minutes. Transfer to a bowl.

4. Add the remaining oil to the skillet and fry the fish pieces, turning once or twice, until golden outside, about 4 minutes total.

5. Add the coconut milk and simmer over low heat, about 5 minutes. Do not stir with a spoon; if needed, stir by shaking the skillet. Very carefully, mix in the vinegar and simmer another 2 to 3 minutes to blend the flavors. (The fish should be just flaky and opaque inside.) Transfer to a serving dish, sprinkle the cilantro on top, and serve.

Goan Fish Curry with Coconut Milk and Tamarind

Goa ki Fish Caldene Kari

Makes 4 to 6 servings

Rosita Dighe gave me this recipe—a popular fish curry from Goa that can be made with any firm variety of fish.

1 cup Coconut Milk (page 44 or store-bought)
2 to 3 tablespoons Tamarind Paste (page 54)
2 tablespoons vegetable oil
1 large onion, finely chopped
4 large cloves fresh garlic, minced
3 dried red chile peppers, such as chile de arbol, broken into pieces
1 teaspoon coriander seeds
1 teaspoon cumin seeds
1/4 teaspoon ground turmeric
1 cup water
1 teaspoon salt, or to taste
1 1/2 pounds any firm fish fillets, such as catfish, salmon, or swordfish, about 1 inch thick, cut into 2-inch pieces
1/4 cup finely chopped fresh cilantro, including soft stems

1. Prepare the coconut milk and tamarind paste. Heat the oil in a large nonstick wok or saucepan over medium-high heat and cook the onion, stirring, until golden, about 5 minutes. Add the garlic and stir 1 minute.

2. In a small spice grinder or coffee grinder, grind together the red chile peppers, coriander, and cumin. Mix in the turmeric, then add the spice mixture to the onions and cook, stirring, about 2 minutes.

3. Add the water and coconut milk and bring to a quick boil, stirring, over high heat. Reduce the heat to medium and simmer about 5 minutes. Add the tamarind paste and salt and simmer another minute.

4. Add the fish pieces and simmer until the fish is flaky and opaque inside, 10 to 15 minutes. Remove to a serving dish, mix in the cilantro, and serve.

Variation: Add 1 large finely chopped tomato to the onion before adding the spices in Step 2.

Hyderabadi Fish Curry with Sesame Seeds and Tamarind

Til aur Imli ki Fish Kari

Makes 4 to 6 servings

A thick, hot, and tangy sauce envelopes the fish pieces in this typical Hyderabadi preparation that is authentically made with flame-roasted onions—though I roast mine in the oven.

1/4 cup Tamarind Paste (page 54)
2 medium onions, with skin on, halved
1 small head garlic, cloves separated but not peeled
1/4 cup finely chopped dried coconut (kopra) or 1 tablespoon finely ground unsweetened dried coconut
2 tablespoons white sesame seeds
1/2 teaspoon hot red pepper flakes, or to taste
1 1/2 tablespoons coriander seeds
2 1/2 teaspoons cumin seeds
1/2 teaspoon fenugreek seeds
2 to 3 tablespoons vegetable oil
15 to 20 fresh curry leaves
1/8 teaspoon ground asafoetida
1 1/2 pounds any firm fish fillets, such as halibut, or swordfish, about 1/2 inch thick, cut into 2-inch pieces
1 teaspoon salt, or to taste
1 1/2 to 2 cups water
1/4 cup finely chopped fresh cilantro, including soft stems
1/4 teaspoon garam masala

1. Prepare the tamarind paste. Then, preheat the broiler. Place the onions and garlic on a cookie sheet and broil on the top rack of the oven or in the broiler, turning once or twice, until completely charred. Let cool, peel off most of the charred skin from the onions (leave a little of the second layer for flavor) and garlic, then process in a food processor or a blender to make a smooth paste. Leave in the work bowl.

2. In a small nonstick skillet over medium heat, dry-roast together the coconut, sesame seeds, and red pepper flakes until golden, and remove to a bowl. Then dry-roast the coriander, 1½ teaspoons cumin, and fenugreek seeds until a few shades darker. Let cool, then grind all the dry-roasted ingredients together in a spice or a coffee grinder to make as fine as possible. Add to the roasted onion-garlic paste and process once again to mix.

3. Heat the oil in a large nonstick wok or saucepan over medium-high heat and add the remaining 1 teaspoon cumin seeds; they should sizzle upon contact with the hot oil. Quickly add the curry leaves and asafoetida, then carefully (in case it splatters) mix in the processed onion-spice paste. Cook, stirring as needed, over medium heat until golden brown, about 10 minutes.

4. Mix in the tamarind paste and cook about 2 minutes. Add the fish pieces and salt and stir carefully about 2 minutes. Then add the water and cilantro and simmer until the fish is flaky and opaque and the oil separates to the sides, about 10 minutes. Transfer to a serving dish, sprinkle the garam masala on top, and serve.

Fish with Bell Peppers and Onions
Sabz-Macchi Masala

Makes 4 to 6 servings

Inspired by Bengali cuisine and its famous panch-phoran *mixture of five spices, this fragrant dish can be made with any oil, but it is mustard oil that packs the punch and really gives it its distinctive taste. The bell peppers and onions add yet another dimension to the flavors.*

2 tablespoons Bengali 5-Spices (Panch-Phoran), page 27 or store-bought
2 pounds any firm white fish, such as halibut or sea bass, about ³/₄-inch thick, cut into 2-inch pieces
1 teaspoon ground turmeric
¹/₂ teaspoon salt, or to taste
2 tablespoons mustard oil or vegetable oil
3 bell peppers (1 red, 1 green, and 1 yellow), cut into ¹/₂-inch pieces
1 medium onion, finely chopped
1 cup water
1 to 2 tablespoons fresh lemon juice
A few sprigs fresh cilantro, including soft stems

1. Prepare the 5-spice mixture. Place the fish pieces in a large bowl, add the turmeric and salt, and mix, making sure all the pieces are well-coated. Cover and marinate in the refrigerator 30 to 40 minutes.

2. Heat the oil in a large nonstick wok or saucepan over medium-high heat and add the 5-spice mixture; they should sizzle upon contact with the hot oil. Quickly add the bell peppers and onion, and stir 1 minute.

3. Add the fish, along with all the marinade, and stir gently to mix. Cook about 2 minutes, then add the water and bring to a boil over high heat. Reduce the heat to medium-low, cover the pan, and simmer until the fish is flaky and opaque and the bell peppers are crisp-tender, 5 to 7 minutes. Transfer to a serving dish, drizzle the lemon juice on top, garnish with the cilantro, and serve.

Rice

Plain and Steamed Rice Dishes 533

Boiled Basmati Rice

Steamed Basmati Rice (Absorption Method)

Steamed Turmeric and Red Peppercorn Basmati Rice

Steamed Basmati Rice with Dry-Roasted Spices

Steamed Green Basmati Rice

Simple Herbs and Spices Pilafs (Pullaos) 535

Simple Cumin Basmati Rice

Roasted Saffron Basmati Rice

Savory Saffron and Almond Rice

Basmati Rice with Whole Spices

Quick Cilantro-Garlic Pilaf with Peas

Ginger-Mint Pilaf with Potatoes and Roasted Cumin Seeds

South and West Indian Vegetarian Rice Dishes 539

South Indian Mustard and Asafoetida Pilaf

Yogurt and Cashew Rice

Coorgi Yogurt Rice

Long-Grain Rice with Roasted Peanuts

Lemon Rice

South Indian Sesame Rice

South Indian Tamarind Rice

Potato, Coconut, and Yogurt Fried Rice

Madras-Style Spicy Eggplant Rice

Tangy South Indian Rice and Pigeon Peas

Goan Coconut Milk Pilaf

Vegetarian Pilafs (Sabzi kae Pullao) 546

Basmati Pilaf with Caramelized Onions and Broccoli

Mixed Cauliflower Pilaf

Roasted Fresh Fenugreek Leaves Pilaf

Morel Mushroom Pilaf with Pistachios and Silver Leaves

Stir-Fried Mushrooms and Red Chard Pilaf

Spinach and Red Bell Pepper Pilaf

Grilled Bell Pepper Fried Rice

Corn, Peas, and Tomato Fried Rice

Mixed Vegetable Pilaf

Kashmiri Mixed Vegetable Pilaf

Tofu and Chickpea Pilaf

Punjabi Green Chickpea Pilaf

Quick Soybean Pilaf

Royal Fresh and Dried Fruit Pilaf

Cranberry Pilaf

Non-Vegetarian Pilafs (*Pullaos*) 555

Spicy Chicken Pilaf

Moist Ground Lamb Pilaf

Simple Lamb Pilaf

Garlic Shrimp Pilaf
with Coconut Milk

Layered Rice Dishes (*Biryanis*) 558

Layered Rice
with Eggplant and Coconut

Hyderabadi Layered Rice
with Mixed Vegetables

Layered Rice with Fragrant Mixed
Nuts and Saffron

Hyderabadi Layered Rice
with Cooked Chicken

Hyderabadi Layered Rice
with Marinated Chicken

Layered Rice
with Lamb and Apricots

Layered Rice
with Fragrant Lamb Chops

Special Grain and Lentil Dishes (*Khichadis*) 564

Creamy Rice and Split Mung Beans
with Cumin Seeds

Pilaf-Style Rice and
Yellow Mung Beans with Ginger

Creamy Rice and Mixed Vegetables
with Spinach Ribbons

Pilaf-Style Tapioca Pearls

Creamy Cracked Wheat, Rice,
and Mung Beans

Creamy Cracked Wheat
with Mixed Lentils and Beans

Other Grain Pilafs 568

Brown Basmati Rice
with Asafoetida

Pressed Rice Flakes
with Peas and Potatoes

Pressed Rice Flakes with Tamarind

Stir-Fried Spicy Semolina

Stir-Fried Indian Vermicelli
with Coconut and Vegetables

Basmati and Wild Rice Pilaf
with Roasted Nuts

*R*ice, a grain cultivated and eaten the world over, plays an integral part in the social, religious, and daily lives of Indian people. In a testament to its place in our culture, in all our religious ceremonies rice is offered to the gods before it is eaten. It is nearly always part of weddings, where it is showered upon the bride as a blessing, and is, in certain families, a part of the bride's trousseau.

Consumed as a staple alongside an array of curries and *dals* (legumes), rice is an indispensable part of our meals. It is quick to make and easy to digest, and even though rice (especially polished white rice) is not as nutrient-rich as other grains, it does deliver a fair amount of protein, carbohydrates, and vitamins A and B. In the north, the wheat basket of India, rice is reserved more for special occasions, while throughout the rest of the country, people eat rice at least twice a day.

India is home to a multitude of rice varieties, differing not only in their shape, size, and color, but also in their intrinsic flavors and aroma. Thus, every day, Indian homes consume a variety of rice grains—long-grain, short-grain, white, red, jasmine, some brown—and within each category there are finer distinctions. For everyday meals, the type of rice used depends on which part of the country you are from, with the south preferring locally available long-grain and also a red rice variety, and the northerners gravitating towards the prized aromatic, long-grain *basmati* rice, which is grown primarily in the foothills of the Himalayas. Of course, throughout the country, when an occasion calls for fancy *pullaos* (seasoned rice dishes) or *biryanis* (layered rice and meat or vegetable dishes), the preference is *basmati*—"queen of fragrance" in Hindi.

Luckily for us in America, today this rice has become easy to find. Most recipes in this chapter use *basmati* rice, but you'll also find samplings of other kinds of rice and rice products, and a few other grains.

Here are a few things to remember while cooking rice: There are three basic ways to cook rice: 1) Boil it in lots of water, then drain out the water (similar to pasta); 2) Steam it in measured amounts of water (also known as the absorption method); or 3) Cook it in a pressure cooker. All exotic Indian *pullaos, biryanis,* and stir-fries are typically started with some form of the boiled or steamed rice preparations.

For each method, particularly when cooking basmati rice: Place the rice in a large bowl and wash it in 3 to 4 changes of water. All the husks and hollow grains float to the top and can be poured out with the water. This does not happen if you wash it in a fine-mesh strainer under running water.

For the steaming (absorption) method of cooking rice, which is very popular in India, it is important before cooking to soak the rice in water at least 30 minutes or longer. Doing so enables the rice grains to soak up moisture and lengthen and, when cooked, the end product—especially in the case of *basmati*—has that prized long, individuated look. Keep in mind that after being soaked, the rice has softened and is very fragile. Treat it gently; do not stir or mix it, or it will break.

When cooking in a pressure cooker, you can soak the rice before cooking for better rice texture, but you can skip that step to save time.

Despite popular Indian belief, rice can be cooked ahead of time and re-heated very successfully. Not only is pre-cooked rice very good, but it saves you last-minute panic and anxiety. Here's how—cook the rice completely, transfer it to a serving dish, cover it with the lid, and set it aside up to 4 hours at room temperature or up to 24 hours in the refrigerator. Reheat in the microwave oven 3 to 5 minutes on high power or in a preheated 375°F oven about 30 minutes. Sprinkle 1 to 2 tablespoons water over the rice, if you reheat it in the oven.

If you do not wish to pre-cook and re-heat the rice, mix together everything that needs to go in the rice, then cook it minutes before serving. Here's how—in a nonstick saucepan, sauté your herbs and spices (if using) until golden, remove the pan from the heat, and mix in the rice and the water. Allow the rice to soak in this up to 8 hours. Then, finish cooking the rice about ½ hour before serving. (In this case, do not pre-soak the rice in a separate bowl.) The rice soaks in the pan in which it is to be cooked.

Indian rice dishes fall into two broad categories—plain and fancy. The first category comprises the unadorned, quick-cooking boiled or steamed dishes and the simpler herb- and spice-enriched *pullao*s (pilafs). In the second group are all the vegetable-, nut- and meat-enhanced stir-fries, *pullao*s and *biryani*s which require some assembly and preparation.

There is yet another set of Indian rice dishes: the soft-cooked, risotto-like or dry-cooked rice and *dal* (legume) combination dishes called *khichadi*s, which, along with certain other delicacies, are the ultimate comfort foods—literally. These dishes are reserved for family only and are almost never served formally. They are light on the stomach, easy to digest, and are often served when you are feeling under the weather.

Each cup of uncooked rice makes 3 cups of cooked rice.

Plain and Steamed Rice Dishes

Boiled Basmati Rice
Khullae Paani mein Ooblae Chaval

Makes 4 to 6 servings, or about 4 cups

All over India, and especially in the southern parts, this method of making rice is probably the first thing taught to anyone who is ready to cook, male or female. Serve it with curries, or use as a base to make stir-fried dishes or biryanis. *(You can even use the drained water to starch clothes—something done in most Indian homes.)*

**1¼ cups basmati rice, sorted and washed
   in 3 to 4 changes of water
5 to 6 cups water**

1. Put the rice and the water in a large pot and bring to a rolling boil over high heat. Reduce the heat to medium, and continue to boil until the rice is ¾ cooked, about 7 minutes. (There will be plenty of water in the pot even after the rice is ready.) Drain the rice through a large fine-mesh strainer and discard the water, or use it as a base for soups, stews, or curries.

2. Return the drained rice to the pot, cover the pot with a small, clean kitchen towel (making sure that the overhang is 1 inch or less, or it may burn on the stove), then place the lid of the pot back on, over the towel.

3. Return the pot to the stove and cook on the lowest heat setting, heat until each grain of rice is fluffy and separate, 10 to 15 minutes. Or, place a griddle (or tava, page 575) on low heat and set the pot of rice on it. (Make sure the towel is well above the flame.) The towel absorbs all the excess moisture and the rice comes out perfectly cooked, with each grain separate. Remove from the heat and let the rice rest undisturbed about 5 minutes. Transfer to a serving platter, fluff lightly with a fork, and serve.

Variation: To salt the rice and finish cooking it in the oven, bring lightly salted water to a rolling boil, then add the rice. Lower the heat, simmer about 7 minutes, then drain and transfer to an oven-safe serving dish. Cover tightly with aluminum foil and cook in a preheated 400°F oven about 15 minutes.

Steamed Basmati Rice (Absorption Method)
Ooblae Chaval

Makes 4 to 6 servings, or about 4 cups

This is another basic and popular way of making rice. With no additional flavors and seasonings, the celebrated flavors of basmati *rice truly shine through—as does its nutrition content, because the nutrients are usually lost when the water is drained away, but here they are absorbed into the rice. It is important to soak the rice before cooking with this method to ensure fluffy, individuated grains.*

**1¼ cups basmati rice, sorted and washed
   in 3 to 4 changes of water
2⅓ cups water
Cilantro sprig, for garnish (optional)**

1. In a medium bowl, soak the rice in the water, about 30 minutes.

2. Put the rice and the water in a medium saucepan and bring to a boil over high heat. Reduce the heat to the lowest setting, cover the pan (partially at first, until the foam subsides, then snugly), and cook until the rice is done, 10 to 15 minutes. Do not stir the rice at all. Remove the pan from the heat and let the rice rest undisturbed about 5 minutes. Transfer to a serving platter, fluff lightly with a fork, and serve with a sprig of cilantro, if you like.

Steamed Turmeric and Red Peppercorn Basmati Rice

Haldi kae Ooblae Chaval

Makes 4 to 6 servings, or 4 cups

Not only is this dish eye-catching with its brilliant yellow color and flecks of red, it also makes for a great conversation piece because not many people think of adding something as simple as turmeric and peppercorns (both Indian culinary contributions to the world) to steamed rice.

Besides color, this dish offers many health benefits—turmeric is considered a natural antiseptic and overall digestive stimulant.

1¼ cups basmati rice, sorted and washed
    in 3 to 4 changes of water
2⅓ cups water
¼ teaspoon ground turmeric
1 teaspoon red or black peppercorns
5 black cardamom pods, crushed lightly
    to break the skin
½ teaspoon salt, or to taste
1 teaspoon dried mint leaves (or 1 tablespoon
    minced fresh)

1. In a medium bowl, soak the rice in the water, about 30 minutes.

2. Put the rice with the water it was soaking in, along with all the other ingredients (except the mint) in a medium saucepan and bring to a boil over high heat. Reduce the heat to the lowest setting, cover the pan (partially at first, until the foam subsides, then snugly), and cook until the rice is done, 10 to 15 minutes. Do not stir the rice while it cooks. Remove from the heat and let the rice rest undisturbed about 5 minutes. Transfer to a serving platter, garnish with the mint leaves, and serve.

Steamed Basmati Rice with Dry-Roasted Spices

Bhunae Masalae ke Ooblae Chaval

Makes 4 to 6 servings

Dry-roasting allows the spices to release their essential oils and gives them a smoky aroma that eventually is infused into each grain of rice. As a result, this speckled rice dish, made with no added fat, tastes a lot richer than it actually is.

1½ cups basmati rice, sorted and washed
    in 3 to 4 changes of water
2¾ cups water
1½ teaspoons cumin seeds
½ teaspoon coarsely ground black pepper
¼ teaspoon saffron threads
5 to 7 green cardamom pods, crushed lightly
    to break the skin
½ teaspoon salt, or to taste
¼ cup finely chopped fresh cilantro,
    including soft stems

1. In a medium bowl, soak the rice in the water, about 30 minutes. Drain, saving the water in a bowl.

2. Put the cumin, black pepper, saffron, and cardamom pods in a medium saucepan and roast, stirring and shaking the pan, over medium-high heat until they are a few shades darker and highly fragrant, about 1 minute. Add the drained rice and continue to roast another 2 to 3 minutes, shaking the pan or turning the rice with a wooden spoon very carefully (washed rice tends to break easily).

3. Add the reserved rice-water and the salt, and bring to a boil over high heat. Reduce the heat to the lowest setting, cover the pan (partially at first, until the foam subsides, then snugly), and cook until the rice is done, 10 to 15 minutes. Do not stir the rice while it cooks. Remove from the heat and let the rice rest undisturbed about 5 minutes. Transfer to a serving platter, gently mix in the cilantro, and serve.

Steamed Green Basmati Rice

Harae Ooblae Chaval

Makes 4 to 6 servings

Whenever my mother got tired of serving plain steamed rice, she puréed some of her favorite seasonal greens (very often fresh fenugreek leaves) and tossed them into the rice. That rice looked lovely, tasted different, and enabled her to feed us a taste of the season. Nowadays, most greens are available year-round and you don't have to wait for the seasons to enjoy this dish.

1¹/₂ cups basmati rice, sorted and washed
    in 3 to 4 changes of water
2³/₄ cups water
1 large bunch fresh spinach, trimmed, washed, dried,
    and coarsely chopped
1 cup fresh fenugreek or watercress leaves,
    washed and dried
1 fresh green chile pepper, such as serrano, stemmed
³/₄ teaspoon salt, or to taste
¹/₂ teaspoon coarsely ground black pepper
¹/₄ teaspoon garam masala

1. In a medium bowl, soak the rice in the water, about 30 minutes.

2. Put the spinach, fenugreek leaves, and green chile pepper in a food processor and pulse until minced. Remove to a large nonstick saucepan and cook, stirring, over medium-high heat until a few shades darker, 2 to 4 minutes.

3. Add the rice with the water it was soaking in, and the salt and black pepper. Mix lightly and bring to a boil over high heat. Reduce the heat to lowest setting, cover the pan (partially at first, until the foam subsides, then snugly), and cook until the rice is done, 10 to 15 minutes. Do not stir the rice while it cooks. Remove from the heat and let the rice rest undisturbed about 5 minutes. Transfer to a serving dish, sprinkle the garam masala on top, and serve.

Simple Herbs and Spices Pilafs (*Pullaos*)

Simple Cumin Basmati Rice

Jeera Chaval

Makes 4 to 6 servings

This is probably one of the simplest everyday pullaos *(pilafs). Made with cumin seeds and coarsely ground black peppercorns that are first sizzled in hot oil or ghee, the naturally fragrant* basmati *rice takes on an exciting flavor.*

1¹/₂ cups basmati rice, sorted and washed
    in 3 to 4 changes of water
2³/₄ cups water
1 tablespoon peanut oil or melted ghee
1¹/₂ teaspoons cumin seeds
¹/₂ teaspoon coarsely ground black pepper,
    or to taste
³/₄ teaspoon salt, or to taste
Finely chopped fresh cilantro

1. In a medium bowl, soak the rice in the water about 30 minutes.

2. Heat the oil (or ghee) in a large saucepan over medium-high heat and add the cumin seeds and black pepper; they should sizzle upon contact with the hot oil. Quickly add the rice with the water it was soaking in. Mix in the salt and bring to a boil over high heat. Reduce the heat to the lowest setting, cover the pan (partially at first, until the foam subsides, then snugly), and cook until the rice is done, 10 to 15 minutes. Do not stir the rice while it cooks. Remove from the heat and let the rice rest undisturbed about 5 minutes. Transfer to a serving platter, garnish with cilantro, and serve.

Variation: For more complex flavors, add 5 black crushed cardamom pods, 2 1-inch sticks cinnamon, and 8 to 10 cloves to the hot oil along with the cumin seeds in Step 2, then continue with the recipe.

Roasted Saffron Basmati Rice

Kesari Pullao

Makes 4 to 6 servings

In a gourmand's fantasy world, this recipe would be currency with its value measured by the spices it contains—some of the most treasured in the world—saffron, black cumin, and cardamom pods. The whole spices and herbs add to the presentation of the dish, but you can take them out or tell guests to push them to the side.

1¹⁄₂ cups basmati rice, sorted and washed
    in 3 to 4 changes of water
2³⁄₄ cups water
¹⁄₃ teaspoon saffron threads
1 tablespoon vegetable oil or melted ghee
1 (1-inch) stick cinnamon, bruised
2 bay leaves
5 to 7 green cardamom pods, lightly crushed
    to break the skin
¹⁄₂ teaspoon black cumin seeds (or 1 teaspoon
    cumin seeds)
³⁄₄ teaspoon salt, or to taste
¹⁄₄ teaspoon garam masala

1. In a medium bowl, soak the rice in the water about 30 minutes. Put the saffron in a small skillet and roast over medium heat, shaking the skillet until the saffron is fragrant and a few shades darker, about 1 minute. Transfer to a bowl and crush lightly with a spoon.

2. Heat the oil (or ghee) in a large saucepan over medium-high heat and cook the cinnamon, bay leaves, and cardamom pods, stirring, until golden, about 1 minute. Add the cumin seeds, then the rice with the water it was soaking in. Mix in the roasted saffron and salt and bring to a boil over high heat. Reduce the heat to the lowest setting, cover the pan (partially at first, until the foam subsides, then snugly), and cook until the rice is done, 10 to 15 minutes. Do not stir the rice while it cooks. Remove from the heat and let the rice rest undisturbed about 5 minutes. Transfer to a serving platter, sprinkle the garam masala on top, and serve.

Savory Saffron and Almond Rice

Kesar-Badaam Pullao

Makes 4 to 6 servings

Replete with saffron and almonds, this is another richly-flavored dish. Don't shy away from using ghee—it truly makes a difference, giving the dish its distinctive edge of decadence.

1¹⁄₄ cups basmati rice, sorted and washed
    in 3 to 4 changes of water
2¹⁄₄ cups water
¹⁄₂ cup sliced or slivered raw almonds
¹⁄₂ teaspoon saffron threads
¹⁄₄ cup warm milk (any kind)
1 tablespoon melted ghee, or vegetable oil
1 tablespoon peeled minced fresh ginger
¹⁄₂ teaspoon black cumin seeds (or 1 teaspoon
    cumin seeds)
6 green cardamom pods, shelled and ground
¹⁄₂ teaspoon freshly ground black pepper, or to taste
1 teaspoon salt, or to taste
¹⁄₄ teaspoon garam masala
2 tablespoons shelled, raw pistachios, thinly sliced

1. In a medium bowl, soak the rice in the water, about 30 minutes. Put the almonds in a small skillet and roast, stirring and shaking the skillet, over medium heat until a few shades darker, about 1 minute. Reserve for garnish. Soak the saffron in the milk about 15 minutes.

2. Heat the ghee (or oil) in a large nonstick saucepan over medium-high heat and sauté the ginger, cumin, cardamom, and black pepper, about 1 minute. Add the rice with the water it was soaking in. Mix in the salt and bring to a boil over high heat. Reduce the heat to lowest setting, cover the pan (partially at first, until the foam subsides, then snugly), and cook until the rice is almost done, 8 to 10 minutes.

3. Uncover the pan, sprinkle the saffron milk over the rice, then cover the pan and cook another 5 minutes to blend the flavors. Do not stir the rice while it cooks. Remove from the heat and let the rice rest undisturbed about 5 minutes. Transfer to a serving platter, lightly mix in the garam masala, then scatter the roasted almonds and the pistachios on top and serve.

Basmati Rice with Whole Spices

Khadha Masala Chaval

Makes 4 to 6 servings

This is another everyday pullao *(pilaf). You simply sizzle a few additional whole spices, along with the typical cumin seeds, and end up with a dish that has a lot more flavor. This* pullao *also looks pretty—the whole spices stand out in the fluffy white rice and continue to spread their fragrance until they are pushed to the side of the guest's plate.*

1¹/₂ cups basmati rice, sorted and washed
    in 3 to 4 changes of water
2³/₄ cups water
1¹/₂ tablespoons peanut oil or melted ghee
1 teaspoon cumin seeds
2 bay leaves
1 (2-inch) stick cinnamon, broken
5 green cardamom pods, crushed lightly
    to break the skin
4 black cardamom pods, crushed lightly
    to break the skin
8 to 10 whole cloves
¹/₂ teaspoon coarsely ground black pepper,
    or to taste
³/₄ teaspoon salt, or to taste
Finely chopped fresh cilantro

1. In a medium bowl, soak the rice in the water about 30 minutes.

2. Heat the oil (or ghee) in a large saucepan over medium-high heat and add the cumin seeds; they should sizzle upon contact with the hot oil. Lower the heat to medium, then quickly add all the remaining spices and cook, stirring, about 1 minute.

3. Add the rice plus the water it was soaking in. Mix in the salt and bring to a boil over high heat. Reduce the heat to low, cover the pan (partially at first, until the foam subsides, then snugly), and cook until the rice is done, 10 to 15 minutes. Do not stir the rice while it cooks. Remove from the heat and let the rice rest undisturbed about 5 minutes. Transfer to a serving platter, garnish with the cilantro, and serve.

Quick Cilantro-Garlic Pilaf with Peas

Hara Dhaniya Lassan, aur Muttar ka Pullao

Makes 4 to 6 servings

Indians routinely make everyday pullaos *(pilafs) like this one in a pressure cooker to save time. You save even more time by not soaking the rice before cooking, as would be done for pan-cooked* pullaos. *The rice will stick together more than is common for* basmati *rice, but it is still satisfying and delicious.*

2 tablespoons canola oil
1¹/₂ teaspoons cumin seeds
3 to 4 whole red chile peppers, such as such as chile
    de arbol
1 (1-inch) stick cinnamon
3 to 5 black cardamom pods, crushed lightly
    to break the skin
1 small onion, cut in half lengthwise and
    thinly sliced
2 large cloves fresh garlic, minced
1 to 3 fresh green chile peppers, such as serrano,
    minced with seeds
1 cup frozen peas
1¹/₂ cups finely chopped fresh cilantro, including
    soft stems + 2 tablespoons for garnish
¹/₂ teaspoon garam masala
1 teaspoon salt, or to taste
1¹/₄ cups basmati rice, sorted and washed
    in 3 to 4 changes of water
2¹/₃ cups water

1. Heat the oil in a pressure cooker over medium-high heat and add the cumin seeds, red chile peppers, cinnamon, and cardamom pods; they should sizzle upon contact with the hot oil. Quickly add the onion and cook, stirring, until golden, about 3 minutes.

2. Add the garlic, green chile peppers, peas, cilantro, garam masala, and salt and cook over high heat, stirring, about 2 minutes.

3. Add the rice and the water, secure the lid of the pressure cooker, place it over high heat and cook until the pressure gauge indicates high pressure. Then remove from the heat and allow the pot to depressurize on its own, 12 to 15 minutes. Carefully open the lid. Do not stir or cook any more, or you will break the rice grains.

Ginger-Mint Pilaf with Potatoes and Roasted Cumin Seeds

Adrak-Pudina Pullao

Makes 4 to 6 servings

This is one of those delightfully light, yet impressive preparations that can be served any time you have access to fresh mint and ginger. Both flavors lend it what I refer to as the "tingle factor."

1¼ cups basmati rice, sorted and washed
    in 3 to 4 changes of water
2⅓ cups water
2 teaspoons cumin seeds
2 tablespoons vegetable oil
1 small onion, cut in half lengthwise and thinly sliced
1 small potato (any kind), finely chopped
1½ tablespoons peeled minced fresh ginger
2 tablespoons minced fresh mint leaves
1 fresh green chile pepper, such as serrano,
    minced with seeds
¾ teaspoon salt, or to taste

1. In a medium bowl, soak the rice in the water, about 30 minutes.

2. Put the cumin seeds in a small skillet and roast, shaking the skillet, over medium heat until fragrant and a few shades darker, about 1 minute. Then coarsely crush the seeds with the back of a spoon and reserve.

3. Heat the oil in a large saucepan over medium-high heat and sauté the onion over medium heat until brown, about 7 minutes. Add the potato, ginger, half the mint, and the green chile pepper and cook, stirring, about 2 minutes.

4. Add the rice with the water it was soaking in, and the salt, and bring to a boil over high heat. Reduce the heat to the lowest setting, cover the pan (partially at first, until the foam subsides, then snugly), and cook until the rice is done, 10 to 15 minutes. Do not stir the rice while it cooks. Remove from the heat and let the rice rest undisturbed about 5 minutes. Transfer to a serving platter, sprinkle the roasted cumin and the remaining mint leaves on top, and serve.

South and West Indian Vegetarian Rice Dishes

South Indian Mustard and Asafoetida Pilaf

Dakshini Raayi aur Hing ka Pullao

Makes 4 to 6 servings

Made with popular south Indian spices, this fragrant pullao *has become a favorite of family and friends. I make it at every opportunity; it is easy and does not require any chopping. Serve it with plain yogurt or present it with a curry such as Mixed Vegetables in Tomato-Cream Sauce (page 414) or Curried Paneer Cheese with Peas and Potatoes (page 332)—rice always elicits rave reviews.*

1¼ cups basmati rice, sorted and washed
   in 3 to 4 changes of water
2⅓ cups water
1 tablespoon canola oil
1 teaspoon cumin seeds
1 teaspoon black mustard seeds
½ teaspoon coarsely ground black pepper
½ teaspoon ground fenugreek seeds
⅛ teaspoon ground asafoetida
1 tablespoon dried curry leaves
1 teaspoon dried mint leaves
½ teaspoon dried fenugreek leaves
¾ teaspoon salt, or to taste
¼ teaspoon ground turmeric
Finely chopped fresh cilantro

1. In a medium bowl, soak the rice in the water about 30 minutes.

2. Heat the oil in a large saucepan over medium-high heat and add the cumin, mustard seeds, and black pepper; they should splutter upon contact with the hot oil, so lower the heat and cover the pan until the spluttering subsides. Quickly stir in the fenugreek seeds, asafoetida, and curry, mint and fenugreek leaves, and then add the rice with the water it was soaking in. Mix in the salt and turmeric and bring to a boil over high heat.

3. Reduce the heat to the lowest setting, cover the pan (partially at first, until the foam subsides, then snugly), and cook until the rice is done, 10 to 15 minutes. Do not stir the rice while it cooks. Remove from the heat and let the rice rest undisturbed about 5 minutes. Transfer to a serving platter, garnish with cilantro, and serve.

Yogurt and Cashew Rice

Dahi-Kaaju Bhath

Makes 4 to 6 servings

*This popular south Indian rice dish, made with non-*basmati *long-grain white rice, comes well moistened with calcium-rich yogurt. Little wonder that it is frequently packed for school lunches and served as a healthy midday meal with a vegetable on the side.*

This is one example of when Indians bend the rule, "fluffy, separate grains make perfect rice." Though long-grain, this rice, when made right, is smooth and creamy, very much like a risotto. In recent years, Thai jasmine rice has been used as a substitute for the similar Indian long-grain rice. Try it if you like.

1¼ cups long-grain white rice, such as jasmine rice,
   sorted
2½ cups water
1 teaspoon salt, or to taste
1½ to 2 cups nonfat plain yogurt, whisked until smooth
2 to 4 seedless cucumber (about ⅓ pound),
   peeled and grated
1 tablespoon peeled minced fresh ginger
1 fresh green chile pepper, such as serrano,
   minced with seeds
1 tablespoon peanut oil
5 to 7 whole dried red chile peppers,
   such as chile de arbol
1 tablespoon black mustard seeds
½ cup coarsely chopped raw cashews
⅛ teaspoon ground asafoetida
1½ tablespoons minced fresh curry leaves
2 tablespoons finely chopped fresh cilantro

1. Bring the rice, water, and salt to a boil in a medium nonstick saucepan over medium-high heat. Reduce the heat to low, cover the pan (partially at first, until the foam subsides, then snugly), and cook until all the water has been absorbed and the rice is tender, 12 to 15 minutes.

2. In a medium bowl, combine the yogurt, cucumber, ginger, and green chile pepper and mix well. Then mix into the rice. Cover and keep warm.

3. Heat the oil in a small saucepan over medium heat and cook the red chile peppers, stirring, about 1 minute. Then add the mustard seeds; they should splutter upon contact with the hot oil, so cover the pan and reduce the heat until the spluttering subsides. Quickly add the cashews, asafoetida, and curry leaves and stir about 2 minutes over medium heat. Transfer to the rice and mix well. Place the rice on a serving platter, garnish with cilantro, and serve.

Coorgi Yogurt Rice
Coorg ka Dahi-Bhath

Makes 4 to 6 servings

From Corgi, in southwestern India, comes this dish, one of the simplest but most pleasing rice preparations. It is often served as a soother (in spite of the green chile pepper) after a spicy meal. Omit the green chile pepper if you wish, and pack it for picnics and potlucks.

1 cup long-grain white rice, sorted

2 cups water

1 tablespoon peanut oil

1 small sweet onion, such as Vidalia or Maui, finely chopped

1 teaspoon peeled minced fresh ginger

1 fresh green chile pepper, such as serrano, minced with seeds

3/4 teaspoon salt, or to taste

1 1/2 to 2 cups nonfat plain yogurt, whisked until smooth

1/4 cup finely chopped fresh cilantro, including soft stems

1/4 teaspoon freshly ground black pepper, or to taste

1/4 teaspoon ground paprika

1. Bring the rice and water to a boil in a medium nonstick saucepan over medium-high heat. Reduce the heat to the lowest setting, cover the pan (partially at first, until the foam subsides, then snugly), and cook until all the water has been absorbed and the rice is tender, 12 to 15 minutes.

2. Heat the oil in a medium nonstick wok or skillet over medium-high heat and cook the onion, ginger, and green chile pepper until heated through, 1 minute. Add the rice and salt and cook, stirring to break any clumps, until well mixed. Mix in the yogurt and the cilantro and remove from the heat. Transfer to a serving dish, garnish with black pepper and paprika, and serve (preferably) at room temperature.

Variation: To serve this rice as a salad, finely chop 3 Roma tomatoes, 1 small seedless cucumber, and 1/2 cup daikon or red radishes, then mix the vegetables and about 1 tablespoon minced fresh ginger into the cooked rice.

Long-Grain Rice with Roasted Peanuts
Moong-Phalli Bhath

Makes 4 to 6 servings

This recipe beautifully combines the delicate crunch of roasted peanuts and dals *(legumes) with the softness of cooked rice. Its flavor is enhanced by the addition of black mustard seeds and fresh curry leaves—a standard southern Indian seasoning.*

2 tablespoons dried yellow split chickpeas (channa dal), sorted

1 tablespoon dried white urad beans (dhulli urad dal), sorted

1 1/4 cups long-grain white rice, sorted

2 1/2 cups water

1/4 teaspoon ground turmeric

1 teaspoon salt, or to taste

1/2 cup shelled raw peanuts, red skin on or removed

2 tablespoons peanut oil

3 to 5 whole dried red chile peppers, such as chile de arbol

1 1/2 teaspoons black mustard seeds

1/8 teaspoon ground asafoetida

1 1/2 tablespoons minced fresh curry leaves

2 to 3 tablespoons fresh lemon juice

2 tablespoons finely chopped fresh cilantro, including soft stems

2 tablespoons finely sliced scallions, green parts only

1. In a small bowl, soak the 2 dals in water to cover by 2 inches, about 30 minutes. Drain well and spread on paper towels to dry.

2. Put the rice, water, turmeric, and salt in a medium nonstick saucepan and bring to a boil over medium-high heat. Reduce the heat to low, cover the pan (partially at first until the foam subsides, then snugly), and cook until all the water has been absorbed and the rice is tender, 12 to 15 minutes.

3. In a small nonstick skillet, roast the peanuts, stirring and shaking the pan, over medium heat until golden, about 2 minutes. Transfer to a bowl. In the same skillet, heat the oil over medium heat and cook the red chile peppers and the 2 dals, stirring, until golden, about 1 minute. (Stand away from the pan in case the peppers burst.) Add the mustard seeds, asafoetida, and curry leaves and cook, stirring, another 30 seconds.

4. Add the roasted peanuts, cook about 1 minute, then transfer everything to the rice pan. Add the lemon juice and mix well. Transfer to a serving platter, garnish with the chopped cilantro and scallion greens, and serve hot. Or refrigerate up to 2 days and serve cold.

Lemon Rice
Nimboo Bhath

Makes 4 to 6 servings

Originally an old classic from Tamilnadu (formerly Madras, in the southeast) that impresses party guests and the lunchbox crowd alike, this dish is a favorite all over southern India. Garnished with red chile peppers and chopped greens, the presentation is enticing and the taste lives up to the promise.

1 1/2 cups long-grain white rice, sorted

3 cups water

1/4 teaspoon ground turmeric

1 teaspoon salt, or to taste

2 tablespoons fresh lemon juice

2 tablespoons peanut oil

3 to 5 dried red chili peppers, such as chile de arbol, broken

1 tablespoon dried yellow split chickpeas (channa dal), sorted

1 tablespoon dried white urad beans (dhulli urad dal), sorted

2 (1-inch) sticks cinnamon

6 to 8 whole cloves

1 1/2 teaspoons brown mustard seeds

1/16 teaspoon ground asafoetida

1/4 cup finely chopped fresh cilantro, including soft stems

1 1/2 tablespoons minced fresh curry leaves

1. In a large bowl, put the rice, water, turmeric, and salt in a medium nonstick saucepan and bring to a boil over medium-high heat. Reduce the heat to low, cover the pan (partially at first until the foam subsides, and then snugly), and cook until all the water has been absorbed and the rice is tender, 12 to 15 minutes. Carefully mix in the lemon juice and transfer the rice to a serving platter. Cover and keep warm.

2. Heat the oil in a small nonstick saucepan over medium-high heat and add the red chile peppers, both the dals, cinnamon, and cloves. Cook, stirring, until the dals are golden, about 1 minute. (Stand away from the pan in case the peppers burst.) Add the mustard seeds, asafoetida, cilantro, and curry leaves and cook, stirring, another minute. Transfer to the rice platter and carefully mix into the rice, taking care that some of this mixture is visible as a garnish. Serve hot.

Variations: To make this dish in the authentic south Indian way, first spread the freshly cooked rice on a tray and break up any clumps. Then mix in the lemon juice and, finally, top it with the sizzling oil (or ghee) and spices. For a flavor change, sauté and mix in some green peas and minced ginger.

South Indian Sesame Rice

Dakshini Til Bhath

Makes 4 to 6 servings

Serve this savory and spicy rice any time of the day, by itself with a yogurt raita *or* pachadi *(yogurt side dish), with a* dal *(legume) dish, or simply pack it for school lunches and picnics.*

1½ cups long-grain white rice, sorted

3 cups water

1 teaspoon salt, or to taste

¼ cup white sesame seeds

1 tablespoon dried split black urad beans (chilkae vaali urad dal), sorted

2 to 5 dried red chile peppers, such as chile de arbol, broken

2 tablespoons peanut oil

½ teaspoon Asian sesame oil

10 to 12 raw cashews, coarsely broken

8 to 10 fresh curry leaves

2 scallions, green parts only, finely chopped

1. Put the rice, water, and salt in a medium nonstick saucepan and bring to a boil over medium-high heat. Reduce the heat to low, cover the pan (partially at first until the foam subsides, and then snugly), and cook until all the water has been absorbed and the rice is tender, 12 to 15 minutes. Let the rice rest undisturbed about 5 minutes.

2. In a small skillet, over medium heat, dry-roast the sesame seeds until golden, remove to a bowl, and set aside about 2 teaspoons for garnish. Then dry-roast the dal and red chile peppers until golden. Transfer to a spice or coffee grinder, along with the sesame seeds, and grind coarsely.

3. Heat both oils in a large nonstick skillet over medium heat and cook the cashews and curry leaves, stirring, until golden, 1 minute. Add the scallion greens and stir about 30 seconds.

4. Add the cooked rice and ground sesame-red chile mixture and mix well. Cover and cook over low heat 3 to 5 minutes. Transfer to a serving dish, garnish with the reserved sesame seeds, and serve.

South Indian Tamarind Rice

Puliyodarai or Puliogore

Makes 4 to 6 servings

Known as puliyodarai *or* puliogore *in the south, this classic is a tribute to its main ingredient—tamarind. It is primarily tart, with a fruity, sweet fragrance. This rice is lovely by itself and pairs deliciously with a yogurt* pachadi, *such as Spicy Yogurt with Mango and Coconut (page 245).*

½ cup Tamarind Paste, or to taste (page 54)

1¼ cups long-grain white rice, sorted

2½ cups water

1 teaspoon salt, or to taste

1½ tablespoons coriander seeds

1 teaspoon white sesame seeds

2 to 4 dried red chile peppers, such as chile de arbol, broken

2 tablespoons vegetable oil or melted ghee

½ cup shelled raw peanuts, without red skin

15 to 20 raw cashews, coarsely chopped

10 to 15 fresh curry leaves

1 teaspoon black mustard seeds

½ teaspoon coarsely ground fenugreek seeds

1 tablespoon dried yellow split chickpeas (channa dal), sorted

¼ teaspoon ground turmeric

1. Prepare the tamarind paste. Then, put the rice, water, and salt in a medium nonstick saucepan and bring to a boil over medium-high heat. Reduce the heat to low, cover the pan (partially at first until the foam subsides, and then snugly), and cook until all the water has been absorbed and the rice is tender, 12 to 15 minutes. Let the rice rest undisturbed about 5 minutes, then transfer to a serving platter. Cover and keep warm.

2. In a small skillet, over medium heat, dry-roast—separately and in order—coriander seeds (about 1 minute), sesame seeds (about 30 seconds), and red chile peppers (about 1½ minutes), until lightly browned, transferring each to a bowl as it is done. Let cool, then grind them all together as fine as possible. Mix into the rice.

3. Heat 1 tablespoon oil in a small nonstick skillet over medium-high heat and cook the peanuts, cashews, and curry leaves until fragrant and lightly browned. Add to the rice.

4. Add the remaining 1 tablespoon oil to the skillet and add the mustard and fenugreek seeds; they should splutter upon contact with the hot oil, so cover the pan and reduce the heat until the spluttering subsides. Quickly add the chickpea dal and turmeric, and cook, stirring, until golden, then add the tamarind paste and cook, stirring, 1 to 2 minutes. Transfer this sauce to the rice platter and mix it into the rice, taking care that some of it is visible as a garnish. Serve.

Variation: To enhance and bring out the sweetness of the dish, sprinkle 2 to 3 tablespoons powdered jaggery (gur) or dark brown sugar over the dish while it's still warm—just after you've transferred it to a platter.

Potato, Coconut, and Yogurt Fried Rice
Aalu-Nariyal ka Dahi Bhath

Makes 4 to 6 servings

This soft-cooked rice dish, with its distinct sweet and tart flavors from the coconut and yogurt, and an extraordinary fragrance from mustard and fenugreek seeds and fresh ginger is another southern Indian specialty. Eat it as a snack or serve it as part of a brunch menu.

4 cups (1 recipe) Steamed Basmati Rice (page 533)
2 medium potatoes (any kind)
1/3 cup fresh, frozen, or unsweetened dried grated coconut
3 tablespoons peeled minced fresh ginger
1 to 3 fresh green chile peppers, such as serrano, minced with seeds
1 tablespoon melted ghee or vegetable oil

1 teaspoon cumin seeds
1 teaspoon black mustard seeds
1/2 teaspoon coarsely ground fenugreek seeds
1/8 teaspoon ground asafoetida
1/2 cup finely chopped fresh cilantro, with soft stems
1/4 teaspoon ground turmeric
1/2 teaspoon salt, or to taste
1 cup nonfat plain yogurt, whisked until smooth

1. Prepare the rice. Meanwhile, boil the potatoes in lightly salted water to cover until tender, about 20 minutes, then peel and cut them into 1/2-inch pieces.

2. Place the coconut in a large nonstick wok or saucepan and stir over medium heat golden, about 1 minute. Then add the ginger and green chile peppers and stir another minute. Remove from the pan.

3. To the pan, add the ghee (or oil), then add the cumin, mustard seeds, and fenugreek seeds; they should splutter upon contact with the hot oil, so cover the pan until the spluttering subsides. Quickly add the asafoetida, potatoes, cilantro (save some for garnish), turmeric, and salt and stir about 5 minutes.

4. Mix in the cooked rice and yogurt, cover, and cook until all the yogurt is absorbed by the rice, 5 minutes. Transfer to a serving dish, garnish with the reserved cilantro, and serve.

Madras-Style Spicy Eggplant Rice
Vangi Bhath

Makes 4 to 6 servings

Vangi is eggplants and bhath *is rice in Tamil, the language of Tamilnadu (formerly Madras). This is a version of the classic dish, which is very popular all over the southern states of India.*

The rice and eggplants are first cooked separately and then together, and the dish is then generally served with paapads *(lentil wafers) and pickles. A* rasam *(a spicy south Indian soup) also makes a nice accompaniment.*

¼ cup Tamarind Paste (page 54)

4 cups (1 recipe) Steamed Basmati Rice (page 533)

1 cup grated fresh or frozen coconut or shredded unsweetened dried coconut

8 to 10 dried red chile peppers, such as chile de arbol, broken

1½ tablespoons coriander seeds

1 tablespoon dried yellow split chickpeas (channa dal), sorted

1 tablespoon dried white urad beans (dhulli urad dal), sorted

1 teaspoon cumin seeds

2 teaspoons sesame seeds

½ teaspoon green cardamom seeds

½ teaspoon black peppercorns

¼ teaspoon ground turmeric

¼ teaspoon ground cloves

¼ teaspoon ground cinnamon

2 tablespoons peanut oil

1 tablespoon black mustard seeds

1 tablespoon minced fresh curry leaves

⅛ teaspoon ground asafoetida

1 large eggplant (about 1 pound), cut in 1-inch pieces

1 teaspoon salt, or to taste

1. Prepare the tamarind paste and then the rice. Then place the coconut, red chile peppers, coriander, both the dals, cumin, sesame seeds, cardamom seeds, and black peppercorns in a medium skillet and dry-roast, stirring and shaking the skillet, over medium heat until golden and fragrant, about 2 minutes. Let cool, then and grind in a spice or coffee grinder until fine. Mix in the turmeric, cloves, and cinnamon.

2. Heat the oil in a large nonstick wok or saucepan over medium-high heat and add the mustard seeds; they should splutter upon contact with the hot oil, so cover the pan until the spluttering subsides. Quickly add the curry leaves, asafoetida, eggplant, salt, and half the ground spice mixture. Cover the pan and cook over medium-high heat the first 2 to 3 minutes, then reduce the heat to medium and cook until the eggplant is quite soft, about 10 minutes.

3. Add the tamarind paste and cook about 5 minutes. Gently mix in the cooked rice and most of the remaining ground spice mixture (save some for garnish). Cover and cook over low heat, 5 to 7 minutes,

to blend the flavors. Transfer to a serving dish, sprinkle the reserved spice mixture on top, and serve.

Variation: To make this dish a biryani, preheat the oven to 400°F, then layer the rice and eggplant in an oven-safe dish, cover, and bake 15 to 20 minutes.

Tangy South Indian Rice and Pigeon Peas
Bise Bele Bhath

Makes 4 to 6 servings

Bise *means hot,* bele *means* dal *(legumes) and* bhath *means rice in Tamil, a south Indian language, and this hot, tangy, spicy rice and* dal *dish is a masterpiece from the south. Meant to be eaten with pickles and* paapads *(lentil wafers),* bisi bele bhath *can also be a main dish, served with a yogurt* raita *or* pachadi *(yogurt side dish).*

¼ cup Tamarind Paste (page 54)

¾ cup dried split pigeon peas (toor dal), sorted and washed in 3 to 4 changes of water

4 cups water

2 to 4 dried red chile peppers, such as chile de arbol, coarsely broken

1 tablespoon coriander seeds

1 teaspoon dried yellow split chickpeas (channa dal), sorted

1 teaspoon dried white urad beans (dhulli urad dal), sorted

¼ teaspoon fenugreek seeds

2 tablespoons unsweetened grated or shredded dried coconut

1 cup long-grain white rice, sorted

3 cups finely chopped mixed fresh or frozen vegetables, such as potatoes, green beans, eggplants, and peas

¼ teaspoon ground turmeric

⅛ teaspoon ground asafoetida

1 teaspoon salt, or to taste

2 tablespoons vegetable oil or melted ghee

1 teaspoon black mustard seeds

8 to 10 fresh curry leaves

¼ cup coarsely chopped raw cashews

1 teaspoon garam masala

¼ cup finely chopped fresh cilantro, including soft stems

1. Prepare the tamarind paste. Place the toor dal and 2 cups water in a large saucepan and bring to a boil over high heat. Reduce the heat to medium-low and simmer, uncovered, stirring occasionally, until the toor dal is very soft and creamy, about 20 minutes.

2. Meanwhile, in a small skillet, dry-roast together the red chile peppers, coriander seeds, channa and urad dals, and fenugreek seeds over medium heat until fragrant and a few shades darker, about 2 minutes. Add the coconut and stir until the coconut is golden, 1 to 2 minutes. Transfer to a small spice or coffee grinder and grind to make as smooth as possible.

3. To the cooked toor dal, add the rice and vegetables, along with the turmeric, asafoetida, salt, tamarind, and the remaining 2 cups water and bring to a boil over high heat. Reduce the heat to low, cover the pan, and cook until the rice and vegetables are tender, 12 to 15 minutes. Mix in the roasted spice mixture and transfer to a serving dish.

4. Heat the ghee (or oil) in a small nonstick saucepan over medium-high heat and add the mustard seeds; they should splutter upon contact with the hot oil, so cover the pan until the spluttering subsides. Quickly add the curry leaves, cashews, and the garam masala and cook, stirring, until the cashews are golden, about 1 minute. Add to the rice and swirl lightly to mix, with parts of it visible as a garnish. Sprinkle the cilantro on top and serve.

Goan Coconut Milk Pilaf
Goan Nariyal Doodh ka Pullao

Makes 4 to 6 servings

Goa is situated on the western coast of India and has a warm climate perfect for growing coconuts. It's no surprise, then, that Goan cuisine uses coconuts generously in dishes. The Goan spice combinations, influenced by Portuguese inhabitants, are also quite different from other parts of India, and that is what marks Goan cuisine.

1/2 to 1 teaspoon Goan Vindaloo Powder (page 28 or store-bought) or garam masala
1 cup Coconut Milk (page 44 or store-bought)
2 tablespoons grated fresh coconut or shredded unsweetened dried coconut
1 to 2 tablespoons peanut oil
1 (1-inch) stick cinnamon
5 whole cloves
6 green cardamom pods, lightly crushed to break the skin
1 large onion, finely chopped
1 1/2 cups basmati rice, sorted and washed in 3 to 4 changes of water
1 3/4 cups water
1 teaspoon salt, or to taste
2 tablespoons finely chopped fresh cilantro

1. Prepare the vindaloo masala and the coconut milk. Then dry-roast the coconut in a small skillet or tava over medium heat until fragrant, but just barely darker, 1 to 2 minutes.

2. Heat the oil in a medium nonstick saucepan over medium-high heat, add the cinnamon, cloves, and cardamom pods, and cook, stirring, until fragrant, about 1 minute.

3. Add the onion and cook until golden, about 5 minutes. Then mix in the rice, coconut milk, water, and salt and bring to a boil over high heat. Reduce the heat to low, cover the pan (partially at first until the foam subsides, and then snugly), and cook until all the water has been absorbed and the rice is tender, 12 to 15 minutes. Do not stir the rice while it is cooking. Remove from the heat and allow the rice to rest about 5 minutes. Then transfer to a serving platter, lightly mix in the roasted coconut, vindaloo powder (or garam masala), and cilantro, and serve.

Variation: For a traditional, even richer flavor, make this recipe with only coconut milk—simply substitute more coconut milk for the water. A similar rice is also made in southern India, but they add 1/4 teaspoon turmeric and 3 to 5 dried red chile peppers along with the cinnamon and cloves.

Vegetarian Pilafs (Sabzi kae Pullao)

Basmati Pilaf with Caramelized Onions and Broccoli

Bhunna Pyaz aur Hari Gobhi ka Pullao

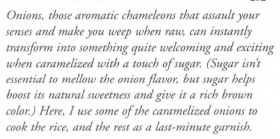

Makes 4 to 6 servings

Onions, those aromatic chameleons that assault your senses and make you weep when raw, can instantly transform into something quite welcoming and exciting when caramelized with a touch of sugar. (Sugar isn't essential to mellow the onion flavor, but sugar helps boost its natural sweetness and give it a rich brown color.) Here, I use some of the caramelized onions to cook the rice, and the rest as a last-minute garnish.

1¹/₂ cups basmati rice, sorted and washed
     in 3 to 4 changes of water
2³/₄ cups water
4 tablespoons peanut oil or melted ghee
6 to 8 green cardamom pods, crushed lightly
     to break the skin
1 (1-inch) stick cinnamon
6 to 8 whole cloves
3 to 4 small onions, cut in half lengthwise and
     thinly sliced
2 teaspoons sugar
1 teaspoon salt, or to taste
1 teaspoon cumin seeds
1 teaspoon black mustard seeds
1 small head broccoli, cut into ¹/₂-inch florets,
     stems cut into ¹/₄-inch pieces

1. In a medium bowl, soak the rice in the water, about 30 minutes.

2. Heat 3 tablespoons oil (or ghee) in a medium nonstick saucepan over medium-high heat and cook the cardamom pods, cinnamon, and cloves, stirring, about 30 seconds. Add the onions and cook, stirring as needed, until golden, about 5 minutes. Sprinkle the sugar over the onions, reduce the heat to medium-low, and continue to cook until they are dark brown. With a slotted spatula, remove half the onions, drain them on paper towels (to make them crisp), and reserve for garnish.

3. To the pan, add the rice, the water it was soaking in, and the salt and bring to a boil over medium-high heat. Reduce the heat to low, cover the pan (partially at first until the foam subsides, and then snugly), and cook until all the water has been absorbed and the rice is tender, 12 to 15 minutes. Do not stir the rice while it is cooking. Remove from the heat and allow the rice to rest about 5 minutes.

4. Meanwhile in a small saucepan, heat the remaining 1 tablespoon oil and add the cumin and mustard seeds; they should splutter upon contact with the hot oil, so lower the heat and cover the pan until the spluttering subsides. Quickly add the broccoli florets and stir about 2 minutes. Transfer the rice to a serving platter and lightly mix in the broccoli, with some of it visible as a garnish, top with the reserved onions, and serve.

Mixed Cauliflower Pilaf
Neelam ka Gobhi Pullao

Makes 4 to 6 servings

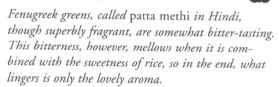

My friend Neelam Rai in Los Angeles makes this pullao *with different members of the cruciferous vegetable family. With a distinctive taste and aroma, and packed with some of nature's best antioxidants, this simply flavored, energizing dish is one that can be repeated again and again. When you cut the cauliflower and broccoli into tiny half-inch florets, they look like jewels in the rice.*

4 cups (1 recipe) Simple Cumin Basmati Rice
    (page 535)
2 tablespoons vegetable oil
1 small onion, cut in half lengthwise and thinly sliced
1 cup finely chopped kohlrabi
1 cup thinly sliced cauliflower florets, stems discarded
1 cup thinly sliced broccoli florets, stems discarded
1/4 head finely shredded green cabbage
1/2 teaspoon salt, or to taste
1/2 teaspoon freshly ground black pepper
1/4 teaspoon hot red pepper flakes, or to taste
1 teaspoon garam masala
1/4 cup finely chopped fresh cilantro,
    including soft stems

1. Prepare the rice and let cool to room temperature. Then, heat the oil in a large nonstick skillet over medium-high heat and cook the onion, stirring, until golden, about 5 minutes.

2. Add the kohlrabi, cauliflower, broccoli, and cabbage, along with the salt, black pepper, red pepper flakes, and half the garam masala, and stir about 2 minutes. Reduce the heat to medium, cover the pan, and cook until the vegetables are crisp-tender, 3 to 5 minutes.

3. Add the rice and the cilantro and mix carefully, trying not to break the rice. Transfer to a serving

dish, sprinkle the remaining garam masala on top, and serve.

Variation: Give your rice more protein by adding about 1 cup paneer cheese (page 43 or store-bought), extra-firm tofu, or cooked chicken, cut into 1/2-inch pieces, along with the vegetables in Step 2.

Roasted Fresh Fenugreek Leaves Pilaf
Bhuni Methi ka Pullao

Makes 4 to 6 servings

Fenugreek greens, called patta methi *in Hindi, though superbly fragrant, are somewhat bitter-tasting. This bitterness, however, mellows when it is combined with the sweetness of rice, so in the end, what lingers is only the lovely aroma.*

4 cups (1 recipe) Simple Cumin Basmati Rice
    (page 535)
1 large russet potato
2 tablespoons vegetable oil
2 to 3 bunches fresh fenugreek leaves (about 4 cups),
    trimmed and finely chopped
1/4 teaspoon ground turmeric
1/2 teaspoon salt, or to taste
1/4 teaspoon garam masala

1. Prepare the rice and keep warm. Meanwhile, boil the potato in lightly salted water to cover until soft, about 20 minutes. Let cool, then peel and chop finely.

2. Place the oil and the fenugreek leaves in a large cast-iron or nonstick skillet and cook, over medium heat, stirring, about 5 minutes. Add the potato, turmeric, and salt and continue to cook until the leaves are dark brown and crisp, about 20 minutes. Transfer the rice to a serving platter and carefully mix in the fenugreek and potatoes. Sprinkle the garam masala on top and serve.

Morel Mushroom Pilaf with Pistachios and Silver Leaves

Gucchi-Pista Pullao

Makes 4 to 6 servings

Morel mushrooms are called gucchi *or* gucchiyan *in Hindi, and this exotic* pullao *is traditionally associated with weddings and special occasions. And that calls for ghee, pistachios, and a garnish of pure silver leaves (found in Indian grocery stores). In place of the morels, try using chanterelles or any other wild mushrooms.*

1 tablespoon Basic Ginger-Garlic Paste
    (page 47 or store-bought)
10 to 12 dried morel mushrooms
1/2 cup blanched raw pistachios
    (Blanching Raw Nuts, page 35)
1 1/4 cups basmati rice, sorted and washed
    in 3 to 4 changes of water
2 1/3 cups water
2 tablespoons vegetable oil or melted ghee
2 (1-inch) sticks cinnamon, broken
5 to 7 green cardamom pods, crushed lightly
    to break the skin
3 black cardamom pods, crushed lightly
    to break the skin
2 bay leaves
1/2 teaspoon black peppercorns
1 teaspoon black cumin seeds
1 medium onion, cut in half lengthwise and
    thinly sliced
1 teaspoon dried mint leaves
1/4 cup finely chopped fresh cilantro,
    including soft stems
6 (4-inch) squares silver leaves (optional)
1/4 teaspoon garam masala

1. Prepare the ginger-garlic paste. Wash then soak the morel mushrooms in water to cover by 2 inches, 1 hour or longer. Drain (saving the water) and wash under running water to remove any loosened dirt. Then slice each mushroom into thin 1/4-inch rings. Meanwhile, blanch the pistachios.

2. Strain the mushroom water through paper towels and use it, cup for cup, in place of plain water to soak

and cook the rice. In a medium bowl, soak the rice in the strained mushroom water, about 30 minutes.

3. Heat the ghee (or oil) in a large nonstick saucepan over medium-high heat and stir-fry the cinnamon, cardamom pods, bay leaves, and black peppercorns until fragrant, 1 minute. Add the cumin, then mix in the onion and cook, stirring, until golden, 3 to 5 minutes.

4. Add the ginger-garlic paste and mint leaves, then mix in the rice with the water it was soaking in, and bring to a boil over high heat. Reduce the heat to low, cover the pan (partially at first until the foam subsides, and then snugly), and cook until all the water has been absorbed but the rice is still not fully cooked, 8 to 10 minutes.

5. Carefully mix in the mushroom rings, cilantro, and half the pistachios, cover the pan, and cook over low heat until the rice is done, 5 to 7 minutes. Remove from the heat and allow the rice to rest undisturbed about 5 minutes. Transfer to a serving platter, fluff with a fork, garnish with the silver leaves (if using), the reserved pistachios and the garam masala, and serve.

Stir-Fried Mushrooms and Red Chard Pilaf

Khumb aur Laal Saag ka Pullao

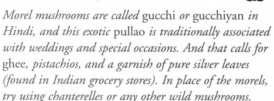

Makes 4 to 6 servings

Here, we cook the rice and vegetables separately and then serve them together on a platter. Don't discard the red stems of the Swiss chard—they add a lovely pink color to the rice. This recipe suggests a special presentation, but you can also just gently mix the rice and mushrooms together. The choice of mushrooms and greens can vary every time you make this dish.

4 cups (1 recipe) Simple Cumin Basmati Rice (page 535)
1 pound medium mushrooms, such as white button,
    washed and quartered
2 tablespoons vegetable oil
1 bunch (about 1 pound) finely chopped red chard or
    beet greens, trimmed, washed, and finely chopped
1 large clove fresh garlic, minced
1 to 3 fresh green chile peppers, such as serrano,
    minced with seeds
1/4 teaspoon salt, or to taste
Freshly ground black pepper

1. Prepare the rice. Then place the mushrooms in a large nonstick skillet (with no oil) and cook, stirring, over medium-high heat until they release their juices. Continue cooking until the juices evaporate and the mushrooms are golden, 5 to 7 minutes. Remove to a bowl.

2. To the same skillet, add the oil and red chard and cook, stirring, over medium-high heat until wilted, about 3 minutes. Add the garlic, green chile peppers, and salt, reduce the heat to medium, cover the skillet, and cook until the leaves are soft, 7 to 10 minutes. Mix in the mushrooms.

3. To serve, arrange the rice in 3 to 4 diagonal rows on a platter, each about 2 inches apart. Fill the empty rows with the mushrooms and chard. Garnish with black pepper and serve.

Spinach and Red Bell Pepper Pilaf

Palak aur Shimla Mirch ka Pullao

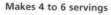

Makes 4 to 6 servings

Brilliantly colored with red, green, and white, this dish is fit to be a centerpiece on any table. Include it on a party menu, serve it at barbecues, or at home with a dal *(legume) dish or curry.*

1 teaspoon Chaat Masala (page 20 or store-bought)
4¹/₂ cups (1 recipe) Simple Cumin Basmati Rice
    (page 535)
1 tablespoon peanut oil
1 large clove garlic, minced
1 to 3 fresh green chile peppers, such as serrano,
    minced with seeds
1 teaspoon ground dried fenugreek leaves
1 large bunch fresh spinach, washed, trimmed,
    and coarsely chopped
1 large red bell pepper, cut into ³/₄-inch dice
¹/₂ teaspoon salt, or to taste
1 tablespoon minced fresh mint leaves
¹/₄ teaspoon garam masala

1. Prepare the chaat masala and the rice. Then heat the oil in a large nonstick wok or saucepan over

medium-high heat. Add the garlic, green chile peppers, fenugreek, and spinach and cook, stirring, until the spinach is wilted.

2. Lower the heat to medium, add the bell pepper, cover the pan, and cook, stirring occasionally, until the bell pepper is crisp-tender, 2 to 3 minutes. Mix in the salt.

3. Add the cooked rice and chaat masala and cook, stirring carefully, to mix. Cover and set aside 3 to 5 minutes to blend the flavors. Transfer to a serving platter, sprinkle the mint and garam masala on top, and serve.

Grilled Bell Pepper Fried Rice

Bhuni Shimla Mirch ka Pullao

Makes 4 to 6 servings

This is one of my inventive recipes, not something normally made in Indian kitchens. I've been making it for years for my family and for parties. Its smoky flavors and lovely colors always earn compliments.

4 to 5 small red and yellow bell peppers, washed
1 pasilla chile or green bell pepper, washed
2 tablespoons olive oil
1 small onion, cut in half lengthwise and thinly sliced
1 large clove fresh garlic, minced
1¹/₄ cups basmati rice, sorted and washed
    in 3 to 4 changes of water
1 tablespoon ground coriander
¹/₂ cup finely chopped fresh cilantro,
    including soft stems
2¹/₃ cups water
³/₄ teaspoon salt, or to taste
Finely chopped scallion, green parts only

1. Roast the peppers as described on page 36. Transfer to a bowl, cover with plastic wrap or foil, and set aside to cool, about 5 to 7 minutes. While they are still a little warm, peel off only the highly charred skin. Discard the stems and seeds and chop the peppers coarsely. Strain and save any juices that may have accumulated in the bowl.

2. Heat the oil in a large nonstick saucepan over medium-high heat and cook the onion, stirring, until golden, 5 minutes. Add the garlic, rice, coriander, and cilantro and cook over medium heat, stirring carefully, until golden, about 5 minutes.

3. Add the water, salt, and any reserved juices from the peppers and bring to a boil over medium-high heat. Reduce the heat to low, cover the pan, and cook until all the water has been absorbed and the rice is tender, 12 to 15 minutes. Gently mix in the roasted peppers, cover the pan, and allow the rice to rest undisturbed about 5 minutes. Transfer to a serving dish, fluff with a fork, garnish with the scallion greens, and serve.

Corn, Peas, and Tomato Fried Rice

Makki, Muttar, aur Tamatar ka Pullao

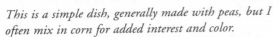

Makes 4 to 6 servings

This is a simple dish, generally made with peas, but I often mix in corn for added interest and color.

4 cups (1 recipe) Steamed Basmati Rice (page 533)
1 teaspoon peanut oil
2 tablespoons peeled minced fresh ginger
1 large clove fresh garlic, minced
1 to 3 fresh green chile peppers, such as serrano, minced with seeds
1 teaspoon cumin seeds
1 teaspoon black mustard seeds
1 tablespoon ground dried curry leaves
1 teaspoon ground dried fenugreek leaves
1 teaspoon ground dried mint leaves
1/4 teaspoon ground turmeric
1/8 teaspoon ground asafoetida
1 1/2 cups frozen peas, thawed,
1 1/2 cups frozen corn kernels, thawed
1 small onion, finely chopped
1 teaspoon salt or to taste
1 large tomato, coarsely chopped
1/2 cup finely chopped fresh cilantro, including soft stems

1. Prepare the rice. Then heat the oil in a large nonstick wok or skillet over medium-high heat and cook the ginger, garlic, and green chile peppers, stirring, about 1 minute. Add the cumin and mustard seeds; they should splutter upon contact with the hot oil, so cover the pan until the spluttering subsides. Quickly add the curry leaves, fenugreek leaves, mint leaves, turmeric, and asafoetida and stir 30 seconds.

2. Add the peas, corn, onion, and salt and stir until golden, about 5 minutes. Add the tomato and cilantro, then carefully mix in the cooked rice. Cover and cook over low heat about 5 minutes to blend the flavors. Transfer to a platter and serve.

Mixed Vegetable Pilaf

Sabzi Pullao

Makes 4 to 6 servings

This old family-style pullao *has as many variations as there are ways to combine vegetables. It is simple enough to be made every day, yet be made fancy, depending upon your choice of fresh vegetables.*

Carrots, peas, cauliflower and other everyday vegetables fall in the simple category; for a fancier version use baby squash, fresh wild mushrooms, orange and yellow bell peppers, and other colorful vegetables.

1 cup basmati rice, sorted and washed in 3 to 4 changes of water
1 3/4 cups water
2 tablespoons canola oil
1 1/2 teaspoons cumin seeds
3 to 5 black cardamom pods, crushed lightly to break the skin
1 small onion, cut in half lengthwise and thinly sliced
1 tablespoon peeled minced fresh ginger
1 to 3 fresh green chile peppers, such as serrano, minced with seeds
2 cups finely chopped fresh or frozen mixed vegetables
1/2 teaspoon garam masala
1 teaspoon salt, or to taste
1/4 cup nonfat plain yogurt, whisked until smooth
2 tablespoons finely chopped fresh cilantro

1. In a medium bowl, soak the rice in the water, about 30 minutes.

2. Heat the oil in a large nonstick saucepan over medium-high heat and add the cumin seeds and black cardamom pods; they should sizzle upon contact with the hot oil. Quickly add the onion and cook, stirring, until lightly browned, 5 to 7 minutes.

3. Add the ginger and green chile peppers, mix in the vegetables, garam masala, and salt and cook, stirring, over high heat, about 2 minutes. Mix in the yogurt and cook another minute.

4. Add the rice with the water it was soaking in and bring to a boil over high heat. Reduce the heat to the lowest setting, cover the pan (partially at first, until the foam subsides, then snugly), and cook until the rice is done, 10 to 15 minutes. Do not stir the rice while it is cooking. Remove from the heat and allow the rice to rest undisturbed about 5 minutes. Transfer to a serving platter, fluff with a fork, garnish with the cilantro, and serve.

Variation: To make this in a pressure cooker: Follow the recipe through Step 3, cooking everything in the pressure cooker. (You may need an extra teaspoon or 2 of oil in case your pressure cooker is not nonstick.) Then add the rice with the water it was soaking in. Secure the lid of the pressure cooker and cook over high heat until it reaches high pressure. Turn off the heat and allow the pot to depressurize on its own, 12 to 15 minutes. Carefully remove the lid, and serve as described in Step 5.

Kashmiri Mixed Vegetable Pilaf

Kashmiri Sabzi Pullao

Makes 4 to 6 servings

Fragrant with Kashmiri flavors of dried ginger and fennel seeds and studded with lots of colorful vegetables, this dish is reminiscent of the lovely gardens of Kashmir, now sadly off-limits to most of us.

1 teaspoon Kashmiri Garam Masala (page 19) or garam masala
2 tablespoons vegetable oil or melted ghee
1 teaspoon black cumin seeds
6 whole cloves
1 teaspoon fennel seeds
2 bay leaves
1/8 teaspoon ground asafoetida
3 small white potatoes, cut into wedges
1 1/4 cups basmati rice, sorted and washed in 3 to 4 changes of water
2 small carrots, cut into 1/2-inch slices
1/2 small cauliflower, cut into florets
1 cup frozen peas, thawed
1 1/2 cups finely chopped tomatoes
1 fresh green chile pepper, such as serrano, minced with seeds
1 tablespoon ground coriander
1/2 teaspoon ground turmeric
1 teaspoon salt, or to taste
2 1/4 cups water
1/2 cup finely chopped fresh cilantro, including soft stems

1. Prepare the Kashmiri masala. Heat the oil (or ghee) in a large nonstick saucepan over medium-high heat and add the cumin, cloves, fennel, bay leaves, and asafoetida; they should sizzle upon contact with the hot oil. Quickly add the potatoes and cook, stirring until golden, about 2 minutes.

2. Add the rice and cook, stirring, about 3 minutes, then add the carrots, cauliflower, and peas. Cook a few minutes, then mix in the tomatoes, green chile pepper, coriander, garam masala, turmeric, and salt and cook, stirring, another 3 to 5 minutes.

3. Add the water and bring to a boil over high heat. Reduce the heat to the lowest setting, cover the pan (partially at first, until the foam subsides, then snugly), and cook until the rice is done, 10 to 15 minutes, adding more water if needed. Do not stir the rice while it is cooking. Remove from the heat, lightly mix in the cilantro, then allow the rice to rest about 5 minutes. Transfer to a serving platter, fluff with a fork, and serve.

Tofu and Chickpea Pilaf

Tofu aur Channae ka Pullao

Makes 6 to 8 servings

This dish is generally made with paneer *cheese, and you can, indeed, do so if you wish to. But of late, I've been making it with tofu, which is made similarly to paneer, but with soy milk. This healthful dish has a lovely combination of textures. The tofu gives it a smooth, silky quality, while the chickpeas offer a satisfying heartiness in every mouthful.*

1¼ cups basmati rice, sorted and washed
    in 3 to 4 changes of water
2⅓ cups water
1 teaspoon cumin seeds, dry-roasted and coarsely
    ground (Dry-Roasting Spices, page 35)
    + 1 teaspoon
2 tablespoons peanut oil
4 whole dried red chile peppers, such as chile de arbol
2 large cloves fresh garlic, thinly sliced
1 (1-inch) stick cinnamon
3 black cardamom pods, crushed lightly
    to break the skin
½ teaspoon coarsely ground ajwain seeds
2 cups canned chickpeas, drained and rinsed
1½ cups extra-firm tofu, or paneer cheese,
    cut into ½-inch pieces
1 teaspoon salt, or to taste
2 to 3 scallions, thinly sliced
1 small tomato, finely chopped

1. In a medium bowl, soak the rice in the water, about 30 minutes. Prepare 1 teaspoon cumin seeds.

2. Heat the oil in a large nonstick saucepan over medium-high heat and stir the red chile peppers, garlic, cinnamon, and cardamom pods, 1 minute. Add the remaining 1 teaspoon cumin seeds and ajwain seeds, then mix in the chickpeas and cook until golden, about 3 minutes.

3. Add the tofu (or paneer cheese) and salt, and cook, stirring, another 2 minutes. Then mix in the rice with the water it was soaking in. Bring to a boil over high heat. Reduce the heat to the lowest setting, cover the pan (partially at first, until the foam subsides, then snugly), and cook until the rice is done, 10 to 15 minutes. Do not stir the rice while it cooks.

4. Remove from the heat and let the rice rest undisturbed about 5 minutes. Transfer to a serving platter, then carefully mix in the scallions and tomatoes, sprinkle the dry-roasted cumin seeds on top, and serve.

Punjabi Green Chickpea Pilaf

Chholia ka Pullao

Makes 4 to 6 servings

Green chickpeas (chholia) *are the young chickpeas still in a pod. They are popular all over north India, but more so in the Punjab. I see them at farmers' markets in Santa Monica, and whenever I do, I buy them by the bundle (they generally come attached to the freshly harvested stems).*

At home, I shell each small pod (like fresh peas) and then cook them in one of many delicious dishes, such as Fresh Green Chickpeas with Lentil Nuggets (page 382), and I freeze some for later use.

Green chickpeas are delicate and mild tasting, and are cooked in much the same way as fresh peas, which you substitute if you can't find green chickpeas.

1¼ cups basmati rice, sorted and washed
    in 3 to 4 changes of water
2⅓ cups water
1 tablespoon peanut oil
3 to 5 black cardamom pods, crushed lightly
    to break the skin
1 (1-inch) stick cinnamon
1 teaspoon cumin seeds
2 small onions, finely chopped
1 tablespoon peeled minced fresh ginger
1 large clove fresh garlic, minced
1 tablespoon ground coriander
½ teaspoon garam masala + ¼ teaspoon for garnish
¼ teaspoon ground turmeric
1 large tomato, finely chopped
1½ cups shelled fresh green chickpeas (chholia)
1 teaspoon salt, or to taste

1. In a medium bowl, soak the rice in the water, about 30 minutes.

2. Heat the oil in a large saucepan over medium-high heat and cook the cardamom pods and cinnamon, stirring, about 30 seconds. Add the cumin seeds; they should sizzle upon contact with the hot oil. Quickly add the onions and cook, stirring, until golden, about 5 minutes. Add the ginger, garlic, coriander, garam masala, and turmeric, stir about 30 seconds, then add the tomato and green chickpeas and cook, stirring, about 5 minutes.

3. Add the rice with the water it was soaking in, and the salt, and bring to a boil over high heat. Reduce the heat to the lowest setting, cover the pan (partially at first, until the foam subsides, then snugly), and cook until the rice is done, 10 to 15 minutes. Do not stir the rice while it cooks. Remove from the heat and let the rice rest undisturbed about 5 minutes. Transfer to a serving platter, sprinkle the garam masala on top, and serve.

Quick Soybean Pilaf
Soyabeans ka Pullao

Makes 4 to 6 servings

Indians routinely make a pullao *(pilaf or seasoned rice dish) with fresh green peas. It is probably one of the most popular rice dishes made for home meals, for parties, and even for banquets. But here I offer an alternate pea* pullao *that is made with shelled fresh green soybeans.*

Although green soybeans (also called edamame, the Japanese name) are not a common bean in Indian households, I often use them in my Santa Monica

kitchen and they work well in this rice dish. Look for them in the frozen section of supermarkets or gourmet markets. If you can't find them, use fresh or frozen peas instead.

1^1/$_4$ cups basmati rice, sorted and washed
    in 3 to 4 changes of water
2^1/$_3$ cups water
2 tablespoons vegetable oil
1 teaspoon cumin seeds
^{1}/$_2$ teaspoon coarsely crushed fenugreek seeds
1 large clove fresh garlic, minced
1 tablespoon ground coriander
1^1/$_2$ cups shelled frozen soybeans
1 large tomato, finely chopped
^{1}/$_4$ teaspoon ground paprika
^{1}/$_4$ teaspoon garam masala
^{1}/$_8$ teaspoon ground asafoetida
1 teaspoon salt, or to taste
1 large red bell pepper, finely chopped

1. In a medium bowl, soak the rice in the water, about 30 minutes.

2. Heat the oil in a pressure cooker over medium-high heat and add the cumin, fenugreek seeds, and garlic; they should sizzle upon contact with the hot oil. Quickly add the coriander, soybeans, tomato, paprika, garam masala, asafoetida, salt, and cook, stirring, until lightly roasted, 5 to 7 minutes.

3. Add the rice with the water with was soaking in, and the red bell pepper. Secure the lid, cook over high heat until the regulator indicates high pressure, then cook about 30 seconds more. Remove from the heat and allow the pot to depressurize on its own, 12 to 15 minutes. Carefully open the lid, transfer to a serving platter, fluff with a fork, and serve.

Royal Fresh and Dried Fruit Pilaf

Shahi Pullao

Makes 4 to 6 servings

A dish fit for royalty, made with some of India's best flavors and nature's nutrients—rich dried fruits and nuts—this lavish, star-studded rice dish is definitely one to talk about. Every bite is a mouthful of sweet and savory flavors and diverse textures, some soft and others chewy or firm. Present it with a simple yogurt raita *or as part of a larger menu, or take it to your holiday potluck. Silver leaves and rose essence are available in Indian markets.*

1/4 teaspoon saffron threads

2 tablespoons milk (any kind)

1 1/2 cups basmati rice, sorted and washed in 3 to 4 changes of water

2 3/4 cups water

1 tablespoon Mughlai Garam Masala with Nutmeg and Mace (page 18) or garam masala

2 tablespoons Dessert Masala (page 32) or coarsely ground raw pistachios and almonds

2 tablespoons melted ghee or vegetable oil

1 cup shelled, raw mixed nuts (such as almonds, walnuts, cashews, peanuts, and pistachios), chopped

1/4 cup each raisins and finely chopped dried peaches, dried nectarines, and dried dates

1/2 cup each finely chopped fresh apples, pineapple, and bananas

1 tablespoon peeled minced fresh ginger

1 large clove fresh garlic, minced

3/4 teaspoon salt, or to taste

2 drops rose essence (optional)

6 to 8 silver leaves (optional)

1/4 teaspoon ground green cardamom seeds

1. In a small bowl, soak the saffron threads in the milk at least 30 minutes. Meanwhile, in a medium bowl, soak the rice in the water, about 30 minutes. Prepare the garam masala and dessert masala.

2. Heat 1 tablespoon ghee (or oil) in a large saucepan over medium-high heat and cook the nuts, stirring, until golden. With a slotted spatula, remove the nuts to a bowl, leaving as much of the ghee as possible behind in the pan. In the same ghee, cook all the dried fruits. Transfer to the bowl with the nuts. Then cook the fresh fruits until golden, about 1 minute, and mix into the nuts.

3. Heat the remaining 1 tablespoon ghee to the pan and cook the ginger, garlic, and garam masala, stirring, until fragrant, about 30 seconds. Add the rice with the water it was soaking in, and the salt, and bring to a boil over medium-high heat. Reduce the heat to the lowest setting, cover the pan (partially at first until the foam subsides, and then snugly), and cook until all the water has been absorbed and the rice is almost tender, 10 to 12 minutes. Do not stir the rice while it is cooking.

4. Lightly mix the fried nuts and fruits, into the cooked rice, then drizzle the saffron milk and the rose essence (if using) over the rice. Cover and cook over medium-low heat until the rice is done, 10 to 12 minutes.

5. Remove from the heat and allow the rice to rest about 5 minutes. Transfer to a serving platter, garnish with the silver leaves (if using), sprinkle the saffron, ground cardamom seeds, and dessert masala (or chopped nuts) on top, and serve.

Cranberry Pilaf
Karonda Pullao

Makes 4 to 6 servings

This recipe is not a tradition passed down to me, but the availability of cranberries in America inspired me to make this one day. Studded with tangy, fresh cranberries, this lovely pink pullao *is savory but with a hint of sweetness from the brown sugar–like jaggery (or* gur *in Hindi).*

1 tablespoon Basic Ginger-Garlic Paste (page 47 or store-bought)
1 tablespoon Bengali 5-Spices (Panch-Phoran), page 27 or store-bought
1¼ cups basmati rice, sorted and washed in 3 to 4 changes of water
2⅓ cups water
2 tablespoons peanut oil
2 (1-inch) sticks cinnamon
3 black cardamom pods, crushed lightly to break the skin
½ teaspoon coarsely ground black pepper
1 large onion, cut in half lengthwise and thinly sliced
2 cups fresh or frozen thawed cranberries
2 tablespoons grated jaggery (gur), or brown sugar
¼ cup finely chopped fresh cilantro, including soft stems

1. Prepare the ginger-garlic paste and 5-spices. In a medium bowl, soak the rice in the water, about 30 minutes.

2. Heat the oil in a large nonstick saucepan over medium-high heat and cook the cinnamon, cardamom pods, panch-phoran, and black pepper until fragrant, about 1 minute. Add the onion and cook, stirring, until golden, about 5 minutes.

3. Mix in the ginger-garlic paste and cranberries and stir about 2 minutes. Then add the rice with the water it was soaking in and bring to a boil over high heat. Reduce the heat to the lowest setting, cover the pan (partially at first until the foam subsides, and then snugly), and cook until all the water has been absorbed and the rice is done, 12 to 15 minutes.

4. Lightly fork in the jaggery and cilantro, and allow the rice to rest undisturbed about 5 minutes. Transfer to a serving platter, fluff with a fork, and serve.

Non-Vegetarian Pilafs (Pullao)

Spicy Chicken Pilaf
Mursh Pullao

Makes 4 to 6 servings

A classic north Indian dish for everyday or for a special occasion, this pullao *is a favorite among children and teenagers. Any leftovers are promptly divvied up for school lunches and college dorms.*

1¼ cups basmati rice, sorted and washed in 3 to 4 changes of water
2⅓ cups water
3 tablespoons vegetable oil
5 to 7 green cardamom pods, crushed lightly to break the skin
3 black cardamom pods, crushed lightly to break the skin
2 (1-inch) sticks cinnamon
1 large onion, cut in half lengthwise and thinly sliced
2 large cloves fresh garlic, minced
2 tablespoons peeled minced fresh ginger
1 to 3 fresh green chile peppers, such as serrano, minced with seeds
1 tablespoon ground coriander
1 teaspoon ground cumin
1 teaspoon dried fenugreek leaves
1 teaspoon garam masala + ¼ teaspoon for garnish
½ teaspoon ground turmeric
1 teaspoon salt, or to taste
1 pound skinless boneless chicken breasts, cut into 1½-inch pieces
1 large tomato, finely chopped
½ cup finely chopped fresh cilantro, including soft stems
1 cup nonfat plain yogurt, whisked until smooth

1. In a medium bowl, soak the rice in the water, about 30 minutes.

2. Heat the oil in a large saucepan over medium-high heat and cook the green and black cardamom pods, and cinnamon, stirring, 30 seconds. Add the onion and cook, stirring, until golden, about 5 minutes.

3. Add the garlic, ginger, and green chile peppers, stir about 1 minute, then add the coriander, cumin, fenugreek leaves, 1 teaspoon garam masala, turmeric, and ½ teaspoon salt, and stir another minute.

4. Add the chicken, tomato, and cilantro, then add the yogurt, a little at a time, stirring constantly to prevent it from curdling until it comes to a boil. Reduce the heat to medium, cover the pan, and cook until the chicken is tender and the sauce is thick, 10 to 15 minutes. Leaving about ½ cup of the sauce in the pan, remove the chicken pieces to a bowl and keep warm.

5. Mix in the rice with the water it was soaking in, and the remaining ½ teaspoon salt, and bring to a boil over high heat. Reduce the heat to the lowest setting, cover the pan (partially at first, until the foam subsides, then snugly), and cook until most of the water has been absorbed but the rice is not yet fully cooked, about 10 minutes.

6. Carefully mix in the cooked chicken. Cover and cook over low heat until the rice is tender, about 10 to 12 minutes. Remove from the heat and allow the rice to rest undisturbed about 5 minutes. Transfer to a serving platter, fluff with a fork, sprinkle the ¼ teaspoon garam masala on top, and serve.

Moist Ground Lamb Pilaf
Keema Pullao

Makes 4 to 6 servings

When I crave my mother's cooking, I often head to the kitchen to make this dish—one of her few meat recipes. For religious reasons, she was and remains a strict vegetarian and before she married my non-vegetarian father, she would not eat at a table where any meats were being served. When her children were born, her outlook changed, because we sometimes wanted to eat meat, so she cooked it for us.

4 cups (1 recipe) Steamed Basmati Rice (page 533)
1 pound ground extra lean lamb or beef
1 large onion, finely chopped
1 large tomato, finely chopped
1 to 3 fresh green chile peppers, such as serrano, minced with seeds
1½ tablespoons peeled minced fresh ginger
2 large cloves fresh garlic, minced
1 tablespoon ground coriander
1 teaspoon garam masala
1 teaspoon dried fenugreek leaves
½ teaspoon ground cumin
½ teaspoon ground turmeric
1 teaspoon salt, or to taste
1½ cups nonfat plain yogurt, whisked until smooth
½ cup finely chopped fresh cilantro, including soft stems
Freshly ground black pepper, or to taste
¼ cup blanched almond slivers

1. Prepare the rice. Then place the ground lamb and everything else (except the cooked rice, yogurt, cilantro, black pepper, and almonds) into a large nonstick saucepan and cook, stirring as needed, over medium-high heat the first 2 to 3 minutes and then over medium heat until all the juices evaporate and the lamb is golden, 25 to 30 minutes.

2. Add the yogurt, a little at a time, stirring constantly to prevent it from curdling, and cook until most of it is absorbed, about 5 minutes.

3. Add the cooked rice and cilantro. Cover the pan and cook over low heat, 5 to 7 minutes, to blend the flavors. Transfer to a serving platter, garnish with black pepper and almonds, and serve.

Simple Lamb Pilaf
Gosht Pullao

Makes 4 to 6 servings

This is about as easy as you can get with a meat pullao. Cook the lamb until it's ¾ done, add the rice, then finish cooking. All is done in 1 pot in 2 simple and easy steps. Serve it just with a yogurt raita and a salad, if you wish.

1¼ cups basmati rice, sorted and rinsed
in 3 to 4 changes of water
2 tablespoons peanut oil
1 large onion, coarsely chopped
1½ pounds boneless leg of lamb, all visible fat
trimmed, cut into 1-inch pieces
2 tablespoons peeled minced fresh ginger
1 large clove fresh garlic, minced
1 to 3 fresh green chile peppers, such as serrano,
minced with seeds
1 large tomato, finely chopped
1 tablespoon ground coriander
2 teaspoons garam masala
1 teaspoon salt, or to taste
1 large russet potato, peeled and cut into 1-inch pieces
1 cup milk (any kind)
½ teaspoon ground green cardamom seeds

1. Soak the rice in water to cover by 2 inches, 30 minutes or longer. Drain, saving 1¼ cups of the water.

2. Heat the oil in a large nonstick saucepan over medium-high heat and sauté the onion until golden, about 5 minutes. Add the lamb, ginger, garlic, green chile peppers, tomato, coriander, garam masala, and salt and cook over medium heat the first 3 to 5 minutes, then over medium heat until the lamb pieces are golden brown and almost done, about 20 minutes.

3. Add the potato and cook, stirring, about 2 minutes. Then add the rice, the reserved 1¼ cups water, and the milk, and bring to a boil over high heat. Reduce the heat to medium-low, cover the pan, and simmer until the rice is done and the lamb and potatoes are tender, 12 to 15 minutes. Transfer to a serving dish, sprinkle the cardamom seeds on top, and serve.

Garlic Shrimp Pilaf with Coconut Milk

Jhinga Pullao

Makes 4 to 6 servings

Spicy shrimp added into cooked rice minutes before serving lend a magical garnish to this colorful pullao.

Have the shrimp and all the other ingredients ready to go, and cook it at the last minute. If shrimp is cooked ahead of time, it will become tough and almost inedible.

4 cups (1 recipe) Steamed Turmeric and Red
Peppercorn Basmati Rice (page 534)
½ cup Coconut Milk (page 44 or store-bought)
2 tablespoons vegetable oil
1 teaspoon cumin seeds
1 large onion, cut in half lengthwise and
thinly sliced
½ cup finely chopped fresh cilantro,
including soft stems
1 fresh green chile pepper, such as serrano,
minced with seeds
2 large cloves fresh garlic, minced
25 to 30 fresh large shrimp (about 1¼ pounds),
shelled, deveined and tails removed
½ teaspoon ajwain seeds
¼ teaspoon garam masala
¼ teaspoon salt, or to taste
2 tablespoons fresh lime or lemon juice
3 to 4 scallions, green parts only, finely chopped

1. Prepare the coconut milk. Then prepare the rice and keep warm. Heat the oil in a large nonstick saucepan over medium-high heat and add the cumin seeds; they should sizzle upon contact with the hot oil. Quickly add the onion and cook, stirring, until golden, about 7 minutes.

2. Add the cilantro, green chile pepper, and garlic, and stir until the cilantro is completely wilted, about 2 minutes. Then add the shrimp, ajwain seeds, garam masala, and salt and cook, stirring, until the shrimp are pink and opaque, about 2 minutes. Add the coconut milk and simmer over medium-low heat, about 5 minutes.

3. Transfer the cooked rice to a serving platter. Very carefully mix in the cooked shrimp, plus any sauce in the pan. Drizzle the lime juice on top, garnish with the scallion greens, cover the platter, and keep warm about 5 minutes before serving.

Layered Rice Dishes (Biryanis)

Biryanis are special Mughlai dishes made by layering cooked rice with cooked vegetables, meats, or *paneer* cheese. All *biryanis* are elaborate affairs, full of enticing flavors, and very much a part of Indian festivities such as weddings and religious occasions, especially in Muslim communities.

For eating at home, they are best enjoyed alone or with simple yogurt *raitas*, such as Tomato Raita with Fresh Mint Leaves (page 224) or Ginger and Scallion Raita (page 222). Or you can serve them with chutneys, such as Cilantro-Lime Chutney (page 59).

Layered Rice with Eggplant and Coconut

Baingan Biryani

Makes 4 to 6 servings

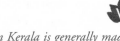

This famous rice dish from Kerala is generally made very hot and spicy, and is served with a soothing yogurt raita. The recipe may seem more complicated than it actually is, since we are cooking two separate dishes and presenting them as one.

2 cups Coconut Milk (page 44 or store-bought)
1¼ cups basmati rice, sorted and washed
    in 3 to 4 changes of water
1¾ cups water
½ cup grated fresh or frozen coconut
1 to 3 dried red chile peppers, such as chile de arbol,
    broken into pieces
1 large clove fresh garlic, peeled
5 quarter-size slices peeled fresh ginger
1 to 3 fresh green chile peppers, such as serrano,
    minced with seeds
1 small onion, coarsely chopped
1 teaspoon ground coriander
1 teaspoon garam masala + ¼ teaspoon for garnish

½ teaspoon ground turmeric
3 tablespoons peanut oil
2 to 3 Chinese eggplants (about 1 pound),
    cut into ¾-inch pieces
1¼ teaspoons salt, or to taste
1 large tomato, finely chopped
2 tablespoons finely chopped fresh mint leaves
½ cup finely chopped fresh cilantro,
    including soft stems
2 to 3 tablespoons fresh lemon juice

1. Prepare the coconut milk. Then, in a medium bowl, soak the rice in the water, 30 minutes or longer.

2. Meanwhile, place the grated coconut and red chile peppers in a small nonstick skillet and dry-roast, stirring and shaking the pan, over medium heat until fragrant and lightly golden, 1 to 2 minutes. Let cool, then transfer to a blender or food processor and process along with the garlic, ginger, green chile peppers, and onion until everything is finely ground. Mix in the coriander, garam masala, and turmeric and process again. Transfer to a large nonstick saucepan. Add 2 tablespoons oil and cook, stirring, over medium-high heat until golden, about 5 minutes.

3. Add the eggplants, half the salt, and ½ cup coconut milk and cook over high heat about 3 minutes. Reduce the heat to medium, cover the pan, and cook until the eggplants are soft, 15 to 20 minutes. Remove to a bowl.

4. To the same pan, add the remaining 1 tablespoon oil, tomato, mint, and cilantro and cook over medium heat, stirring, until most of the juice from the tomato evaporates, about 2 minutes. Add the rice with the water it was soaking in, along with the remaining salt and coconut milk, and bring to a boil over high heat. Reduce the heat to low, cover the pan (partially at first until the foam subsides, and then snugly), and cook until most the water has been absorbed but the rice is not yet fully cooked, about 10 minutes.

5. To assemble the biryani: Remove about half the rice to a bowl. Spread the cooked eggplant mixture over the rice that remains in the saucepan. Cover the eggplant mixture with the reserved rice. Drizzle the lemon juice over the rice, cover the pan, and cook over lowest heat setting, 10 to 15 minutes, to blend the flavors. Sprinkle the garam masala on top and serve from the pan itself, or transfer to a serving platter, fluff the top of the rice with a fork, and serve.

Variation: For a more formal presentation, in Step 7 preheat oven to 300°F. Lightly grease the bottom of a clear oven-safe casserole dish, add half the rice, top with the eggplant mixture, then cover with the remaining rice. Drizzle the lemon juice on top, then bake 15 to 20 minutes.

Hyderabadi Layered Rice with Mixed Vegetables
Sabz Biryani

Makes 4 to 6 servings

This biryani *recipe is from my friend Yasmin AliKhan. Her authentic version calls for the vegetables to be boiled before adding them to the dish—a step I do without, because I find that the raw vegetables cook just fine.*

1 tablespoon Hyderabadi Ginger-Garlic Paste
    (page 48)
4 cups (1 recipe) Steamed Basmati Rice (page 53)
1/4 teaspoon saffron threads
1/4 cup milk (any kind)
1/2 cup coarsely chopped mixed raw nuts, such as
    almonds, pistachios, cashews, and walnuts
2 tablespoons melted ghee, or 1 tablespoon each
    ghee and peanut oil
2 (1-inch) sticks cinnamon
6 whole cloves
5 green cardamom pods, crushed lightly
    to break the skin
2 bay leaves
1 medium onion, cut in half lengthwise and
    thinly sliced

1 to 3 fresh green chile peppers, such as serrano,
    minced with seeds
3 to 4 cups washed and chopped mixed fresh
    vegetables, such as green beans, carrots,
    potatoes, eggplant, and peas
1 cup nonfat plain yogurt, whisked until smooth
1 to 2 tablespoons fresh lime juice
1/2 cup finely chopped fresh cilantro,
    including soft stems
2 tablespoons finely chopped fresh mint leaves
1/2 teaspoon ground green cardamom seeds

1. Prepare the ginger-garlic paste and the rice. Meanwhile, soak the saffron in milk 30 minutes or longer. Place the nuts in a small skillet and dry-roast them over medium heat, stirring and shaking the pan, until golden, about 3 minutes. Reserve.

2. Heat the ghee (or ghee and oil) in a large nonstick wok or saucepan over medium-high heat and add the cinnamon, cloves, cardamom pods, and bay leaves and cook, stirring, until fragrant, about 1 minute. Add the onion and cook, stirring, until browned, about 7 minutes. Mix in the ginger-garlic paste and green chile peppers and cook, stirring, 1 minute.

3. Add the vegetables and cook, stirring, 5 to 7 minutes. Then add the yogurt, a little at a time, stirring constantly to prevent it from curdling, and cook until most of it is absorbed, about 5 minutes. Remove from heat.

4. Preheat the oven to 350°F. To assemble the biryani, baste the bottom of a clear oven-safe dish with some of the juices from the vegetables and spread half the rice in the pan. Layer all the vegetables over the rice and top with the lime juice, cilantro, and mint. Then spread the remaining half of the rice over the vegetables.

5. Drizzle the saffron milk over the rice and cover well with aluminum foil. Bake the rice until the grains are soft and the flavors are well-blended, about 30 minutes. Remove from the oven, fluff the rice lightly with a fork, garnish with the roasted nuts and cardamom seeds, and serve.

Layered Rice with Fragrant Mixed Nuts and Saffron

Dry-Fruit ki Biryani

Makes 4 to 6 servings

In India, a country where nuts are very expensive, this dish signals elegance and sophisticated special-occasion cooking. In America, we can enjoy it more often. Just remember that all nuts are rich in fat, so eat in moderation. Here, I do not soak the rice; instead I fry it until it is lightly golden and then I cook it.

1½ teaspoons Mughlai Garam Masala with Nutmeg and Mace (page 18), or garam masala
¼ teaspoon saffron threads
½ cup light cream, half and half, or whole milk
1½ cups Crispy Fried Onions (page 44)
¼ cup Crispy Fried Fresh Ginger (page 45)
2 tablespoons peanut oil
2 cups coarsely chopped mixed nuts, such as almonds, pistachios, walnuts, peanuts, cashews, and pine nuts
¼ cup raisins
1¼ cups basmati rice, sorted and washed in 3 to 4 changes of water
2¼ cups water
1 teaspoon salt, or to taste
1 teaspoon coarsely ground green cardamom seeds

1. Prepare the garam masala. Soak the saffron in the cream or milk about 30 minutes. Meanwhile, prepare the fried onions and ginger.

2. Heat 1 tablespoon oil in a large nonstick saucepan over medium heat and cook the nuts and the raisins, stirring, until the nuts are golden, 2 to 3 minutes. Transfer to a bowl. In the same pan, heat the remaining 1 tablespoon oil over medium-high heat and add the garam masala; it should sizzle upon contact with the hot oil. Quickly add the rice and cook over high heat, stirring carefully by shaking the pan, until lightly golden, 3 to 5 minutes.

3. Add the water and salt and bring to a boil over high heat. Reduce the heat to low, cover the pan (partially at first until the foam subsides, and then snugly), and cook until most of the water has been absorbed but the rice is not yet fully cooked, about 10 minutes.

4. Preheat the oven to 350°F. To assemble the biryani, lightly grease the bottom of a clear oven-safe dish with some ghee (or butter or oil) and spread half the rice in the dish. Layer the roasted nuts and raisins over the rice, then spread the remaining half of the rice over the nuts.

5. Drizzle the saffron cream over the rice, garnish with the fried onions and ginger, and cover well with aluminum foil. Bake the rice until the grains are soft and the flavors well-blended, about 30 minutes. Remove from the oven, fluff the top of the rice lightly with a fork, making sure that some of the nuts are visible, sprinkle the cardamom seeds on top, and serve.

Hyderabadi Layered Rice with Cooked Chicken

Pukki Murgh Biryani

Makes 4 to 6 servings

This outstanding biryani *from my friend Yasmin AliKhan is as much a work of art as it is an object for greedy consumption. It takes a fair amount of time and assembly, and, if you are like Yasmin's mother and aunt, this dish takes much more—love, precise monitoring of heat, consistency of ground spices, and perfect layering of every element. Needless to say, the dish is worth prefecting.*

This is a one-pot meal to be served with yogurt only, so make a generous allowance for each person.

½ recipe Hyderabadi Chicken Curry (page 466)
¼ teaspoon saffron threads
2 tablespoons milk (any kind)
1 cup Crispy Fried Onions (page 44)
1¼ cups basmati rice, sorted and washed in 3 to 4 changes of water
4 cups water
1 teaspoon salt
1 tablespoon fresh lime juice
¼ cup finely chopped fresh cilantro, including soft stems
1 teaspoon finely chopped fresh mint leaves
½ teaspoon ground green cardamom seeds

1. Prepare the chicken. Meanwhile, in a small bowl, soak the saffron in the milk, 30 minutes or longer. Prepare the fried onions.

2. In a medium bowl, soak the rice in the water and salt, 30 minutes or longer. Drain over a bowl and save the drained water. Put the drained water in a large pot and bring to a rolling boil. Mix in the rice and cook over medium-high heat, uncovered, until most of the water has been absorbed but the rice is not yet fully cooked, about 10 minutes. Drain the rice and discard the water (or use it for soups).

3. Preheat the oven to 350°F. To assemble the biryani, baste the bottom of a large oven-safe dish with a spoonful or two of the sauce from the chicken dish and spread half the rice in the dish. Layer all the chicken over the rice. Top with the lime juice, cilantro, and mint, then spread the remaining rice over the chicken.

4. Drizzle the saffron milk on top, scatter the crispy onions on the rice, and cover well with aluminum foil. Bake until the chicken literally falls off the bone, the rice grains are soft, and the flavors are well-blended, about 1 hour. Remove from the oven, fluff the top of the rice lightly with a fork, sprinkle the cardamom seeds on top, and serve hot.

Hyderabadi Layered Rice with Marinated Chicken
Kacchi Murgh Biryani

Makes 4 to 6 servings

Here, marinated chicken is cooked along with the rice instead of separately, as is common for most other biryanis. *This dish, replete with all the mouthwatering Hyderabadi flavors, is another terrific 1-pot party dish.*

4 large cloves fresh garlic, peeled

8 to 10 quarter-size slices peeled fresh ginger

1 to 3 fresh green chile peppers, such as serrano, stemmed

2 large tomatoes, coarsely chopped

1 cup coarsely chopped fresh cilantro, including soft stems + 1/2 cup finely chopped

2 to 3 tablespoons fresh lime juice

2 cups nonfat plain yogurt, whisked until smooth

1 tablespoon garam masala

1 teaspoon salt, or to taste

1 (2- to 2 1/2-pound) chicken, skinned and cut into serving pieces (discard back and wings)

1/2 teaspoon saffron threads

1/4 cup milk (any kind)

1 1/2 cups basmati rice, sorted and washed in 3 to 4 changes of water

4 cups water

1 1/2 cups (1/2 recipe) Crispy Fried Onions (page 44)

2 tablespoons vegetable oil or melted ghee

4 black cardamom pods, crushed lightly to break the skin

6 green cardamom pods, crushed lightly to break the skin

1 (1-inch) stick cinnamon

2 whole bay leaves

2 teaspoons black cumin seeds

2 tablespoons finely chopped fresh mint

1/2 teaspoon ground green cardamom seeds

1. In a food processor or a blender, process together the garlic, ginger, and green chile peppers until minced. Add the tomatoes, coarsely chopped cilantro, and lime juice and process again to make a smooth purée. Transfer to a large non-reactive bowl and mix in the yogurt, garam masala, and salt. Add the chicken and mix well, making sure all the pieces are well-coated with the marinade. Cover and marinate at least 8 and up to 24 hours in the refrigerator.

2. In a small bowl, soak the saffron in the milk, 30 minutes or longer. In a medium bowl, soak the rice in the water, 30 minutes or longer. Prepare the fried onions.

3. Put the rice and water in a large nonstick saucepan and bring to a boil over high heat. Reduce the heat to medium-low, and cook, uncovered, until the most of the water has been absorbed but the rice is not yet fully cooked, about 10 minutes. Drain the rice and discard the water (or use it for soups).

4. Heat the ghee (or oil) in a large nonstick, oven-safe saucepan (such as a Dutch oven) over medium-high heat. Add the black and green cardamom pods, cinnamon, bay leaves, and cumin seeds; they should sizzle upon contact with the hot oil. Quickly add the marinated chicken, plus all the marinade, and stir well. Remove from the heat.

5. Spread the fried onions (save some for garnish), chopped cilantro, and mint on top of the chicken, then cover everything well with the partially cooked rice. Top the rice with the saffron milk, seal the pan well with aluminum foil and place the lid over the foil. Cook over medium-high heat about 10 minutes. Lower the heat to medium and cook about 15 minutes. Lower the heat further to low, and continue to cook until the chicken literally falls off the bone, the rice grains are soft, and the flavors are well-blended, about 1 hour. Remove from the oven, fluff the top of the rice lightly with a fork, sprinkle the cardamom seeds and the reserved fried onions on top, and serve.

Layered Rice with Lamb and Apricots

Gosht aur Khubani ki Biryani

Makes 4 to 6 servings

Apricots, called khubani *in Hindi, are often added to lamb and chicken dishes. Here is one such authentic dish. Daunting though the promise of authenticity may seem, don't let that deter you from trying out this relatively easy recipe. Its fragrance alone sets the stage for celebration.*

1¹/₂ to 2 pounds boneless leg of lamb, all visible fat trimmed, cut into 1¹/₂-inch pieces

¹/₂ cup coarsely chopped raw cashews

4 to 5 large cloves fresh garlic, peeled

6 to 8 quarter-size slices peeled fresh ginger

1 cup coarsely chopped fresh cilantro, including soft stems

20 to 25 fresh curry leaves

3 to 5 fresh green chile peppers, such as serrano, stemmed

2 large tomatoes, coarsely chopped

2 to 3 tablespoons fresh lime juice

1 tablespoon garam masala

1¹/₂ teaspoons salt, or to taste

1¹/₂ cups nonfat plain yogurt, whisked until smooth

8 to 10 dried apricots, coarsely chopped

2 large potatoes (any kind), peeled and cut into 1-inch pieces

1¹/₄ cups basmati rice, sorted and washed in 3 to 4 changes of water

2¹/₃ cups water

¹/₄ teaspoon saffron threads

¹/₄ cup milk (any kind)

2 tablespoons melted ghee or peanut oil

2 (1-inch) sticks cinnamon

6 to 8 green cardamom pods, crushed lightly to break the skin

3 bay leaves

1 tablespoon cumin seeds

1. Place the meat on a clean cutting board, cover with plastic wrap, then, with the flat side of a meat mallet, lightly pound each piece of lamb a few times to break the fibers.

2. In a food processor or a blender, process together the cashews, garlic, ginger, cilantro, curry leaves, green chile peppers, tomatoes, lime juice, garam masala, and salt to make a smooth paste. Transfer to a large non-reactive bowl, add the yogurt, and mix well. Add the lamb, potatoes, and apricots and mix well, making sure everything is well-coated with the marinade. Cover and marinate at least 4 and up to 24 hours in the refrigerator.

3. In a medium bowl, soak the rice in the water at least 30 minutes. Soak the saffron in the milk at least 30 minutes or longer. Preheat the oven to 450°F. Place the rice in a large nonstick saucepan and bring to a boil over high heat. Reduce the heat to low, cover the pan, and cook until most of the water is absorbed but the rice is not yet fully cooked, about 10 minutes.

4. Lightly grease the bottom of large oven-safe covered dish. Spread half the rice in the dish, spread all the marinated meat, plus the marinade, over the rice, then cover the meat with the remaining rice.

5. Heat the ghee (or oil) in a small nonstick saucepan over medium-high heat and add the cinnamon, cardamom pods, bay leaves, and cumin seeds; they should sizzle upon contact with the hot oil. Remove

from the heat, add the saffron milk, then drizzle everything over the rice. Cover well with aluminum foil, and then with the lid of the dish. Bake the rice about 15 minutes, then lower the heat to 350°F and continue to bake until the lamb is very soft and the flavors are well-blended, about 1 hour. Remove from the oven, fluff the top of the rice lightly with a fork, and serve.

Layered Rice with Fragrant Lamb Chops

Chaamp ki Biryani

Makes 4 to 6 servings

This lamb biryani is made with bone-in lamb chops (called chaampein *in Hindi), and is fragrant with rosewater and saffron, both of which add an incredible flavor and aroma to the* biryani.

1/2 teaspoon saffron threads

1/2 cup milk (any kind)

1 1/2 tablespoons Basic Ginger-Garlic Paste (page 47 or store-bought)

4 cups (1 recipe) Simple Cumin Basmati Rice (page 535)

2 tablespoons melted ghee or peanut oil

2 pounds lamb rib chops with bone, all visible fat trimmed

1 to 3 fresh green chile peppers, such as serrano, minced with seeds

1 teaspoon garam masala

1/8 teaspoon ground asafoetida

1 teaspoon salt, or to taste

1 cup nonfat plain yogurt, whisked until smooth

1 teaspoon ground cumin

1/2 teaspoon ground black cardamom seeds

1/2 teaspoon ground cloves

1/4 teaspoon ground cinnamon

1/4 teaspoon ground nutmeg

1/4 teaspoon ground mace

1 teaspoon rosewater or 2 drops rose essence

2 tablespoons finely chopped fresh mint

1. Soak the saffron in the milk at least 30 minutes or longer. Meanwhile, prepare the ginger-garlic paste and the rice.

2. Heat the ghee (or oil) in a large nonstick wok or saucepan over medium-high heat and add the lamb chops, ginger-garlic paste, green chile peppers, garam masala, asafoetida, and salt and cook, turning once or twice, until the chops are golden, about 2 to 3 minutes per side.

3. Add the yogurt, a little at a time, stirring constantly to prevent it from curdling, until all the yogurt is absorbed, about 7 minutes. Then add the cumin, cardamom seeds, cloves, cinnamon, nutmeg, and mace and continue to cook over medium heat the first 2 to 3 minutes, then over medium heat until the lamb is very tender, about 30 minutes.

4. Preheat the oven to 350°F. To make the biryani, spread half the rice in a large ovenproof covered dish, spread the lamb chops and all the sauce evenly over the rice, then cover the chops well with the remaining half of the rice.

5. Mix the rosewater into the saffron milk and drizzle over the rice. Cover well with aluminum foil and then with the lid of the dish. Bake the rice about 1 hour. Remove from the oven, fluff the top of the rice lightly with a fork, sprinkle the mint leaves on top, and serve.

Variation: This biryani can also be made in the pan in which the lamb is cooked. Remove the cooked lamb from the pan, put half the rice on the bottom, cover with the cooked lamb, then with the rest of the rice. Drizzle the saffron milk and rosewater over the rice, cover the pan well with aluminum foil, and cook over low heat 45 to 50 minutes. Stir, garnish, and serve.

Special Grain and Lentil Dishes (Khichadis)

A *khichadi* is a soft-cooked rice and *dal* dish. One could compare it to a risotto—a risotto made with *basmati* rice and one that always has some form of beans, lentils, or peas. Although this generally holds true, Indian cuisine also has a few *khichadis* that are dry-cooked, and some that are made with other vegetables or grains, for example whole-wheat and tapioca.

Creamy Rice and Split Mung Beans with Cumin Seeds

Chilkae vaali Mung Dal ki Khichadi

Makes 4 to 6 servings

This soft-cooked khichadi *is our family favorite and my ultimate comfort food! It cooks quickly in a pressure cooker and is easy on the stomach. My mother always gave it to us with her homemade lemon pickle whenever we were under the weather, and we loved it. This is a tradition I've continued with my own family in America, and my daughters, Sumi and Supi, have also grown to love it. It's a gift from my mother that I've passed on.*

Made with rice and split mung beans, this khichadi *comes with a* tarka *(a sizzling flavor topping) of fragrant* ghee *and cumin seeds. Serve it with plain yogurt,*

and a lemon pickle such as Sun-Cured Pickled Lime (or Lemon) Wedges (page 82).

1 cup basmati rice, sorted and washed in 3 to 4 changes of water

1/3 cup dried green split mung beans (chilkae vaali mung dal), sorted and washed in 3 to 4 changes of water

5 1/2 to 6 cups water

4 black cardamom pods, crushed lightly to break the skin

1 teaspoon black peppercorns

2 (1-inch) sticks cinnamon

3/4 teaspoon salt, or to taste

2 tablespoons melted ghee or olive oil

1 1/2 teaspoons cumin seeds

1. Place the rice and the dal in a pressure cooker along with 5½ cups water, the cardamom pods, peppercorns, cinnamon, and salt. Secure the lid and cook over high heat until the regulator indicates high pressure, then cook about 1 minute more. Remove from the heat and allow the pot to depressurize on its own, 12 to 15 minutes. Carefully open the lid and stir the rice. The khichadi should be soft and creamy; if not, then add more water, if needed, cover and boil, stirring a few times, until it is soft and creamy, about 5 minutes. Transfer to a serving dish.

2. Heat the ghee (or oil) in a small saucepan over medium-high heat and add the cumin seeds; they should sizzle upon contact with the hot oil. Quickly add the tarka to the khichadi and mix lightly, with parts of it visible as a garnish. Serve.

Variation: To cook in a pan, place everything except the ghee and cumin seeds in the pan and cook over medium-high heat, stirring occasionally, until the dal and rice are soft and creamy, adding another cup of water if the khichadi is dry, about 45 minutes. Top with the tarka and serve.

Pilaf-Style Rice and Yellow Mung Beans with Ginger
Sookhi Dhulli Mung ki Khichadi

Makes 4 to 6 servings

Made in a pressure cooker like most other khichadis, *this is my mother-in-law's special recipe. A little drier than other* khichadis, *this one is made with skinless yellow mung dal and a topping of sizzling fresh ginger, black pepper, and cardamom seeds, and presents more like a pullao (pilaf), in which every grain of rice is separate.*

2/3 cup basmati rice, sorted and washed
    in 3 to 4 changes of water
1/2 cup dried yellow mung beans (dhulli mung dal),
    sorted and washed in 3 to 4 changes of water
5 to 5 1/2 cups water
3 black cardamom pods, crushed lightly
    to break the skin
2 (1-inch) sticks cinnamon
3/4 teaspoon salt, or to taste
2 tablespoons ghee or olive oil
1 1/2 teaspoons cumin seeds
1 tablespoon peeled minced fresh ginger
1 teaspoon coarsely ground black pepper
1 black cardamom pod, seeds only, coarsely ground

1. Place the rice and dal in a pressure cooker along with 5 cups water, cardamom pods, cinnamon, and salt. Secure the lid and cook over high heat until the regulator indicates high pressure, then cook about 30 seconds more. Remove from the heat and allow the pot to depressurize on its own, 12 to 15 minutes. Carefully open the lid and stir the rice and dal. If the rice and dal are not soft, add the remaining 1/2 cup water and cook over low heat another 5 to 7 minutes. (The rice grains should be separate; don't stir to make it creamy.) Transfer to a serving dish.

2. Heat the ghee in a small saucepan over medium-high heat and add the cumin seeds; they should sizzle upon contact with the hot oil. Quickly add the ginger, black pepper, and cardamom seeds and stir a few seconds, then add to the khichadi and mix lightly, with parts of it visible as a garnish. Serve.

Variation: With the same cooking time, this recipe can also be made by replacing the yellow mung beans with any one or a mixture of red lentils (dhulli masoor dal), split pigeon peas (toor dal), and yellow split chickpeas (channa dal).

Creamy Rice and Mixed Vegetables with Spinach Ribbons
Sabzi aur Palak ki Khichadi

Makes 4 to 6 servings

This is a great dish for kids (and adults) to grow on. It's got lots of nutrients—proteins and carbohydrates from the rice and dal, *vitamins from the vegetables, and iron from the spinach, but it's all suitably disguised, mixed together in this creamy rice. And that's not all: The sizzling flavoring that tops it makes the* khichadi *really delicious.*

This dish, cooked in a pressure cooker, goes well with Simple Salt and Pepper Raita (page 222) and a fresh green chutney such as Mint Chutney with Pomegranate Seeds (page 58).

2/3 cup basmati rice, sorted and washed
    in 3 to 4 changes of water
1/3 cup dried yellow mung beans (dhulli mung dal),
    sorted and washed in 3 to 4 changes of water
3 cups finely chopped fresh or frozen vegetables,
    such as carrots, potatoes, green beans,
    cauliflower, peas, or others
1 tablespoon peeled minced fresh ginger
1 teaspoon minced garlic
4 black cardamom pods, crushed lightly
    to break the skin
2 (1-inch) sticks cinnamon
3/4 teaspoon salt, or to taste
5 to 5 1/2 cups water
1 small bunch fresh spinach (8 to 10 ounces),
    trimmed, washed, and cut into thin ribbons
2 tablespoons ghee or olive oil
1 1/2 teaspoons cumin seeds
1 teaspoon coarsely ground black pepper
1/2 teaspoon coarsely ground fenugreek seeds
1/8 teaspoon ground asafoetida
1 black cardamom pod, seeds only, coarsely ground

1. Place the rice and dal in a pressure cooker. Add the vegetables, ginger, garlic, cardamom pods, cinnamon, salt, and water. Secure the lid and cook over high heat until the regulator indicates high pressure, then cook about 1 minute more. Remove from the heat and allow the pot to depressurize on its own, 12 to 15 minutes. Carefully, open the lid, mix in the spinach, and cook over low heat until the spinach is wilted, about 2 minutes. Transfer to a serving dish.

2. To make the tarka, heat the ghee in a small saucepan over medium-high heat and add the cumin seeds; they should sizzle upon contact with the hot oil. Quickly add the black pepper, fenugreek seeds, and asafoetida and stir a few seconds. Transfer to the khichadi in the serving dish, swirl lightly to mix, with parts of it visible as a garnish, sprinkle the cardamom seeds on top and serve.

Variation: To add meat, mix in 8 to 10 ounces finely chopped uncooked chicken tenders along with the vegetables in Step 1.

Pilaf-Style Tapioca Pearls
Sabudana Khichadi

Makes 4 to 6 servings

This savory dish is different from any tapioca dish you may have tried before. It is tangy and spicy, and studded with crunchy peanuts. My sister-in-law Reita Bhalla first introduced me to this delicious khichadi *many years ago, and then shared the recipe.*

Tapioca are little white pearls made from cassava root (also known as tapioca root), which belongs to the potato family. It is served during the sacred Navratrae fasts—9 days of fasting that come twice a year, in March–April and in October–November— when cereal consumption is forbidden.

Tapioca grains comes in three sizes: the smallest are very fine, just a little bigger than semolina; the medium ones are tiny pearls, about ¹⁄₁₆ -inch in diameter; and the largest are ⅛-inch in diameter. The medium grain is the one most commonly used, and can be found in supermarkets or Indian or Asian markets.

1 cup medium-grain tapioca, sorted and washed
     in 3 to 4 changes of water
2 small russet potatoes
1 tablespoon vegetable oil or melted ghee
1¹⁄₂ teaspoons cumin seeds
¹⁄₃ cup shelled raw peanuts, with or without red skin
1 tablespoon peeled and minced or coarsely chopped
     fresh ginger
1 fresh green chile pepper, such as serrano,
     minced with seeds
¹⁄₂ teaspoon salt, or to taste
¹⁄₂ cup finely chopped fresh cilantro, with soft stems
1 tablespoon fresh lime juice

1. Soak the tapioca in the water to cover about 2 hours. Drain well through a fine-mesh strainer and spread on a tray lined with paper towels to dry it completely. (This step is essential, or the khichadi will be soggy.) Meanwhile, boil the potatoes in lightly salted water to cover, about 20 minutes. Let cool, then peel and finely chop.

2. Heat the ghee in a large nonstick wok or skillet and add the cumin seeds; they should sizzle upon contact with the hot oil. Quickly add the peanuts, reduce the heat to medium-low, and cook until golden, about 3 minutes.

3. Add the potatoes, ginger, and green chile pepper and stir 2 more minutes. Then add the tapioca, salt, cilantro, and lime juice, cover the pan, and cook, stirring as needed, about 2 minutes. Remove from the heat and set aside about 5 minutes. Transfer to a serving bowl and serve.

Creamy Cracked Wheat, Rice, and Mung Beans

Gehun, Chaval, aur Dhulli Mung ka Khichada

Makes 4 to 6 servings

This pressure-cooked recipe is a specialty of Hyderabad in the south. The people of Hyderabad often make their khichadi *with cracked wheat instead of rice, and they usually call it* khichada. *This dish is traditionally made by soaking, washing, and coarsely grinding whole-wheat grains. In America we take a shortcut and use cracked wheat instead. This easier version turns out almost as good.*

Soak the grains the night before, then cook and serve this for breakfast with some fresh mangoes and papayas and a glass of buttermilk or lussi *(a cold yogurt drink).*

1 cup cracked wheat or pearl barley, sorted

1/2 cup basmati rice, sorted

1/2 cup dried yellow mung beans (dhulli mung dal), sorted

6 to 7 cups water

1 teaspoon salt, or to taste

2 to 3 tablespoons vegetable oil or melted ghee

1 1/2 teaspoons cumin seeds

1/2 teaspoon ajwain seeds

1/8 teaspoon ground asafoetida

2 tablespoons minced fresh mint leaves

1 to 2 tablespoons fresh lime or lemon juice

1. Mix together the cracked wheat (or barley), rice, and dal and wash in 3 to 4 changes of water. Then soak everything overnight in the 6 cups of the water.

2. Transfer the grains and water to a pressure cooker. Mix in the salt, then secure the lid and cook over high heat until the regulator indicates high pressure, and cook about 30 seconds more. Reduce the heat to low and continue to cook another minute. Remove from the heat and allow the pot to depressurize on its own, 12 to 15 minutes. Carefully open the lid and check to see if the khichadi is soft and creamy; if not, add more water if needed, cover, bring up to pressure, and cook under pressure another minute. Or cover and boil until soft, about 1/2 hour. Stir well and transfer to a serving bowl.

3. Heat the oil (or ghee) in a small saucepan over medium-high heat and add the cumin and ajwain seeds; they should sizzle upon contact with the hot oil. Quickly add the asafoetida, mint, and lime juice and transfer to the khichadi. Swirl lightly to mix, with parts of it visible as a garnish, and serve.

Creamy Cracked Wheat with Mixed Lentils and Beans

Gehun aur Dal ka Khichada

Makes 4 to 6 servings

This is another special khichada *from the southern city of Hyderabad. This one has no rice and is made only with cracked wheat and* dal *(legumes). Khichada is generally cooked with a lot more spices than a* khichadi, *and is very fragrant and substantial. It is normally served for brunch, or on a rainy day with a cup of hot Spicy Chai Tea (page 662).*

3/4 cup cracked wheat, sorted

2 tablespoons each: split pigeon peas (toor dal), yellow split chickpeas (channa dal), white urad beans (dhulli urad dal), yellow mung beans (dhulli mung dal) and red lentils (red masoor dal), sorted and washed in 3 to 4 changes of water

3 to 4 cups water

2 tablespoons Basic Ginger-Garlic Paste (page 47 or store-bought)

1 teaspoon salt, or to taste

1/4 cup vegetable oil or melted ghee

3 small onions, cut in half lengthwise and thinly sliced

1/2 teaspoon cayenne pepper, or to taste

1/2 teaspoon ground turmeric

1/2 teaspoon garam masala

1. Mix together the cracked wheat and dals and soak them in 3 cups of the water overnight. Meanwhile, prepare the ginger-garlic paste.

2. Transfer the softened grains and water to a pressure cooker, add the salt and more water if all of it has been absorbed. Secure the lid and cook over high heat until the regulator indicates high pressure, then cook about 1 minute more. Remove from the heat and allow the pot to depressurize on its own, 12 to 15 minutes. Carefully open the lid and check to see if the khichadi is soft and creamy; if not, add more water if needed, cover, bring up to pressure, and cook under pressure another minute. Or cover and boil until soft, about ½ hour. Stir well and transfer to a serving dish.

3. Heat the oil (or ghee) in a large nonstick wok or saucepan over medium heat and cook the onions until dark brown, about 15 minutes. Set aside some of them for garnish.

4. Add ginger-garlic paste, cayenne pepper, turmeric, and garam masala and stir another minute. Add to dish and swirl lightly to mix, with parts of it visible as a garnish. Top with the reserved fried onions and serve.

Other Grain Pilafs

Brown Basmati Rice with Asafoetida

Hing vaali Brown Basmati

Makes 4 to 6 servings

All rice is first brown, and then it is polished to the white grain we are so familiar with. So even though this type of rice is not what Indians eat routinely, it does exist—as I've happily discovered in America.

Be aware that, like any other brown rice, because it is the whole grain, brown basmati takes a long time to become tender and is thus a great one to cook in a pressure cooker. This rice remains somewhat sticky after cooking.

1¼ cups brown basmati rice, sorted and washed in 3 to 4 changes of water
1 tablespoon Basic Ginger-Garlic Paste (page 47 or store-bought)
3 cups water
2 tablespoons peanut oil
1 teaspoon cumin seeds
1 teaspoon black mustard seeds
1 large onion, finely chopped
1 large tomato, finely chopped
2 tablespoons finely chopped fresh curry leaves
1 teaspoon dried fenugreek leaves
¹/₈ teaspoon ground asafoetida
¹/₂ teaspoon salt, or to taste
2 tablespoons finely chopped fresh cilantro

1. In a medium bowl, soak the rice in the water, 2 to 3 hours. Meanwhile, prepare the ginger-garlic paste.

2. Heat the oil in a medium saucepan over medium-high heat and add the cumin and mustard seeds; they should splutter upon contact with the hot oil, so cover the pan until the spluttering subsides. Quickly add the onions and cook, stirring, until golden, about 5 minutes. Add the tomato, ginger-garlic paste, curry leaves, fenugreek leaves, asafoetida, and salt and stir a few minutes. Transfer to a pressure cooker.

3. Add the rice with the water it was soaking in. Secure the lid and cook over high heat until the regulator indicates high pressure, then cook about 1 minute more. Reduce the heat to low and continue to cook another 3 minutes. Then remove from the heat and allow the pot to depressurize on its own, 12 to 15 minutes. Carefully open the lid and check to see if the rice is very soft; if not, cover, bring up to pressure, and cook under pressure another minute. Or cover and boil until soft, about ½ hour. Transfer to a serving dish, garnish with chopped cilantro, and serve.

Pressed Rice Flakes with Peas and Potatoes
Muttar-Aalu Poha

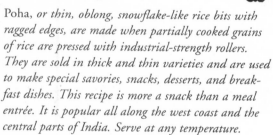

Makes 6 to 8 servings

Poha, or thin, oblong, snowflake-like rice bits with ragged edges, are made when partially cooked grains of rice are pressed with industrial-strength rollers. They are sold in thick and thin varieties and are used to make special savories, snacks, desserts, and breakfast dishes. This recipe is more a snack than a meal entrée. It is popular all along the west coast and the central parts of India. Serve at any temperature.

2 small russet (or any) potatoes
3 cups thick pressed rice flakes, sorted
3 tablespoons peanut oil
¼ cup shelled raw peanuts, with red skin
2 teaspoons black mustard seeds
1 medium onion, cut in half lengthwise and
    thinly sliced
⅛ teaspoon ground asafoetida
1 to 3 fresh green chile peppers, such as serrano,
    minced with seeds
1 cup frozen peas, thawed
¼ teaspoon ground turmeric
1 tablespoon ground coriander
1 teaspoon salt, or to taste
½ cup finely chopped fresh cilantro,
    including soft stems
2 to 3 tablespoons fresh lime or lemon juice
Lime or lemon slices

1. Boil the potatoes in lightly salted water to cover until tender, about 20 minutes. Drain, let cool, then peel and cut into 6 wedges each. Place the rice flakes in a large fine-mesh strainer and wash well under running water. With the rice flakes still in the strainer, soak in a bowl of water about 1 minute, then drain and set aside.

2. Heat the oil in a large nonstick skillet over medium-high heat and cook the peanuts, stirring, until lightly golden. Use a slotted spatula to remove the peanuts to a bowl, leaving all the oil behind.

3. Add the mustard seeds to the oil; they should splutter upon contact with the hot oil, so reduce the heat and cover the pan until the spluttering subsides. Quickly add the onion and cook, stirring, until golden, 3 to 4 minutes. Add the asafoetida and green chile peppers, then mix in the peas and potatoes and cook, stirring, until the potatoes are golden, about 4 minutes.

4. Add the turmeric, coriander, and salt, then add the rice flakes and stir gently to mix. Cover and cook over medium-low heat until fluffy and yellow, 4 to 5 minutes. Mix in the cilantro and lime (or lemon) juice. Transfer to a platter, garnish with lime (or lemon) slices, and serve.

Pressed Rice Flakes with Tamarind

Imli Poha

Makes 4 to 6 servings

Tamarind, with its dark color and a fruity sour taste, gives this pressed rice flakes dish a new flavor.

1 tablespoon sesame seeds, dry-roasted
    (Dry-Roasting Spices, page 35)
3 tablespoons Tamarind Paste (page 54
    or store-bought)
1/2 cup water
1/4 teaspoon ground turmeric
1/2 teaspoon salt
3 cups thick pressed rice flakes, sorted
3 tablespoons peanut oil
2 to 5 dried red chile peppers, such as chile de arbol,
    broken
2 teaspoons black mustard seeds
1 tablespoon dried yellow split chickpeas (channa dal),
    sorted
1 tablespoon dried white urad beans (dhulli urad dal),
    sorted
1 tablespoon finely chopped fresh curry leaves
1/8 teaspoon ground asafoetida
1 to 3 fresh green chile peppers, such as serrano,
    minced or split in half lengthwise
1/2 cup finely chopped fresh cilantro,
    including soft stems

1. Prepare the sesame seeds and the tamarind paste. Then, in a small bowl, mix together the tamarind paste, water, turmeric, and salt.

2. Place the rice flakes in a fine-mesh strainer and wash well under running water. Transfer to a large bowl, mix in the tamarind-water, and set aside until all the water is absorbed and the grains stand separate, about 5 minutes.

3. Heat the oil in a large nonstick skillet over medium-high heat and add the red chile peppers and mustard seeds; they should splutter upon contact with the hot oil, so cover the pan and reduce the heat until the spluttering subsides. Quickly add both the dals, curry leaves, asafoetida, and green chile peppers and cook, stirring, until the dals are golden, about 1 minute.

4. Add the rice flakes and stir gently to mix. Cover and cook over medium-low heat until completely dry and fluffy, 4 to 5 minutes. Mix in the cilantro, sprinkle the sesame seeds on top, and serve.

Stir-Fried Spicy Semolina

Rava Uppma

Makes 4 to 6 servings

Uppma is one of India's quick-cooking and easily digested dishes. With a texture somewhat like couscous and a taste of southern India, uppma is generally served as part of a brunch menu and an anytime snack. Use coarse or fine semolina; the coarse grain results in a pilaf-style rice dish and the finer one will be more lumpy.

1 tablespoon each: yellow split chickpeas (channa
    dal), split black urad beans (chilkae vaali urad
    dal), white urad beans (dhulli urad dal), sorted
    and washed in 3 to 4 changes of water
1 1/2 cups semolina
2 tablespoons vegetable oil
1 teaspoon black mustard seeds
2 tablespoons shelled raw peanuts, with red skin
2 tablespoons chopped raw cashews
1 small onion, finely chopped
1 tablespoon peeled minced fresh ginger
1 to 3 fresh green chile peppers, such as serrano,
    minced with seeds
10 to 15 fresh curry leaves
1 teaspoon salt, or to taste
3 to 3 1/2 cups water
1/2 cup finely chopped fresh cilantro,
    including soft stems
1 to 2 tablespoons fresh lime or lemon juice

1. Soak the dals in water to cover about 30 minutes. Drain. Place the semolina in a large wok or saucepan and dry-roast, stirring over medium-high heat until heated through. Reduce the heat to medium and continue to roast until golden, about 5 minutes. Remove to a bowl.

2. In the same pan, heat the oil and add the mustard seeds; they should splutter upon contact with the hot oil, so lower the heat and cover the pan until the spluttering subsides. Quickly add the drained dals and stir about 30 seconds.

3. With the heat still on medium, add the peanuts and cashews, and cook, stirring, until golden, about 1 minute. Add the onion, ginger, green chile peppers, and curry leaves, and cook, stirring, until the onions are golden, about 5 minutes.

4. Mix in the roasted semolina, salt, and water and bring to a boil over high heat. Reduce the heat to medium-low and simmer until all the water is absorbed and the semolina is soft and fluffy, about 5 minutes. Mix in the cilantro and lime (or lemon) juice, allow to rest about 5 minutes, and serve.

Stir-Fried Indian Vermicelli with Coconut and Vegetables

Sevai Uppma

Makes 4 to 6 servings

Made with an Indian vermicelli called sevai *or* seviyan, *the preparation of this* uppma *is almost exactly like the previous one made with semolina. Indian vermicelli is available as thin, curly ½-inch noodles (much thinner than angel hair pasta) packaged in clear plastic wrap. Do not buy the roasted long, thin ones.*

½ cup semolina
1 tablespoon peanut oil or melted ghee
1 cup Indian vermicelli
1 teaspoon black mustard seeds
¼ teaspoon ground asafoetida
1 small onion, finely chopped
1 tablespoon peeled minced fresh ginger
1 to 3 fresh green chile peppers, such as serrano, minced with seeds
10 to 15 fresh curry leaves
1 tablespoon grated fresh or frozen coconut
1 to 2 cups finely chopped fresh or frozen mixed vegetables, such as carrots, peas, corn, and cauliflower florets
1 teaspoon salt, or to taste
3 to 3½ cups water
¼ cup finely chopped fresh cilantro, including soft stems
1 to 2 tablespoons fresh lime or lemon juice

1. In a large nonstick wok or skillet over medium heat, dry-roast the semolina until fragrant and golden, about 5 minutes. Remove to a bowl. In the same pan, heat 1 teaspoon oil (or ghee) and roast the vermicelli until golden, about 5 minutes. Add to the semolina bowl.

2. In the same pan, heat the remaining ghee (or oil) and add the mustard seeds; they should splutter upon contact with the hot oil, so cover the pan until the spluttering subsides. Quickly mix in the asafoetida, onion, ginger, green chile peppers, curry leaves, and coconut, and cook, stirring, until the onions are golden, about 3 minutes.

3. Add the vegetables and salt and cook, stirring, 3 more minutes, then add the water and bring to a boil over high heat.

4. Mix in the roasted semolina and vermicelli, reduce the heat to medium-low, cover the pan and simmer, until the vegetables are tender and all the water has been absorbed, about 10 minutes. Stir every few minutes. Mix in the cilantro and lime or lemon juice, allow to rest about 5 minutes, then serve.

Basmati and Wild Rice Pilaf with Roasted Nuts

Junglee Pullao

Makes 4 to 6 servings

This is a traditional recipe with a surprise—wild rice. Because wild rice takes a long time to soften, I first cook it separately and then together with the basmati rice to make this inspired dish. To dry-roast the peanuts, almonds, and sesame seeds, see Dry-Roasting Spices, Nuts, and Flours, page 35.

1/3 cup wild rice, sorted and washed
    in 3 to 4 changes of water
31/4 cups water
1 cup basmati rice, sorted and washed
    in 3 to 4 changes of water
1/4 cup coarsely broken raw peanuts,
    without red skin, dry-roasted
1/4 cup sliced raw almonds, dry-roasted
1 tablespoon white sesame seeds, dry-roasted
1 to 2 tablespoons peanut oil
1 teaspoon cumin seeds
2 (1-inch) sticks cinnamon
3 black cardamom pods, crushed lightly
    to break the skin
3 whole dried red chile peppers, such as chile de arbol
2 bay leaves
2 large cloves fresh garlic, minced
1 teaspoon salt, or to taste

1. Place the wild rice in a medium saucepan, add 1¼ cups water, and bring to a boil over high heat. Reduce the heat to medium-low, cover the pan, and cook until the all the water is absorbed and the rice is soft, about 40 minutes.

2. Meanwhile, in a medium bowl, soak the basmati rice in the remaining 2 cups water about 30 minutes. In a small skillet, dry-roast the peanuts, almonds, and sesame seeds, roasting each separately because they cook at different rates. Then, mix them all together and save for garnish.

3. Heat the oil in a large saucepan over medium-high heat and add the cumin seeds; they should sizzle upon contact with the hot oil. Quickly add the cinnamon, cardamom pods, and red chile peppers and cook, stirring, about 1 minute.

4. Add the bay leaves and the garlic and cook, stirring, another minute. Add the cooked wild rice, the basmati rice, plus all the water it was soaking in, and the salt and bring to a boil over high heat. Reduce the heat to lowest heat setting, cover the pan (partially at first, until the foam subsides, then snugly), and cook until the rice is done, 10 to 15 minutes. (Do not stir the rice while it cooks.) Let the rice rest about 5 minutes. Transfer to a serving platter, gently mix in the roasted nuts and sesame seeds, with some of them visible as a garnish, and serve.

Breads and Crepes

Simple Griddle Breads 576

Basic Whole-Wheat Dough

Whole-Wheat Griddle Breads

Multi-Flour Griddle Breads

Griddle-Fried Breads (Paranthas) 579

Basic Griddle-Fried Breads

Griddle-Fried Oat Breads with Ajwain Seeds

Griddle-Fried Legume Breads

Griddle-Fried Spinach and Red Bell Pepper Breads

My Healthy Griddle-Fried Mashed Potato Breads

Griddle-Fried Layered Mint, Ajwain, and Black Pepper Breads

Griddle-Fried Layered Green Chile Pepper Breads

Griddle-Fried Flaky Onion Breads

Griddle-Fried Mughlai Breads with Almonds and Poppy Seeds

Stuffed Griddle-Fried Flatbreads 586

Basic Stuffed Griddle-Fried Breads

Potato Parantha Stuffing

Cauliflower Parantha Stuffing

Daikon Radish Parantha Stuffing

Paneer Cheese Parantha Stuffing

Ground Lamb Parantha Stuffing

Sweet Jaggery-Stuffed Paranthas

Puffed Deep-Fried Breads (Pooriyan) 589

Basic Deep-Fried Puffed Breads

Deep-Fried Puffed Breads with Ajwain Seeds

Deep-Fried Puffed Breads with Mint (or Fenugreek)

Deep-Fried Puffed Breads with Fresh Spinach

Deep-Fried Stuffed Puffed Breads

Deep-Fried Sweet Saffron Puffed Breads

Deep-Fried Bengali-Style Flour Breads

Deep-Fried Leavened Flour Breads

V = Vegan   P = Pressure-Cooker Quick

*W*hether they are humble everyday staples or creatively flavored and artfully prepared, Indian breads are integral to the country's cuisine. With roots well before *Vedic* times (the *Vedas* is a collection of Hindu scriptures believed to have been written about 5,000 years ago), no meal is complete without some form of bread made from dough or from a batter, which are similar to crepes and pancakes. Breads are used as scoops to sop up curries and as wraps for all dry-cooked dishes. Even the rice-eating communities, like those in the south and in the east of India, serve breads along with rice.

Indian breads are great-tasting, quick-cooking, easy enough to be made fresh at every meal, and nutrient-rich, because most are made with whole-grain flours.

Made with whole-grain flours (except for the occasionally consumed *naans*, *kulchas* and *bhaturas*) and flours made from legumes, Indian breads are great-tasting, full of healthful nutrients, quick-cooking, and easy enough to be made fresh at every meal.

Whole-wheat flour (*gehun ka atta* or *atta*) is by far the most popular for breads. The whole-wheat flour used for Indian breads is typically made by stone-grinding the whole kernel of wheat—bran, germ, and endosperm. Although all varieties of whole-wheat can be used to make the flour, Indians generally use a winter variety called durum—the hardest wheat of all. It is white and has a high protein-to-starch ratio and more gluten, which is necessary to bind the breads and give them their characteristic light texture. On the other hand, American whole-wheat flour, the type available in supermarkets, is made with a soft summer wheat and is not best suited for Indian breads. This flour is reddish in color, has a coarser texture, and yields heavier breads.

Stone-ground durum wheat flour is available in most health food markets and in all Indian markets. If you can't find it, mix two parts whole-wheat flour with one part all-purpose flour, although even this leads to heavier and drier breads.

There are many types of Indian breads distinguished mainly by how they are made. Of course, there are variations and exceptions, but this classification generally holds true.

Griddle Breads: Made on the *tava* (concave Indian griddle), these are mostly non-leavened, round, triangular, or square flatbreads called *roti*, *chapati*, *phulka*, *rotli*, and *parantha*.

Deep-Fried Breads: Fried in an Indian wok or deep skillet, these leavened and un-leavened breads are called *poori*, *kulcha*, *lucchi*, or *baati*. They can be as small as 3 inches in diameter or as big as 1 foot across.

Tandoori Breads: Baked by slapping them along the inside wall of a *tandoor* oven, these breads, called *tandoori roti*, *parantha*, *naan*, or *kulcha*, can be round or triangular.

Crepes and Pancakes: Griddle-fried and made with batters rather than a dough, and eaten in place of standard breads; these breads, called *dosas*, *uthapam*, *pudhas*, and *chillas*, are generally round.

Most of the everyday breads such as the *chapatis* (whole-wheat griddle breads) and *paranthas* (griddle-fried breads) are typically made on a *tava*—a round, slightly concave, cast-iron griddle. It looks like an omelet pan, with a gentle, gradual curve to the bottom but without a lip. A *tava* comes in various sizes—anywhere from 10 inches to 3 feet, but only the smaller 10- to 12-inch ones are used in homes. Look for *tava* griddles in Indian markets. *Tava* griddles, though crucial to Indian bread making, can be replaced with a regular square or rectangular cast-iron or nonstick griddle.

To keep your breads from sticking to it, season it every time you wash it. To season, heat the *tava* over medium-high heat until hot but not smoking. Put 2 to 3 drops of melted *ghee* or oil on it, and quickly, with a clean cotton kitchen towel, spread the oil all over the *tava*. There will be a lot of smoke for a minute or two, until you wipe off the oil, so turn on the exhaust fan and open the windows, if you have any in the kitchen.

Do not wash the *tava* with soap and water after each use. As long as you use your *tava* only to make breads, after using it, just let it cool completely, wipe off any excess flour, and store it someplace dust free. I store mine in the oven.

Simple Griddle Breads

Basic Whole-Wheat Dough
Gundha Hua Atta

Makes 10 to 12 breads

In Indian bread making, this whole-wheat flour and water dough, with no other additives, is the most basic.

2 cups stone-ground durum whole-wheat flour
About 1 cup water, or nonfat plain yogurt,
whisked until smooth

To make in a food processor:

1. Place the flour in the work bowl of the food processor fitted with the metal S-blade. Turn the machine on, add the water or yogurt in a thin stream, and process until it just gathers into a ball.

2. Continue to process until the sides of the bowl look clean, 20 to 30 seconds. (Add 1 or 2 tablespoons more flour if the dough sticks to the sides of the work bowl, and some water if the dough seems hard.) Stop the machine, remove the dough to a bowl, cover with plastic wrap or the lid of the bowl, and let rest at least 1 and up to 4 hours. (This allows the gluten to develop.) If keeping for a longer period, refrigerate the dough.

To make by hand:

1. Place the flour in a bowl and add ¾ cup water. Stir lightly in round circular motions with clean fingers until it starts to gather. (Add 1 or 2 tablespoons more flour if the dough seems sticky, or some water if it seems too firm.)

2. Knead for about a minute, pressing your knuckles lightly into the dough, spreading the dough outward, then gathering the ends together toward the center with your fingers and pressing the center down. Repeat kneading a few times until you have a soft and pliable dough that does not stick to your fingers. If, while kneading, the dough sticks to your hands, put a little oil or water on them.

3. Cover with plastic wrap or the lid of the bowl and let rest at least 1 and up to 4 hours at room temperature. (This allows the gluten to develop.) If keeping for a longer period, refrigerate the dough.

Storing and Freezing Indian Breads

Very little compares to the fragrance and taste of freshly made bread, especially when basted with a touch of *ghee* (Indian clarified butter)—a culinary extravagance that I will not part with, even though I do take all other measures to make my cooking more healthful.

Indian breads can also be made, then stored in the refrigerator up to 5 days and in the freezer as long as 2 months. To do this, cook the breads lightly on both sides, then place them on any clean flat surface to cool them completely. Then stack them one on top of the other and wrap in aluminum foil or place in zip closure bags, and refrigerate or freeze.

When ready to use, finish cooking the breads in one of several ways: on the *tava* or griddle; in a single layer on an ungreased broiler-safe tray, 4 to 5 inches from the heat source; or grill them on an outdoor or indoor grill. Leftover breads can be reheated in the toaster oven about 1 minute at 450°F, or in a regular toaster. Do not cook or reheat any breads in the microwave.

Whole-Wheat Griddle Breads

Chapati, Roti, aur Phulkae

Makes 10 to 12 breads

Made with the basic whole-wheat and water dough, chapatis *are also called* roti *and* phulka. *These unleavened flatbreads are the Indian daily bread, a versatile staple all over the country, at just about every meal. Served with vegetables, meats, or just pickles, they can go from being center stage during a major meal to being side dishes during breakfast and tea.*

Typically, chapatis *are rolled out and cooked while people are eating, so everyone gets to enjoy them fresh. As each* chapati *is picked off the griddle, it is lightly basted with melted* ghee *or butter and then crumpled like a piece of paper, before it is deposited in front of a hungry diner. The* chapati *stays crumpled and the* ghee *seeps into the cracks formed by crumpling, spreading the flavor. If you wish to crumple them, first put each on a clean kitchen towel and then do so; they can be very hot on bare hands.*

1 recipe Basic Whole-Wheat Dough (page 576)
1 cup stone-ground durum whole-wheat flour
    in a medium bowl or a pie dish, for coating
    and dusting
Rolling pin
3 to 4 tablespoons melted ghee or butter,
    for basting (optional)

1. Heat the tava or griddle over medium-high heat until a sprinkling of the flour immediately turns dark brown. Wipe off the flour and proceed. While the tava is heating, with lightly oiled hands, divide the dough equally into 10 to 12 round balls and cover with foil to prevent drying.

2. Working with each ball separately, place it in the bowl with the dry flour, flatten it with your fingertips and coat well with the flour. Then transfer it to a cutting board or any other clean flat surface, and, with a rolling pin, roll it into a 6- to 7-inch circle of uniform thickness. If the dough sticks to the rolling surface, dust lightly with more flour. (Chapatis can be rolled on a lightly floured surface also, though this is not a common practice in India.)

3. Place the rolled chapati on the hot tava and turn it over when it is dotted with tiny golden dots on the bottom, about 30 seconds. Once the other side is covered with larger brown dots, turn it over again. Soon the chapati will start to puff up. With the help of a small clean kitchen towel crumpled into a ball, press lightly on the puffed parts and gently guide and push the air into the flatter parts until the whole chapati puffs up into a round ball. (Your first few puffing attempts may not be successful, but don't be disheartened; the taste and texture will still be wonderful.) Transfer to a plate, baste lightly with the ghee, if using (and crumple it if you wish), and serve hot.

Multi-Flour Griddle Breads

Millae-Jullae Aatton ki Chapatiyan

Makes 10 to 12 breads

An array of flours ground from different grains and legumes can be found in health food stores and Indian markets all over the country. Experiment with them; they are easy to use. Make a dough, mix in some flours, and see how delicious the breads turn out. Here, I give you a basic blend of flours, but mix them in any proportions. The bread density may change, but the breads will still be wonderful and nutritious.

1/3 cup whole-wheat flour
1/3 cup oat flour
1/3 cup soy flour
1/3 cup fine-grain semolina
1/4 cup ground flax seeds
1 teaspoon dried fenugreek leaves
1 teaspoon dried mint leaves
1/2 teaspoon coarsely ground carom seeds
1/4 teaspoon salt, or to taste
1/4 teaspoon freshly ground black pepper, or to taste
1 cup finely chopped fresh spinach, or any other greens
2/3 to 3/4 cup water or nonfat plain yogurt,
    whisked until smooth

Working with Whole-Wheat Dough

The whole-wheat flour-and-water dough for breads is traditionally made by hand, though the food processor and mixer are popular in today's kitchens (including mine). One friend even makes her *chapati* dough in an electric bread machine—removing it from the work bowl as soon as the dough is formed. Forming the breads, however, still requires individual attention.

If you really like *chapatis* (whole-wheat griddle breads) and plan to make many of them, consider a *chapati* press, gaining popularity all over India and the West. They are similar to tortilla presses in that they flatten and shape the dough. You place a ball of dough into the press and it turns out a symmetrically round rolled bread—ready to be transferred to a hot griddle. Look for them in Indian markets.

Here are some tips for working with the dough:

1. Make a semi-firm dough that doesn't stick to your fingers. If the dough is too firm, the bread made from it will be hard, and if it is too soft, it will stick to your fingers and you will not be able to work with it.

2. Cover the dough with plastic wrap or the lid of the bowl and let it rest 1 to 4 hours to allow the gluten to develop. This makes breads that are crisp outside and soft inside.

3. Whole-wheat dough stores well about 3 days in an airtight container in the refrigerator. Use it preferably at room temperature, or chilled straight from the refrigerator. Chilled dough will be firm and a little harder to use.

4. Dough can be frozen up to 2 months. Thaw at room temperature. Do not microwave. This cooks the dough, rendering it useless for any breads.

1. In a large bowl, mix together everything except the water (or yogurt). Then add the water (or yogurt), a little at a time, mixing lightly with clean fingers in round circular motions until the flour starts to gather. (Add 1 or 2 tablespoons more flour if the dough seems sticky, or some water if it seems too firm.)

2. Knead for about a minute, pressing your knuckles lightly into the dough, spreading the dough outward, then gathering the ends together toward the center with your fingers. Push down the center, then repeat pressing and gathering a few times until you have a soft and pliable dough that does not stick to your fingers. If, while kneading, the dough sticks to your hands, put a little oil or water on them.

3. Cover with plastic wrap or the lid of the bowl and let it rest at least 1 and up to 4 hours at room temperature. This allows the gluten to develop. If keeping for a longer period, refrigerate the dough.

4. To make the chapati breads, with lightly oiled hands divide the dough equally into 10 to 12 round balls, cover with foil to prevent drying, then follow the directions for Whole-Wheat Griddle Breads (page 577) from Step 2.

Variation: Baste each freshly made chapati with butter or ghee and then top it with 3 to 6 coarse grinds from a peppermill filled with colorful peppercorns. (Finely ground peppercorns do not add as much flavor.) Sprinkle with salt, if you wish. Roll up loosely or cut into wedges and serve.

Griddle-Fried Breads (Paranthas)

Paranthas differ considerably from other Indian breads. They are the enriched, griddle-fried breads that Indians couldn't imagine living without.

The common factor in just about all *paranthas* is some measure of oil, butter, *ghee,* or shortening mixed into the dough, and then some more that is used for individual pan-frying. Authentically, *paranthas* are made on a *tava*-griddle, but they can also be made on an ordinary pancake griddle (of any size).

Unfortunately, these objects of deep affection, especially the more elaborate versions, exemplify the adage: That which tastes so good, must be bad for you. While possibly transcendant for the soul, the heart may not appreciate the fat that is used. So, my recipes use the least amount of fat possible, but if you are watching your health, eat these breads sparingly or save them for when you are allowing yourself some indulgence.

The simplest *paranthas* are made with whole-wheat and water dough and minimal fat, such as Basic Griddle-Fried Breads (page 581). The next kind are slightly more elaborate affairs made with *ghee* (or any other fat), spices, herbs, and vegetables worked into the dough, such as Griddle-Fried Spinach and Red Bell Pepper Breads (page 582). Then come the kind that are layered (*lachaedar*), and flaky (*khasta*), such as Griddle-Fried Layered Green Chile Pepper Breads (page 585) and Griddle-Fried Mughlai Breads with Almonds and Poppy Seeds (page 586).

Requiring a little more work, but well worth the effort, are yet another level of *parantha* breads—the stuffed kind, filled with every imaginable vegetable, *dal,* and meat.

And finally, there are the stuffed sweet *paranthas,* oozing with *ghee* or butter and melted sugars—jaggery (the British term for Indian brown sugar, *gur*), or regular table sugar.

Health notes: *Paranthas* can be cooked like a *chapati*—without any fat in the dough or any frying. Such *paranthas* are lightly basted with butter before serving. This renders a lighter, healthier *parantha,* such as My Healthy Griddle-Fried Mashed Potato Breads (page 583).

All *parantha* breads, even the stuffed kind, can also be made in the oven, like *naan.* Roll out the *paranthas* following any of the recipes, and then, instead of cooking them on the *tava* (griddle), place them on lightly greased baking trays and grill as for Basic Oven-Grilled Leavened Breads (page 594).

Chapati breads can also be made in a similar manner, but you have to roll them much thicker, or they will dry out.

Basic Parantha Breads

Layered *paranthas* are a culinary blessing to the novice Indian bread maker. Because a new daughter-in-law making *chapatis* may be judged by a critical mother-in-law —"they're not round, they didn't puff up," she might say—*paranthas* are an easier choice of bread to work with. They need not be perfect rounds, or puff up like *chapatis.*

However, like all breads, you do need to have a good hand with the dough, so that the resulting bread is all the things *paranthas* should be—soft in the inside, crisp on the outside, with distinct layers. You want each layer to be distinct and adhere to each other, but not disappear into each other, yet you don't want the *parantha* too dry and flaky so the layers are rough on the inside of the mouth. It is customary and a sign of affection to slightly crumple up a freshly made *parantha* before serving. This releases each layer, and allows the *ghee* (or oil) that is used for basting to seep into every crevice. (Use a towel to crumple; the parantha may be too hot.)

Shaping Paranthas

Paranthas can be formed into triangles, squares, or rounds. For each of these, roll the dough into a circle, baste the top of the circle with oil (*ghee* or butter) then fold it (for triangles or squares) or roll and shape it (for circles) into the required shape.

To Make a Layered Triangle

1. With lightly oiled clean hands, divide the dough equally into the required number of portions and cover with foil to prevent drying. Working with each portion separately, flatten into a disc with your fingertips, generously coat with flour, and roll into a 5- to 6-inch circle.

2. Brush the top surface lightly with oil, sprinkle on the spices, herbs, or vegetables, if you are using them, then sprinkle about 1 teaspoon dry flour over the spices and fold in half, forming a semi-circle.

3. Brush the top of the semi-circle with oil and fold in half once again, forming a triangle. Flatten this triangle into a larger triangle with your fingertips, coat it with flour once again, and roll it into a 6- to 7-inch triangle, taking care to maintain its shape.

To Make a Layered Square

1. Divide the dough into the required number of portions. Working with each portion separately, flatten into a disc with your fingertips, coat generously with flour, and roll into a 5- to 6-inch circle.

2. Brush the top surface lightly with oil, sprinkle on the spices, herbs, or vegetables, if you are using them, then sprinkle about 1 teaspoon dry flour on top.

3. In your mind, divide the circle into 3 portions lengthwise. Fold ⅓ over the center portion (making a D-shape), then fold the exposed portion toward the center, placing it on top of the first one. You should now have a long, triple-folded rectangle.

4. Brush the top surface of this rectangle with oil and fold it one more time, bringing the two smaller edges toward the center, placing one over the other, to make a small square. Flatten this square into a larger square with your fingertips, coat it with flour, and roll it out into a 6- to 7-inch square, taking care to maintain its shape.

To Make a Layered Circle

Method 1

1. Divide the dough into the required number of portions. Working with each portion separately, flatten into a disc with your fingertips, coat with flour, and roll it into a 5- to 6-inch circle.

2. Brush the top surface lightly with oil, sprinkle on the spices, herbs, or vegetables, if you are using them, then sprinkle about 1 teaspoon dry flour over the spices, and roll it into a rope 7 to 8 inches long and ½ inch in diameter. Brush the rope with oil.

3. Starting from one end, wind the rope in a spiral fashion into a coil, with all sides touching. Flatten this coil with your fingertips and coat it with flour, then roll it out into a 6- to 7-inch circle.

Method 2

1. Roll the dough into a 5- to 6-inch circle. Brush the top surface lightly with oil, sprinkle on the spices, herbs, or vegetables, if you are using them, then sprinkle about 1 teaspoon dry flour over the spices.

2. Make a cut from the center to the edge (along a radius), then start rolling the dough up from the cut edge sideways around the center, ending at the second edge, forming a cone.

3. Brush the cone lightly with oil, then press the pointed end into the wider, rounder end to form a disc. Coat this disc with flour, and roll into a 6- to 7-inch circle again.

Basic Griddle-Fried Breads
Saada Parantha

Makes 10 to 12 breads

Made with a whole-wheat flour and water dough, this recipe is the perfect example of a parantha *at its most basic. When frying, keep the rhythm going— while one* parantha *is on the griddle being cooked, prepare the next one. This will save you a lot of time, but be sure to watch both.*

Although freshly made paranthas *are best, they can be cooked a few hours before serving. To cook ahead of time, store and reheat following directions in the box Storing and Freezing Indian Breads (page 576). Allow 2 to 3 per person.*

2 cups stone-ground durum whole-wheat flour + 1 cup for coating and dusting

About 1 cup water or nonfat plain yogurt, whisked until smooth

Rolling pin

3 to 4 tablespoons oil or melted ghee or butter, for basting

1. Place the 2 cups flour in a mixing bowl, add ¾ cup water or yogurt, and mix with your clean fingers in round circular motions, until it starts to gather. (Add 1 or 2 tablespoons more flour if the dough seems sticky, or some water if it seems too firm.)

2. Knead for about a minute, pressing your knuckles lightly into the dough, spreading the dough outward, then gathering the ends together toward the center with your fingers. Push down the center, then repeat pressing and gathering a few times until you have a soft and pliable dough that does not stick to the fingers. Cover and let it rest at least 1 and up to 4 hours at room temperature. (This allows the wheat gluten to develop.) If keeping for a longer period, refrigerate the dough.

3. Preheat the tava or griddle over medium-high heat until a sprinkling of the flour immediately turns dark brown. Wipe off the flour and proceed. While the tava is heating, with lightly oiled hands divide the dough into 10 to 12 round balls (depending on the size of the parantha you like). Cover with foil to prevent drying.

4. Working with each ball of dough separately, place in the bowl with the dry flour, flatten it with your fingertips, and coat well with the dry flour. Transfer to a cutting board or any other clean flat surface and, with a rolling pin, roll into a 6- to 7-inch circle of uniform thickness. (If the dough sticks to the rolling surface, dust with more flour.) Baste the top of the dough with ghee and fold into a triangle, square, or circle, as per the directions on page 580.

5. Place the rolled parantha on the hot tava or griddle. Turn over when it is slightly cooked and dotted with tiny golden spots on the bottom, about 1 minute. When the other side is covered with larger brown dots, turn it over, and brush lightly with oil. Flip it over again and fry the oiled side about 30 seconds. Similarly, baste and fry the other side another 30 seconds. There should be a total of 4 turns.

6. Remove from the griddle and serve.

Griddle-Fried Oat Breads with Ajwain Seeds
Jaee aur Ajwain kae Paranthae

Makes 10 to 12 breads

In my continuing effort to eat healthfully, I am always experimenting with different whole-grain flours. This is the result of one of those experiments. This bread is one of my favorites: the whole wheat and oats make it nutritious, the ajwain seeds make it delicious. (It's my favorite spice.)

³/₄ cup stone-ground durum whole-wheat flour

¹/₂ cup oat flour

¹/₄ cup oat bran

2 tablespoons olive oil

¹/₂ teaspoon coarsely crushed ajwain seeds

¹/₂ teaspoon cayenne pepper, or to taste

¹/₃ teaspoon salt, or to taste

¹/₂ cup water, or more if necessary

1. In a bowl, mix together the whole-wheat and oat flours, oat bran, oil, ajwain seeds, cayenne pepper, and salt.

2. Add the water and mix again with your clean fingers in round circular motions until it starts to gather. Knead for about a minute, pressing your knuckles lightly into the dough, spreading the dough outward, then gathering then ends together toward the center with your fingers. Push down the center, then repeat pressing and gathering a few times until you have a soft and pliable dough that does not stick to your fingers. If, while kneading, the dough sticks to your hands, put a little oil or water on them.

3. Cover with plastic wrap or the lid of the bowl and set aside at least 1 and up to 4 hours. (This allows the wheat gluten to develop.) If keeping for a longer period, refrigerate the dough.

4. To roll and cook the paranthas, proceed as per the directions for Basic Griddle-Fried Breads (page 581), from Step 3.

Griddle-Fried Legume Breads

Dal kae Paranthae

Makes 10 to 12 breads

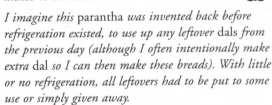

I imagine this parantha *was invented back before refrigeration existed, to use up any leftover* dals *from the previous day (although I often intentionally make extra* dal *so I can then make these breads). With little or no refrigeration, all leftovers had to be put to some use or simply given away.*

These paranthas *are normally served at breakfast with plain or cumin-flavored yogurt and a cup of milky cardamom tea. The quantity of the* dal *needed to make the dough will depend on how thick or thin the cooked* dal *you're using is.*

1¹/₂ cups stone-ground durum whole-wheat flour
2 scallions, minced
¹/₄ cup finely chopped fresh cilantro, including soft stems
1 to 2 tablespoons peeled minced fresh ginger
1 to 3 fresh green chile peppers, such as serrano, minced with seeds
¹/₄ teaspoon salt, or to taste

¹/₄ teaspoon freshly ground black pepper, or to taste
¹/₄ teaspoon coarsely ground ajwain seeds
¹/₄ teaspoon hot red pepper flakes, or to taste
1 cup any leftover cooked dal, such as Yellow Mung Beans with Sautéed Onion and Ginger (page 342), or Yellow Split Chickpeas with Spinach (page 363), or more as needed

1. Place all the ingredients except the dal in a medium bowl and mix well with your clean fingers. Add ⅔ cup dal and stir in round circular motions until it starts to gather into a dough. (Add 1 or 2 tablespoons more flour if the dough seems sticky, or some water if it seems too firm.)

2. Knead for about a minute, pressing your knuckles lightly into the dough, spreading the dough outward, then gathering then ends together toward the center with your fingers. Push down the center, then repeat pressing and gathering a few times until you have a soft and pliable dough that does not stick to your fingers. If, while kneading, the dough sticks to your hands, put a little oil or water on them.

3. Cover with plastic wrap or the lid of the bowl and set aside at least 1 and up to 4 hours. (This allows the wheat gluten to develop.) If keeping for a longer period, refrigerate the dough.

4. To roll and cook the paranthas, proceed as per the directions for Basic Griddle-Fried Breads (page 581), from Step 3.

Griddle-Fried Spinach and Red Bell Pepper Breads

Palak aur Laal Shimla Mirch kae Paranthae

Makes 10 to 12 breads

This bread, with ribbons of spinach and flecks of red bell pepper, has incredible flavor, and is nutritious, too. Make the dough by hand to ensure that the vegetables will remain intact and stand out like a garnish. (The food processor would purée the vegetables into the flour.)

1 1/2 cups stone-ground durum whole-wheat flour,
    or 1 cup whole-wheat flour and 1/2 cup oat bran
1 small bunch fresh spinach (8 to 10 ounces),
    trimmed, washed, and finely chopped
3 to 4 scallions, finely chopped
1 red bell pepper, cut into 1/4-inch pieces
1 tablespoon peeled minced fresh ginger
1 to 3 fresh green chile peppers, such as serrano,
    minced with seeds
1 teaspoon ground dried fenugreek leaves
1/2 teaspoon coarsely ground ajwain seeds
1/2 teaspoon salt, or to taste
Freshly ground black pepper, to taste
2/3 to 3/4 cup water

1. Place everything except the water in a large mixing bowl and mix lightly with clean fingers. Add the water, a little at a time, and mix with your fingers in round circular motions until it starts to gather into a dough. (Add 1 or 2 tablespoons more flour if the dough seems sticky or some water if it seems too firm.)

2. Knead about a minute, pressing your knuckles lightly into the dough, spreading the dough outward, then gathering the ends together toward the center with your fingers. Repeat pressing and gathering a few times until you have a soft and pliable dough that does not stick to your fingers.

3. Cover with plastic wrap or the lid of the bowl and let it rest at least 1 and up to 4 hours at room temperature. (This allows the wheat gluten to develop.) If keeping for a longer period, refrigerate the dough.

4. To roll and cook the paranthas, proceed as per the directions for Basic Griddle-Fried Breads (page 581), from Step 3.

Variation: In place of spinach and red bell pepper, make your paranthas using crushed corn kernels, puréed fresh fenugreek leaves or any other greens, mashed tofu, grated carrots—you name it.

My Healthy Griddle-Fried Mashed Potato Breads
Attae Mein Gundhae Hui Aalu ki Rotiyan

Makes 10 to 12 breads

These are not your traditional stuffed potato parantha *breads. Here, I mix mashed potatoes into the dough along with some aromatics to make one of the easiest and most flavorful potato breads around. It is also much lower in fat than other* paranthas, *because I don't fry it. I make the dough as I would for the griddle-fried breads, but I cook them without oil and then simply baste them lightly with butter while they are warm.*

As far as I know, no one really makes them this way. Even my mother-in-law was surprised and impressed when I gave her this for an afternoon lunch with nonfat plain yogurt and the spicy Cilantro-Lime Chutney (page 59).

2 large russet (or any kind) potatoes
2 tablespoons Basic Ginger and Green Chile Pepper
    Paste (page 48)
1 cup stone-ground durum whole-wheat flour
1/4 cup all-purpose flour
1 tablespoon dried mint leaves
1 teaspoon dried fenugreek leaves
1 fresh green chile pepper, such as serrano,
    minced with seeds
1/2 teaspoon salt, or to taste
1/4 teaspoon freshly ground black pepper, or to taste
1/4 teaspoon coarsely ground ajwain seeds
2 tablespoons vegetable oil
1 tablespoon peeled minced fresh ginger
1/4 cup nonfat plain yogurt, whisked until smooth,
    if needed
Chilled butter, to taste
1 cup stone-ground durum whole-wheat flour
    in a medium bowl or a pie dish, for dusting

1. Boil the potatoes in lightly salted water to cover until tender, about 20 minutes. Drain, let cool, then peel and grate them. Meanwhile, prepare the ginger-chile paste.

2. In a large bowl, with clean fingers, mix together the whole-wheat and all-purpose flours, mint and fenugreek leaves, green chile pepper, salt, black pepper, and ajwain seeds. Then mix in the potatoes, oil, and ginger. (By now there should be enough moisture to make the dough. If not, add up to ¼ cup yogurt to make a semi-firm dough that does not stick to the fingers.) This dough does not require resting time, nor should it be kneaded.

3. With lightly oiled hands, divide the dough equally into 10 to 12 round balls and cover with foil to prevent drying. Working with each ball of dough separately, coat with the dry flour, transfer to a cutting board or any other clean flat surface, and, with a rolling pin, roll into a thin 6- to 7-inch circle. (If the dough sticks to the rolling surface, dust with more flour.)

4. Heat a tava or a griddle over medium-high heat and cook the breads, turning them once or twice until they are speckled with golden dots on both sides, about 1 minute per side. Remove from the griddle, lightly baste with butter, and serve.

Griddle-Fried Layered Mint, Ajwain, and Black Pepper Breads

Pudina, Ajwain aur Kaali Mirch kae Paranthae

Makes 10 to 12 breads

I love the flavors of mint, black pepper, and ajwain together. Paranthas are hearty to start with, and with these three strong flavors this bread is really satisfying— it becomes a simple but great meal with mango pickle and a yogurt raita.

1¼ cups stone-ground durum whole-wheat flour
¼ cup fine-grain semolina
1 to 3 fresh green chile peppers such as serrano, minced with seeds
1 teaspoon black pepper, dry-roasted and coarsely ground (page 35)
1 tablespoon ground dried mint leaves + more for garnish
½ teaspoon coarsely ground ajwain seeds
⅓ teaspoon salt, or to taste
2 to 3 tablespoons canola oil
½ cup nonfat plain yogurt, whisked until smooth, or more if necessary

1. In a bowl, mix together the whole-wheat flour and semolina with clean fingers, then add the green chile peppers, black pepper, mint, ajwain, and salt. Rub in the oil. Add the yogurt and mix again with your fingers in round circular motions until it starts to gather into a dough.

2. Knead about a minute, pressing your knuckles lightly into the dough, spreading the dough outward, then gathering the ends together toward the center with your fingers. Repeat pressing and gathering a few times until you have a soft and pliable dough that does not stick to your fingers. If, while kneading, the dough sticks to your hands, put a little oil or water on them.

3. Cover with plastic wrap or the lid of the bowl and let it rest at least 1 and up to 4 hours. (This allows the wheat gluten to develop.) If keeping for a longer period, refrigerate the dough.

4. To roll and cook the paranthas, proceed as per the directions for Basic Griddle-Fried Breads (page 581), from Step 3. As each parantha is made, sprinkle about ¼ teaspoon dried mint, then serve.

Griddle-Fried Layered Green Chile Pepper Breads

Mirchi ka Lachaedar Paranthae

Makes 10 to 12 breads

Sharp and hot—especially if you add all 3 chile peppers—this parantha *is best served with mild accompaniments, one of which should definitely be a mild yogurt* raita.

1 teaspoon Chaat Masala (page 20 or store-bought)
1 pound (1 recipe) dough for Basic Griddle-Fried Breads (page 581)
1/4 cup finely chopped fresh cilantro, including soft stems
2 tablespoons peeled minced fresh ginger
3 scallions, white parts only, minced
1 to 3 fresh green chile peppers, such as serrano, minced with seeds
1 teaspoon ground dried fenugreek leaves
1/4 teaspoon salt, or to taste
2 to 3 tablespoons vegetable oil
1 cup stone-ground durum whole-wheat flour in a medium bowl or a pie dish, for dusting

1. Prepare the chaat masala. Prepare the dough. Then, in a small bowl, mix together the cilantro, ginger, scallions, green chile peppers, fenugreek leaves, and salt.

2. To roll the paranthas, divide the dough and the herb mixture into 10 to 12 portions. Working with each dough portion separately, make a layered triangle, square, or circle as per the directions for Shaping Paranthas on page 580.

3. To cook the paranthas, proceed as per the directions for Basic Griddle-Fried Breads (page 581), from Step 5.

Griddle-Fried Flaky Onion Breads

Pyaz kae Khasta Paranthae

Makes 10 to 12 breads

With minced onions worked into the dough, each bite of this lovely parantha *is a crunchy mouthful. The dough for this* parantha *should be made with your hands; the delicate crunch of the onions will be lost if the dough is made in a food processor.*

2 cups stone-ground durum whole-wheat flour
3 tablespoons vegetable oil, melted ghee, or butter
1 cup finely chopped red onion
1/4 cup finely chopped fresh cilantro
1 to 3 fresh green chile peppers, such as serrano, minced with seeds
1 teaspoon coarsely ground fennel seeds
1/2 teaspoon kalonji seeds
1/2 teaspoon ground fenugreek seeds
1/2 teaspoon salt, or to taste
2/3 cup nonfat plain yogurt, whisked until smooth

1. Place the flour and oil (or ghee or butter) in a bowl and rub with clean fingers to mix. Then add all the remaining ingredients, except the yogurt, and again, mix well with your fingers. Add the yogurt and mix again with your fingers in round circular motions until it starts to gather into a dough. (Add 1 or 2 tablespoons more flour if the dough seems sticky, or some more yogurt if it seems too firm.)

2. Knead about a minute, pressing your knuckles lightly into the dough, spreading the dough outward, then gathering the ends together toward the center with your fingers. Repeat pressing and gathering a few times until you have a soft and pliable dough that does not stick to your fingers. (If, while kneading, the dough sticks to your hands, put a little oil or water on them.)

3. Cover with plastic wrap or the lid of the bowl and set aside at least 1 and up to 4 hours. (This allows the wheat gluten to develop.) If keeping for a longer period, refrigerate the dough.

4. To roll and cook the paranthas, proceed as per directions for Basic Griddle-Fried Breads (page 581), from Step 3.

Breads and Crepes   585

Griddle-Fried Mughlai Breads with Almonds and Poppy Seeds

Khastae Mughlai Paranthae

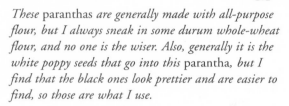

Makes 10 to 12 breads

These paranthas *are generally made with all-purpose flour, but I always sneak in some durum whole-wheat flour, and no one is the wiser. Also, generally it is the white poppy seeds that go into this* parantha, *but I find that the black ones look prettier and are easier to find, so those are what I use.*

25 to 30 raw almonds, shelled

1¹/₂ cups all-purpose flour

¹/₂ cup stone-ground durum whole-wheat flour

1 to 3 fresh green chile peppers, such as serrano, stemmed

3 tablespoons black poppy seeds

2 teaspoons ground dried fenugreek leaves

1 teaspoon coarsely ground black pepper, or to taste

¹/₂ teaspoon salt, or to taste

2 to 3 tablespoons vegetable oil

About ³/₄ cup water

1. Soak the almonds in water to cover overnight. Then, with clean hands, peel the softened brown skin off the almonds. In a food processor, add all the ingredients except the water and process until everything is smooth. Then, with the motor running, add the water in a slow, steady stream until the dough gathers into a smooth ball and cleans the sides of the work bowl. (Add more flour if the dough seems sticky and more water if it seems too dry.)

2. Lightly oil your hands and transfer the dough to a bowl. Cover with plastic wrap or the lid of the bowl and let it rest for 1 to 4 hours. (This allows the gluten to develop.) If keeping for a longer period, refrigerate the dough.

3. To roll and cook the paranthas, proceed as per the directions for Basic Griddle-Fried Breads (page 581), from Step 3.

Stuffed Griddle-Fried Flatbreads

Basic Stuffed Griddle-Fried Breads

Bharae Huae Paranthae

Makes 10 to 12 breads

Although these are fried in the same way as basic paranthas, *their filling technique is a new addition.*

1 recipe stuffing of your choice (pages 587 to 588)

1 pound (1 recipe) Basic Whole-Wheat Dough (page 576)

1 cup whole-wheat flour in a medium bowl or pie dish, for coating and dusting

¹/₄ cup vegetable oil, or melted butter or ghee, for basting

1. Prepare the stuffing. Prepare the dough. Heat the tava or griddle over medium-high heat until a sprinkling of flour immediately turns dark brown. Wipe off the flour and proceed. While the tava is heating, with lightly oiled clean hands, divide the dough equally into 10 to 12 balls and cover with foil to prevent drying. Divide it into 10 to 12 portions, about 3 to 4 tablespoons each.

2. Working with each ball of dough separately, transfer to the bowl with the dry flour, press lightly to form a disc, coat generously with dry flour, and roll into a 4- to 5-inch circle. Place the stuffing in the center. Bring the edges together, pinch to seal, then shape into a ball once again.

3. Flatten and coat this stuffed ball with flour and roll it into a 7- to 8-inch circle of even thickness. As you roll, keep turning and dusting the dough with flour or it may stick to the rolling surface. If the stuffing has excess moisture, the paranthas may develop tiny (or large) holes as they stretch while rolling. If that happens, seal the holes by putting a little dry flour over them (or by pinching them together).

4. Place the rolled parantha on the hot tava. Turn it over when it is slightly cooked and dotted with tiny golden spots on the bottom, about 1 minute. When the other side is covered with larger brown dots, turn it over and brush lightly with oil. Flip it over again and fry the oiled side about 30 seconds. Similarly, baste and fry the other side another 30 seconds. There should be a total of 4 turns. Remove from the griddle and serve.

Stuffings for Parantha Breads

Paranthas can essentially be stuffed with any and every moisture-free, dry-cooked potato, lentil, *paneer* cheese, or meat dish. Any moisture will make it harder to stuff and roll the *paranthas*. As you roll them, the dough shell will absorb the moisture and split in various places, so be sure your filling is dry.

In spite of this, some juicy vegetables, such as cauliflower and daikon radishes, are very popular as stuffings. When using them, keep in mind that salt draws out natural juices, so add salt to individual *paranthas* as you roll them, or first salt the grated vegetable before cooking, allowing the vegetable to sweat. Then squeeze out the juices, and if they are still moist, mix in some dry flour.

Here, then, are some popular *parantha* stuffings. These stuffings can also be used in all types of stuffed breads mentioned in this chapter (such as deep-fried *poories*, baked *kulchas*, and grilled *naans*), and also in Indian snacks such as *samosas* (stuffed triangular pastries).

When you've prepared each of these fillings, proceed with the directions for Basic Stuffed Griddle-Fried Breads (page 586).

Potato Parantha Stuffing

Aalu kae Paranthae

Makes enough for 10 to 12 breads

3 large russet (or any) potatoes (about 1¹/₄ pounds)
1 to 2 tablespoons peeled minced fresh ginger
¹/₄ cup finely chopped fresh cilantro,
    including soft stems

4 to 5 scallions, white parts only, minced (optional)
1 to 2 fresh green chile peppers, such as serrano,
    minced with seeds
2 tablespoons ground coriander
2 teaspoons ground dried pomegranate seeds
1 teaspoon ground dried fenugreek leaves
¹/₂ teaspoon ground cumin
¹/₂ teaspoon garam masala
³/₄ teaspoon salt, or to taste

Boil the potatoes in lightly salted water to cover until tender, about 20 minutes. Then peel and grate or mash them in a medium bowl. Mix all the ingredients together. Use in Basic Stuffed Griddle-Fried Breads (page 586).

Cauliflower Parantha Stuffing

Gobhi kae Paranthae

Makes enough for 10 to 12 breads

5 quarter-size slices peeled fresh ginger
1 to 3 fresh green chile peppers, such as serrano,
    stemmed
¹/₂ cup coarsely chopped fresh cilantro,
    including soft stems
1 small cauliflower (about ³/₄ pound),
    cut into florets
1 tablespoon ground coriander
2 teaspoons ground pomegranate seeds
¹/₂ teaspoon ground cumin
¹/₂ teaspoon coarsely ground ajwain seeds
¹/₂ teaspoon salt, or to taste

In a food processor, process together the ginger, green chile peppers, cilantro, and cauliflower until minced. Transfer to a bowl and mix in the spices, but not the salt. Add the salt only to the individual paranthas as you roll them. (Mixing the salt will cause the cauliflower to release its juices and make it harder to use.) Use in Basic Stuffed Griddle-Fried Breads (page 586).

Daikon Radish Parantha Stuffing

Mooli kae Paranthae

Makes enough 10 to 12 breads

- 1¹/₂ pounds white daikon radishes
- 1 teaspoon salt, or to taste
- 1 to 3 fresh green chile peppers, such as serrano, minced with seeds
- 1 tablespoon peeled minced fresh ginger
- ¹/₄ cup finely chopped fresh cilantro, including soft stems
- ¹/₂ teaspoon coarsely ground ajwain seeds

In a food processor, grate or mince the radishes. Transfer to a bowl, mix in the salt and leave the radishes to sweat, about 30 minutes. Then squeeze out as much water as you can. (This removes much of the strong and bitter juice from the daikons, making them much sweeter. If you wish, use these juices to make the dough for paranthas.) Add the remaining ingredients and mix well. Use in Basic Stuffed Griddle-Fried Breads (page 586).

Paneer Cheese Parantha Stuffing

Paneer kae Paranthae

Makes enough for 10 to 12 breads

- 8 ounces (1 recipe) Paneer Cheese (page 43 or store-bought), crumbled
- ¹/₄ cup grated Monterey Jack or mild cheddar cheese
- 3 quarter-size slices peeled fresh ginger
- 1 large clove fresh garlic, peeled
- 1 to 2 fresh green chile peppers, such as serrano, stemmed
- ¹/₂ cup finely chopped fresh cilantro, with soft stems
- 1 tablespoon ground coriander
- ¹/₂ teaspoon garam masala
- ¹/₄ teaspoon salt, or to taste

Prepare the paneer, then crumble and place in a food processor along with the cheese, ginger, garlic, green chile peppers, and cilantro and process until minced. Add the coriander, garam masala, and salt and pulse a few times to mix. Use in Basic Stuffed Griddle-Fried Breads (page 586).

Ground Lamb Parantha Stuffing

Keemae kae Paranthae

Makes enough for 10 to 12 breads

- 1 pound ground lamb, chicken, or turkey
- 1 small onion, coarsely chopped
- 4 quarter-size slices peeled fresh ginger
- 1 large clove fresh garlic, peeled
- 1 fresh green chile pepper, such as serrano, stemmed
- A few fresh mint leaves
- 1 teaspoon garam masala
- ¹/₂ teaspoon salt, or to taste

Cook the lamb (or poultry) over medium heat until golden, 5 to 7 minutes. Let cool and transfer to a food processor. Add the remaining ingredients and process until minced. If the stuffing seems too moist from the onion, mix in up to 2 tablespoons chickpea or whole-wheat flour. Use in Basic Stuffed Griddle-Fried Breads (page 586).

Variation: Any leftover grilled meat or chicken can be minced in a food processor and used as stuffing.

Sweet Jaggery-Stuffed Paranthas

Gur Bharae Paranthae

Makes 4 breads

These paranthas *are rich, delicious, and comforting. Serve them for a leisurely breakfast or brunch with a cup of hot tea or coffee, to allow for proper digestion.*

As the paranthas *cook, the jaggery and the butter encased inside melt into a thick syrup and occasionally, if the seal is not firm enough, a bit of the syrup may escape and caramelize on the* parantha. *Be careful when you eat them—the syrup inside is very hot. Use* a knife to break open the *parantha, then cool it to the temperature you can tolerate. Take a bite-size piece of the* parantha *and dip it into the oozing syrup.*

*You can substitute an equal amount of Indian brown sugar (*shakkar*) or regular brown sugar in place of the grated jaggery (found in Indian markets). The* parantha *made with* shakkar *will be similar to the jaggery stuffed one, but the brown sugar one will be a lot more syrupy.*

1 pound (1 recipe) Basic Whole-Wheat Dough (page 576)
1 cup grated jaggery (gur)
2 tablespoons unsalted butter, at room temperature
1 cup stone-ground durum whole-wheat flour in a medium bowl or a pie dish, for dusting
2 tablespoons melted ghee

1. With lightly oiled clean hands, divide the dough equally into 8 portions, 4 of them slightly larger than the others. Cover with foil to prevent drying. On a clean work surface, working with 1 large and 1 small portion at a time, roll the larger portion with a rolling pin into a 6- to 7-inch circle, and the smaller one into a 4- to 5-inch circle.

2. Place about ¼ cup jaggery in the center of the larger circle and dot with about 1 teaspoon butter. Then, place the smaller circle on top and press lightly on the edges to seal in the filling. About a ¾-inch rim of the larger circle will remain exposed all around. Fold this exposed portion over the smaller circle, pressing firmly to seal as you go around, until the edges of the smaller circle are completely covered. You now have one thick parantha.

3. Dust lightly with dry flour, then with a rolling pin, roll lightly to make a ¼-inch-thick, 7- to 8-inch circle.

4. Heat the tava or griddle over medium-high heat until a sprinkling of the flour immediately turns dark brown. Wipe off the flour and proceed. Place the rolled parantha on the hot tava, larger side down. Turn over when the bottom is slightly cooked and dotted with tiny golden spots, about 1 minute. When the other side is covered with larger brown dots, turn it over and brush lightly with the ghee. Flip it over again and fry the oiled side about 30 seconds. Similarly baste and fry the other side another 30 seconds. There should be a total of 4 turns. Remove from the griddle, place about ½ teaspoon butter on top, and serve.

Puffed Deep-Fried Breads (Pooriyan)

Poori (or *poodhi*) breads—crisp, balloon-like breads—are one of the many pleasures of Indian culinary life. They are deep-fried, puffed whole-wheat unleavened breads, light and crispy, and best consumed as soon as they come out of the *kadhai* (Indian wok). They lose their puffed appeal when they are fried ahead of time and stacked one on top of the other, but they do keep well and are customarily packed for picnics and long journeys.

Homemade *poories* are delicate, genteel things, not more than 3 to 6 inches across—quite unlike what you get from street vendors, which are usually twice that size.

Essentially, *poories* can be served with all meals, but they are really popular as breakfast and brunch staples along with certain classic accompaniments: potatoes, chickpeas, mint chutney, mango pickles, fresh mangoes, *lussi* (a chilled yogurt drink), and chai teas.

Basic Deep-Fried Puffed Breads

Saadi Pooriyan

Makes 14 to 16 breads

This is my most basic recipe for everyday poori *breads. Most people make their* poories *with just whole-wheat flour, but I prefer to mix in some all-purpose flour, for lighter and crispier* poories.

Just like pasta, poories *can be flavored, and they then change colors. They can be green with the addition of mustard, spinach, or fenugreek greens, deep red with cooked and puréed beets, and orange-red with carrots and red or orange bell peppers; there are many choices. Mix in your favorite herbs and spices (and they don't have to be Indian—rosemary is wonderful) and you can have fun with them.*

1 cup stone-ground durum whole-wheat flour
1/2 cup all-purpose flour
3 tablespoons vegetable oil
1/3 to 1/2 cup water

To make dough in a food processor:

1. Place both the flours in the work bowl of a food processor and process about 30 seconds to mix. With the motor running, add the oil and then the water in a thin stream, and process until the dough gathers into a ball.

2. Continue to process until the sides of the bowl look clean, 20 to 30 seconds. (Add 1 to 2 tablespoons more flour if the dough sticks to the sides of the work bowl, or some water if the dough seems hard.) Stop the machine, transfer the dough to a bowl, cover with plastic wrap or the lid of the bowl, and let rest at least 1 and up to 4 hours. (This allows the wheat gluten to develop.) If keeping for a longer period, refrigerate the dough.

To make dough by hand:

1. Place both the flours in a large bowl, mix together, add ¾ of the water and mix again with your clean fingers in round circular motions until it starts to gather into a dough. (Add 1 or 2 tablespoons more flour if the dough seems sticky, or some more water if it seems too firm.)

2. Knead about a minute, pressing your knuckles lightly into the dough, spreading the dough outward, then gathering the ends together toward the center with your fingers. Push down the center and repeat pressing and gathering a few times until you have a soft and pliable dough that does not stick to your fingers. (If, while kneading, the dough sticks to your hands, put a little oil or water on them.)

3. Cover with plastic wrap or the lid of the bowl and set aside at least 1 and up to 4 hours. (This allows the wheat gluten to develop.) If keeping for a longer period, refrigerate the dough.

To shape and fry the poories:

2 to 3 cups peanut oil for deep-frying
1 recipe Basic Deep-Fried Puffed Breads (left),
    or any other poori bread dough
1 cup stone-ground durum whole-wheat flour
    or all-purpose flour in a medium bowl
    or a pie dish, for dusting
Rolling pin

1. Heat the frying oil in a wok or skillet over high heat until it reaches 350°F to 375°F on a frying thermometer, or until a little piece of the dough dropped into the hot oil bubbles and rises to the top immediately.

2. While the oil is heating, lightly oil your clean hands and divide the dough equally into 14 to 16 balls. Cover with foil to prevent drying, and set aside.

3. Working with each ball of dough separately, place in the bowl with the dry flour, flatten it with your fingertips and coat well with the dry flour. Transfer to a cutting board or any other clean flat surface and, with a rolling pin, roll into a thin 4- to 5-inch circle. (If the dough sticks to the rolling surface, dust with more flour.)

4. Carefully place the rolled poori into the hot oil. Almost instantly the poori will rise to the top and start to puff up. With the back of a large slotted spatula, quickly press lightly on the puffed top surface, submerge the poori back into the oil, then release. This will guide the air toward the flatter portions and cause the poori to balloon into a complete round in about 10 to 15 seconds.

5. Turn the poori over once to cook the other side until golden. (Perfectly fried poories should be crisp and golden, not brown.) With a slotted spatula, remove to paper towels to drain and serve immediately.

Flavored Deep-Fried Puffed Breads

Flavor variation in deep-fried puffed breads, or *poories,* comes mainly from additions to the dough (and occasionally from different frying mediums—*ghee,* mustard oil, coconut oil, or sesame oil). The frying technique, however, remains the same. Here is a selection of some of my favorite flavored *poori* bread doughs. Make the dough in a food processor or by hand, then fry the *poories* according to the directions for Basic Deep-Fried Puffed Breads (page 589).

Deep-Fried Puffed Breads with Ajwain Seeds

Ajwaini Pooriyan

Makes 14 to 16 breads

1 cup stone-ground durum whole-wheat flour
1/2 cup all-purpose flour
1/2 teaspoon coarsely ground ajwain seeds
1 teaspoon dried mint leaves
1/2 teaspoon salt, or to taste
3 tablespoons vegetable oil
1/3 to 1/2 cup water

Prepare the dough in a food processor or by hand (as described on page 590), mixing together all the dry ingredients, then adding the oil to blend, followed by the water, until a dough is formed. Shape and fry the poories (as described on page 590).

Deep-Fried Puffed Breads with Mint (or Fenugreek)

Pudina (ya Methi) ki Pooriyan

Makes 14 to 16 breads

1 cup stone-ground durum whole-wheat flour
1/2 cup all-purpose flour
1/4 teaspoon coarsely ground ajwain seeds
1/4 teaspoon salt, or to taste

10 to 12 fresh mint leaves, or 1 tablespoon dried fenugreek leaves
3 tablespoons vegetable oil
1/3 to 1/2 cup water
1 to 2 tablespoons dried mint leaves

1. Prepare the dough in a food processor or by hand (as described on page 590), mixing together all the dry ingredients and the fresh mint leaves (or fenugreek leaves), then adding the oil to blend, followed by the water, until a dough is formed.

2. Heat the frying oil and shape each poori (Steps 1 to 3, page 590). For each poori, dust one of the sides with the dried mint leaves and press lightly with the rolling pin to make sure that they adhere, then fry the poories (Steps 4 and 5).

Deep-Fried Puffed Breads with Fresh Spinach

Palak ki Pooriyan

Makes 14 to 16 breads

1 small bunch fresh spinach (8 to 10 ounces), trimmed, washed, and coarsely chopped
1 large clove fresh garlic, peeled
1 to 3 fresh green chile peppers, such as serrano, stemmed
1 cup stone-ground durum whole-wheat flour
1/2 cup all-purpose flour
1 teaspoon dried fenugreek leaves
1/2 teaspoon freshly ground black pepper
1/4 teaspoon salt, or to taste
3 tablespoons peanut oil
1/3 to 1/2 cup water

In a food processor, process together the spinach, garlic, and green chile peppers until minced, then add all the dry ingredients and process about 30 seconds to mix. Then add the oil to blend, followed by the water, and process until a dough is formed. Shape and fry the poories (as described on page 590).

Deep-Fried Stuffed Puffed Breads

Bhari Hui Pooriyan

Makes 14 to 16 breads

Like paranthas, poori *breads can also be stuffed and fried. Although all the* parantha *stuffings can be used for* poories, poories *are much smaller and require only about a teaspoon of the filling each. In addition, many dry-cooked dishes, such as paneer cheese, vegetables or a* dal *(legume) dish, or any of the grilled meats, can also be used as fillings. Process them first in the food processor until smooth. If they seem watery, mix in some chickpea or whole-wheat flours to soak up the juices. Here is one such* poori.

- 1/2 cup any skinless dried beans, such as green split pea (muttar dal), yellow split chickpea (channa dal), yellow mung (dhulli mung dal), or white urad (dhulli urad dal), sorted and washed in 3 to 4 changes of water
- 1 recipe dough for Deep-Fried Puffed Breads with Ajwain Seeds (page 591)
- 1 fresh green chile pepper, such as serrano, stemmed
- 1 clove fresh garlic, peeled
- 3 quarter-size slices peeled fresh ginger
- 1/4 cup coarsely chopped fresh cilantro, including soft stems
- 1 teaspoon garam masala
- 1/4 teaspoon salt, or to taste
- 1 cup stone-ground durum whole-wheat flour in a medium bowl or a pie dish, for coating and dusting

1. Soak the dal in water to cover, about 2 hours, then drain. Meanwhile, prepare the dough and set aside at least 30 minutes. In a small food processor or a grinder, process together all the remaining ingredients (except the flour for dusting) to make a paste that is as smooth as possible.

2. Heat the frying oil (Step 1, page 590). With lightly oiled clean hands, divide the dough equally into 14 to 16 balls and cover with foil to prevent drying.

3. Working with each ball of dough separately, transfer to the bowl with the dry flour, press lightly to form a disc, coat well with dry flour and then roll it into a thin 2- to 3-inch circle. Place about 1 teaspoon filling in the center, then bring the edges together and pinch to seal. Shape into a ball and roll into a thin 4 to 5-inch circle once again. (If the dough sticks to the rolling surface, dust with more flour.)

4. Fry the poories (Steps 4 and 5, page 590).

Deep-Fried Sweet Saffron Puffed Breads

Khameeri Kesar Pooriyan

Makes 14 to 16 breads

Khameer *is the Indian word for a fermenting agent such as yeast. This leavened, sweet* poori *bread is a specialty of Kashmir, where it is served with dry-cooked vegetables and meat dishes. The Kashmiris fry* poories *in* ghee, *but I use peanut oil for less saturated fat.*

- 1/2 cup warm milk (any kind), about 110°F
- 1 teaspoon active dry yeast
- 2 tablespoons sugar
- 3/4 cup stone-ground durum whole-wheat flour
- 3/4 cup all-purpose flour
- 1 tablespoon fennel seeds, finely ground
- 1/2 teaspoon salt, or to taste
- 2 tablespoons vegetable oil or melted ghee
- 2 tablespoons nonfat plain yogurt, whisked until smooth
- 1/4 teaspoon saffron threads
- 1 teaspoon white poppy seeds
- 1 cup all-purpose flour in a medium bowl or a pie dish, for coating and dusting

1. In a small bowl, mix together the milk, yeast, and 1 teaspoon sugar and set aside about 5 minutes, or until frothy. Place both the flours, the fennel seeds, the remaining sugar, and the salt in a food processor and process until mixed, about 30 seconds.

2. With the motor running, add first the oil (or ghee) and then the yeast-milk mixture through the feeder tube until the flours gather into a ball and the sides of the work bowl look clean. (If the dough seems too sticky, add some more flour through the feeder tube.) Transfer to a large bowl, cover with plastic wrap or the lid of the bowl, and place in a warm draft-free spot until it doubles in volume, at least 4 and up to 8 hours. (This allows the yeast to ferment and multiply, causing the dough to rise.) If keeping for a longer period, refrigerate the dough.

3. Heat the frying oil (Step 1, page 590). In a small bowl, mix together the yogurt, saffron, and poppy seeds. Then, with lightly oiled clean hands, divide the dough equally into 14 to 16 round balls and cover with foil to prevent drying. Working with each ball of dough separately, place in the bowl with the dry flour, flatten it with your fingertips and coat well with the dry flour from the bowl. Transfer to a cutting board or any other clean flat surface and, with a rolling pin, roll into a thin 4- to 5-inch circle. (If the dough sticks to the rolling surface, dust with more flour.)

4. Then, with a basting brush, lightly coat the top of the rolled poori with the yogurt mixture and fry the poories (Steps 4 and 5).

Deep-Fried Bengali-Style Flour Breads

Lucchiyan

Makes 8 to 10 breads

There are 2 types of deep-fried lucchi *breads. The first type (popular in the northern states of Kashmir and Punjab) are 8- to 9- inches in diameter, paper-thin* poories *made with all-purpose flour. These are almost white and are quite chewy, because the bread is taken out of the oil quickly and not allowed to brown or become crispy in the hot oil. Because of their size and thinness, these breads are usually bought from special eateries. They are not usually made at home.*

The second type of lucchi *breads (a specialty of Bengal), are 4- to 5- inches in diameter and puff up just like* poories, *except they are made with all-purpose flour (instead of whole-wheat) and are usually served at all mealtimes, instead of* chapati *or other flatbreads.*

1 cup all-purpose flour
A pinch of salt
2 to 3 tablespoons peanut oil or melted ghee
About ¹/₂ cup water

1. Place the flour, salt, and oil (or ghee) in the work bowl of a food processor and process about 30 seconds to mix. With the motor running, add the water in a thin stream, and process until it gathers into a ball. Continue to process until the sides of the bowl look clean, 20 to 30 seconds. (Add 1 or 2 tablespoons more flour if the dough sticks to the sides of the work bowl, and some water if the dough seems hard.)

2. Transfer the dough to a large bowl, cover with plastic wrap or the lid of the bowl, and let rest for at least 1 and up to 4 hours. (This allows the wheat gluten to develop.) If keeping for a longer period, refrigerate the dough.

3. Shape and fry the poories (as described on page 590).

Deep-Fried Leavened Flour Breads

Bhaturaae

Makes 14 to 16 breads

A specialty of north India, bhaturas *are another popular type of* poori *bread. Like the* lucchi *breads, they are made with all-purpose flour (plus some semolina) and are deep-fried. But* bhaturas *are leavened and are therefore much thicker, spongier, and have a little more texture.*

1³/₄ cups all-purpose flour
¹/₂ cup fine-grain semolina
1 teaspoon sugar
¹/₂ teaspoon salt, or to taste
2 teaspoons active dry yeast
³/₄ to 1 cup nonfat plain yogurt, whisked until smooth
1¹/₂ to 2 cups peanut oil for deep-frying
1 cup all-purpose flour in a medium bowl or a pie dish for coating and dusting

1. Place the flour, semolina, sugar, salt, and yeast in a food processor and process until mixed, about 30 seconds.

2. With the motor running, add yogurt through the feeder tube until the dough gathers into a ball and the sides of the work bowl look clean, 20 to 30 seconds. (If the dough seems too sticky, add some more flour through the feeder tube.) Transfer to a large bowl, cover with plastic wrap or the lid of the bowl, and place in a warm draft-free spot until it doubles in volume, at least 4 and up to 8 hours. (This allows the yeast to ferment and multiply, causing the dough to rise.) If keeping for a longer period, refrigerate the dough.

3. With lightly oiled clean hands, divide the dough equally into 14 to 16 round balls and cover with foil to prevent drying. Working with each ball of dough separately, place in the bowl with the dry flour, flatten it with your fingertips, and coat well with the dry flour. Then, transfer to a cutting board or any other clean flat surface and, with a rolling pin, roll into 6 to 7-inch circle. (If the dough sticks to the rolling surface, dust with more flour.)

4. Heat the oil in a wok or skillet over high heat until it reaches 350°F to 375°F on a frying thermometer, or until a piece of dough dropped into the hot oil bubbles and rises to the top immediately. Carefully place the rolled bhatura into the hot oil. Almost instantly it will rise to the top and start to puff up. With the back of a large slotted spatula, quickly press lightly on the puffed top surface and submerge it back into the oil, then release. This will guide the air towards the flatter portions, and cause it to balloon into a complete round, 10 to 15 seconds.

5. Turn the bhatura over once to cook the other side until golden. Bhaturas should be lightly golden on both sides, not brown. Remove with a slotted spoon, transfer to paper towels to drain, and serve immediately.

Variation: Like *paranthas* and *poories*, bhaturas can be stuffed. Refer to Stuffings for Parantha Breads (page 587 to page 588) for examples.

Oven-Grilled Naan and Other Breads

Naan breads are the crispy triangular breads so popular in Indian restaurants. Traditionally, they are made with all-purpose flour and are grilled by slapping them against the walls of a super-hot *tandoor*. Once inside the *tandoor,* they absorb some of the intoxicating smoky aroma from the burning coals, cook quickly and simultaneously from the back to the front, and, because they cook so fast, moisture gets locked inside. All this results in extraordinarily moist and flavorful breads that are as good as they sound—crispy on the outside and moist inside, and almost impossible to reproduce without a *tandoor.*

However, making similar breads under the broiler of a conventional oven is the next best thing. For this you can use a baking or broiling tray, or a pizza stone. The stone, of course, is the better alternative, because once heated, it retains its heat and the breads can cook simultaneously from the top and bottom.

Basic Oven-Grilled Leavened Breads
Tandoori Naan

Makes 10 to 12 breads

This basic recipe is made with refined all-purpose flour and is cooked under the broiler. These naans *have yogurt in the dough, for a vegan alternative, use water in its place.*

2 teaspoons active dry yeast
1 teaspoon sugar
1/4 cup warm water (about 110°F)
1/2 cup nonfat plain yogurt, whisked until smooth
2 tablespoons vegetable oil
2 cups all-purpose flour, or bread flour
1/4 teaspoon salt, or to taste
1 cup all-purpose flour in a medium bowl
    or a pie dish, for coating and dusting
1/4 cup melted butter or ghee, for basting (optional)

1. For the dough, dissolve the yeast and sugar in warm water and set aside until frothy, about 5 minutes. Mix in the yogurt and oil.

2. Place the flour and salt in the food processor and process until mixed. With the motor running, pour the yeast mixture into the work bowl in a thin stream and process until the flour gathers into a ball and the sides of the processor are clean. (If the dough seems too sticky, add some more flour through the feeder tube, or add some more yogurt if the dough is dry and hard.) Transfer to a large bowl, cover with plastic wrap or the lid of the bowl, and place in a warm draft-free spot until it doubles in volume, 3 to 4 hours. (This allows the yeast to ferment and multiply, causing the dough to rise.) If keeping for a longer period, refrigerate the dough.

3. To roll and grill the naan breads, with clean, lightly oiled hands, divide the dough equally into 10 to 12 balls and cover with foil to prevent drying. Working with each ball of dough separately, place in the bowl with the dry flour, flatten it with your fingertips and coat well with the dry flour. Then transfer to a cutting board or any other clean flat surface and, with a rolling pin, roll into a 7- to 8-inch triangle. (If the dough sticks to the rolling surface, dust with more flour.)

4. Place on large baking trays or, if you have a separate broiler, place on the broiler trays—3 to 4 per tray. With a basting brush or your fingers, lightly baste the top of each naan with water. (This prevents them from drying out.)

5. Preheat the oven to broil or preheat the broiler, and place the trays, one at a time, 4 to 5 inches below the heating element and broil until small brown spots appear on the top surface, about 1 minute. With a spatula, carefully, turn each naan over and cook until the other side is golden, about 30 seconds. Transfer the naan breads to a platter, baste lightly with butter, if you wish, and serve hot.

Oven-Grilled Breads with Different Flavors

The basic recipe for all *naan* breads essentially stays the same. Variations come from the addition of herbs, spices, and other aromatics. These can be added to the dough before rolling, or they can be pressed onto the surface of the dough after rolling.

The following recipes are some popular flavors to try with the recipe for Basic Oven-Grilled Leavened Breads (page 594):

Oven-Grilled Garlic and Turmeric Breads
Lussan Haldi kae Naan

Makes 10 to 12 breads

Instead of basting the dough with the flavoring, simply put the peeled fresh garlic and turmeric into the work bowl in Step 2 and process along with the rest of the dough ingredients. Then baste the rolled-out naan *with the butter or* ghee.

Basic Oven-Grilled Leavened Breads (page 594)
3 large cloves fresh garlic, peeled
1 teaspoon melted butter or ghee
¼ teaspoon turmeric

1. Prepare the bread dough through Step 4 of Basic Oven-Grilled Leavened Breads. Then, in a small food processor, process together the garlic, butter (or ghee), and turmeric to make a smooth paste.

2. Continue with Step 5 of Basic Oven-Grilled Leavened Breads (left), basting each rolled-out naan with this paste.

Spicy Oven-Grilled Breads with Kalonji or Sesame Seeds

Kalonji ya Til kae Naan

Makes 10 to 12 breads

Here, the flavorings are best integrated into the dough, rather than spread on top. For less heat, remove the chile pepper seeds before mincing.

Basic Oven-Grilled Leavened Breads (page 594)
1 small onion, coarsely chopped
1 to 2 fresh green chile peppers, such as serrano, stemmed
1 tablespoon kalonji or sesame seeds

1. Prepare the bread dough through Step 3 of Basic Oven-Grilled Leavened Breads. Then, in a food processor, process together the onion and green chile pepper until minced, then add to the ingredients to make the dough.

2. Continue with Step 4 of Basic Oven-Grilled Leavened Breads (page 595), after the naans are rolled out and set on trays, sprinkle each one with about ¼ teaspoon kalonji or sesame seeds and press them into the dough to make sure they adhere to the naan. Broil the breads, as described in Step 5.

Oven-Grilled Breads with Dried Herbs and Spices

Sookhae Masalae kae Naan

Makes 10 to 12 breads

These naans are flavored with a simple basting when they are fresh from the oven. Vary the flavorings, if you wish, with your favorite herbs and spices.

Basic Oven-Grilled Leavened Breads (page 594)
1 teaspoon ground dried fenugreek
1 teaspoon ground dried mint
1 teaspoon ground dried curry leaves
¼ teaspoon coarsely ground ajwain seeds
¼ teaspoon cayenne pepper or paprika
1 tablespoon melted ghee or butter

1. Prepare the bread dough through Step 4 of Basic Oven-Grilled Leavened Breads. Before you put the breads in the oven, mix together all the ingredients except the ghee in a small bowl.

2. Broil the breads as described in Step 5 (page 595). Then, as soon as the breads come out of the oven, baste them generously with melted ghee or butter and sprinkle some of the seasoning mixture on them before serving.

Stuffed Pepper Jack Cheese Oven-Grilled Breads

Cheese vaalae Naan

Makes 10 to 12 breads

These naans are really unusual. They come stuffed with spicy Jack cheese—unheard of in India, but delicious all the same. This fun offering from my American kitchen is delicious with grilled foods, can be served with soup and salad, and also with meals that are not necessarily Indian.

Basic Oven-Grilled Leavened Breads (page 594)
1 cup grated Pepper Jack cheese, or more as needed

Prepare the bread dough through Step 3 of Basic Oven-Grilled Leavened Breads, rolling them out with a rolling pin into 4- to 5-inch rounds and place about 1½ tablespoons of grated Pepper Jack cheese in the center. Pick up the edges of the dough, bring them together, and pinch to seal. Then roll out once again and broil the breads as described in Step 5 (page 595).

Oven-Grilled Tofu Breads

Tofu aur Jaee kae Naan

Makes 10 to 12 breads

"Now I've seen everything," said my teenage nephew, Tini, when he saw me alter the naan dough with soy flour and oat bran. "I'm not telling my mom; she'll sneak some into breads and ruin everything." Despite his protests against my healthful additions, in the end, he loved the naans!

2 teaspoons active dry yeast

1 teaspoon sugar

$^1/_4$ cup warm water (about 110°F)

$^1/_4$ cup nonfat plain yogurt, whisked until smooth

$^1/_4$ cup warm lowfat milk (about 130°F)

2 cups all-purpose flour

$^1/_2$ cup soy flour

$^1/_2$ cup oat bran

$^1/_2$ cup soft tofu, crumbled

2 tablespoons vegetable oil + 1 tablespoon
    if making dough by hand

$^1/_4$ teaspoon salt, or to taste

Chaat Masala (page 20 or store-bought), to taste

Melted butter, for basting

1. For the dough, dissolve the yeast and sugar in warm water in a small bowl and set aside until frothy, about 5 minutes. In a medium bowl, mix together the yogurt and milk. (The milk may curdle, but don't be concerned.)

2. In a food processor, process together the flours, oat bran, tofu, 2 tablespoons oil, and salt until mixed. Then, with the motor running, pour through the feeder tube, first the yeast mixture, then the yogurt-milk mixture, and process until the flour gathers into a ball and the sides of the processor are clean. (If the dough seems too sticky, add some more flour through the feeder tube, or add some more yogurt if the dough is dry and hard.)

3. Transfer to a large bowl, cover with plastic wrap or the lid of the bowl, and place in a warm draft-free spot until it doubles in volume, 3 to 4 hours. (This allows the yeast to ferment and multiply, causing the dough to rise.) If keeping for a longer period, refrigerate the dough. Meanwhile, prepare the chaat masala.

4. To roll and grill the naan breads, follow directions for Basic Oven-Grilled Leavened Breads (page 595), from Step 3. Remove the naan breads to a platter, baste lightly with the butter, sprinkle a generous pinch of chaat masala on top, and serve.

Baked Semolina Breads

Kulchae

Makes 10 to 12 breads

Kulchas *are baked pure white, leavened flour and semolina breads. They are more like flat, round slices of bread; nothing like any other Indian bread. They are generally served with chickpea curries and mango or other pickles and green puréed herb chutneys, in most roadside intersections of northern India.*

The kulcha *can be eaten as is, or they can be lightly basted with ghee or oil and reheated on a hot tava or griddle. (Heat them until lightly golden on both sides.) I love to make grilled cheese and vegetable sandwiches (think: warm foccacia sandwiches) using kulchas instead of sliced bread, and have, on occasion, used them as pizza crusts.*

2 teaspoons active dry yeast

1 teaspoon sugar

$^1/_4$ cup warm water (about 110°F)

$^3/_4$ cup nonfat plain yogurt, whisked until smooth

1 cup fine-grain semolina

1 cup all-purpose flour

2 tablespoons unsalted butter, at room temperature

$^1/_4$ teaspoon salt, or to taste

1 cup all-purpose flour in a medium bowl
    or a pie dish, for coating and dusting

1. For the dough, dissolve the yeast and sugar in warm water in a small bowl and set aside until frothy, about 5 minutes. Mix in the yogurt.

2. Place the semolina, flour, butter, and salt in a food processor and process until mixed. With the motor running, pour the yeast mixture into the work bowl in a thin stream and process until the flour gathers into a ball and the sides of the processor are clean. (If the dough seems too sticky, add some more flour through the feeder tube, or add some more yogurt if the dough is dry and hard).

3. Transfer to a large bowl, cover with plastic wrap or the lid of the bowl, and place in a warm draft-free spot until it doubles in volume, 3 to 4 hours. (This allows the yeast to ferment and multiply, causing the

dough to rise.) If keeping for a longer period, refrigerate the dough.

4. Lightly grease 2 or 3 large baking trays. Preheat the oven to the lowest setting, about 10 minutes, then turn it off. Then, with lightly oiled clean hands, divide the dough equally into 10 to 12 balls and cover with foil to prevent drying. Working with each ball of dough separately, place in the bowl with the dry flour, flatten it with your fingertips, and coat well with the dry flour. Transfer to a cutting board or any other clean flat surface and, with a rolling pin, roll into 5 to 6-inch circle and place on the baking trays. (If the dough sticks to the rolling surface, dust with more flour.)

5. With a basting brush or your fingers, lightly baste the top surface of each bread with water. (This prevents them from drying out.) Cover with foil and place the trays in the turned-off oven to rise once more, about 1 hour.

6. Remove the baking trays and preheat the oven to 350°F. Bake until the kulcha breads are still white, but firm, about 10 minutes. They should not brown. Serve.

Variation: Like other Indian breads, kulchas are also made with with various stuffings. All the Stuffings for Parantha Breads (page 587 to page 588) can be used.

Special Breads

Punjabi Griddle-Fried White Corn Breads
Sufaid Makki ki Roti

Makes 8 to 10 breads

This flatbread is generally made with yellow corn flour, perhaps because most of the corn grown in the Punjab is yellow. In America, I use the Mexican white corn flour, which I find results in really sweet and fragrant breads. You could use whichever of the two you prefer (or have in your pantry). Remember to mix in some whole-wheat flour, which binds this easily breakable roti *(bread).*

1¼ cups white corn flour
¼ cup stone-ground durum whole-wheat flour
¾ to 1 cup hot water (only as hot as your hands can tolerate)
3 to 4 tablespoons corn oil or melted ghee, for basting

1. In a bowl, mix together the flours, then add enough hot water to make a semi-soft dough that does not stick to your fingers. (Coat your fingers with some oil if it does stick.) This dough does not require resting time, nor should it be kneaded.

2. With lightly oiled clean hands, divide the dough equally into 8 to 10 balls and cover with foil to prevent drying. Working with each ball separately, place between 2 sheets of wax paper, aluminum foil, or plastic wrap and gently press with your fingertips or a rolling pin to spread it into a 5- to 6-inch circle. If the dough breaks, pinch it together to seal.

3. Heat the tava on medium heat (do not make it too hot—these breads are thicker than the whole-wheat ones and need to cook longer), baste the tava lightly with oil (or ghee), then carefully put the bread on it. Cook until the bottom is flecked with golden dots, about 1 minute, and turn it over.

4. When the other side is golden, flip it once again. Then baste the top with ½ teaspoon oil (or ghee), put that side down onto the tava, and fry until crisp, a few seconds. Similarly, baste and fry the other side until crisp. Repeat with all the other breads. Transfer to a serving plate and serve as hot as possible, topped with a dollop of whipped butter, if you wish.

Variation: Along with the flour in Step 1, also mix in about 1 cup finely chopped fresh fenugreek (or radish) leaves, ½ cup cilantro, and salt and black pepper to taste.

Griddle-Fried Chickpea Flour Breads

Missi Roti

Makes 8 to 10 breads

A classic in their own right, missi roti, *as all chickpea flour breads are called, are quite a culinary delight. On its own, chickpea flour lacks the gluten and elasticity needed to roll out dough. It is generally combined with whole-wheat or all-purpose flour. The following is the most basic recipe for* missi roti *breads.*

1 cup chickpea flour (besan)
½ cup stone-ground durum whole-wheat flour
¼ teaspoon salt, or to taste
½ teaspoon hot red pepper flakes, or to taste
¼ teaspoon ajwain seeds, coarsely ground
½ cup nonfat plain yogurt, or as needed
1 to 2 tablespoons water, as needed

1. In a large bowl, mix together the chickpea and whole-wheat flours with clean fingers. Add the salt, red pepper flakes, and ajwain seeds and mix again. Add the yogurt and mix with your fingers, in round circular motions, until it gathers into a soft, pliable ball that does not stick to your fingers. (Use the water only if you need to.)

2. Knead for about a minute, pressing your knuckles lightly into the dough, spreading the dough outward, then gathering the ends together toward the center with your fingers. Push down the center, then repeat pressing and gathering a few times until you have a soft and pliable dough that does not stick to your fingers. If, while kneading, the dough sticks to your hands, scrape off the dough, put some oil on them, and continue kneading. Cover with plastic wrap or the lid of the bowl and let the dough rest at least 1 and up to 4 hours at room temperature. (This allows the wheat gluten to develop.)

3. To roll and fry the breads, with lightly oiled hands, divide the dough equally into 8 to 10 balls and cover with foil to prevent drying. Then follow the directions for Basic Griddle-Fried Breads (page 581), starting from Step 4.

Variation: Along with the spices in Step 1, add a cup or 2 of finely chopped fresh spinach and about ½ cup minced onion.

Roti

The term *roti* has multiple meanings to Indians. In its broadest sense, symbolically, it implies an entire meal, as in "your daily bread." If someone asks you in Hindi "*Roti khaoge?* (Will you eat *roti?*)," they're inviting you to join them for a meal, not just bread.

Roti is also used generally to refer to any flat (unleavened) breads, such as *chapatis* and *paranthas*. Then there is a whole set of unique and distinctive flatbreads for which the term *roti* simply signifies bread. These breads are named after the flours or the predominant seasonings and vegetables, such as *makki ki roti* (corn bread) or *methi ki roti* (fenugreek bread).

Griddle-Fried Leavened Breads

Khameeri Roti

Makes 8 to 10 breads

A leavened bread, this whole-wheat roti *is light and spongier than most. It's quite possible that this bread came about during hot Indian summers, when any leftover dough, if not carefully watched, fermented very quickly. Today, it is considered a specialty.*

No matter how thin you roll out the dough, the leavening will always make a somewhat soft, puffy, spongy, textured bread. This bread travels well, which makes it a perfect lunch-box or picnic treat with dry-cooked vegetables, such as Mashed Fire-Roasted Eggplant (page 263). Use the bread as a wrap or serve it on the side. For a healthier version, cook the breads as you would chapatis *(Whole-Wheat Griddle Breads, page 577).*

1 teaspoon active dry yeast
1 teaspoon sugar
¼ cup warm water (about 130°F)
1½ cups stone-ground durum whole-wheat flour
½ teaspoon salt, or to taste
½ teaspoon freshly ground black pepper
¼ cup nonfat plain yogurt

1. In a small bowl, mix the yeast and sugar in the water and set aside until frothy, 5 to 7 minutes.

2. Place the flour, salt, and black pepper in a food processor and process until mixed. With the motor running, slowly add the yeast mixture, then the yogurt, through the feeder tube until the flour gathers into a ball and the sides of the work bowl look clean, about 1 minute. (If the dough seems too sticky, add some more dry flour through the feeder tube.) Transfer to a large bowl, cover with plastic wrap or the lid of the bowl, and place in a warm draft-free spot until it doubles in volume, at least 4 and up to 12 hours.

3. With lightly oiled hands, divide the dough equally into 8 to 10 balls and cover with foil to prevent drying.

4. Preheat a tava or griddle over medium-high heat until a sprinkling of flour immediately turns dark brown. Wipe off the flour and proceed. While the tava is heating, working with each ball separately, press into a flat disc in a bowl or pie tin with dry flour, and coat completely with flour. With a rolling pin, on a cutting board or any clean flat work surface, roll each disc into 6- to 7-inch circles.

5. Cook the breads according to directions for Basic Griddle-Fried Breads (page 581), starting from Step 5.

Griddle-Cooked Flour and Potato Bread for Spicy Wraps

Kathi Kabaab ki Aalu Roti

Makes 12 to 16 breads

Kathi kabaabs *made with these breads are the Indian equivalent of burritos. Filled with small pieces of grilled or baked chicken, meat, fish, or* paneer *cheese (see Paneer Cheese Wraps, page 319), and a spicy hot and tangy tomato and onion salad, these wrapped delights make a quick and delicious lunch (or dinner) for people on the go.*

Thinner than packaged corn tortillas, these rotis *are delicately soft, pliable, and silky smooth. To ensure that they remain so, it is crucial to mash and combine the potatoes with the flour while they are still warm. Use a light touch; this dough is ready when everything just starts to gather together. Do not knead.*

This is one bread that works very well (actually, works much better) if you make it in an electric tortilla press than if you roll it with a rolling pin and then cook it on a tava. *The heated tortilla press simultaneously spreads the dough and cooks it, making for a perfect* roti. *Look for an electric tortilla press in most specialty cookware stores.*

2 large russet potatoes (about ³/₄ pounds)
1 cup self-rising flour
1 teaspoon vegetable oil
¹/₂ cup all-purpose flour in a small bowl or a pie dish, for dusting

1. Boil the potatoes in lightly salted water to cover until tender, about 20 minutes. Let cool, then peel them. Coarsely chop them and place them in a food processor along with the flour, and pulse 8 to 10 times (do not process continuously, the potatoes will become starchy) until you have a semi-firm dough, adding 1 to 2 tablespoons hot water only if necessary. This dough does not require resting time, nor should it be kneaded.

2. Transfer to a bowl, add the oil, and mix lightly with clean fingers. Then, with lightly oiled hands, divide the dough equally into 12 to 16 balls and cover with foil to prevent drying. Working with each portion separately, coat with the dry flour and roll into a thin 6- to 8-inch circle.

3. Preheat a tava or a griddle over medium-high heat until a little flour dropped on the surface turns brown. Wipe off the flour and proceed. Cook the roti breads until lightly speckled with golden dots, about 1 minute per side. (These are not like well-cooked breads that are browned.)

Variation: To make the dough by hand, work with the potatoes while they are warm. Mash them, then add the flour and work with your fingers until you get a semi-firm dough. Add about 1 tablespoon oil if the dough sticks to your fingers.

Griddle-Fried Millet Breads with Potatoes

Bajrae ki Roti

Makes 8 to 10 breads

Bajra rotis *are eaten in various parts of the country. In the north, they are 6 to 7 inches in diameter and are called* roti, *but in Gujarat in the west they are much smaller, 4 to 5 inches, and are called* rotla.

Millet flour is gluten-free and crumbly. Therefore, it is routinely mixed with potatoes or whole-wheat flour before any bread can be made. Breads made with millet flour are thick, substantial, and sustaining, and very much a part of the rural villagers' diet, which includes eating them with a tall glass of iced lussi, *a chilled yogurt drink.*

2 large russet (or any kind) potatoes
6 to 8 scallions, white and light green parts only, coarsely chopped
4 quarter-size slices peeled fresh ginger
1 fresh green chile pepper, such as serrano, stemmed
2 cups millet flour
1 tablespoon ground coriander
¹/₂ teaspoon salt, or to taste
2 teaspoons ground pomegranate seeds
3 tablespoons vegetable oil
¹/₃ cup finely chopped fresh cilantro, including soft stems

1. Boil the potatoes in lightly salted water to cover until tender, about 20 minutes. Let cool, then peel and mash. In a food processor, process together the scallions, ginger, and green chile pepper until minced.

2. Add the flour, mashed potatoes, coriander, salt, pomegranate seeds, and oil, and pulse 8 to 10 times (do not process continuously or the potatoes with turn starchy) until everything starts to gather into a ball. Transfer to a bowl.

3. Add the cilantro and mix with clean fingers to make a semi-soft dough that does not stick to them. (Coat your fingers with some oil if that happens.) There is no need to knead this dough or allow for any resting time.

4. Roll and cook the breads according to the directions for Punjabi Griddle-Fried White Corn Breads (page 598), starting from Step 2.

Griddle-Fried Sorghum Breads with Onions

Jowar ka Rotla

Makes 8 to 10 breads

A specialty of Gujarat, rotlas are small, thick rotis. Essentially, they can be made with any flour, but they are popularly made with gluten-free and rustic flours such as sorghum and millet. Because they have low gluten, these flours lack elasticity and are harder to roll into thinner rotis, so people generally make small, thick flatbreads with them. That is the main reason that some whole-wheat flour or potatoes are mixed in.

*Sorghum (*jowar*) is a grain found in plenty around the world, but used sparingly in India and the United States. It does have a loyal following in the Gujarati community of the Mumbai (Bombay) area, and is very nutritious, so try it. This recipe is from my friend Jaywanti Thacker, who lives there.*

1¹⁄₂ cups sorghum flour
¹⁄₄ cup stone-ground durum whole-wheat flour
2 tablespoons vegetable oil or melted ghee
1 cup finely chopped onions
1 to 3 fresh green chile peppers, such as serrano, minced with seeds
1 teaspoon cumin seeds
¹⁄₂ teaspoon salt, or to taste
¹⁄₂ cup water, as needed
Whipped butter

1. In a bowl, mix together the flours, oil (or ghee), onions, green chile peppers, cumin seeds, and salt and then add the water to make to make a semi-soft dough that does not stick to your fingers. (If the dough sticks to your hands, put a little oil or water on them.) This dough does not require resting time, nor should it be kneaded.

2. With lightly oiled hands, divide the dough equally into 8 to 10 balls and cover with foil to prevent drying.

3. To cook, follow the directions for Punjabi Griddle-Fried White Corn Breads (page 598), but make the roti into small 4- to 5-inch circles. Everything else remains the same. Serve with a dollop of whipped butter.

Griddle-Fried Gujarati Fenugreek Breads

Methi Thepla

Makes 12 to 16 breads

Methi theplas, *a specialty of the western states of Gujarat and Maharashtra, are thin and meltingly soft griddle-fried breads (*paranthas*) speckled with chopped fenugreek leaves. They are also spicy, very fragrant and rich from the oil that is added to the dough, plus whatever is used when they are fried.*

*The dough for these breads must be made by hand. If it is made in the food processor the fenugreek leaves will be puréed along with the flour, making the breads green instead of being speckled with the chopped green leaves. Theplas *stay fresh about 2 days at room temperature.*

1 tablespoon Basic Ginger and Green Chile Pepper Paste (page 48)
1¹⁄₄ cups stone-ground durum whole-wheat flour
¹⁄₄ cup chickpea flour (besan)
1 bunch fresh fenugreek leaves, trimmed and finely chopped
2 to 3 tablespoons peanut oil
1 teaspoon sugar
¹⁄₂ teaspoon ground turmeric
1 teaspoon salt, or to taste
¹⁄₈ teaspoon ground asafoetida
¹⁄₂ to ³⁄₄ cup nonfat plain yogurt, whisked until smooth

1. Prepare the ginger-chile paste. Then, in a bowl, add all the ingredients except the yogurt and mix well with clean fingers. Add ¹⁄₂ cup yogurt and mix with your fingers in round circular motions until the dough starts to gather. (Add 1 or 2 tablespoons more flour if the dough seems sticky, or some water if it seems too firm.)

2. Knead for about a minute, pressing your knuckles lightly into the dough, spreading the dough outward, and gathering the ends together toward the center with your fingers. Push the center down and repeat pressing and gathering a few times until you have a soft and pliable dough that does not stick to the fingers. (If, while kneading, the dough sticks to your hands, put a little oil or water on them.)

3. Cover and let rest at least 1 and up to 4 hours at room temperature. (This allows the gluten to develop.) If keeping for a longer period, refrigerate the dough.

4. To make the breads, preheat the tava or griddle over medium-high heat until a sprinkling of the flour immediately turns dark brown. Wipe off the flour and proceed. While the tava is heating, with lightly oiled hands, divide the dough equally into 12 to 16 balls and cover with foil to prevent drying.

5. To roll and cook the breads, follow the directions for Basic Griddle-Fried Breads (page 581), starting from Step 4.

Griddle-Fried Opo Squash Breads

Lauki Ka Thepla

Makes 12 to 16 breads

Opo squash, also known as marrow squash in English or lauki *in Hindi, is a long and large, pale green summer squash with a mild flavor. This squash, like the others in its family, is very watery, so no water or yogurt is needed to make the dough. Zucchini and yellow summer squash are good alternatives here.*

1 cup stone-ground whole-wheat flour
1/4 cup chickpea flour (besan)
1/4 teaspoon turmeric
1/2 teaspoon cayenne pepper, or to taste
1/2 teaspoon salt, or to taste
1/4 teaspoon ajwain seeds
1/8 teaspoon ground asafoetida
1/2 small opo squash (about 1 pound), grated
1 large clove fresh garlic, minced
2 tablespoons vegetable oil
1 to 3 fresh green chile peppers, such as serrano, minced with seeds

1. In a large bowl, add all the dry ingredients and mix well with clean fingers. Add the squash, garlic, oil,

and green chile peppers and mix with your fingers in round circular motions, until it starts to gather into a dough. (Add 1 or 2 tablespoons more flour if the dough seems sticky, or some water if it seems too firm.)

2. Knead for about a minute, pressing your knuckles lightly into the dough, spreading the dough outward, and gathering the ends together toward the center with your fingers. Push the center down and repeat pressing and gathering a few times until you have a soft and pliable dough that does not stick to your fingers. (If, while kneading, the dough sticks to your hands, put a little oil or water on them.)

3. Cover and let rest at least 1 and up to 4 hours at room temperature. (This allows the gluten to develop.) If keeping for a longer period, refrigerate the dough.

4. To make the breads, preheat the tava or griddle over medium-high heat until a sprinkling of the flour immediately turns dark brown. Wipe off the flour and proceed. While the tava is heating, with lightly oiled hands, divide the dough equally into 12 to 16 balls and cover with foil to prevent drying.

5. To roll and cook the breads, follow the directions for Basic Griddle-Fried Breads (page 581), starting from Step 4.

Basic Rajasthani Rolls

Baati

Makes 10 to 12 rolls

Baati *rolls are thick (about 1½ inches), disc-shaped with a slight depression in the center. They are a specialty of the northwestern state of Rajasthan and are made mainly with whole-wheat flour mixed with chickpea flour or fine semolina.*

This recipe comes to me from my son-in-law's mother, Pushpa Khatod, and according to her, the dough for all baaties is best made by hand, as opposed to in a food processor, because any over-processing of the dough reduces the rolls' flakiness.

There are three basic steps to this preparation of these rolls, and several ways to do each. First, you can steam or boil the baaties, as explained in Step 3 of this recipe. Then you brown them (Step 5), either in the oven or on a grill, or you can deep-fry them (page 590). Once done, if baked or grilled, then the baaties are bathed with ghee—you dunk them in a pan of melted ghee, then drain them, or simply baste them as we do in this recipe (basting is not needed if you deep-fry).

If not ghee-*dunked*, baati *rolls are rather dry. They are authentically served with a special* dal (legume dish), *such as Rajasthani Mixed 5 Lentils and Beans (page 367) or with Rajasthani Chickpea Flour Bits in Yogurt Sauce (page 424). A side of potatoes, such as Rajasthani Potatoes with Cashews and Raisins (page 253) completes the meal.*

2 cups stone-ground durum whole-wheat flour

1 cup fine-grain semolina or chickpea flour (besan)

$^1/_2$ teaspoon baking soda

1 teaspoon ajwain seeds

$^1/_2$ teaspoon salt, or to taste

1 teaspoon sugar

$^1/_4$ cup melted ghee (or butter or vegetable oil) + 1 tablespoon ghee for basting

$^2/_3$ to 1 cup water

1. Place the whole-wheat flour and semolina (or chickpea flour) in a large bowl and mix in the baking soda, ajwain seeds, salt, and sugar. With clean fingers, rub in the ghee (or butter or oil), then add the water a little at a time to make a firm but pliable dough that does not stick to your fingers. Cover with plastic wrap or the lid of the bowl and let rest about 1 hour. (This allows the gluten to develop.)

2. With lightly oiled hands, divide the dough equally into 10 to 12 balls and cover with foil to prevent drying. Working with each ball of dough separately, flatten it to make a 3- to 3½-inch disc, then bring the edges up toward the center and pinch together to seal. Press down lightly on the seal with your thumb to make a slight depression, then flatten the rest of the dough once again to make a 2½-inch disc (the depression must show). Repeat with all the remaining balls.

3. To steam: Place the baaties in a metal or bamboo steamer set over or in a pot half-filled with water. (The bottom of the steamer shouldn't touch the water.) Steam them (in 2 batches, if necessary) 7 to 10 minutes, or until a knife inserted in a baati comes out clean.

To boil: Half fill a large pot with water and bring it to a boil. Then place as many of the baaties in the water as will fit comfortably. Cover and simmer until they float to the top, about 10 minutes.

4. Lightly grease a large, heavy baking sheet. Carefully remove the rolls from the steamer or the water and set them on the baking sheet.

5. To brown in the oven: Pre-heat the oven to 400°F. Place the baking sheet on the center rack and bake until the rolls are lightly golden, 15 minutes. After 15 minutes, turn the baaties over with tongs and bake until golden-brown, another 10 minutes. Remove from the oven and place each one individually on a clean pot holder or kitchen towel. Crumple lightly to break open and expose the insides. Return to the oven and bake another 5 to 7 minutes, or until the insides are lightly golden, baste generously with the ghee, and serve.

To brown on a grill: Preheat a grill to medium-high heat (400°F) and grill the baaties, turning them occasionally, until crispy and lightly browned, about 5 minutes. Baste generously with the ghee and serve.

Potato Stuffed Baati Rolls
Aalu Bhari Baati

Makes 10 to 12 rolls

Even though they are made with the same dough as the plain baaties, the stuffed ones take on a new identity because of the stuffing—which can, essentially, be any dry-cooked vegetable, dal, nuts, and, on rare occasions, minced meats. This is from Pushpa Khatod (my daughter's mother-in-law). Pushpa takes a shortcut with these baaties—once stuffed and ready to go, she simply bakes them in the oven.

¹/₂ recipe Rajasthani Potatoes with Cashews and Raisins (page 253)

2 cups stone-ground durum whole-wheat flour

¹/₄ cup fine-grain semolina

1 tablespoon coarsely ground coriander seeds

¹/₂ teaspoon ajwain seeds

¹/₂ teaspoon salt, or to taste

**¹/₄ cup melted warm ghee or butter
+ 1 tablespoon ghee for basting**

About ²/₃ cup water

1. Prepare the potatoes. Then place the whole-wheat flour and semolina in a large bowl and mix in the coriander, ajwain seeds, and salt. With clean fingers, mix in the ghee, then add the water, a little at a time, to make a firm but pliable dough that does not stick to your fingers. Cover with plastic wrap or the lid of the bowl and let rest about 1 hour. (This allows the gluten to develop.)

2. With lightly oiled hands, divide the dough equally into 10 to 12 balls and cover with foil to prevent drying. Divide the potato filling into an equal number of portions.

3. Grease a large, heavy baking sheet. Working with each ball of dough separately, press it to make a thick 4- to 5-inch disc and place 1 portion of the filling in the center. Bring the edges up over the filling and press them together to seal. Pinch off the extra dough above the seal, then shape into a ball once again. Flatten the ball into a thick, 2½-inch disc and press down lightly on the seal with your thumb to make a slight depression (the depression must show). Place on the baking sheet. Repeat with all remaining portions.

4. To bake: Pre-heat the oven to 450°F. Place the baking sheet on the center rack and bake until the rolls are lightly golden, 15 minutes. After 15 minutes, turn the baaties over with tongs and bake until golden-brown, another 10 minutes. Remove from the oven, place each one individually on a clean pot holder or kitchen towel, and crumple lightly to break open and expose the insides. Return to the oven and

bake another 5 to 7 minutes, or until the cracked portions are lightly golden, and serve.

To grill: Preheat a grill to high heat (450°F) and grill the baaties, turning them occasionally, until crispy and lightly browned, about 5 minutes.

5. Baste generously with the ghee and serve.

Baati Rolls

Baaties are delicious breads unique to Rajasthan in the northwest. Being part of the Indian desert area and faced with a constant shortage of fresh produce, the Rajasthani people depend heavily upon different whole-grain flours, *dals* (legumes) and other dried foodstuffs that have a long shelf life. And for them to enjoy the same foods day after day, they have to be creative and inventive. *Baati* bread rolls are a delicious part of that necessity and creativity.

Made mainly with whole-wheat flour and occasionally with chickpea flour, *baati* rolls take many forms—plain, plain with spices, stuffed, then steamed or boiled and then deep-fried, baked in an oven, or grilled over hot coals. No matter how they are cooked, according to tradition, they are then soaked in a melted *ghee* bath for at least 5 minutes—a process that both Pushpa Khatod, my son-in-law's mother (who graciously gave me my *baati* education), and I, do not follow. They should, however, at least be basted.

Rolls with Oat Bran and Fresh Mint

Jaee aur Pudinae ki Double-Roti

Makes 12 to 16 rolls

This is not a traditional Indian recipe, but another of my inventions that I make often. It is healthy and nutritious, it's full of Indian flavors and can be served with just about any meal. Try it with a soup and salad, cut in half and make sandwiches, or serve with grilled fare or curries.

1 tablespoon active dry yeast
1 teaspoon sugar
2¹/₂ cups all-purpose flour
¹/₂ cup warm water (about 110°F)
¹/₄ cup oat flour
¹/₄ cup soybean flour
¹/₂ cup oat bran
1 large clove fresh garlic, peeled
¹/₄ cup chopped fresh mint leaves
1 to 3 fresh green chile peppers, such as serrano, coarsely chopped with seeds
1 teaspoon ajwain seeds
¹/₂ teaspoon salt, or to taste
2 tablespoons olive oil or vegetable oil
1 large egg
¹/₂ cup nonfat plain yogurt, whisked until smooth
1 tablespoon melted butter

1. To make the dough, mix together the yeast, sugar, 1 teaspoon all-purpose flour and water and set aside until frothy, 3 to 4 minutes. (If it doesn't foam, that means the yeast is not active and should be discarded. Start again with fresh yeast.)

2. Put all the flours, oat bran, garlic, mint, green chile peppers, ajwain seeds, and salt in a food processor and process until well mixed. With the motor of the food processor running, pour in the oil through the feeder tube and process until well mixed. Then pour in the egg and the frothy yeast mixture and process until mixed. Finally, add the yogurt and process until the dough gathers into a ball. Continue to process until the sides of the bowl look clean, 20 to 30 seconds. (If the dough seems too sticky, add more flour through the feeder tube; if it seems hard, add more yogurt or water.) Transfer to a large bowl, cover with plastic wrap or the lid of the bowl, and place in a warm draft-free spot until it doubles in volume, 3 to 4 hours.

3. Lightly grease 2 large baking trays. Preheat the oven to 150°F or the lowest setting, about 10 minutes, then turn it off. Then, with lightly oiled clean hands, divide the dough equally into 12 to 16 balls, flatten them lightly with your fingers to make about 3-inch discs, and place them on the trays. With a basting brush or your fingers, lightly baste the top surface of each bread with water. (This prevents them from drying out.) Cover with foil and place them in the turned-off oven to rise once more, about 1 hour.

4. Remove the baking trays and preheat the oven to 350°F. Place the trays in the center of the oven and bake until the tops are golden, about 15 minutes. Check the rolls midway, and if they are browning too quickly, reduce the heat to 300°F and lightly cover the top with aluminum foil. Remove from the oven, baste lightly with the butter, and serve warm. Or let cool completely before storing.

Crepes and Pancakes

Falling into the light meal and substantial snack category are a large array of crepes and pancakes. Made from a vast selection of whole grains and whole-grain flours, plain, spiced, or stuffed with every imaginable dry-cooked vegetable and some meat preparations, these crepe and pancake dishes are popular everywhere.

Belonging to this group are *dosa, pudha, addai, chilla, uthapam,* and many others. All these are pan-fried batters, yet they each have their own identity and a passionate following.

Dosas, a specialty of southern India, are by far the most popular and the most well-known outside of the Indian community. They are the savory, paper-thin, crispy rice and lentil crepes, sometimes about 18-inches long—especially the ones you get in restaurants. They often come with a spicy potato filling and with a side of coconut chutney and a *sambar* (a soupy south Indian lentil dish made with pigeon peas). All the others are basically stand-alones, to be served with one or more of the spicy Indian chutneys.

Basic South Indian Rice and Bean Crepes
Saada Dosa

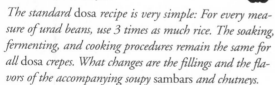

Makes 12 to 16 crepes

The standard dosa *recipe is very simple: For every measure of urad beans, use 3 times as much rice. The soaking, fermenting, and cooking procedures remain the same for all* dosa *crepes. What changes are the fillings and the flavors of the accompanying soupy* sambars *and chutneys.*

Here is a no-fail recipe from my friend Bharti Dhalwala. To make a smooth grain-free batter, use a blender to blend the rice and the dal. *The food processor cannot make it smooth enough.*

**2 cups long-grain white or parboiled rice,
    sorted and washed in 3 to 4 changes of water**
**²/₃ cup dried white urad beans (dhulli urad dal),
    sorted and washed in 3 to 4 changes of water**
¹/₂ teaspoon fenugreek seeds
¹/₂ cup water

¹/₂ teaspoon salt, or to taste
About 3 tablespoons peanut oil

1. Place the rice in one bowl and the dal and fenugreek seeds in another. Soak both overnight in water to cover by about 2 inches. Drain and grind each one separately in a blender (not a food processor), blending to make a smooth and semi-thick batter, adding up to ¹/₄ cup water to each mixture, as needed.

2. In a large bowl, mix both the batters together and add the salt. Cover and place in a warm, dry spot to ferment until fluffy and full of tiny bubbles, at least 24 hours. Mix in up to ²/₃ cup water—just enough to make a semi-thick batter of pouring consistency—then whip with a fork to make it fluffier.

3. To make the dosa, heat a large cast-iron tava or a nonstick griddle or skillet over medium-high heat until a sprinkling of water sizzles immediately. Wipe the tava and baste it lightly with oil. Using a metal soup ladle, pour about ¹/₂ cup of batter onto the hot tava and spread it evenly into a 6- to 7-inch circle by lightly pushing the batter outwards in round, circular motions with the back of the ladle.

4. As the dosa sets and turns lightly golden on the bottom (which happens very quickly), drizzle ¹/₂ to 1 teaspoon oil around the edges and a few drops over the top and cook until the bottom takes on a rich golden hue, about 15 seconds. Turn over once and cook until the other side is barely golden, about 30 seconds. Repeat with remaining batter. Serve as is, or fill in some dry-cooked vegetables or meats and transform it into a Stuffed South Indian Crepe (page 608).

Semolina Crepes
Rava Dosa

Makes 12 to 16 crepes

Made with a batter that is thinner than the plain dosas *of Basic South Indian Rice and Bean Crepes, these* dosa *crepes are very crispy and can have a lot of holes in them, giving them a filigree effect. Make them with plain batter or flavor them with chile peppers, cilantro, and several spices, as I do in this recipe, and serve them as we do the plain* dosas.

Semolina, a product of durum wheat, is available as fine, medium, and coarse grain. Make these dosas with the medium-grain semolina, found in specialty and Indian markets.

1 cup medium-grain semolina

1/2 cup rice flour

2 tablespoons all-purpose flour

1/2 cup nonfat plain yogurt, whisked until smooth

1 to 1 1/2 cups water, as needed

1/2 teaspoon salt, or to taste

1/2 cup finely chopped fresh cilantro, including soft stems

2 tablespoons grated fresh or frozen coconut

1 to 2 fresh green chile peppers, such as serrano, minced with seeds

1 tablespoon dried curry leaves

1/2 teaspoon cumin seeds

1/4 teaspoon ground fenugreek seeds

1. In a medium bowl mix together the semolina, rice flour, all-purpose flour, yogurt, 1 cup water, and salt and set aside until the semolina absorbs all the water, about 30 minutes.

2. Mix in the remaining ingredients and whisk for a few seconds, adding enough of the remaining water to make a thin batter of pouring consistency. (If the batter becomes too thin, mix in some rice flour.)

3. Cook as per the directions for Basic South Indian Rice and Bean Crepes (page 607), starting with Step 3.

Stuffed South Indian Crepes
Masala Dosa

Makes 12 to 16 crepes

Making masala dosas is basically an assembly job. You make the filling, then make the dosa. Once the dosa is made, you place the filling in the center, fold the dosa, and serve.

Although potatoes are the most popular stuffing for masala dosas, *just about any dry-cooked vegetable or meat can be used. Try it with Kerala Coconut Eggplant (page 269) or Basic Paneer Cheese Scramble (page 320).*

12 to 16 (1 recipe) Basic South Indian Rice and Bean Crepes (page 607) or Semolina Crepes (page 607)

1 1/2 pounds russet (or any) potatoes

2 tablespoons peanut oil

2 to 4 dried red chile peppers, such as chile de arbol, with stems

2 tablespoons peeled minced fresh ginger

1 to 3 fresh green chile peppers, such as serrano, minced with seeds

1 tablespoon dried white urad beans (dhulli urad dal), sorted

1 tablespoon dried yellow split chickpeas (channa dal), sorted

1 1/2 teaspoons black mustard seeds

1 teaspoon cumin seeds

1 teaspoon ground fenugreek seeds

1/8 teaspoon ground asafoetida

2 tablespoons dried curry leaves

1/2 teaspoon ground turmeric

1 teaspoon salt, or to taste

1 cup finely chopped fresh cilantro, including soft stems

2 to 3 tablespoons fresh lemon juice

1. Prepare the dosa batter. Then boil the potatoes in lightly salted water to cover until tender, about 20 minutes. Let cool, peel, and coarsely mash.

2. Heat the oil in a large nonstick wok or saucepan over medium-high heat, add the red chile peppers and ginger and cook, stirring, until golden, 1 minute. Reduce the heat to medium and add the green chile peppers, both the dals, mustard seeds, cumin, fenugreek, asafoetida, curry leaves, turmeric, and salt, and stir until golden, about 1 minute.

3. Add the potatoes and cook, stirring lightly, over medium-high heat until heated through. Add the cilantro and lemon juice and cook about 5 minutes to blend the flavors.

4. Cook as per the directions for Basic South Indian Rice and Bean Crepes (page 607), starting with Step 3. As you make each dosa, place about 1/2 cup filling in the center of the softer (whiter) side, then serve open-faced, folded in half, or shaped into a cone.

Rama's Sweet Crepes
Meetha Dosa

Makes 12 to 16 crepes

Instead of frequently making special desserts to satisfy her sweet tooth, my friend Rama Srinivasan decided to sweeten her everyday dosa crepe. This dosa is made with the standard dosa batter, but it comes with a sweet surprise—caramelized sugar. Also try it with a sprinkling of grated jaggery (gur) or brown sugar.

¹/₂ recipe Basic South Indian Rice and Bean Crepes (page 607)
About ¹/₂ cup sugar
1 to 2 tablespoons vegetable oil or melted ghee (optional)

1. Prepare the batter. Then heat a large cast-iron tava or a nonstick griddle over medium-high heat until a sprinkling of water sizzles immediately. Wipe the tava and baste it lightly with oil (or ghee).

2. Using a metal soup ladle, pour about ½ cup batter onto the hot tava and spread it into a 6- to 7-inch circle, spreading and lightly pushing the batter outwards in round, circular motions with the bottom of the ladle.

3. As the dosa sets and turns lightly golden on the bottom (which happens very quickly), drizzle ½ to 1 teaspoon oil (or ghee) around the edges and a few drops on top and cook until the bottom takes on a rich golden hue, about 15 seconds. Then turn it over and cook until the other side is barely golden, 30 seconds.

4. Turn the dosa over once more, sprinkle 2 to 3 teaspoons sugar on top, and fold in half. Baste lightly with the oil (or ghee), if you wish, and press on the dosa with a spatula to seal the two sides, about 30 seconds. (Some of the sugar may seep out and caramelize, giving the dosa a lovely flavor.) Transfer to a serving platter, repeat with remaining batter, and serve hot.

Crispy Chickpea Flour Crepes
Besan kae Pudhae

Makes 12 to 16 crepes

Made with chickpea flour, these crispy crepes require no soaking or fermenting time and are delicious. When we were kids, my mother made them for us very often—not looking at the time of the day. They were as desirable (and quick and easy) for breakfast and brunch as they were with a cup of afternoon tea (hot milk for the kids). Try it with Yogurt Chutney with Puréed Greens (page 68).

1¹/₂ cups chickpea flour (besan)
1 small onion, minced
¹/₂ cup finely chopped fresh cilantro, including soft stems
1 tablespoon peeled minced fresh ginger
1 to 3 fresh green chile peppers, such as serrano, minced with seeds
1 tablespoon ground coriander
1 teaspoon salt, or to taste
¹/₄ teaspoon baking soda
1¹/₂ to 2 cups water, as needed
¹/₄ cup peanut oil

1. In a small bowl, mix together everything except the water and oil. Then add the water as needed to make a semi-thick batter of pouring consistency. Whip with a fork a few seconds to make it fluffy. Set aside about 30 minutes.

2. Heat about 2 teaspoons oil in a tava or a medium nonstick skillet over medium heat until a sprinkling of water sizzles immediately. Using a metal soup ladle, pour about ¼ cup batter onto the hot tava and spread it evenly into a 5- to 6-inch circle by lightly pushing the batter outwards in round, circular motions with the back of the ladle.

3. As the pancake sets and turns lightly golden on the bottom (which happens very quickly), drizzle ½ to 1 teaspoon oil around the edges and a few drops on top and cook until the bottom takes on a rich golden hue, about 30 seconds. Turn over once and cook until the other side takes on a similar color, about 30 seconds. Transfer to a serving platter, repeat with the remaining batter, and serve hot.

Traditional Lentil Pancakes

Addai

Makes 12 to 16 pancakes

Made with a batter similar to that for dosas, *but with a mixture of different* dals *and rice,* addai *crepes are generally smaller and thicker—more like pancakes.*

Serve them with any coconut chutney from the Chutneys and Pickles chapter or with South Indian Tomato Chutney (page 71) and a sambar *(a south Indian soupy dish made with pigeon peas), if you wish.*

²/₃ cup long-grain white rice, sorted

3 tablespoons dried white urad beans (dhulli urad dal), sorted

3 tablespoons dried yellow mung beans (dhulli mung dal), sorted

3 tablespoons dried yellow split chickpeas (channa dal), sorted

3 tablespoons dried split pigeon peas (toor dal), sorted

1¹/₃ cups water, plus more for soaking the dals

1 small onion, coarsely chopped

¹/₄ cup coarsely chopped fresh cilantro, including soft stems

1 to 2 fresh green chile peppers, such as serrano, stemmed

¹/₂ teaspoon salt, or to taste

¹/₄ teaspoon ground asafoetida

3 to 4 tablespoons peanut oil

1. Wash the rice and dals in 3 to 4 changes of water. Then place together in a bowl and soak overnight in water to cover by about 2 inches.

2. Drain and transfer to a blender, add the onion, cilantro, green chile peppers, salt, and asafoetida, and blend until smooth, adding up to 1¹/₃ cups water, as needed, to make a thick and smooth batter. Whip with a fork a few seconds to make the batter fluffy. Set aside 3 to 4 hours. If the batter is too thick, add more water, as needed, to make a semi-thick batter of pouring consistency.

3. Heat a cast-iron tava or a nonstick griddle or skillet over medium-high heat until a sprinkling of water sizzles immediately. Wipe the tava and put about

1 teaspoon in the center. Then, using a metal soup ladle, pour about ¹/₂ cup batter onto the hot tava and spread it evenly into a 5- to 6-inch circle by lightly pushing the batter outwards in round, circular motions with the back of the ladle.

4. As the pancake sets and turns lightly golden on the bottom (which happens very quickly), drizzle ¹/₂ to 1 teaspoon oil around the edges and a few drops on top and cook until the bottom takes on a rich golden hue, about 1 minute. Turn over once and cook until the other side is takes on a similar color, about 1 minute. Transfer to a serving platter, repeat with the remaining batter, and serve hot.

Yellow Mung Bean Pancakes

Mung Dal kae Chillae

Makes 12 to 16 pancakes

Chillas *are a north Indian version of* addai *and other pancakes.* Mung dal *is a popular favorite in the north, so cooks use it in all sorts of recipes, this being just one of them. Serve them with any green, sonth, or tomato chutneys in the Chutneys and Pickles chapter.*

1 cup dried yellow mung beans (dhulli mung dal), sorted

¹/₄ cup dried white urad beans (dhulli urad dal), sorted

3 to 4 quarter-size slices peeled fresh ginger

1 to 2 fresh green chile peppers, such as serrano, minced with seeds

1¹/₂ cups water, as needed

¹/₈ teaspoon ground asafoetida

¹/₄ teaspoon ground turmeric

¹/₄ teaspoon freshly ground black pepper, or to taste

¹/₄ teaspoon baking soda

¹/₄ teaspoon salt, or to taste

¹/₄ cup peanut oil

1. Wash both the dals in 3 to 4 changes of water. Place together in a bowl and soak in water to cover by 2 inches, about 3 hours. Drain and transfer to a food processor, add the ginger, green chile peppers, and

1 cup water and process to make a thick, smooth batter. (It will still have a bit of a grain.) Transfer to a bowl.

2. Add the remaining ½ cup water to the food processor and swirl to remove any batter left in the work bowl and mix it into the batter. Add the asafoetida, turmeric, black pepper, baking soda, and salt, and mix well. Set aside 3 to 4 hours. If the batter is too thick, add more water, as is needed, to make a semi-thick batter of pouring consistency.

3. Cook the pancakes as described in Traditional Lentil Pancakes (page 610), starting from Step 3.

Stuffed Mung Bean Pancake Rolls
Paneer-Bharae Chillae

Makes 12 to 16 pancake rolls

A filling of paneer *cheese moves the everyday* chillas *into party fare, in the finger-foods category. Serve them as my Mumbai (formerly Bombay) friend Jaywanti Thaker does, with Garlic and Fresh Red Chile Pepper Chutney (page 65), or drizzle some Yogurt Chutney with Puréed Greens (page 68) over the* chilla *rolls and sprinkle on a handful of store-bought crispy, spicy potato noodles (aalu bhujia).*

1½ cups Paneer Cheese (page 43 or store-bought), coarsely crumbled
1 recipe Yellow Mung Bean Pancakes (page 610)
1 small onion, coarsely chopped
1 to 3 fresh green chile peppers, such as serrano, stemmed
½ cup coarsely chopped fresh cilantro, including soft stems
1 tablespoon peanut oil
½ teaspoon kalonji seeds
½ teaspoon salt, or to taste
Cilantro sprigs

1. Prepare the paneer cheese. Prepare the pancakes. Then, in a food processor, process together the paneer cheese, onion, green chile peppers, and cilantro until minced.

2. Heat the oil in a small nonstick wok or saucepan over medium-high heat and add the kalonji seeds;

they should sizzle upon contact with the hot oil. Quickly add the processed paneer cheese mixture and the salt and cook, stirring, until lightly golden, about 3 minutes.

3. Working with each chilla separately, place about 2 tablespoons of the filling along one edge of the chilla, then roll it up into a long tube. Cut each roll diagonally into 2 pieces, place on a serving platter, garnish with cilantro sprigs, and serve.

Rice Flour Pancakes with Carrots
Gajjar Utthapam

Makes 12 to 16 pancakes

Thick and soft like regular pancakes, and always studded with vegetables either mixed into the batter or sprinkled on top, uthapams *can be made with rice flour or with semolina, as in Semolina Pancakes with Tomatoes and Bell Peppers (page 612).*

Uthapams are a south Indian treat—quick and easily made for the family as well as for unexpected company. Often, home cooks add chopped vegetables (and some semolina or rice flour, if the batter is too thin) to leftover dosa *crepe batter to make these pancakes.*

Serve them for breakfast or brunch, or as a snack with Peanut and Garlic Chutney (page 65) or South Indian Tomato Chutney (page 71). Urad bean flour can be found in Indian markets.

1 cup rice flour
½ cup urad bean flour
1½ to 2 cups nonfat plain yogurt, whisked until smooth
¼ to ½ cup water, as needed
1 small red onion, finely chopped
2 to 3 small carrots, grated
½ cup finely chopped fresh cilantro, including soft stems
1 to 3 fresh green chile peppers, such as serrano, minced with seeds
2 tablespoons finely chopped fresh dill leaves
½ teaspoon salt, or to taste
¼ cup peanut oil

1. In a bowl, mix together the rice flour, urad bean flour, and yogurt and mix to make a smooth batter. Whip with a fork a few seconds to make the batter fluffy. Set aside 3 to 4 hours. If the batter is too thick, add more water, as is needed, to make a semi-thick batter of pouring consistency. Mix in the onion, carrots, cilantro, green chile peppers, dill leaves, and salt.

2. Heat about ½ teaspoon oil in a nonstick tava or skillet over medium medium-high heat until , until a drop of batter sizzles lightly.

3. Then, using a metal soup ladle, pour about ½ cup batter onto the hot tava and spread it evenly into a 5- to 6-inch circle by lightly pushing the batter outwards in round, circular motions with the back of the ladle.

4. As the pancake sets and turns lightly golden on the bottom (which happens very quickly), drizzle ½ to 1 teaspoon oil around the edges and a few drops on top and cook until the bottom takes on a rich golden hue, about 1 minute. Turn over once and cook until the other side is takes on a similar color, about 1 minute. Transfer to a serving platter, repeat with the remaining batter, and serve hot.

Semolina Pancakes with Tomatoes and Bell Peppers

Tamatar Utthapam

Makes 12 to 16 pancakes

This is another popular uthapam *recipe using semolina instead of rice flour and urad bean flour. These* uthapams *are one of the easiest snacks to make, but can be enhanced as simply or elaborately as you want. You can make these in the same way as* Rice Flour Pancakes, *with the vegetables all mixed into the batter, or top them with vegetables, as I do in this recipe.*

1½ cups fine-grain semolina
1½ cups nonfat plain yogurt, whisked until smooth
³/4 to 1 cup water, as needed
1 teaspoon salt, or to taste
1 tablespoon fresh lemon juice
1 to 3 fresh green chile peppers, such as serrano, minced with seeds
1 small onion, finely chopped
1 cup finely chopped fresh cilantro, including soft stems
2 tablespoons peeled minced fresh ginger
1 large tomato, finely chopped
1 green bell pepper, finely chopped
1 medium zucchini, grated
¹/4 cup peanut oil

1. In a large bowl, mix together the semolina flour, yogurt, ¾ cup water, salt, and lemon juice to make a smooth batter, then whip with a fork a few seconds to make it fluffy. Set aside 3 to 4 hours.

2. When ready to cook, if the batter is too thick, add up to ¼ cup more water to make a semi-thick batter of pouring consistency. Mix in the green chile peppers, onion, cilantro, and ginger.

3. In a separate bowl, mix together the tomato, bell pepper, and zucchini. Heat about ½ teaspoon oil in a nonstick skillet over medium-high heat, until a drop of batter sizzles lightly. With a metal soup ladle, pour about ½ cup batter in the skillet and spread it evenly by tilting and rotating the pan or with the back of the ladle, to make a 5- to 6-inch pancake.

4. Scatter about ⅓ cup mixed vegetables over the pancake. As the pancake sets and turns lightly golden on the bottom (which happens very quickly), drizzle ½ to 1 teaspoon oil around the edges and a few drops on top and cook until the bottom takes on a rich golden hue, about 1 minute. Making sure the vegetables don't fall off, turn over the pancake with 2 large spatulas and cook until the other side takes on a similar color, about 1 minute. Transfer to a serving platter, repeat with the remaining batter, and serve hot or warm.

Desserts

Prasaad Offerings 616

Marzipan Delights

Himachali Nuts

Banana Dumplings

Sweet Roasted Whole-Wheat Flour

Sweet Pastries with Dates and Nuts

Halva 618

Traditional Semolina Halva

Traditional Semolina Halva
with Chickpea Flour and Raisins

Whole-Wheat Flour Halva

Almond and Saffron Halva

Yellow Mung Bean Halva

Simple Carrot Halva

Decadent Carrot Halva
with Evaporated Milk and Jaggery

Plantain Halva

Milk-Based Puddings (Kheer, Payasam, and Payesh) 622

Punjabi Rice Pudding

South Indian Rice Pudding

Bengali Rice Pudding

Parsi Pressed Rice Flakes Pudding

Punjabi Semolina Pudding

Parsi Semolina Pudding

Tapioca Pudding

Indian Vermicelli Pudding

Paneer Cheese Kheer Pudding

Almond and Saffron Kheer Pudding

Yellow Split Chickpea Pudding

Traditional Bread Pudding Bites

French Roll Bread Pudding

Traditional Thickened Milk
Pudding

Microwave Milk Pudding

Creamy Milk Pudding with
Almonds and Saffron

Creamy Milk Pudding
with Summer Fruits

Custards and Mousses 631

Basmati Rice Custard

Corn Custard

Pressure-Cooked Caramel Custard

Caramelized Yogurt

Yogurt Mousse with Saffron

Fresh Fruit in Rose-Flavored Cream

Indian Ice Creams (Kulfi) 634

Quick and Easy Indian Ice Cream

Indian Ice Cream with Pistachios

Indian Ice Cream with Saffron

Indian Ice Cream with Almonds

Indian Ice Cream with Mangoes

Cellophane Noodles
in Cardamom-Saffron Syrup

Indian Ice Cream Desserts 637

Mango Ice Cream Dessert

Lychee Ice Cream Dessert

Pistachio and Cardamom
Ice Cream Dessert

Saffron and Almond
Ice Cream Dessert

 = Vegan   = Pressure-Cooker Quick

Desserts weave a dynamic spell, full of sinful sweetness. They help set the stage for celebration, and some desserts tied to holidays, weddings, and family gatherings make desserts the most memorable and treasured part of the cuisine.

Indian desserts feature unique flavors such as cardamom seeds, saffron, rose essence, almonds, pistachios, cashews, melon seeds, and mangoes. Indian desserts can be simple, homemade affairs like *halvas* (soft-cooked grain or vegetable desserts) and *kheers* (milk-based puddings). Or they can be works of art, such as created by *halvais* (professional sweet makers).

Their presentation is often a visual treat. Artfully served under paper-thin yet edible pure silver leaves, garnished with the thinnest slivers of softened pistachios and almonds, or dusted with coarsely ground nuts and seeds, each dessert tempts the eyes before satisfying the palate.

The allure of desserts is so powerful, they are often hard to resist. Although most Indian desserts are nutritious because they are based on grains and beans, fruits, nuts, and dairy products, they are also calorie-rich so enjoy them, but in moderation.

Prasaad Offerings

Indians are deeply religious people. Part of the worship ritual dictates that foods are a gift from the Gods, and special dishes should be offered back to the Gods to thank him. Such foods are called *prasaad*, or consecreated food, and desserts are the most commonly offered *prasaad* in places of worship.

These offerings are made at home or at or near temples, and certain temples are renowned for their *prasaad*s. For instance, my friend Sohini Baliga has never forgotten the sweets she had from Thirumala Tirupati Devasthanam, a famous south Indian temple. As she puts it, "For a 12-year-old, dragged on a long, wearying pilgrimage along with several prayerful relatives, the reward wasn't seeing the Lord; it was the softball-sized desserts, laden with *ghee*, and studded with raisins, and rock candy. Now *that* was heaven."

Marzipan Delights
Badaam ki Mithai

Makes 15 to 20 pieces

During the celebration of Diwali—the Hindu new year and festival of lights—mothers and grandmothers humor children by shaping this sweet almond dough into little toys, adding chopped nuts and food coloring for special effects.

1/2 pound blanched raw almonds
1 1/2 pounds confectioners' sugar
1 teaspoon almond extract
1 cup coarsely chopped mixed nuts, such as blanched almonds, pistachios, or cashews

1. Process the almonds in a food processor until as fine as possible. Then, add the sugar and almond extract and continue to process until everything comes together into a dough. With clean hands, divide the dough into 15 to 20 portions and roll each portion into a round ball.

2. Roll each dough ball in the chopped nuts and serve, or place in airtight containers and store in the refrigerator about 2 months.

Himachali Nuts
Himachal kae Mithae Mavae

Makes 4 to 6 servings

Served over a bed of freshly cooked basmati *rice, this mixture of fragrant nuts, floating in a thick saffron syrup, is a traditional dessert from the northern hill state of Himachal Pradesh. Try it over vanilla ice cream or frozen yogurt.*

4 cups (1 recipe) Steamed Basmati Rice (page 533)
1/3 cup raw cashews, coarsely chopped
1/3 cup raw almonds, coarsely chopped
1/3 cup raw pistachios, coarsely chopped
1 1/2 cups sugar
1 cup water
1 teaspoon ground green cardamom seeds
1 teaspoon fennel seeds
1/4 teaspoon saffron threads

1. Prepare the rice. Then place all the nuts in a small nonstick skillet and dry-roast, stirring and shaking the skillet, over medium-low heat until fragrant and golden, about 3 minutes. Remove from the heat and cool.

2. Place the sugar, water, cardamom seeds, fennel seeds, and saffron in a medium wok or saucepan and boil over medium-high heat about 2 minutes, then reduce the heat to medium-low and cook until the mixture forms a thick syrup, about 5 minutes.

3. Mix in the cashews, almonds, and pistachios and cook 1 minute. Meanwhile, place the rice in a serving dish. Pour the nuts and the syrup over the rice and serve. Or ladle over individual servings of rice.

Banana Dumplings
Modak

Makes 4 to 6 servings

A specialty along the west coast of India, these bite-sized banana dumplings are a popular tea-time snack. They are also a served as prasaad *at temples and, on occasion, are dedicated to the elephant God, Ganesh. These are typically made with ripe plantains, but firm, ripe bananas also work well.*

2 large firm, ripe bananas
1/2 cup all-purpose flour
1/2 cup sugar, or to taste
2 cups peanut oil for deep-frying

1. In a mixing bowl, peel and mash the bananas with a fork. Add the flour and 1/3 cup sugar and mix well, forming a semi-firm batter.

2. Heat the oil in a large wok over medium-high heat until it reaches 325°F to 350°F on a frying thermometer or until a piece of dough dropped into the hot oil rises to the top after 15 to 20 seconds.

3. With a spoon or clean fingers, carefully drop about 1 tablespoon of the batter into the oil, adding as many spoonfuls as the wok can hold at one time without crowding. Fry, stirring and turning with a slotted spatula, until golden. Remove dumplings to a tray lined with paper towels to drain. Transfer to a serving platter, dust with the remaining sugar, and serve hot.

Sweet Roasted Whole-Wheat Flour
Attae ki Panjeeri

Makes about 4 cups

Called panjeeri, *this is a sweet, fragrant, and powdery Punjabi dessert. It is often served as a* prasaad *during religious ceremonies, especially on* puran-masi—*the day of the full moon, which comes once every month. For best flavor, do not replace the* ghee *with oil. If you prefer to use butter, spend an extra minute to clarify it (page 41).*

1/2 cup shelled raw pistachios
1/2 cup shelled raw almonds
1 teaspoon coarsely ground green cardamom seeds, or more to taste
2 cups stone-ground durum whole-wheat flour
1/4 to 1/3 cup melted ghee (or clarified butter)
1 cup sugar

1. In a food processor, process the pistachios and almonds until coarsely ground. Transfer to a bowl and mix in the cardamom seeds.

2. Place the flour and ghee (or clarified butter) in a large wok (not nonstick) and roast, stirring constantly with a slotted spatula, over medium-high heat until heated through, then over medium-low heat until a very fragrant smoke arises from the wok and the flour turns a rich golden color, 12 to 15 minutes.

3. Mix in the sugar and the nuts and roast, stirring, about 1 minute. Let cool and serve at room temperature, or store in an airtight container about 1 month at room temperature, or about 3 months in the refrigerator.

Variation: For added flavor and enhanced presentation, add 1/4 teaspoon crushed saffron threads and 1/4 cup melon seeds (char magaz, page 12) during the last 3 to 5 minutes of cooking.

Sweet Pastries with Dates and Nuts
Mandi-Pirakari

Makes 12 pieces

This prasaad is typically made and served during Krishna Janamashtami, Lord Krishna's birthday, in late August. Lord Krishna is one of the Hindu Gods. Stored in an airtight container, these pastries will keep fresh for about a month. They make a lovely tea-time snack.

1/4 cup ghee
2 cups all-purpose flour
2 to 3 tablespoons water
1 cup coarsely chopped seedless dates
1 cup finely chopped raisins and raw mixed nuts
1 to 2 tablespoons honey
1 1/2 to 2 cups peanut oil for deep-frying

1. With clean fingers, work the ghee into the flour till it forms a ball without crumbling. Add the water, a little at a time, and keep working the dough with your fingers. Use only as much water as needed to make a semi-firm dough that does not stick to the fingers. Cover and let the dough rest, at least 1 but no more than 4 hours, at room temperature. (This allows the wheat gluten to develop.) If you're keeping the dough longer, refrigerate until ready for use.

2. In another bowl, mix together the dates, nuts, raisins, and honey until the ingredients bind together. Reserve.

3. With lightly oiled hands, divide the dough and the filling each into 12 equal portions. Shape each portion of dough into a ball, and, with a rolling pin, roll each ball into a 4-inch circle. Baste the edges of the circle with water, then place a portion of the filling on one half of the circle. Fold the other half over the filling to form a semi-circle. Press, first with your fingers, then with a fork to seal.

4. Heat the oil in a large wok over medium-high heat until it reaches 325°F to 350°F on a frying thermometer or until a piece of dough dropped into the hot oil rises to the top after 15 to 20 seconds. Add the pastries, in 2 batches, and slowly fry, stirring and turning with a slotted spatula until golden on both sides. Drain on paper towels and serve at room temperature.

Halva

The *halva* (often spelled *halvah*) sold in Indian stores in America is nothing like what is made in Indian homes. While it is true that shops in India sell their share of firm *halvas* with a long shelf life, the fresh homemade versions are much more authentic. With *ghee* or butter and sugar as the common denominators, they are made from grains, flours, *dals* (legumes), and vegetables. These homemade *halvas* are far more perishable than the packaged varieties, so they are made as needed and are always served as hot as they can safely be consumed. (This dessert should not be confused with the dense sesame seed candy called *halvah*.)

Traditional Semolina Halva
Sooji ka Halva

Makes 4 to 6 servings

Served on many happy and auspicious occasions throughout India, every region adds its own special touches to halva. *It is a quick and spontaneously made dessert, especially pleasing to families with children. When my children were young, whenever I made this, they were be suspiciously well-behaved until they got to enjoy it.*

1/3 to 1/2 cup unsalted butter
1 cup fine semolina
3 cups boiling water
1 cup sugar
1/2 teaspoon ground green cardamom seeds
1/4 cup blanched raw almonds, coarsely chopped
2 tablespoons shelled raw pistachios, coarsely chopped
4 (4-inch) silver leaves (optional)

1. In a large wok or saucepan, cook the butter and semolina over medium-low heat, stirring, until it turns a rich brown, 20 to 25 minutes. Standing far from the pan, carefully add the boiling water and stir. (Use caution when adding the water, because as soon as it touches the hot wok, it will steam and splatter for 5 to 10 seconds.) Cover the pan and simmer on low heat, stirring occasionally, until all the water is absorbed, 5 to 7 minutes.

2. Add the sugar, cover, and continue to simmer, stirring occasionally, until it is absorbed, 3 to 5 minutes. Reserving some of the nuts, mix in the cardamom seeds, almonds, and pistachios.

3. Uncover the pan and cook, stirring, until the halvah pulls away from the sides of the pan and a shiny glaze appears on top, 2 to 4 minutes. Transfer to a serving bowl, garnish with the silver leaves and reserved nuts, and serve hot.

Traditional Semolina Halva with Chickpea Flour and Raisins

Sooji—Besan ka Halva

Makes 4 to 6 servings

Very similar to Traditional Semolina Halva (page 618), this recipe, courtesy of my mother-in-law, is enriched with chickpea flour and raisins. It has a unique fragrance, smooth texture, and the occasional crunch of caramelized sugar. It has become a family favorite.

1 to 2 tablespoons Dessert Masala (page 32)
¹/₃ to ¹/₂ cup unsalted butter
²/₃ cup fine semolina
¹/₃ cup chickpea flour
¹/₄ cup golden raisins
1 cup sugar
¹/₂ teaspoon ground green cardamom seeds
¹/₄ cup blanched raw almonds, coarsely chopped
2 tablespoons shelled raw pistachios,
    coarsely chopped
3 cups boiling water
4 (4-inch) silver leaves (optional)

1. Prepare the dessert masala. Then in a large wok or saucepan, mix the butter, semolina, and chickpea flour and cook, stirring, over medium-low heat until the mixture is rich brown, 20 to 25 minutes. During the last 5 minutes of cooking, mix in the raisins.

2. Add the sugar, cardamom seeds, almonds, and pistachios and continue to cook, stirring, about 5 minutes. This process roasts the nuts and lightly caramelizes the sugar. Standing far from the pan, carefully add the boiling water. (Use caution when adding the water, because as soon as it touches the hot wok, it will steam and splatter for 5 to 10 seconds.) Cover the pan and simmer, stirring occasionally, until all the water is absorbed, 5 to 7 minutes.

3. Uncover the pan and cook, stirring, until the halva pulls away from the sides of the pan and a shiny glaze appears on top, 2 to 4 minutes. Transfer to a serving bowl, garnish with the silver leaves and dessert masala, and serve hot.

Whole-Wheat Flour Halva

Kadhaa

Makes 4 to 6 servings

Called kadhaa, *and traditionally served as a* prasaad *in Sikh* gurdwaras *(temples), this* halva *is made with the four basics found in almost all Indian homes: whole-wheat flour, sugar, ghee, and water. Without any nut garnishes or spice additions, its fragrance comes from the* ghee *and the long, slow roasting of the whole-wheat flour. That is why its color is very pale when compared to similar* halvas.

¹/₂ cup melted ghee
1 cup stone-ground durum whole-wheat flour
2 cups water
1 cup sugar

1. In a large wok or saucepan, mix the whole-wheat flour and the ghee and cook, stirring, over medium-low heat, until fragrant and a few shades darker, 30 to 40 minutes.

2. In another saucepan, mix together the water and sugar and bring to a boil over high heat. Standing far from the pan, carefully add the sugar-water to the roasted flour and stir to mix. (Use caution when adding the sugar-water, because as soon as it touches the hot wok, it will steam and splatter for 5 to 10 seconds.) Cover the pan and simmer, stirring occasionally, until all the water is absorbed, 5 to 7 minutes.

3. Uncover the pan and cook, stirring, until the halva pulls away from the sides of the pan and a shiny glaze appears on top, 2 to 4 minutes. Transfer to a serving bowl and serve hot, without garnish.

Almond and Saffron Halva
Kesari Badaam Halva

Makes 4 to 6 servings

Made in much the same way as traditional halvas, here ground almonds replace part of the semolina, and saffron threads lend their unique color and aroma.

1 to 2 tablespoons Dessert Masala (page 32)
¼ teaspoon saffron threads
2 tablespoons whole milk
⅓ to ½ cup melted ghee
½ cup fine semolina
1 cup shelled ground raw almonds
1 cup sugar
½ teaspoon ground green cardamom seeds
2 tablespoons coarsely chopped shelled raw pistachios
3 cups boiling water
4 (4-inch) silver leaves (optional)

1. Prepare the dessert masala. Then, in a small bowl soak the saffron threads in the milk about 30 minutes.

2. In a large wok or saucepan, mix the ghee and semolina and cook, stirring, over medium-low heat, until golden, 12 to 15 minutes. Mix in the ground almonds and cook, stirring, until the nuts turn golden, 5 to 7 minutes.

3. Add the sugar, cardamom seeds, pistachios, and saffron-infused milk (reserving the saffron threads) and continue to roast, stirring, about 5 minutes. This process roasts the pistachios and lightly caramelizes the sugar.

4. Standing far from the pan, carefully, add the boiling water. (Use caution when adding the water, because as soon as it touches the hot wok, it will steam and splatter for 5 to 10 seconds.) Cover the pan and simmer, stirring occasionally, until all the water is absorbed, 5 to 7 minutes.

5. Uncover the pan and cook, stirring, until the halva pulls away from the sides of the pan and a shiny glaze appears on top, 2 to 4 minutes. Transfer to a serving bowl, garnish with the silver leaves (if using), reserved saffron threads, and the dessert masala, and serve hot.

Yellow Mung Bean Halva
Dhulli Mung Dal Ka Halva

Makes 4 to 6 servings

This traditional and decadent recipe from my friend Bharti Dhalwala's Santa Monica kitchen is loaded with ghee. *But if it's cooked properly, a good part of the* ghee *separates from the mixture and can be poured off, leaving behind a perfectly roasted, fragrant* halva.

1 cup dried yellow mung beans (dhulli mung dal),
    sorted and washed in 3 to 4 changes of water
2 tablespoons Dessert Masala (page 32)
¼ cup water
½ cup melted ghee
1 cup sugar
1½ cups whole milk (or any kind)
¼ teaspoon saffron threads
¼ cup raw cashews, coarsely ground
¼ cup shelled raw almonds, coarsely ground
½ teaspoon ground green cardamom seeds

1. In a bowl, soak the beans in water to cover by 2 inches overnight, then drain. Meanwhile, prepare the dessert masala. Then, in a food processor, process the dal, adding the ¼ cup water by the teaspoon as needed, until it is as smooth as you can make it. The consistency should be something between a dough and a thick batter.

2. Heat half the ghee in a medium nonstick wok or saucepan over medium heat. Add the processed dal and roast, stirring, until golden, 15 to 20 minutes.

3. Add the sugar, milk, saffron, cashews, almonds, and cardamom seeds and mix well. Add the remaining half of the ghee and continue to roast, stirring, until the halva is very fragrant and pulls away from the sides of the pan and the ghee separates from the halva, about 30 minutes.

4. Remove from the stove and tilt the pan, keeping it tilted 3 to 5 minutes, allowing the ghee to collect at one end. Then, with a spoon, remove as much of the ghee as you can. (This ghee can be reused.) Transfer to a serving dish, garnish with the dessert masala, and serve hot.

Simple Carrot Halva
Gaajar Halva or Gajjeraela

Makes 4 to 6 servings

The carrot halva I make in my American kitchen tastes almost the same as the Indian version, but it lacks the lovely rich, red color that authentic gajjeraela *has. This is because Indian carrots have more color, and no amount of organic shopping or food coloring can compensate for the difference. Do not peel the carrots (too much is lost), but with a dull knife, simply scrape each one lightly.*

1/4 cup Dessert Masala (page 32)
1 pound carrots, scraped, washed, and grated
7 cups whole milk
1 (14-ounce) can sweetened condensed milk
1 teaspoon coarsely crushed green cardamom seeds
2 tablespoons unsalted butter or melted ghee
4 (4-inch) silver leaves (optional)

1. Prepare the dessert masala. Place the carrots and milk in a large, heavy wok or saucepan and cook, stirring, over high heat until the milk comes to a boil. Reduce the heat to medium and continue to cook, stirring and scraping the sides of the pan often, making sure the milk does not boil over (reduce the heat if that happens), until all the milk is absorbed into the carrots, 30 to 35 minutes.

2. Mix in the condensed milk and cardamom seeds and cook, stirring and scraping, until the mixture is quite dry, 10 to 12 minutes. Add the butter and continue cooking, stirring constantly, until it pulls away from the sides of the pan and is slightly golden, 10 to 12 minutes. Mix in most of the dessert masala, saving some for garnish. Transfer to a serving dish, garnish with the silver leaves (if using), and reserved dessert masala, and serve hot.

Decadent Carrot Halva with Evaporated Milk and Jaggery
Khoa aur Gur Ka Gaajar Halva

Makes 4 to 6 servings

Jaggery (gur or brown, unrefined cane sugar) deepens the color and imparts a smoky richness to this carrot halva, *which is traditionally served hot. If you want to make it ahead of time, keep the cooked carrots and the khoa (thickened milk, Step 3) separate. Then, before serving, mix them together in small portions as needed. This way, your* halva *will always look and taste fresh.*

The khoa I use in this recipe is not the real one, but a shortcut I created. Here, I mix together ricotta cheese, cream, and evaporated milk to make something that is very close to true khoa, but is much easier to make.

1/4 cup raw almond slices
1 tablespoon Dessert Masala (page 32)
1 pound carrots, scraped, washed, and grated
1/2 cup ground or grated jaggery (gur),
    or 1 cup dark brown sugar, or to taste
13/4 cups heavy cream
3 cups nonfat dry milk
1 cup part-skim ricotta cheese
2 tablespoons raw pistachio halves
4 to 6 (4-inch) squares silver leaves (optional)

1. Soak the almonds in water to cover for 30 minutes to soften. Meanwhile, prepare the dessert masala. Drain the almonds.

2. Place the carrots in a large, heavy wok or a saucepan. Cover and cook over medium-high heat about 5 minutes, stirring occasionally. Reduce the heat to low and cook another 5 minutes. Add the jaggery and cook until melted, 2 to 3 minutes. Increase the heat to medium and cook, stirring as needed, until the jaggery is completely absorbed into the carrots, 10 to 12 minutes.

3. While the carrots are cooking, make the khoa: Combine the cream, dry milk, and ricotta cheese in a large nonstick skillet or saucepan and stir over medium heat until smooth, 3 to 5 minutes. Reduce the heat to low and cook, stirring often, until the mixture is almost dry, 7 to 10 minutes.

4. Mix the khoa into the carrots, along with the soaked almonds and the pistachios, and cook over low heat until the halva is completely dry and clumpy, 3 to 5 minutes. Transfer to a serving dish, garnish with the silver leaves and dessert masala, and serve hot.

Plantain Halva
Kaelae ka Halva

Makes 4 to 6 servings

A time-consuming labor of love, my friend Sohini's grandmother made this chewy halva *in large batches over the course of an afternoon. To keep the kids out of her hair, she gave them the job of crushing the cardamom seeds by hand into a fine powder. It kept them busy and introduced them to the kitchen. The following recipe is quick and easy, very much an American adaptation of the original.*

2 large very ripe plantains
2 tablespoons melted ghee
1/2 cup sugar, or to taste
1/2 teaspoon ground green cardamom seeds

1. Peel and, if needed, seed the plantains. In a food processor or a blender, process them until smooth. Transfer to a medium wok or saucepan, add the ghee, and cook, stirring, over moderately high heat, about 5 minutes.

2. Add the sugar and cook until the mixture bubbles vigorously. Reduce heat to medium-low and continue to cook until the halva thickens and pulls away from the sides of the pan, about 30 minutes.

3. Transfer the halva into a lightly greased tray with raised edges and spread to a thickness of 1 inch. Sprinkle the cardamom seeds on top and allow the halva to cool to room temperature. Serve as is, or cut into squares or rectangles.

Milk-Based Puddings (Kheer, Payasam, and Payesh)

With a base of milk and many grains, vegetables, fruits, and nuts defining their character, *kheers, payasams,* and *payeshes* are all names for what is basically the same type of dessert: a soft, creamy pudding. They are found throughout India under different regional names and flavor accents—*kheer* in the north, *payasam* in the south, and *payesh* in the west.

Because these puddings are all made with milk that has been simmered over a long period of time, preparing them requires vigilance and patience. You have to frequently stir and scrape the pan to keep the milk from scalding.

Keep in mind that all *kheers, payasams,* and *payeshes* will thicken as they cool. If your chilled pudding seems too thick, just stir in some boiled milk, garnish once again, and serve.

For best results, use whole milk; lowfat milk can be substituted, but nonfat or skim milk will not. Do not use Silverstone- or Teflon-coated nonstick pans while making any milk-based desserts. The milk will burn, and a thin layer of brown skin will form on the bottom of the pan. As you stir, this skin breaks off and mixes into the milk, ruining the entire dessert.

Punjabi Rice Pudding
Punjabi Chaval ki Kheer

Makes 4 to 6 servings

Even though you can save time by making this kheer *with pre-cooked rice, I strongly believe the best flavors come from the joint simmering of its two main ingredients—milk and basmati rice. For a spectacular visual effect, present this pudding in a silver serving dish and don't skip the garnish of silver leaves.*

1/2 cup Dessert Masala (page 32)
1/2 cup Blanched and Slivered Raw Almonds
    (page 35 or store-bought)
1/4 teaspoon saffron threads
1/2 gallon whole milk
1/2 cup basmati rice, sorted and washed
    in 3 to 4 changes of water
1/2 cup sweetened condensed milk
1/2 teaspoon ground green cardamom seeds
2 drops rose essence
6 (4-inch) silver leaves (optional)

1. Prepare the dessert masala and the almonds. In a small bowl, soak the saffron threads in 1/4 cup milk for about 30 minutes.

2. Place the milk and the rice in a large, heavy wok or saucepan and bring to a boil over high heat. Reduce the heat to medium-low and simmer, stirring and scraping the bottom and the sides of the wok often, until the rice is very soft and the milk is reduced by at least half, about 35 minutes. Stirring and scraping is crucial to prevent the milk from scalding and adding a burned flavor to the pudding.

3. Mix in the almonds, condensed milk, cardamom seeds, and half the dessert masala. Continue to cook, stirring, 5 to 7 minutes. Add the rose essence, saffron and saffron-infused milk, and transfer to a serving dish. Let cool and garnish with the silver leaves and the remaining dessert masala. Refrigerate at least 4 hours and serve chilled.

South Indian Rice Pudding
Paal Payasam

Makes 4 to 6 servings

This south Indian version of rice pudding has far more milk than rice, and is called milk pudding, or paal payasam. Because this dessert is very liquidy, it can even be served as a beverage.

Made on special occasions, especially birthdays (before cake became the standard), payasam is traditionally prepared the day of the event and can be served hot, warm, or at room temperature. Some Indians would consider it improper to serve cold payasam to guests, but I feel even the chilled version is lovely.

1/2 teaspoon saffron threads
1/2 gallon whole milk, plus up to 1 cup more,
    if needed
3 tablespoons long-grain white rice
1/3 cup sugar, or to taste
1/2 teaspoon ground green cardamom seeds

1. In a small bowl, soak the saffron threads in 1/4 cup milk for about 30 minutes.

2. Place the remaining milk in a large, heavy wok or saucepan and bring to a boil over high heat. Reduce the heat to medium-low, add the rice and simmer, stirring and scraping the bottom and sides of the wok often, until the rice is very soft and the milk is reduced by at least half, about 35 minutes. Stirring and scraping is crucial to prevent the milk from scalding and adding a burned flavor to the pudding.

3. Add the sugar, saffron, and saffron-infused milk and continue to simmer, 10 to 12 minutes. If you want a thicker payasam, continue simmering until you reach the desired consistency. For a thinner payasam, add up to a cup of milk to thin it down. Always bring it back to a boil if you add more milk. Transfer to a serving dish, top with cardamom seeds, and serve.

Bengali Rice Pudding
Payesh or Payes

Makes 4 to 6 servings

This Bengali interpretation of rice pudding uses a special Bengali short-grain rice called govindabhog *(meaning food for God; Govind is also the name for Lord Krishna). This rice is hard to come by in America, so you can substitute any commonly available short-grain rice. Try making it with arborio, or Asian short-grain rice.*

1/4 cup short-grain rice, sorted and washed
    in 3 to 4 changes of water
1/2 gallon whole milk
2 bay leaves
1 1/2-inch stick cinnamon
5 to 7 green cardamom pods, crushed lightly
    to break the skin
1/4 cup brown sugar or grated jaggery (gur)
1/2 cup coarsely chopped raw almonds

1. Place the rice, milk, bay leaves, cinnamon, and cardamom pods in a large, heavy wok or saucepan and bring to a boil over high heat. Reduce the heat to medium-low and simmer, stirring and scraping the bottom and sides of the pan often, until the rice is very soft and the milk is reduced by at least half, about 35 minutes. Stirring and scraping is crucial to prevent the milk from scalding and adding a burned flavor to the pudding.

2. Add the brown sugar and almost all the almonds, saving some for garnish, and continue to cook until the pudding is thick and creamy. Transfer to a serving dish, garnish with the reserved almonds, and serve warm or at room temperature.

Parsi Pressed Rice Flakes Pudding
Poha ki Kheer

Makes 4 to 6 servings

This is a very basic kheer *that is quick to make and tastes as delicious warm as it does chilled. If you're serving it warm, stick to the 3 basic ingredients: rice, milk, and sugar. If you serve it as a chilled dessert, dress it with nuts and fragrant spices. Poha are pressed rice flakes, available at Indian markets.*

1 cup pressed rice flakes (poha), sorted
4 cups whole milk
1 to 2 tablespoons sugar, or to taste
2 tablespoons coarsely ground raw cashews
    or almonds
1/4 teaspoon ground green cardamom seeds
1 drop rose essence

1. Place the pressed rice flakes in a fine-mesh strainer and rinse under running water. Set aside to drain until needed.

2. Place the milk in a large, heavy wok or saucepan and bring to a boil over high heat. Reduce the heat to medium-low and simmer, stirring and scraping the sides and bottom of the wok often, until the milk is reduced by about 1/4, 10 to 12 minutes.

3. Add the drained pressed rice and simmer, stirring and scraping the sides of the wok, until the kheer is thick and creamy, 3 to 5 minutes.

4. Add the sugar, nuts, cardamom, and rose essence and cook until the pudding reaches the desired consistency, keeping in mind that it will thicken as it cools. Transfer to a serving dish and serve.

Punjabi Semolina Pudding
Sooji ki Kheer

Makes 4 to 6 servings

This is a quick-cooking kheer, *because the roasted semolina instantly thickens the milk and gives it a smooth consistency almost as soon as it is added. This* kheer *is considered light and easy to digest and is often served in generous portions first thing in the morning.*

As a breakfast, this pudding tends to be served warm and on the thin side; as a dessert, it is generally thick and creamy and always chilled. You do not have to cook it any differently to make it thicker—it will thicken as it chills in the refrigerator.

2 tablespoons Dessert Masala (page 32)
1 tablespoon unsalted butter
1/2 cup fine semolina
2 tablespoons shelled, coarsely chopped raw almonds
4 cups whole milk
1/4 cup sugar, or to taste
1/2 teaspoon ground green cardamom seeds

1. Prepare the dessert masala. Then mix the butter and semolina in a medium heavy wok or saucepan and cook over medium heat until fragrant and a few shades darker, about 5 minutes.

2. Add the almonds and milk and bring to a boil, stirring constantly, over high heat. Reduce the heat to medium-low and simmer until thickened, 3 to 5 minutes. Mix in the sugar, cardamom seeds, and half the dessert masala and cook 1 minute.

3. Transfer to a serving dish, garnish with the remaining dessert masala, and serve hot, or refrigerate at least 4 hours and serve chilled.

Parsi Semolina Pudding

Parsi Ravo Kheer

Makes 4 to 6 servings

Flavored with vanilla extract and dry-roasted or deep-fried nuts and raisins, this creamy pudding, often called white halva, *comes to me from my Parsi sister-in-law, Khushnoor. In her family, this dessert is served on auspicious occasions, like when a member of a family living in America visits home—in other words, me.*

1 tablespoon coarsely chopped almonds, dry-roasted or deep-fried (Dry-Roasting Spices, Nuts, and Flours, page 35)

1 tablespoon cashews, dry-roasted or deep-fried (page 35)

1 tablespoon raisins, dry-roasted or deep-fried (page 35)

4 cups whole milk

¼ cup sugar

2 tablespoons fine semolina

2 tablespoons unsalted butter

4 drops vanilla extract

1. Prepare the almond, cashews, and raisins. Place 3½ cups milk and the sugar in a large, heavy wok or saucepan and bring to a boil, stirring, over high heat. Reduce the heat to medium and simmer, stirring and scraping the bottom and the sides of the wok often, until it is reduced by half, 15 to 20 minutes.

2. In a bowl, mix the semolina and the remaining ½ cup milk, then add to the thickened milk in the wok, stirring constantly to avoid the formation of lumps.

3. Add the butter, 1 teaspoon at a time, stirring constantly until the pudding is thick and creamy, 7 to 10 minutes. Remove from the heat, mix in the vanilla extract, and garnish with the almonds, cashews, and raisins. Serve hot, or refrigerate at least 4 hours and serve chilled.

Tapioca Pudding

Sabudana ki Kheer

Makes 4 to 6 servings

This is another light and easy-to-digest kheer *that makes a delicious breakfast food. Serve chilled as is, or topped with fresh fruit or with puréed berries.*

This is the one kheer *I actually prefer to make in the microwave. Make sure to use a very large bowl—the milk and tapioca need room to bubble up while they cook. The dish can be made on the stove, but be prepared for a lot of clean-up as the combination of tapioca and milk stubbornly sticks to the pot.*

½ cup medium pearl tapioca

1 cup water

4 cups whole milk, plus more as needed

2 tablespoons shelled, coarsely chopped raw pistachios

¾ cup sugar, or to taste

½ teaspoon ground green cardamom seeds

1 to 2 drops rose essence

4 to 6 (4-inch) squares silver leaves (optional)

1 tablespoon ground raw pistachios

1. In a large microwave-safe dish, soak the tapioca in the water, about 2 hours. Then mix in 3 cups milk and cook, uncovered, in the microwave on high power, about 10 minutes. A thin skin will have formed on the surface. Carefully break the skin, being sure to avoid the steam that will escape, and stir well.

2. Stir in the chopped pistachios and the remaining milk, and put the dish back in the microwave. Cook on high power 15 minutes total, stopping to stir at 3-minute intervals, until the pudding is thick and creamy. During the last 3 to 4 minutes, add the sugar. If the pudding becomes too thick, add more milk as needed.

3. Transfer to a serving bowl, mix in the cardamom seeds and rose essence, and bring to room temperature, either uncovered (but stirring often to prevent a skin from forming) or covered with plastic wrap. Garnish with silver leaves and ground pistachios and serve hot, or refrigerate at least 4 hours and serve chilled.

Indian Vermicelli Pudding

Seviyan ki Kheer

Makes 4 to 6 servings

This pudding calls for roasted seviyan vermicelli, which is found only in Indian markets. Seviyan is incredibly delicate and thin—much finer than angel hair pasta—and comes in foot-long lengths, which are broken into smaller pieces before cooking.

1 tablespoon Dessert Masala (page 32)
5 cups whole milk
2 tablespoons golden raisins
**2 tablespoons coarsely chopped blanched
    raw almonds**
2 tablespoons coarsely chopped raw pistachios
1 cup coarsely broken roasted seviyan vermicelli
1/2 cup sugar, or to taste
1/2 teaspoon ground green cardamom seeds

1. Prepare the dessert masala. In a large, heavy wok or saucepan, bring the milk, raisins, almonds, and pistachios to a boil over high heat. Reduce the heat to medium-low and simmer, stirring constantly, 5 to 7 minutes. Add the vermicelli and continue to simmer, stirring and scraping the sides of the wok often until the pudding is thick and creamy, 3 to 5 minutes.

2. Add the sugar and cardamom seeds, and cook until the pudding reaches the consistency you desire, keeping in mind that it will thicken as it cools. Transfer to a serving dish, garnish with the dessert masala, and serve hot, or refrigerate at least 4 hours and serve chilled.

Paneer Cheese Kheer Pudding

Paneer ki Kheer

Makes 4 to 6 servings

This pudding is very similar in flavor to ras-malai (Paneer Cheese Patties in Creamy Thickened Milk, page 645), because it contains all the same ingredients.

The only difference is that the paneer cheese in this dish is broken up and not formed into the traditional mouth-watering patties.

**1 cup Paneer Cheese, coarsely broken (page 43
    or store-bought) or part skim ricotta cheese**
2 tablespoons Dessert Masala (page 32)
1/4 cup sugar, or to taste
1 cup water
4 cups whole milk
1/2 teaspoon coarsely ground green cardamom seeds
2 drops rose essence

1. Prepare the paneer cheese. Prepare the dessert masala. Then, in a food processor process the paneer cheese until finely crumbled. (Do not process too much or it will go beyond crumbling and gather into a ball. If using ricotta cheese, do not process.)

2. Place the sugar and water in a medium wok or saucepan and bring to a boil over high heat. Add the processed paneer cheese (or ricotta cheese), reduce the heat to medium-low, and simmer until most of the water evaporates, 3 to 5 minutes.

3. Add the milk and cook, stirring, over medium-high heat, 2 to 3 minutes. Reduce the heat to medium and cook until the pudding is reduced by about half and is thick and creamy, 30 to 40 minutes.

4. Transfer to a serving dish, mix in the cardamom seeds and rose essence, and let cool to room temperature, about 1 hour. (Stir a few times to prevent a skin from forming on top.) Refrigerate at least 4 hours to serve chilled. Just before serving, swirl in the dessert masala as a garnish.

Almond and Saffron Kheer Pudding

Badaam ki Kheer

Makes 4 to 6 servings

Grainy and pale yellow in color, this delicate kheer is a fragrant ending to a perfect meal. Also, try it with a cup of afternoon tea.

1 tablespoon Dessert Masala (page 32)

2 cups shelled raw almonds

4 cups whole milk

1/3 cup sugar

1/2 teaspoon ground green cardamom seeds

1/4 teaspoon saffron threads

1. Prepare the dessert masala. Soak the almonds overnight in water to cover by 2 inches. Drain and peel the almonds, then transfer to a food processor and process to make a fine paste.

2. Place the milk in a medium wok or saucepan and bring to a boil over high heat. Add the puréed almonds and cook, stirring, over medium heat, 2 to 3 minutes. Reduce the heat to medium-low and cook until the pudding thickens, 20 to 25 minutes.

3. Mix in the sugar, cardamom seeds, and saffron and continue to simmer until the pudding is the consistency you desire, 10 to 20 minutes. Add more milk if the pudding is too thick. Transfer to a serving dish and garnish with dessert masala. Refrigerate at least 4 hours and serve chilled.

Yellow Split Chickpea Pudding

Channa Dal Payasam

Makes 4 to 6 servings

This payasam *is made with yellow split chickpeas (*channa dal*) and coconut milk. Thanks to the nutritional content of the* dal, *this pudding is considered an appropriate way to break a religious fast. Its smoky-sweet taste comes from the jaggery and is so good, it has to be tasted to be believed.*

1/4 cup Coconut Milk (page 44 or store-bought)

3 tablespoons dried yellow split chickpeas (channa dal), sorted and washed in 3 to 4 changes of water

2 tablespoons coarsely chopped raw cashews

1 tablespoon coarsely chopped golden raisins

1/4 cup water

3 cups whole milk

1/4 cup ground jaggery (gur) or dark brown sugar

1/2 teaspoon ground green cardamom seeds

1. Prepare the coconut milk. Then, in a bowl, soak the dal in water to cover by 2 inches, 3 to 4 hours. In a large, heavy wok or saucepan, dry-roast the cashews and raisins over medium heat until golden.

2. Add the dal and the water and bring to a boil over high heat. Reduce the heat to medium-low, cover the pan, and simmer until the dal is soft and the water has evaporated, about 5 minutes.

3. Add the milk and cook, stirring, over medium-high heat until reduced by 2/3, 25 to 30 minutes. Add the coconut milk and jaggery and cook, stirring, until the pudding is thick and creamy, 5 to 7 minutes. Transfer to a serving dish, sprinkle with the cardamom seeds, and serve warm, or refrigerate at least 4 hours and serve chilled.

Traditional Bread Pudding Bites

Shahi Tukri

Makes 24 pieces

Shahi tukri, *the Indian name for this dessert, translates literally as "royal pieces"—the royalty in this case coming from the calorie-rich, creamy interior of each bite-sized morsel. Its richness is the reason why* shahi tukri *is served in small pieces.*

Shahi tukri *is not a true pudding, but I'm calling it one because it has the feel of a pudding due to the addition of* rabdi *(creamy, sweet, thickened milk).*

1/2 cup Dessert Masala (page 32)

1 quart half-and-half

1 teaspoon coarsely ground green cardamom seeds

1 cup sugar, or to taste

2 drops rose essence

2 to 3 cups peanut oil for deep-frying

18 slices thin white sandwich bread, crusts removed, cut into 4 squares

1. Prepare the dessert masala. Then, in a large, heavy wok or saucepan, bring the half-and-half to a boil over medium-high heat. Reduce the heat to medium and simmer, stirring and scraping the sides of the wok often, until the milk is reduced by about half,

25 to 35 minutes. Mix in the cardamom seeds, sugar, rose essence, and all but 1 tablespoon of the dessert masala, and remove from heat.

2. Heat the oil in a large wok over medium-high heat until it reaches 325°F to 350°F on a frying thermometer or until a piece of bread dropped into the hot oil rises to the top after 15 to 20 seconds. Add as many bread squares as the wok can hold at one time without crowding, and fry until golden. (This will happen almost instantly.) Transfer to paper towels to drain.

3. In a large flat-bottomed serving dish, arrange 24 of the fried bread pieces side by side in a single layer. Spoon a little of the thickened half-and-half mixture over each piece. Top each with another piece of fried bread and spoon some half-and-half over once again. Repeat one more time, using up all the bread pieces and the half-and-half mixture, making a total of 3 layers. (The pudding may seem a little watery at first, but the bread with absorb all the sauce as it cools.)

4. Garnish with the reserved dessert masala, cover with plastic wrap or the lid of the dish, and refrigerate at least 4 hours until chilled. Serve straight from the dish, or remove the pieces, keeping the stacks intact, and arrange them on another platter.

French Roll Bread Pudding
Lambi Dubble-Roti kae Shahi Tukrae

Makes 4 to 6 servings

A specialty of my sister-in-law, Reita, this variation of Traditional Bread Pudding Bites (page 627) uses crusty, long, thin French bread instead of regular white bread. The chewy tukris (pieces), piled one on top of the other, create a lovely presentation and taste divine.

Deep-fried and soaked in a fragrant condensed milk syrup, this recipe is what I call a calorie grenade.

1/4 **cup Dessert Masala (page 32)**
1 **(12-ounce) can evaporated milk**
1 **(14-ounce) can sweetened condensed milk**
1/2 **teaspoon ground green cardamom seeds**
2 **to 3 cups peanut oil for deep-frying**
1 **pound long French bread or rolls, cut into
    2-by-1-inch pieces**
1 **cup water**
1 **cup sugar**
4 **to 6 (4-inch) silver leaves**

1. Prepare the dessert masala. Place the evaporated milk in a large microwave-safe bowl and cook on high power 4 minutes, to reduce the milk by about a third. Mix in the condensed milk and cook another 4 minutes on high power. Remove from the microwave and mix in the cardamom seeds.

2. Heat the oil in a large wok over medium-high heat until it reaches 325°F to 350°F on a frying thermometer, or until a piece of bread dropped into the hot oil rises to the top after 15 to 20 seconds. Add the bread pieces, in 2 or 3 batches, and fry, turning each piece until crisp and golden, about 1 minute per batch. Transfer to paper towels to drain.

3. Combine the water and sugar in a small saucepan and boil over high heat, 2 to 3 minutes. Keep the pan on low heat and, using tongs, dip each fried piece of bread in the sugar syrup and transfer to a serving platter. Arrange all the pieces in an overlapping manner, making a mound or a plateau.

4. Pour the thickened milk mixture evenly over the mound in a thin stream, making sure all the pieces are covered. Garnish with silver leaves and dessert masala. Cover with plastic wrap, refrigerate at least 4 hours, and serve chilled.

Traditional Thickened Milk Pudding
Rabdi

Makes 4 to 6 servings

True rabdi is simply milk that has been brought to a boil and then simmered until most of the water evaporates, and it is thick and creamy. Mixed with sugar, nuts such as almonds and pistachios, and flavorings, rabdi is a dessert in itself. It is also used to make other Indian desserts. Rabdi is incredible when served as a sauce over grilled, stewed, or poached fruits—try it with pineapples, apples, pears, mangoes, peaches, and nectarines. When frozen, it transforms into Kulfi *(Indian ice cream, page 634).*

1/2 gallon whole milk
1/4 cup sugar, or to taste
1/2 teaspoon ground green cardamom seeds
2 to 3 tablespoons coarsely chopped raw pistachios

1. Place the milk in a large, heavy wok or skillet and bring to a boil over high heat. Continue to boil, stirring, 2 to 3 minutes. Reduce the heat to medium-low and simmer, stirring and scraping the bottom and sides of the wok often, until the milk is reduced by at least 3/4, about 45 minutes. You should be left with about 2 cups of thickened milk. (It should have a few lumps.)

2. Mix in the sugar and cardamom seeds and cook, stirring, until the sugar melts and thins down the pudding, and then until the pudding thickens again, 5 to 7 minutes. Transfer to a serving dish and garnish with the pistachios. Refrigerate at least 4 hours and serve.

Microwave Milk Pudding
Microwave mein bani Rabdi

Makes 4 to 6 servings

Ever since I discovered the microwave oven, making rabdi has become very easy. You still have to watch carefully and stir, but much less frequently, and there is much less clean-up required.

My modified rabdi still reflects the authentic grainy texture that results when raw milk is used, as it is in India. (Raw milk develops a characteristic light grain as moisture evaporates and the milk thickens.) Here in America, with the widespread use of homogenized milk, I include some ricotta cheese, which adds a grain—or daana *as it is called in Hindi.*

1/4 cup Dessert Masala (page 32) + more for garnish
1/2 gallon whole milk
1 cup part skim ricotta cheese
1/3 cup sugar, or to taste
1/2 teaspoon ground green cardamom seeds
1 drop rose essence

1. Prepare the dessert masala. Place the milk and ricotta cheese in a large microwave-safe bowl and, with an electric mixer or whisk, mix well. Place in the microwave and cook on high power 30 to 45 minutes, stopping first after 15 minutes, and then every 5 to 7 minutes, to stir, scrape the sides of the bowl, and mix everything together. Do this until you are left with about 2 cups of liquid. Every time you stop to stir, a thin skin will have formed on the surface; break it, but carefully, to avoid giving yourself a steam burn.

2. Mix in the sugar, cardamom seeds, and dessert masala, then cook in the microwave on high another 5 minutes.

3. Transfer to a serving dish, let cool, then mix in the rose essence. Garnish with the dessert masala and refrigerate at least 4 hours until chilled. Serve cold.

Creamy Milk Pudding with Almonds and Saffron
Kesari Rabdi

Makes 4 to 6 servings

This dish, called kesari rabdi, *cooks faster than milk rabdi because you start with half-and-half, which is much thicker than milk to begin with. The higher fat content, though worrisome for some in today's health-conscious world, contributes tremendously and imparts a richer flavor.*

About Rabdi (Basundi) and Khoa (Khoya)

Rabdi (*basundi*) and *khoa* (*khoya* and *mawa*), are both made from milk that has been slowly reduced over low heat, but each one is different. *Rabdi* is milk that is simmered and simmered until most of the liquid evaporates, leaving behind a thick, creamy, and somewhat lumpy residue. *Khoa,* on the other hand, takes *rabdi* a step further, cooking it longer and transforming it into a dense ball of milk solids from which all moisture has evaporated.

Sweetened and enhanced with traditional Indian flavors, such as nuts, saffron, rosewater, and cardamom, *rabdi* is sometimes served just by itself as a dessert, as in Traditional Thickened Milk Pudding (page 629), though more often it forms the base of other desserts, such as *ras-malai* (Paneer Cheese Patties in Creamy Thickened Milk, page 645), *kulfi* (Indian Ice Cream page 634), *mal-pudhas* (Creamy Semolina Pancakes with Thickened Milk, page 650), and others. And, it is often served as a

dessert topping—for *gulaab-jamuns* (Traditional Dark Brown Milk Rolls in Saffron Syrup, page 648), and other desserts. *Khoa,* on the other hand, is used as a base for *burfees* (milk fudge pieces), is added to *halvas,* and occasionally, curries, to which it contributes a creamy richness.

Unfortunately, buffalo milk, from which *khoa* is traditionally made, is not readily available in the United States. *Khoa* made from homogenized and pasteurized milk, or even raw cow's milk, is simply not the same. So, I've created various ways to bring about a more authentic consistency to *khoa* in my American kitchen, with the addition of ricotta cheese, dry milk powder, and whipping cream (see Decadent Carrot Halva with Evaporated Milk and Jaggery, Step 3 (page 621). Easily found in grocery stores, these substitute dairy products lend a texture and richness associated with buffalo milk *khoa.*

$^{1}/_{2}$ cup shelled raw almonds
$^{1}/_{3}$ teaspoon saffron threads
$^{1}/_{4}$ cup whole milk
1 quart half-and-half
$^{1}/_{4}$ cup sugar, or to taste
$^{1}/_{4}$ teaspoon ground green cardamom seeds
1 to 2 drops rose essence

1. In a bowl, soak the almonds in water to cover by 2 inches. Drain and peel the almonds and, in a blender or a food processor, coarsely grind them.

Meanwhile, in another bowl, soak the saffron threads in the milk about 30 minutes.

2. Place the half-and-half in a large microwave-safe bowl and cook on high power 25 to 30 minutes, stopping to stir after the first 10 minutes, then every 5 minutes, until the half-and-half is reduced by at least half. Every time you stop to stir, a thin skin will have formed on the surface; break it, but carefully, to avoid giving yourself a steam burn.

3. Mix in the sugar, ground almonds, and saffron-infused milk (reserving the saffron threads for garnish) and cook on high power another 3 to 5 minutes.

4. Transfer to a serving bowl, mix in the cardamom seeds and rose essence, and cool to room temperature, stirring occasionally while it cools. Refrigerate at least 4 hours and serve chilled. If the pudding is thicker than you wish, add more half-and-half or milk until you get the consistency you desire. Scatter the reserved saffron threads as a garnish and serve.

Variation: To give this rabdi another authentic touch, mix in 1 cup part-skim ricotta cheese after the first 10 minutes. Adjust the sugar before serving.

Creamy Milk Pudding with Summer Fruits
Phallon vaali Rabdi

Makes 4 to 6 servings

Make this dessert with a mixture of fruits, as in this recipe, or only with mangoes, as they do in India, where mangoes are in abundance and are beloved. To add more interest to the pudding, grill 1- to 1½-inch chunks or slices of ripe mangoes, ripe peaches, nectarines, or pineapples until golden and lightly caramelized, then cool and mix into the rabdi (thickened milk pudding).

2 tablespoons Dessert Masala (page 32)
2 cups (1 recipe) Creamy Milk Pudding with Almonds and Saffron (page 629)
2 large ripe mangoes
2 large ripe peaches or nectarines, cut into ³/₄-inch pieces
1 cup mixed berries, such as blueberries, blackberries, raspberries, and boysenberries

Prepare the dessert masala. Then prepare the milk pudding. With a vegetable peeler, peel the mangoes and cut the fruit around the center seed into ¾-inch pieces. Place in a serving bowl and mix in all the remaining fruit. Add the pudding and mix well. Sprinkle the dessert masala on top and serve.

Custards and Mousses

Indians make a kind of dessert that is similar to what Americans think of as a custard or mousse. But, unlike Western custards, which use eggs and gelatin as thickening agents, Indian custards are made with whole grains and milk or yogurt (the exception being caramel custard, which comes from the Anglo-Indian tradition).

It goes without saying that a very different set of flavors and garnishes are to be expected in Indian custards and mousses, as well—in particular cardamom, saffron, and rose water along with pistachios, cashews, and almonds. And don't forget the most important, tell-tale Indian ingredient: *verk,* or pure silver leaves.

Basmati Rice Custard
Chaval ki Firni

Makes 4 to 6 servings

The White House served this classic custard from north India when then Prime Minister Rajiv and his wife, Sonia Gandhi, visited the United States in the 1980s. The custard is made with basmati *rice, as opposed to eggs, and is traditionally presented in huge terra cotta bowls, or as individual servings in small terra cotta cups, garnished lavishly with silver leaves, colorful nuts, and saffron. A well-made* firni *will bring exotic flavors to any table.*

1 cup basmati rice, sorted and washed in 3 to 4 changes of water
1¹/₄ cups + ¹/₂ gallon whole milk
¹/₃ teaspoon saffron threads
2 tablespoons Dessert Masala (page 32)
³/₄ cup sugar
¹/₂ teaspoon ground green cardamom seeds
2 drops rose essence
4 to 6 (4-inch) squares silver leaves (optional)

1. Soak the rice overnight in water to cover by 2 inches. Drain and place in a blender (not a food processor) along with 1 cup milk and blend, about 1 minute. The mixture will still appear grainy. Reserve. In a small bowl, soak the saffron threads in ¼ cup milk about 30 minutes. Meanwhile, prepare the dessert masala.

2. Place ½ gallon milk in a large, heavy wok or saucepan and bring to a boil over high heat. Reduce the heat to medium and simmer, stirring and scraping the bottom and sides of the wok often, until the milk has slightly thickened, 5 to 7 minutes.

3. Add the blended rice to the simmering milk in a slow, steady stream, stirring constantly to prevent the formation of lumps. (If any lumps develop, let cool and mix again in the blender until smooth. Then return everything to the pan.) Increase the heat to medium-high and cook, stirring and scraping the bottom and sides of the wok constantly, until the custard is thick and creamy, about 5 minutes.

4. Add the sugar and cardamom seeds, reduce the heat to low, and cook another 5 minutes to blend the flavors. Remove from the heat, add the rose essence, and bring to room temperature, either uncovered (stir often to prevent a skin from forming) or covered with plastic wrap. Transfer to a serving dish and garnish with silver leaves and dessert masala. Sprinkle with the saffron threads and pour the saffron-infused milk over the top. Refrigerate at least 4 hours and serve chilled.

Corn Custard
Makki ki Firni

Makes 4 to 6 servings

My guests are always surprised to find humble corn kernels at the base of a custard dessert. It is an age-old Indian way of eating corn, and the cooking method extracts the corn essence out of each kernel. The resulting custard is very delicate, smooth and creamy, but with just enough texture to give character to each mouthful.

¹/₄ cup Dessert Masala (page 32)
1¹/₂ cups fresh or thawed frozen corn kernels
2 cups whole milk
¹/₂ cup condensed milk
¹/₂ teaspoon ground green cardamom seeds

1. Prepare the dessert masala. Then place the corn kernels and 1 cup milk in a blender or a food processor and process until the mixture is as smooth as possible, about 1 minute.

2. Transfer to a bowl and mix in the remaining 1 cup milk. Pass the mixture through a food mill or a fine-mesh strainer lined with muslin (not cheesecloth, because its weave is too loose). Squeeze out all the juices, then discard whatever remains in the muslin.

3. Transfer to a large, heavy wok or saucepan and bring to a boil over high heat. Reduce the heat to medium and simmer, stirring and scraping the bottom and sides of the wok often, until slightly thickened, 5 to 7 minutes. Mix in the condensed milk and cardamom seeds and continue to cook, stirring, until thick and creamy, 7 to 10 minutes.

4. Transfer to a serving bowl and mix in most of the dessert masala, reserving some for garnish. Serve warm, or refrigerate at least 4 hours, sprinkle the reserved dessert masala on top, and serve chilled.

Pressure-Cooked Caramel Custard
Andae Ki Firni

Makes 4 to 6 servings

A holdover from the Raj and not really an authentic Indian dessert, I'm including this recipe because the subcontinent has taken it to heart. Instead of baking in the traditional water bath, the custard is made in a pressure cooker—a process that takes less time and yields great results. Use pure vanilla extract (not imitation vanilla) for best flavor.

3¹/₂ cups whole milk
5 large eggs, lightly beaten
³/₄ cup sugar
1 teaspoon pure vanilla extract

1. In a large, heavy saucepan, bring the milk to a boil over medium-high heat. Transfer to a bowl and cool, stirring once in awhile to prevent a skin from forming on the surface, about 10 minutes. Mix in the beaten eggs, ½ cup sugar, and the vanilla.

2. Place the remaining ¼ cup sugar in a flat-bottomed pan with no handles and a metal lid; be sure to choose a pan that will fit comfortably inside your pressure cooker. Heat the sugar over low heat, stirring constantly, until the sugar melts and turns golden brown, about 1 minute. Using oven mitts to hold the pan, rotate and swirl it so the caramelized sugar spreads to cover the base of the pan, and allow the sugar to cool until hardened. Or, to speed the hardening, immediately dip the bottom of the pan in a bowl of cold water. This may cause some cracking, but the caramelized sugar will be fine.

3. Pour the prepared milk and egg mixture over the hardened sugar and cover the pan, first with aluminum foil and then with the pan's lid.

4. Pour 2 to 3 cups of water into the pressure cooker, then place the custard pan inside it. (The water should be about ⅓ of the way up the sides of the pan.) Secure the lid of the pressure cooker and cook over high heat until the regulator indicates high pressure, then cook about 40 seconds more. Remove from the heat and allow the pan to depressurize on its own, 12 to 15 minutes. Carefully open the lid of the pressure cooker and remove the custard pan. (If it seems too hot to remove, leave it inside until it is cool enough to handle.) Cool to room temperature, then refrigerate at least 4 hours until chilled.

5. To serve, run a sharp (not serrated) knife around the sides of the pan to loosen the custard. Then place a round serving dish over the top of the pan, and, holding the sides of plate and pan together, invert the custard onto the dish.

Caramelized Yogurt
Mishti-Dhoi

Makes 4 to 6 servings

A Bengali specialty, mishti-dhoi, *or sweetened yogurt, is traditionally made in small terra cotta pots called* matkas. *A* halvai *(professional sweet maker) named K.C. Das, who set up shop in the southern city of Bangalore, made his name and fortune solely on this delicacy.*

3 cups whole milk
⅔ cup sugar, or to taste
¼ cup water
3 tablespoons nonfat plain yogurt,
     whisked until smooth
1 large thick kitchen towel

1. In a heavy, medium wok or saucepan, bring the milk and ⅓ cup sugar to a boil over high heat. Lower the heat to medium and simmer, stirring and scraping the bottom and sides of the wok constantly, until reduced by about a third, 4 to 6 minutes.

2. Meanwhile, in a small nonstick saucepan, add the remaining sugar and cook, stirring, over medium heat until it melts and then caramelizes to a dark brown, 1 to 2 minutes. Quickly, before the caramel burns, add the water and stir until the sugar dissolves in the water, making a brown syrup, 30 seconds.

3. Add the caramel syrup to the pan with the milk and simmer about 5 minutes. Transfer to a bowl and allow the mixture to cool until it registers 118°F to 120°F on a meat thermometer. Mix in the yogurt, and cover the bowl with a loose-fitting lid. Then, fold the kitchen towel in half, wrap it snugly around the milk bowl, and place in a warm, draft-free place (such as the oven or a kitchen cabinet) until firm, 4 to 6 hours. Refrigerate at least 4 hours until chilled, and serve.

Yogurt Mousse with Saffron
Kesari Shrikhand

Makes 4 to 6 servings

A specialty of the Mumbai (Bombay) area, this lowfat dessert, often made by my friend Falguni Jalota (originally from Bombay now living in Los Angeles), can be even more healthy if you start with nonfat yogurt. Unlike ordinary yogurt, shrikhand *is thick and creamy, drained of all whey, until it takes on a mousse-like texture. This traditional and much revered velvety dessert is fragrant and sweet, and is often served in individual terra cotta cups or in a bowl mixed with fresh fruits, such as mangoes, peaches, and pineapples.*

4 cups plain yogurt (any kind), whisked until smooth
½ cup confectioners' sugar
¼ teaspoon saffron threads, ground
¼ teaspoon ground green cardamom seeds
2 to 3 drops rose essence
¼ cup coarsely ground raw pistachios

1. Put the yogurt in a colander lined with 3 layers of cheesecloth, set within another bowl. Refrigerator

overnight to allow the whey to drain from the yogurt. It should be reduced by half. Discard the whey.

2. Transfer the drained yogurt to a serving bowl, and add the sugar, saffron, cardamom, and rose essence. With an electric mixer, whip the yogurt until well mixed, about 1 minute. Add half the pistachios and, using a spoon, mix well. Refrigerate at least 1 hour to allow the saffron to release its color and fragrance. Garnish with the remaining pistachios and serve.

Fresh Fruit in Rose-Flavored Cream
Malai-Phal

Makes 4 to 6 servings

Perfumed with a drop of rose essence, which can be purchased from Indian and Middle-Eastern markets, and garnished with a dusting of ground pistachios, I love my lowfat version of this popular Indian dessert. It is especially good when made with soft summer fruits that literally melt in your mouth. Use apples, Asian pears, or grapes if you prefer a crunch.

2 cups fat-free non-dairy whipped topping, such as Cool Whip
1 tablespoon sugar, or to taste
1 drop rose essence
1 drop red food coloring
4 cups mixed fruit, such as bananas, mangoes, orange or tangerine segments, peaches, and nectarines, cut into 1/2- to 1-inch pieces
2 tablespoons coarsely ground raw pistachios

In a serving bowl, mix together the non-dairy whipped topping, sugar, and rose essence. Lightly fold in the fruit, leaving some visible for a garnish. Sprinkle the pistachios on top and serve.

Variation: For a more authentic version, substitute 1 pint heavy whipping cream for the non-dairy whipped topping. Using an electric mixer, whip the cream until fluffy, then proceed with the recipe.

Indian Ice Creams (Kulfi)

Kulfi is Indian ice cream, and although Indians eat Western ice cream with pleasure, it is *kulfi* that is most beloved. Made with thickened whole milk and, often, cream, it is perfumed with traditional Indian dessert flavors such as cardamom, rosewater, saffron, and screw-pine essence (*ruh-kewra*). *Kulfi* is frozen in conical metal molds (available in Indian markets), traditionally served topped with soft noodles soaked in a fragrant sugar syrup, called *falooda* noodles (page 636).

A well-made *kulfi* is a little denser than Western ice cream, always smooth and creamy, and has no ice particles. To achieve this consistency, some people add cornstarch or fresh bread crumbs to the milk while it is being simmered. But authentic *kulfi* is made as it was by my grandmother—without short-cuts, as a leisurely afternoon project where the milk was thickened over low heat and the *kulfi* was ready only when my grandmother said so.

Here, I've included an instant, no-cook *kulfi* recipe along with the traditional one. And if true *kulfi* molds are hard to find, simply freeze the thickened milk in small disposable plastic cups—a blessing when it comes to clean-up, especially after large gatherings. *Kulfi* can also be frozen in ice cube trays or in cake pans.

Quick and Easy Indian Ice Cream
Jaldi bani Kulfi

Makes 4 to 6 servings

At the base of all kulfi *ice cream is a* rabdi *(creamy, sweet thickened milk). Once you have that, the rest is up to your imagination. However, there are a few additions and flavors that make a more traditional* kulfi*—green cardamom, almonds, and pistachios being the favorites.*

Because making the authentic recipe (starting with Traditional Thickened Milk Pudding) is a time-intensive project, here is quick and easy alternative.

1/4 cup Dessert Masala (page 32)

1 (12-ounce) can evaporated milk

1 (14-ounce) can sweetened condensed milk

3/4 cup fat-free non-dairy whipped topping, such as Cool Whip

1/2 teaspoon ground green cardamom seeds

2 drops rose essence

A few sprigs fresh mint

1. Prepare the dessert masala, then place all the ingredients (except the mint) in a large bowl and whip with either a fork, a whisk, or an electric mixer until smooth.

2. Transfer to traditional kulfi molds or disposable 5½-ounce plastic soufflé cups. Cover and place in the freezer until completely frozen, at least 4 hours.

3. To serve, dip each mold in hot water about 10 seconds, run a knife around the inside of the mold and transfer immediately to a dessert plate. Serve whole or cut into smaller pieces, with mint sprigs on the side, and serve.

Flavored Indian Ice Creams
Kisum-Kisum ki Kulfi

Makes 4 to 6 servings

To make flavored kulfi, *start with the recipe for Traditional Thickened Milk Pudding (page 629) which is more time-consuming but more authentic, or use the recipe for Quick and Easy Indian Ice Cream (page 634) to make an easier and equally tasty version. Then choose any of the following flavors. Freeze as directed in Quick and Easy Indian Ice Cream.*

Indian Ice Cream with Pistachios
Pista Kulfi

Makes 4 to 6 servings

This green-tinted kulfi *is one of the most popular. The ground pistachios add to the overall taste and the chopped ones, a delicate punch.*

2 cups (1 recipe) Traditional Thickened Milk Pudding (page 629) or Quick and Easy Indian Ice Cream (page 634)

1/4 cup blanched pistachios, coarsely chopped (page 35) + 1/4 cup ground

1 to 2 drops green food coloring

Prepare the pudding or the ice cream. Prepare the pistachios. Then, mix everything together and freeze and serve as directed in Quick and Easy Indian Ice Cream (page 634).

Indian Ice Cream with Saffron
Kesari Kulfi

Makes 4 to 6 servings

With the delicate strands of saffron lending their luxurious fragrance and color to this kulfi, *it's no wonder that it is reserved for special occasions.*

2 cups (1 recipe) Traditional Thickened Milk Pudding (page 629) or Quick and Easy Indian Ice Cream (page 634)

1/2 teaspoon saffron threads

2 tablespoons heavy cream or milk

1 drop orange food coloring

Prepare the pudding or the ice cream. In a small bowl, soak the saffron threads in the cream (or milk) about 30 minutes. Then, mix everything together and freeze and serve as directed in Quick and Easy Indian Ice Cream (page 634).

Indian Ice Cream with Almonds
Badaam Kulfi

Makes 4 to 6 servings

Although studded with raw almonds, this kulfi *is white in color, because before they are added, the almonds are soaked and peeled.*

1/2 cup raw shelled almonds

2 cups (1 recipe) Traditional Thickened Milk Pudding (page 629) or Quick and Easy Indian Ice Cream (page 634)

1. Soak the almonds overnight in water to cover, then peel and grind half of them, and coarsely chop the other half.

2. Prepare the pudding or the ice cream. Then, mix in the almonds and the almond essence and freeze as directed in Quick and Easy Indian Ice Cream (page 634).

Indian Ice Cream with Mangoes
Aam ki Kulfi

Makes 4 to 6 servings

If any fruit is associated with India, it is mangoes— so it's no wonder then that we see mangoes in all types of desserts, including this one. (A similar kulfi *can be made using other fruits, especially puréed berries.)*

2 cups (1 recipe) Traditional Thickened Milk Pudding (page 629) or Quick and Easy Indian Ice Cream (page 634)
1/4 cup heavy cream or milk
1 teaspoon cornstarch
1 cup canned mango pulp

1. Prepare the pudding or the ice cream. In a small saucepan, stir together the milk and cornstarch, then add the mango pulp and mix well. Cook, stirring over medium heat until creamy and smooth, about 3 minutes. Let cool.

2. Then, mix everything together and freeze and serve as directed in Quick and Easy Indian Ice Cream (page 634).

Cellophane Noodles in Cardamom-Saffron Syrup
Falooda

Makes 4 to 6 servings

Falooda *noodles, made from arrowroot or cornstarch, are unique to India. They are created by passing a paste-like batter through a cylindrical, hand-held vermicelli press, called a* sev-machine. *As the batter passes through the perforated disc of the press, it falls directly into icy cold water and immediately firms up to become thin, transparent noodles. Serve these noodles over any* kulfi *of your choice, or mix some into* rabdi *(creamy sweet thickened milk).*

Falooda *noodles can be bought at Indian confectioneries (or sweet shops as they are popularly called) in all major cities in America. Failing that, you can purchase dried cellophane or rice noodles from Asian and most well-stocked American markets and soften them in water following the package directions.*

1/2 cup arrowroot powder or cornstarch
2 1/2 cups water
1/2 cup sugar
5 to 6 cups ice cold water
2 to 3 drops screw-pine essence (ruh-kewra), or rose essence
1/2 teaspoon ground green cardamom seeds
1/4 teaspoon saffron threads

1. In a small saucepan, mix together the arrowroot (or cornstarch) and 2 cups water, and cook over medium heat, stirring constantly, about 15 minutes. As it cooks, the mixture will bubble lightly and thicken considerably, then thin down and take on a gelatinous, translucent blue appearance. Remove from the heat.

2. Fill a large bowl with ice cold water. Pour the batter into the vermicelli press, fitted with a perforated disc with holes of about 0.1 inches. Working about 12 inches directly above the bowl of water, turn the handle of the vermicelli press. The batter will pass through the holes and the long noodles will firm up when they come in contact with the water. Keep turning the press until all the batter is used. Drain the noodles and transfer to a serving bowl.

3. In a small saucepan, mix the remaining 1/2 cup water and the sugar and cook over high heat until thick, about 3 minutes. Cool and add to the noodles. Mix in the screw-pine or rose essence, cardamom seeds, and saffron threads and refrigerate at least 1 hour to blend the flavors.

Indian Ice Cream Desserts

Ice cream is very popular in India, especially in the summer months, when the ice cream vendors dominate the dessert business. Indians like their ice cream spiced with nuts and Indian flavorings, fruit-flavored, with fruit on the side, or simply plain. Here are some Indian classics.

Mango Ice Cream Dessert
Aam ki Baraf Malai

Makes 4 to 6 servings

Summertime in India would be unbearable were it not for the mangoes and the various cooling desserts that are made with them. Here is an easy-to-make yet luxuriously satisfying dessert using store-bought vanilla ice cream. Of course, if you've made your own kulfi (Indian ice cream), using it here will create an extra-special dessert.

Select a ripe mango that has a sweet and fragrant aroma, without any hint of sourness, and gives under the light pressure of your fingers when held in your hand. I add canned mango pulp to this dessert because most of the mango varieties found in this country are not as fragrant and flavorful as those in India, and the canned pulp enhances that flavor. If your mangoes are sweetly fragrant, purée the pulp from one in a food processor and use it in place of the canned pulp.

1 large ripe mango
1 cup canned mango pulp
1 to 2 drops mango essence
1 pint vanilla ice cream

1. With a vegetable peeler, peel the mango, then cut the fruit around the center seed into ½-inch pieces. Then, in a medium bowl, mix together the mango pieces, the canned mango pulp, and the mango essence, and chill at least 1 hour.

2. To serve, place rounded scoops of ice cream in a serving platter and top with the prepared mango mixture.

Variation: Mix 1 cup canned mango pulp into 1 pint softened vanilla ice cream and freeze. Peel and cut 2 large mangoes into 1-inch pieces and serve alongside the ice cream.

Lychee Ice Cream Dessert
Leechi ki Baraf Malai

Makes 4 to 6 servings

Shaped like strawberries, but with a bumpy red shell (which can be removed by hand), juicy white pulp, and a large brown center seed, lychees, though Chinese in origin, are also very popular in India. The sweet, delicious fresh lychees are hard to come by in America, so I use canned ones, which are readily available in Asian and Indian markets.

This dish is easy to make, but prepare it in advance to allow the cooked lychees to chill and then the ice cream to freeze.

1 (20-ounce) can lychees, drained
1 teaspoon cornstarch
1 pint vanilla ice cream, softened

1. Finely chop 4 to 5 of the lychees and set aside. In a food processor or a blender, process the remaining lychees to make a smooth purée. Mix in the cornstarch and process once again to combine.

2. Transfer the lychee purée to a medium nonstick saucepan and bring to a boil over high heat. Remove from the heat, let cool, then chill in the refrigerator at least 1 hour.

3. In a food processor or a blender, blend together the chilled lychees and the softened vanilla ice cream, then transfer to an airtight container and freeze, about 2 hours. To serve, place rounded scoops of the ice cream in a serving platter and top with the chopped lychees.

Variation: Purée half the lychees and finely chop the remaining half. Mix together and serve over scoops of store-bought vanilla ice cream.

Pistachio and Cardamom Ice Cream Dessert

Pista Illaichi ki Baraf Malai

Makes 4 to 6 servings

Pistachios and cardamom—two popular flavors in Indian desserts—add fragrant and colorful interest to simple vanilla ice cream to make a dessert that can be put together on the spur of the moment, or when you are running short of time.

This dessert also works well with fruit-flavored ice cream or frozen yogurt, such as strawberry, raspberry, or banana.

1/2 cup shelled raw pistachios
1 pint vanilla ice cream, softened
2 drops green food coloring
1/2 teaspoon ground green cardamom seeds

1. In a food processor or a blender, process the pistachios until coarsely ground. Reserve 2 to 3 tablespoons for garnish, and leave the rest in the work bowl. Then add the ice cream, green food coloring, and cardamom seeds to the food processor and pulse a few times to mix. Transfer to an air-tight container and freeze, about 2 hours.

2. To serve, place rounded scoops of ice cream in a serving platter and top with the reserved pistachios.

Variation: Put scoops of vanilla ice cream on a platter. Mix 2 drops of green food color in 1 tablespoon milk and sprinkle it over the ice cream. Top with the chopped pistachios and ground cardamom seeds.

Saffron and Almond Ice Cream Dessert

Kesar Badaam ki Baraf Malai

Makes 4 to 6 servings

This is another popular Indian dessert flavor combination that tastes great over vanilla ice cream. The saffron lends a delicate flavor and color.

1/4 teaspoon saffron threads
2 tablespoons heavy cream or whole milk
1/4 cup sliced raw almonds
1/4 cup shelled blanched raw almonds
2 tablespoons shelled raw pistachios
1/2 teaspoon ground green cardamom seeds
1 pint vanilla ice cream

1. In a small bowl, soak the saffron threads in the cream (or milk) about 30 minutes. Meanwhile, in a small nonstick skillet, dry-roast the sliced almonds, stirring, over medium heat until golden, about 1 minute. Let cool and reserve for garnish.

2. In a spice or coffee grinder, grind together the blanched almonds, pistachios, and ground cardamom seeds to make as fine as possible. (Or grind each separately, then mix together well.) Place rounded scoops of vanilla ice cream on a platter, top with the ground nut and seed mixture, and drizzle with the saffron milk. Scatter the dry-roasted almonds on top, and serve.

Milk Fudge (Burfee)

Burfee are bite-sized, rich confections, served as a dessert after a meal or as a tea-time snack along with *samosas* (deep-fried triangular pastries) and *pakoras* (chickpea fritters). Think of them as you do fudge in America.

Burfee is made with thickened milk and flavored with spices, nuts, and sweet vegetables. Even though the term *burfee* is a catch-all for a variety of *burfee* fudges, there are many distinct recipes, each different in flavor and technique. Types of *burfee* range from dense and chewy to light and crumbly, and are ubiquitous in Indian sweet shops. Naturally, the homemade versions tend to be simpler and not so brightly colored.

You can serve the *burfees* on a platter or cut large pieces and serve them in a pool of puréed fresh fruits.

Basic White Milk Fudge
Saadi Burfee

Makes 30 to 40 pieces

This is at the base of a good number of my burfees—*a simple recipe that I've made easier and much more accessible for the American kitchen.*

This recipe may be halved, but I suggest making it all. Burfees stay fresh in the refrigerator more than a month and make great hostess gifts during the holiday season. Layer in an airtight container, with a plastic sheet or wax paper separating each layer.

6 tablespoons (³/₄ stick) unsalted butter
2 pounds part-skim ricotta cheese
1 (14-ounce) can sweetened condensed milk
1 teaspoon pure (not artificial) vanilla extract
6 to 8 (4-inch) square silver leaves (optional)

1. Heat the butter in a large, heavy wok or saucepan (not nonstick) over medium-high heat until melted. Add the ricotta cheese and cook, stirring often, over medium heat for the first 2 to 3 minutes, then over medium heat until all the liquid evaporates, 20 to 25 minutes.

2. Add the condensed milk and vanilla extract and continue to cook until all the liquid evaporates and

the mixture thickens and pulls away from the sides of the pan, 10 to 12 minutes. During the last 5 minutes of cooking, mix in the nuts and other flavors of your choice (see pages 640 to 641).

3. Place on an 11- by 8-inch baking or any other tray or dish with raised edges and, with a spatula, flatten into a smooth ½- to ¾-inch-thick layer. Garnish with the silver leaves and refrigerate until somewhat firm, at least 2 hours. (Warm burfee is very soft and does not retain its shape or cut well.) Cut into 1-inch or larger squares, rectangles, or diamonds. Transfer to a platter and serve, or layer in airtight containers with wax paper separating each layer and store in the refrigerator.

Basic White Milk Fudge with Cream
Malai Burfee

Makes 30 to 40 pieces

A recipe from my friend Bharti Dhalwala, this fudge is made with whipping cream instead of butter. It has a much smoother texture than Basic White Milk Fudge (left). However, they can both be used interchangeably.

¹/₂ pint heavy cream
1 cup sugar
1 pound part-skim ricotta cheese
1 cup instant nonfat dry milk
¹/₂ to 1 teaspoon ground green cardamom seeds

1. In a large nonstick wok or saucepan, boil together the cream and sugar over medium-high heat until it bubbles vigorously.

2. Add the ricotta cheese, dry milk, and cardamom seeds, increase the heat to high, and bring to a boil. Reduce the heat to medium-low and simmer, stirring constantly, until the mixture thickens and pulls away from the sides of the pan, about 15 minutes. During the last 5 minutes of cooking, mix in the nuts and other flavors of your choice (from pages 640 to 641).

3. Finish making the burfee according to the directions for Basic White Milk Fudge, starting from Step 3 (above).

Flavored Milk Fudge

Kisum-Kisum ki Burfee

Makes 30 to 40 pieces

Start with the recipe for Basic White Milk Fudge (page 639) or Basic White Milk Fudge with Cream (page 639). Cook until the mixture pulls away from the sides of the pan in Step 2, then add any of the following flavors. Finish the burfee as explained in Step 3 of Basic White Milk Fudge.

Basic White Milk Fudge with Pistachio Bits

Pista Burfee

Makes 30 to 40 pieces

Speckled with bits of brilliantly green pistachios, this is a very basic burfee.

1 recipe Basic White Milk Fudge (page 639)
1/2 cup shelled raw pistachios
1 cup boiling water
1 teaspoon ground green cardamom seeds
1 drop rose essence

1. Soak the pistachios in the boiling water, about 1 hour. Drain the pistachios, place on a kitchen towel and rub vigorously to remove the thin, softened skins. The pistachios will now be brilliant green. Cut each nut in half or quarters. Reserve.

2. Prepare the Basic White Milk Fudge recipe through Step 2. Then mix all the ingredients into the fudge and set the burfee as explained in Step 3.

Saffron Milk Fudge

Kesari Burfee

Makes 30 to 40 pieces

It would truly be a shame to call this burfee *a mere variation of anything. With its tell-tale threads of saffron and lovely yellow-orange color, it is appealing in its own right and deserves a singular place on the table.*

1/2 teaspoon saffron threads
2 tablespoons whole milk
1/2 teaspoon ground green cardamom seeds
2 drops rose essence

Soak the saffron threads in the milk at least 30 minutes. Prepare Basic White Milk Fudge (page 639) or Basic White Milk Fudge with Cream (page 639) through Step 2. Then mix all the ingredients into the fudge and set the burfee as explained in Step 3 of Basic White Milk Fudge.

Layered White and Brown Chocolate Milk Fudge

Chaclate Burfee

Makes 30 to 40 pieces

This recipe, with its origins in the British Raj, is a layered white and brown burfee *with chocolate as its main flavor. Garnished lavishly with pure silver leaves, this* burfee *is a favorite with kids, including mine.*

1/4 cup white chocolate chips
3/4 cup semisweet chocolate chips

1. Prepare Basic White Milk Fudge (page 639) or Basic White Milk Fudge with Cream (page 639) through Step 2. While it is still in the pan, mix in the white chocolate chips and cook, stirring, 1 to 2 minutes.

2. Divide the burfee mixture into 2 parts. Leaving one half in the pan, place the other half on an 11-by-8-inch tray with raised edges (or any other dish) and, with a spatula, smooth and flatten it into a 1/4-inch-thick layer.

3. Add the chocolate chips to the mixture in the wok and cook, stirring, over medium heat until the chocolate melts and the mixture is thick and smooth, about 2 minutes.

4. Spread the chocolate mixture over the white burfee, making a smooth brown top layer. Garnish with the silver leaves. Cool well and cut into 1-inch (or larger) squares. Or, make a long, thin roll with each color, lay them side by side, then roll them together to make one roll about 1½-inches in diameter. Then, with a sharp knife, cut 1/3- to 1/2-inch slices and serve.

White and Pink Coconut Milk Fudge
Nariyal Burfee

Makes 30 to 40 pieces

The layering procedure is the same as for chocolate burfee, *but the flavors here are very different.*

¹/₂ cup sweetened shredded coconut, processed in a food processor until fine
2 to 3 drops red food coloring

1. Prepare Basic White Milk Fudge (page 639) or Basic White Milk Fudge with Cream (page 639), but do not add the vanilla. Instead, mix in all but 2 tablespoons of the shredded coconut.

2. Divide the fudge into 2 parts. Leaving one half in the wok, place the other half on an 11-by-8-inch tray with raised edges (or any other dish) and, with a spatula, smooth and flatten into a ¼-inch-thick layer. Add the red food coloring to the mixture in the wok and cook over medium heat, stirring, 30 seconds.

3. Spread the pink burfee over the white layer, making a smooth pink top layer. Sprinkle the reserved coconut on top and lightly press it into the surface. Cool well and cut into 1-inch (or larger) squares.

Pure Cashew Milk Fudge
Kaaju ki Burfee

Makes 30 to 40 pieces

The authentic way of making cashew burfee *calls for* chashni *(sugar syrup), which can be tricky for the novice. Here is my fail-safe, easy way. This exact same recipe can be made with ground, blanched almonds or walnuts instead of cashews.*

1¹/₂ cups coarsely chopped raw cashews
¹/₂ cup confectioners' sugar
¹/₃ cup instant nonfat dry milk
1 to 2 tablespoons warm water
6 (4-inch) squares silver leaves (optional)

1. In a food processor, process together the cashews, sugar, and dry milk until the mixture becomes a powder. Add the water and continue to process until

the ingredients gather into a smooth dough that does not stick to the sides of the bowl.

2. With lightly oiled clean hands, shape the dough into a round ball and place between 2 large sheets of aluminum foil or wax paper. Then, with a rolling pin, roll on top of the foil to make an 8-by-4-inch rectangle, about ½-inch thick. Remove the top piece of the foil and garnish with silver leaves. Then cut into 30 to 40 pieces. Transfer to a serving platter and serve, preferably at room temperature.

Pure Pistachio Fudge
Pistae ki Burfee

Makes 30 to 40 pieces

Remember all those unnatural green burfees *you've seen in Indian stores? They're all aiming to be colorful like this classic, brilliant green* burfee *fudge. Typically associated with affluence, this fudge has always been among the formal gifts given during weddings and festivals, especially* Diwali, *the Hindu festival of lights.*

2 cups shelled raw pistachios
¹/₂ cup confectioners' sugar
1¹/₂ teaspoons ground green cardamom seeds
2 tablespoons warm water
6 (4-inch) squares silver leaves (optional)

1. In a food processor, process together the pistachios, sugar, and cardamom seeds until the mixture resembles a powder. Add the water and continue to process until the ingredients gather into a dough that does not stick to the sides of the bowl. Do not make the dough too smooth; this burfee should have a grainy texture.

2. With lightly oiled clean hands, shape the dough into a ball and place between 2 large sheets of aluminum foil or wax paper. Then, with a rolling pin, roll on top of the foil to make an 8-by-4-inch rectangle, about ½-inch thick. Remove the top piece of the foil and garnish with silver leaves (if using). Then cut into 30 to 40 pieces. Transfer to a serving platter and serve, preferably at room temperature.

Saffron Milk Patties

Pedhae

Makes 30 to 40 pieces

Associated with the city of Mathura, the home of Lord Krishna, these bite-sized sweets made with khoa *(thickened milk) are different from the typical* burfee *fudge, in that they are crumbly and drier, and are generally shaped into smaller, 1-inch round patties.*

1/3 teaspoon saffron threads
1/4 cup whole milk
1 cup heavy cream
1 1/2 cups nonfat dry milk
1/2 cup part-skim ricotta cheese
2 tablespoons coarsely ground shelled raw pistachios

1. In a small bowl, soak the saffron threads in the milk about 30 minutes. Then, in a large nonstick skillet or saucepan, mix the cream, dry milk, and ricotta cheese and cook, stirring, over medium heat until smooth, 3 to 5 minutes. Reduce the heat to low, mix in the saffron-infused milk and the saffron, and cook, stirring often, until the mixture (*khoa*) is almost dry and pulls away from the sides of the pan, 7 to 10 minutes.

2. Remove from the heat. Let cool about 1 hour and shape the mixture into 1-inch patties. Then, with your thumb, press into the center of each patty to make a slight depression. Press some ground pistachios into the depression and serve, preferably at room temperature.

Authentic Curdled Milk Fudge

Kalaakand

Makes 30 to 40 pieces

This fudge is meant to be pure white with a slight grain, due to the fact it is made with curdled milk.

4 cups whole milk
1 cup plain yogurt (any kind), whisked until smooth
1 (14-ounce) can condensed milk
1/2 teaspoon coarsely ground green cardamom seeds

1. Place the milk in a large saucepan and bring to a boil over high heat. Add the yogurt, stirring constantly; this will cause the milk to curdle and break into tiny curd particles. Keep stirring and boiling over high heat until the curd particles are firm, about 3 minutes. Then pass the mixture through a fine-mesh strainer. The liquid whey will drain out and the curds will remain in the strainer. Discard the whey and return the curds to the pan.

2. Mix in the condensed milk and cardamom seeds and cook, stirring, over medium heat until the mixture pulls away from the sides of the pan and gathers in the center, 15 to 20 minutes.

3. Transfer to a small tray and, with a spatula, spread into a smooth layer, about 3/4-inch thick. Cover with plastic wrap and cool in the refrigerator about 1 hour. Cut into 1 1/2-inch or smaller cubes or rectangles and serve, preferably at room temperature.

Saffron Curdled Milk Patties

Kesari Sandesh

Makes 30 to 40 pieces

Similar to pedhas *in shape and color, these rounds, called* sondesh *or* sandesh, *are a typical Bengali dessert. But instead of* khoa *(thickened milk solids),* sondesh *is made with* chenna, *which, like* paneer, *comes from curdled milk, but it is softer and has a finer grain. (You can substitute* paneer *cheese for the* chenna, *but soften it first in a food processor.)*

1/3 teaspoon saffron threads
4 cups whole milk
2 to 3 tablespoons distilled white vinegar
1/2 pint heavy cream
3/4 cup sugar
3/4 cup instant nonfat dry milk

1. In a small skillet over medium heat, dry-roast half the saffron, stirring and shaking the pan, until crisp and a few shades darker, about 1 minute. Grind in a mortar and pestle or with the back of a spoon.

2. In a heavy saucepan, bring the milk to a boil over high heat. Remove from the heat and cool about 5 minutes. Then add the vinegar and stir lightly until the milk curdles. The curds should be very tiny (unlike the big curds of paneer cheese). Drain through a very fine-mesh strainer about 1 minute. Discard the whey, transfer the curds to a bowl, and mash them with a fork until fine. If the curds are large, process in the food processor until minced.

3. In a large nonstick skillet over medium-high heat, boil together the cream and sugar until it bubbles vigorously, about 3 minutes. Mix in the curds and dry milk and bring to a boil over high heat. Reduce the heat to medium-low and simmer, stirring constantly, until the mixture thickens and pulls away from the sides of the pan, 7 to 10 minutes. Mix in the remaining saffron threads and the roasted saffron during the last 2 to 3 minutes of cooking.

4. Let cool at room temperature about 1 hour. Shape the mixture into 30 to 40 (1-inch) balls. Then, with your thumb, press down in the center of each ball to flatten them and make a slight depression. Serve, preferably at room temperature.

Variation: To make cardamom-flavored *sandesh*, do not add any saffron; instead, fill each depression with a scant pinch of thinly sliced pistachios and ground green cardamom seeds.

Bharti's Milk Cake
Bharti ka Palang-Todh

Makes 8 to 10 servings

My friend Bharti Dhalwala is the only person I know who actually makes her own milk cake. Most people buy it, because it seems complicated to make. I did too until Bharti showed me that it really is not very difficult.

Authentic milk cake is white on the outside and a rich, deep brown inside, and there is a real art to

achieving this beautiful color contrast. The secret is to quickly cool the cake from the outside so it stays white, while making sure the inside remains hot enough for the sugar to caramelize, which gives the cake its dark brown, grainy interior.

It is necessary to buy raw milk for this recipe, as homogenized or pasteurized milk will not work. Raw milk is available in health food stores. The raw milk is boiled then simmered, so it is safe to eat.

¹/₂ gallon raw whole milk
1 pint heavy cream
³/₄ cup plain yogurt (any kind), whisked until smooth
1¹/₄ cups sugar

1. In a large saucepan, boil the milk and cream, over medium-high heat the first 2 to 3 minutes, then over medium heat until reduced by half, 15 to 20 minutes.

2. Add the yogurt, which will cause the milk to curdle, reduce the heat to low, and cook, about 10 minutes. Increase the heat to medium and continue to cook until the whey from the curdled milk has almost evaporated, about 15 minutes. Add the sugar and cook, stirring, until the mixture starts to pull away from the sides of the pan, about 10 minutes.

3. Meanwhile, lightly grease a 6- to 8-inch round container, making sure it has a secure and tight-fitting lid. Have ready a large pot with ice cold water and ice cubes. As soon as the cake mixture is done, transfer it in to the greased container and quickly secure the lid. Then, carefully, place the container in the ice cold water, which will instantly start to cool the cake from the outside. Make sure no moisture gets inside the cake. Allow the cake container to sit in its ice bath 30 to 45 minutes, and add more ice if needed.

4. Carefully remove from the ice bath and bring to room temperature. Invert the cake onto a serving dish and serve as you would any cake.

Ricotta Cheese Cake

Ricotta Paneer ka Cake

Makes 8 to 10 servings

One of the reasons that true cakes will always be a Western concept to many Indians is because they use eggs, which a large number of observant Indian vegetarians don't eat. But they love the symbolism of cakes for birthdays, weddings, and anniversaries.

My Indian invention in America is this egg-less, cake-like dessert, which imitates the flavor of rasgullas (paneer cheese balls in syrup) that all Indians love.

2 tablespoons Dessert Masala (page 32)
2 pounds part-skim ricotta cheese
1 cup sugar, or to taste
1/2 cup coarsely chopped mixed raw almonds and pistachios
1/2 teaspoon ground green cardamom seeds

1. Preheat the oven to 375°F. Prepare the dessert masala. Then, in a bowl, mix the ricotta cheese, all but 1 tablespoon sugar, and the almonds and pistachios. Transfer the mixture to a greased 11-inch pie dish or cake pan. Sprinkle the reserved sugar on the top.

2. Bake until the edges are medium-brown and the center is firm and golden, 1 to 1¼ hours. The sugar on top will caramelize, lending a rich brown color to the cake. If the edges begin to brown too quickly before the cake is done, cover them lightly with a strip of aluminum foil. Remove the cake from the oven and set aside to cool.

3. Run a knife along the insides of the pan to loosen the cake. Place a large plate over the pan, hold the edges together, and invert the cake. Then carefully invert it once again onto a serving platter to expose the caramelized top. Sprinkle with the cardamom seeds, pressing them lightly into the surface, then the dessert masala, and serve. This cake can be served chilled or at room temperature.

Paneer Cheese Specialty Desserts

White Paneer Cheese Balls in Fragrant Syrup

Rasgulla

Makes 25 to 30 pieces

Floating in a cardamom-flavored syrup, these light, spongy, white treats are a specialty from the northeastern state of Bengal and are one of India's most popular desserts. They are very easy to make at home, especially with a pressure cooker.

Typically served chilled, they make for a low-fat and low-sugar dessert—simply drain each rasgulla *of all excess sugar syrup, and you'll have a dessert that is nothing but protein with a hint of sweet.*

8 ounces (1 recipe) Paneer Cheese (page 43 or store-bought), coarsely crumbled, at room temperature
5 1/2 cups water
1 2/3 cups sugar
8 green cardamom pods, crushed lightly to break the skin
1/2 teaspoon coarsely ground green cardamom seeds
2 to 3 drops rose essence

1. Prepare the paneer cheese in advance. Then, place the paneer cheese in a food processor and process until it's smooth and starts to gather into a soft and pliable dough (just before it forms a ball). Divide the dough equally into 25 to 30 portions and shape each into smooth, crack-free balls. This should be done between the palms of your clean hands, applying gentle pressure as you shape them. Cover with a piece of aluminum foil and set aside.

2. Place 5 cups water, 1½ cups sugar, 5 cardamom pods, and the ground cardamom seeds in a pressure cooker and bring to a boil over high heat. Turn off the heat and add half the cheese balls. Secure the lid of the pressure cooker, place it over high heat, and cook until the regulator indicates high pressure, then cook for about 1 more minute. Remove from the heat and allow the pot to depressurize on its own, 12 to 15 minutes. Carefully open the lid of the pressure cooker and let the rasgullas cool about 10 minutes. Do not stir. Transfer to a medium bowl, along with about ½ cup of the syrup in which they were cooked, and set aside.

3. Add the remaining water, sugar, cardamom pods, and cardamom seeds, along with the uncooked rasgulla balls, to the pressure cooker and cook exactly as you did the first batch. Mix the second batch with the first, along with all the syrup, and set aside to cool. Mix in the rose essence, refrigerate at least 6 hours, and serve chilled.

Miniature Multi-Hued Paneer Cheese Balls

Rangeen Rasgullian

Makes 80 pieces

P

This festive version of the traditional rasgullas *(paneer cheese balls in sugar syrup) are also made in the pressure cooker. These dainty, half-inch balls in pastel colors are always a hit at kids' birthday parties—children love their color and size, and the fact that these baby rasgullas look more like candy than food. To make sure they retain their shape and size, they are cooked in a thick sugar syrup, which firms them up.*

8 ounces (1 recipe) Paneer Cheese (page 43 or store-bought), coarsely crumbled, at room temperature

3 drops each red, yellow, and green food coloring

2½ cups sugar

6 cups water

8 green cardamom pods, crushed lightly to break the skin

4 drops rose essence

1. Prepare the paneer cheese in advance. Then, place the paneer cheese in a food processor and process until it's smooth and starts to gather into a soft and pliable dough (just before it forms a ball). Remove and divide the dough equally into 4 portions. Mix 1 portion with 2 drops red food coloring, 1 with 2 drops yellow food coloring, and 1 with 2 drops green food coloring, and leave 1 portion white. Make 20 balls, about ⅓ inch around, from each portion, being sure to keep each ball free from cracks.

2. Dissolve the sugar in the water and divide evenly into 4 portions. Working with each portion separately, place in a pressure cooker, along with 2 cardamom pods and 1 drop of matching food coloring. Secure the lid of the pressure cooker, place it over high heat, and cook until the regulator indicates high pressure, then cook about 30 to 40 seconds. Remove from the heat and allow the pot to depressurize on its own, 12 to 15 minutes.

3. Carefully open the lid of the pressure cooker and bring to a boil once again over high heat. Continue to boil until most of the water evaporates, 4 to 5 minutes. Transfer to a small bowl, add 1 drop rose essence, and set aside to cool. Repeat this procedure with each color, transferring each to a separate bowl. Then cover each bowl and refrigerate 6 hours to chill. Transfer to a serving plate, arranging the colors separately or tossing them together, and serve.

Paneer Cheese Patties in Creamy Thickened Milk

Ras-Malai

Makes 8 pieces

P

I think of this classic as the ultimate Indian dessert. Made with paneer *cheese,* ras-malai *combines the best of texture and flavor. A well-made ras-malai should be a smooth, soft, creamy patty, floating in a thick, sweet* rabdi*, flavored with lots of saffron, cardamom, and a touch of rosewater.*

My trips to India are never complete without a visit to my favorite sweet shop in New Delhi, whose ras-malai I grew up on and remains the gold standard for me.

6 ounces Paneer Cheese (page 43 or store-bought), coarsely crumbled, at room temperature

1/4 teaspoon saffron threads

1/4 cup whole milk

1 to 2 tablespoons Dessert Masala (page 32)

1 tablespoon all-purpose flour

3 cups water + 1 cup boiling water

1 1/2 cups sugar

6 green cardamom pods, crushed lightly to break the skin

1/2 teaspoon coarsely ground green cardamom seeds

1 cup boiling water

1 quart half-and-half

6 silver leaves (optional)

1. Prepare the paneer cheese in advance. Soak the saffron threads in the milk about 30 minutes. Prepare the dessert masala. Then place the paneer cheese and the flour in a food processor and process until it's smooth and starts to gather into a soft and pliable dough (just before it forms a ball). Divide the dough equally into 8 portions and shape each portion into 1 1/2-inch patties that are free from cracks. This should be done between the palms of your clean hands, applying gentle pressure as you shape them. Cover and set aside.

2. Place the water, sugar, cardamom pods, and cardamom seeds in a pressure cooker and bring to a boil over high heat. Turn off the heat and add the cheese patties. Secure the lid of the pressure cooker, place it over high heat, and cook until the regulator indicates high pressure, then cook about 1 minute. Remove from the heat and allow the pot to depressurize on its own, 12 to 15 minutes. Carefully open the lid of the pressure cooker, transfer about 1 cup of the syrup to a saucepan, and simmer until it is reduced by about half. Reserve. Mix 1 cup boiling water into the contents of the pressure cooker and set it aside to cool.

3. Meanwhile, heat the half-and-half in a heavy wok or a saucepan over high heat, stirring constantly, until it comes to a boil. Reduce the heat to medium-low and simmer until reduced by half (or more). Mix in the reduced sugar syrup. Taste and add more sugar, if needed.

4. When the patties are cool enough to handle, lightly squeeze them to remove most of the liquid, and add the patties to the thickened milk sauce. Mix in the saffron-infused milk and the saffron, and bring to a boil over high heat. Reduce the heat to medium-low and simmer another minute. Transfer to a serving dish, garnish with the silver leaves (if using), sprinkle the dessert masala on top, cover, and refrigerate at least 6 hours before serving.

Saffron Paneer Cheese Triangles
Cham-Cham

Makes 15 pieces

A relative of Bengali rasgullas *and also made in a pressure cooker,* cham-cham *triangles have their own following among dessert fans. Pale yellow and topped with* rabdi *(creamy sweet thickened milk), speckled with crushed cardamom seeds and crowned with an emerald pistachio,* cham-cham *are as much a visual delight as they are a delicious dessert.*

8 ounces (1 recipe) Paneer Cheese (page 43 or store-bought), crumbled, at room temperature

2 tablespoons Traditional Thickened Milk Pudding (Rabdi), page 629, or 1 1/2 tablespoons nonfat dry milk mixed with 1 tablespoon heavy cream

15 blanched pistachios (page 35)

4 cups water

1 1/2 cups sugar

8 green cardamom pods, crushed lightly to break the skin

1/2 teaspoon saffron threads

1/2 teaspoon coarsely crushed green cardamom seeds

1. Prepare the paneer cheese in advance. Prepare the milk pudding. Prepare the almonds. Place the paneer cheese in a food processor and process the cheese until it's smooth and starts to gather into a soft and pliable dough (just before it forms a ball). Divide the dough into 15 equal portions and shape each one into a thick, crack-free triangle. This should be done between the palms of your clean hands, applying gentle pressure as you shape them. Cover and set aside.

2. Place the water, sugar, cardamom pods and saffron in a pressure cooker and bring to a boil over high heat. Turn off the heat and add the triangles. Secure the lid of the pressure cooker, place it over high heat, and cook until the regulator indicates high pressure, then cook about 1 minute more. Remove from the heat and allow the pot to depressurize on its own, 12 to 15 minutes. Carefully open the lid of the pressure cooker and let cool, about 10 minutes. Transfer each cham-cham, one by one, to a tray, tilting the tray to one side to allow them to drain, 15 to 20 minutes.

3. Transfer to a serving platter. Place a dollop of the rabdi on each cham-cham, sprinkle with cardamom seeds, then top each with a pistachio. Refrigerate at least 6 hours before serving.

Stuffed Paneer Cheese Rolls in Fragrant Syrup

Raj-Bhog

Makes 15 pieces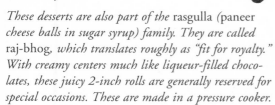

These desserts are also part of the rasgulla *(paneer cheese balls in sugar syrup) family. They are called* raj-bhog, *which translates roughly as "fit for royalty." With creamy centers much like liqueur-filled chocolates, these juicy 2-inch rolls are generally reserved for special occasions. These are made in a pressure cooker.*

8 ounces (1 recipe) Paneer Cheese (page 43 or store-bought), at room temperature

2 tablespoons Dessert Masala (page 32)

1/2 cup heavy cream

1/4 cup finely chopped or slivered raw pistachios

4 cups water

1 1/2 cups sugar

8 green cardamom pods, crushed lightly to break the skin

1/2 teaspoon coarsely ground green cardamom seeds

2 tablespoons shredded sweetened coconut

1. Prepare the paneer cheese in advance. Prepare the dessert masala. Then, in a small nonstick saucepan, mix together the cream and pistachios and bring to a boil over high heat. Reduce the heat to medium-low and simmer until quite thick, 3 to 5 minutes. Set aside to cool and thicken further. Then prepare the dessert masala.

2. Place the paneer cheese in a food processor and process until it's smooth and starts to gather into a soft and pliable dough (just before it forms a ball). Divide the dough into 15 equal portions, and shape each portion into a 2-inch patty. Then, with your thumb, press into the center of each patty to make a slight depression. Place about 1/2 teaspoon of the pistachio-cream mixture into the depression. Fold the patty in half to cover the filling, pressing it lightly between your clean palms, then roll it into a 2-inch log. Repeat with all the dough portions. Cover and set aside.

3. Place the water, sugar, cardamom pods, and cardamom seeds in a pressure cooker and bring to a boil. Turn off the heat and add the logs. Secure the lid of the pressure cooker, place it over high heat, and cook until the regulator indicates high pressure, then cook about 1 minute more. Remove from the heat and allow the pot to depressurize on its own, 12 to 15 minutes. Carefully open the lid of the pressure cooker and simmer over medium heat until the logs are somewhat firm, 3 to 5 minutes. Set aside to cool, about 10 minutes.

4. Transfer each raj-bhog, one by one, to a tray, tilting the tray to one side to allow them to drain, 15 to 20 minutes. Then place them on a large serving platter and sprinkle the dessert masala and coconut on top. Refrigerate at least 6 hours before serving.

Other Desserts

Traditional Dark Brown Milk Rolls in Saffron Syrup
Gulaab Jamun

Makes 15 pieces

Authentic gulaab jamuns *are made with buffalo milk* khoa, *which is very hard to come by or to make at home in America, so I offer this recipe using American substitutes. You'll be pleasantly surprised with it!*

For ideal flavor and texture, do not replace the shortening with oil. You could, however, use ghee *if you wish. Also, monitor the temperature carefully, making sure that it remains between 300°F to 325°F. It is crucial to fry the* gulaab jamuns *at a low temperature for a longer time to ensure that the centers get cooked and the* gulaab jamuns *don't collapse when added to the syrup.*

1 cup instant nonfat dry milk
$^{1}/_{2}$ cup all-purpose flour
$^{3}/_{4}$ teaspoon baking powder
1 teaspoon coarsely ground green cardamom seeds
$1^{1}/_{2}$ cups sugar
$^{1}/_{4}$ cup ($^{1}/_{2}$ stick) unsalted butter, at room temperature
$^{1}/_{3}$ cup plain yogurt (any kind), whisked until smooth
2 to 3 cups melted vegetable shortening,
    for deep-frying
2 cups water
$^{1}/_{2}$ teaspoon saffron threads
1 to 2 tablespoons coarsely chopped raw pistachios

1. In a food processor, add the dry milk, flour, baking powder, $^{1}/_{2}$ teaspoon cardamom seeds, and 1 tablespoon sugar and pulse a few times to mix. Add the butter and process until the mixture resembles bread crumbs, about 30 seconds.

2. With the food processor running, add the yogurt in a thin stream through the feed tube and process until everything gathers into a ball. The dough should be soft and somewhat sticky; if it seems too sticky, add some more dry milk.

3. With lightly buttered clean hands, divide the dough into 15 equal portions. Shape each portion either into a log about $1^{1}/_{2}$ inches long and $^{1}/_{2}$ inch wide, or into a ball. Make sure the pieces are smooth and free of cracks. Cover with a piece of aluminum foil and set aside.

4. Heat the shortening in a large, heavy wok over medium-high heat until it reaches 325°F on a frying thermometer or until a piece of dough dropped into the hot oil rises to the top after 30 to 40 seconds. Do not make the oil any hotter; the gulaab jamuns need to be fried long and slow. (If you can, leave the thermometer in the wok and carefully monitor the temperature as you cook; it should remain between 275°F to 325°F. Turn off the heat if it goes any higher.) Add half the gulaab jamuns and fry, stirring and turning gently with a slotted spatula, until they are dark brown, about 5 minutes. Remove to paper towels to drain.

5. Place the water, saffron, and the remaining sugar and cardamom seeds in a skillet or wok and bring to a boil over high heat. Reduce to medium-low and simmer, about 5 minutes. Add the fried rolls to the syrup and continue to simmer until they soak up the syrup, swell and become soft, and the sugar syrup becomes very thick, 15 to 20 minutes. Transfer to a serving dish, sprinkle the pistachios on top, and serve hot or at room temperature.

Caramelized Milk Balls in Thick Syrup
Kaala Jaam

Makes 20 pieces

Kaala *means black, and the word* jaam *comes from* jamun, *a purple-black, date-like fruit with a long center seed. These words attempt to describe the characteristic eye-catching color of* kaala jaam, *which comes from the sugar coating that caramelizes upon frying, forming a deep, caramel-colored crust.*

These spongy and cake-like caramel-colored balls, a firmer and drier version of authentic gulaab jamuns *(dark brown milk balls in syrup) are popular high-tea items, along with* pakoras *(chickpea flour fritters)*, samosas *(deep-fried triangular pastries), and* burfees *(milk fudge)*.

4 ounces (¹/₂ recipe) Paneer Cheese (page 43 or store-bought), crumbled, at room temperature

1¹/₄ cups (1 recipe) dough for Traditional Dark Brown Milk Rolls in Saffron Syrup (page 648), crumbled

4 cups sugar

2 to 3 cups melted vegetable shortening, for deep-frying

4 cups water

8 to 10 green cardamom pods, crushed lightly to break the skin

¹/₂ teaspoon ground green cardamom seeds

1. Prepare the paneer cheese in advance. Prepare the dough for milk rolls. Then, in a food processor, process the paneer cheese and the milk roll dough until the mixture gathers into a ball that does not stick to the sides of the bowl.

2. Place about 2 tablespoons sugar in a small dish. Then, with lightly buttered clean hands, shape the dough into 15 smooth, crack-free balls. Roll each ball in the sugar.

3. Heat the shortening in a large heavy wok over medium-high heat until it reaches 325°F on a frying thermometer or until a piece of dough dropped into the hot oil rises to the top after 30 to 40 seconds. Do not make the oil any hotter; the kaala jaams need to be fried long and slow. (If you can, leave the thermometer in the wok and carefully monitor the temperature as you cook; it should remain between 275°F to 325°F. Turn off the heat if it goes any higher.) Add half the kaala jaams and fry, stirring and turning gently with a slotted spatula, until they are very dark brown, about 7 minutes. Remove to paper towels to drain.

4. Place the remaining sugar, water, and cardamom pods in a large skillet or wok and bring to a boil over high heat. Reduce to medium-low and simmer, about 5 minutes. Add the fried balls to the syrup and continue to simmer until the kaala jaams soak up the syrup, swell and become soft, and the sugar

syrup becomes very thick and almost evaporates, 20 to 25 minutes. Transfer to a serving dish, sprinkle the cardamom seeds on top and serve hot or at room temperature.

Variation: There are many ways to serve *kaala jaams*: rolled in sweetened shredded coconut; cut in half and dusted on the cut or the round sides with a sprinkling of dessert masala (this gives you twice as many pieces); or cut into halves or quarters and served in a pool of *rabdi* (traditional thickened milk pudding, page 629) garnished with some dessert masala.

Sweet Pretzel-Shaped Desserts
Jalebis

Makes 15 pieces

Sticky and oozing with a sugary syrup, jalebis *are crispy, saffron-colored, pretzel-shaped desserts made from a fermented flour batter. The batter is squeezed through an icing cone straight into the hot oil. The fried batter is then added to hot syrup that gets absorbed, and you are left with these delicious sweets.*

Indians are very passionate about their jalebis, *serving them at tea time and as after-dinner desserts. As if their own calorie content was not enough,* jalebis *are often paired with* rabdi *and* kulfi, *and also dropped in a glass of hot milk.*

1 teaspoon active dry yeast

1 teaspoon sugar

¹/₂ cup warm water (about 110°F)

¹/₂ cup all-purpose flour

¹/₄ teaspoon saffron threads

1 cup sugar

¹/₂ cup water

¹/₂ teaspoon ground green cardamom seeds

1 to 1¹/₂ cups vegetable oil for deep-frying

1 tablespoon melted ghee for deep-frying

Icing cone fitted with a ¹/₈-inch or smaller tip or a small funnel

1. In a large bowl, dissolve the yeast and 1 teaspoon sugar in the warm water and set aside until frothy, about 5 minutes. Add the flour and mix vigorously to make a smooth batter with the consistency of heavy cream. Add up to 3 tablespoons more water, as needed, to achieve the desired consistency. Cover and place in a warm, draft-free spot until the batter is full of bubbles and has doubled in volume, about 2 hours. Then, with a fork or ladle, mix the batter one more time until smooth.

2. In a small saucepan, mix 1 cup sugar, ½ cup water, and the cardamom seeds and bring to a boil over high heat. Reduce the heat to medium-low and simmer about 1 minute. Then reduce the heat to low to keep the syrup warm. Add 1 to 2 tablespoons more water if the syrup begins to thicken too quickly.

3. Heat the oil and the ghee in a large wok over medium-high heat until it reaches 325°F to 350°F on a frying thermometer or until a small piece of dough dropped into the hot oil rises to the top after 15 to 20 seconds. Keeping a finger over the opening, place the batter in an icing cone fitted with a ⅛-inch or smaller tip. Keeping the cone directly over the oil, remove your finger and squeeze the batter into the hot oil in a figure-8, double concentric circles, or the shape of small pretzels. As soon as the batter touches the oil, it will firm up. Cook the jalebis, turning once, until golden on both sides; this happens very quickly, in about 30 seconds.

4. As each one is removed from the oil, dip it directly into the sugar syrup, hold it there for about 10 seconds, and transfer to a serving platter. Serve hot.

Creamy Semolina Pancakes with Thickened Milk
Mal-Pudha

Makes 15 pancakes

Mal-pudhas *are to Indians what pancakes are to Westerners—a comforting breakfast food. But* mal-pudhas *can also be a dessert, especially when*

presented with Traditional Thickened Milk Pudding (Rabdi), page 629.

1 to 2 tablespoons Dessert Masala (page 32)
½ cup fine semolina
¼ cup all-purpose flour
¼ cup instant nonfat dry milk
½ cup sugar
¼ teaspoon ground green cardamom seeds
¼ teaspoon baking powder
1¼ cups water
2 tablespoons vegetable oil

1. Prepare the dessert masala. Then, in a bowl, mix together the semolina, flour, dry milk, 1 tablespoon sugar, cardamom seeds, and baking powder. Add about ¾ cup water and mix well to make batter with the consistency of pancake batter. Set aside about 30 minutes.

2. In a small skillet, mix together the remaining sugar and water. Bring to a boil over high heat. Reduce the heat to medium-low and simmer until the syrup thickens to the consistency of honey, 2 to 4 minutes. If the syrup thickens too much, add some water and return to a boil. Remove from the heat.

3. Heat ½ teaspoon oil in a small nonstick skillet over medium heat. Add about 2½ to 3 tablespoons batter to form a 4-inch pancake. After about 30 seconds, the pancake will firm up and the bottom will be golden (check by lifting the pancake with a spatula). Turn over and cook until the other side is golden, about 30 seconds.

4. As each pancake is done, remove it, and, using tongs, immediately dip it into the sugar syrup, leaving it to rest there about 1 minute. Transfer to a serving platter and arrange the pancakes in an overlapping manner. (Do not stack them.) Sprinkle the dessert masala on top and serve.

Variations: Make these pancakes using only all-purpose flour, or mix in some whole-wheat flour. Add 2 to 3 tablespoons chopped almonds and pistachios to the batter, or add 2 teaspoons fennel seeds and ½ teaspoon ground black pepper.

Hot and Cold Beverages

Yogurt Drinks (Lussi) 653

Sweet Yogurt Cooler

Sweet Mango-Yogurt Cooler

Savory Yogurt Cooler

Spicy Yogurt Cooler

Buttermilk Cooler

Milk Drinks 655

Mango Milkshake

Simple Ice-Blended Almond Milk

Chilled Milk with Almonds,
Melon Seeds, and Saffron

Hot Milk with Pistachios
and Poppy Seeds

Ice-Blended Cold Coffee
with Ice Cream

Spiced Cold Coffee

Teas (Chai) 660

Orange Pekoe Tea

Green Cardamom Tea Latté

Fennel and Black Cardamom Tea

Almond Chai Tea

Spicy Chai Tea

Fresh Mint Chai Tea

Kashmiri Spiced Green Tea

Fruit Coolers 657

Spicy Fresh Lemonade

Fresh Lime Soda with Berries

Sparkling Savory Mint-Lime Cooler

Spicy Pomegranate Juice

Fire-Roasted Green Mango Cooler

Spicy Tamarind Water
with Mint and Roasted Cumin

Savory Carrot Cooler

Drinks in India can be quite different than what you find in the United States. Ever heard of soda water with lemon juice and spices, milky-white tea with cardamom and cinnamon, or yogurt whipped up like a smoothie with dry-roasted cumin seeds? They stretch the imagination, but untraditional though these potions might seem, they are quite popular in India, wonderful with Indian foods (and other cuisines, too), and worth trying.

To Indian people, the flavorful combinations in these beverages are considered very meaningful in terms of purpose and taste. Carefully selected additions to the beverages may aid digestion, counter the effects of heat or chill, or refresh and rejuvenate you.

So be adventurous and try some of these brews; you may find yourself actually loving them. They can be very quick to make if your cupboard is stocked with the seasonings called for. If not, a little extra effort may be necessary to buy the ingredients or prepare them, but that's part of the culinary experience.

Yogurt Drinks (Lussi)

Lussi—often spelled *lassi*, but truthfully pronounced luh-see—is a cold yogurt-and-water drink made throughout India. There are many variations, with northern Indian flavorings often including roasted cumin and southern versions including curry leaves.

Sweet Yogurt Cooler
Meethi Lussi

Makes 2 servings

Always served in tall metal tumblers, this is as Indian as you can get with beverages. Offer it with a breakfast or brunch of parantha breads, by itself on a hot summer afternoon, or as a prelude to a dinner. Make it with nonfat yogurt, adding only as much sugar as necessary to barely sweeten it. Some common variations include adding a few drops of rose water or a pinch of saffron.

2 cups plain yogurt, any kind
1 to 2 cups water
¹/₂ cup crushed ice or ice cubes, + more for serving
¹/₄ cup sugar, or to taste
1 teaspoon minced fresh mint leaves

Place the yogurt, water, ½ cup ice, and sugar in a blender and blend until frothy. Divide into 2 glasses and serve cold over crushed ice with a sprinkling of fresh mint leaves.

Sweet Mango-Yogurt Cooler
Aam Ki Lussi

Makes 2 servings

Before my mother acquired a blender, she made this drink the authentic way—in a deep S-shaped metal pot called gadhvi *(louta) using a wooden, long-handled, four-pronged churner called a* madhaani.

Mango essence may sometimes be sold in Indian markets as mango-milk essence. It is very strong, so add carefully when using it. You can also make this recipe with nectarines, peaches, bananas, strawberries, and any other berries.

2 cups plain yogurt, any kind
1 cup chopped fresh ripe mango or canned mango pulp
¹/₂ cup crushed ice or ice cubes, + more for serving
1 tablespoon sugar
1 drop mango essence (optional)

1. Place the yogurt, mango, ½ cup ice, sugar, and mango essence in a blender and blend until frothy.

2. Divide into 2 glasses and serve cold over crushed ice.

Savory Yogurt Cooler
Patli Masala Lussi

Makes 2 servings

This chilled yogurt drink comes with a last-minute topping of sizzling cumin black pepper oil, typical of North Indian flavoring.

2 cups nonfat plain yogurt
2 cups coarsely crushed ice
1 teaspoon vegetable oil
¹/₄ teaspoon coarsely ground cumin seeds
¹/₄ teaspoon coarsely ground black pepper
¹/₈ teaspoon ground black salt (optional)

1. Place the yogurt and ice in a blender and blend until frothy. Transfer to a serving jar or a punch bowl.

2. Heat the oil in a small saucepan over medium heat and add the cumin seeds and black pepper; they should sizzle upon contact with the hot oil. Quickly add the black salt and then mix the spices into the lussi.

Variation: Make a southern Indian version by using ¼ teaspoon ground black mustard seeds, 1 to 2 teaspoons ground dried curry leaves, and a scant pinch of ground asafoetida in place of the cumin, black pepper, and black salt.

Spicy Yogurt Cooler

Mirchi-vaali Lussi

Makes 2 servings

You've got to try this one to believe it. It comes to me from my friend Neelam Malhotra's kitchen in Bangalore, in the southwestern state of Karnataka.

1/4 teaspoon dry-roasted and coarsely ground cumin seeds (page 35)
2 cups plain yogurt
3 dime-size slices peeled fresh ginger
1/2 to 1 fresh green chile pepper, such as serrano, stemmed
5 small fresh mint leaves
5 small fresh curry leaves
1/4 teaspoon salt, or to taste
1/2 cup water
Crushed ice or ice cubes

1. Prepare the cumin seeds. Then put everything (except the cumin) in a blender and blend until smooth.

2. Divide into 2 glasses and serve cold over crushed ice with a sprinkling of roasted cumin seeds.

Buttermilk Cooler

Chaach

Makes 2 servings

Buttermilk is the liquid byproduct when cream is cultured and whipped to separate the butter solids. Buttermilk coolers are similar to yogurt-based lussi drinks in that they are both made from cultured dairy products, but buttermilk coolers are thinner. In India, buttermilk is traditionally made from scratch for this cooler, but store-bought buttermilk works just fine. Enjoy this on a sultry summer afternoon for its cooling effect.

1/4 teaspoon dry-roasted and coarsely ground cumin seeds (page 35)
2 cups buttermilk
1/4 teaspoon salt, or to taste
1/4 teaspoon freshly ground black pepper
1 cup water
Crushed ice or ice cubes

1. Prepare the cumin seeds. Then place the buttermilk, salt, black pepper, and water in a blender and blend until smooth and frothy.

2. Divide into 2 glasses and serve cold over ice with a sprinkling of roasted cumin seeds.

Milk Drinks

Mango Milkshake
Aam Doodh

Makes about 2 12-ounce servings

This is one milkshake that I just cannot get enough of. Mango essence may sometimes be sold in Indian markets as mango-milk essence. It is very strong, so add carefully, if using.

1 cup fresh chopped ripe mango or canned mango pulp
1¼ cups milk
1 to 3 teaspoons sugar (optional, depending on the sweetness of the mango)
1 drop mango essence (optional)
Crushed ice or ice cubes

In a blender, blend together all the ingredients until frothy and serve.

Simple Ice-Blended Almond Milk
Badaam ka Thanda Doodh

Makes about 2 8-ounce servings

The enticing flavor of green cardamom seeds, along with the delicate essence of almonds, yields a cooling summer beverage—perfect first thing in the morning with breakfast or with brunch.

20 blanched almonds (page 35 or store-bought)
1 teaspoon thinly Slivered Blanched Almonds (page 36), or Dessert Masala (page 32)
½ teaspoon ground green cardamom seeds
1½ cups milk
½ cup crushed ice
1 tablespoon sugar
4 to 6 drops almond or vanilla extract

1. Prepare the raw almonds and the blanched almonds or dessert masala. Then, put everything (except the blanched almonds or dessert masala) in a blender and blend until smooth.

2. Divide into 2 glasses, garnish each with a sprinkling of slivered almonds or dessert masala, and serve immediately.

Chilled Milk with Almonds, Melon Seeds, and Saffron
Thandai

Makes 4 to 6 servings

Fragrant and sweet with an occasional bite of coarsely crushed black pepper, this chilled, nutritious drink is a true part of Indian heritage. In a country where alcohol was, until recently, almost a taboo, this was the beverage of choice at weddings and religious ceremonies.

¾ cup shelled raw almonds
½ cup mixed melon seeds (char-magaz, page 12)
1 tablespoon Dessert Masala (page 32)
1 teaspoon black peppercorns
Seeds from 20 to 25 green cardamom pods
4 cups milk
¼ cup sugar, or to taste
½ teaspoon saffron threads
1 drop rose essence or 1 tablespoon rose water
A few pesticide-free red rose petals (optional)
Crushed ice

1. Soak the almonds overnight in water to cover by 2 inches. Drain and peel off the loosened brown skin. Soak the melon seeds at least 1 hour in water to cover. Meanwhile, prepare the dessert masala.

2. In a blender, process together the almonds, melon seeds, black peppercorns, cardamom seeds, 1 cup milk, and sugar until smooth. Add the remaining milk, saffron, and rose essence, and blend again until smooth and frothy.

3. Refrigerate at least 1 hour to blend the flavors. Garnish with the dessert masala and rose petals, if using, and serve over crushed ice.

Variation: For a quicker and easier version, make a dry blend that can be mixed into the milk as the need arises. Do not soak the almonds; instead, buy blanched raw almonds and grind them together with all the other dry ingredients to make a fine powder. Add to cold milk, along with the rose essence, and serve.

Hot Milk with Pistachios and Poppy Seeds

Badaam aur Khas-khas ka Garam Doodh

Makes 2 servings

This is a perfect night-time drink. The combination of hot milk and poppy seeds is believed in ayurvedics to relax and soothe the body, and thus lead to a good night's sleep. White poppy seeds are available in Indian markets.

Seeds from 5 green cardamom pods
1/4 cup shelled raw pistachios
1/4 cup blanched almonds
2 tablespoons white poppy seeds
1/2 teaspoon saffron threads
8 to 10 black peppercorns, or to taste
3 cups milk
Sugar (optional)

1. Prepare the cardamom seeds. Then, place the pistachios, almonds, poppy and cardamom seeds, saffron, and black peppercorns in a spice grinder and grind to make a fine powder.

2. In a heavy saucepan (not nonstick), mix together the milk and ground spices and bring to a boil over high heat, stirring constantly. Reduce the heat to medium and simmer, stirring, another 5 minutes. Add sugar to taste and serve hot.

Ice-Blended Cold Coffee with Ice Cream

Thandi Kaffee

Makes 2 servings

This British-influenced beverage has become the drink of the masses in India. It's quick to make and delicious.

2 cups milk
1 to 2 teaspoons sugar, or to taste
2 to 3 teaspoons instant coffee
4 to 5 scoops coffee or vanilla ice cream

1. Place the milk, sugar, instant coffee, and 2 scoops ice cream in a blender, and blend until frothy.

2. Divide the remaining ice cream into 2 tall serving glasses and pour the blended coffee over each one. Serve with a straw and a tall spoon.

Spiced Cold Coffee

Masaladar Thandi Kaffee

Makes 2 servings

Indians routinely spice up their chai *teas, but sometimes they serve spiced coffees. This coffee can also be served hot. Add the milk into the coffee pan and bring to a boil, then strain and serve.*

1 cup water
1 (1-inch) stick cinnamon
4 whole cloves
1 black cardamom pod, crushed lightly
  to break the skin
1 1/2 to 2 teaspoons instant coffee
1 1/2 cups milk

1. Put the water, cinnamon, cloves, and cardamom pods in a medium saucepan and bring to a boil over high heat. Then cover the pan, reduce the heat to low, and simmer until the water turns brown and about 3/4 cup of water remains in the pan.

2. Mix in the instant coffee and bring to a boil over high heat. Reduce the heat to medium-low, cover the pan, and simmer about 1 minute. Let cool and . refrigerate 2 hours or up to 2 days.

3. Before serving, strain and discard the whole spices. Divide the coffee into 2 cups, mix in the milk or a combination of milk and water, and serve.

Fruit Coolers

Spicy Fresh Lemonade
Shakanjvi

Makes 2 10-ounce servings

Shakanjvi is the refreshing summer drink of choice in most parts of India. Besides being inexpensive and delicious, on a hot day every sip hydrates the body, replenishes lost salts, and has an overall cooling effect.

1/4 teaspoon dry-roasted and coarsely ground cumin seeds (page 35)
1/4 cup sugar
1 1/2 cups water
2 to 3 tablespoons fresh lime or lemon juice, or to taste
1 teaspoon minced fresh mint leaves
A pinch of ground black salt (optional)
A pinch of freshly ground black pepper
Crushed ice or ice cubes

Prepare the cumin seeds. Then dissolve the sugar in the water. Mix in the lime juice, mint leaves and the spices, and serve over ice.

Variation: Dissolve the sugar in about 1/2 cup water, add 1 cup sparkling mineral water or club soda, and continue with the rest of the recipe.

Fresh Lime Soda with Berries
Beri aur Sodae ki Shakanjvi

Makes 2 servings

Make more concentrate than you need. It keeps about 10 days in the refrigerator and freezes well.

1/2 cup any one or mixed fresh berries, such as blueberries, raspberries, or chopped hulled strawberries
3 tablespoons sugar
2 tablespoons fresh lime juice
1/4 cup water
Crushed ice or ice cubes, and chilled club soda, to taste
Fresh lime slices

1. Place the berries, sugar, and lime juice in a small saucepan and cook over medium heat until the sugar melts and the berries are very soft, about 5 minutes.

2. Pass through a food mill to remove the seeds, or process in a food processor or blender and then pass through a very fine-mesh strainer. Add about 1/4 cup water to the seeds and strain the seeds more to get all the juices. Return all the juice to the pan and bring to a boil once more.

3. Divide into 2 glasses, add ice and, club soda to taste, garnish with lime slices, and serve.

Sparkling Savory Mint-Lime Cooler
Pudina aur Sodae ki Shakanjvi

Makes 2 servings

Made with a purée of fresh green chile pepper, scallion, and fresh herbs, this savory cooler is a delightful thirst quencher on hot summer afternoons.

1 fresh green chile pepper, such as serrano, stemmed
1 scallion, coarsely chopped
1/4 cup coarsely chopped fresh mint leaves
1/2 cup coarsely chopped fresh cilantro leaves
2 to 3 tablespoons fresh lime or lemon juice
1 1/2 cups (or more, to taste) sparkling water or club soda
2 to 3 teaspoons sugar
1/4 teaspoon black salt, or to taste
Freshly ground black pepper, or to taste
Crushed ice or ice cubes

1. In a blender, blend together all the ingredients (except the ice) until smooth.

2. Serve as is or add more sparkling water and adjust seasonings to taste, and serve over ice.

Spicy Pomegranate Juice
Masaladar Anaar ka Rassa

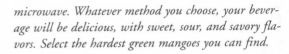

Makes 2 servings

This is best made with fresh pomegranate juice and orange juice. Preparing both is labor-intensive and time-consuming, so look for pomegranate juice at a farmers' market or health food store. Buy fresh orange juice, too.

1/2 teaspoon Chaat Masala (page 20 or store-bought)
1 1/3 cups fresh pomegranate juice
2/3 cup fresh orange juice
1/2 cup plain yogurt (any kind)
2 quarter-size slices peeled fresh ginger
6 fresh mint leaves
1/8 teaspoon ground black salt (optional)
Crushed ice or ice cubes
Fresh mint sprigs

1. Prepare the masala. Then, in a blender, blend together both the juices, yogurt, ginger, mint leaves, chaat masala, and black salt until smooth and frothy.

2. Put crushed ice in 2 glasses, pour the drink into each glass, and garnish with the mint sprigs.

Variation: This recipe can also be made as a smoothie, with chopped mixed fruits, berries, boiled beets, and other vegetables. I often throw in some sprouted beans for texture and added health benefits.

Fire-Roasted Green Mango Cooler
Ammbi-Panna

Makes 4 to 6 servings

Ammbi is the Hindi name for small, unripe mangoes. This drink is traditionally made by roasting the ammbis over direct coals (or in the dying ashes of a coal-burning stove) until the pulp inside turns soft and mushy and takes on an enticing sweet, smoky flavor as the sugars inside caramelize lightly. The mangoes can also be baked, boiled, or softened in the

microwave. Whatever method you choose, your beverage will be delicious, with sweet, sour, and savory flavors. Select the hardest green mangoes you can find.*

2 teaspoons cumin seeds, dry-roasted and coarsely ground (Dry-Roasting Spices, page 35)
2 medium green unripe mangoes (about 12 ounces each)
3 cups water
1/2 cup sugar
5 to 7 fresh mint leaves
1 teaspoon freshly ground black pepper, or to taste
1/2 teaspoon salt, or to taste
1/4 teaspoon ground black salt
Crushed ice or ice cubes
Fresh mint leaves

1. Prepare the cumin seeds. Then, preheat the grill. Place the mangoes on the grill, turning as needed, until they are charred on the outside and very soft inside, about 30 minutes. (Check with the back of a spoon.) Alternately, preheat the oven to 425°F. Wrap the mangoes in aluminum foil and bake in the center of the oven until they are very soft inside, 35 to 40 minutes.

2. Let cool, then peel off the skin and separate the pulp from the center seeds. Transfer the pulp to a blender, mix in 2 cups water, sugar, mint leaves, cumin, black pepper, salt, and black salt, and blend until smooth. Transfer to a saucepan and bring to a boil over high heat. Let cool.

3. Serve as is, or dilute with more water, adjust the seasonings, and pour over crushed ice or ice cubes. Garnish each glass with mint leaves and serve. Keeps refrigerated up to 5 days.

Spicy Tamarind Water with Mint and Roasted Cumin
Imli-paani

Makes 2 servings

Also known as jal-jeera *or* jeera-paani, *this tangy and spicy-hot water is served at all roadside eateries, where it is served alongside Crispy Puffs with Spicy*

Tamarind Water (page 140). It is also a much-beloved summer beverage, because tamarind is considered to have a cooling effect on the body. Serve as prelude to a holiday brunch with fresh fruits, or present it with any of the chaat *snacks or salads. Tamarind pulp can be purchased from Indian, Asian, and Mexican markets.*

2 ounces seedless tamarind pulp

2 to 3 cups water

4 quarter-size slices peeled fresh ginger

1 to 3 fresh green chile peppers, such as serrano, coarsely chopped

2 tablespoons fresh whole mint leaves, + 1 tablespoon minced

2 tablespoons fresh lime or lemon juice

1 1/2 teaspoons ground cumin

1/4 teaspoon cayenne pepper, or to taste

1/8 teaspoon ground asafoetida

1 teaspoon ground black salt

1/2 to 1 teaspoon salt, or to taste

1 to 2 tablespoons sugar

1. Soak the tamarind pulp in 1 cup water until softened, about 2 hours. Rub with clean fingers to release the pulp from the fibers and pass through a fine-mesh strainer or a food mill. Mix another cup water with the pulp in the strainer and extract some more pulp. Discard the fiber. Transfer the pulp to a jar.

2. In a small spice grinder or processor, grind together the ginger, green chile peppers, and whole mint leaves. Transfer to a small bowl and mix well with lime (or lemon) juice to make a paste. Mix into the tamarind pulp.

3. Place the cumin, cayenne pepper, and asafoetida in a small cast-iron skillet, and roast the spices over medium heat, stirring and shaking the skillet, until the spices are highly fragrant are a few shades darker, 1 to 2 minutes. Immediately mix into the tamarind pulp.

4. Add the remaining water, black salt, salt, and sugar, and mix well. Taste, adjust the seasonings, and chill at least 2 hours to allow the flavors to develop. When ready, mix in the minced mint leaves and serve.

Variation: A quick version can be made by mixing 2 to 3 tablespoons Minty Cumin-Water Masala (page 21) into a glass of chilled water.

Savory Carrot Cooler

Kaanji

Makes about 1/2 gallon

This intriguing deep-red-cooler— part of the Punjabi food legacy— is a lunch-time favorite. Its tell-tale color comes from special beet-colored carrots used for this drink. Its spicy and sour taste comes from an enzyme released by the ground mustard seeds as they ferment in the jar of water, a process which continues as the days progress.

Because the deep burgundy carrots are rarely available in America, I use regular carrots and throw in a beet or two for color. If you can't set it outside in the sun, put it near a sunny window for a little longer than a week.

1/2 pound carrots, peeled and cut into thin 2-inch sticks

1 beet, peeled and finely chopped

1/2 cup ground black mustard seeds

1/4 cup salt

1/2 gallon water

Cheesecloth

In a large jar, mix everything together, cover securely with a double-folded sheet of cheesecloth, and set in the sun about a week, bringing it inside every evening. By the end of the week the drink should be very spicy and sour. Serve at room temperature or refrigerate at least 2 hours and serve chilled.

Teas (Chai)

Tea, or *chai* as it is called all over the country, was introduced to India by the Chinese, but Indians have certainly made it their own. Indians consume black tea strong, sweet, milky, and spiced. For most people in India, tea is the first drink of the morning, a mid-day picker-upper, and an afternoon break accompanied by sweet and savory goodies. Even in southern parts of India where coffee is the breakfast drink of choice, it is tea that follows throughout the day.

Indian tea has traditionally been sold in two forms. The gourmet variety of rolled, long-leaf teas have more fragrance than color and a delicate yet assertive flavor. These luxurious teas are quite expensive. Long-leaf teas are brewed with no additions—just boiling hot water and tea leaves. They are then served with milk and sugar on the side, and you pour your own cup.

Then there are the commonly available broken, ash-like leaves called *daana chai.* They tend to have more color than fragrance, and are widely used because they are available everywhere and are much cheaper. These leaves are boiled and simmered along with milk, sugar, and aromatics into a stronger and stronger brew at homes and on street corners.

Teabags are very much a Western concept. If found in India, they are usually filled with tea from the lesser category. In the United States, most of the popular teas can be found in Indian markets. For the color-giving small leaves, look for Brook Bond Red Label. For the gourmet long-leaf varieties, try Lopchu Orange Pekoe or Lipton Green Label or Connoisseur Tea, or sample others.

Traditionally, Indians use whole milk in their teas. But I find that nonfat milk works well (once you get used to it) and is a much healthier choice.

Orange Pekoe Tea
Orange Pekoe Chai

Makes 2 servings

One of the best teas in India is the Orange Pekoe variety of tea leaves. They have a lovely aroma but not much color and can be served straight, without any milk—although most Indians would be appalled by this suggestion. I like my tea light, and tend to add fewer tea leaves. If you prefer a stronger brew, add another spoonful.

Do use a tea-cozy to brew your tea. It maintains the optimum temperature needed for brewing, and you get a perfect, hot cup of tea.

4 cups water
2 teaspoons Orange Pekoe tea leaves
¼ cup hot milk (optional)
Sugar or honey, to taste
Slices of fresh lime (optional)

1. Put the water in a medium saucepan and bring to a boil over high heat. Continue to boil about 30 seconds.

2. Swirl about 1 cup boiling water into the teapot to warm it. Then pour out the water and add the tea leaves to the warmed pot. Pour the remaining 3 cups water over the tea leaves. Cover the pot with a tea-cozy and steep at least 2 minutes for a light brew and up to 4 minutes for a stronger tea. (If you like really strong tea, add another ½ to 1 teaspoon tea leaves.)

3. Pour through a tea or very fine-mesh strainer into 2 teacups. Serve hot with a choice of milk, sugar, honey, and slices of fresh lime on the side.

Green Cardamom Tea Latté
Doodh vaali Illaichi Chai

Makes 2 cups

This is one of the most basic breakfast teas. It goes equally well with parantha *(griddle-fried breads) as it does with eggs and toast. With a generous serving of milk, this tea, like caffe latte, gives you a calcium* boost. If you wish, you can make this tea with hot milk only—no water.

To prevent the milk from boiling over, keep a vigilant eye on the pot and stir it while it heats up, or the milk will stick to the bottom of the pan and may spill over as soon as it comes to a boil.

1 cup water
1 cup milk
2 green cardamom pods, crushed lightly
    to break the skin
1¹/₂ to 2 teaspoons loose black tea leaves
    or 2 teabags (regular or decaffeinated)
¹/₄ teaspoon green cardamom seeds, coarsely ground
Sugar, to taste

1. In a medium saucepan, put the water, milk, and cardamom pods and bring to a boil over high heat. Reduce the heat to low, add the tea leaves and simmer until the color of the tea is to your liking—30 seconds for a lighter tea and about 1 minute for a more robust flavor.

2. Put ¹/₈ teaspoon ground cardamom seeds in each of 2 teacups, and pour the tea through a tea or very fine-mesh strainer into the cups. Discard the pods and the tea leaves. Serve hot, with the sugar on the side.

Fennel and Black Cardamom Tea

Saunf—Illaichi ki Chai

Makes 2 cups

This tea, made with the fennel seeds and black cardamom pods, is very therapeutic. My mother-in-law makes it at every opportunity; so much so that today, my daughters think of it as their comfort tea, asking for it whenever they are feeling low.

1¹/₂ cups water
1 black cardamom pod, broken open to release
    the seeds
1¹/₂ teaspoons fennel seeds
1¹/₂ to 2 teaspoons loose black tea leaves
    or 2 teabags
1 cup milk
Sugar, to taste

1. Put the water, cardamom pod, and fennel seeds in a medium saucepan, and bring to a boil over high heat. Then, cover the pan, reduce the heat to low and simmer until the water turns brown and is reduced by a third. (You should have 1 cup of water in the pan.)

2. Add the tea leaves and turn off the heat. Let the tea steep about 2 minutes, then add milk and bring to a boil once again.

3. Pour through a fine-mesh strainer into 2 teacups, and discard the seeds and tea leaves. Serve hot with sugar on the side.

Variation: For a different flavor, make the tea using a 1-inch stick of cinnamon instead of the fennel seeds.

Almond Chai Tea

Badaam Chai

Makes 2 cups

This tea recipe, from my husband's cousin, Vikram Budhraja, offers drinkers a pleasant surprise: the sweet almonds left at the bottom of the cup after all the fennel-flavored tea has disappeared.

3 cups water
¹/₄ cup milk
1 teaspoon fennel seeds
1¹/₂ teaspoons loose black tea leaves or 2 teabags
6 to 8 shelled, raw almonds, coarsely broken

1. Put the water and fennel seeds in a medium saucepan and bring to a boil over high heat. Then, add the milk and bring to a boil again.

2. Reduce the heat to low, add the tea leaves, and continue to boil, about 30 seconds. Remove from the heat, cover the pan, and let the tea steep about 2 minutes.

3. Divide the almonds into 2 teacups. Pour the tea through a fine-mesh strainer and serve hot, with sugar on the side.

Spicy Chai Tea
Masala Chai

Makes about 2 cups

The flavored teas you find in coffee shops today— tea brewed with a combination of spices—take their inspiration from Indian masala chai. *There are as many variations as there are people and palates in India, and you will never find the same flavor twice, unless you make it at home.*

2 cups water
1/2 cup milk
2 green cardamom pods, broken open to release
   the seeds
8 to 10 black peppercorns
1 1/2-inch stick cinnamon
1/2 teaspoon fennel seeds
1 quarter-size slice of fresh ginger, coarsely crushed
1 teaspoon loose black tea leaves, or 1 teabag
Honey or raw sugar, to taste

1. In a medium saucepan, add everything except the tea leaves and honey and bring to a boil over high heat. Lower the heat and continue to boil another minute to extract maximum flavor from the spices. Add the tea, turn off the heat, cover the pan, and set aside to steep, about 3 minutes.

2. Pour through a tea or very fine-mesh strainer into 2 teacups. Discard the spices and the leaves. Serve hot, with the honey or sugar on the side.

Variations: Instead of using the whole spices, boil the water with about 2/3 teaspoon Chai Tea Masala (page 32).

Fresh Mint Chai Tea
Pudina Chai

Makes about 2 cups

This is a fragrant, luxurious, and elegant addition to a high tea afternoon. For another exotic variation, add 1/4 teaspoon saffron threads along with the mint and ginger.

2 cups water
1/4 cup coarsely chopped fresh mint leaves
1 quarter-size slice of fresh ginger, coarsely ground
   (optional)
1/2 cup milk
1 teaspoon loose black tea leaves, or 1 teabag
Honey or raw sugar, to taste

1. In a medium saucepan, add the water, mint, and ginger and bring to a boil over high heat. Lower the heat to medium and continue to boil another minute to extract maximum flavor. Add the milk and bring to a boil once again. Add the tea leaves (or teabag) turn off the heat, cover the pan, and set aside to steep, about 3 minutes.

2. Pour through a tea or very fine-mesh strainer into 2 teacups. Discard the spices and the leaves. Serve hot, with the honey or sugar on the side.

Kashmiri Spiced Green Tea
Kehwa

Makes 2 cups

This special green tea preparation, called kehwa *or* kahwa, *is very popular in the northern state of Kashmir.*

6 shelled raw almonds
1/2 teaspoon green cardamom seeds
1/4 teaspoon ground cinnamon
1/8 teaspoon saffron threads
2 1/2 cups water
2 teaspoons green tea leaves or 2 teabags
2 teaspoons sugar, or to taste

1. In a spice or a coffee grinder, finely grind 2 almonds and the cardamom seeds. Remove to a bowl and mix in the cinnamon and saffron. Then coarsely grind the remaining 4 almonds and reserve.

2. Place the water, tea leaves, 2 teaspoons sugar, and the almond-cinnamon mixture in a small saucepan, and bring to a boil over high heat. Reduce the heat to medium-low, cover the pan, and boil another 2 minutes to extract maximum flavor from the spices.

3. Meanwhile, divide the reserved coarsely ground almonds into 2 cups. Then pour the tea through a tea or very fine-mesh strainer into the 2 teacups. Discard the spices and tea leaves. Serve hot, with more sugar on the side.

Indian Cooking Glossary

aalu: (also *batata*) potatoes

aalu-bhujia: (also *aloo-bhujia*) thin, wispy, half-inch noodles of spicy potato and chickpea flour batter

aam: mango

achaar: pickle

achaari: dish cooked with pickling spices

addai: crepe made with dal (legumes)

adrak: fresh ginger

ajwain: carom, lovage, omum or Bishop's weed

akoori: Parsi scrambled egg dish with vegetables, generally corn

amchur: mango powder, made from dried, ground, unripe mango pulp

ammavadai: croquettes made with a fermented mixed dal (legume) batter

ammbi: (also *kairi*) raw or unripe green mangoes

ammbi-panna: savory cold beverage made with unripe green mangoes

anaardana: pomegranate seeds

angeethi: (also *chulha, sigri*) an old-fashioned pail-shaped coal-burning stove, used for everyday Indian home cooking

arbi: (also *arvi*) taro root, a starchy underground tuber with fuzzy brown skin and white flesh

atta: whole-wheat flour

avial: south Indian yogurt, coconut, and vegetable soup

Ayurveda: the ancient Indian art of natural medicine

baati or baaties: whole-wheat bread rolls from Rajasthan; about 1½-inch thick disc-shaped rolls with a slight depression in the center

badi, badiyan, or vadiyan: (also *bari, vadi*) lentil nuggets made with spicy lentil paste shaped into nuggets and then dried in the sun

bajra: millet

basmati: fragrant long-grain white rice

bathua: lambs quarters, a type of greens

besan: chickpea (garbanzo bean) flour

besan pudhae: pancakes made with chickpea flour

bhagarae-baingan: spicy tamarind-flavored dish from Hyderabad

bhain: (also *kamal-kakdi*) lotus root

bhaji: vegetables

bhajia or bhajias: chickpea flour and vegetable fritters

bhalla: (plural *bhallae*) white urad bean (*dhulli urad dal*) croquettes

bhartha: mashed roasted vegetables cooked with onions and tomatoes, typically made with eggplants and opo (marrow) squash

bhath: cooked rice

bhatmas: (also *soyabeans*) soybeans

bhatura: (plural *bhaturae*) deep-fried leavened flatbreads

bhindi: okra

bhujia: see **sev**

bhunae channae: roasted black chickpeas

bhuna-masala: roasted spices

bhunna: (pronounced *bhun-na*) to roast

bhurji: scrambled eggs

bhutta: corn-on-the-cob

biryani: (plural *biryanis*) elaborate layered basmati rice dish with meats or vegetables

boondi: deep-fried chickpea flour batter drops

boti: piece of meat with bone

boti kabaabs: marinated and grilled pieces of bone-in meat

bundh gobhi: cabbage

burfee: (plural *burfees*) milk fudge

cachumbar: chopped salad

chaach: buttermilk

chaat: a composed dish infused with complex savory, sweet, salty, tangy, and spicy flavors that is usually eaten as a salad or snack.

chaat masala: special savory spice blend

chaat-wallah: person who makes and sells chaat

chai: tea

cham-cham: paneer cheese dessert flavored with saffron and cardamom

chandi ka verk or vark: edible silver leaves used to garnish desserts; commonly referred to as *verk*

channa: (also *channae, chholae*) chickpeas

chapati: (also *phulka*) whole-wheat flat bread

char-magaz: mixture of four melon seeds

chaval: rice

chenna: soft paneer cheese

chholia: fresh green chickpeas

chilkae vaali: split dal with the skin on

chillas: savory lentil pancakes

chitree vaalae raajma: whole pinto beans

chori dal: adzuki beans, a brown-red dal a little larger than mung beans

daana: grain, generally referring to the spices anaardana (pomegranate seeds) or daana methi (fenugreek seeds)

daana-methi: (also *metharae*) fenugreek seeds

dahi ka paneer: yogurt cheese

dal: (plural *dals*) small and split large beans, lentils, and peas, often categorized as legumes

dalchini: (also *darchini*) cinnamon

dandal: cauliflower stems

degchi: saucepan

degi-mirch: (also *rang vaali mirch*) paprika

desi: from the country or from India

dhaba: (plural *dhabas*) roadside eateries

dhana-jeera: spice mixture of coriander and cumin

dhania: fresh cilantro leaves or coriander seeds

dhansak: "dhan" is dal (legumes) and "sak" is vegetable; dhansak is a dish made with dal and vegetables

dhokla: (plural *dhoklas*) steamed split chickpea cakes

dhulli masoor dal: red lentils

dhulli mung dal: yellow mung beans

dhulli urad dal: white urad beans

Diwali: Indian festival of lights that usually falls in October-November in the Western calendar

dobara-talna: fry a second time, referring to chickpea batter fritters and other snacks

doiyan: small chickpea flour pancakes

dosa: crispy fermented rice and lentil crepe

dum: pot-roast

dum-aalu: pot-roasted potatoes

dum-pukht: special pot-roasted dishes. Traditionally, these dishes were made in a pot that is sealed with a ring of dough and cooked with a hot coal on the lid, for concentrated cooking from heat below and above

falooda: thin, long, soft noodles (like softened cellophane noodles), served with kulfi ice cream

firni: rice custard

gaajar: carrots

gadhvi:(also *louta*) deep S-shaped metal pot traditionally used for making lussi (a yogurt drink)

gajjeraela: carrot halva, a soft-cooked dessert made with grated carrots

ganth gobi: kohlrabi

garam masala: blend of cinnamon, black cardamom, cloves, and black peppercorns

gattae: steamed chickpea flour bites

gehun ka atta: whole-wheat flour

ghee: clarified butter that is further cooked over low heat until the milk solids turn a rich golden color

ghia: (also *lauki*) opo or marrow squash; pale green, bottle-shaped squash

gobi: cauliflower

gol-guppas: (also *paani poories*) crispy, hollow, 1-inch puffed balls

gosht: meat, usually referring to lamb or goat

gucchi: (also *gucchiyan*) morel mushrooms

gujjias: nut- and raisin-filled, crescent-shaped croquettes

gulaab: rose

gulaab jal: rosewater

gulaab jamuns: spongy, reddish-brown milk rolls or balls in fragrant sugar syrup

gur: blocks or pieces of brown, unrefined cane sugar; usually referred to by the British-English term "jaggery"

gushtaaba: meat balls from Kashmir

handwa: (also *haandva*) Gujarati quick-bread made with fermented rice and chickpea flour

halva: soft-cooked Indian dessert, made with semolina, vegetables, legumes or nuts

halvai: person who makes Indian sweets and savories

hara: (also *hari*) green

hari illaichi: green cardamom pods

heeng: (also *hing*) asafoetida

Hindi: north Indian language; also India's national language

iddli: (plural *iddlis*) steamed rice and lentil cakes

illaichi: cardamom pods and seeds

imli: tamarind

imli-paani: savory cold beverage made with tamarind and water

jaiphul: nutmeg

jalebis: pretzel-shaped Indian sweets of fried fermented batter

jal-jeera: (also *jeera-paani*) savory cold beverage made with water and dry-roasted cumin seeds

jau: barley

javitri: mace

jeera: (also *zeera*) cumin

jeera-aalu: cumin potatoes

jhalfraezi: mild restaurant-style mixed vegetable dish with tomatoes and onions

jowar: sorghum

junglee dalchini: wild cinnamon

kaala: black

kaala-jaams: spongy, caramel-colored dried milk balls in sugar syrup; "kaala" means black, and is used because the milk balls turn very dark brown

kaala namak: black salt

kaali illaichi: black cardamom pods

kaali mirch: black pepper

kaanji: savory cold beverage made with beet-colored carrots

kaathi kabaabs: grilled meat or chicken or paneer cheese kabaabs rolled in a special roti bread

kabaab: (also *kabab, kebab*) special grilled or deep-fried finger food

kacchi: raw

kaddu: (also *petha*) pumpkin or gourd, including butternut and acorn squash

kachauri: (also *khasta kachauries*) savory deep-fried pastries made with 2- to 3-inch puffed rounds of pastry dough

kadhai: an Indian round-bottomed wok used for deep-frying and cooking

kadhai masala: a spice blend made with coriander, dried mint, fenugreek leaves, pomegranate seeds, used for wok-cooked foods

kadhi: yogurt curry thickened with chickpea flour

kairi: (also *ammbi*) unripe green mangoes

kakdi: (also *tar*) Armenian cucumber, thin, long (7 to 9 inches), and pale green

kalaakand: milk fudge made by curdling milk and then cooking it with condensed milk

kalaeji: the liver of any animal

kalonji: also nigella seeds; charcoal black, tiny, triangular seeds used in pickles and curries

kamal-kakdi: see **bhain**

kamrak: (also *karambola, carambola*) star fruit

karelae: bitter melon or bitter gourd; long, light green squash with uneven, bumpy skin

kari: curry, a dish with a sauce

kari patta: (also *meethi neem*) fresh curry leaves

kasoori methi: dried fenugreek leaves

katori: small (2½- to 3-inch) metal bowl with straight edges, used as a bowl for saucy dishes

keema: ground meat

kesar: saffron

kesari: with saffron

khada masala: whole spices

khameer: leavening agent, such as yeast

khandvi: Gujarati snack, made with chickpea flour

khus-khus: poppy seeds

khasta: flaky

kheer: (plural *kheers*) milk-based pudding

khichadi: (plural *khichadis*) soft-cooked rice and lentil dish

khichda: grain and lentil preparation from Hyderabad

khoa: (also *khoya, mawa*) milk from which all the liquid has been evaporated

kofta: (plural *koftas*) minced meat, cheese, or vegetable balls, fried or cooked in a sauce

kokum: (also *cocum, cocamful*) black-brown, dried apricot-like fruit, used as a souring agent, sold as halved pieces, like dried apricots

kootupodi: south Indian curry powder mixture of rice, urad beans, coriander, and fenugreek seeds

kopra: (also *copra*) dried coconut

korma: nut-based Mughlai curries where the foods are braised in yogurt and cream and fragrant spices

kothmir: fresh cilantro

kulcha: (plural *kulchas*) baked leavened flour breads

kulfi: Indian ice cream, authentically made by thickening the milk on the stove and freezing it

lachaedar: with layers, referring to layered parantha (griddle-fried breads)

lauki: see **ghia**

laung: (also *lavang*) cloves

lobia: black-eyed peas

lucchi: thin, deep-fried breads made with all-purpose flour

lussan: (also *lahsoon*) fresh garlic

lussi: cold yogurt beverage

macher-jhol: fish curry from Bengal

maha-aushadhi: the biggest medicine reference for Ayurvedic medicine

maharaja: emperor

maida: all-purpose flour

makhani: with butter

makki: corn

makki ki roti: corn flatbread

mal-pudhas: sweet dessert pancakes

manga thoku: south Indian mango pickle

masala: (plural *masalas*) spice blend

masoor dal: red and green lentils

masala chai: spiced tea

mathri: (plural *mathris*) deep-fried Indian pastry crackers

mattha: thin, watered-down yogurt dish

medhu-vadai: special doughnut-shaped croquette made with fermented dal batter

meethi neem: curry leaves

methi: fenugreek

mirch: (also *mirchi*) chiles

mishti: sweet

missi roti: griddle-fried flatbread made with chickpea flour

mooli: radish

moth dal: (pronounced *mo-ath*) dew beans

mulligatawny: pepper-water; a thin, hot South Indian soup flavored with tamarind, chile peppers, mustard seeds, and curry leaves

mung dal: mung beans; whole green, green split, and yellow

murgh: chicken

mutter dal: dried green split peas

naan: (plural *naans*) leavened flour bread made in a tandoor

namak-paarae: (also *nimki*) savory bite-sized pastry crackers

nargisi koftas: meat balls made with hard-boiled eggs and minced meat

Navratrae: 9 auspicious days of fasting

paani-poories: (also *gol-guppas*) round, crispy, hollow, 1-inch puffed deep-fried whole-wheat breads, often filled with spicy potatoes and spicy tamarind-mint water

paapad: (also *paapads, paapadhs, paapadums*) lentil wafers

pachadi: (plural *pachadis*) yogurt side dish with southern flavors of mustard seeds and curry leaves

pakora: (also *pakoras, pakauradha*) fritters made with chickpea flour batter and vegetables or meat

panch-phoran: mixture of 5 seeds—mustard, fenugreek, fennel, kalonji, and cumin—collectively known as Bengali 5-Spices

paneer: homemade curdled-milk cheese

papri chaat: composed, savory street salad made with flour chips, potatoes, yogurt, and special sauces

parantha: (plural *paranthas*) griddle-fried Indian flatbreads

pasandae: (also *pasindae*) flattened pieces of lamb

pateela: saucepan with a ½- to 1-inch lip

patta: leaf, as in kari patta (curry leaves) or tej patta (bay leaves)

pav-bhaji: bread and vegetables, a Mumbai (formerly Bombay) dish made with spicy soft-cooked vegetables and served with grilled breads

payasam: milky rice pudding from southern India, flavored with cardamom

payesh: rice pudding from the northeastern state of Bengal, flavored with cinnamon and bay leaves

pedha: (plural *pedhae*) saffron milk fudge patties

phool-paapadh: sun-dried wafer made with ground rice, then fried

phool-vadis: rice nuggets; same as phool-paapad, but shaped as nuggets

poha: pressed rice flakes with ragged edges, used for savory stir-fried and sweet dishes

poori: (also *poodhi*) deep-fried puffed whole-wheat breads

prasaad: consecrated food offerings to God

pudha: (plural *pudhae*) sweet or savory pancakes

pudina: mint

puliyodarai: (also *puliyogore*) spicy south Indian tamarind rice

pullao: pilaf; a dry-cooked rice dish made with spices and vegetables

raajma: kidney beans

raan: leg of lamb

rabdi: thickened milk pudding

raesham: silk, as in silky kabaabs, long hot-dog shaped kabaabs

ragi: red millet

rai: (also *raayi*) mustard seeds

raita: (plural *raitas*) yogurt dish enhanced with vegetables and spices

rajas: kings

raj-bhog: literally, fit for a king; a paneer cheese dessert with creamy pistachios and saffron centers, much like liqueur chocolates

Ramzan: (also *Ramadan*) a Muslim religious month of fasting from sunrise to sunset

ras-malai: sweet paneer cheese patties floating in a thickened milk sauce

rasam: watery, south Indian soup flavored with mustard seeds and curry leaves

rasgulla: (plural *rasgullas*) steamed paneer cheese balls in fragrant cardamom and rose syrup

rattan: literally, jewels; special ingredients in a dish

rava: (also *sooji*) semolina

roti: (plural *rotis*) general word for chapati and other griddle-cooked flatbreads

rotli: small roti

ruh-gulaab: rose essence

saabut: whole

saabut masala gosht: meat cooked with whole spices

saabut masoor: green lentils

saabut mung dal: green mung beans

saabut urad dal: black urad beans

saalan: Hyderabadi (south Indian) tamarind-flavored spicy and hot vegetable curry

saag: cooking greens, or a dish made with cooking greens

sambar: soupy south Indian dish made with split pigeon peas (toor dal)

samosa: (plural *samosas*) savory stuffed and deep-fried triangular pastries

sandesh: (also *sondesh*) milk fudge made with soft paneer cheese

santara: mandarin orange

sarson: mustard

sarson ka saag: mustard greens

sarson ka tael: mustard oil

satpura: literally, with 7 layers; refers to the layers of samosas (deep-fried filled flaky pastries)

saunf: fennel seeds

seekh: skewer

seekh kabaabs: long, minced-meat or vegetable rolls made on skewers

sev: (also *bhujia*) crispy savory chickpea flour noodles

sevai or seviyan: Indian vermicelli

sev-poori: pastry canapés topped with a mixture of potatoes, onions, sev noodles, and chutneys

shabdegh: Kashmiri dish with meat and turnips

shah-jeera: (also *shahi, siyah jeera*) black cumin seeds; considered a more expensive and exotic alternative to cumin seeds

shahi: fit for royalty

shakanjvi: lemonade

shakkar: granular Indian brown sugar made from sugar cane

shrikhand: thickened yogurt mousse, generally flavored with saffron and cardamom

soae: (also *sowa*) fresh dill greens

sonth: silky smooth, sweet and sour brown chutney made with tamarind or dried unripe mangoes; used in chaats, salads, and finger foods

sookha: (also *sookhi*) dry

sookhae muttar: dried peas

succha: pure, as in extract or essence

sufaid: white

sufaid mirch: white pepper

sufaid mooli: white daikon radishes

sund: dried ginger

taang: leg; cut of meat used for chicken or lamb

taaza: (also *taazi*) fresh

talna: to fry

tandoor: barrel-shaped, coal-burning clay oven

tandoori: relating to a tandoor

tandoori phool: marinated and grilled whole cauliflower, traditionally cooked in a tandoor

tangdhi: chicken drumsticks

tarka: (also *tadka, bhagar vaghar, chaunk*) blend of spices and seasonings fried briefly in hot oil (also called tempering) and used to top dal (legume) and other dishes

tava: concave cast-iron griddle used to make Indian flatbreads

tej patta: (also *tejpat, tej patra*) bay leaves

thali: large metal tray used for serving foods, as well as a dinner plate; usage depends on the size

thandai: chilled milk beverage with almonds, melon seeds, and saffron

tikka: (plural *tikkas*) marinated and grilled boneless pieces of meat

tikki: (plural *tikkis*) pan- or deep-fried potato patties

til: sesame (*gingelly*) seeds

tindora: small summer squash

toor dal: split pigeon peas

tukris: pieces

tulsi: holy basil

ubaalna: to boil

uppma: fluffy, dry-cooked, couscous-like semolina dish

uthapam: rice flour or semolina pancakes

vadae: (also *vadai, vadais, vadas*) deep-fried, fermented white urad beans (dhulli urad dal) croquettes

vangi-bhaat: south Indian rice with eggplants

vendaka: okra

vindaloo: Goan curry made with vinegar and red chile peppers

xacuti: spicy Goan meat or chicken curry with coconut and many spices

yakhni: meat broth

zaffron: (also *kesar*) saffron

zeera: (also *jeera*) cumin

Mail and Internet Sources

Mail-Order Sources

Bharat Bazaar
11510 W Washington
    Boulevard
Los Angeles, CA 90066
(310) 398-6766
Kundanfoods.com

India Sweets & Spices
18110 Parthenia Street
Northridge, CA 91325
(818) 407-1498

India Sweets and Spices
9409 Venice Boulevard
Culver City, CA 90232
(310) 837-5286

Bazaar of India
1810 University Avenue
Berkeley, CA 94703
(510) 548-4110

Neelkamal Spice House
1182 N. Capitol Avenue
San Jose, CA 95132
(408) 923-8742

New India Bazar
1584 Branham Drive
San Jose, CA 95118
(408) 265-6031

Jai-Hind Grocery
4722 N Kedzie Avenue
Chicago IL 60631
(773) 583-6608

Kamdar Plaza
2646 West Devon Avenue
Chicago, IL 60659
(773) 338-8100

Patel Bros.
2600 West Devon Avenue
Chicago IL 60631
(773) 262-7777

Kalustyan Brothers
123 Lexington Avenue
New York, NY
(212) 685-3451
www.kalustyans.com

Little India Stores
128 East 28th Street
New York, NY 10016
(212) 689-5182

Patel Brothers
3727 74th Street
Jackson Heights, NY 11372
(718) 898-3445

India Grocers
15 Richardson Heights Center
    North
Richardson, TX 75080
(972) 234-8051

House of Spices
115 Spring Valley
Richardson, TX, 75080
(972) 783-7544

Links to find Indian markets in the United States:

http://www.indian-shops.com/usa.html

http://www.searchindia.com/search/groc.html

Links to shopping on-line:

http://www.indiangrocerynet.com/

http://www.patelbrothersusa.com/new/

www.mahabazaar.com

www.valueindia.com

www.namaste.com

Index

 = Vegan    = Pressure-Cooker Quick

E

Easy Mashed Spicy Eggplant and Potatoes, 264–65 🌿

Egg(s), 154–55, 216, 293, 436, 437, 442, 443–44, 496–97
  curries, 442–44
  scrambled, 436–37

Egg-Fried Okra Fingers, 293

Eggplant(s), 36–37, 90, 115, 190–91, 230, 231, 263–70, 270, 307–8, 393–94, 400, 543–44, 558–59
  broiling, 37
  Chinese, 231, 265, 270
  mashed, 263–64
  roasting and grilling, 36–37

Eggplant and Malanga Root Pickle, 90 🌿

Eggplant Curry with Sambar Powder, 393–94

Eggplant with Red Potatoes, 268

Egg-Stuffed Meat Balls in Yogurt-Cream Sauce, 496–97

F

Falguni's Gujarati Split Pigeon Peas, 351–52 🌿

Falguni's Steamed Chickpea Flour Cakes, 136 🌿

Fast Black Bean Soup, Indian Style, 182 🅿

Fennel and Black Cardamom Tea, 661

Fennel seeds, about, 10
  and ginger, Kashmiri curry powder with, 16

Fennel-flavored black urad beans with yogurt, Kashmiri, 359–60

Fenugreek, 10–11, 118, 152–53, 159, 255–56, 272–73, 327–28, 408–9, 428, 454–55, 486, 547, 591, 602–3
  leaves, 152–53, 159, 327, 357, 547
  seeds, 10–11, 272–73

Fenugreek Yogurt Curry with Fritters, 428

15-Spice Curry Powder, 15 🌿

Fillings for samosas, 108–11
  green split pea samosa, 109
  meat samosa, 110
  mixed vegetable samosa, spicy, 108
  potato, 108
  spinach samosa, yellow mung bean and, 109
  sprouted green mung bean, 110

Fillings for omelets, 440–41
  oven-roasted vegetable omelet, 440–41
  spicy green chutney, 440
  tomato and paneer cheese, 440

Fillings for Potato Patties, 145 🌿

Fire-Roasted Corn-on-the-Cob, 302 🌿

Fire-Roasted Green Mango Cooler, 658 🌿

Fish
  with Bell Peppers and Onions, 528
  with Bengali 5-Spices, 523
  and chicken soups, 193–96
  curries, 522–28
  with Ground Mustard Seeds, 524
  fillets, pan-fried, with ajwain seeds, 520
  fried, grilled, and baked, 517–21
  fried, Southern Indian, basic, 519
  garam masala, blackened, 521
  grilled, tikka marinade, 166
  kabaabs, spicy batter-coated, 156
  Pakora Fritters, 124–25
  and shellfish, 510–28
  masala, with pearl onions, Cochin, 524–25
  tikka kabaabs, basic, 161
  tikka marinade, sesame, 166
  vinegar-poached, with fresh curry leaves, 517
  whole, pan-fried, with tomatoes and kokum, 519–20

5-spices. See Bengali 5-spices

Flatbreads, stuffed griddle-fried, 586–89

Flattened Lamb Kabaab Skewers with Cardamom Seeds, 150–51

Flattened Lamb Kabaab Skewers with Nuts and Poppy Seeds, 151

Flattened Lamb Strips in Fragrant Yogurt Curry, 507–8

Flavored deep-fried puffed breads, 591–94

Flavored indian ice creams, 635–36

Flavored milk fudge, 640–41

Flavoring pastes, basic, 46–54

Flour, 120, 121, 577–78, 600–601, 611–12, 617. See also Chickpea flour
  breads, 577–78, 593–94
  rice, 120, 121, 611–12

Flour chips, crispy, with vegetables and spicy chutneys, 141–42

Flour Chips with Yogurt and Mango Powder Chutney, 142

Flour halva, whole-wheat, 619–20

Flour mixture, shredded and minced vegetable, fritters, 117–21

Fragrant Baby Turnip Halves, 258 🌿

Fragrant Chicken Curry with Coconut and Sesame Seeds, 465

Fragrant Corn-off-the-Cob, 302 🌿

Fragrant Lamb Chops in Yogurt Curry, 481–82

Fragrant Mango Chutney Preserve, 73 🌿

Fragrant Masala with Nuts, 25 🌿

Fragrant Yogurt Soup, 189–90

French fries with tomatoes, Indian, 127

French Roll Bread Pudding, 628

French toast, 441–42

Fresh Coconut Chutney with Cilantro, 61

Fresh Fenugreek Pakora Fritters with Pomegranate Seeds, 118 🌿

Fresh Fruits in Rose-Flavored Cream, 634

Fresh Green Bean Pakora Fritters with Ginger, 114 🌿

Fresh Green Chickpeas with Lentil Nuggets, 382

Fresh Green Chutney Lamb Tikka Marinade, 163

Fresh Lime Soda with Berries, 657 🌿

Fresh Mint Chai Tea, 662

Fresh Spinach Raita with Ginger-Lime Pickle, 227

Fried. See also Deep-fried; Griddle-fried; Pan-fried; Pot-roasted fried

Fried Cauliflower Florets with Red Chili Flakes, 283 🌿

Fried fish, Southern Indian, basic, 519

Fried Onion Paste, 49

Fritters (Pakorae or Bhajiae), 112, 113–25, 426–27, 428. See also Fritters, pakora
  cheese and meat, 121–25
  frying, (pakorae talna), 112
  shredded and minced vegetable, and flour mixture, 117–21
  sliced, chopped, and stuffed vegetable, 113–17

Fritters, pakora
  baby spinach, 116
  basic batter for, 113
  bell pepper, with ajwain seeds, 114–15
  bread, stuffed with coconut chutney, 117
  cabbage, shredded, with yogurt, 117–18
  cashew, rice flour and, 121

About the Author

Neelam Batra was born in New Delhi, India, and lived there until she got married and moved to Los Angeles with her husband, Pradeep, in 1973.

Living in America, far from home and with no Indian restaurants and no Indian grocery stores in sight, she faced a crucial challenge—how to enjoy the foods she knew and loved. She set out to recreate the dishes with the ingredients she had available to her. Although she learned the basics of Indian cooking at her mother's side as she was growing up, she had no formal training in Indian cuisine. Her knowledge was developed as she recreated dish after dish in her Los Angeles kitchen, as she visited and toured India to understand more about the regional foods and cooking styles, and as she sampled regional dishes and home-cooked favorites and talked about Indian cooking with friends, family, and restaurant chefs from all over India.

Her re-creations of the classics and her own adaptations won raves from her friends and her family, which, over time, included two daughters, Sumita and Supriya and son-in-law Monti. She soon found herself being invited to teach at local cooking schools in Santa Monica, where she has since taught cooking for 18 years.

She has written two cookbooks, *The Indian Vegetarian* and *Chilis to Chutneys*. She has also been a guest and on-air instructor for national TV cooking shows in the United States and India. She continues to live in Santa Monica, California, with her husband, Pradeep.

Afghanistan

Pakistan

China

Nepal

JAMMU AND KASHMIR

HIMACHAL PRADESH

PUNJAB

HARYANA

Delhi ◉

Ganges River

UTTAR PRADESH

Lucknow ●

RAJASTHAN

GUJARAT

MADHYA PRADESH

Bhutan

SIKKIM

Darjeeling ●

ARUNACHAL PRADESH

ASSAM

NAGALAND

MEGHALAYA

MANIPUR

Bangladesh

TRIPURA

MIZORAM

BIHAR

WEST BENGAL

Calcutta ●

Myanmar

ORISSA

MAHARASHTRA

Bay of Bengal

Mumbai (Bombay) ●

ANDHRA PRADESH

GOA

Hyderabad ●

Arabian Sea

KARNATAKA

Mysore ●

Coorg ●

Madras ●

Cochin ●

TAMIL NADU

KERALA

INDIAN OCEAN

Sri Lanka

N